Visual Basic .NET and the .NET Platform: An Advanced Guide

ANDREW TROELSEN

Apress™

Visual Basic .NET and the .NET Platform: An Advanced Guide

ISBN (pbk): 1-893115-26-7

Printed and bound in the United States of America 12345678910

Editorial Directors: Dan Appleman, Gary Cornell, Jason Gilmore, Karen Watterson
Technical Reviewers: Pamela Fanstill, Rob Macdonald, Dan Appleman, William Oellermann
Managing Editor: Grace Wong
Copy Editors: Anne Friedman, Nicole LeClerc
Production Editors: Janet Vail with Kari Brooks and Anne Friedman
Composition and Art Services: Impressions Book and Journal Services, Inc.
Indexer: Carol Burbo
Cover Designer: Tom Debolski
Marketing Manager: Stephanie Rodriguez

Distributed to the book trade in the United States by Springer-Verlag New York, Inc.,175 Fifth Avenue, New York, NY, 10010
and outside the United States by Springer-Verlag GmbH & Co. KG, Tiergartenstr. 17, 69112 Heidelberg, Germany

In the United States, phone 1-800-SPRINGER, email `orders@springer-ny.com`, or visit `http://www.springer-ny.com`.
Outside the United States, fax +49 6221 345229, email `orders@springer.de`, or visit `http://www.springer.de`.

For information on translations, please contact Apress directly at 901 Grayson Street, Suite 204, Berkeley, CA 94710.
Phone 510-549-5930, fax: 510-549-5939, email `info@apress.com`, or visit `http://www.apress.com`.

The source code for this book is available to readers at `http://www.apress.com` in the Downloads section. You will need to answer questions pertaining to this book in order to successfully download the code.

This book is dedicated to the memory of the thousands of people who lost their lives during the tragic events that took place on September 11, 2001. Of exactly equal importance, this book is dedicated to each and every individual who worked around the clock, without limits, to bring some degree of normalcy back to New York, Pennsylvania, and Washington D.C. Thank you for your strength, inspiration, and relentless commitment. Thank you for engaging the unimaginable.

Contents at a Glance

Contents

Chapter 4 Object-Oriented Programming with VB .NET 159

Chapter 5 Interfaces and Collections 227

Chapter 6 Delegates, Events, and Callback Interfaces 263

Chapter 9 Building a Better Window (Introducing Windows Forms) 421

Chapter 10 A Better Painting Framework (GDI+) ...507

Chapter 11 Programming with Windows Form Controls 589

What You Need to Use This Book

THE VERY FIRST THING you must do before you dig in is download the accompanying source code for this book from the Apress Web site (`http://www.apress.com`). As you read over each chapter, you find the following icon has been liberally scattered throughout the text:

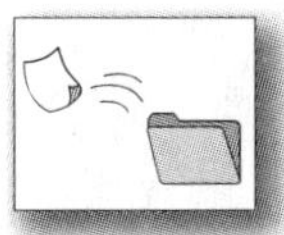

This is your visual cue that the example under discussion may be loaded into Visual Studio .NET for examination.

In addition to the source code, you need to have a copy of .NET Beta 2. In this text, I have chosen to focus primarily on using the Visual Studio .NET development environment. Although you are free to build and compile your code using nothing more than the VB .NET compiler (which is included with the .NET SDK) and Notepad.exe, you will find that VS .NET takes care of a number of low-level details on your behalf.

Finally, understand that this is an advanced text geared toward the seasoned software professional. The goals of this text are *not* to labor over each and every detail of the "For" loop, examine each and every menu selection of the Visual Studio .NET IDE, or describe all ten steps of a given VS .NET wizard. My assumption is that you are well equipped to explore the IDE and have no problem activating menu options. On the other hand, I assume no foreknowledge of VB .NET or the .NET platform. In particular, this book is well suited for individuals possessing the following traits:

- You are an experienced software professional who has solid background in some modern-day programming language (Visual Basic, C++, Java, and so on).

- You are unafraid to consult online Help, build sample programs, and explore .NET on your own terms (and do so often without shame).

Even a book of this size cannot possibly cover each and every aspect of the .NET platform. The online Help that ships with the .NET SDK is incredibly readable, and it provides numerous code examples, white papers, and online tutorials. Once you have read (and understood) these sixteen chapters, you will be in a perfect position to build complete .NET solutions with the VB .NET language. At this point, online Help will become your faithful companion that extends and complements the material presented here.

So, let's get on with the show! It is my sincere hope that this book will guide you safely through the .NET universe and serve as a solid reference during your life as an author of managed code using VB .NET.

Andrew Troelsen
Minneapolis, Minnesota

Acknowledgments

FIRST, MANY THANKS to Gary Cornell and Dan Appleman, who encouraged me to translate my first Apress publication (*C# and the .NET Platform*) into the vernacular of Visual Basic. A solid (and affectionate) thanks to Grace Wong and Stephanie Rodriguez, who again kept me honest and provided a fantastic working environment (see you at the PDC!). A special thanks to Carol Burbo for working with an incredibly tight deadline in order to index this material.

A *mammoth* amount of gratitude to the editorial staff: Anne Friedman (glad to work with you again Anne! See you on book number three?), Nicole LeClerc, Christie Roden, Janet Vail, and Kari Brooks, who all did an outstanding job editing, formatting, and massaging the knots out of my original manuscript. Thanks for your focus and clarity during the course of this project.

I also must offer heartfelt thanks to my primary technical editor, Pam Fanstill. Thanks for laboring over each and every line of syntax and pointing out the lingering C# tokens that escaped my view. Your work was phenomenal (honest). Additional huge thanks are extended to Dan Appleman, Rob Macdonald, and William Oellermann for offering additional technical reviews (and numerous insights). Any remaining faux pas are my sole responsibility.

Thanks to my fellow cohorts at Intertech-Inc.: Steve Close, Gina McGhee, Andrew "Gunner" Sondgeroth, and Tom Barnaby, who, while working on their own books, provided an encouraging, intense, and positive environment. As well, thanks to Tom Salonek for just being Tom (remember, *always* bring more beer).

Finally, thanks and love to Mary and Wally Troelsen (aka Mom and Dad), and my wife, friend, and confidant, Amanda. I hope you all know how much your support means to me.

Introduction

MICROSOFT'S .NET PLATFORM represents an entirely new way to build distributed, desktop, and mobile applications. One thing to be painfully aware of from the outset is that the .NET platform has *nothing* at all to do with classic COM, VB 6.0, ATL, or any other pre-.NET frameworks. For example, as you read over this text, you will find that .NET types do not support IUnknown, are not cataloged in the system registry, and are not described using COM type libraries. Understand that these COM primitives have not simply been hidden away from view—they no longer exist.

Given that .NET is such a radical departure from the current modus operandi of Win32 development, Microsoft has developed a new language named C# (pronounced "see-sharp") specifically for this new platform. C#, like Java, has its syntactic roots in C++. However, C# has *also* been influenced by Visual Basic 6.0, specifically with regard to the use of class properties, "for each"–like iteration, and the IDE itself. Nevertheless, given that C# still uses numerous C++-like tokens (semicolons, colons, and curly brackets), many die-hard VBers may find the syntax of C# a bit unpalatable.

The good news is that in addition to the advent of C#, Microsoft has also shipped a brand-new update of the ever-popular Visual Basic programming language termed *VB .NET,* which is also specifically geared toward the development of .NET applications. As you move through this text, you will see that VB .NET is *not* simply an upgrade from VB 6.0. Rather, VB .NET can best be understood as a brand-new programming language that *just happens* to look suspiciously like earlier iterations of the language. If you feel this last statement is a bit alarmist in nature, consider the following (partial) sampling of new constructs offered by VB .NET:

- Unlike VB 6.0, VB .NET supports class constructors, implementation inheritance, classical polymorphism, and method overloading.

- VB .NET allows developers to natively build multithreaded applications (which could be achieved to some degree in VB 6.0, if you were willing to drop down to the raw Win32 API).

- Unlike previous versions of Visual Basic, VB .NET supports the development of extremely robust graphical-based (as opposed to GUI-based) applications using a facility termed *GDI+*.

- VB .NET supports new data types (System.Object), removes other data types (the Variant), and has reworked current language constructs (class properties, strings, arrays, enumerations, and class types) to bring Visual Basic up to snuff with the .NET architecture.

Despite these (and other) substantial changes, VB .NET still supports the key features that have established Microsoft Visual Basic as the most popular programming language to date. For those of you who have worked with earlier editions of VB, you will notice many key similarities.

On a related note, once you learn the syntax and semantics of VB .NET, you find that the process of learning additional .NET-aware languages (such as C#) is painfully simple. The truth of the matter is that .NET is an extremely language-agnostic platform. You can make use of any .NET-aware language (and possibly numerous .NET-aware languages) during the development of your next coding effort. In this vein, your greatest challenge is not necessarily learning the VB .NET language, but rather coming to terms with the numerous types defined in the .NET base class libraries.

Once you understand how to leverage the existing code base, you find that the concept of "syntax" becomes a nonissue given that all .NET-aware languages make use of the same base class types. This is also a good thing, given that you should be able to move swiftly between various .NET languages with minimal fuss and bother.

The goals of this text are to provide a solid foundation of the syntax and semantics of VB .NET, as well as the architecture of the .NET platform. As you read through the (many) pages that follow, you are exposed to each major facet of the .NET base class libraries. Let's take a high-level overview of each chapter.

Chapter 1: The Philosophy of .NET

Chapter 1 functions as the backbone for this text. The first task of the chapter is to examine the world of Windows development as we know it today and review the shortcomings of the current state of affairs. However, the primary goal is to acquaint you with the meaning behind a number of .NET-centric building blocks, such as the Common Language Runtime (CLR), the Common Type System (CTS), the Common Language Specification (CLS), and the base class libraries. In addition, this chapter introduces you to a set of core tools (ILDasm.exe, WinCV.exe, and so on) that allow you to explore the .NET class libraries at your leisure.

Chapter 2: Building VB .NET Applications

Chapter 2 begins with an examination of how to interact with the VB .NET compiler (vbc.exe) in the raw. As you see later in the text, some advanced aspects of VB .NET (such as building multifile assemblies) are only accessible from the command-line compiler. Given this fact, spending the time to build some simple VB .NET applications by hand will serve you well. The later half of this chapter illustrates the core features of the Visual Studio .NET IDE. To wrap things up, you examine the pros and cons of converting existing VB 6.0 code into the .NET paradigm.

Chapter 3: VB .NET Language Fundamentals

The goal of Chapter 3 is to showcase the core syntax of the VB .NET programming language. As you would hope, you are introduced to the intrinsic data types of VB .NET as well as the set of iteration and decision constructs. More important, you learn about the composition of a VB .NET class, and you make friends with a number of new .NET techniques, such as value and reference types, namespace development, and the role of the mighty System.Object.

Chapter 4: Object-Oriented Programming with VB .NET

Now that you can build complex stand-alone types, Chapter 4 focuses on the pillars of object technology: encapsulation, inheritance ("is-a" and "has-a"), and polymorphism (classical and ad hoc). The chapter begins with a high-level examination of these key terms, and then quickly turns its attention to exploring how VB .NET supports each pillar. Along the way, you are exposed to new syntax used to define class properties, and you learn the ins and outs of developing class hierarchies. Finally, this chapter examines a new mechanism to handle runtime anomalies: Structured Exception Handling. The chapter ends with a discussion of the .NET garbage collection scheme, and you see how to programmatically interact with this service using the System.GC class type.

Chapter 5: Interface and Collections

Like C++, Java, and VB 6.0, VB .NET supports the technique of interface-based programming. In this chapter you learn the role of an interface and understand how to define and implement such a creature in VB .NET. Once you can build types that support multiple interfaces, you learn a number of techniques you can use to obtain an interface reference from a valid type instance. The second half of this chapter examines a number of predefined interfaces defined within the .NET class libraries and illustrates how to make use of the System.Collections namespace to build custom container types. You also learn how to build "cloneable" and "enumerable" types.

Chapter 6: Delegates, Events, and Callback Interfaces

This chapter rounds out your understanding of core OOP using VB .NET. To begin, you review the classic VB 6.0 event protocol, and you quickly see that VB .NET makes use of the same core keywords (Event, WithEvents, and RaiseEvent) to enable bidirectional communication. Under the hood, however, the .NET event architecture is founded on the use of *delegates*. The bulk of this chapter is spent examining the use of this type and several related topics, such as hooking into events dynamically at runtime using the new AddHandler and RemoveHandler statements.

Chapter 7: Assemblies, Threads, and AppDomains

At this point you should be very comfortable building stand-alone VB .NET applications. This chapter illustrates how to break apart a monolithic EXE into discrete code libraries. Here, you learn about the internal composition of a .NET assembly and understand the distinction between "shared" and "private" assemblies. This entails a discussion of the Global Assembly Cache (GAC), XML configuration files, and side-by-side execution. To further illustrate the virtues of the CLR, this chapter also examines cross-language inheritance using C# and (gasp!) C++. The chapter wraps up with an examination of how to construct multithreaded applications using VB .NET.

Chapter 8: Reflection and Attributes

Reflection is the process of runtime type discovery. This chapter examines the details behind the System.Reflection namespace and illustrates how to investigate the contents of an assembly on the fly. On a related note, you learn how to *build* an assembly (and its contained types) at runtime using the System.Reflection.Emit namespace. Chapter 8 also illustrates how to exercise late binding to a .NET type and dynamically invoke its members. Finally, the chapter wraps up with a discussion of attribute-based programming. As you will see, this technique allows you to augment compiler-generated metadata with application-specific information.

Chapter 9: Building a Better Window (Introducing Windows Forms)

Despite its name, the .NET platform has considerable support for building traditional desktop applications. In this chapter, you come to understand how to build a stand-alone main window using the types contained in the System.Windows.Forms namespace. Once you understand the derivation of a Form, you then learn to add support for topmost and pop-up menu systems, toolbars, and status bars. As an added bonus, this chapter also examines how to programmatically manipulate the system registry and Windows 2000 event log.

Chapter 10: A Better Painting Framework (GDI+)

For the first time in VB's rich ten-year history, programmers are given the tools they need to build exotic, graphics-intensive applications. This chapter teaches you how to render geometric images, bitmaps, and complex textual images onto the Form's client area using VB .NET. On a related note, you learn how to drag images within a Form (in response to mouse movement), as well as how to perform hit tests against geometric regions (in response to mouse clicks). This chapter ends with an examination of the .NET resource format which, as you might assume, is based on XML syntax.

Chapter 11: Programming with Windows Form Controls

This final chapter on Windows Forms examines how to program with the suite of GUI widgets provided by the .NET Framework. Here, you discover details behind the Calendar, DataGrid, and input validation controls, in addition to the vanilla-flavored TextBox, Button, and ListBox types (among others). In addition, you learn how to build custom .NET controls (and components) using VB .NET. The chapter wraps up with an examination of how to build custom dialog boxes and MDI applications, and you come to understand a new technique termed *Form inheritance.*

Chapter 12: Input, Output, and Object Serialization

The .NET Framework provides a number of types devoted to IO activities. In this chapter you learn how to save and retrieve simple data types to (and from) files, memory locations, and string buffers. Of greater interest is the use of object serialization services. Using a small set of predefined attributes and a corresponding object graph, the Framework is able to persist related objects using an XML or binary formatter. To illustrate object serialization at work, this chapter wraps up with a Windows Forms application that allows the end user to create and serialize custom class types for use at a later time.

Chapter 13: Interacting with Unmanaged Code

As bizarre as it may seem, Microsoft's Component Object Model (COM) can now be regarded as a *legacy* technology. As you most certainly know by this point in the book, the architecture of COM bears little resemblance to that of .NET. This chapter examines the details of how COM types and .NET types can live together in harmony through the use of COM Callable Wrappers (CCW) and Runtime Callable Wrappers (RCW). Here, you see how various COM constructs such as SAFEARRAYs, COM events, and COM enumerations map into VB .NET code. The chapter concludes by examining how to build .NET types that can take advantage of the COM+ runtime.

Chapter 14: Data Access with ADO.NET

To be perfectly blunt, ADO.NET bears little resemblance to classic ADO proper. As you discover, ADO.NET is a data access model specifically built for the disconnected world. To begin, you learn how to create and populate an in-memory DataSet and establish relationships between the internal DataTables. The second half of this chapter examines how to make use of the OleDb and Sql managed providers to obtain access to relational database management systems such as Microsoft Access and SQL Server. Once you understand how to connect to a given data store, you learn how to insert, update, and remove data records as well as trigger logic contained within stored procedures.

Chapter 15: Web Development and ASP.NET

For the sake of completeness, this chapter begins with an overview of the Web programming model and examines how to build Web front ends (using HTML), how to perform client-side validation (using JavaScript), and how to request a response from a classic ASP Web application. Of course, if you are already "Web aware," you are free to skip these initial pages entirely. The bulk of the chapter provides a solid introduction to the ASP.NET architecture. Here, you learn about Web Controls, server-side event handling, and the core properties of the Page type (including the Request and Response properties). As you would hope, you learn how to build a Web-enabled front end that is able to display (and manipulate) data retrieved using ADO.NET.

Chapter 16: Building (and Understanding) Web Services

In this final chapter of this book, you examine the role of .NET Web services. Simply put, a "Web service" is a unit of code that is activated using standard HTTP. Here you examine the surrounding technologies (WSDL, SOAP, and discovery services) that enable a Web service to take incoming client requests. Once you understand how to construct a VB .NET Web service, you then learn how to build a client-side proxy class, which hides the low-level SOAP logic from view.

CHAPTER 1

The Philosophy of .NET

EVERY FEW YEARS, the modern-day programmer must be willing to perform a self-inflicted knowledge transplant to stay current with new technologies. The languages (C++, Visual Basic 6.0, Java), frameworks (MFC, ATL, STL) and architectures (COM, CORBA) that were touted as the silver bullets of software development eventually become overshadowed by something better or new. Regardless of the frustration you may feel as you upgrade your knowledge base, it is unavoidable. Microsoft's .NET platform represents the next major wave of (positive) changes coming from those kind folks in Redmond.

The point of this chapter is to lay the conceptual groundwork for the remainder of the book. It begins with a high-level discussion of a number of .NET-related atoms such as assemblies, intermediate language (IL), and just-in-time (JIT) compilation. During the process, you will come to understand the relationship between core aspects of the .NET framework, such as the Common Language Runtime (CLR), the Common Type System (CTS), and the Common Language Specification (CLS).

This chapter also provides an overview of the functionality supplied by the .NET base class libraries and examines helpful utilities (such as ILDasm.exe) that you can use to investigate these libraries at your leisure.

Understanding the Current State of Affairs

Before examining the specifics of the .NET universe, it's helpful to consider some of the issues that motivated the genesis of this new platform. To get in the proper mindset, let's begin this chapter with a brief (and painless) history lesson to remember the roots of Windows development and understand the limitations of the current state of affairs (after all, admitting you have a problem is the first step toward finding a solution). After this quick tour of life as we know it, we turn our attention to the numerous benefits provided by the VB .NET programming language and the .NET platform.

Life As a Win32/C Programmer

Traditionally speaking, developing software for the Windows operating system involved using the C programming language in conjunction with the Windows

API (application programming interface). While it is true that numerous applications have been successfully created using this time-honored approach, few would disagree that building applications using the raw API is a complex undertaking.

The first problem is that C is a very terse language. C developers are forced to contend with manual memory management, ugly pointer arithmetic, and awkward syntactical constructs. Furthermore, given that C is a structured language, it lacks the benefits provided by the object-oriented approach (can anyone say *spaghetti code*?). When you combine the thousands of global functions defined by the raw Win32 API to an already formidable language, it is little wonder that there are so many buggy applications floating around today.

Life As a C++/MFC Programmer

One vast improvement over raw C development is the use of the C++ programming language. In many ways, C++ can be thought of as an object-oriented *layer* on top of C. Thus, even though C++ programmers benefit from the famed "pillars of OOP" (encapsulation, polymorphism, and inheritance), they are still at the mercy of the painful aspects of the C language (i.e., memory management, ugly pointer arithmetic, and awkward syntactical constructs).

Despite the inherent complexity, many C++ frameworks exist today. For example, the Microsoft Foundation Classes (MFC) provide the developer with a set of existing C++ classes that facilitate the construction of Windows applications. The main role of MFC is to wrap a "sane subset" of the raw Win32 API behind a number of classes, magic macros, and numerous GUI tools (e.g., AppWizard, ClassWizard, and so forth). Regardless of the helpful assistance offered by the MFC framework (as well as many other windowing toolkits), the fact of the matter is that C++ programming remains a difficult and error-prone process, given its historical roots in C.

Life As a Visual Basic 6.0 Programmer

In an effort to enjoy a simpler lifestyle, many programmers have shifted away from the world of C(++)-based frameworks to kinder, gentler languages such as Visual Basic 6.0 (VB). VB is popular due to its ability to build complex user interfaces, code libraries (e.g., COM servers), and data access logic with minimal fuss and bother. Even more than MFC, VB hides the complexities of the Win32 API from view using a number of integrated GUI tools, intrinsic data types, classes, and VB-centric functions.

The major downfall of VB (at least until the advent of VB .NET) is that it is not a fully object-oriented language, but rather "object aware." For example, VB 6.0 does not allow the programmer to establish "is-a" relationships between types (i.e., no classical inheritance), has no support for parameterized class construction, no intrinsic support for building multithreaded applications, and so on. As this book shows, VB .NET removes all such limitations.

Life As a Java Programmer

Enter Java. The Java programming language is a completely object-oriented entity that has its syntactic roots in C++. As many of you are aware, Java's strengths are far greater than its support for platform independence. Java as a language cleans up the unsavory syntactical aspects of C++. Java as a platform provides programmers with a large number of predefined "packages" that contain various class and interface definitions. Using these types, Java programmers are able to build "100% Pure Java" applications complete with database connectivity, messaging support, Web-enabled front ends and rich-user interfaces (in addition to other services).

Although Java is a very elegant language, one potential problem is that using Java typically means that you must use Java front-to-back during the development cycle. In effect, Java offers little hope of language independence, as this goes against the grain of Java's primary goal (a single programming language for every need). In reality, there are millions of lines of existing code in the world that would like to comingle with newer Java code. Sadly, Java doesn't make this easy.

On a related note, Java alone is not appropriate for every situation. If you are building a graphics intensive product (such as a 3D-rendered video game), you'll find Java's execution speed can leave something to be desired. A better approach is to use a lower-level language (such as C++) where appropriate, and have Java code interoperate with the external C++ binaries. While Java does provide a limited ability to access non-Java APIs, there is little support for true cross-language integration.

Life As a COM Programmer

The truth of the matter is if you are not currently building Java-based solutions, the chances are good that you are investing your time and energy understanding Microsoft's Component Object Model (COM). COM is an architecture that says, in effect, "If you build your classes in accordance with the rules of COM, you end up with a block of reusable binary code."

The beauty of a binary COM server is that it can be accessed in a language-independent manner. Thus, C++ programmers can build coclasses that can be used by VB. Delphi programmers can use coclasses built using C, and so forth. However, as you may be aware, COM's language independence is limited. For example, there is no way to derive a new COM type using an existing COM type (no support for classical inheritance). Rather, you must make use of the less robust "has-a" relationship to reuse existing COM types.

Another benefit of COM is its location-transparent nature. Using constructs such as application identifiers (AppIDs), stubs, proxies, and the COM runtime environment, programmers can avoid the need to work with raw Sockets, RPC (remote procedure calls), and other low-level details. For example, ponder the following Visual Basic 6.0 COM client code:

```
' This block of VB 6.0 code can activate a COM class written in
' any COM aware language, which may be located anywhere
' on the network (including your local machine).
Dim c as MyCOMClass
Set c = New MyCOMClass    ' Location resolved using AppID.
c.DoSomeWork
```

Although COM is a dominant object model, it is extremely complex under the hood (at least until you have spent many months exploring its plumbing. . . especially if you happen to be a C++ programmer). To help simplify the development of COM binaries, numerous COM-aware frameworks have come into existence. For example, the Active Template Library (ATL) provides another set of C++ predefined classes, templates, and macros to ease the creation of classic COM types.

Many other COM-aware languages (such as Visual Basic 6.0) also hide a good part of the COM infrastructure from view. However, framework support alone is not enough to hide the complexity of classic COM. Even when you choose a relatively simply COM-aware language such as Visual Basic 6.0, you are still forced to contend with fragile registration entries and numerous deployment-related issues.

Life As a Windows DNA Programmer

Finally there is a little thing called the Internet. Over the last several years, Microsoft has been adding more Internet-aware features to its family of operating systems. It seems that the popularity of Web applications is ever expanding. Sadly, building a complete Web application using Windows DNA (Distributed iNternet Architecture) is also a very complex undertaking.

Some of this complexity is due to the fact that Windows DNA requires many technologies and languages (ASP, HTML, XML, JavaScript, VBScript, COM(+), and a data access technology such as ADO). One problem is that many of these items are completely unrelated from a syntactic point of view. For example, JavaScript has a syntax much like C, while VBScript is a subset of Visual Basic proper. The COM servers that are created to run under the COM+ runtime have a very different look and feel from the ASP pages that invoke them. The end result is a highly confused mishmash of technologies. Furthermore, each language and/or technology has its own type system (that looks nothing like the other type systems). An "int" in JavaScript is not the same as an "int" in C, which is different from an "Integer" in VB 6.0.

The .NET Solution

So much for the brief history lesson. The bottom line is life as a Windows programmer is tough. The .NET framework is a radical and brute-force approach to making your life easier. The solution proposed by .NET is "Change everything from here on out" (sorry, you can't blame the messenger for the message). As you will see during the remainder of this book, the .NET framework is a completely new model for building systems on the Windows family of operating systems, and possibly non-Microsoft operating systems in the future. To set the stage, here is a quick rundown of core features provided courtesy of .NET:

- *Full interoperability with existing code.* This is (of course) a good thing. As shown in Chapter 13, existing COM binaries can comingle (i.e., interop) with newer .NET binaries and vice versa.
- *Complete and total language integration.* Unlike classic COM, .NET supports cross-language inheritance, cross-language structured exception handling, and cross-language debugging.
- *A common runtime engine shared by all .NET aware languages.* One aspect of this engine is a well-defined set of types that each .NET-aware language "understands."
- *A base class library* that provides shelter from the complexities of raw API calls, and offers a consistent object model used by all .NET-aware languages.
- *No more COM plumbing!* IClassFactory, IUnknown, IDL code, and the evil VARIANT-compliant types (BSTR, SAFEARRAY, and so forth) have no place in a .NET binary.
- *A truly simplified deployment model.* Under .NET, there is no need to register a binary unit into the system registry. Furthermore, the .NET runtime allows multiple versions of the same DLL to exist in harmony on a single machine.

Building Blocks of .NET (CLR, CTS, and CLS)

Although the roles of the CLR, CTS, and CLS are examined in greater detail later in this chapter, you do need to have a working knowledge of these topics to make sense of the .NET universe. From a programmer's point of view, .NET can be understood as a new runtime environment and a common base class library. The runtime layer is referred to as the Common Language Runtime, or CLR. The primary role of the CLR is to locate, load, and manage .NET types on your behalf. The CLR takes care of a number of low-level details such as automatic memory management and language integration. The CLR also assists with simplified deployment (and versioning) of binary code libraries.

Another building block of the .NET platform is the Common Type System, or CTS. The CTS describes all possible data types (and constructs) supported by the runtime, specifies how those types can interact with each other, and details how they are represented in the .NET metadata format (more information on "metadata" later in this chapter).

Understand that a given .NET-aware language might not support each and every data type and/or construct defined by the CTS. The Common Language Specification (CLS) is a set of rules that defines a subset of common types that ensure .NET binaries can be used seamlessly across all languages targeting the .NET platform. Thus, if you build .NET types that only expose CLS-compliant features, you can rest assured that all .NET-aware languages could make use of your custom types.

The .NET Base Class Libraries

In addition to the CLR and CTS/CLS specifications, the .NET platform provides a base class library that is available to all .NET programming languages. Not only does this base class library encapsulate various primitives such as file IO, graphical rendering, and interaction with external hardware devices, but it also provides support for a number of services required by most real world applications.

For example, the base class libraries define types that support database manipulation, XML integration, programmatic security, and the construction of Web-enabled (as well as traditional desktop and console-based) front ends. From a conceptual point of view, you can visualize the relationship between the .NET runtime layer and the corresponding base class library as shown in Figure 1-1.

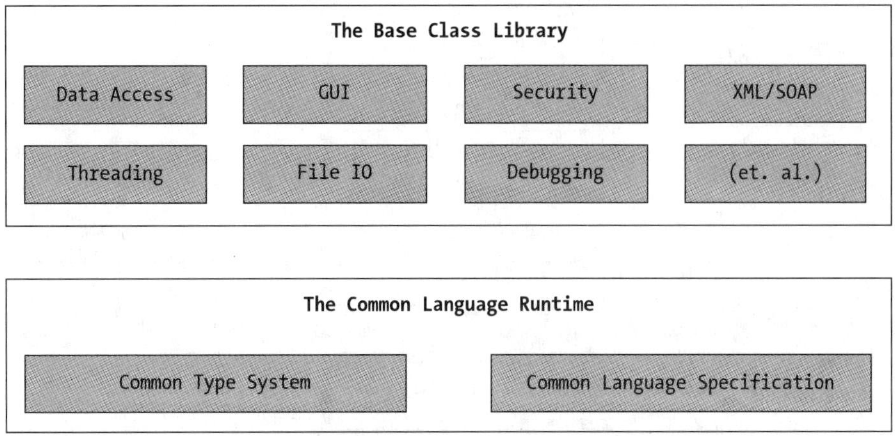

Figure 1-1. A sampling of the functionality provided by the base class libraries

.NET-Aware Programming Languages

When the .NET platform was announced to the general public during the 2000 Professional Developers Conference (PDC), several speakers listed vendors who are busy building .NET-aware versions of their respective compilers. At the time of this writing, more than 30 different languages are slated to undergo .NET enlightenment. In addition to the four languages that ship with Visual Studio .NET (C#, Visual Basic .NET, "Managed C++," and JScript.NET), be on the lookout for .NET versions of Smalltalk, COBOL, Pascal, Python, PL1, and Perl.

Regardless of which language you choose, the end result is a binary DLL or EXE file. The funny thing about the .NET binaries produced by a given compiler is that despite the fact they take the same file extensions (DLL or EXE) as classic COM binaries, they have absolutely no internal similarities. For example, .NET DLLs do not export methods to facilitate communications with the classic COM runtime (given that .NET is *not* COM). Furthermore, .NET binaries are not described using type libraries and are not registered into the system registry. Perhaps most important, unlike classic COM servers, .NET binaries do not contain platform-specific instructions. Instead they include platform-agnostic "intermediate language" officially termed Microsoft Intermediate Language (MSIL) or simply, IL. Conceptually, Figure 1-2 shows the big picture.

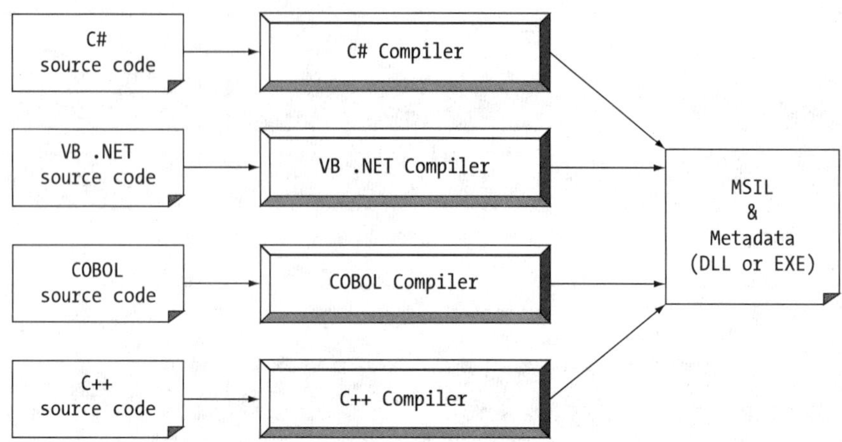

Figure 1-2. All .NET-aware compilers emit IL instructions and metadata.

Given that .NET is such a radical departure from current thinking, it should be clear that the current programming languages (VB 6.0, C++, C, and whatnot) are incapable of producing code that targets the .NET runtime. As time marches on, more and more modern day languages will achieve .NET enlightenment. Recall, Visual Studio .NET already provides you with four languages that are capable of building managed code: VisualBasic .NET, C#, C++ with Managed Extensions, and Jscript .NET. Obviously, my main concern in this text is to come to terms with the syntax and semantics of VB .NET. However, it is worth pointing out the role of C#.

A Brief Word Regarding C#

C# is a brand-new programming language, specifically designed to build .NET binaries. Like Java, C# has roots in the syntax of C++. However, a number of C#'s syntactic constructs are modeled after various aspects of Visual Basic. For example, like Visual Basic 6.0, C# supports the notion of class properties, "for each" like iteration and type indexers. On the other hand, like C++, C# allows you to overload operators for a custom type as well as create "unsafe" code blocks that bypass the CLR. Given that C# is a hybrid of numerous languages, the end result is a product that is as syntactically clean (if not cleaner) than Java, just about as simple as Visual Basic, and provides just about as much power and flexibility as C++ (without the associated ugly bits).

Although an experienced Visual Basic developer should be able to view C# code without too much pain, be aware that the syntax of C# is a bit on the terse side. For example, assume you are using C# to define a class property called FirstName. The code block looks like the following:

```
// C#. Assume fName is a private member
// variable of type string.
public string FirstName()
{
    get{return fName;}
    set{fName = value;}
}
```

The same property is expressed in VB .NET as follows:

```
' VB .NET. Also assume that fName is a private
' String.
Public Property FirstName() as String
    Get
        Return fName
    End Get
    Set(ByVal Value as String)
        FName = Value
    End Set
End Property
```

At this point in the game, do not concern yourself with the exact syntax of the FirstName property (in either language). Do notice, however, that the VB .NET version is constructed using readable, user-friendly keywords (e.g., Property, End Get, End Set) rather than the more C++-like curly brackets ({ and }) and semicolons.

As you see later in this chapter, the underlying IL emitted by each compiler is identical. In this light, the programming language you choose to build your managed application becomes little more than a personal choice. If you have a solid background in the BASIC family of languages, the chances are you will feel much more at home with the syntax of VB .NET. On the other hand, if an individual is already comfortable using languages that come from the C++ family (such as Java or C++ itself), C# is a more natural fit. As you might expect, once you are familiar with the syntax of one .NET-aware programming language, it is relatively simple to read code written in another managed language. While this text focuses on the syntax of VB .NET, I show C# examples where appropriate.

What VB .NET Brings to the Table

Assuming you have decided to adopt VB .NET, you can rest assured that you have made an intelligent choice. Unlike previous editions of Visual Basic, VB .NET provides the same level of syntactic expression found in other object-oriented programming languages. For the first time in VB's 10-year history, you can build complete, feature-rich, OO applications. To wet your appetite, here is a quick rundown of some (but not all) of the features provided by Visual Basic .NET.

- *Complete object orientation.* VB programmers can now make use of classical inheritance, method overloading, and classical polymorphism.
- *Improved error handling.* To be blunt, error handling in earlier versions of VB was awful. Although you are free to make use of the infamous "On Error Goto" syntax, VB .NET now supports structured exception handling (which you get to know in Chapter 4).
- *Parameterized class construction.* No longer are you forced to build ad hoc methods to hydrate your custom types. VB .NET now supports type constructors (which can take any number of parameters).
- *Support for building multithreaded applications.* Attempting to build multithreaded applications in VB 6.0 was a dark, dreary process. Although it was possible to spawn a secondary thread of execution, you were required to bypass the VB runtime layer to do so. Not only was this dangerous, it was unnecessarily complex.
- *Full support for interface-based programming techniques.* Unlike classic COM, the interface is not the only way to manipulate types between binaries. .NET supports true object references that can be passed between boundaries (by reference or by value).
- Finally, VB .NET cleans up many unsavory aspects of VB 6.0's syntax (as you see over the course of this text).

Perhaps the most important point to understand about the VB .NET language is that it is only capable of producing code that can execute within the .NET runtime (you could never use VB .NET to build a classic COM server). Officially speaking, the term used to describe the code targeting the .NET runtime is *managed code.* The conceptual unit that contains the managed code is an *assembly.*

An Overview of .NET Binaries (aka Assemblies)

When a DLL or EXE has been created using a .NET-aware compiler, the resulting module is bundled into an assembly. You examine the complete details of .NET assemblies in Chapter 7. However, to facilitate the discussion of the .NET runtime environment, you need to examine some basic properties of this new file format.

As mentioned, an assembly contains IL code, which is conceptually similar to Java byte code in that it is not compiled to platform-specific instructions until absolutely necessary. "Absolutely necessary" is the point at which a block of IL instructions (such as a method implementation) are referenced for use by the .NET runtime engine.

In addition to IL instructions, assemblies contain metadata that describes in vivid detail the characteristics of every "type" living within the binary. For example, if you have a class named Foo contained in a given assembly, the type metadata describes details such as Foo's base class, which interfaces are implemented by Foo (if any), as well as a full description of each field, method, property, and event supported by the Foo type.

In many respects, .NET metadata is a dramatic improvement to classic COM type information. As you may already know, classic COM binaries are typically described using an associated type library (which is little more than a binary version of IDL code). The problems with COM type information is that it is not guaranteed to be present (depending on your choice of programming tools), and the fact that IDL code has no way to catalog externally referenced servers that are required for the correct operation of the contained coclasses. In contrast, .NET metadata is always present and is automatically generated by a given .NET-aware compiler.

In addition to type metadata, assemblies themselves are also described using metadata, which is officially termed a *manifest*. The manifest contains information about the current version of the assembly, any optional security constraints, locale information, and a list of all externally referenced assemblies that are required for proper execution. You examine tools that can be used to examine an assembly's underlying IL, type metadata, and information listed in the manifest later in this chapter.

Single File and Multifile Assemblies

In a great number of cases, there is a simple one-to-one correspondence between a .NET assembly and the underlying DLL or EXE binary. Thus, if you are building a .NET DLL, it is safe to consider that the binary and the assembly are one and the same. As seen in Chapter 7, however, this is not completely accurate. Technically speaking, if an assembly is composed of a single DLL or EXE module, you have a "single file assembly." Single file assemblies contain all the necessary IL, metadata, and associated manifest in one well-defined package.

Multifile assemblies, on the other hand, may be composed of numerous .NET binaries, each of which is termed a *module*. When building a multifile assembly, one of these modules must contain the assembly manifest (and possibly IL instructions). Related modules contain a *module level manifest*, IL, and type metadata.

So why would you choose to create a multifile assembly? When you partition an assembly into discrete modules, you end up with a more flexible deployment option. For example, if an end user is referencing a remote assembly that needs to be downloaded onto his or her machine, the runtime only downloads the required modules. In contrast, if all your types were placed in a single file assembly, the end user may end up downloading a large chunk of data that is not really needed (which is obviously a waste of time). Thus, as you can see, an assembly is really a *logical* grouping of one or more related modules.

The Role of Microsoft Intermediate Language

Now that you have a better feel for .NET assemblies, let's examine MSIL in a bit more detail. MSIL is a language that sits above any particular platform-specific instruction set. Regardless of which .NET aware language you choose (C#, Visual Basic .NET, Eiffel, and so forth) the associated compiler emits IL instructions. For example, the following VB .NET class definition models a trivial calculator (which is only capable of returning the sum of 10 and 84 . . .). Don't concern yourself with the exact syntax for the time being, but do notice the signature of the Add() method:

```
Module Module1
    ' The VB .NET calc. . .
    Class Calc
        Public Function Add(ByVal x As Integer, _
                            ByVal y As Integer) As Integer
            Return x + y
        End Function
    End Class
    ' The application's entry point
    Sub Main()
        Dim ans As Integer
        Dim c As New Calc()
        ans = c.Add(10, 84)
        Console.WriteLine("10 + 84 is: {0}.", ans)
    End Sub
End Module
```

Once the VB .NET compiler (vbc.exe) compiles this source code file, you end up (by default) with a single file assembly that contains a manifest, IL instructions, and metadata describing each aspect of the module. For example, if you peek inside this binary and investigate the IL instructions for the Add() method (which you learn to do later in this chapter), you find the following:

```
.method public instance int32  Add(int32 x,
                                   int32 y) cil managed
{
  // Code size       10 (0xa)
  .maxstack  2
  .locals init ([0] int32 Add)
  IL_0000:  nop
  IL_0001:  nop
  IL_0002:  ldarg.1
  IL_0003:  ldarg.2
  IL_0004:  add.ovf
  IL_0005:  br.s       IL_0008
  IL_0007:  ldloc.0
  IL_0008:  nop
  IL_0009:  ret
} // end of method Calc::Add
```

Don't worry if you are unable to make heads or tails of the resulting IL for this method. Chapter 8 examines some IL basics in greater detail. The point to concentrate on is that the VB .NET compiler emits IL, not platform-specific instructions. Now, recall that this is true of all .NET-aware compilers. To illustrate, assume you created the Calc class using C# rather than Visual Basic .NET:

```
namespace Calculator
{
    using System;

    public class Calc
    {
        // A single method.
        public int Add(int x, int y)
        { return x + y; }

        public static int Main(string[] args)
        {
            Calc c = new Calc();
            int ans = c.Add(10, 84);
            Console.WriteLine("10 + 84 is {0}.", ans);
            return 0;
        }
    }
}
```

If you examine the IL for the Add() method, you would find the same set of instructions (slightly tweaked by the C# compiler):

```
.method public hidebysig instance int32  Add(int32 x,
int32 y) cil managed
{
  // Code size       8 (0x8)
  .maxstack  2
  .locals ([0] int32 CS$00000003$00000000)
  IL_0000:  ldarg.1
  IL_0001:  ldarg.2
  IL_0002:  add
  IL_0003:  stloc.0
  IL_0004:  br.s       IL_0006
  IL_0006:  ldloc.0
  IL_0007:  ret
} // end of method Calc::Add
```

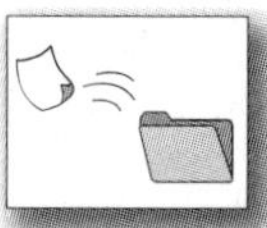

SOURCE CODE *The CSharpCalculator and VBCalculator applications are both included under the Chapter 1 subdirectory.*

Benefits of IL

At this point, you might be wondering exactly what benefits are gained by compiling source code into IL (with the associated metadata) rather than directly to a specific instruction set. One benefit of compiling to IL (with the associated metadata) is language integration. As you have already seen, each .NET-aware language produces the same underlying IL. As you see in the next section, the same holds true with regard to the generated type metadata. Therefore, all languages are able to interact within a well-defined binary arena.

Given that IL is platform agnostic, it is very possible that the .NET runtime will be ported to other (non-Windows) operating systems in the future. In this light, the .NET runtime is poised to become a platform-independent architecture, providing the same benefits Java developers have grown accustomed to (that is, the potential of a single code base running on numerous operating systems). Unlike Java however, .NET allows you to build applications in a language-independent fashion.

Thus, .NET has the potential to allow you to develop an application in *any* language and have it run on *any* platform supporting the .NET runtime.

Again, the crux of the last paragraph is "potential platform independence." At the time of this writing, there is no official word from Microsoft regarding the platform-agnostic nature of .NET. For now, you should assume that .NET is only equipped to run on the Windows family of operating systems (however, the writing seems to be on the proverbial wall).

The Role of Metadata

COM programmers are without a doubt familiar with the Interface Definition Language (IDL). IDL is a "metalanguage" that is used to describe in unambiguous terms the types contained within a given COM server. IDL is compiled into a binary format (termed a type library) using the midl.exe compiler, which can then be consumed by a COM-aware client to understand the contained types.

In addition to describing the types within a COM binary, IDL has minimal support to describe characteristics about the server itself, such as its current version (e.g., 1.0, 2.0, or 2.4) and intended locale (e.g., English, German, Urdu, Russian). The problem with COM metadata is that it may or may not be present and it is often the role of the programmer to ensure the underlying IDL accuracy reflects the internal types. The .NET framework makes no use of IDL whatsoever. However, the spirit of describing the types residing within a particular binary lives on.

In addition to the underlying IL instructions, a .NET assembly contains complete and accurate metadata. Like IDL, .NET metadata describes each and every type (class, structure, enumeration, and so forth) defined in the binary, as well as the members of each type (fields, properties, methods, and events).

Furthermore, the .NET manifest is far more complete than IDL in that it also describes each *externally* referenced assembly that is required by this assembly to operate. Because .NET metadata is so wickedly meticulous, assemblies are completely self-describing entities. In fact, .NET binaries have no need to be registered into the system registry (more on that little tidbit later).

A Quick Metadata Example

As an example, let's take a look at the metadata that has been generated for the Add() method of the C# Calculator class you examined previously (the metadata generated for the VB .NET Calculator class is identical):

```
Method #2
-------------------------------------
MethodName: Add (06000002)
Flags     : [Public] [HideBySig] [ReuseSlot]  (00000086)
RVA       : 0x00002058
ImplFlags : [IL] [Managed]  (00000000)
CallCnvntn: [DEFAULT]
hasThis
ReturnType: I4
2 Arguments
     Argument #1:  I4
     Argument #2:  I4
2 Parameters
     (1) ParamToken : (08000001) Name : x flags: [none] (00000000) default:
     (2) ParamToken : (08000002) Name : y flags: [none] (00000000) default:
```

Here you can see that the Add() method, return type, and method arguments have been fully described by the C# compiler (and yes, you see how to view type metadata and IL later in this chapter).

Metadata is used by numerous aspects of the .NET runtime environment, as well as by development tools. For example, the IntelliSense feature provided by Visual Studio.NET is made possible by reading an assembly's metadata at design time. Metadata is also used by object-browsing utilities, debugging tools, and the VB .NET compiler itself.

Compiling IL to Platform-Specific Instructions

Due to the fact that assemblies contain IL instructions and metadata, rather than platform specific instructions, the underlying IL must be compiled on the fly before use. The entity that compiles the IL into meaningful CPU instructions is termed a just-in-time (JIT) compiler that sometimes goes by the friendly name of "Jitter." The .NET runtime environment supplies a JIT compiler for each CPU targeting the CLR. In this way, developers can write a single body of code that can be JIT-compiled and executed on machines with different architectures.

As the Jitter compiles IL instructions into corresponding machine code it caches the results in memory. In this way, if a call is made to a method named Bar() defined within a class named Foo, the Bar() IL instructions are compiled into platform-specific instructions on the first invocation and retained in memory for later use. Therefore, the next time Bar() is called, there is no need to recompile the IL.

.NET Types and .NET Namespaces

A given assembly (single file or multifile) may contain any number of distinct *types*. In the world of .NET, a type is simply a generic term used to collectively refer to classes, structures, interfaces, enumerations, and delegates. When you build solutions using a .NET aware language (such as VB .NET), you interact with each of these types. For example, your assembly may define a single class that implements some number of interfaces. Perhaps one of the interface methods takes a custom enum type as an input parameter.

As you build your custom types, you have the option of organizing your items into a *namespace*. In a nutshell, a namespace is a logical naming scheme used by .NET languages to group related types under a unique umbrella. When you group your types into a namespace, you provide a simple way to circumvent possible name clashes between assemblies.

For example, if you were building a new Windows Forms application that references two external assemblies, and each assembly contained a type named GoCart, you would be able to specify which GoCart class you are interested in by appending the type name to the target namespace (i.e., "CustomVehicals.GoCart" not "SlowVehicals.GoCart").

Understanding the Common Language Runtime

Now that you have an understanding of types, assemblies, metadata, and IL, you can begin to examine the .NET runtime engine in a bit greater detail. Programmatically speaking, the term *runtime* can be understood as a collection of services that are required to execute a given block of code. For example, when developers make use of the Microsoft Foundation Classes (MFC) to create a new application, they are (painfully) aware that their binary is required to link with the rather hefty MFC runtime library (mfc42.dll). Other popular languages have a corresponding runtime. Visual Basic 6.0 programmers are also tied to a runtime module or two (e.g., msvbvm60.dll). Java developers are tied to the Java Virtual Machine (JVM). You get the picture.

The .NET platform offers yet another runtime system. The key difference between the .NET runtime and the runtimes previously mentioned is the fact that the .NET runtime provides a single well-defined runtime layer that is shared by all languages that are .NET aware. As mentioned earlier in this chapter, the .NET runtime is officially termed the Common Language Runtime, or simply CLR.

The CLR consists of two core entities. First we have the runtime execution engine, mscoree.dll (which, unlike the VB runtime, will eventually become part of the operating system itself). When an assembly is referenced for use, mscoree.dll is loaded automatically, which in turn loads the required assembly into memory. The runtime engine is responsible for a number of tasks. First and foremost, it is the entity in charge of resolving the location of an assembly and finding the requested type (e.g., class, interface, structure) within the binary by reading the supplied metadata. The execution engine compiles the associated IL into platform-specific instructions and performs any (optional) security checks as well as related tasks.

The second major entity of the CLR is the base class library. Although the entire base class library has been broken into a number of discrete assemblies, the primary binary is mscorlib.dll. This .NET assembly contains a large number of core types that encapsulate a wide variety of common programming tasks. When building .NET solutions, you always make use of this particular assembly, and perhaps other .NET binaries (both system supplied and custom).

Figure 1-3 illustrates the basic workflow that takes place between your source code (which is making use of base class library types), a given .NET compiler, and the .NET execution engine.

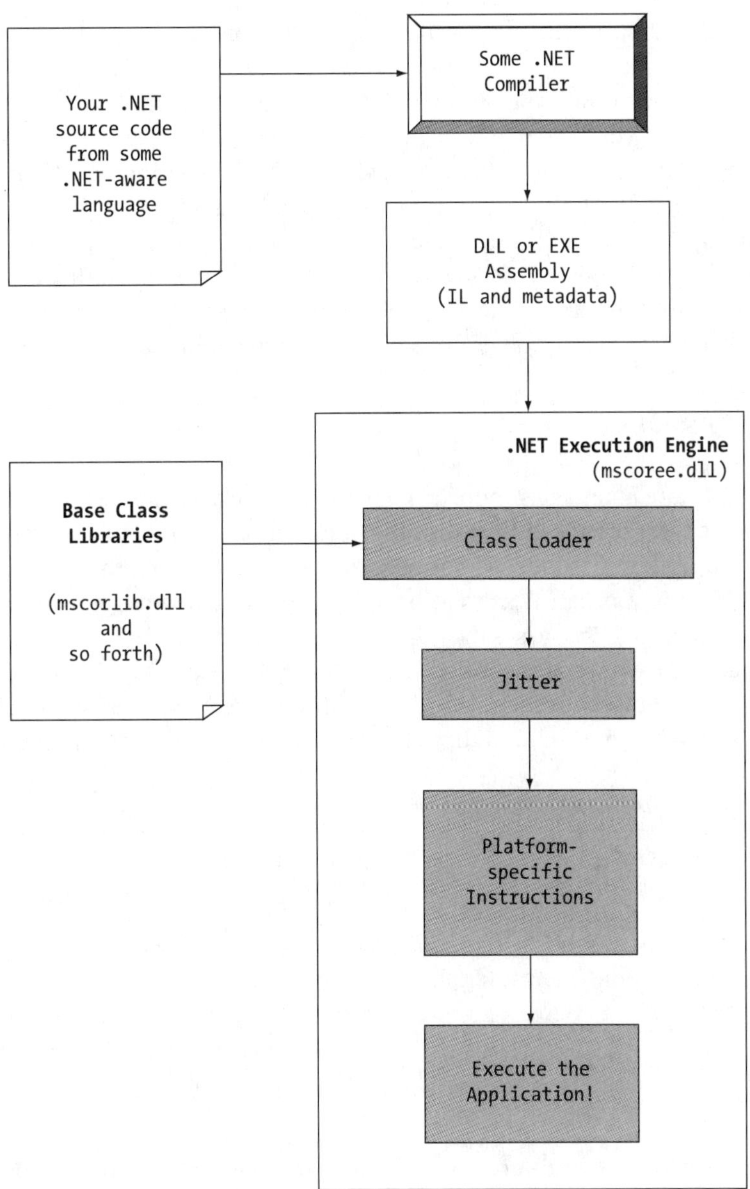

Figure 1-3. mscoree.dll in action

Understanding the Common Type System

Recall that the Common Type System (CTS) is a formal specification that describes how a given type (class, structure, interface, enum, etc.) must be defined to be hosted by the CLR. Also recall that the CTS defines a number of syntactic constructs (such as operator overloading) that may or may not be supported by a given .NET-aware language. When you want to build assemblies that can be used by all possible .NET-aware languages, you need to conform your exposed types to the rules of the CLS (mentioned in just a moment). For the time being, let's preview the formal definitions of various members of the CTS.

CTS Class Types

Every .NET-aware language supports the notion of a "class type," which is the cornerstone of object-oriented programming. A class is composed of any number of fields, properties, methods, and events. As you would expect, the CTS allows a given class to support abstract members that provide a polymorphic interface for any derived classes. CTS classes may only derive from a single base class (multiple inheritance is not allowed for class types). To help you keep your wits about you, Table 1-1 documents a number of characteristics of interest to class types. You see the exact VB .NET syntax behind these terms as you progress throughout the text.

Table 1-1. NET Class Characteristics

CLASS CHARACTERISTIC	MEANING IN LIFE
Is the class "sealed" or not?	Sealed classes are types that cannot function as a base class to other classes.
Does the class implement any interfaces?	An interface is a collection of abstract members that provide a contract between the object and object user. The CTS allows a class to implement any number of interfaces.
Is the class abstract or concrete?	Abstract classes cannot be directly created, but are intended to define common behaviors for derived types. Concrete classes can be created directly.
What is the "visibility" of this class?	Each class must be configured with a visibility attribute. Basically this trait defines if the class may be used by external assemblies, or only from within the containing assembly (e.g., an internal helper class).

CTS Structure Types

The concept of a structure is also formalized by the CTS. Visual Basic 6.0 supports the "Type" keyword, which allows you to construct a user-defined type (UDT) that groups together related points of data. In VB .NET, the "Type" keyword has been replaced by the word "Structure."

In general, a structure is a lightweight value type (as explained in Chapter 3). CTS structures may define any number of parameterized constructors (however, the no-argument constructor is reserved). In this way, you are able to establish the value of each field when it is constructed. While the use of structures is best suited for modeling numerical entities (points, rectangles, complex numbers, and whatnot) the following example offers a bit more pizzazz:

```
' Create a VB .NET structure.
Structure Baby
    'Structures can contain fields.
    Public name As String
    ' Structures may take methods.
    Public Sub Cry()
        Console.WriteLine("Waaaaaaaaaaaah!!!")
    End Sub
    Public Function IsSleeping() As Boolean
        Return False
    End Function
    Public Function IsChanged() As Boolean
        Return False
    End Function
End Structure
```

Here is our structure in action:

```
Dim emma As Baby
Console.WriteLine("Changed?: {0}", emma.IsChanged().ToString())
Console.WriteLine("Sleeping?: {0}", emma.IsSleeping().ToString())
'Show your true colors Emma Close.
Dim i As Integer
For i = 0 To 5
    emma.Cry()    ' Yes you do need () here!
Next
```

All CTS structures are derived from a common base class: System.ValueType. This base class configures a structure to function as a value-based (stack) data type rather than a reference-based (heap) entity. Be aware that the CTS allows structures to implement any number of interfaces; however structures may not derive from other types and are therefore always "sealed."

CTS Interface Types

Interfaces are nothing more than a collection of method, property, and event definitions. Unlike classic COM, .NET interfaces do not derive a common base interface such as IUnknown. On their own, interfaces are of little use. However when a class or structure implements a given interface in its unique way, you are able to request access to the supplied functionality using an interface reference. When you build custom interfaces using a .NET-aware programming language, the CTS permits a given interface to derive from multiple base interfaces. Again, you examine interface-based programming in Chapter 5.

Members of a CTS Type

As you have just seen, classes and structures can take any number of members. Formally speaking, a member is from the set {field, method, property, event}. These are examined in detail over the next several chapters. However, do be aware that the CTS defines the various "adornments" that may be associated with a given member.

For example, each member has a given "visibility" trait (e.g., Public, Private, Protected, and Friend). A member may be declared "MustInherit" to enforce a polymorphic behavior on derived types or using the "Shadows" keyword to hide a base class implementation. Members may also be "Shared" (bound at the class level) or bound at the object level (the default behavior).

CTS Enumeration Types

Enumerations are a handy programming construct that allow you to group name/value pairs under a specific name. For example, assume you are creating a video game application that allows the end user to select one of three player types (Wizard, Fighter, or Thief). Rather than keep track of raw numerical values to represent each possibility, you could build a custom enumeration:

```
'A VB .NET enumeration.
Enum PlayerType
      Wizard = 100
      Fighter = 200
      Thief = 300
End Enum
```

While this looks more or less like a VB 6.0 enumeration, be aware that the CTS demands that enumerated types derive from a common base class, System.Enum. As you discover in Chapter 3, this base class defines a number of interesting members that allow you to extract (and manipulate) the underlying name/value pairs.

CTS Delegate Types

Delegates are the .NET equivalent of a type safe C style function pointer (i.e., a variable that points to some memory location). The key difference is that a .NET delegate is a class that derives from MulticastDelegate, rather than a raw memory address. Given this, .NET delegates are object-oriented, type safe, and secure. These types are useful when you want to provide a way for one entity to forward a call to another entity. As you learn in Chapter 6, delegates provide the foundation for the .NET event protocol.

Intrinsic CTS Data Types

The final aspect of the CTS to be aware of is that it establishes a well-defined set of intrinsic data types. Although a given language may use a unique keyword to declare an intrinsic data type, all languages alias the same type defined in the .NET class libraries. Consider Table 1-2.

Table 1-2. The Intrinsic CTS Data Types

.NET BASE CLASS	VISUALBASIC.NET REPRESENTATION	C# REPRESENTATION	C++ WITH MANAGED EXTENSIONS REPRESENTATION
System.Byte	Byte	byte	char
System.SByte	Not supported	sbyte	signed char
System.Int16	Short	short	short
System.Int32	Integer	int	int or long
System.Int64	Long	long	__int64
System.UInt16	Not supported	ushort	unsigned short
System.UInt32	Not supported	uint	unsigned int or unsigned long
System.UInt64	Not supported	ulong	unsigned __int64
System.Single	Single	float	float
System.Double	Double	double	double
System.Object	Object	object	Object*
System.Char	Char	char	__wchar_t
System.String	String	string	String*
System.Decimal	Decimal	decimal	Decimal
System.Boolean	Boolean	bool	bool

As you can see, not all languages are able to represent the same intrinsic data members of the CTS. This could be a huge bother if you attempt to use an assembly that makes use of CTS features not supported by your language. As you might imagine, it would be very helpful to create a well-known subset of the CTS that defines a common, shared set of programming constructs (and types) for all .NET-aware languages. Enter the CLS.

Understanding the Common Language Specification

Different languages express the same programming constructs in language-specific terms. For example, in C#, string concatenation is denoted using the plus operator (+) and in Visual Basic you make use of the ampersand (&). As well, even when two distinct languages express the same programmatic construct (for example, a method with no return value) the chances are good that the syntax appears quite different on the surface:

```
' VB .NET method with no return value (aka VB subroutines).
Public Sub Foo()
End Sub

// C# method with no return value (aka method returning void)
public void Foo()
{
}
```

As you have already seen, these minor syntactic variations are inconsequential in the eyes of the .NET runtime, given that the respective compilers (vbc.exe or csc.exe in this case) are configured to emit the same IL instruction set. However languages can also differ with regard to their overall levels of functionality. For example some languages allow you to overload operators for a given type while others do not. Some languages may support the use of unsigned data types, which do not map correctly in other languages. What's needed is a baseline to which all .NET aware languages conform.

The Common Language Specification (CLS) is a set of guidelines that describe in detail, the minimal but complete set of features a given .NET-aware compiler must support to produce code that can be hosted by the CLR and be used uniformly between all languages that target the .NET platform. In many ways the CLS can be viewed as a subset of the full functionality defined by the CTS.

Be very aware that VB .NET is only capable of emitting CLS-compliant code (which is a good thing). In this way, VB programmers can rest assured that the code they write can be consumed by any other language targeting the .NET runtime. This is not (necessarily) true of C#. C# programmers have non-CLS compliant features that they may employ for a more exotic solution. However, if a C# developer writes code that falls outside the realm of CLS compliance, they have effectively built an assembly that is not usable across all .NET languages. In Chapter 8, you are introduced to an assembly level attribute that forces all exposed types to jibe with the CLS (which I assume you will tell your C# cohorts to be well aware of).

The CLS is ultimately a set of rules that tool builders must conform to, if they want their products to function seamlessly within the .NET universe. Each rule is assigned a simple name (e.g., "CLS Rule 6"), and the rule describes how it will affect those who build the tools as well as those who (in some way) interact with the tools. For example, the crème de la crème of the CLS is the mighty Rule 1:

- **Rule 1**: CLS rules apply only to those parts of a type that are exposed outside the defining assembly.

Given this statement you can (correctly) infer that the remaining rules of the CLS do not apply to the internal logic used to build the inner workings of a .NET type. For example, assume you are building a .NET tool that exposes its services to the outside world using three classes, each of which defines a single function. Given Rule 1, the only aspect of the classes that must conform to the CLS are the member functions themselves (i.e., the member's visibility, naming conventions, parameters, and return types). The internal implementations of each method can use any number of non-CLS techniques —the outside world won't know the difference.

Of course, the CLS defines other rules. For example, the CLS describes how a given language must represent text strings, how enumerations should be represented internally (the base type used for storage), how to use static types, and so forth. Remember that in most cases these rules do not have to be committed to memory (unless you build the next generation of LISP.NET!).

Working with Namespaces

Now that you have examined various aspects of the .NET runtime, you can turn your attention to the base class libraries. Each of us understands the importance of code libraries. The point of libraries such as MFC or ATL is to give developers a well-defined set of existing code to leverage in their applications. For example, MFC defines a number of C++ classes that provide canned implementations of dialog boxes, menus, and toolbars. This is a good thing for the MFC programmers of the world, as they can spend less time reinventing the wheel, and more time building a custom solution. Visual Basic and Java offer similar notions: intrinsic classes/functions and packages, respectively.

Unlike MFC or Java, the VB .NET language does not come with a predefined set of language-specific classes. Ergo, there is no VB .NET class library. Rather, VB .NET developers leverage existing types supplied by the .NET framework. To keep all the types within this binary well organized, the .NET platform makes extensive use of the namespace concept.

The key difference between this approach and a language-specific library such as MFC, is that any language targeting the .NET runtime makes use of the same namespaces and same types as a C# developer. For example, the following three programs illustrate the ubiquitous "Hello World" application, written in C#, VB .NET, and C++ with managed extensions (MC++):

```
// Hello world in C#
using System;
public class MyApp
```

```
{
     public static void Main()
     { Console.WriteLine("Hi from C#"); }
}

' Hello world in VB .NET
Imports System
Public Module MyApp
     Sub Main()
          Console.WriteLine("Hi from VB .NET")
     End Sub
End Module

// Hello world in Managed C++ (MC++)
#using <mscorlib.dll>
using namespace System;
// Note! The .NET runtime secretly wraps the global
// C++ main function inside a class definition.
void main()
{ Console::WriteLine("Hi from MC++"); }
```

Notice that each language makes use of the Console class defined in the System namespace. Beyond minor syntactic variations, these three applications look and feel alike, both physically and logically. As you can see, the .NET platform has brought a streamlined elegance to the world of software engineering.

A Tour of the .NET Namespaces

Your primary goal as a .NET developer is to get to know the types defined in the base class namespaces. The most critical namespace to get your mind around is named "System." This namespace provides a core body of types that you will leverage time and again as a .NET developer. In fact, you cannot build any working application without at least making reference to the System namespace.

Namespaces are little more than a way to group semantically related types (classes, enumerations, interfaces, delegates, and structures) under a single umbrella. For example, the System.Drawing namespace contains a number of types to assist you in rendering images onto a graphics device. Other namespaces exist for data access, Web development, threading, and programmatic security. From a very high level, Table 1-3 offers a rundown of some (but certainly not all) of the .NET namespaces.

Table 1-3. A Sampling of .NET Namespaces

.NET NAMESPACE	MEANING IN LIFE
System	Within System you find numerous low-level classes dealing with primitive types, mathematical manipulations, garbage collection, and so forth.
System.Collections	This namespace defines a number of stock container objects (ArrayList, Queue, SortedList).
System.Data System.Data.Common System.Data.OleDb System.Data.SqlClient	These namespaces are (of course) used for database manipulations. You examine each of these later in this book.
System.Diagnostics	Here, you find numerous types that can be used by any .NET-aware language to debug and trace the execution of your source code.
System.Drawing System.Drawing.Drawing2D System.Drawing.Printing	Here, you find numerous types wrapping GDI+ primitives such as bitmaps, fonts, icons, printing support, and advanced rendering classes.
System.IO	This namespace is full of IO manipulation types, including file IO, buffering, and so forth.
System.Net	This namespace (as well as other related namespaces) contains types related to network programming (request/response, sockets, etc.).
System.Reflection System.Reflection.Emit	Defines items that support runtime type discovery and dynamic creation and invocation of custom types.
System.Runtime.InteropServices System.Runtime.Remoting	Provides facilities to interact with "unmanaged code" (e.g., Win32 DLLs, COM servers).
System.Security	Security is an integrated aspect of the .NET universe. Here you find numerous classes dealing with permissions, cryptography, and so on.
System.Threading	You guessed it, this namespace deals with threading issues. Here you find types such as Mutex, Thread, and Timeout.
System.Web	A number of namespaces are specifically geared to developing Web applications, including ASP.NET.

Table 1-3. A Sampling of .NET Namespaces (continued)

.NET NAMESPACE	MEANING IN LIFE
System.Windows.Forms	Despite the name, the .NET platform does contain namespaces that facilitate the construction of more traditional Win32 main windows, dialog boxes, and custom widgets.
System.Xml	Contains numerous classes that represent core XML primitives and types to interact with XML based data.

Accessing a Namespace Programmatically

It is worth pointing out that a namespace is nothing more than a convenient way for us mere humans to logically understand and organize related types. For example, consider again the System namespace. From your perspective, you can assume that System.Console represents a class named Console that is contained within a namespace called System. However, in the eyes of the .NET runtime, this is not so. The runtime engine only sees a single entity named System.Console.

In VB .NET, the "Imports" keyword simplifies the process of accessing types defined in a particular namespace. Here is how it works. Let's say you are interested in building a traditional main window. This window renders a pie chart based on some information obtained from a back end database and displays your company logo using a Bitmap type. While learning the types each namespace contains takes time and experimentation, here are some obvious candidates to reference in your program:

```
' Here are all the namespaces used to build this application.
Imports System                          ' General base class library types.
Imports System.Drawing                  ' GDI+ Rendering types.
Imports System.Windows.Forms            ' GUI widget types.
Imports System.Data                     ' General data centric types.
Imports System.Data.OleDb               ' OLE DB access types.
```

Once you have referenced some number of namespaces, you are free to create instances of the types they contain. For example, if you are interested in creating an instance of the Bitmap class (defined in the System.Drawing namespace), you can write:

```
' Explicitly list the namespace. . .
Imports System.Drawing
Public Class MyClass
     Public Sub DoIt()
          ' Create a 20 * 20 pixel bitmap.
          Dim bm as Bitmap =  New Bitmap(20, 20)   ' Calling a constructor!
     End Sub
End Class
```

Because your application is referencing System.Drawing, the compiler is able to resolve the Bitmap class as a member of this namespace. If you did not directly reference System.Drawing in your application, you are issued a compiler error. However, you are free to declare variables using a fully quailed name as well:

```
' Not listing namespace!
Public Class MyClass
    Public Sub DoIt()
         ' Using fully qualified name.
         Dim bm As System.Drawing.Bitmap = _
            New System.Drawing.Bitmap(20, 20)
         . . .
    End Sub
End Class
```

I think you get the general idea: Explicitly specifying namespaces reduces keystrokes.

Referencing External Assemblies

In addition to referencing a namespace via the Imports keyword, you also need to tell the compiler the name of the assembly containing the actual IL. As mentioned, many core .NET namespaces live within mscorlib.dll. System.Drawing is contained in a separate binary named System.Drawing.dll. By default, the system-supplied assemblies are located under <drive>: \WINNT\Microsoft.NET\Framework\<version> as seen in Figure 1-4 (do note that the version identifier may differ, based on your current installation of .NET).

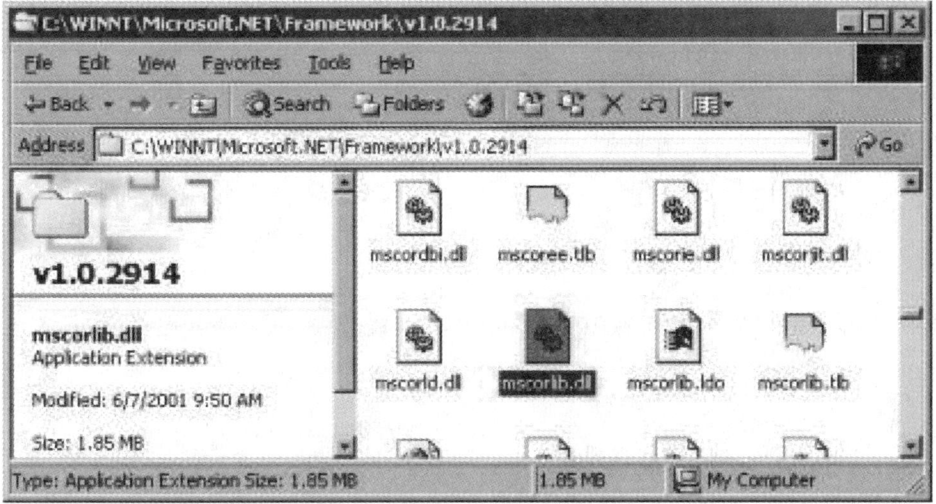

Figure 1-4. The base class libraries

Depending on the development tool you are using to build your .NET types, you have various ways to tell the compiler which assemblies you want to include in the compilation cycle. You examine how to do so in Chapter 2.

Increasing Your Namespace Nomenclature

If you are beginning to feel a tad overwhelmed at the thought of gaining mastery over every nuance of the .NET world, just remember that what makes a namespace unique is that the items it defines are all semantically related. Therefore, if you have no need for a user interface beyond a simple console application, you can forget all about the System.Windows.Forms and System.Drawing namespaces (among others). If you are building a painting application, the database programming namespaces are most likely of little concern. Like any new set of prefabricated code, you learn as you go.

Throughout the course of this book, you are exposed to numerous aspects of the .NET platform and related namespaces. As it would be impractical to detail every type contained in every namespace in a single book, you should be aware of the following techniques that can be used to learn more about the .NET libraries:

- .NET SDK online documentation (MSDN).
- The ILDasm.exe utility.
- The ClassView Web application.
- The WinCV.exe desktop application.
- The Visual Studio.NET Object Browser

I think it's safe to assume you know what to do with the supplied online Help (remember, F1 is your friend). However it is important that you understand how to work with the ILDasm.exe, ClassView and WinCV.exe utilities, each of which is shipped with the .NET SDK. You examine the VS.NET Object Browser in Chapter 2.

Using ILDasm.exe

The Intermediate Language Disassembler utility (ILDasm.exe) allows you to load up any .NET assembly (EXE or DLL) and investigate its contents (including the associated manifest, IL instruction set, and type metadata) using a friendly GUI. By default, this is located under C:\Program Files\Microsoft.NET\FrameworkSDK\bin (as are many other .NET specific tools). Once you launch this tool, proceed to the "File | Open" menu command and navigate to the assembly you want to explore. For the time being, open mscorlib.dll (Figure 1-5). Note the path of the opened assembly is documented in the caption of the ILDasm.exe utility.

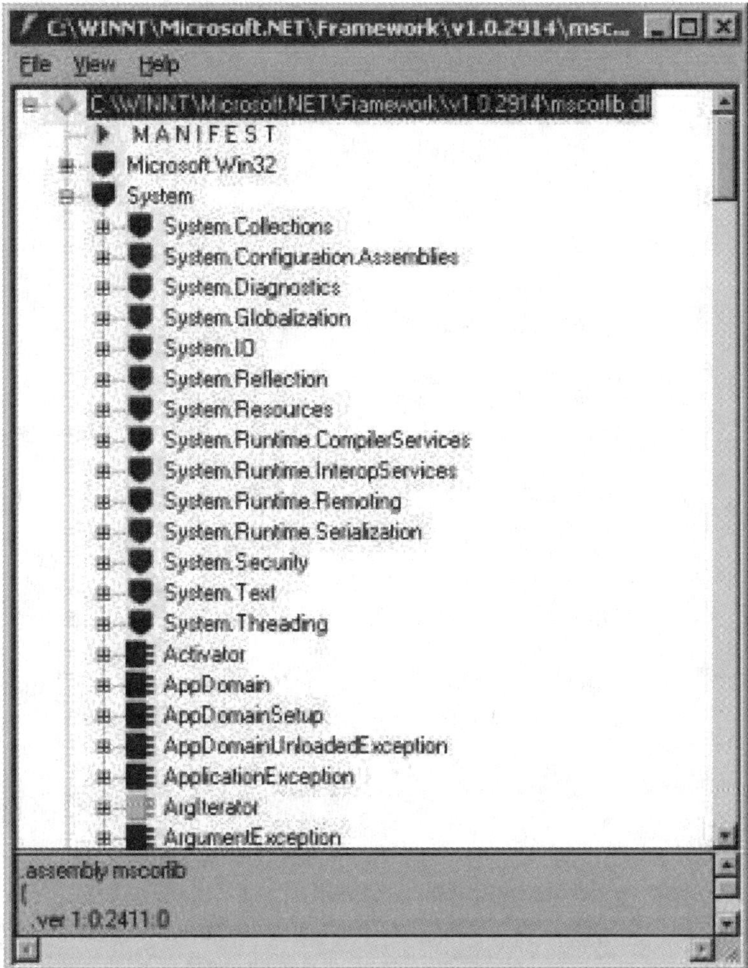

Figure 1-5. Your new best friend, ILDasm.exe

As you can see, the structure of an assembly is presented in a familiar tree view format. While exploring a given type, notice that the methods, properties, and nested classes for a given type are identified by a specific icon. Table 1-4 lists some of the more common iconic symbols and text-dump abbreviations.

Table 1-4. ILDasm.exe Icons

ILDASM.EXE SYMBOL	TEXT DUMP ABBREVIATION	MEANING IN LIFE
	. (dot)	This icon signifies that additional information is available for a given type. In some cases, double-clicking the item will jump to a related node in the tree.
	[NSP]	Represents a namespace.
	[CLS]	Signifies a class type. Be aware that nested classes are marked with the <outer class>$<inner class> notation.
	[VCL]	Represents a structure type.
	[INT]	Represents an interface type.
	[FLD]	Represents a field (e.g., public data) defined by a given type.
	[STF]	Represents a shared (e.g., class level) field defined by a given type.
	[MET]	Represents a method of a given type.
	[STM]	Represents a shared method of a given type.
	[PTY]	Signifies a property supported by the type.

Beyond allowing you to explore the types (and members of a specific type) contained in a given assembly, ILDasm.exe also allows you to view the underlying IL instructions for a given item. To illustrate, locate and double-click the icon for the Close() method of the System.IO.BinaryWriter class. This launches a separate window, displaying the IL shown in Figure 1-6.

```
BinaryWriter::Close : void()
.method public hidebysig newslot virtual
        instance void  Close() cil managed
{
  // Code size       8 (0x8)
  .maxstack  8
  IL_0000:  ldarg.0
  IL_0001:  ldc.i4.1
  IL_0002:  callvirt   instance void System.IO.Binary
  IL_0007:  ret
} // end of method BinaryWriter::Close
```

Figure 1-6. Viewing the underlying IL

Dumping Namespace Information to File

The next point of interest with regard to ILDasm.exe is the very useful ability to dump the relational hierarchy of an assembly into a text file. In this way, you can make hard copies of your favorite assemblies to read at your neighborhood coffeehouse (or brewpub). To do so, select "File | Dump TreeView" and provide a name for the resulting *.txt file. As you look over the dump, notice that the identifying icons have been replaced with their corresponding textual abbreviations (see the previous table). Ponder Figure 1-7.

```
assemblylisting.txt - Notepad
File  Edit  Format  Help
___[MOD] C:\WINNT\Microsoft.NET\Framework\v1.0.2914\msco
   |      M A N I F E S T
   |___[NSP] Microsoft.Win32
   |   |___[CLS] OAVariantLib
   |   |   |       .class private auto ansi sealed beforef
   |   |   |        extends System.Object
   |   |   |___[STF] AlphaBool : public static literal i
   |   |   |___[STF] CV_OBJECT : private static literal
   |   |   |___[STF] CalendarHijri : public static liter
   |   |   |___[STF] ClassTypes : static assembly initon
   |   |   |___[STF] LocalBool : public static literal i
   |   |   |___[STF] NoUserOverride : public static lite
   |   |   |___[STF] NoValueProp : public static literal
   |   |   |___[STF] VARCMP_EQ : private static literal
   |   |   |___[STF] VARCMP_GT : private static literal
   |   |   |___[STF] VARCMP_LT : private static literal
   |   |   |___[STF] VARCMP_NULL : private static litera
```

Figure 1-7. Dumping namespace information to file

Dumping IL Instructions to File

On a related note, you are also able to dump the IL instructions for a given assembly to file, using the "File | Dump" menu option. Once you configure your dump options, you are asked to specify a location for the *.il file. Assuming you have dumped the contents of mscorlib.dll to file you can view its contents. (Figure 1-8 shows the IL for a method you come to know [and love] in Chapter 8, GetType().)

```
test.il - Notepad
File  Edit  Format  Help

    .method /*06000002*/ public hidebysig
            instance class System.Type/* 020000CF */
            GetType() il managed
    // SIG: 20 00 12 83 3C
    {
      // Method begins at RVA 0x20d4
      // Code size       19 (0x13)
      .maxstack  1
      .locals (class System.Type/* 020000CF */ V_0)
      IL_0000:  /* 02   |                  */ ldarg.0
      IL_0001:  /* 28   | (06)000004       */ call
      IL_0006:  /* 0A   |                  */ stloc.0
      IL_0007:  /* 06   |                  */ ldloc.0
      IL_0008:  /* 2D   | 07               */ brtrue.s

      IL_000a:  /* 02   |                  */ ldarg.0
      IL_000b:  /* 28   | (06)000003       */ call
      IL_0010:  /* 0A   |                  */ stloc.0
      IL_0011:  /* 06   |                  */ ldloc.0
      IL_0012:  /* 2A   |                  */ ret
    } // end of method Object::GetType
```

Figure 1-8. Dumping IL to file

Viewing Type Metadata

ILDasm.exe has additional options that can be discovered from the supplied online Help. Although I assume you will investigate these options on your own, one item of interest is the "CTRL + M" keystroke. As you recall, .NET-aware compilers emit IL and metadata that is used by the CLR to interact with a given type. Once you load an assembly into ILDasm.exe, press CTRL + M to view the generated type metadata. Now, be aware that the larger the assembly, the longer it takes to disassemble the binary! To offer a preview of things to come, Figure 1-9 shows the metadata for the TestApp.exe assembly you create in Chapter 2.

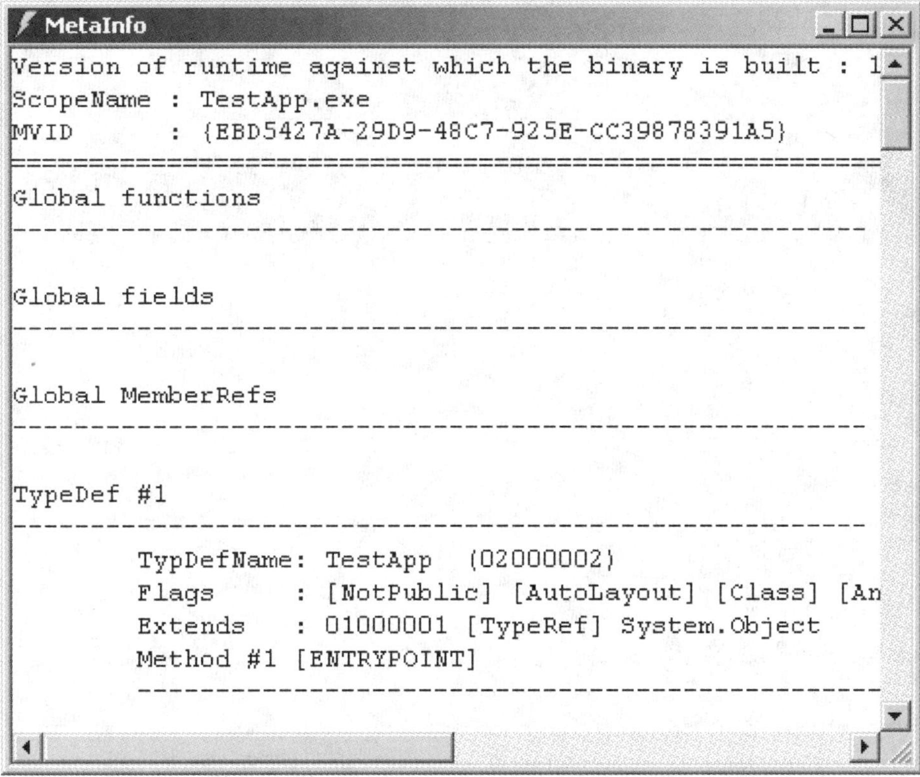

Figure 1-9. Viewing type metadata with ILDasm.exe

If you have not realized it by now, ILDasm.exe is in many ways the .NET equivalent of the OLE/COM Object Viewer utility (oleview.exe). Oleview.exe is the tool of choice to learn about classic COM servers and examine the underlying IDL behind a given binary. ILDasm.exe is the tool of choice to examine .NET assemblies, the underlying IL, and related metadata.

The ClassViewer Web Application

In addition to ILDasm.exe, the ClassViewer sample application (shipped with the .NET SDK) is yet another way to explore the .NET namespaces. Once you have installed the samples shipped with the SDK, launch Internet Explorer and navigate to http://localhost/quickstart/aspplus/samples/classbrowser/vb/classbrowser.aspx (note that the exact location of this Web application may change in future releases of .NET). This enables you to examine the relationship of types in a more Web-savvy manner (Figure 1-10).

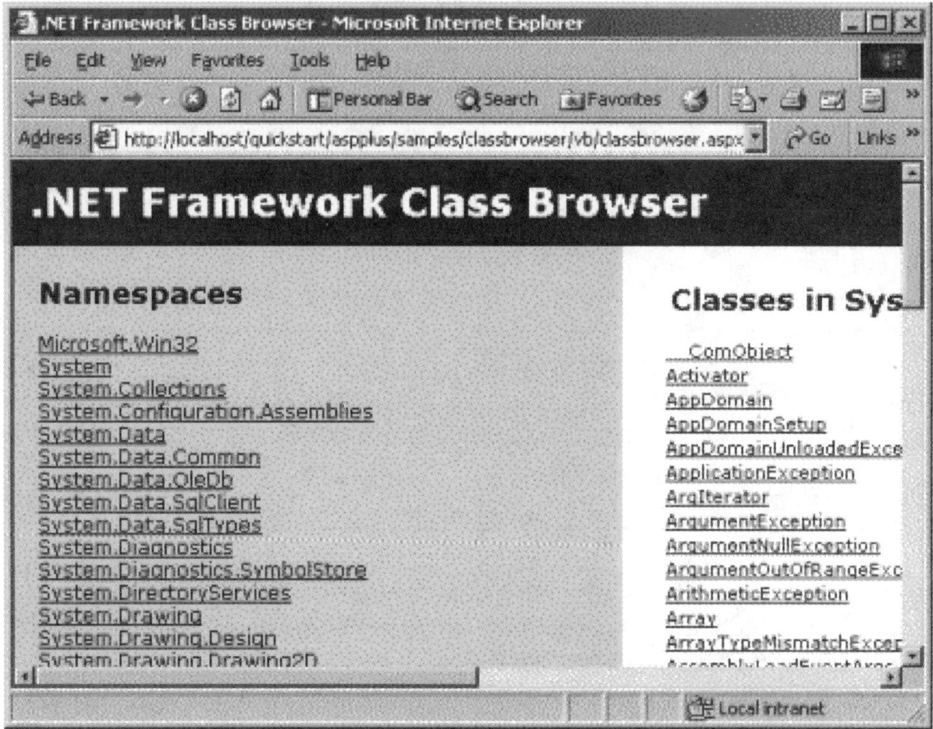

Figure 1-10. Viewing types using the ClassViewer Web application

The WinCV.exe Desktop Application

The final tool to be aware of is WinCV.exe (Windows Class Viewer), located under C:\Program Files\Microsoft.NET\FrameworkSDK\bin. This application allows you to browse the underlying C# type definition in the base class libraries (at the time of this writing, this tool does not support an option to show the equivalent VB .NET definition). Do be aware that the base class libraries were (in fact) written using the C# programming language. Thus, even if you are a die-hard VB programmer, it behooves you to become comfortable viewing C# code.

The GUI of this tool is quite simple: Type the name of the item you want to explore, and the underlying source code definitions are displayed on the right-hand side. Figure 1-11 shows the member set for the System.Windows.Forms.ToolTip class.

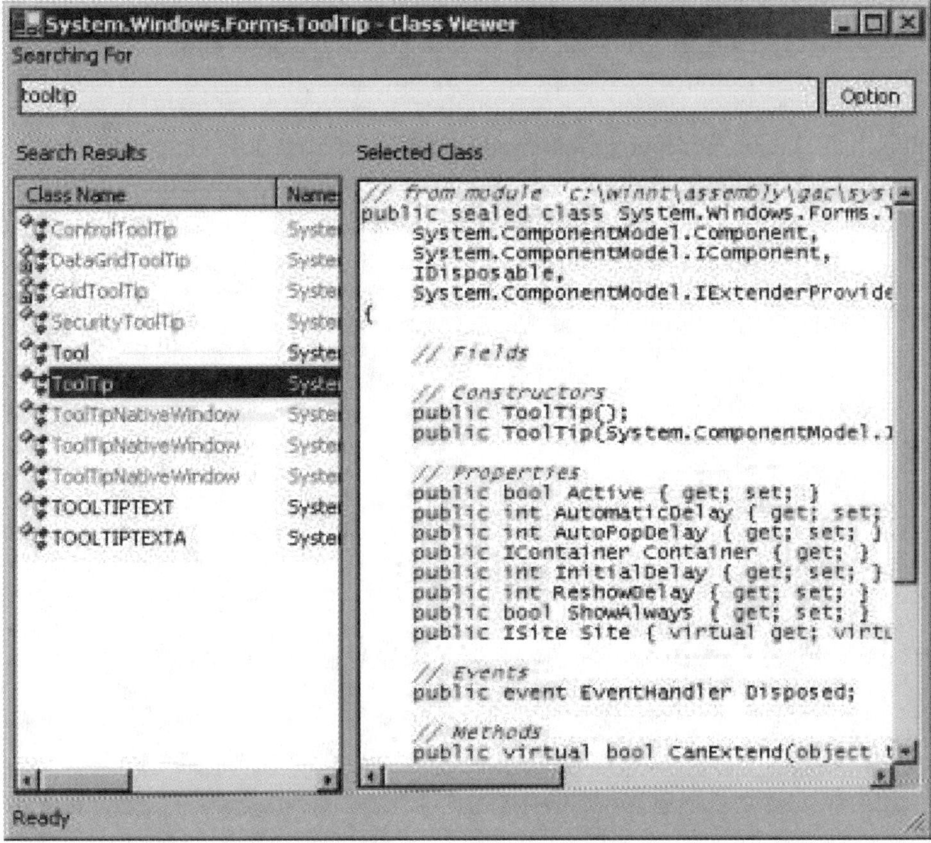

Figure 1-11. Working with WinCV.exe

Now that you have a number of strategies that you can use to explore the entirety of the .NET universe, the time has come to examine how to build some VB .NET applications.

Summary

The point of this chapter was to lay out the conceptual framework necessary for the remainder of this book. It began by examining a number of limitations and complexities found within the technologies that exist today, and followed up with an overview of how .NET and VB .NET attempt to improve on them.

.NET is basically a runtime execution engine (mscoree.dll) and base class library (mscorlib.dll and friends). The Common Language Runtime (CLR) is able to host any .NET binary (aka "assembly") that abides by the rules of managed code. As you have seen, assemblies contain IL instructions (and accompanying metadata) that are compiled to platform-specific instructions using a just-in-time (JIT) compiler. In addition, you explored the role of the Common Language Specification (CLS) and Common Type System (CTS).

CHAPTER 2

Building Visual Basic .NET Applications

VISUAL BASIC .NET IS ONE of many languages hosted by Visual Studio .NET (VS .NET). Unlike previous editions of Microsoft IDEs (Integrated Development Environments), VS .NET provides a common GUI shell that spans across languages. In this chapter, you get a grand tour of the key features of VS .NET IDE, and learn about common configuration options, as well as core design time tools. The chapter opens with an examination of the VB .NET compiler: vbc.exe, wraps up with a discussion of the Microsoft.VisualBasic namespace, and addresses the issue of VB 6.0 / Visual Basic .NET compatibility.

Building VB .NET Applications Using the Command Line Compiler

The first option you have as a VB .NET developer is to compile your assemblies using the stand-alone compiler, vbc.exe (Visual Basic Compiler), which is included in the .NET SDK, and is freely downloadable from Microsoft. While it is true that you may never decide to build an entire application using the raw VB .NET compiler, it is important to understand the basics of how to compile your *.vb files by hand. I can think of two reasons you should get a grip on the basics:

- The most obvious reason is the simple fact that you might not have a copy of Visual Studio .NET (but do have the .NET SDK). If this is the case, you will need to make use of vbc.exe as you move through this text.

- Another reason is this very important fact: Design time editors, wizards, and configuration dialogs do little more than save you typing time. The more you understand what happens "under the hood" the stronger your programming muscle becomes. As you use VS .NET to build applications, you are ultimately instructing the raw VB .NET compiler how to manipulate your *.vb input files. In this light, it's edifying to see what takes place behind the scenes.

Another nice byproduct of working with vbc.exe in the raw, is that you become that much more comfortable manipulating other command line tools included with the .NET SDK. As you will see throughout this book, a number of important tools are only accessible from the command prompt.

Configuring the VB .NET Compiler

Before you can begin to make use of the command line compiler, you need to ensure that your development machine recognizes the vbc.exe tool. Ideally, vbc.exe is configured correctly at the time you install the .NET SDK. However, in my experiences teaching various .NET classes, I have found (the hard way) this is not always the case. If vbc.exe is not configured correctly, you are forced to change to the directory containing vbc.exe before you can compile your programs (which is a massive pain in the neck). To equip your development machine to run vbc.exe from *any* subdirectory, follow these steps:

- Right-click the My Computer icon from your desktop and select Properties from the pop-up menu.
- Select the Advanced tab and click the Environment Variables. . . button.
- Double click the Path variable from the System Variables list box.
- Add the following line to the end of the current value (note each value is separated by a semicolon, as shown in Figure 2-1).

```
C:\WINNT\Microsoft.NET\Framework\v1.0.2914
```

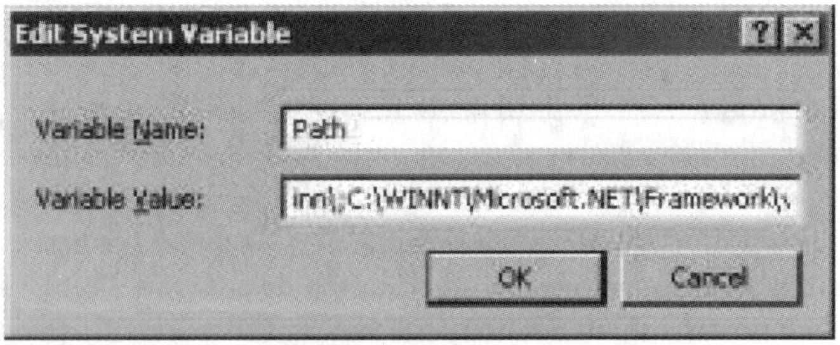

Figure 2-1. Establishing the path to vbc.exe

Of course, the exact path name may need to be adjusted based on your version and location of the .NET SDK. To take a test run, open a Command window and type "vbc." If you set things up correctly, you should see a display of each option supported by the raw command line compiler (Figure 2-2).

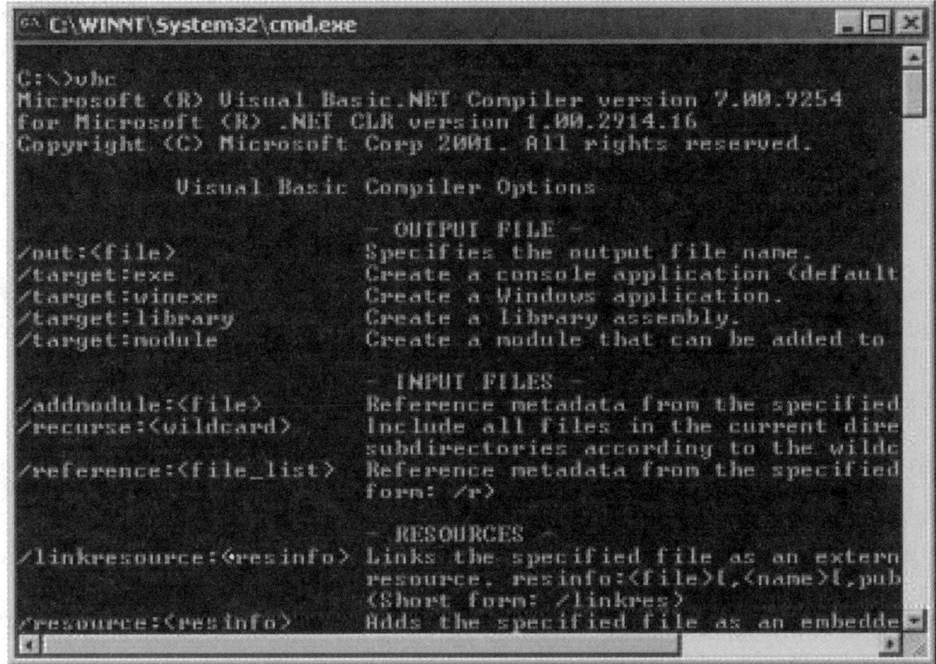

Figure 2-2. Options of the Visual Basic .NET compiler

Building Your First VB .NET Application

The goal in this section is to build a simple single file assembly named TestApp.exe. First, you need some VB .NET source code. Open a text editor (notepad.exe is fine), and enter the code seen in Figure 2-3. Save the file (in a convenient location) as TestApp.vb.

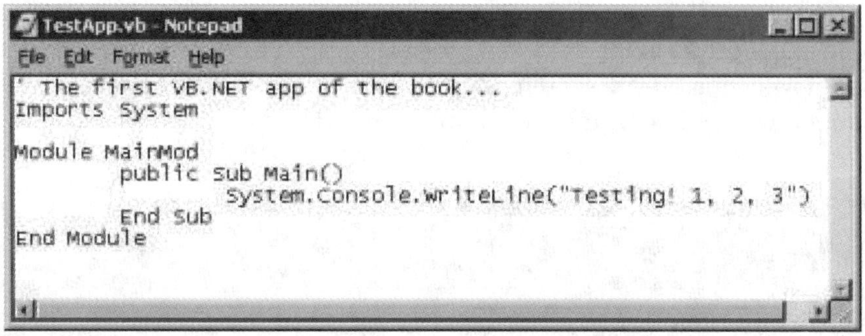

```
TestApp.vb - Notepad
File Edit Format Help
' The first VB.NET app of the book...
Imports System

Module MainMod
        public Sub Main()
                System.Console.WriteLine("Testing! 1, 2, 3")
        End Sub
End Module
```

Figure 2-3. The TestApp class

Now, let's get to know the core options of the VB .NET compiler. The first point of interest is to understand how to specify the sort of output file you are interested in obtaining (e.g., a Console application, a DLL, a Windows EXE application). Each option is represented by a specific flag that is sent into vbc.exe as a command line parameter (Table 2-1).

Table 2-1. Output Options of the VB .NET Compiler

FILE OUTPUT OPTION	MEANING IN LIFE
/out	Used to specify the name of the output file (e.g., MyAssembly.dll, WordProcessingApp.exe, etc.) By default, the name of the output file is the same as the name as the input *.vb file, and thus the /out flag can be omitted.
/target:exe	This option builds an EXE Console application (i.e., a DOS-style application). This is the default file output type, and thus may be omitted when building this application type.
/target:library	This option builds a single file DLL assembly, with a related manifest.
/target:module	This option builds a "module" which, as you recall, is a DLL that does not contain a related assembly manifest (used to build multifile assemblies, as you do in Chapter 7).
/target:winexe	Although you are free to build Windows-based applications using the /target:exe flag, this option hides the console window that appears while the application is running.

Thus, to compile the TestApp.vb file into a console application, you would use the following command set (note that the output flags must come before the name of the VB .NET file not after):

```
vbc /target:exe TestApp.vb
```

Be aware that each of the VB .NET command line flags has an abbreviated version. Such as "/t" rather than "/target":

```
vbc /t:exe TestApp.vb
```

Furthermore, given that the /t:exe flag is the default used by the VB .NET compiler, you could also compile the TestApp.vb file by saying:

```
vbc TestApp.vb
```

To try this for yourself: Open a command window and change to the directory containing your TestApp.vb file. Then, enter the previous command and hit return. This builds TestApp.exe, which can now be run from the command line (see Figure 2-4).

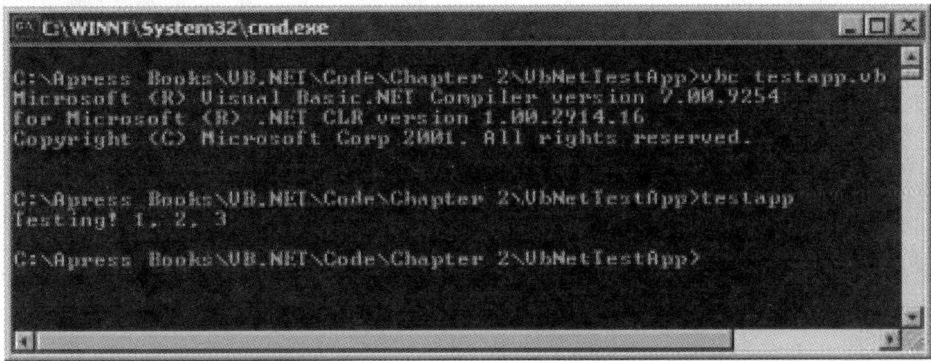

Figure 2-4. The TestApp in action

The first thing that should strike you is the fact that you have just created a Console application using Visual Basic! One of VB's greatest strengths is the fact that it allows you to build complex GUIs with minimal fuss and bother. One limitation of previous versions of Visual Basic is the lack of support for building simple command line applications. VB .NET is the first version that supports this type of UI.

These applications (while far less sexy than a Forms-based or HTML-based front end) can be useful when you need to build a program that requires a minimal graphical user interface. Perhaps the application in question prompts the user for input to perform a calculation or establish machine-wide settings. The initial chapters of this text make use of simple Command window applications to ensure that you are able to focus on the syntax of VB .NET rather than focusing on the complexities of building GUIs using the Windows Forms or ASP.NET namespaces.

Referencing External Assemblies

Next, you need to examine how to build an application that makes use of types defined in a separate .NET assembly. In case you are wondering how the VB .NET compiler understood your reference to the System.Console class, realize that mscorlib.dll is automatically referenced during the compilation process. To illustrate referencing additional .NET assemblies, let's update the TestApp application to launch a Windows Forms message box. Thus, open your TestApp.vb file and update it as shown in Figure 2-5.

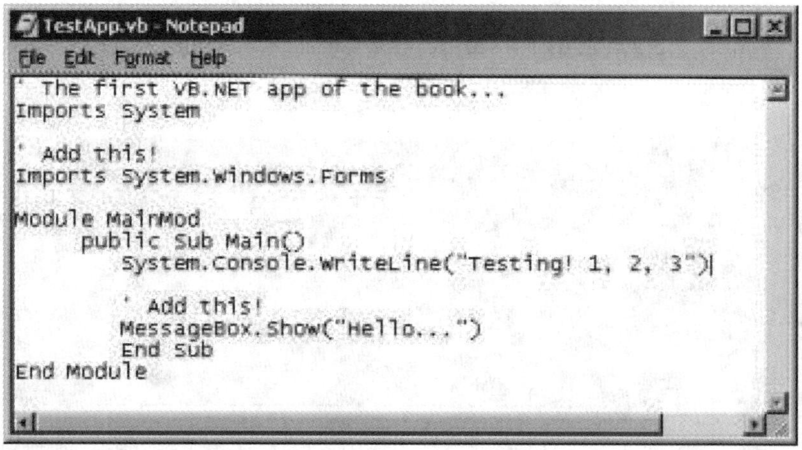
TestApp.vb - Notepad
File Edit Format Help
' The first VB.NET app of the book...
Imports System
' Add this!
Imports System.Windows.Forms
Module MainMod
public Sub Main()
System.Console.WriteLine("Testing! 1, 2, 3")
' Add this!
MessageBox.Show("Hello...")
End Sub
End Module

Figure 2-5. The updated TestApp.vb file

Notice the reference to the System.Windows.Forms namespace using the VB .NET "Import" directive (explained in Chapter 1). In order for the compiler to resolve the MessageBox class, you must specify the System.Windows.Forms.dll assembly as a compiler option by using the /reference flag (which can be abbreviated to /r). Be aware that the /reference flag must not have a space between the colon and assembly name:

```
vbc /r:System.Windows.Forms.dll testapp.vb
```

If you now rerun your application, you should see what appears in Figure 2-6.

Figure 2-6. Your first Windows Forms application

Compiling Multiple Source Files

The current incarnation of the TestApp.exe application was created using a single *.vb source code file (as well as a single external assembly). Of course, most projects are composed of multiple *.vb files. To illustrate, assume you have created the additional class shown in Figure 2-7.

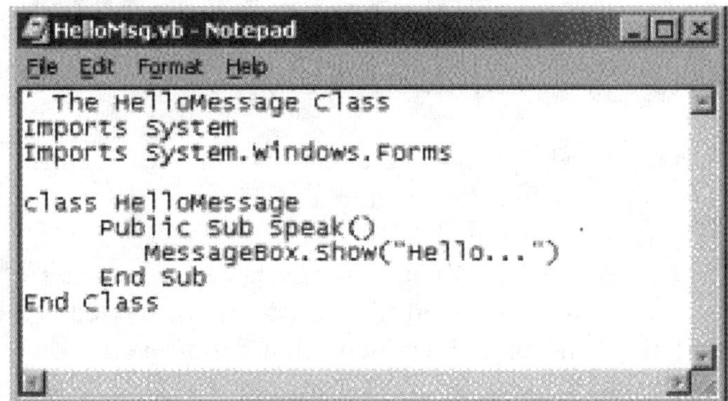

Figure 2-7. The HelloMessage class type

Now, update your previous class to make use of this new type as shown in Figure 2-8.

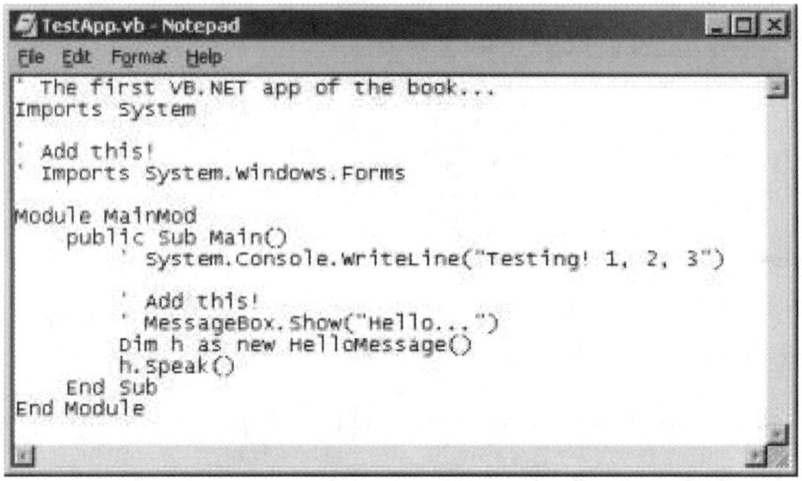


```
' The first VB.NET app of the book...
Imports System

' Add this!
' Imports System.Windows.Forms

Module MainMod
    public Sub Main()
        ' System.Console.WriteLine("Testing! 1, 2, 3")

        ' Add this!
        ' MessageBox.Show("Hello...")
        Dim h as new HelloMessage()
        h.Speak()
    End Sub
End Module
```

Figure 2-8. The updated TestApp.vb file

You can compile this multifile application by listing each *.vb file explicitly:

```
vbc /r:System.Windows.Forms.dll testapp.vb hellomsg.vb
```

When you run the program again, the output is identical. The only difference between the two applications is the fact that the current logic has been split among multiple files.

On a related note, the VB .NET compiler allows you to make use of the wildcard character (*) to inform vbc.exe to add all *.vb files contained in the current directory as part of the current build. When you use this option, you must specify the name of the output file (/out):

```
vbc /r:System.Windows.Forms.dll /out:TestApp.exe *.vb
```

Referencing Multiple External Assemblies

Now, what if you need to reference numerous external assemblies? Simply list each assembly using a comma-delimited list. You don't need to do this for your current example, but some sample usage follows:

```
vbc /r:System.Windows.Forms.dll,System.Drawing.dll testapp.vb hellomsg.vb
```

As you might guess, the VB .NET compiler has many other flags that may be used to control how the resulting binary is generated. You can explore these options on your own using online Help (do a search for "Visual Basic Compiler Options"). You learn additional flags of the vbc.exe compiler during the discussion of multifile assemblies (see Chapter 7).

SOURCE CODE *The VbNetTestApp application is included under the Chapter 2 subdirectory.*

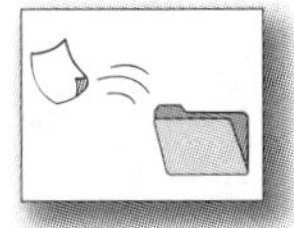

Building VB .NET Applications Using the Visual Studio .NET IDE

Now that you have had the chance to build a VB .NET application in the raw, turn your attention to the Visual Studio.NET IDE. As mentioned, this product allows you to build applications using any number of languages. Thus, you make use of VS .NET when you build VB .NET, C#, MFC, ATL or traditional C-based Win32 applications. The one thing you *cannot* do is build a traditional Visual Basic 6.0 application using VS .NET. If you want to create classic COM servers (or any additional VB 6.0 project types) you need to make use of the Visual Basic 6.0 IDE (and yes, it is safe to have each IDE installed on a single development machine).

Let's take some time to examine the core features of the Visual Studio.NET IDE (the operative word being *core*). You see other aspects of the development environment as necessary throughout this text.

The VS .NET Start Page

By default, the first thing you see when you launch Visual Studio.NET is the Start Page (Figure 2-9). For your purposes now, you need only be concerned with the Get Started and My Profile configuration options (the remaining options allow you to connect to the Internet to view online resources, obtain product updates, and whatnot).

The Get Started view allows you to open existing projects (including the items in the most recent list) and create a brand new project workspace. Be aware that these options are all available from the File menu.

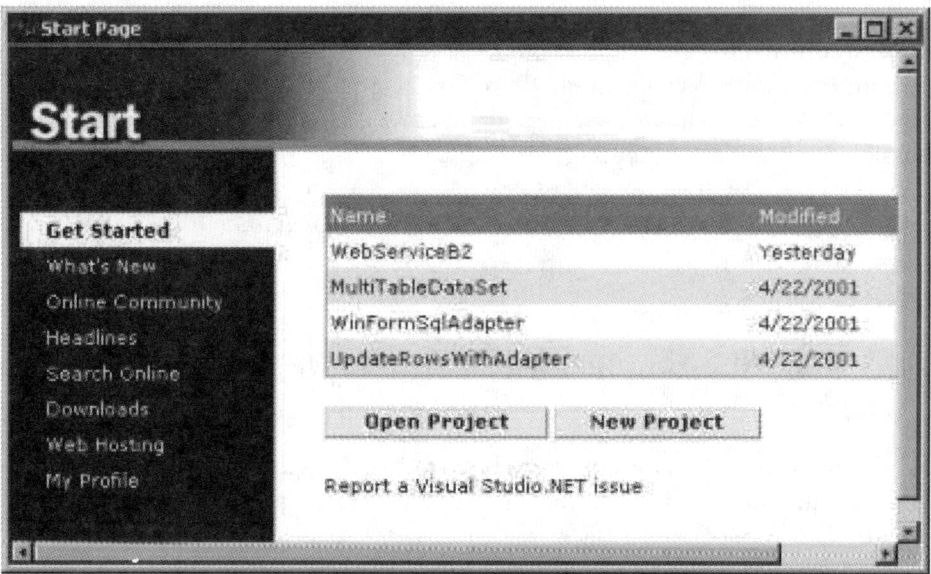

Figure 2-9. The VS .NET Start Page

If you click on the My Profile link, you are shown something like what you see in Figure 2-10.

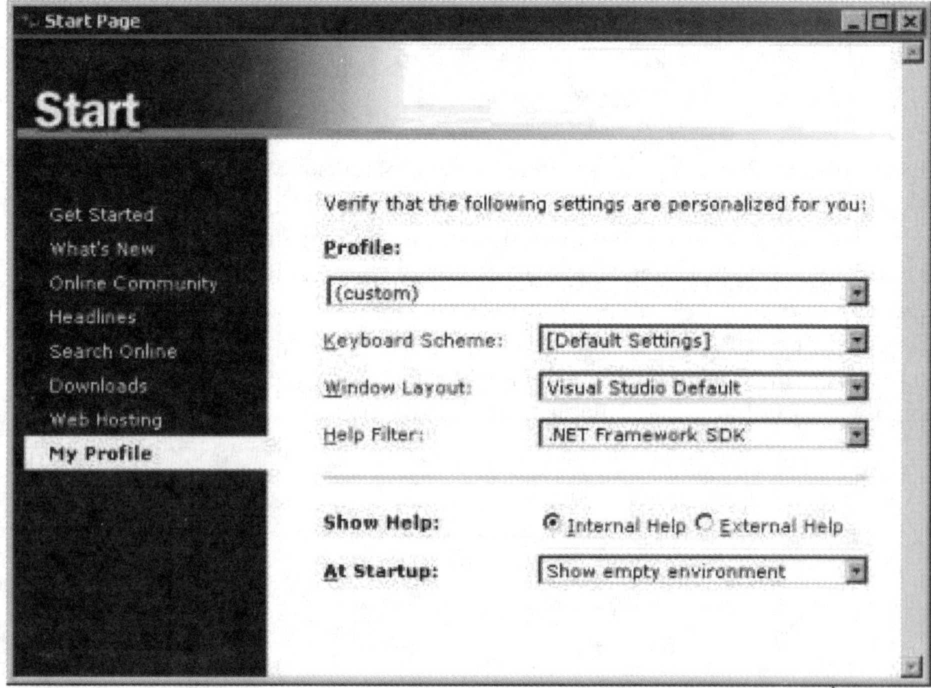

Figure 2-10. The My Profile page

Here, you are able to control how the VS .NET IDE should be configured each time you launch the tool. For example, the Keyboard Scheme drop-down list allows you to control which keyboard mapping should be used. If you want, you can opt to have your shortcut keys configured to work as VB 6.0, Visual C++ 6.0, or the default VS .NET settings.

Other options allow you to configure how online Help should be filtered (and displayed), as well as how the core IDE windows (i.e., Properties, Toolbox, etc.) should display themselves. To check things out first hand, take a moment to select the various options found under the Window Layout drop-down list and find a look and feel you are comfortable with.

Finally, be aware that if you close the Start Page window (and want to get it back), access the Help | Show Start Page menu option. On a related note, if you do not want to see the Start Page, you may disable its automatic display using the At Startup drop-down list from the My Profile section.

Creating a VS .NET Project Solution

Our next stop on the tour is to get to know the various types of VB .NET project workspaces. Open the New Project dialog box by clicking on the New Project button from the Start Page, or by choosing the File | New | Project menu selection. As you can see from Figure 2-11, project types are grouped (more or less) by language.

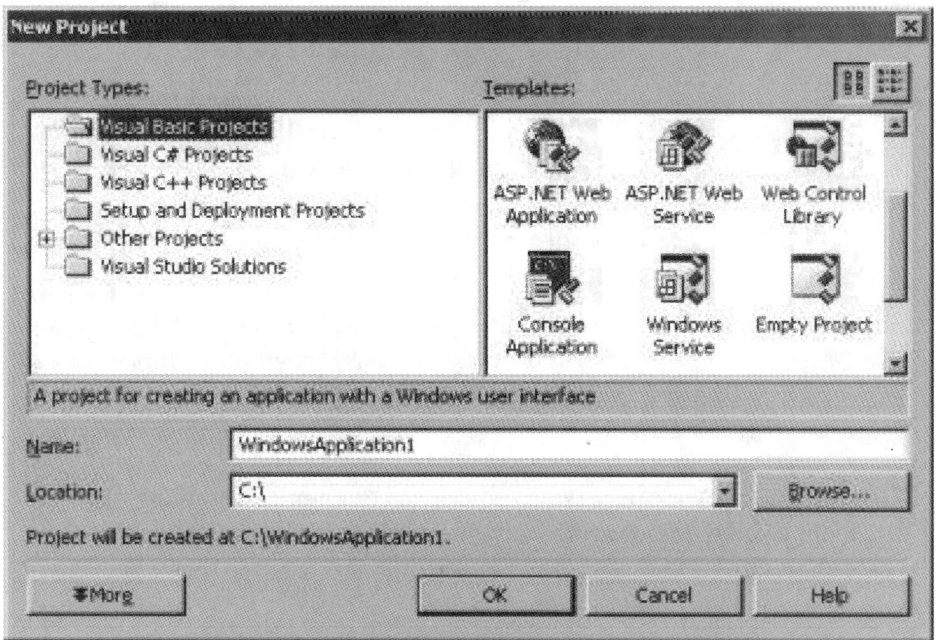

Figure 2-11. The New Project dialog box

Table 2-2 offers an explanation of each possible VB .NET project type.

Table 2-2. Project Workspace Types

PROJECT TYPE	MEANING IN LIFE
Windows Application	This project type represents a Windows Forms application. You begin building GUI-based applications in Chapter 9.
Class Library	This option allows you to build a single file assembly (DLL). Conceptually, this is much like the VB 6.0 ActiveX DLL workspace type (without the COM infrastructure).
Windows Control Library	This type of project allows you to build a single file assembly (DLL) that contains custom Windows Forms Controls. Again, this is analogous to the VB 6.0 ActiveX Control workspace type. You learn how to build custom Windows Forms controls in Chapter 11.
ASP.NET Web Application	Select this option when you want to build an ASP.NET Web application (as you do in Chapter 15).
ASP.NET Web Service	This option allows you to build a .NET Web Service. As shown in Chapter 16, a .NET Web Service is a block of code reachable using HTTP requests.
Web Control Library	VS .NET also allows you to build customized Web controls. As you see in Chapter 16, these GUI widgets are responsible for emitting HTML back to a requesting browser.
Console Application	The good old Command window. As mentioned, you spend the first number of chapters working with this type of project type, just to keep focused on the syntax and semantics of VB .NET.
Windows Services	VB .NET allows you to build NT / 2000 services. As you may know, these are background worker applications which are launched during the OS boot process.

The remaining workspace types require no comment. They simply create empty workspaces that are configured to launch the vbc.exe compiler.

Building Your VS .NET Test Application

To illustrate the basic mechanics of this new IDE, let's build a new Console application that mimics the functionality of the previous TestApp. To get started, create a brand-new VB .NET Console application named VbVsTestApp.

The Solution Explorer Window

VS .NET logically arranges a given project using a solution metaphor. Simply put, a "solution" is a collection of one or more "projects." Each project contains any number of source code files, external references, and resources that constitute the application as a whole. Do be aware that regardless of which project workspace type you create, the *.sln file can be opened using VS .NET to load each project in the workspace. Each VB .NET project is marked with the *.vbproj file extension. Using the Solution Explorer window, you are able to view and open any such item (Figure 2-12). Notice the default name of your initial module is "Module1.vb."

Figure 2-12. The Solution Explorer

One radical difference between VB 6.0 and VB .NET projects is the fact that all of your VB .NET source code is placed in *.vb files. Recall that in VB 6.0, numerous file extensions (*.frm, *.bas, *.cls) were used to contain different types of code. As you will see, VB .NET supplies a new set of keywords (Class, Interface,

Module, and so forth) that are used to designate the type of entity you are building. Given this, the vbc.exe compiler has no need to work with various file extensions to understand the contained code.

Notice as well that the Solution Explorer window provides a Class View tab, which shows the object-oriented view of your project (Figure 2-13). Do note that the Resource View tab is not visible by default, but can be activated using the View menu.

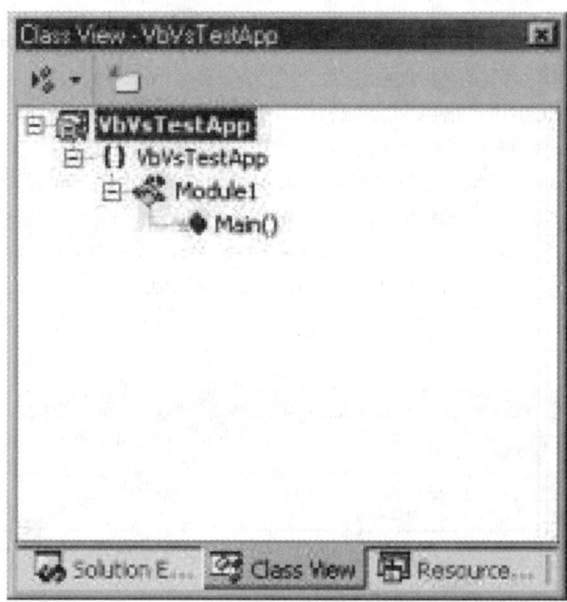

Figure 2-13. Class View

As you would expect, when you right click a given item, you activate a context-sensitive pop-up menu. The menu lets you access a number of tools that allow you to configure the current project settings and sort items in a variety of ways. For example, right-click the Solution node from Class View and check out Figure 2-14.

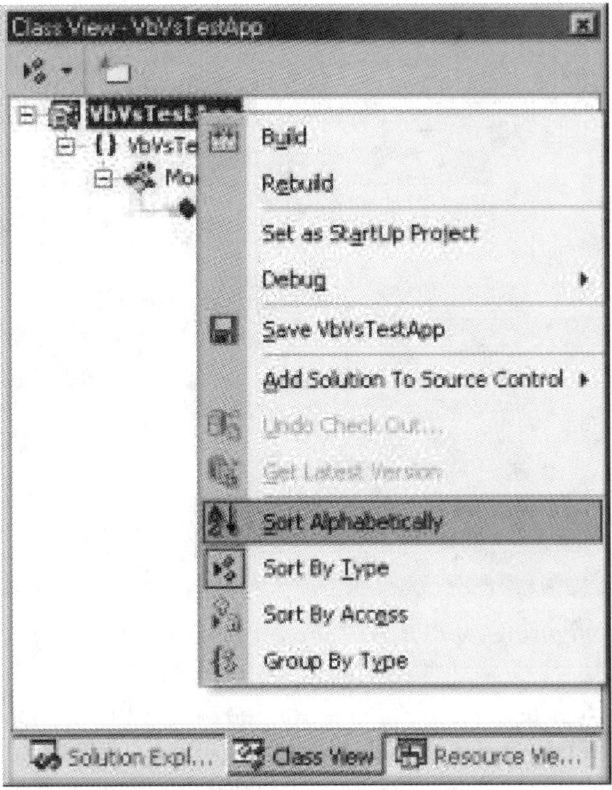

Figure 2-14. Type sorting options

Configuring a VB .NET Project

Now, switch back to the Solution Explorer tab. Right-click the VbVsTestApp project node, and select Properties from the context menu. This launches the all-important Project Property Page (Figure 2-15).

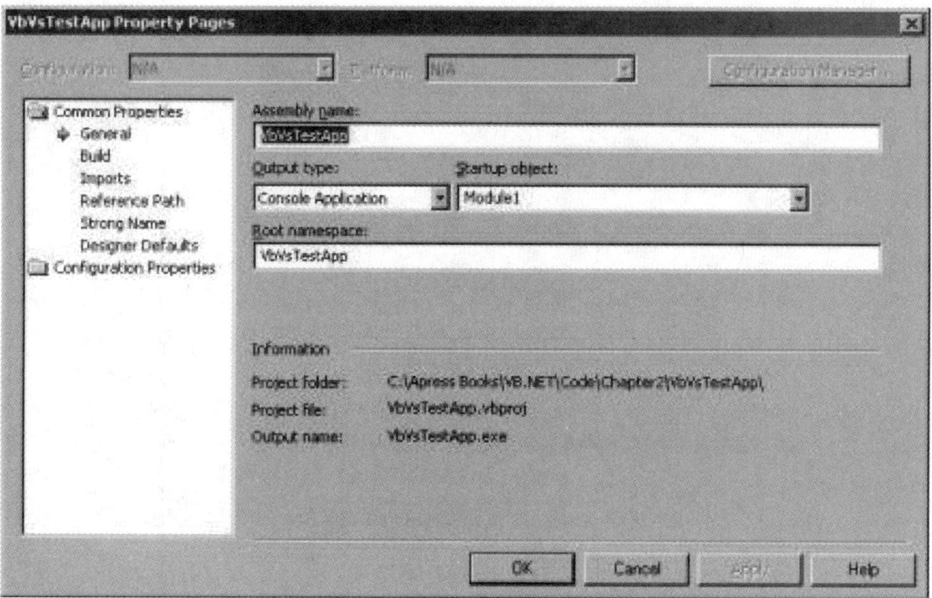

Figure 2-15. Configuring your VB .NET project starts here

This dialog provides a number of intriguing settings. To begin, when you select the General node, you are able to configure the type of output file that should be produced by vbc.exe (as you can guess, this is a GUI-based alternative to specifying the /output: flag). You are also able to configure which item in your application should be marked as the Startup object (meaning, the type in the application that contains the Main() method). Finally, notice that the General node also allows you to configure the root namespace for this particular project (by default this is the same name as your project). You revisit the role of namespaces in Chapter 3, so just make a mental note of this option for now.

Project "Option" Options

Next, select the Build node (Figure 2-16). As you can also see, the Project Properties window allows you to establish project-wide options for your current development effort. Like VB 6.0, VB .NET supports the Option Explicit setting, which ensures that variables are spelled and declared correctly (Unlike VB 6.0, Option Explicit is enabled by default. . .which is a good thing).

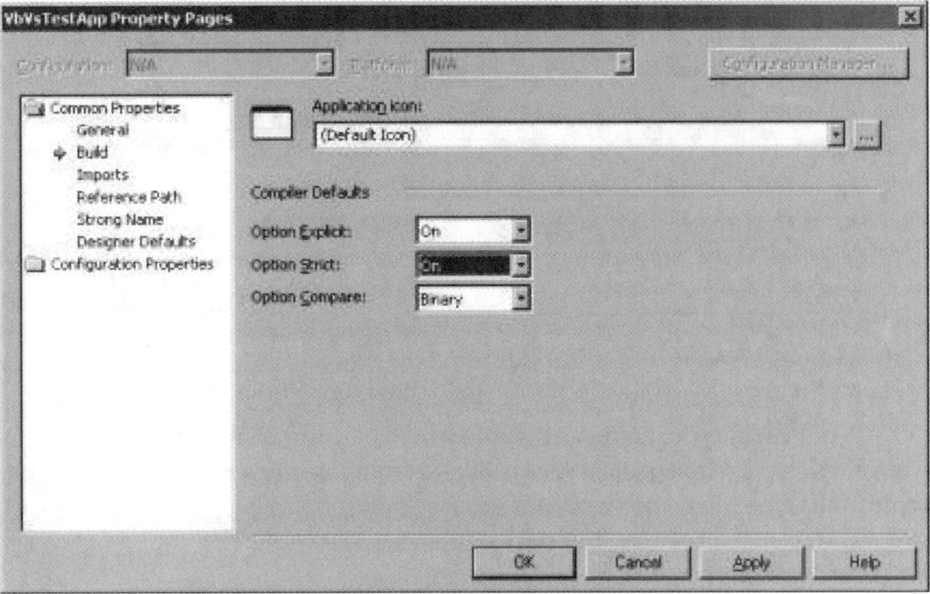

Figure 2-16. Project build options

Option Strict is new. Although this option is turned Off by default (as of Beta 2), let's see why you *always* want to enable this feature (as seen in Figure 2-16). As you already know, the VB language often performs automatic type conversions when needed. For example, assume you have authored the following VB 6.0 code:

```
' VB 6.0 will automatically convert
' a Long into an Integer.
Dim theInt As Integer
theInt = 100
Dim theLong As Long
theLong = 40000
' Data Loss!!
theInt = theLong
```

This is a bad thing, as you just lost a huge amount of data. To prevent this sort of implicit conversion under VB .NET, enable Option Strict. Using this setting, you tell vbc.exe to generate compiler errors whenever a type conversion results in loss of data. Thus if you enable Option Strict and run the previous code within a VB .NET application, you see the following compiler error (Figure 2-17).

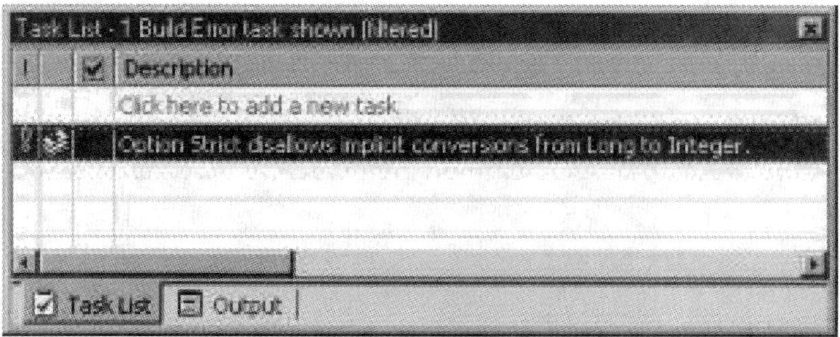

Figure 2-17. Option Strict prevents implicit data loss

As you would expect, VB .NET allows you to perform explicit conversions from larger types into smaller types using a number of conversion functions. The same holds true when you convert base classes to subclasses, subclasses to base classes, and when obtaining interface references. You will see examples of data and class type conversions in Chapters 4 and 5.

Finally, you should also be aware that enabling Option Strict also prevents you from exercising classic COM late binding (given that late binding to COM types requires the use of the loosely typed VB 6.0 Object data type). You revisit this aspect of Option Strict in Chapter 8.

Last but not least, you have the Option Compare. This setting is used to specify if text strings should be compared at a binary level (which is the default and typically what you require) or at a case-insensitive text level (which is based on your system's default locale).

When you configure Option settings using the Project Properties window, you are establishing a behavior for the entire project. However, you are also free to set Option Strict and Option Explicit using the Option keyword:

```
Option Strict On
Option Explicit On
```

When you do, you are able to override the project-wide settings for a particular *.vb file.

Default Imports

Now select the Imports node. Here, you are able to specify the names of any external namespaces that you plan to reference from your *.vb files. This is a nice feature of the IDE, given that when you add additional namespace listings, you are able to make use of the containing types without needing to add explicit

Imports directives in each and every project file. For now, specify the System.Windows.Forms namespace (Figure 2-18). Be aware that this tool does *not* check the validity of the namespace you enter. If you misspell namespaces, you are bound to get compile time errors.

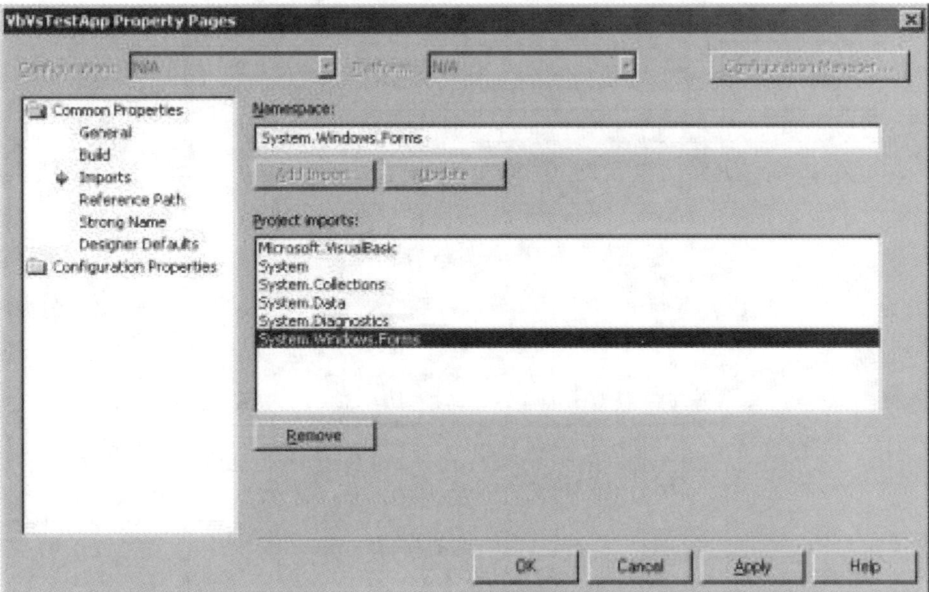

Figure 2-18. Specifying external namespaces

Many of the remaining options of this dialog (such as the Strong Name node) are examined as you progress through the book. However, as always, consult online Help for further details.

The Properties Window

Another important aspect of the IDE is the Properties window. This window details a number of characteristics for the currently focused item. Be aware that this item may be an open source code file, a GUI widget (as you see later when you examine Windows Forms), or the project itself. For example, to change the name of your initial *.vb file, select it from the Solution Explorer and configure the FileName property (Figure 2-19).

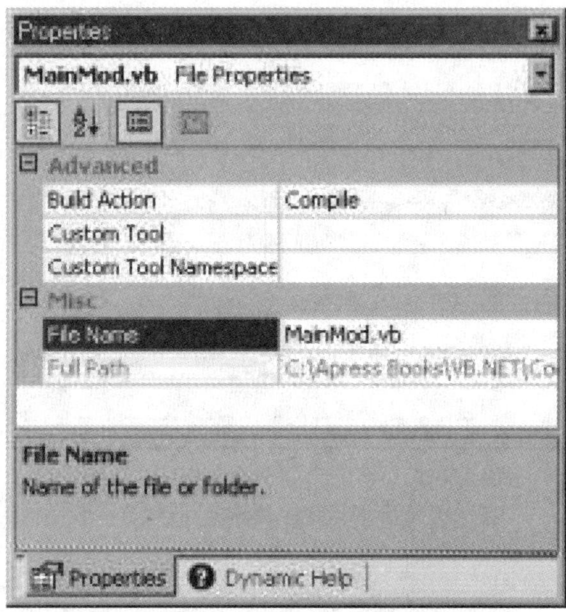

Figure 2-19. File names may be changed using the Properties window

Adding Some Code

Now that you have configured your new VB .NET project workspace, you can add source code. Within the Main() method, add code that prints a line to the console and displays a Windows Forms message box:

```
Module Module1
    Sub Main()
        Console.WriteLine("Hello again!")
        MessageBox.Show("Yo!")
    End Sub
End Module
```

Referencing External Assemblies

As you typed in the previous code example, you may have noticed that the WriteLine() method was displayed through the expected IntelliSense, while the Show() method fails to reveal itself. This may seem odd, given that you specified the System.Windows.Forms namespace using the Project Properties window. The key to keep in mind is that when you specify a namespace using this approach, all you have done is informed the IDE to add a "hidden" Imports statement (in each file) on your behalf. If you did not add a namespace reference using the Project Properties window, you need to explicitly list this namespace in each *.vb file using Windows Forms types with the Imports keyword:

```
Imports System.Windows.Forms
Module Module1
    Sub Main()
        Console.WriteLine("Hello again!")
        MessageBox.Show("Yo!")
    End Sub
End Module
```

Regardless of how you specify the namespaces you are using, the compiler requires that you set a reference to the actual physical assembly. (Just like you learned to do with the command line compiler /r option). When you need to add external references (such as System.Windows.Forms.dll) into your current project, access the Project | Add Reference. . . menu selection (or right-click the References node from the Solution Explorer window). Whichever way you go, you end up with the dialog box shown in Figure 2-20.

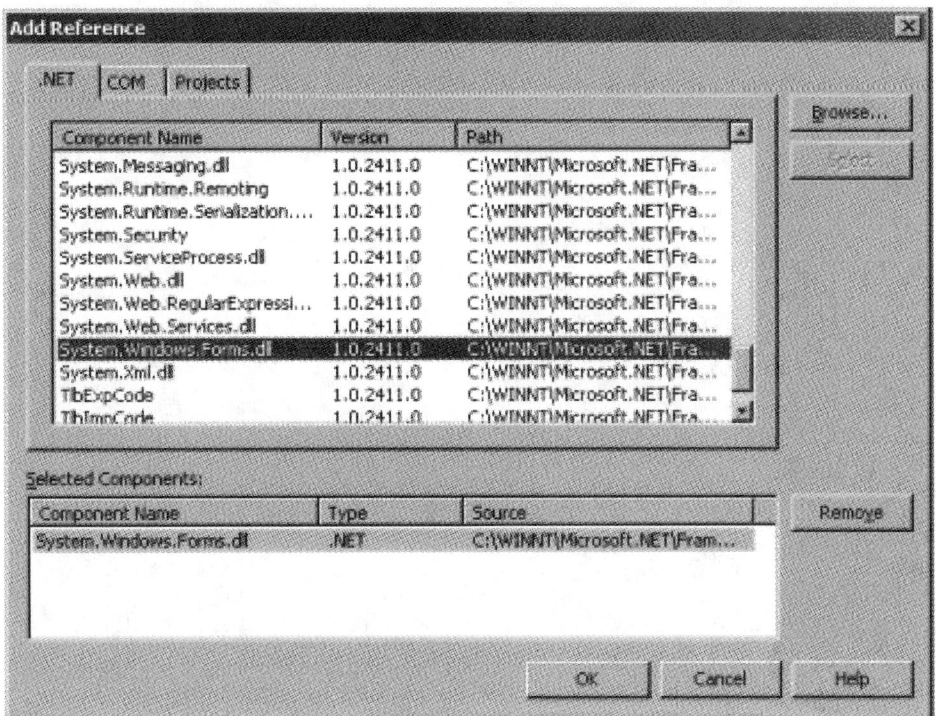

Figure 2-20. The Add References dialog box

As you can see, this dialog box allows you to reference classic COM servers (you examine the gory details of .NET/COM interoperability in Chapter 13). Once you have added the System.Windows.Forms.dll assembly you can compile and run your application.

Adding New Types

When you want to add new types (such as a class) to your current project you are always free to insert a blank *.vb file and manually flesh out the details of the new item. As an alternative, you are also free to use the Project menu and specify the sort of item you want to insert. Activate the Project | Add Class menu selection and insert a new class named HelloClass.vb. As you can see, you are given a skeletal definition of an empty class. Add a simple subroutine named SayHi() (again, don't worry about the syntax at this point):

```
Public Class HelloClass
    Public Sub SayHi()
        MessageBox.Show("Hello from HelloClass. . .")
    End Sub
End Class
```

Now, update your existing Main() method to create a new instance of this type, and call the SayHi() member.

```
Module Module1
    Sub Main()
        Console.WriteLine("Hello again!")
        MessageBox.Show("Yo!")
        ' Make a HelloClass type.
        Dim h As New HelloClass()
        h.SayHi()
    End Sub
End Module
```

Outlining Your Code

One extremely helpful aspect of the IDE is the ability to show or hide blocks of code using the "+" and "-" icons (Figure 2-21). When you place your cursor over the ellipses icon (which represents a collapsed block of code) a pop-up window gives you a snapshot of the member implementation.

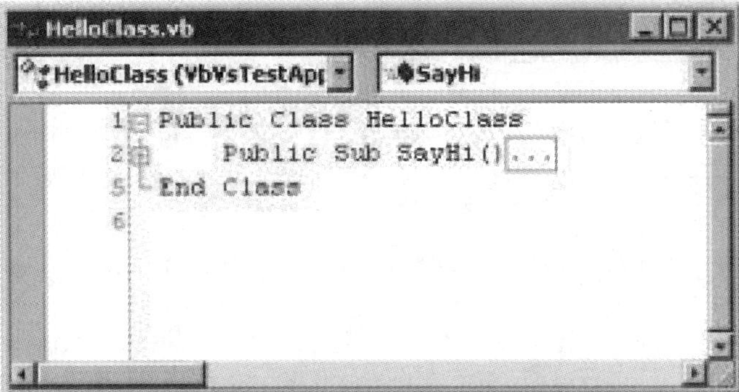

Figure 2-21. Collapsing the SayHi() method

Debugging with the Visual Studio .NET IDE

As you would expect, Visual Studio .NET contains an integrated debugger. To illustrate the basics, begin by clicking in the far left gray column of an active code window to insert a breakpoint (Figure 2-22).

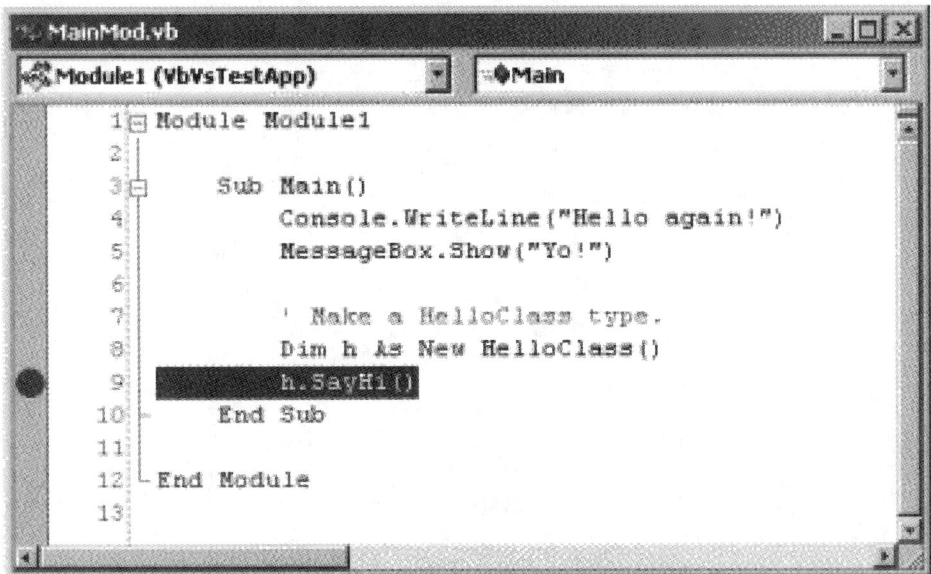

Figure 2-22. Setting breakpoints

When you initiate the debug session, the flow of execution halts at each breakpoint. Using the Debug toolbar, you can step over, step into, and step out of a given line of code. As you would expect, the integrated debugger hosts a number of debug-centric windows (e.g., Call Stack, Autos, Locals, Breakpoints,

Modules, Exceptions, and so forth). To show or hide a particular window, simply access the Debug | Windows menu selection.

SOURCE CODE *The VbVsTestApp project is included under the Chapter 2 subdirectory.*

Examining the Server Explorer Window

At this point, you should have a better feeling about the core features of the IDE. I'll assume you will keep exploring with the IDE as you read through the book. However, to paint a more complete picture, let's quickly check out additional features of VS .NET. One extremely useful aspect of Visual Studio .NET is the Server Explorer window (Figure 2-23), which can be accessed using the View menu.

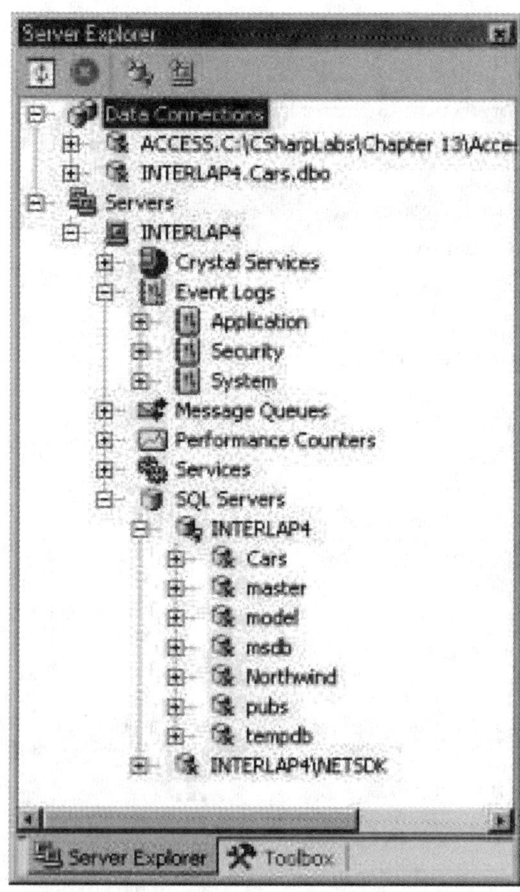

Figure 2-23. The Server Explorer window

This window can be thought of as the command center of a distributed application you may be building. Using the Server Explorer, you can attach to and manipulate local and remote databases (and view any of the given database objects), plug into a message queue, and obtain general machine-wide information (such as seeing what services are running and the event log).

XML-Related Editing Tools

Visual Studio .NET has integrated tools to edit XML-related data (as well as HTML files). Much of this functionality was taken from the legacy Visual InterDev IDE. Once you insert a new XML file into your application, you are able to edit the underlying XML using GUI design-time tools (and related toolbars). For example, Figure 2-24 shows an XML file you will generate during our discussion of ADO.NET.

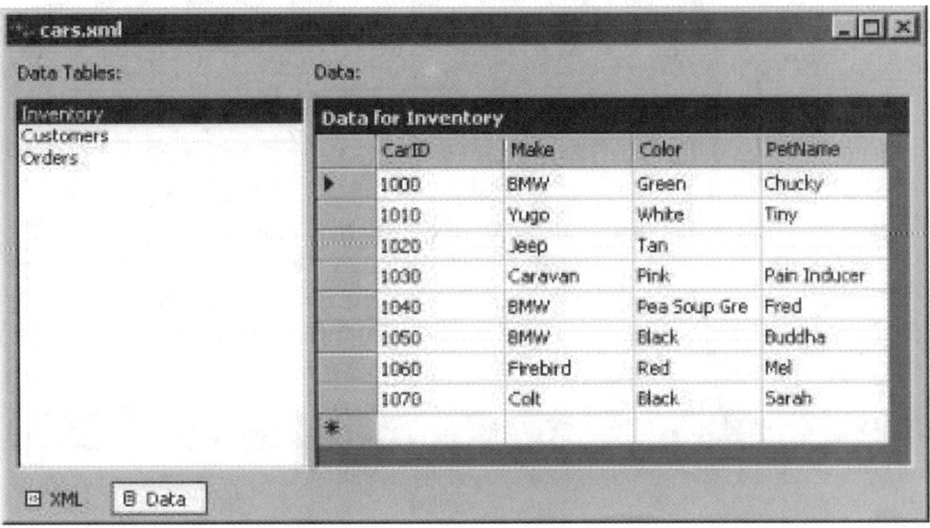

Figure 2-24. The integrated XML editor

The Object Browser Utility

In addition to the type browsing tools you examined in Chapter 1, the Visual Studio .NET IDE also supplies a utility, which looks and feels much like the VB 6.0 Object Browser. If you access the View | Other Windows | Object Browser menu option, you will see the tool displayed in Figure 2-25.

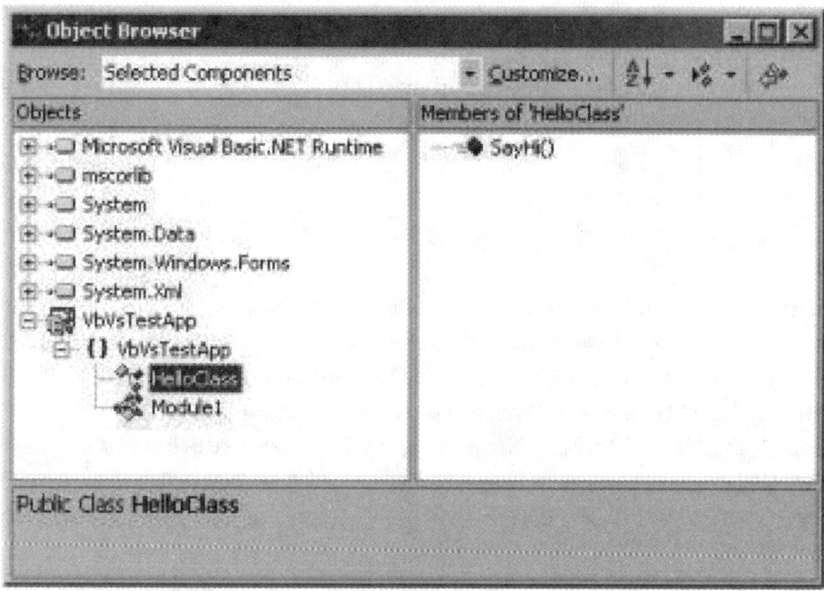

Figure 2-25. The integrated Object Browser

Database Manipulation Tools

Integrated database support is also part of the VS .NET IDE. Once you add a data connection to your application using the Server Explorer window, you can open and examine any database object from within the IDE. For example, Figure 2-26 shows a view of the Inventory table of the Cars database you build in Chapter 14.

dbo.Inventory : Table (INTERLAP4.Cars)

CarID	Make	Color	PetName
0	BMW	Red	Biffy
1	FooFoo	FooFoo	FooFoo
3	BMW	Pink	Chucky
4	Colt	Rust	Mary
444	Escort	Orange	Buddha
666	Jetta	Pink	Cranky
1111	SlugBug	Pink	Pain Inducer

Figure 2-26. Integrated database editors

Integrated Help

The final aspect of the IDE you must be familiar with from the outset is the fully integrated Help system. Rather than having to ALT + TAB between MSDN and the development environment, VS .NET provides the Dynamic Help window, which changes its contents (dynamically!) based on what item (window, menu, source code keyword, etc.) is the current focus. For example, if you place the cursor on Main() method, the Dynamic Help window displays what's shown in Figure 2-27.

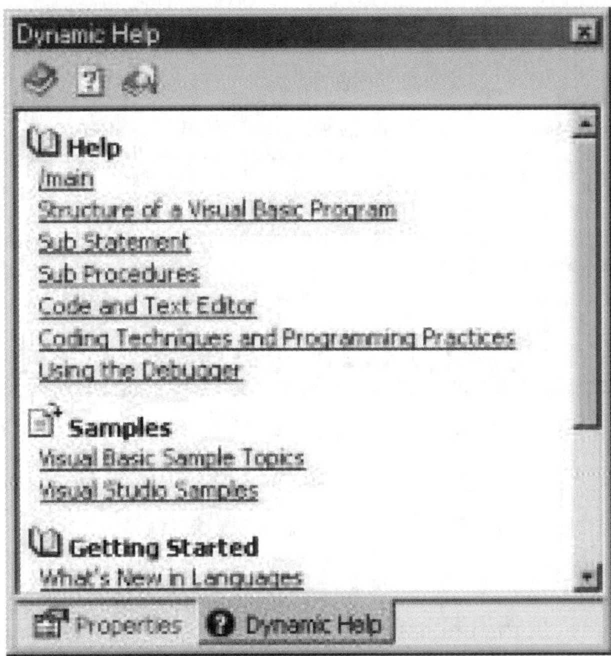

Figure 2-27. Integrated Help

As you would expect, if you select on one of the suggested links (such as /main), you are shown the information that appears in Figure 2-28.

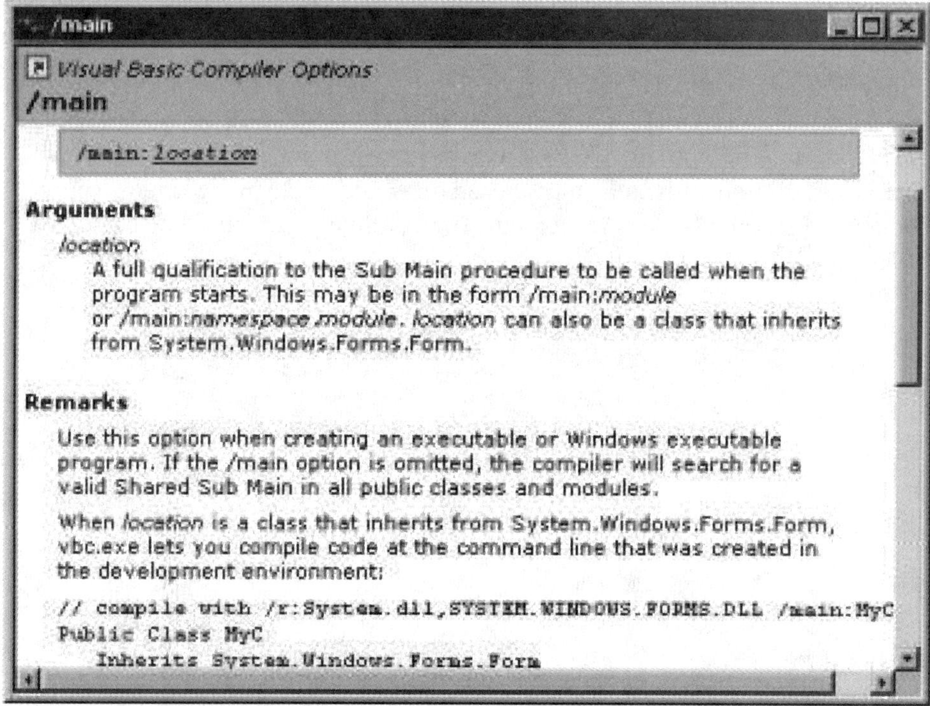

Figure 2-28. Remember, F1 is your friend

What Happened to the World of VB 6.0?

As you can see, you have many new toys at your disposal. Now that you have a solid background in the philosophy of .NET and have seen two approaches to compile your projects (vbc.exe and VS .NET), you are almost ready to begin a formal investigation of the VB .NET language and the .NET platform. To wrap up this chapter, let's spend some time coming to grips with issues of VB 6.0/Visual Basic .NET compatibility.

The approach I take in this text (more or less) is to treat Visual Basic .NET as a brand-new programming language. As you move through each chapter, I venture to guess that you will begin to agree. Nevertheless, Visual Basic .NET does have deep roots in the sixth version of VB, and given this, one of the choices you face is how much functionality of VB 6.0 will creep into your new VB .NET projects.

When you create a new project workspace using VS .NET, you automatically have a listing in your Project Imports node to a namespace called Microsoft.VisualBasic (Figure 2-29).

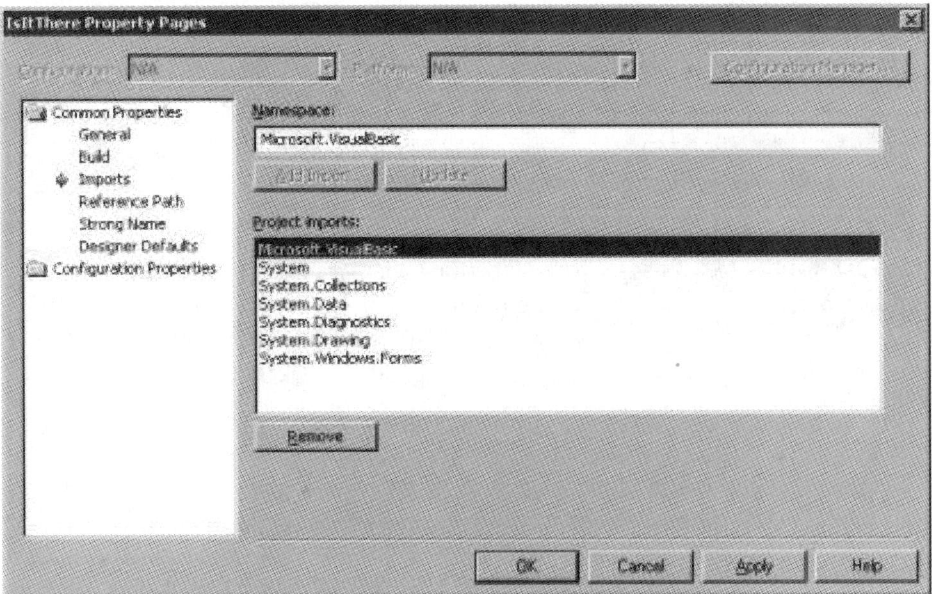

Figure 2-29: VB .NET applications automatically reference the Microsoft.VisualBasic namespace.

If you launch the VS .NET Object Browser, you can check out some of the contained types (Figure 2-30).

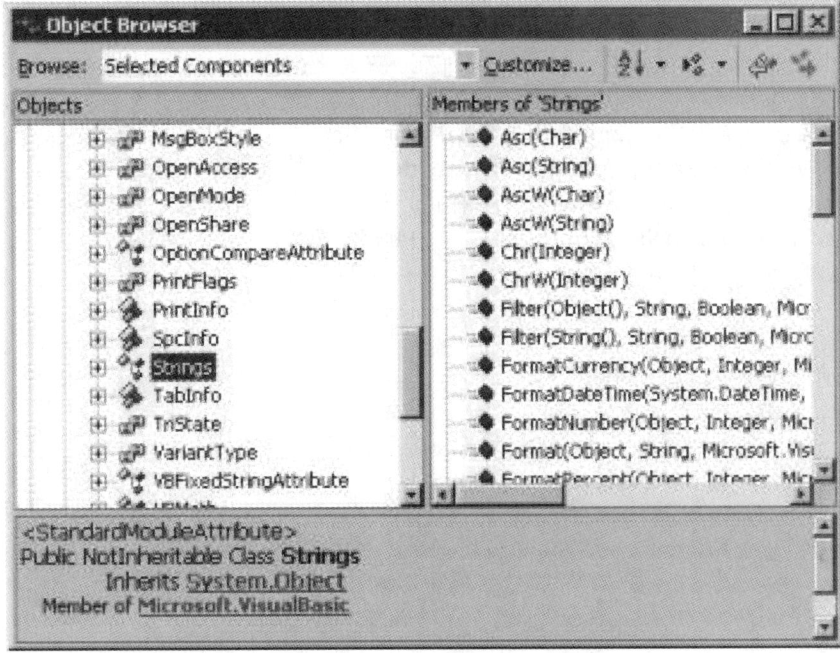

Figure 2-30. Members of the Microsoft.VisualBasic namespace

As you look over the types contained in this namespace, you should recognize that a vast majority of VB 6.0 functions, enumerations, and constants have been wrapped by various .NET types. Table 2-3 lists some (but not all) of the types contained within the Microsoft.VisualBasic namespace.

Table 2-3. Select Members of the Microsoft.VisualBasic Namespace

MICROSOFT.VISUALBASIC TYPE	MEANING IN LIFE
AppWinStyle DateFormat DateInterval FileAttribute MsgBoxResult MsgBoxStyle PrintFlags	These types (as well as many others) are .NET enumerations, which wrap related VB 6.0 constants. For example, MsgBoxResult type defines the VB 6.0 Abort, Cancel, Ignore, No, Ok, Retry and Yes constants.
Collection	Represents the VB 6.0 Collection type.
Constants	This class defines VB 6.0 constants such as VbAbort, VbLf, VbYes, VbNo, and so forth.
Strings	This type wraps the VB 6.0 string manipulation functions (Asc(), Len(), LCase(), and whatnot).
Interaction	This type wraps VB 6.0 commands that require user input (MsgBox(), InputBox(), Beep(), and so on).
VBMath	Wraps the VB 6.0 mathematical functions (i.e., Rnd() and Randomize()).

In a nutshell, the items found within the Microsoft.VisualBasic namespace represent VB 6.0 atoms that are still considered "safe" to use in the .NET universe. To illustrate, assume you have created a brand-new VB .NET Console application named Vb6FromVbNet. Within the Main() method, you may interact with aspects of the VB 6.0 world as follows:

```
Module Module1
    Sub Main()
        ' This is a VB 6.0 message box.
        MsgBox("VB 6.0 MsgBox", MsgBoxStyle.Exclamation, _
               "Microsoft.VisualBasic")
        ' Create a managed string which is
        ' manipulated by VB 6.0 functions.
        Dim s As String = "This is a managed string"
        Console.WriteLine(Strings.StrReverse(s))
```

```
        Console.WriteLine(Strings.LCase(s))
        Console.WriteLine(Strings.UCase(s))
    End Sub
End Module
```

As you expect, the program displays a message box using the VB 6.0 MsgBox() function, and dumps the text in Figure 2-31 to the console window.

Figure 2-31. Triggering VB 6.0 functionality

One intriguing aspect of the Microsoft.VisualBasic namespace is the fact that these types may be used by *any* .NET aware language. To illustrate, assume you have another Console application written using C#. The following C# class makes use of the same VB 6.0 functionality seen in the previous VB .NET application.

```
using System;
// You will also need to explicitly set a reference to Microsoft.VisualBasic.dll
// to run this project (by default this is located under
// C:\WINNT\Microsoft.NET\Framework\
// v1.0.2914\Microsoft.VisualBasic.dll)
using Microsoft.VisualBasic;
namespace CSharpUsingVB
{
    class TheCSharpApp
    {
        static void Main(string[] args)
        {
            // This is a VB 6.0 message box.
            Interaction.MsgBox("VB 6.0 MsgBox",
            MsgBoxStyle.Exclamation,
            "Microsoft.VisualBasic");

            // Create a managed string which is
            // manipulated by VB 6.0 functions.
            string s = "This is a managed string";
```

```
            Console.WriteLine(Strings.StrReverse(s));
            Console.WriteLine(Strings.LCase(s));
            Console.WriteLine(Strings.UCase(s));
        }
    }
}
```

As you would expect, the output of this application is identical to the earlier application.

Although you may feel some warm fuzzies at this point in the game, I challenge you to *avoid* the types contained within the Microsoft.VisualBasic namespace. The most important reason is the fact that the new .NET base class libraries do a far better job manipulating files, strings, printers and other application entities than the VB 6.0 equivalents ever did.

For example, in place of the VB 6.0 string functions, .NET supplies a number of discrete classes devoted to the manipulation of textual information (System.String, System.Text.StringBuilder). Although VB 6.0 provides a handful of members that allow you to interact with an external printer, VB .NET provides an entire .NET namespace devoted to printing (System.Drawing.Printing). The bottom line is that the Microsoft.VisuaBasic namespace is provided as a little bridge connecting the world of yore (VB 6.0) with the universe that is .NET.

SOURCE CODE *The Vb6FromVbNet and CSharpUsingVB applications are included under the Chapter 2 subdirectory.*

Upgrading VB 6.0 Projects into VB .NET

Another issue you have to contend with is whether you should upgrade your existing VB 6.0 projects to the world of VB .NET. To begin, assume that you have an existing VB 6.0 Windows EXE application that contains a single custom class named Car that supports two Public data members (just to keep things simple) and a single subroutine that sets the state of each data point (Figure 2-32).

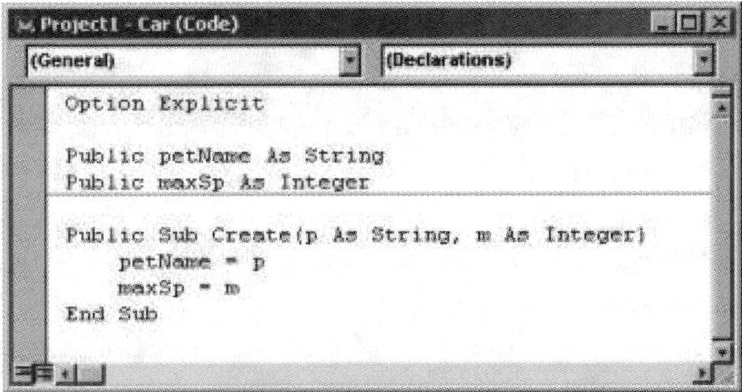

Figure 2-32. A VB 6.0 Class type

Also assume that the main Form allows the user to set each value using TextBox widgets. If you click the "Make Car" button, you create the Car and display the state values (Figure 2-33):

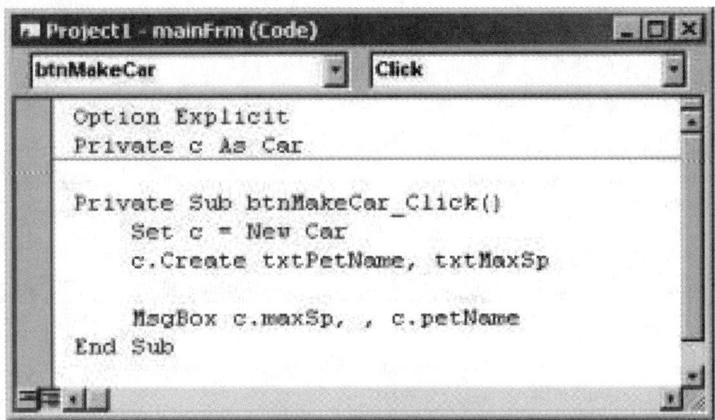

Figure 2-33. The logic behind the Main Form (VB 6.0)

If you attempt to open the VB 6.0 *.vbp file using Visual Studio .NET, you are greeted by the Upgrade Wizard. This process entails a number of steps. First, you are asked if you want to upgrade your project to an EXE or DLL format (obviously Standard EXEs only upgrade to an EXE). Next, you are asked where to store the new VB .NET project. Once you tell the wizard to work its magic, you see that a new *.htm file named _UpgradeReport.htm has been added to your project. As you would guess, this is a log of any and all issues encountered during the upgrade process (Figure 2-34).

Figure 2-34. Upgrade report

If you check the Car.vb file, you find the following (note that Option Strict is *Off,* which I am sure you will turn promptly turn *On*):

```
Option Strict Off  ' Ugh!
Option Explicit On
Friend Class Car
    Public petName As String
    Public maxSp As Short
    Public Sub Create(ByRef p As String, ByRef m As Short)
        petName = p
        maxSp = m
    End Sub
End Class
```

The generated code behind the Main Form is *extremely different* than VB 6.0 GUI logic. So much so, that I do not list the generated code because I'm fearful that you might uninstall the .NET SDK from your development machine (but I encourage you to check out the companion code. . .and you address Windows Forms beginning with Chapter 9).

The Microsoft.VisualBasic.Compatability.VB6 Namespace

When you upgrade a VB 6.0 project to the standards defined by VB .NET, the converted project references a new assembly (Microsoft.VisualBasic.Compatability.VB6.dll). This assembly contains a number of types that are used to convert VB 6.0 constructs into terms of VB .NET. Unlike the types contained within the Microsoft.VisualBasic namespace, the types found within the Compatibility layer are considered obsolete in VB .NET, and are supported only as a crutch for the Upgrade Wizard. More often than not, there's no need to directly interact with these types (and you should avoid them in any new VB .NET project). As is the case with any deprecated code, you cannot be assured that the functionality of the Microsoft.VisualBasic.Compatability.VB6 namespace will remain intact as VS .NET matures.

Should You Upgrade?

Given our simple test case, the Upgrade Wizard did a fine job. However, a real world project might consist of tens of thousands of lines of code, numerous COM DLLs, and may be distributed across many machines. Clearly, the upgrade process is not without its shortcomings. If you have a substantial application that functions just fine as is and choose to upgrade, you may find yourself in the unenviable position of having to sort though the generated upgrade report and making hundreds of code modifications by hand.

The question you need to ask yourself is: what do you gain? In most cases, the answer is not too much. In fact, you may create more work for yourself (and your team) in the long run. The short answer to this question posed by this section is "no". There is no compelling reason to take existing VB 6.0 project workspaces and upgrade them to VB .NET just for the sake of doing so. As you learn in Chapter 13, your new .NET assemblies are able to interact with existing COM code (and visa versa). In fact, Microsoft seems to understand that existing VB 6.0 applications are left well enough alone. Even with the advent of .NET, Microsoft is currently committed to supporting (and updating) VB 6.0.

The approach taken in this book is that you are building *new* applications using VB .NET, and want to make use of the related .NET class libraries.

Given this mindset, I do not address the Microsoft.VisualBasic or Microsoft.VisualBasic.Compatability.VB6 namespaces (or the Upgrade Wizard) beyond this point. If you need additional information, I assume you will check online Help for details.

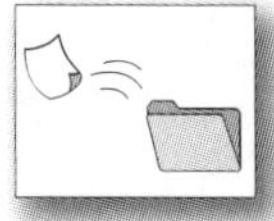

SOURCE CODE *The VB6AppOriginal and VB6AppUpgrade applications are included under the Chapter 2 subdirectory.*

Summary

The point of this chapter was to introduce you to the basic process of building VB .NET applications. As you have seen, the ultimate recipient of your *.vb files is the VB .NET compiler, vbc.exe. You began by learning how to use vbc.exe in the raw, and in the process examined a number of compiler options. The bulk of this chapter however, explored the Visual Studio.NET IDE. As I mentioned, you will continue to see additional functionality of VS .NET where appropriate.

The chapter ended by checking out some issues involved in moving between VB 6.0 and VB .NET. As mentioned, VB .NET is best thought of as a brand-new programming language (which just happens to look similar to VB 6.0). Although Microsoft has designed namespaces that are devoted to VB 6.0 compatibility, you should consider the contained types only as a crutch that can ease the transition to .NET. As you become more proficient working in the .NET universe (as you will during the course of this book), you will find little need to make use of the VB 6.0 centric namespaces.

CHAPTER 3

VB .NET Language Fundamentals

THE MINOR MISSION of this chapter is to survey core syntactic changes that have been introduced to the Visual Basic programming language with the advent of VB .NET. As you will see, a number of language constructs used in earlier versions of VB have been cleaned up, removed, and improved, to produce a more consistent and elegant programming language. However, the main thrust of this chapter is to introduce you to the core aspects of the VB .NET language, including value-based and reference-based data types, the System.Object base class, and basic class construction techniques. Along the way, you also learn how to manipulate modules, strings, arrays, enumerations, and structures.

To illustrate these language fundamentals, you take a deeper programmatic look at the .NET base class libraries, and build a number of sample applications making use of various namespaces. Once you understand how to leverage pre-fabricated namespaces, the chapter closes by showing you how to organize your custom types into discrete user-defined namespaces (and explains why you might want to do so).

The Role of the Module Type

As you have seen in the first two chapters, VB .NET Console applications contain a *.vb file with the following definition:

```
Module Module1
    Sub Main()      ' Public by default.
    End Sub
End Module
```

A Module is a standard class type, with a few notable exceptions. First and foremost, any Public function, subroutine, or member variable defined within the scope of a Module is exposed as a "shared" member that is directly accessible throughout an application (more on shared members later in this chapter). To illustrate, if you compile a Module type containing some number of members and open the resulting assembly using ILDasm.exe, you find that all methods of the Module are marked with the “s” icon, which signifies a shared member (Figure 3-1).

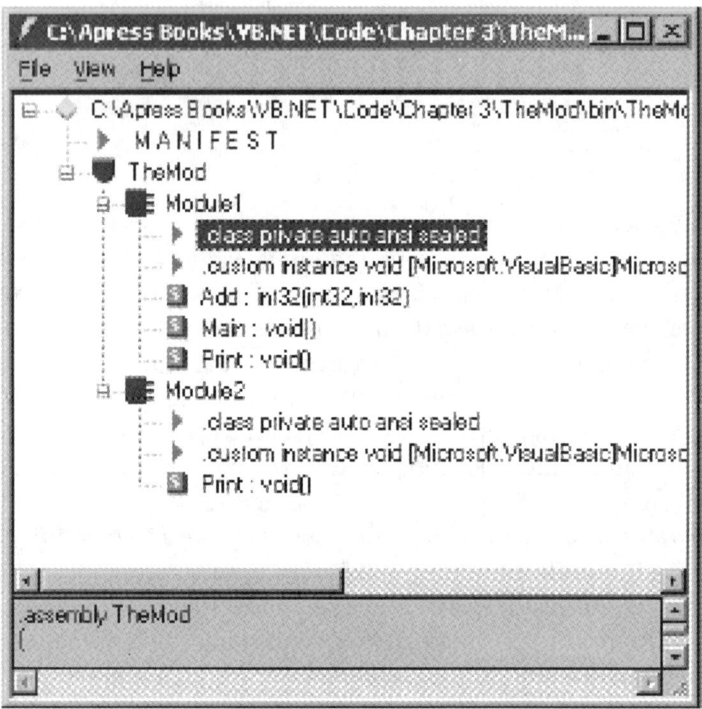

Figure 3-1. All members of a Module are shared.

Given that a Module simulates a global scope, you are not required to prefix the Module’s name when accessing its members. For example:

```
Module Module1
    Sub Main()
        ' Call public members of the mod.
        Print()
        ' The {0} syntax will be explained a bit later. . .
        Console.WriteLine("40 + 3332 is: {0}", _
                       Add(40, 3332))
        Module1.Print()   ' Don't need to prefix.
    End Sub
    Public Sub Print()
        Console.WriteLine("Hello from Print()")
    End Sub
    Public Function Add(ByVal x As Integer, _
```

```
        ByVal y As Integer) As Integer
        ' The Return keyword will also be examinied later in the chapter.
        Return x + y
    End Function
End Module
```

Here, you can see that the Main() method makes calls to the Module level Print() and Add() members. Do notice that the second call to Print() prefixes the name of the Module to the function call. In this case, this is a completely optional bit of syntax. However, if were to define an additional Module as follows:

```
Module Module2
    Public Sub Print()
        Console.WriteLine("Hello from Module2.Print()")
    End Sub
End Module
```

You would now need to specify which version of the Print() method you want to call, as each Module contains a member of the same name [if you do not specify the Module, the Main() method automatically calls the Module1.Print() method, as it is in the defining scope]:

```
Sub Main()
    ' Call public members of the mod.
    Print()
    Console.WriteLine(Add(40, 3332))
    ' Trigger the Print() in Module2.
    Module2.Print()
End Sub
```

Modules Are Not Creatable

Another trait of the Module type is that it cannot be directly created using the VB .NET "New" keyword (any attempt to do so will result in a compiler error). Therefore the following code is illegal:

```
' Nope! Error!
Dim m as New Module1
```

Rather, a Module type simply exposes shared members. In a nutshell, the VB .NET Module type is a rough equivalent to the VB 6.0 standard module (*.bas files). All Public types appear to exist in a global scope. Under the hood however, members of a Module are in fact shared members of the Module class.

The Main Method

Console applications have a shared member named Main(). Every VB .NET application must contain a class defining a Main() subroutine, which is used to signify the entry point of the application. Although it is technically possible for a single VB .NET project to contain multiple classes defining a Main() method, you must specify (to the VB .NET compiler) which Main() method should be used as the application's entry point or you encounter a compile-time error.

Within the scope of your Main() method, you typically create objects that carry out the functionality of your application. For the time being, you'll see Main() within the context of a Console application. Understand, however, that Main() is required of any executable application (such as a Windows Forms application).

Processing Command Line Arguments

It is quite commonplace for Console applications to accept any number of command line arguments. For example, assume you are building a video game that may be started up using command line flags (such as specifying –GODMODE as a cheat code). When you want to process any option command line flags, make use of the shared GetCommandLineArgs() method defined by the System.Environment type. For example:

```
Sub Main()
    ' Get command line args.
    Dim args As String() = Environment.GetCommandLineArgs()
    Dim s As String
    For Each s In args
        Console.WriteLine("Arg: {0}", s)
    Next
...
End Sub
```

Supplying these (optional) arguments is equally as simple (see Figure 3-2). As you can see, the first String in the returned array represents the name of the executable (which you can feel free to ignore).

```
C:\WINNT\System32\cmd.exe
C:\>themod -hello -GODMODE -993
Arg: themod
Arg: -hello
Arg: -GODMODE
Arg: -993
Hello from Module1.Print()
40 + 3332 is: 3372
Hello from Module2.Print()
Hello from Mod2 method
Hello from Mod2 method

C:\>
```

Figure 3-2: Processing command line arguments.

On a related note, the Beta 2 online Help documents state that VB .NET supports a variation of the Main() method that takes an array of String types as an argument. However, I have not been able to configure my VB .NET console applications to recognize them (we will have to wait to see if this feature is supported in the final release).

SOURCE CODE *The TheMod project is located under the Chapter 3 subdirectory.*

Data Types and Variable Declarations

Like any programming language, VB .NET has an intrinsic set of data types, which are used to represent elements in your programs, class field data, and method parameters. One thing to be painfully aware of is that the data types of VB .NET do *not* map directly into VB 6.0 types. Table 3-1 documents the data types of VB .NET (and CLR equivalents).

Table 3-1. The Intrinsic Data Types of VB .NET

VB .NET DATA TYPE	CLR EQUIVALENT	MEANING IN LIFE (RANGE OF VB .NET TYPE)
Boolean (2 bytes)	System.Boolean	True or False
Byte (1 byte)	System.Byte	0 to 255 (unsigned)
Char (2 bytes)	System.Char	0 to 65535 (unsigned)
Date (8 bytes)	System.DateTime	January 1, 0001 to December 31, 9999
Decimal (16 bytes)	System.Decimal	+/-79,228,162,514,264,337,593,543,950,335 with no decimal point. +/-7.9228162514264337593543950335 with 28 places to the right of the decimal; smallest nonzero number is +/-0.0000000000000000000000000001
Double (8 bytes)	System.Double	-1.79769313486231E+308 to -4.94065645841247E-324 for negative values. 4.94065645841247E-324 to 1.79769313486231E+308 for positive values
Integer (4 bytes)	System.Int32	-2,147,483,648 to 2,147,483,647
Long (8 bytes)	System.Int64	-9,223,372,036,854,775,808 to 9,223,372,036,854,775,807
Object (4 bytes)	System.Object	Any type can be stored in a variable of type Object. Consider this type the .NET functional equivalent (but physically very different) of the Variant type.
Short (2 bytes)	System.Int16	-32,768 to 32,767
Single (4 bytes)	System.Single	This single-precision floating-point can take the range of -3.402823E+38 to -1.401298E-45 for negative values; 1.401298E-45 to 3.402823E+38 for positive values.
String	System.String	System.String represents a string of a varying length. The storage required for System.String is platform dependent.

Be aware that each of the numerical types (Short, Integer, and so forth) map to a corresponding *structure* in the System namespace. As you see later in this chapter, structures derive from a common base class type named System.ValueType. The basic role of System.ValueType is to ensure that the structure behaves as a stack-based entity rather than a heap-based entity.

On the other hand, System.String derives directly from System.Object and is thus a "reference type," meaning the type is allocated on the managed heap. You examine full details of value and reference types later in the chapter. For now, the relationship between these core system types (as well as some other soon-to-be-discovered types) can be understood as shown in Figure 3-3.

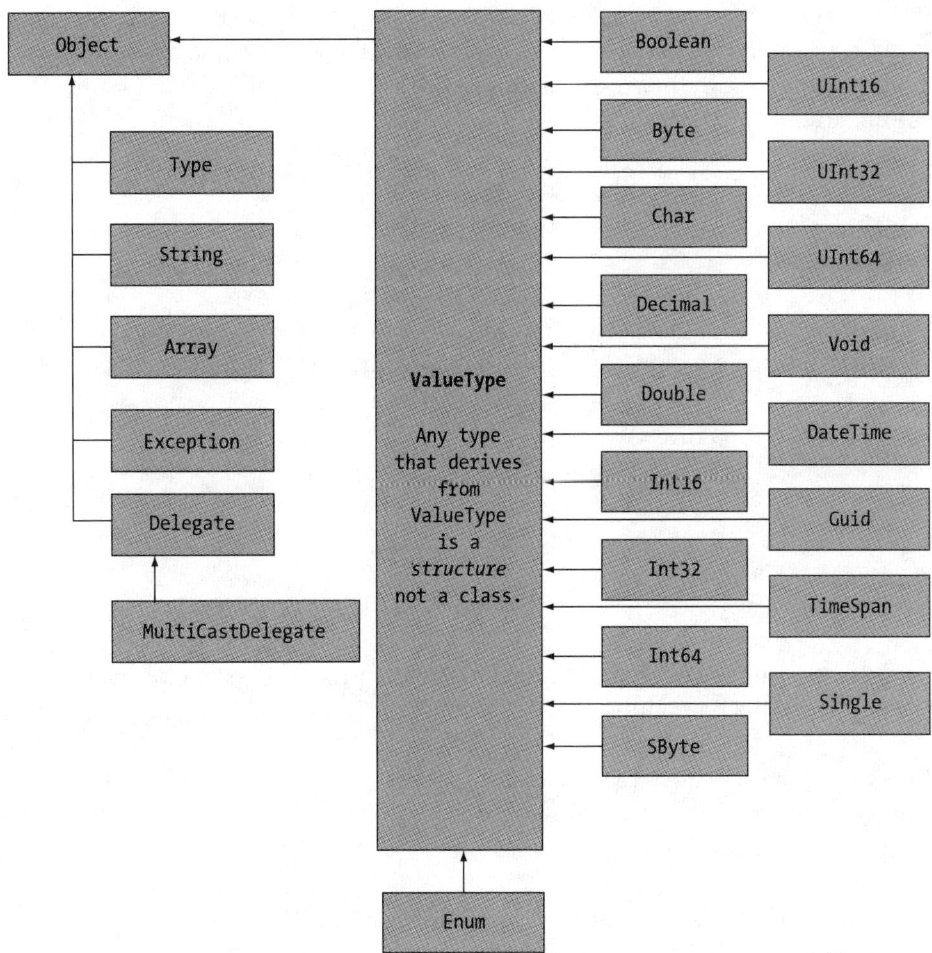

Figure 3-3. The hierarchy of System types

Note that the System namespace defines some "unsigned" types (UInt16, UInt32, UInt64) that are not supported by VB .NET but may be supported in another language targeting the .NET runtime (such as C#). The truth of the matter is that these types are not CLS compliant. Thus, if you happen to have a coworker who makes use of C#, MC++ or another .NET-aware language supporting unsigned types, be painfully aware that if these types are exposed to the outside world (i.e., they show up on a Public member), a VB .NET application is not able to make use of them! When attributes are discussed later in this text (Chapter 8), you learn how to ensure that C# code libraries make exclusive use of CLS compliant features (VB .NET code libraries to do automatically).

Variable Declaration/Initialization

One helpful syntactic change that has occurred in VB .NET is the ability to declare a sequence of variables on a single line of code. Of course, VB 6.0 also supported this ability, but the semantics were a bit nonintuitive and a source of subtle bugs:

```
' In this line of VB 6.0 code, varOne
' is implicitly defined to be of type Variant!
Dim varOne, varTwo as Integer
```

This is a bit annoying, given that the only way you are able to define multiple variables of the same type is to write the following slightly redundant code:

```
Dim varOne as Integer, varTwo as Integer
```

Or even:

```
Dim varOne as Integer
Dim varTwo as Integer
```

While there is nothing too traumatic with the process of explicitly specifying the type of each data member, VB .NET allows the following declaration syntax:

```
' In this line of VB .NET code, varOne
' and varTwo are both of type Integer!
Dim varOne, varTwo as Integer
```

In this line of code, you have created two variables of type *Integer*. On a related note, VB .NET now supports the ability to assign a value to a type directly at the point of declaration. In contrast, in VB 6.0, you were forced to write the following:

```
' VB 6.0 code.
Dim i as Integer
i = 99
```

However, in VB .NET you can use the following notation:

```
' VB .NET code.
Dim i as Integer = 99
```

The same variable initialization is also possible at the class (or structure) level. For example, if you had a simple class with a set of private data members, you could initialize the values as follows:

```
Class Test
    Private myInt As Integer = 90
    Private myStr As String = "My initial value."
    Private viper As HotRod = New HotRod(200, "Chucky", Color.Red)
    . . .
End Class
```

Typically, member data of a class is assigned within the scope of a class "constructor" (that is defined soon enough). In any case, understand that you are not required to make use of this new syntax. You are still free to define and assign on separate lines of code (although I suspect most of you will welcome this change).

Experimenting with the System Data Types

All system data types ultimately derive from System.Object. This master node in the .NET framework defines a small set of members that are common to every type in the hierarchy. One member, named ToString(), returns a "stringified" version of the associated type. Thus, because data types such as "Integer" are simply shorthand notations for the corresponding system type System.Int32, the following is perfectly legal syntax:

```
' Remember! A VB .NET integer is really an alias for System.Int32.
Dim s as String = 12.ToString()
```

As mentioned, most intrinsic VB .NET data types directly alias a related structure derived from ValueType. Functionally, the only purpose of System.ValueType is to override the methods defined by System.Object to work with value-based verse reference-based semantics. In fact, the signatures of the methods defined by ValueType are identical to those of Object. But keep in mind that when you compare two instances of a type derived from ValueType, you are using value-based semantics:

```
' Test value semantics.
Dim intA As System.Int32 = 1001
Dim intB As System.Int32 = 1000
If (intA = intB) Then
    Console.WriteLine("Same value!")
Else
    Console.WriteLine("Not the same value!")
End If
```

Every system value type (e.g., Int32, Char, Boolean) defines a similar set of helpful members. While I assume you will consult online Help for full details, some points of interest are the MaxValue and MinValue properties that provide information regarding the minimum and maximum value a given type can hold. Assume you have created a variable of type System.Int32, and exercised it as follows:

```
' Working with System.Int32.
Dim myInt32 As System.Int32 = 30000
Console.WriteLine("Max for an Int32 is: {0}", myInt32.MaxValue)
Console.WriteLine("Min for an Int16 is: {0}", myInt32.MinValue)
Console.WriteLine("My value is: {0}", myInt32.ToString())
Console.WriteLine("I am a: {0}", myInt32.GetType().ToString())
```

You will seldom (if ever) need to directly declare a variable using the corresponding System type. However, it is important to understand that the intrinsic VB .NET data types map to a corresponding type in the System namespace. Thus, the following code is semantically equivalent to the previous example:

```
' Still Working with System.Int32!
Dim myInt32 As Integer = 30000
Console.WriteLine("Max for an Int32 is: {0}", myInt32.MaxValue)
Console.WriteLine("Min for an Int16 is: {0}", myInt32.MinValue)
Console.WriteLine("My value is: {0}", myInt32.ToString())
Console.WriteLine("I am a: {0}", myInt32.GetType().ToString())
```

Minor Commentary on Select Data Types

To wrap up the discussion of intrinsic data types, there are a few points of interest, especially when it comes to changes between VB 6.0 and VB .NET. As you have already seen in Table 3-1, the maximum and minimum bounds of many types have been retrofitted to be consistent with the rules of the Common Type System (CTS). In addition to this fact, also be aware of the following updates.

- The Boolean data type may only be assigned the values {True | False}. Although under the hood, VB represents False as 0 and True as –1, this is not the case in other .NET-aware languages! As long as you only make use of the {True | False} keywords, you will not have any problems manipulating the Boolean data type between languages.

- As you may have noticed from Figure 3-3, VB .NET does not support a Currency data type. The Decimal data type has replaced this type. In addition to the fact that Decimal is a base class type (and thus can be understood by all .NET-aware languages), Decimal supports far greater precision (and functionality) than the VB 6.0 Currency type.

- As you also may have noticed, the Variant data type (together with the related Variant-centric functions) is history as of VB .NET. Variants in and of themselves were a nice idea, in that a variable of type Variant could hold any [oleautomation] compatible type (which was great for COM). However, Variants are slow and loosely typed, so they are gone.

- VB .NET does not support unsigned data types. As mentioned, unsigned data types are not CLS compliant in the first place, so to this extent, the VB .NET type system guarantees that other languages can interact with the resulting binaries.

- Unlike VB 6.0, VB .NET now supports a Char data type. This type is used to represent a single Unicode character, and can be helpful when iterating over the individual members of a System.String type.

In addition to these data type-centric changes, VB .NET also modifies the behaviors of strings, enumerations, arrays, and structures (i.e., UDTs). You examine the specifics of these topics later in this chapter. To illustrate the final bullet point, ponder the following use of the Char data type. When executed, each character in the String type is printed out to the standard console.

```
Dim s As String
s = "Hello Char"
Dim c As Char
For Each c In s
    Console.WriteLine(c)
Next
```

SOURCE CODE *The DataTypes project is located under the Chapter 3 subdirectory.*

Data Type Conversions

VB 6.0 supported a very lazy approach to type conversion (lovingly referred to as "evil type coercion"). As you have already seen in Chapter 2, VB .NET supports the Option Strict setting, which forces you to explicitly make a conversion (sometimes called a *cast*) whenever it's possible information might be lost:

```
' Loss of information!
' If Option Strict is enabled, this will trigger a
' compiler error.
Dim theInt as Integer = 10000
Dim theLong as Long = 100000
theInt = theLong
```

Of course, if you are performing a cast that does not entail potential data loss, the VB .NET compiler is happy (Option Strict or not). Technically speaking, *widening* is the termed used to define a safe "upward" cast that does not result in a loss of data. Table 3-2 illustrates the safe widening conversions for the numerical types of VB .NET.

Table 3-2. Safe Widening Conversions

VB .NET TYPE	SAFELY WIDENS TO. . .
Byte	Byte, Short, Integer, Long, Decimal, Single, Double
Short	Short, Integer, Long, Decimal, Single, Double
Integer	Integer, Long, Decimal, Single, Double
Long	Long, Single, Decimal, Double
Single	Single, Double
Date	Date, String

Sometimes, you may want to perform a nonwidening cast, and accept a possible loss of data. Given that Option Strict should be enabled for any VB .NET application, you must explicitly make use of the conversion functions defined in Table 3-3.

Table 3-3. VB .NET Conversion Functions

CONVERSION FUNCTION	MEANING IN LIFE
CBool	Makes an expression a Boolean.
CByte	Makes an expression a byte.
CInt	Makes a numeric expression an integer by rounding.
CLng	Makes a numeric expression a long integer by rounding.
CSng	Makes a numeric expression single precision.
CDate	Makes a date expression a date.
CDbl	Makes a numeric expression double precision.
CDec	Makes a numeric expression of the currency type.
CStr	Makes any expression a string.
CChar	Converts the first character in a string to a Char.

Thus, we could convert a Long into an Integer as follows:

```
' OK. We can live with the data loss. . .
Dim theInt As Integer = 10000
Dim theLong As Long = 100000
theInt = CInt(theLong)
```

Later when OOP and interface based programming are discussed, you will also come to know the CType() conversion function, which can be used to explicitly cast between related objects (and their interfaces).

Concatenation Operators

It is worth pointing out that this version of Visual Basic supports a very C++ like notation, which can be helpful when you are attempting to somehow update "type A" using "type B". For example, when you want to increase the value of A by B, you could write the following VB 6.0 code:

```
Dim A as Integer
A = 9
Dim B as Integer
B = 30
A = A + B    ' A = 39
```

VB .NET allows you to shorten this assignment to:

```
Dim A as Integer
A = 9
Dim B as Integer
B = 30
A += B      ' A = 39
```

Here, you are basically saying that the Integer A is equal to itself plus the value of B. This shorthand is not limited to additive operations. In fact, any numerical operator can make use of this notation (e.g., A += B, A *= B, A /= B, A -= B and so forth). A similar notation may be used when concatenating string types (as you would guess, A &= B).

Basic Input and Output with the Console Class

Console is one of many types defined in the System namespace. As its name implies, this class encapsulates input, output, and error stream manipulations. Thus, you are correct to assume that this type is mostly useful when creating console-based applications rather than GUI-based applications (as you begin doing in Chapter 9).

Principal among the methods of System.Console are ReadLine() and WriteLine(), both of which are defined as shared. As you have seen, WriteLine() pumps a text string (including a carriage return) to the output stream. The Write() method pumps text to the output stream, without a carriage return. ReadLine() allows you to receive information from the input stream up until the carriage return, while Read() is used to capture a single character from the input stream.

To illustrate basic IO using the Console class, consider the following program, which prompts the user for some bits of information and echoes each item to the standard output stream.

```
' Make use of the Console class to perform basic IO.
Sub Main()
    ' Echo some stats.
    Console.Write("Enter your name: ")
    Dim s as String
    s = Console.ReadLine()
    Console.WriteLine("Hello, {0}", s)
    Console.Write("Enter your age: ")
    s = Console.ReadLine()
    Console.WriteLine("You are {0} years old", s)
End Sub
```

Introducing VB .NET String Formatting

During these first few examples, you have seen numerous occurrences of the tokens {0}, {1}, and the like. .NET introduces a new style of string formatting, slightly reminiscent of the printf() function used in the C language, without the cryptic "%d" "%s", " "%c" flags. Here is an update to the current example (see the output in Figure 3-4).

```
Module Module1
    Sub Main()
        . . .
        ' Format a simple string. . .
        Dim theInt As Integer = 90
        Dim theDouble As Double = 9.99
        Console.WriteLine("Int is: {0} Double is: {1}", _
                          theInt, theDouble)
        Console.WriteLine()
    End Sub
End Module
```

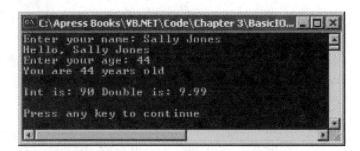

Figure 3-4. Simple format strings

The first parameter to WriteLine() represents a format string that contains optional placeholders designated by {0}, {1}, {2}, and so forth. The remaining parameters to WriteLine() are simply the values to be inserted into the respective placeholders (in this case, an Integer and a Double). Also be aware that WriteLine() also allows you to specify placeholder values as an array of objects. Thus, you can represent any number of items to be plugged into the format string as follows:

```
' Fill placeholders using an array of objects.
' We will examine arrays in greater detail later in this chapter.
Dim stuff() As Object = {"Hello", 20.9, 1, "There", "83", 99.99933}
Console.WriteLine("The Stuff: {0}, {1}, {2}, {3}, {4}, {5}", stuff)
```

It is also permissible for a given placeholder to repeat within a given string. For example if you want to build the string "9Number9Number9" you would write:

```
' John says. . .
Console.WriteLine("{0}Number{0}Number{0}", 9)
```

When you require more elaborate formatting, you should know that each placeholder can optionally contain various format characters (in either uppercase or lowercase), as seen in Table 3-4.

Table 3-4. VB .NET Format Characters

VB .NET FORMAT CHARACTER	MEANING IN LIFE
C or c	Used to format currency. By default, the flag will prefix a dollar sign ($) to the value, however this can be changed using a NumberFormatInfo type.
D or d	Formats decimal numbers. This flag may also specify the minimum number of digits used to pad the value.
E or e	Exponential notation.
F or f	Fixed point formatting.
G or g	General. Used to format a number to fixed or exponential format.
N or n	Basic numerical formatting (with commas).
X or x	Hexadecimal formatting. If you use an uppercase X, your hex format also contains uppercase characters.

These format characters are placed within a given placeholder using a single colon (for example, {0:C}, {1:d}, {2:X}). To illustrate, assume you have updated Main() with the following logic (Figure 3-5 shows a test run):

```
' Now make use of some format tags.
Console.WriteLine("C format: {0:C}", 99989.987)
Console.WriteLine("D9 format: {0:D9}", 99999)
Console.WriteLine("E format: {0:E}", 99999.76543)
Console.WriteLine("F3 format: {0:F3}", 99999.9999)
Console.WriteLine("N format: {0:N}", 99999)
Console.WriteLine("X format: {0:X}", 99999)
Console.WriteLine("x format: {0:x}", 99999)
```

```
C:\Apress Books\VB.NET\Code\Chapter 3\BasicIO\bin\BasicIO...
Enter your name: Mike
Hello, Mike
Enter your age: 2
You are 2 years old

Int is: 90 Double is: 9.99

The Stuff: Hello, 20.9, 1, There, 83, 99.99933
C format: $99,989.99
D9 format: 000099999
E format: 9.999977E+004
F3 format: 100000.000
N format: 99,999.00
X format: 1869F
x format: 1869f
```

Figure 3-5. More complex format strings

Be aware that the use of the VB .NET formatting characters is not limited to the System.Console.WriteLine() method. For example, these flags can be used within the context of the shared String.Format() method. This is helpful when you need to build a string containing numerical values in memory and display it at a later time:

```
' Use the static String.Format() method to build a new string.
Dim formStr As String
formStr = String.Format("Don't you want you had {0:C} in your account?", _
                                                 99989.987)
Console.WriteLine(formStr)
```

SOURCE CODE *The BasicIO project is located under the Chapter 3 subdirectory.*

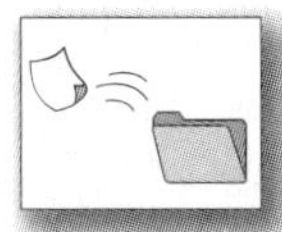

Anatomy of a Simple VB .NET Class

Although it is possible to build applications that contain nothing but a number of Modules, this is not a terribly object-oriented approach (in fact, it has the look and feel of a structured C application!). In the real world, VB .NET programs are composed of class definitions. All object-oriented languages make a clear distinction between *classes* and *objects.* A *class* is a definition of a user-defined type (UDT) which is often regarded as a blueprint for variables of this type. An *object* is simply a term describing a given instance of a particular class. In its simplest form, a VB .NET class can be defined as follows:

```
' Recall, all VB .NET code files end with a *.vb file extension.
Class HelloClass
End Class
```

Notice that VB .NET class definitions are marked using the Class keyword, rather than the VB 6.0 approach of defining a custom class within a *.cls file. In fact, in VB .NET, there is no *.cls extension. All files are simply marked with a *.vb extension, regardless of what they contain (forms, classes, Modules or whatnot). Because you now have specific keywords used to mark your types, you are also able to define multiple classes in a single *.vb file. In fact, you may define any number of types (interfaces, structures, classes, enumerations) within a single file:

```
' MyTypes.vb
Class HelloClass
End Class
Class AnotherClass
End Class
Interface IAmDescribedLater
End Interface
```

Empty type definitions are not very useful (or interesting) on their own. Once you have defined the shell of a class, the next step is to populate it with any number of members. You examine the syntactic details of methods, properties, and events a bit later. For now, let's examine a long overdue feature: parameterized class constructors.

Creating Objects: Constructor Basics

In earlier versions of VB, class designers are provided with the Initialize and Terminate events. Within the handler for the Initialize event, you were able to perform any necessary start-up logic, to ensure the object came to life in a proper state. The problem with this approach was that Initialize did not allow you to pass in any start-up parameters. Without this possibility, the object user needed to establish the state of the object on a member-by-member basis:

```
' VB 6.0 would demand something like so.
Dim obj as CMyType
Set obj = New CMyType ' Initialize fired!
With obj
    .Prop = 90
    .Prop2 = "Chucky"
End With
```

To help the object user along, and reduce the number of hits required on the type, many VB developers created an ad hoc construction routine. For example:

```
' VB 6.0 ad hoc creation method
' CMyType definition
...
Private mProp as Integer
Private mProp2 as String
Public Sub Create(p as Integer, p2 as String)
    mProp = p
    mProp2 = p2
End Sub
```

With this, the object user reduced the number of hits on the object:

```
' A slightly better solution.
Dim obj as CMyType
Set obj = New CMyType ' Initialize fired!
obj.Create 90, "Chucky"
```

Still, this is far from ideal. In a perfect situation, you could allow the object user to specify start-up parameters at the time of creation. In essence, you would *like* to be able to write the following VB 6.0 code:

```
' ILLEGAL VB 6.0 code!!!
Dim obj as New CMyType(90, "Chucky")
```

While illegal in VB 6.0, using VB .NET you are able to do this very thing. For example:

```
' This is LEGAL VB .NET code.
Dim obj as CMyType = New CMyType(90, "Chucky")
```

To understand how this works syntactically, let's see a simple example of creating an object. In VB .NET, the *New* keyword is the de facto way to create an object instance. Observe the following updated Main() method:

```
Class HelloClass
End Class
Module Module1
     Sub Main()
          ' You can declare and create a new object in a single line
          Dim c1 as HelloClass = New HelloClass()
```

```
        ' . . .or break declaration and creation into two lines.
        Dim c2 as HelloClass
        c2 = New HelloClass()     ' Set keyword is now obsolete!
    End Sub
End Module
```

The New keyword is in charge of allocating the correct number of bytes for the specified object and acquiring sufficient memory from the managed heap. Here, you have allocated two objects (c1 and c2) each of which points to an instance of the HelloClass type. Understand that VB .NET class variables are actually a *reference* to the object in memory, not the actual object itself. Thus, in this light, c1 and c2 each reference a distinct HelloClass object allocated on the managed heap (Chapter 4 offers additional details).

Set Is Dead (and New Is Consistent)

In the world of VB 6.0 development, programmers were forced to contend with a rather oddball behavior of object creation. Assume you wrote the following VB 6.0 code block:

```
' Under VB 6.0, this is evil!. . .
Dim myObj as New MyClass
myObj.SomeSub            ' Initialized fired here. . .
myObj.SomeProp = 12      ' CHECKED for null reference!
myObj.SomeFx(39)         ' CHECKED again for null reference!
```

The VB6 oddball behavior is that the object is Initialized the first time the object is referenced in code. Yet each subsequent time the object was referenced a *separate check* had to be performed to see if it had been Initialized. Therefore, when you "declare and New" a variable on a single line of VB 6.0 code, you incur an extra step each time you touch the object. To avoid this, VB 6.0 developers drilled the following object creation pattern into their heads:

```
' Under VB 6.0, this is annoying,
' but not evil.
Dim myObj as MyClass
Set myObj = New MyClass ' Initialized fired here. . .
myObj.SomeSub
myObj.SomeProp = 12
myObj.SomeFx(39)
```

When you use the VB 6.0 Set keyword, you avoid the internal subsequent checks for uninitialized object types.

Under VB .NET this process cleans up quite a bit. First, it makes *no* difference if you "declare and New" on a single line or on two lines. The constructor is triggered at the point of "New-ing." Even better, no internal checks are made to ensure the object has been initialized. As an interesting corollary, VB .NET no longer supports the Set keyword. The short answer is, it makes no difference whatsoever when you choose to make use of the New keyword. Thus, each of the following code blocks are just as efficient (and just as safe):

```
' No Set keyword in VB .NET. . .
Dim myObj as MyClass = New MyClass()    ' constructor called here.
Dim myObj2 as MyClass
MyObj2 = New MyClass()  ' constructor called here.
```

Building Custom Constructors

The previous code block is making calls to the *default constructor* of the type. Every VB .NET class is automatically endowed with a free default constructor, which you may redefine if need be. By definition, default constructors never take arguments. Beyond creating a new object instance, the default constructor ensures that all state data (for example, member variables of the class) is set to an appropriate default value (this behavior is true of all constructors).

Typically, your custom classes provide additional constructors beyond the default. In doing so, you provide the object user with a simple way to initialize the state of an object directly at the time of creation. Here is a type named HelloClass, defined with a custom constructor, a redefined default constructor, and some simple state data:

```
Class HelloClass
    ' Default constructor has been redefined.
    Public Sub New()
        Console.WriteLine("Default ctor called!")
    End Sub
    ' This custom constructor assigns state data to a known value.
    Public Sub New(ByVal x As Integer, ByVal y As Integer)
        Console.WriteLine("Custom ctor called!")
        intX = x
        intY = y
    End Sub
    ' Sample state data.
    Public intX, intY As Integer
    ' Simple member function.
    Public Sub SayHi()
        Console.WriteLine("Hi there!")
```

```
    End Sub
End Class

Module Module1
    Sub Main()
        ' Make instance of HelloClass using
        ' default constructor.
        Dim c1 As HelloClass = New HelloClass()
        c1.SayHi()
        Console.WriteLine("c1.intX = {0} c1.intY = {1}", c1.intX, c1.intY)
        ' Another instance of HelloClass.
        ' using custom constructor.
        Dim c2 As HelloClass
        c2 = New HelloClass(100, 200)
        c2.SayHi()
        Console.WriteLine("c2.intX = {0} c2.intY = {1}", c2.intX, c2.intY)
    End Sub
End Module
```

On examining the program's output you can see that the default constructor has indeed assigned the internal state data to the default values (zero), while the custom constructor has assigned the member data to values specified by the object user (see Figure 3-6).

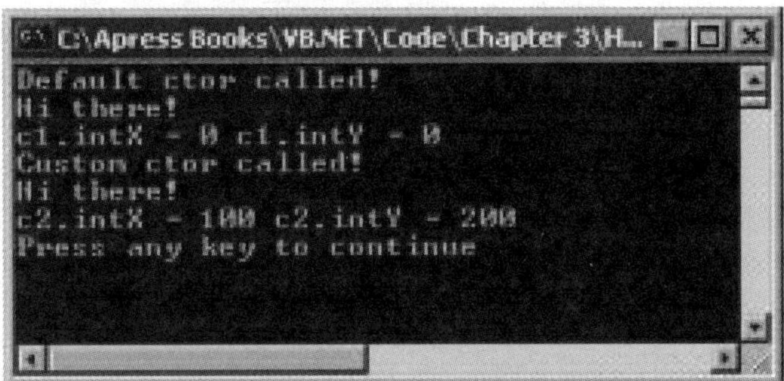

Figure 3-6. Simple constructor logic

As you can see, you have a bit of new syntax to contend with. When you want to equip your custom classes to support constructors, you can add any number of Public subroutines named "New." As suggested by the name of the method, each version of a New method provides the user with a distinct way to establish the state of an object. Chapter 4 discusses the finer points of building class constructors. Until then, simply understand that when you define "New" methods on your custom types, you provide the user with a handy way to create a new object.

Keep in mind that what makes one constructor different from another (in the eyes of vbc.exe) is the number of and type of constructor arguments. Formally speaking, when a class has a member of the same name that differs by its set of arguments, you have *overloaded* the method. Thus, the HelloClass type has *overloaded* the constructor to provide a number of ways to create the object at the time of declaration. As you will see in Chapter 4, VB .NET allows you to overload any method.

SOURCE CODE *The HelloThere project is located under the Chapter 3 subdirectory.*

Default Values

As illustrated in this chapter, all intrinsic .NET data types have a default value. When you create custom types, all member variables are automatically assigned to an appropriate initial value. To illustrate, consider the following Module definition:

```
' VB .NET automatically sets all member variables to a safe default value.
Module Module1
    ' Here are a number of fields. . .
    Public theSignedByte As SByte
    Public theByte As Byte
    Public theShort As Short
    Public theInt As Integer
    Public theLong As Long
    Public theChar As Char
    Public theDouble As Double
    Public theBool As Boolean
    Public theDecimal As Decimal
    Public theStr As String
    Public theObj As Object

     Sub Main()
        ' Print out default values.
        Console.WriteLine("bool: {0}", theBool)
        Console.WriteLine("byte: {0}", theByte)
        Console.WriteLine("char: {0}", theChar)
        Console.WriteLine("decimal: {0}", theDecimal)
        Console.WriteLine("double: {0}", theDouble)
        Console.WriteLine("int: {0}", theInt)
        Console.WriteLine("long: {0}", theLong)
        Console.WriteLine("object: {0}", theObj)
        Console.WriteLine("short: {0}", theShort)
```

```
        Console.WriteLine("signed byte: {0}", theSignedByte)
        Console.WriteLine("string: {0}", theStr)
    End Sub
End Module
```

If you were to now run the application, you would see that each member variable has been automatically assigned to a corresponding default value, as seen in Figure 3-7 (note that String and Char data types default to empty strings, while an object reference begins life as Nothing (not easily seen in this screen shot!)

```
C:\Apress Books\VB.NET\Code\Chapter 3\Defau...
bool: False
byte: 0
char:
decimal: 0
double: 0
int: 0
long: 0
object:
short: 0
signed byte: 0
string:
Press any key to continue
```

Figure 3-7. All types have a safe default value.

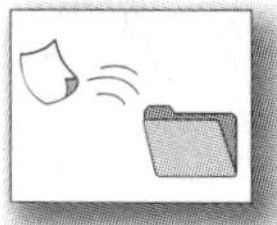

SOURCE CODE *The DefaultValues project is located under the Chapter 3 subdirectory.*

Defining Program Constants

Now that you can create variables, you need to examine the logical opposite: Constants. VB .NET offers the "Const" keyword, to define constant data types. Although it is possible to define constants within a method scope, a more beneficial use of Const is to create class level constant definitions. For example:

```
Public Class MyConstants
    Public Const myIntConst As Integer = 5
    Public Const myStringConst As String = "I'm a const"
End Class
Module Module1
    Sub Main()
        Console.WriteLine(MyConstants.myIntConst)
```

```
        Console.WriteLine(MyConstants.myStringConst)
        'Scoped constant.
        Const localConst As String = "I am a rock, I am an island"
        Console.WriteLine("Local constant: {0}", localConst)
        ' Uncomment below to trigger errors..
        ' MyConstants.myIntConst = 999
        ' localConst = "I am not wishy washy"
    End Sub
End Module
```

Notice that we are referencing the constant data defined by the MyConstants class using a class name prefix. However, if you have a class instance handy, you could write the following code:

```
' Get at constant data from an object variable.
Dim mc as New MyConstants()
Console.WriteLine(mc.myIntConst)
```

If you create a utility class that contains nothing but constant data, you may want to define a *private* constructor. In this way, you ensure the object user cannot make an instance of your class:

```
Public Class MyConstants
    ' These must be accessed at the class level.
    Public Const myIntConst As Integer = 5
    Public Const myStringConst As String = "I'm a const"
    ' Redefine default constructor as private
    ' to stop user from making this class.
    Private Sub New()
    End Sub
End Class
```

The same end result can be achieved by marking your "constant only class" as an abstract type, using the MustInherit class designation. You examine the use of this keyword in the next chapter; however here is some sample usage:

```
'Abstract definition also prevents the creation of a given type.
Public MustInherit Class MyConstants
    ' These must be accessed at the class level.
    Public Const myIntConst As Integer = 5
    Public Const myStringConst As String = "I'm a const"
End Class
```

In either case, if you attempt to create an instance of MyConstants, a compiler error is generated. When you want to gain access to these constants, you need to prefix the class name to the member (i.e., MyConstants.myIntConst).

SOURCE CODE *The Constants project is located under the Chapter 3 subdirectory.*

Understanding Value Types and Reference Types

As you have already seen, intrinsic VB .NET data types alias a specific base class type. One very positive byproduct of this design is the fact that, when you create a data point of type Integer, all .NET-aware languages understand the fixed nature of this type, and all agree on the range it is capable of handling (even though it may be represented by a unique keyword in each language).

Specifically speaking, a VB .NET data type may be *value based* or *reference based.* Value-based types, which include all numerical data types (Integer, Double, etc.) as well as enumerations and structures, are allocated *on the stack.* When you assign one value type to another, a member-by-member copy of the type is achieved. To illustrate, assume you have the following VB .NET structure (you examine structures in greater detail later in this chapter):

```
' Structures are value types.
Structure FOO
    Public x, y as Integer
End Structure
```

Now, observe the following Main() logic (the output can be seen in Figure 3-8).

```
Module Module1
    Sub Main()
        ' The new keyword is optional
        ' when calling the default constructor of a structure.
        Dim f1 As FOO = New FOO()
        f1.x = 100
        f1.y = 100
        ' This results in a copy of f1,
        ' which is stored in f2.
        Dim f2 As FOO = f1
        ' Here is F1.
        Console.WriteLine("F1.x = {0}", f1.x)
        Console.WriteLine("F1.y = {0}", f1.y)
        ' Here is F2.
        Console.WriteLine("F2.x = {0}", f2.x)
        Console.WriteLine("F2.y = {0}", f2.y)
```

```
        ' Change f2.x. This will NOT change f1.x.
        Console.WriteLine("Changing f2.x")
        f2.x = 900
        ' Print again.
        Console.WriteLine("F2.x = {0}", f2.x)
        Console.WriteLine("F1.x = {0}", f1.x)
End Sub
End Module
```

```
Making new Foo STRUCTURE
Assigning f2 to f1
F1.x = 100
F1.y = 100
F2.x = 100
F2.y = 100
Changing f2.x
F2.x = 900
F1.x = 100
Press any key to continue
```

Figure 3-8: Assigning one value type to another results in a member-by-member copy

Here you have created a variable of type FOO (named f1) which is then assigned to another FOO type (f2). Because FOO is a value type, you have two copies of the FOO type on the stack that can be independently manipulated. Therefore, when you change the value of f2.x, the value of f1.x is unaffected.

In stark contrast, reference types (classes) are allocated on the garbage-collected heap. Assigning reference types results in a new reference to an existing type, meaning multiple variables point to the same location in memory. To illustrate, let's change the definition of the FOO type from a VB .NET Structure to a VB .NET Class:

```
' Classes are reference types.
Class FOO
    Public x, y as Integer
End Class
```

If you run your test program once again, notice the change in behavior (Figure 3-9).

```
C:\Apress Books\VB.NET\Code\Chapter 3\ValAnd...
Making new Foo CLASS
Assigning f2 to f1
F1.x = 100
F1.y = 100
F2.x = 100
F2.y = 100
Changing f2.x
F2.x = 900
F1.x = 900
Press any key to continue
```

Figure 3-9. Assigning reference types results in a new reference.

This time around, you have two references to the same object on the managed heap. Therefore, when you change the value of *x* using the *f2* reference, *f1.x* reflects the same value.

Value Types Containing Reference Types

Now that you have a better feeling for the core differences between value types and reference types, let's see a more complex example. Assume you have the following simple reference type:

```
Class TheRefType
    Public x As String
    Sub New(ByVal s As String)
        x = s
    End Sub
End Class
```

Now assume that you want to contain a variable of this reference type within a value type named InnerRef as well as a simple Integer data type. The syntax is as you would expect. Understand however, that the default constructor of a Structure is reserved. Thus, to set the state of the string maintained by TheRefType, you provide a custom constructor:

```
Structure InnerRef
    Public refType As TheRefType ' Ref type.
    Public structData as Integer ' Val type
    Sub New(ByVal s As String)
        refType = New TheRefType(s)
    End Sub
End Structure
```

At this point, you have contained a reference type within a value type. The million dollar question would now be, what happens if you assign one InnerRef type to another? Given what you already know about value types, you would be correct in assuming that the value of the Integer should be an independent entity for each InnerRef variable (as a copy was achieved). But what about the reference type? Will the internal object be fully copied, or will the *reference to that object* be copied? Ponder the following code and check out Figure 3-10 for the answer.

```
' Make val type that contains ref type.
Dim valWithRef As New InnerRef("Initial value")
valWithRef.structData = 666
Dim valWithRef2 As InnerRef
valWithRef2 = valWithRef
valWithRef2.refType.x = "I have been changed by ref 2!"
valWithRef2.structData = 777
Console.WriteLine("valWithRef.refType.x is {0}", valWithRef.refType.x)
Console.WriteLine("valWithRef2.refType.x is {0}", valWithRef2.refType.x)
Console.WriteLine("valWithRef.structData is {0}", valWithRef.structData)
Console.WriteLine("valWithRef2.structData is {0}", valWithRef2.structData)
```

```
C:\Apress Books\VB.NET\Code\Chapter 3\ValAndRef\bin\ValAndRef...
valWithRef.refType.x is I have been changed by ref 2!
valWithRef2.refType.x is I have been changed by ref 2!
valWithRef.structData is 666
valWithRef2.structData is 777
Press any key to continue
```

Figure 3-10. Reference types are not *fully copied*

As you can see, the internal reference type (TheRefType) was not fully copied into new InnerRef value type. By default, when a value type contains any reference types, assignment results in a "shallow copy" of the references. In this way, you have two independent Structures, each of which contains a class pointing to the same memory location! When you want to perform a "deep copy," where the state of your objects are fully copied, you need to implement the ICloneable interface (as you do in Chapter 5).

Value and Reference Types: Further Details

To further understand the distinction between value types and reference types, ponder Table 3-5 which illustrates how each stands up against a number of "intriguing questions" (many of which are examined in greater detail throughout this text):

Table 3-5. Value Types and Reference Types Side-by-Side

INTRIGUING QUESTION	VALUE TYPE	REFERENCE TYPE
Where is this type allocated?	Allocated on the stack	Allocated on the managed heap
How is a variable represented?	Value types variables are local copies.	Reference type variables are pointing to the memory occupied by the allocated instance.
What is the base type?	Must directly derive from System.ValueType	Can derive from any other type (except System.ValueType)
Can this type function as a base to other types?	No. Value types cannot be extended.	Yes. If the type is not 'sealed' (see Chapter 4), it may function as a base to other types.
Able to override Object.Finalize()?	No. Value types are never placed onto the heap and therefore do not need to be finalized.	Yes (more details in Chapter 4).
Can I define constructors for this type?	Yes, but the default constructor is reserved (i.e., your custom constructors must all have arguments).	But of course!
When do variables of this type die?	When it falls out of the defining scope	When the managed heap is garbage collected

Despite their differences, value types and reference types both have the ability to implement standard (i.e., preexisting) and custom (i.e., you made them) interfaces, and may support any number of fields, methods, properties, and events.

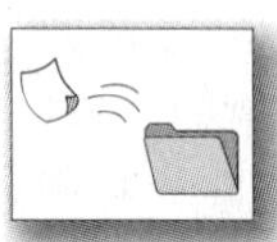

SOURCE CODE *The ValAndRef project is located under the Chapter 3 subdirectory.*

The Master Node: System.Object

In VB .NET, every data type (value or reference based) is ultimately derived from a common base class: System.Object. The Object class defines a common polymorphic behavior for every type in the .NET universe. In the HelloClass type definition seen earlier in this chapter, I did not explicitly indicate that Object was your base class, but this is assumed. If you want to explicitly state System.Object as a type's base class, you are free to define your class definitions as such:

```
' Here we are explicitly deriving from System.Object.
Class HelloClass
    Inherits System.Object
End Class
```

Like any VB .NET class, System.Object defines a set of instance members. In the following formal C# definition, note that some of these items are declared "virtual," which specifies that a given member may be *overridden* (e.g., redefined) by a subclass (to view this definition with your own eyes, make use of the WinCV.exe utility as described in Chapter 1):

```
// The top-most class in the .NET world: System.Object
namespace System
{
     public class Object
     {
          public Object();
          public virtual Boolean Equals(Object obj);
          public virtual Int32 GetHashCode();
          public Type GetType();
          public virtual String ToString();
          protected virtual void Finalize();
          protected Object MemberwiseClone();
     }
. . .
}
```

Table 3-6 offers a rundown of the functionality provided by each method.

Table 3-6. Core Members of System.Object

INSTANCE METHOD OF OBJECT CLASS	MEANING IN LIFE
Equals()	By default this method returns True only if the items being compared refer to the exact same item in memory. Thus, Equals() is used to compare object references, not the state of the object. Typically, this method is overridden to return True only if the objects being compared have the same internal state values (that is, value-based semantics). Be aware that if you override Equals(), you should also override GetHashCode().
GetHashCode()	Returns an Integer that identifies a specific object instance.
GetType()	This method returns a Type object that fully describes the object you are currently referencing. In short, this is a Runtime Type Identification (RTTI) method available to all objects (discussed in greater detail in Chapter 8).
ToString()	Returns a string representation of this object, using the "<namespace>.<class name>" format (termed the "fully qualified name"). This method can be overridden by a subclass to return a tokenized string of name/value pairs that represent the object's internal state, rather than its fully qualified name.
Finalize()	For the time being, you can understand this method (when overridden) is called to free any allocated resources before the object is destroyed. I talk more about the CLR garbage collection services in Chapter 4.
MemberwiseClone()	This method exists to return a member by member copy of the current object. This method cannot be overridden or accessed by the outside world from an object instance. If you need to allow the outside world to obtain deep copies of a given type, implement the ICloneable interface, which you do in Chapter 5.

To illustrate some of the default behavior provided by the Object base class, consider the following (Figure 3-11 shows a test run):

```
' Trivial class definition
Class HelloClass
    Inherits System.Object
End Class
Module Module1
    Sub Main()
        Dim hc As New HelloClass()
        ' Use inherited members of System.Object.
        Console.WriteLine("ToString: {0}", hc.ToString())
        Console.WriteLine("Hash code: {0}", hc.GetHashCode())
        Console.WriteLine("Type: {0}", hc.GetType().ToString())
        ' Make some other references to hc.
        Dim hc2 As HelloClass = hc
        Dim o As Object = hc2
        ' Are all 3 instances pointing to the same object in memory?
        If o.Equals(hc) And hc2.Equals(o) Then
            Console.WriteLine("Same instance!")
        End If
    End Sub
End Module
```

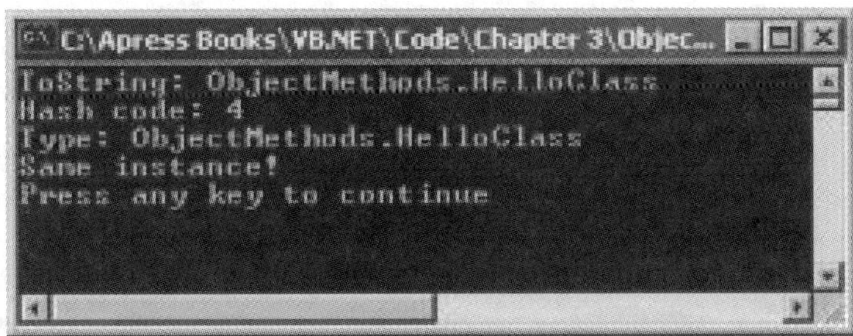

Figure 3-11. Working with select Object methods

First, notice how the default implementation of ToString() simply returns the fully qualified name of the current type (ObjectMethods.HelloClass). In many situations, derived classes override this method to return a string representing the values of its internal state data (as you do in a moment). Now, examine the following block of code:

```
' Compare objects references. . .
Sub Main()
    . . .
    ' Make some other references to hc.
    Dim hc2 As HelloClass = hc
    Dim o As Object = hc2
    ' Are all 3 instances pointing to the same object in memory?
    If o.Equals(hc) And hc2.Equals(o) Then
        Console.WriteLine("Same instance!")
    End If
End Sub
```

The default behavior of Equals() is to compare two objects using *reference semantics* not *value semantics.* Here, you create a new HelloClass variable named hc. At this point, a new HelloClass is placed on the managed heap. Hc2 is also of type HelloClass. However, you are not creating a *new* instance, but rather assigning this variable to reference hc. Therefore, hc and hc2 are both pointing to the same object in memory, as is the variable o (of type Object, which was thrown in for good measure). Given that hc, hc2 and o all point to the same memory location, the equality test succeeds.

Overriding Some Default Behaviors of System.Object

Although the canned behavior of System.Object can fit the bill in a number of cases, it is quite common for your custom types to override some of these inherited methods. For example, assume you have a class named Person, which defines some state data representing an individual's name, social security number, and age:

```
' Remember! All classes implicitly derive from Object.
Class Person
    Public Sub New(ByVal fname As String, ByVal lname As String, _
                   ByVal ssn As String, ByVal a As Byte)
        FirstName = fname
        LastName = lname
        Me.SSN = ssn
        age = a
    End Sub
    ' The state of the person.
    Public FirstName As String
    Public LastName As String
    Public SSN As String
    Public age As Byte
End Class
```

To begin, let's override Object.ToString() to return a textual representation of a person's state. You examine the full details of method overriding in the next chapter. For the time being, just absorb the fact that you are changing the behavior of the ToString() method to work specifically with our Person class:

```
' Need to reference this namespace to access StringBuilder type.
Imports System.Text
' A Person class implements ToString() as so:
Class Person
...
    Public Overrides Function ToString() As String
        Dim sb As StringBuilder = New StringBuilder()
        sb.Append("[FirstName=" & Me.FirstName)
        sb.Append(" LastName=" & Me.LastName)
        sb.Append(" SSN=" & Me.SSN)
        sb.Append(" Age=" & Me.age & "]")
        Return sb.ToString()
    End Function
End Class
```

How you choose to format the string returned from System.Object.ToString() is largely a matter of personal choice. In this example, the name/value pairs have been contained within square brackets ([. . .]). Also notice that this example is making use of a new type, System.Text.StringBuilder (which is also a matter of personal choice). This type is described in greater detail later in the chapter.

Let's also override the behavior of Object.Equals() to work with *value-based semantics*. Recall that by default, Equals() returns True only if the two objects being compared reference the same object instance in memory. For the Person class, it may be helpful to implement Equals() to return True if the two variables being compared contain the same state values (e.g., name, SSN, and age):

```
' A Person class implements Equals() as follows:
Public Overrides Overloads Function Equals(ByVal o As Object) As Boolean
    ' Does the incoming object
    ' have the same values as me?
    Dim temp As Person = o
    If temp.FirstName = Me.FirstName And _
        temp.LastName = Me.LastName And _
        temp.SSN = Me.SSN And _
        temp.age = Me.age Then
        Return True
    Else
        Return False
    End If
End Function
```

Here, you are examining the values of the incoming object against the values of our internal values (note the use of the "Me" keyword). If the name, SSN, and age of each are identical, you have two objects with the exact same state data and therefore return True.

Before you see the output of this new type, you have one final detail to attend to. When a class overrides the Equals() method, you should also override the default implementation of GetHashCode() (if you do not, you are issued a compiler warning). This method returns a numerical value used to identify an object in memory, and is commonly used with hash-based collections.

There are many algorithms that can be used to create a hash code, some fancy, others not so fancy. For our current purposes, let's assume that the hash code of the string representing an individual's SSN is unique enough:

```
' Return a hash code based on the person's SSN.
Public Overrides Function GetHashCode() As Integer
    Return SSN.GetHashCode()
End Function
```

With this, here is our new Person class in action (check out Figure 3-12 for output):

```
Sub Main()
    '  Now make some people and test for equality.
    '  NOTE:  We want these to be identical to test
    '  the Equals() method.
    Dim p1 As Person = New Person("Fred", "Jones", "222-22-2222", 98)
    Dim p2 As Person = New Person("Fred", "Jones", "222-22-2222", 98)

    '  Overridden Equals()
    If (p1.Equals(p2)) Then
        Console.WriteLine("P1 and P2 have same state")
    Else
        Console.WriteLine("P1 and P2 are DIFFERENT")
    End If
    '  Change state of p2.
    p2.age = 2
    '  Test again.
    If (p1.Equals(p2)) Then
        Console.WriteLine("P1 and P2 have same state")
    Else
        Console.WriteLine("P1 and P2 are DIFFERENT")
    End If
```

```
    ' Get stringified version of objects.
    Console.WriteLine(p1.ToString())
    Console.WriteLine(p2.ToString())
End Sub
```

```
C:\Apress Books\VB.NET\Code\Chapter 3\ObjectMethods\bin\Obje...
P1 and P2 have same state
P1 and P2 are DIFFERENT
[FirstName=Fred LastName=Jones SSN=222-22-2222 Age=98]
[FirstName=Fred LastName=Jones SSN=222-22-2222 Age=2]
Press any key to continue
```

Figure 3-12. The result of value-based equality testing

Shared Members of System.Object

In addition to the instance level members you have just examined, System.Object does define two (very helpful) shared members that also test for value-based or reference-based equality. Consider the following code:

```
' Shared members of System.Object.
Dim p3 As Person = New Person("Sally", "Jones", "333-33-3333", 4)
Dim p4 As Person = New Person("Sally", "Jones", "333-33-3333", 4)
Console.WriteLine("P3 and P4 have same state: {0}", Object.Equals(p3, p4))
Console.WriteLine("P3 and P4 are pointing to same object: {0}", _
    Object.ReferenceEquals(p3, p4))
```

Here, you are able to simply send in two objects (of any type) and allow the System.Object class to determine the details automatically.

SOURCE CODE *The ObjectMethods project is located under the Chapter 3 subdirectory.*

VB .NET Iteration Constructs

All programming languages provide ways to repeat blocks of code until a terminating condition has been met. Regardless of which language you are coming from, the VB .NET iteration statements should pose no raised eyebrows and require little explanation. In a nutshell, VB .NET provides the following iteration constructs:

- For/Next loop
- For/Each loop
- Do/While loop
- Do/Until loop

Let's quickly examine each looping construct in turn.

For/Next Loop

When you need to iterate over a block of code a fixed number of times, the "For" statement is the looping construct of champions. In essence, you are able to specify how many times a block of code repeats itself, including the range of the iteration. Without belaboring the point, here is a sample of the syntax:

```
' A basic for loop.
   Dim i As Integer
   For i = 10 To 23     ' Without Step, incrimination is n + 1
       Console.WriteLine("Number is: {0}", i)
   Next
```

All of your old VB 6.0 tricks still hold when you build a VB .NET For statement. You can create nested For loops, build endless loops, and make use of the Step keyword to force an (n + m) incrimination. I'll assume that you will bend this iteration construct as you see fit.

For/Each Loop

Visual Basic programmers have long seen the benefits of the For Each construct. Here is a simple example using For Each to traverse an array of strings that represent possible titles for forthcoming publications. Once this string array has been populated, you iterate over the contents looking for a pattern match (COM or .NET) using String.IndexOf() (you examine further details of System.String later in this chapter):

```
' Digging into an array using For Each.
Dim arrBookTitles() As String = _
```

```
{"Complex Algorithms", _
"COM for the Fearful Programmer", _
"Do you Remember Classic COM?", _
"VB .NET and the .NET Platform", _
"COM for the Angry Engineer"}
Dim COM, NET As Integer ' Remember, we're both integers!
' Assume there are no books on COM and .NET (yet).
Dim s As String
For Each s In arrBookTitles
    If Not (-1 = s.IndexOf("COM")) Then
        COM += 1
    ElseIf Not (-1 = s.IndexOf(".NET")) Then
        NET += 1
    End If
Next
Console.WriteLine("Found {0} COM references and {1} .NET references.", _
                       COM, NET)
```

In addition to iterating over simple arrays, the For Each construct is also able to iterate over system-supplied or user-defined collections. I'll hold off on the details until Chapter 5, as this aspect of the For Each loop entails an understanding of interface-based programming and the system-supplied IEnumerator and IEnumerable interfaces.

Do/While and Do/Until Looping Constructs

You have already seen that the For statement is typically used when you have some foreknowledge of the number of iterations you want to perform (e.g., loop until $j > 20$). The Do statements on the other hand is useful for those times when you are uncertain how long it might take for a terminating condition to be met.

Do/While and Do/Until are (in many ways) interchangeable. Do/While keeps looping until the terminating condition is *false*. On the other hand, Do/Until keeps looping until the terminating condition is *true*. For example:

```
' Keep looping until X is not equal to an empty string.
Do
    ' Some code to loop over.
Loop Until X <> ""
' Keep looping as long as X is equal to an empty string.
Do
    ' Some code to loop over.
Loop While X = ""
```

Note that in these last two examples, the test for the terminating condition was placed at the end of the Loop keyword. Using this syntax, you can rest assured that the code within the loop will be executed at least once (given that the test to exit the loop occurs after the first iteration). If you prefer to allow for the possibility that the code within the loop may never be executed, move the Until or While clause at the beginning of the loop:

```
' Keep looping until X is not equal to an empty string.
Do Until X <> ""
    ' Some code to loop over.
Loop
' Keep looping as long as X is not equal to an empty string.
Do While X = ""
    ' Some code to loop over.
Loop
```

To illustrate the Do looping constructs, take a brief look at .NET file manipulation (which is fully detailed in Chapter 12). The StreamReader class, defined within the System.IO namespace, encapsulates the details of reading from a given file. Notice that you obtain an instance of the StreamReader type as a return value from the shared File.OpenText() method. Notice that the call to OpenText() is wrapped by new VB .NET keywords (Try, Catch, and End Try). As Chapter 4 shows, VB .NET supports a new error-handling mechanism formally called structured exception handling (SEH). In any case, once you have opened the boot.ini file, you are able to iterate over each line in the file using StreamReader.ReadLine(). After the file as been parsed, you ask the user if he or she is ready to terminate the program (The output of the Iteration logic can be seen in Figure 3-13).

```
' A Do While loop, using VB .NET structured
' exception handling (examined fully in Chapter 4)
Try      ' Just in case we can't find the correct file. . .
    ' Open the file named 'boot.ini'.
    Dim strReader As StreamReader = File.OpenText("C:\boot.ini")
    ' Read the next line and dump to the console.
    Dim strLine As String
    Do
        strLine = strReader.ReadLine()
        Console.WriteLine(strLine)
    Loop While Nothing <> strLine
    ' Close the file.
    strReader.Close()
Catch e As FileNotFoundException
    Console.WriteLine(e.Message)
```

```
End Try
' The Do / Until statement
 Dim ans As String
 Do
    Console.Write("Are you done? [yes] [no] : ")
    ans = Console.ReadLine()
Loop Until ans = "yes"
```

```
C:\Apress Books\VB.NET\Code\Chapter 3\Iterations\bin\Iterations.e...
Number is: 22
Number is: 23
Found 3 COM references and 1 .NET references.
[boot loader]
timeout=30
default=multi(0)disk(0)rdisk(0)partition(1)\WINNT
[operating systems]
multi(0)disk(0)rdisk(0)partition(1)\WINNT="Microsoft Wind
/fastdetect

Are you done? [yes] [no] : Nope
Are you done? [yes] [no] : yes
Press any key to continue
```

Figure 3-13. Iteration logic

Finally, understand that VB .NET still supports the raw While loop. However, the Wend keyword has been replaced with a more fitting "End While":

```
Dim j As Integer
While j < 20
    Console.Write(j & ", ")
    j += 1
End While
```

SOURCE CODE *The Iterations project is located under the Chapter 3 subdirectory.*

VB .NET Control Flow Constructs

Now that you can iterate over a block of code, the next related concept is how to control the flow of program execution. The control flow constructs of VB .NET are identical to VB 6.0. First up, you have your good friend, the "If/Then" statement, which typically involves the use of the following VB .NET operators (Table 3-7).

Table 3-7. VB .NET Relational and Equality Operators

VB .NET EQUALITY/RELATIONAL OPERATOR	EXAMPLE USAGE	MEANING IN LIFE
=	If age = 30 Then	Returns true only if each expression is the same.
<>	If "Foo" <> myStr Then	Returns true only if each expression is different.

<
>
<=
>=
	If bonus < 2000 Then
	If bonus > 2000 Then
	If bonus <= 2000 Then
	If bonus >= 2000 Then
		Returns true if expression A is less than, greater than, less than or equal to, or greater than or equal to expression B.

An If statement may be composed of multiple expressions as well. As you would expect, If conditionals can contain *Else* statements to perform more complex testing. To build such a beast, VB .NET offers an expected set of conditional operators (Table 3-8) as well as some additional conditional operators you see in just a moment.

Table 3-8. VB .NET Conditional Operators

VB .NET CONDITIONAL OPERATOR	EXAMPLE USAGE	MEANING IN LIFE
And	If age = 30 _ And name = "Fred" Then	Conditional AND operator.
Or	If age = 30 _ Or name = "Fred" Then	Conditional OR operator.
Not	If Not myBool Then	Conditional NOT operator.

The other selection construct offered by VB .NET is the *Select* statement. As I am sure you are aware, Select statements allow you to handle program flow based on a predefined set of choices. For example, the following application prompts the user for one of three possible values. Based on the user input, act accordingly:

```
Sub Main()
    ' Prompt user with choices.
    Console.WriteLine("Welcome to the world of .NET")
    Console.WriteLine("1 = C#  2 = Managed C++ (MC++) 3 = VB .NET")
    Console.Write("Please select your implementation language:")

    ' Get choice.
    Dim s As String = Console.ReadLine()
    Dim n As Integer = Integer.Parse(s)

    ' Based on input, act accordingly. . .
    Select Case n
        Case Is = 1
            Console.WriteLine("C# is all about managed code.")
        Case Is = 2
            Console.WriteLine("Maintaining a legacy system, are we?")
        Case Is = 3
            Console.WriteLine("VB .NET:  Full OO capabilities. . .")
        Case Else
            Console.WriteLine("Well. . .good luck with that!")
    End Select
End Sub
```

It is worth pointing out that the VB .NET also supports all the expected adornments of the VB 6.0 Select statement. Again, if you require additional examples, check out online Help.

SOURCE CODE *The Selections project is located under the Chapter 3 subdirectory.*

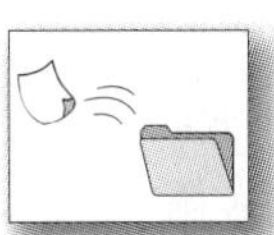

Additional VB .NET Operators

VB .NET defines a number of operators in addition to those you have previously examined. By and large, these operators behave like their VB 6.0 counterparts. Table 3-9 lists the core VB .NET operators.

Table 3-9. VB .NET Operators

OPERATOR CATEGORY	SYMBOL
Exponentiation	^
Unary negation	+, -
Multiplicative	*, /
Integer division	\
Modulus	Mod
Additive	+, -
Concatenation	&
Relational	=, <>, <, >, <=, >=, Like, Is, TypeOf. . .Is
Conditional NOT	Not
Conditional AND	And, AndAlso
Conditional OR	Or, OrElse
Conditional XOR	Xor

Minor Commentary on Select VB .NET Operators

The only operators that you may not be familiar with are AndAlso and OrElse operators. As in VB 6.0, the VB .NET *And* and *Or* operators do not "short circuit" within complex expressions. Thus, if you write the following block of code:

```
If A = 90 And B = 132 And S = "JoJo" Then
    Console.WriteLine("All of the above are true.")
End If
```

each condition is evaluated, even if one expression is evaluated to False. Let's say that in the previous code, (A = 90) is True, but (B = 132) is False. Because you have used the And operator, you have basically gained an unnecessary check. Intuitively, it would be nice to assume that VB would stop processing the complex expression as soon as a given item evaluates to False. To facilitate this approach, VB .NET introduces the *AndAlso* and *OrElse* keywords, for example:

```
If A = 90 AndAlso B = 132 AndAlso S = "JoJo" Then
    Console.WriteLine("All of the above are true.")
End If
```

The *is* and *TypeOf* operators are used to verify at runtime if an object is compatible with a given type (as you discover in Chapter 5). As for the remaining operators, I assume that many (if not all) of them are old hat to you. If you need additional information regarding the VB .NET looping and decision constructs, consult the VB .NET Language Reference using online Help.

Defining Custom Class Methods

Before going much further, let's examine how to define custom methods for a VB .NET type. Every method you implement must be a member of a Class, Module, or Structure. Global methods are not allowed in VB .NET (although as you have seen, members declared at the Module level simulate this). As you know, a method exists to allow the type to perform a unit of work. Custom methods may or may not take parameters, may or may not return values (of any intrinsic or user-defined types), and may or may not be declared as *shared.* Visual Basic has long distinguished between a "subroutine" and "function." While you can collectively refer to each syntactic variation as a "method" the distinction is that subroutines do *not* return a value once the method has completed where functions *do.*

```
' VB 6.0 Code!
' Subroutines return nothing. . .
Public Sub MySub()
End Sub
' Functions do. . .
Public Function MyFunc() as Integer
    MyFunc = 5
End Function
```

Be aware that VB .NET introduces an alternative means for returning a value from a function using the "Return" keyword. Rather than specifying a return value by setting the name of the function to a value, you can now write the following:

```
' VB .NET code!
' Much cleaner!
Public Function MyFunc() as Integer
    Return 5
End Function
```

While I am sure you already are comfortable with the notion of building methods using VB syntax, let's run through a few points of interest.

Method Access Modifiers

To begin, a method (that is, subroutines or functions) must specify its level of accessibility. VB .NET offers the method access modifiers shown in Table 3.10. (You examine the use of Protected and Friend methods in the next chapter during the discussion of class hierarchies.)

Table 3-10. VB .NET Accessibility Keywords

VB .NET ACCESS MODIFIER	MEANING IN LIFE
Public	Marks a method as accessible from an object instance, or any subclass. If you don't say otherwise, Public is assumed (it is the default visibility level).
Private	Marks a method as accessible only by the class that has defined the method.
Protected	Marks a method as usable by the defining class, as well as any child class, but is private as far as the outside world is concerned.
Friend	Defines a method that is publicly accessible by all types in an assembly (but not from outside the assembly).
Protected Friend	Marks a method as usable by any type in the same assembly as well as any derived type.

Here are the implications of each accessibility keyword:

```
' Visibility options.
Class SomeClass
    ' Accessible anywhere.
    Public Sub MethodA()
    End Sub
    ' Accessible only from SomeClass types.
    Private Sub MethodB()
    End Sub
    ' Accessible from SomeClass and any descendent.
    Protected Sub MethodC()
    End Sub
    ' Accessible from within the same assembly.
    Friend Sub MethodD()
    End Sub
```

```
    ' Internal or protected access.
    Protected Friend Sub MethodE()
    End Sub
    ' Public by default.
    Sub MethodF()
    End Sub
End Class
```

Methods that are declared Public are directly accessible from an object instance. Private methods cannot be accessed from an object instance, but instead are called internally by the object to help the instance get its work done (that is, private helper methods).

To illustrate, the Teenager class shown next defines two public methods, Complain() and BeAgreeable(), each of which returns a String to the object user. Internally, both methods make use of a private helper method named GetRandomNumber(), which manipulates a private member variable of type System.Random:

```
Class Teenager
    ' The System.Random type generates random numbers.
    Private r As Random = New Random()
    Public Function Complain() As String
        Dim messages() As String = {"Do I have to?", _
              "He started it!", "I'm too tired. . .", _
              "I hate school!", "You are sooo wrong."}
        Return messages(GetRandomNumber(5))
    End Function
    Public Function BeAgreeable() As String
          dim messages() as string = {"Sure! No problem!", _
              "Uh uh.", "I guess so."}
        Return messages(GetRandomNumber(3))
    End Function
    ' Private function used to grab a random number.
    Private Function GetRandomNumber(ByVal upperLimit As Short) As Integer
        ' Random.Next() returns a random integer between 0 and upperLimit.
        Return r.Next(upperLimit)
    End Function
End Class
```

The obvious benefit of defining GetRandomNumber() as a private helper method is that various parts of the Teenager class can make use of its functionality. The only alternative would be to duplicate the random number logic within the Complain() and BeAgreeable() methods (which in this case would not be too traumatic, but assume GetRandomNumber() contains 20 or 30 lines of code). In any case, here is some logic making use of the Teenager type (Figure 3-14 shows a possible test run).

```
Module Module1
    Sub Main()
        'Let mike complain.
        Dim mike As Teenager = New Teenager()
        Dim i As Integer
        For i = 0 To 10
            Console.WriteLine(mike.Complain())
        Next
    End Sub
End Module
```

Figure 3-14. Random complaints

Note the use of the System.Random type. This class is used to generate and manipulate random numbers. Random.Next() method returns a number between 0 and the specified upper limit. As you would guess, the Random class provides additional members, all of which are documented within online Help.

Optional Arguments

VB has long supported the use of optional arguments. As you would hope, this feature is also part of VB .NET with one important distinction—all optional parameters must now be set to a default value. In Visual Basic 6.0, optional arguments were permitted to ignore default values, given that default values (0 for numerical and "" for strings) were supplied automatically. Assume the Teenager type now has the following additional Public method which supports a single optional Boolean, defaulted to True:

```
Public Sub PerformChores(Optional ByVal groundedIfIgnored As Boolean = True)
    Dim i As Integer
    i = GetRandomNumber(50)
    If i = 43 Then
        Console.WriteLine("Chore response: " & BeAgreeable())
    ElseIf groundedIfIgnored Then
        Console.WriteLine("Response to punishment: " & Complain())
    End If
End Sub
```

In this way, the "bad cop" can simply call this item:

```
mike.PerformChores()    ' groundedIfIgnored is True.
```

while the "good cop" may say:

```
mike.PerformChores(False)
```

Using ParamArrays

In addition to optional parameters, Visual Basic programmers are familiar with the use of ParamArray arguments. In a nutshell, a ParamArray allows you to pass in a variable number of parameters as a *single parameter*. Like optional parameters, VB .NET demands that the underlying type represented by the ParamArray be explicitly marked (because you will always, of course, enable Option Strict). In the following example, the DisplayArrayOfInts() method defines a String message and a single parameter array, which can be a varying number of Integer types.

```
Class SomeClass
    ' ParamArray keyword.
    Public Sub DisplayArrayOfInts(ByVal msg As String, _
                              ByVal ParamArray list() As Integer)
        Console.WriteLine(msg)
        Dim i As Integer
        For i = 0 To UBound(list)
            Console.WriteLine(list(i))
        Next
    End Sub
End Class
```

When calling this method, you may send in an explicitly defined array of Integers, or alternatively, implicitly specify an array of Integers as discrete arguments. For example:

```
' Two ways to represent the ParamArray argument.
Dim s As New SomeClass()
Dim theInts() As Integer = {9, 33, 8323, 9981}
s.DisplayArrayOfInts("Add these for me", theInts)
s.DisplayArrayOfInts("Here are some more integers!", _
                                1, 44, 8, 32, 873223)
```

Method Calling Conventions

The next aspect of building VB .NET methods to be aware of is that *all* methods (subroutines and functions) are now called by wrapping arguments in parentheses. VB 6.0 supported some rather ridiculous calling conventions that forced you to call Subs using a different syntax than Functions. In general, under VB 6.0 Subs do not require parentheses while Functions do. However, the following variations do occur:

```
' VB 6.0 Function calling insanity.
Dim i as Integer
i = myFunction(myArg)   ' Use () to grab return value.
MyFunction myArg        ' Forgo () if you don't care about return value.
Call myFunction(myArg)  ' Same as previous line.
myFunction(myArg)       ' Pass myArg by value.

' VB 6.0 Subroutine calling insanity.
mySub myArg      ' Subs don't take (). . .
mySub (myArg)    ' . . .unless you pass by value.
```

VB .NET stops the madness once and for all by stating that all Functions and all Subs must be called using parentheses. Furthermore, even if a Sub or Function does not define any arguments, parentheses are *still* used:

```
' VB .NET simplicity.
Dim i as Integer
i = AFuncWithNoArgs()                  ' Use ()
ASubWithNoArgs()                       ' Use ()
ASubWithArgs(89, 44, "Ahhh. Better")   ' Use ()
Dim IAmPassedByValue as Boolean
SomeMethod((IAmPassedByValue))         ' Use ()
```

SOURCE CODE *The Methods application is located under the Chapter 3 subdirectory.*

Method Parameter Modifiers (ByRef and ByVal)

Like VB 6.0, VB .NET supports the ByRef and ByVal keywords. In terms of VB 6.0, the distinction between these two parameter-centric keywords is quite clear. If a parameter is marked with the ByVal keyword, a *copy* of the variable is sent into the receiving function. Therefore, if the receiving function modifies the ByVal parameter, changes are not "seen" by the caller as the called function is operating on a copy of the original data. When you want to allow the called function to modify the incoming parameters, you may mark the parameter with the ByRef keyword. In this case, the called function is sent (in effect) a pointer to the memory location of the data point. Thus, modifications of the parameter(s) are seen by the caller.

The short (i.e., incomplete) explanation of this topic is that while VB 6.0 parameters were ByRef by default, VB .NET, all parameters are ByVal by default. If the .NET universe were composed of nothing more than types deriving from System.ValueType you would be able to end the discussion right now. Copies would be copies and references would be references. As you know however, everything in .NET (including VB .NET's intrinsic data types) resolves to either a value type or *reference type*. This is where the fun begins.

Value Types and the ByVal and ByRef Keywords

Recall that a value type is a type that derives from System.ValueType (intrinsic data types and custom structures). Any type that derives from this .NET entity behaves as a stack-based variable. In this case, the ByVal and ByRef keywords are extremely intuitive: ByVal really does make a copy and ByRef really does pass a reference. Consider the following console application:

```
' A value type.
Structure MyValueType
    Public theInt As Integer
End Structure
Class RefValTesterClass
    Public Sub PassStructByVal(ByVal x As MyValueType)
        x.theInt = 30000
    End Sub
    Public Sub PassStructByRef(ByRef x As MyValueType)
        x.theInt = 30000
```

```
    End Sub
End Class
Module Module1
    Sub Main()
        Dim myStruct As MyValueType
        myStruct.theInt = 100
        Console.WriteLine("MyValueType.theInt as declared: {0}", _
                          myStruct.theInt)
        ' Try to change using ByVal.
        Dim t As New RefValTesterClass()
        t.PassStructByVal(myStruct)
        Console.WriteLine("MyValueType.theInt after ByVal : {0}", _
                          myStruct.theInt)
        ' Now ByRef.
        t.PassStructByRef(myStruct)
        Console.WriteLine("MyValueType.theInt after ByRef : {0}", _
                          myStruct.theInt)
    End Sub
End Module
```

The output should be clear. When you pass a variable of type MyValueType into the PassStructVal() method, a copy is of the Structure is made, and therefore the assignment of theInt is not remembered after the invocation. This is the exact opposite behavior of the ByRef pass. Check out Figure 3-15.

Figure 3-15. When using value types, ByVal and ByRef behave as anticipated

Understand that the same behavior is found when passing any value type, including the intrinsic numerical VB .NET data types (Integer, Short, Boolean and whatnot).

Reference Types and the ByVal and ByRef Keywords

So far so good. When you pass a value type into a method using ByRef and ByVal semantics, things behave as you would expect. However, let's update the existing program to pass the following class type:

```
' A reference type
Class MyRefType
    Public theInt As Integer
End Class
Class RefValTesterClass
    . . .
    Public Sub PassClassByVal(ByVal x As MyRefType)
        x.theInt = 30000
    End Sub
    Public Sub PassClassByRef(ByRef x As MyRefType)
        x.theInt = 30000
    End Sub
End Class
```

and call these members as follows (output can be seen in Figure 3-16).

```
Module Module1
    Sub Main()
        ' Same structure logic as before. . .
        Dim myRefType As New MyRefType()
        myRefType.theInt = 100
        Console.WriteLine("MyRefType.theInt as declared: {0}", _
                          myRefType.theInt)
        ' Try to change using by val semantics.
        t.PassClassByVal(myRefType)
        Console.WriteLine("MyRefType.theInt after ByVal : {0}", _
                          myRefType.theInt)
        ' Now by ref.
        t.PassClassByRef(myRefType)
        Console.WriteLine("MyValueType.theInt after ByRef : {0}", _
                          myRefType.theInt)
    End Sub
End Module
```

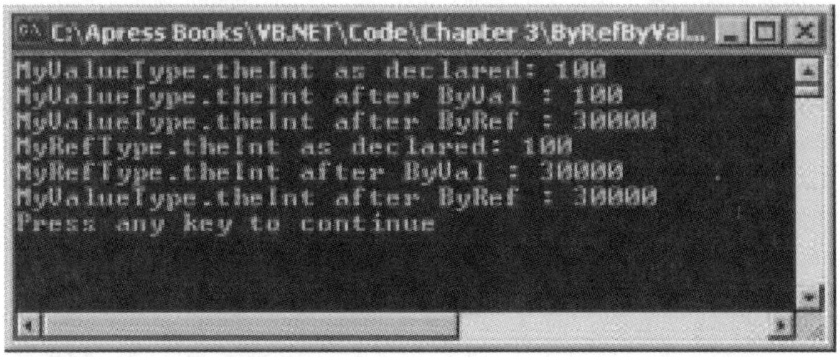

```
C:\Apress Books\VB.NET\Code\Chapter 3\ByRefByVal...
MyValueType.theInt as declared: 100
MyValueType.theInt after ByVal : 100
MyValueType.theInt after ByRef : 30000
MyRefType.theInt as declared: 100
MyRefType.theInt after ByVal : 30000
MyValueType.theInt after ByRef : 30000
Press any key to continue
```

Figure 3-16. Something seems wrong. . .

In this iteration of the application, you would expect that when you pass an object ByVal, a full copy of the type is passed into the method. Again, you would think that any changes to the parameter should NOT be realized in the caller's logic. As you can see however, this is not the case. In fact, the ByVal and ByRef pass of this reference type result in the same output (i.e., the Public theInt field is changed to 30000).

So what happened? Much like the "value type containing a reference type" example seen earlier in this chapter, when you pass reference types into a function using ByVal semantics, what you are saying is "Please make sure that the variable I just passed into this function continues to reference the *same* object when I return from this method". In essence, passing a reference type ByVal locks the reference to the *memory address* in place to make sure that the called function cannot reassign this reference to a new memory location. Assume the RefValTesterClass now supports the following method:

```
Public Sub PassClassByValAndReassign(ByVal x As MyRefType)
    Dim another As New MyRefType()
    another.theInt = 666
    x = another ' This will be forgotten after the call.
    Console.WriteLine("Just tried to reassign ByVal ref type to {0}", x.theInt)
End Sub
```

Here, we are passing a reference type into a method taking a ByVal parameter, which as you recall simply means the variable passed into the function will continue to reference the same object in memory after the call. Thus, when you pass your type into the PassClassByValAndReassign() method as follows:

```
' Try to reassign using ByVal.
Console.WriteLine("theInt before attempted reassignment : {0}", _
    myRefType.theInt)
t.PassClassByValAndReassign(myRefType)
```

```
Console.WriteLine("theInt after attempted reassignment : {0}", _
    myRefType.theInt)
```

you find the result shown in Figure 3-17.

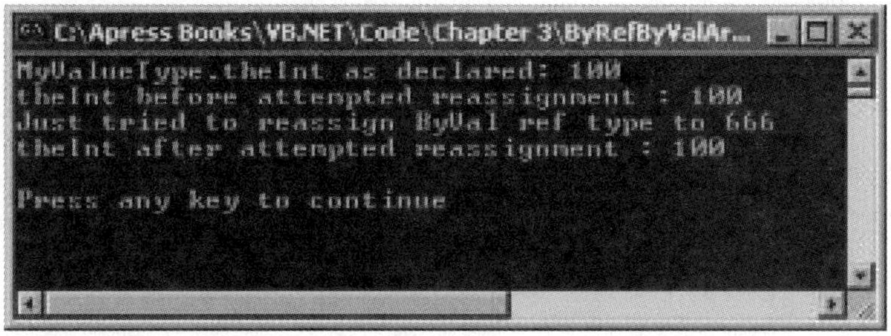

```
C:\Apress Books\VB.NET\Code\Chapter 3\ByRefByValAr...
MyValueType.theInt as declared: 100
theInt before attempted reassignment : 100
Just tried to reassign ByVal ref type to 666
theInt after attempted reassignment : 100

Press any key to continue
```

Figure 3-17. Passing references ByVal locks the reference in place

On the other hand, if you pass a reference type ByRef, you are saying "If the called function wants to reassign this reference to a new memory location, please do." For example:

```
Public Sub PassClassByRefAndReassign(ByRef x As MyRefType)
    Dim another As New MyRefType()
    another.theInt = 666
    x = another ' incoming ref reassigned!
    Console.WriteLine("Just tried to reassign ByVal ref type to {0}", x.theInt)
End Sub
```

When you rerun the application, you now see that the incoming reference has been reassigned to the new object type (see Figure 3-18).

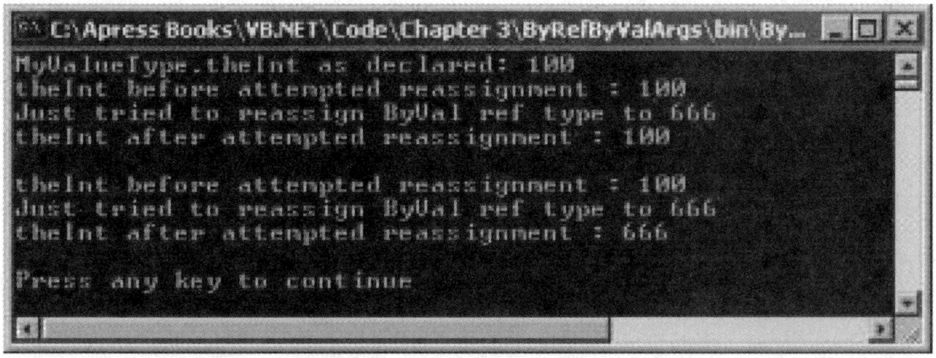

```
C:\Apress Books\VB.NET\Code\Chapter 3\ByRefByValArgs\bin\By...
MyValueType.theInt as declared: 100
theInt before attempted reassignment : 100
Just tried to reassign ByVal ref type to 666
theInt after attempted reassignment : 100

theInt before attempted reassignment : 100
Just tried to reassign ByVal ref type to 666
theInt after attempted reassignment : 666

Press any key to continue
```

Figure 3-18. Passing references ByRef allows the reference to be reassigned

And again, remember that when you pass a reference type ByRef *or* ByVal the receiving function is able to modify the state of the object, and realize those changes after the invocation:

```
Public Sub PassClassByValAndChangeState(ByVal x As MyRefType)
    ' This will work.
    x.theInt = 777
End Sub

    Public Sub PassClassByRefAndChangeState(ByRef x As MyRefType)
    ' This will work too.
    x.theInt = 888
End Sub
```

Passing Arrays and Strings (ByVal and ByRef)

Later in this chapter you take a deeper look at VB .NET arrays. Be aware that when you pass array types into a given method, they follow the *same* behaviors as passing in a custom class type. The truth of the matter is that any time you declare a VB .NET array, you have really created an implicit instance of the System.Array class. It should make sense that arrays are objects and follow the same rules when passing ByVal or ByRef.

Still later in the chapter, you take a deeper look at VB .NET string types. When you create a String type, you actually create a reference variable of type System.String. Strings in VB .NET are immutable (i.e., they can't be changed once assigned). Even though String types are true blue objects, the System.String class changes the behaviors of the type to behave as if it were (in fact) a value type. Again, you see the exact details later in the chapter. For the time being, understand that when you pass String data ByRef, changes are realized by the caller. When you send Strings ByVal, they are not.

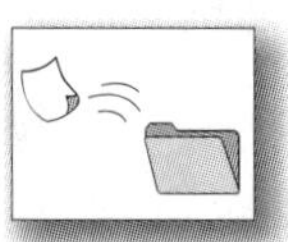

SOURCE CODE *The ByRefByValArgs application is located under the Chapter 3 subdirectory.*

Shared Methods

Type methods can be declared "Shared." So, what does it mean to be a shared method? When a method is marked with the Shared keyword, it may be called directly from the class level, and does not require an active object. Recall that anything defined within a Module is automatically shared. For example, Main() is implicitly shared to allow the runtime to invoke this function without needing to allocate a new instance of the defining type. This is a good thing of course, or else you would need to create an object to create an object to create an object to (. . .).

To illustrate custom Shared methods, assume the Teenager class seen earlier has been modified as so:

```
Class Teenager
    ' Shared members can only reference shared data!
    Private Shared r As Random = New Random()
    Public Shared Function Complain() As String
        . . .
    End Function
    Public Shared Function BeAgreeable() As String
        . . .
    End Function
    Public Shared Function GetRandomNumber() As Integer
        . . .
    End Function
. . .
End Class
```

Given this adjustment, you can now access these members at the class level:

```
    Sub Main()
        Dim i As Integer
        For i = 0 To 10
            Console.WriteLine(Teenager.Complain())
        Next
        For i = 0 To 10
            Console.WriteLine(Teenager.BeAgreeable())
        Next
    End Sub
```

Nonshared (instance) methods are methods that are scoped at the object level. Thus, if Complain() was *not* marked Shared, you would need to create an instance of the Teenager class before you could hear about the gripe of the day.

SOURCE CODE *The SharedMethods application is located under the Chapter 3 subdirectory.*

Defining Shared Data

Recall that a class typically defines a set of state data. This means that each object instance maintains a private copy of the underlying values. Thus, if you have a class defined as follows:

```
' We all love Foo.
Class Foo
     Public intFoo as Integer
End Class
```

you can create any number of objects of type Foo and set the intFoo field to a unique value:

```
' Each Foo reference maintains a copy of the intFoo field.
Dim f1 as Foo = New Foo()
f1.intFoo = 100

Dim f2 as Foo = New Foo()
f2.intFoo = 993

Dim f3 as Foo = New Foo()
f3.intFoo = 6
```

Shared data, on the other hand, is, well, shared among all object instances. Rather than each object holding a copy of a given field, a point of shared data is allocated exactly once. Assume you have a class named Airplane that contains a single point of shared data. In the constructor of the Airplane class you increment this data point. Here is the initial definition:

```
Class Airplane
    ' This shared data member is shared by all Airplane objects.
    Private Shared NumberInTheAir As Integer = 0
    Public Sub New()
        NumberInTheAir += 1
    End Sub
    ' Get shared value.
    Public Shared Function GetNumber() As Integer
        Return NumberInTheAir
    End Function
End Class
```

Notice that the Airplane class is a shared method, GetNumber(), which returns the current number of airplane objects that have been allocated by the application. To illustrate, observe the following usage:

```
Sub Main()
    ' Make some planes.
    Dim a1 As Airplane = New Airplane()
    Dim a2 As Airplane = New Airplane()
    ' How many are in flight?
    Console.WriteLine("Number of planes: {0}", _
                      a1.GetNumber())
    Console.WriteLine("Number of planes: {0}", Airplane.GetNumber())
    ' More planes!
    Dim a3 As Airplane = New Airplane()
    Dim a4 As Airplane = New Airplane()
    ' Now how many?
    Console.WriteLine("Number of planes: {0}", _
                      a3.GetNumber())
    Console.WriteLine("Number of planes: {0}", Airplane.GetNumber())
End Sub
```

Figure 3-19 shows the output.

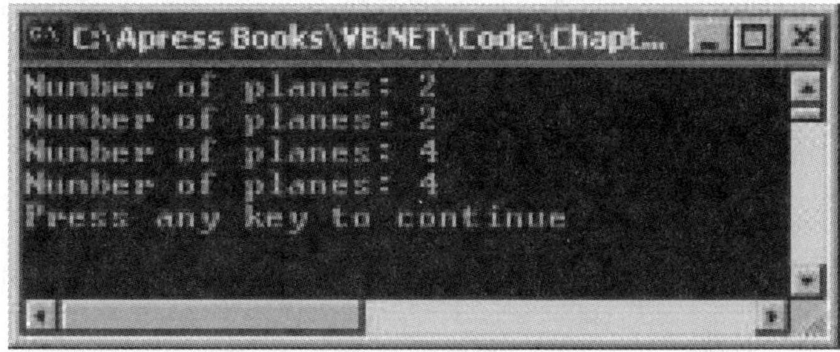

Figure 3-19. Static data is shared among all like objects.

As you can see, all instances of the Airplane class are sharing (i.e., viewing) the same point of data. That's the point of shared data: To allow all objects to share a given value at the class (rather than at the object) level. Do note, however, that shared data may be obtained using an active object (such as a3) as well as through the class itself.

SOURCE CODE *The SharedData project is located under the Chapter 3 subdirectory.*

An Interesting Aside: Some Shared Members of the Environment Class

Environment is yet another class defined within the System namespace. This class represents a type exposing a number of details regarding the operating system currently hosting your .NET application. Each detail is obtained using various shared members. To illustrate, ponder the following (see Figure 3-20 for output):

```
' Here are some (but not all) of the interesting
' shared members of the Environment class.
Module Module1
    Sub Main()
        ' OS?
        Console.WriteLine("Current OS: {0}", Environment.OSVersion)
        ' Directory?
        Console.WriteLine("Current Directory: {0}", _
            Environment.CurrentDirectory)
        ' Here are the drives on this box.
        Dim drives As String() = Environment.GetLogicalDrives()
        Dim i As Integer
        While i < drives.Length
            Console.WriteLine("Drive {0}: {1}", i, drives(i))
            i += 1
        End While
        ' Which version of the .NET platform?
        Console.WriteLine("Current version of .NET: {0}", _
           Environment.Version)
    End Sub
End Module
```

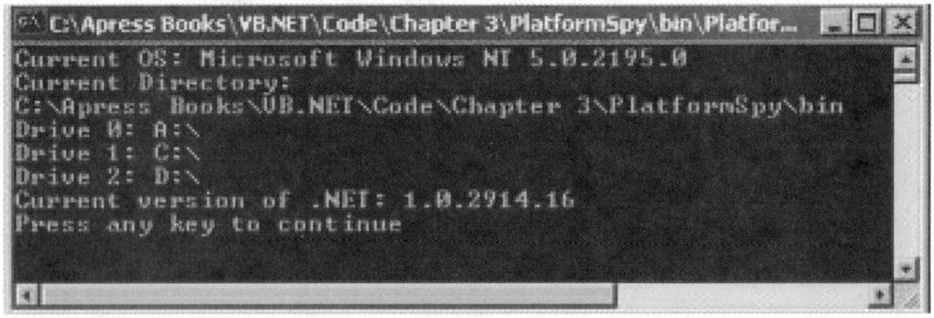

```
C:\Apress Books\VB.NET\Code\Chapter 3\PlatformSpy\bin\Platfor...
Current OS: Microsoft Windows NT 5.0.2195.0
Current Directory:
C:\Apress Books\VB.NET\Code\Chapter 3\PlatformSpy\bin
Drive 0: A:\
Drive 1: C:\
Drive 2: D:\
Current version of .NET: 1.0.2914.16
Press any key to continue
```

Figure 3-20. Basic environment variables

SOURCE CODE *The PlatformSpy example is located under the Chapter 3 subdirectory.*

Static (Not Shared) Data

In VB 6.0, the "Static" keyword is used to define a point of data that is in memory as long as the application is running, but is visible only within the function it was declared. VB .NET also supports the "Static" keyword (with one small variation mentioned momentarily). Assume you have the following class definition:

```
Class StaticTester
    Public Sub CallMe()
        Static IAmRemembered As Integer = 50
        IAmRemembered += 1
        Console.WriteLine(IAmRemembered)
    End Sub
End Class
```

The first time this function is called, the static data is allocated and initialized to its starting value of 50 (if you don't pick an initial value, the type's default value is assigned automatically). The trick is to understand that the previous value is "remembered" between method invocations. Thus, if you use the object as follows:

```
Sub Main()
        Dim i As New StaticTester()
        Dim j As Integer
        For j = 0 To 10
            i.CallMe()
        Next
End Sub
```

you would see the following printout to the console (Figure 3-21).

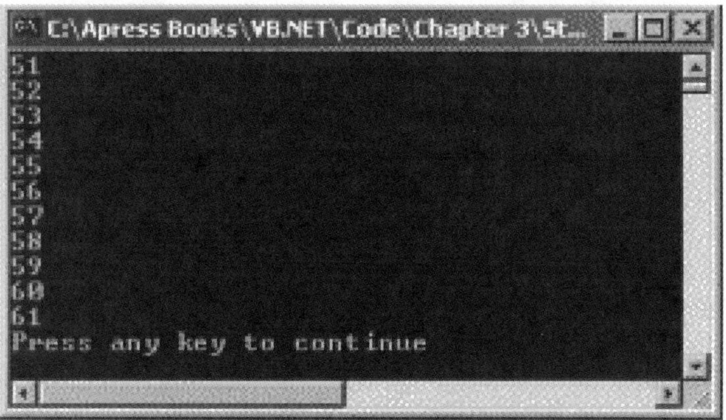

Figure 3-21. Static data is retained between invocations

Of course, if IAmRemembered is not defined as static:

```
Dim IAmRemembered as Integer = 50
```

you would see "51" printed out 11 times, as the Integer is now scoped at the method level and forgotten between calls.

At this point, you can assume that VB .NET used the Static keyword in the exact same manner as VB 6.0. The difference is that VB .NET no longer allows you to create static methods. In VB 6.0, when a method is declared static, *all* data points in the function are declared static. If you require the same behavior from a VB .NET application, you need to explicitly define each data point using the Static keyword.

Be sure you understand the distinction between "Shared" data and "Static" data.

- Shared data is allocated once and is visible from all objects of the defining type (like the Airplane class).
- Static data is allocated once, but is only visible from the method in which it was defined.

This is important to keep straight in your mind, given that other .NET aware languages (such as C#) use a single keyword (static) to describe both concepts.

SOURCE CODE *The StaticData example is located under the Chapter 3 subdirectory.*

Array Manipulation in VB .NET

Formally speaking, an array is a collection of data points (of the same underlying type), that is accessed using a numerical index. As you might assume, arrays can contain any intrinsic type defined by VB .NET, including arrays of objects, interfaces, or structures. In VB .NET, arrays can be single or multidimensional. For example:

```
' A string array containing 11 elements {0, 1, . . .,10}.
Dim booksOnCOM(10) As String
' A 3 item string array, numbered {0, 1, 2}
Dim booksOnPL1(2) As String
' 101 item string array, numbered {0, 1, . . ., 100}
Dim booksOnDotNet(100) As String
```

Look closely at the code comments above. In .NET, all arrays have a lower bound of zero, while the number used in the array declaration represents the upper bound of the array. Thus, as bizarre as it may seem, when you write "Dim x(8) as Integer" you end up with nine elements (0 through 8, inclusive). This oddball behavior is the result of Microsoft's decision to roll back to the way that VB 6.0 (and earlier versions) worked.

The original intention was to have VB .NET work the way that C#, C++, and other .NET aware languages do, where "Dim x(8) as Integer" should in fact yield an array of eight elements (0 through 7). Therefore, you must be extremely careful when passing arrays between assemblies written in distinct .NET languages (and be aware of possible index out of bounds exceptions). Given the fact that all arrays have a lower bound of zero, the LBound() function and the Option Base statement are now obsolete.

Alternative Array Initialization Syntax

One improvement with regard to array syntax, is that like many languages, member initialization can be achieved using curly bracket notation ({}) rather than assigning values member by member. Therefore, the following two arrays are identical in VB .NET:

```
' Initialize items at startup or. . .
Dim firstNames() _
As String = {"Steve", "Gina", "Swallow", "Baldy", "Gunner"}
' . . .go member by member.
Dim firstNames2(4) As String
firstNames2(0) = "Steve"
firstNames2(1) = "Gina"
```

```
firstNames2(2) = "Swallow"
firstNames2(3) = "Baldy"
firstNames2(4) = "Gunner"
```

Also recall that members of VB .NET arrays are automatically set to a default value. For example, if you have an array of numerical types, each member is set to 0, arrays of string begin life as empty strings, and so forth.

Working with Multidimensional Arrays

In addition to the single dimension arrays you have seen thus far, VB .NET also supports multidimensional arrays. To declare and fill a multidimensional array, proceed as follows:

```
Dim myMatrix(6, 6) As Integer  ' makes a 7x7 array
' Populate array.
Dim k As Integer, j As Integer
For k = 0 To 6
    For j = 0 To 6
        myMatrix(k, j) = k * j
    Next j
Next k
' Show array.
For k = 0 To 6
    For j = 0 To 6
        Console.Write(myMatrix(k, j) & "  ")
    Next j
        Console.WriteLine()
Next k
```

The output is seen in Figure 3-22.

Figure 3-22. A rectangular array

Now that you understand how to build and populate VB .NET arrays, you can turn your attention to the ultimate base class of any array, System.Array.

The System.Array Base Class

The most striking difference between VB 6.0 and VB .NET arrays is the fact that every array you create is automatically derived from System.Array. This class defines a number of helpful methods that make working with arrays much more palatable. Table 3-11 gives a rundown of some (but not all) of the more interesting members.

Table 3-11. Select Members of System.Array

MEMBER OF ARRAY CLASS	MEANING IN LIFE
BinarySearch()	This static method is applicable only if the items in the array implement the IComparer interface (see Chapter 5). If so, BinarySearch() finds a given item.
Clear()	This static method sets a range of elements in the array to empty values (0 for value items, null for object references).
CopyTo()	Used to copy elements from the source array into the destination array.
GetEnumerator()	Returns the IEnumerator interface for a given array. I address interfaces in Chapter 5, but for the time being, keep in mind that this interface is required by the construct.
Reverse()	This static method reverses the contents of a one-dimensional array.
Sort()	Sorts a one-dimensional array of intrinsic types. If the elements in the array implement the IComparer interface, you can also sort your custom types (see Chapter 5).

Let's see some of these members in action. The following code makes use of the shared Reverse() and Clear() methods to pump out information about the firstName array to the console:

```
' Create some string arrays and exercise some System.Array members.
Sub Main
    ' Initialize items at startup.
    Dim firstNames() _
        As String = {"Steve", "Gina", "Swallow", "Baldy", "Gunner"}
```

```
    ' Print out names in declared order.
    Console.WriteLine(" -> " & "Here is the array:")
    Dim i As Integer
    For i = 0 To UBound(firstNames)
        ' Print a name
        Console.Write(firstNames(i) & " ")
    Next
    Console.WriteLine()
    ' Reverse them. . .
    Array.Reverse(firstNames)
    Console.WriteLine(" -> " & "The reveresed array")
    ' . . . and print them.
    For i = 0 To UBound(firstNames)
        ' Print a name
        Console.Write(firstNames(i) & " ")
    Next
    Console.WriteLine()
    ' Clear out all but the final member.
    Console.WriteLine(" -> " & "Cleared out all but one. . .")
    Array.Clear(firstNames, 1, 4)
    For i = 0 To UBound(firstNames)
        ' Print a name
        Console.Write(firstNames(i) & " ")
    Next
End Sub
```

The output can be seen in Figure 3-23.

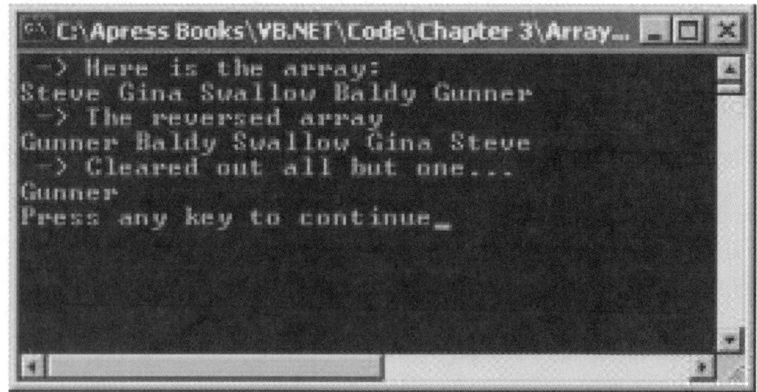

Figure 3-23. Fun with System.Array

Dynamic Arrays

Finally, like VB 6.0, arrays can be resized using the Redim keyword (which destroys the current contents of the array) or using the Redim Preserve keywords (to preserve the values within the current array). However, unlike VB 6.0, you cannot change the underlying type of an array using the As keyword. Once you create an array of Integers, it stays an array of Integers. For example:

```
' Keep Gunner in the array, but add Gina and Joe.
...
ReDim Preserve firstNames(2)
firstNames(1) = "Gina"
firstNames(2) = "Joe"
For i = 0 To UBound(firstNames)
    ' Print a name
    Console.Write(firstNames(i) & " ")
Next
```

SOURCE CODE *The Arrays application is located under the Chapter 3 subdirectory.*

String Manipulation in VB .NET

As you have already seen, String is a native data type in VB .NET. However, like all intrinsic types, string actually aliases a type in the .NET library, which in this case is System.String. System.String provides a number of methods you would expect from such a utility class, including methods that return the length, find substrings, convert to and from uppercase/lowercase, and so forth. Table 3-12 lists some (but by no means all) of the interesting members.

Table 3-12. Select Members of System.String

MEMBER OF STRING CLASS	MEANING IN LIFE
Length	This property returns the length of the current string.
Concat()	This static method of the String class returns a new string that is composed of two discrete strings.
CompareTo()	Compares two strings.
Copy()	This static method returns a fresh copy of an existing string.
Format()	Used to format a string using other primitives (i.e., numerical data, other strings) and the {0} notation examined earlier in this chapter.
Insert()	Used to insert a string within a given string.
PadLeft() PadRight()	These methods are used to pad a string with some character.
Remove() Replace()	Use these methods to receive a copy of a string, with modifications (characters removed or replaced).
ToUpper() ToLower()	Creates a copy of a given string in uppercase or lowercase.

You should be aware of a few aspects of VB .NET string manipulation. First, although the string data type is a reference type, the equality operators (= and <>) are defined to compare the *values* of string objects, not the memory to which they refer. The concatenation operator (&) is a handy shorthand alternative to calling String.Concat():

```
' = and <> are used to compare the values within strings.
' & is used for concatenation.
Sub Main()
    Dim strObj As System.String = "This is a TEST"
    Dim s As String = "This is another TEST"
    ' Test for equality between the strings.
    If (s = strObj) Then
        Console.WriteLine("Same info. . .")
    Else
        Console.WriteLine("Not the same info. . .")
    End If
```

```
    ' Concatenation.
    Dim newString As String
    newString = s & strObj
    Console.WriteLine("s & strObj = " & newString.ToString())
    ' Note!  System.String also defines the Chars() member
    ' to access each character in the string.
    Dim k As Integer
    While k < s.Length
        Console.WriteLine("Char {0} is {1}", k, s.Chars(k))
         k += 1
    End While
End Sub
```

When you run this program, you are able to verify that the two string objects (s and strObj) do not contain the same values, and therefore, the test for equality fails. When you examine the contents of newString, you see it is indeed "This is another TESTThis is a TEST." Finally, notice that you can access the individual characters of a string using the Chars() member.

Using System.Text.StringBuilder

One thing to be very aware of with regard to VB .NET strings: The value of a string cannot be modified once established. Like C# and Java, VB .NET strings are immutable. In fact, if you examine the methods of System.String, you notice that the methods that *seem* to modify a string in fact return a modified *copy* of the string. For example, when you send the ToUpper() message to a string object, you are not modifying the underlying buffer, but are returning a fresh copy of the buffer in uppercase form:

```
' Make changes to this string?  Not really. . .
Dim strFixed As System.String = "This is how I began life"
Console.WriteLine(strFixed)
Dim upperVersion As String = strFixed.ToUpper()
Console.WriteLine(strFixed)
Console.WriteLine(upperVersion)
```

It can be annoying (and inefficient) to have to work with copies of copies of strings. To help ease the pain, the System.Text namespace defines a class named StringBuilder. This class operates much more like an MFC CString or ATL CComBSTR in that any modifications you make to the StringBuilder instance affect the underlying buffer (and is thus more efficient):

```
Imports System.Text  ' StringBuilder lives here!
Sub Main()
    ' Play with the StringBuilder class.
    Dim myBuffer As StringBuilder = New StringBuilder("I am a buffer")
    myBuffer.Append(" that just got longer. . .")
    Console.WriteLine(myBuffer)
    myBuffer.Append("and even longer.")
    Console.WriteLine(myBuffer)
    Dim theReallyFinalString As String = myBuffer.ToString().ToUpper()
    Console.WriteLine(theReallyFinalString)
End Sub
```

As you can see, beyond appending to your internal buffer, the StringBuilder class allows you to replace and remove characters at will. Once you have established the state of your buffer, call ToString() to store the final result into a System.String data type. As you might assume, StringBuilder contains additional methods and properties beyond those examined here. I leave it to you to drill into more specifics at your leisure.

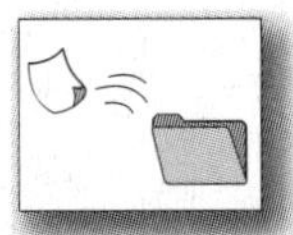

SOURCE CODE *The Strings project is located under the Chapter 3 subdirectory.*

VB .NET Enumerations

Often it is convenient to create a range of symbolic names for underlying numerical values. For example, if you are creating an employee payroll system, you may want to use the constants VP, Manager, Grunt, and Contractor rather than raw numerical values such as {0, 1, 2, 3}. Like other managed languages, VB .NET supports the notion of custom enumerations for this very reason. For example, here is the EmpType enumeration:

```
' A custom enumeration.
Enum EmpType
    Manager     ' = 0
    Grunt       ' = 1
    Contractor  ' = 2
    VP          ' = 3
End Enum
```

The EmpType enumeration defines four named constants, corresponding to discrete numerical values. In VB .NET, the numbering scheme sets the first element to zero (0) by default, followed by an *n+1* progression. You are free to change this behavior as you see fit, thus:

```
' Begin with 102.
Enum EmpType
    Manager = 102
    Grunt        ' = 103
    Contractor   ' = 104
    VP           ' = 105
End Enum
```

Enumerations do not necessarily need to follow a sequential ordering. If (for some reason or another) it makes sense to establish your EmpType as seen here, the compiler continues to be happy:

```
' Elements of an enumeration need not be sequential!
Enum EmpType
    Manager = 10
    Grunt = 1
    Contractor = 100
    VP = 9
End Enum
```

Under the hood, the storage type used for an enumeration automatically maps to an Integer by default; however you are also free to change this to your liking. VB .NET enumerations can be defined in a similar manner for any of the core system types (Byte, Short, Integer, or Long). For example, if you want to set the underlying storage value of EmpType to be a Byte rather than an Integer, write the following:

```
' This time, EmpType maps to an underlying Byte.
Enum EmpType as Byte
     Manager = 10,
     Grunt = 1,
     Contractor = 100,
     VP = 9
End Enum
```

Once you have established the range and storage type of your enumeration, you can use them in place of so-called "magic numbers." Assume you have a Module defining a public method, taking EmpType as the sole parameter:

```
Module Module1
    ' Enums as parameters.
    Public Sub AskForBonus(ByVal e As EmpType)
        Select Case (e)
            Case EmpType.Contractor
                Console.WriteLine("You already get enough cash. . .")
            Case EmpType.Grunt
                Console.WriteLine("You have got to be kidding. . .")
            Case EmpType.Manager
                Console.WriteLine("How about stock options instead?")
            Case EmpType.VP
                Console.WriteLine("VERY GOOD, Sir!")
        End Select
    End Sub
   Sub Main()
       ' Make a contractor type.
       Dim fred as EmpType
       fred = EmpType.Contractor
       AskForBonus(fred)
   End Sub
End Module
```

System.Enum Base Class

The interesting thing about VB .NET enumerations is that they implicitly derive from System.Enum. This base class defines a number of methods that allow you to interrogate and transform a given enumeration. Before seeing some of this functionality first hand, you have a small housekeeping chore. As you know, VB is a case-insensitive language. Therefore in the eyes of vbc.exe, Enum, enum, and ENUM all refer to the intrinsic "Enum" keyword. While this can in fact be helpful (given that the Visual Studio.NET IDE transforms keywords to the correct case), there is one problem. Specifically, to make use of the members of the System.Enum class, you may be tempted to write the following:

```
' Name clash!
Module Module1
Sub Main()
    Dim e as EmpType
    Enum.GetUnderlyingType(e)
End Sub
End Module
```

Here, you attempt to use a shared method of System.Enum defines named GetUnderlyingType(), which resolves (pardon the redundancy) the underlying data type used to represent this enumeration (a Byte in our case). The problem is that vbc.exe assumes that "Enum" refers to its internal keyword, *not* the Enum type! To fix the name clash, you have choices. First, you could explicitly specify System.Enum everywhere in our code:

```
' Better!
Module Module1
Sub Main()
    Dim e as EmpType
    System.Enum.GetUnderlyingType(e.GetType())
End Sub
End Module
```

While this fits the bill, it can be cumbersome to use fully qualified names (especially if the type you want is contained within a nested namespace. . .more later). To help lessen your typing burden, you can make use of a variation of the VB .NET Imports statement:

```
' Build an alias to System.Enum
Imports DotNetEnum = System.Enum
Module Module1
Sub Main()
    Dim e as EmpType
    DotNetEnum.GetUnderlyingType(e.GetType())
End Sub
End Module
```

In this case, you defined an alias to System.Enum, called DotNetEnum. In your code, you can make use of this moniker whenever you want to make use of the members of the Enum type.

Of greater interest than extracting the underlying type of an enumeration, is the ability to extract the string names behind the numerical values. How many times have you had to perform transformational logic between a VB 6.0 enumeration and the underlying strings? In its simplest form, you can call System.Enum.ToString() when you want to suck out the underlying string name.

```
' What is the string value of this EmpType?
Dim fred As EmpType
fred = EmpType.VP
Console.WriteLine("Fred is: {0}", fred.ToString())     ' Prints "Fred is: VP"
```

Using the shared Enum.Format() method, you gain a finer level of formatting options by specifying the desired format flag. In this context "G" is the string value, the hexadecimal value is marked by "x," while the decimal value is obtained using "d". Format() takes two parameters, the first of which is the Enum you want to examine, while the second is the format flag. System.Enum also defines another static method named GetValues(). This method returns an instance of System.Array. Each item in the array corresponds to a member of the specified enumeration. Thus:

```
' Get all stats for EmpType.
Dim obj As Array = DotNetEnum.GetValues(fred.GetType())
Console.WriteLine("This enum has {0} members.", obj.Length)

' Now show the string name and associated value.
Dim e As EmpType
For Each e In obj
    Console.Write("String name: {0}", DotNetEnum.Format(fred.GetType(), e, "G"))
    Console.Write(" ({0})", DotNetEnum.Format(fred.GetType(), e, "D"))
    Console.WriteLine(" hex: {0}", DotNetEnum.Format(fred.GetType(), e, "X"))
Next
```

The output is seen in Figure 3-24.

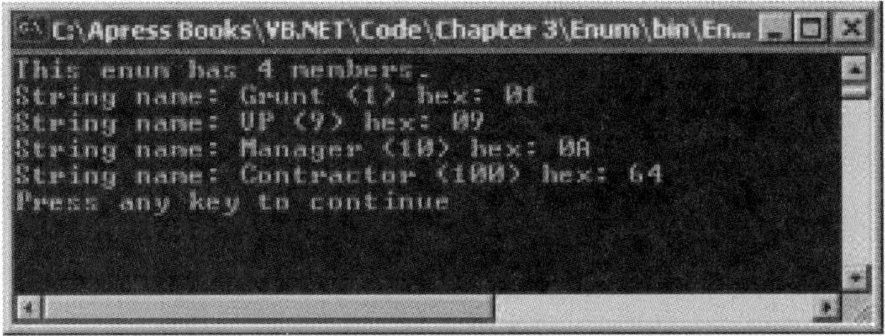

Figure 3-24. Fun with System.Enum

Next, let's explore the IsDefined property. This allows you to determine if a given string name is a member of the current enumeration. For example, assume you want to know if the value "SalesPerson" is part of the EmpType enumeration:

```
' Does EmpType have a SalesPerson value?
If (DotNetEnum.IsDefined(fred.GetType(), "SalesPerson")) Then
```

```
        Console.WriteLine("Yep, we have sales people.")
    Else
        Console.WriteLine("No, we have no profits. . ..")
    End If
```

Last but not least, it is worth pointing out that VB .NET enumerations support the use of various relational operators. For example:

```
' Which of these two EmpType variables has the greatest numerical value?
Dim joe As EmpType = EmpType.VP
Dim fran As EmpType = EmpType.Grunt
If (joe < fran) Then
        Console.WriteLine("Joe's value is less than Fran's")
Else
        Console.WriteLine("Fran's value is less than Joe's")
End If
```

SOURCE CODE *The Enum project is located under the Chapter 3 subdirectory.*

Defining Structures in VB .NET

Structures can take constructors (provided the constructor has arguments), can implement interfaces, and can contain numerous properties, methods, events, and fields. VB .NET structures do not have an identically named alias in the .NET library (that is, there is no System.Structure class), but are implicitly derived from ValueType. Recall that the role of ValueType is to configure the members of System.Object to work with value-based semantics. Here is a simple example:

```
' Here is a custom enum.
Enum EmpType As Byte
    Manager = 10
    Grunt = 1
    Contractor = 100
    VP = 9
End Enum
' And here is a struct using this enum.
Structure EMPLOYEE
    ' Fields.
    Public title As EmpType
    Public name As String
    Public deptID As Short
End Structure
```

```
Module Module1
     Sub Main()
          ' Create and format Fred.
          Dim fred as EMPLOYEE
          fred.deptID = 40
          fred.name = "Fred"
          fred.title = EmpType.Grunt
   End Sub
End Module
```

Here, you created an EMPLOYEE structure on the stack and manipulated each field using the dot operator. To provide a more optimized construction of this type, you are free to define additional custom constructors. Recall that you *cannot* redefine the default constructor for a VB .NET structure, as this is a reserved member. Given this fact, any custom constructors must take some number of parameters:

```
' Structs may define custom constructors (if they have args).
Structure EMPLOYEE
    ' Fields.
    Public title As EmpType
    Public name As String
    Public deptID As Short
    ' Constructor.
    Public Sub New(ByVal et As EmpType, ByVal n As String, ByVal d As Short)
        title = et
        name = n
        deptID = d
    End Sub
End Structure
```

With this, you can create a new employee as follows:

```
' Create and format Mary using a ctor.
Dim mary As EMPLOYEE = New EMPLOYEE(EmpType.VP, "Mary", 10)
```

Structures can, of course, be used as parameters to any member function. For example, assume you have a method named DisplayEmpStats():

```
' Extract interesting information from an EMPLOYEE structure.
Sub DisplayEmpStats(ByVal e As EMPLOYEE)
    Console.WriteLine("Here is {0}'s info:", e.name)
    Console.WriteLine("Department ID: {0}", e.deptID)
    Console.WriteLine("Title: {0}", e.title)
End Sub
```

As I am sure you already understand, structures are types that are well suited for modeling mathematical, geometric, and numerical types. When you are building complete VB .NET solutions, you will most likely make use of Class types (to benefit from the famed pillars of OOP; see Chapter 4). Nevertheless, structures do allow you to build lightweight types that support the bare bones of object technology (i.e., encapsulation).

SOURCE CODE *The Structures project is located under the Chapter 3 subdirectory.*

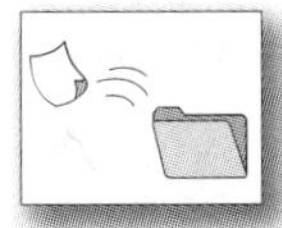

Defining Custom Namespaces

To this point, you have been building small test programs leveraging existing namespaces in the .NET universe. When you build real-life applications, it can be very helpful to group your related types into custom namespaces. In VB .NET, this is accomplished using the "Namespace" keyword.

Recall from Chapter 2 that when you create a brand-new VB .NET project workspace, you are assigned a "root" namespace that logically groups each custom type under a conceptual group. To view this initial namespace, activate the property page for your Project (using the File View tab of the Solutions Explorer). If you create a new Console application named Namespaces, the root namespace would also be Namespaces. This is not a requirement of the .NET architecture. Assume you are building a single file assembly that contained a number of interesting classes modeling geometric types named Square, Circle, and Hexagon. Given their similarities you would like to group them all together into a shared custom namespace. Using the project properties window you could change the name (Figure 3-25).

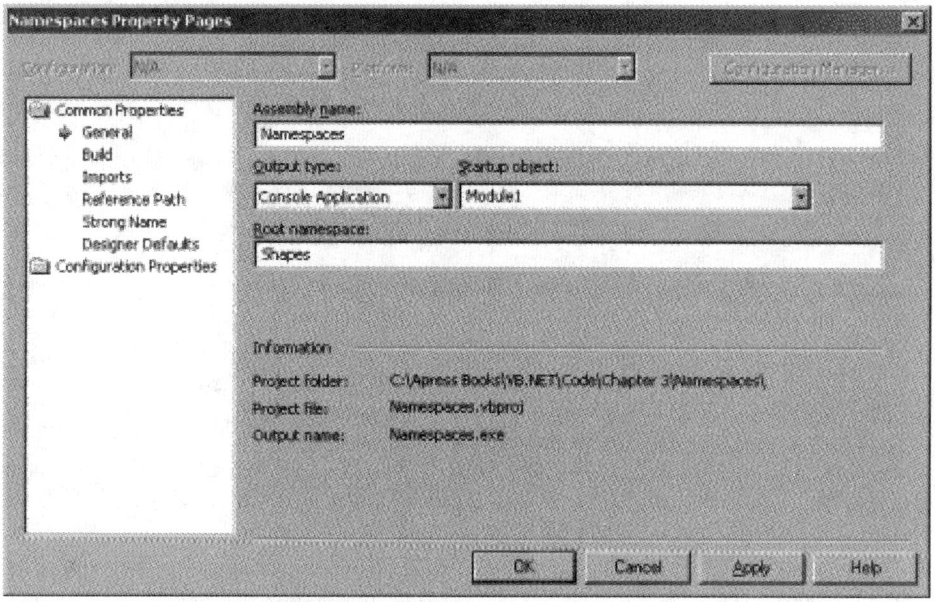

Figure 3-25. Updating the root namespace

Now, as you add more types to your current project, each becomes a member of the Shapes namespace:

```
' Root namespace is Shapes.
Module Module1
    Sub Main()
    End Sub
End Module
' Circle class.
Class Circle
    ' Interesting members.
End Class
' Hexagon class.
Class Hexagon
    ' More interesting members.
End Class
' Square class.
Class Square
    ' Even more interesting members.
End Class
```

Notice how the Shapes namespace acts as the logical "container" of each type. If you open up this assembly using ILDasm.exe, you see the truth of the matter (Figure 3-26):

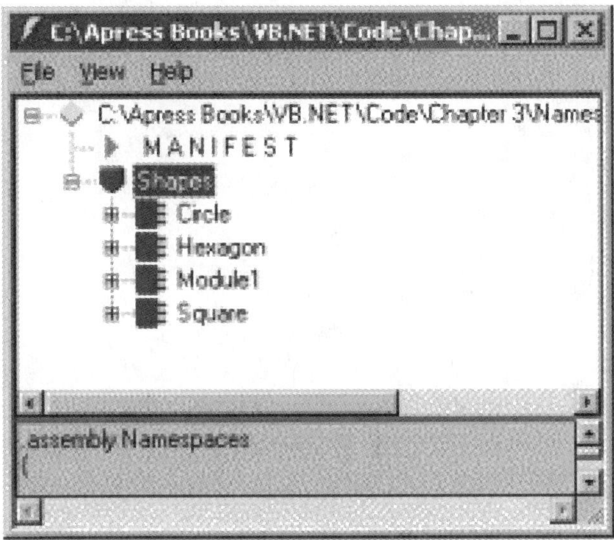

Figure 3-26. The root namespace

As you know, when another assembly you are building wants to use these fine objects from within its namespace, make use of the Imports keyword (and set a reference to the assembly, of course):

```
' Make use of objects defined in another namespace
Imports Shapes
Module ShapeTester
    Sub Main()
        ' All defined in the Shapes namespace.
        Dim h as Hexagon = New Hexagon()
        Dim c as Circle = New Circle()
        Dim s as Square = New Square()
    End Sub
End Module
```

Resolving Name Clashes Across Namespaces

A custom namespace can also be used to avoid nasty name clashes across multiple namespaces (as illustrated in the previous Enum example). Assume you have a new namespace in your current project termed My3DShapes, which defines three additional classes capable of rendering a shape in stunning 3D:

```
' Another shapes namespace. . .
Namespace My3DShapes
    ' Circle class.
    Class Circle
        ' Interesting members.
    End Class
    ' Hexagon class.
    Class Hexagon
        ' More interesting members.
    End Class
    ' Square class.
    Class Square
        ' Even more interesting members.
    End Class
End Namespace
```

With this update, you are not issued any compile-time errors. However, you will find that the classes referenced in the root namespace are automatically activated, as the Module type is in the defining scope. If you want to reference a 3D shape, you may opt to use a fully qualified name:

```
Module Module1
    Sub Main()
        ' Defined in the My3DShapes namespace.
        Dim h As My3DShapes.Hexagon = _
            New My3DShapes.Hexagon()
        ' Defined in root namespace.
        Dim c As Circle = New Circle()
        Dim s As Square = New Square()
    End Sub
End Module
```

An alternative approach to resolving namespace ambiguity is accomplished through aliases. You have already seen this technique during the discussion of System.Enum. Here is another example:

```
' Create a moniker to the 3D hexagon.
Imports The3DHex = My3DShapes.Hexagon
```

Nested Namespaces

The final point of interest with regard to namespaces is the fact that you are free to nest namespaces within other namespaces (including the root namespace). The .NET base class libraries do so in numerous places to provide an even deeper level of type organization. For example, if you want to nest the My3DShapes namespace within the existing root Shapes namespace, you would simply name use of the Namespace keyword from within the project containing the root. If you were to again load the assembly using ILDasm.exe, you would find what's shown in Figure 3-27.

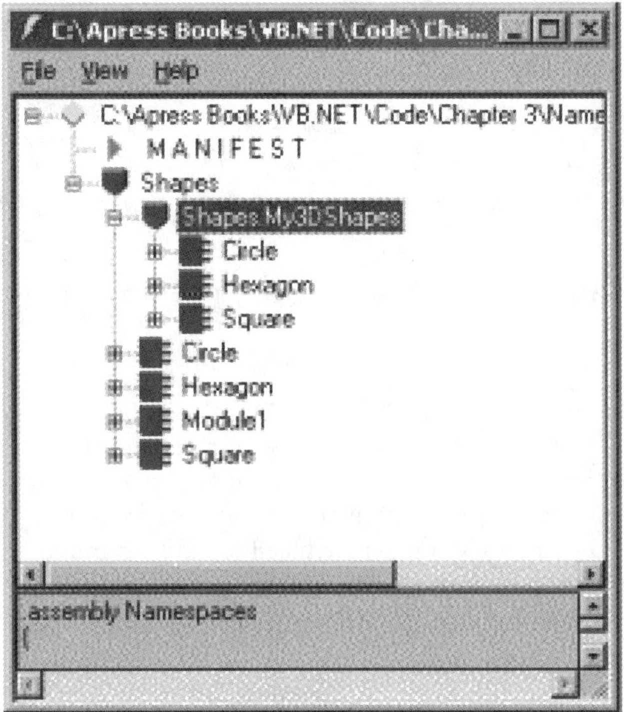

Figure 3- 27. Nested namespaces

If another assembly wanted to make use of these nested types, you would again make use of the fully qualified name (i.e., Shapes.My3DShapes.Square) or build a suitable alias. Finally, understand that namespaces can be arbitrarily deep. If you want to nest another level off the root, you could write:

```
' I live in Shapes.My3DShapes.My3DColoredShapes
Namespace My3DShapes
   Namespace My3DColoredShapes
      Class My3DBrightYellowOctagon
         ' Members. . .
      End Class
   End Namespace
End Namespace
```

Nesting namespaces can also be achieved using the following shorthand notation (which can be quite helpful when defining types in multiple *.vb files that need to be part of the same namespace definition):

```
' OtherClass.vb
Namespace My3DShapes.My3DColoredShapes
    Class My3DDimGreenBox
        ' Members. . .
    End Class
End Namespace
```

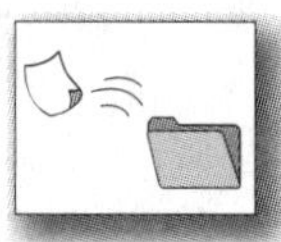

SOURCE CODE *The Namespaces project is located under the Chapter 3 subdirectory.*

Summary

This chapter has exposed you to the core atoms of the VB .NET programming language. The focus was to examine the constructs that will be commonplace in any application you may be interested in building. First, every VB .NET program must have a type defining a Main() method, which serves as the program's entry point. Within the scope of Main(), you typically create any number of objects that work together to breathe life into your application. Recall that the Module type is a specialized class type that defines a set of shared members, and is not directly creatable.

As you have seen, all intrinsic VB .NET data types alias a corresponding type in the System namespace. Ultimately, all types derive from System.Object, which provides a core set of behaviors for every type in the .NET universe. Also examined was the all-important distinction between "value types" and "reference types."

You also peeked inside a number of classes that place an OO spin on common programming constructs, such as arrays, strings, and enumerations, and took a tour of their functionality. Finally, the chapter ends by explaining how to build your own custom namespaces, and why you might want to do so.

CHAPTER 4

Object-Oriented Programming with VB .NET

IN THE PREVIOUS CHAPTER you were introduced to a number of core constructs of the VB .NET language. Here, you spend your time digging deeper into the details of object-based development. You begin by reviewing the famed "pillars of OOP" and then examine exactly how VB .NET contends with the notions of encapsulation, inheritance, and polymorphism. This equips you with the knowledge you need in order to build custom class hierarchies using VB .NET.

During this process, you examine some new constructs such as establishing type (rather than member) level visibility, building custom properties, and designing "sealed" classes. You also gain an understanding of the use of structured exception handling to contend with runtime errors, as opposed to the outdated "On Error Goto" mechanism of VB 6.0. This chapter wraps up with an examination of the "managed heap," including how to programmatically interact with the .NET garbage collector using the members defined by System.GC.

A Catalog of VB .NET OO-Centric Keywords

VB .NET is the first dialect of the VB language that offers full support for object oriented development techniques. Although VB 6.0 supported classes, initialize and terminate events as well as interface based programming techniques, each of these constructs were expressed in far less than ideal terms. For example, interfaces and classes were not declared using a given syntactic construct, but rather were indirectly marked by virtue of being defined within a *.cls file. In VB .NET, these same atoms are expressed using the "Class" and "Interface" keywords.

VB .NET's support for OOP goes far beyond two additional keywords however. As you will see during the course of the next three chapters, VB .NET demands a firm grounding in many OO techniques. Given that VB .NET exposes so many new concepts (especially if your current background is VB 6.0), Table 4-1 provides a high level look at the core keywords you must be ready to contend with.

Table 4-1. A Catalog of VB .NET OO-Centric Keywords

VB.NET OO-CENTRIC KEYWORD	MEANING IN LIFE
Class, Interface	Unlike VB 6.0, VB .NET provides language keywords used to define class and interface types (no more *.cls files).
MustInherit	This keyword marks a class as an "abstract base class" that is used to hold common behaviors for derived types, but is not directly creatable.
Namespace	As you saw in Chapters 2 and 3, namespaces are a way to logically group related types under a shared name.
Property, Sub, Function, Event, Delegate, WithEvents, RaiseEvent	As with VB 6.0, VB .NET class types may support any number of members. For the most part, VB .NET makes use of these keywords in very similar ways. You see the minor differences as you move through the next handful of chapters.
Sub New()	Your custom types (classes and structures) may support any number of overloaded New() methods. As you will see, these members serve as a type's "constructor."
Overridable, Overrides MustOverride, NotOverridable	Unlike VB 6.0, your custom classes may define "overridable" methods that can be "overridden" in a derived class. These keywords are the backbone of VB .NET's support for classic polymorphism.
Me, MyBase, MyClass	These keywords allow you to programmatically reference the current type as well as base class functionality.
Shadows	Derived types can "shadow" (i.e., hide) members of its base class, in order to provide a custom behavior.
Overloads	VB .NET allows you to create types that support multiple methods of the same exact name (but varying parameters). The "Overloads" keyword marks such members, but as you will see, this keyword is technically optional in most cases.
Shared	Shared members are data types and/or methods that are (pardon the redundancy) shared among all objects of the same type.
Public, Private, Protected, Friend	Types (and members of types) support various levels of visibility. These keywords represent the full set visibility options.
Inherits, Implements	These keywords allow you to derive a new class from a specified base class as well as implement any number of interfaces.

Formal Definition of the VB .NET Class

If you have been "doing objects" in another programming language, you are no doubt aware of the roll of class definitions. Formally, a class is nothing more than a custom UDT (user defined type) that is composed of data (often called attributes or properties) and functions that operate on this data (often called methods in OOP-speak). The power of object-based languages is that by grouping data and functionality in a single UDT, you are able to model your software types after real-world entities.

For example, assume you are interested in modeling a generic employee. At minimum, you may want to build a class that maintains the name, current pay, and employee ID for each worker. In addition, the Employee class defines one method named GiveBonus(), which increases an individual's current pay by some amount, and another named DisplayStats(), which prints out the relevant statistics for this individual (Figure 4-1).

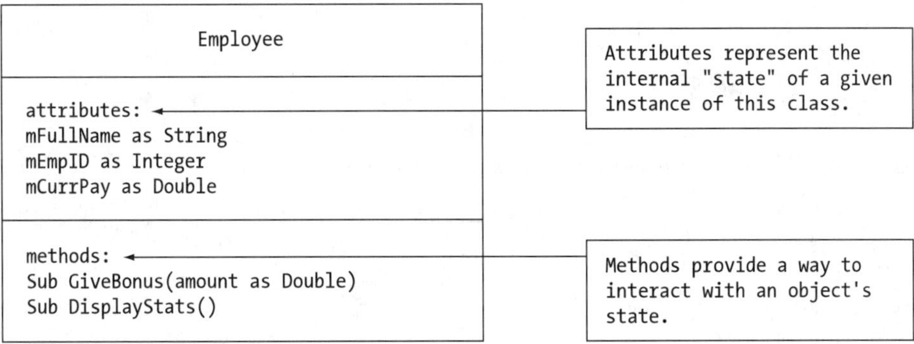

Figure 4-1. A simple class definition

As you recall from Chapter 3, VB .NET classes can define any number of *constructors*. These special class methods provide a simple way for an object user to create an instance of a given class with an initial look and feel. As you know, every VB .NET class is endowed with a freebee default constructor. The role of the default constructor is to ensure that all state data is set to an initial safe value. In addition to the default constructor, you are also free to define as many custom constructors as you feel are necessary. To get the ball rolling, here is our first crack at the Employee class:

```
' The initial class definition.
class Employee
    ' Private state data.
    Private mFullName as String
    Private mEmpID as Integer
```

```
    Private mCurrPay as Double
    ' Constructors.
    Public Sub New()
    End Sub
    Public Sub New(fullName as String, empID as Integer, currPay as Double)
        mFullName = fullName
        mEmpID = empID
        mCurrPay = currPay
    End Sub
    ' Bump the pay for this employee.
    Public Sub GiveBonus(amount as Double)
        mCurrPay += amount
    End Sub
    ' Show stats of this employee.
    Public Sub DisplayStats()
        Console.WriteLine("Name: {0}", mFullName)
        Console.WriteLine("Pay: {0}", mCurrPay)
        Console.WriteLine("ID: {0}", mEmpID)
    End Sub
End Class
```

Notice the empty implementation of the default constructor:

```
Class Employee
    ...
    ' Default constructor.
    Public Sub New()
    End Sub
End Class
```

Recall that in VB .NET, if you choose to include custom constructors in a class definition, the default constructor is *silently removed.* Therefore, if you want to allow the object user to create an instance of your class such as:

```
' Calls the default constructor.
Dim e as New Employee()
```

you need to explicitly redefine the default constructor for your class. If you forget to do so, you generate compile-time errors. Triggering the logic behind a constructor is self-explanatory. Recall that unlike VB 6.0, objects are created at the *exact point* in which the New keyword is used. Therefore, the following Employee declarations behave identically under VB .NET.

```
' Call some custom ctors (two identical approaches)
Sub Main()
    Dim e As Employee = New Employee("Joe", 80, 30000)
    e.GiveBonus(200)
    e.DisplayStats()
    Dim e2 As Employee
    e2 = New Employee("Beth", 81, 50000)
    e2.GiveBonus(1000)
    e2.DisplayStats()
End Sub
```

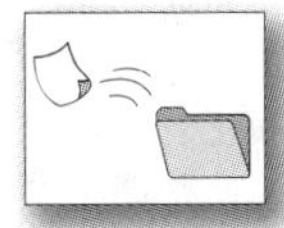

SOURCE CODE *The Employees project that you examine during the course of this chapter is included under the Chapter 4 subdirectory.*

Self-Reference in VB .NET

One common way to name member variables of a class is to attach the letter "m" as a prefix to the data point in question (i.e., mFullName, mEmpID and mCurrPay). Assume for a moment that the private data points of the Employee class are instead named fullName, empID and currPay. In the implementation of your custom constructor, you would suddenly have a name clash, given that the incoming parameter names are exactly the same! Like VB 6.0, VB .NET supports the "Me" keyword, which can be used within a class definition to refer to the members and data points of the defining type. Thus, you could avoid the name clash like so:

```
Class Employee
    ' Private state data.
    Private fullName As String
    Private empID As Integer
    Private currPay As Double
...
    Public Sub New(ByVal fullName As String, ByVal empID As Integer, _
    ByVal currPay As Double)
        Me.fullName = fullName
        Me.empID = empID
        Me.currPay = currPay
    End Sub
    ...
End Class
```

This particular VB .NET keyword is used whenever you want to make reference to the current object instance. C#, Java, and C++ developers can equate the VB .NET "Me" keyword with the "this" keyword, which is used for the same purpose.

In this example, you made use of "Me" in your custom constructor to avoid clashes between the parameter names and names of your internal state variables. Of course, another approach would be to change the names for each parameter (or member variable) and avoid the name clash altogether (but I am sure you get the point). Also, be aware that *shared* type members cannot access the "Me" keyword. This should make perfect sense, given that shared member functions operate on the class (not object) level.

Forwarding Constructor Calls Using "Me"

Another usage of the VB .NET "Me" keyword is to force one constructor to call another. Consider the following example:

```
Class Employee
    Public Sub New(ByVal fullName As String, _
    ByVal empID As Integer, ByVal currPay As Double)
        Me.fullName = fullName
        Me.empID = empID
        Me.currPay = currPay
    End Sub
    ' If the user calls this ctor, forward to the 3-arg version
    ' using arbitrary values. . .
    Public Sub New(ByVal fullName As String)
        Me.New(fullName, IDGenerator.GetNewEmpID(), 3333)
    End Sub
. . .
End Class
```

First, notice that this iteration of the Employee class defines two custom constructors, the second of which requires a single parameter (the individual's name). However, to fully construct a new Employee, you want to ensure you have a proper Employee ID and rate of pay. Assume you have a custom class (IDGenerator) that defines a shared method named GetNewEmpID() for this very purpose. Once you gather the correct set of start-up parameters, you forward the creation request to the three-argument constructor. If you did not forward the call, you would need to add redundant initialization code to each constructor.

Member Overloading

During the last few chapters you have examined the details of VB .NET class constructors. As you have seen, it is quite common for a single class type to support any number of constructors, each of which differs by the number and type of parameters. Technically speaking, when a class defines a member of the same exact name (such as Sub New()) that differs only by the parameter set, you have "overloaded" the member.

As you have already seen, overloaded constructors can be quite helpful when you want to provide a set of construction routines that can each be accessed using the New keyword. When you overload constructors for your class types, you do not have to mark each Sub New() with an additional keyword. As long as each constructor maintains a distinct parameter list, vbc.exe is able to resolve the correct version to call.

Constructors are not the only members that can be overloaded however. In reality, any VB .NET subroutine or function may be overloaded in the same manner. Again, the key is to ensure that each version of the method has a distinct set of arguments (members differing only by return type are *not* unique enough). VB .NET defines the Overloads keyword that can be used when you want to explicitly mark a member as overloaded. This is optional. vbc.exe assumes you are overloading if it finds identically named methods with varying arguments. Assume you have added the following overloaded member to the Employee class:

```
' An overloaded method (Overloads keyword is optional).
Public Overloads Function GetStartDate(ByVal id As Integer) as Integer
    ' Look up start date using employee ID.
End Function
Public Overloads Function GetStartDate(ByVal ssn As String) as String
    ' Look up start date using SSN.
End Function
```

Here, you have a single method, GetStartDate(), which differs only by the incoming argument. This is very helpful in the eyes of the object user, given that he or she can write the following code:

```
' Calling an overloaded member.
fred.GetStartDate("111-11-2233")
jane.GetStartDate(8344)
```

rather than the more VB 6.0-centric approach of having two distinctly named members:

```
fred.GetStartDateUsingSSN("111-11-2233")
jane.GetStartDateUsingEmpID(8344)
```

Another approach taken by many VB 6.0 programmers was to have a discrete method taking a Variant data type. Using this approach, the method was in charge of determining the underlying type and value of said Variant, and acting accordingly. Of course, you are aware that the Variant data type is slow and not very type safe (at all). In fact, under VB .NET, the Variant data type is dead.

Defining the Default Public Interface

Once you have established a class' internal state data and constructor set, your next step is to flesh out the details of the *default public interface* to the class. The term refers to the set of public members that is accessible from an object instance. From an object user's point of view, the default public interface is the set of items that are accessible using the VB .NET dot operator. From the class builder's point of view, the default public interface is any item declared in a class using the Public keyword. In VB .NET, the default interface of a class may be populated by any of the following members:

- Methods: Named units of work that model some behaviors of a class.
- Properties: Accessor and mutator functions in disguise.
- Fields: Public data (although this is typically a bad idea, VB .NET supports them).

As you see in Chapter 6, the default public interface of a class may also be configured to support custom events. For the time being, let's concentrate on the use of properties, methods, and field data.

Specifying Type Level Visibility: Public and Friendly Types

Before you get too far along in your employee example, you must understand how to establish visibility levels for your custom types. In the previous chapter, you were introduced to the following class definition:

```
Class HelloClass
    ' Any number of methods with any number of parameters. . .
    ' Default and/or custom constructors. . .
End Class
```

Recall that each member defined by a class must establish its level of visibility using the Public, Private, Protected, or Friend keywords. In the same vein, VB .NET classes also need to specify their levels of visibility. The distinction is that *method visibility* is used to constrain which members can be accessed from a given object instance, and *class visibility* is used to establish which parts of the system can create the types themselves (in some ways analogous to the VB 6.0 Instancing property).

A VB .NET class can be marked by one of two visibility keywords: Public or Friend. Public classes may be created by any other objects within the same binary (assembly), as well as by other binaries (e.g., another assembly). Therefore, HelloClass could be redefined as follows:

```
' We are now creatable by types outside this assembly.
Public Class HelloClass
    ' Any number of methods with any number of parameters. . .
    ' Default and/or custom constructors. . .
End Class
```

By default, if you do not explicitly mark the visibility level of a class, it is implicitly set to "Friend." Friend classes can only be created by objects living within the same assembly, and are not accessible from outside the assembly's bounds. As you might suspect, internal items can be viewed as "helper types" used by an assembly's types to help the Public classes get their work done:

```
 ' Internal classes can only be used by other types within the same assembly.
Friend Class HelloClassHelper
    . . .
End Class
```

Classes are not the only UDT that can accept a visibility attribute. As you recall, a type is simply a generic term used to refer to classes, structures, enumerations, interfaces, and delegates. Any .NET type can be assigned public or internal visibility. For example:

```
' Any type may be assigned Public or Friend visibility.
Friend Structure X             ' Cannot be used outside this assembly.
    Private myX as Integer
    Public Function GetMyX() as Integer
        Return myX
    End Function
End Structure
Friend Enum Letters    ' Cannot be used outside this assembly.
    a = 0
    b = 1
    c = 2
```

```
End Enum
Public Class HelloClass   ' May be used outside this assembly.
. . .
End Class
```

Logically, the previously defined types can be envisioned as shown in Figure 4-2.

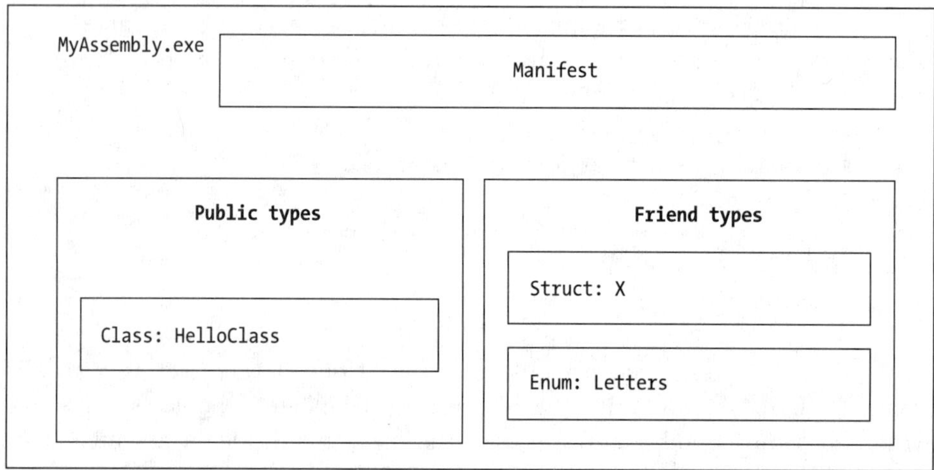

Figure 4-2. Friend and Public types

Chapter 7 drills into the specifics of composing .NET assemblies. Until then, just understand that all of your types may be defined as Public (accessible by the outside world) or Friend (not directly accessible by the outside world).

Pillars of OOP

VB .NET is a newcomer to the world of object-oriented languages (OOLs). Java, C++, Object Pascal, and (to some extent) Visual Basic 6.0 are but a small sample of the popularity of the object paradigm. Regardless of exactly when a given OOL came into existence, all object-based languages contend with three core principles of object-oriented programming, often called the famed "pillars of OOP."

- *Encapsulation:* How well does this language hide an object's internal implementation?
- *Inheritance:* How does this language promote code reuse?
- *Polymorphism:* How does this language let me treat related objects in a similar way?

As you are most likely already aware, VB 6.0 did not support each pillar of object technology. Specifically, VB 6.0 lacked classic inheritance (and therefore lacked classical polymorphism). VB .NET on the other hand supports each aspect of OOP, and is on par with any other modern OO language (such as C#, Java, C++, and Delphi). Before digging into the syntactic details of each pillar, it is important that you understand the basic role of each. Therefore, here is a brisk high-level rundown.

Encapsulation Services

The first pillar of OOP is called *encapsulation.* This trait boils down to the language's ability to hide unnecessary implementation details from the object user. For example, assume you have created a class named DBReader (database reader), which has two primary methods: Open() and Close():

```
' The database reader encapsulates the details of opening and closing a database...
Dim f as DBReader = New DBReader()
f.Open("C:\foo.mdf")
     ' Do something with data file. . .
f.Close()
```

The fictitious DBReader class has encapsulated the inner details of locating, loading, manipulating, and closing the data file. Object users love encapsulation, as this pillar of OOP keeps programming task simpler. There is no need to worry about the numerous lines of code that are working behind the scenes to carry out the work of the DBReader class. All you do is create an instance and send the appropriate messages (e.g., "open the file named foo.mdf").

Closely related to the notion of encapsulating programming logic is the idea of data hiding. As you know, an object's state data should ideally be specified as Private. In this way, the outside world must ask politely in order to change or obtain the underlying value. This is a good thing, as publicly declared data points can easily become corrupted (hopefully by accident rather than intent!)

Inheritance: The "is-a" and "has-a" Relationships

The next pillar of OOP, inheritance, boils down to the languages' ability to allow you to build new class definitions based on existing class definitions. In essence, inheritance allows you to extend the behavior of a base (or "parent") class by inheriting core functionality into a subclass (also called a "child class"). Figure 4-3 shows a simple example.

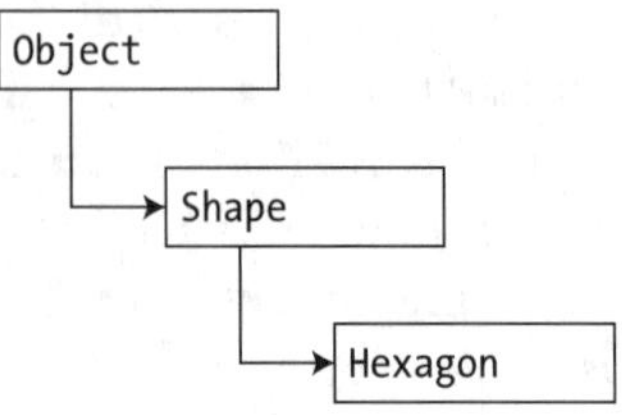

Figure 4-3. The "is-a" relationship

As you are aware, System.Object is always the topmost node in any .NET hierarchy. The Shape class extends Object. You can assume that Shape defines some number of properties, fields, methods, and events that are common to all shapes. The Hexagon class extends Shape, and inherits the core functionality defined by Shape and Object, as well as defines additional hexagon related details of its own (whatever those may be).

You can read this diagram as "A hexagon is-a shape that is-a object." When you have classes related by this form of inheritance, you establish "is-a" relationships between types. The is-a relationship is often termed *classical inheritance.*

There is another form of code reuse in the world of OOP: the containment/delegation model (also known as the "has-a" relationship). This form of reuse (used exclusively by VB 6.0 and classic COM) is not used to establish base/subclass relationships. Rather, a given class can contain another class and expose part or all of its functionality to the outside world.

For example, if you are modeling an automobile, you might want to express the idea that a car "has-a" radio. It would be illogical to attempt to derive the Car class from a Radio, or vice versa (a Car "is-a" Radio? I think not!). Rather, you have two independent classes working together, where the *outer* (or containing) class creates and exposes the *inner* (or contained) class' functionality (Figure 4-4).

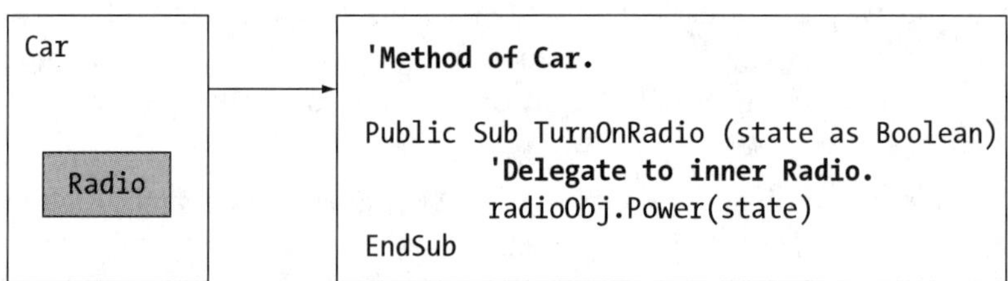

Figure 4-4. The "has-a" relationship

Here, the outer object (Car) is responsible for creating the inner (Radio) object. If the Car wants to make the Radio's behavior accessible from a Car instance, it must extend its public interface. Notice that the object user has no clue that the Car class is making use of an inner object.

```
' The inner Radio is encapsulated by the outer Car class.
Dim viper as New Car()
viper.TurnOnRadio(False)     ' Delegates request to inner Radio object.
```

Polymorphism: Classical and Ad Hoc

The final pillar of OOP is *polymorphism.* This trait captures a language's ability to treat related objects the same way. Like inheritance, polymorphism falls under two camps: Classical and ad hoc. Classical polymorphism can only take place in languages that also support classical inheritance. If this is the case (as it is in VB .NET), it becomes possible for a base class to define a set of members that can be *overridden* by a subclass. When subclasses override the behavior defined by a base class, they are essentially redefining how they respond to the same message.

To illustrate classical polymorphism, let's revisit the shapes hierarchy. Assume that the Shape class has defined a function named Draw(), taking no parameters and returning nothing. Given the fact that every shape needs to render itself in a unique manner, subclasses (such as Hexagon and Circle) are free to reinterpret this method to their own liking (Figure 4-5).

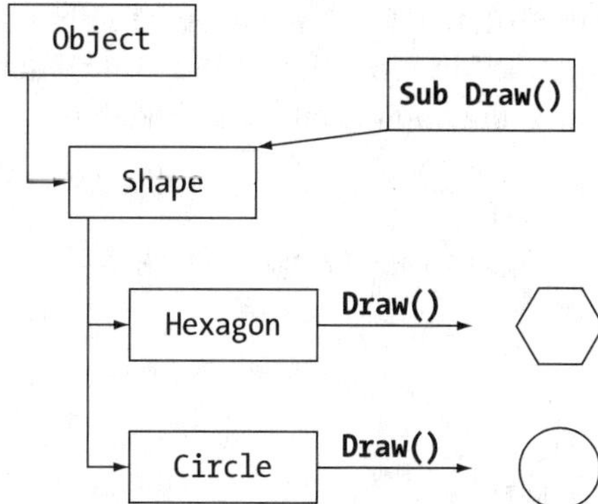

Figure 4-5. Classical polymorphism

Classical polymorphism allows a base class to enforce a given behavior on all descendents. From Figure 4-5 you can assume that any type derived from the Shapes class has the ability to be rendered. This is a great boon to any language because you are able to avoid creating redundant methods to perform a similar operation (e.g., DrawCircle(), DrawRectangle(), DrawHexagon(), and so forth).

Next, you have *ad hoc polymorphism.* This flavor of polymorphism (also used exclusively by VB 6.0) allows objects that are *not* related by classical inheritance to be treated in a similar manner, provided that every object has a method of the exact same signature (that is, method name, parameter list, and return type). Languages that support ad hoc polymorphism employ a technique called *late binding* to discover at runtime the underlying type of a given object. Based on this discovery, the correct method is invoked. As an illustration, first ponder Figure 4-6.

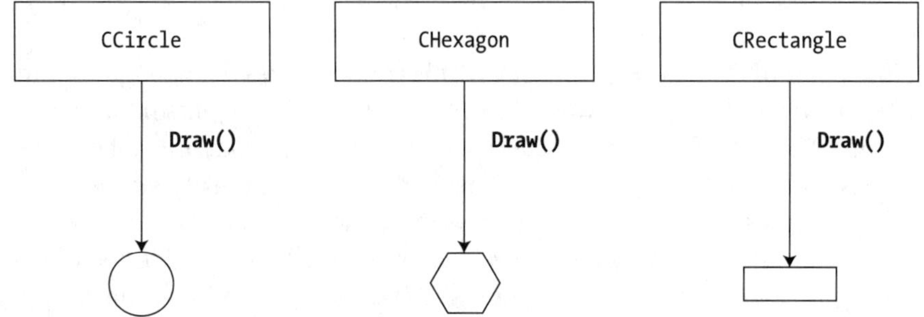

Figure 4-6. Ad hoc polymorphism

Notice how there is no common base class between the CCircle, CHexagon, and CRectangle classes. However, each class supports an identical Draw() method. Until the advent of VB .NET, Visual Basic did not support classical polymorphism (or classical inheritance for that matter), forcing developers to make due with the following ad hoc functionality. To illustrate what this boils down to syntactically, consider the following Visual Basic 6.0 code:

```
' Visual Basic 6.0 code below!
' First create an array of Object data types, setting each to an object reference.
Dim objArr(3) as Object
Set objArr(0) = New CCircle
Set objArr(1) = New CHexagon
Set objArr(2) = New CCircle
Set objArr(3) = New CRectangle

' Now loop over the array, asking each object to render itself.
Dim i as Integer
For i = 0 to 3
     objArr(i).Draw     ' Late binding. . .
Next i
```

In this code block, you begin by creating an array of generic Object data types (which is an intrinsic Visual Basic 6.0 type capable of holding any object reference, and has nothing to do with System.Object). As you iterate over the array at runtime, each shape is asked to render itself. Again, the key difference is that you have no common base class that contains a default implementation of the Draw() method. As an alternative to ad hoc polymorphism, VB 6.0 (as well as VB .NET) support interface-based polymorphism is examined a bit later in this text.

To wrap up this review of the pillars of OOP, recall that every object-oriented language needs to address how it contends with encapsulation, polymorphism, and inheritance. As you may already suspect, VB .NET completely supports each pillar of object technology, including both flavors of inheritance (is-a and has-a) as well as classical and ad hoc polymorphism. Now that you have the theory in your minds, the bulk of this chapter explores the exact VB .NET syntax that represents each trait.

The First Pillar: VB .NET's Encapsulation Services

The concept of encapsulation revolves around the notion that an object's internal data should not be directly accessible from an object instance. Rather, if an object user wants to alter the state of an object, the user does so indirectly using accessor and mutator methods. In VB .NET, encapsulation is enforced at the syntactic level using the Public, Private, Friend, and Protected keywords. To illustrate, assume you have created the following class definition:

```
' A class with a single field.
Public Class Book
    Public numberOfPages as Integer
End Class
```

When a class defines points of public data, these items are termed *fields.* The problem with field data is that the items have no ability to "understand" if the current value to which they are assigned is valid with regard to the current business rules of the system. As you know, the upper range of a VB .NET Integer is quite large (2,147,483,647). Therefore, the compiler allows the following assignment:

```
' Humm. . .
Sub Main()
    Dim miniNovel as New Book()
    miniNovel.numberOfPages = 30000000
End Sub
```

Although you have not overflowed the boundaries of an Integer data type, it should be clear that a mini-novel with a page count of 30,000,000 pages is a bit unreasonable. As you can see, fields do not provide a way to trap logical upper (or lower) limits. If your current system has a business rule that states a book must be between 1 and 2000 pages, you are at a loss to enforce this programmatically.

Because of this, public fields typically have no place in a production level class definition.

Encapsulation provides a way to preserve the integrity of state data. Rather than defining public fields (which can easily foster data corruption), you should get in the habit of defining *private data*, which are indirectly manipulated using one of two main techniques:

- Define a pair of traditional accessor and mutator methods.
- Define a named property.

Additionally, VB .NET supports special keywords "ReadOnly" and "WriteOnly," which also deliver a level of data protection. Whichever technique you choose, the point is that a well-encapsulated class should hide the details of how it operates from the prying eyes of the outside world. This is often termed "black box" programming. The beauty of this approach is that an object is free to change how a given method is implemented under the hood. It does this without breaking any existing code making use of it, provided that the signature of the method remains constant.

Enforcing Encapsulation Using Traditional Accessors and Mutators

Let's return to your existing Employee class. If you want the outside world to interact with your private string representing a worker's full name, tradition dictates defining an *accessor* (get method) and *mutator* (set method). For example:

```
' Traditional accessor and mutator for a point of private data.
Public Class Employee
     Private mFullName as String
...
    ' Accessor.
    Public Function GetFullName() As String
        Return mFullName
    End Function

    ' Mutator
    Public Sub SetFullName(ByVal n As String)
        ' Remove any illegal characters (!,@,#,$,%),
        ' check maximum length or case before making assignment.
        mFullName = n
    End Sub
End Class
```

This technique requires two uniquely named methods to operate on a single data point. The calling logic is as follows:

```
' Accessor/mutator usage.
Sub Main()
     Dim p as new Employee()
     p.SetFullName("Fred")
     Console.WriteLine("Employee is named: {0}", p.GetFullName())
     ' Error! Can't access private data from an object instance.
     ' p.mFullName
End Sub
```

Another Form of Encapsulation: Class Properties

In addition to traditional accessor and mutator methods, classes (as well as structures and interfaces) can also support *properties*. Visual Basic and COM programmers have long used properties to simulate publicly accessible points of data (that is, fields). Under the hood however, properties resolve to a pair of hidden internal methods. Rather than requiring the user to call two discrete methods to get and set the state data, the user is able to call what appears to be a single named field:

```
' Representing a person's ID as a property
Sub Main()
     Dim p as New Employee()
     ' Set the value.
     p.EmpID = 81
     ' Get the value.
     Console.WriteLine("Employee ID is: {0}", p.EmpID)
End Sub
```

Properties always map to "real" accessor and mutator methods. Therefore, as a Class designer you are able to perform any internal logic necessary before making the value assignment (e.g., uppercase the value, scrub the value for illegal characters, check the bounds of a numerical value, and so on). Here is the VB .NET syntax behind the EmpID property:

```
' Custom property for the EmpID data point.
Public Class Employee
...
    Private mEmpID as Integer
   ' Property for the empID.
```

```
        Public Property EmpID() As Integer
            Get
                Return mEmpID
            End Get
            Set(ByVal Value As Integer)
                mEmpID = Value
            End Set
        End Property
    End Class
```

Unlike VB 6.0, a property is not represented by distinct Get and Set methods. A VB .NET property is composed using a Get block (accessor) and Set block (mutator). The "Value" keyword represents the right side of the assignment. As all things in VB .NET, Value is also an object. However, the underlying type of the object depends on which sort of data it represents. In your example, the EmpID property is operating on a private integer, which, as you recall, maps to an Int32:

```
' Calls set, value = 81.
' 81 is an instance of Int32, so 'Value' is an Int32.
p.EmpID = 81
```

To illustrate, assume you have updated your set logic as follows:

```
Public Property EmpID() As Integer
    Get
        Return mEmpID
    End Get
    Set(ByVal Value As Integer)
    ' Just to prove the point.
        Console.WriteLine("value is an instance of: {0}", _
                Value.GetType())
        Console.WriteLine("value as string: {0}", _
                Value.ToString())
        mEmpID = Value
    End Set
End Property
```

When you set the property, you would see the following output (Figure 4-7).

Do be aware that you may only access the Value keyword within the scope of a Set block. Any attempt to do otherwise results in a compiler error.

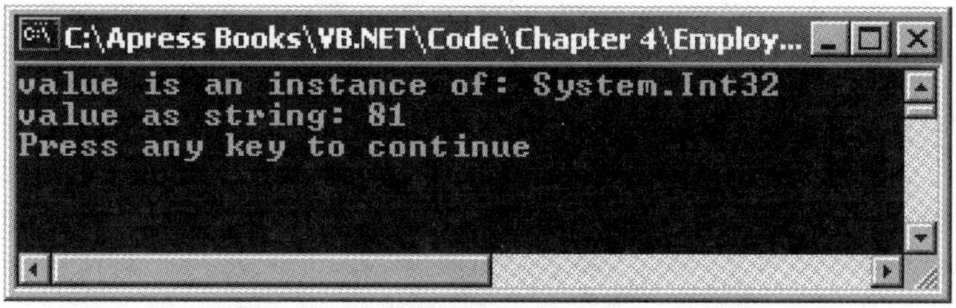

```
value is an instance of: System.Int32
value as string: 81
Press any key to continue
```

Figure 4-7. The value of "Value" when EmpID = 81

Internal Representation of VB .NET Properties

Many programmers tend to design accessor and mutator methods using "get_" and "set_" prefixes (e.g., get_Name() and set_Name()). This naming convention itself is not problematic. However, it is important to understand that under the hood, a VB .NET property is internally represented using these same prefixes. For example, if you open up the Employees.exe assembly using ILDasm.exe you see that each property actually resolves to two discrete (and hidden) methods (Figure 4-8).

Given this, realize that if you defined a class as such, you generate compiler errors:

```
' Remember, a VB .NET property really maps to a get_/set_ pair.
Public Class Employee
...
' Another property.
    Public Property SSN() As String
        Get
            Return mSSN
        End Get
        Set(ByVal Value As String)
            mSSN = Value
        End Set
    End Property
    ' ERROR! These are already defined by SSN property!
    Public Function get_SSN() As String
        Return SSN
    End Function
    Public Sub set_SSN(ByVal newVal As String)
        SSN = newVal
    End Sub
End Sub
```

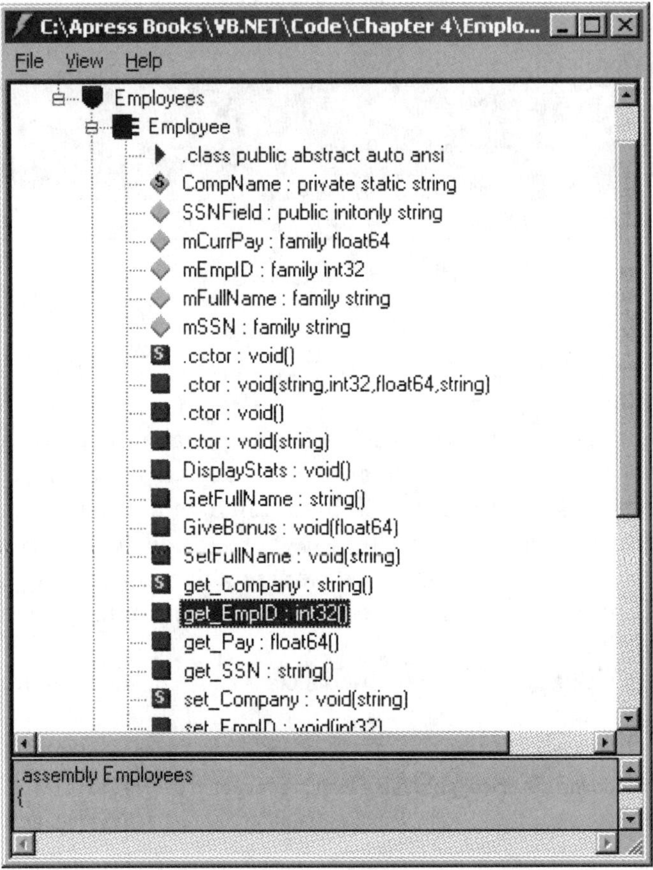

Figure 4-8. Properties map to hidden get_ and set_ methods

On a related note, understand that the reverse of this situation is *not true.* Meaning, if you define two methods named get_X() and set_X() in a given class, you cannot write syntax that references a property named X:

```
' Assume Foo has two methods named get_X() and set_X() but not a
' literal VB .NET property definition.
Dim f as New Foo()
f.X = 100                  ' Error! ! Must be defined as VB .NET property, not
                           ' set_X().
Console.WriteLine(f.X)     ' Error! ! Must also be a VB .NET property, not
                           ' get_X().
```

Read-Only, Write-Only, and Shared Properties

To wrap up our investigation of VB .NET properties, there are a few loose ends to contend with. First, recall that EmpID was established as a read/write property. When building custom properties, you may want to configure a read-only property. To do so, simply build a property without a corresponding Set block, and make use of the ReadOnly keyword. Likewise, if you want to have a write-only property, omit the Get block, and make use of the WriteOnly keyword. Unlike VB 6.0, the ReadOnly and WriteOnly keywords are required in a property definition, in order to enforce readability. To illustrate, here is a read-only property for our Employee class:

```
Public Class Employee
...
    ' Assume this is assigned in the class constructor...
    Private mSSN as String
    ' A read only property.
    Public ReadOnly Property ReadOnlySSN() As String
        Get
            Return mSSN
        End Get
    End Property    ...
End Class
```

VB .NET also supports *shared properties* (which must operate on *shared data*). Recall that shared types are bound to a given class, not an instance (object) of that class. For example, assume that the Employee type defines a point of shared data to represent the name of the organization employing these workers. You may define a shared (e.g., class level) property as follows:

```
' Shared properties must operate on shared data!
Public Class Employee

    ' A shared property.
    Private Shared CompName As String
    Public Shared Property Company() As String
        Get
            Return CompName
        End Get
        Set(ByVal Value As String)
            CompName = Value
        End Set
    End Property
     ...
End Class
```

Shared properties are manipulated in the same manner as shared methods, as seen here:

```
' Set and get the name of the company that employs these people. . .
Public Sub Main()
     Employee.Company = "Intertech, Inc"
     Console.WriteLine("These folks work at {0}", Employee.Company)
     . . .
End Sub
```

Shared Constructors

As an interesting sidebar, consider the use of shared constructors. This may seem strange given that the "constructor" is understood as a method called on a new *object* variable. Nevertheless, VB .NET supports the use of shared constructors that serve no other purpose than to assign initial values to shared data. Syntactically, shared constructors are odd in that they *cannot* take a visibility modifier (but must take the Shared keyword). To illustrate, if you wanted to ensure that the name of the static CompName field was always assigned to "Intertech, Inc" on creation, you would write:

```
' Shared constructors are used to initialize shared data.
Public Class Employee
     Private Shared CompName as String
    . . . .
    Shared Sub New()
        CompName = "Intertech, Inc"
    End Sub
End Class
```

If you invoke the Employee.Company property, there is no need to assign an initial value within the Main() method, as the shared constructor does so automatically:

```
' Automatically set to "Intertech, Inc" via the shared constructor.
Public Sub Main()
. . .
     Console.WriteLine("These folks work at {0}", Employee.Company)
End Sub
```

To wrap up the examination of VB .NET properties, understand that these syntactic entities are used for the same purpose as a classical accessor/mutator pair. The benefit of properties is that the users of your objects are able to manipulate the internal data point using a single named item.

Pseudo-Encapsulation: Creating Read-Only Fields

Closely related to read-only properties is the notion of read-only *fields*. As you know, a field is a point of public data. Typically speaking, public data is a bad thing because the object user has a fairly good chance of making an illogical assignment. Read-only fields offer data preservation that is established using the ReadOnly keyword:

```
Public Class Employee
    ...
    ' Read only field.
    Public ReadOnly SSNField As String = "111-11-1111"
End Class
```

As you can guess, any attempt to make assignments to a field marked ReadOnly results in a compiler error.

Shared Read-Only Fields

Shared read-only fields are also permissible. This can be helpful if you want to create a number of constant values bound to a given class. In this light, ReadOnly seems to be a close cousin to the Const keyword. The difference is that the value assigned to Const must be resolved at compile time. The value of ReadOnly shared fields, however, may be computed at *runtime*.

For example, assume a type named Car that needs to establish a set of tires at runtime. You can create a new class (Tire) that consists of a number of shared ReadOnly fields:

```
' The Tire class has a number of readonly fields.
Public Class Tire
    Public Shared ReadOnly GoodStone As Tire = New Tire(90)
    Public Shared ReadOnly FireYear As Tire = New Tire(100)
    Public Shared ReadOnly ReadyLyne As Tire = New Tire(43)
    Public Shared ReadOnly Blimpy As Tire = New Tire(83)
    Private manufactureID As Integer
    Public ReadOnly Property MakeID() As Integer
```

```
        Get
            Return manufactureID
        End Get
    End Property
    Public Sub New(ByVal ID As Integer)
        manufactureID = ID
    End Sub
End Class

Public Class Car
    ' What sort of tires do I have?
    Public tireType As Tire = Tire.Blimpy ' Returns a new Tire.
End Class
```

Here is an example of working with these new types:

```
' Make use of a dynamically created readonly field.
Module Module1
    Sub Main()
        Dim c As Car = New Car()
        ' Prints out "Manufacture ID of tires: 83
        Console.WriteLine("Manufacture ID of tires: {0}", c.tireType.MakeID)
    End Sub
End Module
```

SOURCE CODE *The SharedReadOnly project is included under the Chapter 4 subdirectory.*

The Second Pillar: VB .NET's Inheritance Support

Now that you understand how to create a single well-encapsulated class, it is time to turn your attention to building a family of related classes. As mentioned, inheritance is the aspect of OOP that facilitates reuse of implementation. Inheritance comes in two flavors: Classical inheritance (the is-a relationship) and the containment/delegation model (the has-a relationship). Let's begin by examining the classical is-a model.

When you establish is-a relationships between classes, you are building a dependency between types. The basic idea behind classical inheritance is that new classes may leverage (and extend) the functionality of other classes. To illustrate, assume that you want to define two additional classes to the Employee project, representing sales people and managers. The hierarchy looks something like what you see in Figure 4-9.

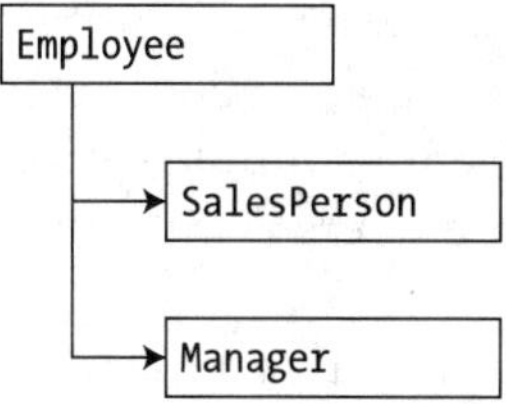

Figure 4-9. The employee hierarchy

As illustrated in Figure 4-9, you can see that a SalesPerson is-a Employee (as is a Manager—at least in a perfect world). In the classical inheritance model, base classes (such as Employee) are used to define general characteristics that are common to all descendents. Subclasses (such as SalesPerson and Manager) extend this general functionality while adding more specific behaviors to the class.

In VB .NET, extending a class is accomplished using the "Inherits" keyword. Therefore, you can syntactically model these relationships as follows:

```
' Add two new subclasses to the Employees namespace.
Public Class Manager
    Inherits Employee
     ' Managers need to know their number of stock options.
     Private numberOfOptions as Long
     Public Property NumbOpts() as Long
        Get
            Return numberOfOptions
        End Get
        Set
            numberOfOptions = Value
        End Set
     End Property
End Class

Public Class SalesPerson
Inherits Employee
    ' Sales people need to know their number of sales.
    Private numberOfSales as Long
    Public Property NumbSales() as Long
        Get
            Return numberOfSales
        End Get
        Set
            numberOfSales = Value
        End Set
    End Property
End Class
```

Notice how each subclass has extended the base class behavior by adding a custom property that operates on an underlying private point of data. Because you have established an is-a relationship, SalesPerson and Manager have *automatically* inherited all public members of the Employee base class. To illustrate:

```
' Create a subclass and access base class functionality.
Public Sub Main()
    ' Make a sales person.
    Dim stan as SalesPerson = New SalesPerson()
    ' These members are inherited from the Employee base class.
    stan.EmpID = 100
    stan.SetFullName("Stan the Man")
    ' This is defined by the SalesPerson subclass.
    stan.NumbSales = 42
End Sub
```

Needless to say, a child class *cannot* directly access private members defined by its parent class. On a related note, when the object user creates an instance of a subclass, encapsulation of private data is ensured:

```
' Error!! Instance of child class cannot allow access to a base class' private data!
Dim stan as SalesPerson = New SalesPerson()
stan.currPay
```

Controlling Base Class Creation

Currently, SalesPerson and Manager can only be created using the default class constructor. With this in mind, consider the following line of code:

```
' Create a subclass using a custom constructor.
Dim chucky as Manager = New Manager("Chucky", 92, 100000, "333-23-2322", 9000)
```

Here, you are creating an instance of the Manager class using a custom constructor. If you look at the argument list, you can clearly see that most of these values should be stored in the member variables defined by the Employee base class. Assuming you have a number of mutator methods (or class properties), you could write the following logic:

```
' If you do not say otherwise, a subclass constructor automatically calls the
' default constructor of its base class.
```

```
Public Sub New(fullName as String, empID as Integer, _
    currPay as Double, ssn as String, numbOfOpts as Long)
    ' This point of data belongs with us!
    numberOfOptions = numbOfOpts
    ' Assume the base class defines the following mutator methods.
    SetEmpID(empID)
    SetFullName(fullName)
    SetSSN(ssn)
    SetPay(currPay)
End Sub
```

Although this is technically permissible, it is not optimal. First, like most OO languages, the base class constructor (in this case the default constructor) is called automatically *before* the logic of the custom Manager constructor is executed. After this point, the current implementation accesses four public members of the employee base class to establish its state. Thus, you have really made six hits during the creation of this derived object!

To help optimize the creation of a derived class, implement your subclass constructors to explicitly call an appropriate custom base class constructor, rather than the default. In this way, you are able to call an appropriate constructor to initialize state data, and increase the efficiency of an object's creation in the process. Let's retrofit the custom constructor to do this very thing:

```
' This time, use the VB .NET 'MyBase' keyword to call
' a custom constructor on the base class.
Public Sub New(ByVal FullName As String, ByVal empID As Integer, _
    ByVal currPay As Double, ByVal ssn As String, ByVal numbOfOpts As Long)
        MyBase.New(FullName, empID, currPay, ssn)
        ' This point of data belongs with us!
        numberOfOptions = numbOfOpts
End Sub
```

Here, you make use of the VB .NET "MyBase" keyword. In this situation, you are explicitly calling the four-argument constructor defined by Employee and saving yourself unnecessary calls during the creation of the child class. The SalesPerson constructor looks almost identical:

```
' As a general rule, all subclasses should explicitly call an appropriate
' base class constructor.
Public Sub New(ByVal fName As String, ByVal empID As Integer, _
    ByVal currPay As Double, ByVal ssn As String, ByVal numbOfSales As Long)
        MyBase.new(fName, empID, currPay, ssn)
        numberOfSales = numbOfSales
End Sub
```

Also be aware that you may use the MyBase keyword any time a subclass wants to access a Public or Protected member defined by a parent class. Use of this keyword is not limited to constructor logic (you see additional examples throughout this chapter).

Regarding Multiple Base Classes

It is important to keep in mind that VB .NET demands that a given class have *exactly one* direct base class. Therefore, it is not possible to have a single type with two or more base classes (this technique is known as multiple inheritance or simply, MI). As you will see in Chapter 5, VB .NET does allow a given type to implement any number of discrete interfaces. In this way, a VB .NET class can exhibit a number of behaviors while avoiding the problems associated with classic MI. On a related note, it is permissible to configure a single *interface* to derive from multiple *interfaces* (again, details to come in Chapter 5).

Keeping Family Secrets: The "Protected" Keyword

As you already know, Public items are directly accessible from any subclass. Private items cannot be accessed from any object beyond the object that has indeed defined the Private data point. VB .NET takes the lead of many other modern day object languages and provides an additional level of accessibility: Protected.

When a base class defines protected data or protected methods, it is able to create a set of members that can be *accessed directly* by each descendent. If you want to allow the SalesPerson and Manager child classes to directly access the data sector defined by Employee, you can update the original Employee class definition as follows:

```
' Protected state data.
Public Class Employee
    ' Child classes can directly access this information. Object users cannot.
    Protected mFullName as String
    Protected mEmpID as Integer
    Protected mCurrPay as Double
    Protected mSSN as String
...
End Class
```

However, as far as the object user is concerned, protected data is private. Therefore, the following is illegal:

```
' Error! Can't access protected data from object instance
Dim emp as Employee = New Employee()
emp.ssn = "111-11-1111"
```

Preventing Inheritance: "Sealed" Classes

Classical inheritance is a wonderful thing. When you establish base class/subclass relationships, you are able to leverage the behavior of existing types. However, what if you want to define a class that cannot (for whatever reason) be subclassed? Classes of this typed are generally called "sealed" in that they prevent the chain of inheritance from continuing. For example, assume you have added yet another class to your employee namespaces, which extends the existing SalesPerson type. Consider Figure 4-10.

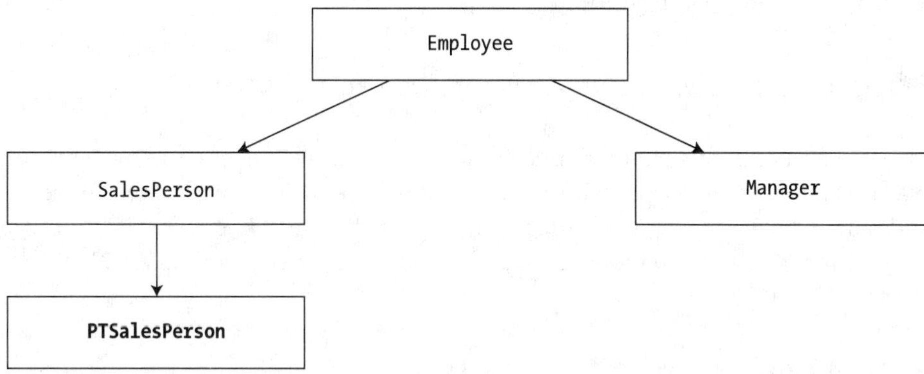

Figure 4-10. The extended employee hierarchy

PTSalesPerson is a class representing (of course) a part-time salesperson. For the sake of argument, let's say that you want to ensure that no other developer is able to subclass from PTSalesPerson (after all, how much more part-time can you get than "part-time"?). To prevent others from extending a class, make use of the VB .NET "NotInheritable" keyword.

```
' Ensure that PTSalesPerson cannot act as a base class to others.
Public NotInheritable Class PTSalesPerson
    Inherits SalesPerson
    ' Other interesting members. . .
    Public Sub New(ByVal FullName As String, ByVal empID As Integer, _
        ByVal currPay As Double, ByVal ssn As String, ByVal numbOfSales As Long)
        MyBase.new(FullName, empID, currPay, ssn, numbOfSales)
    End Sub
End Class
```

Because PTSalesPerson is sealed, it cannot serve as a base class to any other type. For example, if you attempted to extend PTSalesPerson, you receive a compiler error.

```
' Compiler error! PTSalesPerson is sealed and cannot be extended!
Public Class ReallyPTSalesPerson
   Inherits PTSalesPerson ' Error!
End Class
```

By and large, the NotInheritable keyword is most useful when creating standalone utility classes. As an example, the String class defined in the System namespace has been explicitly sealed. Therefore, you cannot create some new class deriving from System.String. If you want to build a class that leverages the functionality of a sealed class your only option is to make use of the containment/delegation model (speaking of which. . .)

Programming for Containment/Delegation

As noted earlier in this chapter, inheritance comes in two flavors. You have just examined the classical is-a relationship. To conclude the exploration of the second pillar of OOP, let's examine the has-a relationship (also known as the containment/delegation model). Assume you have created a simple VB .NET class modeling a radio:

```
' This type will function as a contained class.
Public Class Radio
    Public Sub TurnOn(ByVal state As Boolean)
        If (state) Then
            Console.WriteLine("Jamming. . .")
        Else
            Console.WriteLine("Quiet time. . .")
        End If
    End Sub
End Class
```

Now assume you are interested in modeling an automobile. The Car class maintains a set of state data (the car's pet name, current speed, and maximum speed) all of which may be set using a custom constructor. Here is the initial definition:

```
' This class will function as the 'outer' class.
Public Class Car
    ' Internal state data
    ' (assume related public properties).
    Private currSpeed As Integer
    Private maxSpeed As Integer
    Private petName As String
...
    ' Is the car alive or dead?
    Private dead As Boolean
    Public Sub New()
        maxSpeed = 100
        dead = False
    End Sub
    Public Sub New(ByVal name As String, ByVal max As Integer, _
    ByVal curr As Integer)
        currSpeed = curr
        maxSpeed = max
        petName = name
    End Sub
    Public Sub SpeedUp(ByVal delta As Integer)
        ' If the car is dead, just say so. . .
        If (dead) Then
            Console.WriteLine(petName & " is out of order. . .")
        Else ' Not dead, speed up.
            currSpeed += delta
            If (currSpeed >= maxSpeed) Then
                Console.WriteLine(petName & " has overheated. . .")
                dead = True
            Else
                Console.WriteLine("CurrSpeed = " & currSpeed)
            End If
        End If
    End Sub
End Class
```

At this point you have two independent classes. Obviously, it would be rather odd to establish an is-a relationship between the two entities. However, it should be clear that some sort of relation between the two could be established. In short, you would like to express the idea that the Car 'has-a' Radio. A class that wants to contain another class is often termed the "parent" class. The contained class is termed a "child" class. To begin, you can update the Car class definition as follows:

```
' A Car has-a Radio.
Public Class Car
. . .
     ' The contained Radio.
     Private theMusicBox as Radio
. . .
End Class
```

Notice how the outer Car class has declared the Radio object as Private. This of course is a good thing, as you have preserved encapsulation. However, the next obvious question is: How can the outside world interact with child objects? It should be clear that it is the responsibility of the outer Car class to create the child Radio class. Although the outer class may create any child objects whenever it sees fit, the most common place to do so is in the constructor set:

```
' Outer classes are responsible for creating any child objects.
Public Class Car
. . .
     ' The contained Radio.
     Private theMusicBox as Radio
     Public Sub New()
          maxSpeed = 100
          dead = false
          ' Outer class creates the contained class(es) on start-up.
          ' NOTE:  If we did not, theMusicBox would
          ' begin life as a null reference.
          theMusicBox = New Radio()
     End Sub
     Public Sub New(name as String, max as Integer, curr as Integer)
          currSpeed = curr
          maxSpeed = max
          petName = name
          dead = false
          theMusicBox = New Radio()
     End Sub
. . .
End Class
```

Alternately, you could make use of the VB .NET initializer syntax as follows:

```
' A Car has-a Radio.
Public Class Car
. . .
```

```
    ' The contained Radio.
    Private theMusicBox as Radio = New Radio()
...
End Class
```

At this point, you have successfully contained another object. However, to expose the functionality of the inner class to the outside world requires *delegation.* Delegation is simply the act of adding members to the parent class that make use of the child classes' functionality. For example:

```
' Outer classes extend their public interface to provide access to inner classes.
Public Class Car
...
    Public Sub CrankTunes(ByVal state As Boolean)
        ' Tell the radio play (or not).
        theMusicBox.TurnOn(state)
    End Sub
End Class
```

In the following code, notice how the object user is able to interact with the hidden inner object indirectly, and is totally unaware of the fact that the Car class is making use of a Private Radio instance:

```
' Take this car for a test drive.
Module Module1
    Sub Main()
        ' Make a car.
        Dim c1 As Car
        c1 = New Car("SlugBug", 100, 10)
        ' Jam some tunes.
        c1.CrankTunes(True)
        ' Speed up.
        Dim i As Integer
        For i = 0 To 5
            c1.SpeedUp(20)
        Next
        ' Shut down.
        c1.CrankTunes(False)
    End Sub
End Module
```

Figure 4-11 shows the output.

```
C:\Apress Books\VB.NET\Code\Chapter 4\Containme...
Jamming...
CurrSpeed = 30
CurrSpeed = 50
CurrSpeed = 70
CurrSpeed = 90
SlugBug has overheated...
SlugBug is out of order....
Quiet time...
Press any key to continue
```

Figure 4-11. Our contained Radio in action

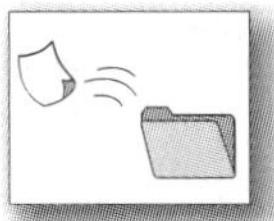

SOURCE CODE *The Containment project is included under the Chapter 4 subdirectory.*

Nested Type Definitions

Before examining the final pillar of OOP (polymorphism), let's explore a programming technique termed *nested classes.* In VB .NET, it is possible to define a type directly within the scope of another type. The syntax is quite straightforward:

```
' Nesting class types.
Public Class MyClass
    ' Members of outer class.
    ...
    Public Class MyNestedClass
        ' Members of nested class.
        ...
    End Class
End Class
```

Although the syntax is clean, understanding *why* you might do this is not readily apparent. Typically, a nested type is regarded only as a helper type of the outer class, and is not intended for use by the outside world. This is slightly along the lines of the "has-a" relationship, however in the case of nested types, you are in greater control of the inner type's visibility. In this light, nested types also help enforce encapsulation services.

To illustrate, you can redesign your current Car application by representing the Radio as a nested type. By doing so, you are assuming the outside world does not need to directly create a Radio. Here is the update:

```
' The Car is nesting the Radio. Everything else is as before.
Public Class Car
. . .
    ' A nested, private radio. Cannot be created by the outside world.
    Private Class Radio
        Public Sub TurnOn(ByVal state As Boolean)
            If (state) Then
                Console.WriteLine("Jamming. . .")
            Else
                Console.WriteLine("Quiet time. . .")
            End If
        End Sub
    End Class
    ' The outer class can make instances of nested types.
    Private theMusicBox as Radio
. . .
End Class
```

Notice that the Car type is able to create object instances of any nested item. Also notice that this class has been declared a *private* type. In VB .NET, nested types may be declared private as well as public. Recall, however, that classes that are directly within a namespace (e.g., nonnested types) cannot be defined as private. As far as the object user is concerned, the Car type works as before. Because of the private, nested nature of the Radio, the following is now illegal:

```
' Can't do it outside the scope of the Car class!
Dim r as Radio = New Radio()
```

SOURCE CODE *The Nested project is included under the Chapter 4 subdirectory.*

The Third Pillar: VB .NET's Polymorphic Support

Assume the Employee base class has implemented the GiveBonus() method as follows:

```
' Employee defines a new method that gives a bonus to a given employee.
Public Class Employee
. . .
    Public Sub GiveBonus(amount as Double)
        mCurrPay += amount
    End Sub
End Class
```

Because this method has been defined as public, you can now give bonuses to salespersons and managers (see Figure 4-12 for output):

```
' Give each child class a bonus.
Dim chucky as Manager= new Manager("Chucky", 92, 100000, "333-23-2322", 9000)
chucky.GiveBonus(300)
chucky.DisplayStats()
Dim fran as SalesPerson = new SalesPerson("Fran", 93, 30000, "932-32-3232", 31)
fran.GiveBonus(200)
fran.DisplayStats()
```

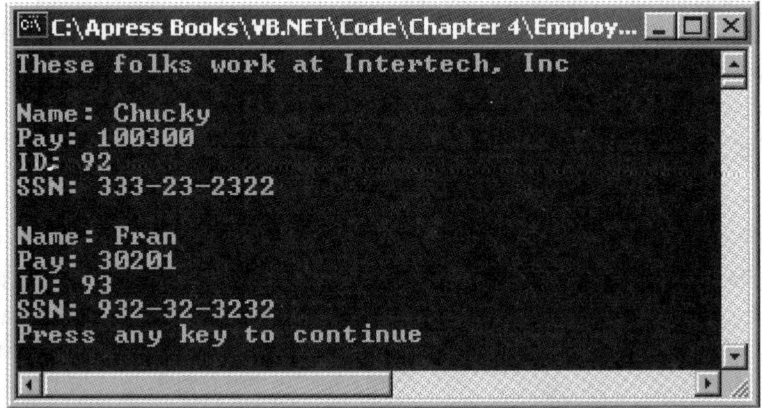

Figure 4-12. The current employee hierarchy does not implement polymorphism

The problem with the current design is that the inherited GiveBonus() method operates *identically* for each subclass. Ideally, the bonus of a salesperson should take into account the number of sales. Perhaps managers should gain additional stock options in conjunction with a monetary bump in salary. Given this, you are suddenly faced with an interesting question: "How can related objects respond differently to the same request?"

Polymorphism is the final pillar of OOP, which provides a way for a subclass to redefine how it responds to a method defined by its base class. To retrofit your current design, you need to understand the use of the VB .NET "Overridable" and "Overrides" keywords. When a base class wants to define a method that may be overridden by a subclass, it must specify the method as Overridable (which is typically referred to as a "virtual method"):

```
Public Class Employee
    ' GiveBonus() has a default implementation, however
    ' child classes are free to override this behavior.
```

```
    Public Overridable Sub GiveBonus(ByVal amount As Double)
        mCurrPay += amount
    End Sub
...
End Class
```

If a subclass wants to redefine a virtual method, it may change the method in question using the Overrides keyword. For example:

```
Public Class SalesPerson
Inherits Employee
     ' A sales person's bonus is influenced by the number of sales.
    Public Overrides Sub GiveBonus(ByVal amount As Double)
        Dim salesBonus As Integer
        If (numberOfSales >= 0 And numberOfSales <= 100) Then
            salesBonus = 10
        ElseIf (numberOfSales >= 101 And numberOfSales <= 200) Then
            salesBonus = 15
        Else
            salesBonus = 20  ' Anything greater than 200.
        End If
        MyBase.GiveBonus(amount * salesBonus)
    End Sub
...
End Class

Public Class Manager
Inherits Employee
     Private r as Random = new Random()
     ' Managers get some number of new stock options, in addition to raw cash.
    Public Overrides Sub GiveBonus(ByVal amount As Double)
        ' Increase salary.
        MyBase.GiveBonus(amount)
        ' And give some new stock options. . .
        numberOfOptions += r.Next(500)
    End Sub
...
End Class
```

Notice how each overridden method is free to leverage the default behavior using the MyBase keyword. In this way, you have no need to completely reimplement the logic behind GiveBonus(), but can reuse (and extend) the default behavior of the parent class.

Also assume that Employee.DisplayStats() has been declared as Overridable, and has been overridden by each subclass to account for displaying the number of sales (for sales folks) and current stock options (for managers). Now that each subclass can interpret what these virtual methods means to itself, each object instance behaves as a more independent entity (see Figure 4-13 for output):

```
' A better bonus system through polymorphism.
Dim chucky as Manager = New Manager("Chucky", 92, 100000, "333-23-2322", 9000)
chucky.GiveBonus(300)
chucky.DisplayStats()
Dim fran as SalesPerson = New SalesPerson("Fran", 93, 3000, "932-32-3232", 31)
fran.GiveBonus(200)
fran.DisplayStats()
```

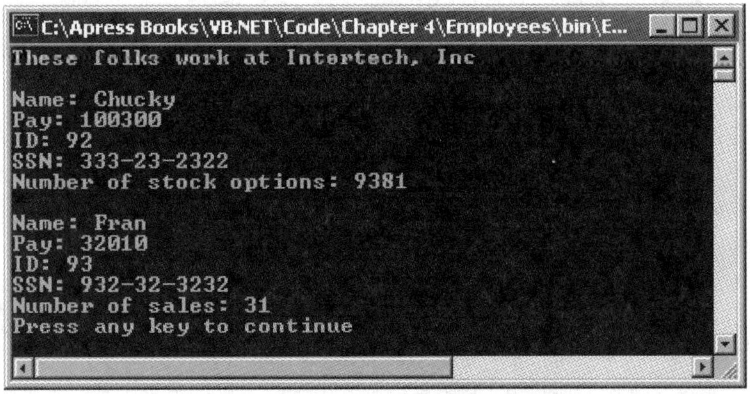

```
C:\Apress Books\VB.NET\Code\Chapter 4\Employees\bin\E...
These folks work at Intertech, Inc

Name: Chucky
Pay: 100300
ID: 92
SSN: 333-23-2322
Number of stock options: 9381

Name: Fran
Pay: 32010
ID: 93
SSN: 932-32-3232
Number of sales: 31
Press any key to continue
```

Figure 4-13. A better bonus system (thanks to polymorphism)

Excellent! At this point you are not only able to establish is-a and has-a relationships among related classes, but also have injected polymorphic activity into your employee hierarchy. As you may suspect, the story of polymorphism goes beyond simply overriding base-class behavior.

Defining (and Understanding) Abstract Classes

Currently, the Employee base class has been designed to supply protected member variables for its descendents, as well as supply two Overridable methods (GiveBonus() and DisplayStats()) that may be overridden by a given descendent. While this is all well and good, there is a rather odd byproduct of the current design: You can directly create instances of the Employee base class:

```
' What exactly does this mean?
Dim X as Employee = New Employee()
```

Now think this one through. The only real purpose of the Employee base class is to define default state data and implementations for a given subclass. In all likelihood, you did not intend anyone to create a direct instance of this class. The Employee type itself is too general a concept. A far better design is to prevent the ability to directly create a new Employee instance. In VB .NET, this is facilitated by using the "MustInherit" keyword (classes that are defined using the MustInherit keyword are termed *abstract base classes*):

```
' Update the Employee class as abstract to prevent direct instantiation.
Public MustInherit Class Employee
     ' Same public interface and state data as before. . .
End Class
```

If you do not attempt to create an instance of the Employee class, you are issued a compile time error.

```
' Error! Can't create an instance of an abstract class.
Dim X as Employee = New Employee()
```

Enforcing Polymorphic Activity: Abstract Methods

Once a class has been defined as an abstract base class, it may define any number of *abstract members.* Abstract methods can be used whenever you want to define a method that *does not* supply a default implementation. By doing so, you enforce a polymorphic trait on each descendent, leaving them to contend with the task of providing the details behind your abstract methods.

The first logical question you might have is: "Why would I ever want to do this?" To understand the role of abstract methods, let's return to the shapes hierarchy seen earlier in this chapter (Figure 4-14).

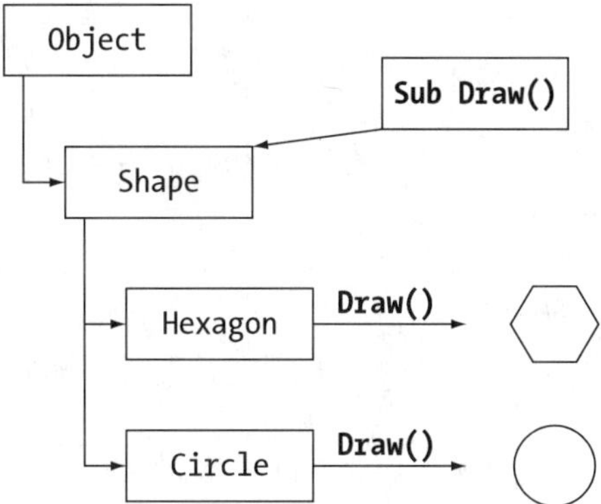

Figure 4-14. Our current shapes hierarchy

Much like the Employee hierarchy, you should be able to tell that you don't want to allow the object user to create an instance of Shape directly. To illustrate, update your initial classes as follows:

```
Public MustInherit Class Shape
    Protected mPetName As String
    ' Constructors.
    Public Sub New()
        mPetName = "NoName"
    End Sub
    Public Sub New(ByVal s As String)
        mPetName = s
    End Sub
    ' Child classes inherit this member.
    Public Overridable Sub Draw()
        Console.WriteLine("Shape.Draw()")
    End Sub
    Public Property PetName() As String
        Get
            Return mPetName
        End Get
        Set(ByVal Value As String)
            mPetName = Value
        End Set
    End Property
End Class

' Circle does NOT override Draw().
Public Class Circle
Inherits Shape
    Public Sub New()
    End Sub
    Public Sub New(name as String)
        MyBase.New(name)
    End Sub
End Class

' Hexagon DOES override Draw().
Public Class Hexagon
    Inherits Shape
    Public Sub New()
    End Sub
    Public Sub New(ByVal name As String)
```

```
        MyBase.New(name)
    End Sub
    Public Overrides Sub Draw()
        Console.WriteLine("Drawing {0} the Hexagon", PetName)
    End Sub
End Class
```

Notice that the Shape class has defined an Overridable method named Draw(). As you have just seen, subclasses are free to redefine the behavior of an Overridable method using the Overrides keyword (as in the case of the Hexagon class). The point of abstract methods becomes crystal clear when you understand that subclasses are *not required* to override virtual methods (as in the case of Circle). Therefore, if you create an instance of the Hexagon and Circle types, you find that the Hexagon understands how to draw itself correctly. The Circle, however, is more than a bit confused (see Figure 4-15 for output):

```
' The Circle object did not override the base class implementation of Draw().
Sub Main()
    ' Make and draw a hex.
    Dim Hex As Hexagon = New Hexagon("Beth")
    Hex.Draw()
    Dim cir As Circle = New Circle("Cindy")
    ' Humm. Using base class implementation.
    cir.Draw()
End Sub
```

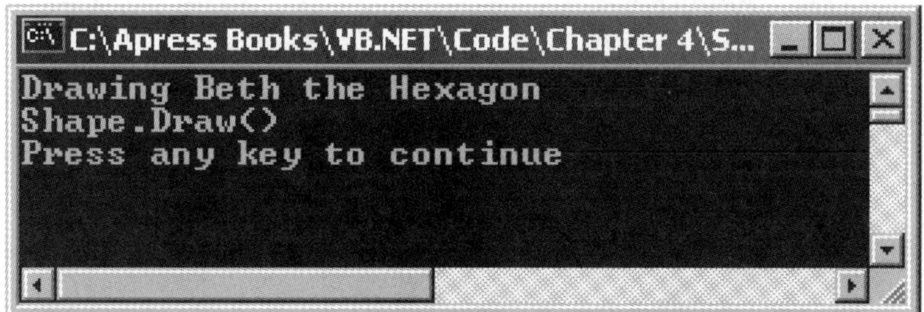

Figure 4-15. Overridable methods do not have to be overridden

Clearly this is not a very intelligent design. To enforce that each child object defines what Draw() means to itself, you can simply establish Draw() as an abstract method of the Shape class using the "MustOverride" keyword, which by definition means you provide no default implementation whatsoever:

```
' Force all kids to figure out how to be rendered.
' Abstract base class.
Public MustInherit Class Shape
    Protected mPetName As String
    ' All child objects must define for themselves what
    ' it means to be drawn.
    Public MustOverride Sub Draw()  ' No 'End Sub' for abstract methods
...
End Class
```

Given this, you are now obligated to implement Draw() in our Circle class:

```
' If we did not implement the abstract Draw() method, Circle would also be
' considered abstract, and could not be directly created!
Public Class Circle
    Inherits Shape
    Public Sub New()
    End Sub
    Public Sub New(ByVal name As String)
        MyBase.New(name)
    End Sub
    Public Overrides Sub Draw()
        Console.WriteLine("Drawing {0} the Circle", PetName)
    End Sub
End Class
```

To illustrate the full story of polymorphism, consider the following code (Figure 4-16 shows the output):

```
' Create an array of various Shapes.
Module Module1
    Sub Main()
        ' The base class reference trick.
        Dim s as Shape() = {New Hexagon(), New Circle(), New Hexagon("Mick"), _
        New Circle("Beth"), New Hexagon("Linda")}
        Dim i As Integer
        For i = 0 To UBound(s)
            s(i).Draw()
        Next
    End Sub
End Module
```

```
C:\Apress Books\VB.NET\Code\Chapter 4\Sh...
Drawing Beth the Hexagon
Drawing Cindy the Circle
Drawing NoName the Hexagon
Drawing NoName the Circle
Drawing Mick the Hexagon
Drawing Beth the Circle
Drawing Linda the Hexagon
Press any key to continue
```

Figure 4-16. Better! Abstract methods must be overridden

This illustrates polymorphism at its finest. Recall that when you mark a class as MustInherit, you are unable to create a *direct instance* of that type. However, you can freely store references to any subclass within an abstract base variable. As you iterate over the array of Shape references, it is at runtime that the correct type is determined. At this point, the correct method is invoked. You may be thinking "hey! This is a lot like interface-based programming!" You are correct. However realize that abstract base classes can do far more than simply define abstract methods. They are also able to define any number of concrete methods that may be leveraged by a subclass.

Shadowing Class Members

VB .NET provides a facility that is the logical opposite of method overriding: method hiding. Assume you are in the process of building a brand new class named Oval. Given that an Oval is-a type of Circle, you may want to extend the Shapes hierarchy as shown in Figure 4-17.

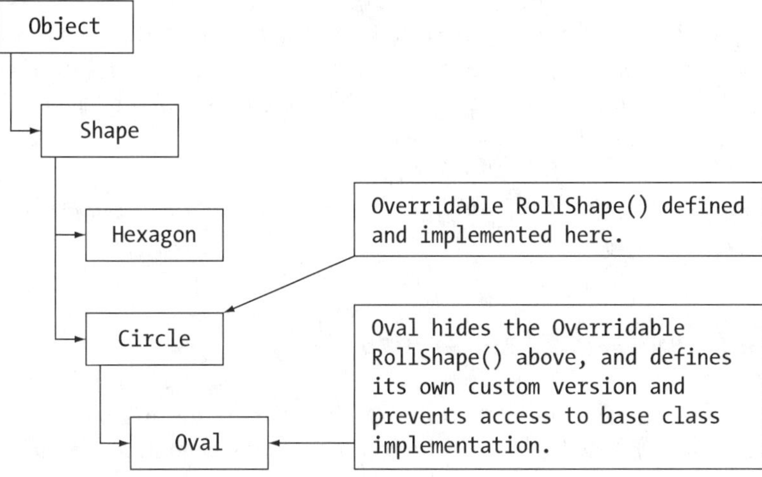

Figure 4-17. Versioning the Draw() method

Now, for the sake of argument, assume that the Oval wants to hide the inherited version of RollShape() and prevent its code base from accessing the base class functionality? Formally, this technique is termed *versioning* a method. Syntactically, this can be accomplished using the Shadows keyword on a method-by-method basis. For example:

```
' This class extends Circle, but hides the inherited RollShape() method.
Public Class Oval
    Inherits Circle
    Public Sub New()
        MyBase.PetName = "Joe"
    End Sub
    ' Hide base class impl if they create an Oval.
    Public Shadows Sub RollShape()
        Console.WriteLine("Rolling an Oval. . .")
        Console.WriteLine("FLOP. . .")
    End Sub
End Class
```

Because you used the Shadows keyword in the definition of RollShape(), you are guaranteed that if an object user makes an instance of the Oval class and calls RollShape(), the most derived version is called. Thus:

```
' The RollShape() defined by Oval will be called.
Dim o As Oval = New Oval()
o. RollShape()
```

At this point, method hiding may seem to be little more than an interesting exercise in class design. However, this technique can be very useful when you are extending types defined within another .NET assembly. Imagine that you want to derive a new class from another class defined in a distinct .NET binary. Now, what if the binary base type defines a Draw() method that is somehow incompatible with your own Draw() method? To prevent object users from triggering a base class implementation, just shadow the member.

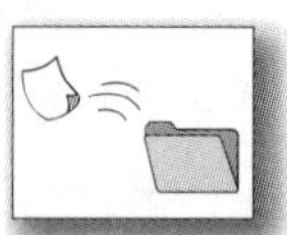

SOURCE CODE *The Shapes hierarchy can be found under the Chapter 4 subdirectory.*

Casting between Class Types (CType)

At this point you have created a number of class hierarchies in VB .NET. Next, you need to examine the laws of *casting* between class types. First, recall the

Employee hierarchy. The topmost member in our hierarchy is System.Object. Given the terminology of classical inheritance, everything "is-a" object. In our example, a part-time salesperson "is-a" salesperson, and so forth. Therefore, the following cast operations are legal.

```
'  A Manager 'is-a' object.
Dim o As Object = New Manager("Frank Zappa", 9, 40000, "111-11-1111", 5)
'  A Manager 'is-a' Employee too.
Dim e As Employee = New Manager("MoonUnit Zappa", 2, 20000, "101-11-1321", 1)
'  A PTSales dude(tte) is a Sales dude(tte)
Dim sp As SalesPerson = New PTSalesPerson("Jill", 834, 100000, "111-12-1119", 90)
```

As seen above, the first law of casting between class types is that when two classes are related by an is-a relationship, it is always safe to reference a derived class using a base class reference. This leads to some powerful programming constructs. For example, if you have a module level method such as:

```
' Fire everyone >:-)
Public Sub FireThisPerson(ByVal e As Employee)
    Console.WriteLine(e.GetFullName() & " has been fired!")
End Sub
```

You can effectively pass any descendent from the Employee class into this method. Thus:

```
' Streamline the staff.
FireThisPerson(sp)
FireThisPerson(e)
```

The following logic works as there is an implicit cast from the base class type (Employee) to the derived types. Now, what if you also wanted to fire your Manager (currently held in a System.Object reference)? If you pass the object reference into the FireThisPerson() method as follows:

```
' A Manager 'is-a' object.
Dim o As Object = New Manager("Frank Zappa", 9, 40000, "111-11-1111", 5)
FireThisPerson(o)      ' Error!
```

you are issued a compiler error (if you have Option Strict enabled, which of course you do)! The reason for the error is because you cannot automatically receive access from a base type (in this case System.Object) to a derived type (in this case Employee) without first performing an explicit cast.

This is the second law of casting: You must explicitly downcast using the VB .NET CType() function. CType() takes two parameters. The first parameter is the base class type you currently have access to. The second parameter is the name of the derived type you want to have access to. The value returned from CType() is the result of the downward cast. Thus, the previous problem can be avoided as follows:

```
' Error! Must explicitly cast when moving from base to derived class!
' FireThisPerson(o) ' No!
' OK.
FireThisPerson(CType(o, Manager))
```

As you will see in the next chapter, CType() is also the safe (and preferred) way of obtaining an interface reference from a type. Furthermore, CType() may operate safely on numerical types but don't forget you have a number of related conversion functions at your disposal (CInt() and so on).

Exception Handling

Error handling among Windows developers has grown into a confused mishmash of techniques over the years. Many programmers roll their own error handling logic within the context of a given application. For example, a development team may define a set of constants that represent known error conditions, and make use of them as method return values. In addition to this ad hoc technique, the Window's API defines a number of error codes that come by way of #defines, HRESULTs, and far too many variations on the simple Boolean. Furthermore, many COM developers have made use of a small set of standard COM interfaces (e.g., ISupportErrorInfo, IErrorInfo, ICreateErrorInfo) to return meaningful error information to a COM client (although VB 6.0 hides the process from view using the "On Error Goto" syntax and intrinsic Err object).

The obvious problem with the previous techniques is the tremendous lack of symmetry. Each approach is tailored to a given technology, a given language, and perhaps a given project. In order to put an end to this madness, the .NET platform provides exactly *one* technique to send and trap runtime errors: Structured Exception Handling (SEH).

The beauty of this approach is that developers now have a well-defined approach to error handling, which is common to all languages targeting the .NET universe. Therefore, the way in which a VB .NET programmer handles errors is conceptually identical to that of a C# programmer, a C++ programmer using managed extensions (MC++), and so forth. As an added bonus it is also possible to throw and catch exceptions across binaries, AppDomains (defined in Chapter 7), and machines in a language-independent manner.

To begin to understand how to program using exceptions, you must first realize that exceptions are indeed objects. All system-defined and user-defined exceptions derive from System.Exception (which in turn derive from System.Object). Here is a breakdown of some of the interesting members defined by the Exception class (Table 4-2):

Table 4-2. Core Members of the System.Exception Type

SYSTEM.EXCEPTION PROPERTY	MEANING IN LIFE
HelpLink	This property returns a URL to a help file describing the error in gory detail.
Message	This read-only property returns the textual description of a given error.
Source	This property returns the name of the object (or possibly the application) that sent the error.
StackTrace	This read-only property contains a string that identifies the sequence of calls that triggered the error.
InnerException	The InnerException property can be used to preserve the error details between a series of exceptions. For example, assume the object user triggers method A. During the invocation of method A, an exception is triggered (and caught). Method A can save this exception using the InnerException property and throw a new (more specific) exception ("method A bombed"). Thus, the caller is able to fully understand the flow of error logic by catching the error and investigate the "inner" exception.

Throwing an Exception

To illustrate the use of System.Exception, let's revisit the Car class defined earlier in this chapter, in particular, the SpeedUp() method. Here is the current implementation:

```
' Currently, SpeedUp() reports errors using console IO.
Public Sub SpeedUp(ByVal delta As Integer)
    ' If the car is dead, just say so. . .
    If (dead) Then
        Console.WriteLine(petName & " is out of order. . .")
    Else ' Not dead, speed up.
        currSpeed += delta
        If (currSpeed >= maxSpeed) Then
            Console.WriteLine(petName & " has overheated. . .")
            dead = True
        Else
```

```
            Console.WriteLine("CurrSpeed = " & currSpeed)
        End If
    End If
End Sub
```

To illustrate, let's retrofit SpeedUp() to throw an exception if the user attempts to speed up the automobile after it has met its maker (dead = True). First, you create and configure a new instance of the Exception class. When you want to pass the error back to the caller, make use of the VB .NET *Throw* keyword. Here is an example:

```
' This time, throw an exception if the user speeds up a trashed automobile.
Public Sub SpeedUp(delta as Integer)
     If(dead) Then
          Throw New Exception("This car is already dead")
     Else
     . . .
End Sub
```

Before examining how to handle this incoming exception, a few points. First of all, when you build custom classes, it is always up to you to decide exactly what constitutes an exception. Here, you are making the assumption that if the program attempts to increase the speed of a car that has expired, the custom Exception should be thrown to indicate the SpeedUp() method cannot continue. Alternately, you could implement SpeedUp() to recover automatically without needing to throw an exception.

By and large, exceptions should be thrown only when a more "terminal" condition has been met (can't connect to a data source, a file that was to be opened is missing, an external device is not responding, or whatnot). Deciding exactly what constitutes throwing an exception is a design issue you must always contend with. For now, assume that asking a doomed automobile to increase its speed justifies a cause for an exception.

Next, understand that the .NET runtime libraries already define a number of predefined exceptions. For example, the System namespace defines numerous exceptions such as ArgumentOutOfRangeException, IndexOutOfRangeException, StackOverflowException, and so forth. Other namespaces define additional exceptions that reflect the behavior of that namespace (e.g., System.Drawing.Printing defines printing exceptions and System.IO defines IO based exceptions).

Catching Exceptions

Because the SpeedUp() method is able to throw an exception object, you need to be ready to handle the error should it occur. When you call a method that may throw an exception, you should establish a Try/Catch block to wrap the call. Here is the simplest form:

```
' Speed up the car safely. . .
Sub Main()
    ' Make a car.
    Dim buddha As Car = New Car("Buddha", 100, 20)
    buddha.CrankTunes(True)
    ' Try to rev the engine hard!
    Try
        Dim i As Integer
        For i = 0 To 10
            buddha.SpeedUp(10)
        Next
    Catch e As Exception
        Console.WriteLine(e.Message)
        Console.WriteLine(e.StackTrace)
    End Try
End Sub
```

In essence, a Try block is a section of code that is on the lookout for any exception that may be encountered during the flow of execution. If an exception is detected, the flow of program execution is sent to the next available Catch block. On the other hand, if the code within a Try block does not trigger an exception, the Catch block is skipped entirely, and all is right with the world. Figure 4-18 shows a test run of the handled error.

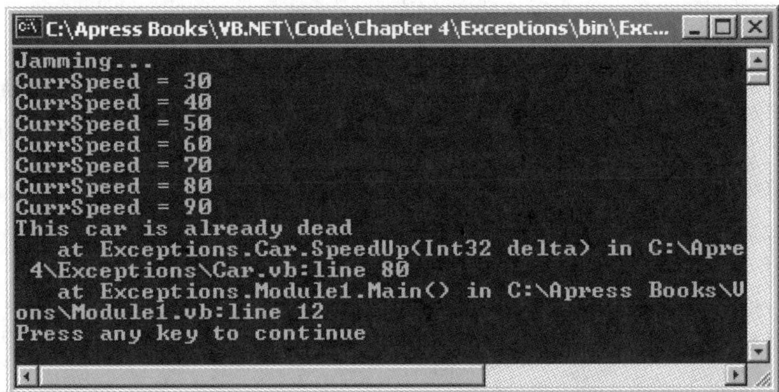

Figure 4-18. Dealing with the error using structured exception handling

Notice how this Catch block explicitly specifies the exception it is willing to catch. In VB .NET (as well as numerous other languages targeting the .NET platform) it is also permissible to configure a Catch block that does not explicitly define a specific exception. Thus, we could implement the Try/Catch block as follows:

```
' A generic catch.
. . .
Catch
    Console.WriteLine("Something bad happened. . .")
. . .
```

Obviously, this is not the most descriptive manner in which to handle runtime exceptions, given that there's no way to obtain meaningful information about the error that occurred. Nevertheless, VB .NET does allow for such a construct.

Building Custom Exceptions

Although you could simply throw instances of System.Exception to signal a runtime error, it is sometimes advantageous to build a custom class that encapsulates the details of your problem. Let's examine two possible approaches.

Take One

Assume you want to build a custom exception to represent the error of speeding up a doomed automobile. To begin, create a new class derived from System.Exception (by convention, custom exceptions should end with an "–Exception" suffix). After this point, you are free to include any custom properties, methods, or fields that can be used from within the catch block of the calling logic. You are also free to override any Overridable members defined by your parent classes:

```
' This custom exception describes the details of the car-is-dead condition.
Public Class CarIsDeadException
    Inherits System.Exception
    ' This custom exception maintains the name of the doomed car.
    Private carName As String
    Public Sub New()
    End Sub
    Public Sub New(ByVal carName As String)
        Me.carName = carName
    End Sub
```

```
    ' Override the Exception.Message property.
    Public Overrides ReadOnly Property Message() As String
        Get
            Dim msg As String = MyBase.Message
            msg &= carName & " has bought the farm. . ."
            Return msg
        End Get
    End Property
End Class
```

Here, the CarIsDeadException type maintains a private data member that holds the name of the car that threw the exception. You have also added two constructors to the class, and overrode the read-only Message property in order to include the pet name of the car in the error description. Throwing this error from within SpeedUp() should be self-explanatory:

```
' Throw the custom exception.
' This time, throw an exception if the user speeds up a trashed automobile.
Public Sub SpeedUp(delta as Integer)
    If(dead) Then
         Throw New CarIsDeadException(Me.petName)
    Else
    . . .
End Sub
```

Catching the error is just as easy:

```
Try
    . . .
 Catch e As CarIsDeadException
       Console.WriteLine(e.Message)
    . . .
End Try
```

In this scenario, you may not need to build a custom exception class, given that you are free to set the Message property directly using the Exception type. Typically, you only need to create custom exceptions when the error is tightly bound to the class issuing the error (for example, a File class that throws a number of file-related errors, a Car class that throws a number of automobile-centric exceptions and so forth). Nevertheless, at this point you should understand the basic process of constructing a custom exception type.

Take Two

Our CarIsDeadException type has overridden the Message property to configure a custom error message. This class also has an overloaded constructor that accepts the pet name of the automobile that has met its maker. When you build custom exceptions, you are able to build the type as you see fit. However, the recommended approach is to build a relatively simple type that supplies three named constructors matching the following signature:

```
Public Class CarIsDeadException
    Inherits System.Exception
    ' Constructors for this exception.
    Public Sub New()
    End Sub
    Public Sub New(ByVal message As String)
        MyBase.New(message)
    End Sub
    Public Sub New(ByVal message As String, ByVal innerEx As Exception)
        MyBase.New(message, innerEx)
    End Sub
End Class
```

Notice that this time you have *not* provided a private string to hold the pet name, and have *not* overridden the Message property. Rather, you are simply passing all the relevant information to your base class. When you want to throw an exception of this type, you would send in all necessary information as a constructor argument (the output would be identical):

```
' If the car is dead, just say so. . .
if(dead)
      ' Pass pet name and message as ctor argument.
      Throw New CarIsDeadException(Me.petName & " has bought the farm!")
End If
```

Using this design, your custom exception is little more than a semantically defined name, devoid of any unnecessary member variables (or overrides).

Handling Multiple Exceptions

As mentioned, in its simplest form, a Try block has a single corresponding Catch block. In reality, you often run into a situation where the code within a Try block could trigger numerous exceptions. For example, assume the car's SpeedUp() method not only throws an exception when you attempt to speed up a doomed automobile, but throws another if you send in an invalid parameter (for example, any number less than zero):

```
Public Sub SpeedUp(ByVal delta As Integer)
    ' Bad param?
    If (delta < 0) Then
        Throw New ArgumentOutOfRangeException("Speed must be greater than zero")
    End If
    ' If the car is dead, just say so. . .
    If (dead) Then
        ' Throw 'Car is dead' exception.
        Throw New CarIsDeadException(petName & " has bought the farm!")
    Else
        currSpeed += delta
        If (currSpeed >= maxSpeed) Then
            dead = True
        Else
            Console.WriteLine("CurrSpeed = {0}", currSpeed)
        End If
    End If
End Sub
```

The calling logic would look something like this:

```
' Here, we are on the lookout for multiple exceptions.
Try
    Dim i As Integer
     For i = 0 To 10
         buddha.SpeedUp(10)
    Next
Catch e As CarIsDeadException
    Console.WriteLine(e.Message)
    Console.WriteLine(e.StackTrace)
Catch e As ArgumentOutOfRangeException
    Console.WriteLine(e.Message)
    Console.WriteLine(e.StackTrace)
End Try
```

It is also worth pointing out that a Catch block may be adorned with a "When" condition. For example, assume you want to handle the CarIsDeadException just a bit differently if the Car that throws the exception is called by a particular pet name. If any other Car type throws a CarIsDeadException, you want to take a different plan of action:

```
Public Sub SpecialErrorForBuddha()
     Dim b As New Car("Buddha", 50, 0)
     Try
         Dim i As Integer
         For i = 0 To 10
             b.SpeedUp(10)
         Next
     Catch e As CarIsDeadException When b.PetName = "Buddha"
         Console.WriteLine("Buddha died. . .")
     Catch
         Console.WriteLine("Some car died. . .")
     End Try
End Sub
```

Given that you did indeed set the pet name of our car as Buddha, the line "Buddha died. . ." will be spit out to the console. If you passed in the string "Bill" as the first argument to the Car's constructor, you would see "Some car died. . ." printed instead. When you make use of a When condition on a Catch block, this does *not* mean you can ignore the error if the condition evaluates to False. What it does mean is you can have a finer level of granularity when handling the error.

The "Finally" Block

A Try/Catch block may also be augmented with an optional "Finally" block. The idea behind a Finally block is to ensure that any acquired resources can be cleaned up, even if an exception interferes with the normal flow of execution. For example, assume you want to always power down the car's radio before exiting Main(), regardless of any errors:

```
' Provide a manner to clean up.
 Sub Main()
    ' Make a simple car.
    Dim buddha As Car = New Car("Buddha", 100, 20)
    buddha.CrankTunes(True)
    ' Try to rev the engine hard!
    Try
        Dim i As Integer
        For i = 0 To 10
            buddha.SpeedUp(10)
        Next
```

```
    Catch e As CarIsDeadException
        Console.WriteLine(e.Message)
        Console.WriteLine(e.StackTrace)
    Catch e As ArgumentOutOfRangeException
        Console.WriteLine(e.Message)
        Console.WriteLine(e.StackTrace)
    Finally
        ' This will always happen regardless.
        buddha.CrankTunes(False)
    End Try
End Sub
```

If you did not include a Finally block, the radio would *not* be turned off if an exception was caught (which may or may not be problematic). If you need to clean up any allocated memory, close down a file, detach from a data source (or whatever), you must add that code within a Finally block to ensure proper clean up. It is important to realize, that the code contained within a Finally block executes *every time* even if the logic within your try clause does not generate an exception.

Final Thoughts Regarding Exceptions

Unlike ad hoc error handling techniques, .NET exceptions cannot be ignored. One obvious question that may be on your mind is what would happen if you do not handle an exception thrown your direction? Assume that the logic in Main() that increases the speed of the Car object has no error-handling logic. The result of ignoring the generated error would be highly obstructive to the end user of your application, as the "last chance exception" dialog is displayed (Figure 4-19).

Now that you see the inherent goodness in catching exceptions, you might ask what you are to do with exceptions once they are caught. Again, this is a design issue based on your current project. In your trivial Car example, you dumped your custom message and call stack to the console. A more realistic scenario can include freeing up acquired resources or writing to a log file. The exception-handling schema is simply a pattern to follow when sending and receiving errors. What you do with them is largely up to you.

Finally, it is important to keep in mind that exceptions should only be thrown if the underlying problem is truly fatal. In other words, if you are able to recover from a user, logical, or general design error without throwing a system defined or custom exception, do so. In this light, the CarIsDeadException may be of arguable necessity. Chapter 6 revisits the SpeedUp() method, and substitutes the custom exception with a more appropriate custom event.

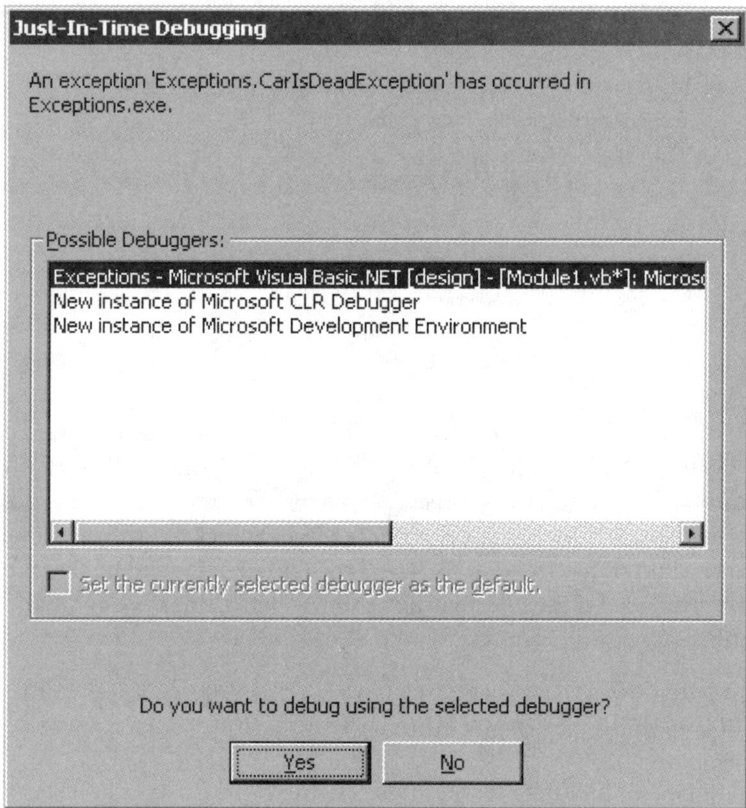

Figure 4-19. Exceptions that are not caught are a major buzz kill.

On Error Goto?

Last but not least, you have the issue of VB 6.0 error handling. To be honest, "On Error Goto" was never a very elegant way to handle runtime anomalies in your code. Nevertheless, VB .NET still supports this syntax for the sake of code migration. If you really wanted to, you are free to define a tag within a given method that can intercept the Err object. Do note that the Err object now has a method named GetException() which returns the underlying System.Exception type. To illustrate:

```
Public Sub OldStyleError()
    On Error Goto OOPS
    Dim c As New Car("Bill", 100, 0)
    Dim i As Integer
    For i = 0 To 10
        c.SpeedUp(10)
    Next
    Exit Sub
```

```
OOPS:
    Console.WriteLine(Err.Description())
    Dim e As Exception = Err.GetException()
    Console.WriteLine(e.Message)
End Sub
```

SOURCE CODE *The Exceptions project is included under the Chapter 4 subdirectory.*

Understanding Object Lifetime

As a VB .NET programmer, the rules of memory management are simple: Use the New keyword to allocate an object onto the managed heap. The .NET runtime destroys the object when it is no longer needed. Next question: How does the runtime determine when an object is no longer needed? The short (i.e., incomplete) answer is that the runtime deallocates memory when there are no longer any outstanding references to an object within the current scope (or if a reference has been explicitly set to Nothing). To illustrate:

```
' Create a local Car variable.
Sub Main()
    ' Place a car onto the managed heap.
    Dim c as Car = New Car("Viper", 200, 100)
End Sub  ' If c is the only reference to the Car object,
         ' it can be reclaimed when it drops out of scope.
```

Now, assume that your application has allocated three Car types. As long as there is enough room on the heap, you are returned a reference to each object in memory. Technically speaking, references to an object on the managed heap are called a *root.* The process can be visualized as illustrated in Figure 4-20.

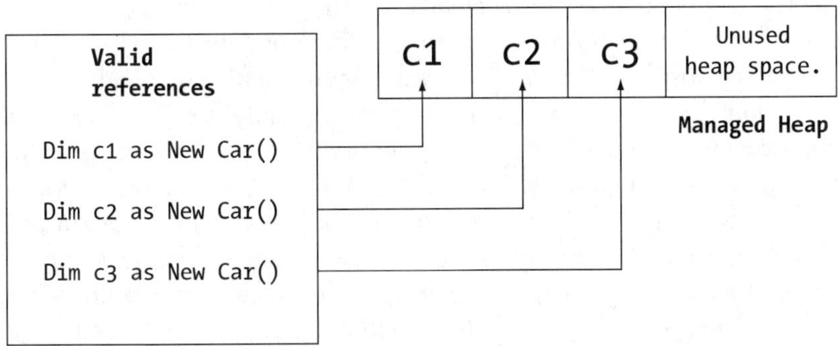

Figure 4-20. Valid references point to a location on the managed heap

As you are busy creating more and more objects, the managed heap may eventually become full. If you attempt to create a new object on a heap plump and full of active object references, an OutOfMemoryException exception is thrown. Therefore, if you want to be extremely defensive in your coding practices, you could allocate an object as follows:

```
' Try to add these cars to the managed heap and check for errors. . .
Public Sub Main()
. . .
   Dim yetAnotherCar as Car
    Try
        yetAnotherCar = New Car()
    Catch e as OutOfMemoryException
        Console.WriteLine(e.Message)
        Console.WriteLine("Managed heap is FULL! Running GC. . .")
    End Try
. . .
End Sub
```

Regardless of how defensive your object allocation logic may be, understand that when the memory allocated to the managed heap runs dry, the garbage collection algorithm kicks in automatically. At this time, all objects on the managed heap are tested for outstanding object references in your application (i.e., active roots). If the garbage collector determines that a given root is no longer used by a given application (i.e., the object has fallen out of scope or was set to Nothing), the object is marked for termination. Once the entire heap has been searched for "severed roots," the heap is swept clean, and the underlying memory is reclaimed.

Finalizing an Object Reference

VB 6.0 supplied a Terminate event, which could be handled on a class-by-class basis in order to ensure that proper clean up of the object occurred. Under VB .NET, the .NET garbage collection scheme is rather nondeterministic. .NET class types do *not* support a Terminate event which is automatically called when the object is no longer in use. In fact, you are typically unable to determine exactly when an object will be deallocated from memory. Although this approach to memory management can simplify coding efforts (allocate and forget) you are left with the unappealing byproduct of your objects possibly holding onto unmanaged resources (Hwnds, database connections, etc.) longer than necessary.

For example, if the Car type was to obtain a connection to a remote database during its lifetime, you would like to ensure that this resource released in a timely manner. One choice you face as a VB .NET class designer is to determine whether or not your classes should override the System.Object.Finalize() method (the default implementation does nothing). To illustrate, let's update our Car type:

```
Public Class Car
    Protected Overrides Sub Finalize()
        Console.WriteLine("In Finalize.")
    End Sub
...
End Class
```

When you place a VB .NET object onto the managed heap using the New keyword, the runtime automatically determines if your object supports a custom Finalize() method. If so, the object is marked as "finalizable." When the runtime determines a finalizable object is no longer referenced, it is placed onto a separate area of the heap named the "finalization queue." If a garbage collection occurs, each object on the finalization queue will have its Finalize() method called before deallocating the memory for the object.

Finalization Details

Assume that you have now defined some additional automobile classes (minivans, sports cars, and jeeps). Also assume that MiniVans and SportsCars do not override Finalize(), while Car and Jeep types do. When Car and Jeeps are no longer referenced, they are moved to the finalization queue and have their Finalize() method called at the next garbage collection. Internally, the process would look something like what you see in Figure 4-21.

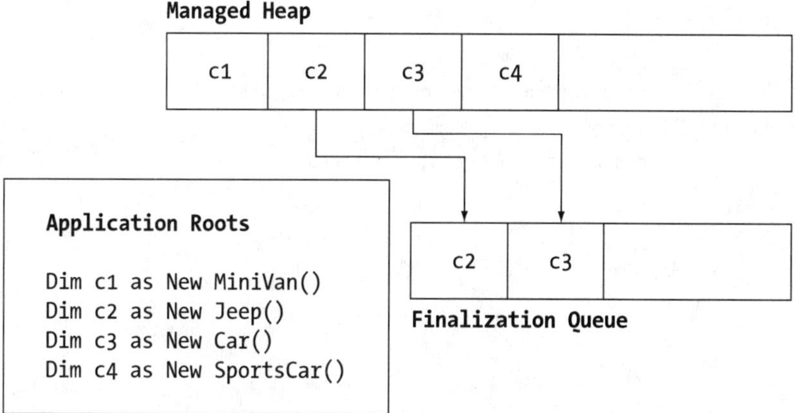

Figure 4-21. Objects that override Finalize() are placed onto the finalization queue

As you may be able to infer, classes that support custom Finalize() methods take longer to remove from memory. C1 and c4 do not override Finalize(), and can therefore be deallocated from memory immediately (if a garbage collection were to occur). C2 and c3 on the other hand, have additional overhead imposed by the call to Finalize(). Nevertheless, when you want to ensure that your objects are given a chance to release any acquired resources, you should support override Finalize() on your custom objects.

Building an Ad Hoc Destruction Method

Again assume the Car class obtains resources during its lifetime. If this type overrides Finalize(), it will take longer to remove from memory than objects that do not (which may or may not be a problem). Given the fact that resources such as database connections are a precious commodity, you may not want to wait for the .NET garbage collector to trigger your Finalize() logic at "some time in the future." A logical question at this point is how you can provide a way for the object user to deallocate the resources held by an object as soon as possible.

One alternative is to define a custom ad hoc method that you can assume all objects in your system implement. Let's call this method Dispose(). The assumption is that when object users are finished using your object, they manually call Dispose() before allowing the object reference to drop out of scope. In this way, your objects can perform any amount of cleanup necessary (i.e., release a database connection) without incurring the hit of being placed on the finalization queue and without waiting for the garbage collector to trigger the class' Finalize() logic:

```
' Equipping our class with an ad hoc destructor.
Public Class Car
...
    ' This is a custom method we expect the object user to call manually.
    Public Sub Dispose()
        ' ... Clean up your Internal resources.
    End Sub
End Class
```

The IDisposable Interface

In order to provide symmetry among all objects that support an explicit destruction routine, the .NET class libraries define an interface named IDisposable which (surprise, surprise) supports a single member named Dispose(). Here is the official C# definition:

```
public interface IDisposable
{
    public void Dispose();
}
```

Now, rest assured that the concepts behind interface-based programming are fully detailed in Chapter 5. Until then, understand that the recommended design pattern to follow is to implement the IDisposable interface for all types that want to support an explicit form of resource deallocation. Thus, you may update the Car type as follows:

```
Public Class Car
   Implements IDisposable
...
    ' This is still a custom method we expect the object user to call manually.
    Public Sub Dispose() Implements IDisposable.Dispose
        ' . . . Clean up your Internal resources.
    End Sub
End Class
```

Again, using this approach, you provide the object user with a way to manually dispose of acquired resources as soon as possible, and avoid the overhead of being placed on the finalization queue. As you may guess, it is possible for a single VB .NET class to support an overridden Finalize() method as well as implement the IDisposable interface. You will see this technique in just a moment.

Interacting with the Garbage Collector

Like everything in the .NET universe, you are able to interact with the garbage collector using an object reference. System.GC is the class that enables you to do so. GC is a sealed class, which, as you recall, means it cannot function as a base class to other types. You access the GC's functionality using a small set of shared members. Here is a rundown of some of the more interesting items (Table 4-3).

Table 4-3. Select Members of the System.GC Type

SYSTEM.GC MEMBER	MEANING IN LIFE
Collect()	Forces the GC to call the Finalize() method for every object on the managed heap. You can also (if you choose) specify the generation to sweep (more on generations soon).
GetGeneration()	Returns the generation to which an object currently belongs.
MaxGeneration	This property returns the maximum of generations supported on the target system.
ReRegisterForFinalize()	Sets a flag indicating that a suppressed object should be reregistered as finalizable. This (of course) assumes the object was marked as nonfinalizable using SuppressFinalize().
SuppressFinalize()	Sets a flag indicating that a given object should not have its Finalize() method called (i.e., it should be taken off the finalization queue).
GetTotalMemory()	Returns the amount of memory (in bytes) currently being used by all objects in the heap, including objects that are soon to be destroyed. This method takes a Boolean parameter, which is used to specify if a garbage collection should occur during the method invocation.

To illustrate programmatic interaction with the .NET garbage collector, let's retrofit our automobile's destruction logic as follows:

```
Public Class Car
    Implements IDisposable
    ' Internal state data. . .
    Private currSpeed As Integer
    Private maxSpeed As Integer
    Private petName As String
    ' Used to mark if we are currently disposed.
    Private disposed As Boolean
    ' Constructors. . . (removed for clarity)
    . . .
    ' This helper function will be called by
    ' explicit and implicit destruction methods.
    Private Sub CleanUpInternalResources()
```

```
        If (disposed = False) Then
            disposed = True
            Console.WriteLine("Cleaning up internal resources. . .")
        End If
    End Sub
    ' This will be called by the runtime when a GC is needed.
    Protected Overrides Sub Finalize()
        Console.WriteLine("In Finalize() for {0}!", petName)
        CleanUpInternalResources()
    End Sub
    ' Called by the client when they are done.
    Public Sub Dispose() Implements IDisposable.Dispose
        Console.WriteLine("In Dispose() for {0}!", petName)
        ' No need to finalize if user
        ' called Dispose() manually.
        CleanUpInternalResources()
        System.GC.SuppressFinalize(Me)
    End Sub
End Class
```

Notice that this iteration of the Car class supports both an overridden implementation of Finalize() as well as the IDisposable interface. In both cases, a call is made to an internal private helper method named CleanUpInternalResources(). Assume this method does some sort of clean up for Car types as long as this method has *not* been called previously (thus the need for the Private Boolean type to check for the "disposedness" of the object).

This time, the Dispose() method has been altered to call GC.SuppressFinalize(), which informs the system that it should remove the specified object from the finalization queue, as the object user has called Dispose() manually (and has therefore cleaned up any internal resources of the Car type).

To illustrate the interplay between explicit and implicit object deallocation, assume the following updated Main() method. GC.Collect() is called to force all objects on the finalization queue to have their Finalize() method triggered before this application shuts down. However, given that two of the Car types have been manually disposed by the object user, these types do not have their Finalize() methods triggered due to the call to GC.SuppressFinalize():

```
' Interacting with the GC.
Public Sub Main()
    Console.WriteLine("Heap memory in use: {0}", _
                      System.GC.GetTotalMemory(false).ToString())
    ' Add these cars to the managed heap.
    Dim c1, c2, c3, c4 as Car
    c1 = New Car("Car one", 40, 10)
```

```
    c2 = New Car("Car two", 70, 5)
    c3 = New Car("Car three", 200, 100)
    c4 = New Car("Car four", 140, 80)
    ' Manually dispose some objects.
    ' This will tell the GC to suppress finialization.
    c1.Dispose()
    c3.Dispose()
    ' Call Finalize() for objects remaining on the finalization queue.
    System.GC.Collect()
End Sub
```

Here is the output (Figure 4-22).

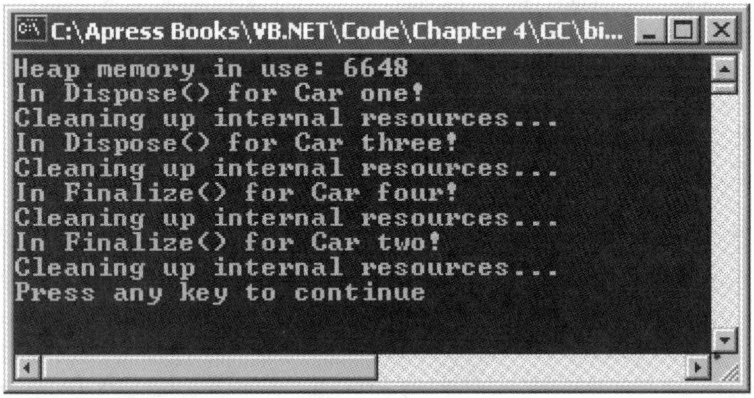

```
C:\Apress Books\VB.NET\Code\Chapter 4\GC\bi...
Heap memory in use: 6648
In Dispose() for Car one!
Cleaning up internal resources...
In Dispose() for Car three!
Cleaning up internal resources...
In Finalize() for Car four!
Cleaning up internal resources...
In Finalize() for Car two!
Cleaning up internal resources...
Press any key to continue
```

Figure 4-22. Cleaning up our resources

Garbage Collection Optimizations

The next topic of interest has to do with the notion of "generations." When the .NET garbage collector is about to mark objects for deletion, is does *not* literally walk over each and every object placed on the managed heap looking for orphaned roots. Doing so would involve considerable time, especially in larger (i.e., real-world) applications.

Recall that the GC forces a collection as soon as it determines there is not enough memory to hold a new object instance. If the GC were to search every single object in memory for severed roots, this could easily entail checking hundreds, if not thousands, of objects. In this case, you could easily envision sluggish performance.

To help optimize the collection process, every object on the heap is assigned to a given "generation." The idea behind generations is simple: The longer an object has existed on the heap, the more likely it is to stay there (such as the application level object). Conversely, objects that have been recently placed on the heap are more likely to be unreferenced by the application rather quickly (e.g., a temporary object created in some method scope). Given these assumptions, each object belongs to one of the following generations:

- Generation 0: Identifies a newly allocated object that has never been marked for collection.
- Generation 1: Identifies an object that has survived a garbage collection sweep (i.e., it was marked for collection, but was not removed due to the fact that the heap had enough free space).
- Generation 2: Identifies an object that has survived more than one sweep of the garbage collector.

Now, when a collection occurs, the GC marks and sweeps all generation 0 objects first. If this results in the required amount of memory, the remaining objects are promoted to the next available generation. If all generation 0 objects have been removed from the heap, but more memory is still necessary, generation 1 objects are marked and swept, followed (if necessary) by generation 2 objects. In this way, the newer objects (i.e., local variables) are removed quickly while an older object is assumed to be in use. In a nutshell, the GC is able to quickly free heap space using the generation as a baseline.

Programmatically speaking, you are able to investigate the generation an object currently belongs to using GC.GetGeneration(). Furthermore, GC.Collect() does allow you to specify which generation should be checked for orphaned roots. Consider the following:

```
' Just how old are you?
Public Sub Main()
    Console.WriteLine("Heap memory in use: {0}", _
                 System.GC.GetTotalMemory(False).ToString())
    ' Add these cars to the managed heap.
    Dim c1, c2, c3, c4 as Car
    c1 = New Car("Car one", 40, 10)
    c2 = New Car("Car two", 70, 5)
    c3 = New Car("Car three", 200, 100)
    c4 = New Car("Car four", 140, 80)
    ' Display generations.
    Console.WriteLine("C1 is gen {0}", System.GC.GetGeneration(c1))
    Console.WriteLine("C2 is gen {0}", System.GC.GetGeneration(c2))
    Console.WriteLine("C3 is gen {0}", System.GC.GetGeneration(c3))
    Console.WriteLine("C4 is gen {0}", System.GC.GetGeneration(c4))
    ' Dispose some cars manually.
```

```
    c1.Dispose()
    c3.Dispose()
    ' Collect all gen 0 objects?
    System.GC.Collect(0)
    ' Display generations again (each will be promoted).
    Console.WriteLine("C1 is gen {0}", System.GC.GetGeneration(c1))
    Console.WriteLine("C2 is gen {0}", System.GC.GetGeneration(c2))
    Console.WriteLine("C3 is gen {0}", System.GC.GetGeneration(c3))
    Console.WriteLine("C4 is gen {0}", System.GC.GetGeneration(c4))
    ' Force memory to be freed for all generations.
    System.GC.Collect()    ' Calls Finalize() for each finalizable object.
    Console.WriteLine("Heap memory in use: {0}", _
                System.GC.GetTotalMemory(False).ToString())
End Sub
```

The output is shown in Figure 4-23. Notice that when you request a collection of generation 0, each object is promoted to generation 1, given that these objects did not need to be removed from memory (as the managed heap was not exhausted):

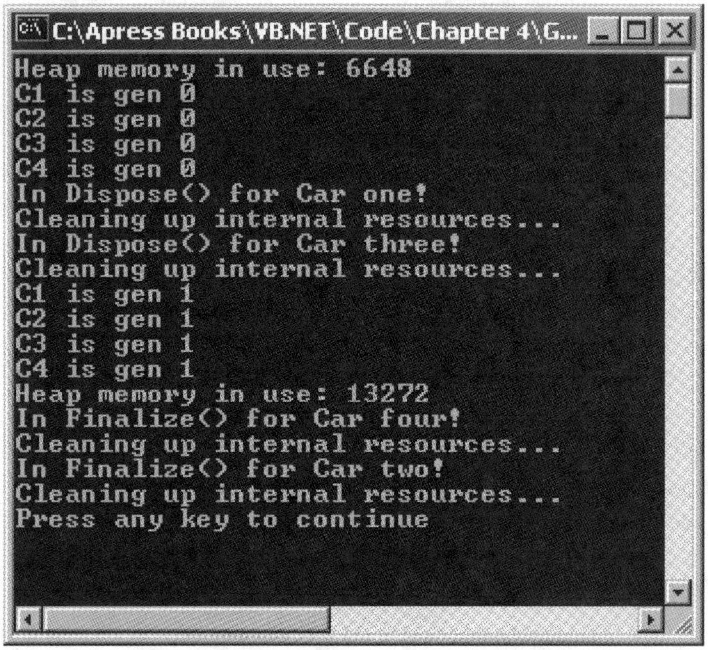

```
C:\Apress Books\VB.NET\Code\Chapter 4\G...
Heap memory in use: 6648
C1 is gen 0
C2 is gen 0
C3 is gen 0
C4 is gen 0
In Dispose() for Car one!
Cleaning up internal resources...
In Dispose() for Car three!
Cleaning up internal resources...
C1 is gen 1
C2 is gen 1
C3 is gen 1
C4 is gen 1
Heap memory in use: 13272
In Finalize() for Car four!
Cleaning up internal resources...
In Finalize() for Car two!
Cleaning up internal resources...
Press any key to continue
```

Figure 4-23. Interacting with the garbage collector

To close, keep in mind that your interactions with the GC should be slim-to-none. The whole point of having a managed heap is to move the responsibility of memory management from your hands into the hands of the runtime. Do remember however, that when you build classes that override Finalize(), your objects will require more time to be removed from the managed heap (due to the extra logic of the finalization queue). If you want to support an implicit means of freeing the resources used by an object, you may implement the IDisposable interface.

SOURCE CODE *The GC project is located under the Chapter 4 subdirectory.*

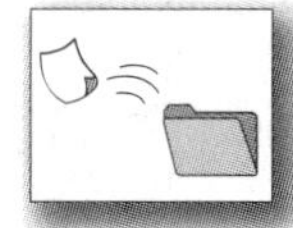

Summary

If you already come to the universe of .NET from another object-oriented language (such as C#, C++, Java, or Delphi), this chapter may have been more of a quick compare and contrast between your current language of choice and VB .NET. On the other hand, those of you who are exploring complete OOP concepts for the first time may have found many of the concepts presented here a bit confounding. Regardless of your background, rest assured that the information presented here is the foundation of any .NET application.

This chapter began with a review of the pillars of OOP: Encapsulation, inheritance, and polymorphism. As you have seen, VB .NET provides full support for each aspect of object orientation. In addition, the use of structured exception handling was introduced, which is *the* way to report and respond to error information in the .NET platform.

Finally, the chapter wrapped up by examining exactly how the .NET runtime frees you from manually cleaning up the memory you allocate by the virtue of a managed heap. You have also explored the interplay between Object.Finalize(), the IDisposable interface and the VB .NET destructor and examined how to programmatically interact with the garbage collector using the System.GC type.

CHAPTER 5

Interfaces and Collections

THIS CHAPTER BUILDS on your current understanding of object-oriented development by introducing the topic of interface-based programming. You learn how to use VB .NET to create and implement custom interfaces, and come to understand the benefits of building types that support multiple behaviors. Along the way, a number of related topics are also discussed, such as obtaining interface references, explicit interface implementation, and the construction of interface hierarchies.

The remainder of this chapter is spent examining some of the standard interfaces defined within the .NET base class libraries. As you will see, your custom types are free to implement these predefined interfaces to support a number of advanced behaviors such as object cloning, object enumeration, and object sorting.

To wrap things up, you get a high-level view of the various predefined interfaces that are implemented by various collection classes (ArrayList, Stack, etc.) defined by the System.Collections namespace.

Understanding Interface-Based Programming

COM programmers have lived and died by the notion of interface-based programming for years. In fact, one of the central tenants of COM is that the only way a client can communicate with a COM class is via an interface pointer (not a direct object reference). Although the .NET universe still honors the use of interfaces, they are not the only means by which two binaries can communicate (as the CLR supports true object references). Be aware however, that this does not in any way imply that interfaces are obsolete! These syntactic entities are still the most elegant means by which you can safely extend the functionality of a custom type without breaking existing code.

First, a formal definition: An interface is nothing more than a collection of semantically related *abstract members*. The exact number of members defined by a given interface always depends on the exact *behavior* you are attempting to model. Yes it's true. An interface expresses a behavior that a given class may want to support. At a syntactic level, an interface is defined using the following

VB .NET keyword (unlike VB 6.0, where interfaces were represented as empty class definitions):

```
Public Interface IPointy
    Function GetNumberOfPoints() As Byte
End Interface
```

.NET interfaces are also able to support any number of properties (and events). For example, you could design the IPointy interface with the following read/write property [if you want to model a read-only or write-only property, make use of the ReadOnly and WriteOnly keywords (see Chapter 4)]:

```
' The pointy behavior as a read / write property.
Public Interface IPointy
    Property Points() As Byte
End Interface
```

In any case, because an interface is nothing more than a named set of abstract members, any class (or structure) that chooses to implement an interface, is obligated to flesh out the details behind each member. Thus, interface-based programming provides yet another way to inject polymorphic behavior into a system: If multiple classes (or structures) implement the same interface in unique ways, you have the power to treat each type in the same manner.

IPointy is a simple interface that expresses the behavior of "having points." As you can tell, this behavior might be useful in the Shapes hierarchy developed in Chapter 4. The idea is simple: Some objects in the Shapes application have points (such as the Hexagon and Triangle) while others (such as the Circle) do not. If you configure the Hexagon and Triangle to support the IPointy interface, you can safely assume that each class supports a common behavior.

At this point, you may be wondering why you need the Interface keyword in the first place. After all, VB .NET allows you to build base classes containing abstract (aka MustOverride) methods. When a child class derives from an abstract base class, it is also under obligation to flesh out the details of the abstract methods. However, abstract base classes typically do far more than define a group of abstract methods. They are free to define Public, Private, and Protected state data, as well as any number of concrete methods that can be accessed (and possibly overridden) by the subclasses.

Interfaces on the other hand, are pure protocol. Interfaces *never* define data members, and *never* provide a default implementation of the methods. Every member of an interface (whether it is a property or method) is automatically abstract. Furthermore, given that VB .NET (and .NET-aware languages in general) only support single inheritance, the interface-based protocol allows a given type to support numerous behaviors, while avoiding the issues that arise when deriving from multiple base classes.

Implementing an Interface

When a VB .NET class (or structure) chooses to extend its functionality by supporting a given interface, it does so using the Implements keyword (which must be listed after any Inherits statement). When you flesh out the details of each member of the interface, you again make use of the Implements keyword to associate the name of the class method to the name of the interface method (the two do not need to be identically named as you learn later). For example:

```
' A given class may implement as many interfaces as necessary, but may have
' exactly 1 base class.
Public Class Hexagon
    Inherits Shape
    Implements IPointy
    Public Sub New()
    End Sub
    Public Sub New(ByVal name As String)
        MyBase.New(name)
    End Sub
    ' override the base class Draw() method.
    Public Overrides Sub Draw()
        Console.WriteLine("Drawing " & PetName & " the Hexagon")
    End Sub
    ' Implementation of IPointy interface.
    Public Function GetNumberOfPoints() As Byte _
            Implements IPointy.GetNumberOfPoints
        Return 6
    End Function
End Class

Public Class Triangle
    Inherits Shape
    Implements IPointy
    Public Sub New(ByVal name As String)
        MyBase.New(name)
    End Sub
    Public Sub New()
    End Sub
```

```
    Public Overrides Sub Draw()
        Console.WriteLine("Drawing " & PetName & " the Triangle")
    End Sub
    Public Function GetNumberOfPoints() As Byte _
            Implements IPointy.GetNumberOfPoints
        Return 3
    End Function
End Class
```

Each class now returns the number of points to the outside world when asked to do so. Notice that implementing an interface is an all-or-nothing proposition. The supporting type is *not* able to selectively choose which methods it will implement. Given that our IPointy interface defines a single method, this is not too much of a burden.

To sum up the story so far, Figure 5-1 illustrates IPointy compatible objects using the popular "COM lollipop" notation. For those coming from a non-Microsoft view of the world, COM objects are graphically represented using a lollipop (aka jack) for each interface supported by a given class. For those who are familiar with the COM lifestyle, notice that the Hexagon and Triangle classes (see Figure 5-1) do *not* implement IUnknown and derive from a common base class (again illustrating the stark differences between COM and .NET).

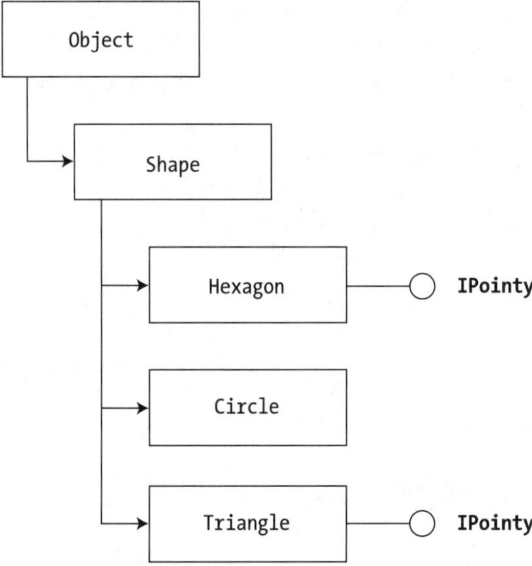

Figure 5-1. The updated Shapes hierarchy

Obtaining Interface References

By default, when a type supports a given interface, the object user is able to directly access the members of an interface from a valid object instance. Therefore, you could make use of the functionality provided by IPointy as follows:

```
' From the obj level. . .
Dim h As New Hexagon()
Console.WriteLine(h.GetNumberOfPoints())
```

Often however, it is desirable to obtain an explicit interface reference from the supporting type. To do so, VB .NET provides several options. First, assume you have created an instance of the Hexagon class, and want to discover if it supports the pointy behavior. One approach is to make use of a direct assignment (recall the Set keyword is obsolete). Thus, you could write the following VB 6.0-like code:

```
' Grab a reference to the IPointy interface using a VB 6.0 style cast.
Dim hex as Hexagon = New Hexagon("Bill")
Dim itfPt as IPointy
ItfPt = hex
Console.WriteLine(itfPt.GetNumberOfPoints())
```

Here, you are asking the Hexagon instance for access to the IPointy interface. If the object does support this interface, you are then able to exercise the behavior accordingly. What if you were to create an instance of the Circle? Given that the Circle class does not support the IPointy interface, you are issued a runtime error! When you attempt to access an interface not supported by a given class using a direct cast, the system throws an InvalidCastException. To safely recover from this error you need to catch this exception:

```
' Obtain IPointy interface?
Dim c As Circle = New Circle("Mitch")
Dim itfPt As IPointy
Try
    itfPt = c
Catch e As InvalidCastException
    Console.WriteLine("OOPS!  Not pointy. . .")
End Try
```

A more type-safe way to obtain an interface reference from a type is to make use of the CType() conversion function:

```
' Obtain IPointy interface?
Dim c As Circle = New Circle("Mitch")
Dim itfPt As IPointy
Try
    itfPt = CType(c, IPointy)
    Console.WriteLine("Got interface using CType(). . .")
Catch e As InvalidCastException
    Console.WriteLine("OOPS!  Not pointy. . .")
End Try
```

Finally, you may also obtain an interface from an object using the TypeOf/Is syntax. If the object in question is not IPointy compatible, the condition fails.

```
' Are you pointy?
Dim t as Triangle = new Triangle()
If(TypeOf(t) is IPointy) Then
    Console.WriteLine(t.GetNumberOfPoints())
Else
    Console.WriteLine("OOPS!  Not pointy. . .")
End If
```

In these previous examples, you could have avoided checking the outcome of asking for the IPointy reference, given that you knew ahead of time which shapes were IPointy-compatible. However, what if you were to create an array of generic Shape references, each of which has been assigned to a given subclass? You may make use of any of the previous techniques to discover at runtime which items in the array support this behavior:

```
' Let's discover which shapes are pointy at runtime. . .
Dim s As Shape() = {New Hexagon(), New Circle(), _
    New Triangle("Joe"), New Circle("JoJo")}
Dim i As Integer
For i = 0 To UBound(s)
    s(i).Draw()
    ' Who's pointy?
         If TypeOf (s(i)) Is IPointy Then
             Dim iPty As IPointy
                 iPty = CType(s(i), IPointy)
                 Console.WriteLine("Points: {0}", iPty.GetNumberOfPoints())
         Else
             Console.WriteLine(s(i).PetName & "'s not pointy!")
         End If
Next
```

The output is shown in Figure 5-2.

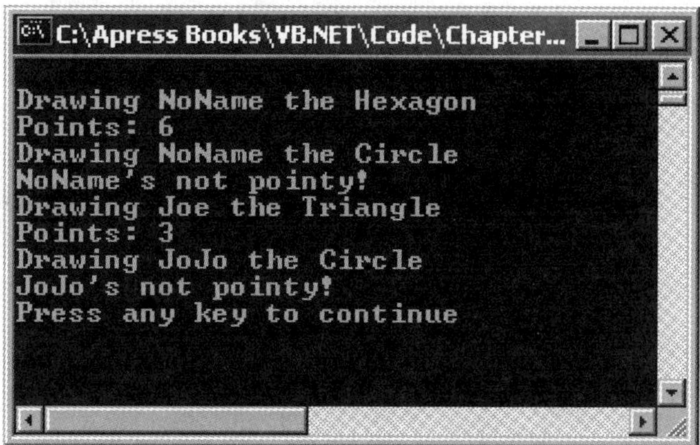

Figure 5-2. Discovering behaviors at runtime

Interfaces As Parameters

Interfaces are strongly typed variables and therefore you can construct methods that take interfaces as parameters as well as return values. To begin, assume you have defined another interface named IDraw3D as follows:

```
' The 3D drawing behavior.
Public Interface IDraw3D
    Sub Draw3D()
End interface
```

Next, assume that two of your three shapes (Circle and Hexagon) have been configured to support this new behavior:

```
' Circle supports IDraw3D.
Public Class Circle
    Inherits Shape
    Implements IDraw3D
...
    Private Sub Draw3D() Implements IDraw3D.Draw3D
        Console.WriteLine("Drawing Circle in 3D!")
    End Sub
End Class
' So does Hexagon.
Public Class Hexagon
    Inherits Shape
```

```
    Implements IPointy, IDraw3D
...
    Private Sub Draw3D() Implements IDraw3D.Draw3D
        Console.WriteLine("Drawing Hexagon in 3D!")
    End Sub
End Class
```

If you now define a method taking an IDraw3D interface as a parameter, you are able to effectively send in *any* object supporting IDraw3D. Consider the following:

```
' I'll Draw anything!
Public Sub DrawThisShapeIn3D(ByVal itf3d As IDraw3D)
    Console.Write("DrawThisShapeIn3D says: ")
    itf3d.Draw3D()
End Sub
Sub Main()
    ' The base class pointer trick.
    Dim s As Shape() = {New Hexagon(), New Circle(), _
                        New Triangle("Joe"), New Circle("JoJo")}
    Dim i As Integer
    For i = 0 To UBound(s)
            ...
        ' Can I draw you in 3D?
        If TypeOf (s(i)) Is IDraw3D Then
            DrawThisShapeIn3D(CType(s(i), IDraw3D))
            Console.WriteLine()
        End If
    Next
End Sub
```

Notice that the triangle is never drawn in 3D as it is not IDraw3D compatible (Figure 5-3).

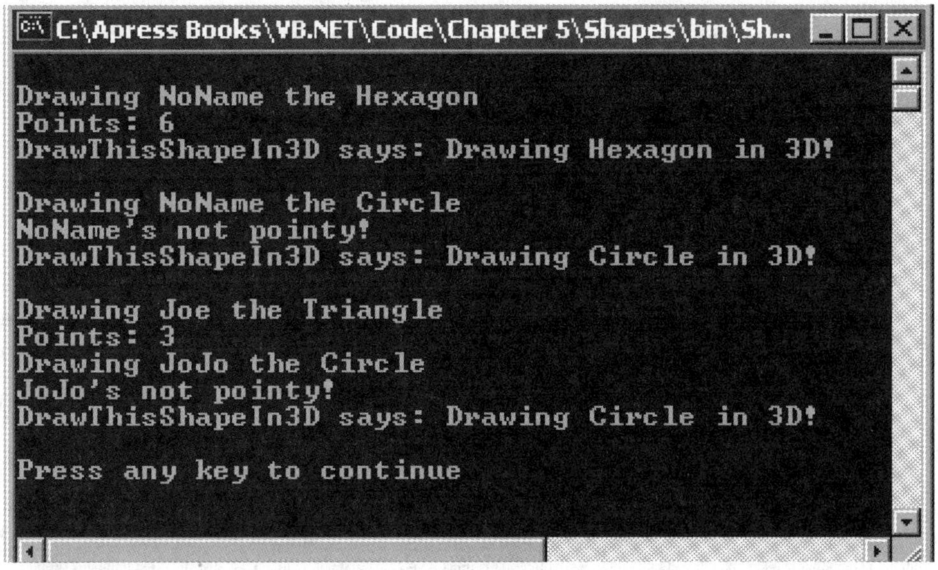

```
C:\Apress Books\VB.NET\Code\Chapter 5\Shapes\bin\Sh...

Drawing NoName the Hexagon
Points: 6
DrawThisShapeIn3D says: Drawing Hexagon in 3D!

Drawing NoName the Circle
NoName's not pointy!
DrawThisShapeIn3D says: Drawing Circle in 3D!

Drawing Joe the Triangle
Points: 3
Drawing JoJo the Circle
JoJo's not pointy!
DrawThisShapeIn3D says: Drawing Circle in 3D!

Press any key to continue
```

Figure 5-3. Discovering all IDraw3D compatible types

Understanding Explicit Interface Implementation

In our previous definition of IDraw3D, you were forced to name your method Draw3D() to avoid clashing with the abstract Draw() method defined in the Shapes base class:

```
' The 3D drawing behavior.
Public Interface IDraw3D
    Sub Draw3D()
End interface
```

While there is nothing horribly wrong with this interface definition, a more natural method name would simply be Draw():

```
' The 3D drawing behavior.
Public interface IDraw3D
    Sub Draw()
End Interface
```

If you create a new class that derives from Shape *and* implements IDraw3D, you are in for some problematic behavior. Assume you have defined the following new class named Line, initially defined as follows:

```
' Problems. . .
Public Class Line
    Inherits Shape
Implements IDraw3D
    Public Sub Draw() Implements IDraw3D.Draw
        Console.WriteLine("Drawing a 3D line. . .")
    End Sub
    Public Overrides Sub Draw()
        Console.WriteLine("Drawing a line. . .")
    End Sub
End Class
```

Given what you already know about the Shapes base class and IDraw3D interface, it looks as if you have implemented two methods named Draw(): one from the IDraw3D interface and one from the Shape base class. However, the VB .NET compiler is unhappy. The problem is that VB .NET does not allow you to override and implement an interface member on the same class, when the member in question is identically named. Even if you attempt to get clever and add the Overloads keyword to each definition, you still will not obtain the result you are hoping for. To resolve the name clash, you are able to rename the method implementing IDraw3D.Draw():

```
Public Class Line
    Inherits Shape
    Implements IDraw3D
    Public Sub itfImplDraw() Implements IDraw3D.Draw
        Console.WriteLine("Drawing a 3D line. . .")
    End Sub
    Public Overrides Sub Draw()
        Console.WriteLine("Drawing a line. . .")
    End Sub
End Class
```

This compiles, but there is one unappealing side effect. When you create an instance of the Line class, you are presented with the following two class members:

```
Dim l As Line = New Line()
l.itfImplDraw() ' Really triggers IDraw3D.Draw()
l.Draw() ' Really triggers overridden Shape.Draw()
```

Of course, if the object user asks for IDraw3D by name, this bit of ugliness is avoided altogether:

```
Dim l As Line = New Line()
Dim i3D As IDraw3D
i3D = CType(l, IDraw3D)
i3D.Draw()   ' Really triggers IDraw3D.Draw()
```

So, how can you ensure that the methods defined by a given interface are only accessible from an interface reference? Recall that by default, interface methods are accessible from the object level as well as from a valid interface reference.

The answer to this question comes by way of *explicit interface implementation.* Using this technique, you are able to ensure that the object user can only access methods defined by a given interface using the correct interface reference. To illustrate, here is the updated Line class:

```
Public Class Line
    Inherits Shape
    Implements IDraw3D
    ' You can only call this using an IDraw3D reference.
    Private Sub itfImplDraw() Implements IDraw3D.Draw3D
        Console.WriteLine("Drawing a 3D line. . .")
    End Sub
    ' You can only call this using a Line reference.
    Public Overrides Sub Draw()
        Console.WriteLine("Drawing a line. . .")
    End Sub
End Class
```

As you can see, the itfImplDraw() method has now been defined as *Private,* not Public. This should make sense. The whole reason to use explicit interface method implementation is to ensure that a given interface method is bound at the interface level. If you use the Public keyword, this would suggest that the method is a member of the public sector of the class, which defeats the point!

Now let's revisit the name clash issue. Given that the name of the method implementing IDraw3D.Draw3D is unique in the class, you are free to update the IDraw3D interface as originally intended:

```
' The 3D drawing behavior.
Public Interface IDraw3D
    Sub Draw()
End Interface
Public Class Line
    Inherits Shape
    Implements IDraw3D
```

```
    Private Sub iftImplDraw() Implements IDraw3D.Draw
        Console.WriteLine("Drawing a 3D line. . .")
    End Sub
    Public Overrides Sub Draw()
        Console.WriteLine("Drawing a line. . .")
    End Sub
End Class
```

Which lends itself to a more natural use of the Line type:

```
Dim l As Line = New Line()
l.Draw()     ' Really triggers overridden Shape.Draw()
Dim i3D As IDraw3D
i3D = CType(l, IDraw3D)
i3D.Draw()
```

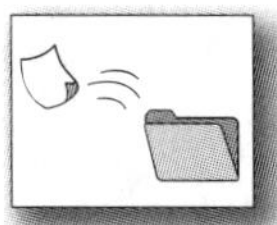

SOURCE CODE *The Shapes project is located under the Chapter 5 subdirectory.*

Building Interface Hierarchies

To wrap up the investigation of custom interfaces, let's examine the topic of interface hierarchies. Just as a class can serve as a base class to other classes (which can in turn function as base classes to yet another class), it is possible to establish derived relationships among interfaces. Like a base class, the topmost interface defines a general behavior, while the most derived interface defines more specific behaviors. Consider the following versioned hierarchy of related interfaces:

```
' The base interface.
Interface IDraw
   Sub Draw()
End Interface
' Derived Interfaces.
Interface IDraw2
    Inherits IDraw
    Sub DrawToPrinter()
End Interface
Interface IDraw3
    Inherits  IDraw2
    Sub DrawToMetaFile()
End Interface
```

The relationships between these custom interfaces can be seen in Figure 5-4.

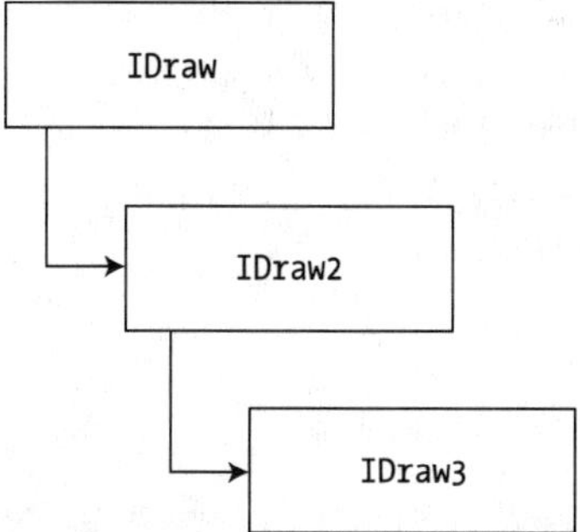

Figure 5-4. Simple interface hierarchy

Now, if a class wanted to support each behavior expressed in this interface hierarchy, it would derive from the *nth-most* interface (IDraw3 in this case). Any methods defined by the base interface(s) are automatically carried into the definition. For example:

```
' Recall, when using explicit interface implementation, you
' force the object user to ask for an interface by name.
Public Class SuperImage
    Implements IDraw3
    Private Sub Draw() Implements IDraw.Draw
        Console.WriteLine("Bland drawing. . .")
    End Sub
    Private Sub DrawToPrinter() Implements IDraw2.DrawToPrinter
        Console.WriteLine("Drawing to the printer. . .")
    End Sub
    Private Sub DrawToMetaFile() Implements IDraw3.DrawToMetaFile
        Console.WriteLine("Drawing to a meta file. . .")
    End Sub
End Class
```

Here is some sample usage (see Figure 5-5 for output):

```
' Exercise the interfaces.
Sub Main()
     ' Make a super image.
     Console.WriteLine("Making a SuperImage:")
     Dim si As SuperImage = New SuperImage()
     ' Get IDraw.
     Dim itfDraw As IDraw
     itfDraw = CType(si, IDraw)
     itfDraw.Draw()
```

```
        ' Now get IDraw3 from super image.
        Dim itfDraw3 As IDraw3 = CType(itfDraw, IDraw3)
        If Not itfDraw Is Nothing Then
            itfDraw3.DrawToMetaFile()
            itfDraw3.DrawToPrinter()
        End If
    End Sub
```

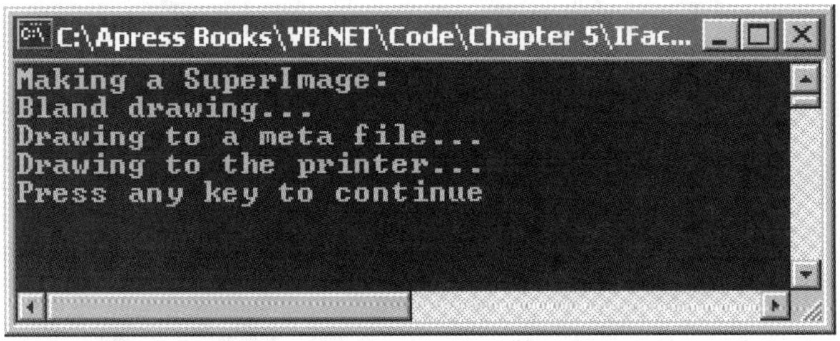

Making a SuperImage:
Bland drawing...
Drawing to a meta file...
Drawing to the printer...
Press any key to continue

Figure 5-5. Using the SuperImage

Specifying Multiple Base Interfaces

As you build interface hierarchies, be aware that it is completely permissible to create an interface that derives from *multiple base interfaces* (unlike classic COM). Recall of course, that it is *not* permissible to build a class that derives from multiple base classes. For example, assume you are building a new set of interfaces that model automobile behaviors:

```
Interface IBasicCar
    Sub Drive()
End Interface
Interface IUnderwaterCar
    Sub Dive()
End Interface
' We are inheriting from TWO base interfaces!
Interface IJamesBondCar
    Inherits IBasicCar, IUnderwaterCar
    Sub TurboBoost()
End Interface
```

What is expressed here is that an IJamesBondCar "is-a" IBasicCar and "is-also-a" IUnderwaterCar. If you were to build a class that implements

IJamesBondCar, you would now be responsible for implementing TurboBoost(), Dive(), and Drive():

```
Public Class JBCar
    Implements IJamesBondCar
    ' Interface impl.
    public Sub Drive() Implements IBasicCar.Drive
        Console.WriteLine("Speeding up. . .")
    End Sub
    Public Sub Dive() Implements IUnderwaterCar.Dive
        Console.WriteLine("Submerging. . .")
    End Sub
    Public Sub TurboBoost() Implements IJamesBondCar.TurboBoost
        Console.WriteLine("Blast off!")
    End Sub
End Class
```

This specialized automobile can now be used as you would expect:

```
Sub Main()
    ' Now make a James Bond car.
    Console.WriteLine()
    Console.WriteLine("Making a JamesBondCar:")
    Dim j As New JBCar()
    Dim itfJBC As IJamesBondCar
    itfJBC = CType(j, IJamesBondCar)
    If Not itfJBC Is Nothing Then
        j.Drive()
        j.TurboBoost()
        j.Dive()
    End If
End Sub
```

SOURCE CODE *The IFaceHierarchy project is located under the Chapter 5 subdirectory.*

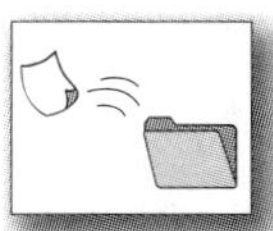

Building a Custom Enumerator (IEnumerable and IEnumerator)

Now that you understand how to work with custom interfaces, you can begin to examine some of the standard (i.e., predefined) interfaces defined in the .NET class libraries. As you dig deeper into the .NET universe, you find that many canned types implement numerous standard interfaces. You are also free to build custom types that support these same interfaces. To illustrate, assume you have developed a class named Cars, which represents a collection of individual Car objects (which you created in Chapter 4). Here is the initial definition:

```
' Cars is a container of Car objects.
Public Class Cars
     Private carArray(3) as Car
     ' Create some Car objects upon start up.
     Public Sub New()
        carArray(0) = New Car("FeeFee", 200, 0)
        carArray(1) = New Car("Clunker", 90, 0)
        carArray(2) = New Car("Zippy", 30, 0)
        carArray(3) = New Car("Fred", 30, 0)
     End Sub
End Class
```

Ideally, it would be convenient from the object user's point of view to iterate over the Cars type using the For Each construct, to obtain each internal sub object:

```
' This seems reasonable. . .
Sub Main()
    Dim carLot As Cars = New Cars()
    Dim c As Car
    For Each c In carLot
        Console.WriteLine("Name: {0}", c.PetName)
        Console.WriteLine("Max speed: {0}", c.MaxSpeed)
    Next
End Sub
```

Sadly, if you attempt to execute this code, the compiler would complain that the Cars class does not implement the "GetEnumerator()" method. This method is defined by the IEnumerable interface, which is found in the System.Collections namespace. To rectify the problem, you may update the Cars definition as follows:

```
' The For Each syntax demands that your
' class support the IEnumerable interface.
Public Class Cars
    Implements IEnumerable
. . .
```

```
    ' IEnumerable defines this method (and only this method).
    Public Function GetEnumerator() As IEnumerator _
      Implements IEnumerable.GetEnumerator
       ' OK, now what?
   End Function
...
End Class
```

So far so good, however as you can see, GetEnumerator() returns yet another interface named IEnumerator. IEnumerator can be obtained from an object to traverse over an internal collection of types. IEnumerator is also defined in the System.Collections namespace and defines the following three methods (shown in C#):

```
// GetEnumerator() returns one of these guys.
public interface IEnumerator
{
     bool MoveNext ();          // Advance the internal position of the cursor.
     object Current {get};      // Get the current item (read-only property).
     void Reset ();             // Reset the cursor to the beginning of the list.
}
```

Now, given that IEnumerable.GetEnumerator() returns an IEnumerator interface, you can update the Cars type as follows:

```
' Getting closer. . .
Public Class Cars
   Implements IEnumerator, IEnumerable
...
    ' IEnumerable defines this method (and only this method).
    Public Function GetEnumerator() As IEnumerator _
      Implements IEnumerable.GetEnumerator
      Return CType(Me, IEnumerator)
   End Function
...
End Class
```

The final detail is to flesh out the implementation of MoveNext(), Current, and Reset(). Here then is the final update of the Cars class:

```
' An enumerable car collection!
Public Class Cars
    Implements IEnumerator, IEnumerable
    ' This class maintains an array of cars.
    Private carArray(3) As Car
    ' Current position in array.
    Private pos As Integer = -1
    Public Sub New()
        carArray(0) = New Car("FeeFee", 200, 0)
        carArray(1) = New Car("Clunker", 90, 0)
        carArray(2) = New Car("Zippy", 30, 0)
        carArray(3) = New Car("Fred", 30, 0)
    End Sub
    ' Implementation of IEnumerator.
    Public Function MoveNext() As Boolean Implements IEnumerator.MoveNext
        If (pos < UBound(carArray)) Then
            pos += 1
            Return True
        Else
            Return False
        End If
    End Function
    Public Sub Reset() Implements IEnumerator.Reset
        pos = 0
    End Sub
    Public ReadOnly Property Current() Implements IEnumerator.Current
        Get
            Return carArray(pos)
        End Get
    End Property
    ' This must be present to let the For Each
    ' loop iterate over our array.
    ' IEnumerable implemtation.
    Public Function GetEnumerator() As IEnumerator _
        Implements IEnumerable.GetEnumerator
        Return CType(Me, IEnumerator)
    End Function
End Class
```

So then, what have you gained by equipping your class to support the IEnumerator and IEnumerable interfaces? First, your custom type can now be traversed using the For Each syntax.

```
' No problem!
Sub Main()
    Dim carLot As Cars = New Cars()
    Dim c As Car
    For Each c In carLot     ' IEnumerable obtained here.
        Console.WriteLine("Name: {0}", c.PetName)
        Console.WriteLine("Max speed: {0}", c.MaxSpeed)
    Next
End Sub
```

In addition, this provides an alternate means for an object user to access the underlying automobiles maintained by the Cars type (which for those of you with a C++ COM background, should look a lot like manipulating the raw COM IEnumXXXX interface):

```
' Now ala IEnumerator
Dim itfEnum As IEnumerator
itfEnum = CType(carLot, IEnumerator)
' Reset the cursor to the beginning.
itfEnum.Reset()
' Advance internal cursor by 1.
itfEnum.MoveNext()
' Cast to a Car and crank some tunes.
Dim curCar As Object = itfEnum.Current
CType(curCar, Car).CrankTunes(True)
```

SOURCE CODE *The ObjEnum project is located under the Chapter 5 subdirectory.*

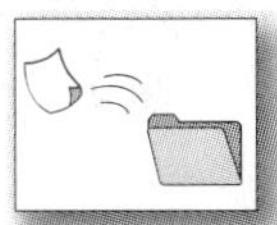

Building Cloneable Objects (ICloneable)

Cloning an object is the process of duplicating the state of an existing object into a new object (of the same type). As you have already seen in Chapter 3, when you assign a value type to a value type, a "shallow copy" is achieved, in that a member-by-member copy of the Structure is returned. If the Structure in question is only composed of other value types, all is fine with the world. Recall however, that if the Structure contains any reference types, the references themselves are copied—not the values they maintain! Likewise, when you assign one reference type to another reference type, you do *not* receive a new copy of the existing object. Rather, you end up with a new variable pointing to the same object in memory.

When you want to build a Class or Structure that is able to return "deep copies" to the outside world (e.g., perform a complete copy of class types, not just a reference to the object in memory), you should implement the ICloneable interface. First, assume you have a simple class named Point:

```
' The classic Point example. . .
Public Class Point
    ' State data.
    Public x, y As Integer
    ' Ctors.
    Public Sub New()
    End Sub
    Public Sub New(ByVal xPos As Integer, ByVal yPos As Integer)
        x = xPos
        y = yPos
    End Sub
    ' Override Object.ToString().
    Public Overrides Function ToString() As String
        Return "X: " & x & " Y: " & y
    End Function
End Class
```

The standard ICloneable interface defines a single method named Clone(). The implementation of the Clone() method varies between objects. However the basic functionality is the same: Copy the values of your member variables into a new object instance, and return it to the user. If the type being cloned contains any reference types, you need to create a brand new instance of each class as well (as you will see in a moment). To start things off, let's retrofit Point to support ICloneable:

```
' The Point class supports ICloneable.
Public Class Point
    Implements ICloneable
    ' State data.
    Public x, y As Integer
    ' Ctors.
    Public Sub New()
    End Sub
    Public Sub New(ByVal xPos As Integer, ByVal yPos As Integer)
        x = xPos
        y = yPos
    End Sub
```

```
    ' The sole method of ICloneable.
    Public Function Clone() As Object _
        Implements ICloneable.Clone
        Return MemberwiseClone()
    End Function
    ' Override Object.ToString().
    Public Overrides Function ToString() As String
        Return "X: " & x & " Y: " & y
    End Function
End Class
```

Notice how the implementation of Clone() simply calls the inherited member System.Object.MemberwiseClone(). This is acceptable for this iteration of the Point class, given that your type only supports internal value types (two Integers). In this way, you can create exact stand-alone copies of the Point type, as illustrated by the following code (note the difference between assignment and cloning, as seen in Figure 5-6):

```
' Notice Clone() returns a generic object type.
' You must perform an explicit cast to obtain the derived type.
Sub Main()
    ' First use assignment operator.
    Dim p1 As Point = New Point(50, 50)
    Dim p2 As Point = p1
    p2.x = 0
    Console.WriteLine("Assigned p2 to p1 and changed p2.x to 0")
    ' Print each obj.
    Console.WriteLine("Point 1: {0}", p1)
    Console.WriteLine("Point 2: {0}", p2)
    ' Now some copies.
    Dim p3 As Point = New Point(100, 100)
    Dim p4 As Point = CType(p3, Point).Clone()
    p4.x = 0
    Console.WriteLine("Cloned p3 into p4 and changed p4.x to 0")
    ' Print each obj.
    Console.WriteLine("Point 3: {0}", p3)
    Console.WriteLine("Point 4: {0}", p4)
End Sub
```

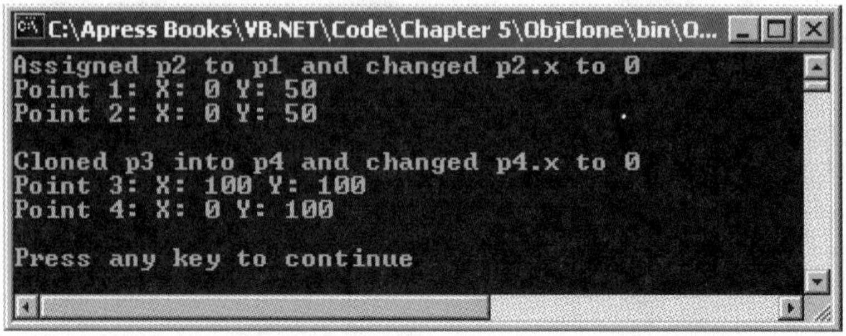

```
C:\Apress Books\VB.NET\Code\Chapter 5\ObjClone\bin\O...
Assigned p2 to p1 and changed p2.x to 0
Point 1: X: 0 Y: 50
Point 2: X: 0 Y: 50

Cloned p3 into p4 and changed p4.x to 0
Point 3: X: 100 Y: 100
Point 4: X: 0 Y: 100

Press any key to continue
```

Figure 5-6. Clones are independent copies.

As you would expect, when you *assign* two reference types, changes made to the object by one reference are visible from all references. On the other hand, when you *clone* an object, you are returned a full copy of the type, which can be independently manipulated.

A More Elaborate Cloning Example

Now assume the Point class contains an internal class that represents a description of a given Point (time of creation and pet name). To represent the time this point came to life, the PointDesc class contains yet another object of type DateTime. Here is the implementation:

```
Public Class PointDesc
   Private mPetName As String
   Private mCreationDate As DateTime
   Public Sub New(ByVal petName As String)
        mPetName = petName
        mCreationDate = DateTime.Now
   End Sub
   Public Property PetName() As String
        Get
            Return mPetName
        End Get
        Set(ByVal Value As String)
            mPetName = Value
        End Set
   End Property
   Public Function CreationDate() As String
        ' Slow things down for a second. . .
        System.Threading.Thread.Sleep(1000)
        Return mCreationDate.ToLongTimeString()
   End Function
End Class
```

The real point of interest is the CreationDate() function, which returns a string that represents the time of creation.

The relevant updates to the Point class itself included modifying ToString() to account for these new bits of state data, as well as defining and creating the PointDesc type. To allow the outside world to establish a pet name for the Point, you also update the arguments passed into the overloaded constructor. Here is the complete code:

```
Public Class Point
    Implements ICloneable
    ' State data.
    Public x, y As Integer
    Public desc As PointDesc
    ' Ctors (allow for PetName)
    Public Sub New()
    End Sub
    Public Sub New(ByVal xPos As Integer, ByVal yPos As Integer, _
                   ByVal name As String)
        x = xPos
        y = yPos
        desc = New PointDesc(name)
    End Sub
    ' The sole method of ICloneable.
    Public Function Clone() As Object _
        Implements ICloneable.Clone
        ' Remember!  MemberwiseClone()
        ' copies the address of reference types!
        Return MemberwiseClone()
    End Function
    ' Override Object.ToString() and allow for PetName and time stamp.
    Public Overrides Function ToString() As String
        Return "[Name: " & desc.PetName & ", X: " & x & ", Y: " & y & _
        ", Created: " & desc.CreationDate() & "]"
    End Function
End Class
```

Notice that you did not yet update your Clone() method. Therefore, when the object user asks for a clone, a shallow (member-by-member) copy is achieved.

Therefore, the Point returned from Clone() references the same PointDesc as the original! To illustrate:

```
Dim p3 As Point = New Point(100, 100, "Jane")
Dim p4 As Point = CType(p3, Point).Clone()
Console.WriteLine("Before modification")
Console.WriteLine("Point 3: {0}", p3)
Console.WriteLine("Point 4: {0}", p4)
p4.desc.PetName = "XXXXX"
Console.WriteLine("Cloned p3 into p4 and changed p4.PetName")
Console.WriteLine("Point 3: {0}", p3)
Console.WriteLine("Point 4: {0}", p4)
```

Figure 5-7 shows the output.

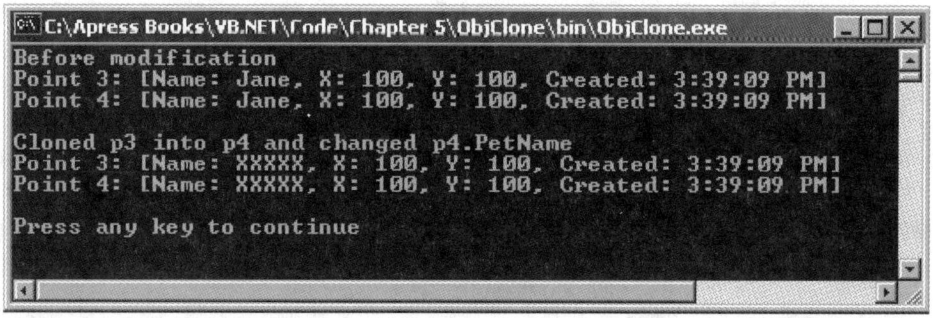

```
C:\Apress Books\VB.NET\Code\Chapter 5\ObjClone\bin\ObjClone.exe
Before modification
Point 3: [Name: Jane, X: 100, Y: 100, Created: 3:39:09 PM]
Point 4: [Name: Jane, X: 100, Y: 100, Created: 3:39:09 PM]

Cloned p3 into p4 and changed p4.PetName
Point 3: [Name: XXXXX, X: 100, Y: 100, Created: 3:39:09 PM]
Point 4: [Name: XXXXX, X: 100, Y: 100, Created: 3:39:09 PM]

Press any key to continue
```

Figure 5-7. MemberwiseClone() copies references, not values!

In order for your Clone() method to make a complete deep copy of the internal reference types, you need to bypass the MemberwiseClone() call with something along the lines of the following:

```
Public Function Clone() As Object _
        Implements ICloneable.Clone
    ' Now we need to adjust for the PointDesc type.
    Dim copyPt As Point = New Point(Me.x, Me.y, Me.desc.PetName)
    copyPt.desc = New PointDesc(Me.desc.PetName)
    Return copyPt
End Function
```

If you rerun the application once again (Figure 5-8), you see that the Point returned from Clone() does indeed reference its own copy of the PointDesc type (note the time stamp and pet name are unique).

```
C:\Apress Books\VB.NET\Code\Chapter 5\ObjClone\bin\ObjClone.exe
Before modification
Point 3: [Name: Jane, X: 100, Y: 100, Created: 3:41:06 PM]
Point 4: [Name: Jane, X: 100, Y: 100, Created: 3:41:07 PM]

Cloned p3 into p4 and changed p4.PetName
Point 3: [Name: Jane, X: 100, Y: 100, Created: 3:41:06 PM]
Point 4: [Name: XXXXX, X: 100, Y: 100, Created: 3:41:07 PM]

Press any key to continue
```

Figure 5-8. Now you have a true deep copy.

To summarize the cloning process, if you have a class or structure that contains nothing but value types, implement your Clone() method using MemberwiseClone(). However, if you have a custom type that maintains other reference types, you need to establish a new type that takes into account each internal class type.

SOURCE CODE *The ObjClone project is located under the Chapter 5 subdirectory.*

Building Comparable Objects (IComparable)

The IComparable interface (defined in the System namespace) specifies a behavior that allows an object to be sorted based on some internal key. Here is the formal C# definition of this interface:

```
// This interface allows an object to specify its
// relationship between other like objects.
interface IComparable
{
    int CompareTo(object o);
}
```

Let's assume you have updated the Car class to maintain an internal ID (of type Integer), as well as an owner supplied pet name (of type String). Object users might create an array of Car types as follows:

```
' Make an array of Car types.
Dim myAutos(4) As Car
myAutos(0) = New Car(123, "Rusty")
myAutos(1) = New Car(6, "Mary")
myAutos(2) = New Car(6, "Viper")
```

```
myAutos(3) = New Car(13, "NoName")
myAutos(4) = New Car(6, "Chucky")
```

Recall that the System.Array class defines a static method named Sort(). When you invoke this method using an array of intrinsic types (e.g., Integer, Long) you are able to sort the items in the array from lowest to highest. However, what if you send an array of Car types into the Sort() method?

```
' Sort my cars?
Array.Sort(myAutos)          ' Nope, not yet. . .sorry!
```

If you run this test, you find that an ArgumentException exception is thrown by the runtime with the following message: "At least one object must implement IComparable." Therefore, when you build custom types, you can implement IComparable to allow arrays of your types to be sorted. When you flesh out the details of CompareTo(), it is up to you to decide what the baseline of the ordering operation will be. For the Car type, the internal ID seems to be the most logical candidate:

```
' The iteration of the Car can be ordered
' based on the CarID.
Public Class Car
    Implements IComparable
. . .
    ' IComparable implementation.
    Private Function CompareTo(ByVal o As Object) _
      As Integer Implements IComparable.CompareTo
        Dim temp As Car = CType(o, Car)
        If (Me.mCarID > temp.mCarID) Then
            Return 1
        ElseIf (Me.mCarID < temp.mCarID) Then
            Return -1
        Else
            Return 0
        End If
    End Function
End Class
```

As you can see, the logic behind CompareTo() is to test a value of the incoming type against the same value of the current instance. The return value of CompareTo() is used to discover if this type is less than, greater than, or equal to the object it is being compared with (Table 5-1).

Table 5-1. CompareTo() Return Values

COMPARETO() RETURN VALUE	MEANING IN LIFE
Any number less than zero	This instance is less than object.
Zero	This instance is equal to object.
Any number greater than zero	This instance is greater than object.

Now that your Car type understands how to compare itself to like objects, you can write the following user code:

```
' Exercise the IComparable interface.
Sub Main()
    ' Make an array of Car types.
    Dim myAutos(4) As Car
    myAutos(0) = New Car(123, "Rusty")
    myAutos(1) = New Car(6, "Mary")
    myAutos(2) = New Car(6, "Viper")
    myAutos(3) = New Car(13, "NoName")
    myAutos(4) = New Car(6, "Chucky")
    ' Dump current array.
    Console.WriteLine("Here is the unordered set of cars:")
    Dim c As Car
    For Each c In myAutos
        Console.WriteLine(c.ID & "  " & c.PetName)
    Next
    Console.WriteLine()
    ' Now, sort them using IComparable.
    Array.Sort(myAutos)
    ' Dump sorted array.
    Console.WriteLine("Ordering by ID:")
    For Each c In myAutos
        Console.WriteLine(c.ID & "  " & c.PetName)
    Next
    Console.WriteLine()
End Sub
```

Figure 5-9 illustrates a test run.

As a side note, if multiple items in the Car array have the same value assigned to the ID member variable, the sort simply lists them according their occurrence in the sort (notice in Figure 5-9 there are three cars with the ID of 6).

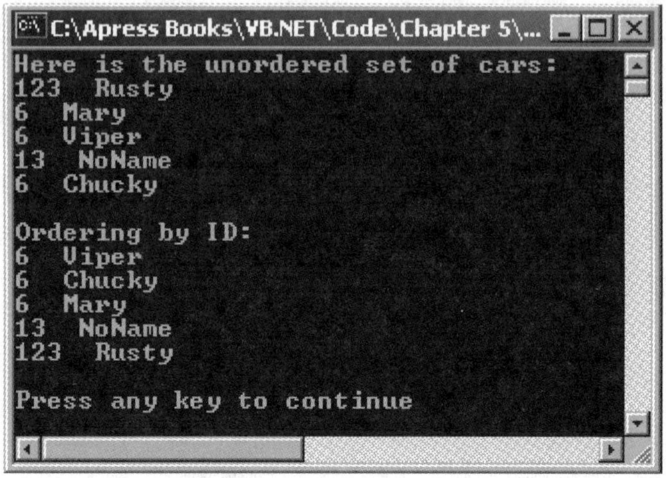

```
C:\Apress Books\VB.NET\Code\Chapter 5\...
Here is the unordered set of cars:
123  Rusty
6  Mary
6  Viper
13  NoName
6  Chucky

Ordering by ID:
6  Viper
6  Chucky
6  Mary
13  NoName
123  Rusty

Press any key to continue
```

Figure 5-9. Sorting Car types by numerical ID

Specifying Multiple Sort Orders (IComparer)

In the previous example, you used the underlying car ID to function as the baseline of the sort order. Another design might have used the pet name of the car as the basis of the sorting algorithm (to list cars alphabetically). Now, what if you wanted to build a Car that could be sorted by ID *as well as* by pet name? If this is the behavior you are interested in, you need to make friends with another standard interface named IComparer. It is defined within the System.Collections namespace as follows:

```
// A generic way to compare two objects.
interface IComparer
{
     int Compare(object o1, object o2);
}
```

Unlike the IComparable interface, IComparer is typically *not* implemented on the type you are trying to sort (i.e., the Car). Rather, you implement this interface on any number of helper objects, one for each sort order (pet name, ID, etc.). Currently, your Car type already knows how to compare itself against other cars based on the internal car ID. Therefore, to allow the object user to sort an array of Car types by pet name requires an additional helper class that implements IComparer. Here's the code:

```
' This helper class is used to sort an array of Cars by pet name.
Public Class SortByPetName
    Implements IComparer
    Public Sub New()
    End Sub
    Private Function Compare(ByVal o1 As Object, ByVal o2 As Object) _
      As Integer Implements IComparer.Compare
        Dim t1 As Car = CType(o1, Car)
        Dim t2 As Car = CType(o2, Car)
        Return String.Compare(t1.PetName, t2.PetName)
    End Function
End Class
```

Now let's make use of this new type. System.Array has a number of overloaded Sort() methods, including one that just happens to take an object implementing IComparer (see Figure 5-10 for output):

```
' Now sort by pet name.
Array.Sort(myAutos, New SortByPetName())
Console.WriteLine("Ordering by pet name:")
For Each c In myAutos
    Console.WriteLine(c.ID & "  " & c.PetName)
Next
```

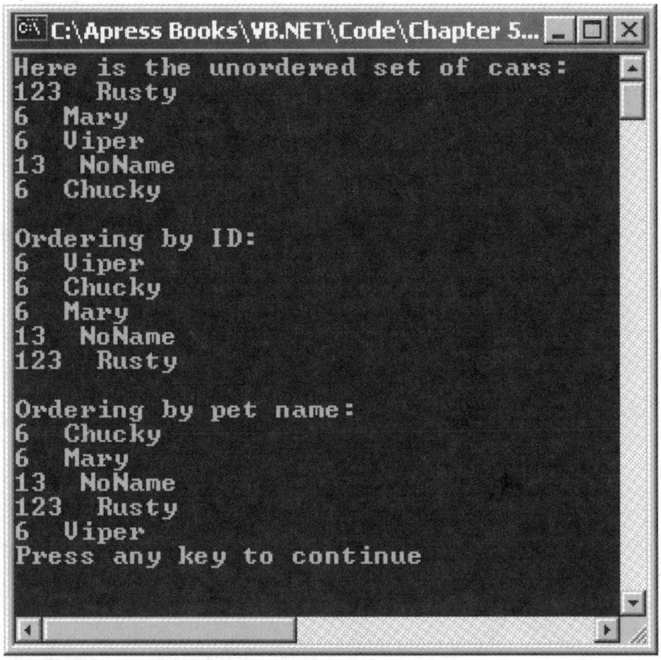

```
C:\Apress Books\VB.NET\Code\Chapter 5...
Here is the unordered set of cars:
123  Rusty
6  Mary
6  Viper
13  NoName
6  Chucky

Ordering by ID:
6  Viper
6  Chucky
6  Mary
13  NoName
123  Rusty

Ordering by pet name:
6  Chucky
6  Mary
13  NoName
123  Rusty
6  Viper
Press any key to continue
```

Figure 5-10. Sorting alphabetically by pet name

Custom Properties, Custom Sort Types

It is worth pointing out that you can make use of a shared property to help the object user along when sorting your Car types by pet name. Assume the Car class has added a shared read-only property named SortByPetName() that returns the correct IComparer interface. To keep things even more tightly encapsulated, you may want to nest the SortByPetName helper type within the Car definition:

```
    Public Class Car
    Implements IComparable
    ' Custom sort type as a nested class!
    Private Class SortByPetNameHelper
        Implements IComparer
        ' IComparer impl.
        Private Function Compare(ByVal o1 As Object, _
        ByVal o2 As Object) As Integer _
        Implements IComparer.Compare
            Dim t1 As Car = CType(o1, Car)
            Dim t2 As Car = CType(o2, Car)
            Return String.Compare(t1.PetName, t2.PetName)
        End Function
    End Class
    ' Property to return the SortByPetNameHelper comparer.
    Public Shared ReadOnly Property SortByPetName() As IComparer
        Get
            Return New SortByPetNameHelper()
        End Get
    End Property
End Class
```

The object user code can now be modified as follows:

```
' This was a bit cumbersome.
' Array.Sort(myAutos, New SortByPetName())
' Cleaner!  Just ask the car for the correct sort object.
Array.Sort(myAutos, Car.SortByPetName)
```

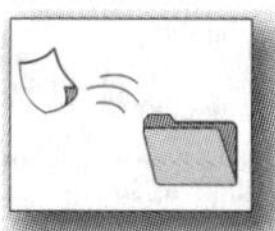

SOURCE CODE *The ObjComp project is located under the Chapter 5 subdirectory.*

Exploring the System.Collections Namespace

The most primitive VB .NET collection construct is System.Array. As you saw in Chapter 3, this class provides quite a number of member functions that offer interesting services (e.g., reversing, sorting, cloning, and enumerating). In a similar vein, this chapter has shown you how to build custom types with many of the same services using standard interfaces. To round out your appreciation of the various .NET collection constructs, the final order of business is to survey the types defined within the System.Collections namespace.

First, System.Collections defines a number of standard interfaces (many of which you have already implemented during the course of this chapter). Most of the classes defined within the System.Collections namespace implement these interfaces to provide access to their contents. Table 5-2 gives a breakdown of the core collection-centric interfaces.

Table 5-2. Interfaces of System.Collections

SYSTEM.COLLECTIONS INTERFACE	MEANING IN LIFE
ICollection	Defines generic characteristics (e.g., read-only, thread safe, etc.) for a collection class.
IComparer	Allows two objects to be compared.
IDictionary	Allows an object to represent its contents using name/value pairs.
IDictionaryEnumerator	Used to enumerate the contents of an object supporting IDictionary.
IEnumerable	Returns the IEnumerator interface for a given object.
IEnumerator	Generally used to support for each style iteration of subtypes.
IHashCodeProvider	Returns the hash code for the implementing type using a customized hash algorithm.
IList	Provides behavior to add, remove, and index items in a list of objects.

As you may suspect, many of these interfaces are related by an interface hierarchy, while others are stand-alone entities. Figure 5-11 illustrates the relationship between each type (recall that it is permissible for a single interface to derive from multiple interfaces).

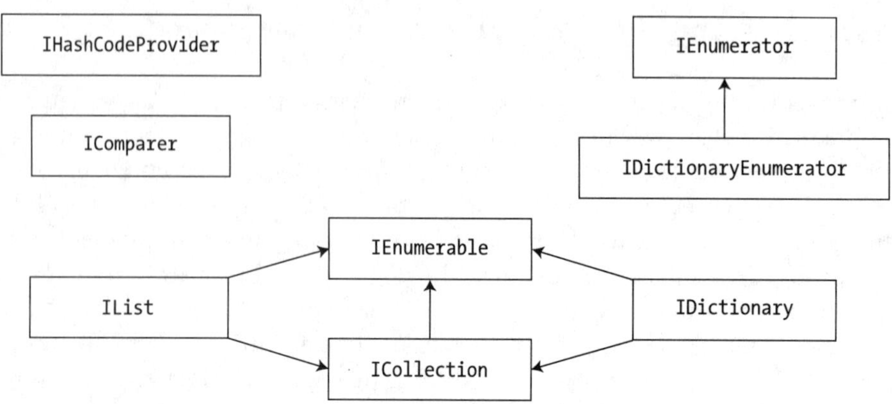

Figure 5-11. The System.Collections interface hierarchy

Now that you understand the basic functionality provided by each interface, Table 5-3 provides a rundown of the core collection classes:

Table 5-3. Classes of System.Collections

SYSTEM.COLLECTIONS CLASS	**MEANING IN LIFE**	**KEY IMPLEMENTED INTERFACES**
ArrayList	A dynamically sized array of objects.	IList, ICollection, IEnumerable and ICloneable.
Hashtable	Represents a collection of associated keys and values that are organized based on the hash code of the key. Types stored in a Hashtable should always override System.Object.GetHashCode().	IDictionary, ICollection, IEnumerable and ICloneable.
Queue	Represents a standard first-in-first-out (FIFO) queue.	ICollection, ICloneable, and IEnumerable.
SortedList	Like a dictionary. The elements can also be accessed by ordinal position (e.g., index).	IDictionary, ICollection, IEnumerable, and ICloneable.
Stack	A last-in-first-out (LIFO) queue providing push, pop (and peek) functionality.	ICollection and IEnumerable.

System.Collections.Specialized Namespace

In addition to the types defined within the System.Collections namespace, you should also be aware that the System.Collections.Specialized namespace provides another set of types that is more (pardon the redundancy) specialized. For example, the StringDictionary and ListDictionary types each provide a stylized implementation of the IDictionary interface. Now the focus is on the generic types defined within System.Collections (see online Help for additional details).

Retrofitting the Cars Type

As you begin to experiment with the System.Collections types, you find they all tend to share common functionality (that's the point of interface-based programming). Thus, rather than listing the members of each and every collection class, the final task of this chapter is to illustrate how to build a custom collection that makes use of a specific .NET collection class: ArrayList. Once you understand this type's functionality, gaining an understanding of the remaining collection classes should naturally follow.

Previously in this chapter, you created the Cars type that was responsible for holding a number of Car objects. Internally, the set of Car objects was represented with an instance of System.Array, and because of this fact, you needed to write a good deal of extra code to allow the outside world to interact with your subobjects. Furthermore, the Car array is defined with a fixed upper limit.

A more intelligent design is to represent the internal set of Car objects as an instance of System.Collections.ArrayList. Given that this class already has a number of methods to insert, remove, and enumerate its contents, the only duty of the Cars type is to supply a set of public functions that delegate to the inner ArrayList (in other words, the Cars type "has-a" ArrayList). As with any containment/delegation scenario, it is up to you to decide how much functionality of the inner object to expose to the object user. Here then, is one possible implementation of the updated Cars type:

```
' Notice we no longer need to implement IEnumerator, given that
' ArrayList already does so.
Public Class Cars
    Implements IEnumerable      ' ,IEnumerator . . . Don't need this anymore!
    ' This class maintains an array of cars.
    Private carList As ArrayList
    ' Make the ArrayList.
    Public Sub New()
        carList = New ArrayList()
    End Sub
    ' Expose select methods of the ArrayList to the outside world.
```

```
    ' Insert a car.
    Public Sub AddCar(ByVal c As Car)
        carList.Add(c)
    End Sub
    ' Remove a car.
    Public Sub RemoveCar(ByVal carToRemove As Integer)
        carList.RemoveAt(carToRemove)
    End Sub
    ' Return number of cars.
    Public ReadOnly Property CarCount() As Integer
        Get
            Return carList.Count
        End Get
    End Property
    ' Kill all cars.
    Public Sub ClearAllCars()
        carList.Clear()
    End Sub
    ' Determine if the incoming car is already in the list.
    Public Function CarIsPresent(ByVal c As Car) As Boolean
        Return carList.Contains(c)
    End Function
    ' Note we simply return the IEnumerator of the ArrayList.
    Public Function GetEnumerator() As IEnumerator Implements _
        IEnumerable.GetEnumerator
        Return carList.GetEnumerator()
    End Function
End Class
```

This new implementation also makes using the Cars type a bit less of a burden for the object user (the output is shown in Figure 5-12):

```
' Use the new Cars container class.
Sub Main()
    Dim carLot As Cars = New Cars()
    ' Add some cars.
    carLot.AddCar(New Car("Jasper", 200, 80))
    carLot.AddCar(New Car("Mandy", 140, 0))
    carLot.AddCar(New Car("Porker", 90, 90))
    carLot.AddCar(New Car("Jimbo", 40, 4))
    Console.WriteLine("You have {0} in the lot:", carLot.CarCount)
    Dim c As Car
    For Each c In carLot
        Console.WriteLine("Name: {0}", c.PetName)
```

```
        Console.WriteLine("Max speed: {0}", c.MaxSpeed)
        Console.WriteLine()
        Next
    ' Kill the third car.
    carLot.RemoveCar(3)
    Console.WriteLine("You have {0} in the lot:", carLot.CarCount)
    ' Add another car and verify it is in the collection.
    Dim temp As Car = New Car("Zippy", 90, 90)
    carLot.AddCar(temp)
    If (carLot.CarIsPresent(temp)) Then
        Console.WriteLine("{0} is already in the lot.", temp.PetName)
    End If
    ' Kill 'em all.
    carLot.ClearAllCars()
    Console.WriteLine("You have {0} in the lot:", carLot.CarCount)
End Sub
```

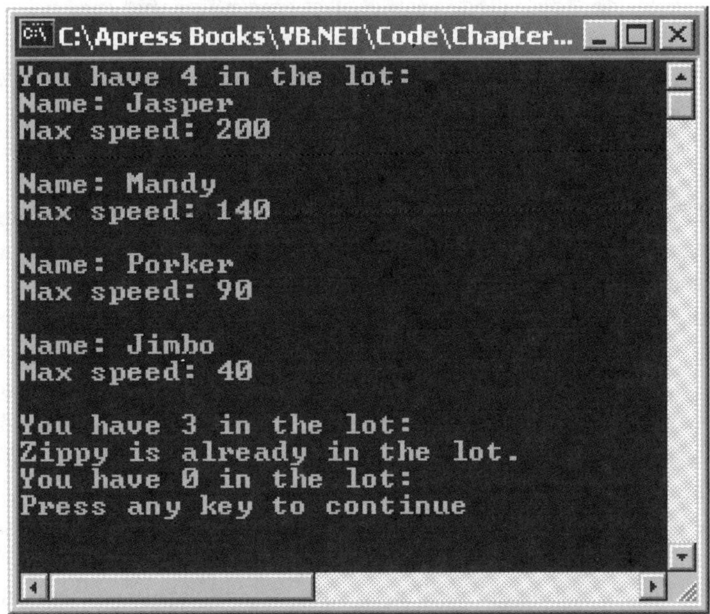

Figure 5-12. The updated Cars container

You may be wondering why you bothered to make the custom Cars type at all, given that the object user could create an ArrayList type directly. The reason is that ArrayList can contain *any* object reference. If you did not create a custom wrapper class such as Cars, the ArrayList instance could contain Cars, Boats, Airplanes, strings, or any other type!

```
Dim ar as ArrayList = New ArrayList()
ar.Add(carLot)
ar.Add("Hello")
ar.Add(New JamesBondCar())
ar.Add(23)
```

Using the containment/delegation model, you are able to leverage the functionality of the ArrayList type, while maintaining control over what can be inserted into the container.

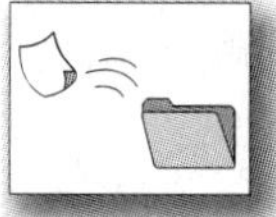

SOURCE CODE *This updated Cars collection (ObjectEnumWithCollection) can be found under the Chapter 5 subdirectory.*

Summary

If you are a COM programmer by trade, this chapter must have given you warm fuzzies. The interface is a collection of abstract members that may be implemented by a given class. Because an interface does not supply any implementation details, it is common to regard an interface as a behavior that may be supported by a given type. When two or more classes implement the same interface, you are able to treat each type the same way (aka interface-based polymorphism). VB .NET provides the interface keyword to allow you to define a new interface. As you have seen, a type can support as many interfaces as necessary using a comma-delimited list. Furthermore, it is permissible to build interfaces that derive from multiple base interfaces.

In addition to building your custom interfaces, the .NET libraries define a number of standard (i.e., framework-supplied) interfaces. This chapter focused on the interfaces defined within the System.Collections namespace. As you have seen, you are free to build custom types that implement these predefined interfaces to gain a number of desirable traits such as cloning, sorting, and enumerating.

Finally, you spent some time investigating the stock collection classes defined within the System.Collections namespace and examined the flexibility that can be obtained when combining the has-a relationship with an existing container class.

CHAPTER 6

Delegates, Events, and Callback Interfaces

UP TO THIS POINT in the text, every sample application you have developed added various bits of code to Main(), which (in some way or another) sent messages *to* a given object. However, you have not yet examined how an object can *talk back* to the entity that created it. In most programs, it is quite common for objects in a system to engage in a "two-way conversation" through the use of events, callback interfaces and other programming constructs. To prime the pump, I begin this chapter by taking you on a quick walk down memory lane to recap the event architecture supported by Visual Basic 6.0.

The bulk of this chapter however, examines various techniques provided by the .NET framework that enable the objects in your system to engage in bidirectional communications. First, you learn about the VB .NET Delegate keyword, which is little more than an object that 'points to' method(s) it is able to make calls on. Once you learn how to create and manipulate delegates, you then investigate the .NET event protocol, which is based on the delegation model. As you will see, VB .NET does a fine job of preserving the syntax of VB 6.0 event handling, while adding increased flexibility.

A Quick Recap of Events a la VB 6.0

Visual Basic 6.0 defines three keywords that allow you to declare, send, and respond to events in your applications: Event, RaiseEvent, and WithEvents. As you may know, the VB 6.0 event protocol is based on the classic COM connection point architecture. The good news is, these intrinsic VB 6.0 event keywords hide the complexity of raw COM connection points from view and take care of the necessary plumbing behind the scenes. While it is true that VB 6.0 events are naturally suited for GUI-based widgets, you can make use of events using standard non-GUI-based class types. For example, assume you have the following VB 6.0 class definition:

```
' TheEventClass class definition (VB 6.0).
Public Event SendMessage(ByVal s As String)
```

```
' When the object user calls this method, the event is fired.
Public Sub TriggerEvent()
    RaiseEvent SendMessage("The event message")
End Sub
```

Under VB 6.0, the *Event* keyword is used to define an event that may be sent at a later time using the *RaiseEvent* keyword. If the object user calls the TriggerEvent() subroutine, the object responds by firing the SendMessage event to whomever happens to be listening.

Now assume you have a VB 6.0 Form that wants to create an instance of the TheEventClass type, and receive the incoming SendMessage event. The first (mandatory) step is to declare the object variable using the *WithEvents* keyword. The next step is to build an event handler (sometimes called an "event sink") that will be called when the event is fired.

VB 6.0 event handlers must conform to a very particular syntax, namely *EventObjVariable_EventName.* In this example, if you create an instance of the TheEventClass type (named ec) the event handler for the SendMessage event must be named "ec_SendMessage" (defined using the same number of, and type of, incoming parameters). Here is the complete code:

```
' The main Form definition (VB 6.0).
Option Explicit
Private WithEvents ec As TheEventClass
Private Sub Form_Load()
    Set ec = New TheEventClass
End Sub
Private Sub btnTriggerEvent_Click()
    ec.TriggerEvent
End Sub
Private Sub ec_SendMessage(ByVal s As String)
    MsgBox s, , "Message sent from TheEventClass"
End Sub
```

Once you run this program, you see the following message shown in Figure 6-1.

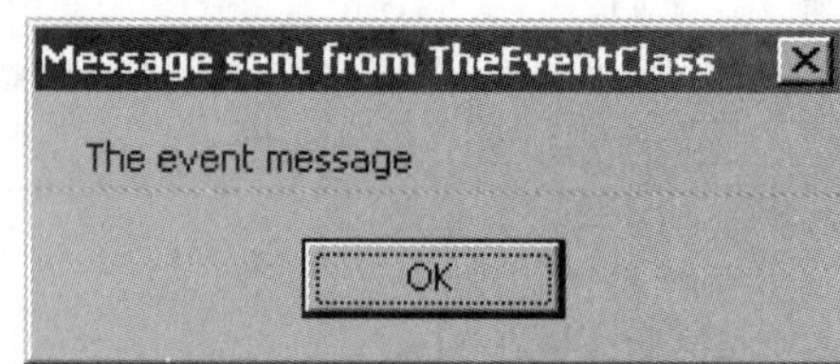

Figure 6-1. Message received

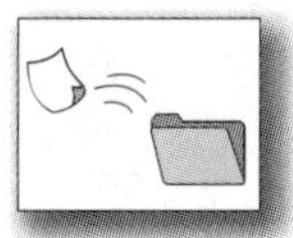

SOURCE CODE *The VB6Events project is located under the Chapter 6 subdirectory.*

A Quick Preview of VB .NET Event Handling

One drawback of the VB 6.0 event handling scheme is the fact that there is very little which marks a given event handler as the recipient of an incoming event. While it is true that experienced VB 6.0 programmers are able to parse the *EventObjVariable_EventName* naming convention with ease, the fact remains that there is nothing that uniquely identifies these oddly named subroutines as an event handler. This can be especially problematic when responding to events sent from a GUI widget.

For example, if you handle the Click event of a Button object before renaming the Button variable using the Properties window, the generated event handler is named Command1_Click(). If you do change the name of this Button type (say, to btnClickMe), the incoming event is no longer handled, as VB is now looking for an event handler named btnClickMe_Click(). At this point, it is up to you to manually relocate the logic contained in the previous event handler into the new event handler.

Ideally, the VB language would provide a specific keyword that programmatically binds a given method to a particular event. Under VB .NET, you are provided the *Handles* keyword for this very reason. For example, if you build the previous VB6Events application using VB .NET, the Form's event logic would look something like the following:

```
Public Class Form1
    Inherits System.Windows.Forms.Form
    ' Note!  You CAN combine New on the same line
    ' as 'WithEvents' under VB .NET (unlike VB 6.0).
    Private WithEvents ec As New TheEventClass()
    Friend WithEvents Button1 As System.Windows.Forms.Button
    . . .
    ' Bind Button1's Click event to the Button1_Click method.
    Private Sub ThisIsTheButton1_Click(ByVal sender As System.Object, _
       ByVal e As System.EventArgs) Handles Button1.Click
        ec.TriggerEvent()
    End Sub
    ' Bind TheEventClass' SendMessage event to the ec_SendMessage
    ' method.
    Private Sub ec_SendMessage(ByVal s As String) _
      Handles ec.SendMessage
        MessageBox.Show(s, "Message sent from TheEventClass")
```

```
    End Sub
End Class
```

You can see VB .NET still supports the WithEvents keyword. The new bit of code is the "Handles" adornment, which is placed after the argument list of the event handler method. As you can see, the Handles statement is qualified by the name of the event that is bound to a given method.

As you would hope, the VS .NET IDE still supports the VB-like drop-down event listbox, which will automatically generate the event handler stub code for any variable declared using the WithEvents keyword (Figure 6-2).

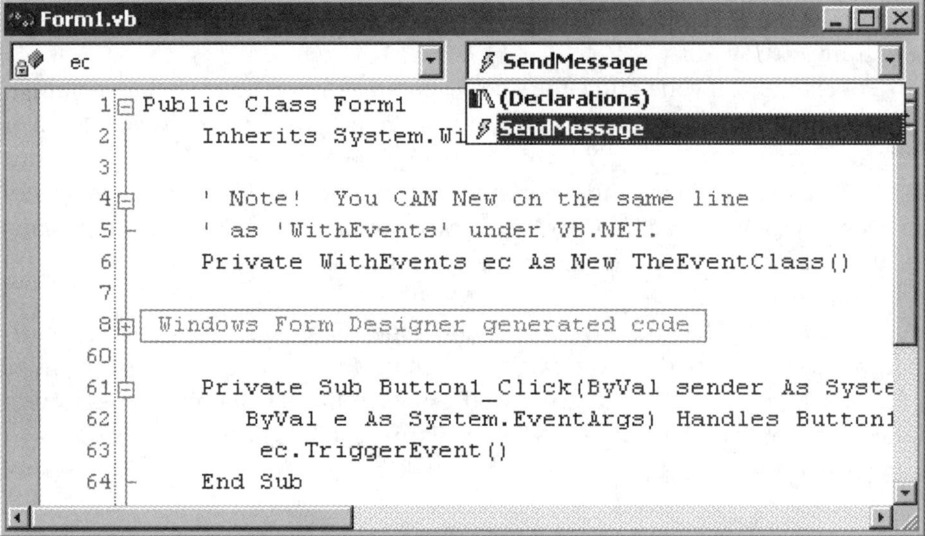

Figure 6-2. The VS .NET IDE still autogenerates event stub code.

The beauty of the Handles keyword is that it syntactically binds the method to a particular event (sent from a particular object). Understand that the name of this method is irrelevant. Thus, even though the IDE names the event handler using the VB 6.0—like *EventObjVariable_EventName* syntax, you are free to change this to whatever name suits your fancy:

```
Private Sub ThisIsTheMethodCalledByTheEventClass(ByVal s As String) _
    Handles ec.SendMessage
    MessageBox.Show(s, "Message sent from TheEventClass")
End Sub
```

As for the definition of TheEventClass itself, things look almost identical under VB .NET:

```
Public Class TheEventClass
    ' VB .NET event syntax.
    Public Event SendMessage(ByVal s As String)
    Public Sub TriggerEvent()
        RaiseEvent SendMessage("The event message")
    End Sub
End Class
```

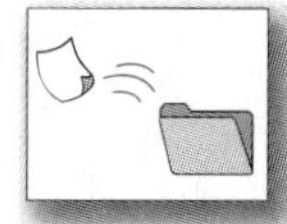

SOURCE CODE *The SimpleVBNetEvents project is located under the Chapter 6 subdirectory.*

Designing an Event Interface

In addition to the VB 6.0 event-centric keywords, you may also be familiar with the notion of defining and implementing "callback interfaces" as an alternative to the official COM connection point protocol. This technique allows a client to receive events from a class by way of a custom interface. As an example of using interfaces as a callback mechanism, let's examine how callback interfaces can be created using VB .NET (which is just about identical to building a callback interface using VB 6.0).

First, assume that the Car type defined in Chapter 4 now wants to inform the outside world when it is about to blow up (current speed is 10 miles below the maximum speed) and has exploded, by firing an event, rather than throwing a custom exception. Here, you will *not* be using the Event or WithEvents keywords, but rather the following custom interface:

```
' The engine event interface.
Public Interface IEngineEvents
    Sub AboutToBlow(ByVal msh As String)
    Sub Exploded(ByVal msg As String)
End Interface
```

This interface is implemented by a client side sink, on which the Car will make calls when a given event has occurred. Here is one possible implementation:

```
Public Class CarEventSink
    Implements IEngineEvents
    Private name As String
    Public Sub New(ByVal sinkName As String)
        name = sinkName
    End Sub
```

```
    Public Sub AboutToBlow(ByVal msg As String) _
        Implements IEngineEvents.AboutToBlow
        Console.WriteLine("{0} reporting: {1}", name, msg)
    End Sub
    Public Sub Exploded(ByVal msg As String) _
        Implements IEngineEvents.exploded
        Console.WriteLine("{0} reporting: {1}", name, msg)
    End Sub
End Class
```

Now that you have an object that implements the event interface, your next task is to pass a reference to this sink into the Car type. The Car holds onto the reference, and makes calls back on the sink when appropriate.

To allow the Car to obtain a reference to the sink, you need to add a method to the Car's public interface. Let's call this method Advise(). When the object user wants to detach from the event source, he or she may call another method, Unadvise(). Furthermore, to allow the object user to register multiple event sinks, the Car will maintain an ArrayList to represent each outstanding connection. Here are the updates to the Car type:

```
Public Class Car
    ' The set of connected sinks.
    Private itfConnections As ArrayList = New ArrayList()
    ' Attach or disconnect from the source of events.
    Public Sub Advise(ByVal itfClientImpl As IEngineEvents)
        itfConnections.Add(itfClientImpl)
    End Sub
    Public Sub Unadvise(ByVal itfClientImpl As IEngineEvents)
        itfConnections.Remove(itfClientImpl)
    End Sub
...
End Class
```

At this point, Car.SpeedUp() can be retrofitted to iterate over the list of connections and fire the correct notification when appropriate (notice that you have removed the previous exception handling code):

```
' Interface based event protocol!
Public Class Car
...
    Public Sub SpeedUp(ByVal delta As Integer)
        ' If the car is dead, send event.
        If (dead) Then
            Dim e As IEngineEvents
```

```
            Dim i As Integer
            For i = 0 To itfConnections.Count - 1
                e = CType(itfConnections(i), IEngineEvents)
                e.Exploded("Sorry, this car is dead. . .")
            Next
        Else
            currSpeed += delta
            ' Almost dead?
            If (10 = maxSpeed - currSpeed) Then
                Dim e As IEngineEvents
                Dim i As Integer
                For i = 0 To itfConnections.Count - 1
                    e = CType(itfConnections(i), IEngineEvents)
                    e.AboutToBlow("Careful buddy!  Gonna blow!")
                Next
            End If
            ' Still OK!
            If (currSpeed >= maxSpeed) Then
                dead = True
            Else
                Console.WriteLine("->CurrSpeed = {0}", currSpeed)
            End If
        End If
    End Sub
End Class
```

Understand, that using event interfaces, the client is able to control exactly when an event sink is established (and terminated). Now that the Car has been configured to maintain a list of connected sinks, here is some client side code that makes the connection:

```
' Make a car and listen to the events.
Module Module1
    Sub Main()
        ' Make a car as usual.
        Dim c1 As Car = New Car("SlugBug", 100, 10)
        ' Make 2 sink objects (just for the heck of it).
        Dim sink As CarEventSink = New CarEventSink("First sink")
        Dim myOtherSink As CarEventSink = New CarEventSink("Other sink")
        ' Hand sinks to Car.
        c1.Advise(sink)
        c1.Advise(myOtherSink)
        ' Speed up (this will generate the events.)
        Dim i As Integer
```

```
            For i = 0 To 10
                c1.SpeedUp(20)
            Next
            ' Detach sink from events.
            Console.WriteLine("->Unadvising from sink. . .")
            c1.Unadvise(sink)
            ' Speed up again (only myothersink will be called.)
            For i = 0 To 10
                c1.SpeedUp(20)
            Next
            ' Detach other sink from events.
            Console.WriteLine("->Unadvising from myOtherSink. . .")
            c1.Unadvise(myOtherSink)
            ' Speed up again (no events sent. . .)
            For i = 0 To 10
                c1.SpeedUp(20)
            Next
            Console.WriteLine("all done.")
        End Sub
    End Module
```

The output can be seen in Figure 6-3.

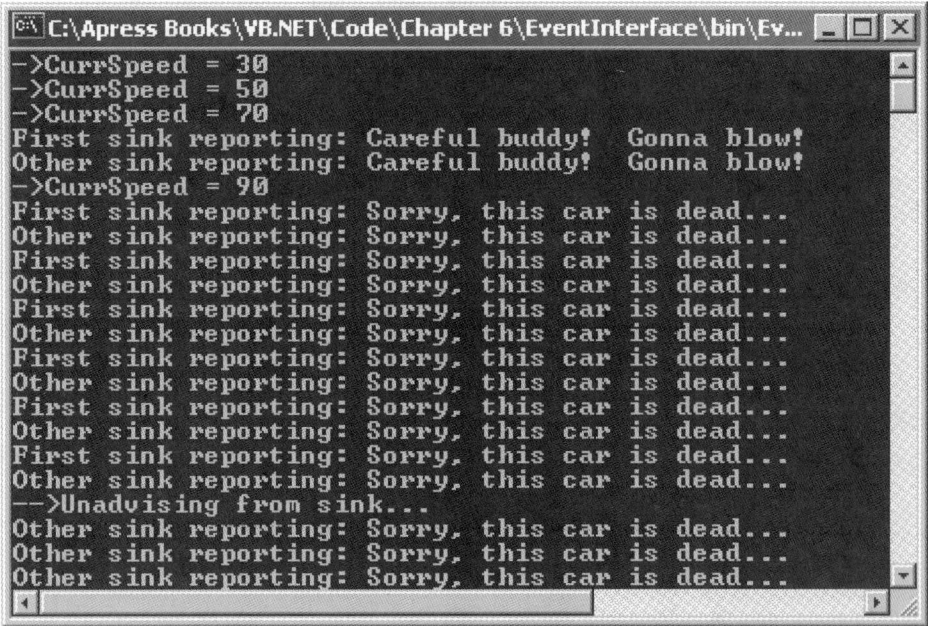

Figure 6-3. Interfaces as an event protocol

Realize that the event interface pattern would work equally well in the world of VB 6.0. However, the major drawback to building and implementing an event interface under VB 6.0 is the dreaded circular reference count phenomenon. For example, given that the Car object holds onto a reference to each client side sink, and the client holds onto a reference to the Car, neither object can be destroyed until one of the two first relinquishes its hold on the other. Under .NET, the circular reference count dilemma is avoided altogether, given that the garbage collection scheme (discussed in Chapter 4) does not make use of COM reference counting.

SOURCE CODE *The EventInterface project is located under the Chapter 6 subdirectory.*

To recap the story thus far, both VB 6.0 and VB .NET support the Event, RaiseEvent, and WithEvents keywords. Both languages support the use of callback interfaces to enable bidirectional communications. In fact at this point, it looks like the VB .NET event protocol is little more than a cleaned up version of its predecessor. However, under the hood things are markedly different. Obviously, under VB .NET these same keywords do *not* make use of the classic COM connection-point protocol (given that .NET is *not* COM). The truth of the matter is, these familiar keywords have undergone a substantial internal retrofitting to work with the .NET event architecture, the key to which is a little concept called a *delegate*.

The VB .NET Delegate Keyword

Before formally defining .NET delegates, you need a bit of perspective. Historically speaking, the Windows API makes frequent use of C style function pointers to create entities termed "callback functions" or simply "callbacks." Using callbacks, programmers were able to configure one function to report back to (call back) another function in the application. Understand that C style callback functions have nothing to do with traditional COM connection points, or event interfaces (however, in many ways the same end result was achieved).

The problem with standard C style callback functions is that they represent little more than a raw address in memory. Ideally, callbacks could be configured to include additional type-safe information such as the number of (and types of) parameters and the return value (if any) of the method pointed to. Sadly, this is not the case in traditional callback functions, and as you may suspect can therefore be a frequent source of bugs, hard crashes, and other runtime disasters.

Callbacks are useful entities. In the .NET framework, callbacks are still possible and their functionality is accomplished in a much safer and more object-oriented manner using "delegates." In essence, a delegate is an object that points to another method in the application. Specifically speaking, a delegate maintains three important pieces of information:

1. The *name* of the method on which it makes calls.
2. The *arguments* (if any) of this method.
3. The *return value* (if any) of this method.

Once a delegate has been created and provided with the aforementioned information, it may dynamically invoke the method it represents at runtime.

When you want to create a delegate in VB .NET, you make use of (surprise, surprise) the Delegate keyword. Under the hood, the Delegate keyword expands to represent a class deriving from System.MulticastDelegate. For example, if you write the following VB .NET code:

```
Public Delegate Sub PlayAcidHouse(ByVal PaulOakenfold As Object, _
ByVal volume As Integer)
```

the VB .NET compiler produces a new class named PlayAcidHouse deriving from System.MulticastDelegate. This class is only capable of calling a method that takes two parameters (of type System.Object and System.Int32) and returns nothing. If you check out how this class type is represented in metadata format using ILDasm.exe (Figure 6-4), you would see that the PlayAcidHouse type derives from System.MulticastDelegate.

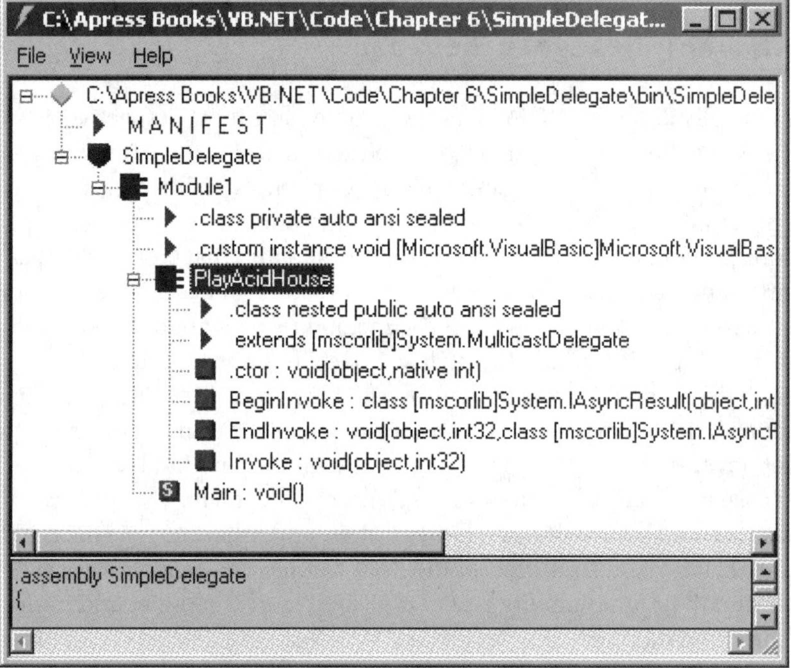

Figure 6-4. The VB .NET Delegate keyword represents a type deriving from System.MulticastDelegate.

As you can see, the PlayAcidHouse class has been endowed with three public methods. Invoke() is perhaps the core method, which may be called to inform the delegate it is time to call the method it is currently pointing to. Notice that the parameters that are sent into Invoke() are identical to the declaration of the PlayAcidHouse delegate. BeginInvoke() and EndInvoke() provide the ability to call the current method asynchronously (Invoke() on the other hand makes synchronous method calls). To keep things simple, you will only focus on the synchronous behavior of the MulticastDelegate.

Members of System.MulticastDelegate

So, when you use the Delegate keyword, you indirectly declare a type that derives from System.MulticastDelegate. The MulticastDelegate type in turn derives from System.Delegate. Together, these two base classes provide the necessary infrastructure to represent and invoke a method on the fly. Table 6-1 illustrates some interesting inherited members to be aware of.

Table 6-1. Select Inherited Members

INHERITED MEMBER	MEANING IN LIFE
Method	This property returns the name of a shared method that is maintained by the delegate.
Target	If the method to be called is defined at the object level (rather than a shared method), Target returns the name of the method maintained by the delegate. If the value returned from Target equals Nothing, the method to be called is a shared member.
Combine()	This shared method adds a method to the list maintained by the delegate.
GetInvocationList()	Returns an array of Delegate types, each representing a particular method that may be invoked.
Remove()	This shared method removes a delegate from the list methods to call.

As you may be able to infer from Table 6-1, Multicast delegates are capable of pointing to multiple methods. Under the hood, the System.Delegate type defines a linked list that is used to hold onto each method maintained by a given delegate. Additional methods can be added to this internal list using the Combine() method. To remove a method from the internal list, call Remove(). As you may know, the ability for a delegate to call multiple functions is termed "multicasting." You see this technique in action a bit later in this chapter.

The Simplest Possible Example

Delegates are the backbone of the .NET event model. For example, when you use the VB .NET Event keyword, you have actually created a new delegate. And when you send an event using the RaiseEvent keyword, the underlying IL automatically calls System.MulticastDelegate.Invoke() on your behalf. Even though VB .NET hides these details from view, delegates can be an extremely helpful construct in and of themselves. To get the ball rolling, let's take a look at a very simple example. Here is the complete code, with analysis to follow:

```
Module Module1
    ' This is the method that will be called
    ' by the delegate.
    Public Sub PlainPrint(ByVal msg As String)
        Console.WriteLine("Msg is: {0}", msg)
    End Sub
    ' Define a delegate.
    Public Delegate Sub AnyMethodTakingAString(ByVal s As String)
    Sub Main()
        ' Make the delegate.
        Dim del As AnyMethodTakingAString
        del = AddressOf PlainPrint
        del.Invoke("Hello there. . .")
        ' Dump info about the delegate.
        Console.WriteLine("I just called: {0}", del.Method)
    End Sub
End Module
```

Here, you begin by declaring a .NET delegate type using the VB .NET Delegate keyword. The AnyMethodWhichTakesAString delegate represents an object that maintains a reference to some method that takes a single String parameter and returns nothing.

When you want to assign the target (i.e., which method to call) of a given delegate, you make use of the VB .NET AddressOf keyword, which returns a brand new instance of the System.MulticastDelegate type, configured to point to the specified method. Finally, when you are ready to inform the delegate it is time to call said method, call Invoke():

```
' Tell the delegate which method to call,
' and do it!
del = AddressOf PlainPrint
del.Invoke("Hello there. . .")
```

Also be aware that you are able to specify the address of the method to call as a constructor parameter. Therefore, you could also declare and configure the delegate on a single line as follows:

```
' Make the delegate (and assign target).
Dim del As AnyMethodTakingAString = _
    New AnyMethodTakingAString(AddressOf PlainPrint)
```

Regardless of how you set the target of the delegate, you will find the output shown in Figure 6-5.

Figure 6-5. Delegating a method invocation

Notice that when you print out the method maintained by the delegate (using the Method property), you see that each parameter (in this case a single VB .NET String) is automatically mapped to the corresponding .NET system type. Also notice the presence of the Void keyword. As you know, when you create a VB .NET subroutine, you are essentially creating a function with no return value. As you may also know, many other languages (such as C#, C++, and Java) do not distinguish between functions and subroutines, but rather make use of the "void" data type to represent methods with no return value. Thus, the Void you see here is nothing more than the internal representation of a VB .NET subroutine (i.e., a method returning nothing).

A delegate object could care less about the actual name of the method it is responsible for invoking. If you want, you could dynamically change the target method as follows:

```
Module Module1
    ' The delegate will now call each of these methods.
    ' Note the signature of the method is identical.
    Public Sub PlainPrint(ByVal msg As String)
        Console.WriteLine("Msg is: {0}", msg)
    End Sub
    Public Sub UpperCasePrint(ByVal msg As String)
```

```
        Console.WriteLine("Msg is: {0}", msg.ToUpper())
    End Sub
    Public Sub XXXXYYYYZZZZ888777aaa(ByVal msg As String)
        Console.WriteLine("Msg is: {0}", msg)
    End Sub
    ' Create a delegate.
    Public Delegate Sub AnyMethodTakingAString(ByVal s As String)
    Sub Main()
        ' Make the delegate and call each method.
        Dim del As AnyMethodTakingAString
        del = AddressOf PlainPrint
        del.Invoke("Hello there. . .")
        Console.WriteLine("I just called: {0}", del.Method)
        del = AddressOf UpperCasePrint
        del.Invoke("YoYoMa")
        Console.WriteLine("I just called: {0}", del.Method)
        del = AddressOf XXXXYYYYZZZZ888777aaa
        del.Invoke("One last test. . .")
        Console.WriteLine("I just called: {0}", del.Method)
    End Sub
End Module
```

The output can be seen in Figure 6-6.

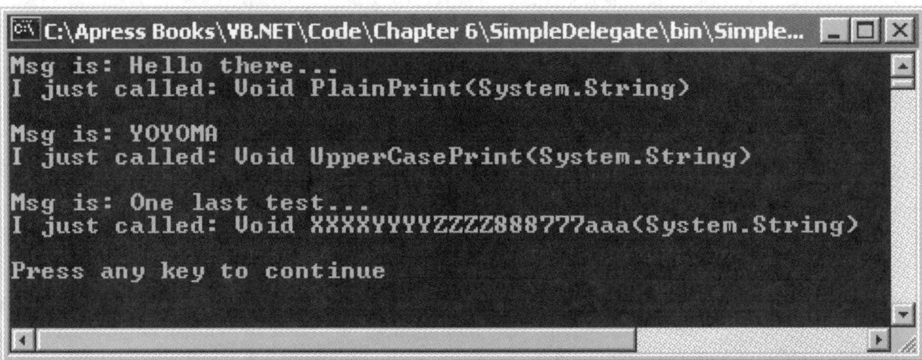

Figure 6-6. Dynamically "pointing to" various methods

If you attempt to assign the address of a method that did not match the delegates declaration:

```
' Bad target!
Public Sub BadTargetForDelegate(ByVal x As Integer, ByVal y As AppDomain)
```

```
    ' Stuff.
End Sub
. . .
' This is not a valid target! Error!
del = AddressOf BadTargetForDelegate
del.Invoke("Huh?!?")
```

you are (thankfully) issued the following compile time error (note the bolded text that highlights the crux of the error):

```
C:\Apress Books\VB .NET\Code\Chapter 6\SimpleDelegate\Module1.vb(45):
Could not find method 'Public Sub BadTargetForDelegate(x As Integer,
y As System.AppDomain)' with the same signature as the delegate
'Delegate Sub AnyMethodTakingAString(s As String)'.
```

SOURCE CODE *The SimpleDelegate project is located under the Chapter 6 subdirectory.*

Building a More Elaborate Delegate Example

Now that you have had a warm-up exercise, let's build a more complex example. To begin, let's retrofit your existing Car class (see Chapter 4) to include two new Boolean member variables. The first (isDirty) is used to determine if your automobile is due for a wash; the other (shouldRotate) represents if the car in question is in need of a tire rotation. To enable the object user to interact with this new state data, Car also defines some additional properties and an updated constructor. Here is the story so far:

```
' Another updated Car class.
Public Class Car
. . .
    ' NEW!  Are we in need of a wash? Need to rotate tires?
    Private isDirty As Boolean
    Private shouldRotate As Boolean
    ' Extra constructor params to set bools.
    Public Sub New(ByVal name As String, ByVal max As Integer, _
    ByVal curr As Integer, ByVal dirty As Boolean, ByVal rotate As Boolean)
        currSpeed = curr
        maxSpeed = max
        petName = name
        dead = False
        isDirty = Dirty
        shouldRotate = rotate
```

```
        theMusicBox = New Radio()
    End Sub
    ' Extra properties to interact with bools.
    Public Property Dirty() As Boolean
        Get
            Return isDirty
        End Get
        Set(ByVal Value As Boolean)
            isDirty = Value
        End Set
    End Property
    Public Property Rotate() As Boolean
        Get
            Return shouldRotate
        End Get
        Set(ByVal Value As Boolean)
            shouldRotate = Value
        End Set
    End Property
End Class
```

Now, assume you have declared the following delegate (which again, is nothing more than an object-oriented type representing a particular method) as a type within the project's root namespace:

```
    Public Delegate Sub CarDelegate(ByVal c As Car)
```

Here, you have created a delegate named CarDelegate. The CarDelegate type represents "some" function taking a Car as a parameter with no return type. Currently, the delegate type is decoupled from its logically related Car type (given that the CarDelegate type is just another type within the root namespace). While there is nothing horribly wrong with the approach, a more enlightened alternative would be to define the CarDelegate directly within the Car type, to keep things more tightly encapsulated:

```
Public Class Car
...
    Public Delegate Sub CarDelegate(ByVal c As Car)
...
End Class
```

Given that the VB .NET Delegate keyword produces a new class deriving from System.MulticastDelegate, the CarDelegate is now in fact a nested type definition! Again, if you check ILDasm.exe (see Figure 6-7), you see the truth of the matter.

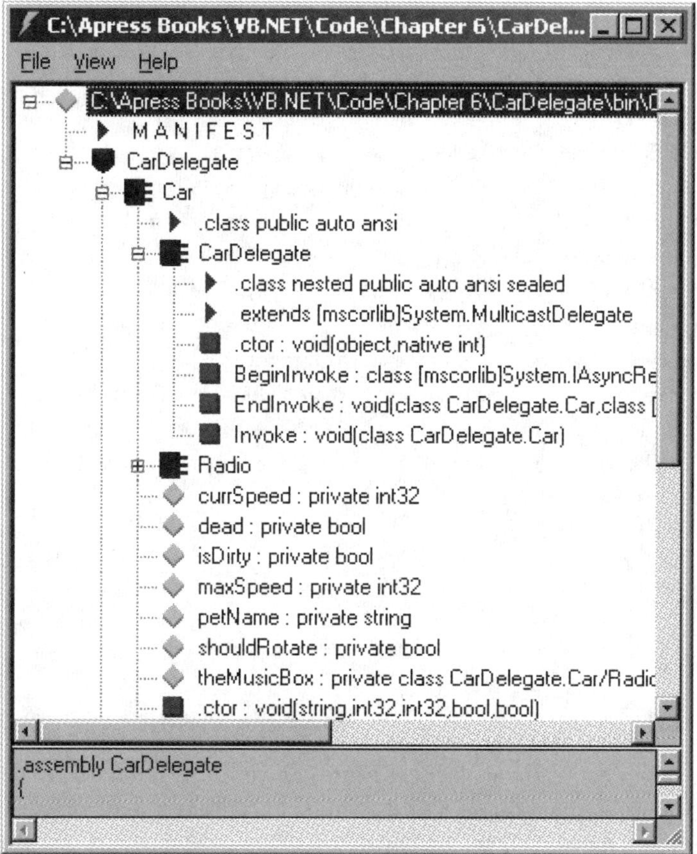

Figure 6-7. Nesting the delegate within the Car type

Using the CarDelegate

Now that you have a delegate that represent a pointer to "some" method taking a Car as a parameter, you can build other methods that take the *delegate* as a parameter. To illustrate, assume you have a new class named Garage. This type maintains a collection of Car types contained in an ArrayList. On creation, the Garage fills the ArrayList with some initial Car types.

More important, the Garage class defines a public ProcessCars() method, which takes a single argument of type Car.CarDelegate (recall that you need to specify the nesting class when referencing a nested type). In the implementation of ProcessCars(), you pass each Car in the collection as a parameter to the "function pointed to" by the delegate parameter. Here, then, is the initial definition of the Garage class:

```
Public Class Garage
    ' We have some cars.
    Private theCars As ArrayList = New ArrayList()
    Public Sub New()
        theCars.Add(New Car("Viper", 100, 0, True, False))
        theCars.Add(New Car("Fred", 100, 0, False, False))
        theCars.Add(New Car("BillyBob", 100, 0, False, True))
        theCars.Add(New Car("Bart", 100, 0, True, True))
        theCars.Add(New Car("Stan", 100, 0, False, True))
    End Sub
    ' This method takes a CarDelegate as a parameter.
    ' Therefore! 'proc' is nothing more than a function pointer. . .
    Public Sub ProcessCars(ByVal proc As Car.CarDelegate)
        ' Send each car into the method pointed to by the delegate.
        Dim c As Car
        For Each c In theCars
            proc(c)
        Next
        Console.WriteLine()
    End Sub
End Class
```

When the object user calls ProcessCars(), it sends in the name of the method that should handle this request. For the sake of argument, assume you have two shared members named WashCar() and RotateTires(). That said, consider the following Main() method:

```
' The garage delegates all work orders to these shared functions
' (finding a good mechanic is always a problem. . .)
Module Module1
    ' A target for the delegate.
    Public Sub WashCar(ByVal c As Car)
        If (c.Dirty) Then
            Console.WriteLine("Cleaning a car")
        Else
            Console.WriteLine("This car is already clean. . .")
        End If
    End Sub
    ' Another target for the delgate.
    Public Sub RotateTires(ByVal c As Car)
        If (c.Rotate) Then
            Console.WriteLine("Tires have been rotated")
        Else
```

```
            Console.WriteLine("Don't need to be rotated. . .")
        End If
    End Sub
    Sub Main()
        ' Make the garage.
        Dim g As Garage = New Garage()
        ' Wash all dirty cars.
        g.ProcessCars(AddressOf WashCar)
        ' Rotate the tires.
        g.ProcessCars(AddressOf RotateTires)
    End Sub
End Module
```

Notice (of course) that the two shared methods are an exact match to the delegate type (no return value and a single Car argument). Also, recall that when you make use of the AddressOf keyword, you are adding a method to the internal list maintained by the System.MulticastDelegate type. Figure 6-8 shows the output of this test run.

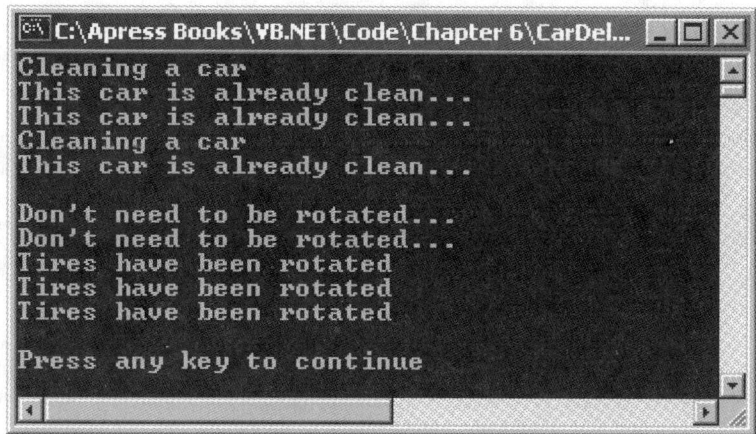

Figure 6-8. Delegate output, take one

Analyzing the Delegation Code

As you can see, the Main() method begins by creating an instance of the Garage type. This class has been configured to delegate all work to other shared functions. Now, when you write the following:

```
' Wash all dirty cars.
g.ProcessCars(AddressOf WashCar)
```

What you are effectively saying is "Add the WashCar() method to the list maintained by CarDelegate type, and pass this delegate to Garage.ProcessCars()." Like most real-world garages, the real work is delegated to another part of the system (which explains why a 30-minute oil change takes 2 hours). Given this, you can assume that ProcessCars() *actually* looks like the following under the hood:

```
' CarDelegate points to the WashCar function:
Public Sub ProcessCars(ByVal proc As Car.CarDelegate)
...
    ' Now call method for each car.
    Dim c As Car
    For Each c In theCars
        proc(c)     ' proc(c) => CarApp.WashCar(c)
    Next
...
End Sub
```

Printing Out the Target Method

To further clarify the fact that the incoming CarDelegate parameter simply points to a particular function, assume you have updated the ProcessCars() method to print out the name of the method currently pointed to. Even though you are only making use of shared functions (which can be identified by reading the Method property of the delegate type) you include the code below to accommodate future use of object level methods. Later in this chapter you will retrofit the CarDelegate's logic to make use of a helper class. You will then be assigning object level methods of the helper class to the Delegate. Object level methods can be identified by reading the Target property:

```
Public Sub ProcessCars(ByVal proc As Car.CarDelegate)
    ' Am I calling an object's method or a shared method?
    If (Not proc.Target Is Nothing) Then
        Console.WriteLine("-->Target: {0}", proc.Target)
    Else
        Console.WriteLine("-->Target is a shared method named {0}", _
                proc.Method)
    End If
    ' Now call method for each car.
    Dim c As Car
    For Each c In theCars
        proc(c)
    Next
    Console.WriteLine()
End Sub
```

The output would now look like what you see in Figure 6-9.

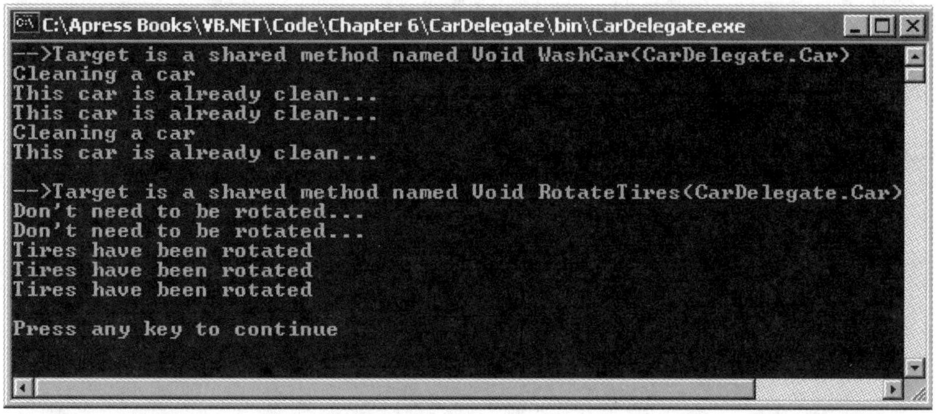

```
C:\Apress Books\VB.NET\Code\Chapter 6\CarDelegate\bin\CarDelegate.exe
-->Target is a shared method named Void WashCar(CarDelegate.Car)
Cleaning a car
This car is already clean...
This car is already clean...
Cleaning a car
This car is already clean...

-->Target is a shared method named Void RotateTires(CarDelegate.Car)
Don't need to be rotated...
Don't need to be rotated...
Tires have been rotated
Tires have been rotated
Tires have been rotated

Press any key to continue
```

Figure 6-9. Printing out the "method pointed to"

Working with Multicasting

Recall that a multicast delegate is an object that is capable of calling any number of methods. In the current example, you did not make use of this feature. Rather, you made two separate calls to Garage.ProcessCars(), specifying a new method address each time. To illustrate multicasting, assume you have updated Main() to now look like the following:

```
' Add two methods to the delegate.
Sub Main()
    ' Make the garage (as before).
    Dim g As Garage = New Garage()
    ' Create two new delegates.
    Dim wash As Car.CarDelegate = AddressOf WashCar
    Dim rotate As Car.CarDelegate = AddressOf RotateTires
    ' Combine each delegate into a single type.
    ' Note we are using the VB [. . .] syntax to specify the
    ' .NET System.Delegate type, not the VB .NET keyword of
    ' the same name.
    Dim d As [Delegate] = [Delegate].Combine(wash, rotate)
    ' Send the multicast delegate into the ProcessCars() method.
    g.ProcessCars(CType(d, Car.CarDelegate))
End Sub
```

Here, you begin by creating two new CarDelegate objects, each of which points to a given method. Next, you create a new Delegate that is holding onto the methods pointed to by the wash and rotate types. Therefore, now when you call ProcessCars(), you are actually passing in a delegate that represents the addresses of two methods (crazy, huh?).

Understand that when you call Delegate.Combine() you are adding a new function pointer to the internal list. If you want to remove a method from the internal list, you can call the static Remove() method. The first parameter marks the delegate you want to remove an item from, while the second parameter marks the item to remove:

```
' Remove the rotate method from the 'd' delegate.
Dim washOnly As [Delegate] = [Delegate].Remove(d, rotate)
g.ProcessCars(CType(washOnly, Car.CarDelegate))
```

Before you view the output of this program, let's also update Garage.ProcessCars() to print out each function pointer stored in the list using Delegate.GetInvocationList(). This method returns an array of Delegate objects, which you iterate over using for each:

```
Public Sub ProcessCars(ByVal proc As Car.CarDelegate)
    ' Where are we passing the call?
    Dim d As [Delegate]
    For Each d In proc.GetInvocationList()
        Console.WriteLine("***** Calling: {0} *****", _
        d.Method.ToString())
    Next
. . .
End Sub
```

The output is shown in Figure 6-10.

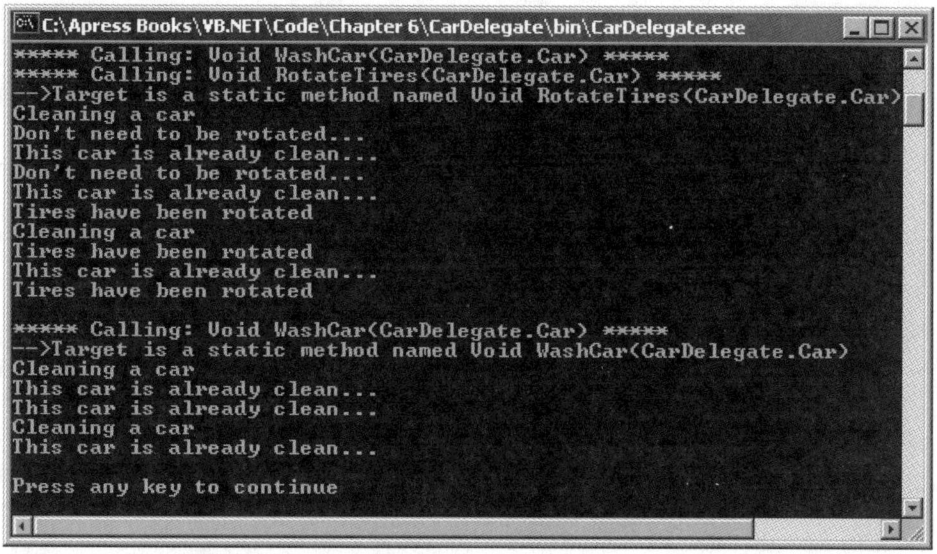

```
C:\Apress Books\VB.NET\Code\Chapter 6\CarDelegate\bin\CarDelegate.exe
***** Calling: Void WashCar(CarDelegate.Car) *****
***** Calling: Void RotateTires(CarDelegate.Car) *****
-->Target is a static method named Void RotateTires(CarDelegate.Car)
Cleaning a car
Don't need to be rotated...
This car is already clean...
Don't need to be rotated...
This car is already clean...
Tires have been rotated
Cleaning a car
Tires have been rotated
This car is already clean...
Tires have been rotated

***** Calling: Void WashCar(CarDelegate.Car) *****
-->Target is a static method named Void WashCar(CarDelegate.Car)
Cleaning a car
This car is already clean...
This car is already clean...
Cleaning a car
This car is already clean...

Press any key to continue
```

Figure 6-10. Delegate output, take two

Instance Methods As Callbacks

Currently, the CarDelegate type is storing pointers to *shared functions*. This is not a requirement of the delegate protocol. It is also possible to delegate a call to a method defined on any *object instance*. To illustrate, assume that the WashCar() and RotateTires() methods have now been moved into a new class named ServiceDept:

```
' A helper class
Public Class ServiceDept
    Public Sub WashCar(ByVal c As Car)
        If (c.Dirty) Then
            Console.WriteLine("Cleaning a car")
        Else
            Console.WriteLine("This car is already clean. . .")
        End If
    End Sub
    Public Sub RotateTires(ByVal c As Car)
        If (c.Rotate) Then
            Console.WriteLine("Tires have been rotated")
        Else
            Console.WriteLine("Don't need to be rotated. . .")
        End If
    End Sub
End Class
```

You could now update Main() as follows:

```
Sub Main()
    ' Make the garage.
    Dim g As Garage = New Garage()
    ' Make the service department.
     Dim sd As ServiceDept = New ServiceDept()
     ' Wash all dirty cars.
     g.ProcessCars(AddressOf sd.WashCar)
     ' Rotate the tires.
     g.ProcessCars(AddressOf sd.RotateTires)
     ' Create two new delegates.
     Dim wash As Car.CarDelegate = AddressOf sd.WashCar
     Dim rotate As Car.CarDelegate = AddressOf sd.RotateTires
     ' Store the new delegate for later use.
     Dim d As [Delegate] = [Delegate].Combine(wash, rotate)
     ' Send the new delegate into the ProcessCars() method.
     g.ProcessCars(CType(d, Car.CarDelegate))
     ' Remove the rotate pointer.
     Dim washOnly As [Delegate] = [Delegate].Remove(d, rotate)
     g.ProcessCars(CType(washOnly, Car.CarDelegate))
End Sub
```

Now notice the output in Figure 6-11 (check out the name of the target).

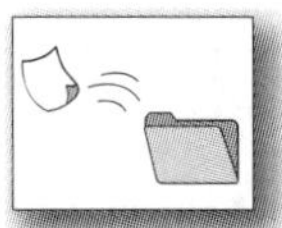

SOURCE CODE *The CarDelegate project is located under the Chapter 6 subdirectory.*

Understanding (and Using) Events

Delegates are fairly interesting constructs because you can resolve the name of a function to call at runtime, rather than at compile time. Admittedly, this syntactic orchestration can take a bit of getting used to. However, because the ability for one object to call back to another object is such a helpful construct, VB .NET provides the Event keyword to allow a simplified way to get this behavior when you do not require the flexibility of using delegates in the raw.

By way of a simple example, let's reconfigure the Car's SpeedUp() method to send custom events, rather than the callback logic seen earlier in this chapter. The first event (AboutToBlow) will be sent when the car's current speed is 10 miles below the maximum speed. The second event (Exploded) will be sent when the user attempts to speed up a car that has already been destroyed.

As seen earlier in this chapter, building a class that is able to send events is two-step process. First, you need to define the event itself using the VB .NET

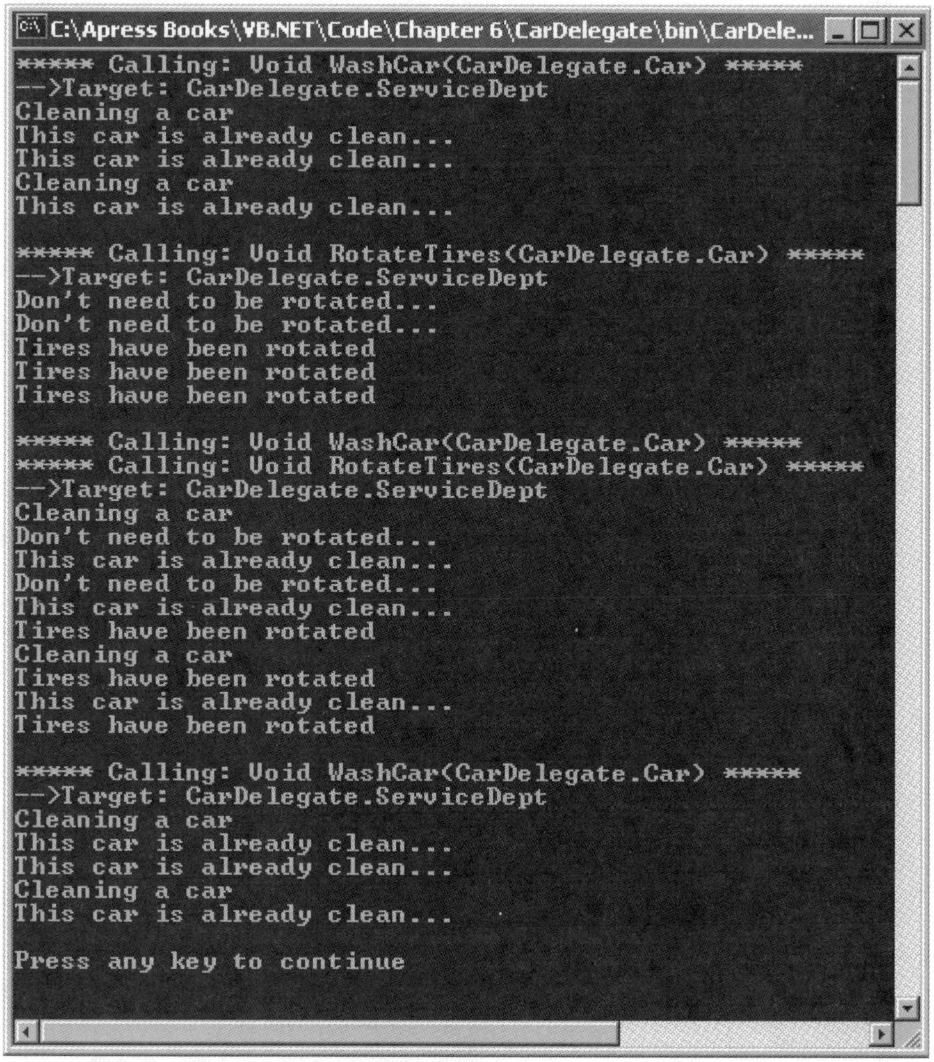

```
C:\Apress Books\VB.NET\Code\Chapter 6\CarDelegate\bin\CarDele...
***** Calling: Void WashCar(CarDelegate.Car) *****
-->Target: CarDelegate.ServiceDept
Cleaning a car
This car is already clean...
This car is already clean...
Cleaning a car
This car is already clean...

***** Calling: Void RotateTires(CarDelegate.Car) *****
-->Target: CarDelegate.ServiceDept
Don't need to be rotated...
Don't need to be rotated...
Tires have been rotated
Tires have been rotated
Tires have been rotated

***** Calling: Void WashCar(CarDelegate.Car) *****
***** Calling: Void RotateTires(CarDelegate.Car) *****
-->Target: CarDelegate.ServiceDept
Cleaning a car
Don't need to be rotated...
This car is already clean...
Don't need to be rotated...
This car is already clean...
Tires have been rotated
Cleaning a car
Tires have been rotated
This car is already clean...
Tires have been rotated

***** Calling: Void WashCar(CarDelegate.Car) *****
-->Target: CarDelegate.ServiceDept
Cleaning a car
This car is already clean...
This car is already clean...
Cleaning a car
This car is already clean...

Press any key to continue
```

Figure 6-11. Delegating to instance methods

Event keyword. Second, when you want to fire the event, you make use of the RaiseEvent keyword and specify the event you want to send. Here are the relevant updates to the Car class:

```
Public Class Car
...
    ' Is the car alive or Dead?
    Private Dead As Boolean

    ' This car can send these events.
    Public Event Exploded(ByVal msg As String)
```

```
    Public Event AboutToBlow(ByVal msg As String)
 . . .
End Class
```

Firing an event is as simple as specifying the event by name and sending out any specified parameters. To illustrate, update the previous implementation of SpeedUp() to send each event accordingly:

```
Public Sub SpeedUp(ByVal delta As Integer)
    ' If the car is Dead, send event.
    If (iDead) Then
        RaiseEvent Exploded("Sorry, this car is Dead. . .")
    Else
        currSpeed += delta
        ' Almost Dead?
        If (10 = maxSpeed - currSpeed) Then
            RaiseEvent AboutToBlow("Careful, approaching terminal speed!")
        End If
        ' Still OK?
        If (currSpeed >= maxSpeed) Then
            Dead = True
        Else ' Just print current speed if not dead.
            Console.WriteLine("--> CurrSpeed = {0}", currSpeed)
        End If
    End If
End Sub
```

With this, you have configured the car to send two custom events (under the correct conditions). You will see the usage of this new automobile in just a moment, but first, let's check the .NET event architecture in a bit more detail.

Events Under the Hood

A given VB .NET Event actually represents a good deal of information. Each time you declare an Event, the following information is generated under the hood:

1. A new hidden, nested delegate is created automatically and added to your class. The name of this delegate is always <EventName>EventHandler.

2. Two hidden public functions, one having an "add_" prefix, the other having a "remove_" prefix, are automatically added to your class. These are used internally to call Delegate.Combine() and Delegate.Remove(), to add and remove methods to/from the list maintained by the delegate.

3. A new hidden member variable is added to your class, which represents a new instance of the hidden System.MulticastDelegate type (see step 1).

Of course, though you are always free to remain blissfully unaware of these facts, it is always edifying to understand what happens under the hood. (Also be aware, that C# programmers must manually define the delegates for their class in addition to the events themselves!). To illustrate, check out Figure 6-12, a screenshot of the Car type as seen through the eyes of ILDasm.exe.

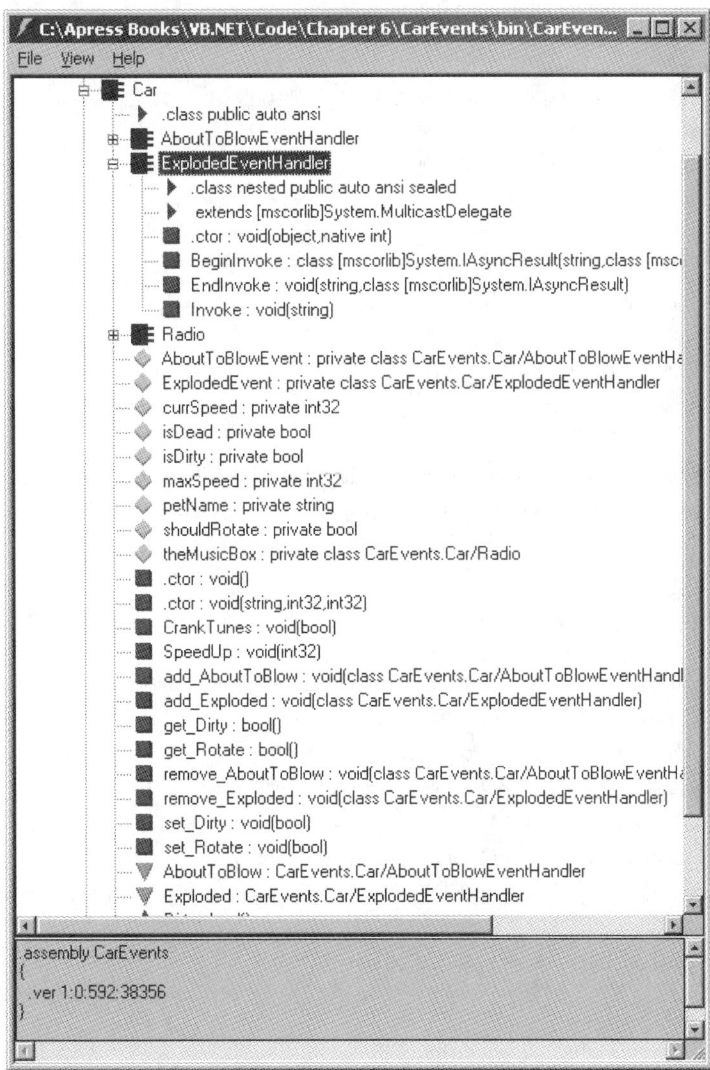

Figure 6-12. Events under the hood

If you check out the IL instructions behind add_AboutToBlow(), you would find the following (note the call to Delegate.Combine() is handled on your behalf):

```
.method public hidebysig specialname static
void  add_AboutToBlow(class CarEvents.Car/EngineHandler 'value') cil managed
synchronized
{
  // Code size       22 (0x16)
  .maxstack  8
  IL_0000:  ldsfld     class CarEvents.Car/EngineHandler CarEvents.Car::AboutToBlow
  IL_0005:  ldarg.0
  IL_0006:  call       class [mscorlib]System.Delegate
  [mscorlib]System.Delegate::Combine(class [mscorlib]System.Delegate,
  class [mscorlib]System.Delegate)
  IL_000b:  castclass  CarEvents.Car/EngineHandler
  IL_0010:  stsfld     class CarEvents.Car/EngineHandler CarEvents.Car::AboutToBlow
  IL_0015:  ret
} // end of method Car::add_AboutToBlow
```

As you may expect, remove_AboutToBlow()makes the call to Delegate.Remove() automatically:

```
.method public hidebysig specialname static
     void  remove_AboutToBlow(class CarEvents.Car/EngineHandler 'value')
                               cil managed synchronized
{
  // Code size        22 (0x16)
  .maxstack  8
  IL_0000:  ldsfld     class CarEvents.Car/EngineHandler CarEvents.Car::AboutToBlow
  IL_0005:  ldarg.0
  IL_0006:  call       class [mscorlib]System.Delegate
[mscorlib]System.Delegate::Remove(class [mscorlib]System.Delegate,
                       class [mscorlib]System.Delegate)
  IL_000b:  castclass  CarEvents.Car/EngineHandler
  IL_0010:  stsfld     class CarEvents.Car/EngineHandler CarEvents.Car::AboutToBlow
  IL_0015:  ret
} // end of method Car::remove_AboutToBlow
```

The IL instructions for the event declarations make use of the [.addon] and [.removeon] tags to establish the correct add_XXX and remove_XXX methods:

```
.event CarEvents.Car/EngineHandler AboutToBlow
{
  .addon
    void CarEvents.Car::add_AboutToBlow(class CarEvents.Car/EngineHandler)
  .removeon
    void CarEvents.Car::remove_AboutToBlow(class CarEvents.Car/EngineHandler)
} // end of event Car::AboutToBlow
```

Perhaps most important, if you check out the IL behind this iteration of the SpeedUp() method, you find that the delegate is invoked on your behalf. Here is a partial snapshot of the intermediate language:

```
.method public instance void  SpeedUp(int32 delta) cil managed
{
  . . .
  IL_000a:  ldfld      class CarEvents.Car/ExplodedEventHandler
  CarEvents.Car::ExplodedEvent
  IL_000f:  ldnull
  IL_0010:  beq.s      IL_0023
  IL_0012:  ldarg.0
  IL_0013:  ldfld      class CarEvents.Car/ExplodedEventHandler
  CarEvents.Car::ExplodedEvent
  IL_0018:  ldstr      "Sorry, this car is Dead. . ."
  IL_001d:  callvirt
    instance void CarEvents.Car/ExplodedEventHandler::Invoke(string)
  IL_0022:  nop
. . .
}
```

As you can see, the VB .NET event keywords are very helpful, given that they build and manipulate raw delegates on your behalf! As you saw earlier in this chapter however, VB .NET allows you to directly manipulate delegates if you so choose. Now that you understand how to build a class that can send events, the next big question is how you can configure an object to receive these events.

Hooking into Incoming Events (WithEvents)

Assume you have now created an instance of the Car class and want to listen to the events it is capable of sending. As you have already seen at the beginning of this chapter, you can hook into an event using the WithEvents/Handles keywords. Thus, you would write the following trivial module definition:

```
Module Module1
    ' Use WithEvents.
    Dim WithEvents c As New Car("NightRider", 50, 0)
    Public Sub MyExplodedHandler(ByVal s As String) _
    Handles c.Exploded
        Console.WriteLine(s)
    End Sub
    Public Sub MyAboutToDieHandler(ByVal s As String) _
    Handles c.AboutToBlow
        Console.WriteLine(s)
    End Sub
    Sub Main()
        Dim i As Integer
        For i = 0 To 10
            c.SpeedUp(10)
        Next
    End Sub
End Module
```

Using this approach, things look more or less like traditional VB 6.0 event logic. The output is seen in Figure 6-13.

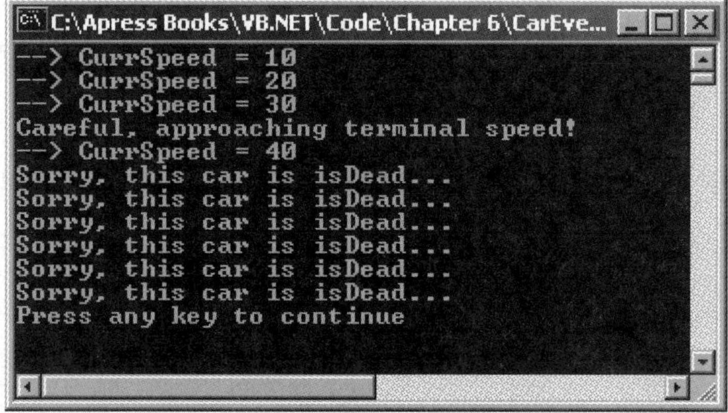

Figure 6-13. Handling events using WithEvents

One extremely useful aspect of the Handles statement is the fact that you are able to configure multiple methods to listen to the same event! For example, if you update your Module as follows:

```
Module Module1
    ' Use WithEvents.
    Dim WithEvents c As New Car("NightRider", 50, 0)
    Public Sub MyExplodedHandler(ByVal s As String) Handles c.Exploded
        Console.WriteLine(s)
    End Sub
    Public Sub MyAboutToDieHandler(ByVal s As String) Handles c.AboutToBlow
        Console.WriteLine("About to die 1: {0}", s)
    End Sub
    Public Sub MyAboutToDieHandler2(ByVal s As String) Handles c.AboutToBlow
        Console.WriteLine("About to die 2: {0}", s)
    End Sub
    Sub Main()
        Dim i As Integer
        For i = 0 To 10
            c.SpeedUp(10)
        Next
    End Sub
End Module
```

You would now find that the AboutToBlow event is sent to both methods configured to handle Car.AboutToBlow! Check out Figure 6-14.

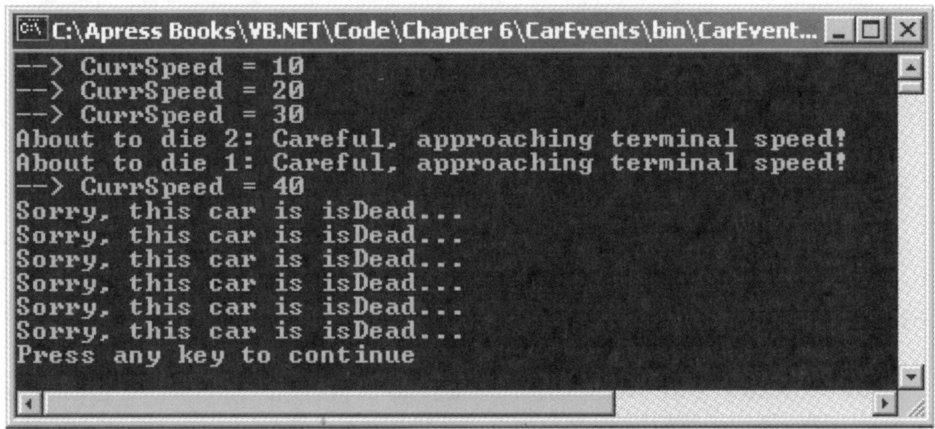

Figure 6-14. Multicasting events using the Handles keyword

Given that GUI widgets are also declared using the WithEvents keyword, you may also configure a GUI-based event to be sent to multiple event sinks.

Hooking into Incoming Events (Dynamically)

The previous approach is simple, well known, and gets the job done just fine in a good number of cases. However, using VB .NET you do have an alternate method that may be used to hook into an event. It is possible to declare an object without using the WithEvents keyword, and dynamically rig together an event handler *at runtime.* To do so, you ultimately need to call the correct add_XXX() method to ensure that your method is added to the list of function pointers maintained by the Car's internal delegate (remember! the Event keyword expands to produce – among other things – a nested delegate). However, you do not call add_XXX() and remove_XXX() directly, but rather use AddHandler and RemoveHandler statements.

Just as when working with raw delegates, you may specify a shared method or an object level method when using the AddHandler/RemoveHandler statements. To keep things interesting, assume you have the following helper class that will be used to represent the event sink (notice the *lack* of the Handles statement):

```
' Car event sink
Public Class CarEventSink
    ' OnBlowUp event sink A.
    Public Sub OnBlowUp(ByVal s As String)
        Console.WriteLine("Message from car: {0}", s)
    End Sub
    ' OnBlowUp event sink B.
    Public Sub OnBlowUp2(ByVal s As String)
        Console.WriteLine("-->AGAIN I say: {0}", s)
    End Sub
    ' OnAboutToBlow event sink.
    Public Sub OnAboutToBlow(ByVal s As String)
        Console.WriteLine("Message from car: {0}", s)
    End Sub
End Class
```

You could now build a new Car type and hook up a new handler on the fly as follows (note the *lack* of the WithEvents keyword):

```
Sub Main()
    Dim i as Integer
    ' Make a car as usual.
    Dim c1 As Car = New Car("SlugBug", 100, 10)
    ' Make sink object.
    Dim sink As CarEventSink = New CarEventSink()
```

```
    ' Hook into events using handlers.
    AddHandler c1.Exploded, AddressOf sink.OnBlowUp
    AddHandler c1.Exploded, AddressOf sink.OnBlowUp2
    AddHandler c1.AboutToBlow, AddressOf sink.OnAboutToBlow
    ' Speed up (this will generate the events.)
    For i = 0 To 10
        c1.SpeedUp(20)
    Next
    ' Detach from events using handlers
    RemoveHandler c1.Exploded, AddressOf sink.OnBlowUp
    RemoveHandler c1.Exploded, AddressOf sink.OnBlowUp2
    RemoveHandler c1.AboutToBlow, AddressOf sink.OnAboutToBlow
    ' No response!
    For i = 0 To 10
        c1.SpeedUp(20)
    Next
    End Sub
End Module
```

As you can see, the AddHandler statement requires the name of the event you want to listen to, and the address of the method that will be invoked when the event is sent. Here, you also enabled multicasting, given that you have associated the Exploded event to two separate methods of the sink. RemoveHandler works in the same manner. The output of this example is seen in Figure 6-15.

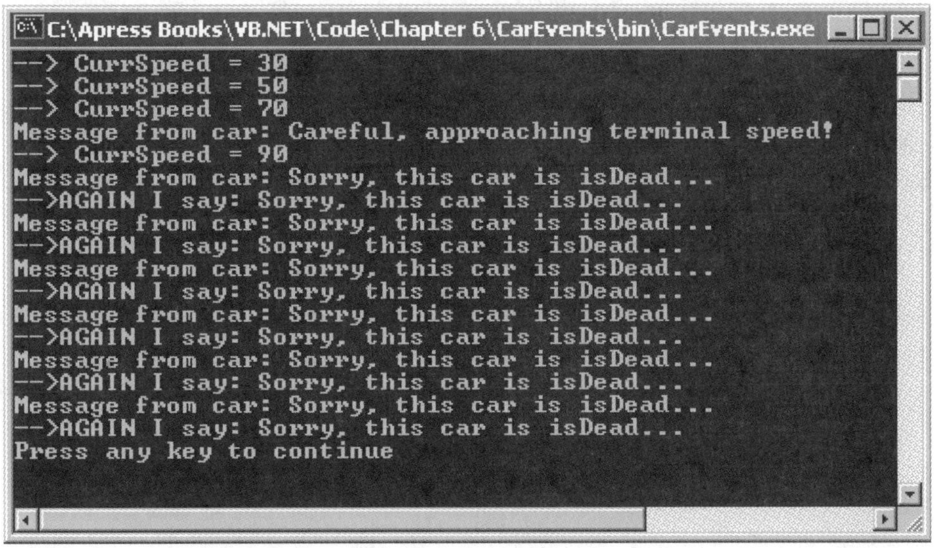

```
C:\Apress Books\VB.NET\Code\Chapter 6\CarEvents\bin\CarEvents.exe
--> CurrSpeed = 30
--> CurrSpeed = 50
--> CurrSpeed = 70
Message from car: Careful, approaching terminal speed!
--> CurrSpeed = 90
Message from car: Sorry, this car is isDead...
-->AGAIN I say: Sorry, this car is isDead...
Message from car: Sorry, this car is isDead...
-->AGAIN I say: Sorry, this car is isDead...
Message from car: Sorry, this car is isDead...
-->AGAIN I say: Sorry, this car is isDead...
Message from car: Sorry, this car is isDead...
-->AGAIN I say: Sorry, this car is isDead...
Message from car: Sorry, this car is isDead...
-->AGAIN I say: Sorry, this car is isDead...
Message from car: Sorry, this car is isDead...
-->AGAIN I say: Sorry, this car is isDead...
Press any key to continue
```

Figure 6-15. Handling your Car's event set

At this point you may wonder when (or if) you would ever need to make use of the AddHandler and RemoveHandler statements, given that VB .NET still supports the WithEvents syntax. Again, understand that this approach is very powerful, given that you have the ability to detach from an event source at will. When you make use of the WithEvent keyword, you will continuously receive events from the source object until the object dies (which typically means until the client application is terminated). Using the RemoveHandler statements, you can simply tell the object "Stop sending me this event" even though the object may be alive and well in memory.

SOURCE CODE *The CarEvents project is located under the Chapter 6 subdirectory.*

Summary

The purpose of this chapter was to round out your understanding of the key features of the VB .NET language. You are now well-equipped to build sophisticated object models that function well within the .NET universe. The chapter began with a quick recap of the event model of VB 6.0, including the use of custom callback interfaces (which are still valid constructs in VB .NET).

You have also seen a number of ways in which multiple objects can partake in a bidirectional conversation under .NET. First, you have the new VB .NET Delegate keyword, which is used to indirectly construct a class derived from System.MulticastDelegate. As you have seen, a delegate is simply an object that maintains a list of methods to call when told to do so (most often using the Invoke() method).

Next, there are the good old Event, RaiseEvent and WithEvents keywords. Although they have been retrofitted under the hood to work with .NET delegates rather than COM connection points, they look and feel much the same. As you have seen, VB .NET now supports the Handles statement, which is used to syntactically associate an event to a given method (the Handles statement allows you to enable multicasting).

Finally, you examined the process of hooking into (and detaching from) an event dynamically using the AddHandler and RemoveHandler statements. This is a very welcome addition to the Visual Basic language, given that you now have a type safe way to dynamically intercept events on the fly.

CHAPTER 7

Assemblies, Threads, and AppDomains

EACH OF THE APPLICATIONS developed during the first six chapters are along the lines of traditional "stand-alone" applications, given that all programming logic was contained within a single (EXE) binary. One aspect of the .NET lifestyle is the notion of binary reuse. Like COM, .NET provides the ability to reuse types among binaries in a language-independent manner. However, the .NET platform provides far greater language integration than classic COM. For example, the .NET platform supports cross-language inheritance (imagine a Visual Basic .NET class *deriving from* a C# class). To understand how this is achieved requires a deeper understanding of assemblies.

Once you understand the logical and physical layout of an assembly (and the related assembly manifest), you then learn to distinguish between "private" and "shared" assemblies. You also examine exactly how the .NET runtime resolves the location of an assembly and come to understand the role of the Global Assembly Cache (GAC). Closely related to location resolution is the notion of application configuration files. As you will see, the .NET runtime can read the XML-based data contained within this file to bind to a specific version of a shared assembly (among other things). You are free to build XML configuration files by hand, or make use of the .NET Administration tool.

This chapter wraps up with an examination of building multithreaded assemblies, using the types defined within the System.Threading namespace. If you come from a Win32 background, you will be pleased to see how nicely thread manipulation has been cleaned up under the .NET Framework.

Problems with Classic COM Binaries

Binary reuse (i.e., portable code libraries) is not a new idea. To date, the most popular way in which a programmer can share types between binaries (and in some respects, across languages) is to build what can now be regarded as "classic COM servers." Although the construction and use of COM binaries is a well-established industry standard, these little blobs have caused each of us a fair share of headaches. Beyond the fact that COM demands a good deal of complex infrastructure (even though VB 6.0 does a fantastic job of hiding the guts), I am sure you have also pondered the following related questions:

- Why is it so difficult to version my COM binary?
- Why is it so difficult to distribute my COM binary?

The .NET Framework greatly improves on the current state of affairs and addresses the versioning and deployment problems head-on using a new binary format termed an *assembly.* However, before you come to understand how the assembly offers a clean solution to these issues, let's spend some time recapping the problems in a bit more detail.

COM Versioning

In COM, you build entities named *coclasses* that are little more than a custom UDT (user defined type) implementing any number of COM interfaces (including the mandatory IUnknown, which VB 6.0 implements automatically). The coclasses are then packaged into a binary home, which is physically represented as a DLL or EXE file. Once all the (known) bugs have been squashed out of the code, the COM binary eventually ends up on some user's computer, ready to be accessed by other programs.

The versioning problem in COM revolves around the fact that the COM runtime offers no intrinsic support to enforce that the correct version of a binary server is loaded for the calling client. It is true that a VB 6.0 COM programmer can modify the version of the type library, establish binary compatibility, and even reengineer the client's code base to reference a particular library. But, the fact remains that these are tasks delegated to *the programmer* and typically require rebuilding the COM client and or COM server. As many of you have learned the hard way, this is far from ideal.

Assume that you have jumped through the necessary hoops to try to ensure the COM client activates the correct version of a COM binary. Your worries are far from over, given that some other application may be installed on the target machine that overrides your carefully configured registry entries (and maybe even replaces a COM server or two with an earlier version during the process). Mysteriously, your client application may now fail to operate.

For example, if you have ten applications that all require the use of MyCOMServer.dll version 1.4, and another application installs MyCOMServer.dll version 2.0, all ten applications are at risk of breaking. This is because you cannot be assured of complete backward compatibility. In a perfect world, all versions of a given COM binary are fully compatible with previous versions. In practice however, keeping COM servers (and software in general) completely backward compatible is extremely difficult.

The lump sum of each of these versioning scenarios is lovingly referred to as "DLL Hell" (which, by the way, is not limited to COM DLLs; traditional C DLLs suffer the same hellish existence). As you'll see during the course of this chapter, the .NET Framework solves this nightmare by using a number of techniques, including private assemblies, side-by-side execution, and a very robust (yet very simple) versioning scheme.

In a nutshell, .NET allows multiple versions of the same binary to be installed on the same target machine. Therefore, under .NET, if client A requires MyDotNETServer.dll version 1.4 and client B demands MyDotNETServer.dll version 2.0, the correct version is loaded for the respective client automatically. You are also able to dynamically bind to a specific version using an XML application configuration file. This is an extremely helpful aspect of .NET, given that you can alter which code library should be used for a given client, *without* the need to recompile the code base or update the system registry.

COM Deployment

The COM runtime is a rather temperamental service. Under the hood, when a COM client wants to make use of a COM object, the first step is to load the COM libraries for use by a given thread by calling CoInitialize(), which is done automatically by VB 6.0 EXE applications. At this point, the client makes additional calls to the COM runtime using the COM mapping provided by a given programming language (e.g., New or CreateObject() for VB programmers, CoCreateInstance() or CoGetClassObject() for C++ developers, and so forth) to load a given binary into memory. The end result is that the COM client receives an interface reference that is then used to manipulate the contained object.

In order for the COM runtime to locate and load a binary, the COM server must be configured correctly on the target machine. From a high level, registering a COM server sounds so simple: Build an installation program (or make use of a system supplied registration tool such as RegSvr32.exe) to trigger the correct logic in the COM binary (DllRegisterServer() for DLLs or WinMain() for EXEs) and call it a day. However, as you may know, a COM server requires a vast number of registration entries to be made. Typically, every COM class (CLSID), interface (IID), type library (LIBID), and application (AppID) must be inserted into the system registry.

The key point to keep in mind is that the relationship between the binary image and the correct registry entries is extremely loose, and therefore extremely fragile. In COM, the location of the binary image (e.g., MyServer.dll) is entirely separate from the massive number of registry entries that completely describe the component. Therefore, if the end user relocated (or renamed) a COM server, the entire system breaks, as the registration entries are now out of sync.

The fact that classic COM servers require a number of external registration details also introduces another deployment difficulty: The same entries must be made on *every machine referencing the server.* Thus, if you have installed your COM binary on a remote machine, and if you have 100 client machines accessing this COM server, this means 101 machines must be configured correctly. To say the least, this is a massive pain in the neck.

The .NET platform makes the process of deploying an application extremely simple given the fact that .NET binaries (i.e., assemblies) are not registered in the system registry at all. Plain and simple. Instead, assemblies are completely self-describing entities. Deploying a .NET application can be (and most often is) as simple as copying the files that compose the application to some location on the machine, and running your program. In short, be prepared to bid a fond farewell to server registration.

An Overview of .NET Assemblies

Now that you understand the problems, let's check out the solution. .NET applications are constructed by piecing together any number of assemblies. Simply put, an assembly is nothing more than a versioned, self-describing binary (DLL or EXE) containing some collection of types (classes, interfaces, structures, and so on) and optional recourses (images, string tables, and whatnot). One thing to be painfully aware of right now is that the internal organization of a .NET assembly is nothing like the internal organization of a classic COM server (regardless of the shared file extensions).

For example, an in-process COM server exports four functions (DllCanUnloadNow(), DllGetClassObject(), DllRegisterServer(), and DllUnregisterServer()) to allow the COM runtime to access its contents (again, all of which are created automatically for VB 6.0 COM DLLs). .NET DLLs, on the other hand, require only one function export: DllMain().

Local COM servers define WinMain() as the sole entry point into the EXE, which is implemented to test for various command-line parameters to perform the same duties as a COM DLL. Not so under the .NET protocol. Although .NET EXE binaries do provide a WinMain() entry point (or main() for console applications), the behind-the-scenes logic is entirely different.

The physical format of a .NET binary is actually more similar to a traditional (non-COM) portable executable (PE) and Common Object File Format (COFF) file formats. The true difference is that a traditional PE/COFF file contains instructions that target a specific platform and specific CPU. In contrast, .NET binaries contain code constructed using Microsoft Intermediate Language (MSIL, or simply IL), which is platform- and CPU-agnostic. At runtime, the internal IL is compiled on the fly (using a just-in-time compiler) to platform and CPU specific instructions. This is a powerful extension of classic COM in that .NET assemblies are poised to be platform neutral entities that are not necessarily tied to the Windows operating system.

In addition to raw IL, recall that an assembly also contains *metadata* that completely describes each type living in the assembly, as well as the full set of members supported by each type. For example, if you created a class named JoyStick using some .NET-aware language, the corresponding compiler emits metadata describing all the fields, methods, properties, and events defined by this custom type. The .NET runtime uses this metadata to resolve the location of types (and their members) within the binary, create object instances, as well as to facilitate remote method invocations. As you will see in the next chapter, you can programmatically obtain metadata from an assembly using a process termed *reflection*.

Unlike traditional file formats or classic COM servers, an assembly must contain an associated *assembly manifest* (also referred to as "assembly metadata"). The manifest documents each module within the assembly, documents the version of the assembly, and also documents any *external* assemblies referenced by the current assembly (unlike a classic COM type library that does not document required external dependencies). Given this, a .NET assembly is completely self-describing.

Single File and Multifile Assemblies

Under the hood, a given assembly can be composed of multiple *modules*. A module is really nothing more than a generic name for a valid file. In this light, an assembly can be viewed as a unit of deployment (often termed a "logical DLL"). In many situations, an assembly is in fact composed of a single module. In this case, there is a one-to-one correspondence between the (logical) assembly and the underlying (physical) binary, as shown in Figure 7-1.

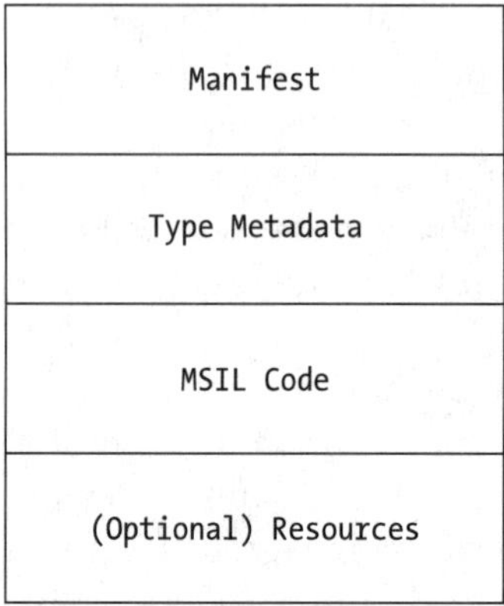

Figure 7-1. A single file assembly

On the other hand, multifile assemblies are composed of (pardon the redundancy) numerous files. A multifile assembly will contain one file that contains the assembly manifest (a *.dll or *.exe file), at least one additional code module (which by convention ends in a *.netmodule file extension) and any optional external resources. Understand that the file containing the assembly manifest records each external *.netmodule. Thus, although multifile assemblies contain a number of individual files, the assembly concept ensures that collectively, each is named and versioned as a *single logical unit.* Also understand that multifile assemblies are not literally linked together into a new (larger) file. Rather, each module in a multifile assembly is logically related by information contained in the corresponding manifest.

Each module in a multifile assembly also contains a *module level* manifest. As you might expect, a module's manifest does not list references to other files in the assembly. It simply lists the external assemblies that are required for it to function correctly. For example, if your *.netmodule makes use of the Console type, the module's manifest will contain a listing for mscorlib.dll. The big picture is shown in Figure 7-2.

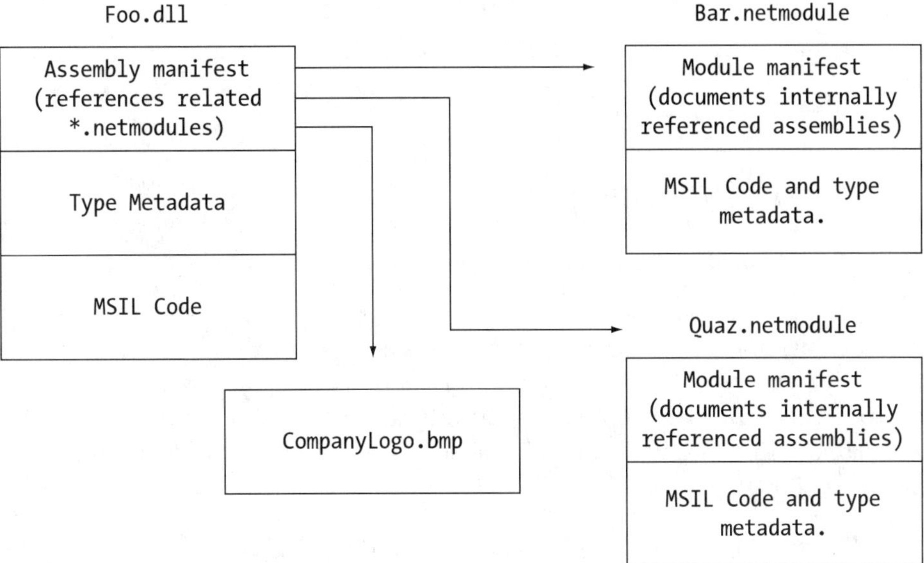

Figure 7-2. A multifile assembly

When you create an assembly that is composed of multiple modules, one benefit is efficient code download. For example, assume you have a remote client that is referencing a multifile assembly composed of three modules. If the remote application references only one of these modules, the .NET runtime only downloads the currently referenced file. In other words, modules in a multifile assembly are loaded on demand. If each module is 1MB in size, I'm sure you can see the benefits. Another benefit is that a multifile assembly can be composed of various *.netmodule files written in different .NET-aware languages. You revisit multifile assemblies later in this chapter.

Two Views of an Assembly: Physical and Logical

As you begin to work with .NET binaries, it can be helpful to regard an assembly (both single file and multifile) as having two conceptual views. When you build an assembly, you are interested in the *physical* view. In this case, the assembly can be realized as some number of files that contain your custom types and resources (see Figure 7-3).

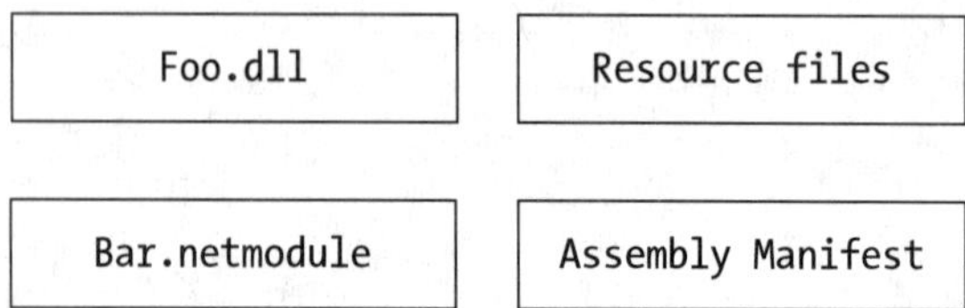

Figure 7-3. Physically, an assembly is a collection of modules

As an assembly consumer, you are interested in a *logical* view of the assembly (see Figure 7-4). In this case, you can understand an assembly as a versioned collection of public types that you can use in your current application (recall that "Friendly" types can only be referenced by the assembly in which they are defined).

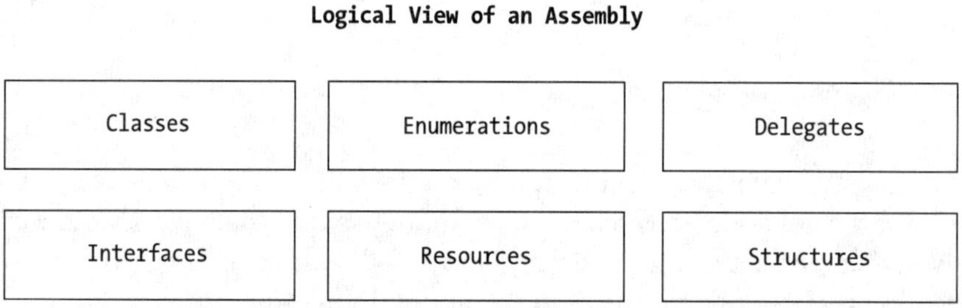

Logical View of an Assembly

Classes

Enumerations

Delegates

Interfaces

Resources

Structures

Figure 7-4. Logically, an assembly is a collection of types

For example, the kind folks in Redmond who developed System.Drawing.dll created a physical assembly for you to consume in your applications. However, although System.Drawing.dll can be physically viewed as a binary DLL, you logically regard this assembly as a collection of related types. Of course, ILDasm.exe is the tool of choice when you are interested in discovering the logical layout of a given assembly (see Figure 7-5).

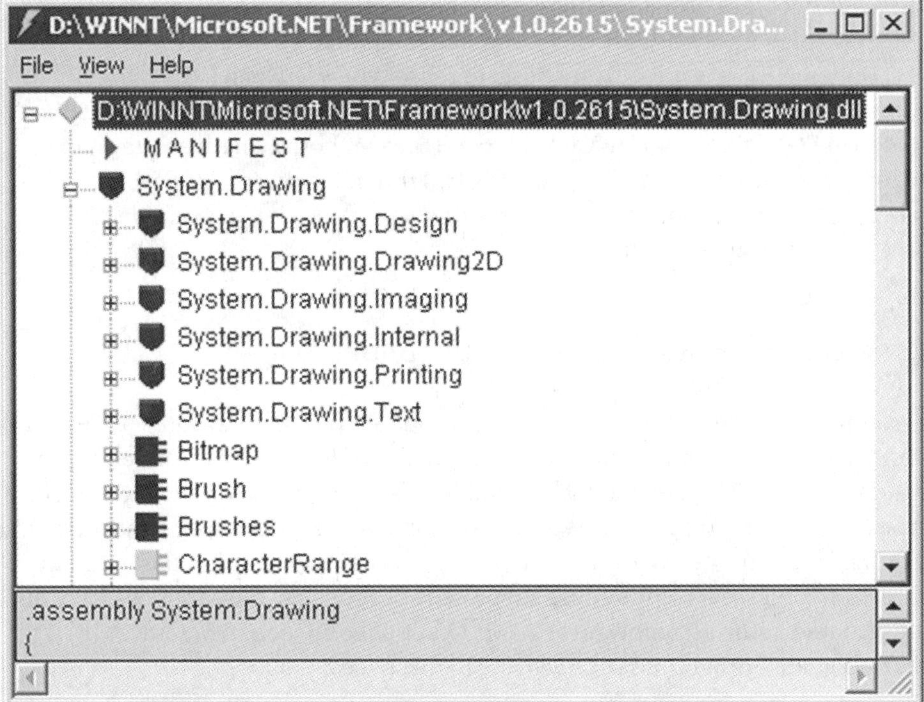

Figure 7-5. Logical view of the physical System.Drawing.dll assembly

The chances are good that you will play the role of both an assembly builder and assembly consumer, as is the case throughout this book. However, before digging into the code, let's briefly examine some of the core benefits of this new file format.

Assemblies Promote Code Reuse

Assemblies contain code that is executed by the .NET runtime. As you might imagine, the types and resources contained within an assembly can be shared and reused by multiple applications, much like a traditional COM binary. Unlike traditional COM, it is also possible to configure "private" assemblies as well (in fact, this is the default behavior). Private assemblies are intended to be used only by a single application on a given machine. As you will see, private assemblies greatly simplify the deployment and versioning of your applications.

Like COM, binary reuse under the .NET platform honors the ideal of language independence. VB .NET is one of numerous languages capable of building managed code, with even more languages to come. When you write code that adheres to the rules of the Common Language Specification (CLS), your choice of language becomes little more than a personal preference (as you recall, the VB .NET compiler always builds CLS-compliant assemblies).

Under .NET, it is not only possible to reuse types between languages, but to extend types across languages as well. In classic COM, developers were unable to derive COM object A from COM object B (even if both types were developed in the same language). In short, classic COM did not support classical inheritance (the "is-a" relationship). Later in this chapter you see an example of cross-language inheritance.

Assemblies Establish a Type Boundary

Assemblies are used to define a boundary for the types (and resources) they contain. In .NET, the identity of a given type is defined (in part) by the assembly in which it resides. Therefore, if two assemblies each define an identically named type (class, structure, or whatnot) they are considered independent entities in the .NET universe. In this way, if you are building a client application that references three assemblies each containing a type called Employee, they are physically disambiguated at the assembly level. As you have already seen, types are disambiguated programmatically using namespaces.

Assemblies Are Versionable and Self-Describing Entities

As mentioned, in the world of COM, the developer is in charge of correctly versioning a binary. For example, to ensure binary compatibility between MyComServer.dll version 1.0 and MyComServer.dll version 2.4, the programmer must use basic common sense to ensure interface definitions remain unaltered or run the risk of breaking client code. While a healthy dose of versioning common sense also comes in handy under the .NET universe, the problem with the COM versioning scheme is that these programmer-defined techniques are *not* enforced by the runtime.

Another major headache with current versioning practices is that COM does not provide a way for a binary server to explicitly list the set of other binaries that must be present for it to function correctly. If an end user mistakenly moves, renames, or deletes a dependency, the solution fails. Under .NET, an assembly's manifest is the entity in charge of explicitly listing all internal and external contingencies.

Each assembly has a version identifier that applies to all types and all resources contained within each module of the assembly. Using a version identifier the runtime is able to ensure that the correct assembly is loaded on behalf of the calling client, using a well defined versioning policy (detailed later).

An assembly's version identifier is composed of two basic pieces: A friendly text string (termed the *informational* version) and a numerical identifier (termed the *compatibility* version). For example, assume you have created a new assembly with an informational string of "MyInterestingTypes." This same assembly would also define a compatibility number, such as 1.0.70.3. The compatibility version number always takes the same general format (four numbers separated by periods). The first and second numbers identify the major and minor version of the assembly (1.0 in this case). The third value (70) marks the build number, followed by the current revision number (3). As you see a bit later in this chapter, an assembly's version is typically established using a system-supplied attribute (if you do not specify a version number, you receive the default version number: 0.0.0.0).

The .NET runtime makes use of an assembly's version to ensure the correct binary is loaded on behalf of the client (provided that the assembly is shared). Because the manifest explicitly lists all external dependencies, the runtime is able to determine the "last known good" configuration (i.e., the set of versioned assemblies that are known to function correctly). Using XML configuration files, you are able to instruct the CLR to override the known configuration to bind to a different version of a given assembly on the fly (as long as the assembly supports a "strong name"—more on this later).

Assemblies Define a Security Context

An assembly may also contain security information. Under the architecture of the .NET runtime, security measures are scoped at the assembly level. For example, if AssemblyA wants to use a class contained within AssemblyB, AssemblyB is the entity that chooses to provide access (or not). The security constraints defined by an assembly are explicitly listed within its manifest. While a treatment of .NET security measures is outside the mission of this text, simply be aware that access to an assembly's contents is verified using assembly metadata.

Assemblies Enable Side-by-Side Execution

Perhaps the biggest advantage of the .NET assembly is the ability of multiple versions of the same assembly to be loaded (and understood) by the runtime. It is also possible to install and load multiple versions of the same assembly on a single machine. In this way, clients are isolated from other incompatible versions of the same assembly.

As you see a bit later in this chapter, assemblies may be "shared" among numerous client programs on a single machine. Shared assemblies are typically placed in a well-known location on a given machine termed the Global Assembly

Cache or GAC. You will come to understand the role of this entity once you come to understand the role of "shared" assemblies.

Building a Single File Test Assembly

Now that you have a better understanding of .NET assemblies, let's build a minimal and complete code library using VB .NET. Physically, this will be a single file assembly named CarLibrary.dll. To build a VB .NET code library using the Visual Studio .NET IDE, you would begin by selecting a new Class Library project workspace (see Figure 7-6).

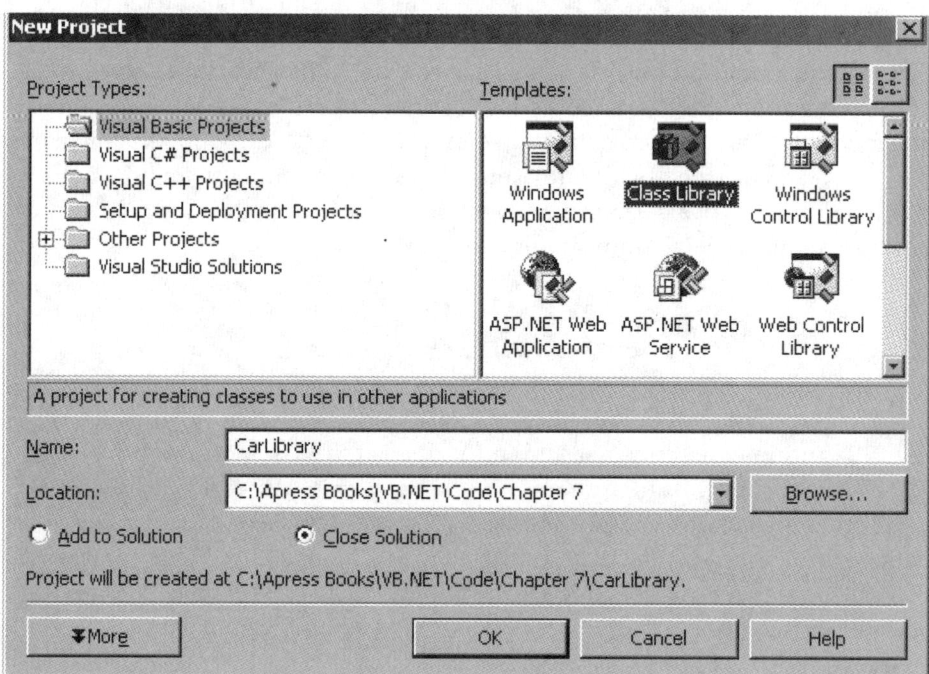

Figure 7-6. Selecting a Class Library project workspace

The design of your automobile library begins with an abstract base class named Car that defines a number of Protected data members exposed to the outside world using custom properties. This class has a single abstract (i.e., MustOverride) method named TurboBoost() and makes use of a custom enumeration (EngineState). Here is the initial definition of the CarLibrary namespace:

```
' Our first code library (CarLibrary.dll)
Imports System.Windows.Forms
```

```
' Holds the state of the engine.
public Enum EngineState
    engineAlive
    engineDead
End Enum
'The abstract base class for the hierarchy.
public MustInherit class Car
    ' State data.
    Protected mPetName As String
    Protected mCurrSpeed As Short
    Protected mMaxSpeed As Short
    Protected egnState as EngineState
    ' Ctors.
    public Sub New()
        egnState = EngineState.engineAlive
    End Sub
    Public Sub New(ByVal name As String, ByVal max As Short, _
    ByVal curr As Short)
        egnState = EngineState.engineAlive
        petName = name
        mMaxSpeed = max
        mCurrSpeed = curr
    End Sub
    ' Properties.
    Public Property PetName() As String
        Get
            Return mPetName
        End Get
        Set(ByVal Value As String)
            mPetName = Value
        End Set
    End Property
    Public Property CurrSpeed() As Short
        Get
            Return mCurrSpeed
        End Get
        Set(ByVal Value As Short)
            mCurrSpeed = Value
        End Set
    End Property
    ' Read only properties.
    Public ReadOnly Property MaxSpeed() As Short
        Get
```

```
            Return mMaxSpeed
        End Get
    End Property
    Public ReadOnly Property EngineState() As EngineState
        Get
            Return egnState
        End Get
    End Property
    ' Abstract member.
    Public MustOverride Sub TurboBoost()
End Class
```

Now assume that you have two direct descendents of the Car type named MiniVan and SportsCar. Each implements the abstract TurboBoost() method in an appropriate manner:

```
' The SportsCar
Public Class SportsCar
    Inherits Car
    ' Ctors.
    Public Sub New()
        MyBase.New()
    End Sub
    Public Sub New(ByVal name As String, ByVal max As Short, _
    ByVal curr As Short)
        MyBase.New(name, max, curr)
    End Sub
    ' TurboBoost impl.
    Public Overrides Sub TurboBoost()
        MessageBox.Show("Ramming speed!", "Faster is better. . .")
    End Sub
End Class

' The MiniVan
Public Class MiniVan
    Inherits Car
    ' Ctors.
    Public Sub New()
        MyBase.New ()
    End Sub
    Public Sub New(ByVal name As String, ByVal max As Short, _
    ByVal curr As Short)
        MyBase.New(name, max, curr)
```

```
    End Sub
    ' TurboBoost impl.
    Public Overrides Sub TurboBoost()
        MessageBox.Show("Time to call AAA!", "Your car is dead. . .")
    End Sub
End Class
```

Notice how each subclass implements TurboBoost() using the MessageBox class, which is defined in the System.Windows.Forms.dll assembly. For your assembly to make use of the types defined within this assembly, the CarLibrary project must include a reference to this binary using the "Project | Add Reference" menu selection, which is simply a GUI-based alternative to supplying the /r: flag to the VB .NET compiler (see Figure 7-7).

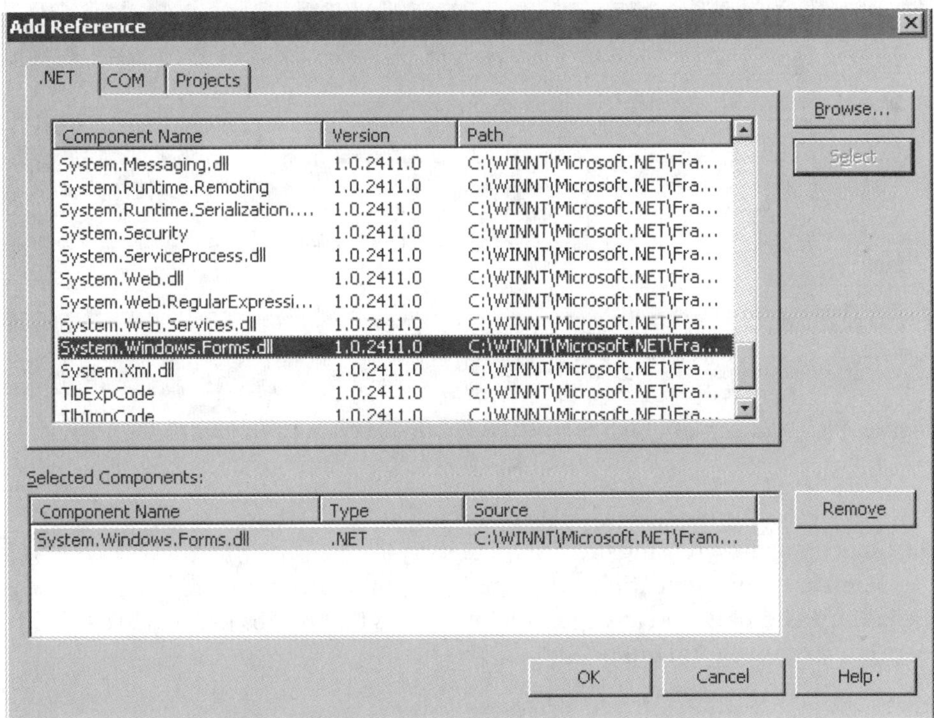

Figure 7-7. Referencing external assemblies

In Chapter 9, the System.Windows.Forms namespace is described in detail. As you can tell by the name of the namespace, this assembly contains numerous types to help you build GUI applications. For now, the MessageBox class is all you need to concern yourself with. If you are following along, go ahead and compile your new code library.

A VB .NET Client Application

Because each of your automobiles has been declared "Public," other binaries are able to use your custom classes. In a moment, you will learn how to make use of these types from other .NET-aware languages such as C#. Until then, let's create a VB .NET client. Begin by creating a new VB .NET Console Application project (VbNetCarClient). Next, set a reference to your CarLibrary.dll, using the Browse button to navigate to the location of your custom assembly (again using the Add Reference dialog box).

Once you add a reference to your CarLibrary assembly, the Visual Studio .NET IDE responds by making a *full copy* of the referenced assembly and placing it into your bin folder (see Figure 7-8).

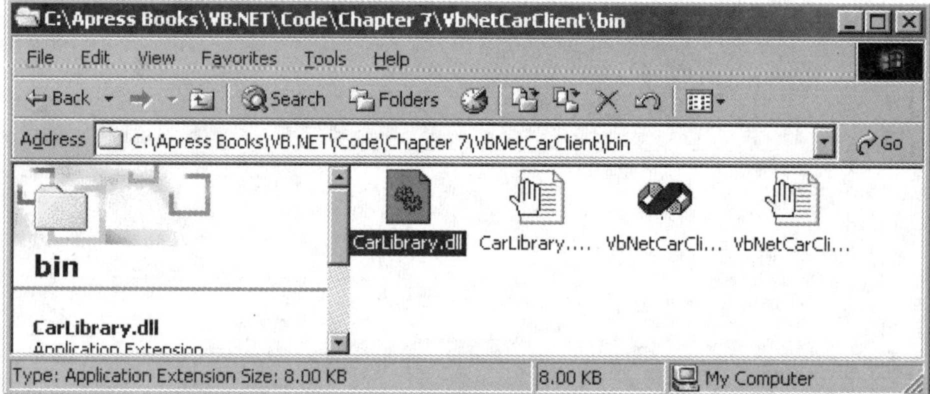

Figure 7-8. Local copies of referenced assemblies are placed in your bin folder

Obviously, this is a huge change from classic COM, where the resolution of the binary is achieved using the system registry.

Now that your client application has been configured to reference the CarLibrary assembly, you are free to create a class that makes use of these types. Here is a test drive (pun intended):

```
' Our first taste of binary reuse.
Imports CarLibrary
Module Module1
    Sub Main()
        ' Make a sports car.
        Dim viper As SportsCar = New SportsCar("Viper", 240, 40)
        viper.TurboBoost()
        ' Make a minivan.
        Dim mv As MiniVan = New MiniVan()
```

```
        mv.TurboBoost()
    End Sub
End Module
```

This code looks just like the other applications developed thus far. The only point of interest is that the client application is now making use of types defined within a unique assembly. Go ahead and run your program. As you would expect, the execution of this program results in the display of two message boxes.

A C# Client Application

When you install Visual Studio .NET, you receive four languages that are capable of building managed code: Jscript .NET, C++ with managed extensions (MC++), C#, and Visual Basic .NET. A nice feature of Visual Studio .NET is that all languages share the same IDE. Therefore, Visual Basic .NET, ATL, C#, and MFC programmers all make use of a common development environment. Given your current understanding of VS .NET, the process of building a C# application making use of the CarLibrary is quite intuitive. Assume you have created a new C# Windows Application project workspace named CSharpCarClient (see Figure 7-9).

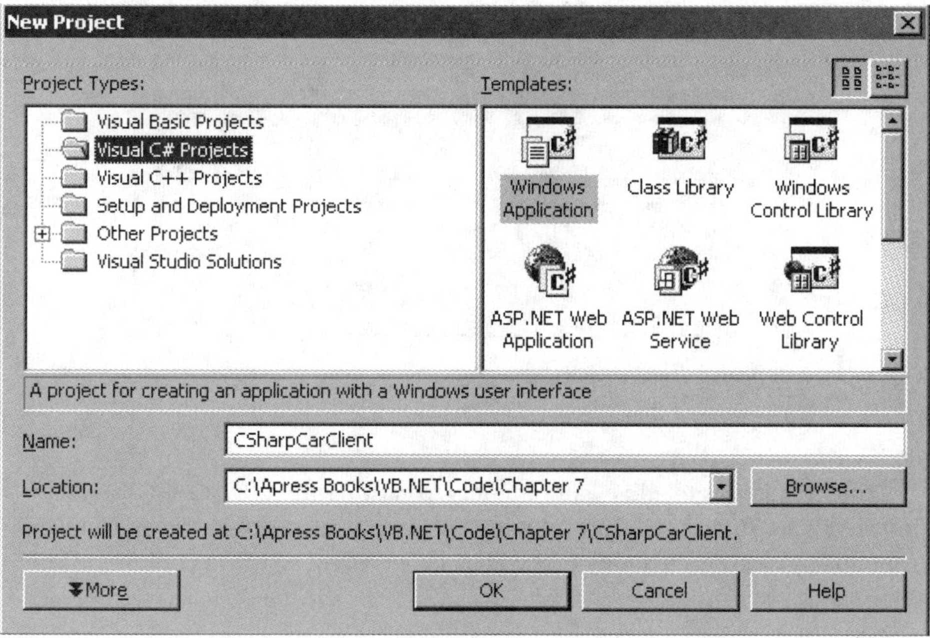

Figure 7-9. Selecting a C# Windows Application project

Similar to Visual Basic 6.0, Windows Forms project workspaces provide a design-time template used to build the GUI of the main window. However, .NET Windows Forms projects are a completely different animal. The template you are looking at is actually a subclass of the Form type, which is quite different from a VB 6.0 Form object (again, more details in Chapter 9).

Now, set a reference to the VB .NET CarLibrary, again using the Add Reference dialog box. Like VB .NET, C# requires you to list each namespace used within your project. However, C# makes use of the "using" keyword rather than the VB .NET "Imports" directive. Thus, open the code window for your Form and add the following (be aware that C# is a *case-sensitive* language—thus, "Using" is not the same as "using"):

```
// Like VB .NET, C# needs to 'see' the namespaces used by a given class.
using System;
using System.Collections;
. . .
using CarLibrary;
```

Using the design-time template, construct a minimal and complete user interface to exercise your automobile types (see Figure 7-10). Two buttons should fit the bill (simply select the Button widget from the Toolbox and draw it on the Form object).

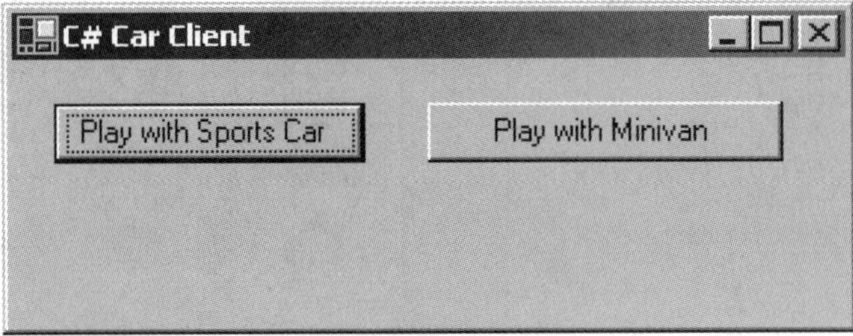

Figure 7-10. A painfully simple UI

The next step is to add event handlers to capture the Click event of each Button object. To do so, simply double-click each button on the Form. The IDE responds by writing stub code that will be called when a button is clicked. Here is some sample code:

```
// A little bit of C#!
private void btnSportsCar_Click(object sender, System.EventArgs e)
{
    SportsCar c = new SportsCar("Zippy", 200, 20);
```

```
    c.TurboBoost();
}

private void btnMiniVan_Click(object sender, System.EventArgs e)
{
    MiniVan mv= new MiniVan("Pokey", 200, 20);
    mv.TurboBoost();
}
```

As you would expect, when you run the program, each automobile responds appropriately.

Cross-Language Inheritance

A very sexy aspect of .NET development is the notion of cross-language inheritance. To illustrate, let's create a new C# class that derives from CarLibrary.SportsCar. Impossible, you say? Well, if you were using classic COM this would be the case. However, with the advent of .NET, programmers are able to subclass types across language boundaries (i.e., establish the "is-a" relationship). To illustrate this feature of .NET, let's extend your current automobile class library as shown in Figure 7-11.

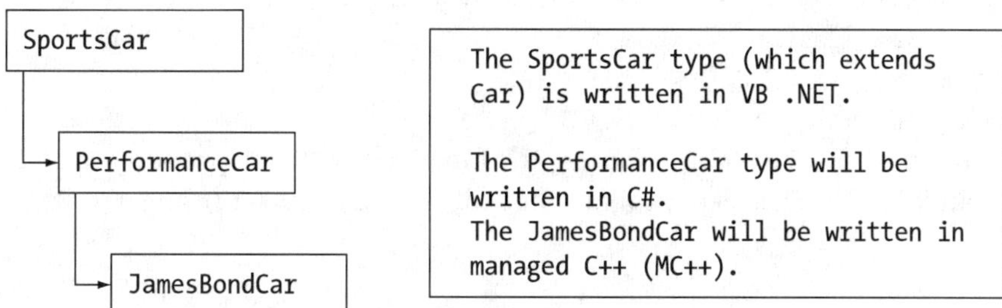

Figure 7-11. Cross-language inheritance

Building the C# Subclass

To begin, add a new class named PerformanceCar to your current C# client application (using the "Project | Add Class" menu selection). In the code that follows, notice you are deriving from the VB .NET Car type using the C# ":" operator. As you recall, the Car class defined an abstract TurboBoost() method, which you implement using the C# "override" keyword:

```
using System;
using CarLibrary;
using System.Windows.Forms;
namespace CSharpCarClient
{
    public class PerformanceCar : Car
    {
        // Default constructor.
        public PerformanceCar() {}
        public override void TurboBoost()
        {
            MessageBox.Show("Blazzing speed. . .");
        }
}
}
```

If you update your existing Form to include an additional Button to exercise the performance car, you could write the following test code:

```
private void btnPerfCar_Click(object sender, System.EventArgs e)
{
    PerformanceCar pc = new PerformanceCar();
    pc.PetName = "Hank";
    MessageBox.Show(pc.GetType().BaseType.ToString(),
        "Base class of Perf car");
}
```

Notice that you are able to access the inherited PetName property and identify your VB .NET base class programmatically (see Figure 7-12).

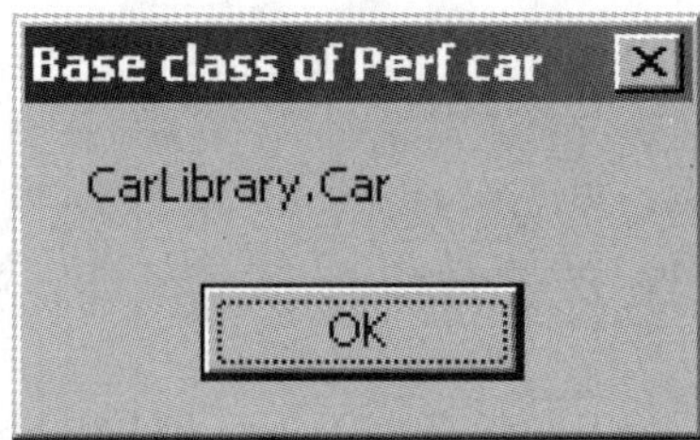

Figure 7-12. Cross-language inheritance (phase one)

Building the MC++ Subclass (Extra Credit Section)

So far, you have a C# class deriving from a VB .NET class. To really drive the point home, let's build a MC++ subclass that derives from the C# class. As you may have guessed, C++ with Managed Extensions (MC++) is Microsoft's augmentation of the C++ language. In order for the C++ programming language to interact with the CLR, several new keywords were introduced. Understand that C++ programmers are *not* required to make use of these new .NET specific keywords when they build C++ projects using Visual Studio .NET. However, when a C++ programmer does want to inject .NET functionality into their programs, VS .NET does include several new project workspaces. To begin, close down your current C# project workspace and create a brand-new Managed C++ Application (see Figure 7-13).

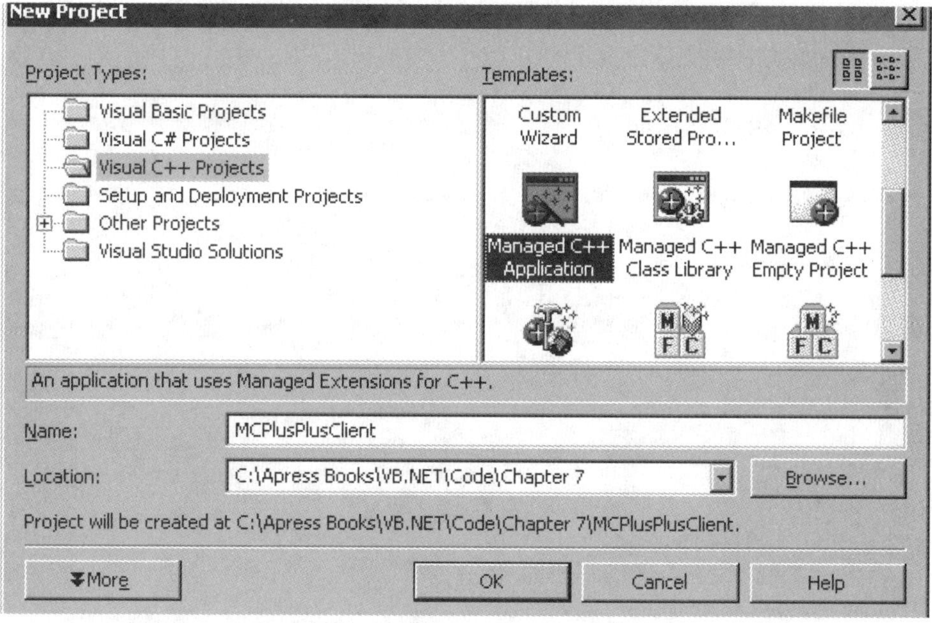

Figure 7-13. A MC++ project workspace

Of all the languages that are able to produce managed code, MC++ is by far the most cryptic. Therefore, in the code that follows, don't fret over each and every line of syntax. The point to focus on is the fact that the MC++ JamesBondCar class is deriving from the C# PerformanceCar (which in turn derives from the VB .NET SportsCar). Here is the complete code (be sure to read the code comments):

```
#pragma once
#include "stdafx.h"
#using <mscorlib.dll>
// '#using' Is much like adding a reference using the 'Add References' dialog.
// Adjust the path to the assemblies If necessary. . .
#using "C:\CSharpCarClient.exe"
#using "C:\CarLibrary.dll"
#using <System.Windows.Forms.dll>
// 'using' Is much like the VB .NET "Imports" keyword.
using namespace CSharpCarClient;
using namespace System;
// __gc (garbage collected) marks this class as managed by the CLR.
__gc class JamesBondCar : public PerformanceCar
{
public:
    JamesBondCar(void){}
    ~JamesBondCar(void){}
    virtual void TurboBoost()
    {
        Console::WriteLine("Diving, flying and drilling. . .");
    }
};
// This is the entry point for this application
#ifdef _UNICODE
int wmain(void)
#else
int main(void)
#endif
{
    // Make a JamesBondCar.
    JamesBondCar* jbc = new JamesBondCar();
    jbc->PetName = S"Jello";
    jbc->TurboBoost();
    Console::Write("Car is called: ");
    Console::WriteLine(jbc->PetName);
    Console::WriteLine(jbc->GetType()->BaseType->ToString());
    return 0;
}
```

Figure 7-14 shows the output.

```
"c:\Apress Books\VB.NET\Code\Chapter 7\MCPlu...
Diving, flying and drilling...
Car is called: Jello
CSharpCarClient.PerformanceCar
Press any key to continue
```

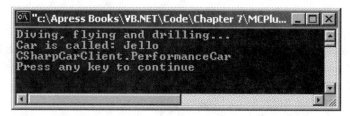

Figure 7-14. Cross-language inheritance (phase two)

Before we move on, a few points of interest. First of all, when an MC++ developer wants to add a reference to an external assembly, he or she makes use of the #using preprocessor directive that will import the assembly's metadata for use in the current application. Here you made four calls to external assemblies, including the VB .NET CarLibrary.dll and CSharpClient.exe binaries. In many respects, the MC++ #using directive is the functional equivalent of adding a reference using the "Add Reference. . ." menu option in VB .NET. Also notice that MC++ supports a "using" keyword, which is the functional equivalent to the VB .NET "Imports" statement.

In addition to some rather arcane pointer syntax (the dreaded "*" symbol), additional preprocessor directives (#ifndef, #else, #endif), and MC++ specific keywords (__gc), the bulk of the application is quite similar in form to the VB .NET and C# applications seen in previous sections. For example, notice that you are able to reference shared members using the "scope resolution operator" (::) and access object level members using the "indirection operator" (->). Again, don't be concerned if this syntax looks offensive. The point here is to notice how the .NET platform truly does support the ability to extend types across diverse languages.

Excellent! At this point you have begun the process of breaking your applications into discrete binary building blocks. Given the language-independent nature of .NET, any language targeting the runtime is able to create (and extend) the types described within a given assembly.

SOURCE CODE *The CarLibrary, CSharpCarClient, VBCarClient and MCPlusPlusClient projects are each included under the Chapter 7 subdirectory.*

Exploring the CarLibrary's Manifest

At this point, you have successfully created several assemblies. Your next order of business is to gain a deeper understanding of how .NET assemblies are constructed under the hood. To begin, recall that every assembly contains an associated manifest, which can be regarded as the Rosetta stone of .NET. An assembly manifest contains metadata that specifies the name and version of the assembly, as well as a listing of all internal and external files that compose the assembly as a whole. Additionally, a manifest may contain culture information (used for internalization), a corresponding "public key" (required by shared assemblies) as well as optional security and resource information (you examine the .NET resource format in Chapter 10).

.NET-aware compilers (such as vbc.exe) automatically create an assembly manifest at compile time. As you see in Chapter 8, it is possible to augment the compiler-generated manifest using attribute-based programming techniques. For now, go ahead and load the VB .NET CarLibrary.dll assembly into ILDasm.exe. As you can see, this tool has read the metadata to display relevant information for each type (see Figure 7-15).

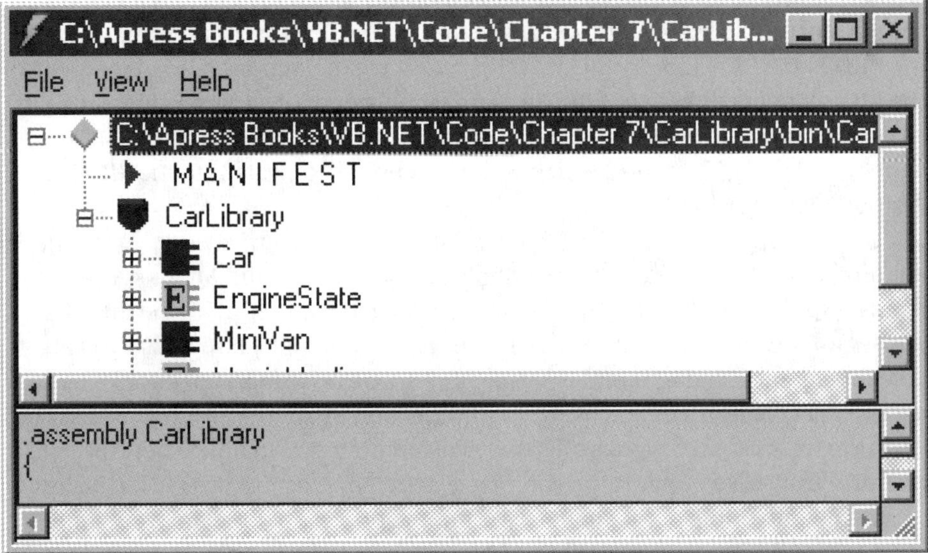

Figure 7-15. Your car library

Now, open the manifest by double-clicking the MANIFEST icon (see Figure 7-16).

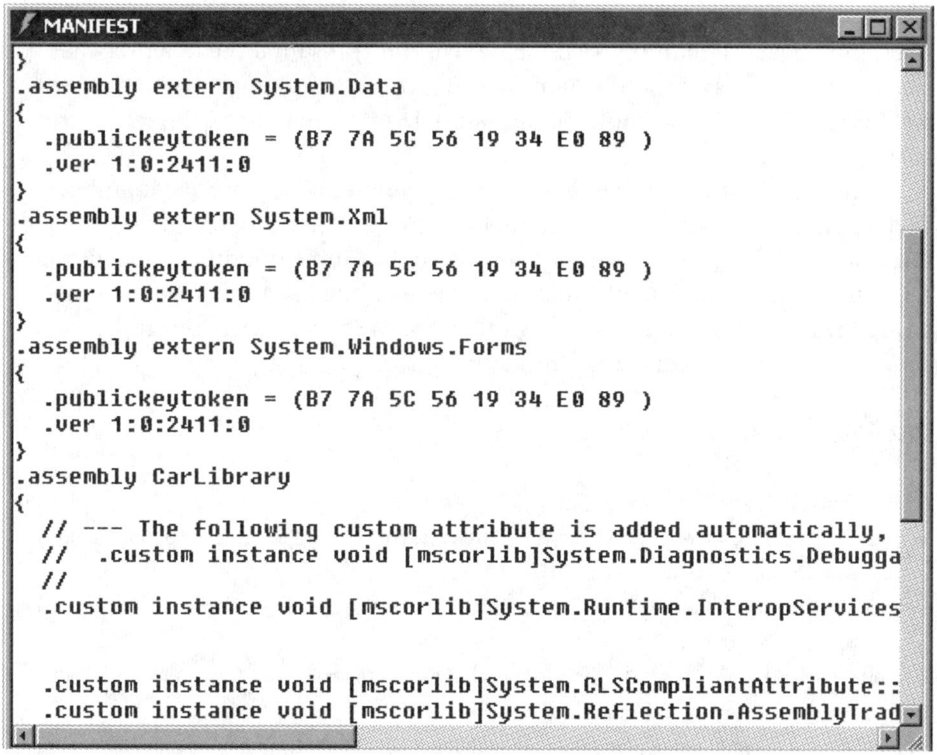

```
MANIFEST
}
.assembly extern System.Data
{
  .publickeytoken = (B7 7A 5C 56 19 34 E0 89 )
  .ver 1:0:2411:0
}
.assembly extern System.Xml
{
  .publickeytoken = (B7 7A 5C 56 19 34 E0 89 )
  .ver 1:0:2411:0
}
.assembly extern System.Windows.Forms
{
  .publickeytoken = (B7 7A 5C 56 19 34 E0 89 )
  .ver 1:0:2411:0
}
.assembly CarLibrary
{
  // --- The following custom attribute is added automatically,
  //   .custom instance void [mscorlib]System.Diagnostics.Debugga
  //
  .custom instance void [mscorlib]System.Runtime.InteropServices


  .custom instance void [mscorlib]System.CLSCompliantAttribute::
  .custom instance void [mscorlib]System.Reflection.AssemblyTrad
```

Figure 7-16. The CarLibrary manifest

The first code block contained in the assembly manifest is used to specify all external assemblies that are required by the current assembly to function correctly. As you recall, CarLibrary.dll made use of mscorlib.dll and System.Windows.Forms.dll, each of which is marked in the manifest using the [.assembly extern] tag (be aware that the exact publickeytoken and version values may differ based on which version of the .NET runtime you are working with):

```
.assembly extern mscorlib
{
  .publickeytoken = (B7 7A 5C 56 19 34 E0 89 )
  .ver 1:0:2411:0
}
.assembly extern System.Windows.Forms
{
  .publickeytoken = (B7 7A 5C 56 19 34 E0 89 )
  .ver 1:0:2411:0
}
```

Here, each [.assembly extern] block is colored by the [.publickeytoken] and [.ver] directives. The [.publickeytoken] tag is only present if the assembly has been configured as a shared assembly and is used to reference the complete public key of the binary (more details later). [.ver] is (of course) the numerical version identifier.

After enumerating each of the external references, the assembly manifest then enumerates each module contained in the assembly. Given that the CarLibrary is a single file assembly, you find exactly one [.module] tag. This manifest also lists a number of attributes (marked with the [.custom] tag) such as company name, trademark, and so forth, all of which are currently empty (more information on these attributes in Chapter 8):

```
.assembly CarLibrary
{
  .custom instance void [mscorlib]
System.Reflection.AssemblyKeyNameAttribute::.ctor(string) = ( 01 00 00 00 00 )
  .custom instance void [mscorlib]
System.Reflection.AssemblyKeyFileAttribute::.ctor(string) = ( 01 00 00 00 00 )
  .custom instance void [mscorlib]
System.Reflection.AssemblyDelaySignAttribute::.ctor(bool) = ( 01 00 00 00 00 )
  .custom instance void [mscorlib]
System.Reflection.AssemblyTrademarkAttribute::.ctor(string) = ( 01 00 00 00 00 )
  .custom instance void [mscorlib]
System.Reflection.AssemblyCopyrightAttribute::.ctor(string) = ( 01 00 00 00 00 )
  .custom instance void [mscorlib]
System.Reflection.AssemblyProductAttribute::.ctor(string) = ( 01 00 00 00 00 )
  .custom instance void [mscorlib]
System.Reflection.AssemblyCompanyAttribute::.ctor(string) = ( 01 00 00 00 00 )
  .custom instance void [mscorlib]
System.Reflection.AssemblyConfigurationAttribute::.ctor(string)=( 01 00 00 00 00 )
  .custom instance void [mscorlib]
System.Reflection.AssemblyDescriptionAttribute::.ctor(string) = ( 01 00 00 00 00 )
  .custom instance void [mscorlib]
System.Reflection.AssemblyTitleAttribute::.ctor(string) = ( 01 00 00 00 00 )
  .hash algorithm 0x00008004
  .ver 1:0:454:30104
}
.module CarLibrary.dll
```

Here, you can see that the [.assembly] tag is used to mark the friendly name of your custom assembly (CarLibrary). As with external declarations, the [.ver] tag defines the version number for this assembly. Do note that the CarLibrary assembly does *not* define a [.publickeytoken] tag, given that CarLibrary has not been configured as a shared assembly. To summarize the tags that dwell in the assembly manifest, ponder Table 7-1.

Table 7-1. Manifest IL Tags

MANIFEST TAG	MEANING IN LIFE
.assembly	Marks the assembly declaration, indicating that the file is an assembly.
.file	Marks extra files in the same assembly.
.class extern	Classes exported by the assembly but declared in another module.
.exeloc	Indicates the location of the executable for the assembly.
.manifestres	Indicates the manifest resources (if any). You see this tag in action in Chapter 9.
.module	Indicates that the file is a module (*.netmodule).
.module extern	Modules of this assembly contain items referenced in this module.
.assembly extern	The assembly reference indicates another assembly containing items referenced by this module.
.publickey	Contains the actual bytes of the public key.
.publickeytoken	Contains a token of the actual public key.

Exploring the CarLibrary's Types

Recall that an assembly does not contain platform specific instructions, but rather platform agnostic intermediate language (IL). When the .NET runtime loads an assembly into memory, the underlying IL is compiled (using the JIT compiler) into instructions that can be understood by the target platform. Also recall that in addition to raw IL and the assembly manifest, an assembly contains metadata that describes the members of each type contained within a given module.

For example, if you double-click the TurboBoost() method of the SportsCar class, ILDasm.exe would open a new window showing the raw IL instructions. Notice in Figure 7-17 that the [.method] tag is used to identify (of course) a method defined by the SportsCar type.

```
SportsCar::TurboBoost : void()
.method public virtual instance void  TurboBoost()
{
  // Code size       19 (0x13)
  .maxstack  8
  IL_0000:  nop
  IL_0001:  ldstr      "Ramming speed!"
  IL_0006:  ldstr      "Faster is better..."
  IL_000b:  call       valuetype [System.Windows.Fc

  IL_0010:  pop
  IL_0011:  nop
  IL_0012:  ret
} // end of method SportsCar::TurboBoost
```

Figure 7-17. IL for the TurboBoost() method

As you might expect, Public data is marked with the [.field] tag. Recall that the Car class defined a set of protected data, such as mCurrSpeed. Note that the "family" tag signifies protected data, as shown in Figure 7-18.

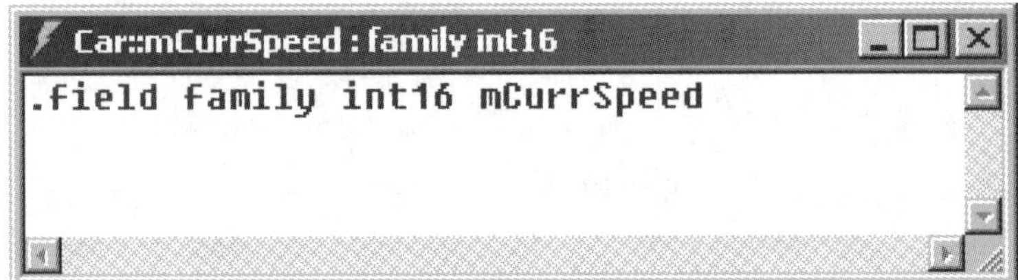
Car::mCurrSpeed : family int16
.field family int16 mCurrSpeed

Figure 7-18. IL for the mCurrSpeed field

Properties are also marked with the [.property] tag, as shown in Figure 7-19. The figure shows the IL describing the public property that provides access to the underlying mCurrSpeed data point (note the read/write nature of the CurrSpeed property is marked by .get and .set tags).

```
Car::CurrSpeed : int16()
.property int16 CurrSpeed()
{
  .get instance int16 CarLibrary.Car::get_CurrSpeed()
  .set instance void CarLibrary.Car::set_CurrSpeed(int16)
} // end of property Car::CurrSpeed
```

Figure 7-19. IL for the CurrSpeed property

If you now select the "Ctrl + M" keystroke, ILDasm.exe would display the metadata for each type (see Figure 7-20).

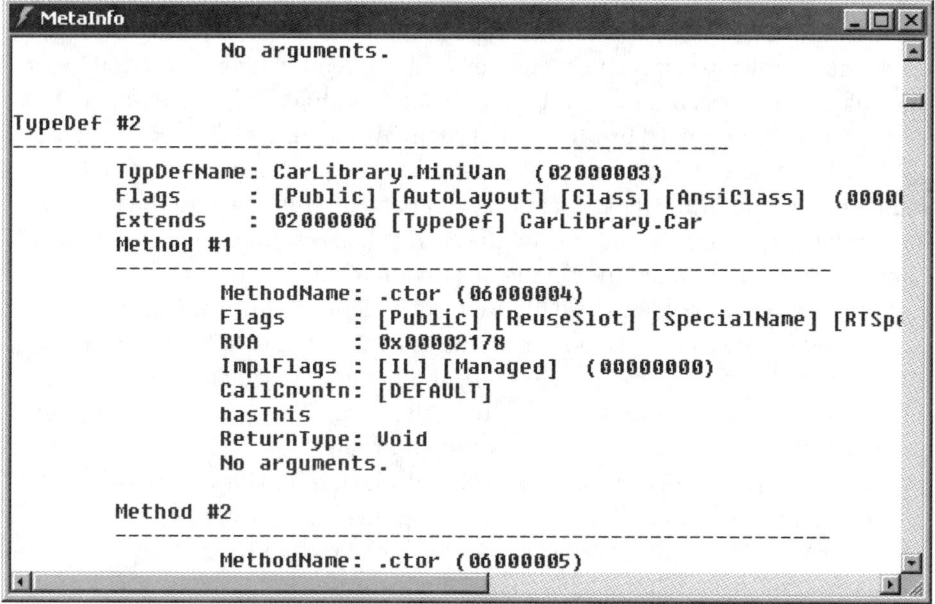

Figure 7-20. Type metadata

Using this metadata, the .NET runtime is able to locate and construct object instances, and invoke methods. Various tools (such as Visual Studio .NET) make use of metadata at design time to validate the number of (and type of) parameters during compilation. To summarize the story so far, make sure the following points are clear in your mind:

- An assembly is a versioned, self-describing set of modules. Each module contains some number of types and optional resources.

- Every assembly contains metadata that describes all types within a given module. The .NET runtime (as well as numerous design-time tools) read the metadata to locate and create objects, validate method calls, activate IntelliSense, and so on.

- Every assembly contains an assembly manifest that enumerates the set of all internal and external files required by the binary, version information, and other assembly-centric details.

Building Multifile Assemblies

Now that you have explored the internals of a single file assembly, let's turn our attention to the process of building a multifile assembly using VB .NET. Recall that a multifile assembly contains a single *.dll or *.exe file that contains MSIL, metadata for the types it contains, as well as the assembly manifest. Additionally, multifile assemblies contain any number of *.netmodule files that are loaded on demand when referenced by an external client. At the time of this writing, Visual Studio .NET does not support a project workspace type that allows you to build standalone *.netmodule files. Therefore, you need to drop down to the level of the raw vbc.exe compiler and specify the correct flags manually (be sure to read Chapter 2 if you happened to skip the discussion of vbc.exe).

To keep things crisp and well focused, you will build some rather simple types. Specifically, you will build a multifile assembly named AirVehicles. The main airvehicles.dll file will contain MSIL and metadata for a single class type named Helicopter. The assembly manifest (also contained in airvehicles.dll) references a stand-alone *.netmodule file named ufos.netmodule, which contains another class type named (of course) UFO. Although both class types are physically contained in separate binaries, you group them into a single namespace named AirVehicles. Finally, both classes are created using VB .NET (although you could certainly mix and match languages if you desire).

To begin, open notepad.exe and create a trivial class definition named UFO (see Figure 7-21). Notice that you are programmatically specifying the namespace to which this class type belongs using the VB .NET Namespace keyword.

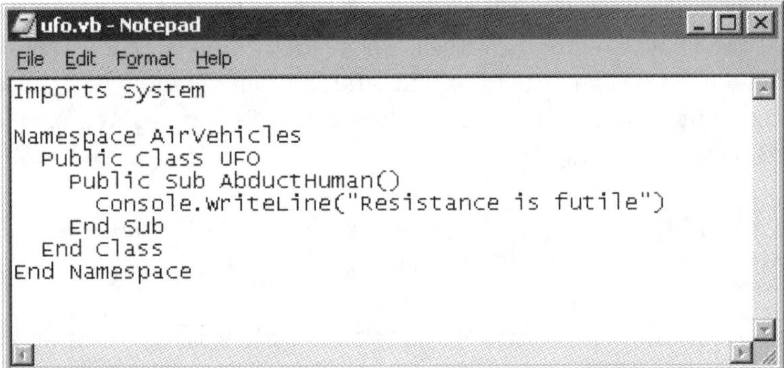

ufo.vb - Notepad
File Edit Format Help
Imports System

Namespace AirVehicles
  Public Class UFO
    Public Sub AbductHuman()
      Console.WriteLine("Resistance is futile")
    End Sub
  End Class
End Namespace

Figure 7-21. The UFO

To compile this class into a .NET module, open a command prompt and issue the following command to the VB .NET compiler (recall the /t: flag is a shorthand notation for the /target: file output option):

```
vbc.exe /t:module ufo.vb
```

If you were to now look in the folder containing the ufo.vb file, you should see a new file named ufo.netmodule (go ahead and take a peek). Next, create a brand-new file (using notepad.exe) named helicopter.vb. The class definition is shown in Figure 7-22.

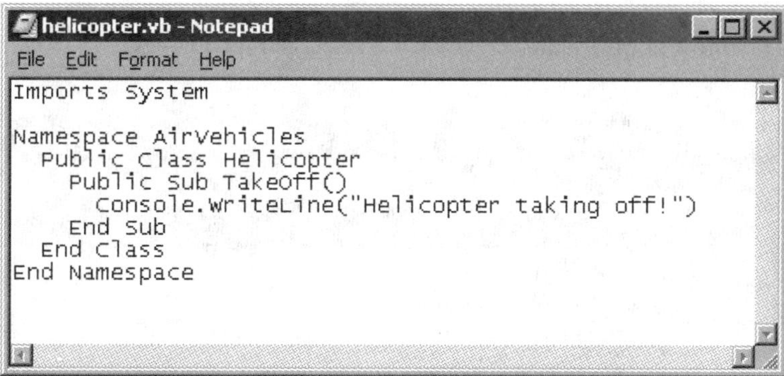

Figure 7-22. Another air vehicle

Given that you want to contain the helicopter type within the AirVehicles.dll, you will need to specify the /t: library flag. However, you also want to encode the ufo.netmodule binary into the assembly manifest, and therefore must specify the /addmodule flag. The following command does the trick:

```
vbc /t:library /addmodule:ufo.netmodule /out:airvehicles helicopter.vb
```

It's not as bad as it looks. Here, you are saying you want a library named AirVehicles that is built using the helicopter.vb file and the ufo.netmodule. Check out the directory containing these files. You should see something like what appears in Figure 7-23.

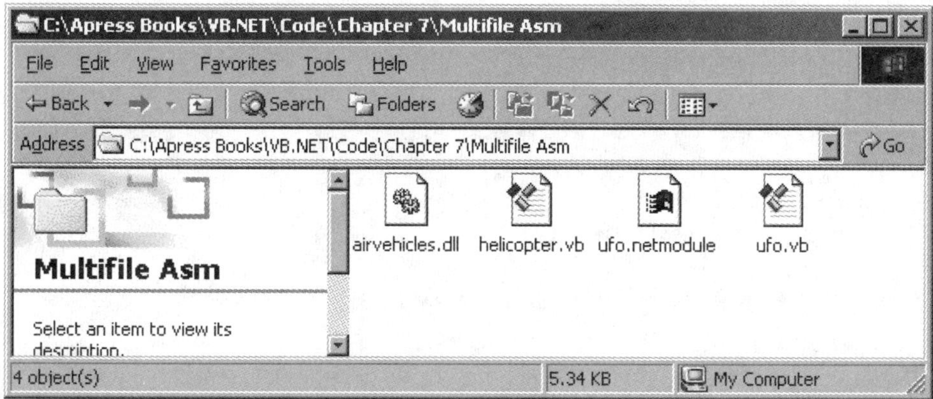

Figure 7-23. Your multifile assembly

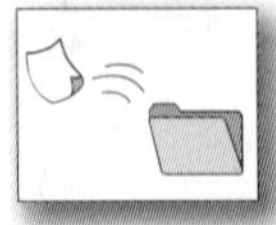

SOURCE CODE *The MultifileAsm project is included under the Chapter 7 subdirectory.*

Exploring the ufo.netmodule

Using ILDasm.exe, open your *.netmodule file (see Figure 7-24).

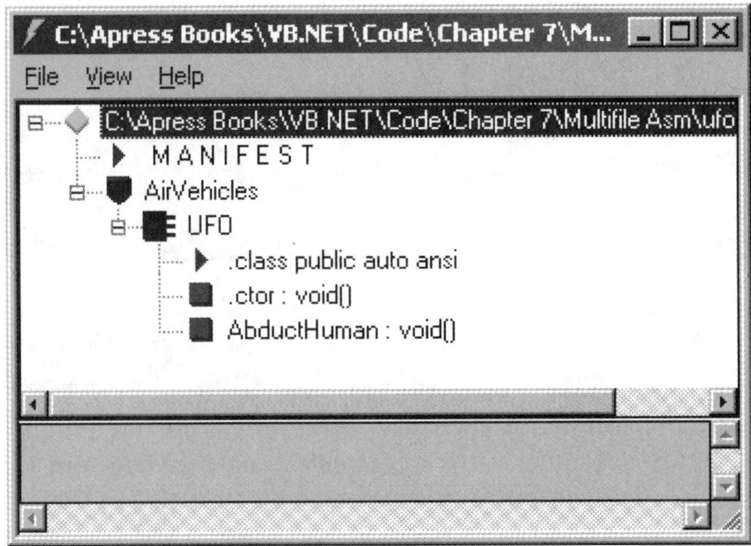

Figure 7-24. The ufo.netmodule

Recall that modules contain a *module level manifest;* however, its sole purpose in life is to list each external assembly referenced within the code base. Given that the UFO class did little more than make a call to System.Console.WriteLine(), you find the following [.assembly extern] tags:

```
.assembly extern mscorlib
{
  .publickeytoken = (B7 7A 5C 56 19 34 E0 89 )
  .ver 1:0:2411:0
}
.assembly extern Microsoft.VisualBasic
{
  .publickeytoken = (B0 3F 5F 7F 11 D5 0A 3A )
  .ver 7:0:0:0
}
.module ufo.netmodule
```

Exploring the airvehicles.dll

Now, using ILDasm.exe, open the assembly manifest contained within airvehicles.dll. As you can see, you now have a [.module extern] reference to the ufo.netmodule (in addition to the various [.assembly extern] tags):

```
.module extern ufo.netmodule
.assembly extern mscorlib
{
  .publickeytoken = (B7 7A 5C 56 19 34 E0 89 )
  .ver 1:0:2411:0
}
.assembly extern Microsoft.VisualBasic
{
  .publickeytoken = (B0 3F 5F 7F 11 D5 0A 3A )
  .ver 7:0:0:0
}
.assembly airvehicles
{
  .hash algorithm 0x00008004
  .ver 0:0:0:0
}
.file ufo.netmodule
    .hash = (8D 6F 59 D1 C2 21 18 50 C9 92 6E 4C 5A AC BF 37
             DD 17 5C 16 )
.module airvehicles.dll
```

Again, realize that the only entity that links together the airvehicles.dll and the ufo.netmodule is the assembly manifest. These two binary files have *not* been merged into a single, larger DLL.

Using the Multifile Assembly

The user of a multifile assembly could care less that the assembly they are referencing is composed of numerous files. To illustrate, build a brand new VB .NET Console application (or if you prefer, a Windows Forms application) and set a reference to the AirVehicles.dll. Within your Module type, create two subroutines that activate a given air vehicle. Within Main(), call each method, placing a message box call between each (in this way you are able to delay the loading of the ufo.netmodule). Here is the complete code:

```
Imports AirVehicles
Imports System.Windows.Forms
Module Module1
    Sub Main()
        UseHelicopter()
        MessageBox.Show("Click to load ufo.netmodule")
        UseUFO()
        MessageBox.Show("Done")
    End Sub
    Sub UseHelicopter()
        Dim h As New AirVehicles.Helicopter()
        h.TakeOff()
    End Sub
    Sub UseUFO()
        ' This will load the *.netmodule on demand.
        Dim u As New UFO()
        u.AbductHuman()
    End Sub
End Module
```

Now, start a debug session and once the first message box is displayed, open the Modules window (using the "Debug | Windows" menu selection). At this point, you should see that airvehicles.dll has been loaded (see Figure 7-25).

Modules

Name	Address	Path	Order
mscorlib.dll	61940000-61B1E000	c:\winnt\microsoft.net\framework\v...	1
MultiFileUser....	11000000-1100A000	C:\Apress Books\VB.NET\Code\Chap...	2
system.windo...	5F060000-5F246000	c:\winnt\assembly\gac\system.wind...	3
airvehicles.dll	02F80000-02F88000	c:\apress books\vb.net\code\chapte...	4
system.dll	5E4B0000-5E61A000	c:\winnt\assembly\gac\system\1.0.2...	5
system.drawi...	5EC00000-5EC70000	c:\winnt\assembly\gac\system.drawi...	6

Figure 7-25. A single module of the multifile assembly

Now, dismiss the message box. You should now find that the related ufo.netmodule has been loaded (see Figure 7-26).

Modules

Name	Address	Path	Order
mscorlib.dll	61940000-61B1E000	c:\winnt\microsoft.net\framework\v...	1
MultiFileUser....	11000000-1100A000	C:\Apress Books\VB.NET\Code\Chap...	2
system.windo...	5F060000-5F246000	c:\winnt\assembly\gac\system.wind...	3
airvehicles.dll	02F80000-02F88000	c:\apress books\vb.net\code\chapte...	4
system.dll	5E4B0000-5E61A000	c:\winnt\assembly\gac\system\1.0.2...	5
system.drawi...	5EC00000-5EC70000	c:\winnt\assembly\gac\system.drawi...	6
ufo.netmodule	03690000-03696000	c:\apress books\vb.net\code\chapte...	7

*Figure 7-26. *.netmodules are loaded on demand*

Again, remember that the point of multifile assemblies is to have a physical collection of files behave as a single named (and versionable) unit. In and of themselves, *.netmodules do not have an individual version number, cannot be loaded directly by the .NET runtime and cannot be used as a stand-alone entity. Individual *.netmodules can only be loaded by the module that contains the assembly manifest.

At this point you should feel comfortable with the process of building both single file and multifile assemblies. To be completely honest, the chances are that 99.99 percent of all your assemblies will be single file entities. Nevertheless, multifile assemblies can prove helpful when you wish to break a large physical binary into more modular units. Next you need to distinguish between private and shared assemblies. If you are coming into the .NET paradigm from a classic COM perspective, be prepared for some significant changes.

SOURCE CODE *The MultiFileAsm and MultiFileUser projects are included under the Chapter 7 subdirectory.*

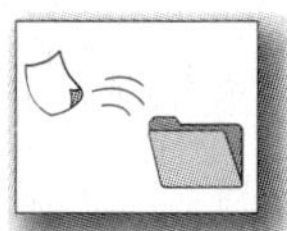

Understanding Private Assemblies

Formally speaking, an assembly is either "private" or "shared." The good news is each variation has the same underlying structure (i.e., some number of modules and an associated assembly manifest). Furthermore, each flavor of assembly provides the same kind of services (access to some number of Public types). The real differences between a private and shared assembly boils down to versioning policies and deployment issues. Let's begin by examining the traits of a private assembly, which is far and away the more common of the two options.

Private assemblies are a collection of types that are only used by the application with which it has been deployed. For example, CarLibrary.dll is a private assembly used by the CSharpCarClient and VBCarClient applications. When you create a private assembly, the assumption is that the collection of types are only accessed by the "using" application, and *not* shared with other applications on the system.

Private assemblies are required to be located within the main directory of the owning application (termed the *application directory*) or a subdirectory thereof. For example, recall that when you set a reference to the CarLibrary assembly (as we did in the CSharpCarClient and VBCarClient applications), the Visual Studio .NET IDE responded by making a full copy of the assembly that was placed in your project's application directory. This is the default behavior, as private assemblies are assumed to be the deployment option of choice.

Note the painfully stark contrast to classic COM. There is no need to register any items under HKEY_CLASSES_ROOT and no need to enter a hard-coded path to the binary using an InprocServer32 or LocalServer32 listing. The resolution and loading of the private CarLibrary happens by virtue of the fact that the assembly is placed in the application directory. In fact, if you moved CSharpCarClient.exe and CarLibrary.dll to a new directory, the application would *still run*. To illustrate this point, copy these two files to your desktop and run the client (see Figure 7-27).

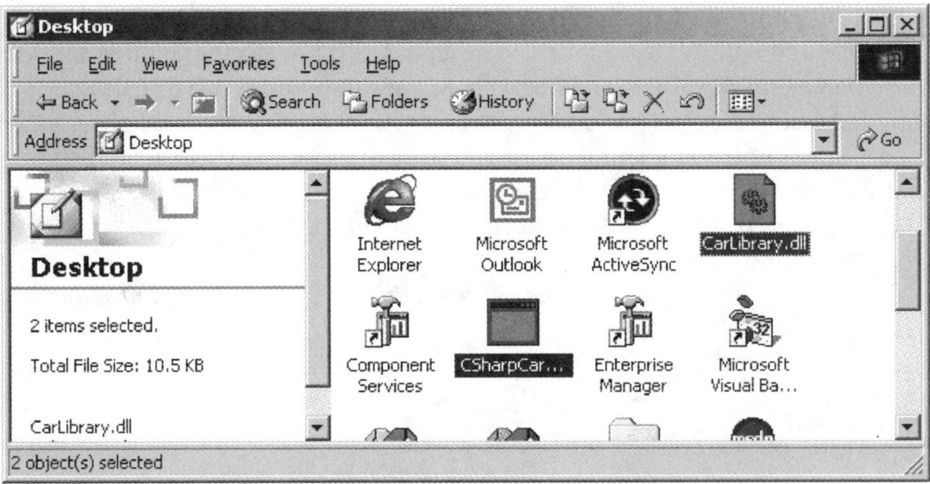

Figure 7-27. Can you say "XCopy installation"?

Uninstalling (or replicating) an application that makes exclusive use of private assemblies is a no-brainer. Delete (or copy) the application folder. Unlike classic COM, you do not need to worry about dozens of orphaned registry settings. More important, you do not need to worry that the removal of private assemblies will break any other applications on the machine!

Probing Basics

Later in this chapter, you are exposed to a number of gory details regarding location resolution of an assembly. Until then, the following overview should help prime the pump. Formally speaking, the .NET runtime resolves the location of an assembly using a technique termed *probing*, which is much less invasive than it sounds. Probing is the process of mapping an external assembly reference (i.e., [.assembly extern]) to the correct corresponding binary file. For example, when the runtime reads the following line from the VBCarClient's manifest:

```
.assembly extern CarLibrary
{
...
}
```

a search is made in the application directory for a file named CarLibrary.dll. If a DLL binary cannot be located, an attempt is made to locate an EXE version (CarLibrary.exe). As you will see a bit later in this chapter, the .NET runtime actually checks the assembly manifest for a [.publickeytoken] tag before examining the application directory. This tag specifies that the assembly is "shared," and will most likely be located within the Global Assembly Cache (GAC). For the time being, it is safe to assume that the runtime engine probes for DLL files first, followed by EXE files in the application directory.

The Identity of a Private Assembly

The identity of a private assembly consists of a friendly string name and numerical version, both of which are recorded in the assembly manifest. The friendly name is typically created based on the name of the binary module that contains the assembly's manifest (but this is only a convention). For example, if you examine the assembly manifest of CarLibrary.dll, you find the following friendly name and version information (your version may vary):

```
.assembly CarLibrary as "CarLibrary"
{
   ...
   .ver 1:0:454:30104
}
```

However, given the nature of a private assembly, it should make sense that the .NET runtime ignores version numbers when loading the assembly. The assumption is that private assemblies do not need to have any elaborate version checking, given that the client application is the only entity that "knows" of its existence. As an interesting corollary you should understand that it is (very) possible for a single machine to have multiple copies of the same private assembly in various application directories.

Private Assemblies and XML Configuration Files

When the .NET runtime is instructed to bind to a private assembly, the first step is to determine the presence of an application configuration file. These optional files contain XML tags that control the binding behavior used by the launching application. By law, configuration files must have the same name as the launching application and take a *.config file extension (for example, TheClient.exe.config).

XML configuration files can be used to specify any optional subdirectories to be searched during the process of binding to private assemblies. As you have seen earlier in this chapter, a componentized .NET application can be deployed simply by placing all assemblies into the same directory as the launching application. Often, however, you may want to deploy an application such that the application directory contains a number of related subdirectories, to give some meaningful structure to the application as a whole.

You see this all the time in commercial software. For example, assume your main directory is called MyRadApplication, which contains a number of subdirectories (\Images, \Bin, \SavedGames, \OtherCoolStuff). Using application configuration files, you can instruct the runtime where it should probe while attempting to locate the set of private assemblies used by the launching application.

To illustrate, let's create a simple configuration file for the previous CSharpCarClient application. The goal is to move the referenced assembly (CarLibrary) from the Debug folder into a new subdirectory named Foo\Bar. Go ahead and move this file now (see Figure 7-28).

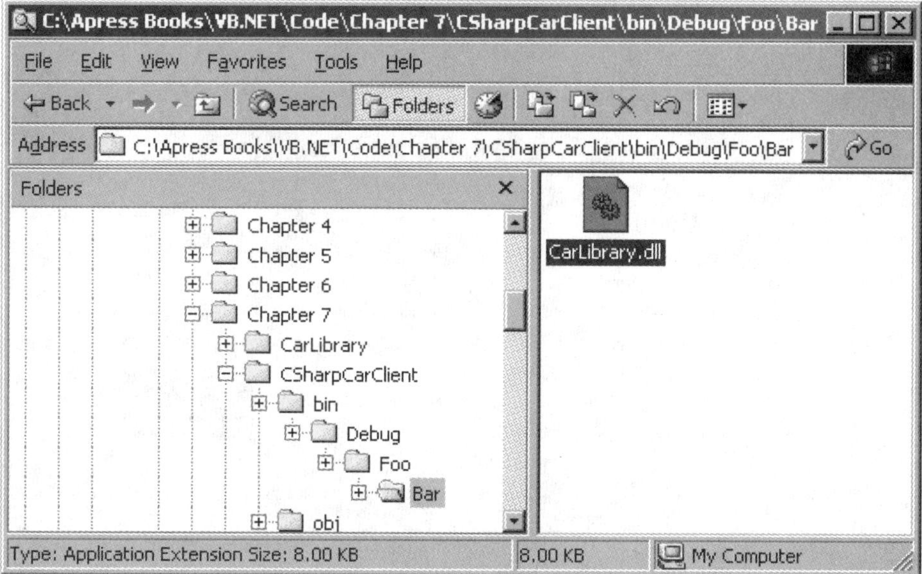

Figure 7-28. Relocating your assembly

Now, create a new configuration file named CSharpCarClient.exe.config (Notepad will do just fine) and save it into the *same* folder containing the CSharpCarClient.exe application. The beginning of an application configuration file is marked with the <Configuration> root element. Before the closing </Configuration> tag, specify an assemblyBinding row, which is used to specify alternative locations to search for a given assembly via the privatePath attribute (FYI, multiple subdirectories can be specified using a semicolon-delimited list). Here is the XML:

```
<!-- CSharpCarClient.exe.config -->
<configuration>
    <runtime>
        <assemblyBinding xmlns="urn:schemas-microsoft-com:asm.v1">
            <probing privatePath="foo\bar"/>
        </assemblyBinding>
    </runtime>
</configuration>
```

Once you are done, save the file and launch the client. You will find that the CSharpCarClient application runs without a hitch. As a final test, change the name of your configuration file and attempt to run the program once again (see Figure 7-29).

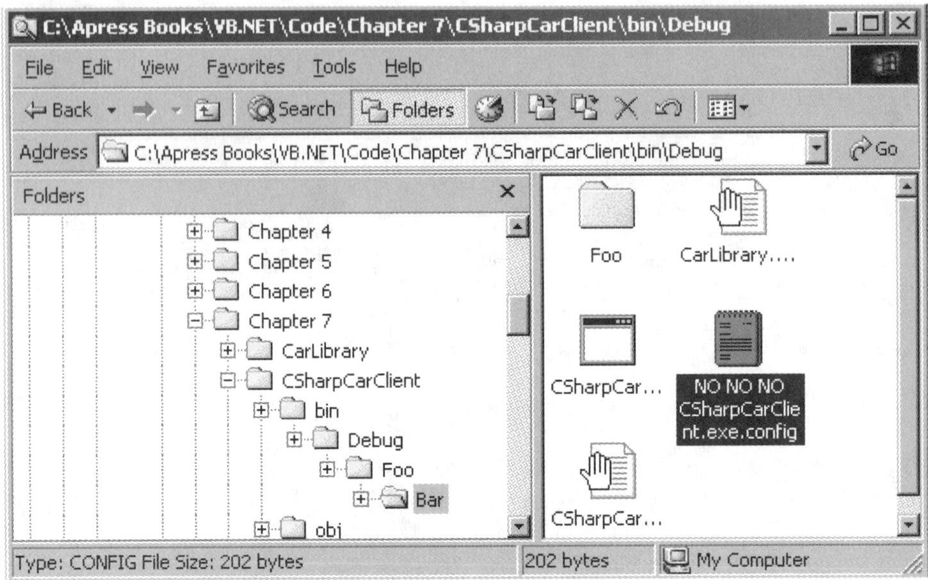

*Figure 7-29. *.config files must have the same name as the launching application*

The client application now fails. Recall that configuration files must have the same name as the launching application. Because you have renamed this file, the .NET runtime assumes you do not have a configuration file, and thus attempts to probe for the referenced assembly in the application directory (which it cannot locate).

In this example, you created an application configuration file for use by an EXE assembly. You should also be aware that ASP.NET applications also make use of application configuration files. Unlike EXE *.config files, ASP.NET web application configuration files are always named simply "web.config." You formally examine ASP.NET in Chapter 15.

Specifics of Binding to a Private Assembly

To wrap up the current discussion, let's formalize the specific steps involved in binding to a private assembly at runtime. First, a request to load an assembly may be either *explicit* or *implicit*. An implicit load request occurs whenever the manifest makes a direct reference to some external assembly. As you recall, external references are marked with the [.assembly extern] instruction:

```
// An implicit load request. . .
.assembly extern CarLibrary
{
        . . .
}
```

An explicit load request occurs programmatically using System.Reflection.Assembly.Load(). The Assembly class is examined in Chapter 8, but be aware that the Load() method allows you to specify the name and various optional aspects such as version and culture information (to specify localized string resources) and the public key token (to identify the public key of a shared assembly). To illustrate, here is a simple example of an explicit load:

```
' An explicit load request. . .
Dim asm as System.Reflection.Assembly = _
    System.Reflection.Assembly.Load("CarLibrary")
```

Collectively, the name, version, public key token and culture information is termed an *assembly reference* (or simply AsmRef). The entity in charge of locating the correct assembly based on an AsmRef is termed the *assembly resolver,* which is a facility of the CLR.

As mentioned earlier, an application directory is nothing more than a folder on your hard drive (for example, C:\MyApp) that contains all the files for a given application. If necessary, an application directory may specify additional subdirectories (e.g., C:\MyApp\Bin, C:\MyApp\Tools, and so on) to establish a more stringent file hierarchy.

When a binding request is made, the runtime passes an AsmRef to the assembly resolver. If the resolver determines the AsmRef refers to a private assembly (meaning there is no public key token recorded in the manifest), the search is as follows:

1. First, the assembly resolver attempts to locate a configuration file in the application directory. As you have seen, this file can specify additional subdirectories to include in the search, as well as establish a version policy to use for the current bind. If a configuration file does exist, any specified subdirectories are searched.

2. If there is no configuration file, the runtime attempts to discover the correct assembly by examining the current application directory.

3. If the assembly cannot be found within the application directory (or a specified subdirectory) the search stops here and a TypeLoadException exception is raised, as private assemblies are always located within the application directory (or a specified subdirectory).

To solidify this sequence of events, Figure 7-30 illustrates the process outlined in the preceding list.

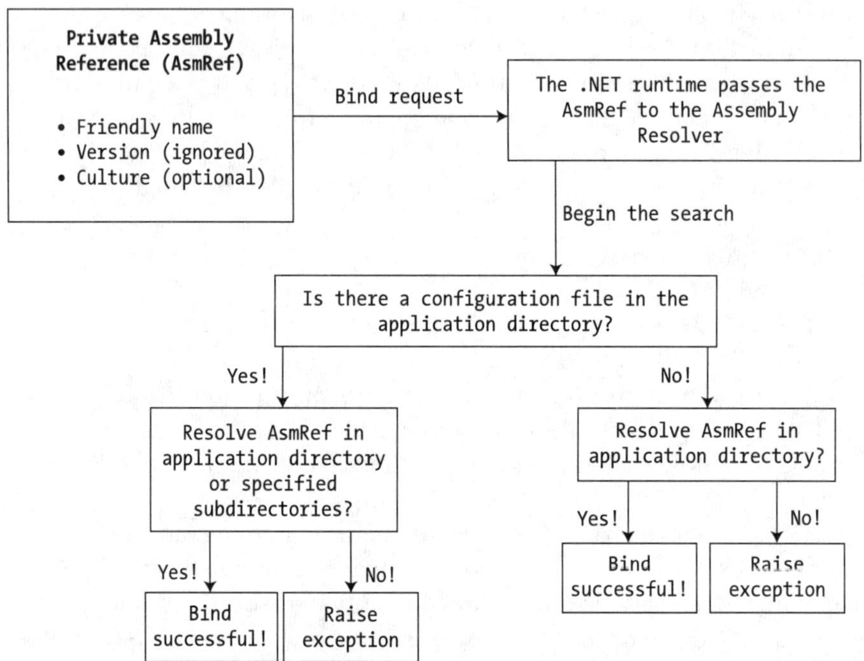

Figure 7-30. Searching for a private assembly

Again, as you can see, the location of a private assembly is fairly simple to resolve. If the application directory does not contain a configuration file, the assembly resolver simply looks for a binary that matches the correct AsmRef. If the application directory does contain a configuration file, any specified subdirectories are also searched.

Understanding Shared Assemblies

Like a private assembly, a "shared" assembly is a collection of types and (optional) resources contained within some number of modules. The most obvious difference between shared and private assemblies is the fact that shared assemblies can be used by several clients on a single machine. Clearly, if you want to create a machine-wide class library, a shared assembly is the way to go.

A shared assembly is typically not deployed within the same directory as the application making use of it. Rather, shared assemblies are installed into a machine-wide Global Assembly Cache, which lends itself to yet another colorful acronym in the programming universe—the GAC. The GAC itself is located under the <drive>:\WinNT\Assembly subdirectory (see Figure 7-31).

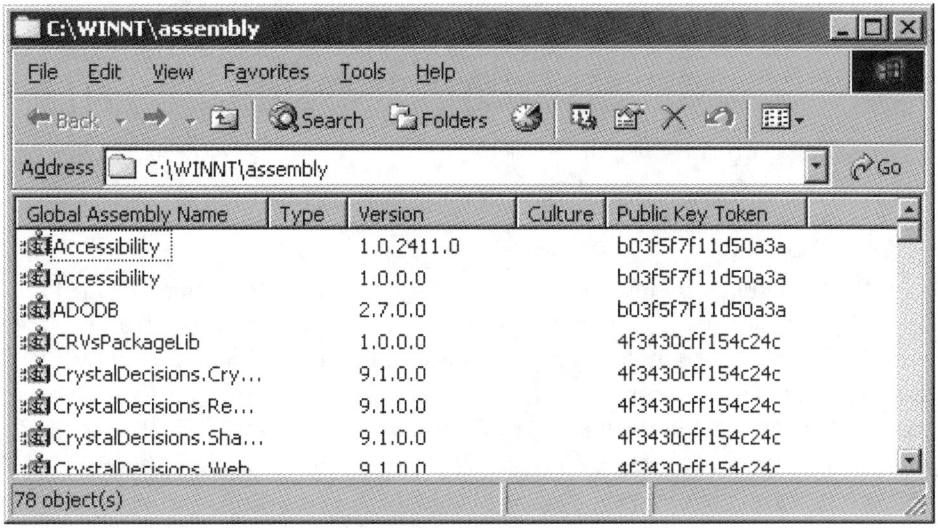

Figure 7-31. The Global Assembly Cache (GAC)

This is yet another major difference between the COM and .NET architectures. In COM, shared applications can reside anywhere on a given machine, provided they are properly registered. Under .NET, shared assemblies are typically placed into a centralized well-known location (the GAC).

Unlike private assemblies, a shared assembly requires additional information beyond the friendly text string. As you may have guessed, the .NET runtime *does* enforce version checking for a shared assembly before it is loaded on behalf of the calling application. In addition, a shared assembly must be assigned a "shared name."

Problems with Your GAC?

By way of a quick side note, I have noticed that some of my development machines are unable to display the GAC correctly under .NET Beta2. The problem is that the GAC is a shell extension that requires the registration of a COM server named shfusion.dll. During installation, this server may fail to register correctly. If you are having problems opening the GAC on your machine, simply register this COM server using regsvr32.exe and you should be just fine.

Understanding Shared Names

When you want to create an assembly that can be used by numerous applications on a given machine, your first step is to create a unique shared name for the assembly. A shared name contains the following information:

- A friendly string name (just like a private assembly)
- A version identifier (that will be used during the bind)
- A public/private key pair
- A digital signature

When creating a shared assembly, an obligatory step is to generate a file that contains a public/private key pair (by convention, these files end with a *.snk file extension). Public keys are used to uniquely identify the individual (or company) that has created a given assembly or set of assemblies. For example, assume your company is in the business of building GUI-based code libraries. Each assembly you ship to the world at large will typically use the same public key, thereby giving your types an identity with the world at large.

The private key is not stored within the assembly, but is stored in a safe location for future use. The private key is used by a .NET-aware compiler to generate a digital signature (which is verified against the public key) of the assembly, which is represented by a hashcode of the assembly manifest (including any optional *.netmodules).

Eventually, the *.snk file is included in the build cycle. The .NET-aware compiler reads this file and writes the full public key into the assembly's manifest (marked with the [.publickey] tag).

Now, assume some client has referenced a shared assembly for use in a given project. When the compiler generates the client binary, a token (represented as an 8-byte hash) of the shared assembly's public key is recorded in the client's assembly manifest. At runtime, the CLR ensures that both the client and the shared assembly are making use of the same public key. If these keys are identical, the client application can rest assured that the correct assembly has been loaded. Figure 7-32 illustrates the basic picture.

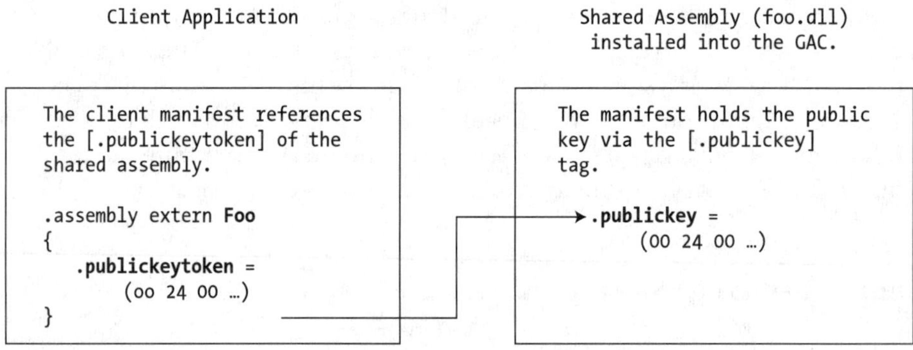

Figure 7-32. Matching public key tokens

As you might guess, there are additional details regarding public/private key pairs. You don't need more details for now, so check out online Help if you desire more information.

Building a Shared Assembly (the Hard Way)

To generate a public/private key, you may make direct use of the sn.exe (strong name) utility. Although this tool has numerous command-line options, all you need to concern ourselves with is the "-k" argument, which instructs the tool to generate a new key pair that will be saved to a specified file (Figure 7-33).

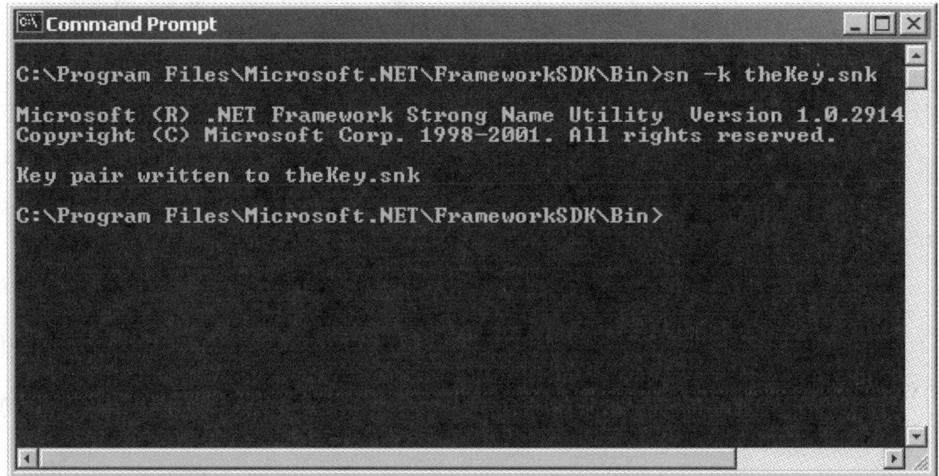

*Figure 7-33. Creating a *.snk file*

If you examine the contents of this new file (theKey.snk) you see the binary markings of the key pair (see Figure 7-34).

```
theKey.snk
2 53 41 32 00 04 00 00   .....$..RSA2....
3 3F 9F 67 59 80 74 AA   .........?.gY.t.
7 D1 4E 41 C0 21 F2 A7   ..~....u$g.NA.!..
A 24 BE AE DF 20 48 20   .Z...gL`.$... H
1 5C 51 B6 C1 EB 63 1F   ....<8..Q\Q...c.
F C6 35 4D 8F A9 67 2C   ~..|..>...5M..g,
3 ED 59 B0 9E 35 13 F5   u..".I.2..Y..5..
C 00 03 BE 9A 45 28 03   ...kP.........E(.
8 D2 5C 00 2E E3 50 F7   .h.?1...(.\...P.
B 10 58 4D 82 8B 50 5F   o.X..d....XM..P_
9 48 C9 12 50 71 FD C8   .,....~^.H..Pq..
9 30 0E F2 52 E5 ED 13   .....ejy.0..R...
0 A7 3B 6F 74 19 12 AB   zz}^......;ot...
E E3 73 7F A2 28 8F 38   .?...{:8..s..(.8
```

*Figure 7-34. The *.snk file, up close and personal*

To continue with the example, assume you have created a new VB .NET Class Library called (of course) MySharedAssembly that contains the following class definition:

```
' Add a ref to System.Windows.Forms.dll
Imports System.Windows.Forms
Public Class VWMiniVan
    Private isBustedByTheFuzz As Boolean = False
    Public Sub Play60sTunes()
        MessageBox.Show("What a loooong, strange trip it's been...")
    End Sub
    Public Property Busted() As Boolean
        Get
            Return isBustedByTheFuzz
        End Get
        Set(ByVal Value As Boolean)
            isBustedByTheFuzz = Value
        End Set
    End Property
End Class
```

The next step is to record the public key in the assembly manifest. The easiest way to do so is to leverage the use of a system-supplied attribute. When you create a new VB .NET project workspace, you will notice that one of your initial project files is named "AssemblyInfo.vb" (see Figure 7-35).

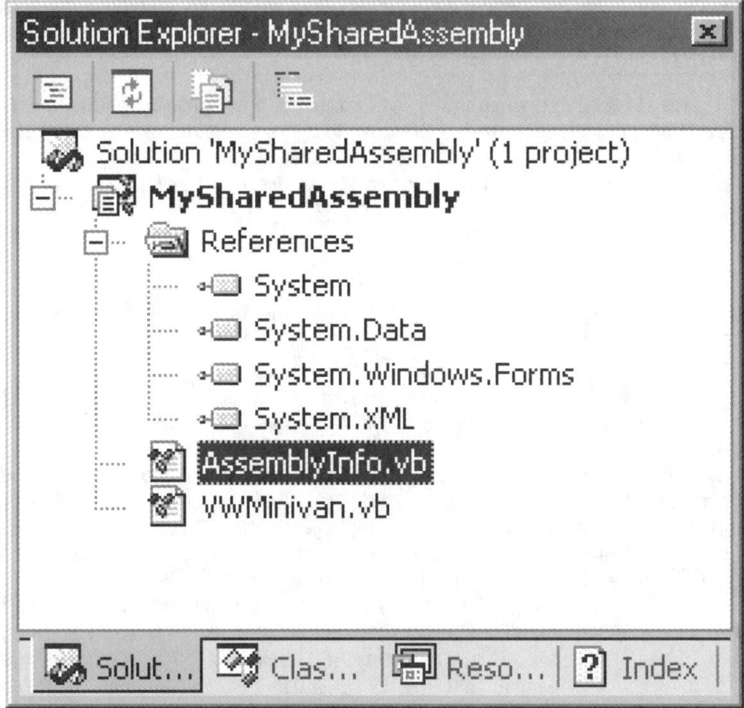

Figure 7-35. The AssemblyInfo.vb file

This file contains a number of (initially empty) attributes that are consumed by a .NET-aware compiler. As well, you are free to add additional attributes as you so choose. One such attribute named AssemblyKeyFile is used to specify the *.snk file used to build a shared assembly. To do so, add the following attribute (and adjust the path to your *.snk file as necessary):

```
<Assembly: AssemblyKeyFile("C:\theKey.snk")>
```

Using this assembly level attribute, the VB .NET compiler now merges the necessary information into the corresponding manifest, as can be seen using ILDasm.exe (note the [.publickey] tag in Figure 7-36).

```
MANIFEST
.assembly MySharedAssembly
{
  // --- The following custom attribute is added automatically,
  //  .custom instance void [mscorlib]System.Diagnostics.Debugg
  //
  .custom instance void [mscorlib]System.Reflection.AssemblyKey



  .custom instance void [mscorlib]System.Runtime.InteropService


  .custom instance void [mscorlib]System.CLSCompliantAttribute:
  .custom instance void [mscorlib]System.Reflection.AssemblyTra
  .custom instance void [mscorlib]System.Reflection.AssemblyCop
  .custom instance void [mscorlib]System.Reflection.AssemblyPro
  .custom instance void [mscorlib]System.Reflection.AssemblyCom
  .custom instance void [mscorlib]System.Reflection.AssemblyDes
  .custom instance void [mscorlib]System.Reflection.AssemblyTit
  .publickey = (00 24 00 00 04 80 00 00 94 00 00 00 06 02 00 00
                00 24 00 00 52 53 41 31 00 04 00 00 01 00 01 00
                B5 CC FA F3 B3 3F 9F 67 59 80 74 AA E8 DA 7E ED
                9D AA 75 24 67 D1 4E 41 C0 21 F2 A7 85 5A EE D6
                F3 67 4C 60 AA 24 BE AE DF 20 48 20 14 C1 1F 1
                3C 38 84 FB 51 5C 51 B6 C1 EB 63 1F 7E BB DD 7C
                0E E1 3E FD 9F C6 35 4D 8F A9 67 2C 75 17 97 22
                E7 49 83 32 A3 ED 59 B0 9E 35 13 F5 92 C2 84 6B
                50 AA 8E C5 8C 00 03 BE 9A 45 28 03 EA 68 9E 3F
                31 E4 9C A2 28 D2 5C 00 2E E3 50 F7 6F 95 58 BB
  .hash algorithm 0x00008004
  .ver 1:0:0:0
}
```

Figure 7-36. The markings of a shared assembly

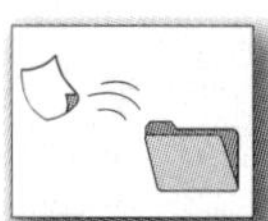

SOURCE CODE *The SharedAssembly project is located under the Chapter 7 subdirectory.*

Building a Shared Assembly (the Easy Way)

In addition to the raw sn.exe application, you are also able to create a *.snk file using the VB .NET IDE. To do so, simply select the access the project Properties window and select the "Strong Name" node (see Figure 7-37).

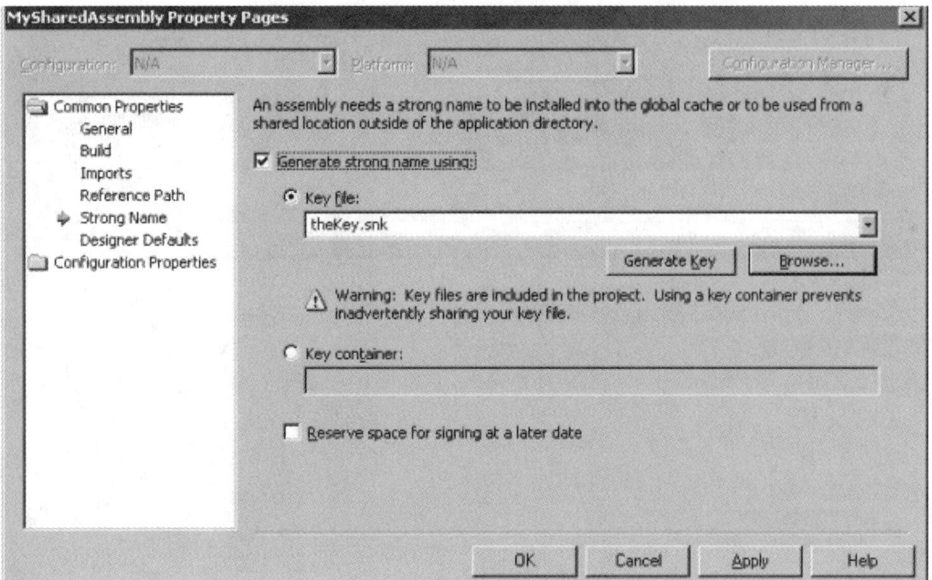

Figure 7-37. Autogenerating key files using VS .NET

Note that you are able to automatically generate a new *.snk file or reference an existing key file. Either way, the file will automatically be included into your project's build cycle (and thus, you will not need to manually edit the AssemblyKeyFile attribute).

Installing Assemblies into the GAC

Once you have established a strong name for your shared assembly, the final step is to install it into the GAC. The simplest approach to install a shared assembly into the GAC is to drag and drop the file(s) onto the active window (you are also free to make use of the gacutil.exe command-line tool; however, I'll let you check that out at your leisure). See Figure 7-38.

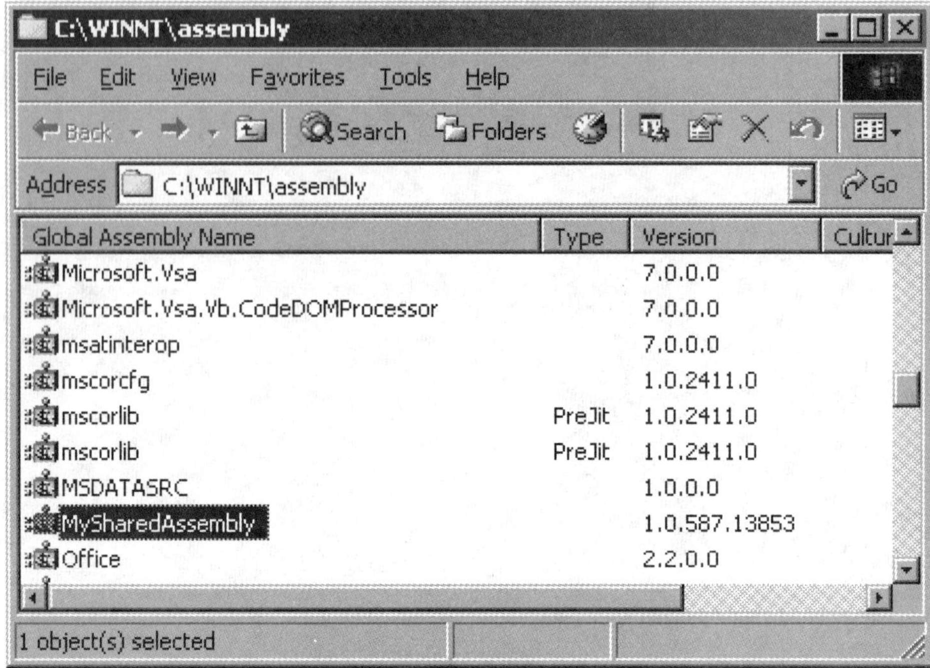

Figure 7-38. Installing your assembly into the GAC

Do be aware that you must have Administrative rights on the computer to install assemblies into the GAC. This is a good thing, in that it prevents the casual user from accidentally breaking existing applications.

The end result is that your assembly has now been placed into the GAC and may be shared by multiple applications on the target machine. On a related note, when you want to remove an assembly from the GAC, you may do so with a simple right-click (just select Delete from the context menu).

Using a Shared Assembly

Now to prove the point, assume you have created a new VB .NET Console application (called SharedAssemblyUser), set a reference to the MySharedAssembly binary, and create the following class definition:

```
Imports MySharedAssembly
Module Module1
    Sub Main()
        Try
            Dim v As VWMiniVan = New VWMiniVan()
```

```
            v.Play60sTunes()
        Catch e As TypeLoadException
            ' Can't find assembly!
            Console.WriteLine(e.Message)
        End Try
    End Sub
End Module
```

Recall that when you reference a shared assembly, IDE automatically creates a local copy of the assembly for use by the client application. However, when you reference an assembly that contains a public key (as is the case with the SharedAssembly.dll), you do not receive a local copy. The assumption is that assemblies containing a public key are designed to be shared (and are therefore placed in the GAC).

Now run the client application once again. If all is well, everything should still function correctly, as the .NET runtime consulted the GAC during its quest to resolve the location of the requested assembly (see Figure 7-39).

Figure 7-39. Strange indeed

SOURCE CODE *The SharedLibUser project can be found under the Chapter 7 subdirectory. Before you run this application, be sure to install SharedAssembly.dll into the GAC.*

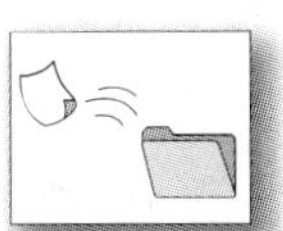

Understanding .NET Version Policies

As you have already learned, the .NET runtime does not bother to perform version checks for private assemblies without a strong name (yes, private assemblies may also be assigned a strong name). The versioning story changes significantly when a request is made to load a shared assembly. Given that the version of a shared assembly is of prime importance, let's review the composition of version numbers. As you recall, a version number is marked by four discrete parts (for example, 2.0.2.11). The first two numbers (2.0) represent the major and minor version of the binary. The third number represents the build number (2) while the final number (11) represents the revision.

Whenever two assemblies differ by either the major or minor version number (e.g., 2.0 versus 2.5) they are considered to be *completely incompatible* with each other as far as the .NET runtime is concerned. When assemblies differ by major or minor numerical markings, you can assume significant changes have occurred (e.g., method name changes, types have been added or removed, parameters have changed, and so forth). Therefore, if a client is requesting a bind to version 2.0 but the GAC only contains version 2.5, the bind request fails (unless overridden by an application configuration file).

If two assemblies have identical major and minor version numbers, but have different build numbers (e.g., 2.5.0.0 vs. 2.5.1.0) the .NET runtime assumes they *might be* compatible with each other (in other words, backward compatibility is assumed, but not guaranteed). By way of a concrete example, a Service Pack release typically involves modifying the build number.

Finally, you have a revision number. When two assemblies differ only by their revision value, the .NET runtime assumes they are fully compatible. Revision numbers are typically modified with the release of a software patch. The idea here is that all calling conventions (e.g., method names, parameters, supported interfaces, and so forth) are identical to previous versions.

Recording Version Information

One question you might be asking yourself at this point is *where* was this version number specified? Recall that every VB .NET project defines a file named AssemblyInfo.vb. If you examine this file, you see an attribute named AssemblyVersion, which is initially set to a string reading "1.0.*":

```
' Version information for an assembly consists of the following four values:
'
'       Major Version
'       Minor Version
'       Build Number
'       Revision
'
' You can specify all the values or you can default the Build and Revision
Numbers
' by using the '*' as shown below:
<Assembly: AssemblyVersion("1.0.*")>
```

Every new VB .NET project begins life versioned at 1.0. As you build new versions of a shared assembly, part of your task is to update the four-part version number. Do be aware that the IDE automatically increments the build and revision numbers using a time stamp (as marked by the "*" tag). If you want to enforce an application-specific value for the assembly's build and/or revision, simply update accordingly:

```
<Assembly: AssemblyVersion("1.0.0.0")>
```

Freezing the Current MySharedAssembly

To really understand .NET versioning policies, you need to have a concrete example. The current goal is to update your previous MySharedAssembly.dll to support additional functionality, update the version number, and then place the new version into the GAC. At this point, you are able to experiment with the use of application configuration files to specify various version policies, as well as side-by-side execution.

To begin, update the constructor of the VWMiniVan class to display a message verifying the *current* version in the class constructor:

```
Sub New()
    MessageBox.Show("Using version 1.0.0.0!", "Shared car")
End Sub
```

Next, update the AssemblyVersion attribute to be fully qualified to version 1.0.0.0 (as seen in the previous section). Go ahead and recompile the project.

The next thing you need to do is ensure that your original SharedAssembly.dll is removed from the GAC (go ahead and delete this assembly now). Next, move your existing 1.0.0.0 assembly into a new folder (I called mine Version1) to ensure you freeze this version (see Figure 7-40).

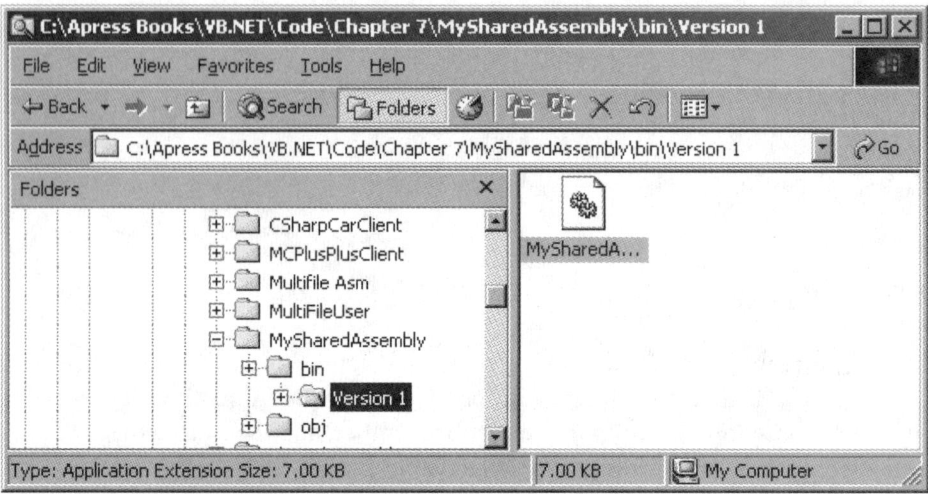

Figure 7-40. Preserving version 1.0.0.0

Now (once again!) place this assembly back into the GAC. Notice that the version of this assembly is <1.0.0.0> (see Figure 7-41).

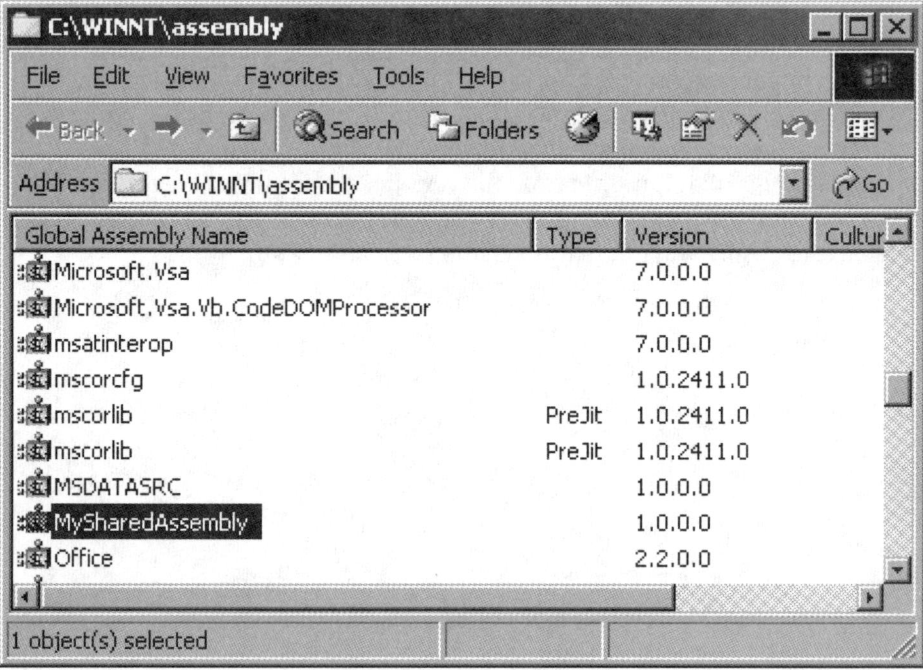

Figure 7-41. Back in the GAC

Once version 1.0.0.0 of the SharedAssembly has been inserted into the GAC, right-click this assembly and select Properties from the context-sensitive pop-up menu. Verify that the path to this binary maps to the Version1 subdirectory. Finally, rebuild and run the current SharedAssemblyUser application. Things should continue to work just fine.

Building SharedAssembly Version 2.0

To illustrate the .NET versioning, let's modify the current SharedAssembly project. Update your VWMiniVan class with a new member (which makes use of a custom enumeration) to allow the user to play more modern musical selections. Also be sure to update the message displayed from within the constructor logic.

```
' Which band do you want?
Public Enum BandName
    TonesOnTail
    SkinnyPuppy
    deftones
    PTP
End Enum
Public Class VWMiniVan
    . . .
    Sub New()
        MessageBox.Show("Using version 2.0.0.0!", "Shared car")
    End Sub
    . . .
    Public Sub CrankGoodTunes(ByVal band As BandName)
        Select Case band
            Case BandName.deftones
                MessageBox.Show("So forget about me. . .")
            Case BandName.PTP
                MessageBox.Show("Tick tick tock. . .")
            Case BandName.SkinnyPuppy
                MessageBox.Show("Water vapor, to air. . .")
            Case BandName.TonesOnTail
                MessageBox.Show("Oooooh the rain. Oh the rain.")
        End Select
    End Sub
End Class
```

Before you compile, let's upgrade this version of this assembly to 2.0.0.0:

```
' Update your assemblyinfo.vb file as follows...
<Assembly: AssemblyVersion("2.0.0.0")>
```

If you look in your project's bin folder, you see that you have a new version of this assembly (2.0) while the previous version is safe in storage under the Version1 directory. Finally, let's install this new assembly into the GAC. Notice that you now have *two* versions of the same assembly (see Figure 7-42).

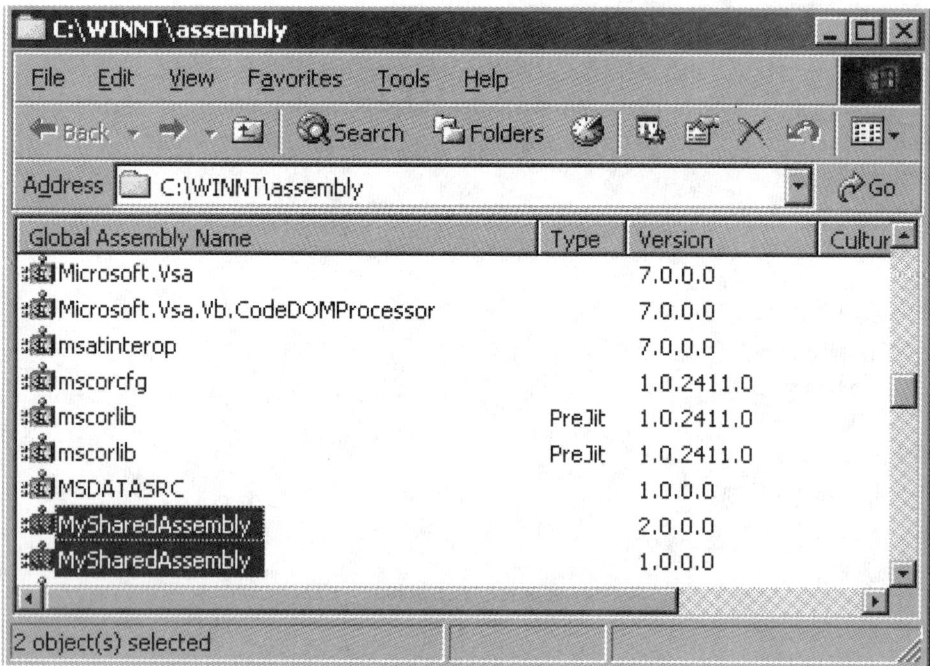

Figure 7-42. Side-by-side execution

Now that you have a distinctly versioned assembly recorded in the GAC, you can begin to work with application configuration files to control how a client binds to a given version.

Specifying Custom Version Policies

When you want to dynamically control how an application binds to an assembly (such as specifying a new version), you need to author an application configuration file. As you have already seen during the discussion of private assemblies, configuration files are blocks of XML that are used to customize the binding process. Recall that these files must have the same name as the owning application (with a *.config extension) and be placed directly in the application directory. In addition to the privatePath tag (used to specify where to probe for private assemblies), a configuration file may specify information for shared assemblies.

The first point of interest is using an application configuration file to specify a specific assembly version that is to be loaded, regardless of what may be listed in the corresponding manifest. When you want to redirect a client to bind to an alternate shared assembly, you make use of the <dependentAssembly> and <bindingRedirect> attributes. For example, the following configuration file forces version 2.0.0.0:

```
<configuration>
    <runtime>
        <assemblyBinding xmlns="urn:schemas-microsoft-com:asm.v1">
            <dependentAssembly>
                <assemblyIdentity name="mysharedassembly"
                    publicKeyToken="6e3828e679a0904"
                    culture=""/>
                <bindingRedirect oldVersion= "1.0.0.0"
                newVersion= "2.0.0.0"/>
            </dependentAssembly>
        </assemblyBinding>
    </runtime>
</configuration>
```

Here, the oldVersion tag is used to specify the version that you want to override (which is typically the version referenced in the client's manifest). The newVersion tag marks a specific version to load.

To test this out for yourself, create the previous configuration file and save it into the directory of the SharedAssemblyUser application (be sure you name this configuration file correctly). Now, run the program. You should see the message that appears in Figure 7-43.

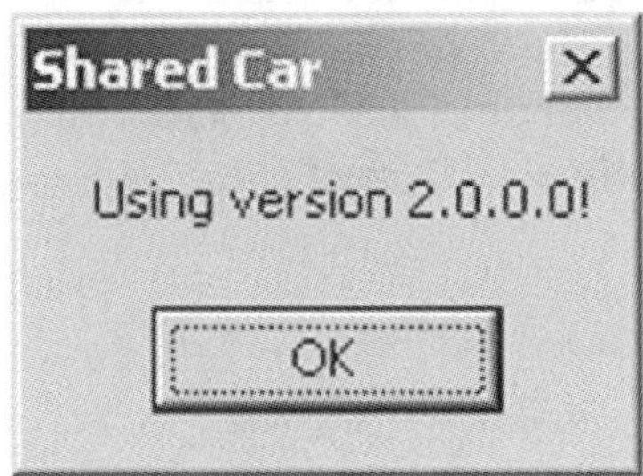

Figure 7-43. Activating version 2.0.0.0

If you update the newVersion attribute to 1.0.0.0:

```
<bindingRedirect oldVersion= "1.0.0.0"
    newVersion= "1.0.0.0"/>
```

you now see a message showing that you have activated version 1.0.0.0. (see Figure 7-44).

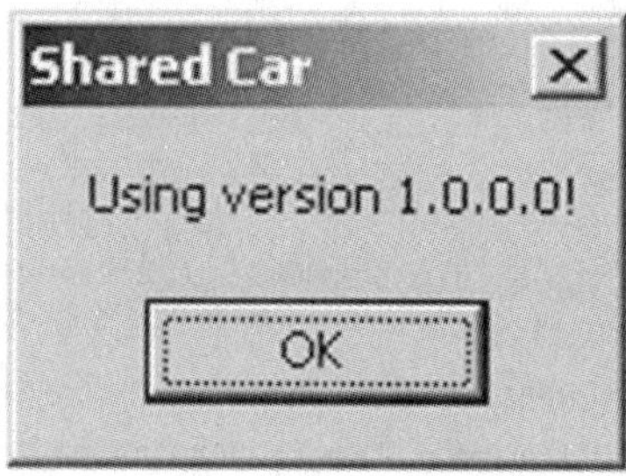

Figure 7-44. Activating version 1.0.0.0

What you have just observed is the notion of side-by-side execution mentioned earlier in the chapter. Because the .NET Framework allows you to place multiple versions of the same assembly into the GAC, you can easily configure custom version policies as you (or a system administrator) see fit. The short answer is that you finally have an elegant solution to DLL Hell.

Using the .NET Administrative Tool (mscorcfg.msc)

In the previous sections you have learned how to build XML application configuration files by hand. While seeing what happens under the hood is edifying, the process of crafting raw XML files is a bit on the verbose side and a rather error-prone endeavor. Given this, the .NET SDK ships with a tool named mscorcfg.msc (yet another MMC snap-in utility) that will generate the correct XML automatically, based on your design-time configurations. Open up the .NET admin tool (which by default is located under C:\WINNT\Microsoft.NET\Framework\<version>) and check out the initial GUI (see Figure 7-45).

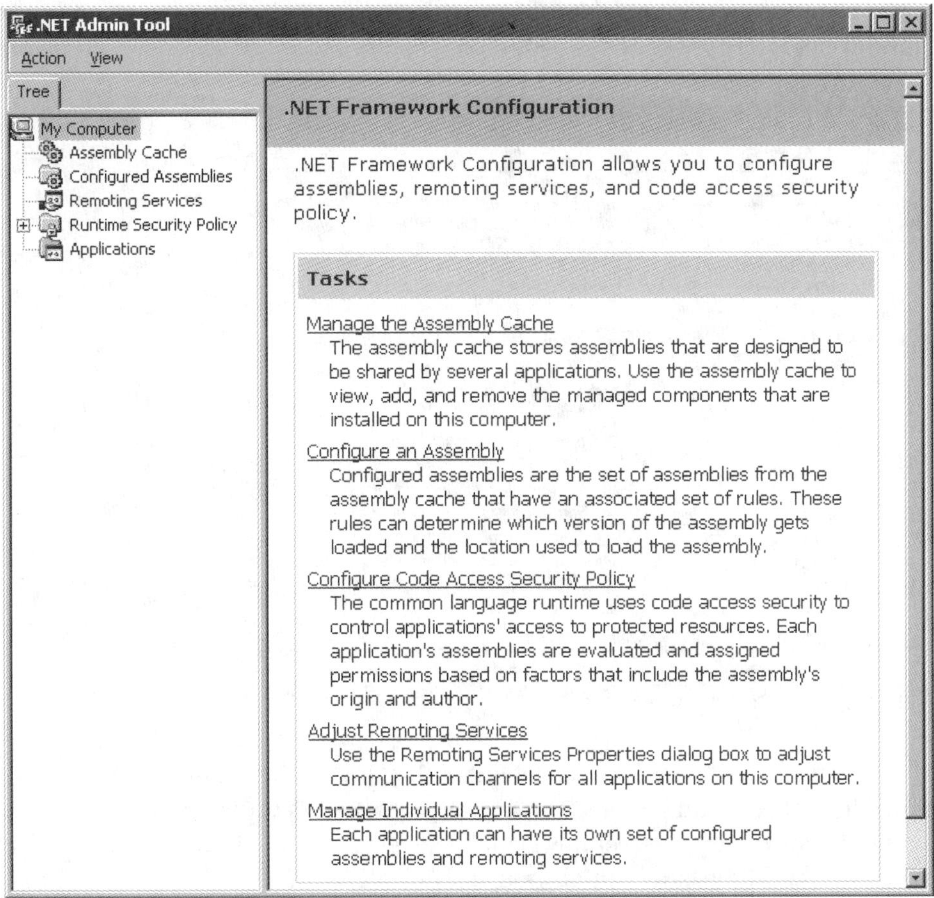

Figure 7-45. The .NET Admin tool allows you to configure assemblies from the safe confines of a GUI tool

To illustrate the use of this tool, you must have a client application you want to configure. To keep things clean, let's build a new console application that makes use of the MySharedAssembly.dll (1.0.0.0), creatively named AnotherSharedAsmUser. Within the Main() loop, simply activate the VWMiniVan and be sure to set a reference to version 1.0.0.0 of your MySharedAssembly.dll. Go ahead and compile the application just to ensure you have activated the correct shared binary.

The first step you need to take is to add AnotherSharedAsmUser.exe into the list of applications that can be configured using the .NET administration tool. To do so, select the Applications node from the left hand tree view, and click the "Add an Application to Configure" link (or as an alternative, right-click the Applications node and select "Add" from the context menu). Once you navigate to the client application, you should see what appears in Figure 7-46, or something like it.

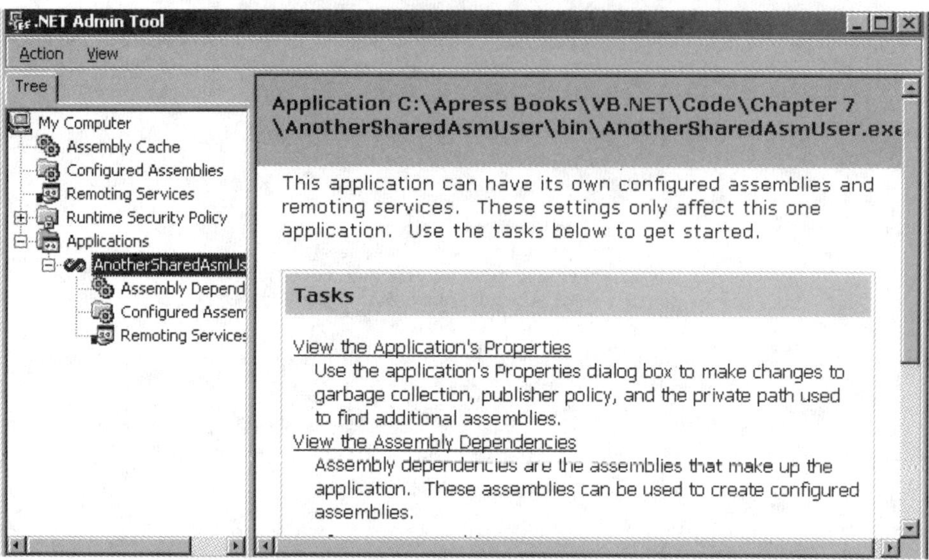

Figure 7-46. Preparing to configure AnotherSharedAsmUser.exe

As you can see, each client listed under the Applications folder has four possible configuration options. The first two options (View the Application's Properties and View the Assembly Dependencies) are rather self-explanatory. When you select the latter option, you are shown a list of all external assemblies that are required by the client application. If you activate this link, you see that MySharedAssembly.dll is present and accounted for (see Figure 7-47).

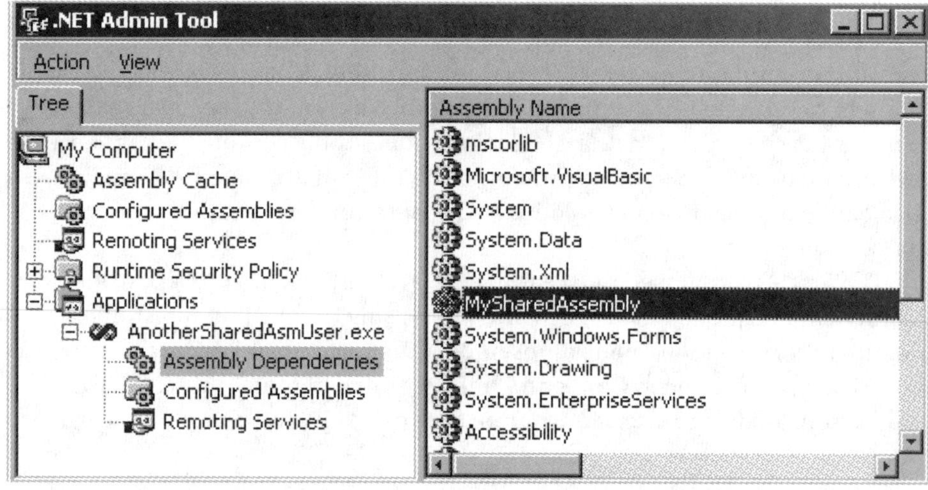

Figure 7-47. Dumping assembly dependencies for a given client

Now, activate the Configured Assemblies node, right-click and select the "Add" option from the context menu. This launches a wizard whose ultimate job is to build an XML configuration file for you automatically. The first step allows you to specify the location of the dependent assembly you want to configure. Given that you are attempting to configure MySharedAssembly.dll, you can leave the default selection (choose an assembly from the GAC) and click "Choose Assembly." From the resulting dialog box, locate MySharedAssembly.dll and click OK. You should now see something like Figure 7-48. Once you are finished, close the dialog box.

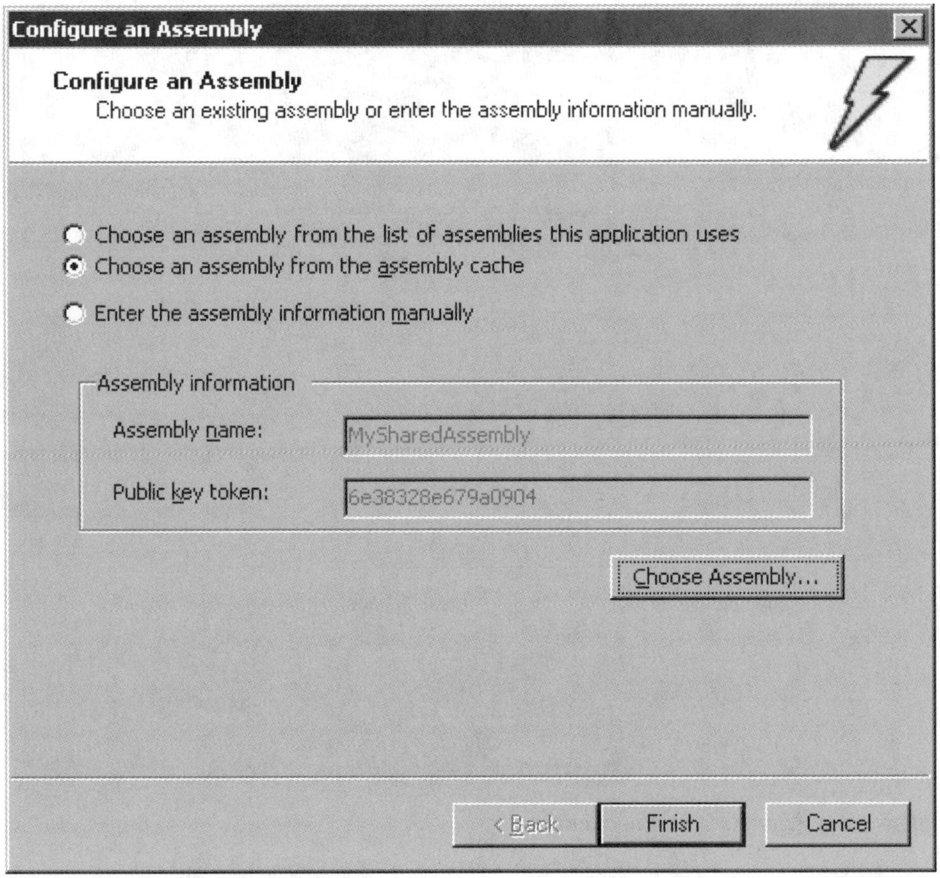

Figure 7-48. Configuring the client

The next step of the wizard allows you to establish a number of probing related details. For your current needs, the interest lies in the "Binding Policy" tab. Here, you are able to specify the oldVersion and newVersion XML elements using a simple GUI interface. Go ahead and redirect the client to version 2.0.0.0 (see Figure 7-49).

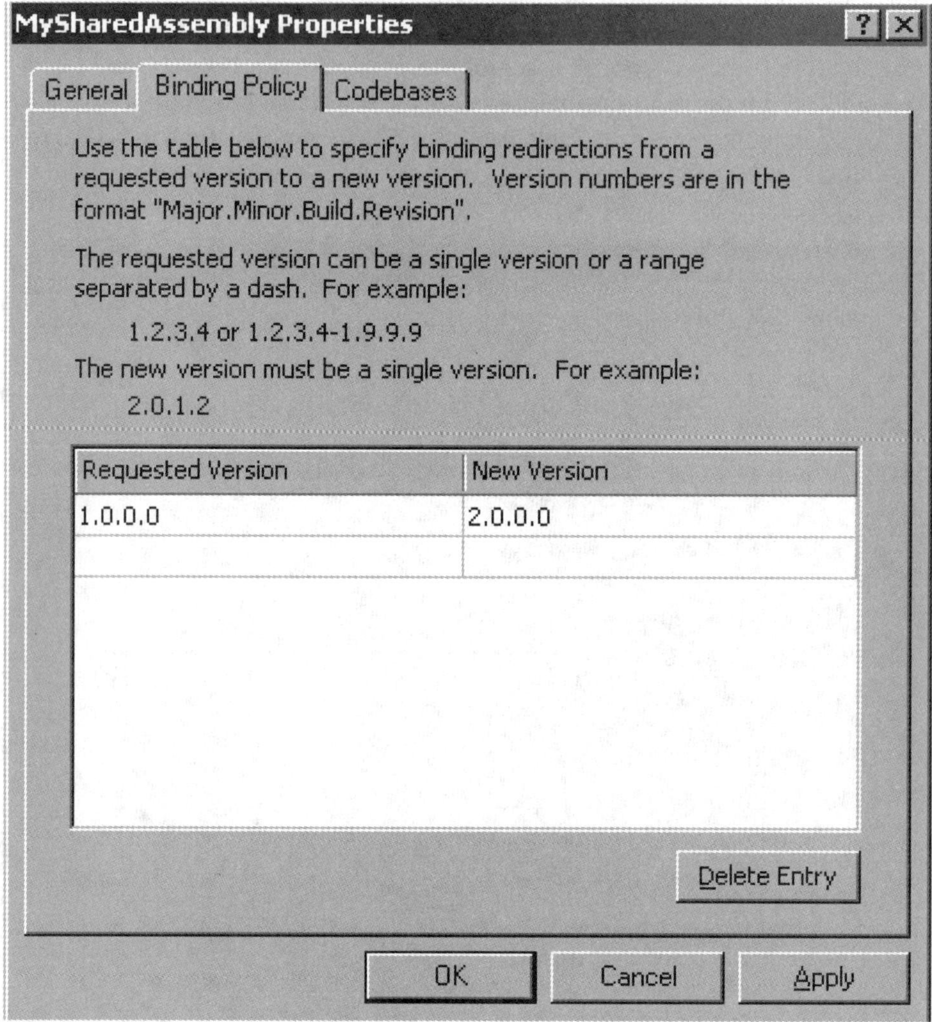

Figure 7-49. Redirecting the client

Once you click OK, notice that a *.config file has been generated and placed in the application directory of the client application (see Figure 7-50). The syntax is identical to the previous raw XML file you wrote by hand (remember, wizards do not perform any magic—they simply save you keystrokes). If you run the client, you now see a message box informing you that you are "Using Version 2.0.0.0."

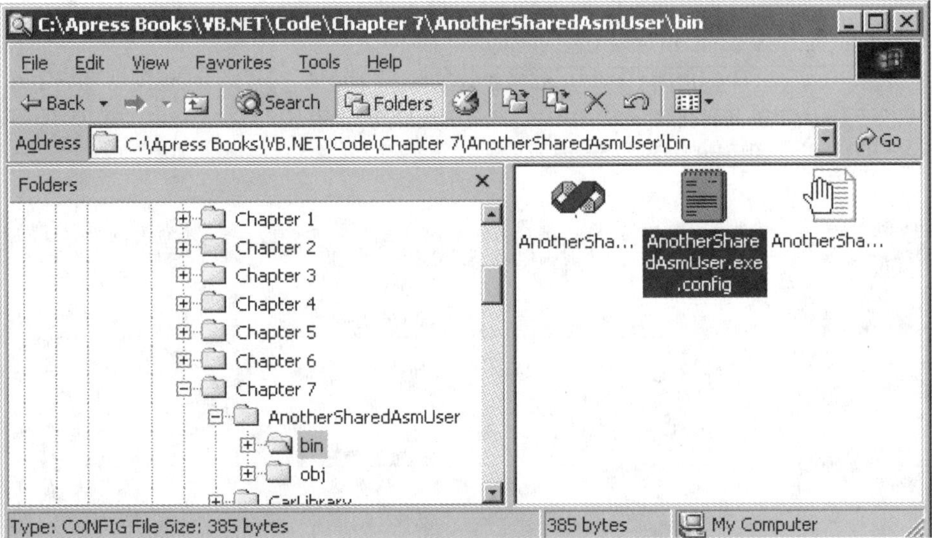

*Figure 7-50. Autogenerated *.config files*

Specifying <Probing> Elements

As you have seen in this chapter, private assemblies are typically located directly in the client's application directory or under a given subdirectory. To illustrate how this tool can also build probing elements in your *.config files, assume that the AnotherSharedAsmUser.exe application has set a reference to the CarLibrary.dll created earlier in this chapter, and exercised a SportsCar as follows:

```
Imports MySharedAssembly
Imports CarLibrary
Module Module1
    Sub Main()
        Dim v As New VWMiniVan()
        v.Busted = True
        v.Play60sTunes()
        Dim c As New CarLibrary.SportsCar()
        c.TurnOnRadio(True, MusicMedia.musicCD)
    End Sub
End Module
```

Because CarLibrary.dll is a private assembly, VS .NET responded by creating a copy of the binary in the client's application directory. Move this copy into a new subdirectory (perhaps \bin\Foo). Now, using the .NET administrative tool, activate the Property page for the AnotherSharedAsmUser.exe client (simply right-click the icon from the tree view).

Notice that the bottom of this Property page allows you to specify additional search paths for a private assembly. Go ahead and add the Foo subdirectory to this list (see Figure 7-51).

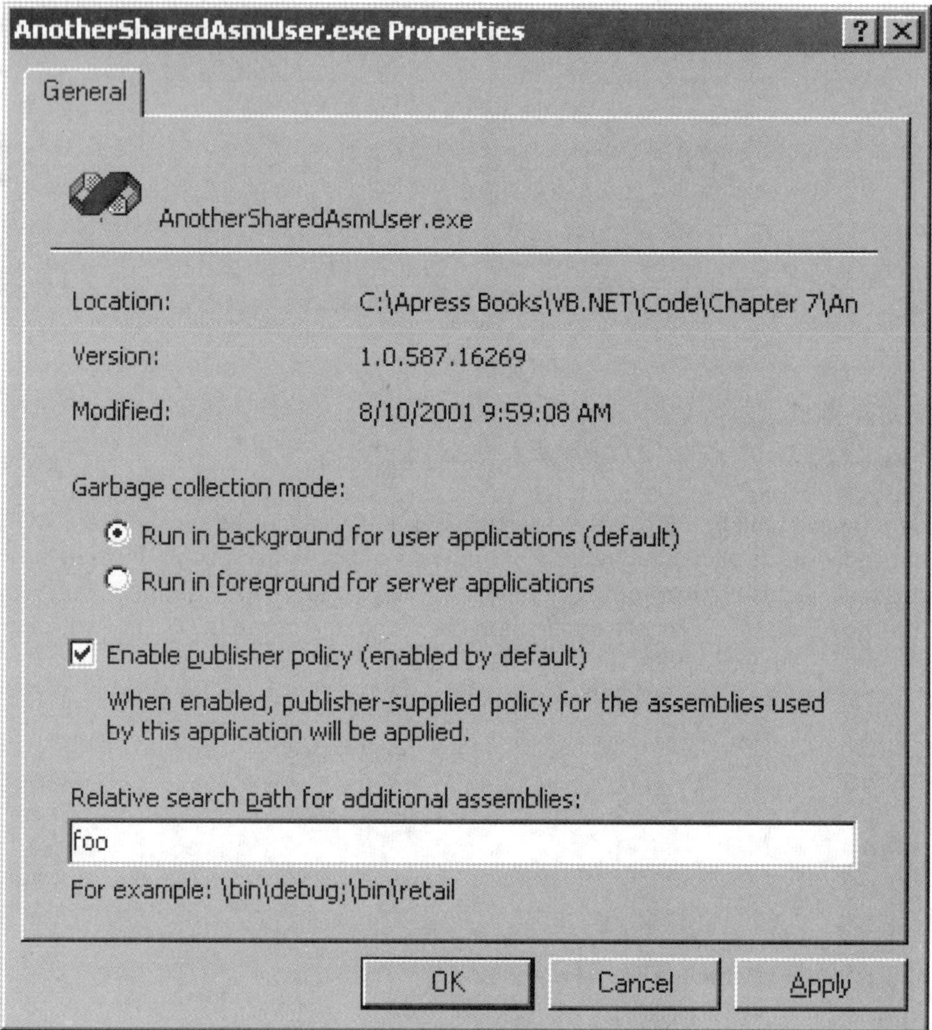

Figure 7-51. Specifying <probing> tags

As you would expect, if you open up the *.config file for this client application, a <probing> tag has been generated on your behalf:

```
<?xml version="1.0"?>
<configuration>
  <runtime>
    <assemblyBinding xmlns="urn:schemas-microsoft-com:asm.v1">
      <dependentAssembly>
        <assemblyIdentity name="MySharedAssembly"
        publicKeyToken="6e38328e679a0904" />
        <bindingRedirect oldVersion="1.0.0.0" newVersion="2.0.0.0" />
      </dependentAssembly>
      <publisherPolicy apply="yes" />
      <probing privatePath="foo" />
    </assemblyBinding>
    <gcConcurrent enabled="true" />
  </runtime>
</configuration>
```

Specifying <Codebase> Elements

The final aspect of application configuration files that you examine at this point is the use of code bases. *.config files can support another XML tag named <Codebase>, which is used by the assembly resolver to locate dependent assemblies that are located at arbitrary locations (including other machines). To illustrate, create a final Console application (CodeBaseAsmUser) that makes use of the MySharedAssembly.dll 2.0.0.0. Once you have created a simple test application, create a new folder under your C drive (perhaps C:\MyAsms) and place a copy of MySharedAssembly.dll 2.0.0.0 under the new directory.

The goal is to build a CodeBaseAsmUser.exe.config file that will force the assembly resolver to probe under C:\MyAsms as it attempts to locate each referenced assembly. To do so, begin by adding this client to the list of configured assemblies (as explained earlier). Next, select the "Configure an Assembly" option, choose "Configure an assembly from the Assembly Cache" and pick the MySharedAssembly.dll from the resulting dialog (as shown earlier). Finally, using the Codebase tab, map version 2.0.0.0 to the C:\MyAsms directory (see Figure 7-52).

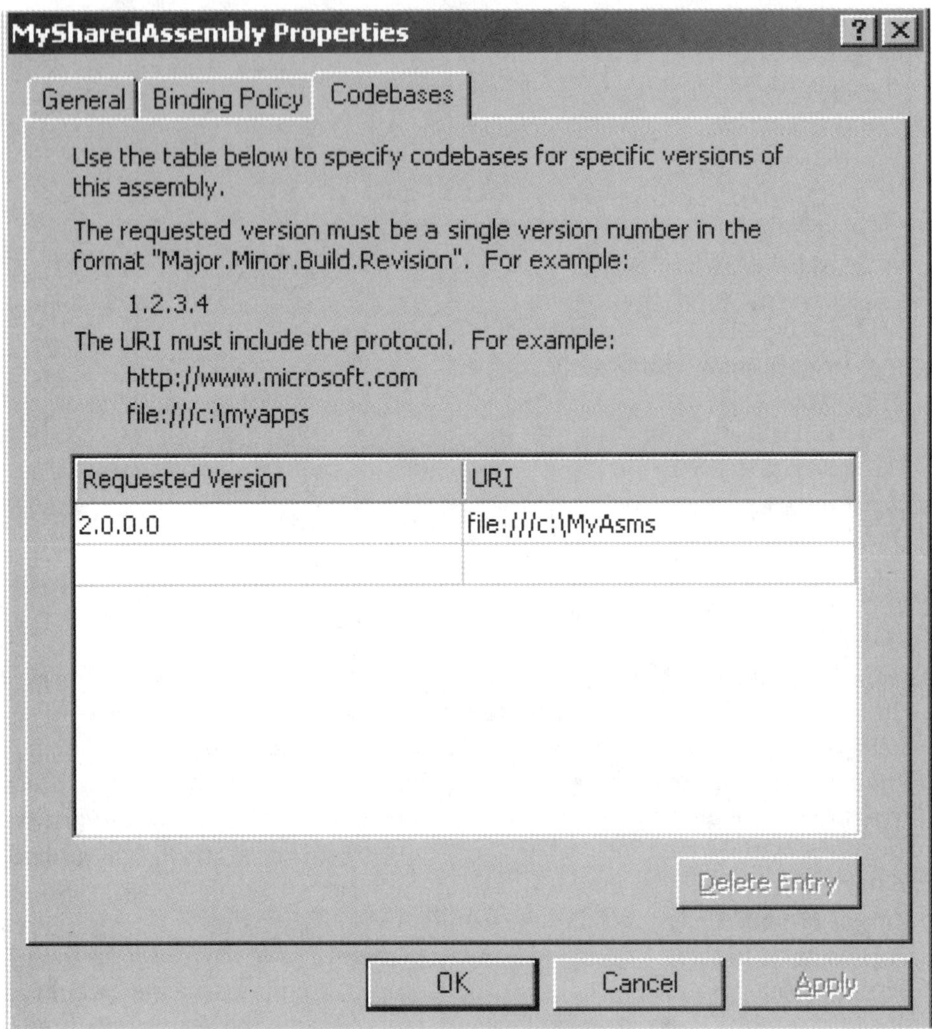

Figure 7-52. Building a Codebase

Note that the URI must specify the protocol used during the probe (local files are marked by file:///). If you check out the generated XML, you find the following:

```
<?xml version="1.0"?>
<configuration>
  <runtime>
    <assemblyBinding xmlns="urn:schemas-microsoft-com:asm.v1">
      <dependentAssembly>
        <assemblyIdentity name="MySharedAssembly"
        publicKeyToken="6e38328e679a0904" />
```

```
        <codeBase version="2.0.0.0" href="file:///c:\MyAsms" />
      </dependentAssembly>
    </assemblyBinding>
  </runtime>
</configuration>
```

SOURCE CODE *The AnotherSharedAsmUser and CodeBaseAsmUser projects are included under the Chapter 7 subdirectory.*

The Ngen.exe Utility

Now that you have an intimate understanding of .NET assemblies, you are just about ready to switch gears completely and examine the topics of application domains and multithreaded assemblies. Although this may seem like a drastic change of content, you will see that assemblies, application domains, and threads are interrelated.

However, before making the gear shift, it is worth mentioning a useful assembly-centric utility named ngen.exe. The role of ngen.exe is to compile IL instructions to platform-specific code during the installation process, and not on client demand (which is the default behavior).

By way of example, while examining the contents of your machine's GAC, you may have noticed that some of the shared assemblies have been marked with the "PreJit" designation. When a shared assembly has been configured as "prejitted," the end result is an assembly that can be loaded faster by the assembly resolver. Notice that I did not say the code within the assembly will *execute* any faster. The truth of the matter is, prejitted code does not necessarily run any faster than just-in-time compiled code, given that the code that is produced during the PreJit process still requires the assemblies metadata to obtain type information at runtime.

PreJitting code is advantageous when you have a shared assembly that you suspect will be used by a great many applications on a given machine (or at least when you suspect the types within this assembly will be used frequently). Reason? Faster load times.

If you determine (through code profiling or an educated guess) that a particular shared assembly may benefit from the PreJit process, you need to make use of the ngen.exe utility that ships with the .NET SDK, and is located (by default) under C:\WINNT\Microsoft.NET\Framework\v1.0.2914 (your version may differ). In any case, from a Console window, run ngen.exe and pass in the name of the assembly you want to bind to the OS. For example, if you were to PreJit MySharedAssembly.dll, issue the following command (note you only specify the friendly name of the assembly in the GAC, and omit the file extension):

```
ngen MySharedAssembly
```

If you check out the statistics of MySharedAssembly.dll within the GAC, you find something similar to Figure 7-53.

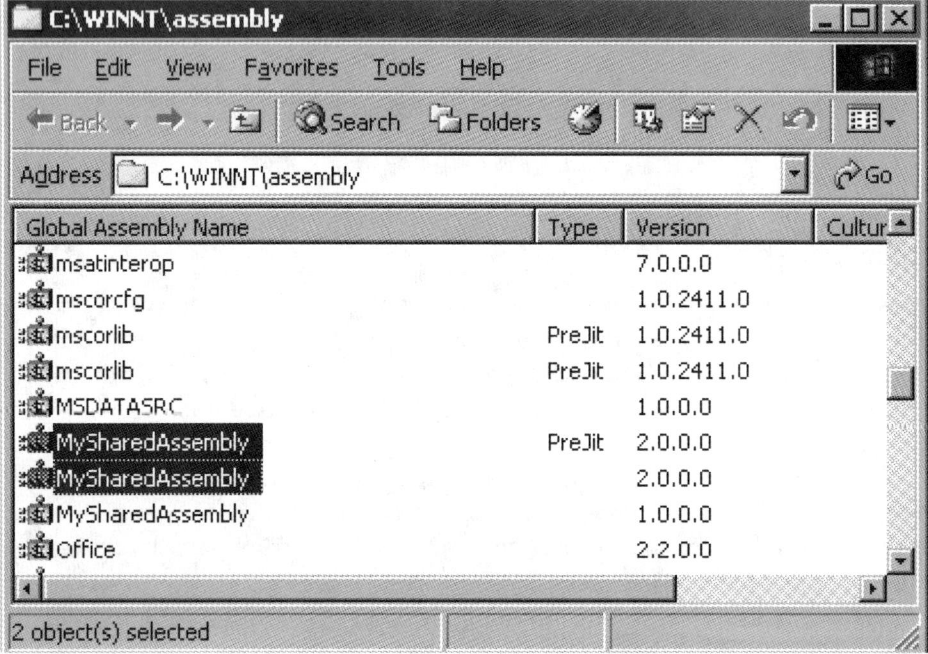

Figure 7-53. The PreJitted shared assembly

Note that you cannot remove the non-prejitted version of the binary after the conversion created by ngen.exe, as the PreJit version must reference the non-prejitted version to obtain the necessary metadata. Be aware that private assemblies may also be prejitted.

Review of Traditional Win32 Thread Programming

Depending on your programming background, you may be extremely interested in building multithreaded binaries, could care less about building multithreaded binaries, or are a little unsure what multithreading means in the first place. To level the playing field, let's take the time to quickly review the basics of multithreading. Once you have reviewed multithreading from a traditional Win32 perspective, you come to understand how things have changed under the .NET platform and learn the basics of building multithreaded VB .NET applications.

To begin, recall that under traditional Win32, each application is hosted by a *process*. Understand that process is a generic term used to describe the set of external resources (such as a COM server) as well as the necessary memory allocations used by a given application. For each EXE loaded into memory, the operating system creates a separate and isolated memory partition (i.e., process) for use during its lifetime.

Every running process has at least one main "thread" that serves as the entry point for the application. Formally speaking, the first thread created in a given process is termed the *primary thread.* Simply put, a thread is a specific path of execution within the Win32 process. A traditional Windows application defines the WinMain() method to function as the application's entry point. On the other hand, Console application provides the main() method for the same purpose.

Applications that contain only a single thread of execution are automatically "thread-safe" given the fact that there is only one thread that can access the data in the application at a given time. On the downside, a single-threaded application can appear a bit unresponsive to the end user if this single thread is performing a complex operation (such as printing out a lengthy text file, performing an exotic calculation, or connecting to a remote server).

Under Win32, it is possible for the primary thread to spawn additional secondary threads in the background, using a handful of Win32 API functions such as CreateThread(). Each thread (primary or secondary) becomes a unique path of execution in the process and has concurrent access to all data in that process. As you may have guessed, developers typically create additional threads to help improve the program's overall responsiveness. Until the advent of VB .NET, the ability to spawn additional threads of execution was not easily accomplished. While a crafty VB 6.0 developer could make use of the Windows API to do so, the creation of multithreaded applications was not intrinsically supported by the Visual Basic language.

Nevertheless, multithreaded applications provide the appearance that numerous activities are happening at more or less the same time. For example, you could spawn a background worker thread to perform a labor-intensive unit of work (again, such as printing a large text file). As this secondary thread is churning away, the main thread is still responsive to user input, which gives the entire process the potential of delivering greater performance. However, this is only a possibility. Too many threads in a single process can actually degrade performance, as the CPU must switch between the active threads in the process (which takes time).

In reality, multithreading is often a simple illusion provided by the operating system. Machines that host a single CPU do not have the ability to literally handle multiple threads at the same exact time. Rather, a single CPU executes one thread for a unit of time (called a *time-slice*) based on the thread's priority level. When a thread's time-slice is up, the existing thread is suspended to allow the other thread to perform its business. In order for a thread to remember what was happening before it was kicked out of the way, each thread is given the ability to write to Thread Local Storage (TLS) and is provided a separate call stack, as illustrated in Figure 7-54.

A Single Win32 Process

Shared Data			
Thread A		Thread B	
TLS	Call Stack	TLS	Call Stack

Figure 7-54. A traditional Win32 process

Problem of Concurrency and Thread Synchronization

Beyond taking time, the process of switching between threads can cause additional problems. For example, assume a given thread is accessing a shared point of data, and in the process begins to modify it. Now assume that the first thread is told to wait, to allow another thread to access the same point of data. If the first thread was not finished with its task, the second thread may be modifying data that is in an unstable state.

To protect the application's data from possible corruption, the Win32 developer must make use of any number of Win32 threading primitives such as critical sections, mutexes, or semaphores to synchronize access to shared data. Given this, multithreaded applications are much more volatile, as numerous threads can operate on the application's data at the same time. Unless the Win32 developer has accounted for this possibility using threading primitives (such as a critical section) the program may end up with a good amount of data corruption.

Although the .NET platform cannot make the difficulties of building robust multithreaded applications completely disappear, the process has been simplified considerably. Using types defined within the System.Threading namespace, you are able to spawn additional threads with minimal fuss and bother. Likewise, when it comes time to lock down shared points of data, you will find additional types that provide the same functionality as the Win32 threading primitives.

Understanding System.AppDomain

Before examining the details of the System.Threading namespace, you need to examine the concept of *application domains*. As you know, .NET applications are created by piecing together any number of related assemblies. However, unlike a traditional (non-.NET) Win32 EXE application, .NET applications are hosted by an entity termed an application domain (aka AppDomain). Be very aware that the term AppDomain is *not* a synonym for a Win32 process.

In reality, a single process can host any number of AppDomains, each of which is fully and completely isolated from other AppDomains within this process (or any other process). Applications that run in different AppDomains are unable to share any information of any kind (global variables or shared data) unless they make use of the .NET remoting protocol. The big picture is shown in Figure 7-55.

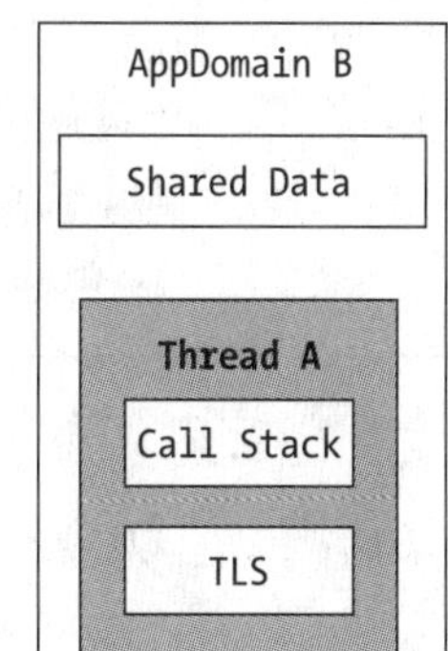

Figure 7-55. A process can contain one or more AppDomains. Each AppDomain can contain one or more threads

Notice the stark difference from a traditional Win32 process. Under .NET, a single process may contain multiple AppDomains. Each AppDomain may contain multiple threads. In some respects, this layout is reminiscent of the "apartment" architecture of classic COM. Of course, .NET AppDomains are managed types whereas the COM apartment architecture is built on an unmanaged (and much more complex) architecture.

AppDomains are programmatically represented by the System.AppDomain type. Some core members to be aware of are shown in Table 7-2.

Table 7-2. Select Members of AppDomain

APPDOMAIN MEMBER	MEANING IN LIFE
CreateDomain()	This static method creates a new AppDomain in the current process.
GetCurrentThreadId()	This static method returns the ID of the current thread.
Unload()	Another static method that unloads the specified AppDomain.
BaseDirectory	This property returns the base directory that the assembly resolver used to probe for assemblies.
CreateInstance()	Creates an instance of a specified type defined in a specified assembly file.
ExecuteAssembly()	Executes the assembly given its file name.
GetAssemblies()	Gets the assemblies that have been loaded into this application domain.
Load()	Loads an assembly into this application domain.

Fun with AppDomains

As you can see, the members of AppDomain provide numerous process-like behaviors, with a .NET flair. To illustrate some of this flair, consider the following namespace definition:

```
Imports DotNetAsm = System.Reflection.Assembly
Imports System.Windows.Forms
Module Module1
    Public Sub PrintAllAssemblies()
        Dim ad As AppDomain = AppDomain.CurrentDomain
        Dim loadedAssemblies() As DotNetAsm
        loadedAssemblies = ad.GetAssemblies()
        Console.WriteLine("Here are the assemblies loaded in this appdomain")
        Dim a As DotNetAsm
        For Each a In loadedAssemblies
            Console.WriteLine(a.FullName)
        Next
    End Sub
    Sub Main()
        MessageBox.Show("This call loaded System.Windows.Forms.dll")
        PrintAllAssemblies()
    End Sub
End Module
```

First of all, notice that you are making use of a new namespace, System.Reflection. Full details of this namespace are seen in Chapter 8. For the time being, just understand that this namespace defines the Assembly type, which you need access to given the role of the PrintAllAssemblies() method.

This method obtains a reference to the hosting AppDomain, and enumerates over the list of loaded assemblies. To make it more interesting, notice that the Main() method launches a message box to force the assembly resolver to load the System.Windows.Forms.dll assembly (which in turn loads other referenced assemblies). Figure 7-56 shows the output.

```
C:\Apress Books\VB.NET\Code\Chapter 7\MyAppDomain\bin\MyAppD...
Here are the assemblies loaded in this appdomain:

mscorlib, Version=1.0.2411.0, Culture=neutral, PublicKeyTo

MyAppDomain, Version=1.0.587.36013, Culture=neutral, Publi

System.Windows.Forms, Version=1.0.2411.0, Culture=neutral,
561934e089

System, Version=1.0.2411.0, Culture=neutral, PublicKeyToke

Press any key to continue
```

Figure 7-56. Investigating loaded assemblies

One question you may have at this point is when (or if) you need to create AppDomains by hand. To be sure, the AppDomain class does provide a CreateInstance() method for this very reason. In reality, you are not very often in the position to create application domains by hand. The .NET runtime will automatically create application domains on an as-needed basis.

SOURCE CODE *The MyAppDomain application is included under the Chapter 7 subdirectory.*

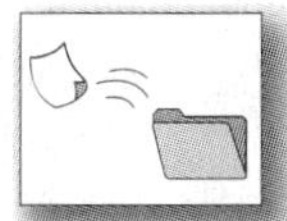

System.Threading Namespace

The System.Threading namespace provides a number of types that enable multithreaded programming. In addition to providing types that represent a specific thread, this namespace also defines types that can manage a collection of threads (ThreadPool), a simple (non-GUI-based) Timer class and numerous types to provide synchronized access to shared data. Table 7-3 lists some (but not all) of the core items.

Table 7-3. Select Types of the System.Threading Namespace

SYSTEM.THREADING TYPE	MEANING IN LIFE
Interlocked	The Interlocked class is used to provide synchronized access to shared data.
Monitor	Provides the synchronization of threading objects using locks and wait/signals.
Mutex	Synchronization primitive that can be used for interprocess synchronization.
Thread	Represents a thread that executes within the CLR. Using this type, you are able to spawn additional threads in the owning AppDomain.
ThreadPool	This type manages related threads in a given process.
Timer	Specifies a delegate to be called at a specified time. The wait operation is performed by a thread in the thread pool.
WaitHandle	Represents all synchronization objects (that allow multiple wait) in the runtime.
ThreadStart	The ThreadStart class is a delegate that points to the method that should be executed first when a thread is started.
TimerCallback	Delegate for the Timers.
WaitCallback	This class is a Delegate that defines the callback method for ThreadPool user work items.

Examining the Thread Class

The most primitive of all types in the System.Threading namespace is Thread. This class represents an object-oriented wrapper around a given path of execution within a particular AppDomain. This type defines a number of methods (both static and shared) that allow you to create new threads from a current thread, as well as suspend, stop, and destroy a given thread. First, consider the list of core shared members given in Table 7-4.

Table 7-4. Shared Members of the Thread Type

THREAD SHARED MEMBER	MEANING IN LIFE
CurrentThread	This (read-only) property returns a reference to the currently running thread.
GetData()	
SetData()	Retrieves the value from the specified slot on the current thread, for that thread's current domain.
GetDomain()	
GetDomainID()	Returns a reference to the current AppDomain (or the ID of this domain) in which the current thread is running.
Sleep()	Suspends the current thread for a specified time.

Thread also supports the object level members shown in Table 7-5.

Table 7-5. Object Methods of the Thread Type

THREAD INSTANCE LEVEL MEMBER	MEANING IN LIFE
IsAlive	This property returns a Boolean that indicates if this thread has been started.
IsBackground	Gets or sets a value indicating whether or not this thread is a background thread.
Name	This property allows you to establish a friendly textual name of the thread.
Priority	Gets or Sets the priority of a thread, which may be assigned a value from the ThreadPriority enumeration.
ThreadState	Gets the state of this thread, which may be assigned a value from the ThreadState enumeration.
Interrupt()	Interrupts the current thread.
Join()	Instructs the thread to wait for a given thread.
Resume()	Resumes a thread that has been suspended.
Start()	Begins execution of the thread that is specified by the ThreadStart delegate.
Suspend()	Suspends the thread. If the thread is already suspended, a call to Suspend() has no effect.

Spawning Secondary Threads

When you want to create additional threads to carry on some unit of work, you need to interact with the Thread class as well as a special threading-related delegate named ThreadStart. The general process is quite simple. To begin, you need to create a method to perform the background work. To keep things well focused, let's build a simple helper class that simply prints out a series of numbers by way of the DoSomeWork() member function:

```
Friend Class WorkerClass
    Public Sub DoSomeWork()
        ' Do the work.
        Console.WriteLine("worker thread. . .")
        Console.Write("Worker says: ")
        Dim i as Integer
        For  i = 0 To 10
          Console.Write(i & ", ");
        Next
        Console.WriteLine()
    End Sub
End Class
```

Now assume the Main() method creates a new instance of the WorkerClass type. In order for Main() to continue processing its workflow, it creates and starts a new Thread that is used by the worker. In the code below, notice the Thread type requests a new ThreadStart delegate type, which as you recall is typically represented in VB .NET using the AddressOf keyword:

```
Sub Main()
    ' Make worker class.
    Console.WriteLine("Primary thread. . .")
    Dim w as WorkerClass = new WorkerClass()
    ' Now make (and start) the background thread.
    Dim backgroundThread As Thread = _
        New Thread(AddressOf w.DoSomeWork)
    backgroundThread.Start()
End Sub
```

Figure 7-57 shows a test run.

```
C:\Apress Books\VB.NET\Code\Chapter 7\SimpleMultiThr...
Primary thread...
worker thread...
Worker says: 0, 1, 2, 3, 4, 5, 6, 7, 8, 9, 10,
Press any key to continue
```

Figure 7-57. Threads at work

Naming Threads

One interesting aspect of the Thread class is that it provides the ability to assign a friendly string name to the underlying path of execution. To do so, make use of the Name property. For example, you could update the MainClass as follows:

```
Sub Main()
    ' Name the current thread.
    Dim primaryThread As Thread = Thread.CurrentThread
    primaryThread.Name = "Boss man"
    Console.WriteLine("Name of primary thread is: {0}", _
        primaryThread.Name)
    ' Same code as before. . .
End Sub
```

The output is now as shown in Figure 7-58.

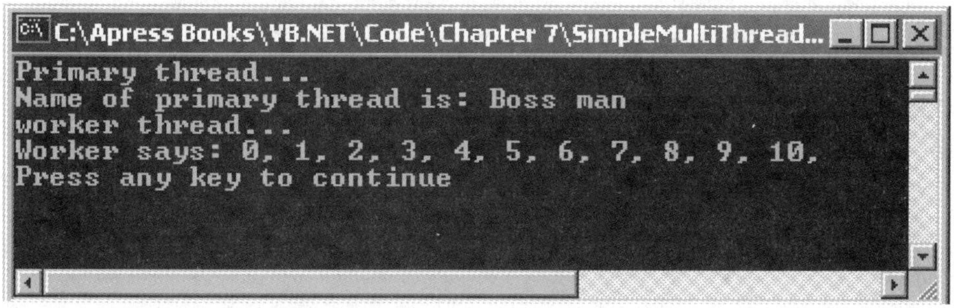

```
C:\Apress Books\VB.NET\Code\Chapter 7\SimpleMultiThread...
Primary thread...
Name of primary thread is: Boss man
worker thread...
Worker says: 0, 1, 2, 3, 4, 5, 6, 7, 8, 9, 10,
Press any key to continue
```

Figure 7-58. Named threads

As you may be thinking, the Name property provides a more user-friendly way to identify the threads in your system.

Clogging Up the Primary Thread

The current application creates a secondary thread to perform a unit of work. The problem is the fact that printing 10 numbers takes no time at all, and therefore you are not really able to appreciate the fact that the primary thread is free to continue processing. Let's update the application to illustrate this very fact. First, let's update the WorkerClass to print out 30,000 numbers (using WriteLine() rather than Write() so you can see the printout more clearly) rather than a mere 10:

```
Friend Class WorkerClass
    Public Sub DoSomeWork()
        Console.WriteLine("worker thread. . .")
        ' Do the work.
        Console.Write("Worker says: ")
        Dim i As Integer
        For i = 0 To 30000
            Console.Write(i & ", ")
        Next
        Console.WriteLine()
    End Sub
End Class
```

Next, let's update Main() such that it launches a message box directly after it creates the background worker thread:

```
Public Sub Main()
    ' Name the current thread.
    . . .
    ' Make worker class.
    . . .
    ' Now make the thread.
    . . .
    ' Now while background thread is working,
    ' do some additional work.
    MessageBox.Show("I'm buzy");
End Sub
```

If you were to now run the application, you would see that the message box is displayed and can be moved around the desktop, while the background worker thread is busy pumping numbers to the console (see Figure 7-59).

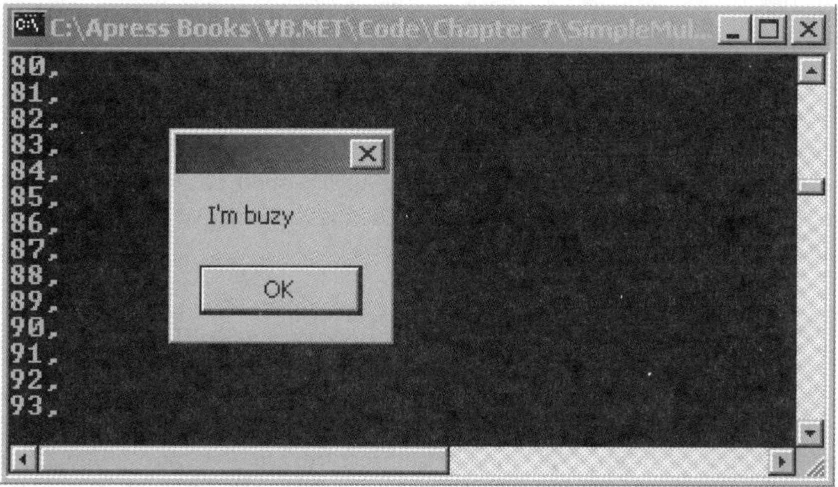

Figure 7-59. Two active threads

Now, contrast this behavior with what you might find if you had a single-threaded application. Assume the Main() method has been updated with logic that allows the user to enter the number of threads used within the AppDomain:

```
Module Module1
    Sub Main()
        Console.WriteLine("Primary thread. . .")
        Console.Write("Do you want [1] or [2] threads? ")
        Dim threadCount As String = Console.ReadLine()

        ' Name the current thread.
        . . .
        ' Make worker class.
        Dim w As WorkerClass = New WorkerClass()

        If (threadCount = "2") Then
            ' Now make the thread (if the user said so. . .)
            Dim backgroundThread As Thread = _
                    New Thread(AddressOf w.DoSomeWork)
            backgroundThread.Start()
        Else
            w.DoSomeWork()
        End If
        ' Do some additional work.
        MessageBox.Show("I'm buzy")
```

```
    End Sub
End Module
```

As you can guess, if the user enters the value "1" he or she must wait for all 30,000 numbers to be printed before seeing the message box appear, given that there is only a single thread in the executing AppDomain. However, if the user enters "2" he or she is able to interact with the message box while the secondary thread spins right along.

Putting a Thread to Sleep

The static Thread.Sleep() method can be used to suspend the current thread for a specified amount of time (specified in milliseconds). To illustrate, let's update the WorkerClass once again. This time around, the DoSomeWork() method does not print out 30,000 lines to the console, but 5 lines. The trick is, between each call to Console.WriteLine(), this background is put to sleep for approximately 5 seconds.

```
Friend Class WorkerClass
    Public Sub DoSomeWork()
        Console.WriteLine("worker thread. . .")
        ' Do the work (and take a nap. . .)
        Console.Write("Worker says: ")
        Dim i As Integer
        For i = 0 To 5
            Console.WriteLine(i & ", ")
            Thread.Sleep(5000)
        Next
        Console.WriteLine()
    End Sub
End Class
```

The output is shown in Figure 7-60.

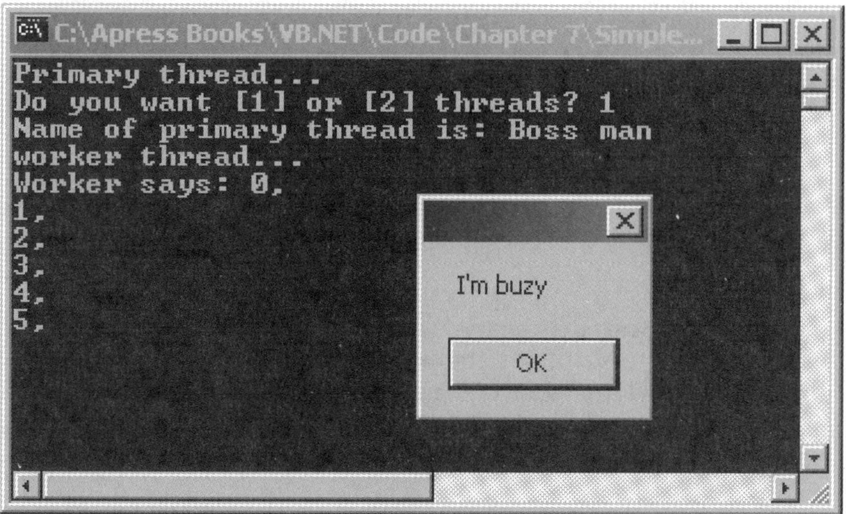

Figure 7-60. Two active threads (one sleeping on the job)

SOURCE CODE *The SimpleMultiThreadApp project is included under the Chapter 7 subdirectory.*

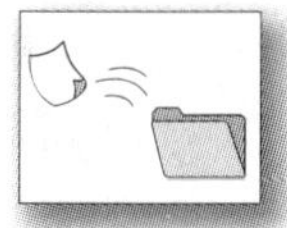

Concurrency Revisited

Given the previous example, you might be thinking that threads are the magic bullet you have been looking for. Simply create threads for each part of your application and the end result will be increased application performance. You already know this is a loaded question, as the previous statement is false. If not used carefully and thoughtfully, too many threads can actually degrade an application's performance.

Perhaps even more important than application performance, is the fact that each and every thread in a given AppDomain has direct access to the shared data of the application. In the current example, this is not a problem. However, imagine what might happen if the primary and secondary threads were both modifying a shared point of data. As you know, the thread scheduler forces threads to suspend their work at random. Since this is the case, what if thread A is kicked out of the way before it has fully completed its work? The answer is thread B is now reading unstable data.

To illustrate, let's build a new multithreaded Console Application named MultiThreadSharedData. This application also has a class named WorkerClass, which is functionally similar to the previous type of the same name:

```
Friend Class WorkerClass
    Public Sub DoSomeWork()
        ' Do the work.
        Dim i As Integer
        For i = 0 To 5
            Console.WriteLine("Worker says: {0},", i)
        Next
    End Sub
End Class
```

In this application, Main() is responsible for creating three distinct secondary threads. The problem is that each of these threads is making calls to the shared instance of the WorkerClass type:

```
Module Module1
    ' Make the shared worker object.
    Public w As WorkerClass = New WorkerClass()
    Sub Main()
        ' Create three secondary threads,
        ' each of which makes calls to the same
        ' shared object.
        Dim workerThreadA As Thread = New Thread(AddressOf w.DoSomeWork)
        Dim workerThreadB As Thread = New Thread(AddressOf w.DoSomeWork)
        Dim workerThreadC As Thread = New Thread(AddressOf w.DoSomeWork)
        ' Now start each one (and slow things down a bit).
        workerThreadA.Start()
        Thread.Sleep(100)
        workerThreadB.Start()
        Thread.Sleep(100)
        workerThreadC.Start()
    End Sub
End Module
```

Now before you see some test runs, let's recap the problem. The primary thread of this AppDomain begins life by spawning three secondary worker threads. Each worker thread is told to make calls on the shared WorkerClass object instance. Given that we have taken no precautions to lock down this shared data, the chances are very good that a given thread will be kicked out of the say before the WorkerClass is able to print out the results for the current thread. Because you don't know when this might happen, you are bound to get a number of strange results. For example, check out Figure 7-61.

```
C:\Apress Books\VB.NET\Code\Chapter 7\...
Worker says: 0,
Worker says: 0,
Worker says: 0,
Worker says: 1,
Worker says: 1,
Worker says: 1,
Worker says: 2,
Worker says: 2,
Worker says: 2,
Worker says: 3,
Worker says: 3,
Worker says: 3,
Worker says: 4,
Worker says: 4,
Worker says: 4,
Worker says: 5,
Worker says: 5,
Worker says: 5,
Press any key to continue
```

Figure 7-61. Bad output—dueling threads

Figure 7-62 shows another run.

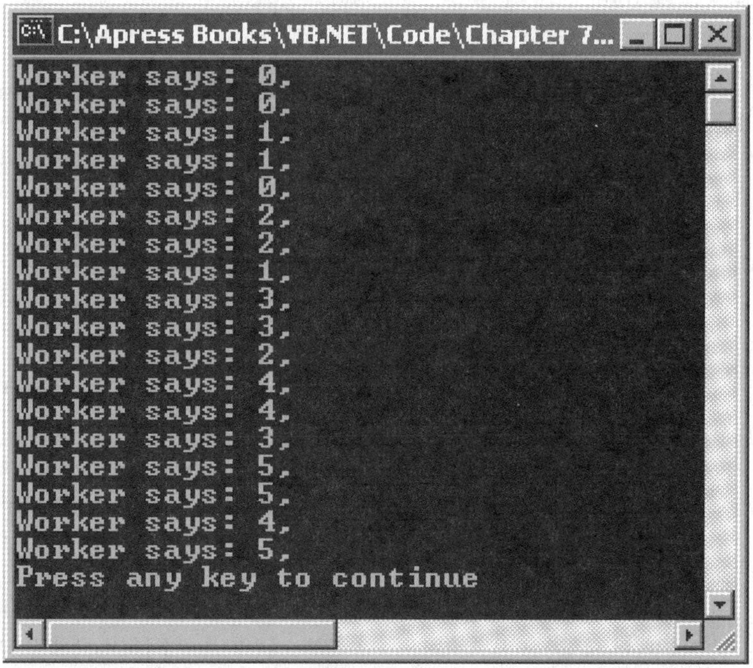

```
C:\Apress Books\VB.NET\Code\Chapter 7...
Worker says: 0,
Worker says: 0,
Worker says: 1,
Worker says: 1,
Worker says: 0,
Worker says: 2,
Worker says: 2,
Worker says: 1,
Worker says: 3,
Worker says: 3,
Worker says: 2,
Worker says: 4,
Worker says: 4,
Worker says: 3,
Worker says: 5,
Worker says: 5,
Worker says: 4,
Worker says: 5,
Press any key to continue
```

Figure 7-62. More bad output—dueling threads

And one more, just for good measure, appears in Figure 7-63.

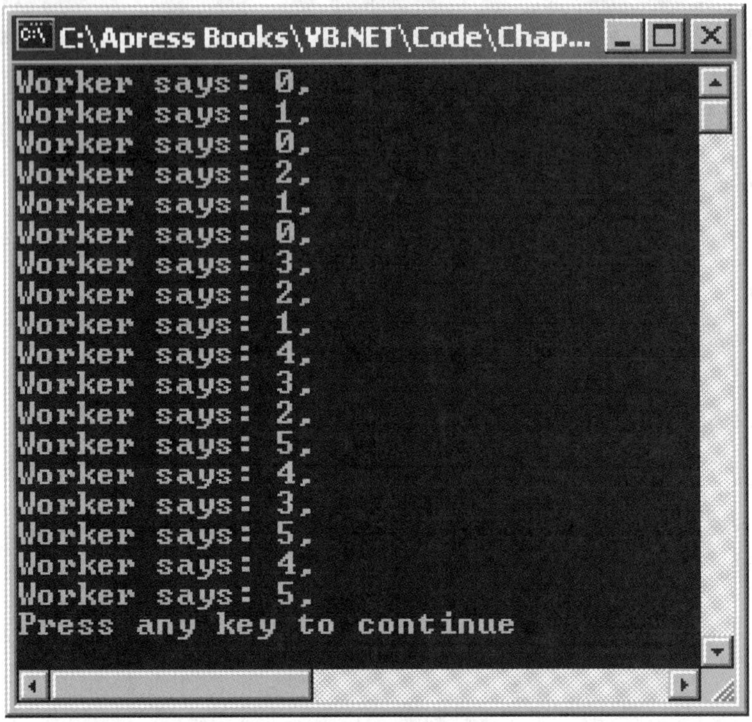

```
C:\Apress Books\VB.NET\Code\Chap...
Worker says: 0,
Worker says: 1,
Worker says: 0,
Worker says: 2,
Worker says: 1,
Worker says: 0,
Worker says: 3,
Worker says: 2,
Worker says: 1,
Worker says: 4,
Worker says: 3,
Worker says: 2,
Worker says: 5,
Worker says: 4,
Worker says: 3,
Worker says: 5,
Worker says: 4,
Worker says: 5,
Press any key to continue
```

Figure 7-63. Even more bad output—dueling threads

Hmm. There are clearly some problems. Given that each thread is telling the WorkerClass to "do some work" in a random way, the output is mangled (to say the least) as a given thread is kicked out of the way before it completely finishes its work. What you need is a way to programmatically enforce synchronized access to the shared type. Like the Win32 API, the .NET base class libraries provide a number of synchronization techniques. Let's examine one possible approach.

The VB .NET "SyncLock" Keyword

The first approach to providing synchronized access to your DoSomeWork() method is to make use of the VB .NET SyncLock statement. This intrinsic keyword allows you to lock down a block of code so that incoming threads must wait in line for the current thread to finish up its work. Using the SyncLock statement is trivial: Pass in a Type class that describes the item currently being locked. You will examine the Type class in detail in the next chapter, but for the time being, simply understand that System.Object.GetType() returns a valid Type instance:

```
Friend Class WorkerClass
    Public Sub DoSomeWork()
        SyncLock Me.GetType
            ' Only one thread at a time can tell the worker
            ' to get busy!
            Dim i As Integer
            For i = 0 To 5
                Console.WriteLine("Worker says: {0},", i)
                Thread.Sleep(100)
            Next
        End SyncLock
    End Sub
End Class
```

If you rerun the application, you can see that the threads are instructed to politely wait in line for the current thread to finish its business in Figure 7-64.

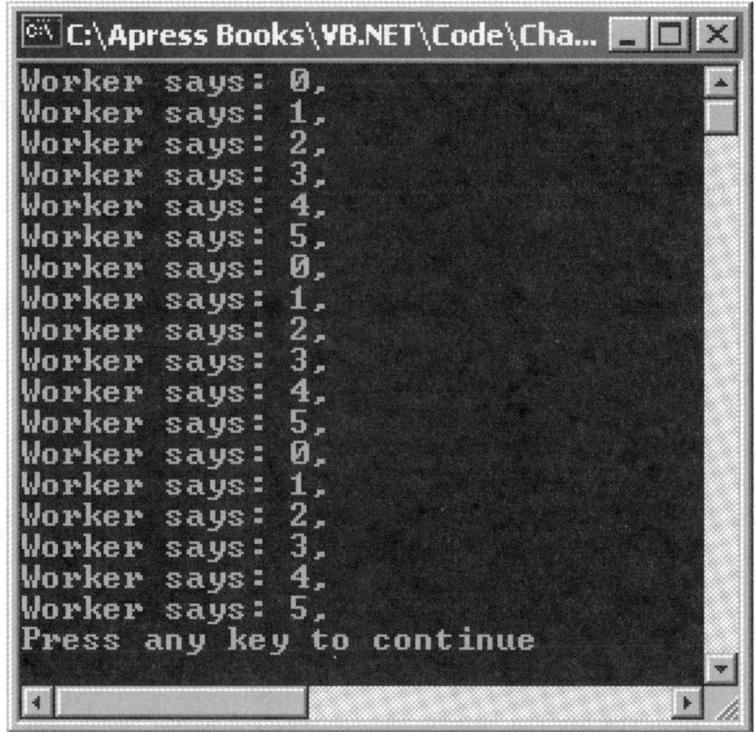

Figure 7-64. Harmonious threads

If you already have a background in Win32 multithreaded programming, understand that working with the VB .NET SyncLock statement is semantically equivalent to working with a raw Win32 CRITICAL_SECTION and related API function calls.

SOURCE CODE *The MultiThreadSharedData application is included under the Chapter 7 subdirectory.*

Using System.Threading.Monitor

The VB .NET SyncLock statement is really just a shorthand notation for working with the System.Threading.Monitor class type. Thus, if you were able to see what a SyncLock block actually resolves to under the hood, you would find the following:

```
Friend Class WorkerClass
    Public Sub DoSomeWork()
        Monitor.Enter(Me)
        Try
            ' Do the work.
            Dim i As Integer
            For i = 0 To 5
                Console.WriteLine("Worker says: {0},", i)
                Thread.Sleep(100)
            Next
        Finally
            Monitor.Exit(Me)
        End Try
    End Sub
End Class
```

If you run the modified application, you would see no changes in the output (which is good). Here, you make use of the static Enter() and Exit() members of the Monitor type, to enter (and leave) a locked block of code.

Using System.Threading.Interlocked

On a related note, the System.Threading namespace also provides a type that allows you to increment or decrement a variable by 1 in a thread-safe manner. To illustrate, assume that you have a class type (named IHaveNoIdea) that maintains an internal reference counter. One method of the class is responsible for incrementing this number by 1, while the other is responsible for decrementing this number by 1 (this may look familiar to the COM developers out there):

```
Public Class MyNetUnknown
    Private refCount  as Long
    Public Sub AddRef()
        refCount += 1
    End Sub
    Public Sub Release()
        refCount -= 1
        If refCount = 0 Then
                GC.Collect()
        End If
    End Sub
End Class
```

If you have numerous threads of execution in the current AppDomain that are all making calls to AddRef() and Release(), the possibility exists that the internal refCount member variable could in fact have a value less than zero before the collection request can be posted to the garbage collector. Imagine threadA calls Release(), and is bumped out of the way by the thread scheduler just after the point at which it decremented the refCount. The next thread calling Release() would decrement the count again, at which point refCount is currently at –1!

To prevent this behavior, you can make use of System.Threading.Interlocked, which atomically increments or decrements a given variable. Notice that a reference to the variable that is being modified is sent in ByRef:

```
Public Class MyNetUnknown
    Private refCount As Long
    Public Sub AddRef()
        Interlocked.Increment(refCount)
    End Sub
    Public Sub Release()
        Interlocked.Decrement(refCount)
        If refCount = 0 Then
            GC.Collect()
        End If
    End Sub
End Class
```

At this point you have just enough information to become dangerous in the world of multithreaded assemblies. While this chapter does not dig into each and every aspect of building multithreaded applications, you should be able to see the benefits (and risks) of the System.Threading namespace, and you should be equipped to investigate additional details as you see fit.

Summary

This chapter drilled into the details behind the innocent looking .NET DLLs and EXEs located on your development machine. You began the journey by examining the core concepts of the assembly: metadata, manifests, and MSIL. Next, you contrasted shared and private assemblies, and investigated the steps taken by the assembly resolver to locate a given binary using application configuration files.

Assemblies are the building blocks of a .NET application. In essence, assemblies can be understood as binary units that contain some number of types that can be used by another application. As you have seen, assemblies may be private or shared. In stark contrast to classic COM, private assemblies are the default. When you want to configure a shared assembly, you are making an explicit choice, and need to generate a corresponding strong name.

As you have also learned, the .NET Framework defines the concept of an AppDomain. In many ways, AppDomains can be viewed as a lightweight process. Within a single AppDomain can exist any number of threads. Using the types defined within the System.Threading namespace, you are able to build thread-safe types that (as you have seen) can provide the end user with a more responsive application.

CHAPTER 8

Type Reflection and Attribute-Based Programming

AS DETAILED IN THE PREVIOUS chapter, assemblies are the basic unit of deployment in the .NET universe. Tools such as Visual Studio .NET have integrated Object Browsers that allow you to examine the internal types of referenced assemblies. Furthermore, external tools such as ILDasm.exe allow you to peek into the underlying IL code, type metadata, and assembly manifest. In addition to the design-time investigation of .NET assemblies, you are also able to *programmatically* obtain this same information using the types defined within the System.Reflection namespace.

Once you understand how to manipulate this namespace to examine an assembly at runtime, the remainder of the chapter examines a number of closely related topics. For example, you explore the types defined within the System.Reflection.Emit namespace, and learn the basics of building a dynamic assembly on the fly. Furthermore, this chapter illustrates how a .NET client may employ "late binding" to activate a given type. As you will see later in this book, late binding is an important aspect of .NET/COM interoperability and also has a direct impact on enabling Option Strict.

The chapter wraps up with an investigation of how to insert custom metadata into your .NET assemblies through the use of system supplied and custom attributes. If you have a background in classic COM, you will be happy to discover that the spirit of IDL attributes has been included (and enhanced) in the .NET architecture.

Understanding Reflection

In the .NET universe, *reflection* is the process of runtime type discovery. Using reflection services, you are able to load an assembly at runtime and discover the same sort of information as ILDasm.exe. For example, you can obtain a list of all types contained within a given module, including the methods, fields, properties, and events defined by a given type. You can also dynamically discover the set of interfaces supported by a given class (or structure), the parameters of a method as well as other related details (base class, namespace information, and so forth).

In order to understand reflection services, you need to come to terms with the Type class (defined in the System namespace) as well as a new namespace, System.Reflection. As you will see, the System.Type class contains a number of methods that allow you to extract valuable information about the current type you happen to be observing. The System.Reflection namespace contains numerous related types to facilitate late binding and dynamic loading of assemblies. To begin, let's investigate System.Type in some detail.

The System.Type Class

Many of the items defined within the System.Reflection namespace make use of the abstract System.Type class. This class provides a number of methods that can be used to discover the details behind a given item. The complete set of members is quite expansive, however Table 8-1 offers a partial snapshot of the members supported by Type.

Table 8-1. Members of the Type Class

TYPE MEMBER	MEANING IN LIFE
IsAbstract	
IsArray	
IsClass	
IsCOMObject	
IsEnum	
IsInterface	
IsPrimitive	
IsNestedPublic	
IsNestedPrivate	
IsSealed	
IsValueType	These properties (among others) allow you to discover a number of basic traits about the Type you are examining (i.e., if it is an abstract method, an array, a nested class, and so forth).
GetConstructors()	
GetEvents()	
GetFields()	

Table 8-1. Members of the Type Class (continued)

TYPE MEMBER	MEANING IN LIFE
GetInterfaces() GetMethods() GetMembers() GetNestedTypes() GetProperties()	These methods (among others) allow you to obtain an array representing the items (interface, method, property, etc.) you are interested in. Each method returns a related array (e.g., GetFields() returns a FieldInfo array, GetMethods() returns a MethodInfo array, etc.). Be aware that each of these methods has a singular form (e.g., GetMethod(), GetProperty()) that allows you to retrieve a specific item by name, rather than an array of all related items.
FindMembers()	Returns an array of MemberInfo types, based on search criteria.
GetType()	This method returns a Type instance given a string name.
InvokeMember()	This method allows late binding to a given item.

Obtaining a Type Object

There are numerous ways in which you can obtain an instance of the Type class. However, the one thing you cannot do is directly create a Type object using the New keyword, as Type is an abstract class. First, as you recall, System.Object defines a method named GetType() that returns an instance of the Type class:

```
' Extract Type using a valid Foo instance.
Dim theFoo As New Foo()
Dim t As Type = theFoo.GetType()
Console.WriteLine("My parent is: {0}", t.BaseType)
```

In addition to the previous technique, you may also obtain a Type using (of all things) the Type class itself. To do so, call the shared GetType() member and specify the textual name of the item you are interested in examining. Do note that Type.GetType() only works on assemblies that are loaded from disk (meaning the type is in a separate binary from the caller).

```
' Get a Type using the shared Type.GetType() method.
Dim t2 As Type
t2 = Type.GetType("System.String")      ' I am in mscorlib.dll
Console.WriteLine("My parent is: {0}", t2.BaseType)
```

Notice that Type.GetType() is helpful in that you do not need to first create an object instance to extract type information. Finally, you may also obtain a Type using the VB .NET GetType() method (which works for types within the defining assembly as well as types in a separate binary):

```
' Use the VB .NET GetType() method.
Dim t3 As Type
t3 = GetType(Foo)
Console.WriteLine("My full name is {0}", t3.FullName)
```

Now that you have a Type reference, let's examine how you can exercise it.

Fun with the Type Class

To illustrate the usefulness of System.Type, assume you have a class named Foo that has been defined as follows (the implementation of the various methods are irrelevant for this example):

```
' Here are the items we are going to
' examine at runtime. . .
' Two interfaces.
Public Interface IFaceOne
    Sub MethodA()
End Interface
Public Interface IFaceTwo
    Sub MethodB()
End Interface

' Foo supports these 2 interfaces.
Public Class Foo
    Implements IFaceOne, IFaceTwo
    'Some public fields.
```

```
    Public myIntField As Integer
    Public myStringField As String
    'A method.
    Public Sub myMethod(ByVal p1 As Integer, ByVal p2 As String)
        Console.WriteLine("Inside myMethod")
    End Sub

    'A read / write property.
    Public Property MyProp() As Integer
        Get
            Return myIntField
        End Get
        Set(ByVal Value As Integer)
            myIntField = Value
        End Set
    End Property

    'IFaceOne and IFaceTwo methods.
    Public Sub MethodA() Implements IFaceOne.MethodA
        Console.WriteLine("Inside method A")
    End Sub
    Public Sub MethodB() Implements IFaceTwo.MethodB
        Console.WriteLine("Inside method B")
    End Sub
End Class
```

Now, let's create a Console program that is able to discover the methods, properties, supported interfaces, and fields for a given Foo object (in addition to some other points of interest). The main Module defines a number of methods that look more or less identical. First you have ListMethods(), which extracts each method from Foo using a Type object. Notice how Type.GetMethods() returns an array of MethodInfo types:

```
' Suck out all method names from Foo.
 Public Sub ListMethods(ByVal f As Foo)
    Console.WriteLine("***** Methods of Foo *****")
    Dim t As Type = f.GetType()
    Dim mi As MethodInfo() = t.GetMethods()
    Dim m As MethodInfo
```

```
    ' Loop over methodinfo array and print names.
    For Each m In mi
        Console.WriteLine("Method: {0}", m.Name)
    Next
    Console.WriteLine("*************************")
End Sub
```

The implementation of ListFields() is similar. The only notable difference is the call to Type.GetFields() and the resulting FieldInfo array:

```
' Suck out all fields from Foo.
Public Sub ListFields(ByVal f As Foo)
    Console.WriteLine("***** Fields of Foo *****")
    Dim t As Type = f.GetType()
    Dim fi As FieldInfo() = t.GetFields()
    Dim field As FieldInfo
    For Each field In fi
        Console.WriteLine("Field: {0}", field.Name)
    Next
    Console.WriteLine("*************************")
End Sub
```

The ListVariousStats(), ListProps(), and ListInterfaces() methods should be self-explanatory at this point:

```
' Suck out some interesting statistics about Foo.
Public Sub ListVariousStats(ByVal f As Foo)
    Console.WriteLine("***** Various stats about Foo *****")
    Dim t As Type = f.GetType()
    Console.WriteLine("Full name is: {0}", t.FullName)
    Console.WriteLine("Base is: {0}", t.BaseType)
    Console.WriteLine("Is it abstract? {0}", t.IsAbstract)
    Console.WriteLine("Is it a COM object? {0}", t.IsCOMObject)
    Console.WriteLine("Is it sealed? {0}", t.IsSealed)
    Console.WriteLine("Is it a class? {0}", t.IsClass)
    Console.WriteLine("***********************************")
End Sub
```

```
'Gather all properties.
Public Sub ListProps(ByVal f As Foo)
    Console.WriteLine("***** Properties of Foo *****")
    Dim t As Type = f.GetType()
    Dim pi As PropertyInfo() = t.GetProperties()
    Dim prop As PropertyInfo
    For Each prop In pi
        Console.WriteLine("Prop: {0}", prop.Name)
    Next
    Console.WriteLine("*****************************")
End Sub
' Dump all interfaces supported by Foo.
Public Sub ListInterfaces(ByVal f As Foo)
    Console.WriteLine("***** Interfaces of Foo *****")
    Dim t As Type = f.GetType()
    Dim ifaces As Type() = t.GetInterfaces()
    Dim i As Type
    For Each i In ifaces
        Console.WriteLine("Interface: {0}", i.Name)
    Next
    Console.WriteLine("*****************************")
End Sub
```

The Main() method simply calls each method (see Figure 8-1 for output):

```
' Needed to gain definitions of MethodInfo, FieldInfo, etc.
Imports System.Reflection
Sub Main()
    Dim theFoo As New Foo()
    Dim t As Type = theFoo.GetType()
    ListVariousStats(theFoo)
    ListMethods(theFoo)
    ListFields(theFoo)
    ListProps(theFoo)
    ListInterfaces(theFoo)
End Sub
```

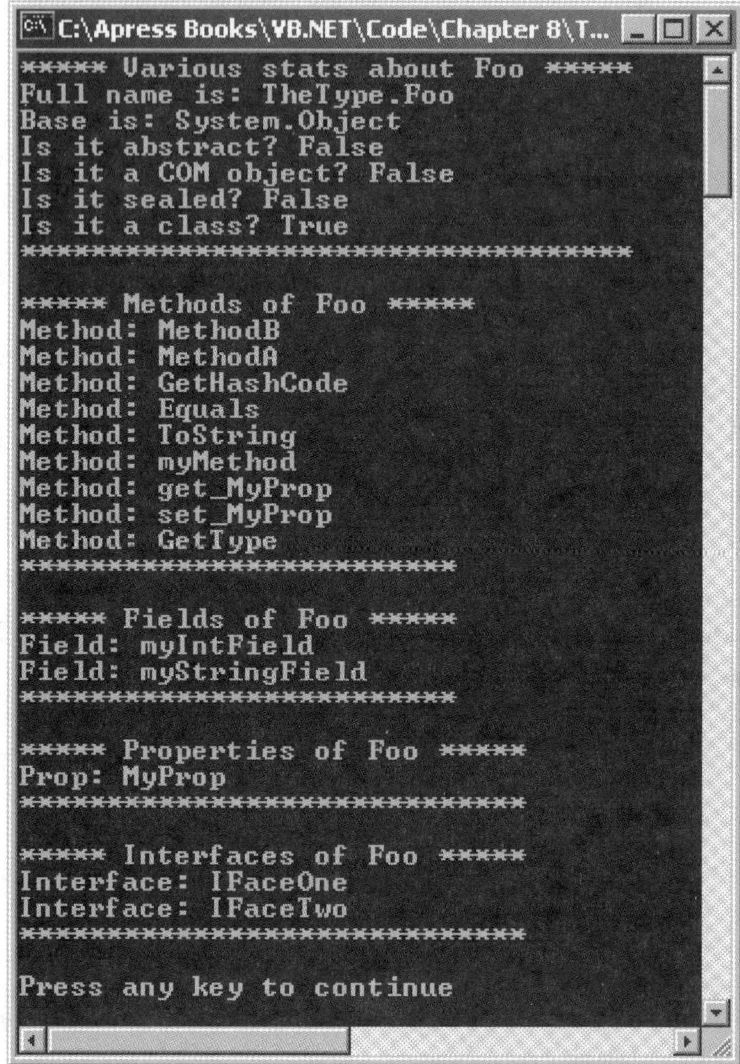

Figure 8-1. Reflecting on Foo

Interesting stuff, huh? Here, we made use of Object.GetType() to gather information about a class (Foo) defined in our current assembly. While the Type class can be very helpful on its own, reflection becomes even more powerful when you make use of the Assembly class defined within the System.Reflection namespace.

SOURCE CODE *The TheType project can be found under the Chapter 8 subdirectory.*

Investigating the System.Reflection Namespace

Like any namespace, System.Reflection contains a number of related types, and like any namespace, some types are of more immediate interest than others. Table 8-2 lists some of the core items you should be familiar with, many of which you have already seen in the previous Foo example.

Table 8-2. Select Members of System.Reflection

SYSTEM.REFLECTION TYPE	MEANING IN LIFE
Assembly	This class (in addition to numerous related types) contains a number of methods that allow you to load, investigate, and manipulate an assembly.
AssemblyName	This class allows you to discover numerous details behind an assembly's identity (version information, culture information, and so forth).
EventInfo	Holds information for a given event.
FieldInfo	Holds information for a given field.
MemberInfo	This is the abstract base class that defines common behaviors for the EventInfo, FieldInfo, MethodInfo, and PropertyInfo types.
MethodInfo	Contains information for a given method.
Module	Allows you to access a given module within a multifile assembly.
ParameterInfo	Holds information for a given parameter.
PropertyInfo	Holds information for a given property.

Dynamically Loading an Assembly

The real workhorse of System.Reflection is the Assembly class. Using this type, you are able to dynamically load an assembly, invoke class members at run-time (a.k.a. late binding), as well as discover numerous properties about the assembly itself.

The first step in investigating the contents of a .NET binary is to load the assembly in memory. Assume you have a new Console project named CarReflector, which has set a reference to the VB .NET CarLibrary assembly created in Chapter 7. The shared Assembly.Load() method can now be called by passing in the friendly string name:

```
Imports System.Reflection
Imports System.IO           ' Needed for FileNotFoundException definition.
' Build alias to reduce typing. . .VB .NET also defines an assembly keyword.
Imports DotNetAssembly = System.Reflection.Assembly
Sub Main()
    ' Use Assembly class to load the CarLibrary.
    Dim a As DotNetAssembly
    Try
        Dim asmName as String
        AsmName = "CarLibrary, Ver=1.0.581.32902," & _
        "PublicKeyToken=null, Culture="""
        a = DotNetAssembly.Load(asmName)
    Catch e As FileNotFoundException
        Console.WriteLine(e.Message)
    End Try
End Sub
```

Notice that the shared Assembly.Load() method has been passed in the friendly name of the assembly you are interested in loading into memory. As you may suspect, this method has been overloaded several times, to provide a number of ways for you to bind to an assembly. Here, you send a String into Assembly.Load(). Beyond the mandatory assembly name, you may choose to specify a version number, public key token and culture information. Also be aware that the Assembly type defines a member named LoadFrom() that allows you to specify the path to the assembly (i.e., C:\myAsm.dll) rather than its friendly name.

Collectively speaking, the set of items identifying an assembly is termed the "display name." The format of a display name is a comma-delimited string that begins with the friendly name, followed by optional qualifiers (that may appear in any order). Here is the template to follow (optional items have been placed in parentheses):

```
Name (,Culture = CultureInfo) (,Ver = Major.Minor.Build.Revision)
(,PublicKeyToken= token)
```

Each element of a display name can be represented by a corresponding type. For example, the System.Reflection.AssemblyName type allows you to represent the string information given above in a handy object instance. Typically, this class is used in conjunction with System.Version, which is an OO wrapper around the assembly's version number. Once you have established the display name, it can then be passed into the overloaded Assembly.Load() method:

```
' Our OO-Aware display name.
Dim asmName As AssemblyName
```

```
asmName = New AssemblyName()
asmName.Name = "CarLibrary"
Dim v As Version = New Version("1.0.581.32902")
asmName.Version = v
a = DotNetAssembly.Load(asmName)
```

Enumerating Types in a Referenced Assembly

Now that you have a reference to the CarLibrary assembly, you can discover the name of each type it contains using Assembly.GetTypes(). Here is a helper method named ListAllTypes() that does this very thing (notice we are passing in a reference to a loaded assembly):

```
' Here are the methods to check out all types.
Private Sub ListAllTypes(ByVal a As DotNetAssembly)
    Console.WriteLine("Listing all types in:")
    Console.WriteLine(a.FullName)
    Dim types() As Type = a.GetTypes()
    Dim t As Type
    For Each t In types
        Console.WriteLine("Type: {0}", t)
    Next
End Sub
```

Enumerating Class Members

Let's now assume you are interested in discovering the full set of members supported by one of our automobiles. To do so, you can make use of the GetMembers() method defined by the Type class. As you recall, the Type class also defined a number of related methods (GetInterfaces(), GetProperties(), GetMethods(), and so forth) that allow you to specify a specific kind of member. GetMembers() returns an array of MemberInfo types. Here is an example that lists the type and signature of each method defined by the MiniVan (the output is shown in Figure 8-2):

```
' Another static method of the CarReflector class.
Private Sub ListAllMembers(ByVal a As DotNetAssembly)
    Dim miniVan As Type = a.GetType("CarLibrary.MiniVan")
    Console.WriteLine("Listing all members for {0}", _
        miniVan.FullName)
```

```
    Dim mi() As MemberInfo = miniVan.GetMembers()
    Dim m As MemberInfo
    For Each m In mi
        Console.WriteLine("Type {0}: {1} ", _
             m.MemberType.ToString(), m)
    Next
End Sub
```

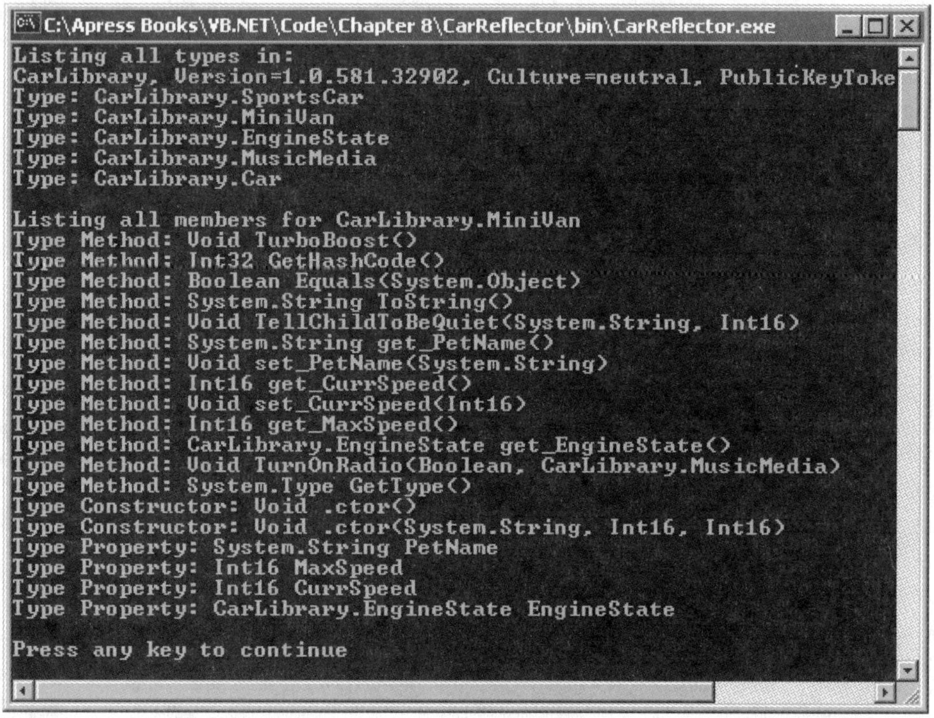

```
C:\Apress Books\VB.NET\Code\Chapter 8\CarReflector\bin\CarReflector.exe
Listing all types in:
CarLibrary, Version=1.0.581.32902, Culture=neutral, PublicKeyToke
Type: CarLibrary.SportsCar
Type: CarLibrary.MiniVan
Type: CarLibrary.EngineState
Type: CarLibrary.MusicMedia
Type: CarLibrary.Car

Listing all members for CarLibrary.MiniVan
Type Method: Void TurboBoost()
Type Method: Int32 GetHashCode()
Type Method: Boolean Equals(System.Object)
Type Method: System.String ToString()
Type Method: Void TellChildToBeQuiet(System.String, Int16)
Type Method: System.String get_PetName()
Type Method: Void set_PetName(System.String)
Type Method: Int16 get_CurrSpeed()
Type Method: Void set_CurrSpeed(Int16)
Type Method: Int16 get_MaxSpeed()
Type Method: CarLibrary.EngineState get_EngineState()
Type Method: Void TurnOnRadio(Boolean, CarLibrary.MusicMedia)
Type Method: System.Type GetType()
Type Constructor: Void .ctor()
Type Constructor: Void .ctor(System.String, Int16, Int16)
Type Property: System.String PetName
Type Property: Int16 MaxSpeed
Type Property: Int16 CurrSpeed
Type Property: CarLibrary.EngineState EngineState

Press any key to continue
```

Figure 8-2. The MiniVan type under the microscope

Enumerating Method Parameters

Not only can you use reflection to gather information for the members of a type, you can also obtain information about the parameters of a given member. To illustrate, let's assume that the Car class has defined the following additional method named TurnOnRadio():

```
' A new member of the Car class.
Public Sub TurnOnRadio(state as Boolean, mm as MusicMedia)
     If(state) Then
```

```
            MessageBox.Show("Jamming with {0}", mm.ToString())
        Else
            MessageBox.Show("Quiet time. . .")
    End If
End Sub
```

TurnOnRadio() takes two parameters, the second of which is a custom enumeration:

```
' Holds source of music.
Public Enum MusicMedia
    musicCD
    musicTape
    musicRadio
End Enum
```

Extracting information for the parameters of TurnOnRadio() requires the use of MethodInfo.GetParameters(). This method returns a ParameterInfo array. Each item in this array contains numerous properties for a given parameter. Here is another shared method of the CarReflector class, GetParams(), which displays various details for each parameter of the TurnOnRadio() method. Check it out:

```
' Get parameter information for the TurnOnRadio() method.
Private Sub GetParams(ByVal a As DotNetAssembly)
    Dim miniVan As Type = a.GetType("CarLibrary.MiniVan")
    Dim mi As MethodInfo = miniVan.GetMethod("TurnOnRadio")
    Console.WriteLine("Here are the params for {0}", mi.Name)
    ' Show number of params.
    Dim myParams() As ParameterInfo = mi.GetParameters()
    Console.WriteLine("Method has {0} params", myParams.Length)
    ' Show info about param.
    Dim pi As ParameterInfo
    For Each pi In myParams
        Console.WriteLine("Param name: {0}", pi.Name)
        Console.WriteLine("Position in method: {0}", pi.Position)
        Console.WriteLine("Param type: {0}", pi.ParameterType)
    Next
End Sub
```

Figure 8-3 displays the output.

```
C:\Apress Books\VB.NET\Code\Chapter 8\Car...
Here are the params for TurnOnRadio
Method has 2 params
Param name: state
Position in method: 0
Param type: System.Boolean
Param name: mm
Position in method: 1
Param type: CarLibrary.MusicMedia
Press any key to continue_
```

Figure 8-3. Parameter information

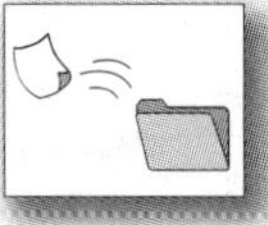

SOURCE CODE *The CarReflector project is included under the Chapter 8 subdirectory.*

Understanding Dynamic Invocation (Late Binding)

At this point you understand how to use some of the core items defined within the System.Reflection namespace to discover a wealth of information at runtime. And, maybe you are already envisioning the code behind ILDasm.exe. Our examples have dumped information to a console window. ILDasm.exe obtains the same information, and places it within the various nodes of a tree view control.

The System.Reflection namespace provides additional functionality beyond runtime type discovery. Reflection also provides the ability to exercise late binding to a type. Late binding is a technique in which you are able to resolve the existence of (and name of) a given type and its members at runtime (rather than compile time). Once the presence of a type has been determined, you are then able to dynamically invoke methods, access properties, and manipulate the fields of a given entity.

The value of late binding may not be immediately understood. It is true that if you can bind early to a type (e.g., use the New keyword) you should opt to do so. Early binding allows you to determine errors at compile time, rather than runtime. Late binding however, does have a place among tool builders as well as COM/.NET interoperability. For example, using late binding, a .NET programmer is able to obtain a COM object's IDispatch interface. You examine interoperability issues later in the book.

Late Binding Using VB 6.0

Visual Basic 6.0 developers interact with the IDispatch interface (and hence late binding) using the Object data type (which has nothing to do with System.Object) in conjunction with the CreateObject() function which takes a *ProgID* (Programmatic Identifier) as the first parameter. Classic COM servers are assigned a ProgID, which is a textual representation of a given coclass contained in a given server. Thus, when you write the following VB 6.0 code:

```
' VB 6.0 late binding.
Dim o as Object
Set o = CreateObject("MyCOMServer.MyCoClass")
```

the system registry is consulted to determine the location of a COM server named MyCOMServer. At this point, the MyCoClass type is created, and the IDispatch interface is returned and stored in the Object variable.

The problem with this approach is that when you reference a COM type using an Object variable, you have no hope of catching type-related errors at compile time. For example, if the MyCoClass type defines a single method named MethodOne(), but you call the following:

```
' There is no method of this name!
o.NothingIsBetterThanRunTimeErrors
```

You will compile just fine, but die at runtime. Sure, you could wrap your late bound calls within an On Error Goto handler, but the fact remains that the error will not be resolved at compile time.

As you have seen in Chapter 2, VB .NET supplies the Option Strict setting. When this setting is enabled, you are telling vbc.exe to force you to declare all variables before use, enforce explicit type conversion and *disable implicit VB 6.0 style late binding.* Thus, when Option Strict is set to True, the following VB .NET code does not compile:

```
' Option Strict = True will not allow this.
' Option Strict = False will. . .
Dim o As Object
o.FFFXXX7737()     ' No such method in System.Object!
```

Now, you are still able to invoke a type's members at runtime under .NET when Option Strict is enabled. The difference is that you make use of (much safer) types in the System.Reflection namespace rather than the VB 6.0 CreateObject()/Object data type combo. To understand how to exercise late binding under VB .NET, let's begin by examining the System.Activator class.

The Activator Class

The System.Activator class is the key to .NET late binding. Beyond the methods inherited from Object, Activator only defines a small set of members. The shared Activator.CreateInstance() method creates an instance of a type at runtime. This method has been overloaded numerous times to provide a good deal of flexibility. One variation of the CreateInstance() member takes a valid Type object. In the code below, notice you are making use of the Assembly.LoadFrom() method, just for a change of pace (you are also free to call the shared Load() method as you did in the previous example).

```
' Create a type dynamically.
Imports System.IO
Imports System.Reflection
Imports DotNetAssembly = System.Reflection.Assembly
Module Module1
    Sub Main()
        ' Use Assembly class to load the CarLibrary.
        Dim a As DotNetAssembly
        Try
            ' Adjust your path accordingly!
            Dim path As String = "C:\ CarLibrary.dll"
            a = DotNetAssembly.LoadFrom(path)
        Catch e As FileNotFoundException
            Console.WriteLine(e.Message)
        End Try
        ' Get the Minivan type.
        Dim miniVan As Type = a.GetType("CarLibrary.MiniVan")
        ' Create the Minivan on the fly.
        Dim obj As Object = Activator.CreateInstance(miniVan)
    End Sub
End Module
```

At this point, the "obj" variable is pointing to a MiniVan instance in memory that has been created indirectly using the Activator class. Now assume you wish to invoke the TurboBoost() method of the MiniVan. As you recall, this sets the state of the engine to "dead" and displays an informational message box.

The first step is to obtain a MethodInfo type for the TurboBoost() method using Type.GetMethod(). From a MethodInfo type, you are then able to call the method using Invoke(). MethodInfo.Invoke() requires you to send in all parameters that are to be given to the method represented by MethodInfo. These parameters are represented by an array of Objects. Given that TurboBoost() does not require any parameters, you can simply pass "Nothing" (meaning "this method has no parameters"):

```
Public Sub Main()
    ' Use Assembly class to load the CarLibrary...
    ' Get the Minivan type....
    '  Create the Minivan on the fly....
    ...
    ' Get info for TurnOnRadio.
    Dim mi As MethodInfo = miniVan.GetMethod("TurboBoost")
     ' Invoke method (no params).
     mi.Invoke(obj, Nothing)
End Sub
```

At this point you are happy to see Figure 8-4.

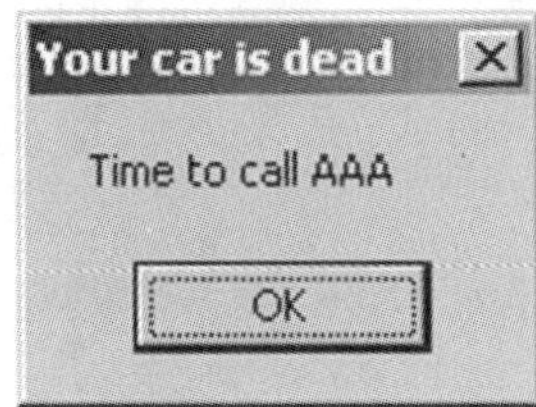

Figure 8-4. Late binding

Now assume you wish to call the following new method defined by MiniVan using late binding:

```
' Quiet down the kids...
Public Sub TellChildToBeQuiet(ByVal kidName As String, _
    ByVal shameIntensity As Integer)
    Dim i As Integer
    For i = 0 To shameIntensity
        MessageBox.Show("Be quiet " & kidName & "!!")
    Next
End Sub
```

TellChildToBeQuiet() takes two parameters. In this case, the array of parameters must be fleshed out as follows:

```
' Create array of params.
Dim MyParamArray(1) As Object  ' Remember, this is {0, 1}
```

```
MyParamArray(0) = "Fred"
MyParamArray(1) = 4
mi = miniVan.GetMethod("TellChildToBeQuiet")
mi.Invoke(obj, MyParamArray)
```

If you run this program, you will see four message boxes popping up, shaming young Fredrick (Figure 8-5).

Figure 8-5. Late binding with parameters

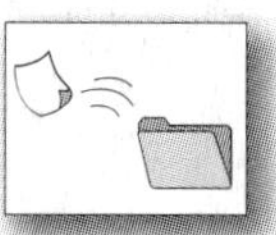

SOURCE CODE *The LateBinding project is included under the Chapter 8 subdirectory.*

Understanding (and Building) Dynamic Assemblies

The next point of interest is the distinction between *static* and *dynamic* assemblies. Static assemblies are what you have been (and for the most part, will be) referring to in this book. Simply put, static assemblies are loaded directly from disk storage, meaning they are located somewhere on a hard drive in a physical file.

On the other hand, a dynamic assembly is created *in memory* on the fly using the functionality provided by the System.Reflection.Emit namespace. This namespace makes it possible to create an assembly, its modules, manifest, and any associated types at *runtime.* Once you have done so, you are then free to dynamically save your new types (again at runtime) to disk. This of course, results in a new static assembly! Furthermore, using the System.Reflection.Emit namespace, it is possible to dynamically add new types and members to the runtime representation of an existing assembly.

Understanding the System.Reflection.Emit Namespace

The types defined within the System.Reflection.Emit namespace are of greatest use to individuals who are in the tool building or language development business. For example, imagine that you have been assigned the rather exotic task of creating a version of QuickBasic that targets the .NET runtime (does anyone use QuickBasic anymore?).

Using System.Reflection.Emit, you could take the raw BASIC code and emit corresponding .NET intermediate language (IL) which is then stored in a dynamically created assembly. While this task might seem unlikely, ASP.NET employs this very same technique. First, Table 8-3 gives a rundown of some (but not all) of the types defined within the System.Reflection.Emit namespace.

Table 8-3. Select Members of System.Reflection.Emit

SYSTEM.REFLECTION.EMIT TYPE	MEANING IN LIFE
AssemblyBuilder	Used to create an assembly at runtime. This type may be used to create either a DLL or EXE binary assembly. EXEs must call the ModuleBuilder. SetEntryPoint() method must set the method that is the entry point to the module. If no entry point is specified, a DLL is generated.
ModuleBuilder	Used to create a module within an assembly at runtime.
EnumBuilder	
TypeBuilder	Creates a type (e.g., class, interface) within a module at runtime.
MethodBuilder	
EventBuilder	
LocalBuilder	
PropertyBuilder	
FieldBuilder	
ConstructorBuilder	
CustomAttributeBuilder	These (and other) items are used to create a given member of a type (methods, local variables, properties, constructors, attributes) at runtime.
ILGenerator	Used to create the underlying intermediate language (IL) of a member at runtime.

Emitting a Dynamic Assembly

As you might guess, if you were to build anything other than a trivial dynamic assembly, you would suddenly need to be very comfortable with the intricacies of raw IL code. Although full coverage of raw IL is beyond the scope of this book, you can most certainly take the System.Reflection.Emit namespace out for a test drive (if you desire additional information, check out the official IL documentation in the *Tool Developers Guide* section of the .NET SDK).

The goal of this section is to create a single file assembly (thus the name of the module is the same as the assembly itself). Within this module, is a single class named (of course) HelloWorld. The HelloWorld type supports a Public field (Msg) of type String. In addition, let's support a Public method named SayHello(), which prints a greeting to the standard IO stream, and another method named GetMsg() which returns the internal string (yes, it would make more sense to declare the internal String as Private, but this would increase the code base quite a bit to account for a custom constructor). In effect, you are going to programmatically build the following class:

```
' This class will be built at runtime using System.Reflection.Emit.
Public Class HelloWorld
    Public Msg as String
    Public Function GetMsg() as String
        Return Msg
    End Function
    Public Sub SayHello()
        System.Console.WriteLine("Hello there!")
    End Sub
End Class
```

Assume you have created a new Console Application project workspace named DynAsmBuilder. The first class within the project (MyAsmBuilder) has a single method (CreateMyAsm) which is in charge of building the dynamic assembly, establishing the HelloClass, and saving the type to disk. Here is the complete code, with analysis to follow:

```
' This class builds an assembly on the fly,
' adds a class
' and saves it to disk.
Imports System.Reflection
Imports System.Reflection.Emit
Imports DotNetAssembly = System.Reflection.Assembly

Public Class MyAsmBuilder
```

```
Public Sub CreateMyAsm(ByVal curAppDomain As AppDomain)
    ' Create a name for the assembly.
    Dim asmName As AssemblyName = New AssemblyName()
    asmName.Name = "MyAssembly"
    asmName.Version = New Version("1.0.0.0")
    ' Create the assembly in memory.
    Dim asm As AssemblyBuilder _
         = curAppDomain.DefineDynamicAssembly(asmName, _
         AssemblyBuilderAccess.Save)
    ' Here, we are building a single file
    ' assembly, so the name of the module
    ' is the same as the assembly.
    Dim myModule as ModuleBuilder = _
        asm.DefineDynamicModule("MyAssembly", "MyAssembly.dll")
    ' Define a public class named "HelloWorld".
    Dim helloWorldClass As TypeBuilder = _
    myModule.DefineType("MyAssembly.HelloWorld", _
     TypeAttributes.Public)
    ' Define a Public String member variable named "Msg":
    Dim msgField As FieldBuilder = helloWorldClass.DefineField("Msg", _
            Type.GetType("System.String"), _
            FieldAttributes.Public)
    ' Now created the GetMsg method:
    ' Public Function GetMsg() as String
    Dim getMsgMethod As MethodBuilder = _
       helloWorldClass.DefineMethod("GetMsg", MethodAttributes.Public, _
       Type.GetType("System.String"), Nothing)
    Dim methodIL As ILGenerator = getMsgMethod.GetILGenerator()
    methodIL.Emit(OpCodes.Ldarg_0)
    methodIL.Emit(OpCodes.Ldfld, msgField)
    methodIL.Emit(OpCodes.Ret)
    ' Create the SayHello method:
    ' Public Sub SayHello()
    Dim sayHiMethod As MethodBuilder = _
     helloWorldClass.DefineMethod("SayHello", _
            MethodAttributes.Public, Nothing, Nothing)
    methodIL = sayHiMethod.GetILGenerator()
    methodIL.EmitWriteLine("Hello there!")
    methodIL.Emit(OpCodes.Ret)
    ' Bake the class HelloWorld.
    ' (baking a type is a cute way to say,
    ' "make it so!").
    helloWorldClass.CreateType()
```

```
        ' Save the assembly to disk.
        asm.Save("MyAssembly.dll")
    End Sub
End Class
```

Code Analysis

Now that you have seen the entire code base necessary to build our dynamic assembly, let's walk through the highlights step-by-step.

Establish the Assembly

The method body begins by establishing a small set of characteristics about your assembly, using the AssemblyName class. Next, we create the assembly in memory using the AppDomain type, which was described in Chapter 7 (note that the CreateMyAsm() helper function takes an incoming AppDomain variable).

```
' Create a name for the assembly.
Dim asmName As AssemblyName = New AssemblyName()
asmName.Name = "MyAssembly"
asmName.Version = New Version("1.0.0.0")
' Create the assembly in memory.
Dim asm As AssemblyBuilder _
    = curAppDomain.DefineDynamicAssembly(asmName, _
    AssemblyBuilderAccess.Save)
```

When calling AppDomain.DefineDynamicAssembly(), you must specify the access mode, which can be any of the values shown in Table 8-4.

Table 8-4. Values of the AssemblyBuilderAccess Enumeration

ASSEMBLYBUILDERACCESS VALUE	MEANING IN LIFE
Run	Represents that a dynamic assembly can be executed but not saved.
RunAndSave	Represents that a dynamic assembly can be executed and saved.
Save	Represents that a dynamic assembly can be saved but not executed.

Insert the Module

The next task is to insert the module into the assembly. Recall that your assembly is a single file unit. If you build a multifile assembly using the DefineDynamicModule() method, you can specify an optional second parameter, which represents the name of a given module (e.g., myMod.netmodule). When you wish to make a single file assembly, the name of the module (and the binary file) is identical to the name of the assembly itself:

```
' Here, we are building a single file
' assembly, so the name of the module
' is the same as the assembly.
Dim myModule as ModuleBuilder = _
   asm.DefineDynamicModule("MyAssembly", "MyAssembly.dll")
```

Build the Class Type

Now for the real fun! Making use of the ModuleBuilder.DefineType() method, you are able to insert a class, structure, or interface into the module, and receive a TypeBuilder reference that represents the new item (in this case, a class named HelloWorld) in reply. At this point, you can insert the public string data member, as seen here:

```
' Define a public class named "HelloWorld".
Dim helloWorldClass As TypeBuilder = _
    myModule.DefineType("MyAssembly.HelloWorld", _
    TypeAttributes.Public)
' Define a Public String member variable named "Msg":
Dim msgField As FieldBuilder = helloWorldClass.DefineField("Msg", _
    Type.GetType("System.String"), _
    FieldAttributes.Public)
```

The GetMsg() method makes use of the MethodBuilder type, which you are able to obtain from the DefineMethod() member of the TypeBuilder class. In addition to setting up the characteristics of the function itself, you need to drop down to some raw IL to return the String variable. Ponder the following:

```
' Now created the GetMsg method:
' Public Function GetMsg() as String
Dim getMsgMethod As MethodBuilder = _
    helloWorldClass.DefineMethod("GetMsg", MethodAttributes.Public, _
    Type.GetType("System.String"), Nothing)
```

```
Dim methodIL As ILGenerator = getMsgMethod.GetILGenerator()
methodIL.Emit(OpCodes.Ldarg_0)
methodIL.Emit(OpCodes.Ldfld, msgField)
methodIL.Emit(OpCodes.Ret)
```

Now let's examine the SayHello() method:

```
' Create the SayHello method:
' Public Sub SayHello()
Dim sayHiMethod As MethodBuilder = _
    helloWorldClass.DefineMethod("SayHello", _
MethodAttributes.Public, Nothing, Nothing)
methodIL = sayHiMethod.GetILGenerator()
methodIL.EmitWriteLine("Hello there!")
methodIL.Emit(OpCodes.Ret)
```

Here, you have established a Public method (MethodAttributes.Public) that takes no parameters and returns nothing (note the "Nothing" entries contained in the DefineMethod() call. Also note the EmitWriteLine() call. This member of the ILGenerator class automatically writes a line to the standard output with minimal fuss and bother. I leave it as an exercise to you to examine the remaining underlying IL in whatever detail you desire.

Using the Dynamically Generated Assembly

Now that you have the logic in place to create and save our assembly, all that's needed is a class to trigger the logic. The logic in Main() creates an AppDomain to send into the CreateMyAsm() method. Once this call returns, you can exercise some late binding to load this assembly into memory, and call each method of the HelloWorld class:

```
Imports System.Threading
Imports System.Reflection
Imports DotNetAssembly = System.Reflection.Assembly
Module Module1
    Sub Main()
        ' Whip up a new assembly.
        Dim a As New MyAsmBuilder()
        Dim curAppDomain As AppDomain = Thread.GetDomain()
        a.CreateMyAsm(curAppDomain)

        ' Now use it!
```

```
        Dim asm As DotNetAssembly
        Try
            asm = DotNetAssembly.Load("MyAssembly")
        Catch
            Console.WriteLine("Can't find assembly. . .")
        End Try
        ' Get the HelloWorld type.
        Dim hello As Type = asm.GetType("MyAssembly.HelloWorld")
        ' Create HelloWorld object.
        Dim obj As Object = Activator.CreateInstance(hello, Nothing)
        Dim fi As FieldInfo = hello.GetField("Msg")
        fi.SetValue(obj, "This is sooo sweet. . .")
        Dim mi As MethodInfo = hello.GetMethod("SayHello")
        mi.Invoke(obj, Nothing)
        mi = hello.GetMethod("GetMsg")
        Console.WriteLine(mi.Invoke(obj, Nothing))
    End Sub
End Module
```

Figure 8-6 shows the output.

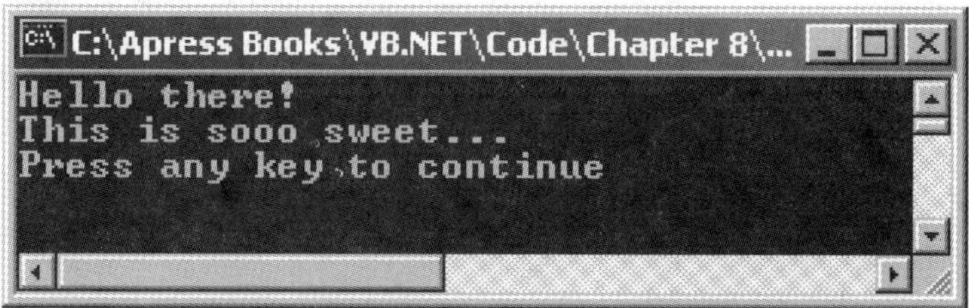

Figure 8-6. Calling members of the dynamically created assembly

Here, we are making use of late binding to load and manipulate the assembly. Understand that other applications could simply set a reference to the binary and make use of it just like any other .NET assembly.

But wait! It gets even better given the fact that you can locate the new assembly in your project's directory. If you open your assembly using ILDasm.exe you will be extremely pleased to see what appears in Figure 8-7 (notice that we received a freebee default constructor).

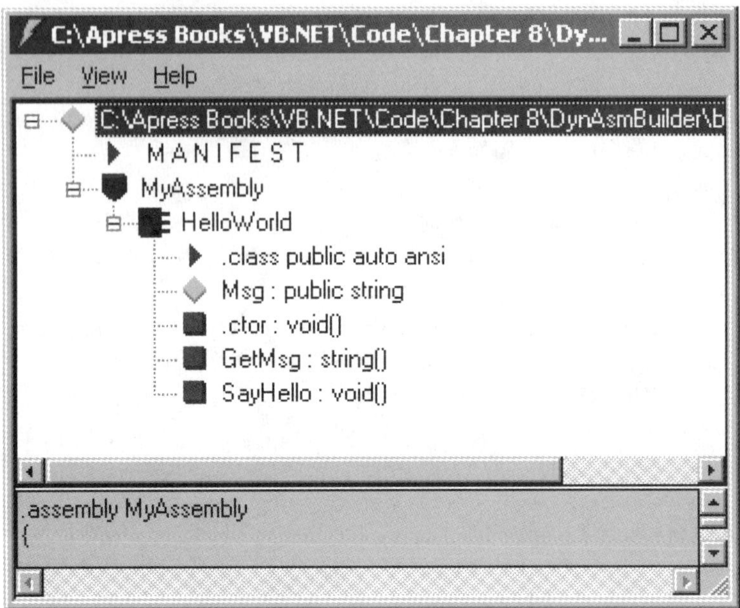

Figure 8-7. Hello dynamic assembly!

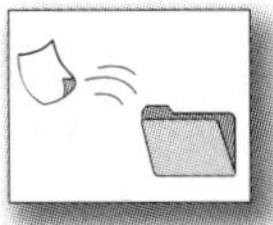

SOURCE CODE *The DynAsmBuilder application is included under the Chapter 8 subdirectory.*

Understanding Attributed Programming

The official meta language of the COM is IDL. As you may know, IDL is used to describe the set of types defined within a given classic COM server. In order to describe these types in unambiguous terms, IDL makes use of "attributes," which are simply IDL keywords placed within square brackets. A given attribute block always applies to the very next thing. For example, when you compile an ActiveX DLL, the VB 6.0 compiler generates a type library (which is simply a binary version of IDL code) that contains a complete description of each item in your COM server.

If you used OleView.exe, you would be able to reverse-engineer the type library into the original IDL code. IDL code makes substantial use of "attributes" to unambiguously describe the internal COM types. For example, COM interfaces are marked with the [uuid] and [object] attributes (at minimum). Parameters can be specified using the [in], [out], [in, out] and [out, retval] attributes. By way of example, here is a classic COM interface defined in IDL, making use of various

IDL attributes (FYI, you dig deeper into IDL and the OleView.exe utility in Chapter 13 during your examination of COM/.NET interoperability):

```
[ object, uuid(4CB8B79A-E991-4AA4-8DB8-DD5D8751407D), oleautomation]
interface IRememberCOM : IUnknown
{
     [helpstring("If you send me a string, I will change it. . .")]
     HRESULT TextManipulation([in] BSTR myStr, [out, retval] BSTR* newStr)
}
```

Notice how the TextManipulation() method has been assigned a [helpstring] attribute, which is used to document how a given item is to be used. Once a COM type has been assigned various attributes, it can be discovered at runtime programmatically, or at design time using various tools. For example, if you examine this COM method using the Visual Basic 6.0 Object Browser utility, you see the custom [helpstring] is automatically extracted and displayed (Figure 8-8).

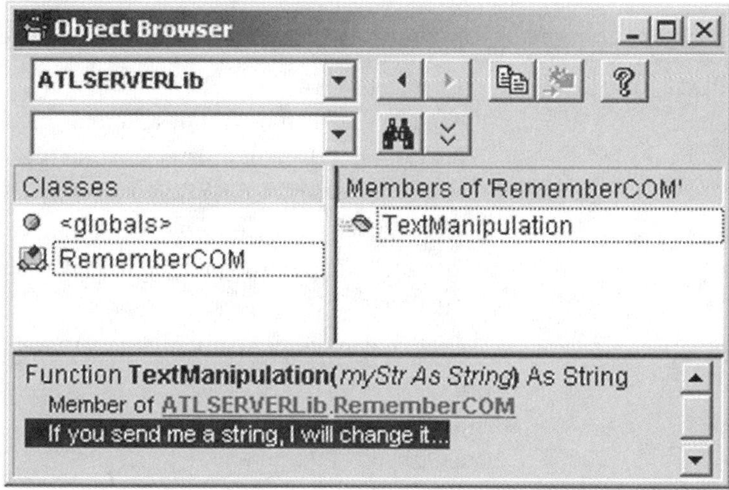

Figure 8-8. COM IDL as seen in Visual Basic 6.0

IDL attributes have proven to be so helpful, that VB .NET (as well as other .NET aware languages) has integrated them as official aspects of the language. Using attributes, you are able to extend the metadata generated by a given .NET compiler with custom information.

As you explore the .NET namespaces, you find that there are many predefined attributes to make use of in your applications. Furthermore, you are free to build custom attributes to further qualify the behavior of your types. Keep in mind that .NET attributes (predefined or custom) are actually *objects* all of which extend System.Attribute (contrast this to IDL, in which attributes are nothing more than simple keywords).

Working with Existing Attributes

Like IDL, VB .NET attributes are objects that can be applied to a given type (class, interface, structure, etc), member (property, method, etc) assembly, or module. As mentioned, the .NET library defines a number of predefined attributes in various namespaces. Many of the predefined attributes are most useful in the context of COM and .NET interoperability, Component Services, remoting, debugging and other “exotic” aspects of building managed code. Table 8-5 gives a snapshot of some (but by no means all) predefined attributes.

Table 8-5. A Tiny Sampling of Predefined Attributes

PREDEFINED .NET ATTRIBUTE	MEANING IN LIFE
CLSCompliant	Ensures that all types in the assembly conform to the Common Language Specification (CLS) and is always the case in VB.NET.
DllImport	While VB.NET still supports the Declare syntax, this attribute can also be used to make calls to the native OS.
StructLayout	Used to configure the underlying representation of a structure.
Dispid	Specifies the DISPID for a member in a COM dispinterface.
Serializable	Marks a class or structure as being serializable.
NonSerialized	Specifies that a given field in a class or structure is not serializable.
WebMethod	Specifies that a given method is reachable via HTTP requests.

As an example, assume that you wish to assign the <Serializable> attribute to a given item. The Motorcycle class that follows has assigned the attribute at the class level. As well, the <NonSerialized> attribute has been attributed to a field named temp. As you can see, VB .NET attributes are enclosed within angled brackets. Somewhat annoyingly, VB .NET demands that an attribute be immediately followed by a type definition, which can lead to some very long lines of code (thus the use of the line continuation character):

```
' This class can be saved to disk.
<Serializable()> Public _
Class Motorcycle
    Public hasRadioSystem As Boolean
    Public hasHeadSet As Boolean
    Public hasSissyBar As Boolean
    ' But when you do, don't bother with this field.
    <NonSerialized()> Private _
    weightOfCurrentPassengers As Short
End Class
```

Using ILDasm.exe (Figure 8-9), you can see that these attributes are now specified within the type definition.

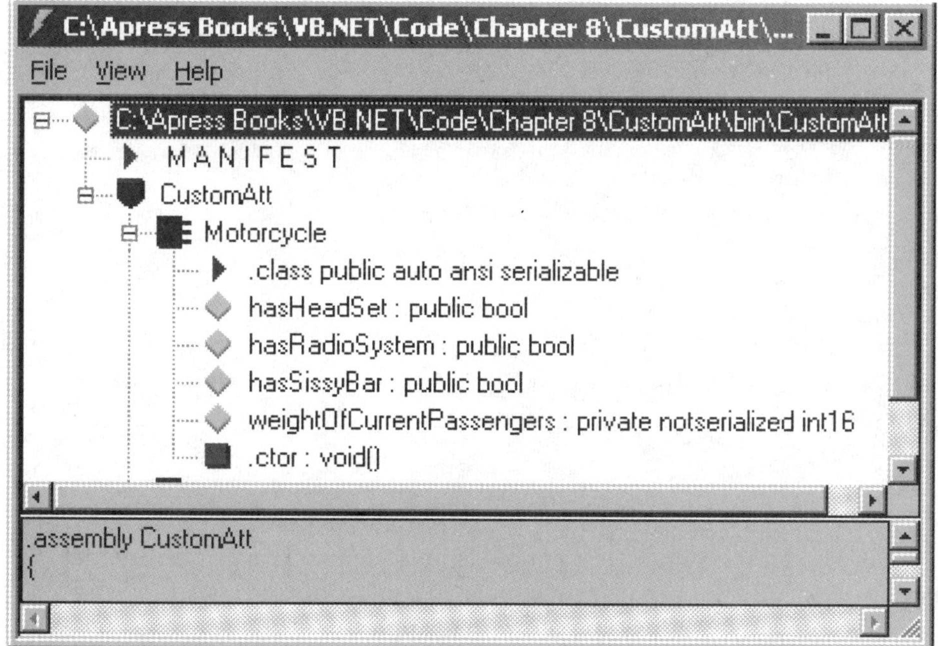

Figure 8-9. Attributes are represented by metadata

Now at this point, don't concern yourself with who or what is on the lookout for the presence of these attributes. Just understand that attributed programming allows you to extend an assembly's metadata with various custom annotations.

Building Custom Attributes

VB .NET (as well as other .NET aware languages) allows you to build custom attributes. Recall that attributes are in fact instances of a class derived from System.Attribute. Thus, when you applied the <Serializable> attribute to the Motorcycle class, you in fact applied the System.SerializableAttribute type. From a design point of view, an attribute is a class instance that can be applied to some other type. In the world of OOP, this approach is termed *aspect-oriented programming*.

The first step to building your custom attribute is to create a new class derived from System.Attribute. The naming convention you should follow is to suffix "-Attribute" to the new type. Here is a basic custom attribute named VehicleDescriptionAttribute that allows a programmer to inject a string into the type metadata describing a particular automobile:

```
' A custom attribute.
Public Class VehicleDescriptionAttribute
    Inherits System.Attribute
    Private description As String
    Public Property Desc() As String
        Get
            Return description
        End Get
        Set(ByVal Value As String)
            description = Value
        End Set
    End Property
    Public Sub New()
    End Sub
    Public Sub New(ByVal desc As String)
        description = desc
    End Sub
End Class
```

As you can see, VehicleDescriptionAttribute maintains a private internal string (description) that can be manipulated using a custom constructor and a named property. Now assume you wish to apply this attribute to a new class named Winnebago. Notice how the constructor signature determines the exact syntax of the attribute:

```
' This class using a custom attributes.
<VehicleDescription("A very long, slow but feature rich auto")> Public _
Class Winnebago
```

```
    ...
End Class
```

Now, let's see your new type in action. The VehicleDescriptionAttribute attribute (or any attribute) makes use of parentheses to pass arguments to the constructor of the associated System.Attribute-derived class. As you have already seen, one of the constructors does indeed take a string parameter. Now, using ILDasm.exe, you find your string message has been injected into the assembly's metadata (Figure 8-10).

```
Winnebago::.class public auto ansi

6F 6E 67 2C 20     // ..'A very long,
61 74 75 72 65     // slow but feature
00 )               //  rich auto..
```

Figure 8-10. Your custom message

If you look at the IL itself (Figure 8-11), you notice that custom attributes are marked using the IL instruction ".custom."

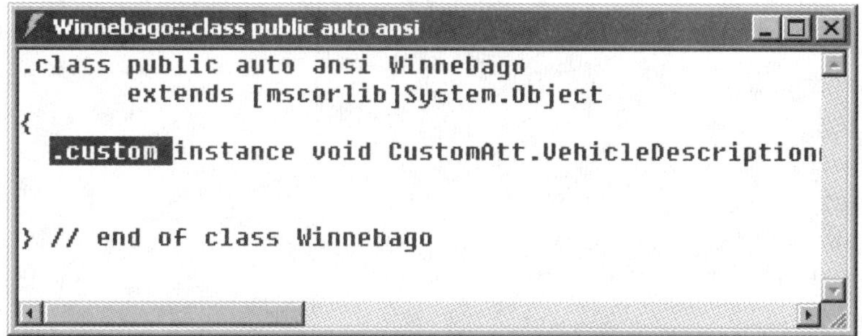

Figure 8-11. The internal representation of your custom attribute

The VB .NET language does offer a shorthand notation for assigning an attribute to a given item (the same is true of C#). If the name of your custom attribute class does indeed have a "-Attribute" suffix, you are allowed to omit this same suffix in the code base. Be aware that not all .NET-enabled languages support this feature.

Restricting Attribute Usage

Currently, your custom attribute has no mechanism to prevent a developer from making illogical aspect specifications. For example, the following is syntactically correct, but semantically out of whack:

```
' OK, but an odd use of this custom attribute. . .
<VehicleDescriptionAttribute("A very long, slow but feature rich auto")> _
Public Class Winnebago
    <VehicleDescriptionAttribute> _
    Public Sub TurnOnRadio()
    End Sub
End Class
```

Ideally, it would be nice to enforce the fact that this particular custom attribute should only be allowed to modify a class (and perhaps a structure) but nothing else. If you wish to constrain your attributes in this way, you need to make use of the AttributeTargets enumeration, defined in C# as follows:

```
// This enumeration is used to control how a custom attribute can be applied.
public  enum AttributeTargets
{
    All,
    Assembly,
    Class,
    Constructor,
    Delegate,
    Enum,
    Event,
    Field,
    Interface,
    Method,
    Module,
    Parameter,
    Property,
    ReturnValue,
    Struct
}
```

These values are passed as a parameter to the AttributeUsage attribute. This predefined attribute is used by the VB .NET compiler to enforce the correct application of a custom attribute. The first parameter is an OR-ing together of members from the AttributeTarget enumeration. The second (optional) parameter is typically a named argument (AllowMultiple), which specifies if the custom attribute can be used more than once on the same type. The final (optional) Boolean parameter determines if the attribute should be inherited by derived classes.

Thus, you can now configure the VehicleDescriptionAttribute to only apply to classes or structures as follows:

```
' This time, we are using the predefined AttributeUsage attribute
' to modify our custom attribute!
<AttributeUsage(AttributeTargets.Class _
Or AttributeTargets.Struct)> Public _
Class VehicleDescriptionAttribute
    Inherits System.Attribute
    Private description As String
    Public Property Desc() As String
        Get
            Return description
        End Get
        Set(ByVal Value As String)
            description = Value
        End Set
    End Property
    Public Sub New()
    End Sub
    Public Sub New(ByVal desc As String)
        description = desc
    End Sub
End Class
```

If you recompile your project, you are (thankfully) issued compile time errors if you apply your attribute on the method level.

Assembly (and Module) Level Attributes

It is also possible to apply attributes on all types within a given module, or all modules within a given assembly. Doing so requires the use of the predefined attribute specifiers, <Assembly: > and <Module: >.

As you recall, VB .NET always compiles code that is CLS compliant. However, the C# language supports various features that do not work correctly in other

.NET aware languages. For example, assume you are building a C# application, and wish to ensure that every type defined within your assembly is compliant. To do so, you would specify the following assembly-level attribute (note that attributes are specified using *square* brackets in C#):

```
// Enforce CLS compliance In C#!
using System
[assembly:System.CLSCompliantAttribute(true)]
namespace MyAttributes
{
[VehicleDescriptionAttribute("A very long, slow but feature rich auto")]
public class Winnebago
{
    public Winnebago(){}
    public ulong notCompliant
}
}
```

Because the use of ulong types falls outside of the CLS, you are now issued a compiler error.

The VB .NET "AssemblyInfo.vb" File

Recall that, VB .NET projects define a file called AssemblyInfo.vb. This file is a handy place to place all assembly level attributes. Here is a quick run-through of some (but not all) assembly level attributes to be aware of (Table 8-6).

Table 8-6. Select Assembly-Level Attributes

ASSEMBLY-LEVEL ATTRIBUTE	MEANING IN LIFE
AssemblyCompanyAttributes	Holds basic company information.
AssemblyConfigurationAttribute	Build information, such as “retail” or “debug.”
AssemblyCopyrightAttribute	Holds any copyright information for the product or assembly.
AssemblyDescriptionAttribute	A friendly description of the product or modules that make up the assembly.
AssemblyInformationalVersionAttribute	Additional or supporting version information, such as a commercial product version number.
AssemblyProductAttribute	Product information.

Table 8-6. Select Assembly-Level Attributes (continued)

ASSEMBLY-LEVEL ATTRIBUTE	MEANING IN LIFE
AssemblyTrademarkAttribute	Trademark information.
AssemblyCultureAttribute	Information on what cultures or languages the assembly supports.
AssemblyKeyFileAttribute	Specifies the name of the file containing the key pair used to sign the assembly (i.e., establish a shared name).
AssemblyKeyNameAttribute	Specifies the name of the key container. Instead of placing a key pair in a file, you can store it in a key container in the CSP. If you choose this option, this attribute will contain the name of the key container.
AssemblyOperatingSystemAttribute	Information on which operating system the assembly was built to support.
AssemblyProcessorAttribute	Information on which processors the assembly was built to support.
AssemblyTitleAttribute	Specifies the title of the given assembly.
AssemblyVersionAttribute	Specifies the assembly's version information.
CLSCompliant	Enforces all types in this assembly to be CLS compliant.

Discovering Attributes at Runtime

And now the final topic of the chapter! It is possible to obtain attributes at runtime using the Type class. Assume you have set a reference to the CustomAtt assembly and added the following code to Main() (see Figure 8-12 for output):

```
Imports CustomAtt
Module Module1
    Sub Main()
        ' Get the Type of winnebago.
        Dim w As New Winnebago()
        Dim t As Type = w.GetType()
        ' Get all attributes in the assembly.
        Dim customAtts() As Object = t.GetCustomAttributes(False)
        ' List all info.
```

```
        Dim v As VehicleDescriptionAttribute
        For Each v In customAtts
            Console.WriteLine(v.Desc)
        Next
    End Sub
End Module
```

```
C:\Apress Books\VB.NET\Code\Chapter 8\AttReade...
A very long, slow but feature rich auto
Press any key to continue
```

Figure 8-12. Reflecting on your custom attribute

As the name implies, Type.GetCustomAttributes() returns an array (of object types) that represent all the attributes applied to the member represented by the Type. From this array you are able to determine a specific attribute on the fly. What you do with this information is (of course) up to you.

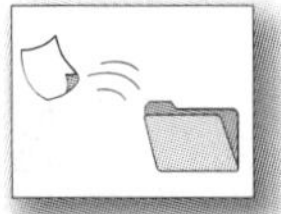

SOURCE CODE *The CustomAtt and AttReader applications are included under the Chapter 8 subdirectory.*

Summary

Reflection is a very interesting aspect of a robust OO environment. In the world of .NET, the keys to reflection services revolve around the System.Type class and the System.Reflection namespace. As you have seen, reflection is the process of placing a type under the magnifying glass at runtime to understand the "who, what, where, why, and how" of a given item.

On a related note, you explored the System.Reflection.Emit namespace, and gained a taste of creating an assembly (and the raw IL) on the fly. Assemblies that are constructed dynamically in memory (and possibly saved to file) are termed "dynamic assemblies."

I closed this chapter with an examination of attribute-based programming. When you adorn your type with attributes, the result is the augmentation of the underlying metadata. While you may never find yourself in the position of *absolutely* having to build custom attributes, you are bound to find the predefined attributes invaluable, especially when building a bridge between your classic COM servers and .NET assemblies.

CHAPTER 9

Building a Better Window (Introducing Windows Forms)

IF YOU HAVE READ the previous eight chapters, you should have a solid handle on the VB .NET programming language as well as the core aspects of the .NET architecture. While you could take your newfound knowledge and begin building the next generation of Console applications (boring!) you are more likely to be interested in building an attractive graphical user interface (GUI) to allow the outside world to interact with your system.

This chapter introduces you to the System.Windows.Forms namespace. Here, you learn the details of building a highly stylized main window (using a custom Form-derived type). In the process, you learn about a number of window-related classes, including Application, MenuItem, ToolBar, and StatusBar. This chapter also examines how to capture and respond to user input (i.e., handling mouse and keyboard events) within the context of a GUI environment. As you will quickly discover, Windows Forms directly exposes much more code (and with that code, much more power) than VB 6.0 GUI development.

This chapter also illustrates a more exotic Windows Forms example that stores user preferences in the system registry (using .NET types) and interacts with the Windows 2000 Event Log. Finally, the chapter wraps up by examining the construction of a basic MDI application. The information presented here prepares you for the material presented in Chapters 10 and 11 (GDI+ and programming with Windows Forms controls). Once you complete these chapters, you are in a perfect position to build sophisticated user interfaces using the .NET Framework and VB .NET.

A Tale of Two GUI Namespaces

The .NET universe supplies two GUI toolkits: Windows Forms and Web Forms. The System.Windows.Forms namespace contains a number of types that allow you to build traditional desktop applications as well as feature-rich presentation layers (or "fat clients") for use in a distributed enterprise application. As you expect, Windows Forms (much like VB 6.0) hides the raw Win32 APIs from view, allowing you to focus on the functionality of your application using the familiar .NET-type system.

Web Forms, on the other hand, is a GUI toolkit used during ASP.NET development. The bulk of the Web Forms types are contained in the System.Web.UI and System.Web.UI.WebControls namespaces. Using these types, you are able to build browser-independent front ends based on various industry standards (HTML, HTTP, and so forth). You examine ASP.NET (as well as the related topic of Web services) in Chapters 15 and 16. This chapter focuses on building traditional desktop applications using the Windows Forms namespace.

As a relevant side note, it is worth pointing out that while Windows Forms and Web Forms contain a number of identically named types (e.g., Button and CheckBox) with similar members (e.g., BackColor and Text), they do *not* share a common implementation and *cannot* be treated identically. Nevertheless, as you become comfortable with the Windows Forms namespace, you should find the process of learning Web Forms far more palatable.

Overview of the Windows Forms Namespace

The System.Windows.Forms namespace contains a large number of types to aid in the process of building rich user interfaces. Like any namespace, System.Windows.Forms is composed of a number of classes, structures, interfaces, and enumerations. Over the next couple of chapters, you will drill into the specifics of a good number of these types. While it is redundant to list every member of the Windows Forms family (as they are all documented in online Help), Table 9-1 lists some (but by no means all) of the core classes.

Building a Windows Forms Application by Hand

When you are building a Windows Forms application, you may choose to write all the relevant code by hand (using Notepad, perhaps) and send the resulting *.vb file into the VB .NET compiler using the /target:winexe flag. Taking time to build some Windows Forms applications by hand is not only a great learning experience, but it also helps you understand the code generated by various GUI wizards provided by VS .NET.

Visual Studio .NET supplies a number of great wizards, starter templates, and configuration tools that make working with Windows Forms extremely simple. The only downside of wizard-generated code is that if you do not understand exactly what the code is doing on your behalf, you have a much tougher time fully understanding the underlying .NET types and the richness of the Windows

Table 9-1. Core Windows Forms Types

WINDOWS FORMS CLASS	MEANING IN LIFE
Application	This class represents the guts of a Windows Forms application. Using the methods of Application, you are able to process Windows messages, start and terminate a Windows Forms application, and so forth. Typically, this type runs silently in the background and does not require direct manipulation.
ButtonBase, Button, CheckBox, ComboBox, DataGrid, GroupBox, ListBox, LinkLabel, PictureBox	These classes (in addition to many others) represent types that correspond to various GUI widgets. You examine many of these items in detail in Chapter 11.
Form	This type represents a main window (or dialog box) of a Windows Forms application.
ColorDialog, FileDialog, FontDialog, PrintPreviewDialog	As you might expect, Windows Forms defines a number of canned dialog boxes. If these don't fit the bill, you are free to build custom dialog boxes.
Menu, MainMenu, MenuItem, ContextMenu	These types are used to build topmost and context-sensitive (pop-up) menu systems.
Clipboard, Help, Timer, Screen, ToolTip, Cursors	Various utility types to facilitate interactive GUIs.
StatusBar, Splitter, ToolBar, ScrollBar	Various types used to adorn a Form with common child controls.

Forms namespace. To ensure you do not become a victim of wizard code paralysis, write as much "wizard-free" code as possible and make use of the integrated tools where appropriate.

Prepping the Project Workspace

To begin understanding Windows Forms programming, let's build a simple main window by hand. While you could make use of vbc.exe directly, simply create a new, *empty* VB .NET project workspace named "MyRawWindow" using the VS. NET IDE. Next, insert a new VB .NET class definition (resist the temptation to insert a new Windows Form class) from the "Project | Add Class. . ." menu option (see Figure 9-1). Go ahead and name this class "MainWindow."

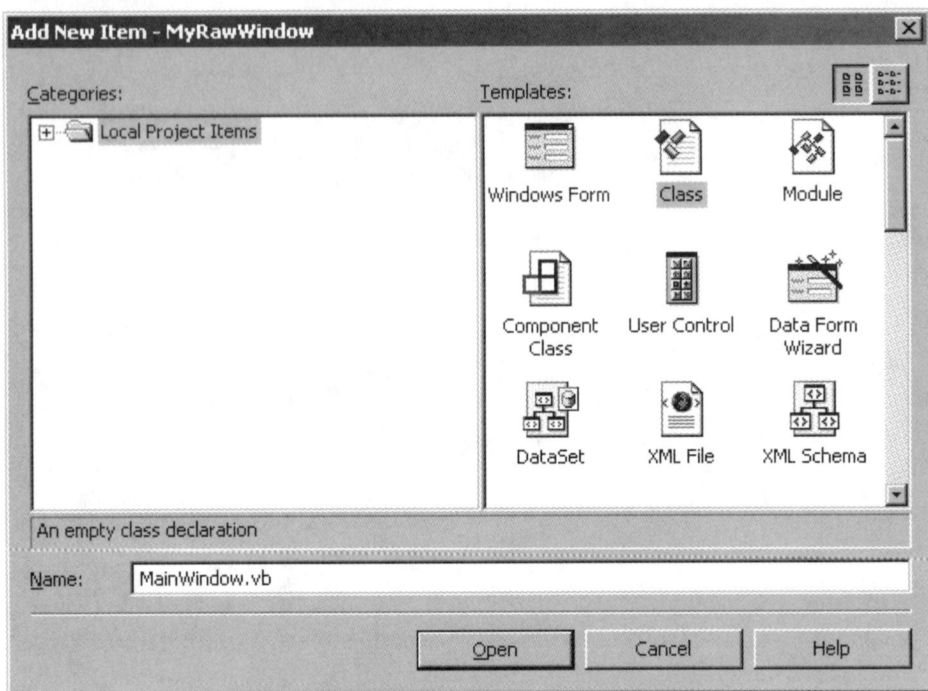

Figure 9-1. Inserting a new VB .NET class type

When you build a main window by hand, you need to use the Form and Application types (at a minimum), both of which are contained in the System.Windows.Forms.dll assembly. A Windows Forms application also needs to reference System.dll given that some Windows Forms types make use of types in the System.dll assembly. Add references to these assemblies now using the Add Reference dialog box (see Figure 9-2).

Building a Main Window

In the world of Windows Forms, the *Form* object is used to represent any window in your application. This includes a topmost main window in a Single Document Interface (SDI) application, modeless and modal dialog boxes, and the parent and child windows of a Multiple Document Interface (MDI) application. When you are interested in creating a new main window by hand, you must perform the following two steps:

1. Derive a new class from System.Windows.Forms.Form.

2. Configure the application's shared Main() method to call Application.Run(), passing an instance of your new Form-derived class as an argument.

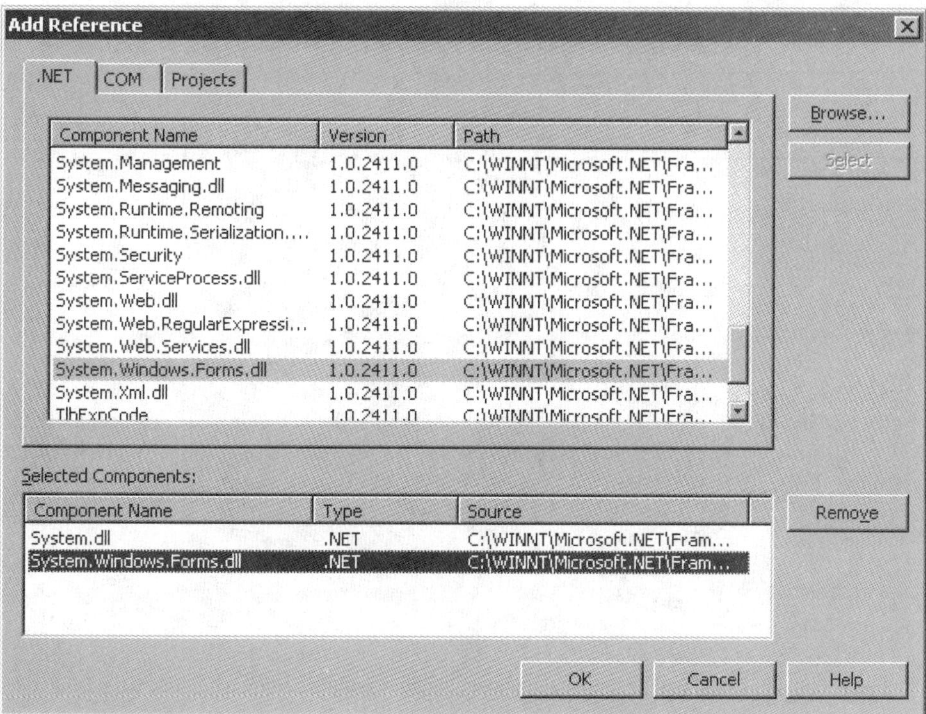

Figure 9-2. You must reference System.dll and System.Windows.Forms.dll.

With these steps in mind, update your empty class definition as follows:

```
' Need to import the Windows Forms namespace.
Imports System.Windows.Forms
Public Class MainWindow
    Inherits Form    ' Derive from Form.
    Public Shared Sub Main()
        ' Launch the window!
        Application.Run(New MainWindow())
    End Sub
End Class
```

Figure 9-3 shows a test run.

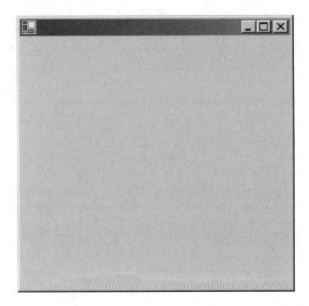

Figure 9-3. A basic Form

Now you have a minimizable, maximizable, resizable, and closable main window (with a default system-supplied icon to boot). Granted, your MainWindow does not do too much at this point. However, you build Forms with enhanced functionality as you move through the chapter.

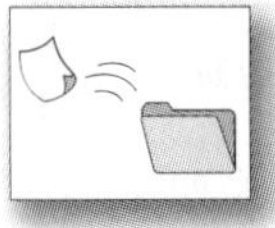

SOURCE CODE *You can find the MyRawWindow application under the Chapter 9 subdirectory.*

Building a Visual Studio .NET Windows Forms Project Workspace

The benefit of building Windows Forms applications using Visual Studio .NET is that the integrated CASE tools can take care of a number of mundane coding details by delegating them to a number of wizards, configuration windows, and so forth. To illustrate how to make use of such assistance, close your current workspace. Now, select a new VB .NET Windows Application project type (see Figure 9-4).

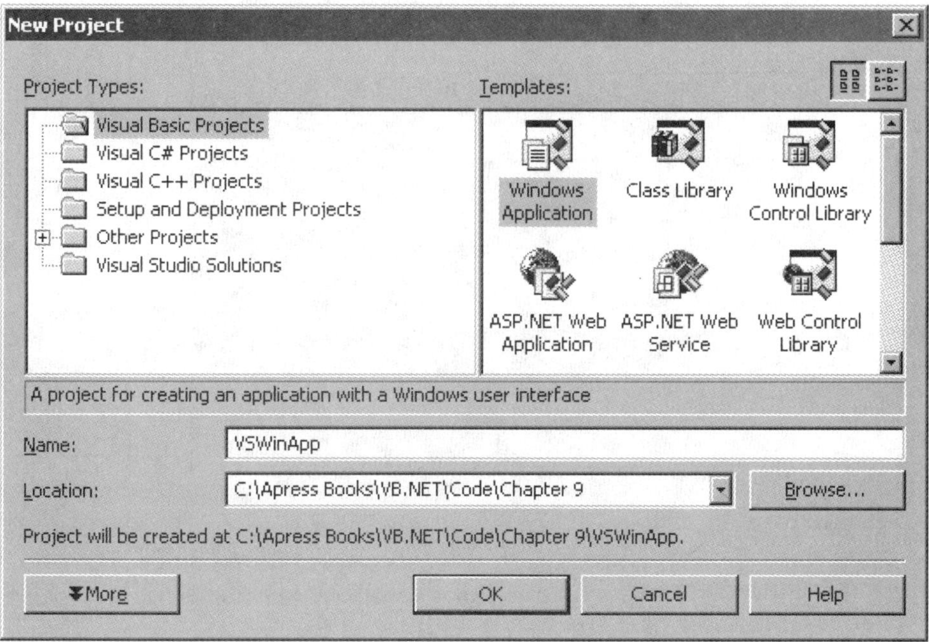

Figure 9-4. Selecting a Windows Application workspace

When you click OK, you find that you are automatically given a new class derived from System.Windows.Forms.Form and have references set to each required assembly (as well as some additional assemblies). Notice, however, that you do *not* directly see a Main() method calling the shared Application.Run() method. This is because the initial Form in a Windows Application is configured (by default) to behave as the startup object (which can be confirmed by viewing the Project Properties window). Given that the main Form is the bootstrapper of the entire executable, Application.Run() is called automatically on your behalf.

Much like VB 6.0, Windows Forms applications offer a design-time template that you can use to assemble the user interface of your Form (see Figure 9-5). Understand that as you update this design-time template, you are indirectly adding code to the associated Form-derived class (named Form1.vb by default). This is quite a change from VB 6.0, where the changes you made to a GUI type with the properties window were never realized directly in the code window (although similar information was stored in the corresponding VB 6.0 *.frm file).

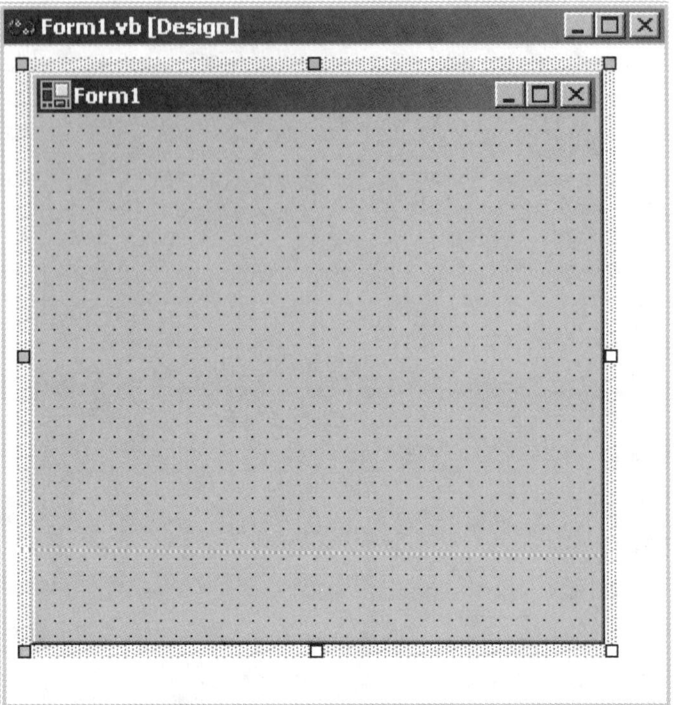

Figure 9-5. The design-time template

Using the Solution Explorer window, you are able to alternate between this design-time template and the underlying VB .NET code. To view the code that represents your current design, simply right-click the *.vb file and select View Code, as shown in Figure 9-6.

You can also open the code window by double-clicking anywhere on the design-time Form; however, this has the (possibly undesirable) effect of writing an event handler for the Form's Load event (more on GUI event processing later in this chapter). In any case, once you open the code window, you see a class looking very much like the following (note that the "Windows Form Designer generated code" region has been fully expanded):

```
Public Class Form1
    Inherits System.Windows.Forms.Form
#Region " Windows Form Designer generated code "
    Public Sub New()
        MyBase.New()
        'This call is required by the Windows Form Designer.
        InitializeComponent()
        'Add any initialization after the InitializeComponent() call
```

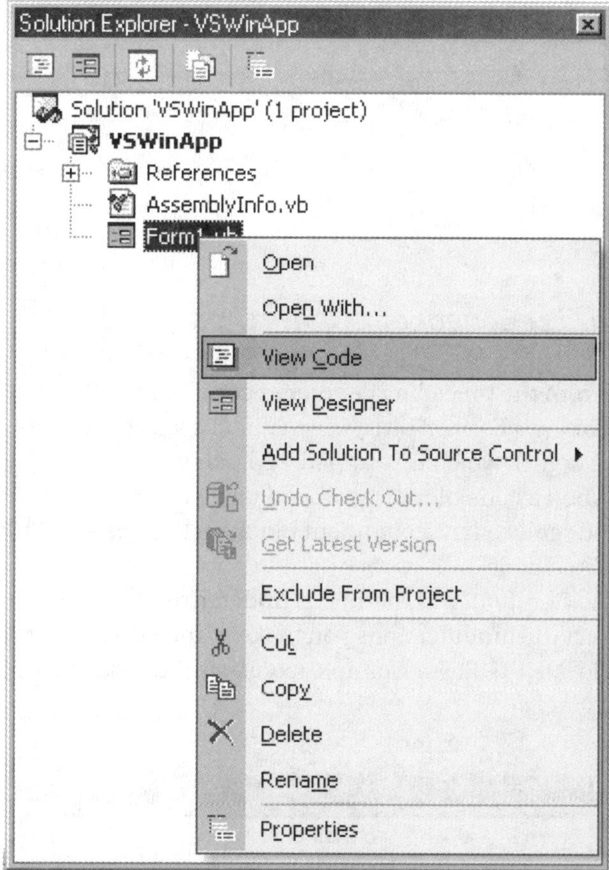

Figure 9-6. Activating the code behind the form

```
End Sub
'Form overrides dispose to clean up the component list.
Protected Overloads Overrides Sub Dispose(ByVal disposing As Boolean)
    If disposing Then
        If Not (components Is Nothing) Then
            components.Dispose()
        End If
    End If
    MyBase.Dispose(disposing)
End Sub
'Required by the Windows Form Designer
Private components As System.ComponentModel.Container
'NOTE: The following procedure is required by the Windows Form Designer
'It can be modified using the Windows Form Designer.
'Do not modify it using the code editor.
```

```
    <System.Diagnostics.DebuggerStepThrough()> _
    Private Sub InitializeComponent()
        components = New System.ComponentModel.Container()
        Me.Text = "Form1"
    End Sub
#End Region
End Class
```

The InitializeComponent() Method

As you can see from the preceding generated code, your class type still derives from System.Windows.Forms.Form. The major change is a new method named InitializeComponent(), which is wrapped by a pair of directives, #Region and #End Region. When a code block is wrapped using the #Region directives, it may be collapsed and replaced by a comment block (in this case, "Windows Form Designer generated code").

The InitializeComponent() method is updated automatically by the form designer to reflect the modifications you make to the Form and its controls using the Visual Studio .NET IDE. For example, consider the Properties window in Figure 9-7.

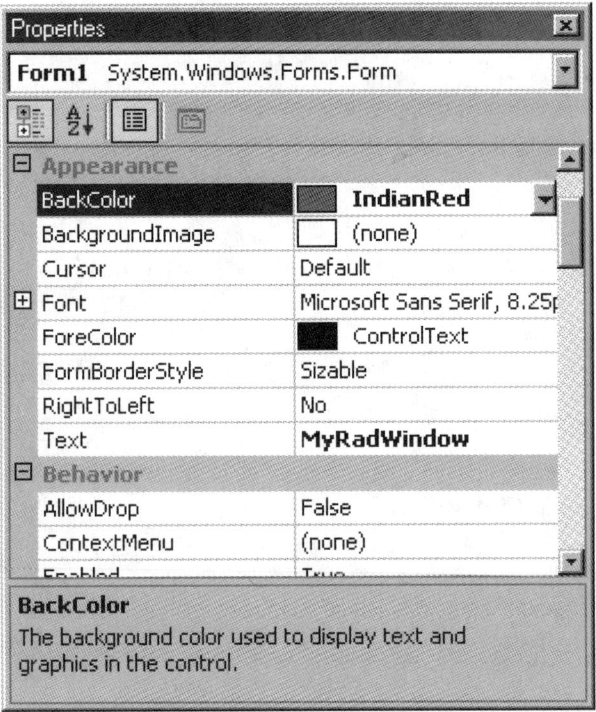

Figure 9-7. The VS .NET IDE Properties window

If you use the Properties window to modify the Form's Text and BackColor properties, you find that InitializeComponent() has been modified accordingly:

```
<System.Diagnostics.DebuggerStepThrough()> _
Private Sub InitializeComponent()
    '
    'Form1
    '
    Me.AutoScaleBaseSize = New System.Drawing.Size(5, 13)
    Me.BackColor = System.Drawing.Color.IndianRed
    Me.ClientSize = New System.Drawing.Size(292, 273)
    Me.Name = "Form1"
    Me.Text = "MyRadWindow"
End Sub
```

The Form-derived class calls InitializeComponent() within the scope of the default constructor. In this way, your Form and any contained widgets begin life with the correct look and feel:

```
Public Sub New()
    MyBase.New()
    'This call is required by the Windows Form Designer.
    InitializeComponent()
    'Add any initialization after the InitializeComponent() call
End Sub
```

Understand that the "safest" way to update the code that appears within the InitializeComponent() method is to make use of the VS .NET Properties window rather than directly manipulating the code contained within the method itself. If you add some bogus code within the InitializeComponent() method, you may cripple the IDE's capability to display the Form at design time. On a related note, also understand that the role of InitializeComponent() is to document your design-time code modifications. If you would rather (for example) set the background color of your Form at runtime, you are free to add code to the Form's constructor directly.

The Dispose() Method

The final point of interest is the overridden (and overloaded) Dispose() method. This method is called automatically when your Form is about to be destroyed, and it is a safe place to destroy any allocated resources. You revisit this method in just a bit, but here is the relevant code blurb:

```
'Form overrides dispose to clean up the component list.
Protected Overloads Overrides Sub Dispose(ByVal disposing As Boolean)
    If disposing Then
        If Not (components Is Nothing) Then
            components.Dispose()
        End If
    End If
    MyBase.Dispose(disposing)
End Sub
```

Now that you have seen how to build an initial Form using two approaches, you can spend a bit of time looking deeper into the functionality of the Application type.

The System.Windows.Forms.Application Class

The Application type defines members that allow you to control various low-level behaviors of a Windows Forms application. In addition, the Application class defines a set of events that allow you to respond to application-level events such as application shutdown and idle processing. Although the shared Run() method is called automatically for the startup Form, let's examine some of its behavior. To begin, ponder the core methods (all of which are shared) listed in Table 9-2.

Table 9-2. Core Methods of the Application Type

METHOD OF THE APPLICATION CLASS	MEANING IN LIFE
AddMessageFilter() RemoveMessageFilter()	These methods allow your application to intercept messages for any necessary preprocessing. When you add a message filter, you must specify a class that implements the IMessageFilter interface (as you will do shortly).
DoEvents()	This method provides the capability for an application to process messages currently in the message queue during a lengthy operation (such as a looping construct).
Exit()	This method terminates the application.
Run()	This method begins running a standard application message loop on the current thread. As you have seen, VB .NET Windows Forms applications hide this call by marking a given Form as the startup object.

The Application class also defines a number of shared properties, many of which are read-only. As you examine the following table, realize that each property represents some "application-level" trait such as company name, version number, and so forth. In fact, given what you already know about .NET attributes (see Chapter 8), many of the properties in Table 9-3 should look vaguely familiar.

Table 9-3. Core Properties of the Application Type

PROPERTIES OF APPLICATION CLASS	MEANING IN LIFE
CommonAppDataRegistry	Retrieves the registry key for the application data that is shared among all users
CompanyName	Retrieves the company name associated with the current application
CurrentCulture	Gets or sets the locale information for the current thread
CurrentInputLanguage	Gets or sets the current input language for the current thread
ProductName	Retrieves the product name associated with this application
ProductVersion	Retrieves the product version associated with this application
StartupPath	Retrieves the path for the executable file that started the application

Notice that some properties, such as CompanyName and ProductName, provide a handy way to retrieve assembly-level metadata. As you recall from Chapter 8, a manifest may be extended using any number of attributes. Thus, if you specify a value for the <Assembly:AssemblyCompany("")> attribute, you may obtain this information using Application.CompanyName without the need to make direct use of the types defined within System.Reflection.

Fun with the Application Class

To illustrate some of the functionality of the Application class, enhance your current VS. NET project to perform the following tasks:

- Display some basic information about the application on startup.
- Perform some "preprocessing" of a standard Windows message.

To begin, assume that you have updated your AssemblyInfo.vb file by specifying the name of this fine application and the company that created it (this process was defined in Chapter 8, so refer to that chapter if you need a refresher):

```
' Some attributes regarding this assembly.
<Assembly:AssemblyCompany("Intertech, Inc.")>
<Assembly:AssemblyProduct("A Better Window")>
```

The default constructor of the main Form class can obtain this information using properties of the Application type, which are displayed using a standard MessageBox type:

```
Public Class MainForm
    Inherits System.Windows.Forms.Form
#Region " Windows Form Designer generated code "
    Public Sub New()
        MyBase.New()
        'This call is required by the Windows Form Designer.
        InitializeComponent()
        'Add any initialization after the InitializeComponent() call
        GetStats()
    End Sub
...
#End Region
    Private Sub GetStats()
        MessageBox.Show(Application.CompanyName, "Company:")
        MessageBox.Show(Application.ProductName, "App Name:")
        MessageBox.Show(Application.StartupPath, "I live here:")
    End Sub
End Class
```

When you run this application, you see various message boxes that display the relevant information (as shown in Figure 9-8).

Figure 9-8. Extracting information using the Application type

Preprocessing Messages with the Application Class

As you most certainly know, Windows is an event-driven operating system. In VB 6.0, you respond to the events in a GUI-based application by choosing a specific event from the code window and adding your code to the generated event handler. Of course, you can take this same approach using Visual Studio .NET, as you will see in just a bit. However, to showcase some of the more exotic uses of the Application class, let's extend the current example to "preprocess" a message.

To begin, understand that in Windows programming each and every message (such as Click, MouseUp, KeyDown, and so forth) is represented by a numerical constant (which by convention is in all capital letters). For example, when you handle the MouseDown event in VB, you are actually responding to a predefined message named WM_LBUTTONDOWN, which just happens to be assigned the value of 513.

The good news is that VB quietly and secretly maps these internal constants to a given event on your behalf. However, using the Application type, you are able to intercept a given message before it is fully dispatched to its established event handler. When you want to filter messages in this manner, your first task is to create a new class that implements the standard IMessageFilter interface. This is extremely simple, given that IMessageFilter defines only one method, PreFilterMessage(). Return True to filter the message and prevent it from being dispatched or False to allow the message to continue on its way.

Within the scope of your implementation, you may examine the incoming Message.Msg field to extract the numerical value of the Windows message (again in this case, WM_LBUTTONDOWN, which is the value 513). Once you discover which message is being routed to a given event handler, you are able to perform any necessary preprocessing logic. For this example, simply display the ID of the message you are attempting to filter. For example:

```
' Must reference this namespace!
Imports Microsoft.Win32
' Create a message filter.
Public Class MyMessageFilter
    Implements IMessageFilter
    Public Function PreFilterMessage(ByRef m As Message) As Boolean _
        Implements IMessageFilter.PreFilterMessage
        ' Intercept the left mouse button down message.
        If (m.Msg = 513) Then      ' WM_LBUTTONDOWN = 513.
            MessageBox.Show("WM_LBUTTONDOWN is: " & m.Msg.ToString())
            Return True
        End If
        Return False  'All other messages are ignored. . .
    End Function
End Class
```

Once you have created the class that is equipped to filter the incoming messages, you must register a new instance of this type using the shared Application.AddMessageFilter() method. When you want to remove the filter from incoming messages, call Application.RemoveMessageFilter(). Here is the update to your existing MainForm class, which illustrates the process:

```
Public Class MainForm
    Inherits System.Windows.Forms.Form
    ' The type which will filter message.
    Private msgFilter As MyMessageFilter = New MyMessageFilter()
...
    Public Sub New()
        ...
        Application.AddMessageFilter(msgFilter)
    End Sub
    'Form overrides dispose to clean up the component list.
    Protected Overloads Overrides Sub Dispose(ByVal disposing As Boolean)
        If disposing Then
            If Not (components Is Nothing) Then
                components.Dispose()
            End If
        End If
        MyBase.Dispose(disposing)
        Application.RemoveMessageFilter(msgFilter)
    End Sub
End Class
```

When you run this application and click the left mouse button on the Form, you see the message box that appears in Figure 9-9. Again, understand that the need to filter Windows messages is not a task you need to perform all that often (if at all). Nevertheless, using VB .NET, you are able to drop down to this level of detail if you so choose.

Figure 9-9. Filtering messages

SOURCE CODE *You can find the VSWinApp project under the Chapter 9 subdirectory.*

The Anatomy of a Form

Now that you have a better understanding of the role of the Application object, your next task is to examine the functionality of the Form class itself. As you have seen, when you create a new window (or dialog box), you need to define a new class deriving from System.Windows.Forms.Form. This class gains a great deal of functionality from the types in its inheritance chain, as shown in Figure 9-10.

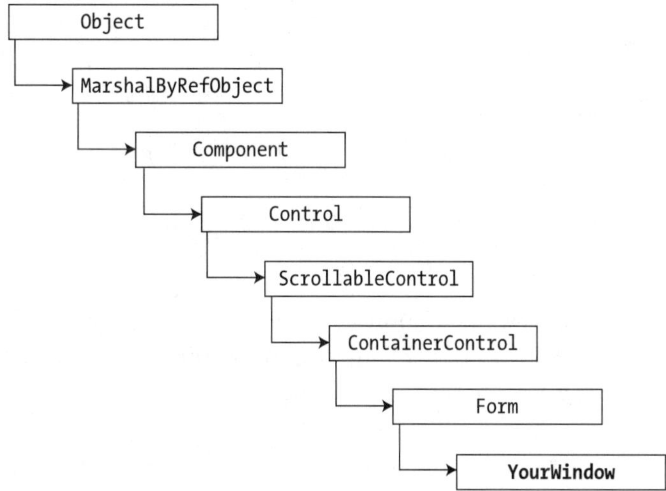

Figure 9-10. The derivation of the Form type

Detailing each and every member of each class in the Form's inheritance chain would require a small book in itself. However, it is important to understand the core behavior supplied by each base class. I assume that you will spend time examining the full details behind each class at your leisure.

Basic Form Functionality

Before I get into the real meat of the Form's inheritance chain, understand that like any type in the .NET universe, Form ultimately derives from System.Object (which should be no surprise to you at this point). MarshalByRefObject defines the behavior to marshal this type by reference, rather than by value. Thus, if you remotely instantiate a Form across the wire, you are manipulating a *reference* to the Form on the remote machine (not manipulating a local copy of the Form).

The System.ComponentModel.Component Class

The first base class of immediate interest is Component. This type provides the capability for a Form to host additional child controls, as well as be hosted within another container. The Component type provides a canned implementation of the IComponent interface. This predefined interface defines a property named Site, which returns (surprise, surprise) an ISite interface. Furthermore, IComponent inherits a single event from the IDisposable interface named Disposed. Here is the official C# definition of IComponent:

```
public interface IComponent : IDisposable
{
     // The Site property.
     public ISite Site {  virtual  get;  virtual  set; }
     // The Disposed event.
     public  event EventHandler Disposed;
}
```

The ISite interface defines a number of properties that allow a Control-derived type to interact with the hosting container (for example, a Form hosting a Button widget). Again, here is the C# definition:

```
public interface ISite : IServiceProvider
{
     // Properties of the ISite interface.
     public IComponent Component {  virtual  get; }
     public IContainer Container {  virtual  get; }
     public  bool DesignMode {  virtual  get; }
     public  string Name {  virtual  get;  virtual  set; }
}
```

By and large, the properties defined by the ISite interface are only of interest to you if you are attempting to build a widget that can be manipulated at design time (such as a custom control).

In addition to the Site property, Component also provides an implementation of the Dispose() method (as seen earlier in this chapter). Recall that the Dispose() method is called when a component is no longer required. For example, when a Form has been closed, the Dispose() method is called automatically on the Form, which in turn calls Dispose() for all widgets contained within that Form.

You are free to override Dispose() in your Form-derived class to free large resources in a timely manner and to remove references to other objects so that they can be garbage collected (Dispose() is overridden on your behalf when you create VS .NET Windows Application project workspaces):

```
Public Overrides Overloads Sub Dispose()
     MyBase.Dispose()
     ' Do your work. . .
End Sub
```

The Control Class

The next base class of interest is System.Windows.Forms.Control, which establishes the common behaviors required by any GUI-centric type. The core members of System.Windows.Forms.Control allow you to configure the size and position of a control, extract the underlying window handle (HWND) for this type, and capture keyboard and mouse input. Table 9-4 defines some of the properties to be aware of.

Table 9-4. Core Properties of the Control Type

CONTROL PROPERTY	MEANING IN LIFE
Top, Left, Bottom, Right, Bounds, ClientRectangle, Height, Width	Each of these properties specifies various attributes about the current dimensions of the Control-derived object. Bounds returns a Rectangle that specifies the size of the control. ClientRectangle returns a Rectangle that corresponds to the size of the client area of the Control.
Created, Disposed, Enabled, Focused, Visible	These properties each return a Boolean that specifies the state of the current Control.
Handle	This property returns a numerical value (integer) that represents the underlying handle (i.e., HWND) of this Control.
ModifierKeys	This shared property checks the current state of the modifier keys (Shift, Ctrl, and Alt) and returns the state in a Keys type.
MouseButtons	This shared property checks the current state of the mouse buttons (left, right, and middle mouse buttons) and returns this state in a MouseButtons type.

Table 9-4. Core Properties of the Control Type (continued)

CONTROL PROPERTY	MEANING IN LIFE
Parent	This property returns a Control object that represents the parent of the current Control.
TabIndex, TabStop	These properties are used to configure the tab order of the Control.
Text	This property specifies the current text associated with this Control.

The Control base class also defines a number of methods that allow you to interact with any Control-derived type. A partial list of some of the more common members appears in Table 9-5.

Table 9-5. Core Methods of the Control Type

CONTROL METHOD	MEANING IN LIFE
GetStyle() SetStyle()	These methods are used to manipulate the style flags of the current Control using the ControlStyles enumeration.
Hide(), Show()	These methods indirectly set the state of the Visible property.
Invalidate()	This method forces the Control to redraw itself by forcing a paint message into the message queue. This method is overloaded to allow you to specify a specific Rectangle to refresh, rather than the entire client area.
OnXXXX()	The Control class defines numerous methods that can be overridden by a subclass to respond to various events (e.g., OnMouseMove(), OnKeyDown(), OnResize(), and so forth). As you will see later in this chapter, when you want to intercept a GUI-based event, you have two approaches. One approach is to simply override one of the existing event handlers. The other approach is to add a custom event handler to a given delegate.
Refresh()	This method forces the Control to "invalidate" and immediately "repaint" (this process is fully described in Chapter 10). As you will see in the next chapter, GDI+ defines an *entirely* new rendering paradigm.
SetBounds(), SetLocation(), SetClientArea()	Each of these methods is used to establish the dimensions of the Control-derived object.

Setting a Form's Styles

Let's examine two interesting methods of the Control type: GetStyle() and SetStyle(). C++ Win32 programmers are no doubt familiar with the WNDCLASSEX structure and the dozens of oddball styles that can be used to fill the various fields. VB programmers indirectly interact with these same fields of the underlying WNDCLASSEX structure by interacting with various Form-level properties exposed through the IDE's Properties window. Much like earlier versions of VB, Windows Forms hides this sort of Windows "goo" from view—however, you are able to modify the default styles of your Form if necessary. First, check out the related ControlStyles enumeration, formally defined in C# as follows:

```
public  enum ControlStyles
{
     AllPaintingInWmPaint,
     CacheText,
     ContainerControl,
     EnableNotifyMessage,
     FixedHeight,
     FixedWidth,
     Opaque,
     ResizeRedraw,
     Selectable,
     StandardClick,
     StandardDoubleClick,
     SupportsTransparentBackColor,
     UserMouse,
     UserPaint
}
```

The values of the ControlStyle enumeration may OR-ed together if you want to specify multiple styles, and as you may expect, a Form has a default style set (I'll assume you will reference online Help for full details of each value). Once you establish the set of styles for a given widget (including the Form itself), you pass the set into the inherited SetStyle() method.

ResizeRedraw is one value you typically want to explicitly add to a given Form (which is the .NET equivalent to the VB 6.0 AutoRedraw property). By default, this style is not active and, thus, a Form does not automatically redraw itself when resized. This means if you intercept a Paint event (which you do a bit later) and resize the Form, the drawing logic is not refreshed correctly. Understand, however, that any GUI widgets that reside on the Form are always updated automatically. However, if you want to ensure that your custom drawing logic refreshes whenever the user resizes the Form, be sure to specify the ResizeRedraw style using SetStyle().

To illustrate the usefulness (and necessity) of the RedrawResize value, assume you have a Form containing two Button types (as mentioned, GUI widgets are always redrawn correctly). In the Click event handler of the first Button, set the value of the ResizeRedraw style to True:

```
Private Sub btnRedrawMe_Click(ByVal sender As System.Object, _
    ByVal e As System.EventArgs) Handles btnRedrawMe.Click
        SetStyle(ControlStyles.ResizeRedraw, True)
End Sub
```

In the other Button's Click handler, set ResizeRedraw to False:

```
Private Sub btnDontRedrawMe_Click(ByVal sender As System.Object, _
    ByVal e As System.EventArgs) Handles brnDontRedrawMe.Click
        SetStyle(ControlStyles.ResizeRedraw, False)
End Sub
```

Although you tackle the topics of GDI+, paint sessions, and GUI widgets in the chapters to come, to illustrate the effect of setting the ResizeRedraw style, assume the Form's Paint event handler attempts to draw a dashed black line around the client area:

```
Private Sub MainForm_Paint(ByVal sender As Object, _
    ByVal e As System.Windows.Forms.PaintEventArgs) Handles MyBase.Paint
        ' A custom dash pattern for the Pen. . .
        Dim customDashPen As Pen = New Pen(Color.Black, 10)
        Dim myDashes() As Single = {5F, 2F, 1F, 3F}
        customDashPen.DashPattern = myDashes
        e.Graphics.DrawRectangle(customDashPen, ClientRectangle)
    End Sub
```

If you run the application and set the ResizeRedraw bit to False, you find the ugliness shown in Figure 9-11 as you resize the Form (again, note that the contained GUI widgets are redrawn correctly).

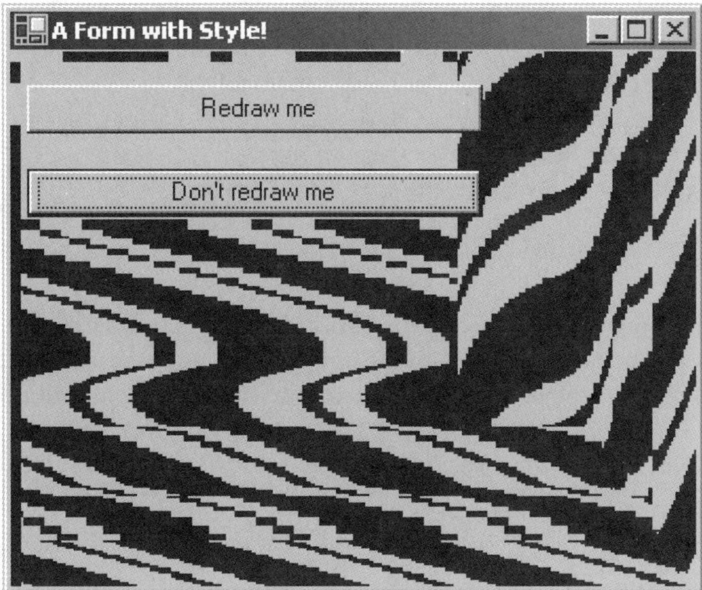

Figure 9-11. ResizeRedraw is a bit off.

If you set ResizeRedraw to True, you have correct rendering of the Forms border (see Figure 9-12).

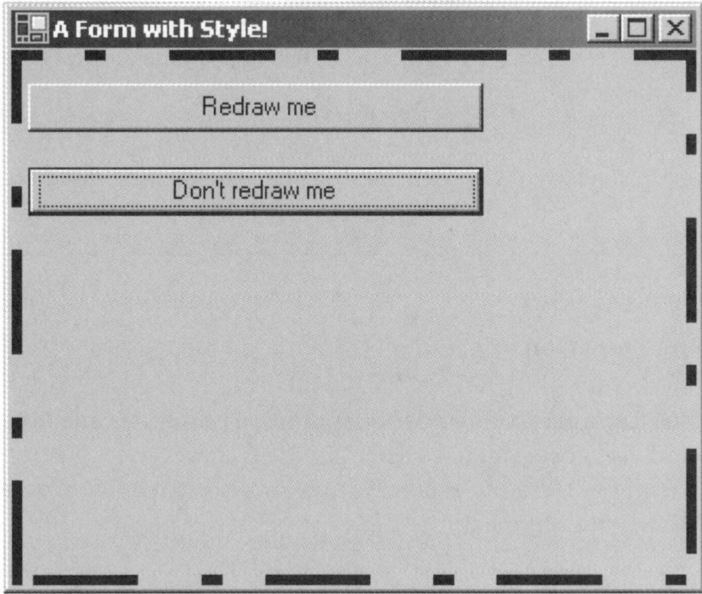

Figure 9-12. ResizeRedraw is correct.

Another (equally valid) alternative to repaint a Form correctly is to intercept the Form's Resize event and call the Invalidate() method directly (and thus bypass the need to set the ResizeRedraw bit manually):

```
Private Sub MainForm_Resize(ByVal sender As Object, _
    ByVal e As System.EventArgs) Handles MyBase.Resize
        Invalidate()    ' This forces a repaint (more details later. . .)
End Sub
```

Typically, you want to intercept the Resize() event when you have *additional* work to do beyond refreshing a paint session. If you do not have extra resize logic to attend to, simply set the ResizeRedraw bit to True when your application starts up.

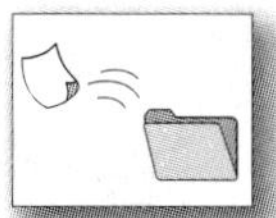

SOURCE CODE *The FormStyles project is under the Chapter 9 subdirectory.*

Control Events

The Control class also defines a number of events that can logically be grouped into two major categories: mouse events and keyboard events (see Table 9-6).

Table 9-6. Core Events of the Control Type

CONTROL EVENT	MEANING IN LIFE
Click, DoubleClick, MouseEnter, MouseLeave, MouseDown, MouseUp, MouseMove, MouseHover, MouseWheel	The Control class defines numerous events triggered in response to mouse input.
KeyPress, KeyUp, KeyDown	The Control class also defines numerous events triggered in response to keyboard input.

Fun with the Control Class

To be sure, the Control class does define additional properties, methods, and events beyond the subset you have just examined. However, to illustrate some of these core members, let's build a new Form type (also called MainForm) that provides the following functionality:

- Sets the initial size of the Form to some arbitrary dimensions
- Interacts with the Dispose() method

- Responds to the MouseMove and MouseUp events (using two approaches)
- Captures and processes keyboard input

To begin, assume you have a new VB .NET class derived from Form. First, update the default constructor to set the top, left, bottom, and right coordinates of the Form using various properties of the Control class. To confirm these changes, make use of the Bounds property and display the string version of the current dimensions. Be aware that Bounds returns a Rectangle type that is defined in the System.Drawing namespace. Therefore, be sure to set an assembly reference (to System.Drawing.dll) if you are building this Form by hand (Visual Studio .NET Windows Forms projects do so automatically):

```
' Need this for Rectangle definition.
Imports System.Drawing
...
Public Class MainForm
Inherits Form
    Public Sub New()
        MyBase.New()
        'This call is required by the Windows Form Designer.
        InitializeComponent()
        'Add any initialization after the InitializeComponent() call
        Top = 100
        Left = 75
        Height = 100
        Width = 500
        MessageBox.Show(Bounds.ToString(), "Current rect")
    End Sub
...
End Class
```

When you run this application, you are able to confirm the coordinates of your Form, as shown in Figure 9-13.

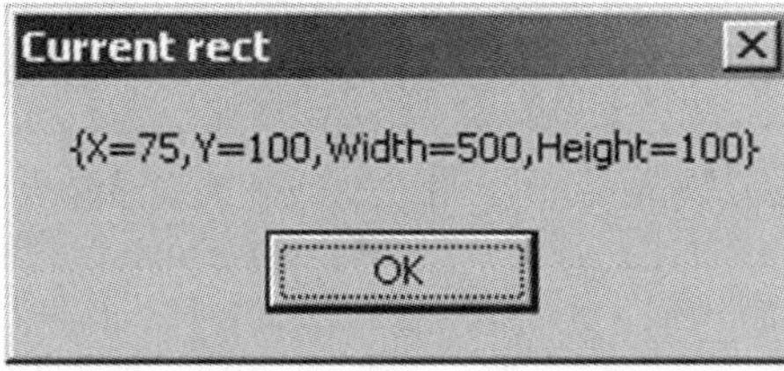

Figure 9-13. The Bounds property

Once you dismiss the message box, you are presented with the rather elongated main window shown in Figure 9-14.

Figure 9-14. The Top, Left, Height, and Width properties in action

Now, retrofit your class to override the inherited Component.Dispose() method. By default, Windows Forms applications created using the VS .NET IDE automatically provide a default implementation of this method on your behalf. Note that you should call your base class' Dispose() method before exiting:

```
' Visual Studio .NET Windows Forms projects automatically support this method.
Protected Overloads Overrides Sub Dispose(ByVal disposing As Boolean)
        If disposing Then
            If Not (components Is Nothing) Then
                components.Dispose()
            End If
        End If
        MyBase.Dispose(disposing)
        MessageBox.Show("Disposing this Form")
End Sub
```

Responding to Mouse Events: Take One

Next, you need to intercept the MouseUp event. The goal is to display the *(x, y)* position at which the MouseUp event occurred. When you want to respond to events from within a Windows Forms application, you have two general approaches. The first approach should be familiar to you at this point in the game: Make use of the VB .NET event mechanism, which as you recall from Chapter 6 is based on the System.MulticastDelegate type. The second approach is to override the appropriate base class method defined by Control. Let's examine each technique, beginning with standard VB .NET event handling.

Much like VB 6.0, VB .NET support two drop-down list boxes mounted at the top of the code window. When you declare an object using the WithEvents keyword, you are able to find the name of this variable listed in the left-hand list.

Once you select the widget you want to work with, the right-hand drop-down list allows you to choose the event(s) you want to handle for that item.

When you want to respond to events on the Form itself, you take the same general approach. However, the Form is not listed by name in the object drop-down list. Rather, you want to select (Base Class Events). Figure 9-15 illustrates the process of handling the MouseUp event for the main Form.

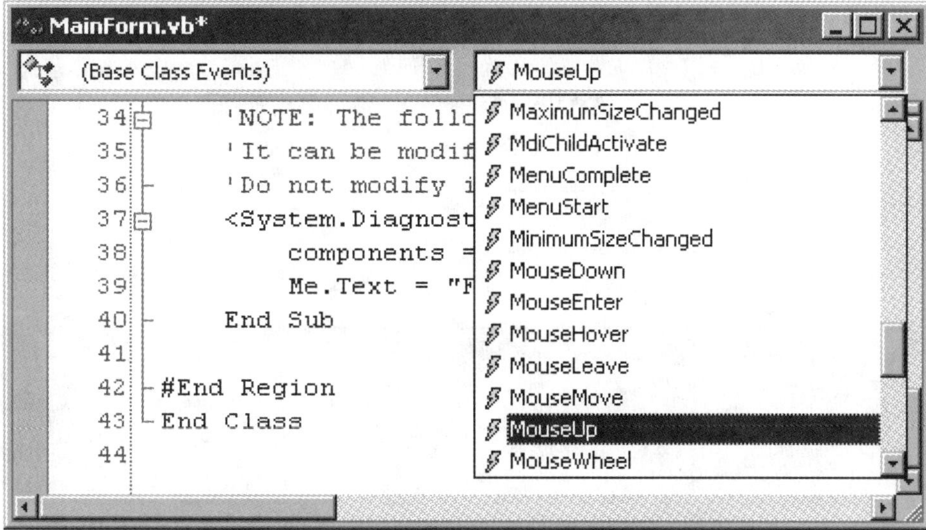

Figure 9-15. Responding to GUI-based events

As you would hope, this tool generates event handler stub code. Here is the code update that places the *(x, y)* of the mouse click in the Form's caption:

```
Private Sub Form1_MouseUp(ByVal sender As Object, _
    ByVal e As System.Windows.Forms.MouseEventArgs) _
    Handles MyBase.MouseUp
        Me.Text = "Clicked at: (" & e.X & ", " & e.Y & ")"
End Sub
```

Now, recall that GUI-based delegates take an EventArgs type (or a derivative thereof) as the second parameter. When you process mouse events, the second parameter is of type MouseEventArgs. This type (defined in the System.Windows.Forms namespace) defines a number of interesting properties that may be used to gather various statistics regarding the state of the mouse, as Table 9-7 shows.

Table 9-7. Properties of the MouseEventArgs Type

MOUSEEVENTARGS PROPERTY	MEANING IN LIFE
Button	Gets which mouse button was pressed, as defined by the MouseButtons enumeration
Clicks	Gets the number of times the mouse button was pressed and released
Delta	Gets a signed count of the number of detents the mouse wheel has rotated
X	Gets the *x*-coordinate of a mouse click
Y	Gets the *y*-coordinate of a mouse click

Figure 9-16 shows a possible test run.

Figure 9-16. Capturing MouseUp events

To make things even more interesting, you can also capture a MouseMove event and display the same (*x, y*) position data in the caption of the Form. In this way, the current location of the cursor is tracked whenever the mouse cursor is moved within the client area. Again, using the (Base Class Events) option, generate a handler and plug in the following:

```
Private Sub Form1_MouseMove(ByVal sender As Object, _
ByVal e As System.Windows.Forms.MouseEventArgs) _
Handles MyBase.MouseMove
        Me.Text = "Clicked at: (" & e.X & ", " & e.Y & ")"
End Sub
```

Determining Which Mouse Button Was Clicked

One thing to be aware of is that the MouseUp (or MouseDown) event is sent whenever *any* mouse button is clicked. If you want to determine exactly which button was clicked (left, right, or middle), you need to examine the Button property of the MouseEventArgs class. The value of Button is constrained by the MouseButtons enumeration. For example:

```
Private Sub Form1_MouseUp(ByVal sender As Object, ByVal e As MouseEventArgs) _
Handles MyBase.MouseUp
    ' Which mouse button was clicked?
    If (e.Button = MouseButtons.Left) Then
        MessageBox.Show("Left click!")
    ElseIf (e.Button = MouseButtons.Right) Then
        MessageBox.Show("Right click!")
    Else ' MouseButtons.Middle
        MessageBox.Show("Middle click!")
    End If
End Sub
```

Thus, if you click the left button you see the box in Figure 9-17.

Figure 9-17. Which mouse button was clicked?

Responding to Mouse Events: Take Two

The other approach to capture events in a Control-derived type is to override the correct base class method, which in your case is OnMouseUp() and OnMouseMove(). The Control type defines a number of overridable methods that are called automatically when the corresponding event is triggered. To override a base class method using the VS .NET IDE, select the (Overrides) option from the left down-drop list. Once you do, the right-hand list displays all of the Overridable members you may handle in your derived class (see Figure 9-18).

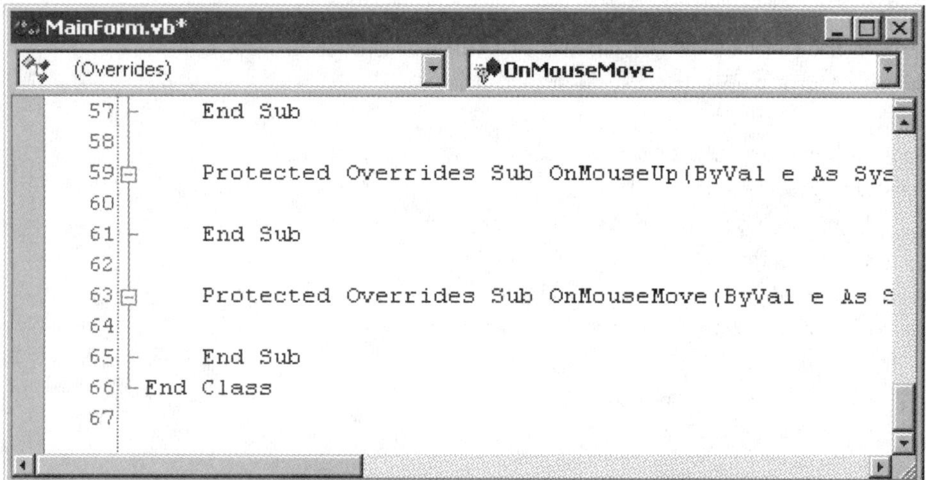

Figure 9-18. Overriding the base class method

If you update your Form using this technique, you have no need to manually specify a custom event handler, and you may instead write the following:

```
Protected Overrides Sub OnMouseUp(ByVal e As System.Windows.Forms.MouseEventArgs)
    ' Which mouse button was clicked?
    If (e.Button = MouseButtons.Left) Then
        MessageBox.Show("Left click!")
    ElseIf (e.Button = MouseButtons.Right) Then
        MessageBox.Show("Right click!")
    Else ' MouseButtons.Middle
        MessageBox.Show("Middle click!")
    End If
    MyBase.OnMouseUp(e)
End Sub
Protected Overrides Sub OnMouseMove(ByVal e As
System.Windows.Forms.MouseEventArgs)
    Me.Text = "Clicked at: (" & e.X & ", " & e.Y & ")"
    MyBase.OnMouseMove(e)
End Sub
```

Notice how the signatures of each method take a single parameter of type MouseEventArg, rather than two parameters that conform to the MouseEventHandler delegate. If you run the program again, you see no change whatsoever (which is good).

So you may be wondering which technique you should use when you want to handle a Form-level event. Typically you only need to override an "OnXXXX()"

method if you have *additional* work to perform before the event is fired. The preferred approach (and the one used by default with Visual Studio .NET) is to handle the event directly using the Handles keyword as you did in the first mouse example.

Responding to Keyboard Events

Processing keyboard input is almost identical to responding to mouse activity. The following code captures the KeyUp event and displays the textual name of the character that was pressed. Here, you capture this event using the delegation technique (there is a method named OnKeyUp() that can be overridden as an alternative):

```
Private Sub Form1_KeyUp(ByVal sender As Object, _
    ByVal e As System.Windows.Forms.KeyEventArgs) _
    Handles MyBase.KeyUp
    MessageBox.Show(e.KeyCode.ToString(), "Key Pressed!")
End Sub
```

As you can see, the KeyEventArgs type maintains an enumeration named KeyCode that holds the ID of the keypress. In addition, the KeyEventArgs type defines the useful properties listed in Table 9-8.

Table 9-8. Properties of the KeyEventArgs Type

KEYEVENTARGS PROPERTY	MEANING IN LIFE
Alt	Gets a value indicating if the Alt key was pressed
Control	Gets a value indicating if the Ctrl key was pressed
Handled	Gets or sets a value indicating if the event was handled
KeyCode	Gets the keyboard code for a System.Windows.Forms.Control.KeyDown or System.Windows.Forms.Control.KeyUp event
KeyData	Gets the key data for a System.Windows.Forms.Control.KeyDown or System.Windows.Forms.Control.KeyUp event
Modifiers	Indicates which modifier keys (Ctrl, Shift, and/or Alt) were pressed
Shift	Gets a value indicating if the Shift key was pressed

Figure 9-19 shows a possible keypress.

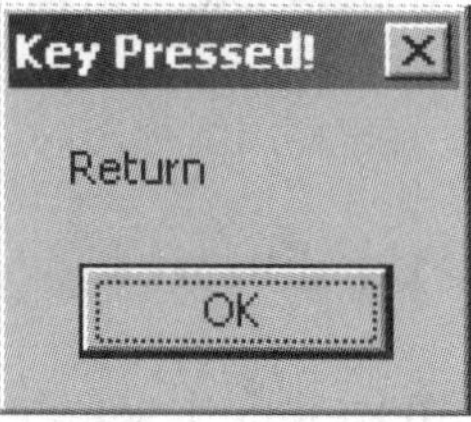

Figure 9-19. Which key was pressed?

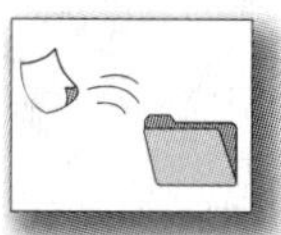

SOURCE CODE *The ControlBehaviors project is included under the Chapter 9 subdirectory.*

The Control Class Revisited

The Control class defines further behaviors to configure background and foreground colors, background images, font characteristics, drag-and-drop functionality, and support for context (i.e., pop-up) menus. This class also provides docking and anchoring behaviors for the derived types (which you examine in Chapter 10). Perhaps the most important duty of the Control class is to establish a mechanism to render images, text, and various geometric patterns onto the client area via the OnPaint() method. To begin, consider the additional properties of the Control class in Table 9-9.

Table 9-9. Additional Control Properties

CONTROL PROPERTY	MEANING IN LIFE
AllowDrop	If AllowDrop is set to True, this control allows drag-and-drop operations and events to be used.
Anchor	The anchor property determines which edges of the control are anchored to the container's edges.
BackColor, BackgroundImage, Font, ForeColor, Cursor	These properties configure how the client area should be displayed.
ContextMenu	This property specifies which context menu (e.g., pop-up menu) is shown when the user right-clicks the control.

Table 9-9. Additional Control Properties (continued)

CONTROL PROPERTY	MEANING IN LIFE
Dock	The dock property controls to which edge of the container this control is docked. For example, when docked to the top of the container, the control is displayed flush at the top of the container, extending the length of the container.
Opacity	This property determines the opacity of the control in percentages (0.0 is completely transparent, and 1.0 is completely opaque).
Region	This property configures a Region object that specifies the outline/silhouette/boundary of the control.
RightToLeft	This property is used for international applications where the language is written from right to left.

The Control class also defines a number of additional methods and events used to configure how the Control should respond to drag-and-drop operations and to painting operations, as shown in Table 9-10.

Table 9-10. Additional Control Methods

CONTROL METHOD/EVENT	MEANING IN LIFE
DoDragDrop() OnDragDrop() OnDragEnter() OnDragLeave() OnDragOver()	These methods are used to monitor drag-and-drop operations for a given Control descendent.
ResetFont() ResetCursor() ResetForeColor() ResetBackColor()	These methods reset various UI attributes of a child control to the corresponding value of the parent.
OnPaint()	Inheriting classes may override this method to handle the Paint event.
DragEnter DragLeave DragDrop DragOver	These events are sent in response to drag-and-drop operations.
Paint	This event is fired whenever the Control has become "dirty" and needs to be repainted.

More Fun with the Control Class

To illustrate some of the additional Control members, the following class sets the background color of the Form object to "Tomato" (you just have to love the names of these colors), sets the opacity to 50 percent, and configures the mouse cursor to display an hourglass icon. More important, it handles the Paint event in order to render a text string into the Form's client area. Here is the update:

```
Imports System.Drawing        ' Needed for Color, Brush, and Font types.

Public Class Form1
    Inherits System.Windows.Forms.Form
#Region " Windows Form Designer generated code "
    Public Sub New()
        MyBase.New()
        'This call is required by the Windows Form Designer.
        InitializeComponent()
        'Add any initialization after the InitializeComponent() call
        Me.Opacity = 0.5D
        Me.Cursor = Cursors.WaitCursor
        Me.BackColor = Color.Tomato
    End Sub
...
Private Sub Form1_Paint(ByVal sender As Object, _
ByVal e As System.Windows.Forms.PaintEventArgs) Handles MyBase.Paint
        Dim g As Graphics = e.Graphics
        g.DrawString("What a head trip. . .", _
             New Font("Times New Roman", 20), _
             New SolidBrush(Color.Black), 40, 10)
    End Sub
End Class
```

If you run this application, you see that the Form is indeed transparent, as shown in Figure 9-20. In fact, my screen shot illustrates this point quite clearly (note the code in the background).

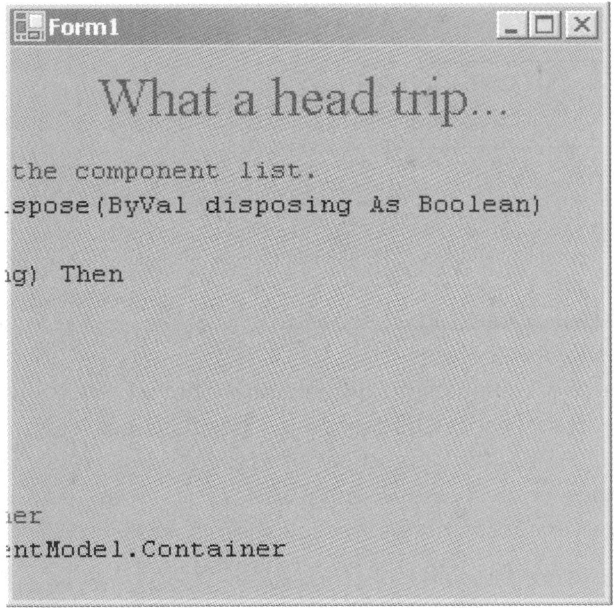

Figure 9-20. Painting with the Opacity property

Painting Basics

The most important aspect of this application is the handling of the Paint event. Notice that the delegate defines a method that takes a parameter of type PaintEventArgs. This type defines two properties to help you configure the current paint session for the Control, as shown in Table 9-11.

Table 9-11. Additional Control Properties

PAINTEVENTARGS PROPERTY	MEANING IN LIFE
ClipRectangle	Gets the rectangle in which to paint
Graphics	Gets the Graphics object used during a paint session

The critical property of PaintEventArgs is Graphics, which is called to retrieve a Graphics object to use during the painting session. You examine this class (and GDI+ in general) in greater detail in Chapter 10. For now, understand that the Graphics class defines a number of members that allow you to render text, geometric shapes, and images onto a Control-derived type.

Finally, in this example you also configure the Cursor property to display an hourglass symbol whenever the mouse cursor is within the bounding rectangle of this Control. The Cursors type can be assigned to any member of the Cursors enumeration (e.g., Arrow, Cross, UpArrow, or Help):

```
Public Sub New()
    ...
    Me.Cursor = Cursors.WaitCursor
End Sub
```

SOURCE CODE *The MoreControlBehaviors project is included under the Chapter 9 subdirectory.*

The ScrollableControl Class

ScrollableControl is used to define a small number of members that allow your widget to support vertical and horizontal scroll bars. The most intriguing members of the ScrollableControl type are the AutoScroll property and the related AutoScrollMinSize property. For example, assume you want to ensure that if an end user resizes your Form, horizontal and vertical scroll bars are automatically inserted if the size of the client area is less than or equal to 300 x 300 pixels. Programmatically, your task is simple:

```
' This could be set in the class constructor or InitializeComponent().
' Note that you need to reference the System.Drawing assembly
' to gain access to the Size type.
Me.AutoScroll = True
Me.AutoScrollMinSize = New System.Drawing.Size (300, 300)
```

The ScrollableControl class takes care of the rest. For example, if you have a Form that contains a number of child objects (e.g., buttons or labels), you find that the scrolling logic ensures the entire Form real estate is viewable as the user resizes. To illustrate, simply render a large block of text (contained within a Label type) onto the form's client area (see Figure 9-21).

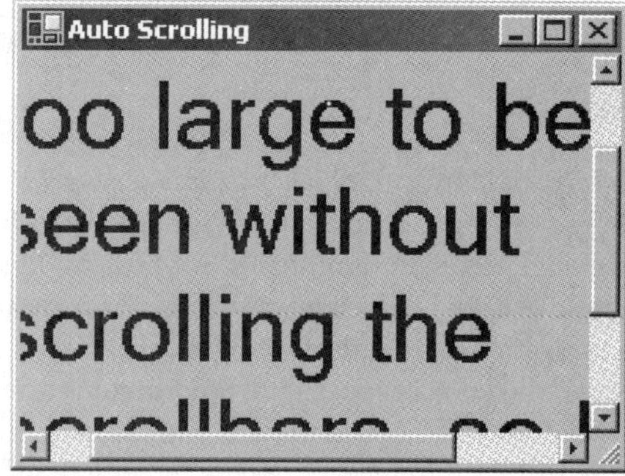

Figure 9-21. Autoscrolling

The ScrollableControl class defines a number of additional members beyond AutoScroll and AutoScrollMinSize, but not many. Also be aware that when you want to take greater control over the scrolling process, you are able to create and manipulate individual ScrollBar types (such as HScrollBar and VScrollBar). I'll leave it to you to find out about the remaining members using online Help.

SOURCE CODE *The ScrollForm project is included under the Chapter 9 subdirectory.*

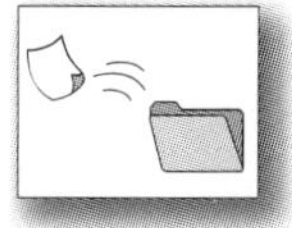

ContainerControl Class

ContainerControl defines support to manage the focus of a given GUI item. In practice, the behavior defined by System.Windows.Forms.ContainerControl is useful when you are building a Form that contains a number of child controls and you want to allow the user to use the Tab key to alternate focus. Using a small set of members, you can programmatically obtain the currently selected control, force another to receive focus, and so forth. Table 9-12 gives a rundown of some of the more interesting members.

Table 9-12. Members of the ContainerControl Type

CONTAINERCONTROL MEMBER	MEANING IN LIFE
ActiveControl ParentForm	These properties allow you to obtain and set the active control, as well as retrieve a reference to the Form that is hosting the item.
ProcessTabKey()	This method allows you to programmatically activate the Tab key to set focus to the next available control.

On a related note, recall that all descendents of System.Windows.Forms.Control inherit the TabStop and TabIndex properties. As you may be able to guess, these items are used to set the tab order of controls maintained by a parent container and are used in conjunction with the members supplied by the ContainerControl class. You revisit the issue of tab order during the discussion of programming controls in Chapter 11.

The Form Class

This brings us to the Form class itself, which is typically the direct base class for your custom Form types. In addition to the large set of members inherited from the Control, ScrollableControl, and ContainerControl classes, the Form type adds even greater functionality. Table 9-13 provides the core properties.

Table 9-13. Properties of the Form Type

FORM PROPERTY	MEANING IN LIFE
AcceptButton	Gets or sets the button on the form that is clicked when the user presses the Enter key.
ActiveMDIChild IsMDIChild IsMDIContainer	Each of these properties is used within the context of an MDI application.
AutoScale	Gets or sets a value indicating if the form adjusts its size to fit the height of the font used on the form and scale its controls.
BorderStyle	Gets or sets the border style of the form. Used in conjunction with the FormBorderStyle enumeration.
CancelButton	Gets or sets the button control to be clicked when the user presses the Esc key.
ControlBox	Gets or sets a value indicating if the form has a control box.
Menu MergedMenu	Gets or sets the (merged) menu for the Form.
MaximizeBox MinimizeBox	Used to determine if this Form enables the maximize and minimize boxes.
ShowInTaskbar	Answers the question "Should this Form be seen on the Windows taskbar?"
StartPosition	Gets or sets the starting position of the form at runtime, as specified by the FormStartPosition enumeration.
WindowState	Configures how the Form is to be displayed on startup. Used in conjunction with the FormWindowState enumeration.

The truth of the matter is that the Form class does not define a great deal of additional methods. The bulk of a Form's functionality comes from the base classes you have already examined. However, Table 9-14 gives a partial list of some additional methods to be aware of.

Table 9-14. Methods of the Form Type

FORM METHOD	MEANING IN LIFE
Activate()	Activates a given Form and gives it focus
Close()	Closes a Form
CenterToScreen()	Places the Form dead center on the screen
LayoutMDI()	Arranges each child Form (as specified by the LayoutMDI enumeration) within the parent Form
OnResize()	May be overridden to respond to Resize events
ShowDialog()	Displays a Form as a Modal dialog box (more on dialog box programming in Chapter 11)

Finally, the Form class defines a number of Events that you should be aware of. Table 9-15 gives a sampling.

Table 9-15. Select Events of the Form Type

FORM EVENT	MEANING IN LIFE
Activate	Sent when a Form is brought to the front of the active application.
Closed, Closing	These events are used to determine when the Form is about to close or has closed.
MDIChildActive	Sent when a child window is activated.

Building Menus with Windows Forms

Now that you understand the composition of the Form class, the next task is to learn how to establish a menu system to provide some degree of user interaction. The System.Windows.Forms namespace provides a number of types that facilitate the building of main menus (i.e., menus mounted at the top of a Form), as well as context-sensitive pop-up menus (i.e., "right-click" menus). To begin, let's examine what it takes to build a simple topmost menu (by hand) that allows the end user to exit the application using a standard "File | Exit" menu command (see Figure 9-22).

Figure 9-22. A simple menu system

The first class to be aware of is System.Windows.Forms.Menu, which functions as the base class for all other menu-related classes (MainMenu, MenuItem, and ContextMenu). Be aware that System.Windows.Forms.Menu is an abstract class, and therefore you cannot create a direct instance of this type. Rather, you create instances of one (or more) of the derived types. The Menu class defines basic menu-centric behaviors, such as providing access to an individual menu item, cloning menus, merging menus (for MDI applications), and so forth. Figure 9-23 shows the relationships among these core types.

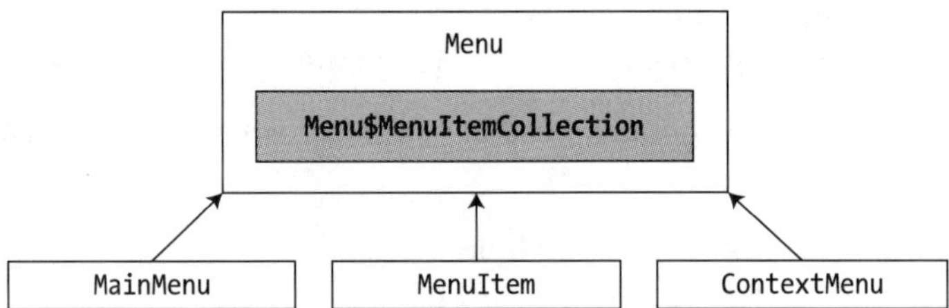

Figure 9-23. The Windows.Form's menu hierarchy

Note that the Menu class defines a nested class (denoted by the "$" syntax) named MenuItemCollection, which is inherited by the MainMenu, MenuItem, and ContextMenu subclasses. As you expect, this collection holds onto a set of related menu items, which is accessed using the Menu.MenuItems property (more details in a moment). The Menu base class defines the core members shown in Table 9-16.

Table 9-16. Members of the Menu Type

MENU MEMBER	MEANING IN LIFE
Handle	This property provides access to the underlying handle that represents this menu.
IsParent	This property specifies whether this menu contains any items or is the topmost item.
MdiListItem	This property returns the MenuItem that contains the list of MDI child windows.
MenuItems	Another property. Returns an instance of the nested Menu.MenuItemCollection type, which represents the submenus owned by the Menu derived class.
GetMainMenu()	Returns the MainMenu item that contains this menu.
MergeMenu()	Merges another menu's items with this one's as specified by their mergeType and mergeOrder properties. Used to merge an MDI container's menu with that of its active MDI child.
CloneMenu()	Sets this menu to be an identical copy of another menu.

Menu$MenuItemCollection Type

Perhaps the most immediately important member of the Menu class is the MenuItems property, which returns a nested Menu$MenuItemCollection type (again, recall that the "$" notation represents a nested type). Nested classes can be helpful when you want to establish a logical relationship between related types. Here, the Menu$MenuItemCollection type represents the set of all submenus owned by a Menu-derived object.

For example, if you create a MainMenu to represent the topmost "File" menu, you add MenuItems (for example, Open, Save, Close, and Save As) into the collection. As you expect, Menu$MenuItemCollection defines members to add and remove MenuItem types, obtain the current count of MenuItems, and access a particular member in the collection. Table 9-17 lists some (but not all) of the core members.

Table 9-17. The Nested MenuItemCollection Type

MENU$MENUITEMCOLLECTION MEMBER	MEANING IN LIFE
Count	Returns the number of MenuItems in the collection.
Add() AddRange() Remove()	Inserts (or removes) a new MenuItem into the collection. Be aware that the Add() method has been overloaded numerous times to allow you to specify shortcut keys, delegates, and so forth. AddRange() is helpful in that it allows you to add an array of MenuItems in a single call.
Clear()	Removes all items from the collection.
Contains()	Used to determine if a given MenuItem is inside the collection.

Building Your Menu System

Now that you understand the functionality of the abstract Menu class (and the nested MenuItemCollection type), you can build your simple File menu. The process begins when you create a MainMenu object. The MainMenu class represents the collection of topmost menu items (e.g., File, Edit, View, Tools, and Help).

```
Public Class Form1
    Inherits System.Windows.Forms.Form
    ' The Form's main menu.
    Private mnuMain As MainMenu = New MainMenu()
...
End Class
```

Once you create a MainMenu object, you make use of Menu$MenuItemCollection.Add() to insert the topmost item (the "File" menu). Menu$MenuItemCollection.Add() returns a new MenuItem class that represents the newly inserted File menu.

To insert the subitems (e.g., Exit), you insert additional MenuItems into the Menu$MenuItemCollection maintained by the File MenuItem. Finally, when you are finished constructing your menu system, attach it to the owning Form using (of course) the Menu property. Here is the complete code:

```
Public Class Form1
    Inherits System.Windows.Forms.Form
    ' The Form's main menu.
    Private mnuMain As MainMenu = New MainMenu()
#Region " Windows Form Designer generated code "
    Public Sub New()
        MyBase.New()
        'This call is required by the Windows Form Designer.
        InitializeComponent()
        ' Create the 'File' Menu and add it to the MenuItemCollection.
        Dim miFile As MenuItem = mnuMain.MenuItems.Add("&File")
        ' Now make the Exit submenu and add it to the File Menu.
        ' This version of Add() takes:
        ' 1) A new MenuItem.
        ' 2) A new delegate (EventHandler).
        ' 3) An optional shortcut key.
        miFile.MenuItems.Add(New MenuItem("E&xit", _
                              New EventHandler(AddressOf FileExit_Clicked), _
                              Shortcut.CtrlX))
        ' Attach main menu to the Form object.
        Me.Menu = mnuMain
    End Sub
...
End Class
```

Notice that if you embed an ampersand (&) within the string name of a menu item, this marks which letter should be underlined to designate the Alt key access combination. Thus, when you specify "&File," you allow the end user to activate the File menu by selecting Alt+F.

When you add the Exit submenu item, you specify an optional shortcut flag. The System.Windows.Forms.Shortcut enumeration is fully detailed in the online Help. As you might guess, this enumeration provides fields that specify traditional shortcut keys (Ctrl+C, Ctrl+V, F1, F2, and Insert) as well as more exotic combinations.

Also notice that the second parameter to the Add() method is the address of the method that is called when a given menu item is selected. As an alternative, you could have declared a new MenuItem (named miFile) WithEvents and passed this item in as a parameter (this is the approach taken by VS .NET). Here then, is the final code for the simple menu application. Just for kicks, notice how you are able to set the BackColor property of the hosting Form using the MainMenu.GetForm() method:

```
Private Sub FileExit_Clicked(ByVal sender As Object, ByVal e As EventArgs)
    mnuMain.GetForm().BackColor = Color.Black
    MessageBox.Show("Changed form's background color via menu object.")
    Me.Close() 'Just close the application. . .
End Sub
```

Adding Another Topmost Menu Item

Now, what if you want to add another topmost menu named "Help" that contains a single subitem named "About" (as in Figure 9-24)?

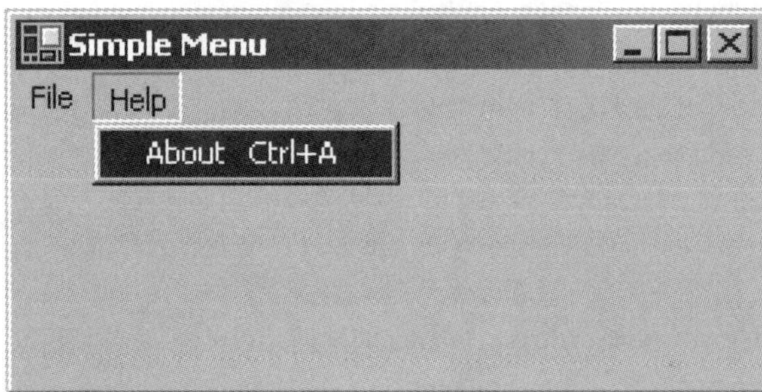

Figure 9-24. Extending the menu system

The code models the "File | Exit" menu logic almost exactly: Begin by adding a new MenuItem to the MainMenu object ("Help"). From here, add a new subitem ("About"). Here is the updated constructor:

```
Public Sub New()
    MyBase.New()
    'This call is required by the Windows Form Designer.
    InitializeComponent()
    ' Create the 'File | Exit' menu.
    Dim miFile As MenuItem = mnuMain.MenuItems.Add("&File")
    miFile.MenuItems.Add(New MenuItem("E&xit", _
            New EventHandler(AddressOf FileExit_Clicked), _
            Shortcut.CtrlX))
    ' Now create a 'Help | About' menu.
    Dim miHelp As MenuItem = mnuMain.MenuItems.Add("Help")
    miHelp.MenuItems.Add(New MenuItem("&About", _
            New EventHandler(AddressOf HelpAbout_Clicked), _
            Shortcut.CtrlA))
```

```
    ' Attach main menu to the Form object.
    Me.Menu = mnuMain
End Sub
```

Finally, here is the event handler logic:

```
Private Sub HelpAbout_Clicked(ByVal sender As Object, ByVal e As EventArgs)
    MessageBox.Show("The amazing menu app. . .")
End Sub
```

SOURCE CODE *The SimpleMenu application is located under the Chapter 9 subdirectory.*

Creating a Pop-Up Menu

Let's now examine the process of building a context-sensitive pop-up (i.e., "right-click") menu. The ContextMenu class represents the pop-up menu itself. Like the process of building a MainMenu, your goal is to add individual MenuItems to the MenuItemCollection to represent the possible selectable subitems. The following Form makes use of a pop-up menu to allow the user to configure the font size of a string rendered to the client area. To represent the range of font sizes, make use of a custom Enum. Here is the code:

```
' Helper enum for font size.
Enum TheFontSize
    Huge = 30
    Normal = 20
    Tiny = 8
End Enum
Public Class Form1
    Inherits System.Windows.Forms.Form
    ' Current size of font.
    Private currFontSize As Integer = TheFontSize.Normal
    ' The Form's pop-up menu.
    Private popUpMenu As ContextMenu
#Region " Windows Form Designer generated code "
    Public Sub New()
        MyBase.New()
        'This call is required by the Windows Form Designer.
        InitializeComponent()
        ' First make the context menu.
        popUpMenu = New ContextMenu()
```

```
        ' Now add the subitems & attach context menu.
        popUpMenu.MenuItems.Add("Huge", _
            New EventHandler(AddressOf PopUp_Clicked))
        popUpMenu.MenuItems.Add("Normal", _
            New EventHandler(AddressOf PopUp_Clicked))
        popUpMenu.MenuItems.Add("Tiny", _
            New EventHandler(AddressOf PopUp_Clicked))
        Me.ContextMenu = popUpMenu
    End Sub
. . .
    Private Sub PopUp_Clicked(ByVal sender As Object, ByVal e As EventArgs)
        ' Figure out the string name of the selected item.
        Dim miClicked As MenuItem = CType(sender, MenuItem)
        Dim item As String = miClicked.Text
        If (item = "Huge") Then
            currFontSize = TheFontSize.Huge
        End If
        If (item = "Normal") Then
            currFontSize = TheFontSize.Normal
        End If
        If (item = "Tiny") Then
            currFontSize = TheFontSize.Tiny
        End If
        Invalidate()
    End Sub
    Private Sub Form1_Paint(ByVal sender As Object, _
    ByVal e As System.Windows.Forms.PaintEventArgs) Handles MyBase.Paint
        Dim g As Graphics = e.Graphics
        g.DrawString("Please click on me. . .", _
            New Font("Times New Roman", currFontSize), _
            New SolidBrush(Color.Black), _
            10, 10)
    End Sub
End Class
```

Notice that as you add the subitems to the ContextMenu, you typically assign the *same* event handler to each. When a given item is clicked, the flow of logic brings you to the PopUp_Clicked() method. Using the "sender" argument, you are able to determine the name of the MenuItem (i.e., the text string it has been assigned) and take an appropriate course of action (which works just fine, assuming you are not interested in localizing the application).

Also notice that once you create a ContextMenu, you associate it to the Form using the Control.ContextMenu property. Be aware that *any* control can be assigned a context menu. For example, you can create a Button object on a dialog box that responds to a particular context menu. In this way, the menu is only displayed if the mouse button is clicked while within the bounding rectangle of the button itself.

Adorning Your Menu System

The MenuItem class also defines a number of members that allow you to check, enable, and hide a given menu item. Table 9-18 gives a rundown of some of the interesting properties of MenuItem.

Table 9-18. More Details of the MenuItem Type

MENUITEM MEMBER	MEANING IN LIFE
Checked	Gets or sets a value indicating if a check mark appears beside the text of the menu item
DefaultItem	Gets or sets a value indicating if the menu item is the default
Enabled	Gets or sets a value indicating if the menu item is enabled
Index	Gets or sets the menu item's position in its parent menu
MergeOrder	Gets or sets the relative position of the menu item when its menu is merged with another
MergeType	Gets or sets a value that indicates the behavior of this menu item when its menu is merged with another
OwnerDraw	Gets or sets a value indicating whether code that you provide draws the menu item or Windows draws the menu item
RadioCheck	Gets or sets a value that indicates whether the menu item, if checked, displays a radio-button mark instead of a check mark
Shortcut	Gets or sets the shortcut key associated with the menu item
ShowShortcut	Gets or sets a value that indicates if the shortcut key that is associated with the menu item is displayed next to the menu item caption
Text	Gets or sets the text of the menu item

To illustrate, extend the current pop-up menu to display a check mark next to the currently selected menu item. Setting a check mark on a given menu item is not at all difficult (just set the Checked property to True). However, tracking which menu item should be checked requires some additional logic. One possible approach is to define distinct MenuItem objects to track each submenu item and an additional MenuItem that represents the currently selected item:

```
Public Class Form1
    Inherits System.Windows.Forms.Form
    ' Current size of font.
    Private currFontSize As TheFontSize = TheFontSize.Normal
    ' The Form's pop-up menu.
    Private popUpMenu As ContextMenu
    ' Used to keep track of the current checked item.
    Private currentCheckedItem As MenuItem       ' Marks the item checked.
    Private checkedHuge As MenuItem
    Private checkedNormal As MenuItem
    Private checkedTiny As MenuItem
...
End Class
```

The next step is to associate each of these MenuItems to the correct submenu. Thus, you update the constructor as follows:

```
' Construct the form.
Public Sub New()
    MyBase.New()
    'This call is required by the Windows Form Designer.
    InitializeComponent()
    ' First make the context menu.
    popUpMenu = New ContextMenu()
    ' Now add the subitems & attach context menu.
    popUpMenu.MenuItems.Add("Huge", _
             New EventHandler(AddressOf PopUp_Clicked))
    popUpMenu.MenuItems.Add("Normal", _
             New EventHandler(AddressOf PopUp_Clicked))
    popUpMenu.MenuItems.Add("Tiny", _
             New EventHandler(AddressOf PopUp_Clicked))
    Me.ContextMenu = popUpMenu

    ' Set each MenuItem to the correct submenu.
    checkedHuge = Me.ContextMenu.MenuItems(0)
    checkedNormal = Me.ContextMenu.MenuItems(1)
    checkedTiny = Me.ContextMenu.MenuItems(2)
    ' Now check the Normal menu item.
    currentCheckedItem = checkedNormal
    currentCheckedItem.Checked = True
End Sub
```

At this point, you have a way to programmatically identify each subitem as well as the currently checked item (which has been initially set to checkedNormal). The last step is to update the PopUp_Clicked() event handler to check the correct MenuItem in response to the user selection (see Figure 9-25 for a test run):

```
Private Sub PopUp_Clicked(ByVal sender As Object, ByVal e As EventArgs)
    ' Uncheck the currently checked item.
    currentCheckedItem.Checked = False
    ' Figure out the string name of the selected item.
    Dim miClicked As MenuItem = CType(sender, MenuItem)
    Dim item As String = miClicked.Text
    If (item = "Huge") Then
        currFontSize = TheFontSize.Huge
        currentCheckedItem = checkedHuge
    End If
    If (item = "Normal") Then
        currFontSize = TheFontSize.Normal
        currentCheckedItem = checkedNormal
    End If
    If (item = "Tiny") Then
        currFontSize = TheFontSize.Tiny
        currentCheckedItem = checkedTiny
    End If
   ' Now check it.
    currentCheckedItem.Checked = True
    Invalidate()
End Sub
```

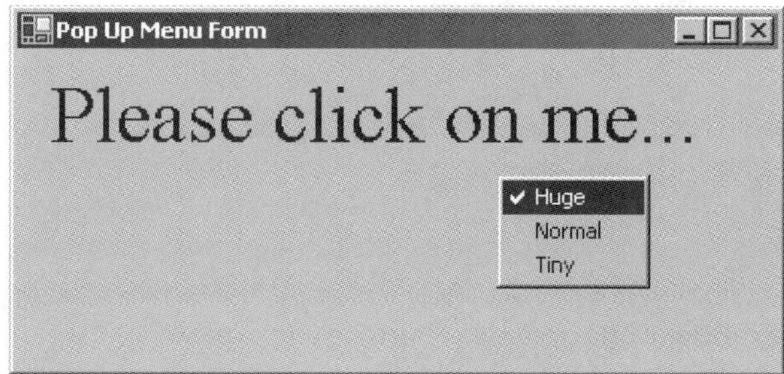

Figure 9-25. Checking menu items

SOURCE CODE *The PopUpMenu project is contained under the Chapter 9 subdirectory.*

Building a Menu Using Visual Studio .NET

Indeed, knowledge is power. However, as you have seen, writing raw menuing code can be a bit on the verbose side. Thus, now that you understand how to write raw VB .NET code to create and configure a menu system, let's examine how Visual Studio .NET can offer some welcome design-time assistance (which is a *huge* improvement over the rather lame menu editor in previous editions of VB). To begin, assume that you have created a new VB .NET Windows Application project workspace. Using the Toolbox window, double-click the MainMenu icon (see Figure 9-26).

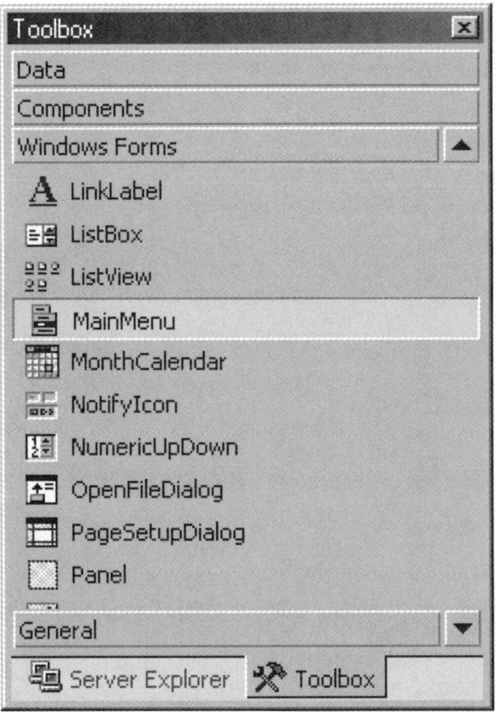

Figure 9-26. Adding menus at design time

Once you double-click the MainMenu icon, you see a new icon appear in the icon tray of the design-time template. Furthermore, you should see a design-time representation of your menu attached to the top of your Form. To add new MenuItem types to the project, simply select a slot and type away (see Figure 9-27).

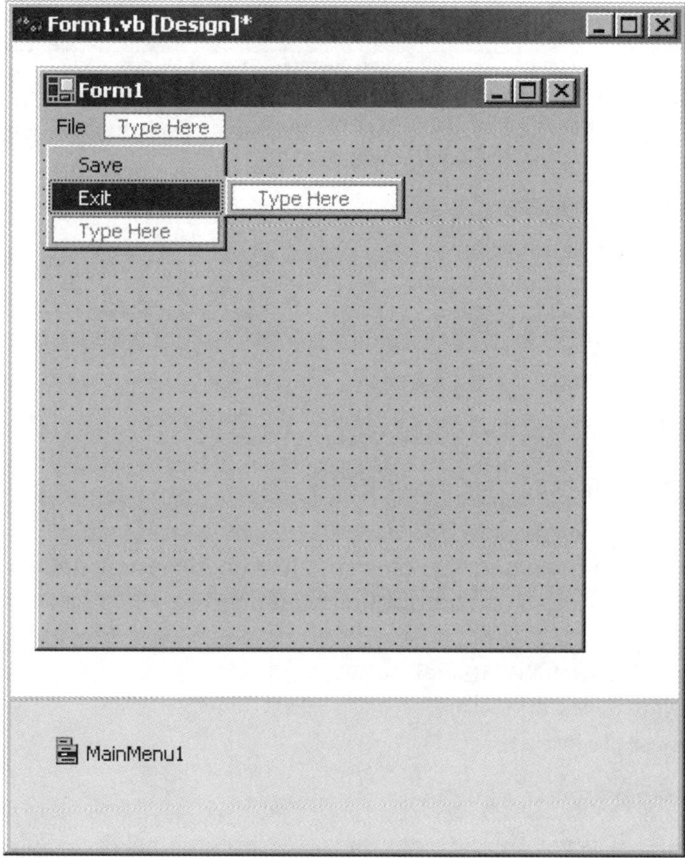

Figure 9-27. Building menus at design time

As far as handling events for a given item, understand that each of the new MenuItems will be declared WithEvents in the owning Form:

```
Friend WithEvents MainMenu1 As System.Windows.Forms.MainMenu
Friend WithEvents mnuFile As System.Windows.Forms.MenuItem
Friend WithEvents mnuFileSave As System.Windows.Forms.MenuItem
Friend WithEvents mnuFileExit As System.Windows.Forms.MenuItem
```

Therefore, to configure events for a given MenuItem, simply make use of the Visual Studio .NET code window shown in Figure 9-28.

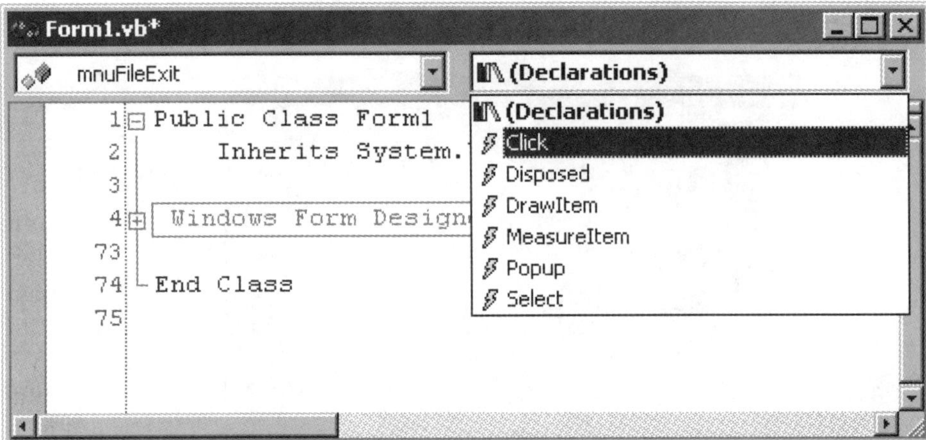

Figure 9-28. Responding to menu events at design time

Once you enter the name of your event handler, the Visual Studio .NET IDE automatically generates stub code for the event handler:

```
Private Sub mnuFileExit_Click(ByVal sender As Object, _
ByVal e As System.EventArgs) Handles mnuFileExit.Click
    ' Code for File | Exit
End Sub
```

Be aware that as you modify your menus at design time, the IDE is updating the InitializeComponent() helper function, as well as adding member variables to represent the types you are manipulating at design time. Even though you took an alternative approach to intercepting the menu item's events (by way of delegates), if you examine the generated code, things (I hope) look very familiar.

Understanding Status Bars

In addition to a menu system, many Forms also maintain a status bar. Status bars may be divided into any number of "panes." Panes hold some textual (or graphical) information such as menu help strings or other application-specific information. The StatusBar type derives directly from System.Windows.Forms.Control. In addition to the inherited members, StatusBar defines the core properties shown in Table 9-19.

Table 9-19. Select StatusBar Properties

STATUSBAR PROPERTY	MEANING IN LIFE
BackgroundImage	Gets or sets the image rendered on the background of the StatusBar control
Font	Gets or sets the font the StatusBar control uses to display information
ForeColor	Gets or sets the foreground color of the control
Panels	Returns a nested StatusBarPanelCollection type that contains each Panel maintained by the StatusBar (much like the menu pattern)
ShowPanels	Gets or sets a value indicating if panels should be shown
SizingGrip	Gets or sets a value indicating whether a sizing grip is rendered on the corner of the StatusBar control

Once you create a StatusBar type, your next task is to add any number of panels (represented by the StatusBarPanel class) into the nested StatusBar$StatusBarPanelCollection. Be aware that the constructor of StatusBarPanel automatically configures the new panel with a default look and feel (therefore, if you are happy with this initial configuration, your programming task is made even simpler). Table 9-20 lists the core members of the StatusBarPanel type (and their default values).

Table 9-20. Properties of the StatusBarPanel Type

STATUSBARPANEL PROPERTY	MEANING IN LIFE
Alignment	Determines the alignment of text in the pane. The default value is HorizontalAlignment.Left.
AutoSize	Determines if this pane should automatically resize (and how). The default value is StatusBarPanelAutoSize.None.
BorderStyle	Configures border style. The default value is StatusBarPanelBorderStyle.Sunken.
Icon	Answers the question "Is there an icon in the pane?" No icon is the default.
MinWidth	The default is 10.

Table 9-20. Properties of the StatusBarPanel Type (continued)

STATUSBARPANEL PROPERTY	MEANING IN LIFE
Style	Answers the question "What does this pane contain?" The default is StatusBarPanelStyle.Text, but there may be other types as specified by the StatusBarPanelStyle enumeration.
Text	Caption of pane. The default is an empty string.
ToolTipText	Answers the question "Are there any tool tips?" An empty string is the default.
Width	The default is 100.

Building a Status Bar (by Hand)

To illustrate, enhance your Simple Menu application by adding a StatusBar object that is divided into two panes. The first pane shows helpful prompts describing the functionality of each menu selection. The second pane displays the current system time. Place a small icon on the extreme left-hand side of the first pane (just to keep things interesting). Figure 9-29 displays the result.

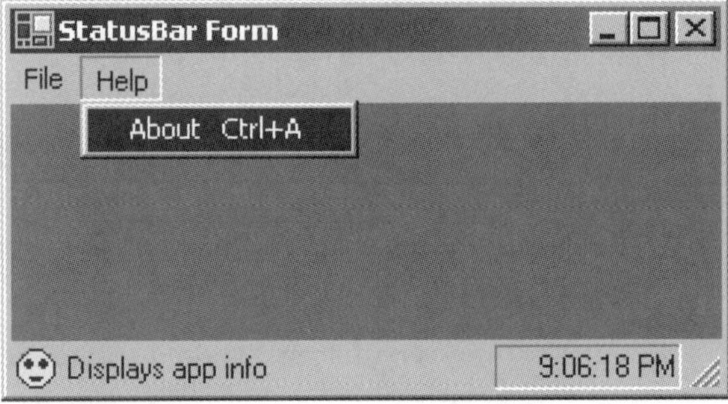

Figure 9-29. Your simple status bar

Like any Control-derived type, the StatusBar needs to be added to the Form's Controls collection (just like in VB 6.0). As you might guess, this collection contains an entry for any GUI widget mounted on the client area, including StatusBars types. Here is the status bar logic:

```
Public Class Form1
    Inherits System.Windows.Forms.Form
    ' Member data for the status bar, and each pane.
    Private statBar As StatusBar = New StatusBar()
    Private sbPnlPrompt As StatusBarPanel = New StatusBarPanel()
    Private sbPnlTime As StatusBarPanel = New StatusBarPanel()
    Public Sub New()
        MyBase.New()
        Me.BackColor = Color.DodgerBlue
        'This call is required by the Windows Form Designer.
        InitializeComponent()
        ' Do all the status bar stuff
        BuildStatBar()
        ' You will move your menu building logic into
        ' a helper function (seen in just a bit)
        BuildMenuSystem()
    ....
    End Sub

    Private Sub BuildStatBar()
        ' Configure the status bar.
        statBar.ShowPanels = True
        statBar.Size = New System.Drawing.Size(212, 20)
        statBar.Location = New System.Drawing.Point(0, 216)
        ' AddRange() allows you to add a set of panes at once.
        statBar.Panels.AddRange(New StatusBarPanel() _
            {sbPnlPrompt, sbPnlTime})
        ' Configure prompt panel.
        sbPnlPrompt.BorderStyle = StatusBarPanelBorderStyle.None
        sbPnlPrompt.AutoSize = StatusBarPanelAutoSize.Spring
        sbPnlPrompt.Width = 62
        sbPnlPrompt.Text = "Ready"
        ' Configure time pane.
        sbPnlTime.Alignment = HorizontalAlignment.Right
        sbPnlTime.Width = 76
        ' Add an icon (more details in Chapter 10).
        Try
            ' This icon must be in the same app directory.
            ' Chapter 10 will illustrate how to embed
            ' resources into your assembly!
            Dim i As Icon = New Icon("status.ico")
            sbPnlPrompt.Icon = i
        Catch e As Exception
```

```
            MessageBox.Show(e.Message)
        End Try
        ' Now add this new status bar to the Form's Controls collection.
        Me.Controls.Add(statBar)
    End Sub
End Class
```

The BuildStatBar() helper function has a similar look and feel to the process of building a menu system. You begin by configuring the basic characteristics of your StatusBar and promptly add each configured StatusBarPanel type. Most important, you add the completed StatusBar type to the Form's Controls collection.

Working with the Timer Type

Recall that the second pane of the status bar should display the current time. The first step to take to achieve this design goal is to add a Timer member variable to the Form. If you have a Visual Basic background, you should understand this object quite well. C++ programmers also understand the notion of timers given the WM_TIMER message. Regardless of your background, a Windows Forms Timer object is simply a type that calls some method (specified by the Tick event) at a given interval (specified by the Interval property). Table 9-21 lists some core members.

Table 9-21. The Timer Type

TIMER MEMBER	MEANING IN LIFE
Enabled	This property enables or disables the Timer's ability to fire the Tick event. You may also use Start() and Stop() to achieve the same effect.
Interval	Sets the number of milliseconds between ticks.
Start() Stop()	Like the Enabled property, these methods control the firing of the Tick event.
OnTick()	This member may be overridden in a custom class deriving from Timer.
Tick	The Tick event adds a new event handler to the underlying MulticastDelegate.

Thus, you can update your class as follows:

```
Public Class Form1
    Inherits System.Windows.Forms.Form
...
    ' The timer (declared with events).
    Private WithEvents timer1 As Timer = New Timer()
    Public Sub New()
        MyBase.New()
...
        ' Configure the timer.
        timer1.Interval = 1000
        timer1.Enabled = True
    End Sub
     ' This method will be called (roughly) every second.
    Private Sub GetTime(ByVal sender As Object, _
    ByVal e As EventArgs) Handles timer1.Tick
        Dim t As DateTime = DateTime.Now
        Dim s As String = t.ToLongTimeString()
        ' Change text of pane to current time.
        sbPnlTime.Text = s
    End Sub
End Class
```

Notice that the Timer event handler makes use of the DateTime type. Here, you simply find the current system time using the Now property and use it to set the Text property of the correct StatusBarPanel object.

Displaying Menu Selection Prompts

Finally, you must configure the first pane to hold menu help strings. As you know, most applications send a small bit of text information to the first pane of a status bar whenever the end user selects a menu item (e.g., "This terminates the application").

Assume the menu system for this application is identical to the Simple Menu application. This time, however, you need to respond to the Select event of each subitem. When the user selects "File | Exit" or "Help | About" you tell the first StatusBarPanel object to display a given text message. You also handle the Form's MenuComplete event to ensure that when the user has finished manipulating the menu, a default message is placed in the first pane of the status bar.

Recall that the Simple Menu application did *not* make use of the WithEvents keyword when declaring the MenuItem member variables. Rather, you dynamically associated a delegate to the address of a given event handler and passed this value into the Menu$MenuCollection.Add() method. The question you now face is this: How can you associate a new Select event for your MenuItems that were not declared WithEvents?

As you may recall from Chapter 6, VB .NET provides the AddHandler statement for just such an occasion. To keep all of your menu handling logic in one place, assume that you have moved the menu building logic into a new helper function named BuildMenuSystem(). Here is the complete update (assume that these dynamic event handlers have been removed using RemoveHandler in the Form's Dispose() method):

```
Public Class MainForm
    Inherits Form . . .
    ' Build this event handler using the code window (Base Class Events)
    Private Sub Form1_MenuComplete(ByVal sender As Object, _
    ByVal e As System.EventArgs) Handles MyBase.MenuComplete
        ' The MenuComplete event is sent when the user clicks off
        ' the menu. You want to capture this event in order to
        ' set the text of the first pane to "Ready." If you did not,
        ' the StatusBarPanel text would always be based on the last menu
        ' selected!
        sbPnlPrompt.Text = "Ready"
    End Sub
    ' These handlers added dynamically using AddHandler
    ' (see BuildMenuSystem() method below)
    Private Sub FileExit_Selected(ByVal sender As Object, ByVal e As EventArgs)
        sbPnlPrompt.Text = "Terminates this app"
    End Sub
    Private Sub HelpAbout_Selected(ByVal sender As Object, ByVal e As EventArgs)
        sbPnlPrompt.Text = "Displays app info"
    End Sub
     ' Move all the menu logic here.
    Private Sub BuildMenuSystem()
        ' Create the 'File | Exit' Menu.
        Dim miFile As MenuItem = mnuMain.MenuItems.Add("&File")
        miFile.MenuItems.Add(New MenuItem("E&xit", _
                                   New EventHandler(AddressOf FileExit_Clicked), _
                                   Shortcut.CtrlX))
        ' Dynamically had a handler for the Select event!
        AddHandler miFile.MenuItems(0).Select, AddressOf FileExit_Selected
        ' Now create a 'Help | About' menu.
        Dim miHelp As MenuItem = mnuMain.MenuItems.Add("Help")
        miHelp.MenuItems.Add(New MenuItem("&About", _
                New EventHandler(AddressOf HelpAbout_Clicked), _
```

```
            Shortcut.CtrlA))
        ' Dynamically add a handler for the Select event!
        AddHandler miHelp.MenuItems(0).Select, AddressOf HelpAbout_Selected
        ' Attach main menu to the Form object.
        Me.Menu = mnuMain
    End Sub
...
End Class
```

Excellent! If you now run your application, you find that the first pane of the status bar is updated automatically as you select each menu item. As you may guess, the Visual Studio .NET IDE also provides some design-time assistance to facilitate the building of status bar objects.

SOURCE CODE *The MyStatusBar project is included under the Chapter 9 subdirectory.*

Building a Status Bar Using Visual Studio .NET

When you want to leverage the VS .NET IDE to build a status bar, the first step is to select the StatusBar widget from the Toolbar. Once you do so, you see a default status bar mounted on the bottom of the Form's design-time template (see Figure 9-30).

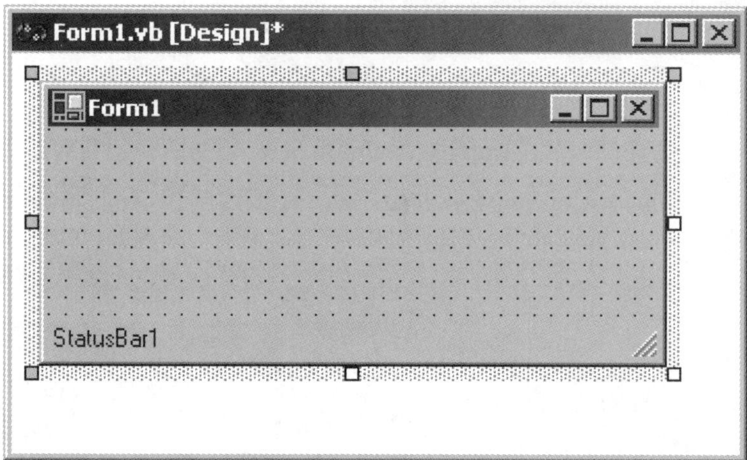

Figure 9-30. Design-time StatusBar manipulation

To add panels to the StatusBar type, open the Panels dialog box using the Properties window (see Figure 9-31).

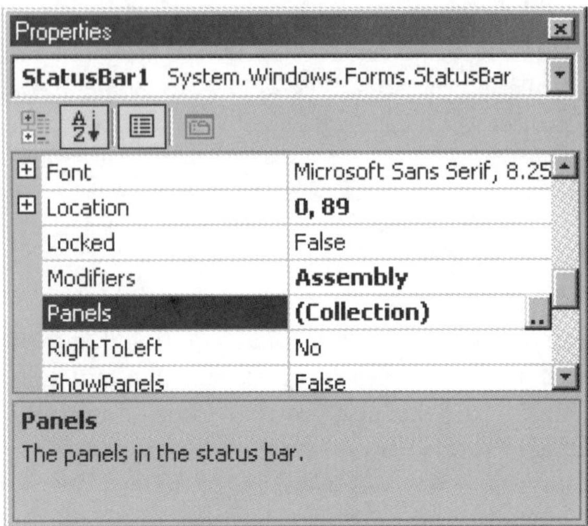

Figure 9-31. Adding Panels at design time

Using the Panels dialog box, you are able to add StatusBarPanel types into the StatusBar in much the same way you add discrete MenuItems to a MainMenu type (see Figure 9-32).

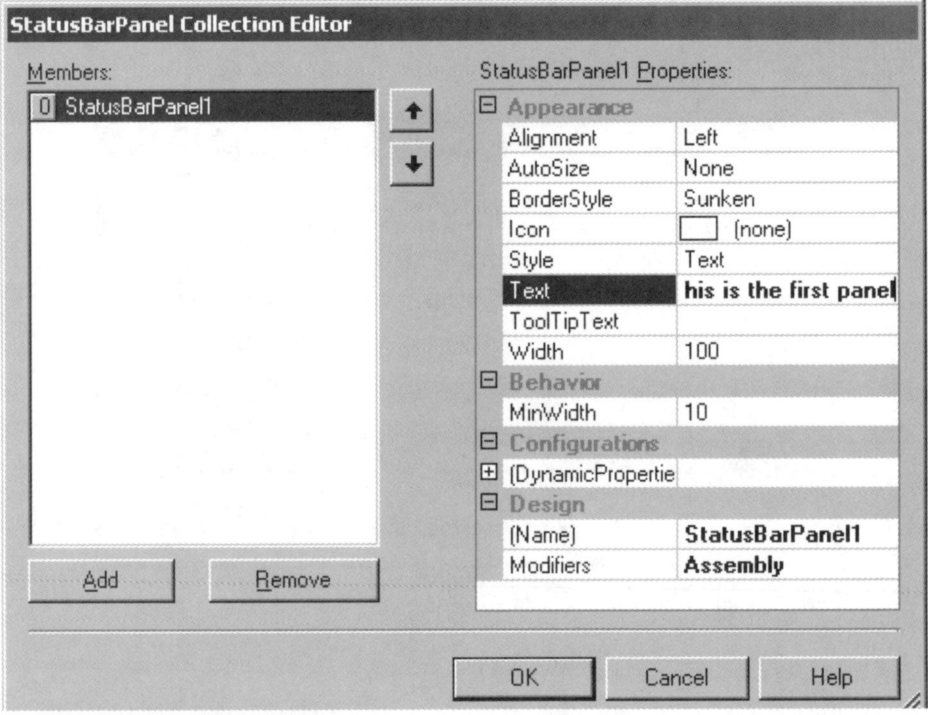

Figure 9-32. Adding panels to a StatusBar

As you expect, these tools help to reduce keystrokes. If you examine the code generated within the InitializeComponent() method, things should look very familiar. One oddball behavior of the default StatusBar configuration is that it is not configured to show the individual panels until you set the ShowPanels property to True (either programmatically or via the Properties window). At this point, you are able to manipulate each panel programmatically, using the same techniques used during the previous example.

Building a ToolBar

The final Form-level GUI item to examine in this chapter is the ToolBar type. As you know, toolbars typically provide an alternate means to activate a given menu item. Thus, if the user clicks a Save button, this has the same effect as selecting "File | Save." In the Windows Forms namespace, a handful of types are defined to allow you to build such a beast. To begin, start with the ToolBar class itself. Table 9-22 lists the core properties.

Table 9-22. Properties of the ToolBar Type

TOOLBAR PROPERTY	MEANING IN LIFE
BorderStyle	The kind of border around this control, as specified by the BorderStyle enumeration.
Buttons	The collection of buttons belonging to the toolbar (e.g., ToolBar$ToolBarButtonCollection).
ButtonSize	Determines the size of a button in the ToolBar.
ImageList	Returns the ImageList control that maintains the images for this ToolBar.
ImageSize	This method returns the size of the images within the ToolBar's image list.
ShowToolTips	Indicates whether or not the ToolBar shows tool tips for each button.
Wrappable	ToolBar buttons can "wrap" to the next line when the ToolBar becomes too narrow to include all buttons on the same line.

When a Form maintains a ToolBar, the goal is to create some number of individual ToolBarButton objects and add them to the ToolBar$ToolBarButtonCollection type. (Are you beginning to see a pattern here?) Each button may contain text, images, or both. To keep things simple, let's begin by building a toolbar containing two buttons displaying text prompts only. Table 9-23 presents some important members of the ToolBarButton type.

Table 9-23. Properties of the ToolBarButton Type

TOOLBARBUTTON PROPERTY	MEANING IN LIFE
DropDownMenu	ToolBarButtons can specify a pop-up menu that is shown whenever the drop-down button is pressed. This property enables you to control just which menu is shown. Note that this is only shown if the Style property is set to DropDownButton.
ImageIndex	Returns the index of the image that this ToolBarButton is using. The index comes from the parent ToolBar's ImageList.
Style	Returns the style of the ToolBar button. This will form the ToolBarButtonStyle enumeration.
Text	The caption that is displayed in this ToolBar button.
ToolTipText	If the parent ToolBar has the ShowToolTips property turned on, this property describes the text that is displayed for this button.
Visible	Indicates whether the button is visible or not. If the button is not visible, it is not shown and is unable to receive user input.

Your custom toolbar contains two buttons: Save and Exit. Here is the code update:

```
Public Class Form1
    Inherits System.Windows.Forms.Form
    ' ToolBar items.
    Private WithEvents tbSaveButton As ToolBarButton = New ToolBarButton()
    Private WithEvents tbExitButton As ToolBarButton = New ToolBarButton()
    Private WithEvents myToolBar As ToolBar = New ToolBar()
    Public Sub New()
        MyBase.New()
        'This call is required by the Windows Form Designer.
        InitializeComponent()
        'Build the ToolBar.
        BuildToolBar()
    End Sub
```

```
    ...
    Private Sub BuildToolBar()
        ' Configure each button.
        tbSaveButton.Text = "Save"
        tbSaveButton.ToolTipText = "Save"
        tbExitButton.Text = "Exit"
        tbExitButton.ToolTipText = "Exit"
        ' Configure ToolBar and add buttons.
        myToolBar.BorderStyle = System.Windows.Forms.BorderStyle.Fixed3D
        myToolBar.ShowToolTips = True
        myToolBar.Buttons.AddRange(New ToolBarButton() _
                                   {tbSaveButton, tbExitButton})
        ' Add the new bar to the Controls collection.
        Me.Controls.Add(myToolBar)
    End Sub
    ' Button click handler.
    Private Sub myToolBar_ButtonClick(ByVal sender As Object, _
        ByVal e As System.Windows.Forms.ToolBarButtonClickEventArgs) _
        Handles myToolBar.ButtonClick
        MessageBox.Show(e.Button.ToolTipText)
    End Sub
End Class
```

Figure 9-33 shows a test run.

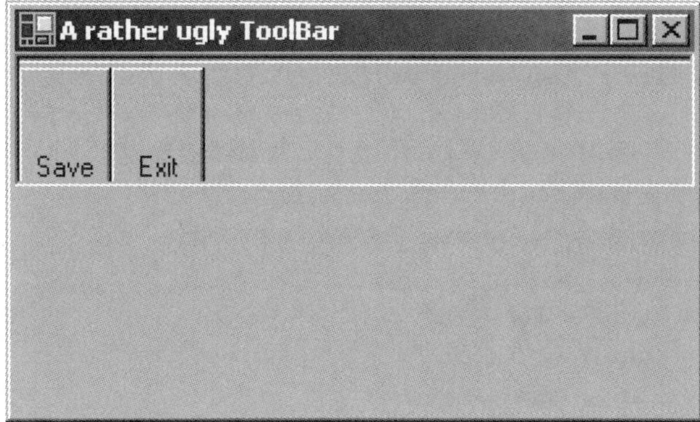

Figure 9-33. A very simple toolbar

Bland, isn't it? You will add some images in just a moment, but first let's analyze some code. The BuildToolBar() helper function begins by configuring some basic properties for each ToolBarButton. Next, add them to the ToolBar collection using the AddRange() method (rather than calling Add() multiple times). To handle the click events for a given button, you must handle the ButtonClick event.

The name of the new ToolBarButtonClickEventHandler delegate must have a signature such that the second parameter is of type ToolBarButtonClickEventArgs. This type may be examined to determine which button sent the event, using the Button property:

```
Private Sub myToolBar_ButtonClick(ByVal sender As Object, _
    ByVal e As System.Windows.Forms.ToolBarButtonClickEventArgs) _
    Handles myToolBar.ButtonClick
    MessageBox.Show(e.Button.ToolTipText)
End Sub
```

Adding Images to Your Toolbar Buttons

Real toolbar buttons contain images. When you want to configure your buttons to contain images, the first step is to have the Form create an ImageList type. This class represents a set of images that are consumed by some other type (such as a ToolBar). If you have ever created a toolbar using Visual Basic 6.0, you should feel right at home with this aspect of Windows Forms. Update your existing ToolBarForm to make use of two icons for display purposes, in addition to simple text strings. Here is the relevant update:

```
Public Class Form1
    Inherits System.Windows.Forms.Form
    ' ToolBar items.
    Private WithEvents tbSaveButton As ToolBarButton = New ToolBarButton()
    Private WithEvents tbExitButton As ToolBarButton = New ToolBarButton()
    Private WithEvents myToolBar As ToolBar = New ToolBar()
    ' Contains the images used by the toolbar.
    Private toolBarIcons As ImageList = New ImageList()
     ...
     Private Sub BuildToolBar()
          ' Configure save button.
          tbSaveButton.ImageIndex = 0
          tbSaveButton.ToolTipText = "Save"
          ' Configure exit button.
          tbExitButton.ImageIndex = 1
          tbExitButton.ToolTipText = "Exit"
          ' Create ToolBar and add buttons.
          toolBar.ImageList = toolBarIcons
          . . .
```

```
        ' Load images (again, the icons need to be in the app dir).
        toolBarIcons.ImageSize = new System.Drawing.Size(32, 32)
        toolBarIcons.Images.Add(New Icon("filesave.ico"))
        toolBarIcons.Images.Add(New Icon("fileexit.ico"))
        toolBarIcons.ColorDepth = ColorDepth.Depth16Bit
        toolBarIcons.TransparentColor = System.Drawing.Color.Transparent
        ...
    End Sub
End Class
```

Notice that you must take the following steps to configure a ToolBar to display images for its individual button types:

- You must tell each ToolBarButton which image to use via the ImageIndex property.
- You add new images to the ImageList class using the Images.Add() method.
- The ToolBar itself must be told which ImageList it is associated to using the ImageList property.

If you now run the application (see Figure 9-34), you see a much more pleasing end result (if you want these buttons to look more standard, simply adjust the size to 16 x 16).

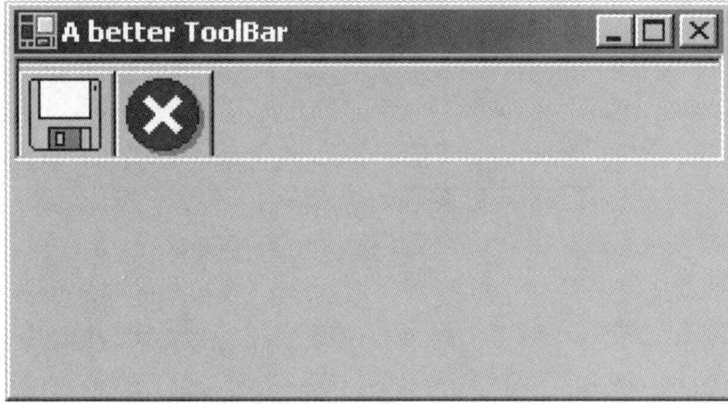

Figure 9-34. A more interesting ToolBar

SOURCE CODE *The SimpleToolBar project is included under the Chapter 9 subdirectory.*

Building ToolBars at Design Time

Again, while it is helpful to understand how ToolBars work under the hood, VS .NET provides numerous tools that make the process of building a ToolBar almost trivial. First assume you have created a brand-new VB .NET Windows Application. Next, add a new ToolBar to your main Form using the Toolbox window (see Figure 9-35). Once you do, you have a new ToolBar member variable listed in your main Form declared WithEvents.

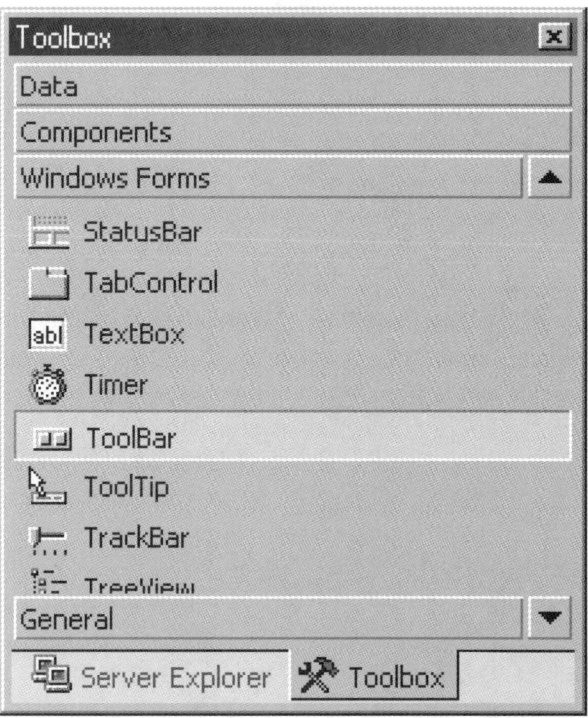

Figure 9-35. Adding new Toolbar types

Design-time configuration of the ToolBar is also accomplished using the Properties Window. For example, when you want to add buttons to the ToolBar type, select the Buttons property, as shown in Figure 9-36.

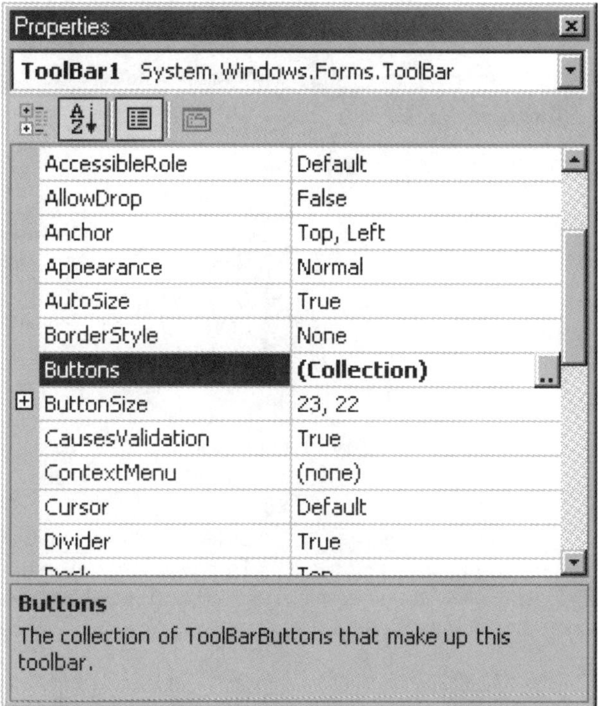

Figure 9-36. Adding ToolBar buttons at design time

Selecting the Buttons property opens a dialog box that allows you to add, remove, and configure the individual ToolBarButton items, as shown in Figure 9-37.

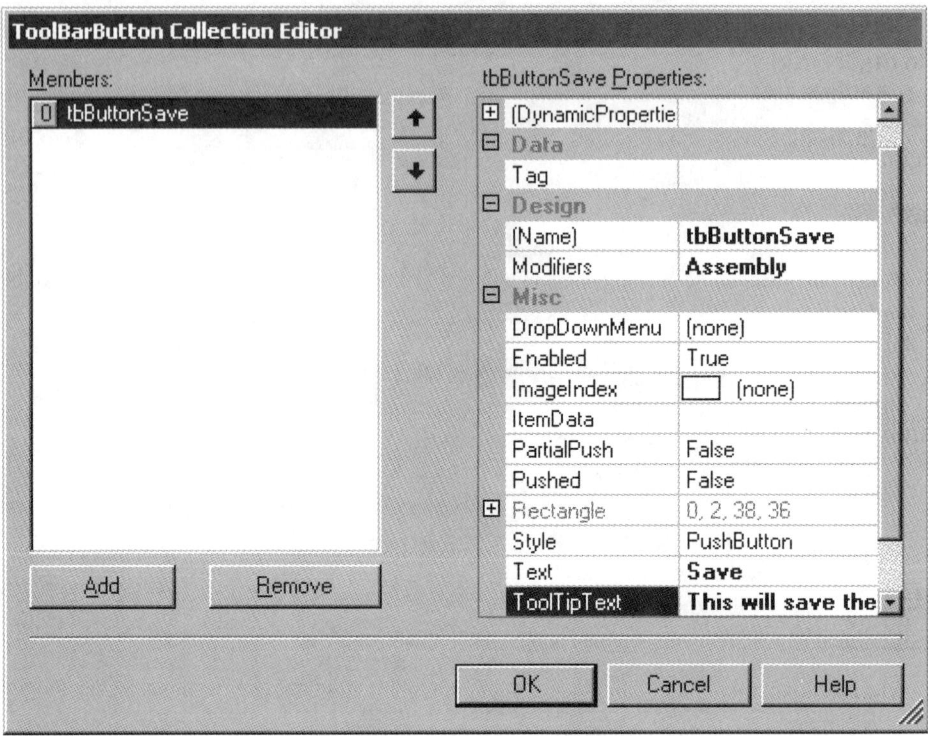

Figure 9-37. Configuring Button types at design time

Adding an ImageList at Design Time

Notice how the dialog box in Figure 9-37 also allows you to assign an iconic image to each button using the ImageIndex property. However, this property is useless until you add an ImageList type to your current project. To add an ImageList member to a Form at design time, return to the Toolbox window and select the ImageList icon.

At this point, you can use the Properties window to add the individual images using the Images property (see Figure 9-38).

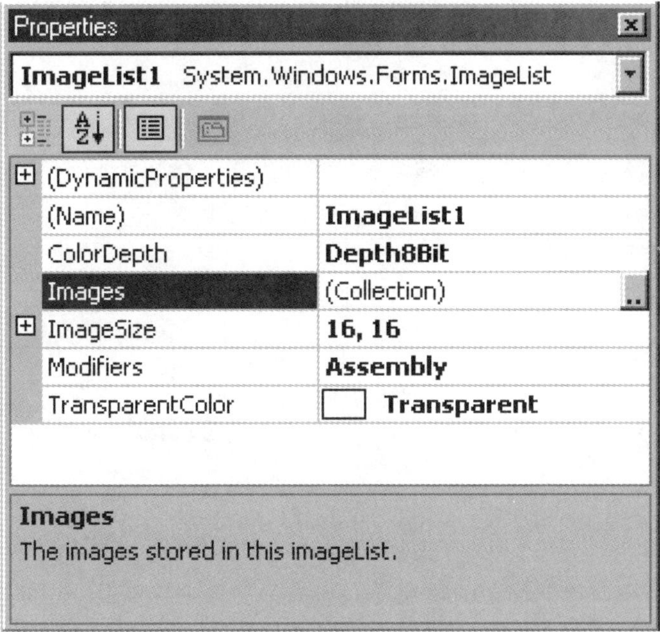

Figure 9-38. Adding Images to your ImageList

Once you have added each image file to the ImageList, inform the ToolBar which ImageList it is to make use of using the Properties window (see Figure 9-39).

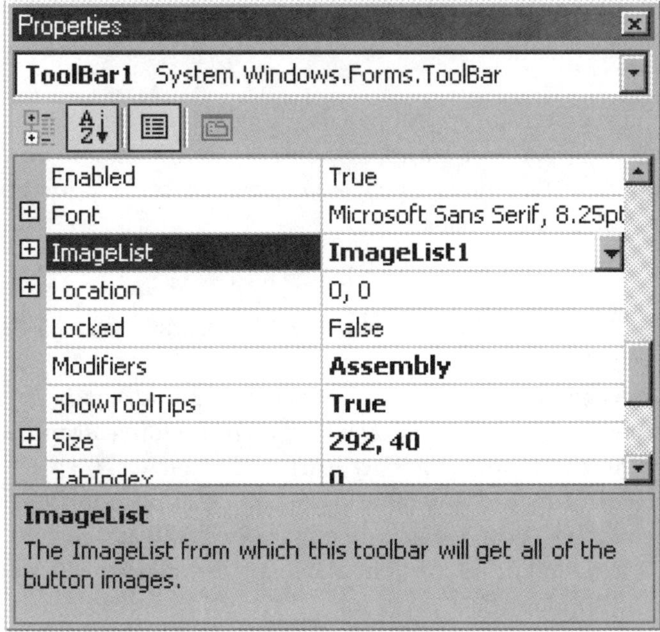

Figure 9-39. Associating an ImageList to a ToolBar

At this point, you return to the ToolBar button editor and map a given image in the ImageList to each button (see Figure 9-40).

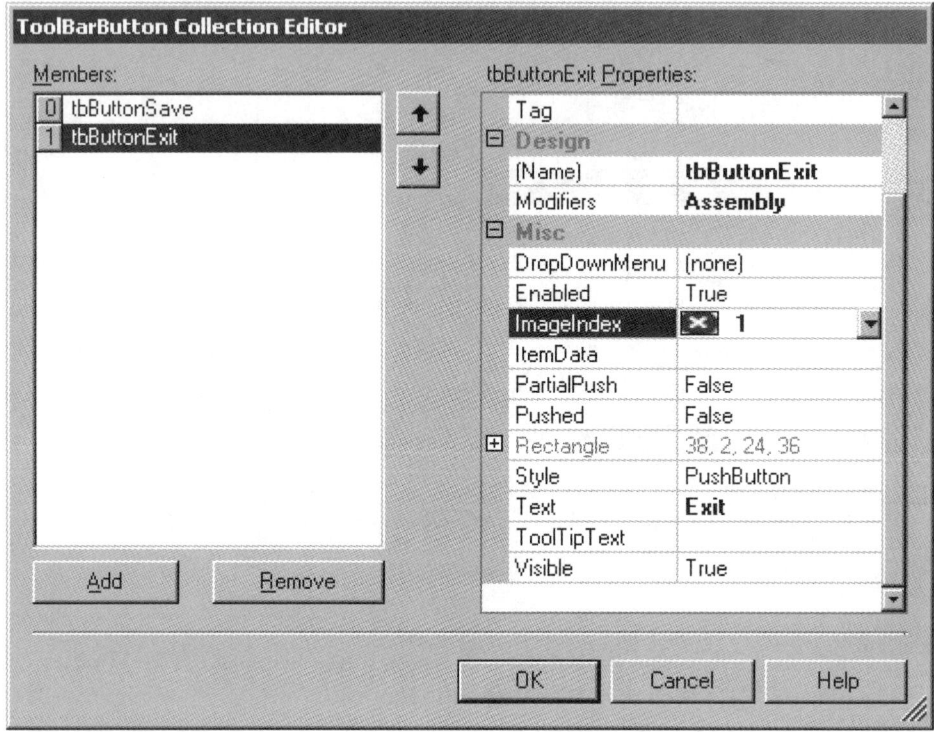

Figure 9-40. Mapping images to buttons

The graphical end result appears on the design-time Form, while the code that represents these design-time adjustments is safely tucked away within the InitializeComponent() method (which, as you might assume, is just about identical to the code you wrote by hand).

A Minimal and Complete Windows Forms Application

At this point you can build a Form that hosts a main menu, a pop-up menu, a status bar and a toolbar. This chapter wraps up by building an application that pulls together the information you have learned thus far.

Let's extend the functionality of the MyStatusBar application you created earlier. In addition to the existing logic, you add code to read and write your application data to (and from) the system registry as well as to illustrate how to interact with the Windows 2000 event log.

First, create a new topmost menu item ("Background Color") that allows the user to select the background color of the client area from a set of possible choices. Each color submenu has an associated help string to be displayed in the first pane of the StatusBar object. The Clicked event for each Color subitem is handled by the *same* event handler (ColorItem_Clicked). Likewise, the Selected event for each subitem is handled by a method named ColorItem_Selected. Here is the code update:

```
Private Sub BuildMenuSystem()
...
 ' Create the 'Background Color' menu.
 Dim miColor As MenuItem = mnuMain.MenuItems.Add("&Background Color")
 miColor.MenuItems.Add("&DarkGoldenrod", _
    New EventHandler(AddressOf ColorItem_Clicked))
 miColor.MenuItems.Add("&GreenYellow", _
    New EventHandler(AddressOf ColorItem_Clicked))
 miColor.MenuItems.Add("&MistyRose", _
    New EventHandler(AddressOf ColorItem_Clicked))
 miColor.MenuItems.Add("&Crimson", _
    New EventHandler(AddressOf ColorItem_Clicked))
 miColor.MenuItems.Add("&LemonChiffon", _
    New EventHandler(AddressOf ColorItem_Clicked))
 miColor.MenuItems.Add("&OldLace", New EventHandler(AddressOf ColorItem_Clicked))

 ' All color menu items have the same selected handler.
 Dim i As Integer
 For i = 0 To miColor.MenuItems.Count - 1
    AddHandler miColor.MenuItems(i).Select, _
        New EventHandler(AddressOf ColorMenuItem_Selected)
 Next
...
End Sub
```

When the end user selects a given subitem from the Background Color menu, the Select event occurs. In the event handler, your task is to extract the text name of the selected menu item (e.g., OldLace, GreenYellow, and so on) and display it in the first panel of your existing status bar. Here is the code:

```
' Color | X Menu selected item handler
Private Sub ColorMenuItem_Selected(ByVal sender As Object, ByVal e As EventArgs)
    ' Figure out the string name of the selected item.
    Dim miClicked As MenuItem = CType(sender, MenuItem)
    Dim item As String = miClicked.Text.Remove(0, 1)
```

```
    sbPnlPrompt.Text = "Select " & item
End Sub
```

When the user clicks a given color menu item, you simply set the Form's BackColor based on the MenuItem's Text property. Notice that you are "remembering" this color by storing the value in a string member variable named currColor:

```
' Color | X Menu clicked item handler
Private Sub ColorItem_Clicked(ByVal sender As Object, ByVal e As EventArgs)
    'Figure out the string name of the color selected.
    Dim miClicked As MenuItem = CType(sender, MenuItem)
    Dim item As String = miClicked.Text.Remove(0, 1)
    BackColor = Color.FromName(item)
    currColor = BackColor
End Sub
```

So far, so good. As you can tell, this is just basic menu logic. Next, let's save the user preferences into the system registry.

Interacting with the System Registry

If you are a COM programmer by trade, there is no escaping the (pain of the) Windows registry. When you live in the world of .NET, your reliance on the system registry dwindles away to little more than a convenient place to store user preferences. The Microsoft.Win32 namespace defines a handful of types that make reading from (and writing to) the system registry a piece of cake. Table 9-24 presents the Microsoft.Win32 types.

Table 9-24. Registry Manipulation Types

MICROSOFT.WIN32 TYPE	MEANING IN LIFE
Registry	A high-level abstraction of the registry itself and all associated hives.
RegistryKey	This is the core type, which allows you to insert, remove, and update information stored in the registry.
RegistryHive	A simple enumeration of each hive in the registry.

As you may already know, previous editions of VB provided two very simple methods (SaveSettings() and GetSettings()) that allowed developers to move information into (and out of) the registry with minimal fuss and bother (the limitation being that these methods only allow you to interact with HKEY_CURRENT_USER). Although these methods are still useful and valid, under VB .NET, you are able to take full control over how your applications interact with the Window's registry, without the need to drop down to raw API calls. The goal for the current application is to allow end users to save their preferences (e.g., font size and background color) to the registry for later use. To do so, you must make use of the RegistryKey class, which provides the core members shown in Table 9-25.

Table 9-25. Properties of the RegistryKey Type

REGISTRYKEY MEMBERS	MEANING IN LIFE
Name	This property retrieves the name of the key.
SubKeyCount	This property retrieves the count of subkeys.
ValueCount	This property retrieves the count of values in the key.
Close()	Closes this key and flushes it to disk if the contents have been modified.
CreateSubKey()	Creates a new subkey or opens an existing subkey. The string subKey is not case-sensitive.
DeleteSubKey()	Deletes the specified subkey. To delete child subkeys, use DeleteSubKeyTree. The string subKey is not case-sensitive.
DeleteSubKeyTree()	Recursively deletes a subkey and any child subkeys. The string subKey is not case-sensitive.
GetSubKeyNames()	Retrieves an array of strings containing all the subkey names.
GetValue()	Overloaded. Retrieves the specified value.
GetValueNames()	Retrieves an array of strings containing all the value names.
OpenRemoteBaseKey()	Opens a new RegistryKey that represents the requested key on a foreign machine.
OpenSubKey()	Overloaded. Retrieves a subkey.
SetValue()	Sets the specified value. The string SubKey is not case-sensitive.

Assume you have added a new "File | Save" menu item. When this is selected you create a RegistryKey object and insert the current background color and font size under HKEY_CURRENT_USER\Software\Intertech\Chapter9App. Also assume your Form has two member variables (currFontSize and currColor) to hold the current font size as well as the current background color. Here is the relevant code (note the use of RegistryKey.SetValue()):

```
' Assume the following state data.
' Private currColor As Color = Color.MistyRose
    ' Private currFontSize As Integer = TheFontSize.Normal
' File | Save Menu clicked handler
Private Sub FileSave_Clicked(ByVal sender As Object, ByVal e As EventArgs)
    ' Save user prefs to reg.
    Dim regKey As RegistryKey = Registry.CurrentUser
    regKey = regKey.CreateSubKey("Software\\Intertech\\Chapter9App")
    regKey.SetValue("CurrSize", currFontSize)
    regKey.SetValue("CurrColor", currColor.Name)
    MessageBox.Show("Settings saved in registry")
End Sub
```

If the user were now to set the current color to LemonChiffon and the current font size to 30 (and save these settings), you would find the information presented in Figure 9-41 inserted into the system registry.

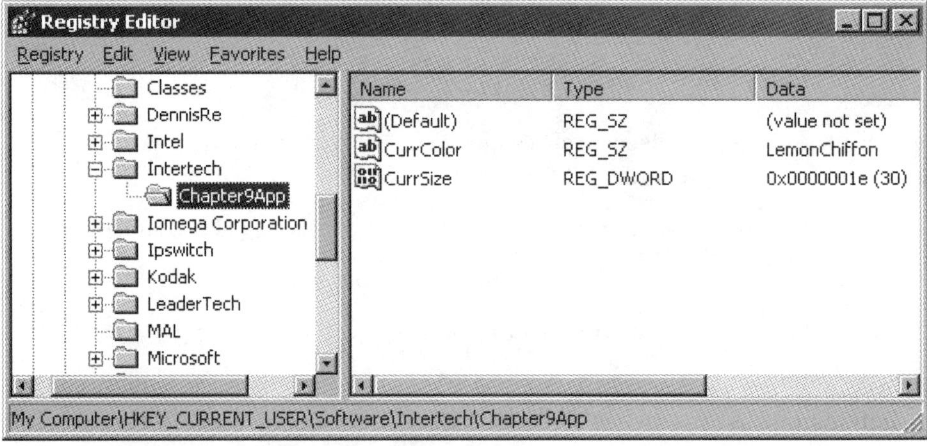

Figure 9-41. Saving application data to HKCU

Reading this information from the registry also makes use of the RegistryKey type. Now retrofit the constructor of your Form-derived class to read the background color and font size from the registry, to assign the corresponding member data to the correct values. In this way, the application starts up having the same look and feel as the previous session (note the use of RegistryKey.GetValue()):

```
Public Sub New()
    MyBase.New()
    . . .
    ' Build the form's initial UI.
    BuildMenuSystem()
    BuildStatBar()
    ' Get Reg values to set state data.
    Dim regKey As RegistryKey = Registry.CurrentUser
    regKey = regKey.CreateSubKey("Software\\Intertech\\Chapter9App")
    currFontSize = CInt(regKey.GetValue("CurrSize", currFontSize))
    Dim c As String = CStr(regKey.GetValue("CurrColor", currColor.Name))
    currColor = Color.FromName(c)
    BackColor = currColor
    . . .
End Sub
```

The following question might pop into your mind: "What if there are currently no entries for these data points in the registry?" For example, assume the user launched the application for the very first time and has not yet saved any settings. In this case, when the constructor logic is hit, the RegistryKey object is unable to locate existing data.

The good news is that the GetValue() method may take an optional second parameter (as seen in the previous code). This parameter specifies the value to use in place of an empty registry entry. Notice that you have sent in currFontSize and currColor member variables. Given that the Form sets these variables to an initial value, these are used in place of any absent registry entries.

The final touch is to update the BuildMenuSystem() helper function to check the correct subitem on the pop-up menu based on the information read in from the registry. In the previous PopUpMenu application, you specified that the currently selected item was TheFontSize.Normal. This may not be the case anymore, given that the user can save preferences to the registry. Here is the update:

```
Private Sub BuildMenuSystem()
. . .
    ' Check the correct pop-up item
    If (currFontSize = TheFontSize.Huge) Then
        currentCheckedItem = checkedHuge
    ElseIf (currFontSize = TheFontSize.Normal) Then
        currentCheckedItem = checkedNormal
    Else
        currentCheckedItem = checkedTiny
    End If
    ' Now check it.
    currentCheckedItem.Checked = True
End Sub
```

Interacting with the Event Viewer

The Windows 2000 operating system supplies a Microsoft Management Console (MMC) snap-in called the Event Viewer. The Event Viewer maintains three separate logs (Application, Security, and System) that provide a way for you to gather information about hardware, software, and system problems, and to monitor various security events (see Figure 9-42).

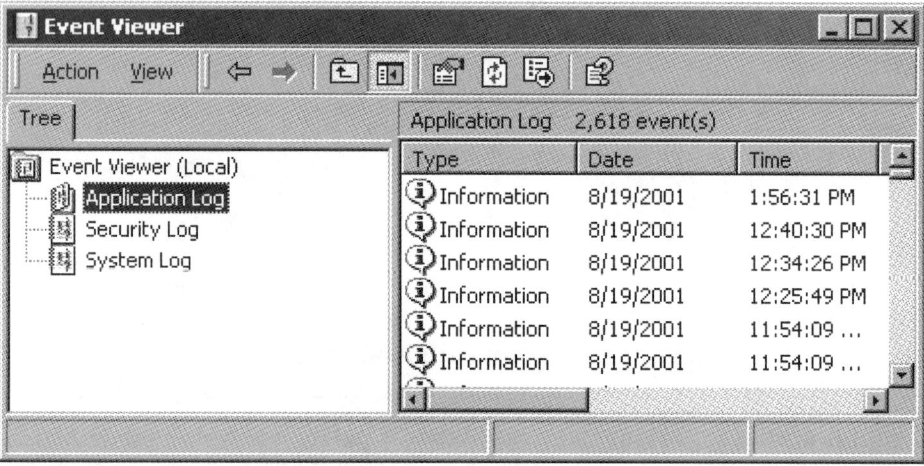

Figure 9-42. The Windows 2000 Event Viewer

When you want to programmatically manipulate the Event Viewer using .NET types, you want to make use of various types defined within the System.Diagnostics namespace. Table 9-26 gives a rundown of the core items you must be aware of.

Table 9-26. Types of the System.Diagnostics Namespace

SYSTEM.DIAGNOSTICS TYPE	MEANING IN LIFE
EventLog	This class is your entry point to manipulate the Windows 2000 Event Viewer.
EventLog.EventLogEntryCollection	Holds individual EventLogEntry types that represent an entry in a given event log.
EventLogEntry	The EventLogEntry type represents a single record in the event log.
EventLogNames	This sealed type provides fields to define the log you want to manipulate (Application, Security, or System).

Using the EventLog class, you can read from existing logs (Application, Security, and System), write entries to logs, delete logs, and react to entries your log receives. If you so desire, you can even create new custom logs when creating an event source. Table 9-27 lists some core members.

Table 9-27. Members of the EventLog Type

EVENTLOG MEMBER	MEANING IN LIFE
Entries	Gets the contents of the event log, held in an EventLog.EventLogEntryCollection type. As you would expect, this collection contains individual EventLogEntry items.
Log	Gets or sets the name of the log to read from and write to. This can be "Application," "System," "Security," an application-specific log, or a custom log name.
MachineName	Gets or sets the name of the computer on which to read or write events. If you do not specify the MachineName, the local computer (".") is assumed.
Source	Gets or sets the application name (source name) to register and use when writing to the event log.
Clear()	Clears all entries from an event log.
Close()	Closes a log and releases read and write handles.
CreateEventSource()	Establishes an application as an event source.
GetEventLogs()	Creates an array containing the event logs.
WriteEntry()	Inserts an entry in the event log.

As mentioned, your application writes an entry to the Application log when the application is terminated. As a simple example, you might write the following logic in your FileExit_Clicked() event handler:

```
' File | Exit clicked handler.
Private Sub FileExit_Clicked(ByVal sender As Object, ByVal e As EventArgs)
    ' Just for kicks, let's log this event to
    ' the Event Log. . .
    Dim log As EventLog = New EventLog()
    log.Log = "Application"
    log.Source = Me.Text
    log.WriteEntry("Hey dude, this app shut down. . .")
    log.Close()
    Me.Close()
End Sub
```

If you were now to examine the Application log, you would find the entry displayed in Figure 9-43 had been inserted.

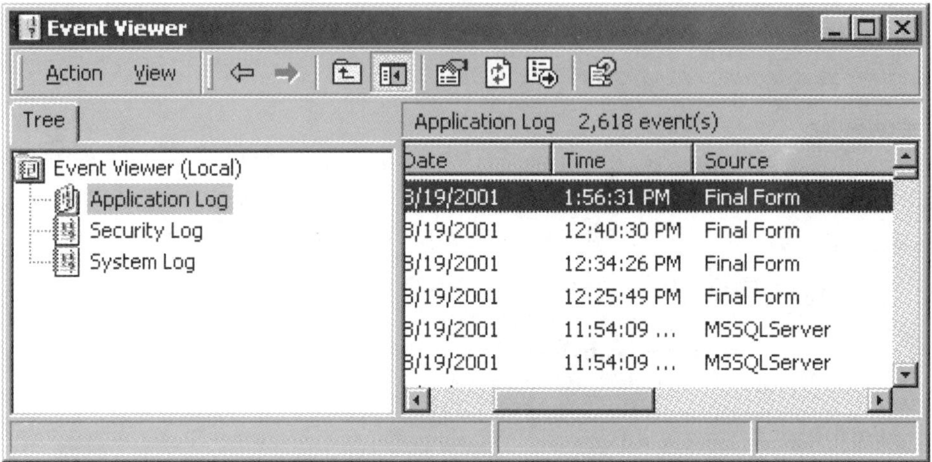

Figure 9-43. Your custom application log

To examine your very helpful message entry (e.g., "Hey dude, this app shut down. . ."), double-click the log entry (see Figure 9-44).

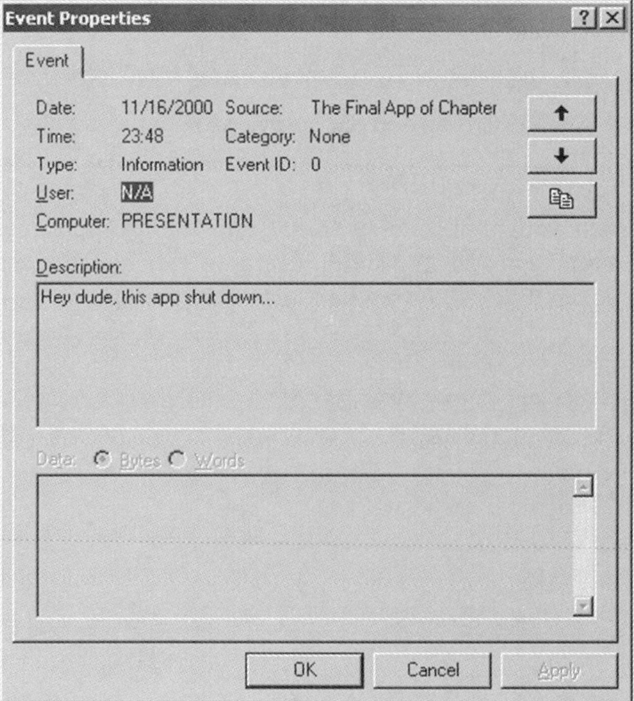

Figure 9-44. Your message

Reading Data from the Event Log

Now assume you want to read some information from a given log. This too is quite simple. Recall that the EventLog class defines a property named Entries. This item returns an instance of EventLog.EventLogEntryCollection. This collection contains some number of indexable EventLogEntry types, each of which represents an entry in a given log (see Table 9-28).

Table 9-28. The EventLogEntry Type

EVENTLOGENTRY MEMBER	MEANING IN LIFE
Category	Gets the text associated with the CategoryNumber for this entry
CategoryNumber	Gets the application-specific category number for this entry
Data	Gets the binary data associated with the entry
EntryType	Gets the type of this entry
EventID	Gets the application-specific event identifier of this entry
MachineName	Gets the name of the computer on which this entry was generated
Message	Gets the localized message corresponding to this event entry
Source	Gets the name of the application that generated this event
TimeGenerated	Gets the time at which this event was generated
TimeWritten	Gets the time at which this event was written to the log, in local time
UserName	Gets the name of the user responsible for this event

If you then update the FileExit_Clicked() method as follows:

```
' File | Exit clicked handler.
Private Sub FileExit_Clicked(ByVal sender As Object, ByVal e As EventArgs)
    ...
    ' Display the first 5 entries in the Application log.
    Dim i As Integer
    For i = 0 To 4
        MessageBox.Show("Message: " & log.Entries(i).Message & vbLf & _
                 "Box: " & log.Entries(i).MachineName & vbLf & _
                 "App: " & log.Entries(i).Source & vbLf & _
```

```
                    "Time entered: " & log.Entries(i).TimeWritten, _
                    "Application Log entry:")
    Next
    log.Close()
    Me.Close() 'Just close the application. . .
End Sub
```

you would see five messages pop up (what they are depends on exactly what is in your current event log). Figure 9-45 shows your complete Windows Forms application in action.

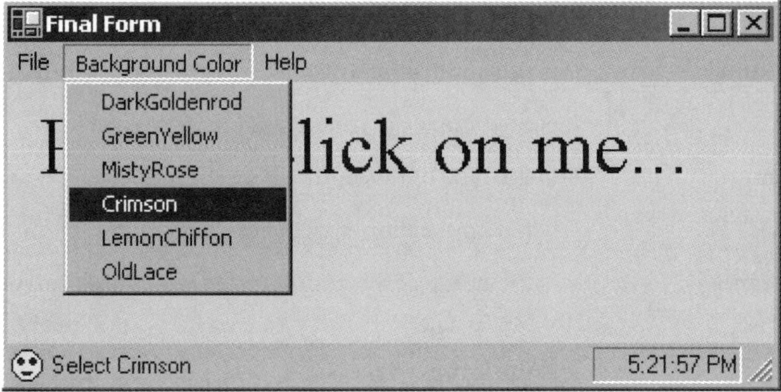

Figure 9-45. The final product

SOURCE CODE *The FinalFormsApp project is included under the Chapter 9 subdirectory.*

Building an MDI Application

To wrap up your initial look at Windows Forms, I close this chapter by examining how to configure a Form to function as a parent to any number of child windows (i.e., an MDI container). MDI applications allow the user to have multiple windows open at a single time, with each window representing a given "document" of the application. By way of an example, VS .NET is an MDI application in that you are able to have multiple documents open from within an instance of the application.

When you are building MDI applications using Windows Forms, your first task is to (of course) create a brand-new Windows Application. The initial Form of the application typically hosts a menuing system that allows the user to create new documents (such as File | New) as well as arrange existing open windows (cascade, vertical tile, and horizontal tile).

The child windows are interesting in that you typically have a prototypical Form that functions as a basis for each child window. Given that Forms are class types, any private data defined in the child Form will be unique to a given instance. For example, if you were to create an MDI word processing application, you might create a child Form that maintained a collection of Strings to represent a given line of text. If the user created five new child windows, each Form would maintain its own copy of the underlying collection and could be treated individually.

Additionally, MDI applications allow you to "merge menus." As mentioned previously, parent windows typically have a menu system that allows the user to spawn and organize additional child windows. However, what if the child window also maintains a menuing system? If the user maximizes a particular child window, you need to merge the child's menu system within the parent Form to allow the user to activate items from each menu system. The Windows Forms namespace defines a number of properties, methods, and events that allow you to programmatically merge menu systems. In addition, there is a "default merge" system, which works in a good number of cases. I leave it as a task for the interested reader to investigate this aspect of MDI applications.

Building the Parent Form

To illustrate the basics of building an MDI application, begin by creating a brand-new VB .NET Windows Application named MDIApp. Almost all of the MDI infrastructure can be assigned to your initial Form using various design-time tools. To begin, locate the IsMdiContainer property in the Property window and set it to True. If you look at the design-time Form, you see that the client area has been modified to visually represent a container of child windows.

Next up, place a new MainMenu widget on your main Form. This menu specifies three topmost MenuItems named "File," "Window," and "Arrange Windows." The File menu contains two subitems named "New" and "Exit." The Window does not contain any subitems, as you programmatically add new items as the user creates additional child windows. Finally, the Arrange Window menu defines three subitems named "Cascade," "Vertical," and "Horizontal." Figure 9-46 offers a high-level design-time view.

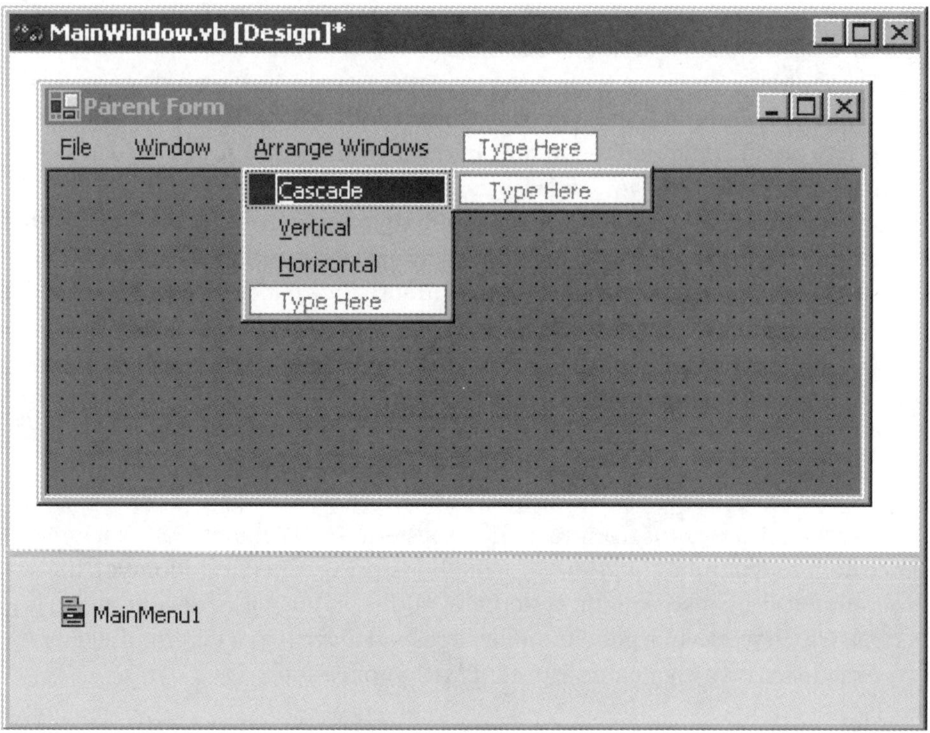

Figure 9-46. Building the Parent's menu system

Given that you already dove into the muck of coding raw menu logic during this chapter, simply use the IDE to generate event handlers for each submenu. You add the code to the File | New handler in the next section—however, here is the code behind the remaining menu selections (remember, the Window menu does not have any subitems just yet):

```
' Lay out all child windows.
Private Sub mnuCascade_Click(ByVal sender As System.Object, _
    ByVal e As System.EventArgs) Handles mnuCascade.Click
    LayoutMdi(MdiLayout.Cascade)
End Sub
Private Sub mnuVert_Click(ByVal sender As System.Object, _
    ByVal e As System.EventArgs) Handles mnuVert.Click
    LayoutMdi(MdiLayout.TileVertical)
End Sub
Private Sub mnuHorizontal_Click(ByVal sender As System.Object, _
    ByVal e As System.EventArgs) Handles mnuHorizontal.Click
    LayoutMdi(MdiLayout.TileHorizontal)
End Sub
```

```
Private Sub mnuFileExit_Click(ByVal sender As System.Object, _
    ByVal e As System.EventArgs) Handles mnuFileExit.Click
        Me.Close()
End Sub
```

The main point of interest here is the use of the LayoutMdi() method and the corresponding MdiLayout enumeration. The code behind each menu select handler should be quite clear. When the user selects a given arrangement, you tell the parent Form to automatically reposition any and all child windows.

Before you move on to the child Form, you need to add one design-time property to the topmost Window menu item. The MdiList property may be set to True for a given topmost menu, which informs the hosting Form to automatically list the name of each child window as a possible menu selection (see Figure 9-47). By default, this list is the value of the child's Text property followed by a numerical suffix (i.e., Form1, Form2, Form3, and so on).

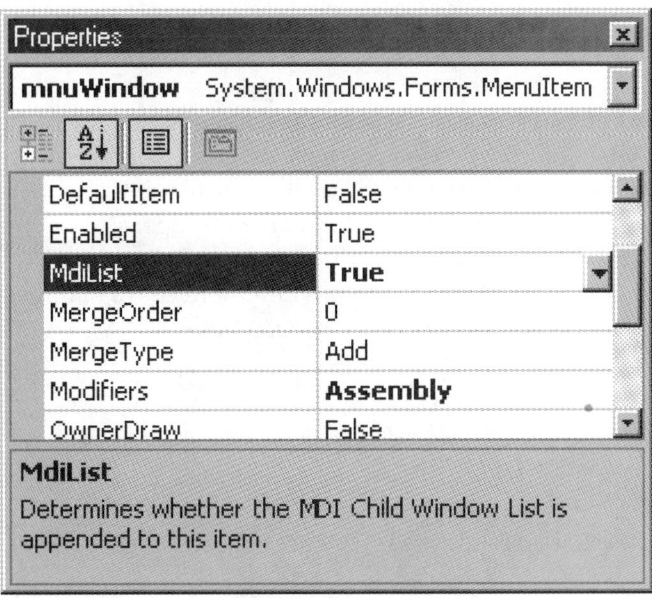

Figure 9-47. Establishing a topmost menu as a MDI list

Building the Child Form

Now that you have the shell of an MDI container Form, you need to build up an additional Form that functions as a given child window. Begin by inserting a new Form type into your current project, and handle the Click event. In the generated event handler, randomly set the background color of the client area. In addition, print out the stringified value of the new Color object into the child's caption bar. The following logic should do the trick:

```
Private Sub ChildWindow_Click(ByVal sender As Object, _
    ByVal e As System.EventArgs) Handles MyBase.Click
    ' Get three random numbers
    Dim r, g, b As Integer
    Dim ran As New Random()
    r = ran.Next(0, 255)
    g = ran.Next(0, 255)
    b = ran.Next(0, 255)
    Dim currcolor As Color = Color.FromArgb(r, g, b)
    Me.BackColor = currcolor
    Me.Text = currColor.ToString()
End Sub
```

Spawning Child Windows

Your final order of business is to flesh out the details behind the parent Form's "File New" event handler. Now that you have defined a child Form, the logic is simple: Create and show a new instance of the ChildForm type. Furthermore, you need to set the value of the child Form's MdiParent property to point to the containing Form (in this case, your main window). Note that the child Form may also access the MdiParent property directly whenever it needs to manipulate (or communicate with) its parent window. Here is the update:

```
Private Sub mnuFileNew_Click(ByVal sender As System.Object, _
    ByVal e As System.EventArgs) Handles mnuFileNew.Click
    ' Make a new child window.
    Dim newChild As New ChildWindow()
    'Set the Parent Form of the Child window.
    newChild.MdiParent = Me
    'Display the new form.
    newChild.Show()
End Sub
```

Now, if you take this application out for a test drive, you may begin by creating a set of new child windows and click on each one to establish a unique background color (see Figure 9-48).

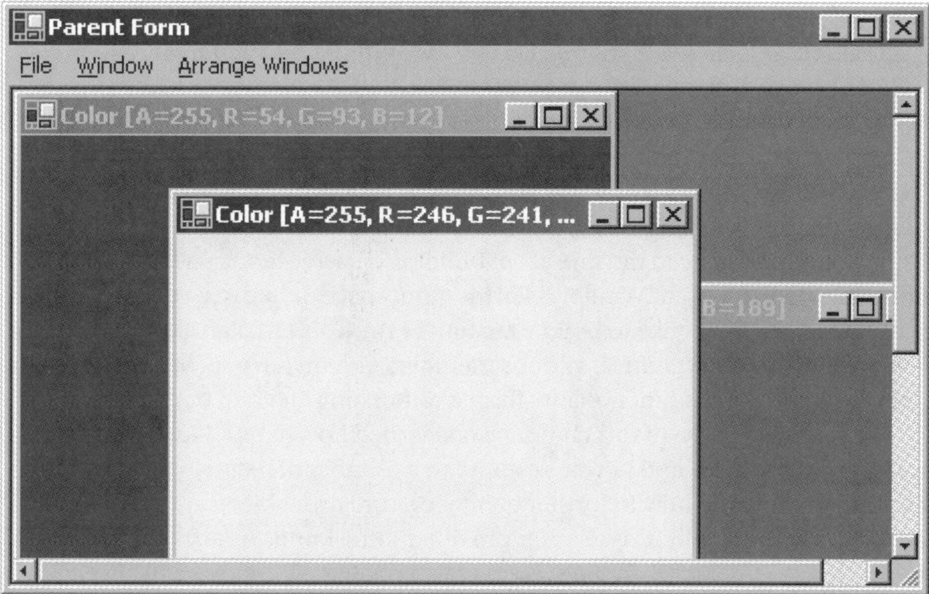

Figure 9-48. Generating child windows

If you access the Arrange Window menu items, you can instruct the parent Form to vertically tile, horizontally tile, or cascade the child Forms. Figure 9-49 shows the result of selecting the vertical tile option.

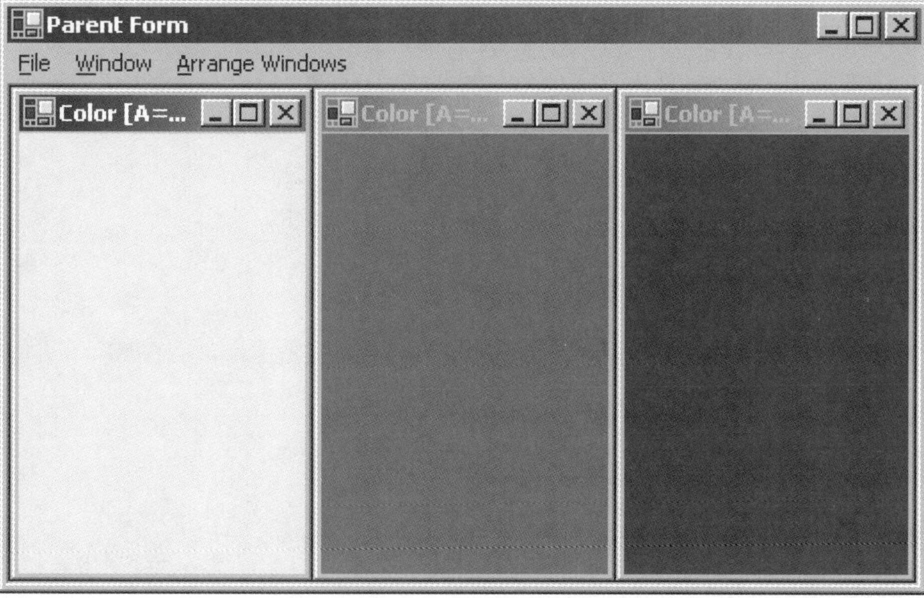

Figure 9-49. Vertically tiling child windows

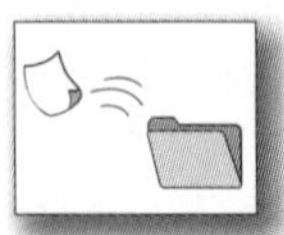

SOURCE CODE *The MDIApp project is included under the Chapter 9 subdirectory.*

Summary

This chapter introduced the fine art of building a user interface with the types contained in the System.Windows.Forms namespace. It began by examining the basic steps you must take to build a custom Form. This entailed a discussion of the Application object and its various members. As you have seen, the Form type gains a majority of its functionality from a rather long chain of base types.

During the course of this chapter, you learned how to build topmost menus (and pop-up menus) and how to respond to a number of menu events. You also came to understand how to further enhance your Form objects using toolbars and status bars. Finally, this chapter provided some bonus information, illustrating how to interact with the system registry and the Windows 2000 Event Viewer, as well as the basic process of building MDI applications.

CHAPTER 10

A Better Painting Framework (GDI+)

THE PREVIOUS CHAPTER introduced you to the fine art of building a traditional main window using various types contained within the System.Windows.Forms namespace. Now that you can assemble a Form to represent the shell of your GUI-based applications, the next task is to learn the details of rendering geometric images (including text and bitmaps) onto the Form's client area.

This chapter begins by taking a high-level overview of the numerous drawing-related namespaces, and examining the process of responding to (and initiating) paint sessions. As well, you will discover various ways of obtaining (and configuring) a Graphics object. Once you understand the general layout of the GDI+ landscape, the remainder of this chapter covers how to manipulate colors, fonts, geometric shapes, and bitmap images. This entails understanding a number of related types such as Brush, Pen, Color, Point, and Rectangle (among others). This chapter also explores a number of GDI+-related programming techniques such as nonrectangular hit testing and GUI drag-and-drop logic.

The chapter concludes by exploring the new .NET resource format, and you learn how to embed your application's external resources into a .NET assembly. During the process, you explore the System.Resources namespace and learn how to perform read/write operations on the underlying *.resx file by hand (and via VS .NET), as well as pull resources from an assembly at runtime using the ResourceManager type.

Remembering the World of VB 6.0 Graphics Programming

Despite the fact that Visual Basic has always been an exceptional tool for building graphical user *interfaces,* the language has lacked support for high-powered graphical *rendering.* In VB 6.0, programmers were provided a limited number of GUI control types (such as the Shape control) as well as a small (rather awkward) set of GDI functions. In addition, previous versions of VB made substantial use of a graphics mode called "twips," whereas most other languages of the world rendered images using the more common "pixel" format. By and large, if you needed to do any sort of advanced rendering operations in VB, you were required to go outside the language to do so (i.e., interact with the Windows API).

Under VB .NET, you are now able to build extremely high-powered drawing-centric applications. In fact, VB .NET programmers are now able to produce graphical applications that are of the same caliber as equivalent projects built using C++. As you may suspect, VB .NET makes use of a number of .NET namespaces to provide programmatic rendering services. The truth of the matter is that none of the old familiar VB 6.0 rendering commands (or controls) has survived in the world of .NET. In their place is a new technology named "GDI+" that is used by all languages targeting .NET. The goal of this chapter is to introduce you to the richness of GDI+. Be aware that this is one area where VB 6.0 and VB .NET differ *markedly.* To begin, let's explore the GDI+-centric namespaces.

Survey of the GDI+ Namespaces

The .NET Framework provides a number of namespaces devoted to two-dimensional graphical rendering. In addition to the basic functionality you would expect to find in a graphics package (color, font, pen, brush, and image manipulation), you also find types that enable geometric transformations, antialiasing, palette blending, and document printing support. Collectively speaking, these namespaces make up the .NET facility called GDI+. Table 10-1 gives a high-level view of each major player.

Table 10-1. The Core GDI+ Namespaces

GDI+NAMESPACE	MEANING IN LIFE
System.Drawing	This is the core GDI+ namespace, which defines numerous types for basic rendering (fonts, pens, basic brushes, and so on) as well as the almighty Graphics type.
System.Drawing.Drawing2D	This namespace offers types used for more advanced two-dimensional graphics functionality (e.g., gradient brushes and geometric transforms).
System.Drawing.Imaging	This namespace defines types that allow you to directly manipulate graphical images (e.g., change the palette, extract image metadata, and manipulate metafiles).
System.Drawing.Printing	This namespace defines types that allow you to render images to the printed page, interact with the printer itself, and format the appearance of a given print job.
System.Drawing.Text	This namespace allows you to manipulate collections of fonts. For example, as you see in this chapter, the FontCollection type allows you to dynamically discover the set of installed fonts on the target machine.

Overview of the System.Drawing Namespace

A vast majority of the types used when programming GDI+ applications are found within the System.Drawing namespace. As you would expect, there are classes that represent images, brushes, pens, and fonts. Furthermore, System.Drawing defines a number of related types such as Color, Point, and Rectangle. Table 10-2 lists some (but not all) of the core types.

Table 10-2. Core Members of the System.Drawing Namespace

SYSTEM.DRAWING TYPE	MEANING IN LIFE
Bitmap	Encapsulates a given image and defines a number of methods to manipulate the underlying graphical data.
Brush Brushes SolidBrush SystemBrushes TextureBrush	Brush objects are used to fill the interiors of graphical shapes such as rectangles, ellipses, and polygons. These types represent a number of brush variations, with Brush functioning as the abstract base class to the remaining types. Additional Brush types are defined in the System.Drawing.Drawing2D namespace.
Color SystemColors ColorTranslator	As you saw in the previous chapter, the Color structure defines a number of fields that can be used to configure the color of fonts, brushes, and pens. The ColorTranslator type allows you to build a new .NET Color type from other color representations (Win32, the OLE_COLOR type, HTML color constants, and so on).
Font FontFamily	The Font type encapsulates the characteristics of a given font (i.e., type name, bold, italic, point size, and so forth). FontFamily provides an abstraction for a group of fonts having a similar generic design but having certain variations in styles.
Graphics	This core class represents a valid drawing surface, as well as a number of methods to render text, images, and geometric patterns. Consider this type the .NET equivalent of a Win32 HDC.
Icon SystemIcons	These classes represent custom icons, as well as the set of standard system-supplied icons.
Image ImageAnimator	Image is an abstract base class that provides functionality for the Bitmap, Icon, and Cursor types. ImageAnimator provides a way to iterate over a number of Image-derived types at some specified interval.

Table 10-2. Core Members of the System.Drawing Namespace (continued)

SYSTEM.DRAWING TYPE	MEANING IN LIFE
Pen Pens SystemPens	Pens are objects used to draw lines and curves. The Pens type defines a number of shared properties that return a new Pen of a given color.
Point PointF	These structures represent an (*x*, *y*) coordinate mapping to an underlying integer or float (respectively).
Rectangle RectangleF	These structures represent a rectangular dimension (again mapping to an underlying integer or float).
Size SizeF	These structures represent a given height/width (again mapping to an underlying integer or float).
StringFormat	This type is used to encapsulate various features of textual layout (i.e., alignment, line spacing, and so on).
Region	Describes the interior of a geometric image composed of rectangles and paths.

Many of these core types make substantial use of a number of related enumerations, most of which are also defined within the System.Drawing namespace. As you can guess, many of these enumerations are used to configure the look and feel of brushes and pens. For example, ponder the types listed in Table 10-3.

Table 10-3. Enumerations in the System.Drawing Namespace

SYSTEM.DRAWING ENUMERATION	MEANING IN LIFE
ContentAlignment	Specifies how to align content on a drawing surface (center, left, right, and so forth)
FontStyle	Specifies style information applied to text (bold, italic, and so on)
GraphicsUnit	Specifies the unit of measure for the given item (much like the Win32 mapping mode constants)
KnownColor	Specifies friendly names for the known system colors
StringAlignment	Specifies the alignment of a text string relative to its layout rectangle
StringFormatFlags	Specifies the display and layout information for text strings (e.g., NoWrap, LineLimit)

Table 10-3. Enumerations in the System.Drawing Namespace (continued)

SYSTEM.DRAWING ENUMERATION	MEANING IN LIFE
StringTrimming	Specifies how to trim characters from a string that does not completely fit into a layout shape
StringUnit	Specifies the units of measure for a text string

If you have a background using graphics toolkits found in other frameworks (especially Java), you should feel right at home with the functionality provided by the System.Drawing namespace. If your background is in VB 6.0 exclusively, be prepared to roll up your sleeves and start coding.

Configuring a GDI+ Project Workspace

When you want to make use of GDI+, you must set a reference to the System.Drawing.dll assembly. This single binary contains types for each of the core GDI+ namespaces. Be aware that if you select a new Windows Application Project Workspace using VS .NET, this reference is set on your behalf automatically. Once you have set this reference, just make use of the VB .NET "Imports" keyword and you are ready to render. To begin the journey, let's examine the utility type defined by the System.Drawing namespace. Then, let's examine the set of basic utility types that are commonly used in GDI+ programming.

Examining the System.Drawing Utility Types

Many of the drawing methods defined by the Graphics object require you to specify the position or area in which you want to render a given item. For example, the DrawString() method requires you to specify the location to render the text string on the Control-derived type. Given that DrawString() has been overloaded a number of times, this positional parameter may be specified using an (x, y) coordinate or the location of a "box" to draw within. Other GDI+ type methods may require you to specify the width and height of a given item or the internal bounds of a geometric image.

To specify such information, the System.Drawing namespace defines the Point, Rectangle, Region, and Size types. Obviously, a Point represents some (x, y) coordinate. Rectangle types capture a pair of points representing the upper-left and bottom-right bounds of a rectangular region. Size types are similar to Rectangles—however, these structures represent a given dimension using a given height and width. Regions provide a way to represent and manipulate nonrectangular drawing surfaces.

The member variables used by the Point, Rectangle, and Size types are internally represented as integer data types. However, if you need a finer level of granularity, you are free to make use of the corresponding PointF, RectangleF, and SizeF types, which (as you might guess) map to an underlying floating point number (representing as a VB .NET Single data type). Regardless of the underlying data representation, each type has an identical set of members. A quick run-through follows.

Point(F) Type

The first utility type you should be aware of is System.Drawing.Point(F). A breakdown of some core members is shown in Table 10-4.

Table 10-4. Members of the Point(F) Types

POINT AND POINTF MEMBER	MEANING IN LIFE
X Y	These properties allow you to get and set the underlying (*x, y*) values.
IsEmpty	This property returns true if *X* and *Y* are both set to 0.
Offset()	This method translates a given Point type by a given amount.

Although this type is most commonly used when working with GDI+ and user interface applications, be aware that you may make use of any utility type from any application. To illustrate, here is a console application that makes use of the System.Drawing.Point type (see Figure 10-1 for output):

```
' Need this to access GDI+ utility types!
Imports System.Drawing
Module Module1
    Sub Main()
        ' Create and offset a point.
        Dim pt As Point = New Point(100, 72)
        System.Console.WriteLine(pt)
        pt.Offset(20, 20)
        System.Console.WriteLine(pt)
        ' Are points equal?
        Dim pt2 As Point = pt
        If pt.Equals(pt2) Then
            Console.WriteLine("Points are the same")
        Else
            Console.WriteLine("Different points")
        End If
```

```
        ' Change pt2's X value.
        pt2.X = 4000
        ' Now show each X:
        Console.WriteLine("First point: {0}", pt.ToString())
        Console.WriteLine("Second point: {0}", pt2.ToString())
    End Sub
End Module
```

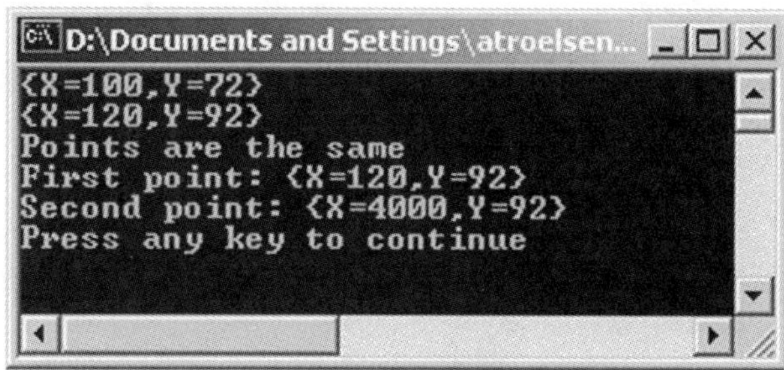

Figure 10-1. Working with basic utility types

Rectangle(F) Type

Rectangles, like Points, are useful in any application (GUI-based or otherwise). Table 10-5 lists some core members to be aware of.

Table 10-5. Members of the Rectangle(F) Types

RECTANGLE AND RECTANGLEF MEMBER	MEANING IN LIFE
Inflate() Intersect() Union()	These shared methods allow you to expand a rectangle, as well as create new rectangles that are a result of an intersection or union operation.
Top Left Bottom Right	These properties set the dimensions of a new Rectangle type.
Height Width	Configures the height and width of a given Rectangle.
Contains()	This method can be used to determine if a given Point (or Rectangle) is within the bounds of the current Rectangle. Great for hit testing a point within a rectangle.
X Y	These properties return the *x* or *y* coordinate of the Rectangle's upper-left corner.

One of the most useful methods of the Rectangle type is Contains(). This method allows you to determine if a given Point or Rectangle is within the current bounds of another Rectangle object. Later in this chapter, you see how to make use of this method to reform hit testing of GDI+ images. Until then, here is a simple example:

```
Module Module1
    Sub Main()
     ...
        Dim r1 As Rectangle = New Rectangle(0, 0, 100, 100)
        Dim pt3 As Point = New Point(101, 101)
        If (r1.Contains(pt3)) Then
            Console.WriteLine("Point is within the rect!")
        Else
            Console.WriteLine("Point is not within the rect!")
        End If
        ' Now place point in rectangle's area.
        pt3.X = 50
        pt3.Y = 30
        If (r1.Contains(pt3)) Then
            Console.WriteLine("Point is within the rect!")
        Else
            Console.WriteLine("Point is not within the rect!")
        End If
    End Sub
End Module
```

Size(F) and Region Types

The Size and SizeF types are quite simple to manipulate and require little comment. Beyond the inherited members, these types each define a small set of members (such as the Height and Width properties).

The Region Class

Finally, you have the Region class. This type represents the interior of a geometric shape. Given this last statement, it should make sense that the constructors of the Region class require you to send an instance of some existing geometric pattern. For example, assume you have created a rectangle 100 x 100 pixels. If you want to gain access to the rectangle's interior region, you could write the following:

```
' Get the interior of this rectangle.
Dim r as Rectangle = New Rectangle(0, 0, 100, 100)
Dim rgn as Region = New Region(r)
```

Once you have the interior dimensions of a given shape (including more complex geometric shapes), you may manipulate the shape using the core members shown in Table 10-6.

Table 10-6. Members of the Region Class

REGION MEMBER	MEANING IN LIFE
Complement()	Updates this Region to the portion of the specified graphics object that does not intersect with this Region.
Exclude()	Updates this Region to the portion of its interior that does not intersect with the specified graphics object.
GetBounds()	Returns a RectangleF that represents a rectangular region that bounds this Region.
Intersect()	Overloaded. Updates this Region to the intersection of itself with the specified graphics object.
IsEmpty() MakeEmpty()	Tests whether this Region has an empty interior on the specified drawing surface (or sets the current Region empty).
IsInfinite() MakeInfinite()	Tests whether this Region has an infinite interior on the specified drawing surface (or sets the current Region infinite).
Transform()	Transforms this Region by the specified Matrix.
Translate()	Offsets the coordinates of this Region by the specified amount.
Union()	Updates this Region to the union of itself and the specified graphics object.
Xor()	Updates this Region to the union minus the intersection of itself with the specified graphics object.

I'm sure you get the general idea behind these coordinate primitives. You have a chance to work with each of them during the course of this chapter (and any time you program against GDI+).

SOURCE CODE *The UtilTypes project is included under the Chapter 10 subdirectory.*

Understanding Paint Sessions

As you saw in the previous chapter, the Control class defines an overridable method named OnPaint(). When a Form (or any descendent of Control) wants to render graphical content, one approach is to override this method and extract a "Graphics" object from the incoming PaintEventArgs parameter (using, of course, the Graphics property):

```
Public Class Form1
    Inherits System.Windows.Forms.Form
    Public Sub New()
        MyBase.New()
        'This call is required by the Windows Form Designer.
        InitializeComponent()
        CenterToScreen()
        Me.Text = "Basic Paint Form (click on me)"
    End Sub
    Protected Overrides Sub OnPaint(ByVal e As _
    System.Windows.Forms.PaintEventArgs)
        Dim g As Graphics = e.Graphics
        ' Render a string directly onto the form using a given font and color.
        g.DrawString("Hello GDI+", New Font("Times New Roman", 20), _
         New SolidBrush(Color.Black), 0, 0)
    End Sub
End Class
```

Recall that when responding to GUI-based events, you actually have two options at your disposal. In this last example, you overrode the OnPaint() method directly. The other approach (the default behavior of VS .NET) is to directly handle the Paint event. Thus, you could retrofit the previous class definition as follows:

```
Public Class Form1
    Inherits System.Windows.Forms.Form
...
    ' Note the signature of the event handler...
    Private Sub Form1_Paint(ByVal sender As Object, _
    ByVal e As System.Windows.Forms.PaintEventArgs) Handles MyBase.Paint
        Dim g As Graphics = e.Graphics
        g.DrawString("Hello GDI+", New Font("Times New Roman", 20), _
            New SolidBrush(Color.Black), 0, 0)
    End Sub
End Class
```

Regardless of how you respond to the Paint event, be aware that whenever a window becomes "dirty," a paint message is placed into the application's message queue. As you may be aware, a window is "dirty" whenever it is resized, covered by another window (partially or completely), or minimized and then restored. Eventually, the flow of logic is routed to the method that handles repainting the window. In these cases, the .NET Framework ensures that when your Form needs to be redrawn, the Paint handler is called automatically.

Invalidating Your Client Area

You may need to explicitly inform a window that it needs to redraw itself (in other words, you need to place a paint message into the message queue programmatically). For example, suppose you have a program that allows the end user to select from a number of bitmap images using a custom dialog box. Once the dialog box is dismissed, you need to draw the newly selected image directly onto the client area (as opposed to placing the image onto a GUI widget). If you wait for the window to become "naturally dirty," the user does not see the change take place until it is resized or covered by another window. When you need to force a window to repaint itself programmatically, call Invalidate(). For example:

```
Public Class Form1
    Inherits System.Windows.Forms.Form
...
    Private Sub Form1_Paint(ByVal sender As Object, _
    ByVal e As System.Windows.Forms.PaintEventArgs) Handles MyBase.Paint
          Dim g as Graphics = e.Graphics
          ' Logic to render a bitmap onto the form...
     End Sub
     Private Sub GetNewBitmap()
          ' Show dialog and get new image...
          ' Now repaint the client area.
          Invalidate()
     End Sub
End Class
```

Be aware that the Invalidate() method has been overloaded to allow you to specify a specific rectangular region to repaint, rather than the entire client area (which is the default). If you only want to update the extreme upper-left rectangle of the client area, you could write the following:

```
' Repaint a given rectangular area of the Form.
Private Sub UpdateUpperArea()
```

```
    Dim myRect as Rectangle = New Rectangle(0, 0, 75, 150)
    Invalidate(myRect)
End Sub
```

Rendering GDI+ Objects Outside Paint Handlers

On a related note, you may find yourself in the position of needing to render some image *outside* the scope of a standard Paint event handler. For example, assume you wish to draw a small circle at the (*x*, *y*) position where the mouse has been clicked. The first step (of course) is to obtain a valid Graphics object, which can be obtained using the shared Graphics.FromHwnd() method. Notice that you are passing your current Handle as the sole parameter (recall that the Handle property is inherited from the Control class):

```
Private Sub Form1_MouseDown(ByVal sender As Object, _
ByVal e As System.Windows.Forms.MouseEventArgs) _
Handles MyBase.MouseDown
    ' Grab a new Graphics object.
    Dim g As Graphics = Graphics.FromHwnd(Me.Handle)
    ' Now draw a 10*10 circle at mouse click.
    g.DrawEllipse(New Pen(Color.Green), e.X, e.Y, 10, 10)
End Sub
```

Now, while this logic renders a circle outside an OnPaint() event handler, it is very important to understand that if the form is invalidated (and thus redrawn), *each of the circles is erased.* This should make sense, given that this rendering only happens within the context of a mouse click.

A better approach is to have the MouseUp logic add a new Point to an internal collection (such as an ArrayList) of Point types followed by a call to Invalidate(). At this point, the OnPaint() method can simply iterate over the collection and draw each item:

```
Public Class Form1
    Inherits System.Windows.Forms.Form
    ' Used to hold all the points.
    Private myPts As ArrayList = New ArrayList()      ...
...
    Private Sub Form1_MouseDown(ByVal sender As Object, _
    ByVal e As System.Windows.Forms.MouseEventArgs) _
    Handles MyBase.MouseDown
        ' Grab a new Graphics object.
        ' Dim g As Graphics = Graphics.FromHwnd(Me.Handle)
```

```
        ' Now draw a 10*10 circle at mouse click.
        ' g.DrawEllipse(New Pen(Color.Green), e.X, e.Y, 10, 10)
        ' Add to points collection.
        myPts.Add(New Point(e.X, e.Y))
        Invalidate()
    End Sub
    Private Sub Form1_Paint(ByVal sender As Object, _
    ByVal e As System.Windows.Forms.PaintEventArgs) _
    Handles MyBase.Paint
        Dim g As Graphics = e.Graphics
        g.DrawString("Hello GDI+", New Font("Times New Roman", 20), _
        New SolidBrush(Color.Black), 0, 0)
        ' Draw each Point in the array list.
        Dim p As Point
        For Each p In myPts
            g.DrawEllipse(New Pen(Color.Green), p.X, p.Y, 10, 10)
        Next
    End Sub
End Class
```

In any case, realize that the Graphics.FromHwnd() method provides a handy way to obtain a Graphics object outside of a registered paint handler. Figure 10-2 shows a test run of this initial GDI+ application.

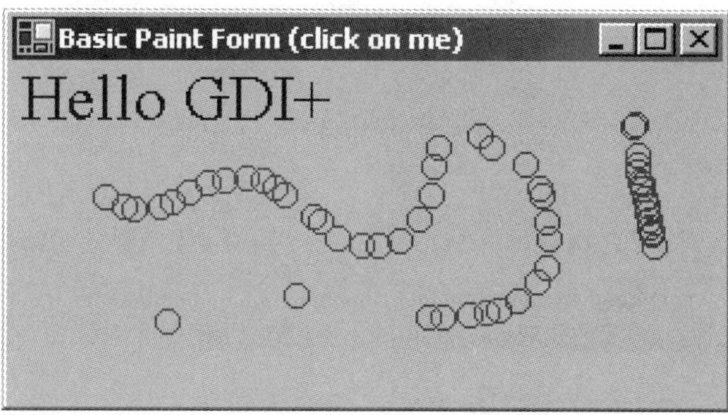

Figure 10-2. A basic GDI+ application

SOURCE CODE *The BasicPaintForm project is included under the Chapter 10 subdirectory.*

Understanding the Graphics Class

Now that you know how to obtain a Graphics object, you need to understand exactly how to manipulate it. The System.Drawing.Graphics object is your gateway to GDI+ rendering functionality. This class represents a valid device context (e.g., a raw Win32 HDC) coupled with a slew of methods that allow you to render text, images (icons, bitmaps, and so on), as well as various geometric patterns. Table 10-7 gives a partial list of intriguing members.

Table 10-7. Members of the Graphics Class

GRAPHICS METHODS	MEANING IN LIFE
FromHdc() FromHwnd() FromImage()	These shared methods provide a way to obtain a valid Graphics object from a given image (e.g., icon, bitmap, and so on) or GUI widget.
Clear()	Fills a Graphics object with a specified color, erasing the current drawing surface in the process.
DrawArc() DrawBezier() DrawBeziers() DrawCurve() DrawEllipse() DrawIcon() DrawLine() DrawLines() DrawPie() DrawPath() DrawRectangle() DrawRectangles() DrawString()	These methods (among others) are used to render a given image or geometric pattern.
FillEllipse() FillPath() FillPie() FillPolygon() FillRectangle()	These methods (among others) are used to fill the interior of a given geometric shape.
MeasureString()	Returns a Size structure that represents the bounds of a given block of text.

As well as providing a number of rendering methods, the Graphics class defines additional members that encapsulate details regarding how the current rendering operation will look and feel. In more concrete terms, the Graphics type allows you to configure the state of the Graphics object using the property set in Table 10-8.

Table 10-8. Stateful Properties of the Graphics Class

GRAPHICS PROPERTY	MEANING IN LIFE
Clip ClipBounds VisibleClipBounds IsClipEmpty IsVisibleClipEmpty	These properties allow you to set the clipping options used with the current Graphics object.
Transform	Allows you to transform "world coordinates" (more on this later).
PageUnit PageScale DpiX DpiY	These properties allow you to configure the point of origin for your rendering operations, as well as configure the unit of measurement.
SmoothingMode PixelOffsetMode TextRenderingHint	These properties allow you to configure the smoothness of geometric objects and text. These are set with corresponding enumerations defined in the System.Drawing and System.Drawing.Drawing2D namespaces.
CompositingMode CompositingQuality	The CompositingMode property determines whether drawing overwrites the background or is blended with the background. The value is set with the corresponding CompositingMode enumeration defined in the System.Drawing.Drawing2D namespace. The CompositingQuality property specifies the complexity of the blending process. It makes use of the CompositingQuality enumeration, which is also in System.Drawing.Drawing2D.
InterpolationMode	Specifies how data is interpolated between endpoints using a related enumeration.

During the course of this chapter you configure a number of these state properties.

Default GDI+ Coordinate System

Before you learn the ins and outs of rendering GDI+ objects, you need a bit of background regarding the underlying coordinate system. Like the raw Win32 API, GDI+ allows you to choose from a variety of coordinate systems. Unlike VB 6.0, the default unit of measurement of GDI+ is *pixel*-based (not twips). The point of origin is the upper-left corner, with the *x*-axis increasing to the right and the *y*-axis increasing downward, as shown in Figure 10-3.

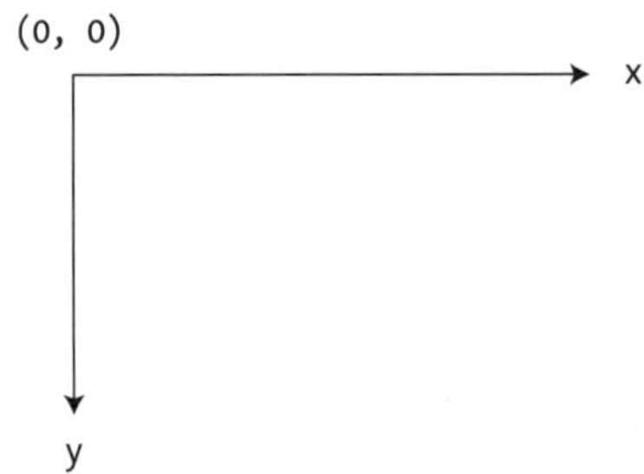

Figure 10-3. The default coordinate system

For example, if you render a Rectangle as follows:

```
Private Sub Form1_Paint(ByVal sender As Object, _
ByVal e As System.Windows.Forms.PaintEventArgs) _
Handles MyBase.Paint
        ' Draw a rectangle using the default coordinate system.
        e.Graphics.DrawRectangle(New Pen(Color.Red, 5), 10, 10, 100, 100)
End Sub
```

you see a square rendered 10 pixels down and in from the top-left client edge, which spans 90 pixels in both directions (see Figure 10-4).

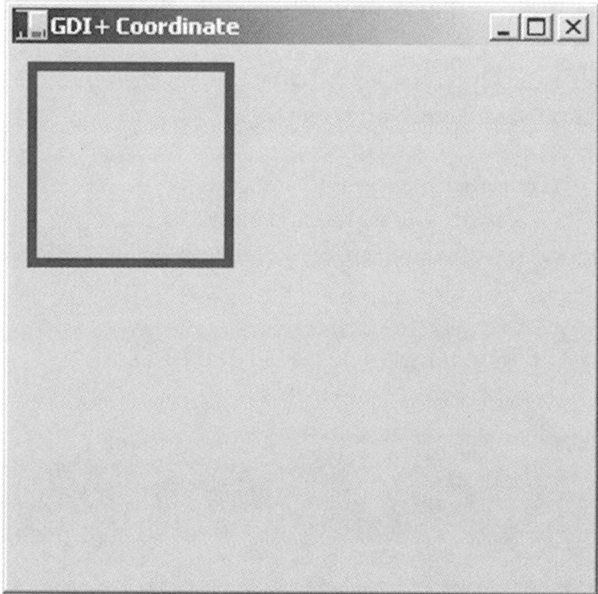

Figure 10-4. Pixel-based rendering

The default GDI+ coordinate system will most likely be your mapping mode of choice. However, like most things in the .NET Framework, you are able to configure the GDI+ mapping mode to your liking should the need arise.

Specifying an Alternative Unit of Measurement

As described in the previous section, the default graphics unit is the pixel. However, you are able to change this default by setting the PageUnit property of the Graphics object. The PageUnit property can be assigned any member of the GraphicsUnit enumeration (see Table 10-9).

Table 10-9. The GraphicsUnit Enumeration

GRAPHICSUNIT ENUMERATION VALUE	DESCRIPTION
Display	Specifies 1/75 inch as the unit of measure.
Document	Specifies the document unit (1/300 inch) as the unit of measure.
Inch	Specifies the inch as the unit of measure.
Millimeter	Specifies the millimeter as the unit of measure.
Pixel	Specifies a device pixel as the unit of measure.
Point	Specifies a printer's point (1/72 inch) as the unit of measure.

For example, if you update your previous rendering code as follows:

```
Private Sub Form1_Paint(ByVal sender As Object, _
ByVal e As System.Windows.Forms.PaintEventArgs) _
Handles MyBase.Paint
        ' Draw a rectangle in inches. . .not pixels.
        e.Graphics.PageUnit = GraphicsUnit.Inch
        e.Graphics.DrawRectangle(New Pen(Color.Red, 5), 0, 0, 100, 100)
End Sub
```

you find a *radically* different rectangle (see Figure 10-5).

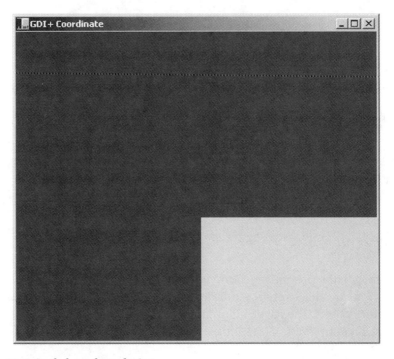

Figure 10-5. Inch-based rendering

The reason that 85 percent (or so) of the Form's client area is now bright red (as you see when you run the application) is a result of the fact that you configured a Pen with a 5-inch nib. The rectangle itself is now 100 x 100 *inches* in size! In fact, the small gray box you see in the lower-right corner is the upper-left interior of the rectangle.

Specifying an Alternative Point of Origin

Recall that when you make use of the default mapping mode, point (0, 0) is at the extreme upper-left of the client area. Again, this is typically what you want. However, what if you want to alter the location where rendering begins? For example, assume that your application always needs to reserve a 100-pixel boundary around the Form's client area (for whatever reason). You need to ensure that all GDI+ operations take place somewhere within this internal region.

One approach you could take is to offset all your rendering code manually. This, of course, is a huge bother. It would be far better (and simpler) if you could set a property that says in effect "Although *I* might say render a rectangle with a point of origin at (0, 0), make sure *you* begin at point (100, 100)." This would simplify your life a great deal, as you could continue to specify your plotting points without modification.

In GDI+, you can adjust the point of origin by setting the transformation value using the TranslateTransform() method of the Graphics class. For example, the following code allows you to keep your logical mapping at (0, 0) while modifying the device view to begin at (100, 100):

```
Private Sub Form1_Paint(ByVal sender As Object, _
ByVal e As System.Windows.Forms.PaintEventArgs) _
Handles MyBase.Paint
    ' Configure graphics unit.
    e.Graphics.PageUnit = GraphicsUnit.Point
    ' Configure device origin to (100, 100).
    e.Graphics.TranslateTransform(100, 100)
    ' World origin is still (0, 0).
    e.Graphics.DrawRectangle(New Pen(Color.Red, 1), 0, 0,100, 100)
End Sub
```

To help you experiment with some of the ways to alter the default GDI+ coordinate system, the companion code contains a sample application named (of course) CoorSystem. Using two topmost menu items, you are able to alter the point of origin as well as the unit of measurement. Figure 10-6 presents an example.

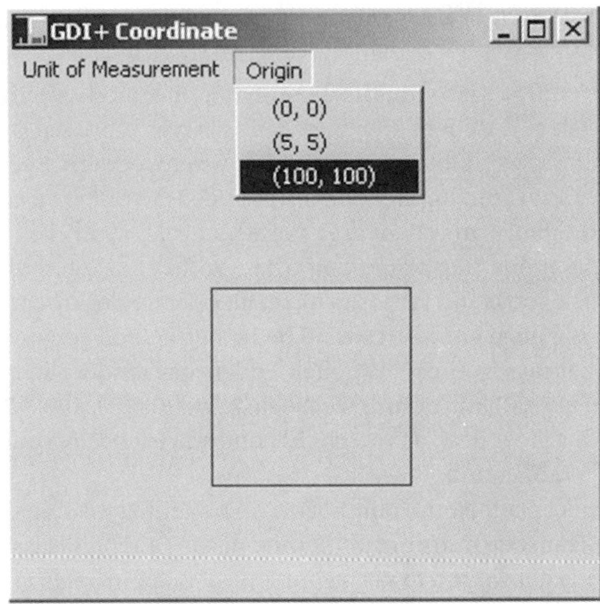

Figure 10-6. The coordinate test application

The next order of business is to examine more details of GDI+ color manipulation.

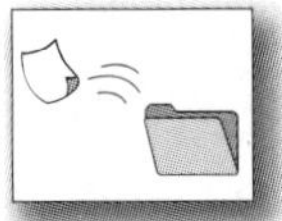

SOURCE CODE *The CoorSystem project is located under the Chapter 10 subdirectory.*

Establishing an Active Color

Many of the rendering methods defined by the Graphics class require you to specify the color that should be used during the drawing process. The Color structure represents an alpha-red-green-blue (ARGB) color constant. Most of the Color type's functionality comes by way of a number of shared properties, which return a new (correctly configured) Color type:

```
' One of many predefined colors. . .
Color c = Color.PapayaWhip
```

As shown in Table 10-9, there are other ways you can create a Color type. Regardless of the method you use, you are then able to extract relevant information using any of the members listed in Table 10-10.

Table 10-10. Members of the Color Type

COLOR MEMBER	MEANING IN LIFE
FromArgb()	Returns a new Color object based on numerical red, green, and blue values.
FromKnownColor()	Returns a new Color object based on a member of the KnownColor enumeration.
FromName()	Returns a new Color object based on a string name (e.g., "Red").
A, R, G, B	These properties return the value assigned to the alpha, red, green, and blue aspect of a Color object.
IsNamedColor() Name	These members can be applied to a Color object to determine if the current ARGB values have a predefined name (e.g., "Red") and, if so, retrieve it via the Name property.
GetBrightness() GetHue() GetSaturation()	GDI+ Color types have an associated Hue-Saturation-Brightness (HSB) value. These methods retrieve the specifics.
ToArgb() ToKnownColor()	Returns the ARGB value of the Color type or the KnownColor enumeration value based on a valid Color object.

Examining the ColorDialog Class

On a related note, the System.Windows.Forms namespace provides a predefined dialog box class (ColorDialog) that can be used to prompt the end user for his or her color selection (see Figure 10-7). Note that the RGB and HSB values can be adjusted using a slider control or directly via a given edit field.

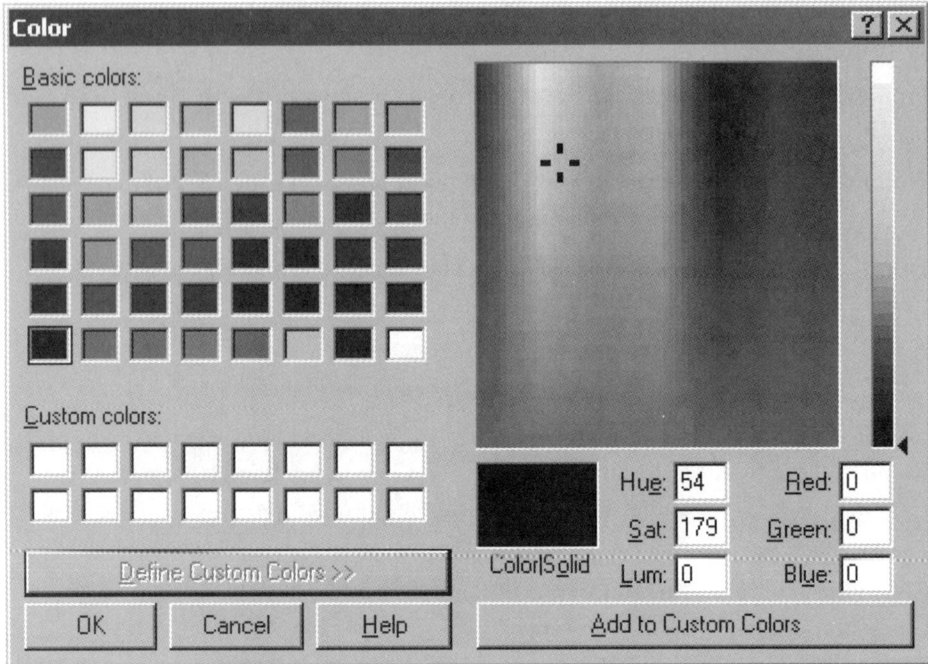

Figure 10-7. The canned Color dialog box

Working with this dialog box is simple given that is it more or less identical to the CommonDialogControl. From a valid instance of the ColorDialog type, call ShowDialog() to display the dialog box modally. Once the user has closed the dialog box, you can extract the corresponding Color object using the ColorDialog.Color property.

For example, assume you want to allow the user to configure the background color of the client area using the ColorDialog. To keep things simple, assume that when the user clicks anywhere on the client area, you show the ColorDialog object and act accordingly. Here is the code:

```
Public Class Form1
    Inherits System.Windows.Forms.Form
    ' Hold onto current color
    Private colorDlg As ColorDialog
    Private currColor As Color
    Public Sub New()
    . . .
        colorDlg = New System.Windows.Forms.ColorDialog()
        colorDlg.AnyColor = True
        colorDlg.ShowHelp = True
```

```
        Text = "Click on me to change the Color"
        currColor = Color.BlueViolet
    End Sub
...
    Private Sub Form1_MouseUp(ByVal sender As Object, _
    ByVal e As System.Windows.Forms.MouseEventArgs) _
    Handles MyBase.MouseUp
        If (colorDlg.ShowDialog() <> DialogResult.Cancel) Then
            currColor = colorDlg.Color
            Me.BackColor = currColor
            ' Show current color.
            Dim strARGB As String = colorDlg.Color.ToString()
            MessageBox.Show(strARGB, "Color is:")
        End If
    End Sub
End Class
```

Figure 10-8 shows a test run.

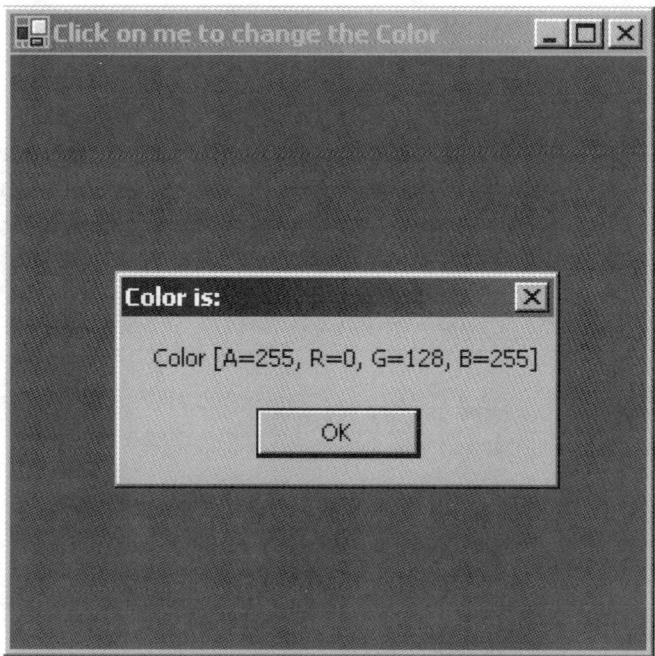

Figure 10-8. Reading ARGB values

Although there has not yet been a formal discussion of how to manipulate dialog boxes, the previous code should not raise too many eyebrows. Notice that you are able to determine which button has been clicked (OK or Cancel) by testing the return value of ShowDialog() against the DialogResult enumeration. You see additional stock dialog boxes used in this chapter. Later, in Chapter 11, you learn how to build custom dialog boxes to gather (and validate) user input.

SOURCE CODE *The ColorDlg application is included under the Chapter 10 subdirectory.*

Manipulating Fonts

Although you have been rendering text since Chapter 9, you have yet to examine the specifics of the Font class (and related types). The System.Drawing.Font type represents a given font installed on the user's machine. While the Font class defines a number of overloaded constructors, here are some common options:

```
' Create a Font of a given type, name, and size.
Dim f as Font= New Font("Times New Roman", 12)

' Create a Font with a given name, size, and style set.
Dim f2 as Font = New Font("WingDings", 50, FontStyle.Bold Or _
FontStyle.Underline)
```

Here, f2 has been created using a set of FontStyle flags. The members of this enumeration allow you to configure a number of properties of the Font object such as bold or italic (if you require more than one FontStyle, simply OR each item together). Table 10-11 lists your choices.

Table 10-11. The FontStyle Enumeration

FONTSTYLE ENUMERATION MEMBER	MEANING IN LIFE
Bold	Bold text
Italic	Italic text
Regular	Normal text
Strikeout	Text with a line through the middle
Underline	Underlined text

Once you have configured the look and feel of your Font object, the next obvious task is to pass it as a parameter to the Graphics.DrawString() method. Although DrawString() has also been overloaded a number of times, each variation typically requires the same basic information: a string to draw, the font to draw it in, a brush used for rendering, and a location to place it. For example:

```
' Sub DrawString(String, Font, Brush, Point)
g.DrawString("My string", New Font("Pop", 25), _
              New SolidBrush(Color.Black), New Point(0,0))

' Sub DrawString(String, Font, Brush, Single, Single)
g.DrawString("Another string", New Font("Times New Roman", 16), _
              New SolidBrush(Color.Red), 40, 40)
```

In each of these examples, you made use of a SolidBrush type (of a particular color). However, it is possible to configure a number of brush types. For the time being, a solid brush fits the bill (you see more exotic brush types a bit later in this chapter).

Once you have created a valid Font type, you are able to extract its current settings using a number of properties (e.g., Bold, Italic, Unit, Height, Size, and FontFamily).

Understanding Font Metrics

If you have not worked with Fonts using this level of detail before, here are a few words regarding character measurements. The dimensions of a given Font are all based on the baseline value, which is the imaginary line on which each character "sits." Some characters (such as "j," "y," or "g") have a portion that drops below this baseline. This is called the *descending value.* The *ascending value* represents the amount a given character rises above the baseline. The *leading value* represents the difference between the height and ascent, where height is the total distance between the leading and descending values.

To keep all this information fixed in your mind, ponder Figure 10-9 (the baseline is identified by the thick line toward the bottom).

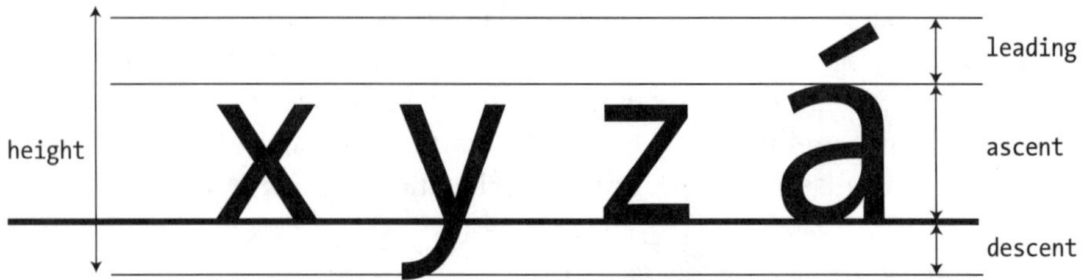

Figure 10-9. The anatomy of a font

Working with Font Families

The System.Drawing namespace also defines the FontFamily type, which abstracts a group of typefaces with a similar basic design but with certain style variations (such as point size). A family of fonts, like Verdana, can include several fonts that differ in style and size. For example, Verdana 12-point bold and Verdana 24-point italic are different fonts in the Verdana font family.

The constructor of the FontFamily type takes a string representing the name of the font family you are attempting to capture. Once you create the generic family, you are then able to create a more specific Font object:

```
' Make a family of fonts.
Dim myFamily As System.Drawing.FontFamily = _
    New System.Drawing.FontFamily("Verdana")
' Pass family into ctor of Font.
Dim myFont As Font = New Font(myFamily, 12)
e.Graphics.DrawString("Hello?", myFont, Brushes.Blue, 10, 10)
```

Of greater interest is the ability to gather various statistics regarding a given family of fonts. For example, say you are building a text-processing application and you want to determine the average width of a character in a particular FontFamily. What if you want to understand the ascending and descending values for a given character? To answer such questions, the FontFamily type defines the members shown in Table 10-12. Note that each requires you to specify the font style using the FontStyle enumeration.

Table 10-12. Members of the FontFamily Type

FONTFAMILY MEMBER	MEANING IN LIFE
GetCellAscent()	Returns the ascender metric for the members in this family
GetCellDescent()	Returns the descender metric for members in this family
GetEmHeight()	Gets the size of the em square for the specified style
GetLineSpacing()	Returns the distance between two consecutive lines of text for this FontFamily with the specified FontStyle
GetName()	Returns the name of this FontFamily in the specified language
IsStyleAvailable()	Indicates if the specified FontStyle is available

To illustrate, here is a Paint handler that prints a number of characteristics of the Verdana font family:

```
Private Sub Form1_Paint(ByVal sender As Object, _
    ByVal e As PaintEventArgs) _
    Handles MyBase.Paint
    Dim g As Graphics = e.Graphics
    Dim myFamily As System.Drawing.FontFamily = New _
    System.Drawing.FontFamily("Verdana")
    Dim myFont As Font = New Font(myFamily, 12)
    Dim y As Integer    ' Y offset.
    Dim fontHeight As Integer = myFont.Height
    ' Show units of measurement.
    Me.Text = "Measurements are in GraphicsUnit." & myFont.Unit.ToString()
    g.DrawString("The Verdana family.", myFont, Brushes.Blue, 10, y)
    y += 20
    ' Print our Family ties. . .
    g.DrawString("Ascent for bold Verdana: " & _
    myFamily.GetCellAscent(FontStyle.Bold), _
    myFont, Brushes.Black, 10, y + fontHeight)
    y += 20
    g.DrawString("Descent for bold Verdana: " _
    & myFamily.GetCellDescent(FontStyle.Bold), _
    myFont, Brushes.Black, 10, y + fontHeight)
    y += 20
    g.DrawString("Line spacing for bold Verdana: " _
    & myFamily.GetLineSpacing(FontStyle.Bold), _
    myFont, Brushes.Black, 10, y + fontHeight)
    y += 20
```

```
    g.DrawString("Height for bold Verdana: " _
    & myFamily.GetEmHeight(FontStyle.Bold), _
    myFont, Brushes.Black, 10, y + fontHeight)
    y += 20
End Sub
```

Figure 10-10 shows the result. Note that these members of the FontFamily type return values using GraphicsUnit.Point (not Pixel) as the unit of measurement, which corresponds to 1/72 inch. You are free to transform these values to other units of measurement as you see fit.

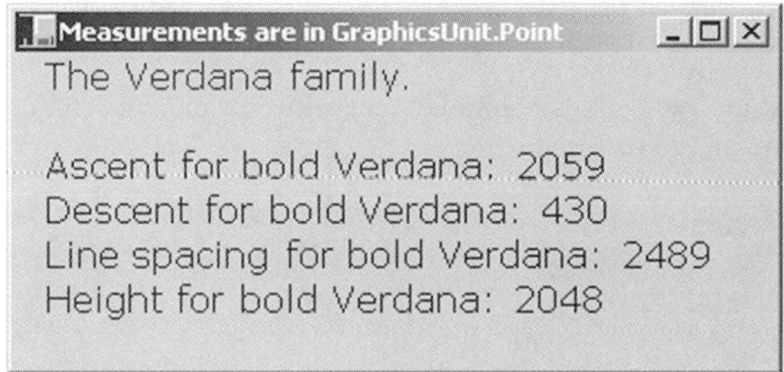

Figure 10-10. Font matrix

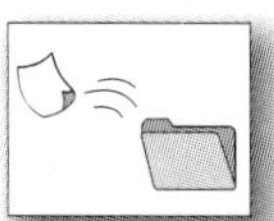

SOURCE CODE *The FontFamily application is included under the Chapter 10 subdirectory.*

Building a Font Application

Now let's build a more complex application that allows the end user to manipulate a Font object. The application will allow the user to select the current font face using the "Configure | Font Face" menu selection. Figure 10-11 shows the layout.

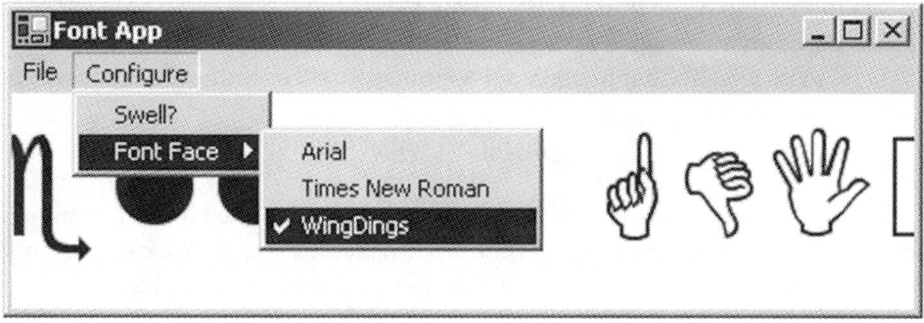

Figure 10-11. The menu system of the Font App

You allow the user to indirectly control the size of the Font object using a Windows Forms Timer object. If the user activates the Timer using the "Configure | Swell?" menu item, the size of the Font object increases at regular intervals (checking for a maximum upper limit) using a Timer object. In this way, the text appears to swell and thus provides a simple animation cycle of "breathing" text.

To begin, you need to derive a new class from System.Windows.Forms.Form. Next, you need some data members to represent your Timer object, the current font face, and an integer (swellValue) to hold the amount to adjust the font size:

```
Public Class Form1
    Inherits System.Windows.Forms.Form
    Private WithEvents theTimer As Timer
    Private swellValue As Integer
    Private fontFace As String = "WingDings"' Default font face.
...
     Public Sub New()
        MyBase.New()
        'This call is required by the Windows Form Designer.
        InitializeComponent()
        theTimer = New Timer()
        Text = "Font App"
        Width = 425
        Height = 150
        BackColor = Color.Honeydew
        CenterToScreen()
        ' Configure timer.
        theTimer.Enabled = True
        theTimer.Interval = 100
    End Sub
End Class
```

In this example, the InitializeComponent() method is used to create and attach the main menu system. The code behind this method is standard menu logic (as described in Chapter 9), and I assume you will examine the companion code for complete details.

Of greater importance is the manipulation of the Timer object. You also saw the use of this type in Chapter 9.

In the Tick event handler, increase the value of the swellValue data member, and refresh your client area. Recall that the swellValue value is added to the current font size to provide a simple animation (notice the swellValue has a maximum upper limit of 50). In order to help reduce the flicker that can occur when redrawing the entire client area, you only refresh the minimum dirty rectangular region:

```
Private Sub theTimer_Tick(ByVal sender As Object, ByVal e As System.EventArgs) _
Handles theTimer.Tick
    ' Increase swellValue by 5 and check
    ' for wrap around.
    swellValue += 5
    If swellValue >= 50 Then
        swellValue = 0
    End If
    'Just invalidate the "minimal dirty rectangle" to help reduce flicker.
    Invalidate(New Rectangle(0, 0, ClientRectangle.Width, 100))
End Sub
```

Now that the upper 100 pixels of your client area are refreshed with each tick of the Timer, you had better have something to render! In the Form's Paint handler, create a Font object based on the user-defined font face (as selected from the appropriate menu item) and current swellValue (as dictated by the timer). Once you have your Font object fully configured, render a message into the center of the dirty rectangle:

```
Private Sub Form1_Paint(ByVal sender As Object, ByVal e As PaintEventArgs) _
Handles MyBase.Paint
    Dim g As Graphics = e.Graphics
    ' The font size can be between 12 and 62,
    ' based on the current swellValue.
    Dim theFont As Font = New Font(fontFace, 12 + swellValue)
    Dim message As String = "Hello GDI+"
    ' Display message in the center of the window!
    Dim windowCenter As Double = Me.DisplayRectangle.Width / 2
    Dim stringSize As SizeF = e.Graphics.MeasureString(message, theFont)
    Dim startPos As Double = windowCenter - (stringSize.Width / 2)
```

```
    g.DrawString(message, theFont, _
         New SolidBrush(Color.Blue), startPos, 10)
End Sub
```

The remaining logic of the Form class that deserves comment is the menu handler for the Swell menu item. If the user wants to stop or start the swelling of the text (i.e., enable or disable the animation), you must configure the Clicked handler to enable or disable the Timer as follows:

```
Private Sub mnuConfigSwell_Click(ByVal sender As Object, _
ByVal e As System.EventArgs) _
Handles mnuConfigSwell.Click
    ' Enable / disable time and check menu.
    theTimer.Enabled = Not theTimer.Enabled
    mainMenu.MenuItems(1).MenuItems(0).Checked = theTimer.Enabled
End Sub
```

Enumerating Installed Fonts (System.Drawing.Text)

Next, let's expand FontApp to programmatically discover the set of installed fonts on the target machine. Doing so gives you a chance to explore another namespace of GDI+: System.Drawing.Text. This namespace contains a handful of useful types that you can use to discover and manipulate the set of fonts installed on the user's machine. The highlights are shown in Table 10-13.

Table 10-13. The Text Type

SYSTEM.DRAWING.TEXT TYPE	MEANING IN LIFE
InstalledFontCollection	Represents the set of all fonts installed on the target system.
PrivateFontCollection	Encapsulates a collection of specific Font types.
LineSpacing	This enumeration specifies the spacing between lines of text in a text string that spans more than a single line.
TextRenderingHint	Another enumeration that allows you to specify the quality of the current text-rendering operation. For example, the Text value represents a fast (but low quality) rendering. AntiAliased marks better quality but a slower rendering cycle.

To illustrate, assume your current application has an additional menu item named "List Installed Fonts" (see Figure 10-12).

Figure 10-12. Enumerating all installed fonts

When the user selects this menu item, the corresponding Clicked handler creates an instance of the InstalledFontCollection class. This class maintains an array named FontFamily, which represents the set of all fonts on the target machine and may be obtained using the InstalledFontCollection.Families property. Using the FontFamily.Name property, you are able to extract the font face (e.g., Times New Roman, Arial, and so on) for each font.

Here, you have added a private string data member named installedFonts to hold each font face. The logic in the "List Installed Fonts" menu handler creates an instance of the InstalledFontCollection type, reads the name of each string, and adds the new font face to the private installedFonts data member:

```
Imports System.Drawing.Text
Public Class Form1
    Inherits System.Windows.Forms.Form
...
    Private installedFonts As String

    ' Menu handler to get the list of installed fonts.
    Private Sub ListFonts_Click(ByVal sender As Object, _
    ByVal e As System.EventArgs) Handles ListFonts.Click
        Dim fonts As InstalledFontCollection = New InstalledFontCollection()
        Dim i As Integer
        For i = 0 To fonts.Families.Length - 1
            installedFonts += fonts.Families(i).Name & "  "
        Next
        ' This time, you need to invalidate the entire client area,
        ' as you will paint the installedFonts string on the lower half
```

```
        ' of the client rectangle.
        Invalidate()
    End Sub
End Class
```

The final task is to render the installedFonts string to the client area, directly below the screen real estate that is used for your swelling text:

```
Private Sub Form1_Paint(ByVal sender As Object, _
ByVal e As System.Windows.Forms.PaintEventArgs) Handles MyBase.Paint
     Dim g As Graphics = e.Graphics
     ' The font size can be between 12 and 62,
     ' based on the current swellValue.
     Dim theFont As Font = New Font(fontFace, 12 + swellValue)
     Dim message As String = "Hello GDI+"
     ' Display message in the center of the window!
     Dim windowCenter As Double = Me.DisplayRectangle.Width / 2
     Dim stringSize As SizeF = e.Graphics.MeasureString(message, theFont)
     Dim startPos As Double = windowCenter - (stringSize.Width / 2)
     g.DrawString(message, theFont, _
     New SolidBrush(Color.Blue), startPos, 10)
     ' Show installed fonts.
     Dim myRect As RectangleF = New RectangleF(0, 100, _
     ClientRectangle.Width, ClientRectangle.Height)
     g.FillRectangle(New SolidBrush(Color.Black), myRect)
     g.DrawString(installedFonts, New Font("Arial", 12), _
     New SolidBrush(Color.White), myRect)
End Sub
```

Recall that the size of the "dirty rectangle" has been mapped to the upper 100 pixels of the client rectangle. Because your Tick handler only invalidates a portion of the Form, the remaining area is not redrawn when the Tick event has been fired (to help optimize the rendering of the client area).

As a final touch to ensure proper redrawing, handle the Resize event to make sure that if the user resizes the Form, the lower part of client rectangle is redrawn correctly:

```
Private Sub Form1_Resize(ByVal sender As Object, ByVal e As System.EventArgs) _
    Handles MyBase.Resize
        Dim myRect As Rectangle = New Rectangle(0, 100, _
            ClientRectangle.Width, ClientRectangle.Height)
    Invalidate(myRect)
End Sub
```

With that, Figure 10-13 shows the final result.

Figure 10-13. Displaying all installed fonts

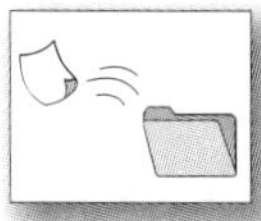

SOURCE CODE *The FontApp application is included under the Chapter 10 subdirectory.*

The FontDialog Class

As you might assume, there is a default font dialog box (FontDialog), which is shown in Figure 10-14.

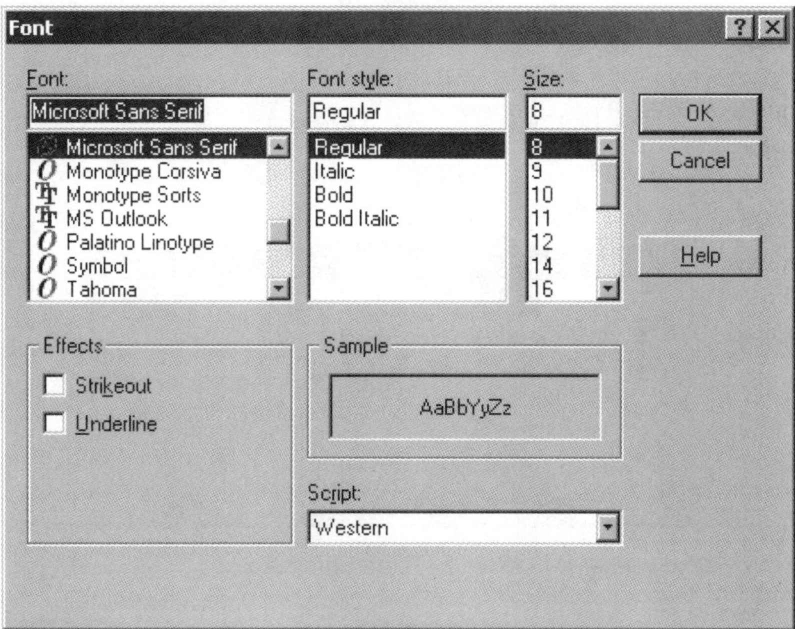

Figure 10-14. The canned Font dialog box

As with the ColorDialog type examined earlier in this chapter, when you want to work with the FontDialog, simply call the ShowDialog() method (as in VB 6.0). Using the Font property, you may extract the characteristics of the current selection for use in the application. To illustrate, here is a new Form that mimics the logic of the previous ColorDlgForm (i.e., click the form to launch the File dialog box). Figure 10-15 shows the output.

```
Public Class Form1
    Inherits System.Windows.Forms.Form
    Private fontDlg As New FontDialog
    Private currFont As Font
...
    Private Sub Form1_Paint(ByVal sender As Object, ByVal e As PaintEventArgs) _
    Handles MyBase.Paint
        Dim g As Graphics = e.Graphics
        g.DrawString("Testing. . .", currFont, _
         New SolidBrush(Color.Black), 0, 0)
    End Sub
    Private Sub Form1_MouseUp(ByVal sender As Object, ByVal e As _
    MouseEventArgs) Handles MyBase.MouseUp
        If (fontDlg.ShowDialog() <> DialogResult.Cancel) Then
```

```
                currFont = fontDlg.Font
                Invalidate()
            End If
        End Sub
    End Class
```

Figure 10-15. Extracting data from the Font dialog box

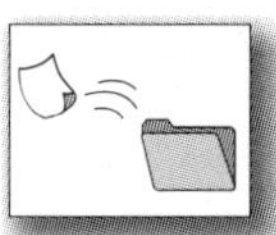

SOURCE CODE *The FontDlgForm application is included under the Chapter 10 subdirectory.*

Survey of the System.Drawing.Drawing2D Namespace

Your next task is to examine how to manipulate Pen and Brush objects to render geometric patterns. While you could do so making use of nothing more than the types found in the System.Drawing namespace, you should be aware that many of the more "sexy" pen and brush configurations (for example, gradient brushes) require types defined within the System.Drawing.Drawing2D namespace.

This additional GDI+ namespace (which is substantially smaller than System.Drawing) provides a number of classes that allow you to modify the line cap (triangle, diamond, and so on) used for a given pen, build textured brushes, and work with vector graphic manipulations. Some core types to be aware of are shown in Table 10-14, grouped by related functionality.

Table 10-14. The Classes of System.Drawing.Drawing2D

SYSTEM.DRAWING.DRAWING2D CLASS	MEANING IN LIFE
AdjustableArrowCap CustomLineCap	Pen caps are used to paint the beginning and end points of a given line. These types represent adjustable arrow-shaped and user-defined caps.
Blend ColorBlend	Used to define a blend pattern (and colors) used in conjunction with a LinearGradientBrush.
GraphicsPath GraphicsPathIterator PathData	A GraphicsPath object represents a series of connected lines and curves. This class allows you to insert just about any type of geometrical pattern (arcs, rectangles, lines, strings, polygons, and so on) into the path. PathData holds the graphical data that makes up a path.
HatchBrush LinearGradientBrush PathGradientBrush	Exotic brush types.

Also be aware that the System.Drawing.Drawing2D namespace defines another set of enumerations that are used in conjunction with these core types. Table 10-15 gives a quick rundown.

Table 10-15. The Enumerations of System.Drawing.Drawing2D

SYSTEM.DRAWING.DRAWING2D ENUMERATION	MEANING IN LIFE
DashStyle	Specifies the style of dashed lines drawn with a Pen
FillMode	Specifies how the interior of a closed path is filled
HatchStyle	Specifies the different patterns available for HatchBrush objects
LinearGradientMode	Specifies the direction to apply a linear gradient
LineCap	Specifies the current cap styles used by a Pen
PenAlignment	Specifies the alignment of a Pen in relation to the line being drawn
PenType	Specifies the type of fill a Pen uses to fill lines
QualityMode SmoothingMode RenderingHint	Specifies the overall quality used to render a graphic image

Establishing the Rendering Quality

Notice that some of the enumerations defined in the System.Drawing.Drawing2D namespace (such as QualityMode and SmoothingMode) allow you to configure the overall quality of the current rendering operation. When you obtain a Graphics object, it has a default rendering mode, which is a middle-of-the-road combination of speed and overall quality. Let's examine one way to tweak a Graphics object to override these default values.

The SmoothingMode enumeration (see Table 10-16) is typically used to control how the GDI+ objects being rendered with the current Graphics object are antialiased (or not).

Table 10-16. Possible Smoothing Values

SMOOTHINGMODE VALUE	MEANING IN LIFE
AntiAlias	Specifies antialiased rendering. The AntiAlias mode uses shades of gray or color to smooth the edges of lines and curves, and it is effective on CRT screens as well as LCD screens.
HighQuality	Specifies high quality, lower performance rendering. The high-quality mode uses more sophisticated techniques that take advantage of the subpixel resolution of LCD screens. A single pixel on an LCD screen is divided into three stripes that are set to various shades in order to produce the line or curve that appears the most smooth to the human eye.
HighSpeed	Specifies low quality, high performance rendering.

When you want to override the default rendering quality for a current GDI+ rendering operation, make use of the SmoothingMode property of the Graphics object:

```
' Set quality of GDI+ object rendering.
Graphics g = e.Graphics
g.SmoothingMode = SmoothingMode.AntiAlias
```

Be aware that the SmoothingMode property is only used to control the quality of rendering GDI+ objects, not textual information. If you want to modify the rendering quality for Font types, you need to set the TextRenderingHint property using the related System.Drawing.TextRenderingHint enumeration.

Working with Pens

GDI+ Pen objects are used to draw lines (not too much of a stretch there!). However, a pen in and of itself is of little value. When you need to render a geometric shape onto a Control-derived type, you send a valid Pen type to any number of render methods defined by the Graphics class. In general, the DrawXXXX() methods are used to render some set of lines to a graphics surface and are typically used with Pen objects. The Graphics class also defines a number of FillXXXX() methods that render an image using some sort of Brush-derived type (more on those in just a minute).

Although you have seen many drawing members earlier in the chapter, here they are again in Table 10-17 in a bit more detail (be aware that each of these methods has been overloaded a number of times).

Table 10-17. Drawing Members of the Graphics Class

DRAWING METHOD OF GRAPHICS CLASS	MEANING IN LIFE
DrawArc()	This method renders an arc given a pen and ellipse on which to base the angle of the arc.
DrawBezier() DrawBeziers()	Given four points, this method draws a cubic Bezier curve (or a number of Bezier curves).
DrawCurve()	Draws a curve defined by an array of points.
DrawEllipse()	Draws the outline of an ellipse within the scope of a bounding rectangle.
DrawLine() DrawLines()	Given a Point (or an array of Point types), these methods connect the dots (if you will).
DrawPath()	Using the GraphicsPath type defined in the System.Drawing.Drawing2D namespace, this method renders a collection of lines/curves as specified by the path.
DrawPie()	Draws the outline of a pie section defined by an ellipse and two radial lines.
DrawPolygon()	Draws the outline of a polygon defined by an array of Point types.
DrawRectangle() DrawRectangles()	Renders a box, or a whole bunch of boxes, based on top-left-bottom-right coordinates. This can be specified using Rectangle types, integers, or floating point numbers.

Now that you understand the core methods used to render geometric images, you can examine the Pen class itself. This class defines a small set of constructors that allow you to determine the initial color and width of the Pen's nib (you can also construct a new Pen based on an existing Brush object). Most of a Pen's functionality comes by way of its supported properties. Table 10-18 gives a partial list of those properties.

Table 10-18. Pen Properties

PEN PROPERTY	MEANING IN LIFE
Brush	Determines the Brush used by this Pen.
Color	Determines the Color type used by this Pen.
CompoundArray	Gets or sets an array of custom dashes and spaces.
CustomStartCap CustomEndCap	Gets or sets a custom cap style to use at the beginning or end of lines drawn with this Pen. "Cap style" is simply the term used to describe how the initial and final stroke of the pen should look and feel. These properties allow you to build custom caps for your Pen types.
DashCap	Gets or sets the cap style used at the beginning or end of dashed lines drawn with this Pen.
DashOffset	Gets or sets the distance from the start of a line to the beginning of a dash pattern.
DashPattern	Gets or sets an array of custom dashes and spaces. The dashes are made up of line segments.
DashStyle	Gets or sets the style used for dashed lines drawn with this Pen.
LineJoin	Gets or sets the join style for the ends of two overlapping lines drawn with this Pen.
PenType	Gets the style of lines drawn with this Pen.
StartCap EndCap	Gets or sets the predefined cap style used at the beginning or end of lines drawn with this Pen. Set the cap of your Pen using the LineCap enumeration defined in the System.Drawing.Drawing2D namespace.
Width	Gets or sets the width of this Pen.

Remember that in addition to the Pen type, GDI+ also provides a Pens collection. Using a number of shared properties, you are able to retrieve a Pen (or a given color) on the fly, rather than creating a custom Pen by hand. Be aware, however, that the Pen types returned will always have a Width of 1. If you require a more exotic pen, you need to build a Pen type by hand.

First, let's render some geometric images using simple Pen types. Assume you have a main Form object, which is capable of responding to paint requests. The implementation is as follows:

```
Private Sub Form1_Paint(ByVal sender As Object, _
ByVal e As System.Windows.Forms.PaintEventArgs) _
Handles MyBase.Paint
    Dim g As Graphics = e.Graphics
    ' Make a big blue pen.
    Dim bluePen As Pen = New Pen(Color.Blue, 20)
    ' Get a stock pen from the Pens type.
    Dim pen2 As Pen = Pens.Firebrick
    ' Render some shapes with the pens.
    g.DrawEllipse(bluePen, 10, 10, 100, 100)
    g.DrawLine(pen2, 10, 130, 110, 130)
    g.DrawPie(Pens.Black, 150, 10, 120, 150, 90, 80)
    ' Draw a purple dashed polygon as well. . .
    Dim pen3 As Pen = New Pen(Color.Purple, 5)
    pen3.DashStyle = DashStyle.DashDotDot
    g.DrawPolygon(pen3, New Point() {New Point(30, 140), _
              New Point(265, 200), _
              New Point(100, 225), _
              New Point(190, 190), _
              New Point(50, 330), _
              New Point(20, 180)})
    ' And a rect with some text. . .
    Dim r As RectangleF = New RectangleF(150, 10, 130, 60)
    g.DrawRectangle(Pens.Blue, 150, 10, 130, 60)
    g.DrawString("Hello out there. . .How are ya?", _
    New Font("Arial", 12), Brushes.Black, r)
End Sub
```

The output is shown in Figure 10-16. While not earth shattering, it should drive the point home.

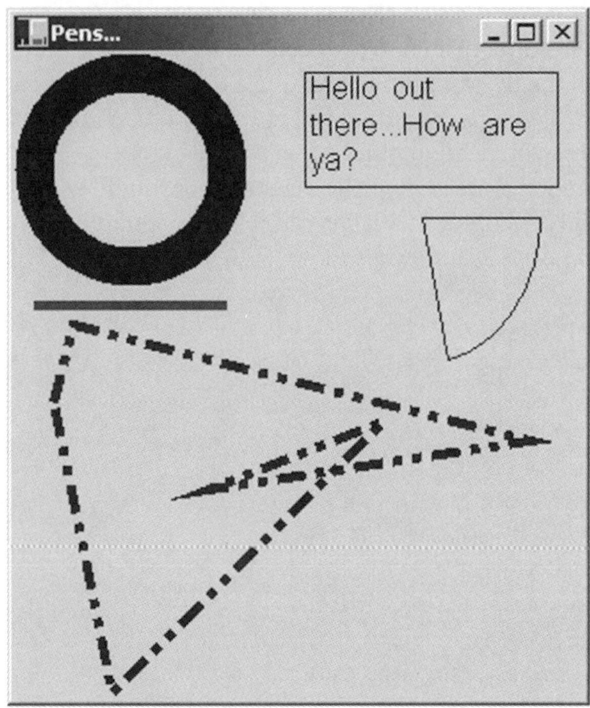

Figure 10-16. Working with Pen types

Notice that the Pen that is used to render your polygon makes use of the DashStyle enumeration (defined in System.Drawing.Drawing2D). Table 10-19 lists your choices.

Table 10-19. Dash Styles

DASHSTYLE VALUE	MEANING IN LIFE
Custom	Specifies a user-defined custom dash style
Dash	Specifies a line composed of dashes
DashDot	Specifies a line composed of an alternating pattern of dash-dot-dash-dot
DashDotDot	Specifies a line composed of an alternating pattern of dash-dot-dot-dash-dot-dot
Dot	Specifies a line comprised of dots
Solid	Specifies a solid line

In addition to the preconfigured DashStyles, you are also able to define custom dash types using the DashPattern property of the Pen type (see Figure 10-17).

```
' Draw custom dash pattern all around the boarder of the form.
Dim customDashPen As Pen = New Pen(Color.BlueViolet, 5)
Dim myDashes As Single() = {5F, 2F, 1F, 3F}
customDashPen.DashPattern = myDashes
g.DrawRectangle(customDashPen, ClientRectangle)
```

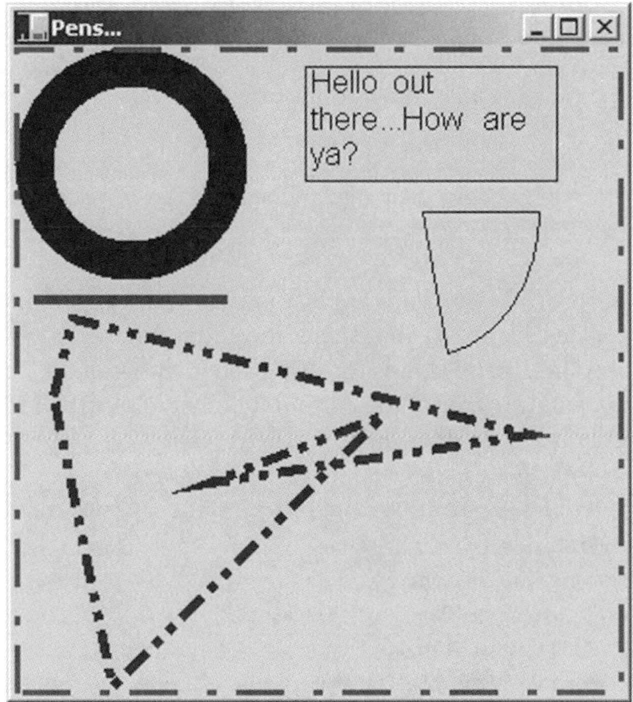

Figure 10-17. Working with dash styles

SOURCE CODE *The PenApp project is included under the Chapter 10 subdirectory.*

Working with Pen Caps

If you examine the output of the previous pen example, you should notice that the beginning and end of each line was rendered using a standard pen protocol (an end cap composed of 90-degree angles). Using the LineCap enumeration, however, you are able to build Pens that exhibit a bit more flair. Table 10-20 provides the core values of this enumeration.

Table 10-20. LineCap Values

LINECAP VALUES	MEANING IN LIFE
ArrowAnchor	Specifies an arrow-shaped cap
DiamondAnchor	Specifies a diamond anchor cap
Flat	Specifies a flat line cap
Round	Specifies a round line cap
RoundAnchor	Specifies a round anchor cap
Square	Specifies a square line cap
SquareAnchor	Specifies a no line cap
Triangle	Specifies a triangular line cap

To illustrate, the following Pens application draws a series of lines using each of the LineCap styles. Figure 10-18 displays the end result.

The painting code simply loops through each member of the LineCap enumeration, prints out the name of the current member (e.g., ArrowAnchor), and then configures and draws a line with the current cap:

```
Private Sub Form1_Paint(ByVal sender As Object, ByVal e As.PaintEventArgs) _
Handles MyBase.Paint
    Dim g As Graphics = e.Graphics
    Dim thePen As Pen = New Pen(Color.Black, 10)
    Dim yOffSet As Integer = 10
    ' Get all members of the LineCap enum.
    Dim lc As LineCap
    Dim obj As Array = System.Enum.GetValues(lc.GetType())
    ' Draw a line with a LineCap member.
    Dim x As Integer
    For x = 0 To obj.Length - 1
        ' Get next cap and configure pen.
        Dim temp As LineCap = CType(obj.GetValue(x), LineCap)
        thePen.StartCap = temp
        thePen.EndCap = temp
```

```
        ' Print name of LineCap enum.
        g.DrawString(temp.ToString(), New Font("Times New Roman", 10), _
            New SolidBrush(Color.Black), 0, yOffSet)
        ' Draw a line with the correct cap.
        g.DrawLine(thePen, 100, yOffSet, Width - 50, yOffSet)
        yOffSet += 40
    Next
End Sub
```

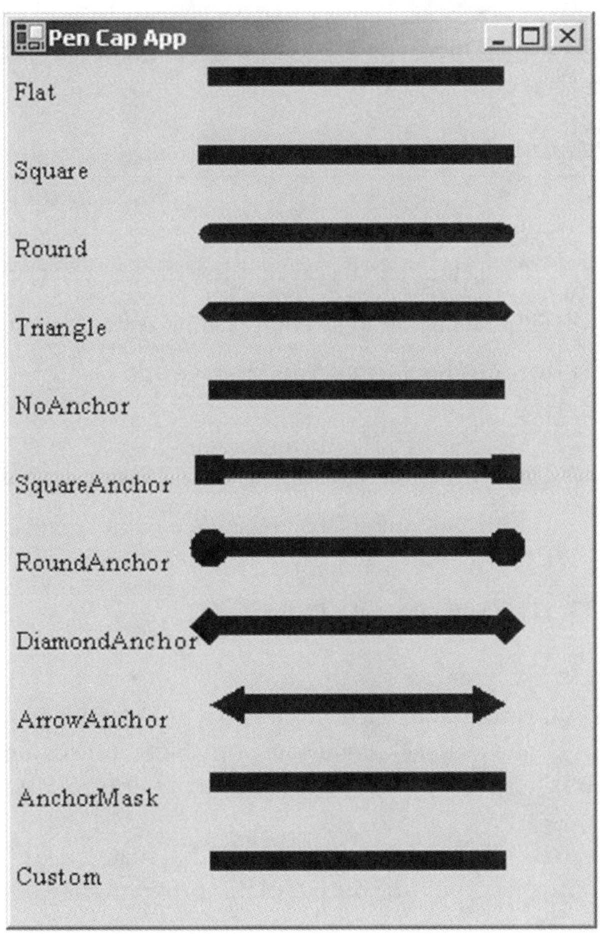

Figure 10-18. Pen caps

SOURCE CODE *The PenCapApp project is included under the Chapter 10 subdirectory.*

Working with Solid Brushes

So much for drawing lines. GDI+ Brush-derived types are used to fill the space between the lines with a given color, pattern, or image. Recall that the Brush class is an abstract type and cannot be directly created. Rather, this type serves as a base class to the other related brush types (e.g., SolidBrush, HatchBrush, LinearGradientBrush, and so forth). In addition to the aforementioned Brush-derived types, the System.Drawing namespace also defines two types that return a configured brush using a number of shared properties: Brushes and SystemBrushes. Using a properly configured brush, you are able to call any number of methods (such as DrawString()), as well as the set of FillXXXX() methods in Table 10-21.

Table 10-21. Fill Methods of the Graphics Type

FILL METHOD OF GRAPHICS CLASS	MEANING IN LIFE
FillClosedCurve()	Fills the interior of a closed curve defined by an array of points
FillEllipse()	Fills the interior of an ellipse defined by a bounding rectangle
FillPath()	Fills the interior of a path
FillPie()	Fills the interior of a pie section
FillPolygon()	Fills the interior of a polygon defined by an array of points
FillRectangle() FillRectangles()	Fills the interior of a rectangle (or a number of rectangles) with a Brush
FillRegion()	Fills the interior of a Region

Also, recall that you can build a custom Pen type by making use of a given brush. In this way, you are able to build some brush of interest (for example, a brush that paints a bitmap image) and render geometric patterns with a configured Pen.

To illustrate, here is a small sample program that makes use of the SolidBrush and Brushes types (the output of this program shown in Figure 10-19 should look familiar).

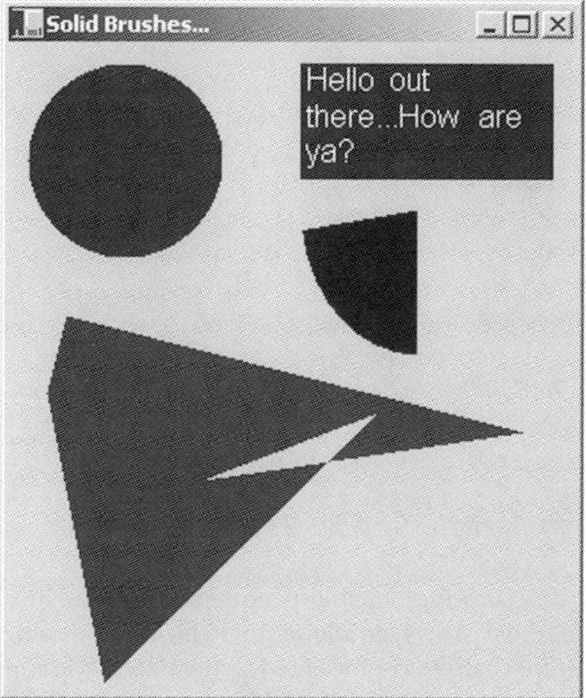

Figure 10-19. Working with Brush types

If you can't tell, this application is little more than the original Pens application that makes use of the FillXXXX() methods and SolidBrush types rather than the Pens and DrawXXXX() methods. Here is the implementation of the paint handler:

```
Private Sub Form1_Paint(ByVal sender As Object, ByVal e As PaintEventArgs) _
Handles MyBase.Paint
    Dim g As Graphics = e.Graphics
    ' Make a blue SolidBrush.
    Dim blueBrush As SolidBrush = New SolidBrush(Color.Blue)
    ' Get a stock brush from the Brushes type.
    Dim brush2 As SolidBrush = CType(Brushes.Firebrick, SolidBrush)
    ' Render some shapes with the brushes.
    g.FillEllipse(blueBrush, 10, 10, 100, 100)
    g.FillPie(Brushes.Black, 150, 10, 120, 150, 90, 80)
    ' Draw a filled polygon as well. . .
    Dim brush3 As SolidBrush = New SolidBrush(Color.Purple)
    g.FillPolygon(brush3, New Point() {New Point(30, 140), _
        New Point(265, 200), _
```

```
            New Point(100, 225), _
            New Point(190, 190), _
            New Point(50, 330), _
            New Point(20, 180)})
        ' And a rect with some text. . .
        Dim r As RectangleF = New RectangleF(150, 10, 130, 60)
        g.FillRectangle(Brushes.Blue, 150, 10, 130, 60)
        g.DrawString("Hello out there. . .How are ya?", _
        New Font("Arial", 12), Brushes.White, r)
End Sub
```

SOURCE CODE *The SolidBrushApp project is included under the Chapter 10 subdirectory.*

Working with Hatch Style Brushes

The System.Drawing.Drawing2D namespace defines another Brush-derived type named HatchBrush. This type allows you to fill a region using a (very large) number of predefined patterns represented by the HatchStyle enumeration. Table 10-22 presents some (but not all) of the hatch values.

Table 10-22. Hatch Styles

HATCHSTYLE ENUMERATION VALUE	MEANING IN LIFE
BackwardDiagonal	Creates a brush consisting of backward diagonal lines
Cross	Creates a brush consisting of horizontal and vertical crossing lines
DiagonalCross	Creates a brush consisting of diagonal crossing lines
ForwardDiagonal	Creates a brush consisting of forward diagonal lines
Hollow	Configures a “hollow” brush that doesn’t paint anything
Horizontal	Creates a brush consisting of horizontal lines
Pattern	Creates a brush with a pattern consisting of a custom bitmap
Solid	Creates a solid colored brush (as an alternative to using the SolidBrush type directly)
Vertical	A brush consisting of vertical lines

In addition, when you construct a HatchBrush, you need to specify the foreground and background colors to use during the fill operation. To illustrate, let's rework the logic seen previously in the PenCapApp example. The output renders a filled oval for a subset of all possible hatch values (see Figure 10-20).

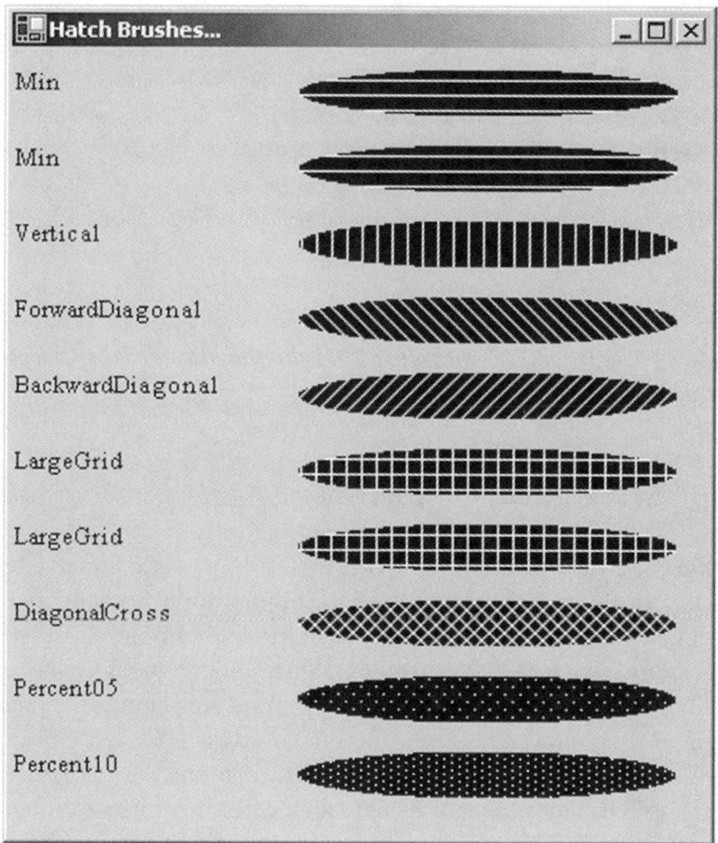

Figure 10-20. Hatch styles

Here is the code behind the Form:

```
Private Sub Form1_Paint(ByVal sender As Object, ByVal e As PaintEventArgs) _
Handles MyBase.Paint
    Dim g As Graphics = e.Graphics
    Dim yOffSet As Integer = 10
    ' Get all members of the HatchStyle enum.
    Dim lc As HatchStyle
    Dim obj As Array = System.Enum.GetValues(lc.GetType())
    ' Draw an oval with a HatchStyle member 0-10.
```

```
    Dim x As Integer
    For x = 0 To 10
        ' Configure Brush.
        Dim temp As HatchStyle = CType(obj.GetValue(x), HatchStyle)
        Dim theBrush As HatchBrush = New HatchBrush(temp, _
        Color.White, Color.Black)
        ' Print name of HatchStyle enum.
        g.DrawString(temp.ToString(), New Font("Times New Roman", 10), _
        New SolidBrush(Color.Black), 0, yOffSet)
        ' Fill a rectangle with the correct brush.
        g.FillEllipse(theBrush, 150, yOffSet, 200, 25)
        yOffSet += 40
    Next
End Sub
```

SOURCE CODE *The BrushStyles application is included under the Chapter 10 subdirectory.*

Working with Textured Brushes

Next, you have the TextureBrush type. This type allows you to attach a bitmap image to a brush, which can then be used in conjunction with a fill operation. In just a few pages, you learn about the details of the GDI+ Image class. For the time being, understand that a TextureBrush is assigned an Image reference for use during its lifetime. The image itself is typically found stored in some local file (*.bmp, *.gif, or *.jpg) or as a resource embedded into a .NET assembly.

Let's build a sample application that makes use of the TextureBrush type. One brush is used to paint the entire client area with the image found in a file named "clouds.bmp," while the other brush is used to paint text with the image found within "soap bubbles.bmp." (Yes, you can use TextureBrush types to render text as well.) The output is shown in Figure 10-21.

The code is very simple. To begin, your Form-derived class maintains two abstract Brush types, which are assigned to a new TextureBrush in the constructor. Notice that the constructor of the TextureBrush type requires an Image object reference:

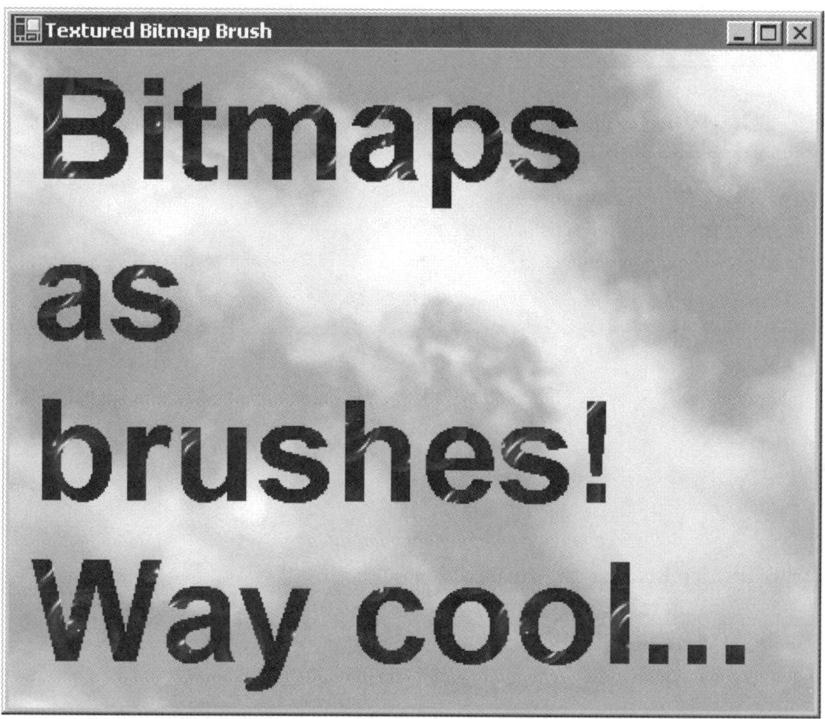

Figure 10-21. Bitmap brushes

```
Public Class Form1
    Inherits System.Windows.Forms.Form
    ' Data for the image brush.
    Private texturedTextBrush As Brush
    Private texturedBGroundBrush As Brush
    Public Sub New()
        MyBase.New()
        'This call is required by the Windows Form Designer.
        InitializeComponent()
        ' Load image for background brush.
        Dim BGroundBrushImage As Image = New Bitmap("Clouds.bmp")
        texturedBGroundBrush = New TextureBrush(BGroundBrushImage)
        ' Now load image for text brush.
        Dim textBrushImage As Image = New Bitmap("Soap Bubbles.bmp")
        texturedTextBrush = New TextureBrush(textBrushImage)
        CenterToScreen()
    End Sub
. . .
End Class
```

Now that you have two TextureBrush types to render with, the paint handler should be a no-brainer:

```
Private Sub Form1_Paint(ByVal sender As Object, ByVal e As PaintEventArgs) _
Handles MyBase.Paint
    Dim g As Graphics = e.Graphics
    ' Paint the clouds on the client araa.
    Dim r As Rectangle = Me.ClientRectangle
    g.FillRectangle(texturedBGroundBrush, r)
    ' Need to translate for DrawString(). . .
    Dim rf As RectangleF
    rf.X = r.X
    rf.Y = r.Y
    rf.Height = r.Height
    rf.Width = r.Width
    ' Some big bold text with a textured brush.
    g.DrawString("Bitmaps as brushes!  Way cool. . .", _
         New Font("Arial", 60, _
         FontStyle.Bold), _
         texturedTextBrush, _
         rf) ' Draws text In bounds of Form.
End Sub
```

Not bad at all. For those of you who have spent time achieving the same effects using the raw Win32 API, you should be quite pleased with the minimal amount of work required to achieve rather complex end results. Now, before I move on to a discussion of image manipulation, there is one final brush type to consider.

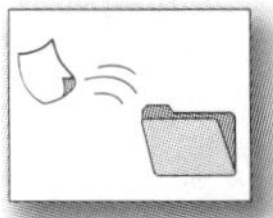

SOURCE CODE *The TexturedBrushes application is included under the Chapter 10 subdirectory.*

Working with Gradient Brushes

Last but not least, there is the LinearGradientBrush type, which can be used whenever you want to blend two colors together in a gradient pattern. Working with this type is just as simple as working with the other brush types. The only point of interest is that when you build a LinearGradientBrush, you need to specify the direction of the blend using a value from the LinearGradientMode enumeration (see Table 10-23).

Table 10-23. LinearGradientMode Enumeration

LINEARGRADIENTMODE VALUE	MEANING IN LIFE
BackwardDiagonal	Specifies a gradient from upper-right to lower-left
ForwardDiagonal	Specifies a gradient from upper-left to lower-right
Horizontal	Specifies a gradient from left to right
Vertical	Specifies a gradient from top to bottom

To test each type, make use of the System.Enum class yet again and draw a series of rectangles using a LinearGradientBrush. The output is shown in Figure 10-22.

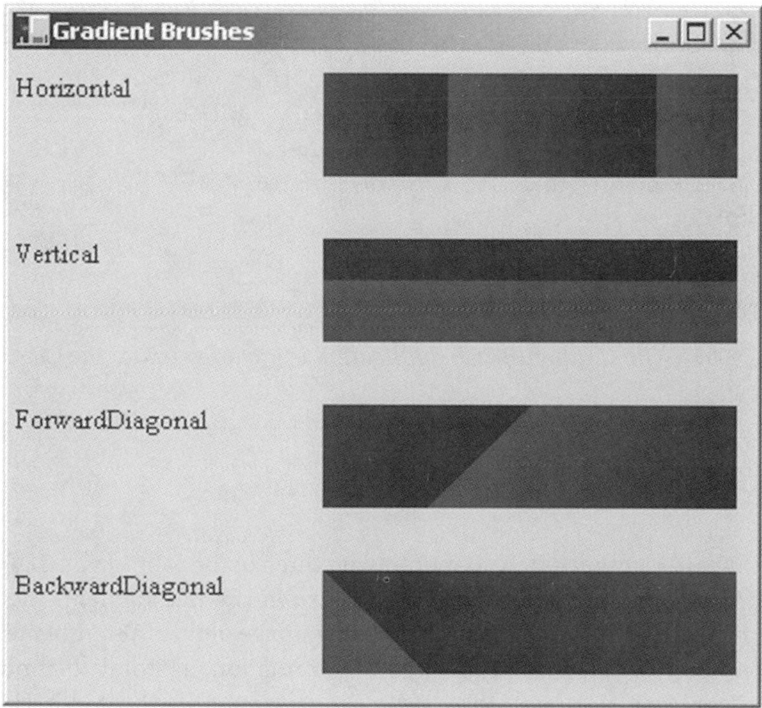

Figure 10-22. Gradient brushes

Now the code, which I assume requires little comment at this point:

```
Private Sub Form1_Paint(ByVal sender As Object, ByVal e As PaintEventArgs) _
Handles MyBase.Paint
    Dim g As Graphics = e.Graphics
```

```
    Dim r As Rectangle = New Rectangle(10, 10, 100, 100)
    ' A gradient brush.
    Dim theBrush As LinearGradientBrush
    Dim yOffSet As Integer = 10
    ' Get all members of the LinearGradientMode enum.
    Dim lgm As LinearGradientMode
    Dim obj As Array = System.Enum.GetValues(lgm.GetType())
    ' Draw an oval with a LinearGradientMode member.
    Dim x As Integer
    For x = 0 To obj.Length - 1
        ' Configure Brush.
        Dim temp As LinearGradientMode = CType(obj.GetValue(x), _
        LinearGradientMode)
        theBrush = New LinearGradientBrush(r, Color.Aquamarine, _
            Color.Black, temp)
        ' Print name of LinearGradientMode enum.
        g.DrawString(temp.ToString(), New Font("Times New Roman", 10), _
                    New SolidBrush(Color.Black), 0, yOffSet)
        ' Fill a rectangle with the correct brush.
        g.FillRectangle(theBrush, 150, yOffSet, 200, 50)
        yOffSet += 80
    Next
End Sub
```

SOURCE CODE *The GradientBrush application is included under the Chapter 10 subdirectory.*

Rendering Images

So far, you have examined how to manipulate three of the four major GDI+ types: fonts, pens, and brushes. The final type you examine in this chapter is the Image class and its related subtypes. System.Drawing.Image defines a number of methods and properties that hold various bits of information regarding the underlying pixel set it represents. For example, the Image class supplies the Width, Height, and Size properties to retrieve the dimensions of the image. Other properties allow you to gain access to the underlying palette.

In addition, a number of types defined within the System.Drawing.Imaging namespace define a whole slew of types that facilitate a number of advanced image transformations. The truth of the matter is that a separate book could be written on the topic of GDI+ image manipulation. This is not that book. The goal here is to provide you with a number of imaging techniques you are likely to use on a day-to-day basis (with some extra eye candy thrown in for good measure). If you require additional information, refer to online Help.

With that disclaimer out of the way, the Image class defines the core members shown in Table 10-24, many of which are abstract (some of which are shared).

Table 10-24. Members of the Image Type

IMAGE MEMBER NAME	MEANING IN LIFE
FromFile()	This shared method creates an Image from the specified file.
FromHbitmap()	Creates a Bitmap from a Windows handle (also shared).
FromStream()	Creates an Image from the specified data stream (also shared).
Height Width Size PhysicalDimensions HorizontalResolution VerticalResolution	These properties return information regarding the dimensions of this Image.
Palette	This property returns a ColorPalette data type that represents the underlying palette used for this Image.
GetBounds()	Returns a Rectangle that represents the current size of this Image.
Save()	Saves an Image to file.

Given that the abstract Image class cannot be directly created, you typically assign objects of type Image to a new instance of the Bitmap class (or simply make a direct instance of the Bitmap type). For example, assume you have some Form-derived class that renders three bitmaps into the client area. To begin, you may create three private Image data members, each of which is assigned to a given Bitmap on startup:

```
Public Class Form1
    Inherits System.Windows.Forms.Form
    ' The images.
    Private bMapImageA As Image
    Private bMapImageB As Image
        Private bMapImageC As Image
    Public Sub New()
        MyBase.New()
        . . .
        ' Fill the images with bitmaps.
        bMapImageA = New Bitmap("imageA.bmp")
        bMapImageB = New Bitmap("imageB.bmp")
        bMapImageC = New Bitmap("imageC.bmp")
    End Sub
. . .
End Class
```

Rendering these items from within the context of a paint handler is easy as could be, given that the Graphics class has a member named (appropriately enough) DrawImage(). This method has been overloaded numerous times to provide various ways to place the image onto the drawing surface. For example, you may specify optional ImageAttributes and GraphicsUnit enumerations. For most purposes, all you need to do is specify the location at which to render each image (which may be defined using Point, Rectangles, or Integers):

```
Private Sub Form1_Paint(ByVal sender As Object, ByVal e As PaintEventArgs) _
Handles MyBase.Paint
    Dim g As Graphics = e.Graphics
    ' Render all three images.
    g.DrawImage(bMapImageA, rectA)
    g.DrawImage(bMapImageB, rectB)
    g.DrawImage(bMapImageC, rectC)
End Sub
```

Figure 10-23 shows the end result.

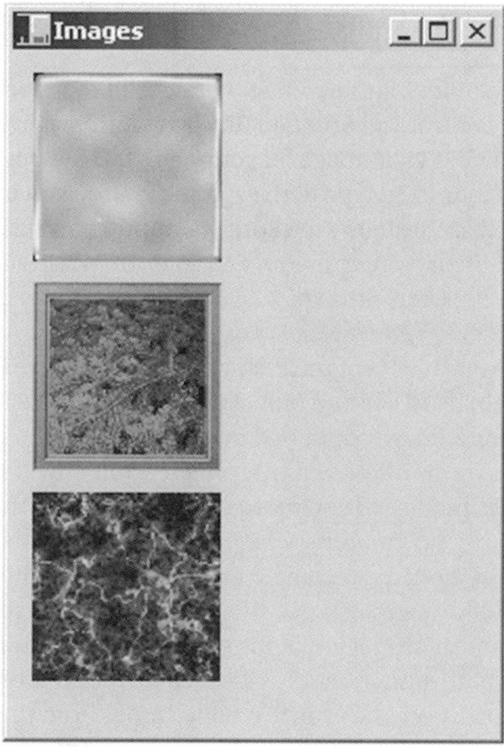

Figure 10-23. Rendering images

Also be aware that regardless of the name given to the Bitmap type, you are able to load in images stored in any number of file formats. For example:

```
' The Bitmap type can hold any number of file formats!
Dim myBMP as Bitmap = New Bitmap("CoffeeCup.bmp")
Dim myGIF as Bitmap = New Bitmap("Candy.gif")
Dim myJPEG as Bitmap = New Bitmap("Clock.jpg")
Dim myPNG as Bitmap = New Bitmap("Speakers.png")
Dim myTIFF as Bitmap = New Bitmap("FooFighters.tif")
' Now render each onto the Graphics context.
g.DrawImage(myBMP, 10, 10)
g.DrawImage(myGIF, 220, 10)
g.DrawImage(myJPEG, 280, 10)
g.DrawImage(myPNG, 150, 200)
g.DrawImage(myTIFF, 300, 200)
```

SOURCE CODE *The Images application is included under the Chapter 10 subdirectory.*

Dragging, Hit Testing, and the PictureBox Control

While you are free to render Bitmap images directly onto a Control-derived type, you gain far greater control and functionality if you instead choose to create a PictureBox type to hold your image on your behalf. There are many reasons to do so. Because the PictureBox type derives from Control, you inherit a great deal of functionality, such as the ability to capture a number of events for a particular image, assign a tool tip or context menu, and so forth. While you can achieve similar behaviors using a raw Bitmap, you are required to add a fair amount of boilerplate code.

To illustrate the usefulness of the PictureBox type, let's create an application that illustrates the ability to capture MouseUp, MouseDown, and MouseMove events from a graphical image contained in a PictureBox.

If the user clicks the mouse down somewhere within the bounds of the image, they are in "dragging" mode and can move the image around the Form. To make things more interesting, let's monitor where they release the image. If it is within the bounds of a GDI+-rendered rectangle, you take some additional course of action (seen shortly). As you may know, the process of testing for mouse click events within the context of a region of the screen is termed "hit testing."

When it comes to the functionality provided by the PictureBox type, there is little to say, as all of the necessary functionality comes from the Control base class. Given that you have already explored a number of the members for these types, you can quickly turn your attention to the process of assigning an image to the PictureBox member variable:

```
Public Class Form1
    Inherits System.Windows.Forms.Form
     ' This holds an image of a smiley face.
     Private WithEvents happyBox As PictureBox
     Public Sub New()
        MyBase.New()
        'This call is required by the Windows Form Designer.
        InitializeComponent()
        CenterToScreen()
        ' Configure the PictureBox.
        happyBox = New PictureBox()
        happyBox.SizeMode = PictureBoxSizeMode.StretchImage
        happyBox.Location = New System.Drawing.Point(64, 32)
        happyBox.Size = New System.Drawing.Size(50, 50)
        happyBox.Image = New Bitmap("happy.bmp")
        happyBox.Cursor = Cursors.Hand
```

```
        ' Now add to the Form's Controls collection.
        Controls.Add(happyBox)
    End Sub
     . . .
End Class
```

The only point of interest is the SizeMode property, which makes use of the PictureBoxSizeMode enumeration. This type is used to control how the associated image should be rendered within the bounding rectangle of the PictureBox. Here, you assigned StretchImage, indicating that you want to skew the image over the entire area of the PictureBox. Table 10-25 presents other possible values.

Table 10-25. The PictureBoxSizeMode Enumeration

PICTUREBOXSIZEMODE MEMBER NAME	MEANING IN LIFE
AutoSize	The PictureBox is sized equal to the size of the image that it contains.
CenterImage	The image is displayed in the center if the PictureBox is larger than the image. If the image is larger than the PictureBox, the picture is placed in the center of the PictureBox and the outside edges are clipped.
Normal	The image is located in the upper-left corner of the PictureBox. If the PictureBox is smaller than the image, it will be clipped.

Now that you have configured the initial look and feel of the PictureBox, you need to hook up some handlers for the MouseMove, MouseUp, and MouseDown events.

The logic behind MouseDown stores the incoming (*x*, *y*) location of the mouse click for later use, and sets a Boolean member variable (isDragging) to True to indicate that a drag operation is process.

```
' Mouse event handler to initiate dragging the pictureBox around.
Private Sub happyBox_MouseDown(ByVal sender As Object, _
ByVal e As System.Windows.Forms.MouseEventArgs) _
Handles happyBox.MouseDown
        isDragging = True
        ' Save the (x, y) of the mouse down click,
        ' because you need them as an offset when
        ' dragging the image.
        oldX = e.X
        oldY = e.Y
End Sub
```

The MouseMove handler simply relocates the position of the PictureBox (using the Top and Left properties) by offsetting the current cursor location with the (x, y) position captured when the mouse went down.

```
' If the user clicks on the image and moves the mouse,
' redraw the image at the new location.
Private Sub happyBox_MouseMove(ByVal sender As Object, _
  ByVal e As System.Windows.Forms.MouseEventArgs) _
  Handles happyBox.MouseMove
    If isDragging Then
        ' Need to figure new Y value based on where the mouse
        ' down click happened.
        happyBox.Top = happyBox.Top + (e.Y - oldY)
        ' Same deal for X (use oldX as a base line).
        happyBox.Left = happyBox.Left + (e.X - oldX)
    End If
End Sub
```

Finally, MouseUp sets the isDragging Boolean to False to signal the end of the drag operation. Recall that this application has one extra point of logic. If the MouseUp event occurs when the PictureBox is contained within a GDI+ Rectangle object, you can assume the user has won the game (albeit a rather lame game). That said, here is the remainder of the Form's logic:

```
' When the mouse goes up, they are done dragging.
' See if they dropped the image in the rectangle. . .
Private Sub happyBox_MouseUp(ByVal sender As Object, _
ByVal e As System.Windows.Forms.MouseEventArgs) _
Handles happyBox.MouseUp
    isDragging = False
    If dropRect.Contains(happyBox.Bounds) Then
        MessageBox.Show("You win!", "What an amazing test of skill. . .")
    End If
End Sub
' Assume you have a private Rectangle configured as follows:
' Private dropRect as Rectangle = New Rectangle(100, 100, 150, 150)
Private Sub Form1_Paint(ByVal sender As Object, _
ByVal e As System.Windows.Forms.PaintEventArgs) _
Handles MyBase.Paint
    Dim g As Graphics = e.Graphics
    g.FillRectangle(Brushes.AntiqueWhite, dropRect)
    ' Display instructions.
    g.DrawString("Drag the happy guy in the box. . .", _
```

```
    New Font("Times New Roman", 15), _
    Brushes.Black, 0, 0)
End Sub
```

As a reminder, it is worth pointing out that the Rectangle type defines the Contains() method that has been overloaded to test for a contained Rectangle, Point, or two integer values. This member can be quite helpful when calculating if a mouse click has occurred within a given rectangular region (as seen in the MouseUp event handler). When you run the application, you are presented with the box in Figure 10-24.

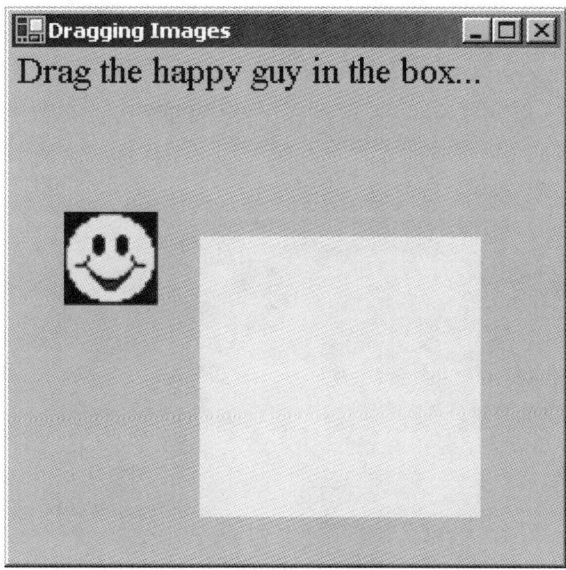

Figure 10-24. Dragging, dropping, and hit testing images

If you have what it takes to win the game, you are rewarded with the message shown in Figure 10-25.

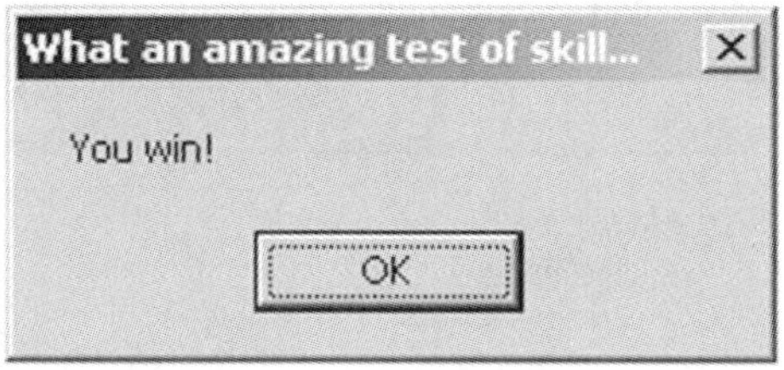

Figure 10-25. A true test of skill

SOURCE CODE *The DraggingImages application is included under the Chapter 10 subdirectory.*

More Hit Testing Details

Validating a hit test against a Control-derived type (such as a PictureBox) is very simple, as each can respond to mouse events directly. However, what if you want to perform a hit test on a geometric shape such as a region rendered on the screen using a GDI+ pen? To illustrate, let's revisit the Images application and add some additional functionality.

The goal is to determine when the user clicks a given image (which as you recall was *not* rendered within a PictureBox control). Once you discover which image was clicked, adjust the Text property of the Form and highlight the image with a red outline. Figure 10-26 shows an example.

Figure 10-26. Highlighting images

The first step is to intercept the MouseDown event for the Form itself. When the event occurs, you need to programmatically figure out if the incoming (*x*, *y*) coordinate is somewhere within the bounds of the Rectangles used to represent the dimension of each Image. If the user clicks a given image, you set a private Boolean member variable (isImageClicked) to True and indicate which image was selected via another member variable (of type integer):

```
Imports System.Drawing.Drawing2D
Public Class Form1
    Inherits System.Windows.Forms.Form
...
    ' Did the user click on an image?
    Private isImageClicked As Boolean = False
    Private imageClicked As Integer
    Private Sub Form1_MouseUp(ByVal sender As Object, _
    ByVal e As System.Windows.Forms.MouseEventArgs) _
    Handles MyBase.MouseUp
        ' Get (x, y) of mouse click.
        Dim mousePt As Point = New Point(e.X, e.Y)
        ' See if the mouse is anywhere in the 3 regions...
        If (rectA.Contains(mousePt)) Then
            isImageClicked = True
            imageClicked = 0
            Me.Text = "You clicked image A"
        ElseIf (rectB.Contains(mousePt)) Then
            isImageClicked = True
            imageClicked = 1
            Me.Text = "You clicked image B"
        ElseIf (rectC.Contains(mousePt)) Then
            isImageClicked = True
            imageClicked = 2
            Me.Text = "You clicked image C"
        Else ' Not in any shape, set defaults.
            isImageClicked = False
            Me.Text = "Images"
        End If
        ' Redraw the client area.
        Invalidate()
    End Sub
```

Notice that the final conditional check sets the isImageClicked member variable to False, indicating that the user did not click one of your three images. This is important, as you want to erase the red outline of the previously selected image. Once all items have then been checked, you invalidate the client area. Here is the updated Paint handler:

```
Private Sub Form1_Paint(ByVal sender As Object, _
ByVal e As PaintEventArgs) Handles MyBase.Paint
    Graphics g = e.Graphics
    ' Render all three images.
     . . .
     ' Draw outline (if clicked. . .)
     If (isImageClicked = True) Then
         Dim outline As Pen = New Pen(Color.Red, 5)
         Select Case (imageClicked)
                Case 0
                    g.DrawRectangle(outline, rectA)
                Case 1
                    g.DrawRectangle(outline, rectB)
                Case 2
                    g.DrawRectangle(outline, rectC)
         End Select
    End If
End Sub
```

Hit Testing Nonrectangular Images

Now, what if you want to perform a hit test in a nonrectangular region, rather than in a simple square? Assume you updated your application to render an oddball geometric shape that will also sport a red outline when clicked, as shown in Figure 10-27.

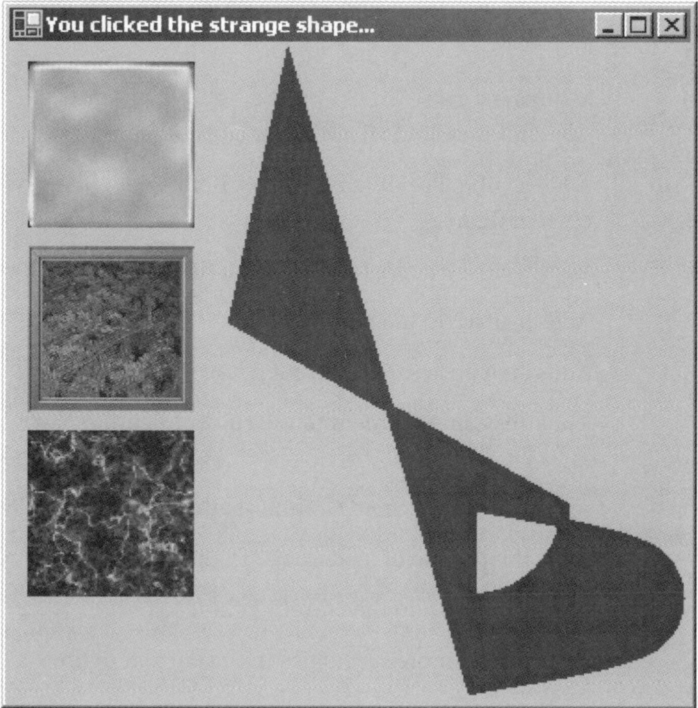

Figure 10-27. Highlighting oddball shapes

This geometric image was rendered on the Form using the FillPath() method of the Graphics type. This method takes an instance of a GraphicsPath object, which was mentioned earlier during your examination of the System.Drawing.Drawing2D namespace. The GraphicsPath object encapsulates a series of connected lines, curves, and (interestingly enough) stings. Adding new items to a GraphicsPath instance is achieved using a number of related "add" methods, which are described in Table 10-26.

Table 10-26. Add-Centric Methods of the GraphicsPath Class

GRAPHICSPATH "ADD" METHOD	MEANING IN LIFE
AddArc()	Appends an elliptical arc to the current figure
AddBezier() AddBeziers()	Adds a cubic Bezier curve (or a set of Bezier curves) to the current figure
AddClosedCurve()	Adds a closed curve to the current figure
AddCurve()	Adds a curve to the current figure
AddEllipse()	Adds an ellipse to the current figure
AddLine() AddLines()	Appends a line segment to the current figure
AddPath()	Appends the specified GraphicsPath to the current figure
AddPie()	Adds the outline of a pie shape to the current figure
AddPolygon()	Adds a polygon to the current figure
AddRectangle() AddRectangles()	Adds one or more rectangles to the current figure
AddString()	Adds a text string to the current figure

Assume that you have added a private GraphicsPath member variable to your current Images application. In the Form's constructor, build the set of items that represent your path as follows:

```
Public Class Form1
    Inherits System.Windows.Forms.Form
    ' A polygon region.
    Private myPath As GraphicsPath = New GraphicsPath()
    Public Sub New()
        MyBase.New()
          ' Create an interesting region.
          myPath.StartFigure()
               myPath.AddLine(New Point(150, 10), New Point(120, 150))
               myPath.AddArc(200, 200, 100, 100, 0, 90)
               Point point1 = New Point(250, 250)
               Point point2 = New Point(350, 275)
               Point point3 = New Point(350, 325)
               Point point4 = New Point(250, 350)
```

```
                Point[] points = {point1, point2, point3, point4}
                myPath.AddCurve(points)
            myPath.CloseFigure()
        . . .
        End Sub
End Class
```

Notice the calls to StartFigure() and CloseFigure(). When you call StartFigure(), you are able to insert a new item into the current path you are building. A call to CloseFigure() closes the current figure and begins a new figure (if you require one). If the figure contains a sequence of connected lines and curves (as in the case of the myPath instance), the loop is closed by connecting a line from the endpoint to the starting point.

Although additional members exist for System.Drawing.Drawing2D.GraphicsPath, let's keep focused on the hit-testing logic. The next step is to update your existing MouseDown event handler to test for the presence of the cursor's (*x*, *y*) position within the bounds of the GraphicsPath. Like a Region type, this can be discovered using the IsVisible() member:

```
Private Sub Form1_MouseUp(ByVal sender As Object, ByVal e As MouseEventArgs) _
Handles MyBase.MouseUp
    ' Get (x, y) of mouse click.
    Dim mousePt As Point = New Point(e.X, e.Y)
    ' See if the mouse is anywhere in the 3 regions. . .
     . . .
            ElseIf (myPath.IsVisible(mousePt)) Then
            isImageClicked = True
            imageClicked = 3
            Me.Text = "You clicked the strange shape. . ."
. . .
End Sub
```

Finally, you can update the Paint handler as follows:

```
Private Sub Form1_Paint(ByVal sender As Object, ByVal e As PaintEventArgs) _
Handles MyBase.Paint
    Dim g As Graphics = e.Graphics
     . . .
     ' Draw the graphics path.
     g.FillPath(Brushes.AliceBlue, myPath)
. . .
```

```
    ' Draw outline (if clicked. . .)
    If (isImageClicked = True) Then
        Dim outline As Pen = New Pen(Color.Red, 5)
            Select Case (imageClicked)
                Case 0
                    g.DrawRectangle(outline, rectA)
                Case 1
                    g.DrawRectangle(outline, rectB)
                Case 2
                    g.DrawRectangle(outline, rectC)
                Case 3
                    g.DrawPath(outline, myPath)
            End Select
        End If
End Sub
```

SOURCE CODE *The Images project is included under the Chapter 10 subdirectory.*

Understanding the .NET Resource Format

Up to this point, each application that made use of external resources (such as bitmaps) assumed that they were located in a separate, stand-alone file. For example, the previous Images application rendered three bitmap images, which as you recall were loaded directly from file:

```
' Fill the images with bitmaps.
bMapImageA = New Bitmap("imageA.bmp")
bMapImageB = New Bitmap("imageB.bmp")
bMapImageC = New Bitmap("imageC.bmp")
```

This logic, of course, demands that the application directory does indeed contain three files named "imageA.bmp," "imageB.bmp," and "imageC.bmp" (see Figure 10-28).

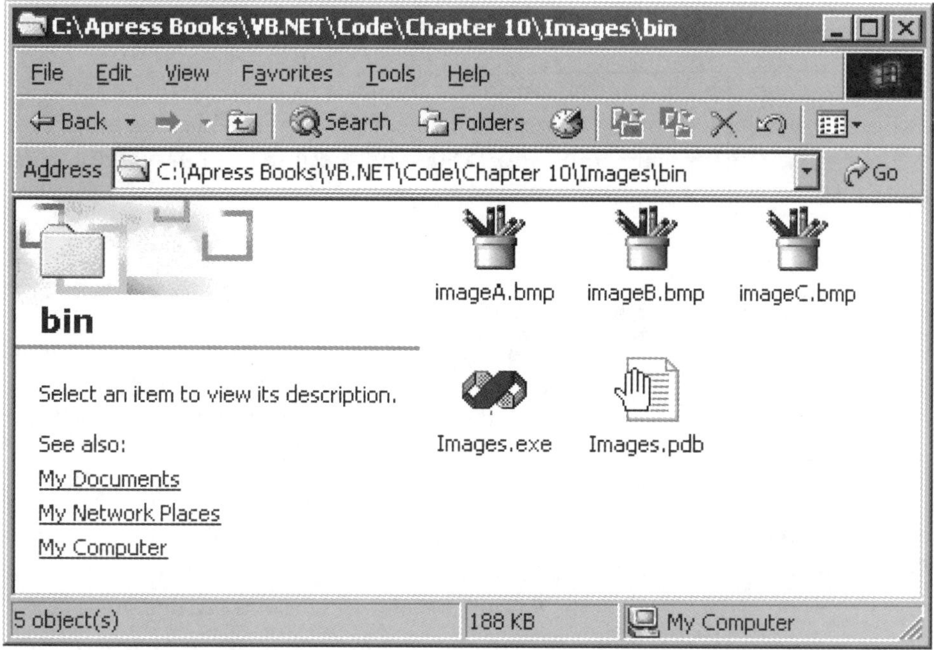

Figure 10-28. Stand-alone external resources

If any of these files are deleted, renamed, or relocated outside of the application directory, the program fails to execute (give it a try just for verification's sake). Now, as you recall from Chapter 7, an assembly is a collection of types and *optional resources.* The time has now come to learn how to bundle external resources (such as image files and strings) into the assembly itself. In this way, your .NET binary is truly self-contained. In a nutshell, bundling external resources into a .NET assembly by hand involves the following steps:

1. Create an *.resx file that establishes name/value pairs for each resource in your application using XML syntax.

2. Use the resgen.exe utility to convert your XML-based *.resx file into a binary equivalent (a *.resources file).

3. Using the /resource flag (or the shorthand /res flag) of the VB .NET compiler, embed the binary *.resources file into your assembly.

As you might suspect, these steps are followed automatically when you use the Visual Studio .NET IDE. You examine how the IDE will assist you in just a bit. For now, let's take the time to work with the .NET resource format in the raw.

System.Resources Namespace

The key to understanding the .NET resource format is to know the types defined within the System.Resources namespace. This set of types provides the programmatic means to manipulate both *.resx (XML) and *.resources (binary) files. Table 10-27 provides a rundown of the core types.

Table 10-27. Members of the System.Resources Namespace

SYSTEM.RESOURCES TYPE	MEANING IN LIFE
IResourceReader IResourceWriter	These interfaces are implemented by types that understand how to read and write .NET resources (in various formats). You do not need to implement these interfaces yourself unless you are interested in building a custom resource reader/writer.
ResourceReader ResourceWriter	These classes provide an implementation of the IResourceReader and IResourceWriter interfaces. Using the ResourceReader and ResourceWriter types, you are able to read from and write to binary *.resources files.
ResXResourceReader ResXResourceWriter	These classes also provide an implementation of the IResourceReader and IResourceWriter interfaces. Using the ResXResourceReader and ResXResourceWriter types, you are able to read from and write to XML *.resx files. This file may be turned into a binary equivalent (the *.resources file) using the resgen.exe utility.
ResourceManager	Provides easy access to culture-specific resources (BLOBs and string resources) at runtime.

*Programmatically Creating an *.resx File*

As mentioned, an *.resx file is a block of XML data that assigns name/value pairs for each resource in your application. The ResXResourceWriter class provides a set of members that allow you to create the *.resx file, add binary and string-based resources, and commit those resources to storage. To illustrate, assume you have a simple application (directly using the VB .NET compiler) whose job in life is to build an *.resx file containing an entry for the happy.bmp image seen earlier in this chapter and a single string resource. The GUI is as simple as possible (see Figure 10-29).

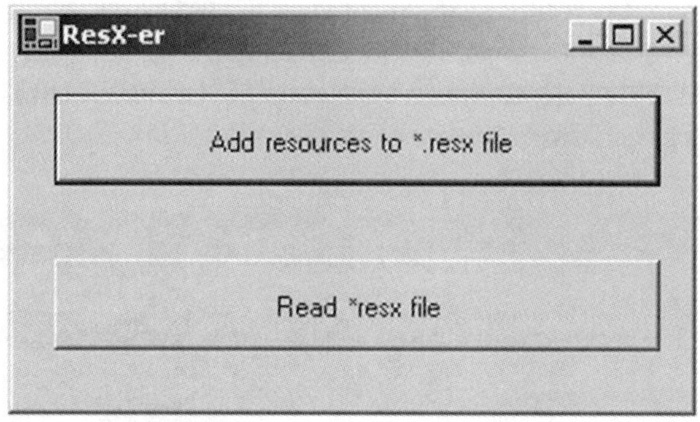

Figure 10-29. The simple UI

The Click event handler for the "Add resources" button does the grunt work of adding the happy.bmp and string resource to the *.resx file. Here is the code:

```
Protected Sub button1_Click (sender as object, e as System.EventArgs ) _
Handles button1.Click
    ' Make a resx writer & specify the file
    ' to write to.
    Dim w as ResXResourceWriter = _
        New ResXResourceWriter("ResXForm.resx")
    ' Add happy dude.
    Dim i as Image = New Bitmap("happy.bmp")
    w.AddResource("happyDude", i)
    ' Add a string.
    w.AddResource("welcomeString", "Hello new resource format!")
    ' Commit it and close.
    w.Generate()
    w.Close()
End Sub
```

The member of interest is ResXResourceWriter.AddResource(). This method has been overloaded a few times to allow you to insert binary BLOB data (as you did with the happy.bmp image), as well as textual data (as you have done for your test string). Notice that each version takes two parameters: the name of a given resources in the *.resx file and the data itself. The Generate() method commits the information to file.

Understand that you are not the one in charge of writing the raw XML that describes your resources. Rather, the logic within the ResXResourceWriter class is responsible for building the XML description of the inserted items. To prove the point, load the new *.resx file using Visual Studio .NET and peek inside the contents (see Figure 10-30). To do so, simply access the "Project | Add Existing Item" menu command and navigate to the *.resx data file (which of course is not present until you click the correct button of your application).

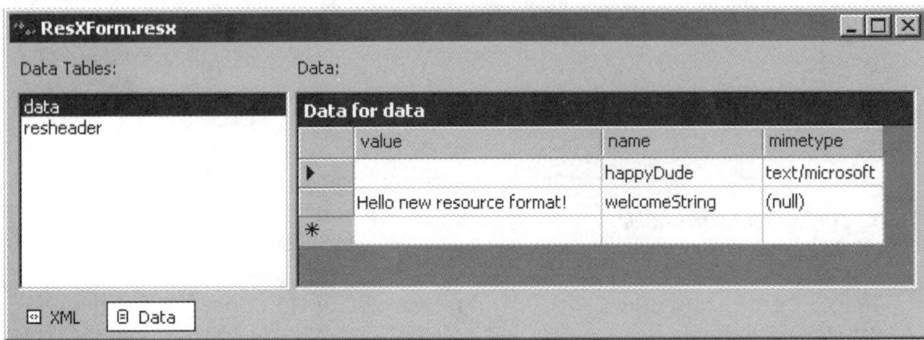

Figure 10-30. The XML representation of your external resources

The XML syntax used to represent your name/value pairs is as follows (note the binary representation of the "happy dude" bitmap):

```
< data name="happyDude" mimetype="text/microsoft-urt/binary-serialized/base64" >
<value>AAEAAAD''/AQAAAAAAAAAMAgAAADxTeXNOZWOuRHJhd2luZywgVmVyPTEuMC4yMjAOLjIxLCBM
b2M9IiIsIFNOPTAzNjg5MTE2ZDNhNGFlMzMFAQAAABVTeXNOZWOuRHJhd2luZy5CaXRtYXABAAAABERhd
GEDDVN5c3RlbS5CeXRlW1OCAAAACQMAAAAHAwAAAAABAAAATgEAAAACiVBORwOKGgoAAAANSUhEUgAAAC
AAAAAgBAMAAACBVGfHAAAAAXNSROIArs4c6QAAAARnQU1BAACxjwv8YQUAAAAgYOhSTQAAeiYAAICEAAD
6AAAAgOgAAHUwAADqYAAAOpgAABdwnLpRPAAAADBQTFRFAAAAgAAAAIAAgIAAAACAgACAAICAgICAwMDA
/wAAAP8A'8AAAD'wD/AP'''ex+xxAAAAAlwSFlzAAAOxAAADsQBlSsOGwAAAHtJREFUKM+FkUEOwCAIBL
kaPu+VX3Dnc21Bt6A2JfHgAMK6ROewO9KVzUNLPteYVcIvOKVglKzg6VCO4z2RiOMlv4ArOA+AKQNMcZ9
A554cIMs/tZChh7GpYjZW9+eGFlfdidqU74kmOsuPqQgDQB6cWW3Yjdqt3MzOcQEjV+MdZ/YPNQAAAABJ
RU5ErkJgggsAAAAAAAAAAAAAAAAAAAAA= </value>
</data>
<data name="welcomeString">
<value>Hello new resource format!</value>
</data>
```

Programmatically Reading an *.resx File

To illustrate how you can load and investigate an *.resx file programmatically, let's examine the code behind the "Read *.resx" button. This time, make use of a ResXResourceReader type. Once the correct file has been opened, ask the reader for a reference to its IDictionaryEnumerator interface, and loop over each name/value pair:

```
Protected Sub button2_Click (sender as object, e as System.EventArgs) _
Handles button2.Click
    ' Make a resx reader.
    Dim r as ResXResourceReader = _
        New ResXResourceReader("ResXForm.resx")
    ' Grab the IDictEnum interface and show everything.
    Dim en as IDictionaryEnumerator = r.GetEnumerator()
    While (en.MoveNext())
        MessageBox.Show("Value:" & en.Value.ToString(), _
            "Key: " & en.Key.ToString())
    End While
    r.Close()
End Sub
```

When you click the button, you see a pair of message boxes pop up, as the ResXResourceReader type loops through the XML file for each named value. For example, Figure 10-31 offers the listing for the happy dude.

Figure 10-31. Extracting the name/value pair

Building the *.resources File

Now that you understand how to build and manipulate an *.resx file, you can make use of the resgen.exe utility to produce the binary equivalent. As you recall from Chapter 2, you must register .NET SDK command-line tools (such as resgen.exe) to run from the command prompt. In this case, the value you must add to your current system variables is as follows:

```
C:\Program Files\Microsoft.NET\FrameworkSDK\Bin
```

Go ahead and add this value to the current Path before continuing. Again, although Visual Studio .NET will generate *.resource files automatically, just for the love of learning here is the raw command (notice you specify the *.resx file as an incoming flag):

```
resgen resxform.resx resxform.resources
```

Of course, you must open a command prompt in the directory containing the *.resx file before you run resgen.exe. If all is well, you should see the window in Figure 10-32.

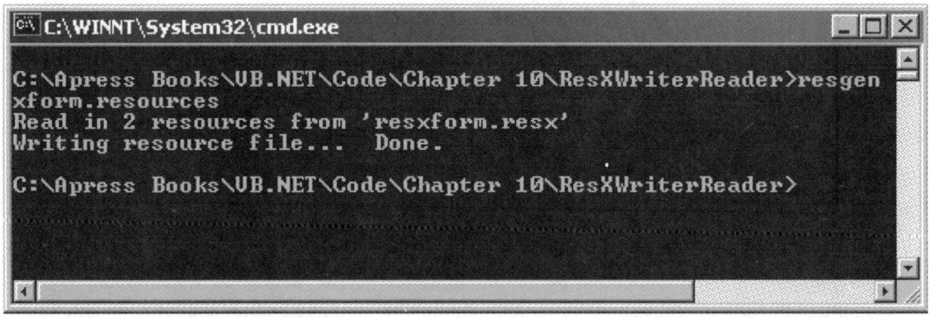

Figure 10-32. Running resgen.exe

At this point, you are able to open the new *.resources file and check out the binary (see Figure 10-33).

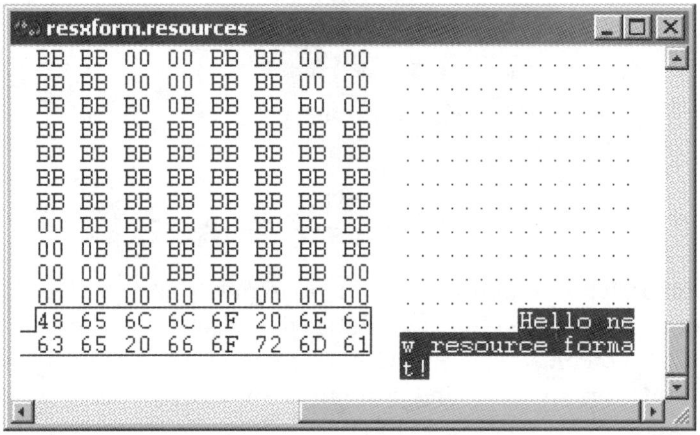

Figure 10-33. The binary *.resources file

*Binding the *.resources File into the Owning Assembly*

At this point, you are able to add the *.resources file as a command-line argument to the VB .NET compiler (again using the /res flag). Recall that doing so also requires you to reference each external assembly (i.e., System.Drawing.dll and so forth):

```
vbc /res:resxform.resources /r:System.Drawing.dll,
System.Windows.Forms.dll,System.dll *.vb
```

If you now open your new assembly using ILDasm.exe, you find the entry shown in Figure 10-34 in the assembly metadata.

```
MANIFEST
  .ver 0:0:0:0
}
.mresource public resxform.resources
{
}
.module ResXForm.exe
// MVID: {28D0A951-5677-4DB7-A3ED-7FD02476D828}
.imagebase 0x00400000
.subsystem 0x00000003
```

Figure 10-34. The updated manifest

As you can see, the manifest has recorded the name of the binary resources that are now contained in the owning assembly. In just a bit you will see how to programmatically read this information from an assembly to make use of it in your application.

SOURCE CODE *The ResXWriterReader project is included under the Chapter 10 subdirectory.*

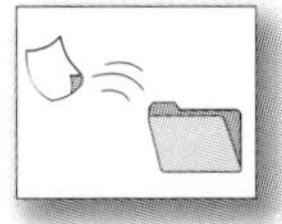

Working with ResourceWriters

The previous example made use of the ResXResourceReader and ResXResourceWriter types to generate an XML file that contains name/value pairs for each application resource. The resulting *.resx file was then run through the resgen.exe utility. Finally, the *.resources file was bound into the owning assembly using the /res flag. The truth of the matter is that you do not need to build an *.resx file (although having an XML representation of your resources can come in handy).

If you do not require an *.resx file, you can make use of the ResourceWriter type to directly create a *.resources file. To illustrate, assume you have created a new VB .NET Console application named ResourceTest. The Main() method uses the ResourceWrite type to directly generate the myResources.resources file:

```
' Manually set resources. . .
Imports System.Resources
Imports System.Windows.Forms
Imports System.Drawing
Module Module1
    Sub Main()
        ' Make a new *.resources file.
        Dim rw As ResourceWriter
        rw = New ResourceWriter("myResources.resources")
        ' Add 1 image and 1 string.
        rw.AddResource("happyDude", New Bitmap("happy.bmp"))
        rw.AddResource("welcomeString", "Welcome to .NET resources.")
        rw.Generate()
        rw.Close()
    End Sub
End Module
```

Compile and run the application to generate the *.resource file. Now you can bind the contained binary data to the owning assembly as before (you may have to relocate some source files into your application directory before running the VB .NET compiler):

```
vbc /res:myresources.resources /r:System.Windows.Forms.dll,
System.dll, System.Drawing.dll Module1.vb
```

If you want to read the raw name/value data from the binary *.resources file, you are free to make use of the ResourceReader class. This is almost identical to working with the ResXResourceReader type.

Working with ResourceManagers

Rather than working with the ResourceReader class directly, you will most likely use the ResourceManager type. The reason is simple: It is easier to work with. Using the ResourceManager, you are able to extract binary and textual data from an assembly for use in your application.

To illustrate, assume you have added a new class to the current project named MyResourceReader. This type uses a ResourceManager type to pull the happyDude and welcomeString resources from the assembly and dump them into a PictureBox and Label object using the GetObject() and GetString() members. Be aware, however, that the double quoted strings you send into these methods are *case-sensitive.* Here is the code:

```
Class MyResourceReader
    Public Sub ReadMyResources()
        ' Open the resources file.
        Dim rm As ResourceManager = New ResourceManager("myResources", _
                  System.Reflection.Assembly.GetExecutingAssembly())
        ' Load image resource.
        Dim p As PictureBox = New PictureBox()
        Dim b As Bitmap = CType(rm.GetObject("happyDude"), Bitmap)
        p.Image = b
        p.Height = b.Height
        p.Width = b.Width
        p.Location = New Point(10, 10)
        ' Load string resource.
        Dim label1 As Label = New Label()
        label1.Location = New Point(50, 10)
        label1.Font = New Font(label1.Font.FontFamily, 12, FontStyle.Bold)
        label1.AutoSize = True
        label1.Text = rm.GetString("welcomeString")
        ' Build a Form to display both resources.
        Dim f As Form = New Form()
        f.Height = 100
        f.Width = 370
        f.Text = "These resources are embedded in the assembly!"
        ' Add controls and show Form.
        f.Controls.Add(p)
        f.Controls.Add(label1)
        f.ShowDialog()
    End Sub
End Class
```

Before you run the application, be sure to update Main() to call the ReadMyResources() method:

```
Dim r As MyResourceReader = New MyResourceReader()
r.ReadMyResources()
```

When you run this application, the box in Figure 10-35 should appear.

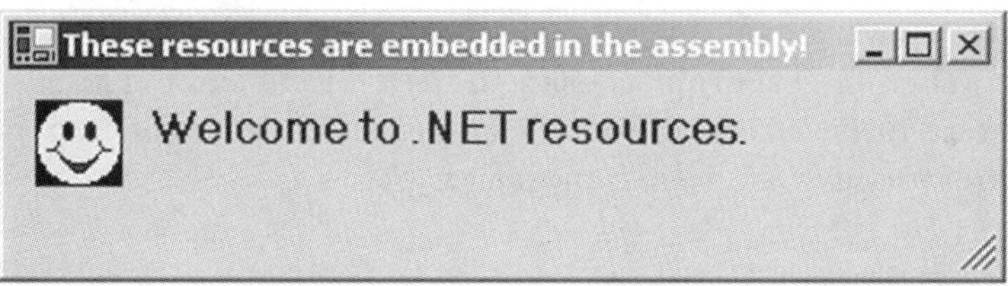

Figure 10-35. Extracting resources with the ResourceManager

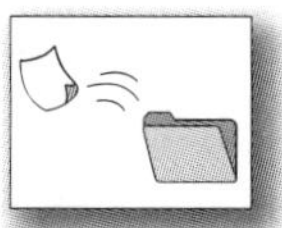

SOURCE CODE *The ResourceTest project is included under the Chapter 10 subdirectory.*

Automatic Resource Configuration a la Visual Studio .NET

Now, let's look at how the Visual Studio .NET IDE gets you up and running with the correct resource file configuration automatically.

When you create a new Windows Forms project workspace using Visual Studio .NET, the IDE automatically defines an *.resx file for your application. Furthermore, when you insert new resources into the project, the name/value pairs contained in the *.resx file are updated on your behalf. You can view the project's *.resx file by selecting the "Show all files" option from the Solution Explorer window (as highlighted in Figure 10-36).

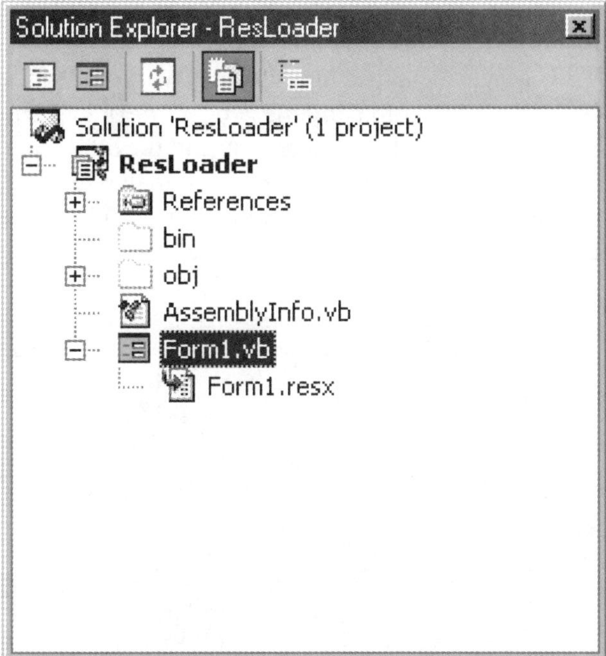

*Figure 10-36. Viewing the freebie *.resx file*

Select this file and look at the Properties window. You will see that the build action for this file has been configured as "Embedded Resource," as shown in Figure 10-37.

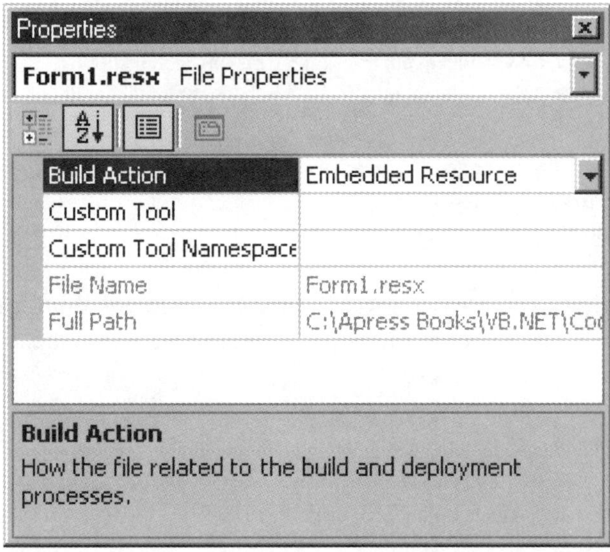

*Figure 10-37. Configuring the Build Action for the *.resx file*

This option compiles the *.resx file to produce the corresponding *.resources file, which is then embedded into your assembly.

To illustrate this process, create a new VB .NET Windows Application workspace named ResLoader. The Form contains two PictureHolder types: One type has its Image property set to the happy.bmp file, and the other type is initially empty. In addition, a single button type will be used to dynamically read this happy dude from file and place it into the empty PictureHolder. The GUI is shown in Figure 10-38.

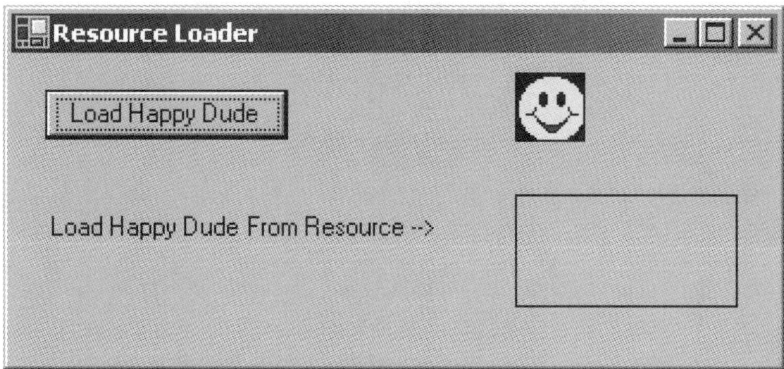

Figure 10-38. Before loading happy dude

As you insert resources (such as a bitmap) into the project, the IDE responds by creating an instance of the ResourceManager type within the scope of your InitializeComponent() method:

```
<System.Diagnostics.DebuggerStepThrough()> Private Sub InitializeComponent()
    Dim resources As System.Resources.ResourceManager = New  _
    System.Resources.ResourceManager(GetType(Form1))
. . .
        Me.PictureBox1.Image = CType(resources.GetObject("PictureBox1.Image"), _
        System.Drawing.Bitmap)
 End Sub
```

Needless to say, you are free to add a private ResourceManager member variable for use throughout your application. To illustrate, here is the code behind the button's Click event:

```
' Be sure to specify "System.Resources"
Private Sub Button1_Click(ByVal sender As System.Object, _
ByVal e As System.EventArgs) Handles Button1.Click
    ' Make a RM.
```

```
Dim resources As System.Resources.ResourceManager = _
    New System.Resources.ResourceManager(GetType(Form1))
' Suck out the image and place in the PictureBox.
PictureBox2.Image = _
    CType(resources.GetObject("PictureBox1.Image"), _
    System.Drawing.Image)
End Sub
```

If you run the application and click the button, you find that the image has been extracted from the assembly and placed into the second PictureBox (see Figure 10-39).

Figure 10-39. After loading happy dude

SOURCE CODE *The ResLoader project is included under the Chapter 10 subdirectory.*

Summary

GDI+ is the name given to a number of related .NET namespaces, each of which is used to render graphic images to a Control-derived type. The chapter began by examining the core types defined within the System.Drawing namespace (including a number of useful utility types), and you learned how to intercept paint events. A key aspect to GDI+ is, of course, the Graphics object.

The bulk of this chapter was spent examining how to work with core GDI+ object types. The Pen and Brush types provide a good deal of specialized functionality, especially when making use of the more exotic types defined in System.Drawing.Drawing2D. Font types require a fair amount of information (a Brush type, Color type, location to render the text, and so on)—however, this does offer a good deal of functionality.

This chapter wrapped up by examining the new .NET resource format. As you have seen, an application does not *need* to bundle its external resources into the containing assembly; however, if this is the case, the binary image is far more portable. The *.resx file is used to describe (in XML syntax) a set of name/value pairs. This file is fed into the resgen.exe utility, resulting in a binary format (*.resources) that can then be embedded into the owning assembly. The ResourceManager type is your key to programmatically obtaining this information.

CHAPTER 11

Programming with Windows Form Controls

THIS CHAPTER IS CONCERNED with providing a road map of the suite of GUI widgets defined in the System.Windows.Forms namespace. If you have been reading this book from the beginning, you have already had a chance to work with some Form-level Control types such as MainMenu, MenuItem, StatusBar, and ToolBar (see Chapter 9). In this chapter, I am interested in examining the types that tend to exist within the boundaries of a Form's client area (e.g., Buttons, TrackBars, TextBoxes, Panels, and the like).

In addition to giving you a formal grounding in the Windows Forms Control set, this chapter also details a number of related topics, such as establishing the tab order for your widgets, and configuring the "docking" and "anchoring" behaviors for your family of GUI types.

The chapter includes a discussion of building custom dialog boxes, as well as techniques for responding to (and validating) user input. In addition, you examine a new facility offered by the .NET Windows Forms architecture: Form inheritance. As you will see, it is now possible to establish "is-a" relationships between related Forms. Finally, the chapter wraps up by examining how to build custom .NET controls (which is almost identical to the process of building an ActiveX control type under VB 6.0) and .NET components.

Understanding the Windows Forms Control Hierarchy

The System.Windows.Forms namespace contains a number of types that represent common GUI widgets. Using these types, you can respond to user input in a Windows Forms application. Because .NET is a system of types built on standard OO principles, these Controls are arranged in a hierarchy of related types. Figure 11-1 illustrates the big picture. (Note that Control is the common base class for all widgets.)

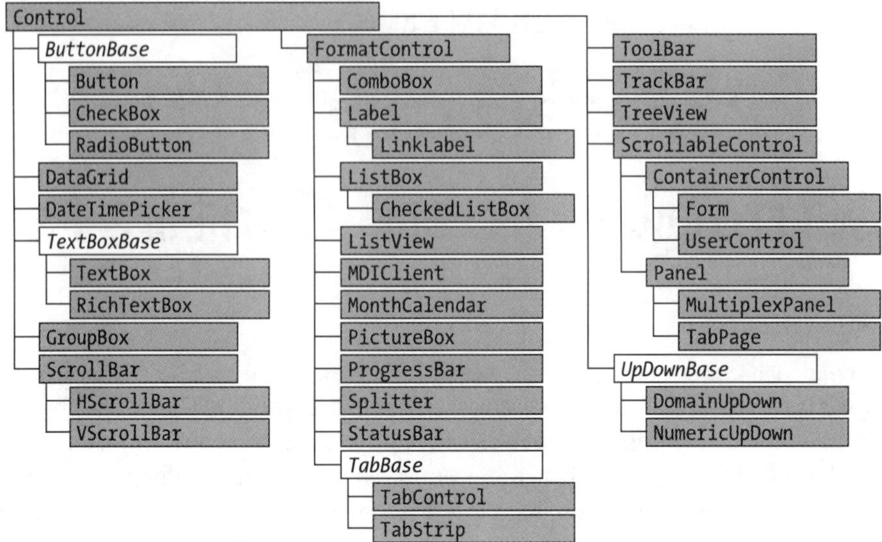

Figure 11-1. The Windows Forms Control hierarchy

As you learned in Chapter 9, the Control type is the base class that provides a minimal and complete set of behaviors for all descending widgets. This includes the ability to process mouse and keyboard events, establish the physical dimensions of the widget using various properties (Height, Width, Left, Right, Location, and so on), manipulate background and foreground colors, establish the active font, and so forth.

As you read through this chapter, remember that the Controls you examine gain most of their functionality from the Control base class. Here I focus (more or less) on a given type's unique members. (I assume you will explore the base class functionality on your own.) And now, on to the show!

Adding Controls to Forms (the Hard Way)

Regardless which type of Control you choose to place on a Form, you follow a similar set of steps (all of which are automated using VS .NET). First of all, create any number of member variables that represent the GUI items maintained by the Form. Next, inside the Form's constructor (or in the InitializeComponent() method), configure the look and feel of each Control using the provided properties, methods, and events. Finally (and most important), once the Control has been set to its initial state, add it to the Form's Controls collection (using the Control property). If you forget this final step, your Control will *not* be visible at runtime! To illustrate the process, assume you have an Empty project workspace, and added a class named MyForm, shown here:

```
' Don't forget to add a reference to System.Windows.Forms.dll.
Public Class Form1
    Inherits System.Windows.Forms.Form
...
    ' 1) Add the private data member.
    ' (with or without events)
    ' TextBox could also be declared as Friend...
    Private WithEvents firstNameBox As TextBox = New TextBox()
    Public Sub New()
        MyBase.New()
        Me.Text = "Controls in the raw"
        ' 2) Configure new TextBox.
        firstNameBox.Text = "Chucky"
        firstNameBox.Size = New Size(150, 50)
        firstNameBox.Location = New Point(10, 10)
        ' 3) Add new Controls to the Form's Controls collection.
        Me.Controls.Add(firstNameBox)
    End Sub
End Class
```

Notice that you do not need to implement an InitializeComponent() method to build the look and feel of the TextBox type. This method is really nothing more than a helper method used by VS .NET and has nothing to do with a "proper" Form implementation.

The Control$ControlCollection Type

While the process of adding a new widget to a Form is quite simple, I'd like to discuss the Controls property in a bit more detail. In a similar vein as VB 6.0, this property returns a reference to a nested class named ControlCollection defined by the Control class (i.e., Control$ControlCollection). The Control$ControlCollection type maintains an entry for each widget placed on the Form. You can obtain a reference to this collection any time you want to "walk the list" of child widgets, as shown here:

```
' Get access to the Control$ControlCollection type for this Form.
Dim coll as Control.ControlCollection = Me.Controls
```

Once you have a reference, you can call any of the members described in Table 11-1 (which should look quite familiar, given your work in Chapter 5).

Be aware that, by default, Controls are placed in the ControlCollection type using an $(n + 1)$ insertion policy.

Table 11-1. Nested ControlCollection Properties

CONTROL$CONTROLCOLLECTION MEMBERS	MEANING IN LIFE
Add() AddRange()	Used to insert a new Control-derived type (or array of types) in the collection
Clear()	Removes all entries in the collection.
Count	Returns the number of items in the collection.
GetChildIndex() SetChildIndex()	Returns (or sets) the index value for a specified item in the collection.
GetEnumerator()	Returns the IEnumerator interface for this collection.
Remove()	Removes a given Control from the collection, given its index.

To illustrate programmatic manipulation of this very important collection, assume you have now added another widget (a Button) to the Form's collection. Also assume you have added an event handler for the Button's Click event. In the implementation of this method, you loop over each item in the Controls collection and print out some relevant information about the current Control, as shown here:

```
Public Class Form1
    Inherits System.Windows.Forms.Form
. . .
    ' Could also be declared as Friend. . .
    Private WithEvents firstNameBox As TextBox = New TextBox()
    Private WithEvents btnShowControls As Button = New Button()

    Public Sub New()
        MyBase.New()
   . . .
        btnShowControls.Text = "Examine Controls collection"
        btnShowControls.Size = New Size(90, 90)
        btnShowControls.Location = New Point(10, 70)
```

```
        Me.Controls.Add(firstNameBox)
        Me.Controls.Add(btnShowControls)
    End Sub

    Private Sub TheButtonWasClicked(ByVal sender As Object, _
    ByVal e As EventArgs) Handles btnShowControls.Click
        ' Display information for each item in the collection.
        Dim coll As Control.ControlCollection = Me.Controls
        Dim c As Control
        For Each c In coll
            ' Second parameter of GetChildIndex() enables or disables
            ' the throwing of an exception if the item is not present.
            If (Not c Is Nothing) Then
                MessageBox.Show(c.Text, "Index numb: " & _
                                coll.GetChildIndex(c, False))
            End If
        Next
    End Sub
End Class
```

Figure 11-2 shows the complete GUI. Notice how the default behavior of the Button.Text property is to wrap text in the display rectangle.

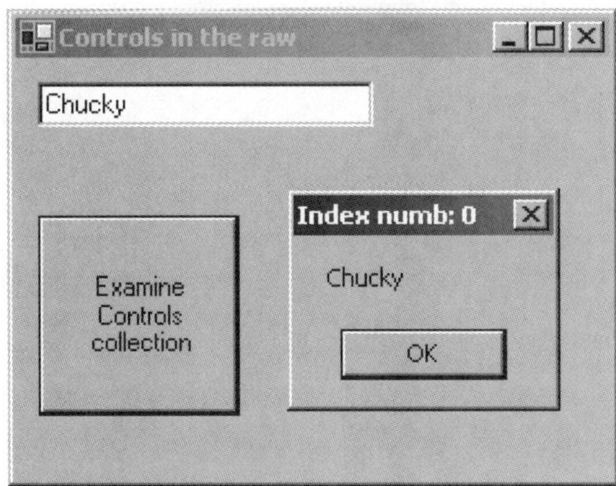

Figure 11-2. Form Controls

Clicking the Button widget results in two messages, which identify the Controls in the internal collection (as seen in Figure 11-2).

SOURCE CODE *The ControlsByHand project is included under the Chapter 11 subdirectory.*

Adding Controls to Forms (the Easy Way)

Although you are always free to write Windows Forms code "in the raw," you will probably choose to use the Visual Studio .NET IDE instead. When you drop a widget on the design time Form, the IDE responds by adding a member variable (declared WithEvents) on your behalf. Of course, typically you want to change the name of this new variable to represent its overall functionality (e.g., "btnFirstName" rather than the default "button1").

As you design the look and feel of the widget using the IDE's Properties window (Figure 11-3), the underlying code changes are added to the InitializeComponent() member function.

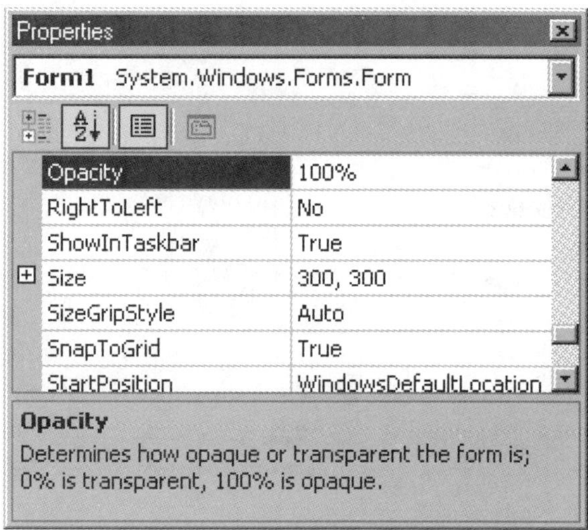

Figure 11-3. Configuring Controls at design time

As you recall from Chapter 6, when you wish to handle events for a given GUI widget, you typically make use of the WithEvents keyword (although you are also free to dynamically intercept events using the AddHandler() method). Once a widget has been declared WithEvents, you may generate an event handler using the VB .NET code window (Figure 11-4).

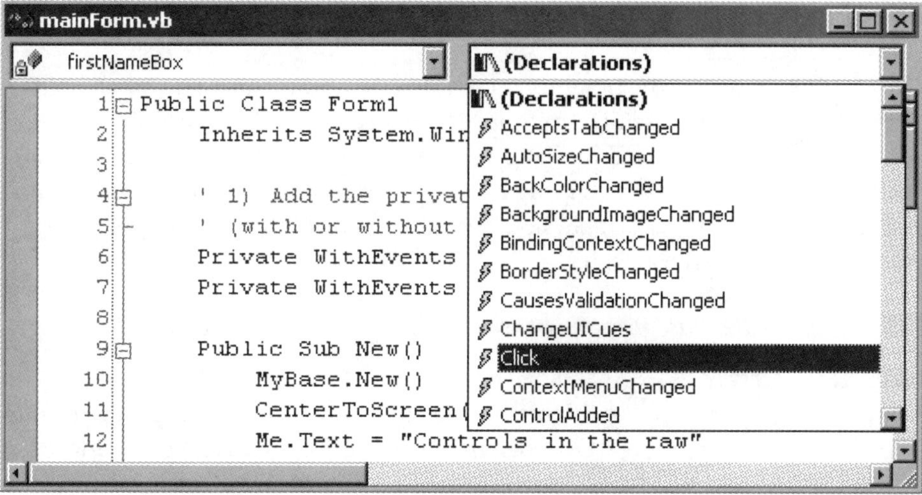

Figure 11-4. Building event handlers at design time

If you examine the code generated in the InitializeComponent() method, you find something like the following (note that the new GUI item is inserted in the Form's Controls collection on your behalf using the AddRange() method, which takes an array of Controls, rather than calling AddControl() numerous times):

```
Private Sub InitializeComponent()
     Me.firstNameBox = new System.Windows.Forms.TextBox()
     Me.firstNameBox.Location = new System.Drawing.Point(32, 40)
     Me.firstNameBox.TabIndex = 0
     Me.firstNameBox.Text = "Chucky"
     Me.AutoScaleBaseSize = new System.Drawing.Size(5, 13)
     Me.ClientSize = new System.Drawing.Size(292, 273)
     Me.Controls.AddRange(new System.Windows.Forms.Control() _
                              {Me.firstNameBox})
     . . .
End Sub
```

The remainder of this chapter focuses on a number of behaviors offered by numerous GUI widgets by examining the "raw" code behind the scenes. If you decide to use the VS .NET IDE, be sure to examine the code generated inside the IntializeComponent() method to gain a deeper understanding of Windows Forms control programming.

The TextBox Control

The TextBox Control is the first item under investigation. This GUI widget holds some blurb of text or possibly multiple lines of text. A TextBox Control can also be configured as read-only and may support scroll bars. The immediate base class of TextBox is TextBoxBase, which provides many common behaviors for the TextBox and RichTextBox Controls. Table 11-2 describes some of the core properties provided by the TextBoxBase type.

Table 11-2. TextBoxBase Properties

TEXTBOXBASE PROPERTY	MEANING IN LIFE
AcceptsTab	Indicates if pressing the Tab key in a multiline TextBox Control tabs in the Control itself, rather than moving the focus to the next Control in the tab order.
AutoSize	Determines if the size of the Control automatically adjusts when the assigned font is changed.
BackColor ForeColor	Gets or sets the background or foreground color of the Control.
HideSelection	Gets or sets a value indicating whether the selected text in the TextBox Control remains highlighted when the Control loses focus.
MaxLength	Configures the maximum number of characters that can be entered in the TextBox Control.
Modified	Gets or sets a value that indicates that the TextBox Control has been modified by the user since the Control was created or its contents were last set.
Multiline	Specifies if this TextBox can contain multiple lines of text.
ReadOnly	Marks this TextBox as read only.
SelectedText SelectionLength	Contains the currently selected text (or some number of characters) in the Control.
SelectionStart	Gets or sets the starting point of text selected in the TextBox.
WordWrap	Indicates whether a multiline TextBox Control automatically wraps words to the beginning of the next line when necessary.

The TextBoxBase type also defines a number of methods, which allow the derived type to handle clipboard operations (via the Cut(), Copy(), and Paste() methods), undo operations (Undo(), of course), and carry out other related functionality (Clear(), AppendText(), and so on).

As for the events defined by TextBoxBase, the item of interest is TextChange. This event is fired whenever the content in a TextBoxBase derived type is modified. This can be very helpful when you wish to block the user from entering certain types of characters (e.g., numerical data only or alphabetic data only).

In addition to the behavior inherited by TextBoxBase, the TextBox type grabs a good deal of functionality from the Control base class. In fact, the properties defined by TextBox alone are quite limited (Table 11-3).

Table 11-3. TextBox Properties

TEXTBOX PROPERTY	MEANING IN LIFE
AcceptsReturn	Gets or sets a value indicating whether pressing Enter in a multiline TextBox Control creates a new line of text in the Control or activates the default Button for the Form.
CharacterCasing	Gets or sets whether the TextBox Control modifies the case of characters as they are typed.
PasswordChar	Gets or sets the character used to mask characters in a single-line TextBox Control used to enter passwords.
ScrollBars	Gets or sets which scroll bars should appear in a multiline TextBox Control.
TextAlign	Gets or sets how text is aligned in a TextBox Control, using the HorizontalAlignment enumeration.

The HorizontalAlignment enumeration used in conjunction with the TextAlign property offers the values described in Table 11-4.

Table 11-4. HorizontalAlignment Values

HORIZONTALALIGNMENT VALUE	MEANING IN LIFE
Center	The object or text is aligned in the center of the Control element.
Left	The object or text is aligned on the left of the Control element.
Right	The object or text is aligned on the right of the Control element.

Fun with TextBoxes

To illustrate some of the more exotic aspects of the TextBox, build a multiline text area that has been configured to accept Return and Tab keystrokes and supports a vertical scroll bar. Here is the configuration code (assume you have already created a member of type TextBox named multiLineBox):

```
' Your first TextBox.
Me.multiLineBox.AcceptsReturn = True
Me.multiLineBox.AcceptsTab = True
Me.multiLineBox.Location = New System.Drawing.Point(152, 8)
Me.multiLineBox.Multiline = True
Me.multiLineBox.Name = "multiLineBox"
Me.multiLineBox.ScrollBars = System.Windows.Forms.ScrollBars.Vertical
Me.multiLineBox.Size = New System.Drawing.Size(240, 104)
Me.multiLineBox.TabIndex = 0
Me.multiLineBox.Text = "Type some stuff here."
```

Notice that the ScrollBars property is assigned a value from the ScrollBars enumeration, which defines the values Vertical, Horizontal, None, and Both.

Now assume you have placed a simple Button on the Form and added an event handler for the Button's Click event. The implementation of this method simply places the TextBox's text in a message box (just to illustrate grabbing values from a TextBox Control). The current UI is shown in Figure 11-5.

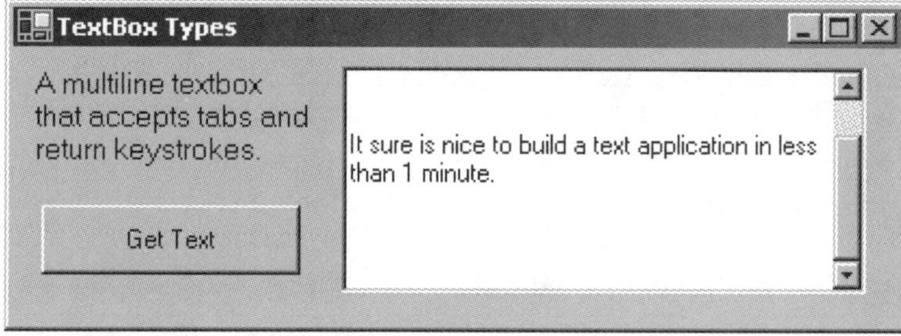

Figure 11-5. The TextBoxes Form

The code behind the Button Click event is simple, as shown here:

```
Private Sub btnGetMultiLineText_Click(ByVal sender As System.Object, _
ByVal e As System.EventArgs) Handles btnGetMultiLineText.Click
    MessageBox.Show(multiLineBox.Text, "Here is your text")
End Sub
```

Next, add some additional TextBoxes to the Form, this time focusing on the masking capabilities of the widget (Figure 11-6). The second TextBox (capsOnlyBox) forces all keystrokes to be converted to uppercase. The third TextBox (passwordBox) forces all keystrokes to be converted to a password character (for which I have chosen "$," signifying how your financial life as a .NET developer should pan out).

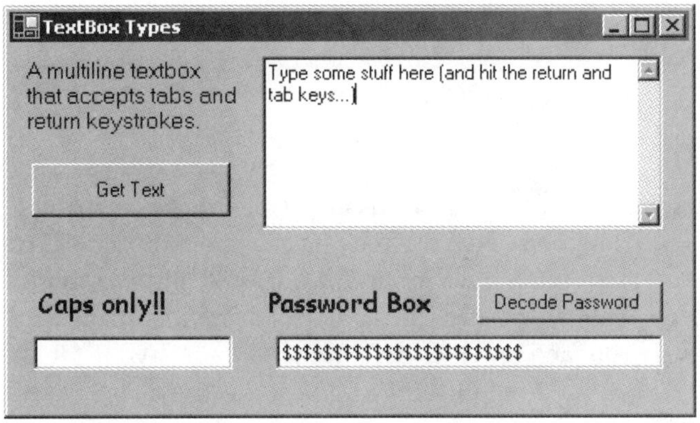

Figure 11-6. Masking capabilities of the TextBox

The additional Button (btnPasswordDecoderRing) supports a Click event handler that extracts the real keystrokes typed in the passwordBox TextBox, as shown here:

```
Private Sub btnPasswordDecoderRing_Click(ByVal sender As System.Object, _
ByVal e As System.EventArgs) Handles btnPasswordDecoderRing.Click
    MessageBox.Show(passwordBox.Text, "Your password is:")
End Sub
```

Here is the relevant code that configures these new TextBox types:

```
' The 'Caps Only!' TextBox.
' Note that CharacterCasing is established by an associated enumeration,
' which can be assigned Upper, Lower, or Normal.
capsOnlyBox.Location = New System.Drawing.Point (14, 176)
capsOnlyBox.CharacterCasing = System.Windows.Forms.CharacterCasing.Upper
capsOnlyBox.Size = New System.Drawing.Size (120, 20)

' The password TextBox
passwordBox.Location = New System.Drawing.Point (160, 176)
Me.passwordBox.PasswordChar = ChrW(36)
```

As mentioned, TextBoxBase defines an additional derived type named RichTextBox. This class is a Control that supports the display and manipulation of (highly) formatted text. For example, you can configure multiple font selections in a single widget, URLs, bulleted text, and so forth. I assume interested readers will consult online Help for further details.

SOURCE CODE *The TextBoxes application is included under the Chapter 11 subdirectory.*

The Mighty Button Type (and the ButtonBase Parent Class)

Of all user interface widgets, the Button can be regarded as the simplest, but most well-respected GUI input device. The role of the System.Windows.Forms.Button type is to provide a simple vehicle for user input, typically in response to a mouse click or key press. The Button class immediately derives from an abstract type named ButtonBase, which provides a number of key behaviors for all Button-related types (CheckBox, RadioButton, and Button). Table 11-5 describes some (but by no means all) core ButtonBase properties.

Table 11-5. ButtonBase Properties

BUTTONBASE PROPERTY	MEANING IN LIFE
FlatStyle	Gets or sets the flat style appearance of the Button Control, using members of the FlatStyle enumeration.
Image	Configures which (optional) image is displayed somewhere within the bounds of a ButtonBase derived type. Recall that Control also defines a BackgroundImage property, which is used to render an image over the entire surface area of a widget.
ImageAlign	Sets the alignment of the image on the Button Control, using the ContentAlignment enumeration.
ImageIndex ImageList	Work together to set the image list index value of the image displayed on the Button Control, from the corresponding ImageList Control.
IsDefault	Specifies whether the Button Control is the default Button (i.e., receives focus in response to pressing of the Enter key).
TextAlign	Gets or sets the alignment of the text on the Button Control, using the ContentAlignment enumeration.

The FlatStyle property controls the general appearance of the Button itself and can be assigned any member of the related FlatStyle enumeration (Table 11-6).

Table 11-6. FlatStyle Values

FLATSTYLE ENUMERATION VALUE	MEANING IN LIFE
Flat	The Control appears flat, with no three-dimensional rendering. When the cursor is over the Button, the text color changes to indicate it has the current focus.
Popup	A Control appears flat until the cursor moves over it, at which point it appears three dimensional.
Standard	The Control appears three dimensional, like the familiar standard push-button.
System	The appearance of the Control is determined by the user's operating system.

The Button class itself defines almost no additional functionality beyond that inherited by the ButtonBase base class, with the core exception of the DialogResult property. As you see later in this chapter, a dialog box makes use of this property to return a value that represents which Button was clicked (e.g., OK, Cancel, and so on) when the dialog box was terminated.

Configuring the Content Position

Most people assume that the text contained in a Button is always placed on the middle of the Button, equidistant from all sides. While this can be a well-established standard, the TextAlign property of the ButtonBase type makes it extremely simple to position text at just about any location. To set the position of your Button's caption, use the ContentAlignment enumeration (Table 11-7). Be aware that this same enumeration is used to configure the location of any optional Button image (as you will see).

Table 11-7. ContentAlignment Values

CONTENTALIGNMENT VALUE	MEANING IN LIFE
BottomCenter	Content is vertically aligned at the bottom and horizontally aligned at the center.
BottomLeft	Content is vertically aligned at the bottom and horizontally aligned on the left.
BottomRight	Content is vertically aligned at the bottom and horizontally aligned on the right.

Table 11-7. ContentAlignment Values (continued)

CONTENTALIGNMENT VALUE	MEANING IN LIFE
MiddleCenter	Content is vertically aligned in the middle and horizontally aligned at the center.
MiddleLeft	Content is vertically aligned in the middle and horizontally aligned on the left.
MiddleRight	Content is vertically aligned in the middle and horizontally aligned on the right.
TopCenter	Content is vertically aligned at the top and horizontally aligned at the center.
TopLeft	Content is vertically aligned at the top and horizontally aligned on the left.
TopRight	Content is vertically aligned at the top and horizontally aligned on the right.

Fun with Buttons

To illustrate working with this most primitive of user input widgets, the following application uses the FlatStyle, ImageAlign, and TextAlign properties. The most interesting aspect of the underlying code is in the Click event handler for the btnStandard type (which is the Button in the middle of the Form). This illustration cycles through each member of the ContentAlignment enumeration and changes the Button's caption text and caption location based on the current value.

Also, the fourth Button on the Form (btnImage) supports a background image and a small bull's-eye icon, which is also dynamically relocated based on the current value of the ContentAlignment enumeration. Figure 11-7 shows the program in action.

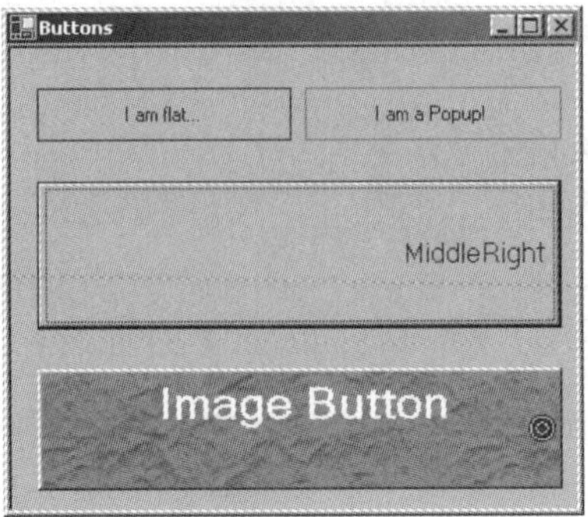

Figure 11-7. ContentAlignment in action

Here is the relevant code:

```
Public Class Form1
    Inherits System.Windows.Forms.Form
    ' Four buttons.
    Private WithEvents btnImage As System.Windows.Forms.Button
    Private WithEvents btnStandard As System.Windows.Forms.Button
    Private WithEvents btnPopup As System.Windows.Forms.Button
    Private WithEvents btnFlat As System.Windows.Forms.Button
    ' Hold the current text alignment
    Private currAlignment As ContentAlignment = ContentAlignment.MiddleCenter
    Private currEnumPos As Integer
    ' InitializeComponent() omitted. . .
    Private Sub btnStandard_Click(ByVal sender As System.Object, _
    ByVal e As System.EventArgs) Handles btnStandard.Click
        ' Get all possible values
        ' of the ContentAlignment enum.
        Dim values As Array = [Enum].GetValues(currAlignment.GetType())
        ' Bump the current position in the enum.
        ' & check for wrap around.
        currEnumPos += 1
        If (currEnumPos >= values.Length) Then
            currEnumPos = 0
        End If
        ' Bump the current enum value.
        currAlignment = CType(values.GetValue(currEnumPos), ContentAlignment)
        btnStandard.TextAlign = currAlignment
        ' Paint enum value name on button.
        btnStandard.Text = currAlignment.ToString()
        ' Now assign the location of the ICON on
        ' btnImage. . .
        btnImage.ImageAlign = currAlignment
    End Sub
End Class
```

SOURCE CODE *The Buttons application is included under the Chapter 11 subdirectory.*

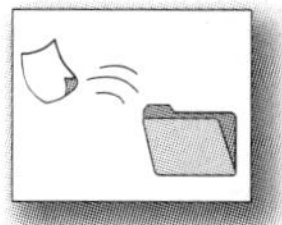

Working with CheckBoxes

The other two ButtonBase-derived types of interest are CheckBox (which can support up to three possible states) and RadioButton (which can be either selected or not selected). Like the Button, these types also receive most of their functionality from the Control base class. However, each class defines some additional functionality. First, consider the core properties of the CheckBox widget described in Table 11-8.

Table 11-8. CheckBox Properties

CHECKBOX PROPERTY	MEANING IN LIFE
Appearance	Configures the appearance of a CheckBox Control, using the Appearance enumeration.
AutoCheck	Gets or sets a value indicating whether the Checked or CheckState value and the CheckBox's appearance are automatically changed when it is clicked.
CheckAlign	Gets or sets the horizontal and vertical alignment of a CheckBox on a CheckBox Control, using the ContentAlignment enumeration (see the Button type for a full description).
Checked	Returns a Boolean value representing the state of the CheckBox (checked or unchecked). If the ThreeState property is set to true, the Checked property returns true for either checked or indeterminately checked values.
CheckState	Gets or sets a value indicating whether the CheckBox is checked, using a CheckState enumeration, rather than a Boolean value. This is very helpful when working with tristate CheckBoxes.
ThreeState	Configures whether the CheckBox supports three states of selection (as specified by the CheckState enumeration) rather than two.

The ThreeState property is configured using the CheckState enumeration (Table 11-9).

Table 11-9. CheckState Values

CHECKSTATE VALUE	MEANING IN LIFE
Checked	The Control is checked.
Indeterminate	The Control is indeterminate. An indeterminate Control generally has a shaded appearance.
Unchecked	The Control is unchecked.

You have probably seen examples of Controls with these check states. For example, imagine a TreeView Control supporting a main node that expands to 10 checkable subnodes. If the user selects 6 of the 10 subnodes, the main node is in an indeterminate state (as 4 items are left unchecked).

Working with RadioButtons and GroupBoxes

The RadioButton type really requires little comment, given that it is (more or less) just a slightly redesigned CheckBox. In fact, the members of a RadioButton are almost identical to those of the CheckBox type. The only notable difference is the CheckedChanged event, which is fired when the Checked value changes. Also, the RadioButton type does not support the ThreeState property, as a RadioButton must be on or off.

Typically, multiple RadioButton objects are logically and physically grouped together to function as a whole. For example, if you have a set of four RadioButton types representing the color choice of a given automobile, you may wish to ensure that only one of the four types can be checked at a time. Rather than writing code programmatically to do so, use the GroupBox Control. Like the RadioButton, there is little to say about the GroupBox Control, given that it receives all of its functionality from the Control base class.

Fun with RadioButtons (and CheckBoxes)

To illustrate working with the CheckBox, RadioButton, and GroupBox types, create a new Windows Form Application named CarConfig. The main Form allows users to enter in (and confirm) information about a new vehicle they intend to purchase. Figure 11-8 shows the initial user interface.

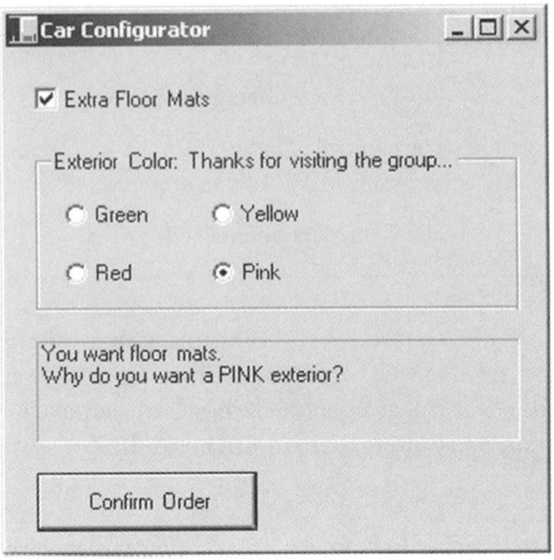

Figure 11-8. Grouped RadioButtons

Assume you have initialized a number of private member variables representing each GUI widget. First, you have your CheckBox, constructed as shown here:

```
' Create your CheckBox.
checkFloorMats.Location = new System.Drawing.Point (16, 16)
checkFloorMats.Text = "Extra Floor Mats"
checkFloorMats.Size = new System.Drawing.Size (136, 24)
checkFloorMats.FlatStyle = System.Windows.Forms.FlatStyle.Popup

' Add to Control collection.
Me.Controls.Add (Me.checkFloorMats)
```

Programmatically speaking, when you wish to place a widget under the ownership of a related GroupBox, you want to add each item to the GroupBox's Controls collection (in the same way you add widgets to the Form's Controls collection). To make things a bit more interesting, respond to the Enter and Leave events sent by the GroupBox object as shown here:

```
' Yellow RadioButton.
radioYellow.Location = new System.Drawing.Point (96, 24)
radioYellow.Text = "Yellow"
radioYellow.Size = new System.Drawing.Size (64, 23)

' Green, Red and Pink Buttons configured in a similar vein. . . .
```

```
' Now build the group of radio items.
groupBox1.Location = new System.Drawing.Point (16, 56)
groupBox1.Text = "Exterior Color"
groupBox1.Size = new System.Drawing.Size (264, 88)
groupBox1.Controls.Add (Me.radioPink)
groupBox1.Controls.Add (Me.radioYellow)
groupBox1.Controls.Add (Me.radioRed)
groupBox1.Controls.Add (Me.radioGreen)
' Add to Control collection.
Me.Controls.Add (Me.groupBox1)
```

The final GUI widgets on this Form (the Label and Button types) also need to be configured and inserted in the Form's Controls collection. The Label is used to display the order confirmation, which is formatted in the Click event handler of the order Button, as shown here:

```
Private Sub btnOrder_Click(ByVal sender As System.Object, _
ByVal e As System.EventArgs) Handles btnOrder.Click
    ' Build a string to display information.
     Dim orderInfo as String
    If(checkFloorMats.Checked) Then
          orderInfo &= "You want floor mats." & vbLf
    End If
    If(radioRed.Checked) Then
          orderInfo &= "You want a red exterior." & vbLf
    End If
    If(radioYellow.Checked) Then
          orderInfo &= "You want a yellow exterior." & vbLf
    End If
    If(radioGreen.Checked) Then
          orderInfo &= "You want a green exterior." & vbLf
    End If
    If(radioPink.Checked) Then
          orderInfo &= "Why do you want a PINK exterior" & vbLf
    End If
    ' Send this string to the Label.
     infoLabel.Text = orderInfo
End Sub
```

Notice that both the CheckBox and RadioButton support the Checked property, which allows you to investigate the state of the widget. Recall that if you have configured a tristate CheckBox, you want to check the state of the widget using the CheckState property (and the corresponding CheckState enumeration).

Examining the CheckedListBox Control

Now that you have explored the basic Button-centric widgets, you move on to the set of list selection-centric types. Specifically, the CheckedListBox, ListBox, and ComboBox types. The CheckedListBox widget allows you to group together related CheckBox options in a scrollable list Control. Assume you have added such a Control to your CarConfig application, which allows the user to configure a number of options for the automobile's sound system (Figure 11-9).

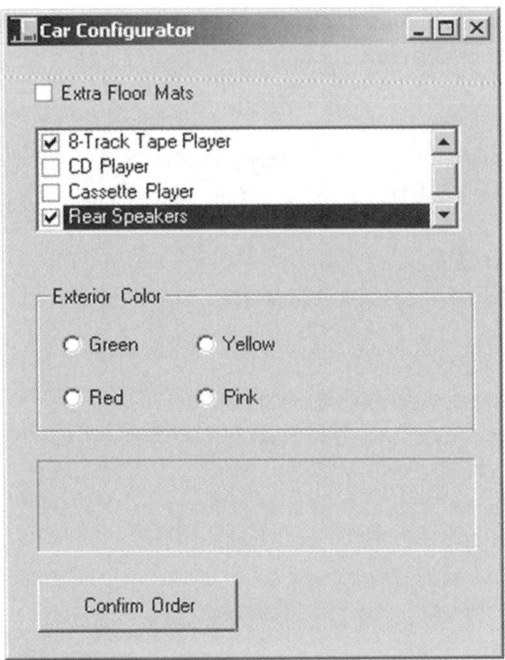

Figure 11-9. The CheckedListBox type

Like the Controls examined thus far, the CheckedListBox type gains most of its functionality from the Control base class type. Also, the CheckedListBox type inherits additional functionality from its direct base class, ListBox (examined later in this chapter).

To insert new items in a CheckedListBox, call Add() for each item or use the AddRange() method and send in an array of objects (strings, to be exact) that represent the full set of checkable items. Here is the configuration code (be sure to check out online Help for details about these new properties):

```
' Configure the CheckedListBox.
checkedBoxRadioOptions.Location = new System.Drawing.Point (16, 48)
checkedBoxRadioOptions.Cursor = Cursors.Hand
checkedBoxRadioOptions.Size = new System.Drawing.Size (256, 64)
checkedBoxRadioOptions.CheckOnClick = True

' Add items to the CheckedListBox.
checkedBoxRadioOptions.Items.AddRange(New Object(5) _
                        {"Front Speakers", "8-Track Tape Player", _
                        "CD Player", "Cassette Player", _
                        "Rear Speakers", "Ultra Base Thumper"})
' As always, add the new widget to the Controls collection.
Me.Controls.Add (Me.checkedBoxRadioOptions)
```

Now update the logic behind the Click event for the Order Button. Ask the CheckedListBox which of its items are currently selected and add them to the orderInfo string. Here is the relevant code:

```
Private Sub btnOrder_Click(ByVal sender As System.Object, _
ByVal e As System.EventArgs) Handles btnOrder.Click
    ' Build a string to display information.
     . . .
        ' For each item in the CheckedListBox. . .
        Dim i As Integer
        For i = 0 To checkedBoxRadioOptions.Items.Count - 1
            ' Is the current item checked?
            If (checkedBoxRadioOptions.GetItemChecked(i)) Then
                ' Get text of current item.
                orderInfo &= "Radio Item: "
                orderInfo &= checkedBoxRadioOptions.Items(i).ToString()
                orderInfo &= vbLf
            End If
        Next
End Sub
```

The final note regarding the CheckedListBox type is that it supports the use of multiple columns through the inherited MultiColumn property. Thus, if you make the following update:

```
checkedBoxRadioOptions.MultiColumn = True
```

you see the multicolumn CheckedListBox shown in Figure 11-10.

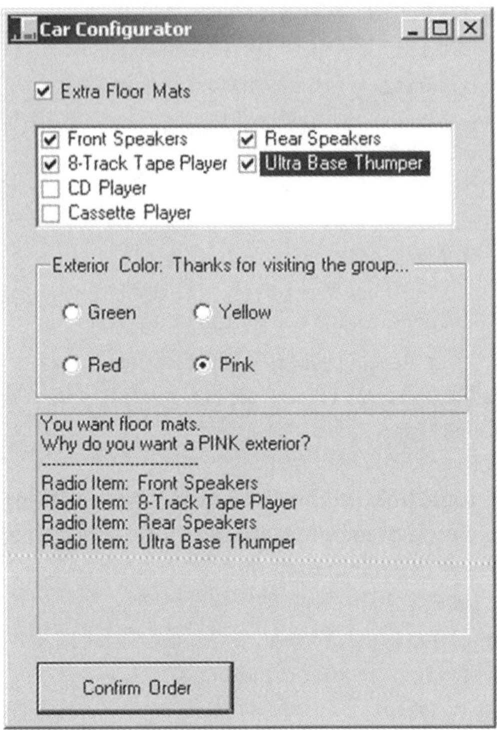

Figure 11-10. A multicolumn CheckedListBox

ListBoxes and ComboBoxes

As mentioned, the CheckedListBox type inherits most of its functionality from the ListBox type. The same holds true for the ComboBox class. Some core properties provided by System.Windows.Forms.ListBox are described in Table 11-10.

Table 11-10. ListBox Properties

LISTBOX PROPERTY	MEANING IN LIFE
ScrollAlwaysVisible	Determines if the associated scroll bar is shown at all times.
SelectedIndex	The index of the currently selected item in the list (if any). The value of –1 indicates "no selection." If the value is 0 or greater, the value is the index of the currently selected item.
SelectedIndices	A collection of the indices of the selected items in the list box. If no selected items are in the list box, the result is an empty collection.
SelectedItem	The value of the currently selected item in the list. If the value is null, there is currently no selection.

Table 11-10. ListBox Properties (continued)

LISTBOX PROPERTY	MEANING IN LIFE
SelectedItems	Returns a collection of all selected items (for a multiselection list box).
SelectionMode	Controls how many items at a time can be selected in the list box, using the SelectionMode enumeration.
Sorted	Indicates if the ListBox is sorted (alphabetically) or not.
TopIndex	Returns the index of the first visible item in a list box.

In addition to this property set, the ListBox also defines a number of methods. As most of them echo the functionality in various class properties, I leave it to you to check things out on your own.

To illustrate using the ListBox type, add another feature to the current CarConfig application: the ability to select the make (BMW, Yugo, and so on) of the automobile. Figure 11-11 shows the desired UI.

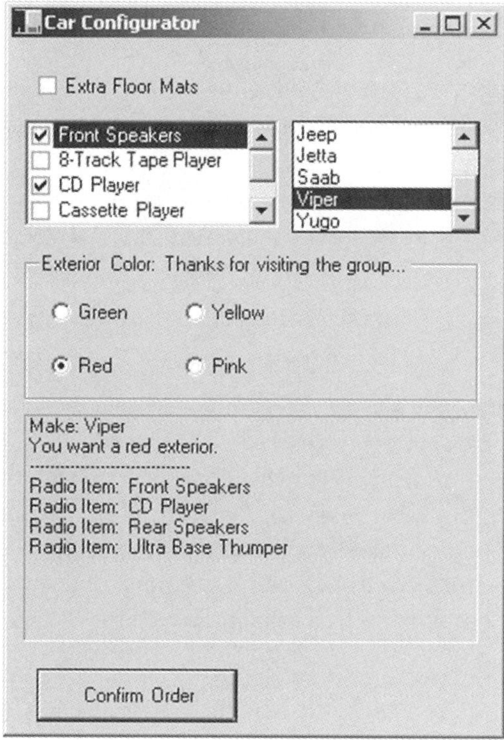

Figure 11-11. The ListBox type

As always, begin by creating a member variable to manipulate your type (in this case a ListBox type). Next, configure the look and feel and insert the new widget in the Form's Controls collection, as shown here:

```
' Configure the list box.
carMakeList.Location = new System.Drawing.Point (168, 48)
carMakeList.Size = new System.Drawing.Size (112, 67)
carMakeList.BorderStyle = System.Windows.Forms.BorderStyle.FixedSingle
carMakeList.ScrollAlwaysVisible = True
carMakeList.Sorted = True
' Populate the listBox using the AddRange() method.
carMakeList.Items.AddRange( New Object(8) {"BMW", "Caravan", "Ford", _
   "Grand Am", "Jeep", "Jetta", "Saab", "Viper", "Yugo"})
' Add new widget to Form's Control collection.
Me.Controls.Add (Me.carMakeList)
```

The update to the btnOrder_Click() event handler is also simple, as shown here:

```
Private Sub btnOrder_Click(ByVal sender As System.Object, _
ByVal e As System.EventArgs) Handles btnOrder.Click
     ' Build a string to display information.
     Dim orderInfo As String
      . . .
     ' Get the currently selected item (not index of the item).
     If (Not carMakeList.SelectedItem Is Nothing) Then
         orderInfo &= "Make: " & carMakeList.SelectedItem.ToString() & vbLf
     End If
End Sub
```

Fun with ComboBoxes

Like a ListBox, a ComboBox allows the user to make a selection from a well-defined set of possibilities. However, the ComboBox type is unique in that the user can also insert additional items. Recall that ComboBox derives from ListBox (which then derives from Control). Beyond this mass of functionality, ComboBox offers the additional properties described in Table 11-11.

Table 11-11. ComboBox Properties

COMBOBOX PROPERTY	MEANING IN LIFE
DroppedDown	Indicates whether the drop-down portion of the combo is dropped down.
MaxDropDownItems	Indicates the maximum number of items to be shown in the drop-down portion of the ComboBox. This number can be from 1 to 100.
MaxLength	Indicates the maximum length of the text the user can type in the edit Control of a combo box.
SelectedIndex	Indicates the zero-based index of the selected item in the combos list. If the value of index is –1, there is no selected item.
SelectedItem	Indicates the handle to the object selected in the combos list.
SelectedText	Indicates the selected text in the edit component of the ComboBox.
SelectionLength	Indicates the length, in characters, of the selection in the edit box portion of the ComboBox.
DropDownStyle	Indicates the type of combo. The value comes from the ComboBoxStyle enumeration.
Text	Gives access to whatever is in the edit box. The inherited Text property is generally most useful when working with ComboBoxes.

A given ComboBox has an associated style that is specified using the ComboBoxStyle enumeration (Table 11-12).

Table 11-12. ComboBox Styles

COMBOBOX STYLE	MEANING IN LIFE
DropDown	The text portion is editable. The user must click the Arrow Button to display the list portion.
DropDownList	The user cannot directly edit the text portion. The user must click the Arrow Button to display the list portion.
Simple	The text portion is editable. The list portion is always visible.

To illustrate, add yet another GUI widget to the CarConfig application, which allows a user to enter the name of a preferred salesperson. If the salesperson in question is not on the list, the user can enter a custom name. The GUI update is shown in Figure 11-12 (this time with a more attractive output Label).

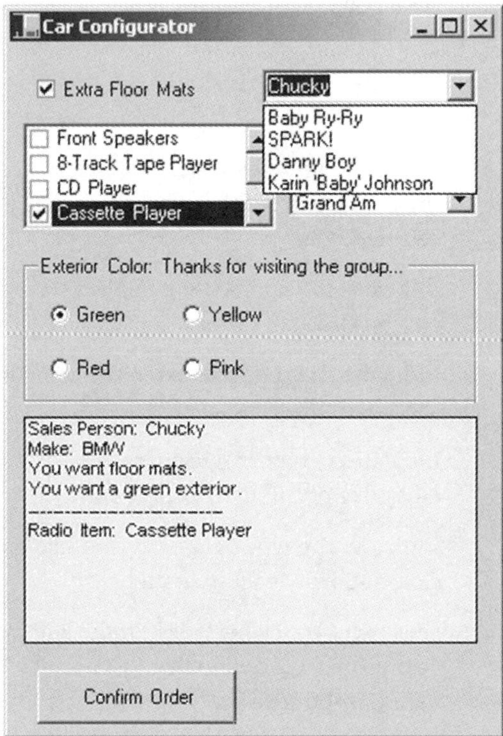

Figure 11-12. The ComboBox type

This modification begins with configuring the ComboBox itself. As you can see here, the logic looks identical to that for the ListBox:

```
' ComboBox configuration.
comboSalesPerson.Location = New System.Drawing.Point (152, 16)
comboSalesPerson.Size = New System.Drawing.Size (128, 21)
comboSalesPerson.Items.AddRange( New object(3) {"Baby Ry-Ry", "SPARK!", _
"Danny Boy", "Karin 'Baby' Johnson"})
Me.Controls.Add (Me.comboSalesPerson)
```

The update to the btnOrder_Click() event handler is again simple, as shown here:

```
Private Sub btnOrder_Click(ByVal sender As System.Object, _
ByVal e As System.EventArgs) Handles btnOrder.Click
    ' Build a string to display information.
    Dim orderInfo As String
      . . .
    If (comboSalesPerson.Text <> "") Then
         orderInfo &= "Sales Person: " & comboSalesPerson.Text & vbLf
    Else
         orderInfo &= "You did not select a salesperson!" & vbLf
    End If
      . . .
End Sub
```

Configuring the Tab Order

To finish up this first attempt at functional user interface, let's address the issue of tab order. As you know, when a Form or dialog box contains multiple GUI widgets, users expect to be able to shift focus using the Tab key. Configuring the tab order for your set of Controls requires that you understand two properties: TabStop and TabIndex.

The TabStop property can be set to true or false, based on whether or not you wish this GUI item to be reachable using the Tab key. Assuming the TabStop property has been set to true for a given widget, the TabOrder property is then set to establish its order of activation in the tabbing sequence. Consider this example:

```
' Configure tabbing properties.
radioRed.TabIndex = 2
radioRed.TabStop = True
```

As you would expect, these properties can be set using the Properties window (Figure 11-13).

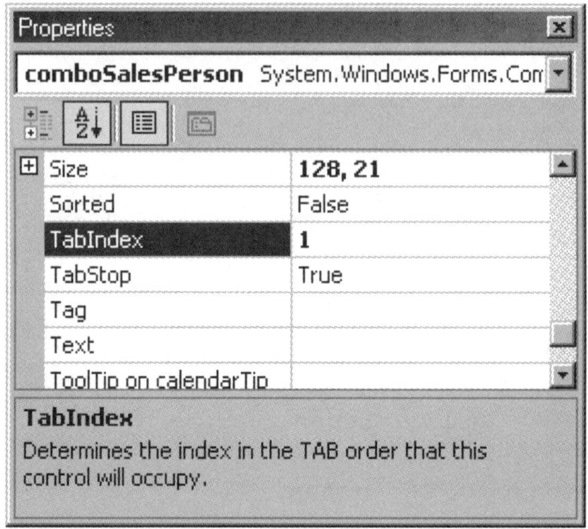

Figure 11-13. Configuring Tab properties

The Tab Order Wizard

The Visual Studio.NET IDE supplies a Tab Order Wizard, accessed using the View|Tab Order menu selection. Once activated (Figure 11-14), your design time Form displays the current TabIndex value for each widget. To change these values, click each item in the order you choose. (Notice that Controls added to a GroupBox's Control collection function as a collective.) To exit the Tab Order mode, just hit the Esc key.

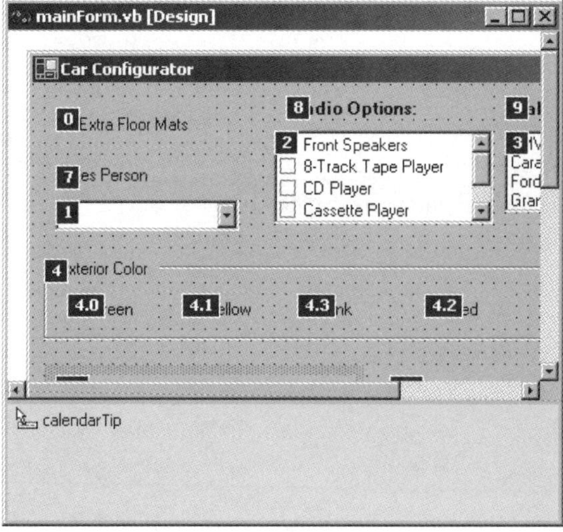

Figure 11-14. The TabOrder Wizard

Excellent! At this point you have learned about some very common GUI types. Now that you have the basics in mind, you can begin to examine more exotic widgets.

SOURCE CODE *The CarConfig project is included under the Chapter 11 subdirectory.*

The TrackBar Control

The TrackBar Control allows users to select from a range of values, using a scroll bar-like input mechanism. In many respects a TrackBar is functionally similar to a traditional scroll bar. When working with this type, you need to set the minimum and maximum range, the minimum and maximum change increments, and the starting location of the slider's thumb. Each of these aspects can be set using the properties described in Table 11-13.

Table 11-13. TrackBar Properties

TRACKBAR PROPERTY	MEANING IN LIFE
LargeChange	The number of ticks by which the TrackBar changes when an event considered a large change occurs (e.g., clicking the mouse button while the cursor is on the sliding range and using the Page Up or Page Down key.
Maximum Minimum	Configure the upper and lower bounds of the TrackBar's range.
Orientation	The orientation for this TrackBar. Valid values are from the Orientation enumeration (i.e., horizontally or vertically).
SmallChange	The number of ticks by which the TrackBar changes when an event considered a small change occurs (e.g., using the arrow keys).
TickFrequency	Indicates how many ticks are drawn. For a TrackBar with an upper limit of 200, it is impractical to draw all 200 ticks on a Control 2 inches long. If you set the TickFrequency property to 5, the TrackBar draws 20 total ticks (each tick represents 5 units).

Table 11-13. TrackBar Properties (continued)

TRACKBAR PROPERTY	MEANING IN LIFE
TickStyle	Indicates how the TrackBar Control draws itself. This affects both where the ticks are drawn in relation to the movable thumb and how the thumb itself is drawn (using the TickStyle enumeration).
Value	Gets or sets the current location of the TrackBar. Use this property to obtain the numeric value contained by the TrackBar for use in your application.

Now you can build an application that makes use of three TrackBars. Each widget has an upper range of 255 and a lower range of 0. As the user slides each thumb, the application intercepts the Scroll event and dynamically builds a new Color type based on the value of each slider. In this way, the user is able to view the underlying RGB value (and see the color) for a given selection. (Of course, the System.Windows.Forms namespace already provides a ColorDialog type for this purpose.) Figure 11-15 shows the GUI for this application.

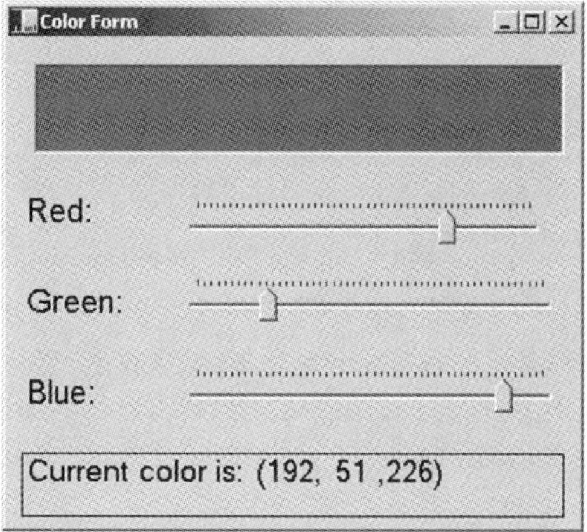

Figure 11-15. TrackBars

First you need to configure each TrackBar. Assume your Form contains three private TrackBar member variables (redTrackBar, greenTrackBar, and blueTrackBar). Here is the relevant code for blueTrackBar (the remaining bars look almost identical, with the exception of the name of the Scroll event handler):

```
' Here is the blue TrackBar.
blueTrackBar.TickFrequency = 5
```

```
blueTrackBar.Location = new System.Drawing.Point (104, 200)
blueTrackBar.TickStyle = System.Windows.Forms.TickStyle.TopLeft
blueTrackBar.Maximum = 255
```

Note that the default minimum value of the TrackBar is 0 and thus does not need to be explicitly set. In the event handlers for each TrackBar, you make a call to an internal private helper function named UpdateColor(), which does the real grunt work, as shown here:

```
Private Sub blueTrackBar_Scroll(ByVal sender As System.Object, _
ByVal e As System.EventArgs) Handles blueTrackBar.Scroll
    UpdateColor()
End Sub
```

UpdateColor() is responsible for two major tasks. First you read the current value of each TrackBar and send this state data to a new Color variable (using the FromArgb() member). Once you have the newly configured color, you update a Form-level member variable of type PictureBox (named colorBox), which in this case does not hold an actual bitmap image, but simply maintains the current background color. Finally, the UpdateColor() method formats this information in a string placed on the Form's color display label (lblCurrColor), as shown here:

```
Private Sub UpdateColor()
    ' Get the new color.
    Dim c As Color = Color.FromArgb(redTrackBar.Value, _
        greenTrackBar.Value, _
        blueTrackBar.Value)
    ' Change the color in the PictureBox.
    colorBox.BackColor = c
    ' Set color label.
    lblCurrColor.Text = "Current color is: " & "(" & _
        redTrackBar.Value & ", " & _
        greenTrackBar.Value & " ," & _
        blueTrackBar.Value & ")"
End Sub
```

The final details are to set the initial values of each slider when the Form comes to life and to render the current color, as shown here:

```
Public Sub New()
    MyBase.New()
    'This call is required by the Windows Form Designer.
```

```
    InitializeComponent()
    CenterToScreen()
    ' Set initial position of each slider.
    redTrackBar.Value = 100
    greenTrackBar.Value = 255
    blueTrackBar.Value = 0
    UpdateColor()
End Sub
```

SOURCE CODE *The Tracker application can be found under the Chapter 11 subdirectory.*

The MonthCalendar Control

The System.Windows.Forms namespace provides an extremely useful widget, which allows the user to select a date (or range of dates) using a friendly user interface: the MonthCalendar Control. To showcase this new Control, update the existing CarConfig application to allow the user to enter in the new vehicle's delivery date. Figure 11-16 shows the updated (and slightly rearranged) Form.

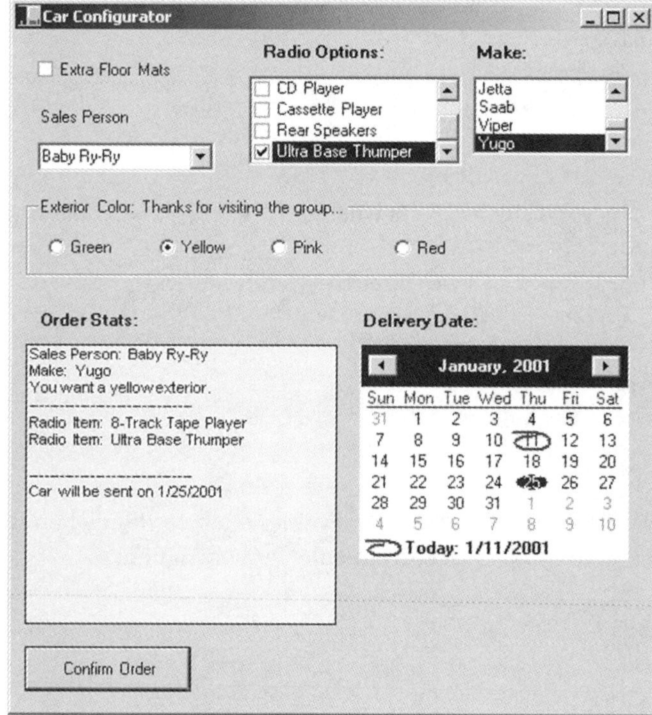

Figure 11-16. The MonthCalendar Control

To begin understanding this new type, examine the core MonthCalendar properties described in Table 11-14.

Table 11-14. MonthCalendar Properties

MONTHCALENDAR PROPERTY	MEANING IN LIFE
BoldedDates	The array of DateTime objects that determines dates is shown in bold.
CalendarDimensions	The number of columns and rows of months displayed in the MonthCalendar Control.
FirstDayOfWeek	The first day of the week for the MonthCalendar Control.
MaxDate	The maximum allowable date that can be selected. (The default is no maximum date.)
MaxSelectionCount	The maximum number of days that can be selected in a MonthCalendar Control.
MinDate	The minimum allowable date that can be selected. (The default is no minimum date.)
MonthlyBoldedDates	The array of DateTime objects that determines which monthly days to bold.
SelectionEnd	Indicates the end date of the selected range of dates.
SelectionRange	Retrieves the selection range for a MonthCalendar Control.
SelectionStart	Indicates the start date of the selected range of dates.
ShowToday ShowTodayCircle	Indicates whether the MonthCalendar Control displays the today date at the bottom of the Control, as well as circles the current date. (What's different about current date and the date in the earlier phrase?)
ShowWeekNumbers	Indicates whether the MonthCalendar Control displays the week numbers (1–52) to the left of each row of days.
TodayDate	The date shown as Today in the MonthCalendar Control. By default, Today is the current date at the time the MonthCalendar Control is created.
TodayDateSet	Indicates whether the TodayDate property has been explicitly set by the user. If TodayDateSet is true, TodayDate returns whatever the user has set it to.

Although the MonthCalendar Control offers a fair bit of functionality, it is very simple to programmatically capture the range of dates selected by the user. The default behavior of this type is to always select (and circle) today's date automatically. To obtain the currently selected date programmatically, you can update the Click event handler for the order Button, as shown here:

```
Private Sub btnOrder_Click(ByVal sender As System.Object, _
ByVal e As System.EventArgs) Handles btnOrder.Click
        ' Build a string to display information.
        Dim orderInfo As String
     . . .
        ' Get ship date.
        Dim startD As DateTime = monthCalendar.SelectionStart
        Dim dateStartStr As String = startD.Month & " / " & _
            startD.Day & " / " & _
            startD.Year()
. . .
End Sub
```

Notice that you can ask the MonthCalendar Control for the currently selected date by using the SelectionStart property. This property returns a DateTime reference, which you store in a local variable (startD). Using a handful of properties of the DateTime type, you can extract the information you need in a custom format. (Note that this type returns the clock time as well, which you are not interested in.)

At this point I assume the user will specify exactly one day on which to deliver the new auto. But what if you want to allow the user to select a range of possible delivery dates? In that case all the user needs to do is drag the cursor across the range of possible delivery dates (Figure 11-17).

You already have seen that you can obtain the start of the selection using the SelectionStart property. The end of the selection can be determined using the SelectionEnd property. Here is the code update:

```
' Get ship date.
Dim startD As DateTime = monthCalendar.SelectionStart
Dim endD As DateTime = monthCalendar.SelectionEnd
Dim dateStartStr As String = startD.Month & " / " & _
    startD.Day & " / " & _
    startD.Year()
Dim dateEndStr As String = endD.Month & " / " & _
    endD.Day & " / " & _
    endD.Year()
```

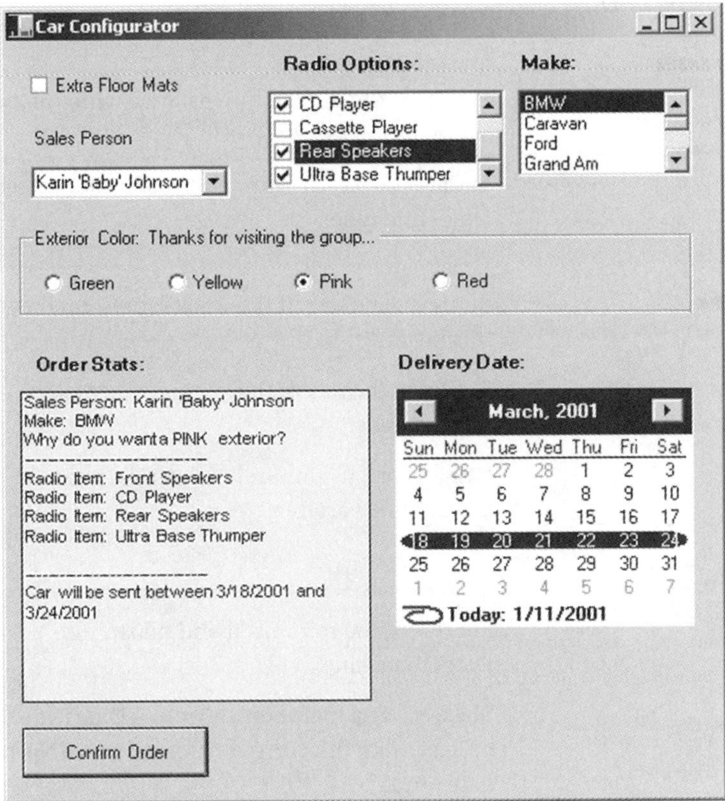

Figure 11-17. Multiple date selection

More on the System.DateTime Type

In the current example, you extracted a DateTime type from the MonthCalendar widget using the SelectionStart and SelectionEnd properties, as shown here:

```
' Get a DateTime (or two).
Dim startD as DateTime = monthCalendar.SelectionStart
Dim endD as DateTime = monthCalendar.SelectionEnd
```

After this point, you used the Month, Day, and Year properties to build a custom format string. While this is permissible, it is not optimal, given that the DateTime type has a number of built-in formatting options (Table 11-15).

Table 11-15. DateTime Members

DATETIME MEMBER	MEANING IN LIFE
Date	Retrieves the date of the instance with the time value set to midnight.
Day Month Year	Extract the day, month, and year of the current DateTime type.
DayOfWeek	Retrieves the day of the week represented by this instance.
DayOfYear	Retrieves the day of the year represented by this instance.
Hour Minute Second Millisecond	Extract various time-related details from a DateTime variable.
MaxValue MinValue	Represent the minimum and maximum DateTime value.
Now Today	These shared members retrieve a DateTime type representing the current date and time (Now) or date (Today).
Ticks	Retrieves the 100-nanosecond tick count for this instance.
ToLongDateString() ToLongTimeString() ToShortDateString() ToShortTimeString()	Convert the current value of the DateTime type to a string representation.

Using these members, you can replace the previous formatting you programmed by hand with the following (you don't see any change in the program's output):

```
' Ditch the custom formatting!
Dim dateStartStr As String = startD.Date.ToShortDateString()
Dim dateEndStr As String = endD.Date.ToShortDateString()
```

The Spin Controls: DomainUpDown and NumericUpDown

Windows Forms provide two widgets that function as "spin controls" (also know as up/down controls). Like the ComboBox and ListBox types, these new items also allow the user to choose an item from a range of possible selections. The difference is that when using a DomainUpDown or NumericUpDown Control, the information is selected using a small pair of up and down arrows. For example, check out Figure 11-18.

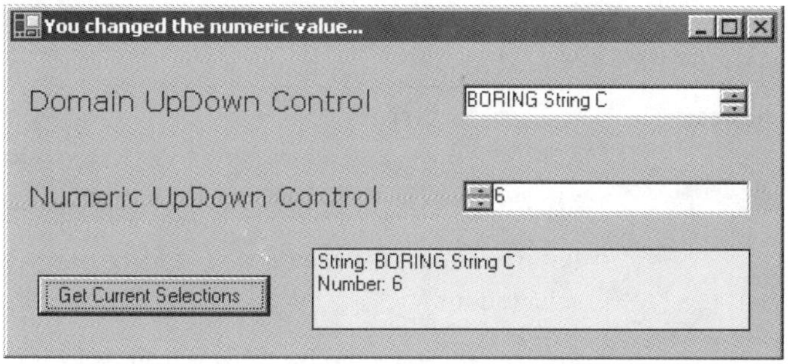

Figure 11-18. Spin Controls

Given your work with previous (and similar) types, you should find working with the UpDown Controls painless. The DomainUpDown widget allows the user to select from a set of string data. NumericUpDown allows selections from a range of numeric data points. Each widget derives from a common direct base class: UpDownBase. Table 11-16 describes some important properties of this class.

Table 11-16. UpDownBase Properties

UPDOWNBASE PROPERTY	MEANING IN LIFE
InterceptArrowKeys	Gets or sets a value indicating whether the user can use the Up Arrow and Down Arrow keys to select values.
ReadOnly	Gets or sets a value indicating whether the text can only be changed by the use of the up or down arrows and not by typing in the Control to locate a given string.
Text	Gets or sets the current text displayed in the spin Control.
TextAlign	Gets or sets the alignment of the text in the spin Control.
UpDownAlign	Gets or sets the alignment of the up and down arrows on the spin Control, using the LeftRightAlignment enumeration.

The DomainUpDown Control adds a small set of properties (Table 11-17), which allow you to configure and manipulate the textual data in the widget.

Table 11-17. DomainUpDown Properties

DOMAINUPDOWN PROPERTY	MEANING IN LIFE
Items	Allows you to gain access to the set of types stored in the widget.
SelectedIndex	Returns the zero-based index of the currently selected item.
SelectedItem	Returns the selected item itself (not its index).
Sorted	Configures whether or not the strings should be alphabetized.
Wrap	Controls if the collection of items continues to the first or last item if the user continues past the end of the list.

The NumericUpDown type is just as simple (Table 11-18).

Table 11-18. NumericUpDown Properties

NUMERICUPDOWN PROPERTY	MEANING IN LIFE
DecimalPlaces ThousandsSeparator Hexadecimal	Used to configure how the numerical data is to be displayed.
Increment	Sets the numerical value to increment the value in the Control when the up or down arrow is clicked. The default is to advance the value by 1.
Minimum Maximum	Sets the upper and lower limits of the value in the Control.
Value	Returns the current value in the Control.

Here is the code behind the sample application. Each Control is configured using a subset of all possible properties:

```
' Configure DomainUpDown widget.
domainUpDown.Sorted = True
domainUpDown.Wrap = True
domainUpDown.Items.AddRange( New object(3) {"Another Boring String named B", _
"Boring String A", "BORING String C", "Final Boring string (D)"})
domainUpDown.SelectedIndex = 2
' Configure NumericUpDown widget.
numericUpDown.Maximum = New Decimal (5000)
numericUpDown.ThousandsSeparator = true
numericUpDown.UpDownAlign = LeftRightAlignment.Left
```

The Click event handler for the Form's Button type simply asks each type for its current value and places it in the appropriate Label as a formatted string, as shown here:

```
Private Sub btnGetSelections_Click(ByVal sender As System.Object, _
ByVal e As System.EventArgs) Handles btnGetSelections.Click
    ' Get info from updowns. . .
    lblCurrSel.Text = "String: " & _
    domainUpDown.Text & _
    vbLf & _
```

```
    "Number: " & _
    numericUpDown.Value
End Sub
```

Of course, the DomainUpDown and NumericUpDown types support a number of events. If you ever need to capture when the selection changes, you can use SelectedItemChanged (for DomainUpDown types) or ValueChanged (for NumericUpDown types).

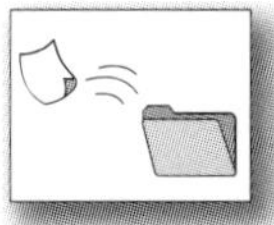

SOURCE CODE *The UpAndDown application is included under the Chapter 11 subdirectory.*

Working with Panel Controls

As you have seen earlier in this chapter, the GroupBox Control can be used to logically bind a number of Controls (such as RadioButtons) to function as a collective. Closely related to the GroupBox is the Panel Control. Panels are also used to group related Controls in a logical unit. One difference is that the Panel type derives from the ScrollableControl class, and thus it can support scroll bars, which is not possible with a GroupBox. Another subtle difference is that a Panel does not support an automatic caption (unlike a GroupBox).

Panels can be used to conserve screen real estate. For example, if you have a group of Controls that take up the entire bottom half of a Form, you can contain them in a Panel that is half the size and set the AutoScroll property to true. In this way, the user can use the scroll bar(s) to view the hidden items. To illustrate, update the previous TrackBar application. This time, each TrackBar is contained in a single Panel. Figure 11-19 shows the update.

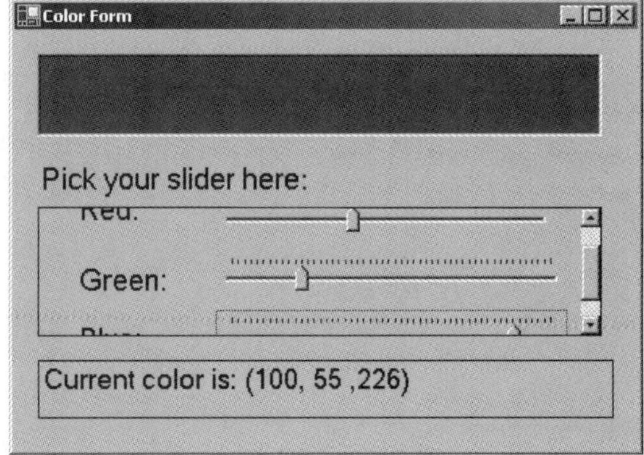

Figure 11-19. The Scrollable Panel type containing other widgets

The underlying code looks almost identical to that of a GroupBox. Begin by declaring a Panel data member (panel1) and add each item using the Controls property, as shown here:

```
' Configure the panel.
panel1.AutoScroll = True
panel1.Controls.Add (Me.label2)
panel1.Controls.Add (Me.blueTrackBar)
panel1.Controls.Add (Me.label3)
panel1.Controls.Add (Me.greenTrackBar)
panel1.Controls.Add (Me.redTrackBar)
panel1.Controls.Add (Me.label1)
```

Assigning ToolTips to Controls

Most modern user interfaces support tool tips. In the System.Windows.Forms namespace, the ToolTip type represents this functionality. These widgets are simply small floating windows that display a helpful message when the cursor hovers over a given item. Table 11-19 describes the core properties of the ToolTip type.

Table 11-19. ToolTip Members

TOOLTIP MEMBERS	MEANING IN LIFE
Active	Configures if the tool tip is activated or not. For example, perhaps you have a menu item that disables all tool tips for advanced users. This property allows you to turn off the pop-up text.
AutomaticDelay	Gets or sets the time (in milliseconds) that passes before the ToolTip appears.
AutoPopDelay	The period of time (in milliseconds) that the ToolTip remains visible when the cursor is stationary in the ToolTip region. The default value is 10 times the AutomaticDelay property value.
GetToolTip()	Returns the tool tip text assigned to a specific Control.
InitialDelay	The period of time (in milliseconds) that the cursor must remain stationary in the ToolTip region before the ToolTip text is displayed. The default is equal to the AutomaticDelay property.

Table 11-19. ToolTip Members (continued)

TOOLTIP MEMBERS	MEANING IN LIFE
ReshowDelay	The length of time (in milliseconds) that it takes subsequent ToolTip instances to appear as the cursor moves from one ToolTip region to another. The default is 1/5 of the AutomaticDelay property value.
SetToolTip()	Associates a tool tip to a specific Control.

To illustrate, add a tool tip to the CarConfig application. Specifically, you want to add the tool tip for the MonthCalendar widget shown in Figure 11-20.

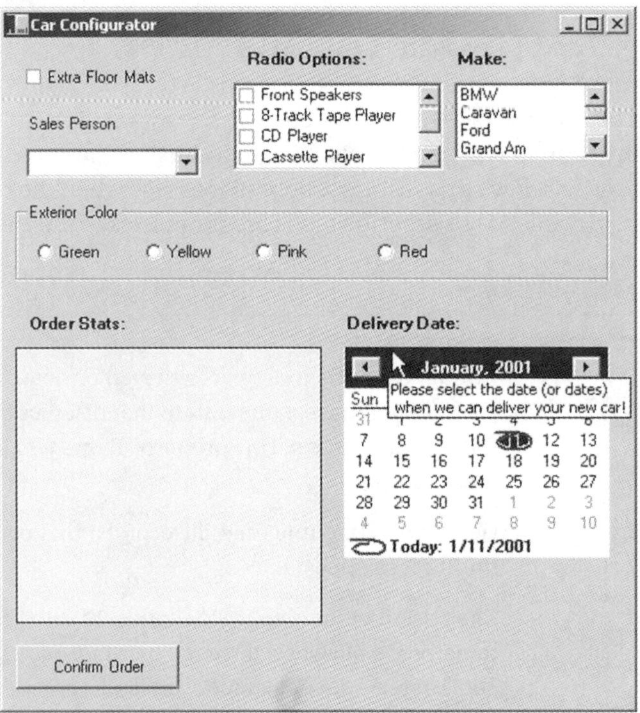

Figure 11-20. Tool tip

Like with any widget, begin by creating a new member variable, this time type ToolTip. Next, configure the set of properties for the new item. Notice that you make a call to SetToolTip(), which configures not only the text to be displayed, but also the widget to which it is assigned:

```
' Create and associate a tool tip to the calendar
calendarTip.Active = True
calendarTip.SetToolTip (monthCalendar, _
"Please select the date (or dates) when we can deliver your new car!")
```

Adding ToolTips at Design Time

If you use the Visual Studio.NET IDE to build your tool tips, begin by adding a ToolTip widget to your Form using the Toolbox window (Figure 11-21).

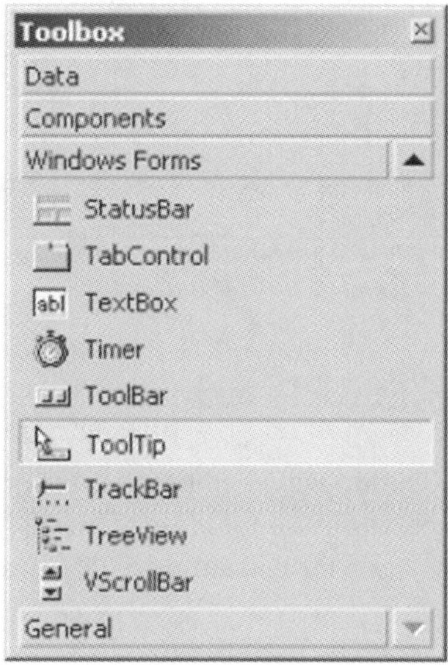

Figure 11-21. Adding ToolTip types at design time

At this point, you can configure the ToolTip using the Properties window. To associate the new tip with a given widget, select the widget that should activate the tip and set the "ToolTip on. . ." property (Figure 11-22).

Figure 11-22. Associating a ToolTip with a widget

Working with the ErrorProvider

Your Windows Forms application will need to validate user input. This is especially true with dialog boxes, as you should inform users if they make a processing error before continuing forward. (You examine dialog box programming later in this chapter.)

The ErrorProvider type can be used to provide a visual cue of user input error. For example, assume you have a Form containing a TextBox and Button widget. If the user enters more than five characters in the TextBox, the error information shown in Figure 11-23 is displayed.

Figure 11-23. The ErrorProvider

Here, you have detected that the user entered more than five characters and responded by placing a small error icon (!) next to the TextBox object. When the user places the cursor over this icon, the descriptive error text appears as a pop-up. Also, this ErrorProvider is configured so the icon blinks a number of times to strengthen the visual cue (which of course you can't see without running the application).

If you wish to support this type of input validation, the first step is to understand the properties of the Control class (Table 11-20).

Table 11-20. Control Properties

CONTROL PROPERTY	MEANING IN LIFE
CausesValidation	Indicates whether selecting this Control causes validation on the Controls requiring validation.
Validated	Occurs when the Control is finished performing its validation logic.
Validating	Occurs when the Control is validating user input (e.g., when the Control loses focus).

Every GUI widget can set the CausesValidation property to True or False. If you set this bit of state data to true, the Control forces the other Controls on the Form to validate themselves when it receives focus (provided the CausesValidation property is also set to true).

Once a validating Control has received focus, the Validating and Validated events are fired for each Control. It is in the scope of the Validating event handler where you configure a corresponding ErrorProvider. Optionally, the Validated event can be handled to determine when the Control has finished its validation cycle.

To begin, assume you have set the CausesValidation property to true for the Button and TextBox and have added a member variable of type ErrorProvider. Here is the configuration code:

```
' Configure the error provider.
errorProvider1.BlinkStyle = System.Windows.Forms.ErrorBlinkStyle.AlwaysBlink
errorProvider1.BlinkRate = 500
```

The ErrorProvider type has a small set of members. The most important item for your purposes is the BlinkStyle property, which can be set to any of the values of the ErrorBlinkStyle enumeration described in Table 11-21.

Table 11-21. ErrorBlinkStyle Properties

ERRORBLINKSTYLE PROPERTY	MEANING IN LIFE
AlwaysBlink	Blinks the error icon when the error is first displayed or when a new error description string is set for the Control and the error icon is already displayed.
BlinkIfDifferentError	Blinks only if the error icon is already displayed, but a new error string is set for the Control.
NeverBlink	Never blinks the error icon.

The ErrorProvider also has additional members beyond BlinkStyle and BlinkRate. For example, if you wish to associate a custom icon to the error, you can do so using the Icon property. Nevertheless, once you have configured how the ErrorProvider looks and feels, you bind the error to the TextBox within the scope of its Validating event handler, as shown here:

```
Private Sub txtInput_Validating(ByVal sender As Object, _
ByVal e As System.ComponentModel.CancelEventArgs) Handles txtInput.Validating
    ' Check if the text length is greater than 5.
    If (txtInput.Text.ToString().Length > 5) Then
        errorProvider1.SetError(txtInput, _
        "Can't be greater than 5!")
    Else
        errorProvider1.SetError(txtInput, "")
    End If
End Sub
```

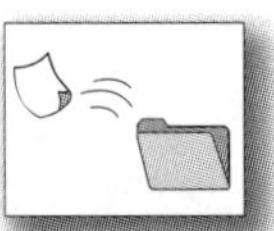

SOURCE CODE *The ErrorProvider application is included under the Chapter 11 subdirectory.*

Configuring a Control's Anchoring Behavior

When you are creating a Form containing widgets, you need to decide whether the Form should be resizable. Typically speaking, main windows are resizable, whereas dialog boxes are not. To configure the resizability of your Form, adjust the FormBorderStyle property to any of the values described in Table 11-22.

Table 11-22. FormBorderStyle Properties

FORMBORDERSTYLE PROPERTY	MEANING IN LIFE
Fixed3D	A nonresizable, three-dimensional border.
FixedDialog	A thick, nonresizable dialog box–style border.
FixedSingle	A nonresizable, single-line border.
FixedToolWindow	A tool window border that is not resizable.
None	No border at all.
Sizable	A resizable border.
SizableToolWindow	A resizable tool window border.

Assume that you have configured your Form to be resizable. This brings up some interesting questions regarding the contained Controls. For example, if the user makes the Form smaller than the rectangle needed to display each Control, should the Controls adjust their size (and possibly location) to morph correctly with the Form?

In the Windows Forms worldview, the Anchor property is used to define a relative fixed position in which the Control should always be rendered. Every Control-derived type has an Anchor property that can be set to any of the values from the AnchorStyles enumeration described in Table 11-23.

Table 11-23. AnchorStyles Values

ANCHORSTYLES VALUE	MEANING IN LIFE
Bottom	The Control is anchored to the bottom edge of its container.
Left	The Control is anchored to the left edge of its container.
None	The Control is not anchored to any edges of its container.
Right	The Control is anchored to the right edge of its container.
Top	The Control is anchored to the top edge of its container.

To anchor a widget at the upper left corner, you are free to OR styles together (e.g., AnchorStyles.Top|AnchorStyles.Left). Again, the idea behind the Anchor property is to configure which edges of the Control are anchored to the edges of its container. For example, if you configure a Button with the following Anchor value:

```
' Anchor this widget relative to the right position.
myButton.Anchor = AnchorStyles.Right
```

you are ensured that as the Form is resized, this Button maintains its position relative to the right side of the Form (which is not very easy to visualize on the printed page).

Configuring a Control's Docking Behavior

Another aspect of Windows Forms programming is establishing the docking behavior of your Controls. If you so choose, you can set a widget's Dock property to configure which side (or sides) of a Form the widget should be attached to. The value you assign to a Control's Dock property is honored, regardless of the Form's current dimensions. Table 11-24 describes possible options.

Table 11-24. DockStyle Values

DOCKSTYLE VALUE	MEANING IN LIFE
Bottom	The Control's bottom edge is docked to the bottom of its containing Control.
Fill	All the Control's edges are docked to the all edges of its containing Control and sized appropriately.
Left	The Control's left edge is docked to the left edge of its containing Control.
None	The Control is not docked.
Right	The Control's right edge is docked to the right edge of its containing Control.
Top	The Control's top edge is docked to the top of its containing Control.

So, for example, if you want to ensure that a given widget is always docked on the left side of a Form, you would write:

```
' This item is always located on the left of the Form, regardless
' of the Form's current size.
myButton.Dock = DockStyle.Left
```

Figure 11-24 shows the output.

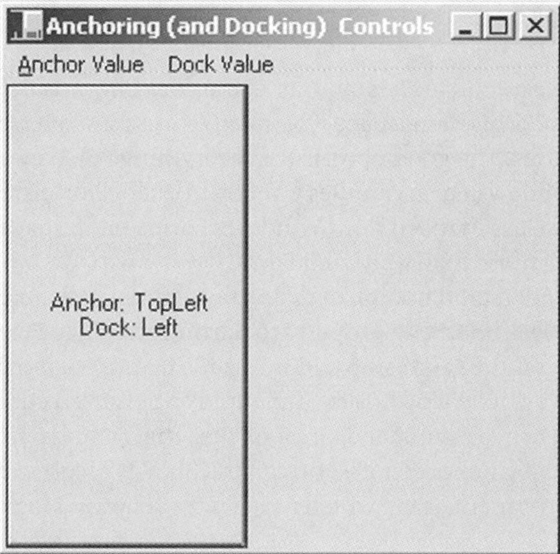

Figure 11-24. Anchoring behaviors

To explore the various anchor and docking styles, check out the AnchoringControls application (under the Chapter 10 subdirectory). Using the topmost menu system, you can select from a set of AnchorStyles and DockStyles values and observe the change in behavior of the Button type (Figure 11-25).

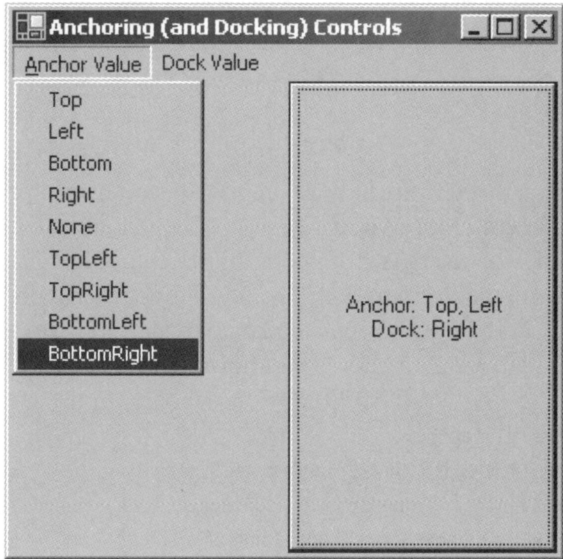

Figure 11-25. Docking and anchoring behaviors

Building Custom Dialog Boxes

Now that you have a solid understanding of the core Controls defined in the System.Windows.Forms namespace, you need to examine the construction of custom dialog boxes. The good news is that everything you have already learned about System.Windows.Forms applies directly to dialog box programming. There is no Dialog base class in the System.Windows.Forms namespace. Rather, a dialog box is nothing more than a stylized Form.

First of all, understand that most dialog boxes are nonsizable. Therefore, you will want to set the BorderStyle property to FormBorderStyle.FixedDialog. Also, you will typically set the ControlBox, MinimizeBox, and MaximizeBox properties to False. In this way the dialog box is configured to be a fixed constant.

To launch a Form as a modal dialog box (i.e., the owning Form cannot receive focus until the dialog box is dismissed), call the ShowDialog() method. Assume you have a topmost menu item, which triggers the following logic:

```
' Launch a modal dialog box.
Private Sub mnuModalBox_Click(ByVal sender As System.Object, _
ByVal e As System.EventArgs) Handles mnuModalBox.Click
    Dim myDlg As MyDialogBox = New MyDialogBox()
    ' Could assign in the ctor of SomeCustomForm as well.
    myDlg.FormBorderStyle = FormBorderStyle.FixedDialog
    myDlg.ControlBox = False
    myDlg.MinimizeBox = False
    myDlg.MaximizeBox = False
' Passing in a reference to the parent Form.
myDlg.ShowDialog(Me)
DoSomeMoreWork()
End Sub
```

Notice that directly after the ShowDialog() call, you have a private helper function named DoSomeMoreWork(). Be aware that when you show a modal dialog box, the flow of processing is stopped until the ShowDialog() method returns. (After all, that is what makes it modal!) To show a modeless dialog box (i.e., the launching window and dialog box can alternate focus), substitute the ShowDialog() call with a call to Show(), as shown here:

```
' Launch a modeless dialog box.
Private Sub mnuModalBox_Click(ByVal sender As System.Object, _
ByVal e As System.EventArgs) Handles mnuModalBox.Click
    Dim myDlg As MyDialogBox = New MyDialogBox()
    myDlg.BorderStyle = FormBorderStyle.FixedDialog
    myDlg.ControlBox = False
    myDlg.MinimizeBox = False
```

```
    myDlg.MaximizeBox = False
    myDlg.Show()
    DoSomeMoreWork()
EndSub
```

In this case, DoSomeMoreWork() would be hit immediately after the call to Show().

A Dialog Box Example Application

Assume you have a Form named mainForm, which supports a topmost menu, allowing the user to launch a modal dialog box (Figure 11-26).

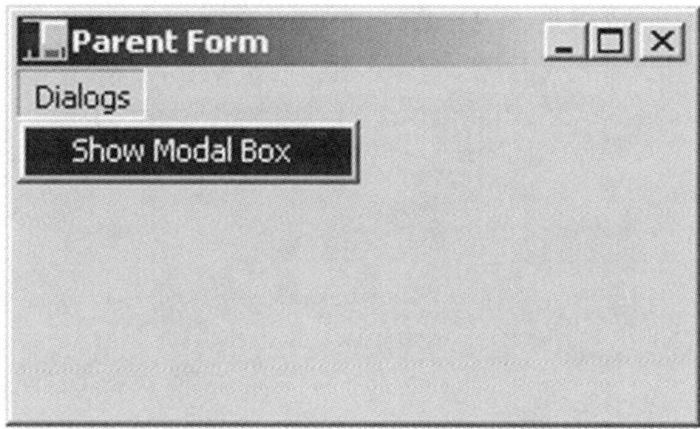

Figure 11-26. Launching your dialog box

When the user selects this option, a simple dialog box is displayed. The goal is to allow the user to type some text, which is then painted on the parent Form (but only if the OK Button is selected). Figure 11-27 shows the UI of your dialog box.

Figure 11-27. The simple dialog box

When the user clicks the OK Button, the end result is that the string is extracted from the TextBox maintained by the custom dialog box and painted in the parent Form's client area (Figure 11-28).

Figure 11-28. Using dialog box data

Moreover, if the user reactivates the dialog box, the parent Form assigns the previous text message to the dialog box's TextBox (Figure 11-29).

Figure 11-29. Prepping the dialog box

The code representing the custom dialog box should be of no surprise, given that a dialog box is nothing more than a Form with minor modifications. Here is the relevant code:

```
' Your dialog box.
Public Class MyDialogBox
    Inherits System.Windows.Forms.Form
    Private WithEvents btnCancel As System.Windows.Forms.Button
    Private WithEvents btnOK As System.Windows.Forms.Button
    Private WithEvents label1 As System.Windows.Forms.Label
    Private WithEvents txtMessage As System.Windows.Forms.TextBox
```

```
    Public Sub New()
        MyBase.New()
...
        Me.StartPosition = FormStartPosition.CenterParent
    End Sub
     ...
<System.Diagnostics.DebuggerStepThrough()> _
Private Sub InitializeComponent()
          ...
    ' btnOK
    Me.btnOK.DialogResult = System.Windows.Forms.DialogResult.OK
    Me.btnOK.Location = New System.Drawing.Point(16, 104)
    Me.btnOK.Name = "btnOK"
    Me.btnOK.Size = New System.Drawing.Size(96, 24)
    Me.btnOK.TabIndex = 2
    Me.btnOK.Text = "OK"
    ' btnCancel
    Me.btnCancel.DialogResult = System.Windows.Forms.DialogResult.Cancel
    Me.btnCancel.Location = New System.Drawing.Point(152, 104)
    Me.btnCancel.Name = "btnCancel"
    Me.btnCancel.Size = New System.Drawing.Size(96, 24)
    Me.btnCancel.TabIndex = 3
    Me.btnCancel.Text = "Cancel"
    ' Form configured to function as dialog box.
    Me.Text = "Some Custom Dialog"
    Me.MaximizeBox = False
    Me.ControlBox = False
    Me.MinimizeBox = False
    ...
    End Sub
End Class
```

The first point of interest is in the constructor of the Form. Notice that you are setting the StartPosition property on start-up. Earlier you directly called CenterToScreen() to ensure that the Form was centered correctly. Using the StartPosition property (and the FormStartPosition enumeration), you can gain a finer level of granularity. Usually you should use FormStartPosition.CenterParent to ensure that the location of the dialog box is centered with regard to the parent (regardless of the parent's location on the screen), as shown here:

```
Me.StartPosition = FormStartPosition.CenterParent
```

Another important aspect of dialog box programming is to assign the termination Buttons to a value defined by the DialogResult enumeration. As you know, most dialog boxes define an OK Button that says, in effect, "I am happy with my selections. Please use them in the program." Furthermore, most dialog boxes have a Cancel Button that allows the user to back out of a selection. To configure how the dialog box's Button should respond with respect to dialog box processing, use the DialogResult property, as shown here:

```
Private Sub InitializeComponent()
    ...
    ' OK Button configuration.
    btnOK.DialogResult = System.Windows.Forms.DialogResult.OK

    ' Cancel Button configuration.
    btnCancel.DialogResult = System.Windows.Forms.DialogResult.Cancel
    ...
End Sub
```

Validating Form Data with the DialogResult Property

What exactly does it mean to assign a Button's DialogResult value? First, when a Button has been set to DialogResult.OK or DialogResult.Cancel, the Form *automatically* closes. Also, you can query this property back in the code that launched this dialog box to see which Button the user selected, as shown here:

```
Private Sub mnuModalBox_Click(ByVal sender As System.Object, _
ByVal e As System.EventArgs) Handles mnuModalBox.Click
    Dim myDlg As MyDialogBox = New MyDialogBox()
...
    myDlg.Message = dlgMsg
    myDlg.ShowDialog(Me)
    If (myDlg.DialogResult = DialogResult.OK) Then
        ' User hit OK, do whatever...
    End If
    DoSomeMoreWork()
End Sub
```

Table 11-25 describes the possible values of the DialogResult enumeration. (Remember, in the dialog box itself you assign these values to the Button widgets. In the launching code you ask the dialog box itself for the value!)

Table 11-25. DialogResult Values

DIALOGRESULT VALUE	MEANING IN LIFE
Abort	The dialog box's return value is Abort (usually sent from a Button labeled Abort).
Cancel	The dialog box's return value is Cancel (usually sent from a Button labeled Cancel).
Ignore	The dialog box's return value is Ignore (usually sent from a Button labeled Ignore).
No	The dialog box's return value is No (usually sent from a Button labeled No).
None	Nothing is returned from the dialog box. This means that the modal dialog box continues running.
OK	The dialog box's return value is OK (usually sent from a Button labeled OK).
Retry	The dialog box's return value is Retry (usually sent from a Button labeled Retry).
Yes	The dialog box's return value is Yes (usually sent from a Button labeled Yes).

Grabbing Data from a Dialog Box

Now that you can configure, launch, and test for a dialog box's Button click, you need to understand how to obtain the information from the dialog box. Your current dialog box allows the user to enter a custom string, which is used in the parent Form. Thus, the first step you need to take is to add some number of member variables that represent the data the dialog box is responsible for, as shown here:

```
Public Class MyDialogBox
    Inherits System.Windows.Forms.Form
...
    ' The dialog box's state data (and a way to get it).
    Private strMessage As String
    Public Property Message() As String
        Get
            Return strMessage
        End Get
```

```
        Set(ByVal Value As String)
            strMessage = Value
            txtMessage.Text = strMessage
        End Set
    End Property
End Class
```

Now, to transfer the value in the TextBox to this private member variable requires that you intercept the Click event for the OK Button. Remember that the DialogResult.OK assignment already ensures that your Form is destroyed when this Button is clicked. This time, however, you need to do some additional work, as shown here:

```
Private Sub btnOK_Click(ByVal sender As System.Object, _
ByVal e As System.EventArgs) Handles btnOK.Click
     ' OK Button clicked! Configure new message.
     strMessage = txtMessage.Text
End Sub
```

That's it! Of course, if you had a more elaborate dialog box (such as the CarConfig Form), you would no doubt need a number of custom properties to represent the full set of user selections.

One aspect of the OK Click event handler that you have not yet pondered is how to validate the values of the widgets before closing the dialog box. For example, assume that you wish to check the value of the txtMessage TextBox for an empty string. If the string value in the widget is empty, you can prevent closing the dialog by setting the *Form's* DialogResult value to DialogResult.None. This effectively nullifies the termination of the dialog (at which point you may want to make use of an ErrorProvider, launch an error message box or whatnot). Here is the update.

```
Private Sub btnOK_Click(ByVal sender As System.Object, _
ByVal e As System.EventArgs) Handles btnOK.Click
    ' Empty text box?
    If txtMessage.Text <> "" Then
        strMessage = txtMessage.Text
    Else
        Me.DialogResult = DialogResult.None
        MessageBox.Show("You need to enter some data!")
    End If
End Sub
```

To complete your example dialog box application, you can update the code that launched this dialog box to extract the internal message and use it in the program. Here is the complete menu selection logic:

```
Private Sub mnuModalBox_Click(ByVal sender As System.Object, _
ByVal e As System.EventArgs) Handles mnuModalBox.Click
    ' Set dialog styles in constructor.
    Dim myDlg As MyDialogBox = New MyDialogBox()
    myDlg.Message = dlgMsg
    ' Passing in a reference to the launching dialog is optional.
    myDlg.ShowDialog(Me)
    If (myDlg.DialogResult = DialogResult.OK) Then
        dlgMsg = myDlg.Message
        Invalidate()  ' Repaint string message.
    End If
    DoSomeMoreWork()
End Sub
```

The extracted string is then painted on the client area using standard GDI+ logic, as shown here:

```
Private Sub Form1_Paint(ByVal sender As Object, _
ByVal e As System.Windows.Forms.PaintEventArgs) Handles MyBase.Paint
    Dim g As Graphics = e.Graphics
    g.DrawString(dlgMsg, New Font("times New Roman", 24), _
         Brushes.Blue, 0, 0)
End Sub
```

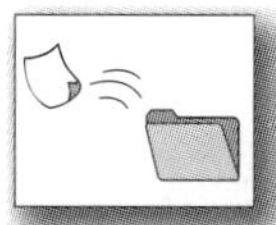

SOURCE CODE *The SimpleDialog application is included under the Chapter 11 subdirectory.*

Form Inheritance

The next topic of this chapter is Form inheritance. As you recall, inheritance is the pillar of OOP that allows one class to extend the functionality of another class. Typically, when you speak of inheritance, you envision one non-GUI type deriving from another non-GUI type. However, in the world of Windows Forms it is possible for one Form to derive from another Form, bringing with it all the previously configured widgets and base class functionality.

For the sake of illustration, assume you have placed your CarConfigForm class in a new VB .NET Code Library application (CarConfigLib) and compiled the binary. Once this is done, create a brand-new Windows Application project workspace. To derive one Form from another, the first step is to set a reference to the external assembly (in this case, the new DLL). Next, specify the base Form using standard VB .NET syntax, as shown here:

```
' The namespace of the base Form.
Imports CarConfigLib
' Your new Form is really a subclass of CarConfigForm!
Public Class Form1
    Inherits CarConfigForm
...
End Class
```

If you now save and reopen the DerivedForm type, you see that the new class has inherited all the widgets! Also be aware that any Controls that have been declared Private by the parent Form may not be modified. If you specify Friend members, you can relocate these items using the design time template. At this point, you are free to extend this Form any way you choose. For test purposes, simply add a new MainMenu that allows the user to exit this application (Figure 11-30).

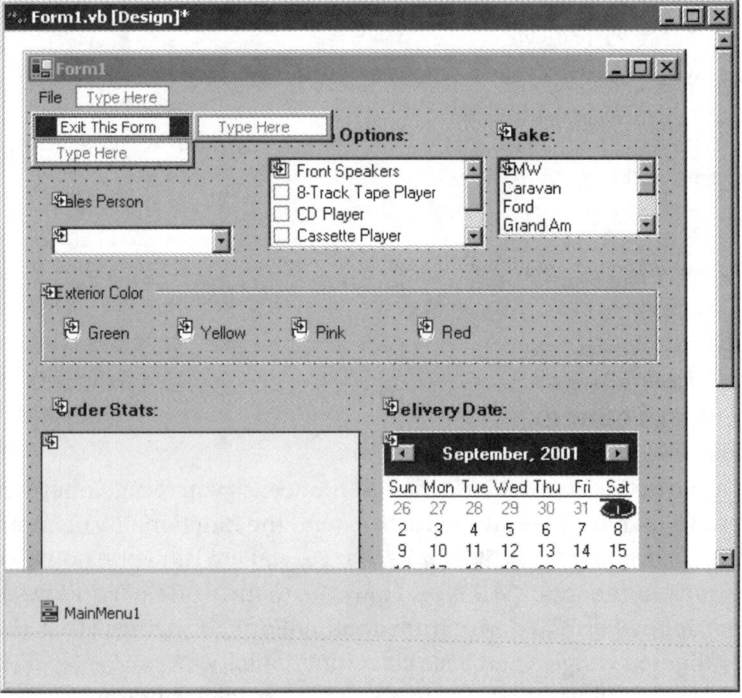

Figure 11-30. Derived form support for a topmost menu

The Click event handler simply shuts down the application, as shown here:

```
Private Sub MenuItem2_Click(ByVal sender As System.Object, _
ByVal e As System.EventArgs) Handles MenuItem2.Click
    Me.Close()
End Sub
```

Finally, it is worth pointing out that the Visual Studio.NET IDE provides an integrated Wizard to create derived forms. To access its functionality, activate the "Project|Add Inherited Form" menu item. Once you provide a name for your new class, you are asked to specify the name of the DLL assembly that contains the base class Form.

SOURCE CODE *The MyDerivedForm and CarConfigLib applications are included under the Chapter 11 subdirectory.*

Understanding Custom Controls

At this point in the game, you should have a firm understanding of the core set of intrinsic Windows Forms controls. As you would expect, the remaining widgets expose their unique set of properties, methods and events, which I assume you will examine at your leisure. To close this chapter, you now spend some time learning how to create *custom* controls.

If you have a background in classic COM, you are no doubt aware of the use of ActiveX controls. These coclasses are simply types that implement a number of COM interfaces, which provide behaviors for rendering graphical content, persisting the state of the coclass between sessions, and enabling control/container communication (among other duties). Like many aspects of COM, VB 6.0 does a fantastic job of hiding the complex underbelly of ActiveX controls from view. However building controls using VB 6.0 has the undesirable byproduct of preventing experienced developers from building more complex solutions (such as tweaking the underlying IDL code). When you require more finite control over the underlying COM infrastructure, the Active Template Library (ATL) provides the required horsepower; however building ActiveX controls with ATL is insidiously complicated.

The .NET framework defines a number of types that allow you to have the best of both worlds. In its simplest form, building a custom Windows Forms control is identical to building a typical VB .NET class. Thus, given your current understanding of object-based and GUI-based development, you could simply fire up a new Windows Control Library workspace and build a reusable GUI type. Unlike VB 6.0, you are also free to dig deeper and build more sophisticated widgets using various system-supplied attributes. In a nutshell, building a custom

.NET control offers the ease of use Visual Basic 6.0 developers have enjoyed for years, while exposing more powerful features using the familiar .NET type system. To begin our journey, let's start by defining some new terminology.

The Class, Control, UserControl, and Component Distinction

As you are already aware, a *class* is a User Defined Type (UDT) that serves as a blueprint for discrete variables of this type. In VB .NET, your custom classes can derive from other types, implement any number of interfaces, serve as the basis for additional types, and typically support any number of properties, methods, and events. In addition to this (obvious) definition, generic classes are unique in that they do not support any design time manipulation. For example, if you have a simple VB .NET class named Car, you are unable to interact with the members of its default public interface using the VS.NET Properties window. Furthermore, when you are building solutions using generic class types, you do not drag the item onto a Form-derived type as you would a Windows Form Button control. In essence, a class is a non-GUI type, that is directly manipulated through code.

A *control* is also a class type. Meaning, it derives from a parent class (typically System.Windows.Forms.Control) and inherits a good deal of functionality in the process. Each of the GUI widgets you have examined during this chapter is considered a control type. Like a simple class, controls support a public interface and can be manipulated directly by code. In addition, controls do support a GUI, and are typically configured using various design time Wizards, the VS.NET Properties window, and are "drawn" onto the owning host using the Toolbox. Obviously, like any intrinsic Windows Forms controls, your custom controls inherit the same set of behaviors from each class in the inheritance chain.

Next you have *user controls.* Like a control type, user controls also support a runtime GUI and are fully configurable at design time. The key difference is that user controls do not derive directly from System.Windows.Forms.Control. Rather, user controls derive from System.Windows.Forms.UserControl, which in turn derives directly from ContainerControl. As you recall from Chapter 8, ContainerControl (and its base class ScrollableControl) provide additional members that allow you to configure scrolling, tab order, and focus logic. When you wish to build a reusable GUI widget that maintains numerous related widgets that need to work together as a whole, you will want to derive your custom class directly from UserControl (in fact, this is the default base class from which your custom controls derive). However, if you are not interested in building a widget that hosts interrelated composite controls, you are free to change the Wizard generated code to derive directly from Control itself.

Finally, you have *components*. Components can best be thought of as a middle of the road alternative between a simple class and a full-fledged (user)control. Meaning, like a simple class, components do not support a runtime user interface. However, components can be selected from the VS.NET Toolbox window and configured using the integrated Property window. For example, check out the Components tab in Figure 11-31.

Figure 11-31. The Components Selection Tab

As you can see, these intrinsic components are not necessarily GUI in nature, but they do lend themselves well to a design time environment. If you drop a component (such as the EventLog) onto your hosting Form-derived type, you will notice that the design time representation is placed in the designer's icon tray (Figure 11-32). Once you select the component, you are able to set various properties using the Properties Window.

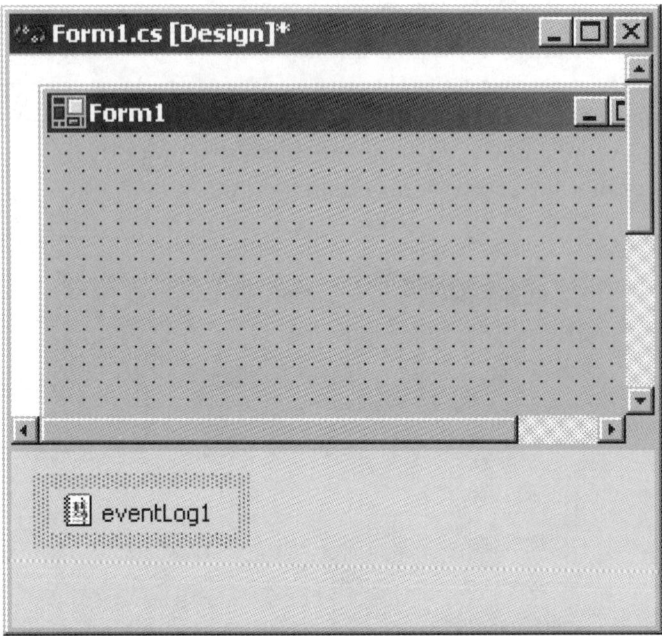

Figure 11-32. Components are hosted by the Icon Tray

The distinction between a control and a component may seem superficial at best. The key difference to keep in mind however, is that a control is visible on the host at design time and *runtime*, whereas a component is visible only at *design time.*

Programmatically speaking, what marks a type as a component is the fact that it implements the System.ComponentModel.IComponent interface (see Chapter 9). Most of the time however, you will not directly flesh out the details of this interface by hand, but rather derive your type from System.ComponentModel.Component (and thus receive the canned implementation).

Building a Custom UserControl

During the next several pages, you construct a custom UserControl named (of course) CarControl, and learn about numerous control-centric .NET types in the process. To begin, fire up Visual Studio.NET and select a new Windows Control Library workspace named MyControlLib (Figure 11-33). When you are finished, rename the initial VB .NET class to CarControl (note that the base class of your type is UserControl).

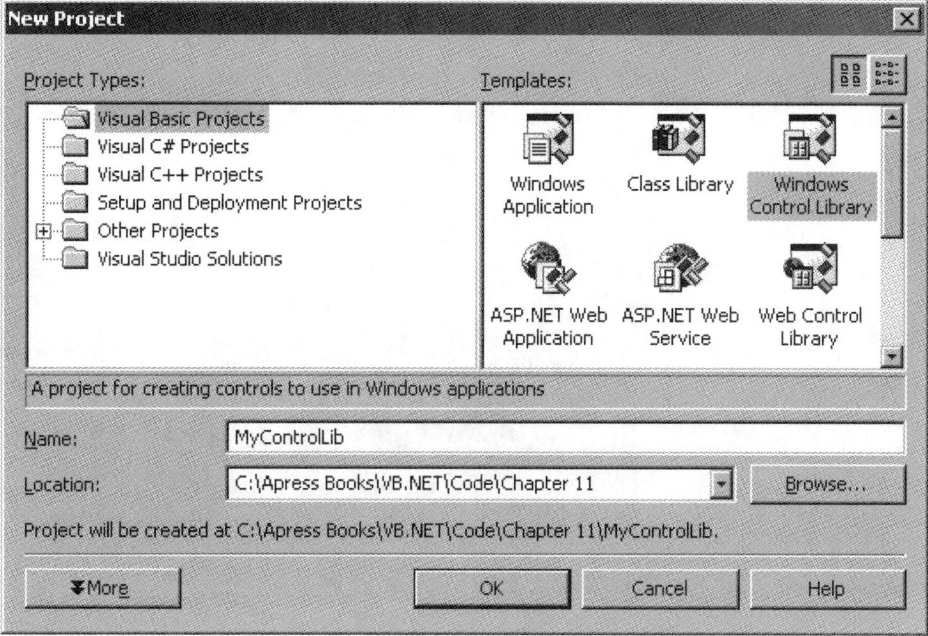

Figure 11-33. Creating a new Windows Control Library workspace

Before you build this custom type, let's establish the big picture of where you are going with this example. The CarControl type is responsible for animating through a series of bitmaps, which will change based on the internal state of the automobile. If the car's current speed is safely under the car's maximum speed limit, the CarControl loops through three bitmap images that render an automobile driving safely along. If the current speed is 10 miles below the maximum speed, the CarControl loops through four images, with the fourth image showing the car breaking down. Finally, if the car has surpassed its maximum speed, the CarControl loops over five images, where the fifth image renders a doomed automobile.

Creating the Images

Given our design notes, the first order of business is to create a set of five *.bmp files for use by the animation loop. If you wish to create custom images, begin by activating the "Project|Add New Item . . ." menu selection and insert five new Bitmap resources. If you would rather not showcase your artistic abilities, feel free to use the images that accompany this sample application (keep in mind, I in *no way* consider myself a graphics artist). The first of these three images (Figures 11-34 through 11-36) illustrate a (very well rendered) car navigating down the road:

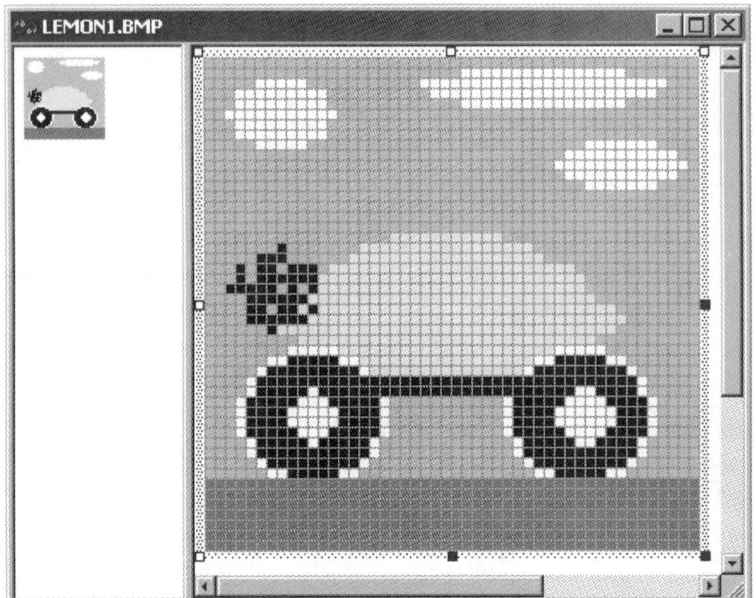

Figure 11-34. Lemon1.bmp

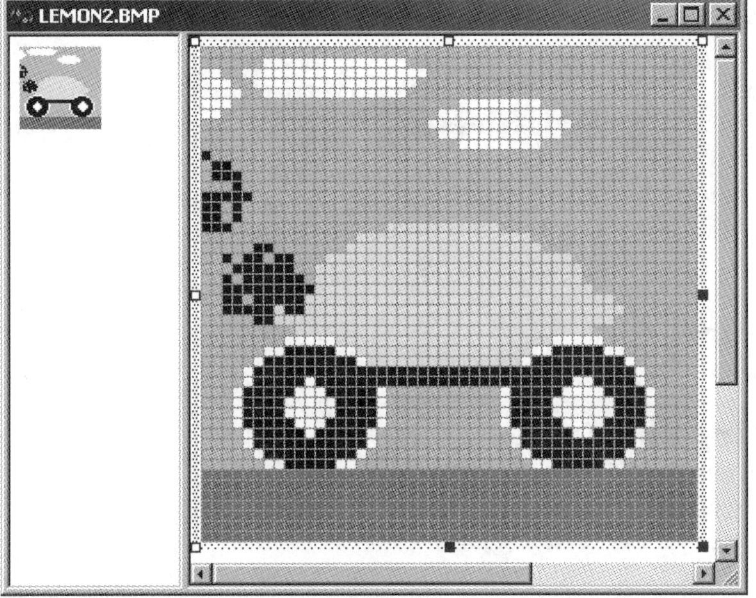

Figure 11-35. Lemon2.bmp

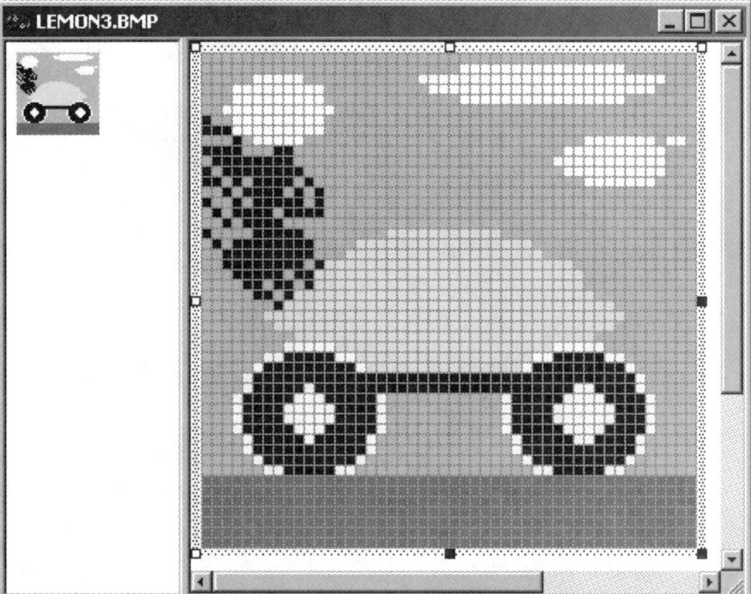

Figure 11-36. Lemon3.bmp

The final two bitmap images (Figure 11-37 and Figure 11-38) represent a car approaching its maximum upper limit and as well its demise.

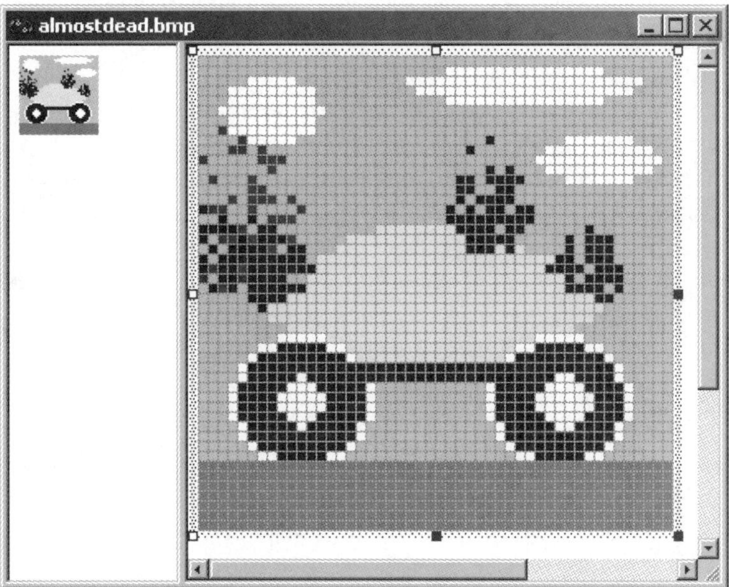

Figure 11-37. AlmostDead.bmp

Figure 11-38. Dead.bmp

Building the Design Time GUI

Now that we have our images, the next step is to open the design time editor for the CarControl type. As you can see, you are presented with a Form-like template, that serves as the client area of the control under construction. Using the Toolbox window, add an ImageList type (to hold each of the bitmaps), a Timer type (to control the animation cycle), and a PictureBox (to hold the current image). Don't worry about configuring the size or location of the PictureBox type, as you will programmatically position this widget within the bounds of the CarControl. Figure 11-39 shows the story thus far.

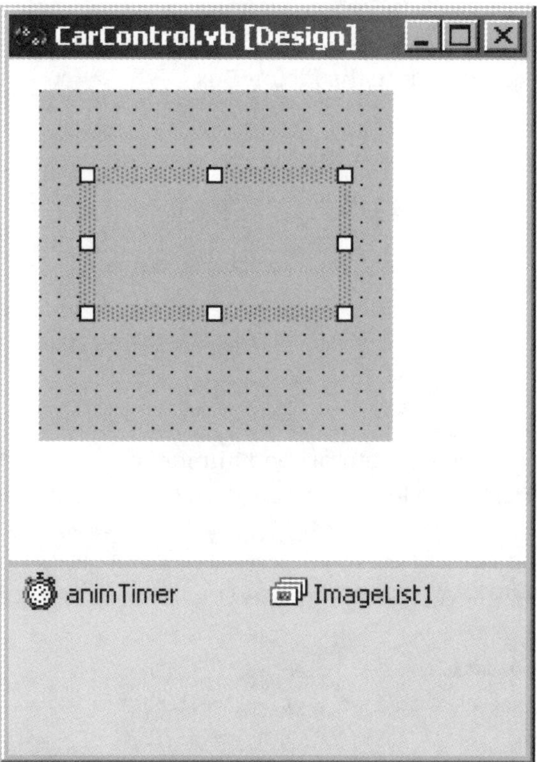

Figure 11-39. Creating the design time GUI

Now, using the Properties Window, configure the ImageList's Images collection by adding each bitmap to the list. Be aware that you will want to add these items sequentially (Lemon1.bmp, Lemon2.bmp, . . . , Dead.bmp) to ensure a linear animation loop. As you recall from Chapter 10, when you incorporate resources (such as bitmaps) into your VS.NET solutions, the underlying *.resx file is automatically updated. Therefore, the images will be embedded into your assembly with no extra work on your behalf. Also be aware that the default width and height of *.bmp files inserted using VS.NET are 47 * 47 pixels. Thus, the ImageSize of the ImageList should also be set to 47 * 47 (or else you will have with some skewed rendering). Finally, configure the state of your Timer type such that the Interval property is set to 200 and is initially disabled.

Establishing the Default Public Sector

With this GUI prep work out of the way, you can now turn your attention to the more exciting world of code. To begin, create a new public enumeration named

AnimFrame, which has a member representing each item maintained by the ImageList. As you will see, you make use of this enumeration to determine the current frame to render into the PictureBox:

```
' Enum for images.
Public Enum AnimFrame
    Lemon1
    Lemon2
    Lemon3
    AlmostDead
    Dead
End Enum
```

The CarControl type maintains a good number of private data points to represent the animation logic. Here is the rundown of each member:

```
Public Class CarControl
    Inherits System.Windows.Forms.UserControl
...
    ' All the state data.
    Private currFrame As AnimFrame = AnimFrame.Lemon1
    Private currMaxFrame As AnimFrame = AnimFrame.Lemon3
    Private IsAnim As Boolean
    Private currSp As Integer
    Private WithEvents pictureBox As System.Windows.Forms.pictureBox
    Private maxSp As Integer = 100
    Private WithEvents animTimer As System.Windows.Forms.Timer
    Private carPetName As String = "NoName"
    Private bottomRect As RectangleF = New RectangleF()
    Friend WithEvents ImageList1 As System.Windows.Forms.ImageList
    Private txtPaneColor As Color
...
End Class
```

As you can see, you have data points that represent the current and maximum speed, the pet name of the automobile, and two members of type AnimFrame. The currFrame variable is used to specify which member of the ImageList is to be rendered. The currMaxFrame variable is used to mark the current upper limit in the ImageList (recall, the CarControl loops through three to five images based on the current speed). The IsAnim data point is used to determine if the car is currently in animation mode. Finally, you have a Rectangle member (bottomRect) that is used to represent the bottom region of the CarControl type. Later, you render the pet name of the automobile into this piece of screen real estate.

To divide the CarControl into two rectangular regions, create a private helper function named StretchBox(). The role of this member is to calculate the correct size of the bottomRect member as well as to ensure that the PictureBox widget is stretched out over the upper 2/3rds (or so) of the CarControl type.

```
Private Sub StretchBox()
    ' Configure picture box.
    pictureBox.Top = 0
    pictureBox.Left = 0
    pictureBox.Height = Me.Height - 50
    pictureBox.Width = Me.Width
    pictureBox.Image = ImageList1.Images(CType(AnimFrame.Lemon1, Integer))
    ' Figure out size of bottom rect.
    bottomRect.X = 0
    bottomRect.Y = Me.Height - 50
    bottomRect.Height = Me.Height - pictureBox.Height
    bottomRect.Width = Me.Width
End Sub
```

Once you have carved out the dimensions of each rectangle, call StretchBox() from the default constructor.

Defining the Custom Events

The CarControl type supports two events, which are fired back to the host Form based on the current speed of the automobile. The first event, AboutToBlow, is sent out when the CarControl's speed approaches the upper limit. BlewUp is sent to the container when the current speed is greater than the allowed maximum. You fire these events in just a moment, but for the time being, add the following members to the public sector of the CarControl.

```
' Car events.
Public Event AboutToBlow()
Public Event BlewUp()
```

Supporting Custom Properties

Like any class type, custom controls may define any number of properties to allow the outside world to interact with the state of the widget. For your current purposes, you are only interested in defining three properties. First, you have Anim. This property enables or disables the Timer type:

```
' Used to configure the internal Timer type.
Public Property Anim() As Boolean
    Get
        Return IsAnim
    End Get
    Set(ByVal Value As Boolean)
        IsAnim = Value
        animTimer.Enabled = IsAnim
    End Set
End Property
```

The PetName property is as you would expect, and requires no comment. Do notice however, that when the user sets the pet name, you make a call to Invalidate() to render the name of the CarControl into the bottom rectangular area of the widget (you do this step in just a moment):

```
' Configure pet name.
Public Property PetName() As String
    Get
        Return carPetName
    End Get
    Set(ByVal Value As String)
        carPetName = Value
        Invalidate()
    End Set
End Property
```

Finally, you have the Speed property. In addition to simply modifying the currSp data member, Speed is also the entity that fires the AboutToBlow and BlewUp events based on the current speed of the CarControl. Here is the complete logic:

```
' Adjust currSp, currMaxFrame and fire our events.
Public Property Speed() As Integer
    Get
        Return currSp
    End Get
    Set(ByVal Value As Integer)
        currSp = Value
        currFrame = currMaxFrame
        ' About to explode?
        If ((maxSp - currSp) <= 10) Then
            RaiseEvent AboutToBlow()
```

```
            currMaxFrame = AnimFrame.AlmostDead
        End If
        ' Maxed out?
        If (currSp >= maxSp) Then
            currSp = maxSp
            RaiseEvent BlewUp()
            currMaxFrame = AnimFrame.Dead
        End If
    End Set
End Property
```

As you can see, if the current speed is 10 miles below the maximum upper speed, you fire the AboutToBlow event and adjust the upper frame limit to AnimFrame.AlmostDead. If the user has pushed the limits of your automobile, you fire the BlewUp event and set the upper frame limit to AnimFrame.Dead.

Controlling the Animation

The next detail to attend to is ensuring that the Timer type advances the current frame to render within the PictureBox. Again, recall that the number of frames to loop through depends on the current speed of the automobile. You only want to bother adjusting the image in the PictureBox if the Anim property has been set to true. Begin by handling the Interval event for the Timer type, and flush out the details as follows:

```
Private Sub animTimer_Tick(ByVal sender As Object, _
ByVal e As System.EventArgs) Handles animTimer.Tick
    If (IsAnim) Then
        ' Here we are loading from the ImageList
        ' thus, these items are embedded into the
        ' assembly.
        pictureBox.Image = ImageList1.Images(CType(currFrame, Integer))
    End If
    ' Bump frame.
    Dim s As String = [Enum].Format(GetType(AnimFrame), currFrame, "D")
    Dim i As Integer = Integer.Parse(s)
    Dim nextFrame As Integer = i + 1
    currFrame = CType(nextFrame, AnimFrame)
    If (currFrame > currMaxFrame) Then
        currFrame = AnimFrame.Lemon1
    End If
End Sub
```

Rendering the Pet Name

Before you can take your control out for a spin, you have one final detail to attend to: displaying the car's moniker. To do this, handle the Paint event for your CarControl, and within the handler, render the CarControl's pet name into the bottom rectangular region of the client area:

```
Private Sub CarControl_Paint(ByVal sender As Object, _
ByVal e As System.Windows.Forms.PaintEventArgs) Handles MyBase.Paint
    ' Render the pet name on the bottom of the control.
    Dim g As Graphics = e.Graphics
    g.FillRectangle(New SolidBrush(txtPaneColor), bottomRect)
    g.DrawString(PetName, New Font("Times New Roman", 15), Brushes.Black,
bottomRect)
End Sub
```

At this point, the initial CarControl is complete! Go ahead and rebuild your project.

Building a VB .NET Client Application

Like all .NET types, you are now able to make use of your custom control from any language targeting the CLR. For your current purposes, build a VB .NET tester application. Begin by closing down the current workspace and creating a new Windows Forms project named CarCtrlClient. To allow your current project to reference auxiliary controls, right-click your Toolbox window and select the "Customize Toolbox . . ." menu selection. Using the "Browse . . ." button on the .NET Framework Components tab, navigate to your MyControlLib library, and then select the CarControl type (Figure 11-40).

At this point you will find a new icon on the Toolbox named, of course, CarControl. Begin building your GUI by placing a CarControl onto the Form designer. Notice that the Anim, PetName, and Speed properties are all exposed through the Properties window. Also notice that the control is in-place active. Thus, if you set the Anim property to true at design time, you will find your car is animating on the Form designer.

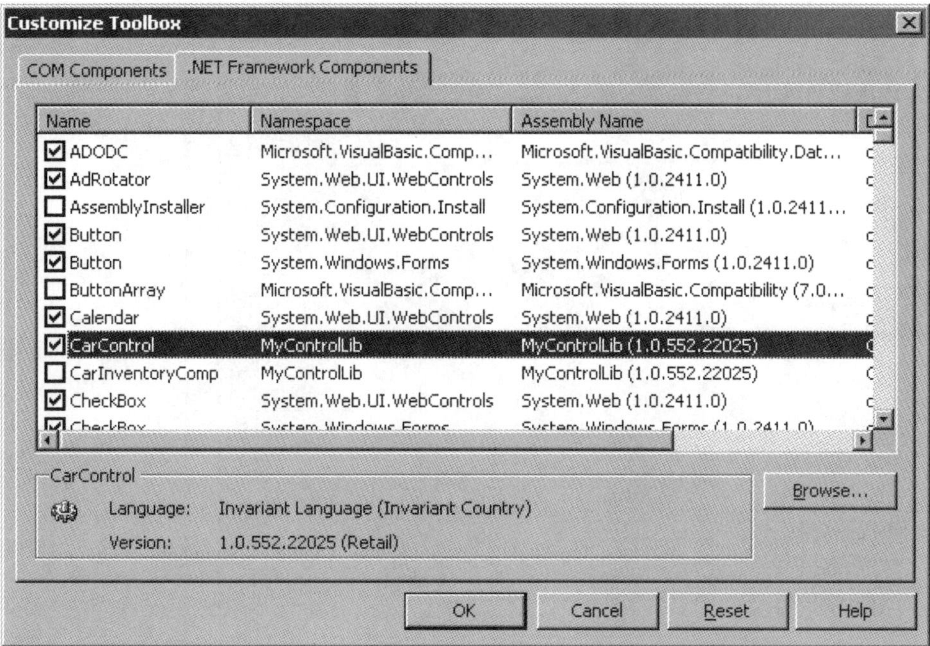

Figure 11-40. Selecting your custom CarControl

Once you have configured the initial state of your CarControl, add additional GUI widgets that allow the user to increase the speed of the automobile, stop and start the animation cycle, and view the incoming events (a Label widget should do nicely). Here is one possible design (Figure 11-41).

The logic behind the Anim Me and Stop It buttons are that they set the Anim property to True or False, and display the current speed of the CarControl in the Label widget:

```
Private Sub btnAnimMe_Click(ByVal sender As System.Object, _
ByVal e As System.EventArgs) Handles btnAnimMe.Click
    carControl1.Anim = True
    lblCurrSp.Text = "Current Speed:" & carControl1.Speed.ToString()
End Sub
Private Sub btnStopIt_Click(ByVal sender As System.Object, _
ByVal e As System.EventArgs) Handles btnStopIt.Click
    carControl1.Anim = False
End Sub
```

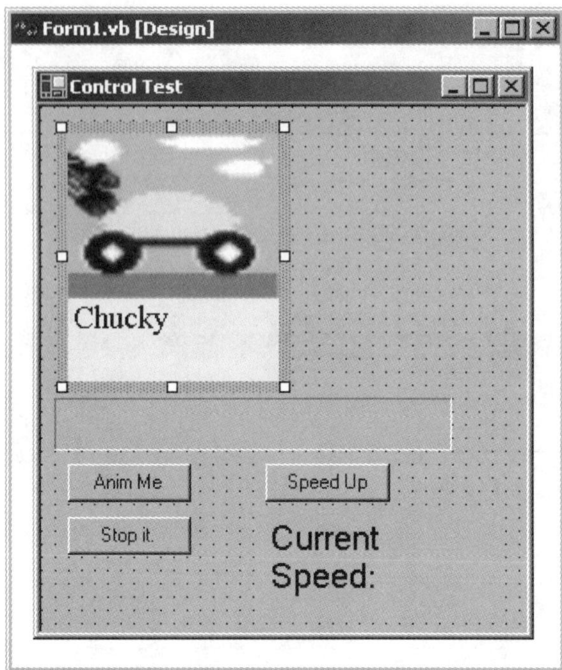

Figure 11-41. The client-side GUI

The "Speed Up" adds 10 to the speed of the CarControl type and prints the current speed to the output Label:

```
Private Sub btnSpeedUp_Click(ByVal sender As System.Object, _
ByVal e As System.EventArgs) Handles btnSpeedUp.Click
    carControl1.Speed += 10
    lblCurrSp.Text = "Current Speed:" & carControl1.Speed.ToString()
End Sub
```

The final aspect of our client-side design is to capture the incoming events from the CarControl widget. Like all other Windows Forms GUI types, you are able to handle events using the Properties window. Handle the AboutToBlow and BlewUp events, and write some informative message to the output Label:

```
' Client side event handlers.
Private Sub carControl1_AboutToBlow() Handles CarControl1.AboutToBlow
    lblCarMsg.Text = "Careful! About to blow!"
End Sub
Private Sub carControl1_BlewUp() Handles CarControl1.BlewUp
    lblCarMsg.Text = "You're toast dude. . ."
End Sub
```

At this point, you are able to run your client application and interact with the CarControl. Consider Figure 11-42.

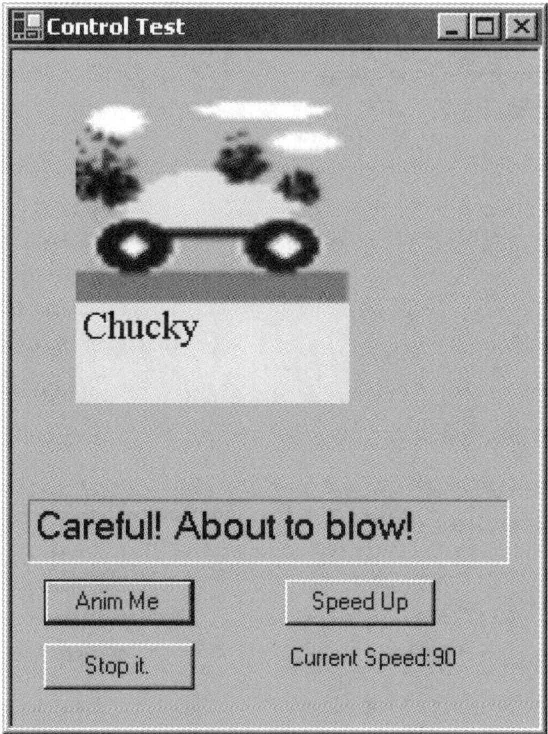

Figure 11-42. Your CarControl in action

As you can see, building and using custom controls is a fairly simple endeavor. Given what you already know about OOP, GDI+, and Windows Forms, the bulk of your work is simply designing the type itself.

Select Members of the System.ComponentModel Namespace

Building a custom control (or component) is unique in that you have one additional programmatic aspect to contend with: Design time functionality. Currently, each of the CarControl's custom properties is displayed within the Property window in a rather disorganized fashion. To allow the end user to interact with your control in a more orderly fashion, it is helpful to incorporate some simple enhancements. For example, you may wish to supply a string that offers a description of each property and group each of your members into a common category.

The System.ComponentModel namespace defines a number of types that allow you to configure how your custom controls and components should display themselves at design time. When you are interested in making the sorts of modifications previously mentioned, you will want to make use of the following core attributes (Table 11-26).

Table 11-26. Select Members of System.ComponentModel

SYSTEM.COMPONENTMODEL ATTRIBUTE	APPLIED TO	MEANING IN LIFE
BrowsableAttribute	Properties and events	Specifies whether a property or an event should be displayed in the property browser. By default, all custom properties and events can be browsed.
CategoryAttribute	Properties and events	Specifies the name of the category in which to group a property or event.
DescriptionAttribute	Properties and events	Defines a small block of text to be displayed at the bottom of the property browser when the user selects a property or event.
DefaultPropertyAttribute	Properties	Specifies the default property for the component. This property is selected in the property browser when a user clicks on the control.
DefaultValueAttribute	Properties	Sets a simple default value for a property.
LocalizableAttribute	Properties	Specifies that a property may be localized. Any properties that have this attribute are automatically persisted into the resources file when a user chooses to localize a form.
DefaultEventAttribute	Events	Specifies the default event for the component. When a user double-clicks the control type, stub code is automatically written for the default event.

Enhancing the Design Time Appearance of CarControl

To illustrate the use of some of these new attributes, assume you want to create a custom category to which each property and event of the CarControl belong (called CarConfig), as well as to supply a description of each member. To do so, simply update your members to support the <Category> and <Description> attributes. For example:

```
Imports System.ComponentModel
Public Class CarControl
    Inherits System.Windows.Forms.UserControl
   . . .
    ' Car events.
    <Category("Car Configuration"), _
    Description("Sent when your car is approaching terminal speed.")> _
    Public Event AboutToBlow()
   . . .
    ' Controls current speed.
    <Category("Car Configuration"), _
    Description("Configure speed of auto"), _
    DefaultValue(50)> _
    Public Property Speed() As Integer
        . . .
    End Property
End Class
```

Once you select an instance of the CarControl at design time, users can now interact with your control as seen in Figure 11-43 (note the description appears in the bottom pane of the Properties window).

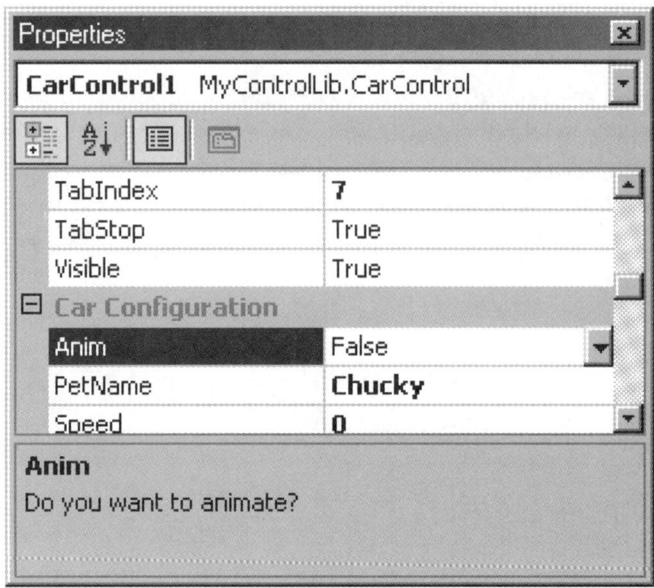

Figure 11-43. The custom design time category

Defining a Default Property and Default Event

In addition to describing and grouping like members into a common category, you may also want to configure your controls (or components) to support default behaviors. A given control may support a default property. Now, if you are coming from a Visual Basic 6.0 background, be very aware that default properties do *not* allow you to write VB .NET code such as:

```
' Illegal! Default properties are not
' supported at the code level!
MyCarControl = 50 ' Default Speed property?
```

Rather, .NET default properties are a design time only feature. When you define the default property for a class using the <DefaultProperty> attribute as follows:

```
' Mark the default property for this control.
<DefaultProperty("Anim")> _
Public Class CarControl
    Inherits System.Windows.Forms.UserControl
...
End Class
```

you ensure that when the user selects this control at design time, the Anim property is automatically highlighted in the Properties window. Likewise, when you configure your control to have a default event:

```
' Mark the default event and property for this control.
<DefaultEvent("BlewUp"), DefaultProperty("Anim")> _
Public Class CarControl
    Inherits System.Windows.Forms.UserControl
...
End Class
```

you ensure that when the user double-clicks the widget at design time, stub code is automatically written for the default event.

The Final Integration

Currently, the CarControl supports properties that expose simple intrinsic types (strings, Booleans, integers). Be aware however that when your custom types support more complex types (such as a Color structure), the IDE responds by intelligently displaying an appropriate design time editor.

To wrap things up, assume CarControl supports one additional property named TextPaneColor. This property wraps a private Color variable that is used to configure the brush that paints the bottom rectangular region of the type:

```
' Configure color of text pane.
<Category("Car Configuration"), _
Description("Set color of text area")> _
Public Property TextPaneColor() As Color
    Get
        Return txtPaneColor
    End Get
    Set(ByVal Value As Color)
        txtPaneColor = Value
        Invalidate()
    End Set
End Property
```

When manipulated using the Property window, the IDE displays the expected color configuration drop-down list (Figure 11-44).

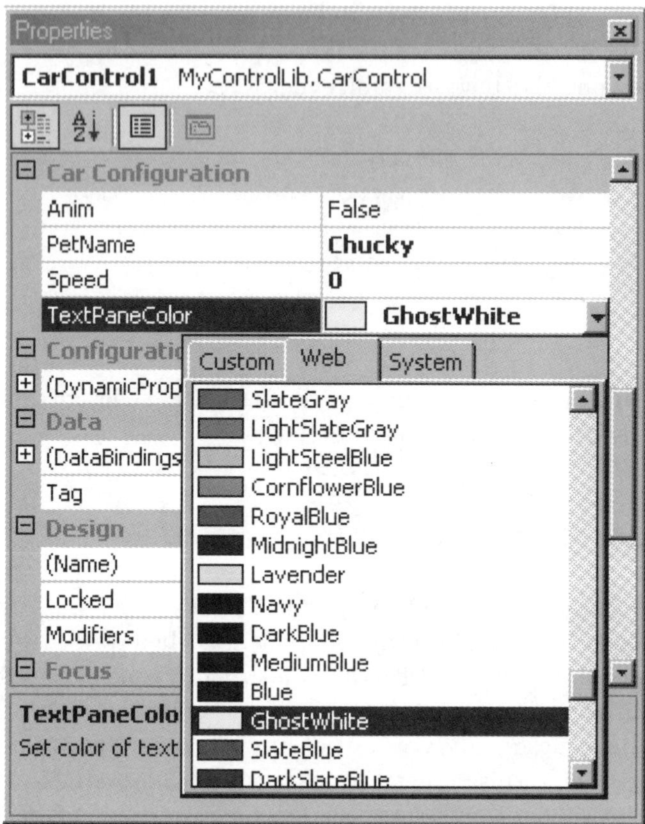

Figure 11-44. Manipulating the TextPaneColor property

Building a .NET (Data) Component

Recall that a *component* is a type that is configurable at design time, but invisible at runtime. In general, components are concerned with containing other types, and exposing a small subset of their overall functionality to the object user (thereby decreasing the complexity of working with the internal types). Components in the .NET framework typically derive from System.ComponentModel.Component, which provides a default implementation of the IComponent interface (which has already been examined in Chapter 9).

To illustrate the construction of custom components (as well as preview ADO.NET), you close this chapter by creating a simple .NET component that wraps up logic that reads a specific table of the Cars database (investigated formally in Chapter 14). To build the component that follows, you need to run the supplied SQL script located under the "Chapter 14 \ SQL Script" subdirectory. If you wish to do so, turn to Chapter 14 for instructions on configuring the Cars database. You are also free to modify the example that follows to work with an existing SQL database such as Pubs.

In any case, the goal is to allow the user of the CarInventoryComp type to obtain a populated DataSet using the GetCars() method. This method (by default) establishes a connection with the Cars database and pulls over every record from the Inventory table. You also allow the user to apply a filter to the underlying SQL query, that is used to fetch automobiles of a specific color (e.g., all red cars).

Begin by inserting a new Component type to your current MyControlLib project using the "Project | Add Component . . ." menu option (go ahead and name your type CarInventoryComp). As you can see, component types have a design time element. Unlike a Form or UserControl-derived type, the design time interface of a Component-derived type is nothing more than an Icon Tray in disguise. Therefore you do not use this template to build a GUI or render images using GDI+. As mentioned, custom components consume and expose functionality of other related components. The sole purpose of the component designer is to contain the related types.

The next order of business is to make reference to a new ADO.NET-centric namespace: System.Data.SqlClient. Again, Chapter 14 documents ADO.NET in detail. For the time being, simply understand that this namespace defines the types that are necessary to pull data from databases managed by Microsoft SQL Server.

```
' Sql database access.
Imports System.Data.SqlClient
Imports System.ComponentModel
Public Class CarInventoryComp
    Inherits System.ComponentModel.Component
...
End Class
```

Connecting to the Cars Database

Now, before you pull data out of the Inventory table, you need to establish a connection with the data source. To do so, select the Data tab of the Toolbox, and place a SqlConnection component onto the design time template (Figure 11-45).

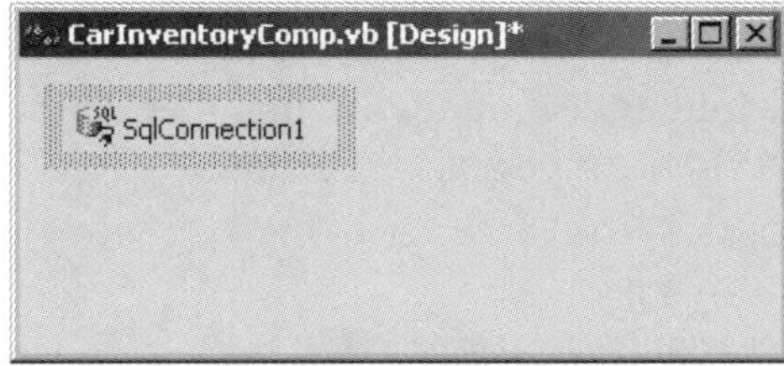

Figure 11-45. Containing a component

Using the Properties window, select the ConnectionString property and choose New Connection. The resulting dialog box is likely a familiar sight to Visual Basic 6.0 developers. Using the Connection tab, enter the name of your local machine and select the Cars database (or whichever database you happen to be working with). Figure 11-46 captures the highlights.

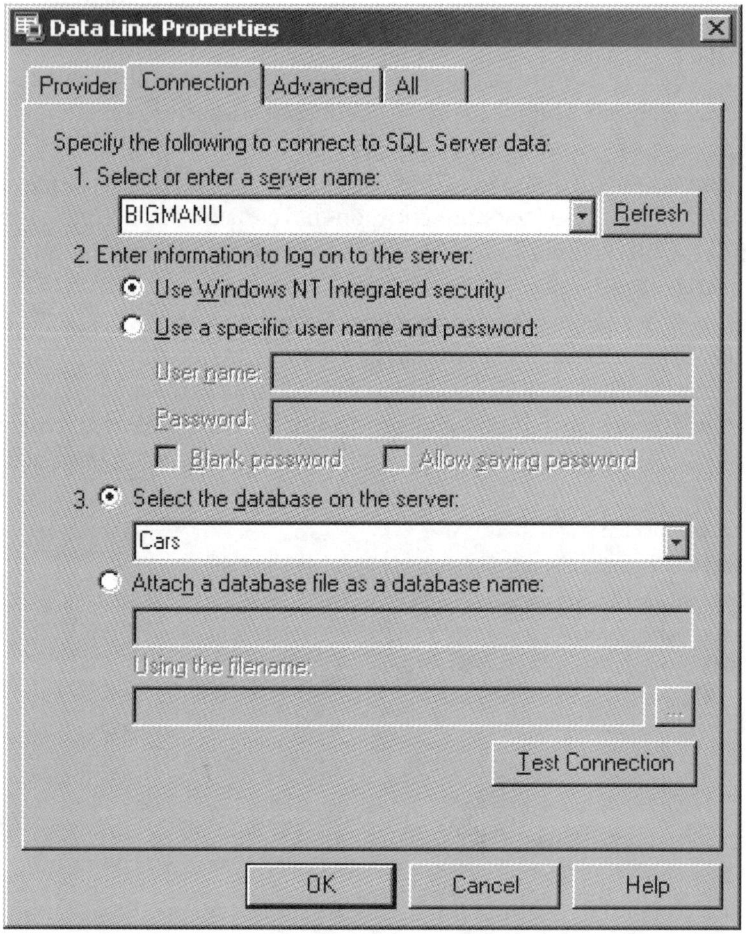

Data Link Properties

Provider | Connection | Advanced | All

Specify the following to connect to SQL Server data:

1. Select or enter a server name:

BIGMANU | Refresh

2. Enter information to log on to the server:

Use Windows NT Integrated security

Use a specific user name and password:

User name:

Password:

Blank password | Allow saving password

3. Select the database on the server:

Cars

Attach a database file as a database name:

Using the filename:

Test Connection

OK | Cancel | Help

Figure 11-46. Configuring your connection

Once you select OK you see that the underlying connection string has been established within the InitializeComponent() member. Your class now contains a new private data member of type SqlConnection:

```
Public Class CarInventoryComp
    Inherits System.ComponentModel.Component
```

```
    Friend WithEvents SqlConnection1 As System.Data.SqlClient.SqlConnection
...
    <System.Diagnostics.DebuggerStepThrough()> Private Sub InitializeComponent()
        Me.SqlConnection1 = New System.Data.SqlClient.SqlConnection()
        '
        'SqlConnection1
        '
        Me.SqlConnection1.ConnectionString = "data source=(local);" & _
        initial catalog=Cars;integrated security=SSPI;persist securit" & _
        "y info=False;workstation id=INTERLAP4;packet size=4096"
    End Sub
End Class
```

Exposing the Data Connection

The first member of our Component derived class is a custom property named ColorFilter. This item allows the user to specify the color of automobile (which as mentioned is merged into the underlying SQL query). Assuming you have a Private data member of type string (named filter), the property logic is a no-brainer:

```
<Category("Car Component"), _
Description("Which Color of Car do you want?")> _
Public Property ColorFilter() As String
    Get
        Return filter
    End Get
    Set(ByVal Value As String)
        filter = Value
    End Set
End Property
```

Finally, the GetCars() method does the dirty work of populating the DataSet based on the filter. If no filter has been specified, the query returns all rows in the Inventory table:

```
Public Function GetCars() As DataSet
    ' Account for optional filter.
    Dim sql As String = "SELECT * FROM Inventory"
    If filter <> "" Then
            sql &= " WHERE Color = '" & filter & "'"
    End If
```

```
    ' Open connection and fill the DataSet.
    Dim ds As DataSet = New DataSet("CarsDS")
    Dim da As SqlDataAdapter = New SqlDataAdapter(sql, SqlConnection1)
    da.Fill(ds, "Inventory")
    Return ds
End Function
```

Here, you make use of the System.Data.SqlClient.SqlDataAdapter type to fill your DataSet based on the SQL query and active connection. Again, you will drill into the specifics of data access using ADO.NET at a later time. For now, recompile your MyControlLib project and squash any typos.

Using Your Custom Component

To test your custom component, you first must reference this new type from the Toolbox. Access the Customize Toolbox dialog and *uncheck* your current reference to the MyControlLib assembly and close the dialog. Now, access the same dialog and (once again) navigate to the location of the MyControlLib binary. Once you have done so, you see a new selection (CarInventoryComp) is available. Select both types contained in the control library and select OK (Figure 11-47).

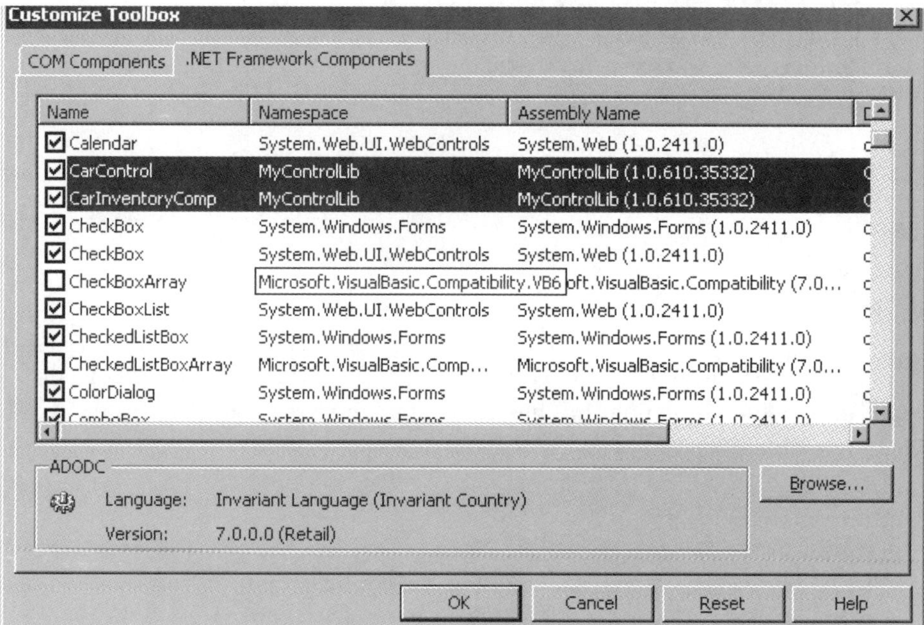

Figure 11-47. Selecting multiple .NET components

Now, drag a CarInventoryComp component onto your main Form. As you can see, the Icon Tray has been activated with a new instance of your custom component. At this point, update the GUI to support a DataGrid widget and a means to gather the filter value from the user. Figure 11-48 shows one possible design.

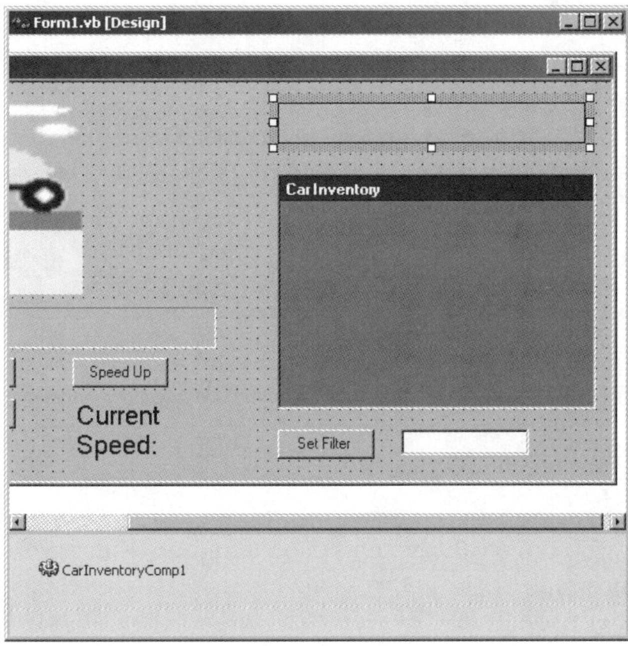

Figure 11-48. The updated client side GUI

Using the component is trivial. Add a private helper function named UpdateGrid() which calls the GetCars() method, taking into account the applied filter. Once you have added the following code, call this member from within the Form's constructor and in response to the Click event of the Set Filter button.

```
Private Sub UpdateGrid()
    ' Load the DataGrid using our Component.
    CarInventoryComp1.ColorFilter = txtColorFilter.Text
    DataGrid1.DataSource = CarInventoryComp1.GetCars().Tables("Inventory")
    lblColorFilter.Text = "Color filter is: " & CarInventoryComp1.ColorFilter
End Sub
```

When the Form loads, you find the DataGrid is populated on start-up. If you were to specify a specific color, you find something like the following (Figure 11-49).

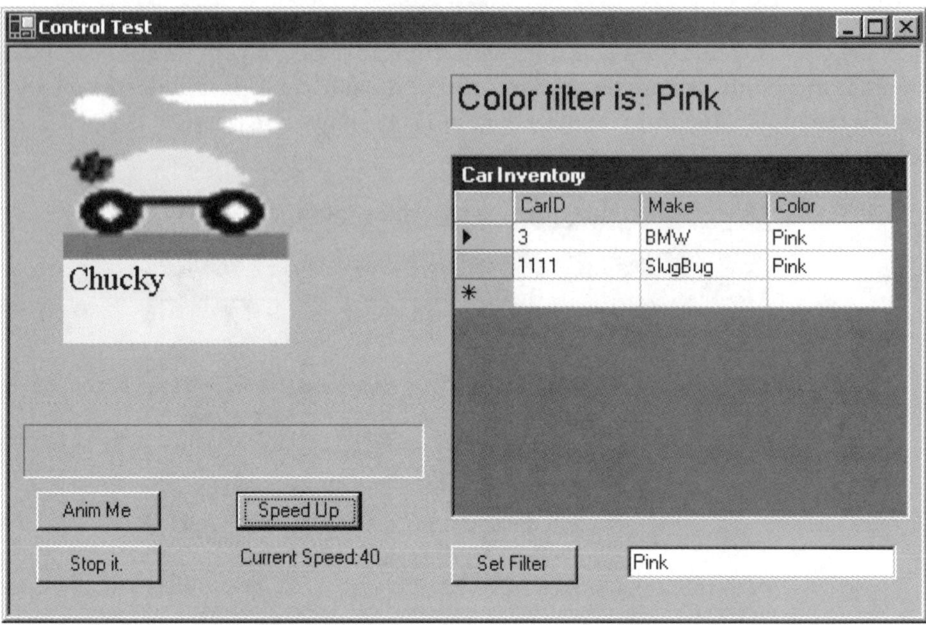

Figure 11-49. Filtering the SQL query

Hopefully, you can see the benefits of building and using custom components. Here our simple CarInventoryComp hides the data access logic from view and allows the end user to specify search criteria. Imagine if our type also provided members that allowed the user to specify the name of the machine to connect to, a specific table to interact with, and so forth. From an object users point of view, he or she is unconcerned with the inner details of the data access logic. Furthermore, the type may be easily manipulated using the design time interface of Visual Studio .NET. For example, notice in Figure 11-50 that your Filter property is editable from the VS .NET Property window.

Best of all, given that components may be placed into a reusable binary assembly, any .NET aware language is able to make use of its functionality.

SOURCE CODE *The MyControlLib and CarCtrlClient projects are located under the Chapter 11 subdirectory.*

Figure 11-50. Design time component manipulation

Summary

This chapter rounded off your current understanding of Windows Forms by examining the programmatic manipulation of numerous GUI widgets from the simple (Button) to the exotic (MonthCalendar). Of course, there are some remaining types for you to explore on your own. Given your current understanding of these core types, you are in the perfect position to do so. You also explored the various anchoring and docking behaviors that can be used to enforce a specific layout of your GUI types, regardless of the size of the owning Form.

In the later half of this chapter, you learned how to build custom dialog boxes and examined a number of issues related to dialog boxes such as the DialogResult property and dialog widget validation. Finally you learned how you can now derive a new Form from an existing Form type using Form inheritance and examined the process of building custom .NET controls.

CHAPTER 12

Input, Output, and Object Serialization

WHEN YOU CREATE full-blown desktop applications, the ability to save information between user sessions is imperative. This chapter examines a number of IO-related topics as seen through the eyes of the .NET Framework. The first order of business is to explore the core types defined in the System.IO namespace and come to understand how to programmatically modify a machine's directory and file structure. Once you can do so, your next task is to explore various ways to read to and write from character-based, binary-based, string-based, and memory-based data stores.

The second half of this chapter examines the .NET serialization schema. Serialization is the process of transforming the state of an object (or set of related objects) into a corresponding byte (or XML) pattern, which can then be placed into (and later recovered from) a stream. During this discussion, you learn the role of the <Serializable> and <NonSerialized> attributes. You also see how to take more control over the serialization process through the implementation of the ISerializable interface.

Finally, to showcase some of these concepts from a real-world point of view, I conclude this chapter with a complete Windows Forms application, which allows the end user to manage a collection of Car types that can be persisted to (and recovered from) a file. As an interesting bonus, the application in question also examines the use of the DataGrid widget (used extensively during the examination of ADO.NET).

Exploring the System.IO Namespace

In the framework of .NET, the System.IO namespace is the region of the base class libraries devoted to file-based (and memory-based) input and output services. Like any namespace, System.IO defines a set of classes, enumerations, structures, and delegates, all of which are contained in mscorlib.dll. Figure 12-1 shows a partial ILDasm.exe dump.

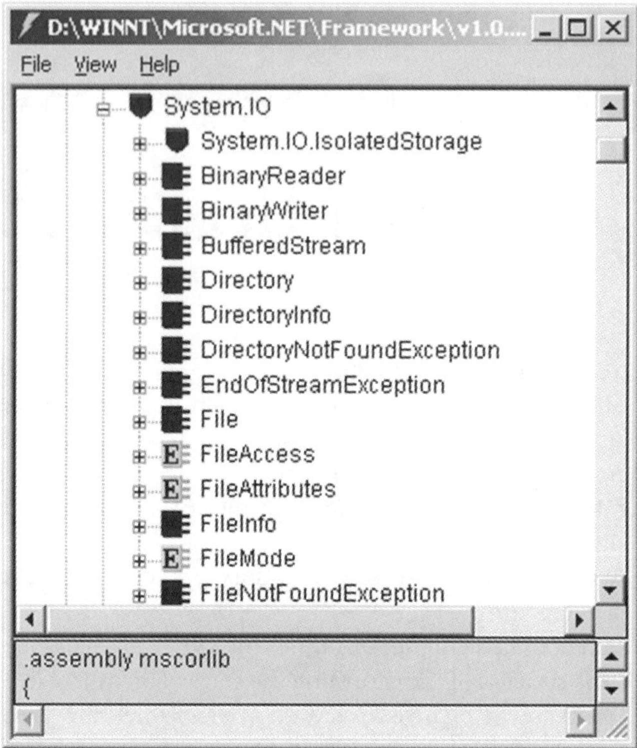

Figure 12-1. The System.IO namespace

As you see during this chapter, the classes in the System.IO namespace typically focus on the manipulation of physical directories and files. However, additional types provide support to read data from and write data to string buffers as well as raw memory locations. To give you a roadmap of the functionality in System.IO, Table 12-1 outlines the core (nonabstract) classes.

Table 12-1. System.IO Namespace Core Types

CREATABLE IO TYPE	MEANING IN LIFE
BinaryReader BinaryWriter	Allows you to store and retrieve primitive data types (integers, Booleans, strings, and so on) as binary values.
BufferedStream	Provides temporary storage for a stream of bytes, which can be committed to storage later.
Directory DirectoryInfo File FileInfo	Used to manipulate the properties for a given directory or physical file as well as create new files and extend the current directory structure. The Directory and File types expose their functionality primarily as shared methods. The DirectoryInfo and FileInfo types expose similar functionality from a valid object instance.
FileStream	Allows for random file access (i.e., seeking capabilities) with data represented as a stream of bytes.
MemoryStream	Allows random access to streamed data stored in memory rather than in a physical file.
StreamWriter StreamReader	Used to store (and retrieve) textual information to (or from) a file. These types do not support random file access.
StringWriter StringReader	Like the StreamReader/StreamWriter types, these classes also work with textual information. However, the underlying storage is a string buffer rather than a physical file.

In addition to these creatable types, there are a number of enumerations and abstract classes (Stream, TextReader, TextWriter, and so forth) that define a shared polymorphic interface to all descendents. You learn about many of these types in this chapter.

The Directory(Info) and File(Info) Types

System.IO provides four types that allow you to manipulate individual files as well as interact with a machine's directory structure. The first two types, Directory and File, expose creation, deletion, and manipulation operations using various shared members. The closely related FileInfo and DirectoryInfo types expose similar functionality as instance-level methods. In Figure 12-2, notice that the Directory and File types directly extend System.Object, while DirectoryInfo and FileInfo derive from the abstract FileSystemInfo type.

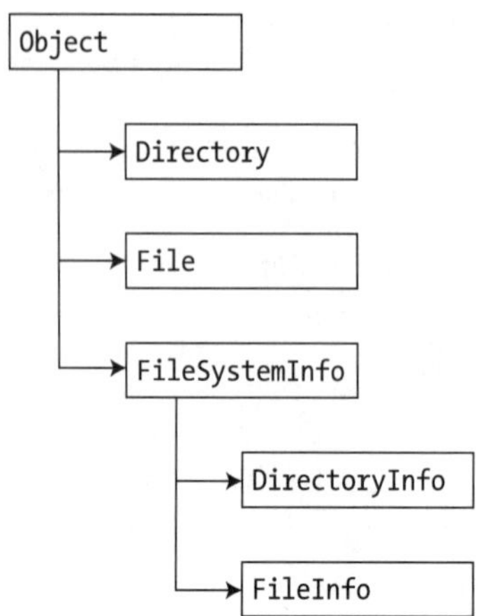

Figure 12-2. The File- and Directory-centric types

The Abstract FileSystemInfo Base Class

The DirectoryInfo and FileInfo types receive many behaviors from the abstract FileSystemInfo type. By and large, the members of the FileSystemInfo class can be used to discover general characteristics (such as the time of creation and various attributes) about a given file or directory. Table 12-2 lists some core properties of interest.

Table 12-2. FileSystemInfo Properties

FILESYSTEMINFO PROPERTY	MEANING IN LIFE
Attributes	Gets or sets the attributes associated to the current file, which are represented by the FileAttributes enumeration.
CreationTime	Gets or sets the time of creation for the current file or directory.
Exists	Can be used to determine if a given file or directory exists.
Extension	Used to retrieve a file's extension.
FullName	Gets the full path of the directory or file.
LastAccessTime	Gets or sets the time the current file or directory was last accessed.
LastWriteTime	Gets or sets the time when the current file or directory was last written to.
Name	Returns the name of a given file; is a read-only property. For directories, gets the name of the last directory in the hierarchy if possible; otherwise, retrieves the fully qualified name.

The FileSystemInfo type also defines the Delete() method. This is implemented by derived types to delete a given file or directory from the hard drive. As well, Refresh() can be called prior to obtaining attribute information to ensure that the information is not outdated.

Working with the DirectoryInfo Type

The first nonabstract type you must understand is the DirectoryInfo class. This class contains a set of members used for creating, moving, deleting, and enumerating over directories and subdirectories. In addition to the functionality provided by the FileSystemInfo base class, DirectoryInfo offers the members presented in Table 12-3.

Table 12-3. Directory Members

DIRECTORYINFO MEMBERS	MEANING IN LIFE
Create() CreateSubdirectory()	Creates a directory (or subdirectories) given a path name.
Delete()	Deletes a directory and all its contents.
GetDirectories()	Returns an array of strings that represent all subdirectories in the current directory.
GetFiles()	Gets the files in the specified directory (as an array of FileInfo types).
MoveTo()	Moves a directory and its contents to a new path.
Parent	Retrieves the parent directory of the specified path.

You begin working with the DirectoryInfo type by specifying a specific directory path (e.g., "C:\," "C:\WinNT," "\\CompanyServer\\Utils," or "A:\") as a constructor parameter. If you want access to the active directory (i.e., the directory of the executing application), use the "." notation. Here are some examples:

```
' Create a new directory bound to the current directory.
Dim dir1 as DirectoryInfo = New DirectoryInfo(".")

' Create a new directory bound to C:\Foo\Bar.
Dim dir2 as DirectoryInfo = New DirectoryInfo("C:\Foo\Bar")
```

If you attempt to programmatically manipulate a nonexistent directory, you are thrown a System.IO.DirectoryNotFoundException. Assuming that this error has not been thrown, you can investigate the underlying directory contents using any of the properties inherited from FileSystemInfo. To illustrate, the following class creates a new DirectoryInfo type mapped to "C:\WinNT" (adjust your letter drive if need be) and dumps out a number of interesting statistics (see Figure 12-3 for output):

```
Module Module1
    Sub Main()
        ' Create a new directoryinfo object.
        Dim dir As DirectoryInfo = New DirectoryInfo("C:\WinNT")
        ' Dump directory information.
        Console.WriteLine("***** Directory Info *****")
        Console.WriteLine("FullName: {0}", dir.FullName)
        Console.WriteLine("Name: {0}", dir.Name)
        Console.WriteLine("Parent: {0}", dir.Parent)
        Console.WriteLine("Creation: {0}", dir.CreationTime)
        Console.WriteLine("Attributes: {0}", dir.Attributes.ToString())
        Console.WriteLine("Root: {0}", dir.Root)
        Console.WriteLine("**************************")
    End Sub
End Module
```

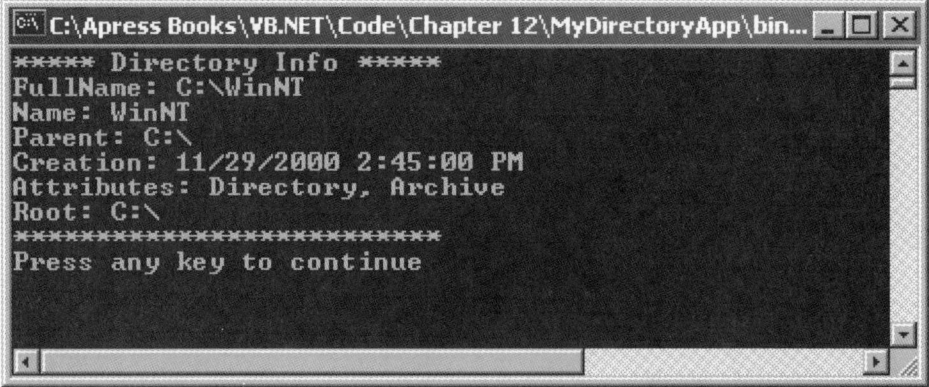

Figure 12-3. C:\WinNT directory information

The FileAttributes Enumeration

As shown in the previous code sample, the Attributes property obtains various traits for the current directory or file, all of which are represented by the FileAttributes enumeration. Table 12-4 describes some core values.

Table 12-4. Select FileAttributes Values

FILEATTRIBUTES ENUMERATION VALUE	MEANING IN LIFE
Archive	The file's archive status. Applications use this attribute to mark files for backup or removal.
Compressed	The file is compressed.
Directory	The file is a directory.
Encrypted	The file is encrypted.
Hidden	The file is hidden and thus is not included in an ordinary directory listing.
Normal	The file is normal and has no other attributes set. This attribute is valid only if used alone.
Offline	The file is offline. The data of the file is not immediately available.
ReadOnly	The file is read-only.
System	The file is a system file. The file is part of the operating system or is used exclusively by the operating system.

Enumerating Files with the DirectoryInfo Type

You can extend the current Main() method to use some methods of the DirectoryInfo type. First, use the GetFiles() method to read all *.bmp files located under the "C:\WinNT" directory. This method returns an array of FileInfo types, which you can iterate over using the foreach construct (more on the FileInfo type later in this chapter), as shown here:

```
Module Module1
    Sub Main()
        ' Create a new directory info object.
        Dim dir As DirectoryInfo = New DirectoryInfo("C:\WinNT")
...
        ' Examine the contents of C:\WinNT,
        ' and look for bitmap files.
        Dim bitmapFiles() As FileInfo = dir.GetFiles("*.bmp")
        Console.WriteLine("Found {0} *.bmp files", bitmapFiles.Length)
        Dim f As FileInfo
        For Each f In bitmapFiles
```

```
            ' Now print out info for the file.
            Console.WriteLine("***************************")
            Console.WriteLine("File name: {0}", f.Name)
            Console.WriteLine("File size: {0}", f.Length)
            Console.WriteLine("Creation: {0}", f.CreationTime)
            Console.WriteLine("Attributes: {0}", f.Attributes.ToString())
            Console.WriteLine("***************************")
        Next
    End Sub
End Module
```

Once you run the application, you see a listing similar to the one shown in Figure 12-4. (Your bitmaps may vary.)

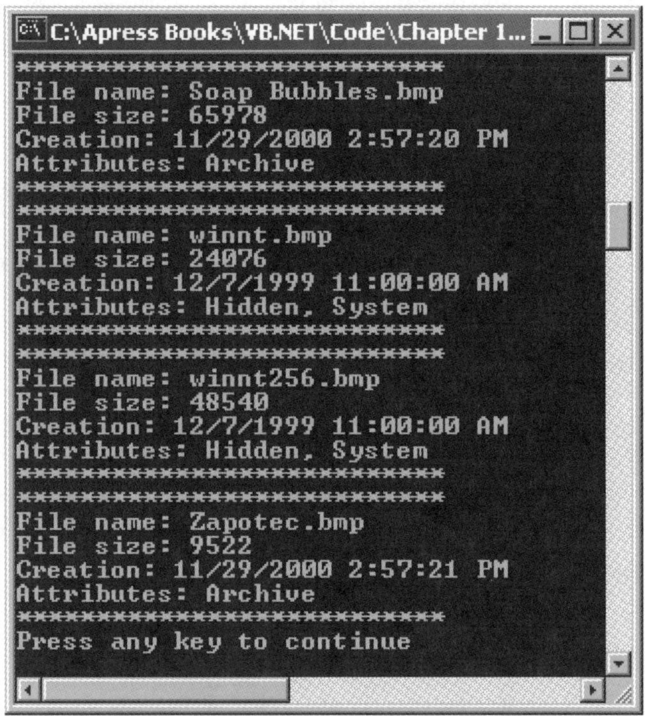
C:\Apress Books\VB.NET\Code\Chapter 1...
****
File name: Soap Bubbles.bmp
File size: 65978
Creation: 11/29/2000 2:57:20 PM
Attributes: Archive
****
****
File name: winnt.bmp
File size: 24076
Creation: 12/7/1999 11:00:00 AM
Attributes: Hidden, System
****
****
File name: winnt256.bmp
File size: 48540
Creation: 12/7/1999 11:00:00 AM
Attributes: Hidden, System
****
****
File name: Zapotec.bmp
File size: 9522
Creation: 11/29/2000 2:57:21 PM
Attributes: Archive
****
Press any key to continue

*Figure 12-4. Enumerating *.bmp files*

Creating Subdirectories with the DirectoryInfo Type

You can programmatically extend a directory structure using the CreateSubdirectory() method. This method can create a single subdirectory on the root, as well as multiple nested subdirectories. To illustrate, here is a block of code that extends the directory structure of "C:\WinNT" with some custom subdirectories:

```
Module Module1
    Sub Main()
        ' Create a new directory info object.
        Dim dir As DirectoryInfo = New DirectoryInfo("C:\WinNT")
...
        ' Now make a new directory on the C:\WinNT root:
        Try
            ' Create C:\WinNT\MyFoo
            Dim d As DirectoryInfo = dir.CreateSubdirectory("MyFoo")
            Console.WriteLine("Created: {0}", d.FullName)
            ' Create C:\WinNT\MyBar\MyQaaz
            d = dir.CreateSubdirectory("MyBar\MyQaaz")
            Console.WriteLine("Created: {0}", d.FullName)
        Catch e As IOException
            Console.WriteLine(e.Message)
        End Try
    End Sub
End Module
```

If you examine your WinNT folder using Windows Explorer, you see the new subdirectories are alive and well (see Figure 12-5).

Figure 12-5. Creating subdirectories

Although you are not required to capture the return value of the CreateSubdirectory() method, be aware that a Directory type is passed back on successful execution, as shown here:

```
' CreateSubdirectory() returns a Directory representing the new item.
Try
    Dim d as Directory = dir.CreateSubdirectory("MyFoo")
    Console.WriteLine("Created: {0}", d.FullName)
    d = dir. CreateSubdirectory("MyBar\MyQaaz")
    Console.WriteLine("Created: {0}", d.FullName)
Catch e as IOException
    Console.WriteLine(e.Message)
End Try
```

The Shared Members of the Directory Class

Now that you have seen the DirectoryInfo type in action, you can learn about the Directory type. By and large, the members of the Directory mimic the same functionality provided by the instance-level members defined by DirectoryInfo, with a few notable exceptions [GetLogicalDrives() for one]. As a result of the common public interface of each type, I assume you will consult online Help to view each member of the Directory class.

The final iteration of this example lists the names of all drives mapped to the current computer and uses the shared Delete() method to remove the "\MyFoo" and "\MyBar\MyQaaz" subdirectories:

```
Module Module1
    Sub Main()
        ' Create a new directory info object.
        Dim dir As DirectoryInfo = New DirectoryInfo("C:\WinNT")
. . .
        ' Now call some shared members of the Directory class.
        Dim drives() As String = Directory.GetLogicalDrives()
        Console.WriteLine("Here are your drives:")
        Dim s As String
        For Each s In drives
            Console.WriteLine("—> {0}", s)
        Next
        ' Now delete what you made.
        Console.WriteLine("Going to delete -> {0}\MyBar\MyQaaz.", _
            dir.FullName)
        Console.WriteLine("and -> {0}\MyFoo.", dir.FullName)
```

```
        Console.WriteLine("Press a key to continue!")
        Console.Read()
        ' Blow em away. . .
        Try
            Directory.Delete("C:\WinNT\MyFoo")
            Directory.Delete("C:\WinNT\MyBar", True)
        Catch e As IOException
            Console.WriteLine(e.Message)
        End Try
    End Sub
End Module
```

Figure 12-6 shows the final output of the application.

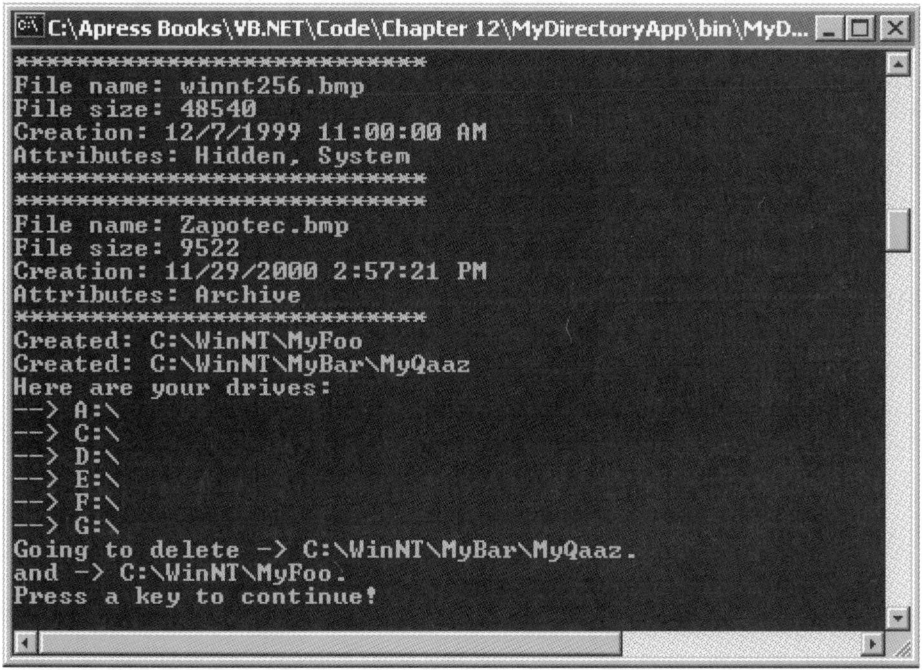

C:\Apress Books\VB.NET\Code\Chapter 12\MyDirectoryApp\bin\MyD...
****
File name: winnt256.bmp
File size: 48540
Creation: 12/7/1999 11:00:00 AM
Attributes: Hidden, System
****
****
File name: Zapotec.bmp
File size: 9522
Creation: 11/29/2000 2:57:21 PM
Attributes: Archive
****
Created: C:\WinNT\MyFoo
Created: C:\WinNT\MyBar\MyQaaz
Here are your drives:
--> A:\
--> C:\
--> D:\
--> E:\
--> F:\
--> G:\
Going to delete -> C:\WinNT\MyBar\MyQaaz.
and -> C:\WinNT\MyFoo.
Press a key to continue!

Figure 12-6. Working with the static members of a directory

Great! At this point you have investigated some core behaviors of the Directory and DirectoryInfo types. Next, you need to learn how to create, open, close, and destroy the files that populate a given directory.

SOURCE CODE *The MyDirectoryApp project is located under the Chapter 12 subdirectory.*

The FileInfo Class

The role of the FileInfo class is to encapsulate a number of details regarding existing files on your hard drive (time created, size, file attributes, and so forth) as well as aid in the creation and destruction of new files. In addition to the set of functionality inherited by FileSystemInfo, Table 12-5 describes some core members unique to the FileInfo class.

Table 12-5. FileInfo Core Members

FILEINFO MEMBER	MEANING IN LIFE
AppendText()	Creates a StreamWriter type (described later) that appends text to a file
CopyTo()	Copies an existing file to a new file
Create()	Creates a new file and returns a FileStream type (described later) to interact with the created file
CreateText()	Creates a StreamWriter type that writes a new text file
Delete()	Deletes the file to which a FileInfo instance is bound
Directory	Gets an instance of the parent directory
DirectoryName	Gets the full path to a file
Length	Gets the size of the current file or directory
MoveTo()	Moves a specified file to a new location, providing the option to specify a new filename
Name	Gets the name of the file
Open()	Opens a file with various read/write and sharing privileges
OpenRead()	Creates a read-only FileStream
OpenText()	Creates a StreamReader type (described later) that reads from an existing text file
OpenWrite()	Creates a read/write FileStream type

First, you should be aware that many methods defined by FileInfo return a specific type (FileStream, StreamWriter, StreamReader, and so forth) that allows you to begin reading and writing data to (or from) the associated file in a variety of ways. You examine these types later in this chapter. Until then, the following class illustrates the most generic (and least flexible) way to create a file programmatically:

```
Imports System.IO
Module Module1
    Sub Main()
        ' Make a new FileInfo.
        Dim f As FileInfo = New FileInfo("C:\Test.txt")
        Dim fs As FileStream = f.Create()
        ' Print some basic traits.
        Console.WriteLine("Creation: {0}", f.CreationTime)
        Console.WriteLine("Full name: {0}", f.FullName)
        Console.WriteLine("Full atts: {0}", f.Attributes.ToString())
        Console.WriteLine("Press a key to delete file")
        Console.Read()
        fs.Close()
        f.Delete()
    End Sub
End Class
```

Notice that the Create() method returns a FileStream type that allows you to close the new file before removing it from the hard drive. (You will see additional uses of FileStream later in the chapter.) When you run this application, you can see your new file at the specified directory (see Figure 12-7) given the call to Create().

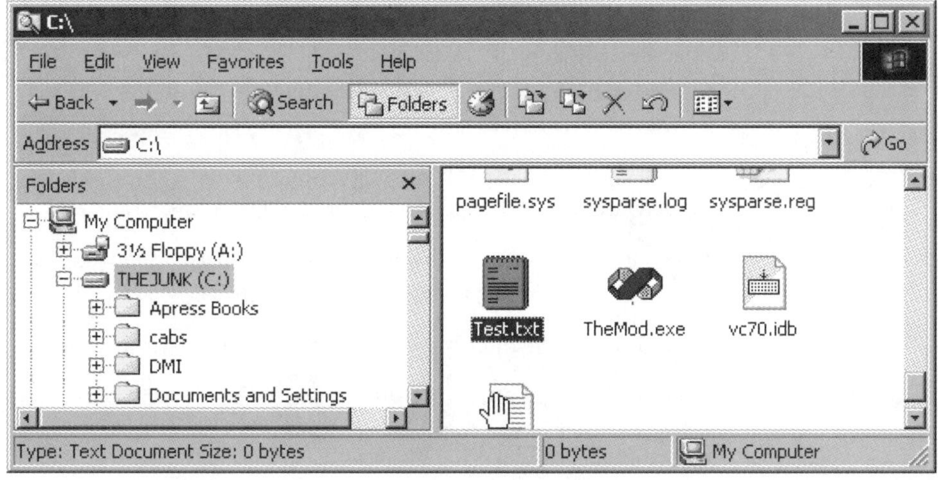

Figure 12-7. Programmatically creating a physical file

Examining the FileInfo.Open() Method

The Open() method of the FileInfo type can be used to open existing files as well as create new files with far more precision than the FileInfo.Create() method. To illustrate, ponder the following logic:

```
' Open (or create) a file with read/write attributes (no sharing),
' and store file handle in a FileStream object.
Dim f2 As FileInfo = New FileInfo("C:\HelloThere.ini")
Dim s As FileStream = f2.Open(FileMode.OpenOrCreate, _
              FileAccess.ReadWrite, _
              FileShare.None)
s.Close()
f2.Delete()
```

This version of the overloaded Open() method requires three parameters. The first parameter specifies the general flavor of the open request (e.g., make a new file, open an existing file, or append to a file), which is specified using the FileMode enumeration. Table 12-6 lists the FileMode enumeration values.

Table 12-6. FileMode Enumeration Values

FILEMODE ENUMERATION VALUE	MEANING IN LIFE
Append	Opens the file if it exists and seeks to the end of the file. If the specified file does not exist, a new file is created. Be aware that FileMode.Append can only be used in conjunction with FileAccess.Write.
Create	Specifies that the operating system should create a new file. Be very aware that if the file already exists, it is overwritten.
CreateNew	Specifies that the operating system should create a new file. If the file already exists, an IOException is thrown.
Open	Specifies that the operating system should open an existing file.
OpenOrCreate	Specifies that the operating system should open a file if it exists; otherwise, a new file should be created.
Truncate	Specifies that the operating system should open an existing file. Once opened, the file should be truncated so that its size is 0 bytes.

The second parameter, FileAccess, is used to determine the read/write behavior of the underlying stream. Table 12-7 lists the FileAccess enumeration values.

Table 12-7. FileAccess Enumeration Values

FILEACCESS ENUMERATION VALUE	MEANING IN LIFE
Read	Specifies read-only access to the file (i.e., data can only be obtained from the file).
ReadWrite	Specifies read and write access to the file (i.e., data can be added to or obtained from the file).
Write	Specifies write access to the file (i.e., data can only be added to the file).

Finally, the third parameter, FileShare, specifies how the currently open file is to be shared among other file handles. Table 12-8 lists the FileShare enumeration values.

Table 12-8. FileShare Enumeration Values

FILESHARE ENUMERATION VALUE	MEANING IN LIFE
None	Declines sharing of the current file. Any request to open the file (by this process or another process) fails until the file is closed.
Read	Allows subsequent opening of the file for reading. If this flag is not specified, any request to open the file for reading (by this process or another process) fails until the file is closed.
ReadWrite	Allows subsequent opening of the file for reading or writing. If this flag is not specified, any request to open the file for writing or reading (by this process or another process) fails until the file is closed.
Write	Allows subsequent opening of the file for writing. If this flag is not specified, any request to open the file for writing (by this process or another process) fails until the file is closed.

The FileInfo.OpenRead() and FileInfo.OpenWrite() Members

In addition to the Open() method, the FileInfo class also has members named OpenRead() and OpenWrite(). As you can imagine, these methods return a read-only or write-only FileStream type. Here is an example:

```
' Get a FileStream object with read-only permissions.
Dim f3 as FileInfo = New FileInfo("C:\boot.ini")
Dim readOnlyStream as FileStream = f3.OpenRead()
readOnlyStream.Close()

' Now get a FileStream object with write-only permissions.
DIm f4 as FileInfo = New FileInfo("C:\config.sys")
Dim writeOnlyStream as FileStream = f4.OpenWrite()
writeOnlyStream.Close()
```

The FileInfo.OpenText(), FileInfo.CreateText(), and FileInfo.AppendText() Members

Another "open-centric" member of the FileInfo type is OpenText(). Unlike Open(), OpenRead(), and OpenWrite(), the OpenText() method returns an instance of the StreamReader type, rather than a FileStream derived type, as shown here:

```
' Get a StreamReader object.
Dim f5 as FileInfo = New FileInfo("C:\bootlog.txt")
Dim sreader as StreamReader = f5.OpenText()
sreader.Close()
```

The final two methods of interest at this point are CreateText() and AppendText(), both of which return a StreamWriter reference, as shown here:

```
' Get some StreamWriters.
Dim f6 as FileInfo = New FileInfo("D:\AnotherTest.txt")
f6.Open(FileMode.Create, FileAccess.ReadWrite)
Dim swriter as StreamWriter = f6.CreateText()
swriter.Close()

Dim f7 as FileInfo = New FileInfo("D:\FinalTest.txt")
f7.Open(FileMode.Create, FileAccess.ReadWrite)
DIm swriterAppend as StreamWriter = f7.AppendText()
swriterAppend.Close()
```

You should now have a good feel for the functionality provided by the FileInfo type. (You will see exactly what to do with the FileStream, StreamReader, and StreamWriter types shortly.) Be aware that the File type provides almost identical functionality using a number of shared members. You see the File type in action where appropriate, but be sure to check out online Help for an exhaustive listing of each member.

SOURCE CODE *The BasicFileApp project is included under the Chapter 12 subdirectory.*

The Abstract Stream Class

In the world of IO manipulation, a *stream* is an entity that is able to obtain or produce chunks of data. The abstract System.IO.Stream class defines a number of members that provide support for synchronous and asynchronous interactions with the storage medium (e.g., an underlying file or memory location). Figure 12-8 shows the basic stream hierarchy.

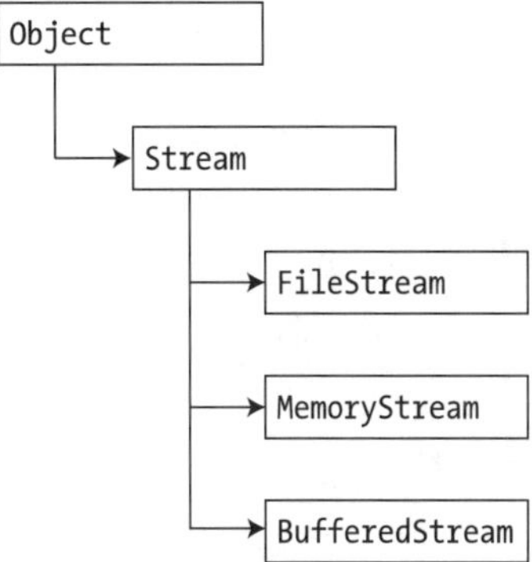

Figure 12-8. Stream-derived types

Stream descendents represent data as a raw stream of bytes (rather than text-based data). Also, Stream-derived types support *seeking*, which refers to the process of obtaining and adjusting the current position in a stream. To begin to understand the functionality provided by the Stream class, take note of the core members described in Table 12-9.

Table 12-9. Abstract Stream Members

STREAM MEMBER	MEANING IN LIFE
CanRead CanSeek CanWrite	Determines whether the current stream supports reading, seeking, and/or writing.
Close()	Closes the current stream and releases any resources (such as sockets and file handles) associated with the current stream.
Flush()	Updates the underlying data source or repository with the current state of the buffer and then clears the buffer. If a stream does not implement a buffer, this method does nothing.
Length	Returns the length of the stream, in bytes.
Position	Determines the position in the current stream.
Read() ReadByte()	Reads a sequence of bytes (or a single byte) from the current stream and advances the current position in the stream by the number of bytes read.
Seek()	Sets the position in the current stream.
SetLength()	Sets the length of the current stream.
Write() WriteByte()	Writes a sequence of bytes (or a single byte) to the current stream and advances the current position in this stream by the number of bytes written.

Working with FileStreams

The FileStream class provides implementations for the abstract Stream members in a manner appropriate for file-based streaming. Like the DirectoryInfo and FileInfo types, FileStream provides the ability to open existing files as well as create new files. FileStreams are usually created using the FileMode, FileAccess, and FileShare enumerations. For example, the following logic creates a new file (test.dat) in the application directory:

```
' Create a new file in the working directory.
Dim myFStream As FileStream = New FileStream("test.dat", _
    FileMode.OpenOrCreate, _
    FileAccess.ReadWrite)
```

To take things out for a test drive, let's experiment with the synchronous read/write capabilities of the FileStream type. To write a stream of bytes to a file, make calls to the inherited WriteByte() or Write() method, both of which advance the internal file pointer automatically. To read the bytes back from a file, simply call Read() or ReadByte(). Here is an example:

```
' Write bytes to the dat file...
Dim i As Byte
For i = 0 To 20
    myFStream.WriteByte(i)
Next
' Reset internal position.
myFStream.Position = 0
' Read 20 bytes from the dat file...
For i = 0 To 20
    Console.Write(myFStream.ReadByte())
Next
Console.WriteLine()
myFStream.Close()
```

If you open this new file from the Visual Studio .NET IDE, you can see the underlying byte stream (see Figure 12-9).

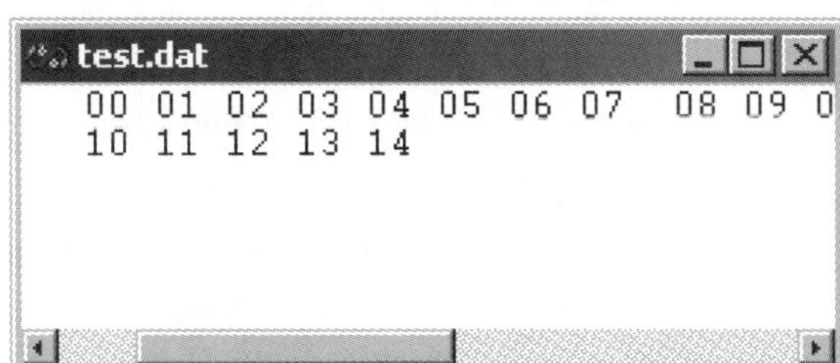

Figure 12-9. The binary dump

Working with MemoryStreams

The MemoryStream type works much like FileStream, with the obvious difference that you are now writing to memory rather than a physical file. Given that each of these types derives from Stream, you can update the previous FileStream logic as shown here:

```
' Create a memory stream with a fixed capacity.
Dim myMemStream As MemoryStream = New MemoryStream()
myMemStream.Capacity = 256
' Write to memory.
```

```
For i = 0 To 200
    myMemStream.WriteByte(i)
Next
Console.WriteLine()
' Reset internal position.
myMemStream.Position = 0
' Read bytes from memory.
For i = 0 To 200
    Console.Write(myMemStream.ReadByte())
Next
myMemStream.Close()
```

The output of this logic is identical to that of the previous FileStream example. The only difference is where you stream the information (file or memory). In addition to the inherited members, MemoryStream supplies other members. For example, the previous code used the Capacity property to specify how much memory to carve out for the streaming operation. Table 12-10 shows the core MemoryStream type members.

Table 12-10. MemoryStream Core Members

MEMORYSTREAM MEMBER	MEANING IN LIFE
Capacity	Gets or sets the number of bytes allocated for this stream
GetBuffer()	Returns the array of unsigned bytes from which this stream was created
ToArray()	Writes the entire stream contents to a byte array, regardless of the Position property
WriteTo()	Writes the entire contents of this MemoryStream to another Stream-derived type (such as a file)

Notice the possible interplay between the MemoryStream and FileStream types. Using the WriteTo() method, you can easily transfer data stored in memory to a file. Furthermore, you can also retrieve the memory stream as a byte array:

```
' Dump memory data to file.
Dim dumpFile As FileStream = New FileStream("Dump.dat", FileMode.Create, _
            FileAccess.ReadWrite)
myMemStream.WriteTo(dumpFile)
Dim bytesinMemory() As Byte = myMemStream.ToArray()
myMemStream.Close()
```

Working with BufferedStreams

The final Stream-derived type to consider is BufferedStream. This type can be used as a temporary location to read or write information, which can later be committed to permanent storage. For example, assume you have opened a data file and need to write out a large series of bytes. While you could stuff each item directly to file using FileStream.Write(), you may want to help optimize the process by storing the new items in a BufferedStream type and making a final commit when each addition has been accounted for. In this way, you can reduce the number of times you must hit the physical file. Here is an example:

```
Dim myFileBuffer As BufferedStream = New BufferedStream(dumpFile)
' Add some bytes to the buffer.
Dim str() As Byte = {127, 22, 2, 12, 98}
myFileBuffer.Write(str, 0, str.Length)
Console.WriteLine()
' commit changes to file.
myFileBuffer.Close() ' Flushes.
myMemStream.Close() ' Flushes.
```

SOURCE CODE *The Streamer project illustrates working with the FileStream, MemoryStream, and BufferedStream types, and is located under the Chapter 12 subdirectory.*

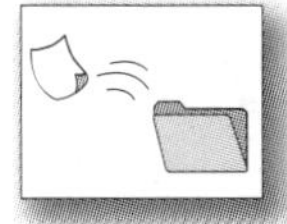

Working with StreamWriters and StreamReaders

The StreamWriter and StreamReader classes are useful whenever you need to read or write character-based data (e.g., strings). Both of these types work by default with Unicode characters; however, you can change this by supplying a properly configured System.Text.Encoding object reference. To keep things simple, let's assume that the default Unicode encoding fits the bill. (Be sure to refer to the System.Text namespace for other possibilities.)

StreamReader derives from an abstract type named TextReader, as does the related StringReader type (discussed later in this chapter). The TextReader base class provides a very limited set of functionality to each of these descendents—specifically, the capability to read and peek into a character stream.

The StreamWriter type (and StringWriter, also examined later in this chapter) derives from a base class named TextWriter. This class defines members that allow derived types to write textual data to a given character stream. Figure 12-10 shows the relationship between each of these new IO-centric types.

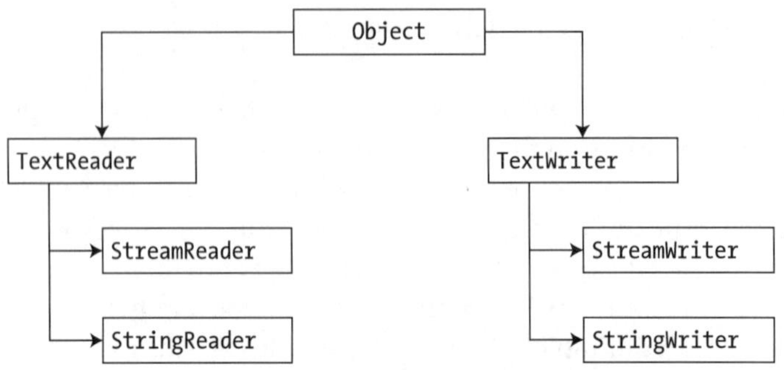

Figure 12-10. Readers and writers

To understand the writing capabilities of the StreamWriter class, you need to examine the base class functionality inherited from the TextWriter type. This abstract class defines the members described in Table 12-11.

Table 12-11. System.IO Namespace Core Types

TEXTWRITER MEMBER NAME	**MEANING IN LIFE**
Close()	Closes the writer and frees any associated resources. In the process, the buffer is automatically flushed.
Flush()	Clears all buffers for the current writer and causes any buffered data to be written to the underlying device, but does not close the writer.
NewLine	Used to make the new line constant for the derived writer class. The default line terminator is a carriage return followed by a linefeed ("\r\n").
Write()	Writes a line to the text stream, without a new line constant.
WriteLine()	Writes a line to the text stream, with a new line constant.

The last two members of the TextWriter class probably look familiar to you. Recall that the System.Console type has similar members that write textual data to the standard output device. Here, TextWriter moves the information to a specified file.

The derived StreamWriter class provides an appropriate implementation for the Write(), Close(), and Flush() methods, and defines the additional AutoFlush property. This property, when set to True, forces StreamWriter to flush all data every time you perform a write operation. Be aware that you can gain better performance by setting AutoFlush to False, provided you always call Close() when you are done writing with a StreamWriter.

Writing to a Text File

Now for an example of working with the StreamWriter type. The following class creates a new file named thoughts.txt using the FileInfo class. Using the CreateText() method, you can obtain a valid StreamWriter. At this point, you add some textual data to the new file, as shown here:

```
Module Module1
    Sub Main()
        ' Make a file.
        Dim f As FileInfo = New FileInfo("Thoughts.txt")
        ' Get a StreamWriter and write some stuff.
        Dim writer As StreamWriter = f.CreateText()
        writer.WriteLine("Don't forget Mother's Day this year. . .")
        writer.WriteLine("Don't forget Father's Day this year. . .")
        writer.WriteLine("Don't forget these numbers:")
        Dim i As Integer
        For i = 0 To 10
            writer.Write(i & " ")
        Next
        writer.Write(writer.NewLine)
        ' Closing automatically flushes!
        writer.Close()
        Console.WriteLine("Created file and wrote some thoughts. . .")
    End Sub
End Module
```

If you locate this new file, you should be able to double-click it to open it in Notepad. Figure 12-11 shows the content of your new file.

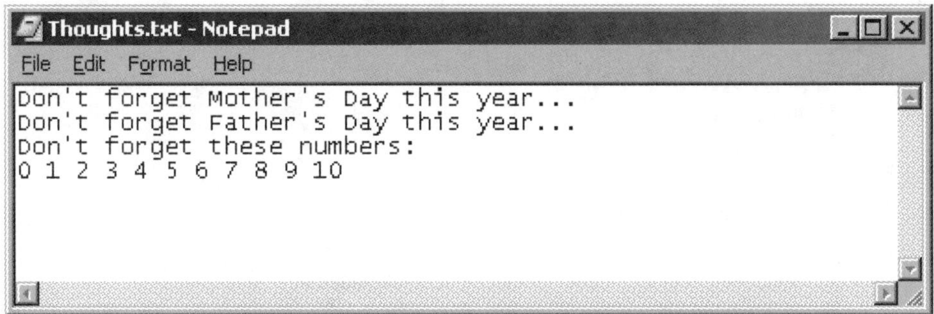

*Figure 12-11. The content of your *.txt file*

As you can see, the StreamWriter has written your data to a file. The Write() and WriteLine() methods have each been overloaded numerous times to provide a number of ways to add textual and numeric data (which defaults to Unicode encoding).

Reading from a Text File

Now you need to understand how to programmatically read data from a file using the corresponding StreamReader type. As you probably recall, this class derives from TextReader, which offers the functionality described in Table 12-12.

Table 12-12. TextReader Core Members

TEXTREADER MEMBER NAME	MEANING IN LIFE
Peek()	Returns the next available character without actually changing the position of the reader.
Read()	Reads data from an input stream.
ReadBlock()	Reads a maximum of count characters from the current stream and writes the data to a buffer, beginning at index.
ReadLine()	Reads a line of characters from the current stream and returns the data as a string. (A null string indicates EOF.)
ReadToEnd()	Reads all characters from the current position to the end of the TextReader and returns them as one string.

If you now extend the current MyStreamWriterReader class to use a StreamReader, you can read in the textual data from the thoughts.txt file, as shown here:

```
Module Module1
    Sub Main()
        ' Make a file.
        Dim f As FileInfo = New FileInfo("Thoughts.txt")
        ' Get a StreamWriter and write some stuff.
...
        ' Now read it all back in using a StreamReader.
        Console.WriteLine("Here are your thoughts")
        Dim sr As StreamReader = File.OpenText("Thoughts.txt")
        Dim input As String
        Do
```

```
            input = sr.ReadLine()
            Console.WriteLine(input)
        Loop While (input <> Nothing)
    End Sub
End Module
```

If you run the program, you see the output shown in Figure 12-12.

```
C:\Apress Books\VB.NET\Code\Chapter 12\StreamWrit...
Created file and wrote some thoughts...
Here are your thoughts
Don't forget Mother's Day this year...
Don't forget Father's Day this year...
Don't forget these numbers:
0 1 2 3 4 5 6 7 8 9 10

Press any key to continue
```

Figure 12-12. Reading from a file

Here, you obtained a valid StreamReader using the shared File.OpenText() method. The read logic makes use of StreamReader.Peek() to ensure that you have an additional character ahead of the reader's current position. If so, you read the next line and pump it to the console. To obtain the contents of the entire file, you could avoid the "peeking" and simply call ReadToEnd(), as shown here:

```
' I want it all!
sr.BaseStream.Position = 0
Dim allOfTheData As String = sr.ReadToEnd()
MessageBox.Show(allOfTheData, "Here it is:")
sr.Close()
```

As you can see, the StreamReader and StreamWriter types provide a custom implementation of the abstract members defined by their respective base classes. Just remember that these two types are concerned with moving text-based data to and from a specified file.

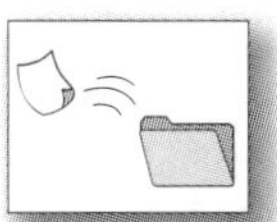

SOURCE CODE *The StreamWriterReaderApp project is included under the Chapter 12 subdirectory.*

Working with StringWriters

Using the StringWriter and StringReader types, you can treat textual information as a stream of in-memory characters. This can prove helpful when you want to append character-based information to an underlying buffer. To gain access to the underlying buffer from an instance of a StringWriter type, you can call the overridden ToString() method (to receive a System.String type) or the GetStringBuilder() method, which returns an instance of StringBuilder. Recall from Chapter 3 that the System.Text.StringBuilder type allows you to directly modify a string buffer.

To illustrate, let's reengineer the previous example to write the character information to a StringWriter instance rather than a generated file. As you should notice, the two programs are nearly identical, given that both StringWriter and StreamWriter inherit the same base class functionality, as shown here:

```
Imports System.IO
' For StringBuilder type (used shortly).
Imports System.Text
Module Module1
    Sub Main()
        ' Get a StringWriter and write some stuff.
        Dim writer as StringWriter = new StringWriter()
        writer.WriteLine("Don't forget Mother's Day this year. . .")
        writer.WriteLine("Don't forget Father's Day this year. . .")
        writer.WriteLine("Don't forget these numbers:")
        Dim i As Integer
        For i = 0 To 10
            writer.Write(i & " ")
        Next
        writer.Write(writer.NewLine)
        ' Closing automatically flushes!
        writer.Close()
        Console.WriteLine("Stored thoughts in a StringWriter. . .")
        ' Get a copy of the contents (stored in a string) and pump
        ' to console.
        Console.WriteLine("Contents: {0}", writer.ToString())
    End Sub
End Module
```

Running this program (of course) dumps out textual data to the console (see Figure 12-13).

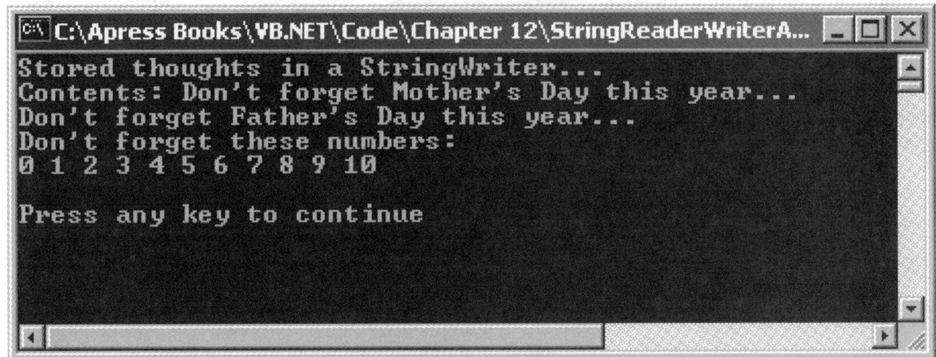

Figure 12-13. Dumping the StringWriter

Now gain access to the underlying StringBuilder maintained by the StringWriter and add the following logic:

```
' Get the internal StringBuilder.
Dim Str As StringBuilder = writer.GetStringBuilder()
Dim allOfTheData As String = Str.ToString()
Console.WriteLine("StringBuilder says: {0}", allOfTheData)
' Insert item to buffer.
Str.Insert(20, "INSERTED STUFF")
allOfTheData = Str.ToString()
Console.WriteLine("New StringBuilder says: {0}", allOfTheData)
' Remove the inserted string.
Str.Remove(20, "INSERTED STUFF".Length)
allOfTheData = Str.ToString()
Console.WriteLine("Original says: {0}", allOfTheData)
```

Here, you write some character data to a StringWriter type and extract and manipulate a copy of the contents using the GetStringBuilder() member function. Figure 12-14 shows the output.

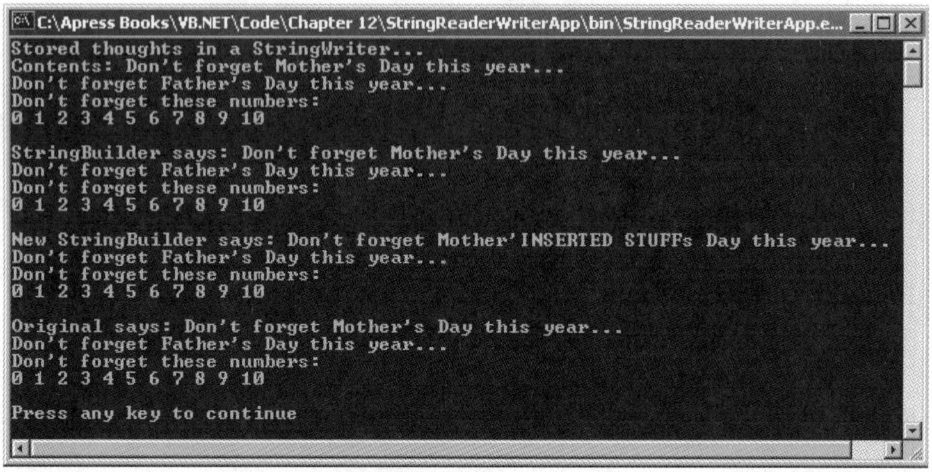

```
C:\Apress Books\VB.NET\Code\Chapter 12\StringReaderWriterApp\bin\StringReaderWriterApp.e...
Stored thoughts in a StringWriter...
Contents: Don't forget Mother's Day this year...
Don't forget Father's Day this year...
Don't forget these numbers:
0 1 2 3 4 5 6 7 8 9 10

StringBuilder says: Don't forget Mother's Day this year...
Don't forget Father's Day this year...
Don't forget these numbers:
0 1 2 3 4 5 6 7 8 9 10

New StringBuilder says: Don't forget Mother'INSERTED STUFFs Day this year...
Don't forget Father's Day this year...
Don't forget these numbers:
0 1 2 3 4 5 6 7 8 9 10

Original says: Don't forget Mother's Day this year...
Don't forget Father's Day this year...
Don't forget these numbers:
0 1 2 3 4 5 6 7 8 9 10

Press any key to continue
```

Figure 12-14. Manipulating the StringBuilder

Working with StringReaders

Next is the StringReader type, which (as you would expect) functions identically to the related StreamReader class. In fact, the StringReader class does nothing more than override the inherited members to read from a block of character data, rather than a file, as shown here:

```
' Now dump using a StringReader.
Console.WriteLine("Here are your thoughts:")
Dim sr As StringReader = New StringReader(writer.ToString())
Dim input As String
Do
    input = sr.ReadLine()
    Console.WriteLine(input)
Loop While (input <> Nothing)
sr.Close()
```

If you were paying attention to the previous sample applications, you may have noticed one limitation of the TextReader and TextWriter descendents. None of these types has the ability to provide random access to its contents (e.g., seeking). For example, StreamReader has no members that allow you to reset the internal file cursor or jump over some number of characters and begin reading from that point. To gain this sort of functionality, you need to use various descendents of the Stream type.

SOURCE CODE *The StringReaderWriterApp is included under the Chapter 12 subdirectory.*

Working with Binary Data (BinaryReaders and BinaryWriters)

The final two core classes provided by the System.IO namespace are BinaryReader and BinaryWriter, both of which derive directly from Object, as shown in Figure 12-15.

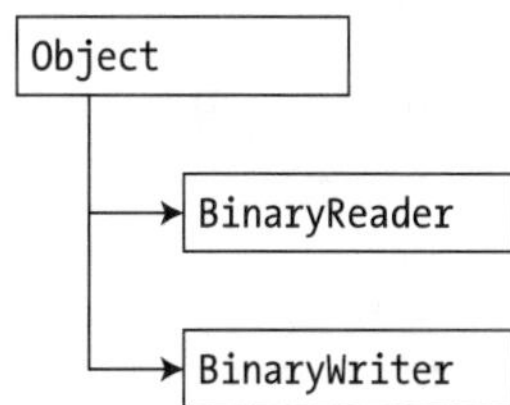

Figure 12-15. Binary readers and writers

These types allow you to read and write discrete data types to an underlying stream. The BinaryWriter class defines a highly overloaded method named (of course) Write() to place a data type in the corresponding stream. The BinaryWriter class also provides some other familiar-looking members (see Table 12-13).

Table 12-13. BinaryWriter Core Members

BINARYWRITER MEMBER	MEANING IN LIFE
BaseStream	Represents the underlying stream used with the binary reader
Close()	Closes the binary stream
Flush()	Flushes the binary stream
Seek()	Sets the position in the current stream
Write()	Writes a value to the current stream

The BinaryReader class complements the functionality offered by BinaryWriter with the members described in Table 12-14.

Table 12-14. BinaryReader Core Members

BINARYREADER MEMBER	MEANING IN LIFE
BaseStream	Enables access to the underlying stream.
Close()	Closes the binary reader.
PeekChar()	Returns the next available character without actually advancing the position in the stream.
Read()	Reads a given set of bytes or characters and stores them in the incoming array.
ReadXXXX()	The BinaryReader class defines numerous ReadXXXX methods, which grab the next type from the stream (ReadBoolean(), ReadByte(), ReadInt32(), and so forth).

The following class writes a number of character types to a new *.dat file created and opened using the FileStream class. Once you have a valid FileStream, pass this object to the constructor of the BinaryWriter type. Understand that the constructor of BinaryWriter takes any Stream-derived type (for example, FileStream, MemoryStream, or BufferedStream). Once the data has been written, a corresponding BinaryReader reads each byte back, as shown here:

```
Module Module1
    Sub Main()
        Console.WriteLine("Creating a file and writing binary data. . .")
        ' Open a bitmap file.
        Dim myFStream As FileStream _
            = New FileStream("temp.dat", _
            FileMode.OpenOrCreate, _
            FileAccess.ReadWrite)
        ' Write some binary info.
        Dim binWrit As BinaryWriter = New BinaryWriter(myFStream)
        binWrit.Write("Hello as binary info. . .")
        Dim myInt As Integer = 99
        Dim myDouble As Double = 9984.823
        Dim myBool As Boolean = False
        Dim myCharArray() As Char = {"H", "e", "l", "l", "o"}
        binWrit.Write(myInt)
        binWrit.Write(myDouble)
        binWrit.Write(myBool)
        binWrit.Write(myCharArray)
```

```
        ' Reset internal position.
        binWrit.BaseStream.Position = 0
        ' Read the binary info as raw bytes.
        Console.WriteLine("Reading binary data. . .")
        Dim binRead As BinaryReader = New BinaryReader(myFStream)
        Dim temp As Integer
        Dim input As String
        Do
            Console.Write(binRead.ReadByte())
            temp = temp + 1
            If (temp = 5) Then
                temp = 0
                Console.WriteLine()
            End If
        Loop While (binRead.PeekChar() <> -1)
        ' Clean things up.
        Console.WriteLine()
        binWrit.Close()
        binRead.Close()
        myFStream.Close()
    End Sub
End Module
```

Figure 12-16 shows the output.

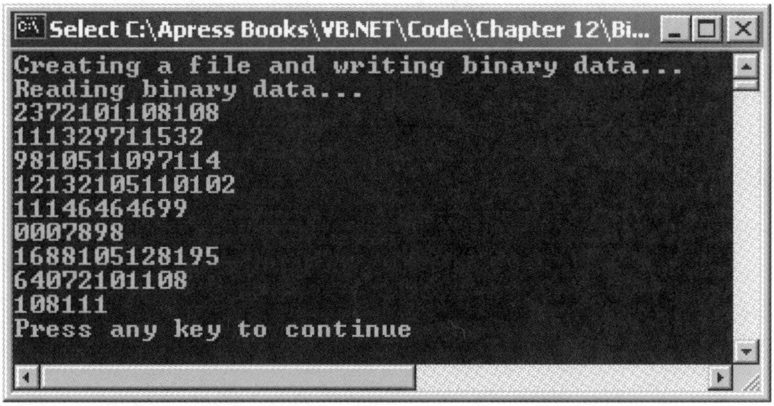

```
Select C:\Apress Books\VB.NET\Code\Chapter 12\Bi...
Creating a file and writing binary data...
Reading binary data...
2372101108108
111329711532
9810511097114
12132105110102
11146464699
0007898
1688105128195
64072101108
108111
Press any key to continue
```

Figure 12-16. A binary read/write session

An Interesting Side Note

Although you may never need to read and write individual bytes to a stream, you should know that other types in the .NET namespaces use these same IO primitives behind the scenes. For example, the System.Windows.Forms.Bitmap type supports a member named Save(), which writes binary data to a new file. It is also possible to construct a new Bitmap type by passing in a Stream-derived type. Given these aspects of the Bitmap type, it is possible to modify the underlying pixel information at runtime. While you could calculate these (*x*, *y*) coordinates by hand, it is far simpler to use the SetPixel() method, as shown here:

```
' Build a Bitmap based on a stream.
Console.WriteLine("Modifying a bitmap in memory")
myFStream = New FileStream("Paint Splatter.bmp", _
    FileMode.Open, _
    FileAccess.ReadWrite)
Dim rawBitmap As Bitmap = New Bitmap(myFStream)
' Draw a white 'X' over the image.
' (This logic assumes the height and width of the image are identical.)
Dim i As Integer
For i = 0 To rawBitmap.Width - 1
    rawBitmap.SetPixel(i, i, Color.White)
    rawBitmap.SetPixel((rawBitmap.Width - i) - 1, _
        i - 1, Color.White)
Next
' Now save the modified image to file.
Console.WriteLine("Saving modified bitmap to file")
rawBitmap.Save("newImage.bmp")
myFStream.Close()
```

Figure 12-17 shows how the paint splatter.bmp file looks before the pixel modification.

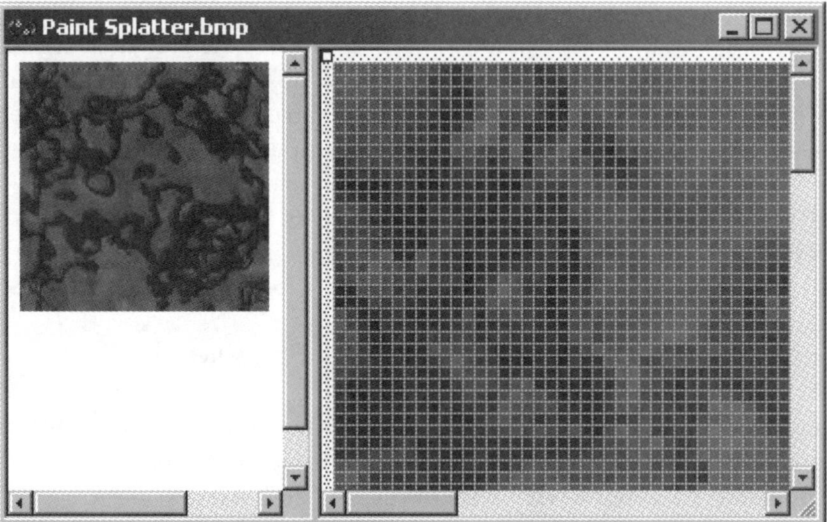

Figure 12-17. The unmodified image

Figure 12-18 shows how the newImage.bmp file looks after new pixels are rendered.

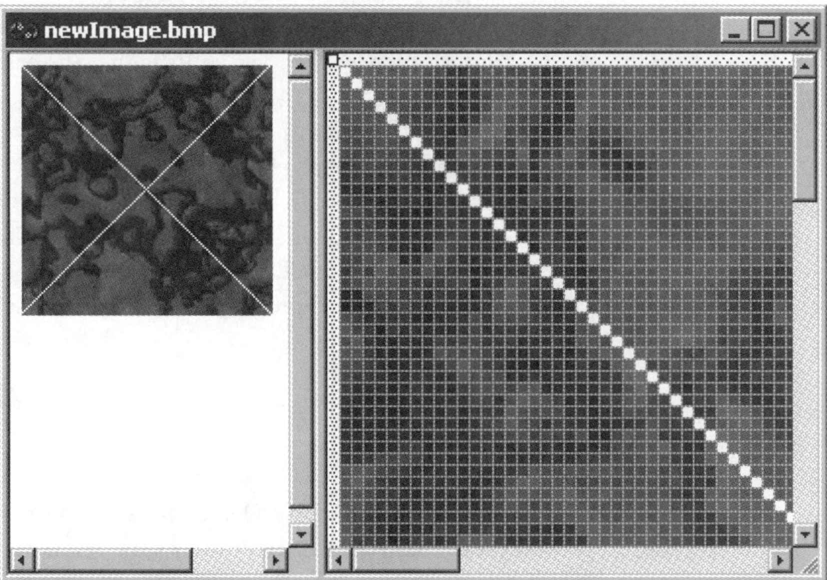

Figure 12-18. The modified image

That wraps up the investigation of the core types in the System.IO namespace. At this point, you are in a position to read and write textual, binary, and intrinsic data types. This chapter concludes with an examination of how the .NET Framework supports the serialization of custom types.

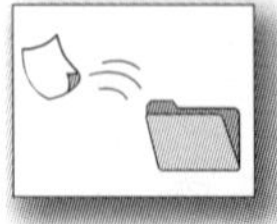

SOURCE CODE *The BinaryReaderWriter application is included under the Chapter 12 subdirectory.*

Object Persistence in the .NET Framework

As you have seen, the System.IO namespace defines a number of types that allow you to send binary and character-based data to some storage device (such as a file or memory location). What has not yet been addressed is how to save instances of custom class types to a stream and how to read instances back from storage.

In the .NET Framework, *serialization* is the term that describes the process of converting the state of an object to a linear sequence of bytes. This byte stream contains all necessary information to reconstruct (or *deserialize*) the state of the object for use later. The .NET serialization services are quite sophisticated: When an object is serialized to a stream, any additional object references required by the root object are serialized as well. For example, when a derived class is serialized, each object up the chain of inheritance is able to write its own custom state data to the byte stream.

Once a set of objects has been saved to a stream, the byte pattern can be relocated as necessary. For example, imagine you have serialized a stream of objects to a MemoryStream. This stream could be forwarded to a remote computer or the Windows clipboard, burned to a CD, or simply stored in a file. The byte stream itself does not care where it is stored. All that matters is the fact that this stream of 1's and 0's (or XML data) correctly represents the state of the serialized objects.

The Role of Object Graphs

The chain of related objects serialized to a stream is collectively referred to as an *object graph*. In essence, graphs are a construct that documents the relationships of a set of related items. Object graphs provide a simple way to document how a set of objects refer to each other and are *not* intended to directly model classic OO relationships (such as the "is-a" or "has-a" relationship). To establish the relations among objects in a graph, each object is assigned a unique numerical value followed by a graph of all related items. Keep in mind that the numbers assigned to the members in an object graph are arbitrary and have no real meaning to the outside world.

As a simple example, assume you have created a set of classes that model (of course) some automobiles. You have a topmost type named Car, which "has-a" Radio. Another class named JamesBondCar extends the basic Car type. Figure 12-19 presents an object graph that models these relationships.

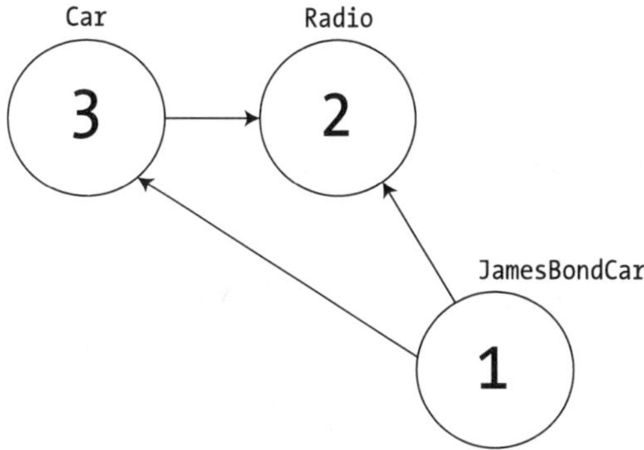

Figure 12-19. A simple object graph

In Figure 12-19 you can see that the Car class refers to the Radio class (given the "has-a" relationship). The JamesBondCar refers to the Car (as it is a subclass) as well as the Radio (as it inherits this protected member). Given that each object reference has been assigned an arbitrary number, you can build the following formula:

```
<Car 3, ref 2>, <Radio 2>, <JamesBondCar 1, ref 3, ref 2>
```

This formula is the pattern that is serialized to a stream, along with the values for each member variable in the Car, Radio, and JamesBondCar types. You can see that the Car type has a dependency on item 2 (the Radio). Also, the JamesBondCar has a dependency on item 3 (the Car) as well as item 2 (the Radio). If you serialize an instance of JamesBondCar to a stream, the object graph ensures that the Radio and Car types also participate in the process. The beautiful thing about the serialization process is that the graph representing the relationships among your objects is established automatically behind the scenes.

Configuring Objects for Serialization

To make an object available for serialization, you mark each class with the <Serializable> attribute. That's it (really). If you determine that a given class has some member data that should not participate in the serialization scheme, you can mark such fields with the <NonSerialized> attribute. This can be helpful if you have member variables (or properties) in a serializable class that do not need to be "remembered" (e.g., constants, transient data, and so on). For example, here is the Radio class, which has been marked as serializable (except for a single member variable):

```
' The Radio class can participate in the .NET serialization scheme.
Imports System.Windows.Forms
<Serializable()> Public Class Radio
    <NonSerialized()> _
    Private objectIDNumber As Integer = 9
    Public Sub TurnOn(ByVal state As Boolean)
        If (state = True) Then
            MessageBox.Show("Music is on. . .")
        Else
            MessageBox.Show("No tunes. . .")
        End If
    End Sub
End Class
```

These attributes are marked in the type's metadata, as seen from ILDasm.exe (see Figure 12-20).

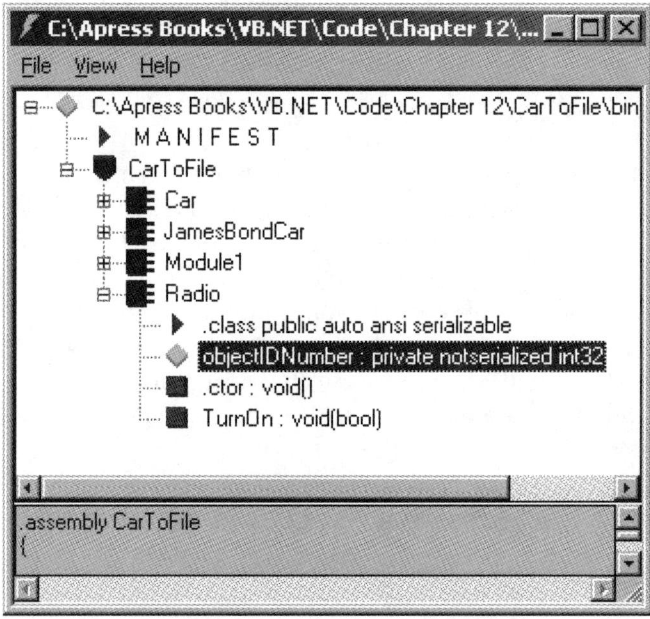

Figure 12-20. The Serializable and NonSerialized attributes

To finish the coding of this car hierarchy, here are the definitions for the Car base class and JamesBondCar subtype, each marked with the <Serializable> attribute:

```
' The Car class is serializable!
<Serializable()> Public Class Car
    ' State data.
    Protected mPetName As String
    Protected mMaxSpeed As Integer
    Protected mTheRadio As Radio = New Radio()
    ' Ctors.
    Public Sub New(ByVal petName As String, ByVal maxSpeed As Integer)
        mPetName = petName
        mMaxSpeed = maxSpeed
    End Sub
    Public Sub New()
    End Sub
    ' Some properties.
    Public Property PetName() As String
        Get
            Return PetName
        End Get
        Set(ByVal Value As String)
            mpetName = value
        End Set
    End Property
    Public Property MaxSpeed() As Integer
        Get
            Return mMaxSpeed
        End Get
        Set(ByVal Value As Integer)
            mMaxSpeed = Value
        End Set
    End Property
    ' A simple method.
    Public Sub TurnOnRadio(ByVal state As Boolean)
        mTheRadio.TurnOn(state)
    End Sub
End Class

' The JamesBondCar class is also serializable!
<Serializable()> _
Public Class JamesBondCar
```

```
    Inherits Car
    Protected isFlightWorthy As Boolean
    Protected isSeaWorthy As Boolean
    Public Sub New(ByVal petName As String, ByVal maxSpeed As Integer, _
    ByVal canFly As Boolean, ByVal canSubmerge As Boolean)
        MyBase.New(petName, maxSpeed)
        isFlightWorthy = canFly
        isSeaWorthy = canSubmerge
    End Sub
    Public Sub New()
    End Sub
    Public Sub Fly()
        If (isFlightWorthy) Then
            MessageBox.Show("Taking off!")
        Else
            MessageBox.Show("Falling off cliff!")
        End If
    End Sub
    Public Sub GoUnderWater()
        If (isSeaWorthy) Then
            MessageBox.Show("Diving. . ..")
        Else
            MessageBox.Show("Drowning!!!")
        End If
    End Sub
End Class
```

Choosing a Formatter

Once you have configured your types to participate in the .NET serialization scheme, your next step is to choose which format to use to persist your object graph. The System.Runtime.Serialization.Formatters namespace contains two additional nested namespaces (*.Binary and *.Soap) that provide two default formatters. As you can guess, the BinaryFormatter type serializes your object graph to a stream using a compact binary format. The SoapFormatter type represents your graph as a Simple Object Access Protocol (SOAP) message (which is expressed in XML format).

The BinaryFormatter type is defined in the mscorlib.dll assembly. Therefore, to serialize your objects to a binary format, all you need to do is specify the following imports directive:

```
' Need to send objects to a binary format!
Imports System.Runtime.Serialization.Formatters.Binary
```

However, the SoapFormatter type is defined in a separate assembly. To format your object graph as a SOAP message, begin by setting a reference to the System.Runtime.Serialization.Formatters.Soap.dll assembly and make the following imports directive:

```
' Need to send objects to a SOAP format!
Imports System.Runtime.Serialization.Formatters.Soap
```

The Role of the System.Runtime.Serialization Namespace

If you ever need to build a custom formatter, you need to use a number of types defined in the System.Runtime.Serialization namespace. Also, if you want to configure your objects to employ custom serialization, these types are also of interest. Although building a custom formatter is outside the scope of this book, Table 12-15 describes some (but not all) of the core classes to be aware of.

Table 12-15. System.Runtime.Serialization Namespace Core Types

TYPES OF THE SYSTEM.RUNTIME.SERIALIZATION NAMESPACE	MEANING IN LIFE
Formatter	An abstract base class that provides base functionality for runtime serialization formatters.
ObjectIDGenerator	Generates IDs for objects in an object graph.
ObjectManager	Keeps track of objects as they are being deserialized.
SerializationBinder	An abstract base class that provides functionality to serialize a type to a stream.
SerializationInfo	Used by objects that have custom serialization behavior. SerializationInfo holds together all of the data needed to serialize or deserialize an object. In essence, this class is a “property bag” that allows you to establish name/value pairs to represent the state of an object.

In addition to these types, there are two core interfaces to be aware of: IFormatter and ISerializable. Later this chapter revisits the ISerializable interface and the issue of custom serialization.

Regardless which formatter you choose (including any custom formatter you dream up), the formatter is in charge of transmitting all of the information required to persist the object during the serialization process. The necessary information includes the full type name of the object (e.g., MyProject.MyClasses.Foo), the name of the assembly containing the object (e.g., friendly name, version, and an optional strong name), as well as any stateful information represented by the SerializationInfo type.

During the deserialization process, the formatter uses this information to build an identical copy of the object, using the information extracted from the underlying stream. Figure 12-21 shows the "big picture" of the process.

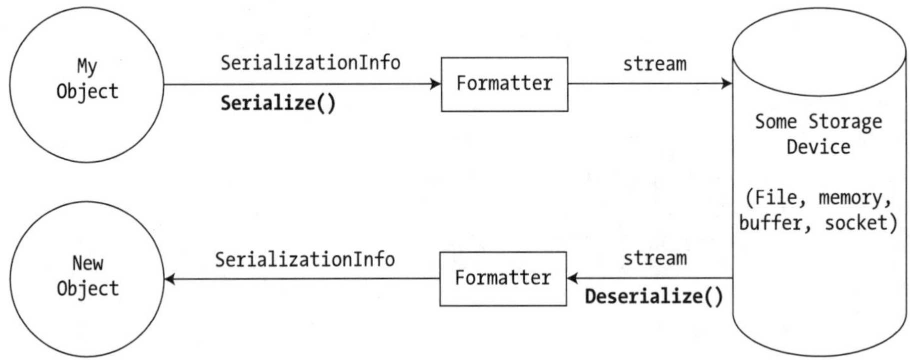

Figure 12-21. The serialization process

Serialization Using a Binary Formatter

Recall that the BinaryFormatter type is a member of the System.Runtime.Serialization.Formatters.Binary namespace, which is located in the mscorlib.dll assembly. BinaryFormatter defines two core methods that read and write an object graph to a stream, as described in Table 12-16.

Table 12-16. BinaryFormatter Members

BINARYFORMATTER MEMBER	MEANING IN LIFE
Deserialize()	Deserializes a stream of bytes to an object graph
Serialize()	Serializes an object or graph of connected objects to a stream

In addition, the BinaryFormatter type defines a number of properties that configure specific details regarding the (de)serialization process. By and large, the default configuration of BinaryFormatter is all you need to concern yourself with.

To illustrate, assume you have created an instance of JamesBondCar, modified some state data, and want to persist your spymobile in a *.dat file, as shown here:

```
Imports System.Runtime.Serialization.Formatters.Binary
Module Module1
   Sub Main()
         ' Make a car and listen to the tunes.
         Console.WriteLine("Made a James Bond Car. . .")
         Dim myAuto As JamesBondCar = New JamesBondCar("Fred", 50, False, True)
         myAuto.TurnOnRadio(True)
         myAuto.GoUnderWater()
         ' Now save this car to a binary stream.
         Dim myStream As FileStream = File.Create("CarData.dat")
         Dim myBinaryFormat As BinaryFormatter = New BinaryFormatter()
         myBinaryFormat.Serialize(myStream, myAuto)
         myStream.Close()
         Console.WriteLine("Saved car to cardata.dat.")
 . . .
End Module
```

As you can see, the BinaryFormatter.Serialize() method is the member responsible for composing the object graph and moving the byte sequence to some Stream-derived type. In this case, the stream happens to be a physical file. However, you could also serialize your object types to any Stream-derived type (such as a memory location, given that MemoryStream is a descendent of the Stream type). If you open the underlying binary file, you can peek inside the byte sequence (see Figure 12-22).

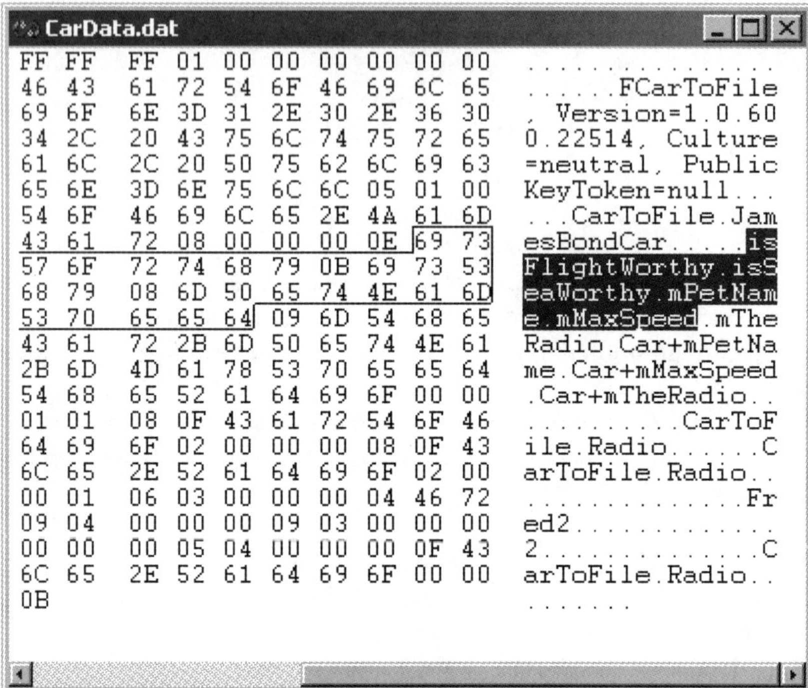

Figure 12-22. JamesBondCar serialized using a BinaryFormatter

Suppose you want to read the persisted JamesBondCar back to an object variable. To do so, use the BinaryWriter.Deserialize() method. Be aware that Deserialize() returns a generic System.Object type, and therefore you need to impose an explicit cast, as shown here:

```
' Read in the Car from the binary stream.
Console.WriteLine("Reading car from binary file.")
myStream = File.OpenRead("CarData.dat")
Dim carFromDisk As JamesBondCar = _
    CType(myBinaryFormat.Deserialize(myStream), JamesBondCar)
Console.WriteLine(carFromDisk.PetName + " is alive!")
carFromDisk.TurnOnRadio(True)
myStream.Close()
```

Notice that when you call Deserialize(), you pass the Stream-derived type that represents the location of the persisted objects (a file stream in this case). Now if that is not painfully simple, I'm not sure what is. In a nutshell, mark each class you want to persist to a stream with the <Serializable> attribute. After this point, use the BinaryFormatter type to move your object graph to and from a stream.

Serialization Using a SOAP Formatter

The other available formatter for serializing your types is SoapFormatter. To use this type, you need to set a reference to the containing assembly, System.Runtime.Serialization.Formatters.Soap.dll. The following block of code extends the previous serialization example to persist the JamesBondCar using the SoapFormatter type (Chapter 16 describes SOAP messages in greater detail):

```
Imports System.Runtime.Serialization.Formatters.Soap
' Save the same car into SOAP format.
Console.WriteLine("Now saving car to XML file")
myStream = File.Create("CarData.xml")
Dim myXMLFormat As SoapFormatter = New SoapFormatter()
myXMLFormat.Serialize(myStream, myAuto)
myStream.Close()
' Read in the Car from the XML file.
Console.WriteLine("Reading car from XML file.")
myStream = File.OpenRead("CarData.xml")
Dim carFromXML As JamesBondCar = _
    CType(myXMLFormat.Deserialize(myStream), JamesBondCar)
Console.WriteLine(carFromXML.PetName + " is alive!")
carFromXML.TurnOnRadio(True)
myStream.Close()
```

As you can see, the SoapFormatter type has the same public interface as the BinaryFormatter. As before, use Serialize() and Deserialize() to move the object graph in and out of the stream. If you open the resulting *.xml file (see Figure 12-23), you can locate the XML tags that mark the stateful values of the current JamesBondCar (as well as the relationship maintained by the graph).

CarData.xml


```
<SOAP-ENV:Envelope xmlns:xsi="http://www.w3.org/2001/XMLSc
    <SOAP-ENV:Body>
        <a1:JamesBondCar id="ref-1">
            <isFlightWorthy>false</isFlightWorthy>
            <isSeaWorthy>true</isSeaWorthy>
            <mPetName id="ref-3">Fred</mPetName>
            <mMaxSpeed>50</mMaxSpeed>
            <mTheRadio href="#ref-4" />
            <Car_x002B_mPetName href="#ref-3" />
            <Car_x002B_mMaxSpeed>50</Car_x002B_mMaxSpeed>
            <Car_x002B_mTheRadio href="#ref-4" />
        </a1:JamesBondCar>
        <a1:Radio id="ref-4"></a1:Radio>
    </SOAP-ENV:Body>
</SOAP-ENV:Envelope>
```


XML Data

Figure 12-23. JamesBondCar serialized using a SoapFormatter

SOURCE CODE *The CarToFile application (demonstrating both binary and SOAP formatting) is located under the Chapter 12 subdirectory.*

Custom Serialization (and the ISerializable Interface)

The default approach to persist a custom type is simple: Mark a class with the <Serializable> attribute. When a formatter is passed the object graph, all referenced objects are sent to the stream. While this is typically exactly the behavior you desire, the System.Runtime.Serialization namespace provides ways to customize how the serialization process occurs.

When you want to "get involved" with the serialization process, your first step is to implement the standard ISerializable interface on the class that will use custom serialization. Here is the official C# definition:

```
// When you wish to tweak the serialization process, implement ISerializable.
public  interface ISerializable
{
     public  virtual  void GetObjectData(SerializationInfo info,
                                         StreamingContext context);
}
```

This interface defines a single method named GetObjectData(), which is called by the formatter during the serialization process. The implementation of this method populates the incoming SerializationInfo parameter with a series of name/value pairs. The SerializationInfo type is essentially a "property bag," which is no doubt familiar to classic COM programmers.

In addition to implementing the ISerializable interface, all objects implementing custom serialization must provide a special constructor taking the following signature:

```
' You must supply a custom constructor with this signature
' to allow the runtime engine to set the state of your object.
Class SomeClass
   Private Sub New(si as SerializationInfo, ctx as StreamingContext)
      ...
   End Sub
End Class
```

Notice that the visibility of this constructor is set as *Private*. This is permissible given that the formatter will have access to this member regardless of its visibility. These special constructors tend to be marked as Private to ensure that the casual object user never creates an object in this manner.

As you can see, the first parameter of this constructor is an instance of the SerializationInfo type, which allows you to configure a set of name/value pairs representing thc state of your object. The SerializationInfo type defines a member named AddValue(), which has been overloaded numerous times to allow you to specify any type of data (strings, integers, floats, Booleans, and so on). Also, numerous GetXXXX() methods are supplied to extract information from the SerializationInfo type to populate the object's member variables. You will see these in action in just a moment.

The second parameter to this special constructor is a StreamingContext type, which contains information regarding the source or destination of the bits. The most informative member of this type is the State property, which represents a value from the StreamingContextStates enumeration (see Table 12-17).

Table 12-17. StreamingContextStates Enumeration Members

STREAMINGCONTEXTSTATES MEMBER NAME	MEANING IN LIFE
All	Specifies that the serialized data can be transmitted to or received from any of the other contexts.
Clone	Specifies that the object graph is being cloned.
CrossAppDomain	Specifies that the source or destination context is a new AppDomain.
CrossMachine	Specifies that the source or destination context is a different machine.
CrossProcess	Specifies that the source or destination context is a different process on the same machine.
File	Specifies that the source or destination context is a file.
Other	Specifies that the serialization context is unknown.
Persistence	Specifies that the source or destination context is a persisted store. This could include databases, files, or other backing stores. Users should assume that persisted data is more long-lived than the process that created the data and not serialize objects in such a way that deserialization requires accessing any data from the current process.
Remoting	Specifies that the source or destination context is remoting to an unknown location. Users cannot make any assumptions about if this is on the same machine.

A Simple Example

Let me reiterate that you typically do not need to bypass the default serialization mechanism provided by the .NET runtime. However, to illustrate, the following is an updated version of the Car type that has been configured to take part in custom serialization. You are not doing anything special in the implementation of GetObjectState() or the custom constructor. Rather, each method dumps out information regarding the current context and manipulates the incoming SerializationInfo type:

```
<Serializable()> _
    Public Class CustomCarType
        Implements ISerializable
        Public petName As String
        Public maxSpeed As Integer
        Public Sub New(ByVal s As String, ByVal i As Integer)
            petName = s
            maxSpeed = i
        End Sub
    ' Impl of ISerializable interface
    Public Sub GetObjectData(ByVal si As SerializationInfo, _
       ByVal ctx As StreamingContext) _
        Implements ISerializable.GetObjectData
        ' What context is the stream?
        Console.WriteLine("[GetObjectData] Context State: {0}",_
        ctx.State.ToString())
        ' Fill the SerializationInfo type with info.
        si.AddValue("CapPetName", petName)
        si.AddValue("maxSpeed", maxSpeed)
    End Sub

    ' You must supply a custom ctor with this signature
    ' to allow the runtime engine to
    ' set the state of your object.
    Private Sub New(ByVal si As SerializationInfo,_
    ByVal ctx As StreamingContext)
        ' What context is the stream?
        Console.WriteLine("[ctor] Context State: {0}", ctx.State.ToString())
        ' Re-hydrate a new object based on incoming
        ' SerializationInfo type.
        petName = si.GetString("CapPetName")
        maxSpeed = si.GetInt32("maxSpeed")
    End Sub
End Class
```

Now that the type has been configured with the correct infrastructure, you will be happy to see that the serialization and deserialization process remains unaltered (see Figure 12-24 for output):

```
Module Module1
    Sub Main()
        ' Make a car and listen to the tunes.
        Console.WriteLine("Making car. . .")
```

```
        Dim myAuto As CustomCarType = New CustomCarType("Siddhartha", 50)
        ' Create a file stream.
        Console.WriteLine("Making *.dat file. . .")
        Dim myStream As Stream = File.Create("CarData.dat")
        ' ISerializable interface obtained!
        Console.WriteLine("Saving to file.")
        Dim myBinaryFormat As BinaryFormatter = New BinaryFormatter()
        myBinaryFormat.Serialize(myStream, myAuto)
        myStream.Close()
        Console.WriteLine("Reading from file.")
        myStream = File.OpenRead("CarData.dat")
        Dim carFromDisk As CustomCarType = _
           CType(myBinaryFormat.Deserialize(myStream), CustomCarType)
        Console.WriteLine(carFromDisk.petName + " is alive!")
        myStream.Close()
    End Sub
End Module
```

```
C:\Apress Books\VB.NET\Code\Chapter 12\CustomSe...
Making car...
Making *.dat file...
Saving to file.
[GetObjectData] Context State: All
Reading from file.
[ctor] Context State: All
Siddhartha is alive!
Press any key to continue
```

Figure 12-24. Custom serialization

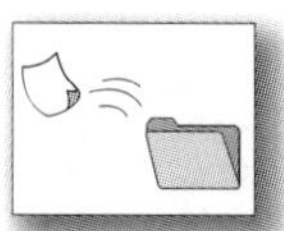

SOURCE CODE *The CustomSerialization project is included under the Chapter 12 subdirectory.*

A Windows Forms Car Logger Application

To wrap up this examination of object serialization, the remainder of this chapter walks you through a minimal and complete Windows Forms application that uses many of the techniques examined thus far. The CarLogApp allows the end user to create an inventory of Car types (contained in an ArrayList), which are displayed in yet another Windows Form control, the DataGrid (see Figure 12-25). To keep focused on the serialization logic, this grid is read-only.

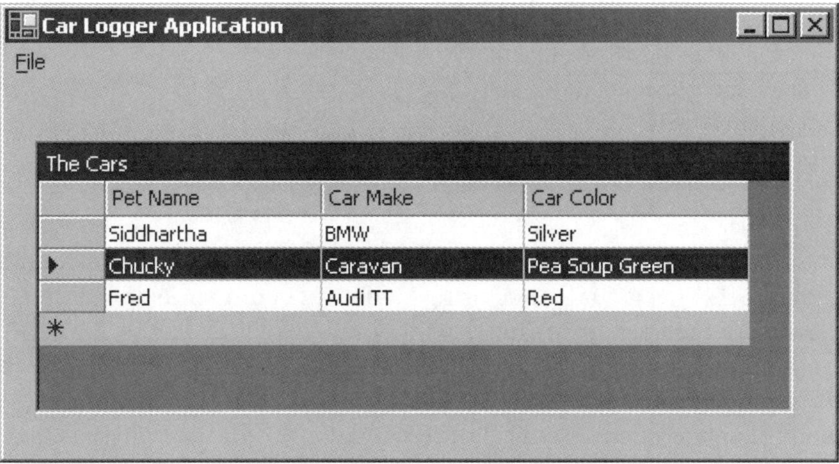

Figure 12-25. The car logger application

The topmost File menu provides a number of choices that operate on the underlying ArrayList. Table 12-18 describes the possible selections.

Table 12-18. The CarLogApp Menu System

FILE SUBMENU ITEM	MEANING IN LIFE
Clear All Cars	Empties the ArrayList and refreshes the DataGrid.
Exit	Terminate the application.
Make New Car	Displays a custom dialog box that allows the user to configure a new Car and refreshes the DataGrid.
Open Car File	Allows the user to open an existing *.car file and refreshes the DataGrid. This file is the result of a BinaryFormatter.
Save Car File	Saves all cars displayed in the DataGrid to a *.car file.

I don't bother to detail the menu construction logic, as you have already seen these steps during the formal discussion of Windows Forms. The first task is to define the Car type itself. This is the class that represents not only a unique row in the DataGrid, but also an item in the serialized object graph. There are numerous iterations of the Car class throughout this book, so this version is brutally bland:

```
<Serializable()> Public Class Car
    ' Make public for easy access. . .
    Public mPetName, mMake, mColor As String
    Public Sub New(ByVal petName As String, _
```

```
    ByVal make As String, ByVal color As String)
        mPetName = petName
        mColor = color
        mMake = make
    End Sub
End Class
```

Next, you need to add a few members to the main Form class. The overall UI of the DataGrid type is configured using a small set of properties, all of which have been assigned using the Property window of the Visual Studio .NET IDE. The most important property for this example is the ReadOnly member (set to True), which prevents the user from editing the cells in the DataGrid. The remaining configurations establish the type's color scheme and physical dimensions (which you can explore at your leisure).

In addition, the main Form maintains a private ArrayList type, which holds each of the Car references. The Form's constructor adds a number of default cars to allow the user to view some initial items in the grid. Once these Car types have been added to the collection, you call a helper function named RefreshGrid(), as shown here:

```
Public Class Form1
    Inherits System.Windows.Forms.Form
    ' List for object serialization.
    Private arTheCars As ArrayList
    Public Sub New()
        MyBase.New()
        'This call is required by the Windows Form Designer.
        InitializeComponent()
        CenterToScreen()
        ' Add some cars.
        arTheCars = New ArrayList()
        arTheCars.Add(New Car("Siddhartha", "BMW", "Silver"))
        arTheCars.Add(New Car("Chucky", "Caravan", "Pea Soup Green"))
        arTheCars.Add(New Car("Fred", "Audi TT", "Red"))
        UpdateGrid()
    End Sub
...
End Class
```

The UpdateGrid() method is responsible for creating a System.Data.DataTable type that contains a row for each Car in the ArrayList. Once the DataTable has been populated, you then bind it the DataGrid type.

Chapter 14 examines the ADO.NET types (such as the DataTable) in much greater detail, so I focus on the basics for the time being. Here is the code:

```
Private Sub UpdateGrid()
    If (Not arTheCars Is Nothing) Then
        '  Make a DataTable object named Inventory.
        Dim inventory As DataTable = New DataTable("Inventory")
        Create DataColumn objects.'
        Dim make As DataColumn = New DataColumn("Car Make")
        Dim petName As DataColumn = New DataColumn("Pet Name")
        Dim color As DataColumn = New DataColumn("Car Color")
        ' Add columns to data table.
        inventory.Columns.Add(petName)
        inventory.Columns.Add(make)
        inventory.Columns.Add(color)
        ' Iterate over the array list to make rows.
        Dim c As Car
        For Each c In arTheCars
            Dim newRow As DataRow
            newRow = inventory.NewRow()
            newRow("Pet Name") = c.mPetName
            newRow("Car Make") = c.mMake
            newRow("Car Color") = c.mColor
            inventory.Rows.Add(newRow)
        Next
        ' Now bind this data table to the grid.
        carDataGrid.DataSource = inventory
    End If
End Sub
```

Here, you begin by creating a new DataTable type named Inventory. In the world of ADO.NET, a DataTable is an in-memory representation of a single table of information. While you might assume that a DataTable would be created as a result of some SQL query, you can also use this type as a stand-alone entity.

Once you have a new DataTable, you need to establish the set of columns that should be listed in the table. The System.Data.DataColumn type represents a single column. Given that this iteration of the Car type has three public fields (make, color, and pet name), create three DataColumns and insert them in the table using the DataTable.Columns property.

Next, you need to add each row to the table. Recall that the main Form maintains an ArrayList that contains some number of Car types. Given that ArrayList implements the IEnumerable interface, you can fetch each Car from the collection, read each public field, and compose and insert a new DataRow in the table.

Finally, the new DataTable is bound to the GUI DataGrid widget using the DataSource property.

If you run the application, you find that the grid is indeed populated with the default automobiles. This is a good start, but you can do better.

Implementing the Add New Car Logic

The CarLogApp project defines another Form-derived type (AddCarDlg), which functions as a modal dialog box (see Figure 12-26). Because you already examined the construction of custom dialog boxes in Chapter 11, I'll hold off on the details. However, from a GUI point of view, this type is composed of a TextBox (to hold the pet name) and two ListBox types (to allow the user to select the car's color and make).

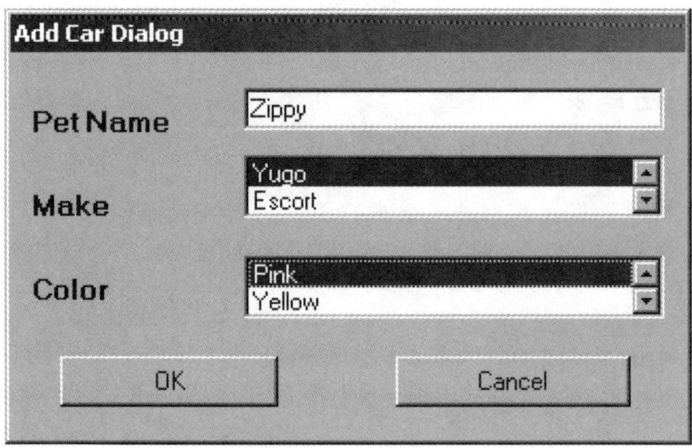

Figure 12-26. The Add Car dialog box

As far as the code behind the Form, the OK button as been assigned the DialogResult property DialogResult.OK. As you recall from Chapter 11, this value marks a Button type to function as a standard OK button. Also, this Form maintains a public Car type (for easy access), which is configured when the user clicks the OK button. The remainder of the code is nothing more than some GUI control prep work. The relevant logic is as follows:

```
Public Class AddCarDlg
    Inherits System.Windows.Forms.Form
    ' Make public for easy access.
    Public theCar As Car
     ...
    Protected Sub btnOK_Click(ByVal sender As Object, _
    ByVal e As System.EventArgs) Handles btnOK.Click
        theCar = New Car(txtName.Text, listMake.Text, listColor.Text)
    End Sub
End Class
```

The main Form displays this dialog box when the user selects the Make New Car menu item. Here is the code behind that object's Clicked event:

```
Private Sub menuItemNewCar_Click(ByVal sender As System.Object, _
 ByVal e As System.EventArgs) Handles menuItemNewCar.Click
    Dim d As AddCarDlg = New AddCarDlg()
    If (d.ShowDialog() = DialogResult.OK) Then
        '  Add new car to arraylist.
        arTheCars.Add(d.theCar)
        UpdateGrid()
    End If
End Sub
```

No surprises here. You just show the Form as a modal dialog box, and if the OK button has been clicked, you read the public Car member variable, add it to the ArrayList, and refresh your grid.

The Serialization Logic

The core logic behind the Save Car File and Open Car File Click event handlers should pose no problems at this point. When the user chooses to save the current inventory, you create a new file and use a BinaryFormatter to serialize the object graph. However, just to keep things interesting, the user can establish the name and location of this file using a System.Windows.Forms.SaveFileDialog type. This type is yet another standard dialog box and is illustrated in Figure 12-27.

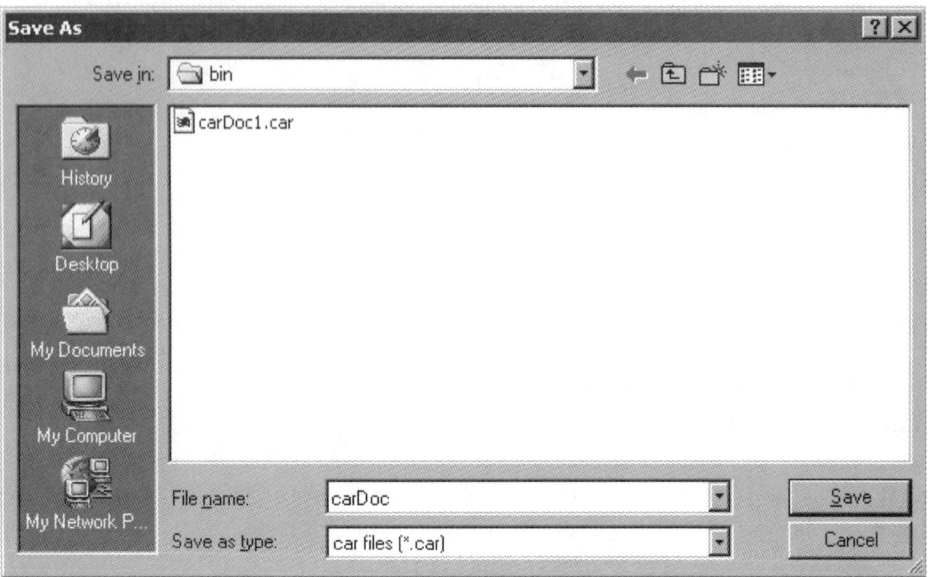

Figure 12-27. The standard Save As dialog box

Notice that the SaveFileDialog is listing a custom file extension (*.car). While I leave the task of investigating the complete functionality of the SaveFileDialog in your capable hands, it is worth pointing out that this has been assigned using the Filter property. This property takes an OR-delimited string that represents the text to be used in the drop-down "File name" and "Save as type" combo boxes. Here is the full implementation:

```
Private Sub menuItemSave_Click(ByVal sender As System.Object, _
  ByVal e As System.EventArgs) Handles menuItemSave.Click
    ' Configure look and feel of save dlg.
    Dim mySaveFileDialog As SaveFileDialog = New SaveFileDialog()
    mySaveFileDialog.InitialDirectory = "."
    mySaveFileDialog.Filter = "car files (*.car)|*.car|All files (*.*)|*.*"
    mySaveFileDialog.FilterIndex = 1
    mySaveFileDialog.RestoreDirectory = True
    mySaveFileDialog.FileName = "carDoc"
    ' Do you have a file?
    If (mySaveFileDialog.ShowDialog() = DialogResult.OK) Then
        Dim myStream As Stream
        myStream = mySaveFileDialog.OpenFile()
            If (Not myStream Is Nothing) Then
                ' Save the cars!
                Dim myBinaryFormat As BinaryFormatter = New BinaryFormatter()
```

```
                myBinaryFormat.Serialize(myStream, arTheCars)
                myStream.Close()
            End If
        End If
End Sub
```

Also note that the OpenFile() member of the SaveFileDialog type returns a Stream that represents the specified file selected by the end user. As you saw earlier in this chapter, this is the very thing needed by the BinaryFormatter type.

The logic behind the Open Car File Click event handler looks very similar. This time you create an instance of the System.Windows.Forms OpenFileDialog type, configure accordingly, and obtain a Stream reference based on the selected file. Next you dump the contents of the ArrayList and read in the new object graph using the BinaryFormatter.Deserialize() method, as shown here:

```
Private Sub menuItemOpen_Click(ByVal sender As System.Object, _
 ByVal e As System.EventArgs) Handles menuItemOpen.Click
    ' Configure look and feel of open dlg.
    Dim myOpenFileDialog As OpenFileDialog = New OpenFileDialog()
    myOpenFileDialog.InitialDirectory = "."
    myOpenFileDialog.Filter = "car files (*.car)|*.car|All files (*.*)|*.*"
    myOpenFileDialog.FilterIndex = 1
    myOpenFileDialog.RestoreDirectory = True

    ' Do you have a file?
    If (myOpenFileDialog.ShowDialog() = DialogResult.OK) Then
        ' Clear list.
        arTheCars.Clear()
        Dim myStream As Stream
        myStream = myOpenFileDialog.OpenFile()
        If (Not myStream Is Nothing) Then
            ' Get the cars!
            Dim myBinaryFormat As BinaryFormatter = New BinaryFormatter()
            arTheCars = CType(myBinaryFormat.Deserialize(myStream), ArrayList)
            myStream.Close()
            UpdateGrid()
        End If
    End If
End Sub
```

At this point, the application can save and load the entire set of Car types held in the ArrayList using a BinaryFormatter. The final menu items are self-explanatory, as shown here:

```
Private Sub menuItemClear_Click(ByVal sender As System.Object, _
ByVal e As System.EventArgs) Handles menuItemClear.Click
    arTheCars.Clear()
    UpdateGrid()
End Sub
Private Sub menuItemExit_Click(ByVal sender As System.Object, _
ByVal e As System.EventArgs) Handles menuItemExit.Click
    Application.Exit()
End Sub
```

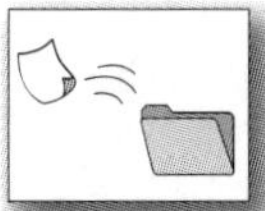

SOURCE CODE *The CarLogApp project is included under the Chapter 12 subdirectory.*

Summary

This chapter began by examining the use of the Directory(Info) and File(Info) types. As you have seen, these classes allow you to manipulate a physical file or directory on your hard drive.

The chapter then examined a number of types derived from the abstract Stream class, including FileStream, MemoryStream, and BufferedStream. Given that each of these types has (more or less) the same public interface, you can easily swap them in and out of your code to alter the ultimate location of your byte array. When you are interested in persisting textual data, the StreamReader and StreamWriter types usually fit the bill.

This chapter concluded by examining how the .NET Framework provides the necessary infrastructure needed to persist your objects in a binary or SOAP message format. Although the <Serializable> and <NonSerialized> attributes are typically all you need to concern yourself with, you also saw how to configure a class to support custom serialization (e.g., the ISerializable interface).

CHAPTER 13

Interacting with Unmanaged Code

BY NOW, YOU HAVE GAINED a solid foundation in the VB .NET language and the core services provided by the .NET platform. I suspect that when you contrast the object model provided by .NET to that of classic COM, you are no doubt on your way to becoming a .NET-head. Sadly, few of us are in a position to completely abandon the ways of COM, Visual Basic 6.0, and classic Windows DNA. The truth is that people have spent hundreds of thousands of hours building systems that make substantial use of these technologies. If .NET is to succeed as a platform, it must have a way to interact gracefully with the legacy systems of today.

The chapter begins by examining the process of .NET to COM interoperability and the related Runtime Callable Wrapper (RCW). The later part of this chapter examines the opposite situation: a COM type communicating with a .NET type using a COM Callable Wrapper (CCW). Once you see how to get COM types and .NET types communicating, you examine how to build managed types that can interact with the services provided by the COM+ runtime layer (e.g., object pooling, object constructor strings, and so on).

Understanding Interoperability Issues

When you build assemblies using a .NET-aware compiler, you are creating "managed code" that can be hosted by the Common Language Runtime (CLR). Managed code offers a number of benefits such as automatic memory management, a unified type system (CTS), self-describing assemblies, and so forth. As you have seen, .NET assemblies have a particular internal composition. In addition to IL instructions and type metadata, assemblies contain a manifest that fully documents any required external assemblies.

On the other side of the spectrum are classic COM servers (which are, of course, "unmanaged code"). These binaries bear no relationship to .NET assemblies beyond a shared file extension (DLL or EXE). First, COM servers contain platform-specific machine code, not platform-agnostic IL instructions. COM servers work with a unique set of data types (BSTRs, VARIANTs, and so forth) that are mapped very differently between COM-aware languages. In addition to the necessary COM "goo" required by all COM binaries (such as registry entries and IUnknown) is the fact that COM types demand to be reference counted. Mismanaged reference counting can lead to memory leaks, as coclasses are not allocated on a managed heap.

Given that .NET types and COM types have so little in common, you may wonder how these two architectures can coexist. Unless you are lucky enough to work for a company dedicated to "100% Pure .NET" development, you will most likely need to build .NET solutions that use legacy COM types. The chances are quite high that you will still need to build a COM server or two that need to communicate with a shiny new .NET assembly.

The bottom line is that for some time to come, COM and .NET must learn how to get along. This chapter examines the issues that arise when managed and unmanaged types attempt to live together in harmony. In general, the .NET Framework supports the following flavors of interoperability:

- .NET types calling COM types
- COM types calling .NET types
- .NET types using COM+ services

As you see throughout this chapter, the .NET SDK supplies a number of tools that help bridge the gap between these unique architectures. As well, the .NET base class libraries define a number of types dedicated solely to the issue of interoperability. However, before diving in too far under the hood, let's look at a painfully simple example and get acquainted with some additional wizards provided by VS .NET.

A Painfully Simple Example: VB .NET Applications Communicating with VB 6.0 COM Types

To begin our exploration of interoperability issues, let's see just how simple things appear on the surface. The goal of this section is to build a VB 6.0 ActiveX DLL server, which is then exercised by a VB .NET application. Fire up VB 6.0, and create a new ActiveX DLL project named SimpleVB6ComServer. Likewise, rename your initial default *.cls file to VBCalc. As you may know, this will define the programmatic identifier (ProgID) of the COM binary (SimpleVB6ComServer.VBCalc). Finally, in the spirit of painful simplicity, add a single function named Add().

```
' The VB 6.0 COM object
Option Explicit
Public Function Add(x As Integer, y As Integer) As Integer
```

```
    Add = x + y
End Function
```

At this point, compile your DLL and, just to keep things peaceful in the world of COM, set binary compatibility before you exit the VB 6.0 IDE.

Building the VB .NET Client

Now open up VS .NET and create a new VB .NET client application. Feel free to make use of a Windows Forms application if you choose; however, to keep the code concise, I opted for a Console application named VBNetSimpleComClient.

The next step is to somehow gain access to the existing ActiveX DLL server. Without going into too many details at this point, simply access the "Project | Add Reference" menu selection and select the COM tab from the Add Reference dialog box. The name of your COM server will be listed alphabetically. Go ahead and select the DLL (see Figure 13-1) and close the dialog box.

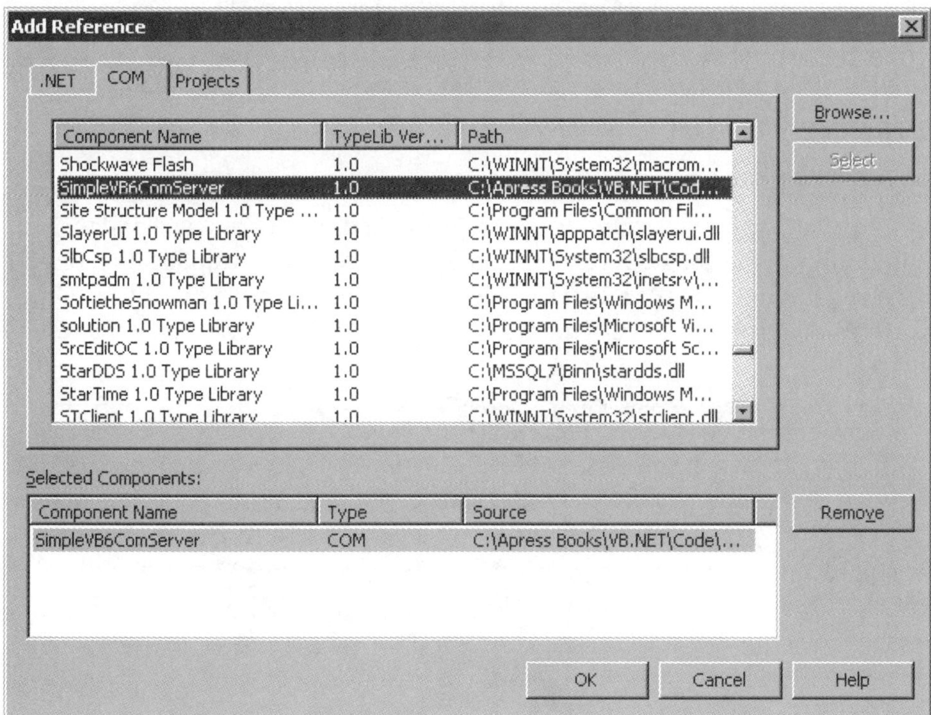

Figure 13-1. Referencing a classic COM server from a .NET project workspace

As soon as you click the OK button, you are greeted with a message saying that a "Primary Interop Assembly" has not been established. Just click OK and move on. Now, if you examine the Solution Explorer, you see what looks to be a new .NET assembly reference added to your project, as shown in Figure 13-2.

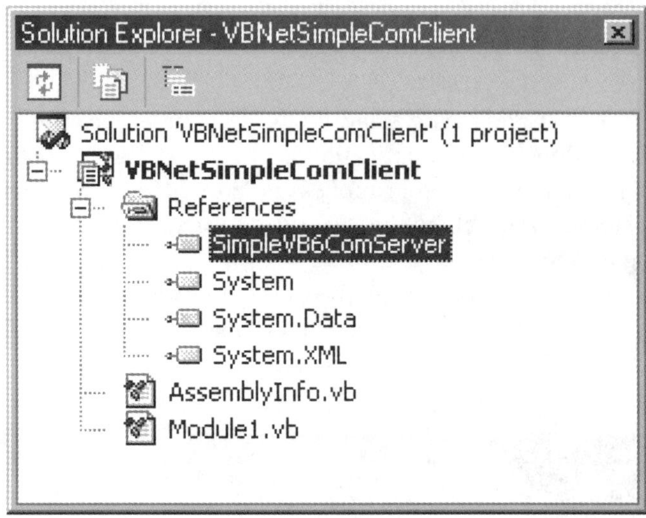

Figure 13-2. A new .NET assembly?

Furthermore, if you examine the project's bin directory, you will find that a local copy of the generated assembly has been placed in the application directory (see Figure 13-3). (Be aware that by convention, generated interoperability assemblies are prefixed with "Interop.-"—however, this is only a convention.)

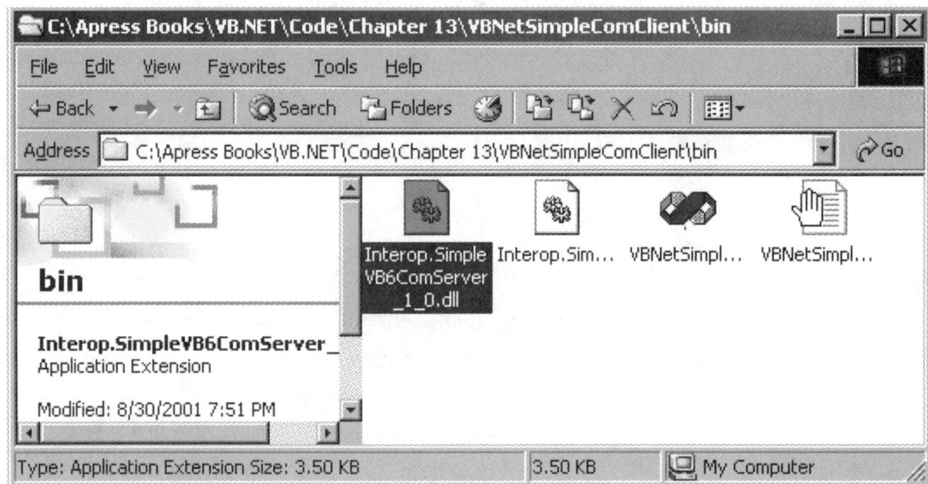

Figure 13-3. The generated assembly

Finally, edit the Main() method of your Module type to simply call the Add() method and display the result. For example:

```
Imports SimpleVB6ComServer
Module Module1
    Sub Main()
        Dim comObj As New VBCalc()
        Console.WriteLine("COM server says 10 + 832 is {0}", _
          comObj.Add(10, 832))
    End Sub
End Module
```

The output shown in Figure 13-4 is as you would expect.

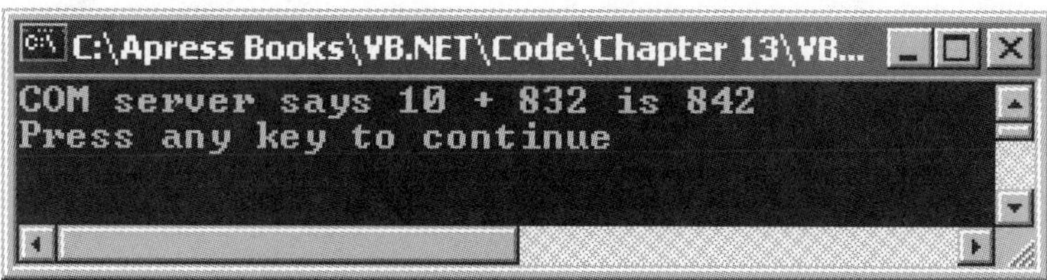

Figure 13-4. .NET to COM interoperability

As you can see, things look extremely simple from the outset. Calling a COM type from within a .NET application is a very transparent operation. As you can imagine, a number of details are occurring behind the scenes to make this communication possible. You explore a number of gory details throughout this chapter. Your next task is to get to know the core .NET namespace, which makes interoperability possible.

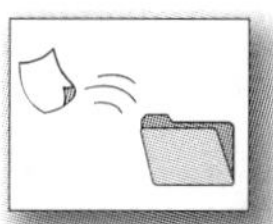

SOURCE CODE *The SimpleVB6ComServer and VBNetSimpleComClient projects are located under the Chapter 13 subdirectory.*

The System.Runtime.InteropServices Namespace

When you use .NET interoperability services, you directly or indirectly (typically indirectly) interact with the types defined in the System.Runtime.InteropServices namespace. Table 13-1 offers a high-level overview of some (but not all) core types.

Table 13-1. Select Members of the System.Runtime.InteropServices Namespace

SYSTEM.RUNTIME.INTEROPSERVICES TYPE	MEANING IN LIFE
ClassInterfaceAttribute	Used to control how a managed type exposes its public members to COM clients.
ComRegisterFunctionAttribute ComUnregisterFunctionAttribute	May be attributed to managed methods to indicate that they should be called when an assembly is registered (or unregistered) for use by COM.
ComSourceInterfacesAttribute	Identifies the list of interfaces that are sources of events for the class.
DispIdAttribute	Custom attribute that specifies the COM DISPID (dispatch identifier) of a method, field, or property.
DllImportAttribute	Used by the platform invoke service (PInvoke) to call unmanaged code.
GuidAttribute	Used to define a specific GUID for a class, interface, or type library.
IDispatchImplAttribute	Indicates which IDispatch implementation the CLR should use when exposing dual interfaces and dispinterfaces.
InterfaceTypeAttribute	Controls how a managed interface is exposed to COM clients (dual, IDispatch-derived, or IUnknown-derived).
OutAttribute InAttribute	Used on a parameter or field to indicate that data should be marshaled out from callee back to caller or from caller to callee.
Marshal	This type is used to handle unmanaged memory allocations (including interacting with COM reference counting) as well as to interact with the marshaling process.
ProgIdAttribute	Custom attribute that allows the user to specify the programmatic identifier (ProgID) of a .NET type.

As you may have noticed, most of these types are attributes used to help move data between .NET types and COM types. Of course, the System.Runtime.InteropServices namespace also defines a number of interfaces, enumerations, and structures. (Examples are given where appropriate.)

Understanding .NET to COM Interoperability

.NET applications are able to make use of COM types with minimal fuss and bother. However, it should be clear that there must be some intervening layer that correctly exposes COM types as .NET equivalents. As shown in the previous example, this mapping is extremely transparent.

The proverbial "black box" to which I am referring is the Runtime Callable Wrapper (RCW). The RCW can be understood as a proxy to the real COM class (or *coclass*). Every coclass accessed by a .NET client requires a corresponding RCW. Thus, if you have a single .NET application that uses three COM coclasses, you end up with three distinct RCWs that map .NET calls into COM requests. Figure 13-5 illustrates the big picture.

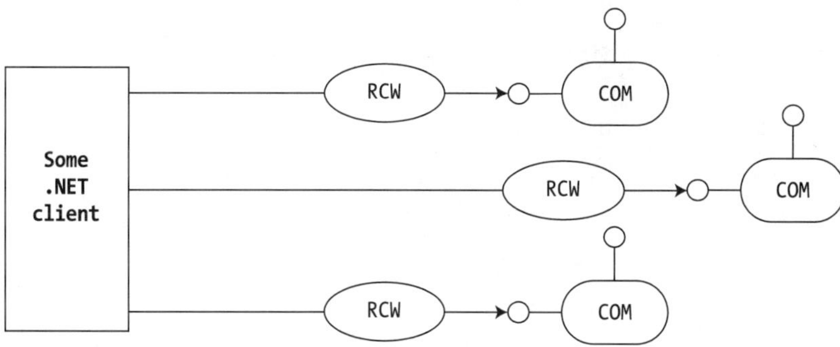

Figure 13-5. The RCW acts as a proxy to the coclass.

Be aware that there is a single RCW per COM object, regardless of how many individual interfaces the .NET client has obtained from a given COM class (you examine a multi-interfaced VB 6.0 COM type a bit later in this chapter). Using this technique, the RCW can maintain the correct COM identity (and reference count) of the COM type.

The good news is that the code used to build the RCW is generated automatically using a tool named tlbimp.exe (type library importer). The other bit of good news is that legacy COM classes do not require any modifications to be consumed by a .NET-aware language. The intervening RCW takes care of the internal work. To see how this is achieved, let's formalize the responsibilities of the RCW.

The RCW: Exposing COM Types As .NET Equivalents

The RCW is in charge of exposing COM data types as managed equivalents. As a simple example, assume you have a VB 6.0 COM method defined as shown here:

```
' VB 6.0 COM method definition.
Public Sub DisplayThisString(s as String)
```

The RCW exposes this method to a .NET client as follows:

```
' VB.NET mapping of COM method.
Public Sub DisplayThisString(ByVal s as System.String)
```

All VB 6.0 COM data types have a corresponding .NET equivalent. To help you gain your bearings, Table 13-2 documents the mapping between COM (IDL) data types and the correct .NET system data types and the corresponding VB .NET alias.

Table 13-2. Mapping Intrinsic COM Types to .NET Types

IDL (TYPE LIBRARY) DATA TYPE	SYSTEM TYPES	VISUAL BASIC .NET DATA TYPE
wchar_t, short	System.Int16	Short
long, int	System.Int32	Integer
hyper	System.Int64	Long
unsigned char, byte	System.Byte	Byte
single	System.Single	Single
double	System.Double	Double
VARIANT_BOOL	System.Boolean	Boolean
BSTR	System.String	String
VARIANT	System.Object	Object
DECIMAL	System.Decimal	Decimal
DATE	System.DateTime	DateTime
GUID	System.Guid	Guid
CURRENCY	System.Decimal	Decimal
IUnknown *	System.Object	Object
IDispatch *	System.Object	Object

In addition to these COM primitives, you examine how other (more exotic) COM types map into .NET equivalents as you move through this chapter.

The RCW: Managing a Coclass' Reference Count

Another important duty of the RCW is to manage the reference count of the underlying coclass. The COM reference-counting scheme is a joint venture between coclass and client and revolves around the proper use of AddRef() and Release() calls. COM classes self-destruct when they detect that they have no outstanding references.

However, .NET types do not use the COM reference-counting scheme, and therefore a .NET client should not be forced to call Release() on the COM types it uses. To keep each participant happy, the RCW caches all interface references internally and triggers the final release when the type is no longer used by the .NET client. The bottom line is that similar to VB 6.0, .NET clients never explicitly call AddRef(), Release(), or QueryInterface().

The RCW: Hiding Low-Level COM Interfaces

The final role of the RCW is to consume a number of select COM interfaces. Because the RCW tries to do everything it can to fool the .NET client into thinking it is using a .NET type, the RCW must hide various low-level COM interfaces from view. In many respects, the RCW takes the same approach as VB 6.0.

For example, when you build a COM class that supports IConnectionPointContainer (and maintains a subobject or two supporting IConnectionPoint), the coclass in question is able to fire events back to the COM client. VB 6.0 hides this entire process from view using the Event and RaiseEvent keywords. In the same vein, the RCW also hides such COM "goo" from the .NET client. Because the RCW hides these low-level interfaces, the external .NET client only sees (and interacts with) the set of custom interfaces implemented by the coclass. Table 13-3 outlines some of these hidden COM interfaces.

Table 13-3. Hidden COM Interfaces

HIDDEN COM INTERFACE	MEANING IN LIFE
IConnectionPointContainer IConnectionPoint	Enables a coclass to send events back to an interested client. VB 6.0 automatically provides a default implementation of each of these interfaces.
IDispatch IProvideClassInfo	Used to facilitate "late binding" to a coclass. Again, when you are building VB 6.0 COM types, these interfaces are automatically supported by a given COM type.
IErrorInfo ISupportErrorInfo ICreateErrorInfo	These interfaces enable COM clients and COM objects to send and respond to COM errors.
IUnknown	The granddaddy of COM. Manages the reference count of the COM object and allows clients to obtain interfaces from the coclass.

The Role of COM IDL

At this point you hopefully have a solid understanding of the role of the RCW. Before you go much further into the COM to .NET conversion process, it is necessary to review some of the finer details of COM IDL (Interface Definition Language). Understand, of course, that is chapter is *not* intended to function as a complete COM tutorial. If you require additional details regarding COM itself as well as the VB 6.0/COM language mapping, I assume you will consult additional texts.

As you saw in Chapter 7 (as well as numerous other places in this text), a .NET assembly contains *metadata*. Formally speaking, metadata is used to describe each and every aspect of a .NET assembly, including the internal types (their members, base class, and so on), assembly version, and optional assembly level information (strong name, culture, and so on).

In many ways, .NET metadata is the big brother of an earlier metadata format used to describe classic COM servers. As you may know, classic ActiveX COM servers (DLLs or EXEs) document their internal types using a *type library*, which may be realized as a stand-alone *.tlb file or bundled into the COM server as an internal resource (which is the default behavior of VB 6.0). COM type libraries are themselves created using a metadata language called IDL (the Interface Definition Language) and a special compiler named midl.exe (the Microsoft IDL compiler).

VB 6.0 does a fantastic job of hiding raw type libraries, IDL, and the MIDL compiler from view. In fact, many skilled VB COM programmers can live a happy and productive life ignoring the syntax of IDL altogether. Nevertheless, whenever you compile ActiveX project workspace types, VB automatically generates and embeds the type library within the physical *.dll / *.exe COM server. Furthermore, VB 6.0 ensures that the type library is automatically registered under a very particular part of the system registry: KKEY_CLASSES_ROOT\TypeLib (see Figure 13-6).

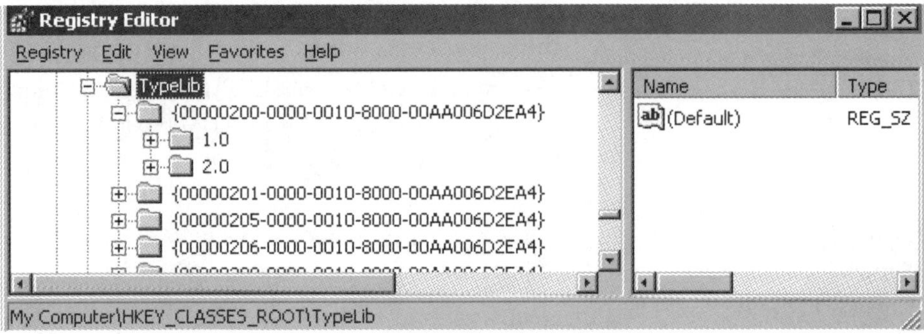

Figure 13-6. HKCR\TypeLib lists all registered type libraries on a given machine.

Type libraries are referenced all the time. Whenever you access the "Project | References" menu selection, the VB 6.0 IDE reads HKCR\TypeLib to determine each and every registered type library. Figure 13-7 shows the end result of this task.

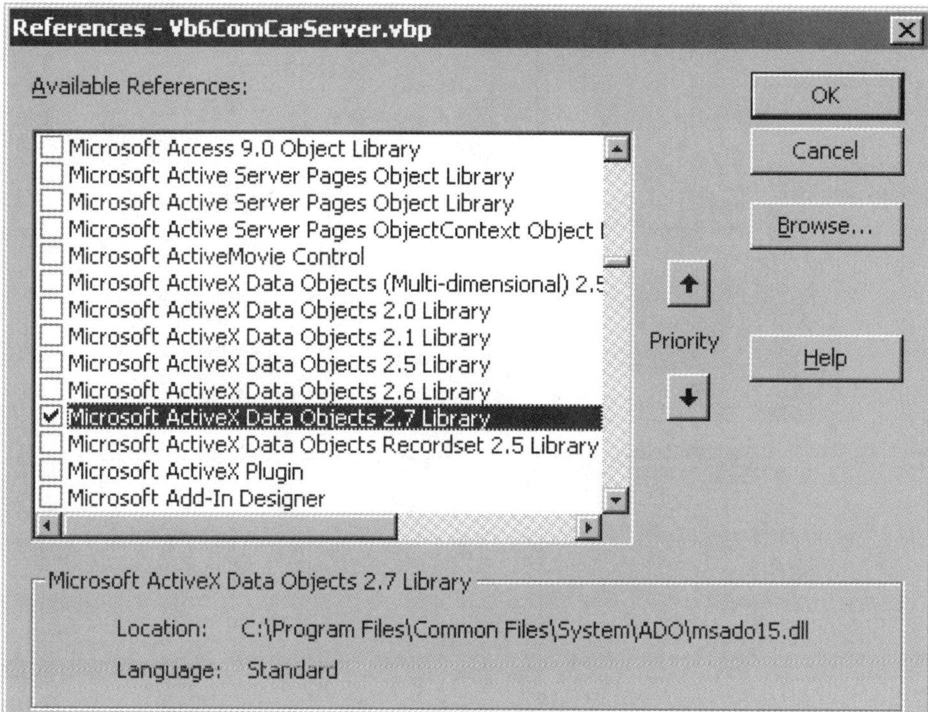

Figure 13-7. Referencing COM type information

Likewise, when you open the VB 6.0 Object Browser, the VB 6.0 IDE reads the type information and displays the contents of the COM server using a friendly GUI (see Figure 13-8).

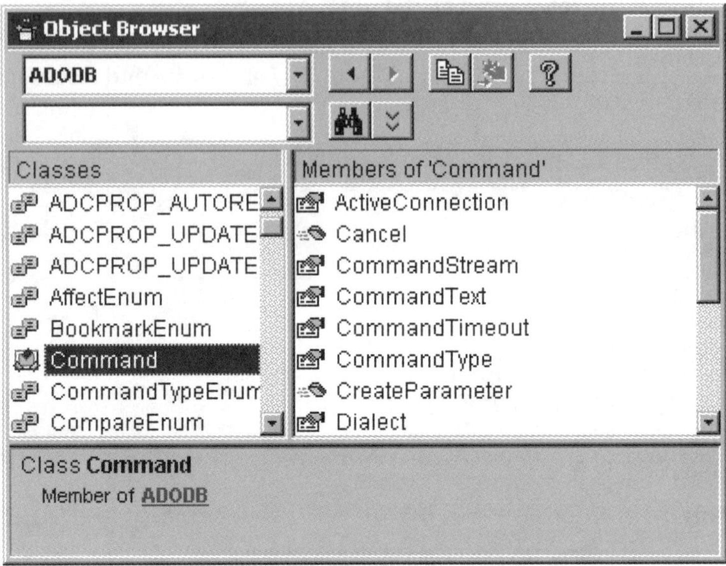

Figure 13-8. Viewing type libraries

Observing the Generated IDL for Your VB COM Server

Although the VB 6.0 Object Browser displays all COM types contained within a type library, the OLE/COM Object Viewer (oleview.exe) allows you to view the underlying IDL syntax used to build the corresponding type library.

To begin the journey, open the OLE/COM Object Viewer and hunt down the ProgID of the SimpleVB6ComServer project (see Figure 13-9). You should see the name of your default custom interface (VBCalc) as well as a number of other COM interfaces implemented by VB on your behalf.

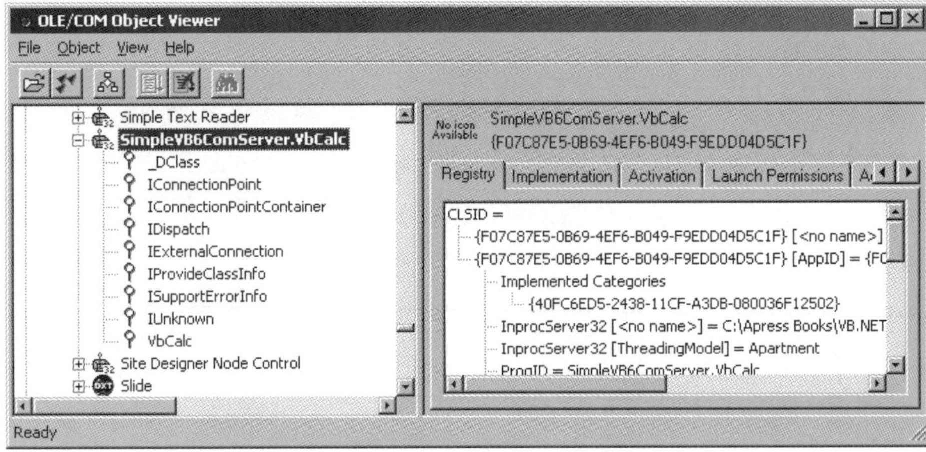

Figure 13-9. Hunting down the coclass using the OLE/COM object viewer

To view the underlying IDL, right-click the coclass and select the "View Type Information" menu option. Here is the relevant IDL (your uuid values will differ):

```
[ uuid(6ED6D94A-EB24-41F3-BF19-22937C74BC81), version(1.0)]
library SimpleVB6ComServer
{
...
    [ odl,
    uuid(8754F18E-0525-47C6-915E-2276038D9B0D), version(1.0),
    hidden, dual, nonextensible, oleautomation]
    interface _VBCalc : IDispatch
    {
        [id(0x60030000)]
        HRESULT Add(  [in, out] short* x,   [in, out] short* y,
                       [out, retval] short* );
    };
    [ uuid(F07C87E5-0B69-4EF6-B049-F9EDD04D5C1F), version(1.0) ]
    coclass VBCalc
    {
        [default] interface _VBCalc;
    };
};
```

IDL Attributes

To begin parsing out this IDL, notice that IDL syntax contains blocks of code placed in square brackets ([. . .]). Within these brackets is a comma-delimited set of IDL keywords, which are used to disambiguate the "very next thing" (the item to the right of the block or the item directly below the block). As you may already know, these blocks are IDL *attributes* that serve the same purpose as .NET attributes (i.e., they describe something). One key IDL attribute is [uuid], which is used to assign the globally unique identifier (GUID) of a given COM type. As you may already know, just about everything in COM is assigned a GUID (interfaces, COM classes, type libraries, and so on), which is used to uniquely identify a given item.

The IDL Library Statement

Starting at the top, you have the COM "library statement," which is marked using the IDL *library* keyword. Contained within the library statement are each and every interface and COM class, and any enumeration (through the VB 6.0 Enum keyword) and user-defined type (through the VB 6.0 Type keyword). In your case, the type library lists exactly one COM class, VBCalc, which is marked using the *coclass* (i.e., COM class) keyword.

The Role of the [default] Interface

According to the laws of COM, the only possible way in which a COM client can communicate with a COM class is to use an interface reference (not an object reference). If you have created C++-based COM clients, you are well aware of the process of querying for a given interface, releasing the interface when it is no longer used, and so forth. However, when you make use of VB 6.0 to build COM clients, you receive an initial interface on the COM class automatically.

When you build VB 6.0 COM servers, any member declared as Public (such as your Add() function) is placed onto the "default public interface" of the COM class. Now, if you examine the class definition of VBCalc, you can see that the name of the default interface is _VBCalc:

```
coclass VBCalc
{
    [default] interface _VBCalc;
};
```

In case you are wondering, when you build VB 6.0 ActiveX COM servers, the name of the [default] interface is always *_NameOfTheClass* (the underscore is a naming convention used to specify a hidden interface). Thus, if you have a class named Car, the default interface is _Car, a class named DataConnector has a default interface named _DataConnector, and so forth.

Under VB 6.0, the default interface is completely hidden from view. Therefore, when you write the following:

```
' VB 6.0 COM client code.
Dim c as VBCalc
Set c = New VBCalc    ' [default] _VBCalc interface returned automatically!
```

the VB runtime automatically queries the object for the [default] interface (as specified by the type library) and returns it to the client. Because VB always returns the default interface on a COM class, you can pretend that you have a true object reference. However, this is only a bit of syntactic sugar provided by Visual Basic. In COM, there is no such thing as an object reference. You always have an interface reference (even if it happens to be the default).

The Role of IDispatch

If you examine the IDL description of the default _VBCalc interface, you see that this interface derives from a standard COM interface named IDispatch. While a full discussion concerning the role of IDispatch is outside of the scope of this book, simply understand that this is the interface that makes it possible to interact with COM objects on the Web from within an Active Server Page, as well as anywhere else where late binding is employed. When you use VB proper (as opposed to VBScript), 99 percent of the time you want to avoid the use of IDispatch (it is slower, and errors are discovered at runtime rather than at compile time). However, just to illustrate, say you call the CreateObject() method as follows:

```
' VB 6.0 late binding.
Dim o as Object
Set o = CreateObject("SimpleVB6ComServer.VBCalc")
```

You have actually instructed the VB runtime to query the COM type for the IDispatch interface. Note that calling CreateObject() alone does not trigger a query for IDispatch. In addition, you must store the return value in a VB 6.0 Object data type. In just a bit, you examine how .NET clients are able to interact with IDispatch using reflection services.

IDL Parameter Attributes

The final bit of IDL that you need to be aware of is how VB 6.0 parameters are expressed under the hood. As you know, under VB 6.0 all parameters are passed by reference, unless the ByVal keyword is used explicitly. In COM IDL, all ByRef parameters are represented using the [in, out] attributes. Furthermore, a function's return value is marked using the [out, retval] attribute pair. Thus

```
// VB 6.0: Public Function Add(x as Integer, y as Integer) as Integer
HRESULT Add(  [in, out] short* x,   [in, out] short* y, [out, retval] short* );
```

when you mark a parameter using the VB 6.0 ByVal keyword:

```
Public Function Subtract(ByVal x As Integer, ByVal y As Integer) _
As Integer
    Subtract = x - y
End Function
```

you find the underlying IDL makes use of the [in] attribute:

```
HRESULT Subtract( [in] short x,  [in] short y,  [out, retval] short* );
```

Importing the Type Library

To be sure, the VB 6.0 compiler generates many other IDL attributes under the hood, and you see additional bits and pieces where appropriate. However, at this point, I am sure you are wondering exactly why I spent the last several pages describing the COM IDL. The reason is simple: When you add a reference to a COM server using VS .NET, the IDE reads the underlying IDL code to build a corresponding .NET assembly that contains the necessary information used to create the RCW. The tool responsible for building the proxy is named tlbimp.exe (type library importer).

Of course when you add COM references using VS .NET, tlbimp.exe is run automatically. To illustrate running this utility at the command line, begin by navigating to the location of the COM binary from a Command Prompt window. Next, specify the name of the COM server and the name of the resulting RCW assembly (using the /out: flag). Here is the command:

```
tlbimp SimpleVB6ComServer.dll /out: CalcInteropAsm.dll
```

At this point, you can open the generated assembly using ILDasm.exe (see Figure 13-10). The details of what the underlying IL actually boils down to are discussed later in this chapter. For the time being, just notice that the [default] _VBCalc interface as well as the VBCalc coclass have each been mapped as .NET equivalents.

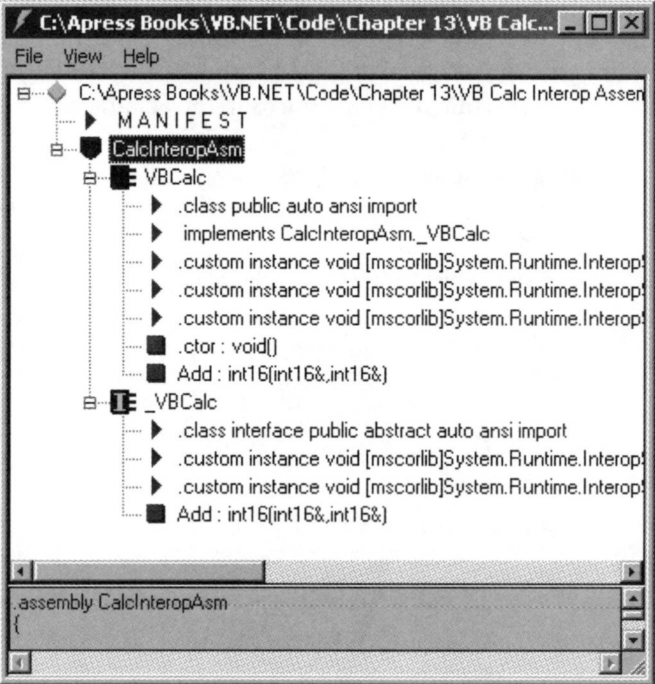

Figure 13-10. Types in the generated assembly

Early Binding to the CoCalc COM Class

Given that you have added a direct reference to the generated interop assembly, you can manipulate the VBCalc using "early binding." As you have already created an early bound VB .NET client application earlier in this chapter, let's build a C# client name CSharpCalcClient (just for kicks). Assume you have created a brand-new C# Console application, and set a reference to the generated interop assembly (or simply make use of the Add Reference dialog box). In the following code, notice that as far as the .NET client is concerned, VBCalc is nothing more than a .NET type contained in a valid assembly. In reality, the RCW is intercepting calls and forwarding them to the registered COM class (note the use of the C# "ref" keyword, which is analogous to ByRef):

```
namespace CSharpCalcClient
{
    using System;
    // You need to reference the namespace containing the proxy.
    using CalcInteropAsm;
    public class CalcClient
    {
        public static int Main(string[] args)
        {
            // Make the VB 6.0 calc!
            VBCalc c = new VBCalc();
            // Add some numbers!
            short x = 30, y = 99;
            Console.WriteLine("30 + 99 is: " + c.Add(ref x,  ref y));
            return 0;
        }
    }
}
```

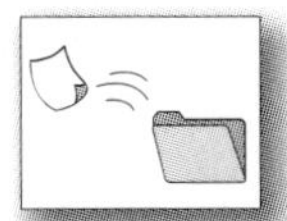

SOURCE CODE *The CSharpCalcClient project is included under the Chapter 13 subdirectory.*

Late Binding to the CoCalc Coclass

As you recall from Chapter 8, the System.Reflection namespace provides a way for you to programmatically inspect the types contained in a given assembly at runtime. In COM, the same sort of functionality is supported through the use of a set of standard interfaces (e.g., ITypeLib, ITypeInfo, and so on). When a client binds to a member at runtime (rather than compile time), the client is said to exercise "late" binding.

By and large, you should always prefer the early binding technique just examined. There are times, however, when you must use late binding to a coclass. For example, some legacy COM servers may have been constructed in such a way that they provide no type information whatsoever. If this is the case, it should be clear that you cannot run the tlbimp.exe utility in the first place. For these rare occurrences, you can access classic COM types using .NET reflection services.

The process of late binding begins with a client obtaining the IDispatch interface from a given coclass. This standard COM interface defines a total of four methods, only two of which you need to concern yourself with at the moment. First, you have GetIDsOfNames(). This method allows a late bound client to obtain the numerical value (called the DISPID) used to identify the method it is attempting to invoke.

In COM IDL, a member's DISPID is assigned using the [id] attribute. If you examine the IDL code generated by Visual Basic (using the OLE/COM Object Viewer), you will see that the DISPID of the Add() method has been assigned a DISPID such as the following:

```
[id(0x60030000)]
HRESULT Add( [in] short x, [in] short y, [out, retval] short* );
```

This is the value that GetIDsOfNames() returns to the late bound client. Once the client obtains this value, it makes a call to the next method of interest, Invoke(). This method of IDispatch takes a number of arguments, one of which is the DISPID obtained using GetIDsOfNames().

In addition, the Invoke() method takes an array of COM VARIANT types that represent the parameters passed to the function. In the case of the Add() method, this array contains two shorts (of some value). The final argument of Invoke() is another VARIANT that holds the return value of the method invocation (again, a short).

Although a .NET client using late binding does not directly use the IDispatch interface, the same general functionality comes through using the System.Reflection namespace. To illustrate, the following is another VB .NET client that uses late binding to trigger the Add() logic. Notice that this application does *not* make reference to the assembly in any way and therefore does not require the use of the tlbimp.exe utility.

```
Imports System.Reflection
Module Module1
    Sub Main()
        ' First get IDispatch reference from coclass.
        Dim calcObj As Type = _
```

```
            Type.GetTypeFromProgID("SimpleVB6COMServer.VBCalc")
        Dim calcDisp As Object = Activator.CreateInstance(calcObj)
        ' Make the array of args.
        Dim addArgs() As Object = {100, 24}
        ' Invoke the Add() method and obtain summation.
        Dim sum As Object
        sum = calcObj.InvokeMember("Add", BindingFlags.InvokeMethod, _
                                    Nothing, calcDisp, addArgs)
        ' Display result.
        Console.WriteLine("Late bound adding: 100 + 24 is: {0}", sum)
    End Sub
End Module
```

SOURCE CODE *The VbNetLateBoundCalcClient application is included under the Chapter 13 subdirectory.*

Examining the Generated Assembly Manifest

Now that you understand how to activate a COM type from managed code, let's take a look at some specific details. To begin, load the interop assembly into ILDasm.exe and open the manifest. Like in any assembly, you first notice an external reference to mscorlib.dll (the core .NET class library) followed by the necessary version information. The real gems of information appear as a number of .NET attributes. When you examine the manifest, you find use of the GuidAttribute and ImportedFromTypeLibAttribute types:

```
.assembly CalcInteropAsm
{
  .custom instance void [mscorlib]
  System.Runtime.InteropServices.GuidAttribute::.ctor(string) . . .
  .custom instance void [mscorlib]
  System.Runtime.InteropServices.ImportedFromTypeLibAttribute::.ctor(string) . . .
  .hash algorithm 0x00008004
  .ver 1:0:0:0
}
```

The value contained in the GuidAttribute is the GUID Visual Basic assigned to the type library (LIBID). If you open the OLE/COM Object Viewer and examine the assigned LIBID, you find an exact match (see Figure 13-11).

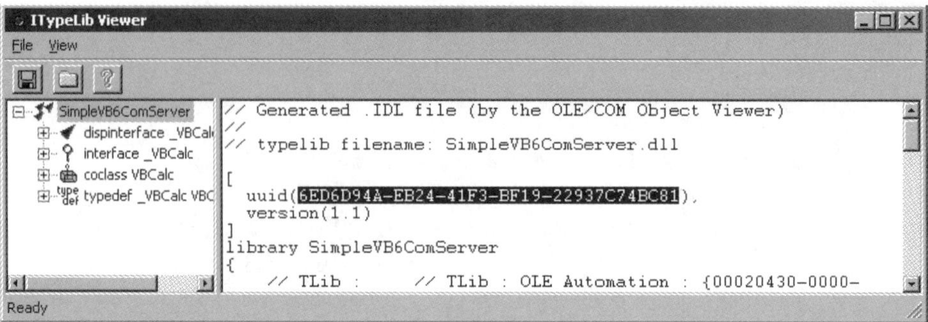

Figure 13-11. Verifying the GUID

The value assigned to ImportedFromTypeLibAttribute holds the string name of the source of the type information (in this case, SimpleVB6ComServer).

Examining the Generated Class Type

Next you have the VBCalc class type itself. In addition to the Add() method, the VBCalc has been supplied with a freebie default constructor. This should make sense, given that the RCW is attempting to expose the raw coclass as a .NET type, and thus you need a constructor to activate it. Also, if you examine the definition of the VBCalc type using ILDasm.exe, you see various IL instructions marking the VBCalc's base class (System.Object) and implemented interfaces (the default _VBCalc), as follows:

```
.class public auto ansi import VBCalc
       extends [mscorlib]System.Object
       implements CalcInteropAsm._VBCalc
{
...
} // end of class VBCalc
```

To further solidify the COM to .NET type conversion, here is an updated Main() method that interrogates your COM type using members of System.Object and System.Type:

```
Module Module1
    Sub Main()
        Dim comObj As New VBCalc()
        Console.WriteLine("COM server says 10 + 832 is {0}", _
          comObj.Add(10, 832))
        ' Extract out some type info.
        Dim t As Type = comObj.GetType()
```

```
        Console.WriteLine("-> COM class? : {0}", t.IsCOMObject)
        Console.WriteLine("-> Full name? : {0}", t.FullName)
        Console.WriteLine("-> CLSID? : {0}", t.GUID.ToString())
    End Sub
End Module
```

Figure 13-12 shows the output.

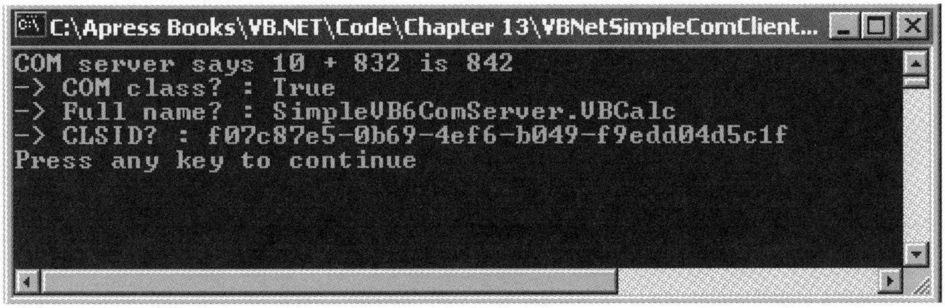

Figure 13-12. Interrogating your COM type

Building a More Interesting VB 6.0 COM Server

So much of Math 101. It's time to build a more exotic VB 6.0 ActiveX server that makes use of more elaborate COM techniques. Create a brand-new ActiveX DLL workspace named Vb6ComCarServer. Rename your initial class CoCar, and add the following members to the default public interface. Note that you are making use of a COM enumeration that contains the make of the automobile, and you have defined a single COM event named BlewUp.

```
Option Explicit
' COM enum.
Enum CarType
    Viper
    Colt
    BMW
End Enum
' Events.
Public Event BlewUp()
' Member variables.
Private currSp As Integer
Private maxSp As Integer
Private Make As CarType
' *****Default Interface! *****'
```

```
Public Property Get CurrentSpeed() As Integer
    CurrentSpeed = currSp
End Property
Public Property Get CarMake() As CarType
    CarMake = Make
End Property
Public Sub SpeedUp()
    currSp = currSp + 10
    If currSp >= maxSp Then
        RaiseEvent BlewUp   ' Fire event If you max out the engine.
    End If
End Sub
Private Sub Class_Initialize()
        MsgBox "Init COM car"
End Sub
Public Sub Create(max As Integer, cur As Integer, t As CarType)
    maxSp = max
    currSp = cur
    Make = t
End Sub
```

Supporting an Additional COM Interface

Now that you have fleshed out the details of building a COM class with a single [default] interface, insert a new *.cls file that defines the following IDriverInfo interface:

```
Option Explicit
' Driver has a name
Public Property Let driverName(s As String)
End Property
Public Property Get driverName() As String
End Property
```

If you have created COM objects supporting multiple interfaces, you are aware that VB 6.0 provides the *Implements* keyword. Once you specify the interfaces implemented by a given COM class, you are able to make use of the VB 6.0 code window to build the method stubs. Assume you have added a Private String variable (driverName) to the CoCar class type and implemented the IDriverInfo interface as follows:

```
' Implemented interfaces
' [General][Declarations]
```

```
Implements IDriverInfo
. . .
' ***** IDriverInfo impl ***** '
Private Property Let IDriverInfo_driverName(RHS As String)
    driverName = RHS
End Property
Private Property Get IDriverInfo_driverName() As String
    IDriverInfo_driverName = driverName
End Property
```

To wrap up this interface implementation, set the Instancing property of IDriverInfo to PublicNotCreatable (given that the outside world should not be able to "New" an interface reference).

Exposing an Inner Object

Under VB 6.0 (as well as COM itself), you do not have the luxury of classic implementation inheritance. Rather, you are limited to the use of the containment/delegation model (the has-a relationship). To test how this sort of design is represented in terms of .NET, add a final *.cls file to your current VB 6.0 ActiveX project named CoEngine, and set its instancing property to PublicNotCreatable (as you want to prevent the user from directly creating an engine).

The default public interface of CoEngine is short and sweet. Define a single function that returns an array of strings to the outside world representing pet names for each cylinder of the engine (okay, no right-minded person gives friendly names to his or her cylinders, but hey . . .):

```
Option Explicit
Public Function GetCylinders() As String()
    Dim c(3) As String
    c(0) = "Grimey"
    c(1) = "Thumper"
    c(2) = "Oily"
    c(3) = "Crusher"
    GetCylinders = c
End Function
```

Finally, add a method to the default interface of CoCar named GetEngine(), which returns an instance of the contained CoEngine (I assume you will create a Private member variable of type CoEngine for this purpose):

```
' Return the CoEngine to the world.
Public Function GetEngine() As CoEngine
```

```
    Set GetEngine = eng
End Function
```

At this point you have an ActiveX server that contains a COM class supporting two interfaces. As well, you are able to return an internal COM type using the [default] interface of the CoCar and interact with some common programming constructs (Enums and COM arrays). Go ahead and compile your sever (setting binary compatibility, of course), and then close down your current workspace.

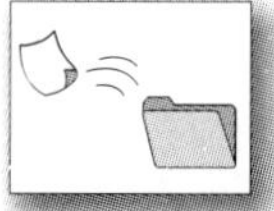

SOURCE CODE *The Vb6ComCarServer project is included under the Chapter 13 subdirectory.*

Examining the Interop Assembly

Using VS .NET, create a brand-new VB .NET Windows Application project workspace and set a reference to the Vb6ComCarServer.dll. Now, load this assembly into ILDasm.exe and examine the generated types, as shown in Figure 13-13. As you see, the CarType, CoCar, and CoEngine COM types have all been mapped to .NET equivalents (the remaining types will be examined soon).

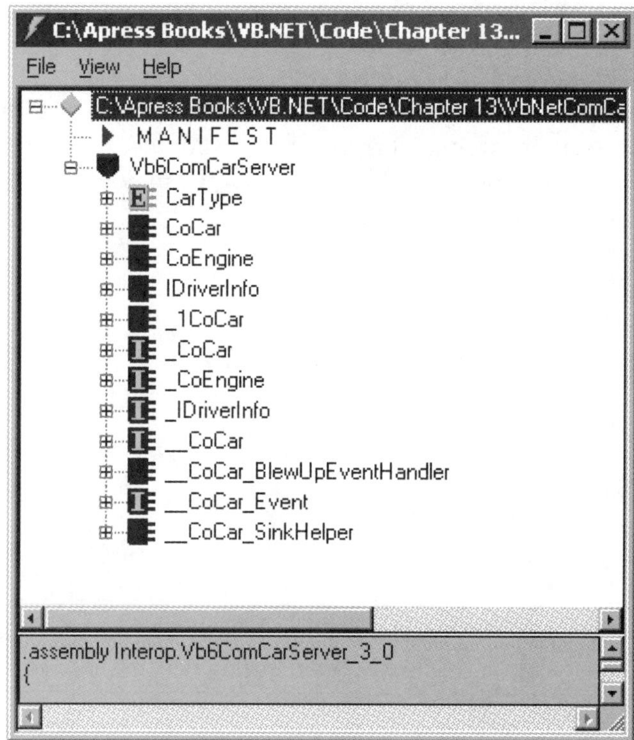

Figure 13-13. The managed types

COM Interface Conversion

When a COM interface is represented as a .NET type, it is qualified using various attributes from the System.Runtime.InteropServices namespace. First is the GuidAttribute type, which is used in this case to document the interface's IID, as specified by the [uuid] attribute in the IDL file.

Next is the InterfaceTypeAttribute type, which is used to catalog how the interface was originally defined in IDL syntax (custom, dual, or dispinterface). This attribute can be assigned any value from the ComInterfaceType enumeration, as Table 13-4 describes.

Table 13-4. COM Interface Types

COMINTERFACETYPE MEMBER NAME	MEANING IN LIFE
InterfaceIsDual	Indicates that the interface should be exposed to COM as a dual interface
InterfaceIsIDispatch	Indicates that an interface should be exposed as a dispinterface
InterfaceIsIUnknown	Indicates that an interface should be exposed as an IUnknown-derived interface, as opposed to a dispinterface or a dual interface Oddly enough, if the proxy is representing a dual interface (as in this case), this attribute is omitted. Instead, dual interfaces are marked using the TypeLibTypeAttribute, which is used to document various aspects of the [dual] interface.

Coclass (and COM Properties) Conversions

As illustrated by the previous VB COM server example, when the assembly is generated using the tlbimp.exe utility, you receive .NET types for each stand-alone interface as well as the coclass itself. Thus, you can exercise a new CoCar type using two approaches. First, you can create a direct instance of the coclass that provides access to each interface member, as shown here:

```
' Here, you are really working with the [default] interface.
Dim viper as CoCar = New CoCar()
viper.SpeedUp(30)
```

Given that CoCar now supports two custom interfaces, you might wonder exactly how this is represented in terms of managed code. As you might suspect, the managed class supports each member defined by the supported interfaces. In other words, if you now create an instance of CoCar, you can call SpeedUp(), GetCurrentSpeed(), GetEngine(), and GetCarType(), as well as manipulate the DriverName property, as shown here:

```
' Notice you can get access to the property defined by IDriverInfo
' directly from the supporting coclass.
CoCar viper as CoCar = New CoCar()
viper.DriverName = "Fred"
Console.WriteLine(viper.DriverName)
```

If you examine the CoCar type using ILDasm.exe, you may be surprised to find that the CoCar type does not directly define these members. If you examine the situation a bit more closely, however, you notice that CoCar derives from a generated type named _1CoCar. This intermediate type defines the members of the default _CoCar and IDriverInfo interfaces.

```
.class public auto ansi import _1CoCar
       extends [mscorlib]System.Object
       implements Vb6ComCarServer._CoCar,
                  Vb6ComCarServer._IDriverInfo
{   ...
}
```

COM Enumeration Conversions

COM enumerations are mapped to managed types deriving from System.Enum. Therefore, you can use any of the (very helpful) supported members. For example:

```
Private Sub btnIDCar_Click(ByVal sender As System.Object, _
ByVal e As System.EventArgs) Handles btnIDCar.Click
    Dim en As [Enum]
    en = comCar.CarMake
    MessageBox.Show(en.ToString())
End Sub
```

Working with the COM Arrays

Next, you examine how the COM array is represented as managed code. As you recall, the CoEngine supports a single method named GetCylinders(), which returns an array of COM strings (BSTRs). The outside world accesses the default interface of CoEngine by calling the GetEngine() method of an existing CoCar (see Figure 13-14 for output).

```
Private Sub btnGetCyl_Click(ByVal sender As System.Object, _
ByVal e As System.EventArgs) Handles btnGetCyl.Click
    ' Declare a variable of type _CoEngine.
    Dim eng As Vb6ComCarServer._CoEngine
    ' Get the engine!
    eng = comCar.GetEngine()
    ' Get the array of strings.
    Dim c As Array = eng.GetCylinders()
    Dim i As Integer
    ' List each string.
    For i = 0 To UBound(c)
        lstCylinders.Items.Add(c.GetValue(i).ToString())
    Next
End Sub
```

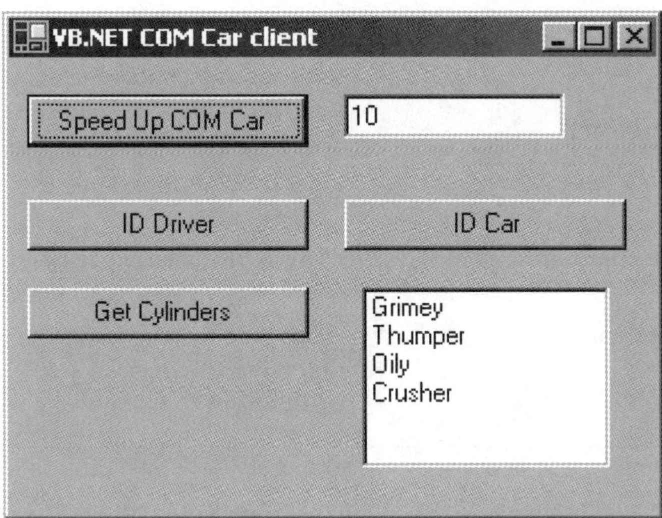

Figure 13-14. Iterating over your COM array

The next point of interest is to look at the process of hooking into the CoCar's Exploded event.

Intercepting COM Events

In Chapter 5 you learned about the .NET event model. Recall that this architecture is based on delegating the flow of logic from one part of the application to another. The entity in charge of forwarding a request is a type deriving from System.MulticastDelegate.

When the tlbimp.exe utility encounters event definitions in the COM server's type library, it responds by creating a number of managed types that wrap the low-level COM connection point architecture. Using these types, you can pretend to add a member to a System.MulticastDelegate's internal linked list. Under the hood, of course, the proxy is mapping the incoming COM event to their managed equivalents.

Table 13-5 briefly describes these types.

Table 13-5. COM Event Helper Types

GENERATED TYPE	MEANING IN LIFE
__ICoCarEvents	This is the managed definition for the outbound interface. It is generally not directly used.
__ICoCar_Event	This is a managed interface that defines the add and remove members used to add (or remove) a method to (or from) the System.MulticastDelegate's linked list. This type is also not generally used directly.
__ICoCar_BlewUpEventHandler	This is the managed delegate (which derives from System.MulticastDelegate).
__ICoCar_SinkHelper	This generated class implements the outbound interface in a .NET-aware sink object.

As you would hope, the VB .NET language does not require you to make direct use of these types. Rather, you are able to handle the incoming COM events in the same way you handle events based on the .NET delegation architecture. Simply declare the COM type WithEvents, and use the Handles keyword to map the event to a given method.

```
Public Class Form1
    Inherits System.Windows.Forms.Form
```

```
    ' The COM type.
    Private WithEvents comCar As New Vb6ComCarServer.CoCar()
. . .
    Public Sub CarIsDead() Handles comCar.BlewUp
        MessageBox.Show("Sorry, COM car is dead. . .")
    End Sub
End Class
```

The Complete VB .NET Client

Now that you have seen how each COM atom is expressed in the terms of .NET, here is the complete VB .NET client code that uses the generated interop assembly:

```
Public Class Form1
    Inherits System.Windows.Forms.Form
    ' member variables.
    Private WithEvents comCar As New Vb6ComCarServer.CoCar()
    Friend WithEvents btnSpeedUp As System.Windows.Forms.Button
    Friend WithEvents txtCurSp As System.Windows.Forms.TextBox
    Friend WithEvents btnGetDriverName As System.Windows.Forms.Button
    Friend WithEvents btnGetCyl As System.Windows.Forms.Button
    Friend WithEvents btnIDCar As System.Windows.Forms.Button
    Friend WithEvents lstCylinders As System.Windows.Forms.ListBox
    Private itfDriverInfo As Vb6ComCarServer.IDriverInfo
    . . . ' InitializeComponent() removed. . .

    Public Sub CarIsDead() Handles comCar.BlewUp
        MessageBox.Show("Sorry, COM car is dead. . .")
    End Sub
    Private Sub btnSpeedUp_Click(ByVal sender As System.Object, _
    ByVal e As System.EventArgs) Handles btnSpeedUp.Click
        comCar.SpeedUp()
        txtCurSp.Text = comCar.CurrentSpeed.ToString()
    End Sub
    Private Sub btnGetDriverName_Click(ByVal sender As System.Object, _
    ByVal e As System.EventArgs) Handles btnGetDriverName.Click
        MessageBox.Show(comCar.driverName)
    End Sub
    Private Sub btnGetCyl_Click(ByVal sender As System.Object, _
    ByVal e As System.EventArgs) Handles btnGetCyl.Click
        Dim eng As Vb6ComCarServer._CoEngine
```

```
        eng = comCar.GetEngine()
        Dim c As Array = eng.GetCylinders()
        Dim i As Integer
        For i = 0 To UBound(c)
            lstCylinders.Items.Add(c.GetValue(i).ToString())
        Next
    End Sub
    Private Sub btnIDCar_Click(ByVal sender As System.Object, _
    ByVal e As System.EventArgs) Handles btnIDCar.Click
        Dim en As [Enum]
        en = comCar.CarMake
        MessageBox.Show(en.ToString())
    End Sub
End Class
```

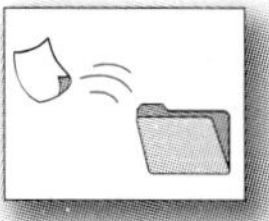

SOURCE CODE *The VbNetComCarClient project is included under the Chapter 13 subdirectory.*

Understanding COM to .NET Interoperability

The next topic of this chapter is the logically opposite interoperability scenario of what you just examined: a COM class calling a .NET type. As you might imagine, this situation is less likely to occur than .NET to COM communications, but it is still worth exploring.

For a COM class to use a .NET type, you need to fool the coclass into believing that the managed type is in fact *unmanaged*. In essence, you need to allow the coclass to interact with the type using the functionality provided by the COM architecture. For example, the COM type should be able to obtain new interfaces through QueryInterface() calls, simulate unmanaged memory management using AddRef() and Release(), make use of the COM connection point protocol, and so on.

Beyond fooling the COM client, COM to .NET interoperability also involves fooling the COM runtime. As you know, a classic COM server is activated using the COM runtime. For this to happen, the runtime must look up numerous bits of information in the system registry (ProgIDs, CLSIDs, IIDs, and so forth). The problem, of course, is that .NET assemblies are not registered (at all).

In a nutshell, to make your .NET assemblies available to classic COM clients, you must take the following steps:

1. Register your .NET assembly into the system registry to allow the COM SCM to locate it.

2. Generate a COM type library (*.tlb) file (based on the .NET metadata) to allow the COM client to interact with the exposed types.

3. Deploy the assembly in the same directory as the COM client or (more typically) install it into the GAC.

You examine the tool that automates these steps in just a moment. For now, you look at exactly how COM clients interact with .NET types using a CCW.

The Role of the CCW

When the COM client accesses a .NET type, the CLR uses a proxy called the COM Callable Wrapper (CCW) to negotiate the COM to .NET conversion (see Figure 13-15).

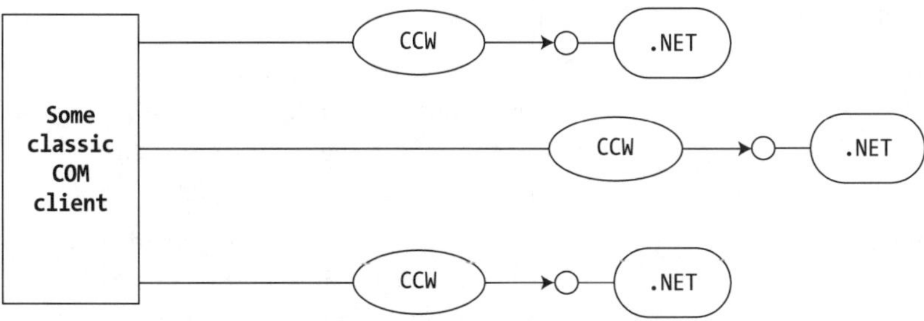

Figure 13-15. COM types talk to .NET types using a CCW.

Understand that the CCW is a reference-counted entity. This should make sense, given that the COM client is assuming that the CCW is a real COM type and thus must abide by the rules of AddRef() and Release(). When the COM client has issued the final release, the CCW releases its reference to the real .NET type, at which point it is ready to be garbage collected.

The CCW implements a number of COM interfaces automatically to further the illusion that the proxy represents a genuine coclass. In addition to the set of custom interfaces defined by the .NET type (including an entity named the class interface that you examine in just a moment), the CCW provides support for the standard COM behaviors described in Table 13-6.

Table 13-6. The CCW Supports Many Core COM Interfaces

CCW-IMPLEMENTED INTERFACE	MEANING IN LIFE
IConnectionPointContainer IConnectionPoint	If the .NET type supports any events, they are represented as COM connection points.
IEnumVariant	If the .NET type supports the IEnumerable interface, it appears to the COM client as a standard COM enumerator.
ISupportErrorInfo IErrorInfo	These interfaces allow coclasses to send COM error objects.
ITypeInfo IProvideClassInfo	These interfaces allow the COM client to pretend to manipulate an assembly's COM type information. In reality, the COM client is interacting with .NET metadata.
IUnknown IDispatch IDispatchEx	These core COM interfaces provide support for early and late binding to the .NET type. IDispatchEx can be supported by the CCW if the .NET type implements the IExpando interface.

Understanding the "Class Interface"

In classic COM, the only way a COM client can communicate with a COM object is to use an interface reference. In contrast, .NET types do not need to support any interfaces. It is possible to build a complete solution using nothing but object references. However, given that classic COM clients cannot work with object references, another responsibility of the CCW is to support a class interface to represent each property, method, field, and event defined by the type's public sector. As you can see, the CCW is taking the same approach as Visual Basic 6.0.

Defining a Class Interface

The ClassInterface attribute is an optional but very important type. By default, any method defined on a .NET class is exposed to COM as a raw dispinterface (i.e., a given implementation of IDispatch). Thus, all COM clients that want to use class-level methods must exercise late binding to manipulate your .NET types. To alter this default behavior, use the ClassInterfaceAttribute type, which can be assigned any value of the ClassInterfaceType enumeration (see Table 13-7).

Table 13-7. Values of the ClassInterfaceType Enumeration

CLASSINTERFACETYPE MEMBER NAME	MEANING IN LIFE
AutoDispatch	Indicates that a dispatch-only interface be generated for the class
AutoDual	Indicates that a dual interface be generated for the class
None	Indicates that no interface be generated for the class

In the next example, you specify ClassInterfaceType.AutoDual as the class interface designation. In this way, late binding clients such as VBScript can access the Add() and Subtract() methods using IDispatch, while early bound clients (such as VB proper and C++) can use the class interface (named _VbDotNetCalc). Like in VB 6.0, the name of your class interface is always based on your type name and prefixed with an underscore.

Building Your .NET Type

To illustrate a COM type communicating with managed code, assume you have created a simple VB .NET Class Library that defines a single class named VbDotNetCalc, which supports two methods named Add() and Subtract(). Also, assume you have defined (and implemented) another interface named IAdvancedMath to allow multiplication and division. The logic behind the class is simple; however, notice the use of the ClassInterface attribute, as shown here:

```
Imports System.Runtime.InteropServices
Public Interface IAdvancedMath
    Function Multiply(ByVal x As Integer, ByVal y As Integer) As Integer
    Function Divide(ByVal x As Integer, ByVal y As Integer) As Integer
```

```
End Interface
<ClassInterface(ClassInterfaceType.AutoDual)> _
Public Class VbNetCalc
    Implements IAdvancedMath
    Public Function Add(ByVal x As Integer, ByVal y As Integer)
        Return x + y
    End Function
    Public Function Subtract(ByVal x As Integer, ByVal y As Integer)
        Return x - y
    End Function
    ' ***** IAdvancedMath Impl ***** '
    Public Function Multiple(ByVal x As Integer, _
     ByVal y As Integer) As Integer Implements IAdvancedMath.Multiply
        Return x * y
    End Function
    Public Function Divide(ByVal x As Integer, _
     ByVal y As Integer) As Integer Implements IAdvancedMath.Divide
        If (y = 0) Then
            ' Intercepted as COM error object.
            Throw New DivideByZeroException()
        End If
        Return x / y
    End Function
End Class
```

On a related note, open up your assemblyInfo.vb file. As you can see, all VS .NET project workspaces are provided with a GUID attribute used to identify the TypeLib of this .NET server (if exposed to COM).

```
'The following GUID is for the ID of the typelib if this project is exposed to
' COM
<Assembly: Guid("EB268C4F-EB36-464C-8A25-93212C00DC89")>
```

Finally, before you build the project, generate an *.snk file to establish a strong name for your .NET code library (see Figure 13-16).

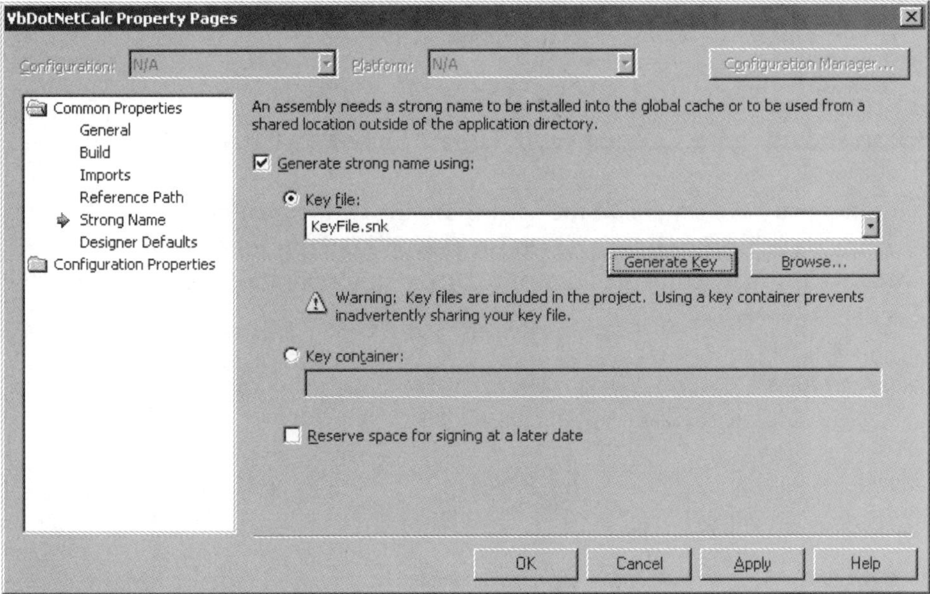

Figure 13-16. Generating a strong name

Once you have compiled your project, install VbDotNetCalc.dll into the GAC.

Generating the Type Library and Registering the .NET Types

Once you compile the project, you have two approaches you can take to generate the type information and register the assembly in the system registry. Your first approach is to use the regasm.exe utility shipped with the .NET SDK. The default functionality of this tool is to enter the necessary COM registration "goo" into the system to allow the COM SCM to locate and load the assembly on behalf of the COM client. However, if you specify the /tlb flag, this tool also generates the required type library, as shown here:

```
regasm VbDotNetCalc.dll /tlb:VbDotNetCalc.tlb
```

As an alternative, you can use regasm.exe to register the correct information in the system registry and generate the type information using a separate tool named tlbexp.exe. (See online Help for command-line options.) In either case, the end result is that your .NET assembly has been configured in the system registry, and you have a COM type library that describes its contents.

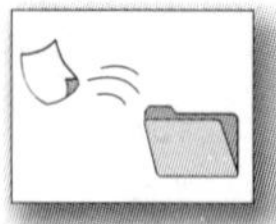

SOURCE CODE *The VbDotNetCalc application and VbDotNetCalc.tlb file are included under the Chapter 13 subdirectory.*

Examining the Exported Type Information

Now that you have generated the corresponding COM type library, you can view its contents using the OLE/COM Object Viewer by simply loading the *tlb file. From there, you will find the following IDL definition for the VbNetCalc class interface (_VbNetCalc):

```
[odl, uuid(60BA5D79-80B7-3116-918A-E1A27367FEAF),
  hidden, dual, nonextensible, oleautomation,
  custom(
    {0F21F359-AB84-41E8-9A78-36D110E6D2F9},
    "VbDotNetCalc.VbNetCalc") ]
interface _VbNetCalc : IDispatch {
    [id(00000000), propget]
    HRESULT ToString([out, retval] BSTR* pRetVal);
    [id(0x60020001)]
    HRESULT Equals(  [in] VARIANT obj,
                     [out, retval] VARIANT_BOOL* pRetVal);
    [id(0x60020002)]
    HRESULT GetHashCode([out, retval] long* pRetVal);
    [id(0x60020003)]
    HRESULT GetType([out, retval] _Type** pRetVal);
    [id(0x60020004)]
    HRESULT Multiple( [in] long x,  [in] long y,  [out, retval] long* pRetVal);
    [id(0x60020005)]
    HRESULT Divide( [in] long x,  [in] long y,  [out, retval] long* pRetVal);
    [id(0x60020006)]
    HRESULT Add( [in] long x,  [in] long y,  [out, retval] VARIANT* pRetVal);
    [id(0x60020007)]
    HRESULT Subtract( [in] long x,  [in] long y,
    [out, retval] VARIANT* pRetVal);
};
```

As specified by the ClassInterface attribute, the [default] has been configured as a [dual]. (Notice that the members have been assigned automatic DISPIDs.) As you can see, the class interface also has explicit listings for the members of System.Object. (More on this in just a bit.)

The generated type library also contains an IDL definition of the IAdvancedMath interface, as shown here:

```
interface IAdvancedMath : IDispatch
{
     [id(0x60020000)] HRESULT Multiple( [in] long x,  [in] long y,
                                        [out, retval] long* pRetVal);

     [id(0x60020001)] HRESULT Divide( [in] long x, [in] long y,
                                      [out, retval] long* pRetVal);
};
```

If you had not used explicit interface inheritance, you would still have a stand-alone definition for IAdvancedMath. However, you would also find that the default class interface would be populated with the Multiply() and Divide() members.

The _Object Interface

The generated IDL contains an interface named _Object. This interface is the unmanaged representation of System.Object. Thus, COM types that consume .NET types can use the core members of this supreme base class. Here is the definition:

```
[ uuid(98417C7D-32E8-3FA0-A54B-0F0B2EFBE91F), hidden, dual,
  nonextensible, custom({0F21F359-AB84-41E8-9A78-36D110E6D2F9},
 "System.Object")]
dispinterface _Object
{
     properties:
     methods:
     [id(00000000), propget] BSTR ToString();
     [id(0x60020001)] VARIANT_BOOL Equals([in] VARIANT obj);
     [id(0x60020002)] long GetHashCode();
     [id(0x60020003)] _Type* GetType();
};
```

The IDL coclass definition automatically adds support for this interface type, as shown here:

```
coclass VbNetCalc {
    [default] interface _VbNetCalc;
    interface _Object;
    interface IAdvancedMath;
};
```

You see the _Object interface in action soon.

The Generated Library Statement

The final point of interest regarding the generated type information is the configuration of the library statement. In classic COM, the library statement is used to represent every IDL type that should be placed in the binary *.tlb file. This file is nothing more than a binary equivalent of the underlying IDL and is the key to COM's language independence (and it plays a major role in marshaling types between boundaries). The rules used by tlbexp.exe are simple. .NET namespaces are populated based on the COM library statement.

You have already seen the definitions of the .NET types (class interface, IAdvancedMath, coclass, and so on). However, it is interesting to note that in addition to the import of the standard OLE type information, your library statement also imports type information that describes mscorlib.dll (the core .NET base class library assembly), as shown here:

```
[ uuid(5C202075-222E-30A4-BF50-4EFC20DDCD27), version(1.0) ]
library VbDotNetCalc           // Based on namespace name.
{
     // TLib: {BED7F4EA-1A96-11D2-8F08-00A0C9A6186D}
     importlib("mscorlib.tlb");
     . . .
}
```

Viewing the Type Using the OLE/COM Object Viewer

COM supports the idea of component categories. Ultimately, a COM category is a GUID (termed a CATID) that identifies a collection of related coclasses. The OLE/COM Object Viewer allows you to browse the registered CATIDs on your machine from a friendly GUI Tree View control. One new category that has been added given the advent of the CLR is the .NET Category, as shown in Figure 13-17.

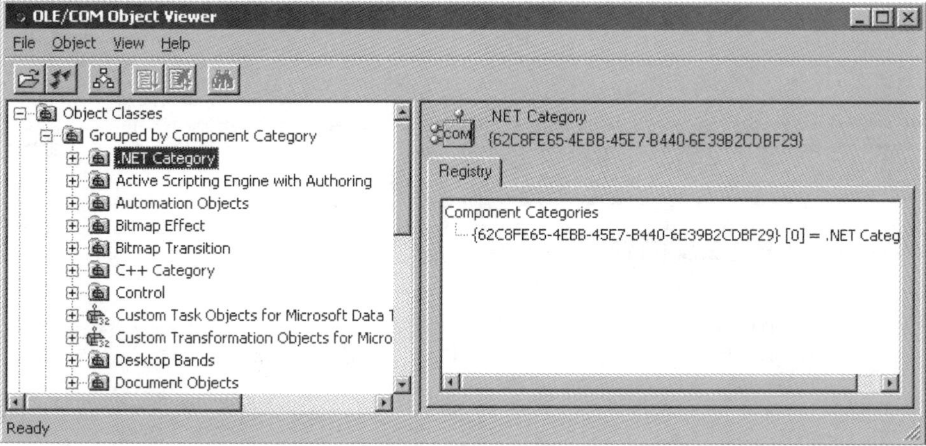

Figure 13-17. All registered assemblies gain membership to the .NET Category.

If you search for the ProgID of your VbDotNetCalc assembly, you are able to examine the interfaces supported by the proxy (see Figure 13-18). Be aware that if your interop assembly has not been installed into the GAC, you are not able to view the interfaces behind your types (unless you place a copy of the assembly into the same folder containing oleview.exe).

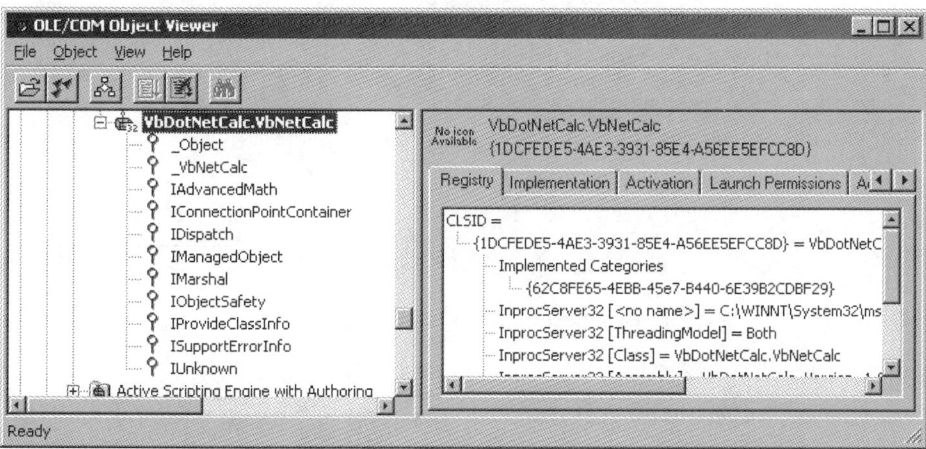

Figure 13-18. Interfaces implemented by the CCW

Examining the Registration Entries

The final details to examine before you can use your assembly from a COM client are the registration entries installed by the regasm.exe utility. First and foremost, you receive the mandatory ProgID for each coclass defined in the assembly (see Figure 13-19).

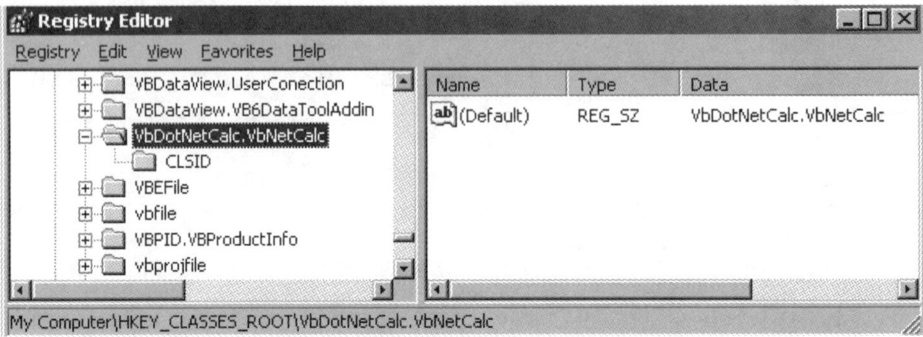

Figure 13-19. The registered ProgID

From the ProgID, you can navigate to the next item of interest, the CLSID (see Figure 13-20).

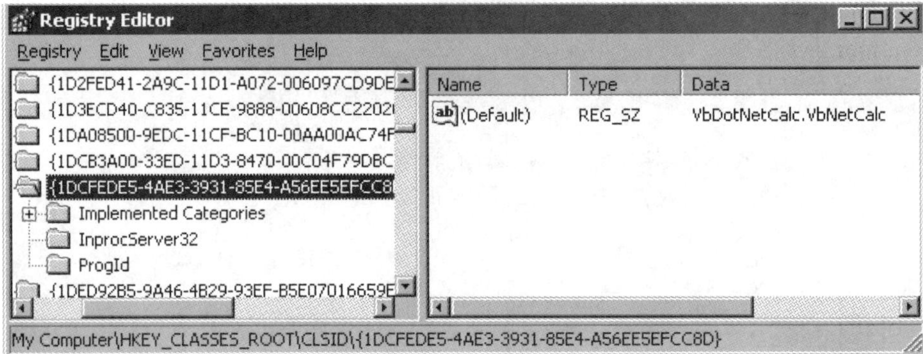

Figure 13-20. The registered CLSID

When a COM client makes an activation request to the runtime, it responds by consulting HKCR\CLSID to resolve the location of the registered server. The most important subdirectory for your current purpose is InprocServer32, which holds the path to the binary to be loaded for the client. However, you don't find a listing for the DotNetClassLib.dll (as a result of the fact that it is not a COM server). Rather, you find the path points to the CLR execution engine (see Figure 13-21).

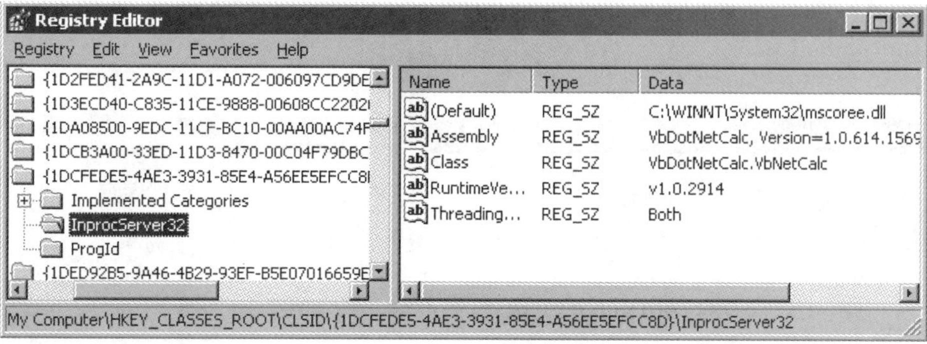

Figure 13-21. InprocServer32 points to the .NET execution engine.

Also listed under the InprocServer32 subdirectory is a new entry named Assembly. This value holds the fully quantified name of the assembly (see Figure 13-22).

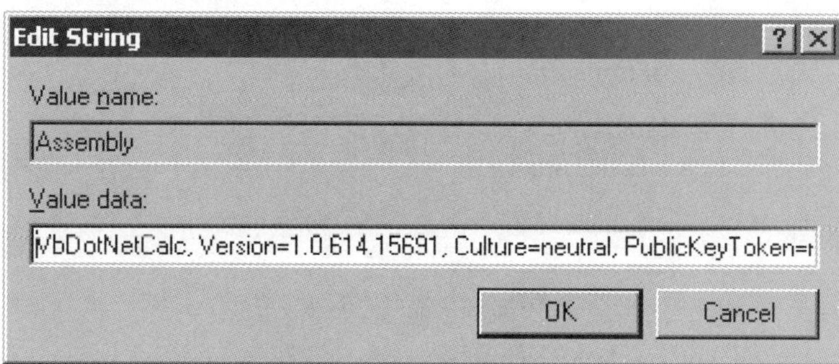

Figure 13-22. The value of the assembly entry

Of course, there are other entries made by regasm.exe. For example, given that .NET types always come through as IDispatch-based interfaces, each interface is configured to use oleaut32.dll. The type information itself is registered under HKCR\TypeLib. The end result is that as far as the COM SCM is concerned, it can load and manipulate the contents of the .NET assembly. Under the hood, the CLR execution engine loads the assembly from the GAC, constructs the CCW, and takes over the show.

Building a Visual Basic 6.0 Test Client

Now that the .NET assembly has been properly configured to interact with the COM runtime, you can build some COM clients. You can create a simple VB 6.0

Standard EXE project type and set a reference to the new generated type library (see Figure 13-23).

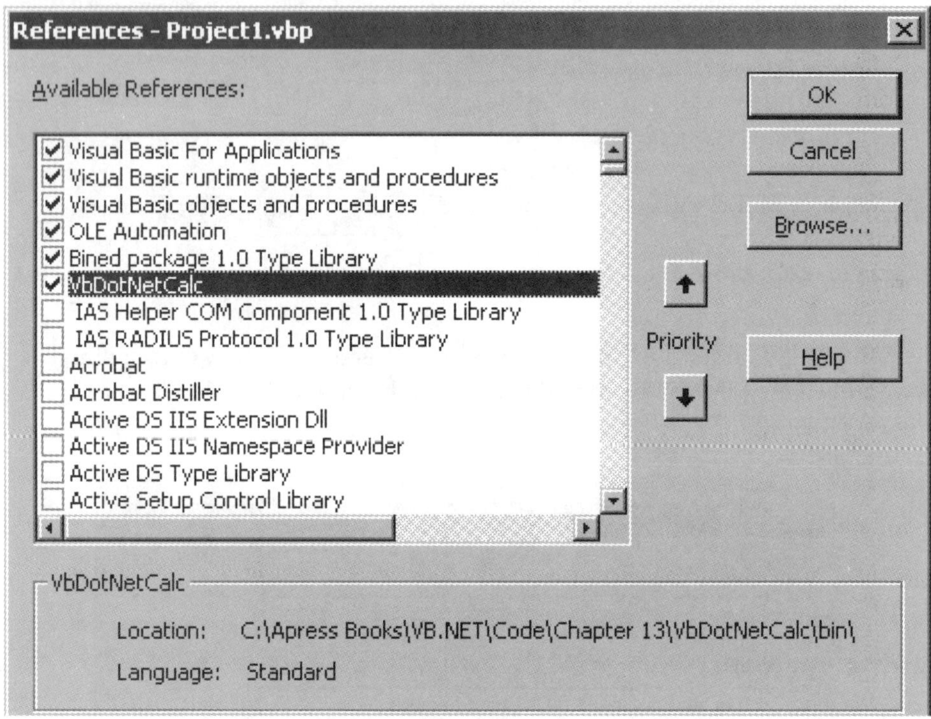

Figure 13-23. Referencing your .NET server from VB 6.0

As for the GUI front end, keep things really simple. A single Button object will be used to manipulate the .NET type. However, recall that when you created your VB .NET calculator, you configured the Divide() method of the IAdvancedMath interface to send out a DivideByZeroException under the correct circumstances. Thus, you can trap this .NET exception as a classic COM error object. Here is the code (notice that you are also using some inherited methods defined by the _Object interface):

```
Private Sub btnDoEverything_Click()
On Error GoTo OOPS:
    ' Make .NET type and add some numbers.
    Dim o As New CSharpCalc
    MsgBox o.Add(30, 30), , "Adding"
    ' Call some members of _Object.
    MsgBox o.ToString, , "To String"
    MsgBox o.GetHashCode, , "Hash code"
```

```
    Dim t As Object
    Set t = o.GetType()
    MsgBox t, , "Type"
    ' Get new interface (and trigger exception).
    Dim i As IAdvancedMath
    Set i = o
    MsgBox i.Multiply(4, 22), , "Multiply"
    MsgBox i.Divide(20, 2), , "Divide"
    MsgBox i.Divide(20, 0)  ' Throw error.
OOPS:
MsgBox Err.Description, , "Error!"      ' Print out exception.
End Sub
```

Notice that VB 6.0 does not allow you to gain access to the _Type interface returned from _Object.GetType(), as it has been marked as a [hidden] interface. The best you can do under VB 6.0 is hold it in a generic object variable (which makes things far less exciting).

SOURCE CODE *The VBDotNetClient application is included under the Chapter 13 subdirectory.*

.NET to COM Mapping Issues

Always keep in mind the fact that the Common Type System (CTS) defines a number of constructs that simply cannot be represented in classic COM. For example, VB .NET class types can support any number of constructors, overloaded operators, and overloaded methods, and can derive from each other using classical inheritance. None of these programming atoms can be understood by classic COM. Therefore, as you might imagine, some under-the-hood voodoo needs to occur when tlbexp.exe builds the COM type library.

To understand these issues, you need a test case. Assume you have a VB .NET code library that contains one base and one derived class. The base class defines some public field data, a constructor set, and a single virtual method, as shown here:

```
Imports System.Runtime.InteropServices
<ClassInterface(ClassInterfaceType.AutoDual)> _
Public Class BaseClass
    ' State data.
    Public memberVar As Integer
    Public fieldOne As String
    ' Constructors.
```

```
    Public Sub New()
    End Sub
    Public Sub New(ByVal m As Integer, ByVal f As String)
        memberVar = m
        fieldOne = f
    End Sub
    ' Virtual method.
    Public Overridable Sub VirMethod()
        Console.WriteLine("Base VirMethod impl")
    End Sub
End Class
```

The derived type overrides the virtual member and declares an overloaded method, as shown here:

```
<ClassInterface(ClassInterfaceType.AutoDual)> _
Public Class DerivedClass
    Inherits BaseClass
    ' State data.
    Public fieldTwo As Double
    ' Constructor.
    Public Sub New(ByVal m As Integer, ByVal f As String)
        MyBase.New(m, f)
    End Sub
    ' Overridden method.
    Public Overrides Sub VirMethod()
        Console.WriteLine("Derived VirMethod impl")
        MyBase.VirMethod()
    End Sub
    ' Overloaded member.
    Public Sub SomeMethod()
    End Sub
    Public Sub SomeMethod(ByVal x As Integer)
    End Sub
    Public Sub SomeMethod(ByVal x As Integer, ByVal o As Object)
    End Sub
    Public Sub SomeMethod(ByVal x As Integer, ByVal f As Double)
    End Sub
End Class
```

Go ahead and create a strong name of your new .NET class library and build the project. Once you are finished, generate a type library using regasm.exe and install the server into the GAC. Obviously, you don't really care what these methods are doing. At this point, you are only interested in how the tlbexp.exe utility maps these .NET-centric types to COM primitives.

Examining the BaseClass Type Information

First, examine the coclass definition for the managed BaseClass type (load the generated *.tlb file into the OLE/COM Object Viewer to check things out first-hand), as shown here:

```
coclass BaseClass {
    [default] interface _BaseClass;
    interface _Object;
};
```

Not too much to say here, as you already understand the concept of a class interface and the role of the _Object interface definition. The real meat is contained in the definition of the class interface itself, as shown here:

```
interface _BaseClass : IDispatch
{
     // _Object methods. . .

     [id(0x60020004)] HRESULT VirMethod();
     [id(0x60020005), propget] HRESULT fieldOne([out, retval] BSTR* pRetVal);
     [id(0x60020005), propput] HRESULT fieldOne([in] BSTR pRetVal);
};
```

Notice that Public field data is represented as a COM property. This should make sense, given that the COM client never has an object-level reference and is forced to work with a type on an interface-by-interface level. Now take a look at the derived class.

Examining the DerivedClass Type Information

Because classic COM does not support classical inheritance between types, it should be clear that tlbexp.exe is unable to model the is-a relationship between the base and derived type. However, you get the next best thing: interface implementation.

```
coclass DerivedClass {
    interface IManagedObject;
```

```
    [default] interface _DerivedClass;
    interface _BaseClass;
    interface _Object;
};
```

Notice that the derived type implements the class interface of its parent. In this way, the derived type can remain functionally equivalent to the base class type. The class interface of the DerivedClass is also of interest. Recall that the managed implementation of this type supported a single overloaded member. Given that COM does not support this syntactical construct, the tlbexp.exe tool hacked out the following solution:

```
interface _DerivedClass : IDispatch
{
     // _Object methods. . .

     // 'Inherited' methods of base type.
     [id(0x60020004)] HRESULT VirMethod();
     [id(0x60020005), propget] HRESULT fieldOne([out, retval] BSTR* pRetVal);
     [id(0x60020005), propput] HRESULT fieldOne([in] BSTR pRetVal);

     // 'Overloaded' method.
     [id(0x60020007)] HRESULT SomeMethod();
     [id(0x60020008)] HRESULT SomeMethod_2([in] long x);
     [id(0x60020009)] HRESULT SomeMethod_3([in] long x, [in] VARIANT o);
     [id(0x6002000a)] HRESULT SomeMethod_4([in] long x,  [in] single f);

     // Field data.
     [id(0x6002000b), propget] HRESULT fieldTwo([out, retval] single* pRetVal);
     [id(0x6002000b), propput] HRESULT fieldTwo([in] single pRetVal);
};
```

Here, you can see that a simple numerical suffix is used to signify overloaded methods. Although some hacking takes place when converting .NET types into COM types, the process is not all that offensive to my eyes. Other possible mappings that you may encounter include nested namespaces, abstract base classes, value types (enums and structs), and so forth. I assume you will take matters into your own hands at this point and convert some VB .NET code into a COM type library. (One very enlightening task is to send the CarLibrary.dll assembly you developed in Chapter 6 to the tlbexp.exe utility [hint, hint].)

SOURCE CODE *The NetToComIssuesServer project is included under the Chapter 13 subdirectory.*

Controlling the Generated IDL (or Influencing Tlbexp.exe)

As you have seen, when you use the tlbimp.exe utility to create a proxy, the generated metadata is automatically adorned with various attributes. When you build .NET types that you expect to be used by classic COM clients, you can also make direct use of these attributes (such as the ClassInterfaceAttribute type) in your managed code. Typically, this is done only to override the default mappings produced by the tlbexp.exe utility.

To illustrate the process of gaining some control over the generated COM type information, here is a new namespace (AttribDotNetObjects) that defines a single interface (IBasicMath) as well as a single class type (Calc). Notice that you are using various attributes to control the generated GUID of the types as well as the underlying definition of the IBasicMath interface and Add() method. In addition, notice that the Calc class defines two static functions that are also adorned with specific attributes (which I mention shortly):

```
Imports System.Runtime.InteropServices
Imports System.Windows.Forms
' This .NET interface has been adorned with various attributes
' that will be used by the tlbimp.exe utility.
<GuidAttribute("47430E06-718D-42c6-9E45-78A99673C43C"), _
 InterfaceTypeAttribute(ComInterfaceType.InterfaceIsDual)>
Public Interface IBasicMath
    <DispId(777)> Function Add(ByVal x As Integer, ByVal y As Integer) As
Integer
end interface
<GuidAttribute("C08F4261-C0C0-46ac-87F3-EDE306984ACC")> _
Public Class DotNetCalc
    Implements IBasicMath
    Function Add(ByVal x As Integer, _
    ByVal y As Integer) As Integer Implements IBasicMath.Add
        Return y + x
    End Function
    ' This attribute configures this method
    ' to be called during the registration of the assembly.
    <ComRegisterFunctionAttribute()> _
    Public Shared Sub AddExtraRegLogic(ByVal regLoc As String)
        ' Do any extra logic when registration occurs.
        MessageBox.Show("Inside AddExtraRegLogic f(x)", _
                        ".NET assembly says:")
    End Sub
    ' This attribute configures this method
```

```
    ' to be called during the unregistration of the assembly.
    <ComUnregisterFunctionAttribute()> _
      Public Shared Sub RemoveExtraRegLogic(ByVal regLoc As String)
        ' Do any extra logic when unregistration occurs.
        MessageBox.Show("Inside RemoveExtraRegLogic f(x)", _
                        ".NET assembly says:")
    End Sub
End Class
```

Examining the Generated COM Type Information

If you run this assembly through the tlbexp.exe utility, you find that the IID and CLSID are the same values as listed here and also that your IBasicMath interface has been configured as a [dual]. Here is the IDL for the IBasicMath interface:

```
// In the assembly you wrote the following attributes:
// <GuidAttribute("47430E06-718D-42c6-9E45-78A99673C43C"), _
// InterfaceTypeAttribute(ComInterfaceType.InterfaceIsDual)>

// Generated IDL.
[ odl, uuid(47430E06-718D-42C6-9E45-78A99673C43C), dual, oleautomation,
custom({0F21F359-AB84-41E8-9A78-36D110E6D2F9},
"AttribDotNetObjects.IBasicMath")]
interface IBasicMath : IDispatch
{
     [id(0x00000309)]       // We wrote: [DispId(777)]
     HRESULT Add( [in] long x, [in] long y, [out, retval] long* pRetVal);
};
```

Interacting with Assembly Registration

Next, you need to examine the use of the ComRegisterFunctionAttribute and ComUnregisterFunctionAttribute types. Classic COM DLL servers export two functions (DllRegisterServer and DllUnregisterServer), which are called by various registration utilities to insert (or remove) the required COM registration information. .NET binaries do not export such functions—however, by declaring shared methods with these attributes, you can simulate the same behavior. To illustrate, if you now register the .NET assembly using regasm.exe, you see the message box shown in Figure 13-24.

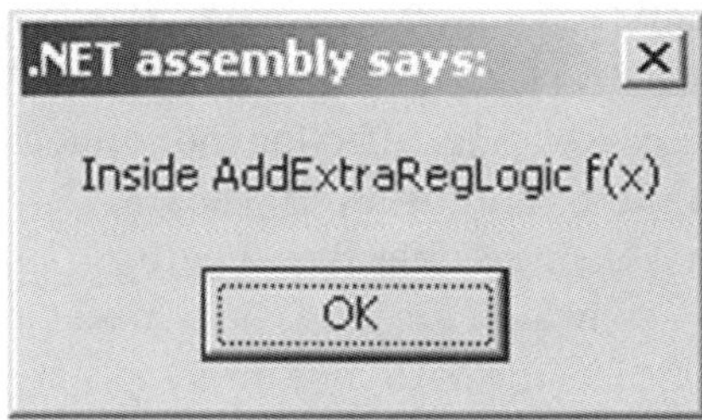

Figure 13-24. Interacting with COM registration

I am sure you can think of more useful logic to write in the method taking the ComRegisterFunctionAttribute attribute, but I think you get the general idea. A few final points on these two registration attributes: First, the name of the method makes no difference whatsoever. However, it must take a single string argument that holds the current location of the registry being updated. Also, if you configure a shared method that takes the ComRegisterFunctionAttribute, you should also configure a method that takes the ComUnregisterFunctionAttribute. In this way, you can simulate a self-registering COM server.

Interacting with COM+ Component Services

The final topic of this chapter is an examination of how the base class libraries make it possible to build .NET types that can be configured to take advantage of the COM+ runtime layer. Before illustrating the general process, I begin with a high-level overview regarding the role of COM+. Again, if you require additional information, I assume you will refer to an appropriate resource.

You may be aware of the product Microsoft Transaction Server (MTS). MTS is an application server that provides the ability to host classic COM DLLs in a manner fitting for an enterprise-level, *n*-tier environment. For example, assume you create a classic COM binary that is in charge of connecting to a data source (perhaps using ADO) to update a number of related tables. Once this COM server has been installed under MTS, it inherits a number of core traits, such as support for declarative transactions, JIT activation, and ASAP deactivation (to increase scalability) as well as a very nice role-based security model. The end result is that you can configure how the MTS-aware type should behave in a declarative manner, rather than with hard-coded logic.

Every MTS-aware COM class has an associated context object used to hold a number of specific traits about how the MTS object is being used. For example, the context may contain information about the security credentials of the caller, about this object's transactional outcome (i.e., the happy bit), and about if the object is ready to be reclaimed from memory (i.e., the done bit).

By and large, MTS COM types are created to be stateless entities. This simply refers to the fact that the object can be created and destroyed by the MTS runtime (to reclaim system resources) without affecting the connected base client (i.e., the entity making calls to the MTS runtime layer). Thus, MTS types are GUI-less and play the role of traditional business objects that perform a unit of work for the base client and quietly pass away. If the base client makes a call on the object it *thinks* it still has a reference to, the MTS runtime simply creates a new copy.

While MTS opened the door to building highly scalable and very reliable distributed systems, it had an ugly side. Specifically, the MTS and COM runtimes were not very well integrated. For example, both architectures wrote to unique parts of the registry, which could prevent the COM DLL from functioning as a typical in-proc server. Also, the object-creation mechanism used by COM was not the same model used by MTS. When objects are installed under MTS, they must create other MTS-hosted COM types using a specific method supported by their associated context.

COM+ is in many respects a cleaned-up version of MTS proper. Under COM+, classic COM and classic MTS have been unified into a single system to take care of the registration and object-creation inconsistencies. COM+ applications still inherit the same core MTS traits (declarative transactions, role-based security, and so on) and some additional traits. Here is a quick rundown of some of these COM+-specific behaviors:

- Support for object pooling. The COM+ runtime layer can maintain a collection of active coclasses that can be quickly handed off to the base client. This trait can help decrease the time the base client needs to wait to be returned an interface reference from the COM+ type. However, this places additional memory demands on COM+ server machine(s).

- A new event model termed Loosely Coupled Events (LCE). The LCE event model of COM+ allows clients and COM+ types to communicate in a disconnected manner. This means that a given COM+ class can send out an event without any foreknowledge of who (if anyone) is listening. Also, a COM+ client can receive events without needing to be connected to the sender.

- Support for object construction strings. Given that classic COM does not allow the client to trigger constructor logic, COM+ introduced a standard interface (IObjectConstruct) that gives the coclass the ability to be send any start-up parameters in the form of a String (which may be parsed internally by the type).

- The ability to control the queuing behavior of a COM+ type in a declarative manner. Microsoft Message Queue (MSMQ) is an enterprise-level messaging service that entails lots of boilerplate "grunge." COM+ introduces Queued Components (QC), which hide much of this grunge from view.

As you can see, the services provide by COM+ can greatly simplify the development of distributed applications. The only problem is that these traits were originally intended to be used by classic COM objects. To allow .NET developers to obtain these same benefits, the base class libraries provided numerous .NET equivalents defined in the System.EnterpriseServices namespace.

Understanding the System.EnterpriseServices Namespace

To build managed types that can be configured to function under the COM+ runtime, you need to equip your .NET entities with numerous attributes defined in the System.EnterpriseServices namespace. If you already have a background in classic MTS and/or COM+, you will find most of these items very familiar. Table 13-8 offers a brief rundown.

Table 13-8. Select Types of the System.EnterpriseServices Namespace

SYSTEM.ENTERPRISESERVICES TYPE	MEANING IN LIFE
ApplicationActivationAttribute	Allows you to specify if the components contained in the assembly run in the creator's process (library application) or in a system process (server application).
ApplicationIDAttribute	Specifies the assembly's application ID (as a GUID).
ApplicationQueuingAttribute InterfaceQueuingAttribute	Used to enable Queued Component (QC) support.
AutoCompleteAttribute	Marks the attributed method as AutoComplete. If the function terminates properly, SetComplete() is called automatically. If an exception is thrown during the course of the method, SetAbort() is called automatically.
ComponentAccessControlAttribute	Enables security checking on calls to a given component.
ConstructionEnabledAttribute	Enables COM+ object construction support.

Table 13-8. Select Types of the System.EnterpriseServices Namespace (continued)

SYSTEM.ENTERPRISESERVICES TYPE	MEANING IN LIFE
ContextUtil	Is the preferred method for obtaining information about the COM+ 1.0 object context. This type defines a number of static members that allow you to obtain COM+-centric contextual information.
DescriptionAttribute	Set this description on an assembly (application), component, method, or interface.
EventClassAttribute EventTrackingEnabledAttribute	Used to interact with the COM+ LCE event model.
JustInTimeActivationAttribute	Turns JIT activation on or off.
SecurityCallContext SecurityCallers SecurityIdentifier SecurityIdentity SecurityRoleAttribute	Used to allow your .NET types to interact with the role-based security model used by MTS/COM+.
SharedPropertyGroupManager SharedPropertyGroup SharedProperty	Provide access to the MTS/COM+ shared property manager (SPM).
TransactionAttribute	Specifies the type of transaction that should be available to this object. Permissible values are members of the TransactionOption enumeration.

Building COM+-Aware Types

To create a .NET assembly that can be hosted by the COM+ runtime, you need to follow a cookbook approach to build the exposed types. To begin, each .NET class type will derive from System.ServicedComponent. This base class provides default implementations of the classic MTS interface, IObjectControl (Activate(), Deactivate(), and CanBePooled()). If you want to override these default implementations, you are free to do so.

Once you add any number of additional COM+-centric attributes to your .NET types, you need to compile the assembly. However, to place this assembly under control of the COM+ runtime, you need to use a new .NET utility, regsvcs.exe. As you see in just a bit, this tool is responsible for a number of steps beyond installing your type in the COM+ catalog.

Finally, and perhaps most important, you should install your assembly into the GAC. The reason is simple. Given that the dllhost.exe (the COM+ surrogate) needs to locate your assembly to host it in a given activity, it must be able to locate this binary. As I am sure you agree, installing your assemblies in the GAC is the most logical choice for this situation. Once you perform each of these steps, you can build any number of base clients.

Building a COM+-Aware VB .NET Type

To illustrate how to build a .NET type that can use the COM+ runtime, build a new managed code library named DotNetCOMPlusServer. (Remember, the COM+ runtime can only host types contained in DLLs.) Configure the single class (ComPlusType) with the following COM+ properties:

- The class supports an object constructor string.
- The class is poolable, with an upper pool limit of 100 and an initial pool size of 5 (and yes, you can build poolable types with VB.NET!).
- The class supports a single method, which may succeed or fail. To inform the runtime about its current state of affairs, this method supports the AutoComplete attribute.

Here is the complete listing:

```
' Need to set a reference to System.EnterpriseServices.dll!
Imports System.Windows.Forms
Imports System.Runtime.InteropServices
imports System.EnterpriseServices
' This object is poolable and supports a ctor string.
<ObjectPooling(True, 5, 100), _
 ConstructionEnabledAttribute(True), _
 ClassInterface(ClassInterfaceType.AutoDual)> _
Public Class ComPlusType
    Inherits ServicedComponent
    ' Override Construct to gain object constructor string.
    Public Overrides Sub Construct(ByVal msg As String)
        MessageBox.Show(msg, "Ctor string is")
    End Sub
    ' Override Activate and Deactivate and CanBePooled.
```

```
    Public Overrides Sub Activate()
        MessageBox.Show("In activate!")
    End Sub
    Public Overrides Sub Deactivate()
        MessageBox.Show("In deactivate!")
    End Sub
    Public Overrides Function CanBePooled() As Boolean
        Return True
    End Function
    ' The sole method of the COM+ aware .NET type.
    Public Sub DeleteCar(ByVal id As Integer)
        MessageBox.Show("Deleting car number " & id.ToString(), "Delete car")
    End Sub
End Class
```

Of course, this object is rather simplistic, because it really does not perform any enterprise-level functionality (such as deleting a car from a data store). This is just fine for this purpose, as you are currently only studying the basics of .NET/COM+ interaction.

You must take one additional step before you install this assembly in a new COM+ application. Given that this binary will eventually end up in the GAC, you need to build a strong name for the assembly. Also, you may want to freeze the autogenerated build and revision numbers, as shown here:

```
<Assembly: AssemblyVersion("1.0.0.0")>
```

Adding COM+-Centric Assembly-Level Attributes

At this point your .NET assembly is ready to be installed into the COM+ catalog. As you will see soon, the regsvcs.exe utility generates an AppID and application name automatically. However, if you want to specify certain aspects of the containing COM+ application, you can add the following assembly-level attributes (simply place them in your AssemblyInfo.vb file):

```
<Assembly: ApplicationActivation(ActivationOption.Server)>
<Assembly: ApplicationID("4fb2d46f-efc8-4643-bcd0-6e5bfa6a174c")>
<Assembly: ApplicationName("DotNetComPlusServer")>
<Assembly: Description("This app really kicks.")>
```

The ApplicationID attribute should be self-explanatory. This is the GUID of the resulting COM+ application. ApplicationName and Description should also make sense. The one attribute of special interest is ApplicationActivation. Recall that MTS and COM+ applications can be hosted as a library (e.g., activated in the caller's process) or server (e.g., in a new instance of dllhost.exe). Given that the default setting is to configure your COM+ application as a library, you typically want to explicitly specify ActivationOption.Server.

Configuring the Assembly in the COM+ Catalog

To configure a .NET assembly into the COM+ catalog, you still need to generate a COM type library (tlbexp.exe) and register the type in the system registry (regasm.exe). You also need to enter the correct information into the COM+ catalog (RegDB). Rather than using these utility tools individually, the .NET SDK ships with an additional tool, regsvcs.exe. This utility simplifies the process by taking care of each necessary detail in a single step. Specifically, the following operations are performed:

- The assembly is loaded into memory.
- The assembly is registered correctly (e.g., as with regasm.exe).
- A type library is generated and registered (e.g., as with tblexp.exe).
- The type library is installed in a specified COM+ application.
- The components are configured according to the attributes specified in the type definitions.

While this tool provides a number of optional arguments, the simplest syntax is as follows:

```
regsvcs /fc DotNetComPlusServer.dll
```

Here, you are specifying the /fc (find or create) flag to instruct the regsvcs.exe tool to build a new COM+ application if one does not currently exist. Alternately, you can specify the name of the COM+ application as a command-line parameter. If you omit this item (as shown here), the name is based on the name of the binary assembly. Finally, place the assembly into the GAC.

Examining the Component Services Explorer

Once you execute the command, you can open up the Windows 2000 Component Services Explorer and find that your .NET assembly is now recognized as a valid COM+ type (see Figure 13-25).

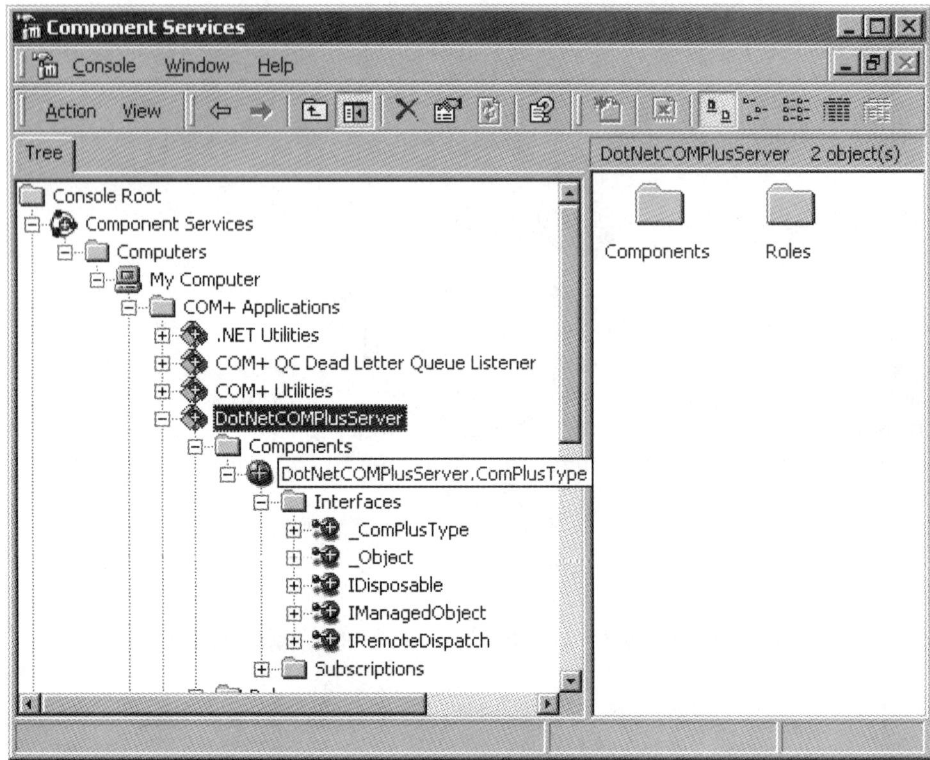

Figure 13-25. The famous COM+ aspirin icon

If you explore the various property windows for your new type, you notice that the various attributes you specified in the VB .NET class have been used to configure your type correctly in the COM+ catalog. For example, right-click the installed component and examine the Activation tab (see Figure 13-26).

These settings have been configured based on the following class-level attribute set:

```
// This object is poolable and supports a ctor string.
<ObjectPooling(5, 100), _
 ConstructionEnabledAttribute(True)>
Public Class MyCOMPlusType
  Inherits ServicedComponent
...
End Class
```

SOURCE CODE *The DotNetComPlusServer project is included under the Chapter 13 subdirectory.*

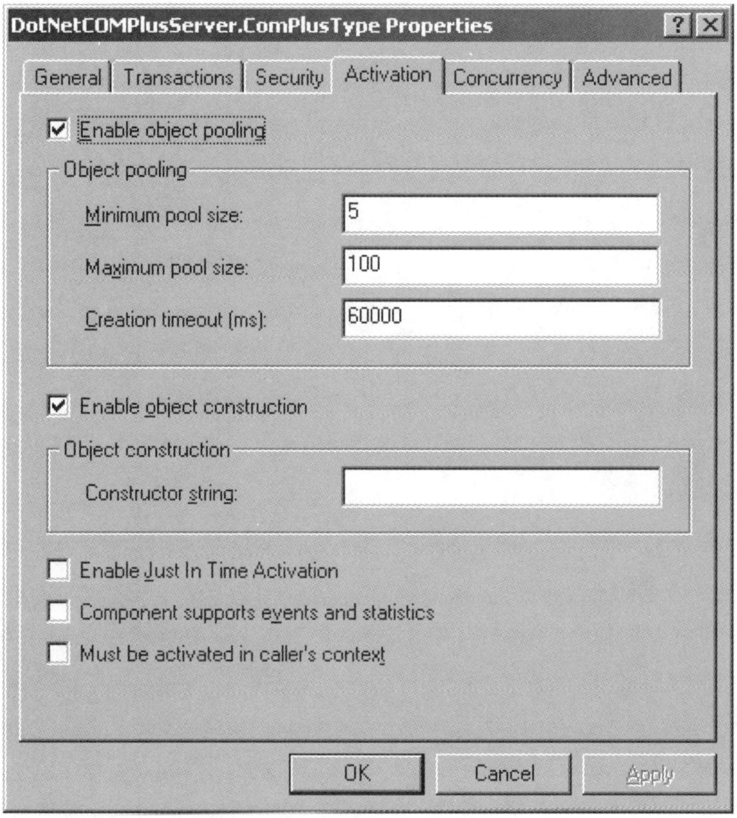

Figure 13-26. The configured component

Summary

.NET is a wonderful thing. Nevertheless, managed and unmanaged code must learn to work together for some time to come. Given this fact, the .NET platform provides various techniques that allow you to blend the best of both worlds.

A major section of this chapter focused on the details of .NET types using legacy COM components. As you have seen, the process begins by generating an assembly proxy for your COM types. The RCW forwards calls to the underlying COM binary and takes care of the details of mapping COM types to their .NET equivalents.

The chapter concluded by examining how COM types can call on the services of newer .NET types. As you have seen, this requires that the creatable types in the .NET assembly are registered to point to the CLR execution engine. Finally, this chapter introduced you to the types defined in System.EnterpriseServices. Using this namespace, you can build types that can take advantage of the COM+ runtime layer.

CHAPTER 14
Data Access with ADO.NET

UNLESS YOU ARE A video game developer by trade, you are probably interested in database manipulation. As you would expect, the .NET platform defines a number of types (in a handful of related namespaces) that allow you to interact with local and remote data stores. Collectively speaking, these namespaces are known as ADO.NET, which as you will see is a major overhaul of the classic ADO object model.

This chapter begins by examining some core types defined in the System.Data namespace—specifically DataColumn, DataRow, and DataTable. These classes allow you to define and manipulate a local in-memory table of data. Next, you spend a good deal of time learning about the centerpiece of ADO.NET, the DataSet. As you discover, the DataSet is an in-memory representation of a *collection* of interrelated tables. During this discussion, you learn how to programmatically model table relationships, create custom views from a given table, and submit queries against your in-memory DataSet.

After discussing how to manipulate a DataSet in memory, the remainder of this chapter illustrates how to obtain a populated DataSet from a Database Management System (DBMS) such as MS SQL Server, Oracle, or MS Access. This entails an examination of .NET "managed providers" and the OleDbDataAdapter and SqlDataAdapter types. You wrap things up by examining various integrated tools that can be used to interact with the ADO.NET types with minimal fuss and bother.

The Need for ADO.NET

The very first thing you must understand when learning ADO.NET is that it is *not* simply the latest and greatest version of classic ADO. While it is true that there is some symmetry between the two systems (e.g., each has the concept of "connection" and "command" objects), some familiar types (e.g., the Recordset) no longer exist. Furthermore, there are a number of new ADO.NET types that have no direct equivalent under classic ADO (e.g., the DataSet).

ADO.NET is a new database access technology specifically geared to facilitate the development of disconnected systems using the .NET platform. *N*-tier applications (especially Web-based applications) are fast becoming the norm, rather than the exception, for most new development efforts.

Unlike classic ADO, which was primarily designed for tightly coupled client/server systems, ADO.NET greatly extends the notion of the primitive ADO disconnected recordset with a new creature named the DataSet. This type represents a *local* copy of any number of related tables. Using the DataSet, the client is able to manipulate and update its contents while disconnected from the data source and submit the modified data back for processing using a related "data adapter."

Another major difference between classic ADO and ADO.NET is that ADO.NET has full support for XML data representation. In fact, the data obtained from a data store is internally represented, and transmitted, as XML. Given that XML is transported between layers using standard HTTP, ADO.NET is not limited by firewall constraints.

As you might be aware, classic ADO makes use of the COM marshalling protocol to move data between tiers. While this was appropriate in some situations, COM marshalling poses a number of limitations. Specifically, most firewalls are configured to reject COM RPC packets, which makes moving data between machines tricky.

Perhaps the most fundamental difference between classic ADO and ADO.NET is that ADO.NET is a managed library of code and therefore plays by all the same rules as any managed library. The types that comprise ADO.NET use the CLR memory management protocol, adhere to the same programming model, and work with many languages. Therefore, the types (and their members) are accessed in the same exact manner, regardless of which .NET-aware language you use.

ADO.NET: The Big Picture

The types that compose ADO.NET work together for a common goal: populate a DataSet, disconnect from the data store, and return the DataSet to the caller. A DataSet is a very interesting data type, given that it represents a local collection of tables (as well as the relationships between these tables) used by the client application. In some respects, this may remind you of the classic ADO disconnected recordset. The key difference is that a disconnected recordset represents a single table of data, whereas ADO.NET DataSets can model a collection of related tables. In fact, it is completely possible to have a client-side DataSet that represents the *entire* remote database.

Once you have obtained a DataSet, you can perform queries against the local tables to obtain specific subsets of information as well as navigate between related tables programmatically. As you would expect, you can add new rows to a given table in the DataSet as well as remove, filter, or update existing records. Once the modifications have been made, the client then submits the modified DataSet back to the data store for processing.

An obvious question at this point is "How do I get the DataSet?" Under the ADO.NET model, DataSets are populated through a managed provider, which is a collection of classes that implement a set of core interfaces defined in the System.Data namespace; specifically IDbCommand, IDbDataAdapter, IDbConnection, and IDataReader (see Figure 14-1).

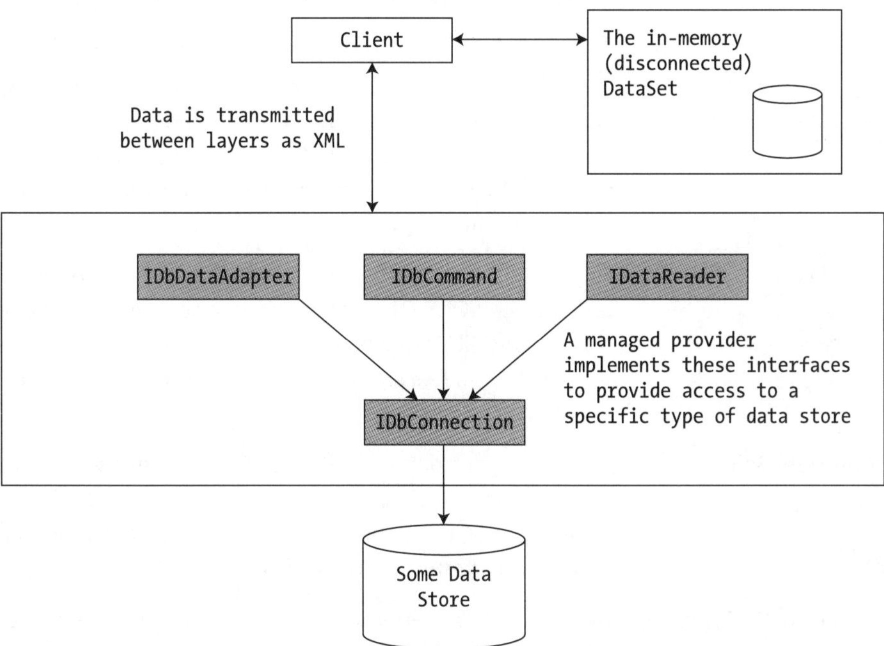

Figure 14-1. Clients interacting with managed providers

ADO.NET ships with two managed providers out of the box. First is the SQL provider, which provides highly optimized interactions with data stored in MS SQL Server (7.0 or higher). If the data you desire is not in a SQL Server data file, you can use the OleDb provider, which allows access to any data store that supports the OLE DB protocol. Be aware, however, that the OleDb provider uses native OLE DB (and therefore requires COM Interop) to enable data access.

As you might suspect, this is always a slower process than talking to a data store in its native tongue. Other vendors will soon begin shipping custom-managed providers for their proprietary data stores. Until then, the OleDb provider does the trick.

Understanding the ADO.NET Namespaces

Like other aspects of the .NET universe, ADO.NET is defined in a handful of related namespaces. Table 14-1 gives a quick rundown of each.

Table 14-1. ADO.NET Namespaces

ADO.NET NAMESPACE	MEANING IN LIFE
System.Data	This is the core namespace of ADO.NET. It defines types that represent tables, rows, columns, constraints, and DataSets. This namespace does not define types to connect to a datasource. Rather, it defines the types that represent the data itself.
System.Data.Common	This namespace contains the types shared between managed providers. Many of these types function as base classes to the concrete types defined by the OleDb and SqlClient managed providers.
System.Data.OleDb	This namespace defines the types that allow you to connect to an OLE DB-compliant data source, submit SQL queries, and fill DataSets. The types in this namespace have a look and feel similar (but not identical) to that of classic ADO.
System.Data.SqlClient	This namespace defines the types that constitute the SQL-managed provider. Using these types, you can talk directly to Microsoft SQL Server and avoid the level of indirection associated with the OleDb equivalents.
System.Data.SqlTypes	These types represent native data types used in Microsoft SQL Server. Although you are always free to use the corresponding CLR data types, the SqlTypes are optimized to work with SQL Server.

All these ADO.NET namespaces are in a single assembly named System.Data.dll (Figure 14-2). Thus, like in any project referencing external assemblies, you must be sure to set a reference to this .NET binary.

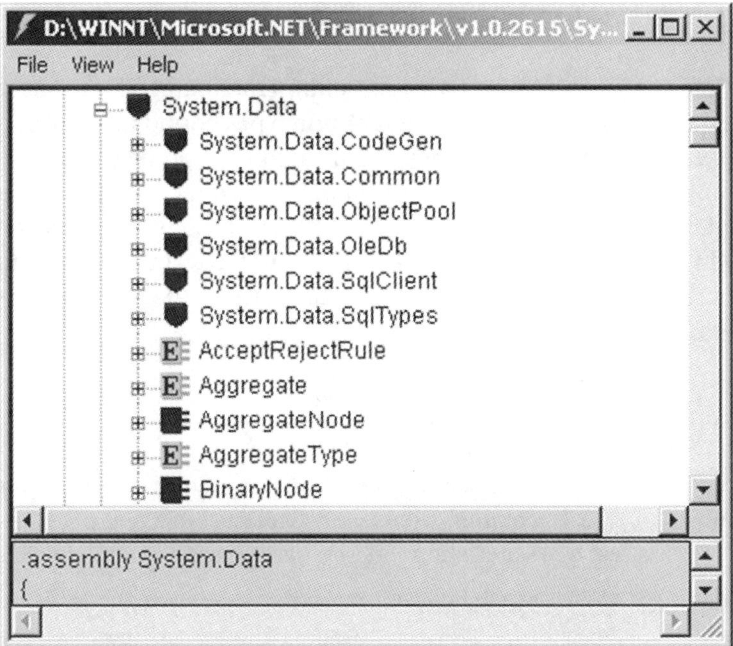

Figure 14-2. The System.Data.dll assembly

Of all the ADO.NET namespaces, System.Data is the lowest common denominator. You simply cannot build ADO.NET applications without specifying this namespace in your data access applications. In addition, when you want to establish a connection with a data store, you also need to specify an Imports directive for the System.Data.OleDb or System.Data.SqlClient namespaces. The exact reasons for this are discussed soon enough. For now, let's get to know some of the core types defined in System.Data.

The Types of System.Data

As mentioned, this namespace contains types that represent the data you obtain from a data store, but not the types that make the literal connection. In addition to a number of database-centric exceptions (NoNullAllowedException, RowNotInTableException, MissingPrimaryKeyException, and the like), these types are little more than OO representations of common database primitives (tables, rows, columns, constraints, and so on). Table 14-2 lists some of the core types, grouped by related functionality.

To get the ball rolling, the first half of this chapter discusses how to manipulate these items in a disconnected mode by hand. Once you understand how to build a DataSet in the raw, you have no problem manipulating a DataSet populated by a managed provider.

Examining the DataColumn Type

The DataColumn type represents a single column maintained by a DataTable. Collectively speaking, the set of all DataColumn types bound to a given DataTable represents the table's schema. For example, assume you have a table named Employees with three columns (EmpID, FirstName, and LastName). Programmatically, you would use three ADO.NET DataColumn objects to represent them in memory. As you see in just a moment, the DataTable type maintains an internal collection (which is accessed using the Columns property) to maintain its DataColumn types.

Table 14-2. Types of the System.Data Namespace

SYSTEM.DATA TYPE	MEANING IN LIFE
DataColumnCollection DataColumn	DataColumnCollection is used to represent all the columns used by a given DataTable. DataColumn represents a specific column in a DataTable.
ConstraintCollection Constraint	The ConstraintCollection represents all constraints (foreign key constraints, unique constraints) assigned to a given DataTable. Constraint represents an OO wrapper around a single constraint assigned to one or more DataColumns.
DataRowCollection DataRow	These types represent a collection of rows for a DataTable (DataRowCollection) and a specific row of data in a DataTable (DataRow).
DataRowView DataView	DataRowView allows you to carve out a predefined view from an existing row. DataView represents a customized view of a DataTable that can be used for sorting, filtering, searching, editing, and navigating.
DataSet	Represents an in-memory cache of data, which may consist of multiple related DataTables.
ForeignKeyConstraint UniqueConstraint	ForeignKeyConstraint represents an action restriction enforced on a set of columns in a primary key/foreign key relationship. The UniqueConstraint type represents a restriction on a set of columns in which all values must be unique.
DataRelationCollection DataRelation	This collection represents all relationships (i.e., DataRelation types) between the tables in a DataSet.
DataTableCollection DataTable	DataTableCollection represents all the tables (i.e., DataTable types) for a particular DataSet.

If you have a background in relational database theory, you know that a given column in a data table can be assigned a set of constraints (e.g., configured as a primary key, assigned a default value, configured to contain read-only information, and so on). Also, every column in a table must map to an underlying data type (int, varchar, and so forth). For example, the Employees table's schema may demand that the EmpID column maps to an integer, while FirstName and LastName map to an array of characters. The DataColumn class has numerous properties that allow you to configure these very things. Table 14-3 provides a rundown of some core properties.

Table 14-3. Properties of the DataColumn

DATACOLUMN PROPERTY	MEANING IN LIFE
AllowDBNull	Used to indicate if a row can specify null values in this column. The default value is true.
AutoIncrement AutoIncrementSeed AutoIncrementStep	These properties are used to configure the autoincrement behavior for a given column. This can be helpful to ensure unique values in a given DataColumn (such as a primary key). By default, a DataColumn does not support autoincrementation.
Caption	Gets or sets the caption to be displayed for this column (for example, what the end user sees in a DataGrid).
ColumnMapping	This property determines how a DataColumn is represented when a DataSet is saved as an XML document using the DataSet.WriteXml() method.
ColumnName	Gets or sets the name of the column in the Columns collection (meaning how it is represented internally by the DataTable). If you do not set the ColumnName explicitly, the default values are Column with (*n+1*) numerical suffixes (i.e., Column1, Column2, Column3, and so forth).
DataType	Defines the data type (Boolean, string, float, and so on) stored in the column.
DefaultValue	Gets or sets the default value assigned to this column when inserting new rows. This is used if not otherwise specified.
Expression	Gets or sets the expression used to filter rows, calculate a column's value, or create an aggregate column.
Ordinal	Gets the numerical position of the column in the Columns collection maintained by the DataTable.

Table 14-3. Properties of the DataColumn (continued)

DATACOLUMN PROPERTY	MEANING IN LIFE
ReadOnly	Determines if this column can be modified once a row has been added to the table. The default is false.
Table	Gets the DataTable that contains this DataColumn.
Unique	Gets or sets a value indicating whether the values in each row of the column must be unique or if repeating values are permissible. If a column is assigned a primary key constraint, the Unique property should be set to true.

Building a DataColumn

To illustrate the basic use of the DataColumn, assume you need to model a column named FirstName, which internally maps to an array of characters. Furthermore, assume this column (for whatever reason) must be read-only. Programmatically, you can write the following logic:

```
Private Sub btnColumn_Click(ByVal sender As System.Object, _
ByVal e As System.EventArgs) Handles btnColumn.Click
        ' Build the FirstName column.
        Dim colFName As System.Data.DataColumn = _
        New System.Data.DataColumn("FirstName", _
             Type.GetType("System.String"))
        ' Set a bunch of values.
        colFName.ReadOnly = True
        colFName.Caption = "First Name"
        colFName.ColumnName = "FirstName"
        ' Get a bunch of values.
        Dim temp As String = "Column type: " & _
        colFName.DataType.ToString() & vbLf & _
        "Read only? " & colFName.ReadOnly & vbLf & _
        "Caption: " & colFName.Caption & vbLf & _
        "Column Name: " & colFName.ColumnName & vbLf & _
        "Nulls allowed? " & colFName.AllowDBNull
        ' Now show all stats.
        MessageBox.Show(temp, "Column properties")
End Sub
```

This gives the result shown in Figure 14-3.

Figure 14-3. Select properties of the DataColumn

Given that the DataColumn provides several overloaded constructors, you can specify a number of properties directly at the time of creation, as relisted here:

```
' Build the FirstName column (take two).
Dim colFName As DataColumn = New DataColumn("FirstName", _
                                        Type.GetType("System.String"))
colFName.ReadOnly = True
colFName.Caption = "First Name"
```

In addition to the properties already examined, the DataColumn does have a small set of methods, which I assume you will check out on your own.

Adding a DataColumn to a DataTable

The DataColumn type does not typically exist as a stand-alone entity, but is instead inserted in a DataTable. To do so, begin by creating a new DataTable type (fully detailed later in the chapter). Next insert each DataColumn in the DataTable.DataColumnCollection type using the Columns property. Here is an example:

```
' Build the FirstName column.
Dim myColumn as DataColumn = New DataColumn()
' Create a new DataTable.
Dim myTable as DataTable = New DataTable("MyTable")
' The Columns property returns a DataColumnCollection type.
' Use the Add() method to insert the column in  the table.
myTable.Columns.Add(myColumn)
```

Configuring a DataColumn to Function As a Primary Key

One common rule of database development is that a table should have at least one column that functions as the primary key. A primary key constraint is used to uniquely identify a record (row) in a given table. In keeping with the current Employees example, assume you want to build a new DataColumn type to represent the EmpID field. This column will be the primary key of the table, and thus should have the AllowDBNull and Unique properties configured as shown here:

```
' This column is functioning as a primary key.
Dim colEmpID as DataColumn = New DataColumn("EmpID", _
   Type.GetType("System.Int32"))
colEmpID.Caption = "Employee ID"
colEmpID.AllowDBNull = False
colEmpID.Unique = True
```

Once the DataColumn has been correctly set up to function as a primary key, the next step is to assign this DataColumn to the DataTable's PrimaryKey property. You will see how to do this in the discussion of the DataTable, so put this on the back burner for the time being.

Enabling Auto-Autoincrementing Fields

One aspect of the DataColumn you may choose to configure is its ability to autoincrement. Simply put, autoincrementing columns are used to ensure that when a new row is added to a given table, the value of this column is assigned automatically, based on the current step of the incrementation. This can be helpful when you want to ensure that a column has no repeating values (such as a primary key). This behavior is controlled using the AutoIncrement, AutoIncrementSeed, and AutoIncrementStep properties.

To illustrate, build a DataColumn that supports autoincrementation. The seed value is used to mark the starting value of the column, where the step value identifies the number to add to the seed when incrementing, as shown here:

```
' Create a data column.
Dim myColumn as DataColumn = new DataColumn()
myColumn.ColumnName = "Foo"
myColumn.DataType = System.Type.GetType("System.Int32")

' Set the autoincrement behavior.
myColumn.AutoIncrement = True
```

```
myColumn.AutoIncrementSeed = 500
myColumn.AutoIncrementStep = 12
```

Here, the Foo column has been configured to ensure that as rows are added to the respective table, the value in this field is incremented by 12. Because the seed has been set at 500, the first five values should be 500, 512, 524, 536, and 548.

To prove the point, insert this DataColumn in a DataTable. Then add a number of new rows to the table, which of course automatically bumps the value in the Foo column, as shown here:

```
Private Sub btnAutoCol_Click(ByVal sender As System.Object, _
ByVal e As System.EventArgs) Handles btnAutoCol.Click
    ' Make a data column that maps to an Integer
    Dim myColumn As System.Data.DataColumn = New System.Data.DataColumn()
    myColumn.ColumnName = "Foo"
    myColumn.DataType = System.Type.GetType("System.Int32")
    ' Set the auto increment behavior.
    myColumn.AutoIncrement = True
    myColumn.AutoIncrementSeed = 500
    myColumn.AutoIncrementStep = 12
    ' Add this column to a new DataTable.
    Dim myTable As DataTable = New DataTable("MyTable")
    myTable.Columns.Add(myColumn)
    ' Add 20 rows.
    Dim r As DataRow
    Dim i As Integer
    For i = 0 To 19
        r = myTable.NewRow()
        myTable.Rows.Add(r)
    Next
    ' Now list the value in each row.
    Dim temp As String = ""
    Dim rows As DataRowCollection = myTable.Rows
    For i = 0 To myTable.Rows.Count - 1
        Dim currRow As DataRow = rows(i)
        temp += currRow("Foo") & " "
    Next
    MessageBox.Show(temp, "These values brought ala auto-increment")
End Sub
```

If you run the application (and click the corresponding Button), you see the message shown in Figure 14-4.

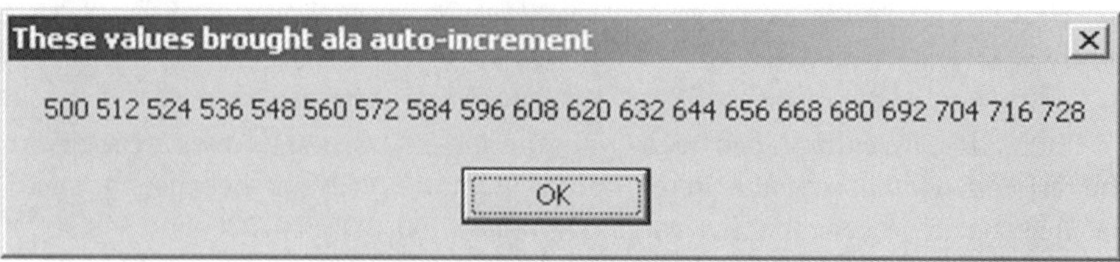

Figure 14-4. An auto autoincremented column

Configuring a Column's XML Representation

While many of the remaining DataColumn properties are rather self-explanatory (provided you are comfortable with database terminology), I would like to discuss the ColumnMapping property. The DataColumn.ColumnMapping property is used to configure how this column should be represented in XML, if the owning DataSet dumps its contents using the WriteXml() method. The value of the ColumnMapping property is configured using the MappingType enumeration (Table 14-4).

Table 14-4. Values of the MappingType Enumeration

MAPPINGTYPE ENUMERATION VALUE	MEANING IN LIFE
Attribute	The column is mapped to an XML attribute.
Element	The column is mapped to an XML element (the default).
Hidden	The column is mapped to an internal structure.
TableElement	The column is mapped to a table value.
Text	The column is mapped to text.

The default value of the ColumnMapping property is MappingType.Element. Assume that you have instructed the owning DataSet to write its contents to a new file stream as XML. Using this default setting, the EmpID column would appear as shown here:

```
<Employee>
    <EmpID>500</EmpID>
</Employee>
```

However, if the DataColumn's ColumnMapping property is set to MappingType.Attribute, you see the following XML representation:

```
<Employee EmpID = "500"/>
```

This chapter examines the ADO.NET/XML integration in greater detail when discussing the DataSet. Nevertheless, at this point, you understand how to create a stand-alone DataColumn type. Now for an examination of the basic behavior of the DataRow.

SOURCE CODE *The DataColumn application is included under the Chapter 14 subdirectory.*

Examining the DataRow Type

As you have seen, a collection of DataColumn objects represents the schema of a table. A DataTable maintains its columns using the internal DataColumnCollection type. In contrast, a collection of DataRow types represents the actual data in the table. Thus, if you have 20 listings in a table named Employees, you can represent these entries using 20 DataRow types. Using the members of the DataRow class, you are able to insert, remove, evaluate, and manipulate the values in the table.

Working with a DataRow is a bit different from working with a DataColumn, because you do not create a direct instance of this type, but rather obtain a reference from a given DataTable. For example, assume you want to insert a new row in the Employees table. The DataTable.NewRow() method allows you to obtain the next slot in the table, at which point you can fill each column with new data, as shown here:

```
' Build a new Table.
Dim empTable as DataTable = New DataTable("Employees")
' . . .Add EmpID, FirstName and LastName columns to table. . .
' Build a new Employee record.
Dim row as DataRow = empTable.NewRow()
row("EmpID") = 102
row("FirstName") = "Joe"
row("LastName") = "Blow"
' Add it to the Table's DataRowCollection.
empTable.Rows.Add(row)
```

Notice how the DataRow class defines an indexed property that can be used to gain access to a given DataColumn by numerical position as well as column name. Also notice that the DataTable maintains another internal collection (DataRowCollection) to hold each row of data. The DataRow type defines the following core members, grouped by related functionality in Table 14-5.

Table 14-5. Members of the DataRow

DATAROW MEMBER	MEANING IN LIFE
AcceptChanges() RejectChanges()	Commits or rejects all the changes made to this row since the last time AcceptChanges was called.
BeginEdit() EndEdit() CancelEdit()	Begins, ends, or cancels an edit operation on a DataRow object.
Delete()	Marks a row to be removed when the AcceptChanges() method is called.
HasErrors GetColumnsInError() GetColumnError() ClearErrors() RowError	The HasErrors property returns a Boolean value indicating if there are errors in a column's collection. If so, the GetColumnsInError() method can be used to obtain the offending members, GetColumnError() can be used to obtain the error description, while the ClearErrors() method removes each error listing for the row. The RowError property allows you to configure a textual description of the error for a given row.
IsNull()	Gets a value indicating whether the specified column contains a null value.
ItemArray	Gets or sets all of the values for this row using an array of objects.
RowState	Used to pinpoint the current state of the DataRow using values of the RowState enumeration.
Table	Use this property to obtain a reference to the DataTable containing this DataRow.

Understanding the DataRow.RowState Property

Most of the methods of the DataRow class only make sense in the context of an owning DataTable. You will see the process of inserting, removing, and updating rows in just a moment; first, however, you should get to know the RowState property. This property is useful when you need to programmatically identify the set of all rows in a table that have changed, have been newly inserted, and so forth. This property may be assigned any value from the DataRowState enumeration (Table 14-6).

Table 14-6. Values of the DataRowState Enumeration

DATAROWSTATE ENUMERATION VALUE	MEANING IN LIFE
Deleted	The row was deleted using the Delete method of the DataRow.
Detached	The row has been created but is not part of any DataRowCollection. A DataRow is in this state immediately after it has been created and before it is added to a collection, or if it has been removed from a collection.
Modified	The row has been modified, and AcceptChanges() has not been called.
New	The row has been added to a DataRowCollection, and AcceptChanges() has not been called.
Unchanged	The row has not changed since AcceptChanges() was last called.

To illustrate the various states a DataRow may have, the following class documents the changes to the RowState property as a new DataRow is created, inserted in, and removed from a DataTable:

```
Module Module1
    Sub Main()
        Console.WriteLine("Illustrating RowState property:")
        ' Build a single column DataTable
        Dim myTable As DataTable = New DataTable("Employees")
        Dim colID As DataColumn = New DataColumn("empID", _
                Type.GetType("System.Int32"))
        myTable.Columns.Add(colID)
        ' The DataRow.
        Dim myRow As DataRow
        ' Create a new (detached) DataRow.
        myRow = myTable.NewRow()
        Console.WriteLine(myRow.RowState.ToString())
        ' Now add it to table.
        myTable.Rows.Add(myRow)
        Console.WriteLine(myRow.RowState.ToString())
        ' Trigger an accept.
        myTable.AcceptChanges()
        Console.WriteLine(myRow.RowState.ToString())
        ' Modify it and see state.
```

```
        myRow("empID") = 100
        Console.WriteLine(myRow.RowState.ToString())
        ' Now delete it.
        myRow.Delete()
        Console.WriteLine(myRow.RowState.ToString())
        myRow.AcceptChanges()
    End Sub
End Module
```

The output should be clear (Figure 14-5).

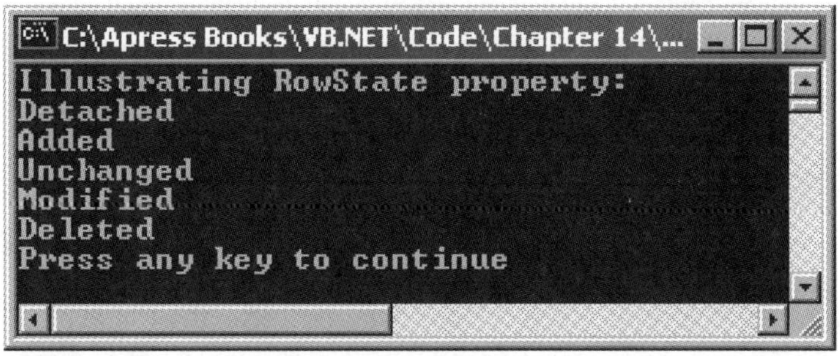

```
C:\Apress Books\VB.NET\Code\Chapter 14\...
Illustrating RowState property:
Detached
Added
Unchanged
Modified
Deleted
Press any key to continue
```

Figure 14-5. Changes in row states

As you can see, the ADO.NET DataRow is smart enough to remember its current state of affairs. Given this, the owning DataTable is able to identify which rows have been modified. This is a key feature of the DataSet, given that when it comes time to send updated information to the data store, only the modified values are submitted. Clearly this behavior helps optimize trips between the layers of your system.

The ItemArray Property

Another helpful member of the DataRow is the ItemArray property. This method returns a complete snapshot of the current row as an array of System.Object types. Also, you can insert a new row using the ItemArray property, rather than listing each DataColumn explicitly. Assume the current table now has two DataColumns (EmpID and FirstName). The following logic adds some new rows by assigning an array of objects to the ItemArray property and then promptly prints the results (see Figure 14-6).

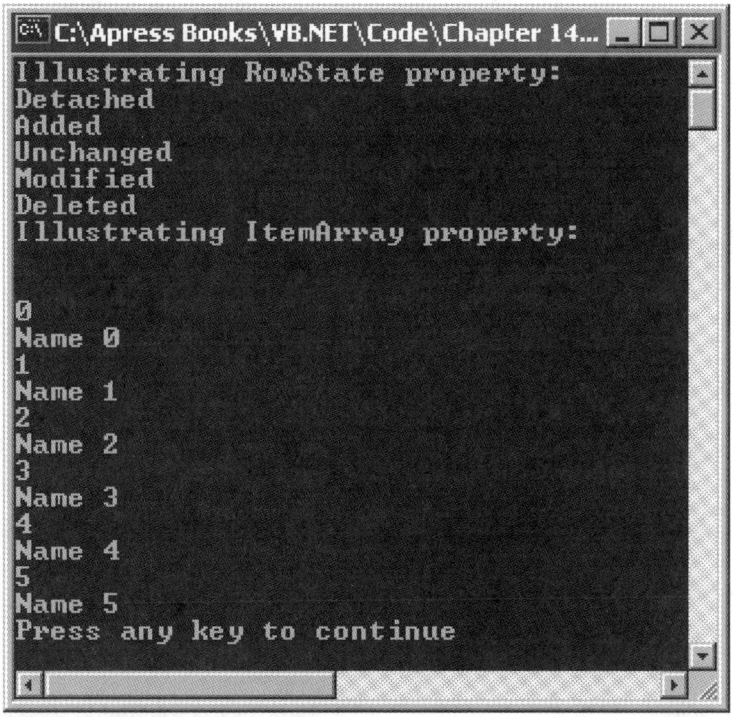

```
C:\Apress Books\VB.NET\Code\Chapter 14...
Illustrating RowState property:
Detached
Added
Unchanged
Modified
Deleted
Illustrating ItemArray property:


0
Name 0
1
Name 1
2
Name 2
3
Name 3
4
Name 4
5
Name 5
Press any key to continue
```

Figure 14-6. Using the ItemArray property

```
' Declare the array variable.
Dim myVals(1) As Object
Dim dr As DataRow
' Create some new rows and add to RowsCollection.
Dim i As Integer
For i = 0 To 5
    myVals(0) = i
    myVals(1) = "Name " & i
    dr = myTable.NewRow()
    dr.ItemArray = myVals
    myTable.Rows.Add(dr)
Next
' Now print each value.
Dim r As DataRow
For Each r In myTable.Rows
    Dim c As DataColumn
    For Each c In myTable.Columns
        Console.WriteLine(r(c))
    Next
Next
```

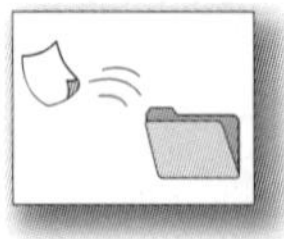

SOURCE CODE *The DataRowState is included under the Chapter 14 subdirectory.*

Details of the DataTable

The DataTable is an in-memory representation of a tabular block of data. While you can manually compose a DataTable programmatically, you more commonly obtain a DataTable dynamically using a DataSet and the types defined in the System.Data.OleDb or System.Data.SqlClient namespaces. Table 14-7 describes some core properties of the DataTable.

Table 14-7. Properties of the DataTable

DATATABLE PROPERTY	MEANING IN LIFE
CaseSensitive	Indicates whether string comparisons in the table are case-sensitive (or not). The default value is false.
ChildRelations	Returns the collection of child relations (DataRelationCollection) for this DataTable (if any).
Columns	Returns the collection of columns that belong to this table.
Constraints	Gets the collection of constraints maintained by the table (ConstraintCollection).
DataSet	Gets the DataSet that contains this table (if any).
DefaultView	Gets a customized view of the table that may include a filtered view, or a cursor position.
MinimumCapacity	Gets or sets the initial number of rows in this table. (The default is 25.)
ParentRelations	Gets the collection of parent relations for this DataTable.
PrimaryKey	Gets or sets an array of columns that function as primary keys for the data table.
Rows	Returns the collection of rows that belong to this table.
TableName	Gets or sets the name of the table. This same property may also be specified as a constructor parameter.

To help visualize the key components of a DataTable, consider Figure 14-7. Be aware that this is *not* a traditional class hierarchy that illustrates the is-a relations between these types (e.g., the DataRow *does not* derive from DataRowCollection). Rather, this diagram points out the logical has-a relationships between the DataTable's core items (e.g., the DataRowCollection has a number of DataRow types).

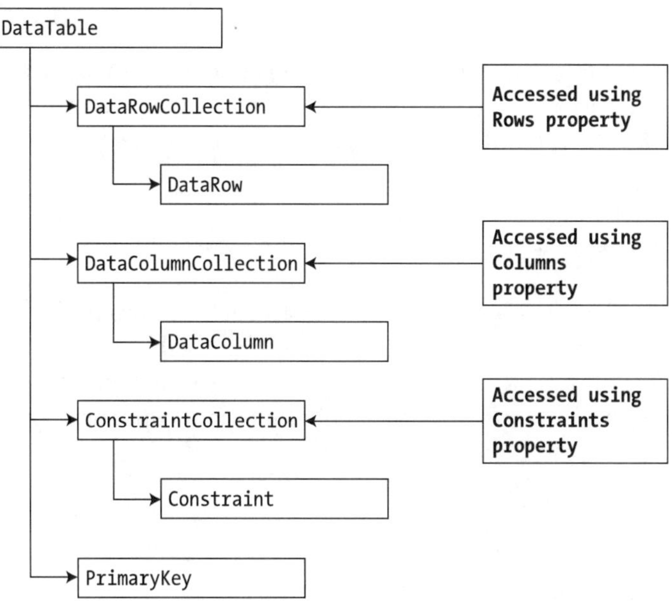

Figure 14-7. Collections of the DataTable

Building a Complete DataTable

Now that you have been exposed to the basics, let's see a complete example of creating and manipulating an in-memory data table. Assume you are interested in building a DataTable representing the current inventory in a database named Cars. The Inventory table will contain four columns: CarID, Make, Color, and PetName. Also, the CarID column will function as the table's primary key (PK) and support autoincrementation. The PetName column will allow null values. (Sadly, not everyone loves his or her automobiles as much as you might!) Figure 14-8 shows the overall schema.

CarID (PK)	Make	Color	PetName
0	BMW	Green	Chucky
1	Yugo	White	Tiny
2	Jeep	Tan	(null)
3	Caravan	Pink	Pain Inducer

Figure 14-8. The Inventory DataTable

The process begins by creating a new DataTable type. You specify the friendly name of the table as a constructor parameter. This friendly name can be used to reference this table from the containing DataSet, as shown here:

```
' Create a new DataTable.
Dim inventoryTable as DataTable = New DataTable("Inventory")
```

The next step is to programmatically insert each column using the Add() method of the DataColumnCollection (accessed using the DataTable.Columns property). The following logic adds the CarID, Make, Color, and PetName columns to the current DataTable (recall that the underlying data type of each column is set using the DataType property):

```
' DataColumn var.
Dim myDataColumn As DataColumn
' Create ID column and add to table.
myDataColumn = New DataColumn()
myDataColumn.DataType = Type.GetType("System.Int32")
myDataColumn.ColumnName = "ID"
myDataColumn.ReadOnly = True
myDataColumn.AllowDBNull = False
myDataColumn.Unique = True
' Set the auto increment behavior.
myDataColumn.AutoIncrement = True
myDataColumn.AutoIncrementSpeed = 1000
myDataColumn.AutoIncrementStep = 10
inventoryTable.Columns.Add(myDataColumn)
' Create Make column and add to table.
myDataColumn = New DataColumn()
myDataColumn.DataType = Type.GetType("System.String")
myDataColumn.ColumnName = "Make"
inventoryTable.Columns.Add(myDataColumn)
' Create Color column and add to table.
```

```
myDataColumn = New DataColumn()
myDataColumn.DataType = Type.GetType("System.String")
myDataColumn.ColumnName = "Color"
inventoryTable.Columns.Add(myDataColumn)
' Create PetName column and add to table.
myDataColumn = New DataColumn()
myDataColumn.DataType = Type.GetType("System.String")
myDataColumn.ColumnName = "PetName"
myDataColumn.AllowDBNull = True
inventoryTable.Columns.Add(myDataColumn)
```

Before you add the rows, take the time to set the table's primary key. To do so, set the DataTable.PrimaryKey property to whichever column is necessary. Because more than a single column can function as a table's primary key, be aware that the PrimaryKey property requires an array of DataColumn types. For the Inventory table, assume the CarID column is the only aspect of the primary key, as shown here:

```
' Make the ID column the primary key column.
Dim PK(0) As DataColumn
PK(0) = inventoryTable.Columns("ID")
inventoryTable.PrimaryKey = PK
```

Last but not least, you need to add valid data to the table. Assuming you have an appropriate ArrayList maintaining Car types, you can fill the table as shown here:

```
' Iterate over the array list to make rows
' (remember, the ID is auto-autoincremented).
Dim c As Car
For Each c In arTheCars
    Dim newRow As DataRow
    newRow = inventoryTable.NewRow()
    newRow("Make") = c.mMake
    newRow("Color") = c.mColor
    newRow("PetName") = c.mPetName
    inventoryTable.Rows.Add(newRow)
Next
```

To display your new local in-memory table, assume you have a Windows Forms application with a main Form displaying a DataGrid. As you saw in Chapter 11, the DataSource property is used to bind a DataTable to the GUI. The output is shown in Figure 14-9.

Figure 14-9. Binding the DataTable to a DataGrid

Here, you added rows by specifying the string name of the column to modify. However, you may also specify the numerical index of the column, which can be very helpful when you need to iterate over each column. Thus, the previous code could be updated as shown here (and still achieve the same end result):

```
' Iterate over the array list to make rows.
Dim c As Car
For Each c In arTheCars
    Dim newRow As DataRow
    newRow = inventoryTable.NewRow()
    newRow(1) = c.mMake
    newRow(2) = c.mColor
    newRow(3) = c.mPetName
    inventoryTable.Rows.Add(newRow)
Next
```

Manipulating a DataTable: Deleting Rows

What if you want to remove a row from a data table? One approach is to call the Delete() method of the DataRowCollection type. Simply specify the index (or DataRow) representing the row to remove. Assume you update your GUI as shown in Figure 14-10.

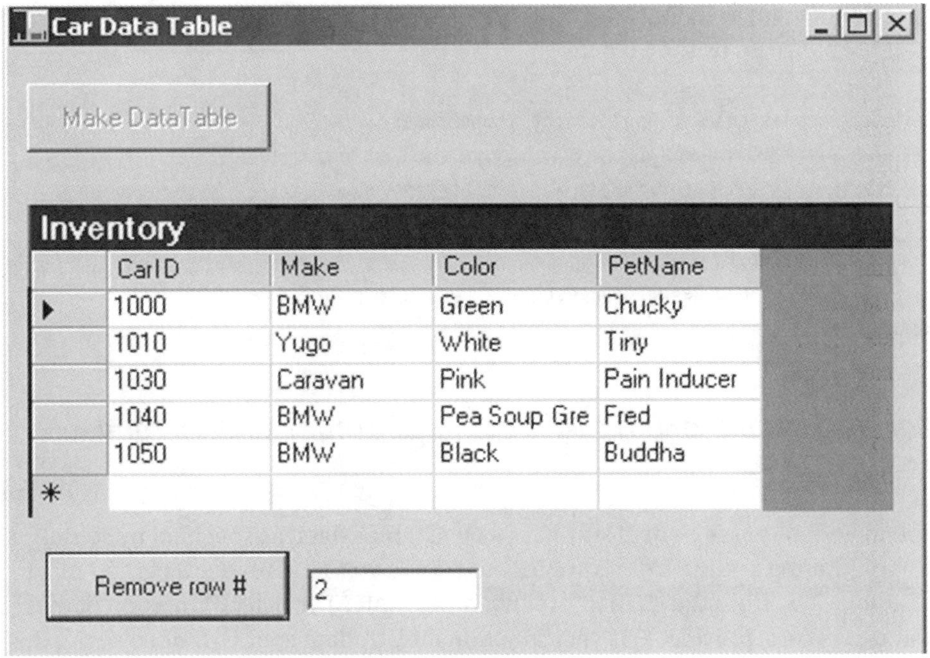

Figure 14-10. *Removing rows from a DataTable*

If you look at the previous screen shot, you will notice that you specified the second row in the DataTable, and therefore CarID 1020 has been blown away. The following logic behind the new Button's Click event handler removes the specified row from your in-memory DataTable:

```
' Remove this row from the DataRowCollection.
Private Sub btnRemoveRow_Click(ByVal sender As System.Object, _
   ByVal e As System.EventArgs) Handles btnRemoveRow.Click
    Try
        inventoryTable.Rows((Integer.Parse(txtRemove.Text))).Delete()
        inventoryTable.AcceptChanges()
    Catch ex As Exception
        MessageBox.Show(ex.Message)
    End Try
End Sub
```

The Delete() method might have been better named MarkedAsDeletable() given that the row is typically not removed until the DataTable.AcceptChanges() method has been called. In effect, the Delete() method simply sets a flag that says "I am ready to die when my table tells me." Also understand that if a row has been marked for deletion, a DataTable may reject those changes before calling AcceptChanges(), as shown here:

```
' Mark a row as deleted, but reject the changes.
Private Sub btnRemoveRow_Click(ByVal sender As System.Object, _
   ByVal e As System.EventArgs) Handles btnRemoveRow.Click
     inventoryTable.Rows((Integer.Parse(txtRemove.Text))).Delete()
    ' Do more work. . .
     inventoryTable.RejectChanges()       ' Restore RowState.
End Sub
```

Manipulating a DataTable: Applying Filters and Sort Orders

You may want to see a small subset of a DataTable's data, as specified by some sort of filtering criteria. For example, what if you want to only see a certain make of automobile from the in-memory Inventory table? The Select() method of the DataTable class provides this very functionality. Update your GUI once again, this time allowing users to specify a string that represents the make of the automobile they are interested in viewing (Figure 14-11).

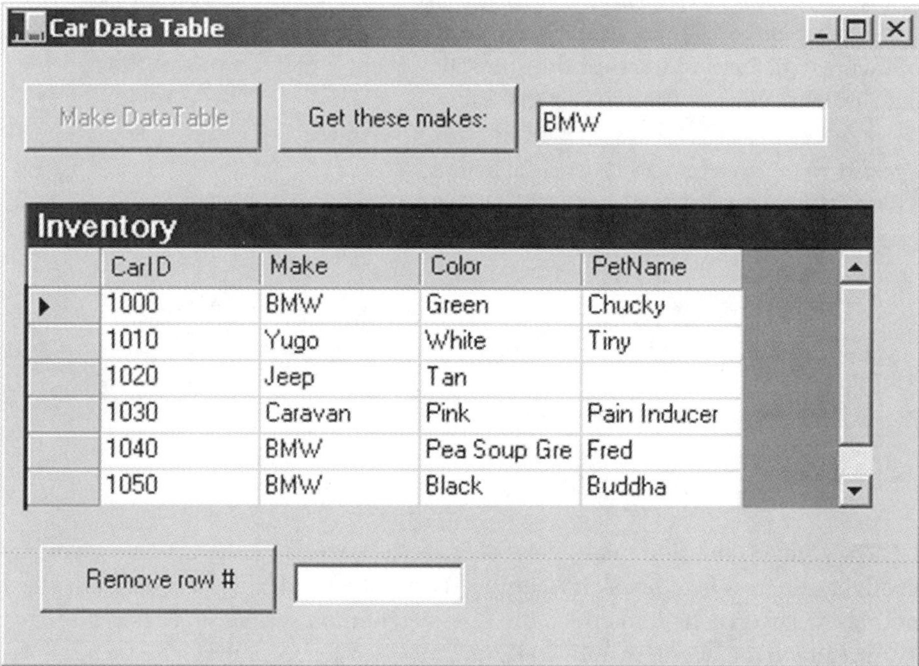

Figure 14-11. Specifying a filter

The Select() method has been overloaded a number of times to provide different selection semantics. At its most basic level, the parameter sent to Select() is a string that contains some conditional operation. To begin, observe the following logic for the Click event handler of your new Button:

```
Private Sub btnGetMake_Click(ByVal sender As System.Object, _
ByVal e As System.EventArgs) Handles btnGetMake.Click
    ' Build a filter based on user input.
    Dim filterStr As String = "Make='" & txtMake.Text & "'"
    Dim strMake As String
    ' Find all rows matching the filter.
    Dim makes() As DataRow = _
    inventoryTable.Select(filterStr)
    Dim i As Integer
    ' Show what we got!
    If (makes.Length = 0) Then
        MessageBox.Show("Sorry, no cars. . .", "Selection error!")
    Else
        For i = 0 To makes.Length - 1
            Dim temp As DataRow = makes(i)
            strMake &= temp("PetName").ToString() & vbLf
        Next
        MessageBox.Show(strMake, txtMake.Text & " type(s):")
    End If
End Sub
```

Here, you first build a simple filter criteria based on the value in the associated TextBox. If you specify BMW, your filter is Make = 'BMW'. When you send this filter to the Select() method, you get back an array of DataRow types, which represent each row that matches the filter criteria (Figure 14-12).

Figure 14-12. Filtered data

A filter string can be composed of any number of relational operators. For example, what if you wanted to find all cars with an ID greater than 1030? You could write the following (see Figure 14-13 for output):

```
' Now show the petnames of all cars
' with carID greater than 1030.
Dim properIDs As DataRow()
Dim newFilterStr As String = "ID > '1030'"
properIDs = inventoryTable.Select(newFilterStr)
Dim strIDs As String

Dim I as Integer
For i = 0 To properIDs.Length - 1
    Dim temp As DataRow = properIDs(i)
    strIDs &= temp("PetName").ToString() _
      & " is ID " & temp("ID") & vbLf
Next
MessageBox.Show(strIDs, "Pet names of cars where ID > 1030")
```

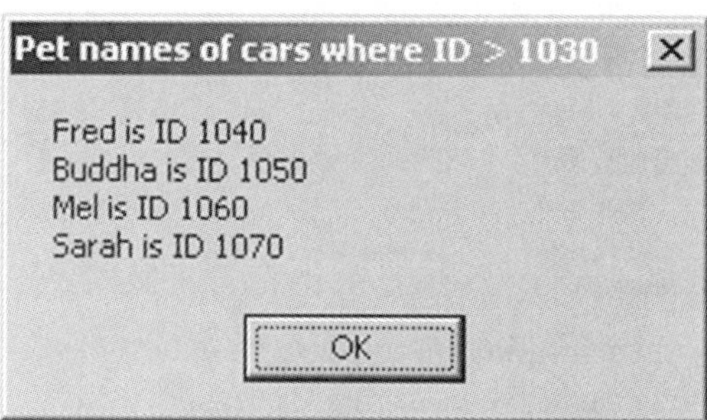

Figure 14-13. Specifying a range of data

Filtering logic is modeled after standard SQL syntax. To prove the point, assume you want to obtain the results of the previous Select() command alphabetically based on pet name. In terms of SQL, this translates into a sort based on the PetName column. Luckily the Select() method has been overloaded to send in a sort criterion, as shown here:

```
properIDs = inventoryTable.Select(newfilterStr, "PetName")
```

This returns something like what is shown in Figure 14-14.

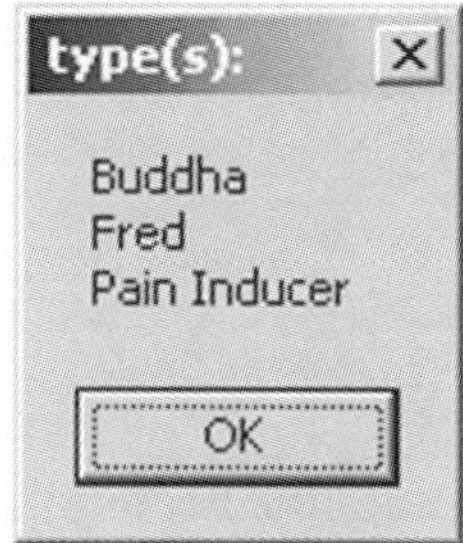

Figure 14-14. Ordered data

I changed the above to make it more clear that the Select with the added parameter could replace the simple Select in the previous code.

If you want the results in descending order, call Select(), as shown here:

```
' Return results in descending order.
properIDs = inventoryTable.Select(newfilterStr, "PetName DESC")
```

In general, the sort string contains the column name followed by "ASC" (ascending, which is the default) or "DESC" (descending). If necessary, multiple columns can be separated by commas.

Manipulating a DataTable: Updating Rows

The final aspect of the DataTable you should be aware of is the process of updating an existing row with new values. One approach is to first obtain the row(s) that match a given filter criterion using the Select() method. Once you have the DataRow(s) in question, modify them accordingly. For example, assume you have a new Button that (when clicked) searches the DataTable for all rows where Make is equal to BMW. Once you identify these items, you change the Make from "BMW" to "Colt":

```
Private Sub btnChange_Click(ByVal sender As System.Object, _
ByVal e As System.EventArgs) Handles btnChange.Click
    ' Build a filter.
    Dim filterStr As String = "Make='BMW'"
    ' Find all rows matching the filter.
    Dim makes() As DataRow = _
            inventoryTable.Select(filterStr)

    ' Change all!
    Dim i As Integer
```

```
    For i = 0 To makes.Length - 1
        Dim temp As DataRow = makes(i)
        temp("Make") = "Colt"
        makes(i) = temp
    Next
End Sub
```

The DataRow class also provides the BeginEdit(), EndEdit(), and CancelEdit() methods, which allow you to edit the content of a row while temporarily suspending any associated validation rules. In the previous logic, each row was validated with each assignment. (Also, if you capture any events from the DataRow, they fire with each modification.) When you call BeginEdit() on a given DataRow, the row is placed in edit mode. At this point you can make your changes as necessary and call either EndEdit() to commit these changes or CancelEdit() to roll back the changes to the original version. For example:

```
' Assume you have obtained a row to edit.
' Now place this row in edit mode.
rowToUpdate.BeginEdit()

' Send the row to a helper function, which returns a Boolean.
If ChangeValuesForThisRow(rowToUpdate)
     rowToUpdate.EndEdit()       ' OK!
Else
     rowToUpdate.CancelEdit()    ' Forget it.
End If
```

Although you are free to manually call these methods on a given DataRow, these members are automatically called when you edit a DataGrid widget that has been bound to a DataTable. For example, when you select a row to edit from a DataGrid, that row is automatically placed in edit mode. When you shift focus to a new row, EndEdit() is called automatically. To test this behavior, assume you have manually updated each car to be of a given Make using the DataGrid (Figure 14-15).

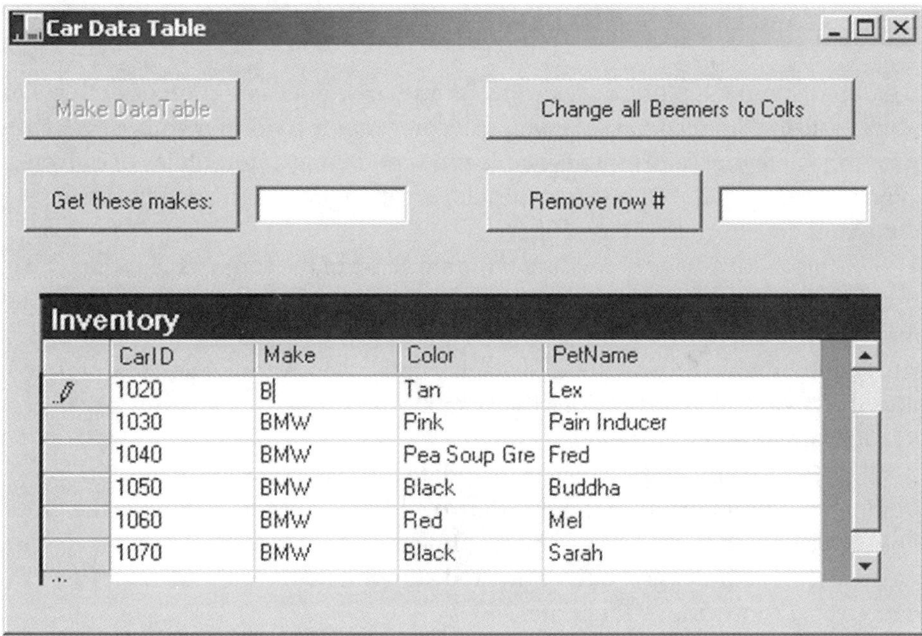

Figure 14-15. Editing rows in a DataGrid

If you now request all BMWs, the message box correctly returns *all* rows, as the underlying DataTable associated to the DataGrid has been automatically updated (Figure 14-16).

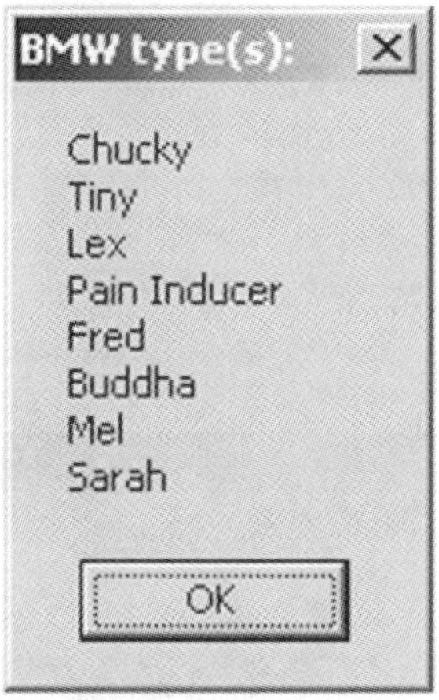

BMW type(s):

Chucky
Tiny
Lex
Pain Inducer
Fred
Buddha
Mel
Sarah

OK

Figure 14-16. The Inventory DataTable

Understanding the DataView Type

In database nomenclature, a *view object* is a stylized representation of a table. For example, using Microsoft SQL Server, you could create a view for your current Inventory table that returns a new table only containing automobiles of a given color. In ADO.NET, the DataView type allows you to programmatically extract a subset of data from the DataTable.

One great advantage of holding multiple views of the same table is that you can bind these views to various GUI widgets (such as the DataGrid). For example, one DataGrid might be bound to a DataView showing all autos in the Inventory, while another may be configured to display only green automobiles. On a related note, the DataTable type provides the DefaultView property that returns the default DataView for the table.

Here is an example. Your goal is to update the user interface of the current Windows Forms application to support two additional DataGrid types. One of these grids only shows the rows from the Inventory that match the filter Make='Colt'. The other grid only shows red automobiles (i.e., Color='Red'). Figure 14-17 shows the GUI update.

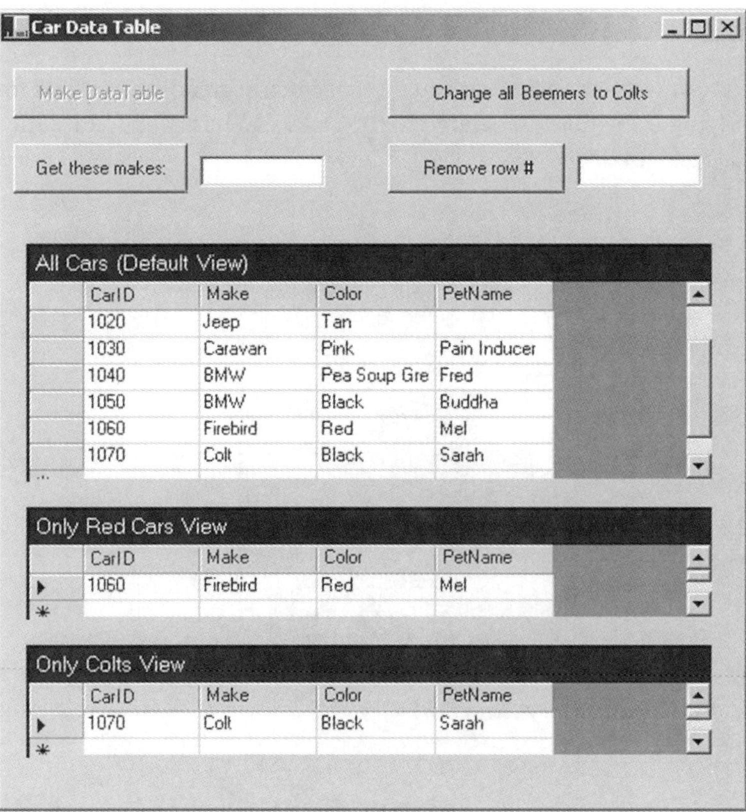

Figure 14-17. Creating multiple views for the Inventory table

To begin, you need to create two member variables of type DataView:

```
Public Class Form1
    Inherits System.Windows.Forms.Form
    ' Views of the DataTable.
    Private redCarsView As DataView  ' I only show red cars.
    Private coltsView As DataView  ' I only show colts
     . . .
End Class
```

Next, assume you have a new helper function named CreateViews(), which is called directly after the DataTable has been fully constructed, as shown here:

```
Private Sub btnMakeDataTable_Click(ByVal sender As System.Object, _
ByVal e As System.EventArgs) Handles btnMakeDataTable.Click
    ' Make a data table.
    MakeTable()
    ' Make Views.
    CreateViews()
    ' Done. Disable button.
    btnMakeDataTable.Enabled = False
End Sub
```

Here is the implementation of this new helper function. Notice that the constructor of each DataView has been passed to the DataTable that will be used to build the custom set of data rows:

```
Private Sub CreateViews()
    ' Set the table which is used for these views.
    redCarsView = New DataView(inventoryTable)
    coltsView = New DataView(inventoryTable)
    ' Now configure the views. . .
    redCarsView.RowFilter = "Color = 'red'"
    coltsView.RowFilter = "Make = 'colt'"
    ' Bind to grids. . .
    RedCarViewGrid.DataSource = redCarsView
    ColtsViewGrid.DataSource = coltsView
End Sub
```

As you can see, the DataView class supports a property named RowFilter, which contains the string representing the filtering criteria used to extract matching rows. Once you have your view established, set the grid's DataSource property accordingly. That's it! Because DataGrids are smart enough to detect changes to their underlying data source, if you click the Make Beemers Colts button, the ColtsViewGrid is updated automatically.

In addition to the RowFilter property, Table 14-8 describes some additional members of the DataView class.

Table 14-8. Members of the DataView Type

DATAVIEW MEMBER	MEANING IN LIFE
AddNew()	Adds a new row to the DataView.
AllowDelete AllowEdit AllowNew	Configure whether the DataView allows deleting, inserting, or updating its rows.
Delete()	Deletes a row at the specified index.
RowFilter	Gets or sets the expression used to filter which rows are viewed in the DataView.
Sort	Gets or sets the sort column or columns and sort order for the table.
Table	Gets or sets the source DataTable.

SOURCE CODE *The complete CarDataTable project is included under the Chapter 14 subdirectory.*

Understanding the Role of the DataSet

You have been examining how to build a DataTable to represent a single table of data held in memory. Although DataTables can be used as stand-alone entities, they are more typically contained in a DataSet. In fact, most data access types supplied by ADO.NET only return a populated DataSet, not an individual DataTable.

Simply put, a DataSet is an in-memory representation of any number of tables (which may be just a single DataTable) as well as any (optional) relationships between these tables and any (optional) constraints. To gain a better understanding of the relationship among these core types, consider the logical hierarchy shown in Figure 14-18.

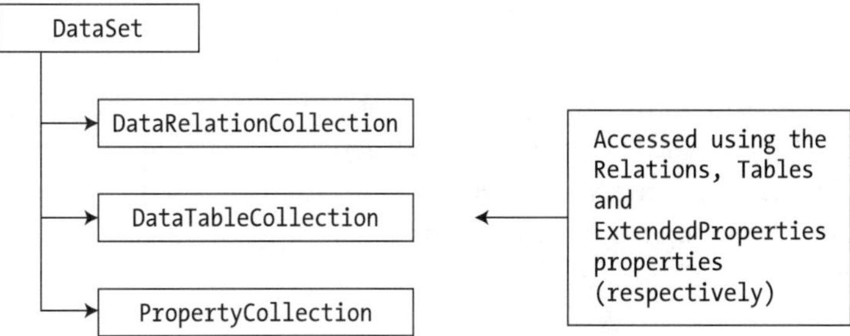

Figure 14-18. Collections of the DataSet

The Tables property of the DataSet allows you to access the DataTableCollection that contains the individual DataTables. Another important collection used by the DataSet is the DataRelationCollection. Given that a DataSet is a disconnected version of a database schema, it can programmatically represent the parent/child relationships between its tables.

For example, a relation can be created between two tables to model a foreign key constraint using the DataRelation type. This object can then be added to the DataRelationCollection through the Relations property. At this point, you can navigate between the connected tables as you search for data. You see how this is done a bit later in the chapter.

The ExtendedProperties property provides access to the PropertyCollection type, which allows you to associate any extra information to the DataSet as name/value pairs. This information can literally be anything at all, even if it has no bearing on the data itself. For example, you can associate your company's name to a DataSet, which can then function as in-memory metadata, as shown here:

```
' Make a DataSet and add some metadata.
Dim ds as DataSet = New DataSet("MyDataSet")
ds.ExtendedProperties.Add("CompanyName", "Intertech, Inc")

' Print out the metadata.
Console.WriteLine(ds.ExtendedProperties("CompanyName").ToString())
```

Other examples of extended properties might include an internal password that must be supplied to access the contents of the DataSet, a number representing a data refresh rate, and so forth. Be aware that the DataTable itself also supports the ExtendedProperties property.

Members of the DataSet

Before exploring too many other programmatic details, take a look at the public interface of the DataSet. The properties defined by the DataSet are centered on providing access to the internal collections, producing XML data representations and providing detailed error information. Table 14-9 describes some core properties of interest.

Table 14-9. Properties of the Mighty DataSet

DATASET PROPERTY	MEANING IN LIFE
CaseSensitive	Indicates whether string comparisons in DataTable objects are case-sensitive (or not).
DataSetName	Gets or sets the name of this DataSet. Typically this value is established as a constructor parameter.
DefaultViewManager	Establishes a custom view of the data in the DataSet.
EnforceConstraints	Gets or sets a value indicating whether constraint rules are followed when attempting any update operation.
HasErrors	Gets a value indicating whether there are errors in any of the rows in any of the tables of this DataSet.
Relations	Get the collection of relations that link tables and allow navigation from parent tables to child tables.
Tables	Provides access to the collection of tables maintained by the DataSet.

The methods of the DataSet mimic some of the functionality provided by the aforementioned properties. In addition to interacting with XML streams, other methods exist to allow you to copy the contents of your DataSet, as well as establish the beginning and ending points of a batch of updates. Table 14-10 describes some core methods.

Table 14-10. Methods of the Mighty DataSet

DATASET METHOD	MEANING IN LIFE
AcceptChanges()	Commits all the changes made to this DataSet since it was loaded or the last time AcceptChanges() was called.
Clear()	Completely clears the DataSet data by removing every row in each table.
Clone()	Clones the structure of the DataSet, including all DataTables, as well as all relations and any constraints.
Copy()	Copies both the structure and data for this DataSet.
GetChanges()	Returns a copy of the DataSet containing all changes made to it since it was last loaded, or since AcceptChanges() was called.
GetChildRelations()	Returns the collection of child relations that belong to a specified table.
GetParentRelations()	Gets the collection of parent relations that belong to a specified table.
HasChanges()	Overloaded. Gets a value indicating whether the DataSet has changes, including new, deleted, or modified rows.
Merge()	Overloaded. Merges this DataSet with a specified DataSet.
ReadXml() ReadXmlSchema()	Allow you to read XML data from a valid stream (file-based, memory-based, or network-based) to the DataSet.
RejectChanges()	Rolls back all the changes made to this DataSet since it was created or the last time DataSet.AcceptChanges was called.
WriteXml() WriteXmlSchema()	Allow you to write out the contents of a DataSet to a valid stream.

Now that you have a better understanding of the role of the DataSet (and some idea what you can do with one), let's run through some specifics. Once this discussion of the ADO.NET DataSet is complete, the remainder of this chapter focuses on how to obtain DataSet types from external sources (such as a relational database) using the types defined by the System.Data.SqlClient and System.Data.OleDb namespaces.

Building an In-Memory DataSet

To illustrate the use of a DataSet, create a new Windows Forms application that maintains a single DataSet, containing three DataTable objects named Inventory, Customers, and Orders. The columns for each table will be minimal but complete, with one column marking the primary key for each table. Most importantly, you can model the parent/child relationships between the tables using the DataRelation type. Your goal is to build the database shown in Figure 14-19 in memory.

Here, the Inventory table is the parent table to the Orders table, which maintains a foreign key (CarID) column. Also, the Customers table is the parent table to the Orders table. (Again note the foreign key, CustID.) As you soon see, when you add DataRelation types to your DataSet, they may be used to navigate between the tables to obtain and manipulate the related data.

To begin, assume you have added a set of member variables to your main Form, representing the individual DataTables and containing DataSet, as shown in Figure 14-19.

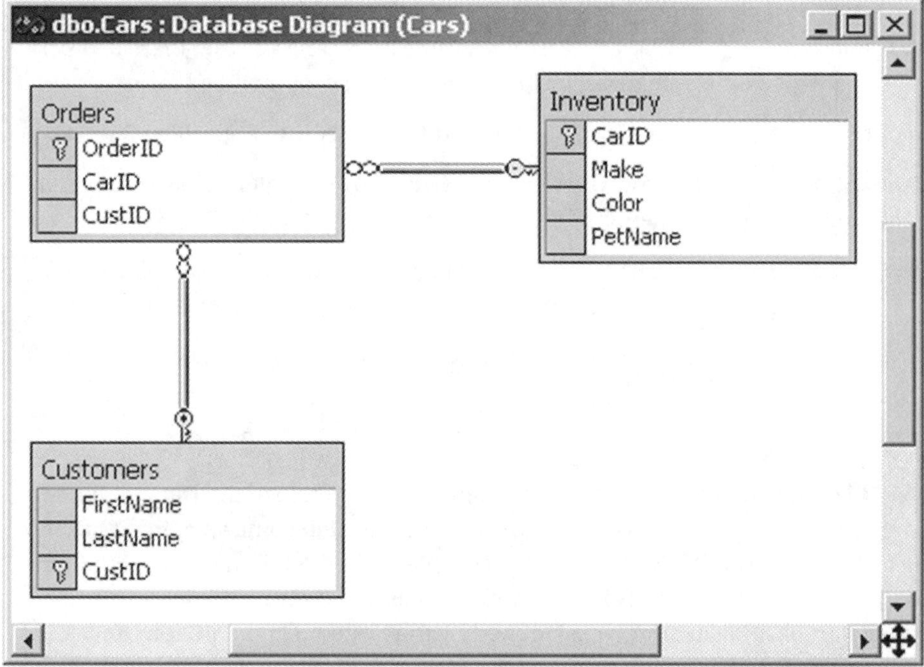

Figure 14-19. The In-Memory Cars database

```
Public Class Form1
    Inherits System.Windows.Forms.Form
    ' Inventory DataTable.
    Private inventoryTable As DataTable = New DataTable("Inventory")
    ' Customers DataTable.
    Private customersTable As DataTable = New DataTable("Customers")
    ' Orders DataTable.
    Private ordersTable As DataTable = New DataTable("Orders")
    ' Our DataSet
    Private carsDataSet As DataSet = New DataSet("CarDataSet")
...
End Class
```

Now, to keep things as OO as possible, build some (very) simple wrapper classes to represent a Car and Customer in the system. Note that the Customer class maintains a field that identifies the car a customer is interested in buying, as shown here:

```
Public Class Car
    ' Make public for eazy access...
    Public mPetName, mMake, mColor As String

    Public Sub New(ByVal petName As String, ByVal make As String, _
    ByVal color As String)
        Me.mPetName = petName
        Me.mColor = color
        Me.mMake = make
    End Sub
    End Class
    Public Class Customer
    Public Sub New(ByVal fName As String, ByVal lName As String, _
    ByVal currentOrder As Integer)
        Me.firstName = fName
        Me.lastName = lName
        Me.currCarOrder = currentOrder
    End Sub
    ' K.I.S.S.
    Public firstName, lastName As String
    Public currCarOrder As Integer
End Class
```

The main Form maintains two ArrayList types that hold a set of cars and customers, which are populated with some sample data in the scope of the Form's constructor. Next, the constructor calls a number of private helper functions to build the tables and their relationships. Finally, this method binds the Inventory and Customer DataTables to their corresponding DataGrid widgets. Notice that the following code binds a given DataTable in the DataSet using the SetDataBinding() method:

```
' Our list of Cars & Customers.
Private arTheCars, arTheCustomers As ArrayList
Public Sub New()
    MyBase.New()
...
    ' Fill the array list with some cars.
    arTheCars = New ArrayList()
    arTheCars.Add(New Car("Chucky", "BMW", "Green"))
    arTheCars.Add(New Car("Tiny", "Yugo", "White"))
    ...
    ' Fill the array list with some customers.
    arTheCustomers = New ArrayList()
    arTheCustomers.Add(New Customer("Dave", "Brenner", 1020))
    ....
    ' Make data tables.
    MakeInventoryTable()
    MakeCustomerTable()
    MakeOrderTable()
    ' Add relation.
    BuildTableRelationship()
    ' Add foreign key constraints.
    AddConstraints()
    ' Bind to grids.
    CarDataGrid.SetDataBinding(carsDataSet, "Inventory")
    CustomerDataGrid.SetDataBinding(carsDataSet, "Customers")
End Sub
```

Each DataTable is constructed using the techniques examined earlier in this chapter. To keep focused on the DataSet logic, I will not repeat every detail of the table-building logic here. However, be aware that each table is assigned a primary key that is autoincremented. Here is some partial table-building logic (check out same code for complete details):

```
Private Sub MakeOrderTable()
    ' Add to the DataSet...
    carsDataSet.Tables.Add(ordersTable)
    ' Create OrderID, CustID, CarID columns and add to table...
...
```

```
    ' Make the ID column the primary key column. . .
    ' Add some orders.
    Dim i As Integer
    For i = 0 To arTheCustomers.Count - 1
        Dim newRow As DataRow
        newRow = ordersTable.NewRow()
        Dim c As Customer = CType(arTheCustomers(i), Customer)
        newRow("CustID") = i
        newRow("CarID") = c.currCarOrder
        carsDataSet.Tables("Orders").Rows.Add(newRow)
    Next
End Sub
```

The MakeInventoryTable() and MakeCustomerTable() helper functions behave almost identically.

Expressing Relations Using the DataRelation Type

The really interesting work happens in the BuildTableRelationship() helper function. Once a DataSet has been populated with a number of tables, you can *optionally* choose to programmatically model the parent/child relationships. Be aware that this is not mandatory. You can have a DataSet that does little else than hold a collection of DataTables in memory (even a single DataTable). However, when you do establish the interplay between your DataTables, you can navigate between them on the fly and collect any sort of information you may be interested in obtaining, all while disconnected from the data source.

The System.Data.DataRelation type is an OO wrapper around a table-to-table relationship. When you create a new DataRelation type, specify a friendly name, followed by the parent table (for example, Inventory) and the related child table (Orders). For a relationship to be established, each table must have an identically named column (CarID) of the same data type (Int32 in this case). In this light, a DataRelation is basically bound by the same rules as a relational database. Here is the complete implementation of the BuildTableRelationship() helper function:

```
Private Sub BuildTableRelationship()
    ' Create a DR obj.
    Dim dr As DataRelation _
            = New DataRelation("CustomerOrder", _
            carsDataSet.Tables("Customers").Columns("CustID"), _
            carsDataSet.Tables("Orders").Columns("CustID"))
    ' Add to the DataSet.
```

```
    Try
        carsDataSet.Relations.Add(dr)
    Catch ex As Exception
        MessageBox.Show(ex.Message)
    End Try
    ' Create another DR obj.
    dr = New DataRelation("InventoryOrder", _
          carsDataSet.Tables("Inventory").Columns("CarID"), _
          carsDataSet.Tables("Orders").Columns("CarID"))
    ' Add to the DataSet.
    Try
            carsDataSet.Relations.Add(dr)
    Catch ex As Exception
            MessageBox.Show(ex.Message)
    End Try
End Sub
```

As you can see, a given DataRelation is held in the DataRelationCollection maintained by the DataSet. The DataRelation type offers a number of properties that allow you to obtain a reference to the child and/or parent table that is participating in the relationship, specify the name of the relationship, and so on. (See Table 14-11.)

Table 14-11. Properties of the DataRelation Type

DATARELATION PROPERTY	MEANING IN LIFE
ChildColumns ChildKeyConstraint ChildTable	Obtain information about the child table in this relationship as well as the table itself.
DataSet	Gets the DataSet to which the relations' collection belongs.
ParentColumns ParentKeyConstraint ParentTable	Obtain information about the parent table in this relationship, as well as the table itself.
RelationName	Gets or sets the name used to look up this relation in the parent data set's DataRelationCollection.

Navigating Between Related Tables

To illustrate how a DataRelation allows you to move between related tables, you will extend your GUI to include a new Button type and a related TextBox. The end user is able to enter the ID of a customer and obtain all the information about that customer's order, which is placed in a simple message box (Figure 14-20).

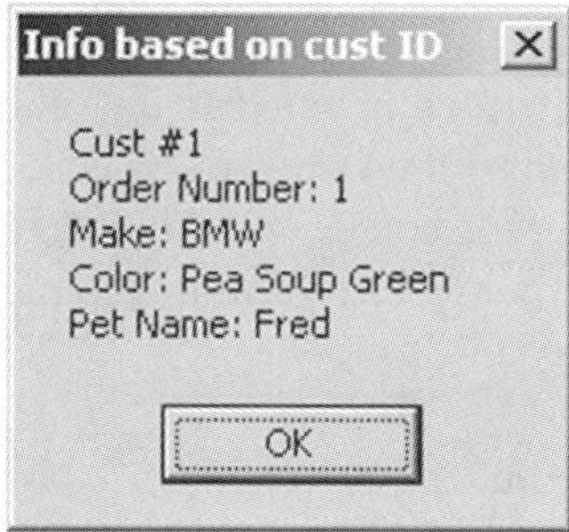

Figure 14-20. Navigating data relations

The Button's Click event handler is as shown here (error checking removed for clarity):

```
Private Sub btnGetInfo_Click(ByVal sender As System.Object, _
ByVal e As System.EventArgs) Handles btnGetInfo.Click
    Dim strInfo As String
    Dim drCust As DataRow
    Dim drsOrder() As DataRow
    ' Get the specified CustID from the TextBox.
    Dim theCust As Integer = Integer.Parse(Me.txtCustID.Text)
    ' Now based on CustID, get the correct row in Customers table.
    drCust = carsDataSet.Tables("Customers").Rows(theCust)
    strInfo &= "Cust #" & drCust("CustID").ToString() & vbLf
    ' Navigate from customer table to order table.
    drsOrder = drCust.GetChildRows(carsDataSet.Relations("CustomerOrder"))
    ' Get customer name.
    Dim r As DataRow
    For Each r In drsOrder
        strInfo &= "Order Number: " & r("OrderID").ToString() & vbLf
    Next
    ' Now navigate from order table to inventory table.
    Dim drsInv() As DataRow = _
        drsOrder(0).GetParentRows(carsDataSet.Relations("InventoryOrder"))
    ' Get Car info.
    For Each r In drsInv
        strInfo &= "Make: " & r("Make").ToString() & vbLf
        strInfo &= "Color: " & r("Color").ToString() & vbLf
```

```
        strInfo &= "Pet Name: " & r("PetName").ToString() & vbLf
    Next
    MessageBox.Show(strInfo, "Info based on cust ID")
End Sub
```

As you can see, the key to moving between data tables is to make use of a handful of methods defined by the DataRow type. Let's break this code down step by step. First, you obtain the correct customer ID from the text box, and use it to grab the correct row in the Customers table (using the Rows property, of course), as shown here:

```
' Get the specified CustID from the TextBox.
Dim theCust As Integer = Integer.Parse(Me.txtCustID.Text)
' Now based on CustID, get the correct row in Customers table.
Dim drCust As DataRow
drCust = carsDataSet.Tables("Customers").Rows(theCust)
strInfo &= "Cust #" & drCust("CustID").ToString() & vbLf
```

Next, you navigate from the Customers table to the Orders table, using the CustomerOrder data relation. Notice that the DataRow.GetChildRows() method allows you to grab rows from your child table, and once you do, you can read information out of the table, as shown here:

```
' Navigate from customer table to order table.
Dim drsOrder() As DataRow
drsOrder = drCust.GetChildRows(carsDataSet.Relations("CustomerOrder"))
' Get customer name.
Dim r As DataRow
For Each r In drsOrder
    strInfo &= "Order Number: " & r("OrderID").ToString() & vbLf
Next
```

Your final step is to navigate from the Orders table to its parent table (Inventory), using the GetParentRows() method. At this point, you can read information from the Inventory table using the Make, PetName, and Color columns, as shown here:

```
' Now navigate from order table to inventory table.
Dim drsInv() As DataRow = _
        drsOrder(0).GetParentRows(carsDataSet.Relations("InventoryOrder"))
' Get Car info.
```

```
For Each r In drsInv
    strInfo &= "Make: " & r("Make").ToString() & vbLf
    strInfo &= "Color: " & r("Color").ToString() & vbLf
    strInfo &= "Pet Name: " & r("PetName").ToString() & vbLf
Next
```

As a final example of navigating relations programmatically, the following code prints out the values in the Orders table that is obtained indirectly using the InventoryOrders relationship:

```
Private Sub btnGetChildRels_Click(ByVal sender As System.Object, _
ByVal e As System.EventArgs) Handles btnGetChildRels.Click
    ' Ask the CarsDataSet for the child relations of the inv. table.
    Dim relCol As DataRelationCollection
    Dim arrRows() As DataRow
    Dim info As String
    relCol = carsDataSet.Tables("inventory").ChildRelations
    info &= "Relation is called: " & relCol(0).RelationName + vbLf
    ' Now loop over each relation, and print out info.
    Dim dr As DataRelation
    For Each dr In relCol
        Dim r As DataRow
            For Each r In inventoryTable.Rows
                arrRows = r.GetChildRows(dr)
                ' Print out the value of each column in the row.
                Dim i As Integer
                    For i = 0 To arrRows.Length - 1
                        Dim dc As DataColumn
                        For Each dc In arrRows(i).Table.Columns
                            info &= "      " & arrRows(i)(dc).ToString()
                        Next
                    info += vbLf
                Next
            Next
            MessageBox.Show(info, _
                    "Data in Orders Table obtained by child relations")
    Next
End Sub
```

Figure 14-21 shows the output.

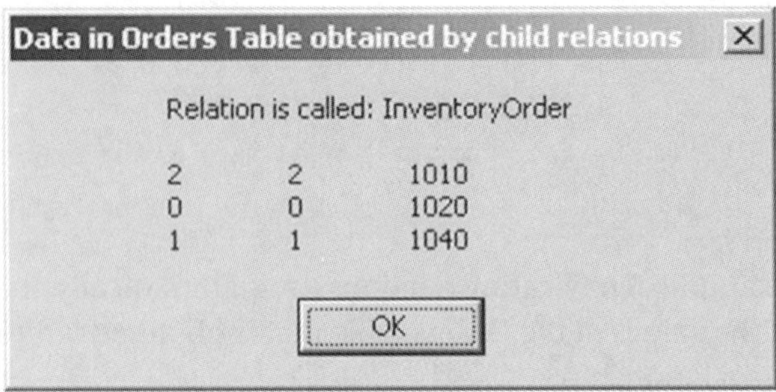

Figure 14-21. Navigating parent/child relations

I hope this last example has you convinced of the usefulness of the DataSet type. Given that a DataSet is completely disconnected from the underlying datasource, you can work with an in-memory copy of data and navigate around each table to make any necessary updates, deletes, or inserts. Once this is done, you can submit your changes to the data store for processing. Of course you don't yet know how to get connected! There is one final item of interest regarding the DataSet before addressing this issue.

Reading and Writing XML-Based DataSets

A major design goal of ADO.NET was to apply a liberal use of XML infrastructure. Using the DataSet type, you can write an XML representation of the contents of your tables, relations, and other schematic details into a given stream (such as a file). To do so, call the WriteXml() method, as shown here:

```
Private Sub btnToXML_Click(ByVal sender As System.Object, _
ByVal e As System.EventArgs) Handles btnToXML.Click
    carsDataSet.WriteXml("cars.xml")
    MessageBox.Show("Wrote CarDataSet to XML file in app directory")
    btnReadXML.Enabled = True
End Sub
```

If you open your new file in the Visual Studio.NET IDE (Figure 14-22), you see that the entire DataSet has been transformed into XML. (If you are not comfortable with XML syntax, don't sweat it. The DataSet understands XML just fine.)

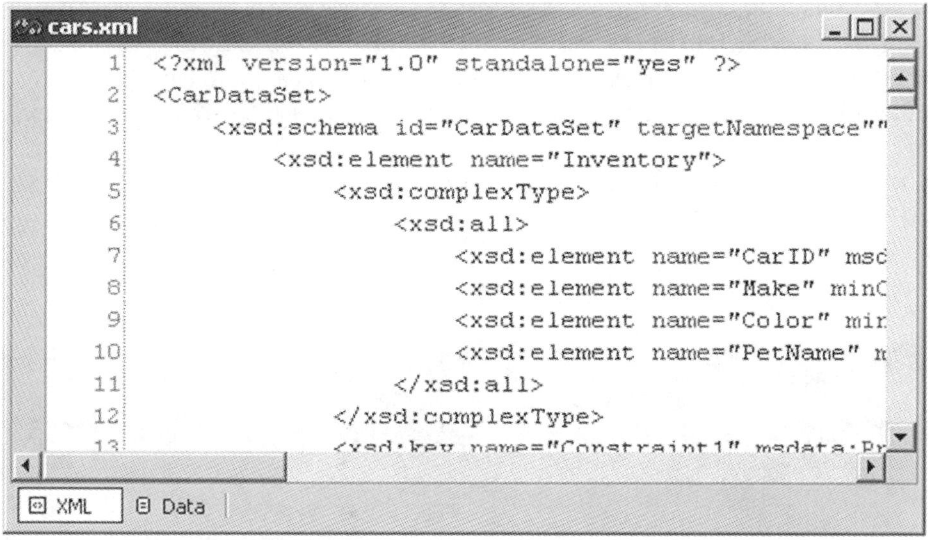

Figure 14-22. The DataSet as XML

To test the ReadXml() method of the DataSet, perform a little experiment. The CarDataSet application has a Button that clears out the current DataSet completely (including all tables and relations). After the in-memory representation has been gutted, instruct the DataSet to read in the cars.xml file, which, as you would guess, restores the entire DataSet, as shown here:

```
Private Sub btnReadXML_Click(ByVal sender As System.Object, _
ByVal e As System.EventArgs) Handles btnReadXML.Click
    ' Kill current DataSet.
    carsDataSet.Clear()
    carsDataSet.Dispose()
    MessageBox.Show("Just cleared data set. . .")
    carsDataSet = New DataSet("CarDataSet")
    ' Build using XML.
    carsDataSet.ReadXml("cars.xml")
    MessageBox.Show("Reconstructed data set from XML file. . .")
    btnReadXML.Enabled = False
    ' Bind to grids.
    CarDataGrid.SetDataBinding(carsDataSet, "Inventory")
    CustomerDataGrid.SetDataBinding(carsDataSet, "Customers")
End Sub
```

Be aware that under the hood, these XML-centric methods are making use of using types defined in the System.Xml.dll assembly (specifically the XmlReader and XmlWriter classes). Therefore, in addition to setting a reference to this binary, you will also need to make explicit reference to its types, as shown here:

```
' Need this namespace to call ReadXml() or WriteXml()!
Imports System.Xml
```

Figure 14-23 shows your final product.

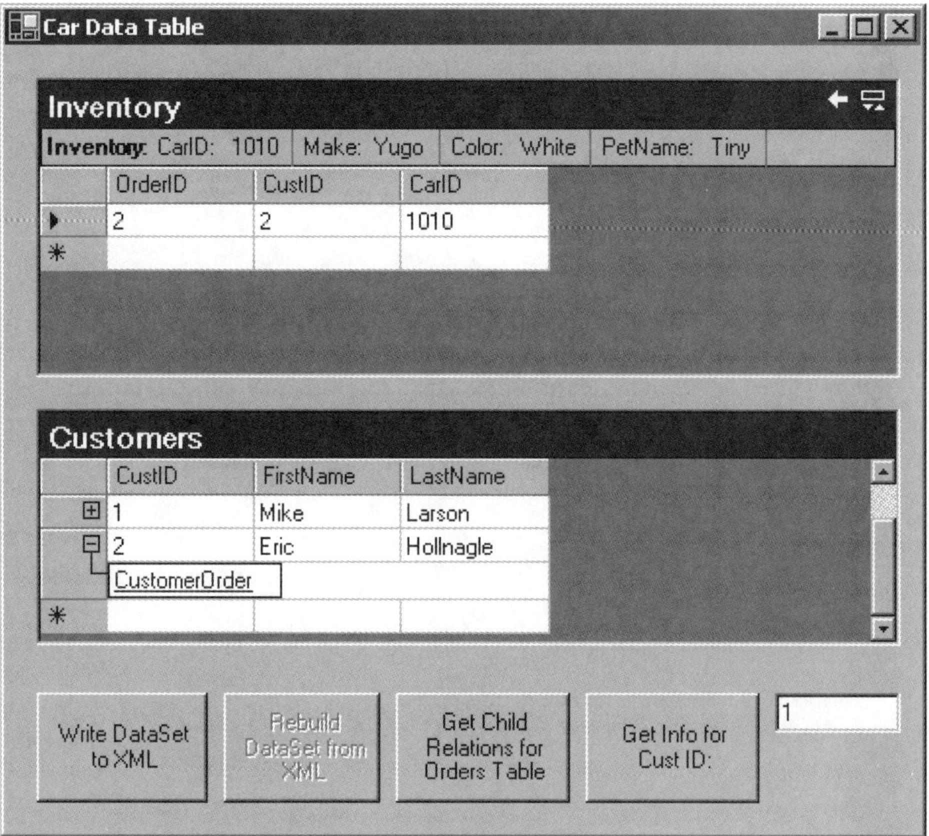

Figure 14-23. The final in-memory DataSet application

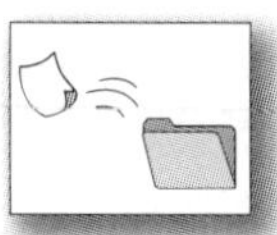

SOURCE CODE *The CarDataSet application is included under the Chapter 14 subdirectory.*

Building a Simple Test Database

Now that you understand how to create and manipulate a DataSet in memory, you can get down to the business of making a data connection and seeing how to obtain a populated DataSet. In keeping with the automotive theme used throughout this text, I have included two versions of a sample Cars database (available for download at www.apress.com) that models the Inventory, Orders, and Customers tables examined in the chapter.

The first version is a SQL script that builds the tables (including their relationships) and is intended for users of SQL Server 7.0 (and greater). To create the Cars database, begin by opening the Query Analyzer utility that ships with SQL Server. Next, connect to your machine and open the cars.sql file. Before you run the script, be sure that the path listed in the SQL file points to *your installation* of MS SQL Server. Thus, be sure you edit the following DDL (in bold) as necessary:

```
CREATE DATABASE [Cars]  ON (NAME = N'Cars_Data',
FILENAME = N' C:\MSSQL7\Data \Cars_Data.MDF' ,
SIZE = 2, FILEGROWTH = 10%)
LOG ON (NAME = N'Cars_Log',
FILENAME = N' C:\MSSQL7\Data\Cars_Log.LDF' ,
SIZE = 1, FILEGROWTH = 10%)
```

Now run your script. Once you do, open up the SQL Server Enterprise Manager (Figure 14-24). You should see the Cars database with all three interrelated tables (with some sample data to boot).

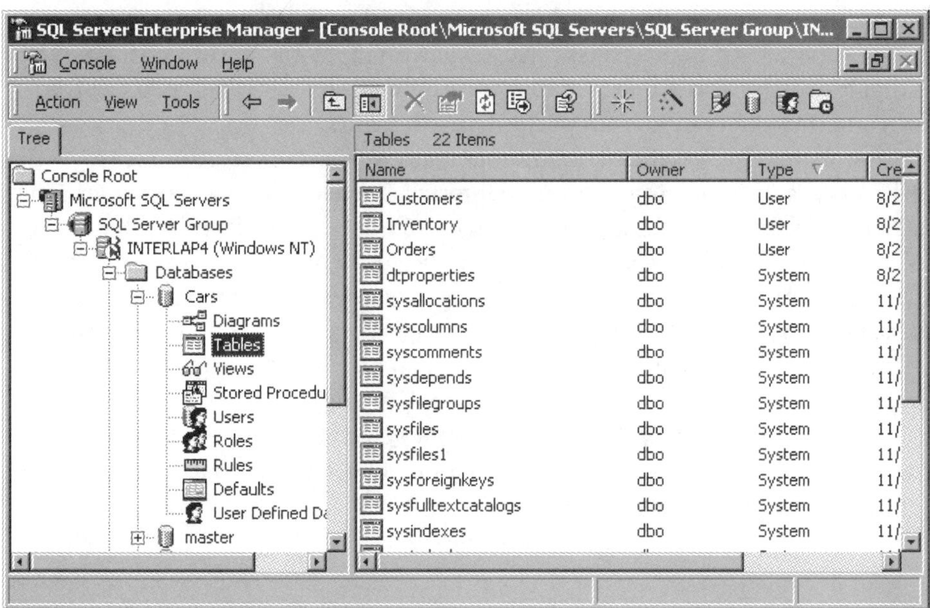

Figure 14-24. The SQL Server Cars database

The second version of the Cars database is for users of MS Access. Under the Access DB folder you will find the cars.mdb file, which contains the same information and underlying structure as the SQL Server version. During the remainder of this chapter, I will assume that you are connecting to the SQL Server Cars database rather than the Access equivalent. In just a bit, however, you see how to configure an ADO.NET connection string to hook into an *.mdb file.

ADO.NET Managed Providers

If you are coming to ADO.NET from a classic ADO background, you can assume that a managed provider is the .NET equivalent of an OLE DB provider. In other words, the managed provider is your gateway between a raw data store and a populated DataSet.

As mentioned earlier in this chapter, ADO.NET ships with two canned managed providers. The first of these is the OleDb managed provider, which is composed of the types defined in the System.Data.OleDb namespace. The OleDb provider allows you to access data located in any data store that supports the OLE DB protocol. Thus, like with classic ADO, you may use the ADO.NET managed provider to access SQL Server, Oracle, or MS Access databases. Because the types in the System.Data.OleDb namespace must communicate with unmanaged code (e.g., the OLE DB providers), you need to be aware that a number of .NET to COM translations occur behind the scenes, which can affect performance.

The other managed provider (the SQL provider) offers direct access to MS SQL Server data stores, and *only* SQL Server data stores (version 7.0 and greater). The System.Data.SqlClient namespace contains the types used by the SQL provider, and provides the same functionality as the OleDb provider. In fact, for the most part, both namespaces have similarly named items. The key difference is that the SQL provider does not make use of the OLE DB or classic ADO protocols, and thus offers numerous performance benefits.

Recall that the System.Data.Common namespace defines a number of abstract types that provide a common interface for each managed provider. First, each defines an implementation of the IDbConnection interface, which is used to configure and open a session with the data store. Objects that implement the IDbCommand interface are used to issue SQL queries against the database. Next is IDataReader, which allows you to read data using a forward-only, read-only cursor. Last but not least are types that implement IDbDataAdapter, which are responsible for populating a DataSet on behalf of the interested client.

For the most part you do not need to interact with the System.Data.Common namespace directly. However, to use either provider requires that you specify the proper using directive, as shown here:

```
' Going to access an OLE DB compliant data source.
Imports System.Data
Imports System.Data.OleDb


' Going to access SQL Server (7.0 or greater).
Imports System.Data
Imports System.Data.SqlClient
```

Working with the OleDb Managed Provider

Once you are comfortable with one managed provider, other providers are easily manipulated. Begin by examining how to connect using the OleDb managed provider. When you need to connect to any data source other than MS SQL Server, you will use the types defined in System.Data.OleDb. Table 14-12 provides a walkthrough of the core members.

Table 14-12. Types of the System.Data.OleDb Namespace

SYSTEM.DATA.OLEDB TYPE	MEANING IN LIFE
OleDbCommand	Represents a SQL query command to be made to a data source.
OleDbConnection	Represents an open connection to a data source.
OleDbDataAdapter	Represents a set of data commands and a database connection used to fill the DataSet and update the data source.
OleDbDataReader	Provides a way of reading a forward-only stream of data records from a data source.
OleDbErrorCollection OleDbError OleDbException	OleDbErrorCollection maintains a collection of warnings or errors returned by the data source, each of which is represented by an OleDbError type. When an error is encountered, an exception of type OleDbException is thrown.
OleDbParameterCollection OleDbParameter	Much like classic ADO, the OleDbParameterCollection collection holds onto the parameters sent to a stored procedure held in the database. Each parameter is of type OleDbParameter.

Establishing a Connection Using the OleDbConnection Type

The first step to take when working with the OleDb managed provider is to establish a session with the data source using the OleDbConnection type. Much like the classic ADO Connection object, OleDbConnection types are provided with a formatted connection string, containing a number of name/value pairs. This information is used to identify the name of the machine you want to connect to, required security settings, the name of the database on that machine, and, most importantly, the name of the OLE DB provider. (See online Help for a full description of each name/value pair.)

The connection string may be set using the OleDbConnection.ConnectionString property, or as a constructor argument. Assume you want to connect to the Cars database on the local machine using the SQL OLE DB provider. The following logic does the trick:

```
' Build a connection string.
Dim cn as OleDbConnection = New OleDbConnection()
cn.ConnectionString = "Provider=SQLOLEDB.1;" & _
"Integrated Security=SSPI;" & _
"Persist Security Info=False;" & _
"Initial Catalog=Cars;" & _
"Data Source=(local);"
```

As you may be able to infer from the preceding code, the Initial Catalog name refers to the database you are attempting to establish a session with (Pubs, Northwind, Cars, and so on). The Data Source name identifies the name of the machine that maintains the database. The final point of interest is the Provider segment, which specifies the name of the OLE DB provider that will be used to access the data store. Table 14-13 describes some possible values. (Table 14-13).

Table 14-13. Core OLE DB providers

PROVIDER SEGMENT VALUE	MEANING IN LIFE
Microsoft.JET.OLEDB.4.0	You want to use the Jet OLE DB provider to connect to an Access database.
MSDAORA	You want to use the OLE DB provider for Oracle.
SQLOLEDB	You want to use the OLE DB provider for MS SQL Server.

Once you have configured the connection string, the next step is to open a session with the data source, do some work, and release your connection to the data source, as shown here:

```
' Build a connection string (can specify User ID and Password if needed).
Dim cn as OleDbConnection = New OleDbConnection()
cn.ConnectionString = "Provider=SQLOLEDB.1;" & _
"Integrated Security=SSPI;" & _
"Persist Security Info=False;" & _
"Initial Catalog=Cars;" & _
"Data Source=(local);"
cn.Open()
      ' Do some interesting work here.
cn.Close()
```

In addition to the ConnectionString, Open(), and Close() members, the OleDbConnection class provides a number of members that let you configure attritional settings regarding your connection, such as timeout settings and transactional information. Table 14-14 gives a partial rundown.

Table 14-14. Members of the OleDbConnection Type

OLEDBCONNECTION MEMBER	MEANING IN LIFE
BeginTransaction() CommitTransaction() RollbackTransaction()	Used to programmatically commit, abort, or roll back a current transaction.
Close()	Closes the connection to the data source. This is the preferred method.
ConnectionString	Gets or sets the string used to open a session with a data store.
ConnectionTimeout	Gets or sets the time to wait while establishing a connection before terminating the attempt and generating an error. The default value is 15 seconds.
Database	Gets or sets the name of the current database or the database to be used once a connection is open.
DataSource	Gets or sets the name of the database to connect to.
Open()	Opens a database connection with the current property settings.
Provider	Gets or sets the name of the provider.
State	Gets the current state of the connection.

Building a SQL Command

The OleDbCommand class is an OO representation of a SQL query, which is manipulated using the CommandText property. Many types in the ADO.NET namespace require an OleDbCommand as a method parameter, to send the request to the data source. In addition to holding the raw SQL query, the OleDbCommand type defines other members that allow you to configure various characteristics of the query (Table 14-15).

Table 14-15. Members of the OleDbCommand Type

OLEDBCOMMAND MEMBER	MEANING IN LIFE
Cancel()	Cancels the execution of a command.
CommandText	Gets or sets the SQL command text or the provider-specific syntax to run against the data source.
CommandTimeout	Gets or sets the time to wait while executing the command before terminating the attempt and generating an error. The default is 30 seconds.
CommandType	Gets or sets how the CommandText property is interpreted.
Connection	Gets or sets the OleDbConnection used by this instance of the OleDbCommand.
ExecuteReader()	Returns an instance of an OleDbDataReader.
Parameters	Gets the collection of OleDbParameterCollection.
Prepare()	Creates a prepared (or compiled) version of the command on the data source.

Working with the OleDbCommand type is very simple, and like with the OleDbConnection object, there are numerous ways to achieve the same end result. As an example, note the following (semantically identical) ways to configure a SQL query using an active OleDbConnection object. In each case, assume you already have an OleDbConnection named cn:

```
' Specify a SQL command (take one).
Dim strSQL1 as String = "Select Make from Inventory where Color='Red'"
Dim myCommand1 as OleDbCommand = New OleDbCommand(strSQL1, cn)

' Specify SQL command (take two).
Dim strSQL2 as String = "Select Make from Inventory where Color='Red'"
Dim myCommand2 as OleDbCommand = New OleDbCommand()
```

```
MyCommand2.Connection = cn
MyCommand2.CommandText = strSQL2
```

Working with the OleDbDataReader

Once you have established the active connection and SQL command, the next step is to submit the query to the data source. There are a number of ways to do so. The OleDbDataReader type is the simplest, fastest, (but least flexible) way to obtain information from a data store. This class represents a read-only, forward-only stream of data returned one record at a time as a result of a SQL command.

The OleDbDataReader is useful when you need to iterate over large amounts of data very quickly, and have no need to work an in-memory DataSet representation. For example, if you request 20,000 records from a table to store in a text file, it would be rather memory intensive to hold this information in a DataSet. A better approach would be to create a data reader that spins over each record as rapidly as possible. Be aware however, that DataReaders (unlike DataSets) maintain a connection to their data source until you explicitly close the session.

To illustrate, the following class issues a simple SQL query against the Cars database, using the ExecuteReader() method of the OleDbCommand type. Using the Read() method of the returned OleDbDataReader, dump each member to the standard IO stream:

```
Module Module1
    Sub Main()
        ' open a connection.
        Dim cn As OleDbConnection = New OleDbConnection()
        cn.ConnectionString = "Provider=SQLOLEDB.1;" & _
         "Integrated Security=SSPI;" & _
         "Persist Security Info=False;" & _
         "Initial Catalog=Cars;" & _
         "Data Source=(local);"
        cn.Open()
        ' Create a SQL command.
        Dim strSQL As String = "SELECT Make FROM Inventory WHERE Color='Red'"
        Dim myCommand As OleDbCommand = New OleDbCommand(strSQL, cn)
        ' Obtain a data reader ala ExecuteReader().
        Dim myDataReader As System.Data.OleDb.OleDbDataReader
        myDataReader = myCommand.ExecuteReader()
        ' Loop over the results.
        While (myDataReader.Read())
            Console.WriteLine("Red car: {0}", myDataReader("Make").ToString())
        End While
```

```
        myDataReader.Close()
        cn.Close()
    End Sub
End Module
```

The result is the listing of all red automobiles in the Cars database (Figure 14-25).

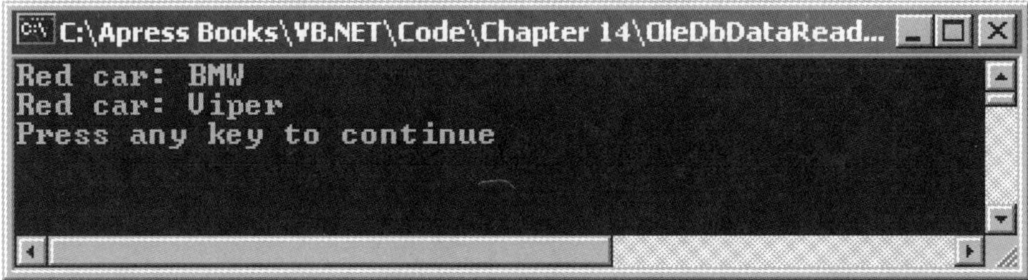

Figure 14-25. The OleDbDataReader in action

Recall that DataReaders are forward-only, read-only streams of data. Therefore, there is no way to navigate around the contents of the OleDbDataReader. All you can do is read each record and make use of it in your application:

```
' Get the value in the 'Make' column.
Console.WriteLine("Red car: {0}", myDataReader("Make").ToString())
```

When you are finished using the DataReader, make sure to terminate the session using the appropriately named method, Close(). In addition to the Read() and Close() methods, there are a number of other methods that allow you to obtain a value from a specified column in a given format (e.g., GetBoolean(), GetByte(), and so forth). Also, the FieldCount property returns the number of columns in the current record, and so forth.

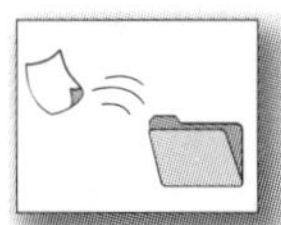

SOURCE CODE *The OleDbDataReader application is included under the Chapter 14 subdirectory.*

Connecting to an Access Database

Now that you know how to pull data from an SQL Server, let's take a moment to see how to obtain data from an Access database. To illustrate, let's modify the previous OleDbDataReader application to read from the cars.mdb file.

Much like classic ADO, the process of connecting to an Access database using ADO.NET requires little more than retrofitting your construction string. First, set the Provider segment to the JET engine, rather than SQLOLEDB. Beyond this adjustment, set the data source segment to point to the path of your *.mdb file, as shown here:

```
' Be sure to update the data source segment if necessary!
Dim cn As OleDbConnection = New OleDbConnection()
cn.ConnectionString = "Provider=Microsoft.JET.OLEDB.4.0;" & _
"data source = C:\Apress Books\VB .NET\Code\Chapter 14\Access DB\cars.mdb"
cn.Open()
```

Once the connection has been made, you can read and manipulate the contents of your data table. The only other point to be aware of is that, given that the use of the JET engine requires OLEDB, you must use the types defined in the System.Data.OleDb namespace (e.g., the OleDb managed provider). Remember, the SQL provider only allows you to access MS SQL Server data stores!

Executing a Stored Procedure

When you are constructing a distributed application, one of the design choices you face is where to store the business logic. One approach is to build reusable binary code libraries, which may be managed by a surrogate process such as the Windows 2000 Component Services manager. Another approach is to place the system's business logic on the data layer in the form of stored procedures. Yet another approach is to supply a blend of each technique.

A stored procedure is a named block of SQL code stored at the database. Stored procedures may be constructed to return a set of rows (or native data types) to the calling component, and may take any number of optional parameters. The end result is a unit of work that behaves like a typical function, with the obvious difference of being located on a data store rather than a binary business object.

Let's add a simple stored procedure to our existing Cars database called GetPetName, which takes an input parameter of type integer. (If you ran the supplied SQL script, this stored proc is already defined.) This is the numerical ID of the car for which you are interested in obtaining the pet name, which is returned as an output parameter of type char. Here is the syntax:

```
CREATE PROCEDURE GetPetName
     @carID int,
     @petName char(20) output
AS
SELECT @petName = PetName from Inventory where CarID = @carID
```

Now that you have a stored procedure in place, let's see the code necessary to execute it. Begin as always by creating a new OleDbConnection, configure your connection string, and open the session. Next, you need to create a new OleDbCommand type, making sure to specify the name of the stored procedure and setting the CommandType property accordingly, as shown here:

```
' Open connection to data store.
Dim cn As OleDbConnection = New OleDbConnection()
cn.ConnectionString = "Provider=SQLOLEDB.1;" & _
                "Integrated Security=SSPI;" & _
                "Persist Security Info=False;" & _
                "Initial Catalog=Cars;" & _
                "Data Source=(local);"
cn.Open()

' Make a command obj for the stored proc.
Dim myCommand As OleDbCommand = New OleDbCommand("GetPetName", cn)
myCommand.CommandType = CommandType.StoredProcedure
```

The CommandType property of the OleDbCommand class can be set using any of the values specified in the related CommandType enumeration (Table 14-16).

Table 14-16. Values of the CommandType Enumeration

COMMANDTYPE ENUMERATION VALUE	MEANING IN LIFE
StoredProcedure	Used to configure an OleDbCommand that triggers a stored procedure.
TableDirect	The OleDbCommand represents a table name whose columns are all returned.
Text	The OleDbCommand type contains a standard SQL text command. This is the default value.

When you issue basic SQL queries (e.g., "SELECT * FROM Inventory") to the data source, the default CommandType.Text setting is appropriate. However, to issue a command to hit a stored procedure, specify CommandType.StoredProcedure.

Specifying Parameters Using the OleDbParameter Type

The next task is to establish the parameters used for the call. The OleDbParameter type is an OO wrapper around a particular parameter passed to (or received from) the stored procedure. This class maintains a number of properties that allow you to configure the name, size, and data type of the parameter, as well as its direction of travel. Table 14-17 describes some key properties of the OleDbParameter type.

Table 14-17. Members of the OleDbParameter Type

OLEDBPARAMETER PROPERTY	MEANING IN LIFE
DataType	Establishes the type of the parameter, in terms of .NET.
DbType	Gets or sets the native data type from the data source, using the OleDbType enumeration.
Direction	Gets or sets whether the parameter is input only, output only, bidirectional, or a return value parameter.
IsNullable	Gets or sets whether the parameter accepts null values.
ParameterName	Gets or sets the name of the OleDbParameter.
Precision	Gets or sets the maximum number of digits used to represent the Value.
Scale	Gets or sets the number of decimal places to which Value is resolved.
Size	Gets or sets the maximum parameter size of the data.
Value	Gets or sets the value of the parameter.

Given that you have one input and one output parameter, you can configure your types as so. Note that you then add these items to the OleDbCommand type's ParametersCollection (which is, of course, accessed via the Parameters property):

```
' Create the parameters for the call.
Dim theParam As OleDbParameter = New OleDbParameter()
' Input.
theParam.ParameterName = "@carID"
theParam.OleDbType = OleDbType.Integer
theParam.Direction = ParameterDirection.Input
theParam.Value = 1   ' Car ID = 1.
```

```
myCommand.Parameters.Add(theParam)
' Output.
theParam = New OleDbParameter()
theParam.ParameterName = "@petName"
theParam.OleDbType = OleDbType.Char
theParam.Size = 20
theParam.Direction = ParameterDirection.Output
myCommand.Parameters.Add(theParam)
```

The final step is to execute the command using OleDbCommand.ExecuteNonQuery(). Notice that the Value property of the OleDbParameter type is accessed to obtain the returned pet name, as shown here:

```
' Execute the command!
myCommand.ExecuteNonQuery()

' Display the result.
Console.WriteLine("Stored Proc Info:")
Console.WriteLine("Car ID: {0}", myCommand.Parameters("@carID").Value)
Console.WriteLine("PetName: {0}", myCommand.Parameters("@petName").Value)
```

Figure 14-26 shows the output.

```
C:\Apress Books\VB.NET\Code\Chapter 14\OleDbStore...
Stored Proc Info:
Car ID: 1
PetName: Snake
Press any key to continue
```

Figure 14-26. Triggering the stored procedure

SOURCE CODE *The OleDbStoredProc project is included under the Chapter 14 subdirectory.*

The Role of the OleDbDataAdapter Type

At this point you should understand how to connect to a data source using the OleDbConnection type, issue a command (using the OleDbCommand and

OleDbParameter types), and work with the OleDbDataReader. This is just fine when you want to iterate over a batch of data very quickly or trigger a stored procedure. However, the most flexible way to obtain a complete DataSet from the data store is through the use of the OleDbDataAdapter.

In a nutshell, this type pulls information from a data store, and populates a DataTable contained in a DataSet using the OleDbDataAdapter.Fill() method, which has been overloaded a number of times. Here are a few possibilities (FYI, the Integer return type holds the number of records returned):

```
' Fills the data set with records from a given source table.
Public Fill(yourDS as DataSet, tableName as String) as Integer

' Fills the data set with the records located between
' the given bounds from a given source table.
Public Fill(yourDS as DataSet, tableName as String, _
                startRecord as Integer, maxRecord as Integer) as Integer
```

Before you can call this method, you need a valid OleDbDataAdapter object reference. The constructor has also been overloaded a number of times, but in general you need to supply the connection information and the SQL SELECT statement used to fill the DataTable.

The OleDbDataAdapter type not only is the entity that fills the tables of a DataSet on your behalf, but is also in charge of maintaining a set of core SQL statements used to push updates back to the data store. Table 14-18 describes some of the core members of the OleDbDataAdapter type.

Table 14-18. Core Members of the OleDbDataAdapter

OLEDBDATAADAPTER MEMBER	MEANING IN LIFE
DeleteCommand InsertCommand SelectCommand UpdateCommand	Used to establish SQL commands that will be issued to the data store when the Update() method is called. Each of these properties is set using an OleDbCommand type.
Fill()	Fills a given table in the DataSet with some number of records.
GetFillParameters()	Returns all parameters used when performing the select command.
Update()	Calls the respective INSERT, UPDATE, or DELETE statements for each inserted, updated, or deleted row for a given table in the DataSet.

The key properties of the OleDbDataAdapter (and as well as the SqlDataAdapter) are DeleteCommand, InsertCommand, SelectCommand, and UpdateCommand. A data adapter understands how to submit changes on behalf of a given DataTable. For example, when you call Update(), the data adapter uses the SQL commands stored in each of these properties automatically. As you will see, the amount of code required to configure these properties is a bit on the verbose side. Before you check these properties out firsthand, let's begin by learning how to use a data adapter to fill a DataSet programmatically.

Filling a DataSet Using the OleDbDataAdapter Type

The following code populates a DataSet (containing a single table) using an OleDbDataAdapter:

```
Sub Main()
    ' Step 1: Open a connection.
    Dim cn As OleDbConnection = New OleDbConnection()
    cn.ConnectionString = "Provider=SQLOLEDB.1;" & _
         "Integrated Security=SSPI;" & _
         "Persist Security Info=False;" & _
         "Initial Catalog=Cars;" & _
         "Data Source=(local);"
    cn.Open()
    ' Step 2: Create SELECT command.
    ' Create a SELECT command.
    Dim selectCmd As OleDbCommand = New OleDbCommand _
    ("SELECT * FROM Inventory", cn)
    ' Step 3: Make a data adapter & associate commands.
    Dim dAdapt As OleDbDataAdapter = New OleDbDataAdapter()
    dAdapt.SelectCommand = selectCmd
    ' Step 4: Create and fill the DataSet, close connection.
    Dim myDS As DataSet = New DataSet("CarsDataSet")
    Try
        dAdapt.Fill(myDS, "Inventory")
    Catch ex As Exception
        Console.WriteLine(ex.Message)
    Finally
        cn.Close()
    End Try
    ' Helper function.
    PrintTable(myDS)
End Sub
```

Notice that unlike your work during the first half of this chapter, you did *not* manually direct a DataTable type and add it to the DataSet. Rather, you specified the Inventory table as the second parameter to the Fill() method. Internally, Fill() builds the DataTable given the name of the table in the data store using the SELECT command. In this iteration, the connection between the given SQL SELECT statement and the OleDbDataAdapter was established as a constructor parameter:

```
' Create a SELECT command as string type.
Dim sqlSELECT as String = "SELECT * FROM Inventory"
Dim dAdapt as OleDbDataAdapter = New OleDbDataAdapter(sqlSELECT, cn)
```

As a more OO-aware alternative, you can use the OleDbCommand type to hold onto the SELECT statement. To associate the OleDbCommand to the OleDbDataAdapter, use the SelectCommand property, as shown here:

```
' Create a SELECT command object.
Dim selectCmd as OleDbCommand = New OleDbCommand("SELECT * FROM Inventory", cn)
' Make a data adapter and& associate commands.
Dim dAdapt as OleDbDataAdapter = New OleDbDataAdapter()
dAdapt.SelectCommand = selectCmd
```

Notice that in this case, you attach the active OleDbConnection as a parameter to the OleDbCommand. Figure 14-27 shows the end result.

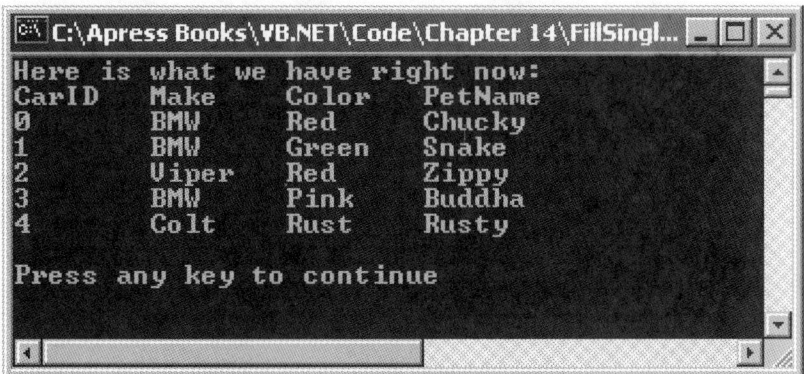

Figure 14-27. The OleDbDataAdapter in action

The PrintTable() method is little more than some formatting razzle-dazzle:

```
Public Sub PrintTable(ByVal ds As DataSet)
    ' Print out results from table.
    Console.WriteLine("Here is what we have right now:")
    Dim invTable As DataTable = ds.Tables("Inventory")
    ' Print the Column names.
    Dim curCol As Integer
    For curCol = 0 To invTable.Columns.Count - 1
        Console.Write(invTable.Columns(curCol).ColumnName.Trim() & vbTab)
    Next
    Console.WriteLine()
    ' Print each cell.
    Dim curRow As Integer
    For curRow = 0 To invTable.Rows.Count - 1
        For curCol = 0 To invTable.Columns.Count - 1
        Console.Write(invTable.Rows(curRow)(curCol).ToString().Trim() & vbTab)
        Next
        Console.WriteLine()
    Next
        Console.WriteLine()
    End Sub
```

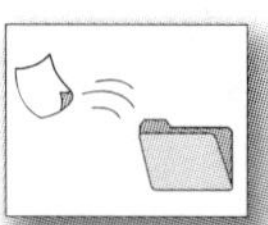

SOURCE CODE *The FillSingleDSWithAdapter project is under the Chapter 14 subdirectory.*

Working with the SQL Managed Provider

Before you see the details of inserting, updating, and removing records using a data adapter, I would like to introduce the SQL managed provider. As you recall, the OleDb provider allows you to access any OLE DB compliant data store, but is less optimized than the SQL provider.

When you know that the data source you need to manipulate is MS SQL Server, you will find performance gains if you use the System.Data.SqlClient namespace directly. Collectively, these classes constitute the functionality of the SQL managed provider, which should look very familiar given your work with the OleDb provider (Table 14-19).

Table 14-19. Core Types of the System.Data.SqlClient Namespace

SYSTEM.DATA.SQLCLIENT TYPE	MEANING IN LIFE
SqlCommand	Represents a Transact-SQL query to execute at a SQL Server data source.
SqlConnection	Represents an open connection to a SQL Server data source.
SqlDataAdapter	Represents a set of data commands and a database connection which are used to fill the DataSet and update the SQL Server data source.
SqlDataReader	Provides a way of reading a forward-only stream of data records from a SQL Server data source.
SqlErrors SqlError SqlException	SqlErrors maintains a collection of warnings or errors returned by SQL Server, each of which is represented by a SQLError type. When an error is encountered, an exception of type SQLException is thrown.
SqlParameterCollection SqlParameter	SqlParametersCollection holds onto the parameters sent to a stored procedure held in the database. Each parameter is of type SQLParameter.

Given that working with these types is almost identical to working with the OleDb managed provider, you should already know what to do with these types, as they have the same public interface. To help you get comfortable with this new set of types, the remainder of the examples use the SQL managed provider.

The System.Data.SqlTypes Namespace

When you use the SQL managed provider, you also have the luxury of using a number of managed types that represent native SQL server data types. Table 14-20 gives a quick rundown.

Table 14-20. Types of the System.Data.SqlTypes Namespace

SYSTEM.DATA.SQLTYPES WRAPPER	NATIVE SQL SERVER
SqlBinary	binary, varbinary, timestamp, image
SqlInt64	bigint
SqlBit	bit
SqlDateTime	datetime, smalldatetime
SqlNumeric	decimal
SqlDouble	float
SqlInt32	int
SqlMoney	money, smallmoney
SqlString	nchar, ntext, nvarchar, sysname, text, varchar, char
SqlNumeric	numeric
SqlSingle	real
SqlInt16	smallint
System.Object	sql_variant
SqlByte	tinyint
SqlGuid	uniqueidentifier

Inserting New Records Using the SqlDataAdapter

Now that you have flipped from the OleDb provider to the realm of the SQL provider, you can return to the task of understanding the role of data adapters. Let's examine how to insert new records in a given table using the SqlDataAdapter (which would be nearly identical to using the OleDbDataAdapter). As always, begin by creating an active connection, as shown here:

```
Sub Main()
    ' Step 1: Create a connection and adapter.
    Dim cn As SqlConnection = New _
    SqlConnection("server=(local);uid=sa;pwd=;database=Cars")
    Dim dAdapt As SqlDataAdapter = _
    New SqlDataAdapter("Select * from Inventory", cn)
```

```
    'Step 2: Kill record you inserted (mentioned in a moment)
    cn.Open()
   Dim killCmd as SqlCommand = _
   New SqlCommand("Delete from Inventory Where CarID = '1111'", cn)
   KillCmd.ExecuteNonQuery()
   cn.Close()
End Sub
```

You can see that the connection string has cleaned up quite a bit. In particular, notice that you do not need to define a Provider segment (as the SQL types only talk to a SQL server!). Next, create a new SqlDataAdapter and specify the value of the SelectCommand property as a constructor parameter (just like with the OleDbDataAdapter).

The second step is really more of a good housekeeping chore. Here, you create a new SqlCommand type that destroys the record you are about to enter (to avoid a primary key violation). The next step is a bit more involved. Your goal is to create a new SQL statement that will function as the SqlDataAdapter's InsertCommand. First, create the new SqlCommand and specify a standard SQL insert, followed by SqlParameter types describing each column in the Inventory table, as shown here:

```
' Create a connection and adapter.
. . .
' Build the insert Command
dAdapt.InsertCommand = _
New SqlCommand("INSERT INTO Inventory (CarID, Make, Color, PetName)" & _
" VALUES (@CarID, @Make, @Color, @PetName)", cn)

' Build parameters for each column in Inventory table.
Dim workParam As SqlParameter
workParam = dAdapt.InsertCommand.Parameters.Add _
(New SqlParameter("@CarID", SqlDbType.Int))
workParam.SourceColumn = "CarID"
workParam.SourceVersion = DataRowVersion.Current

workParam = dAdapt.InsertCommand.Parameters.Add _
(New SqlParameter("@Make", SqlDbType.VarChar))
workParam.SourceColumn = "Make"
workParam.SourceVersion = DataRowVersion.Current
```

```
workParam = dAdapt.InsertCommand.Parameters.Add _
(New SqlParameter("@Color", SqlDbType.VarChar))
workParam.SourceColumn = "Color"
workParam.SourceVersion = DataRowVersion.Current

workParam = dAdapt.InsertCommand.Parameters.Add _
(New SqlParameter("@PetName", SqlDbType.VarChar))
workParam.SourceColumn = "PetName"
workParam.SourceVersion = DataRowVersion.Current
```

Now that you have formatted each of the parameters, the final step is to fill the DataSet and add your new row (note that the PrintTable() helper function has carried over to this example):

```
' Fill data set
Dim myDS As DataSet = New DataSet()
dAdapt.Fill(myDS, "Inventory")
PrintTable(myDS)
' Add new row.
Dim newRow As DataRow = myDS.Tables("Inventory").NewRow()
newRow("CarID") = 666
newRow("Make") = "SlugBug"
newRow("Color") = "Pink"
newRow("PetName") = "Cranky"
myDS.Tables("Inventory").Rows.Add(newRow)
' Send back to database and reprint.
Try
    dAdapt.Update(myDS, "Inventory")
    myDS.Dispose()
    myDS = New DataSet()
    dAdapt.Fill(myDS, "Inventory")
    PrintTable(myDS)
Catch e As Exception
    Console.Write(e.ToString())
End Try
```

When you run the application, you see the output shown in Figure 14-28.

```
C:\Apress Books\VB.NET\Code\Chapter 14\InsertRow...
Here is what we have right now:
CarID   Make    Color   PetName
0       BMW     Red     Chucky
1       BMW     Green   Snake
2       Viper   Red     Zippy
3       BMW     Pink    Buddha
4       Colt    Rust    Rusty

Here is what we have right now:
CarID   Make    Color   PetName
0       BMW     Red     Chucky
1       BMW     Green   Snake
2       Viper   Red     Zippy
3       BMW     Pink    Buddha
4       Colt    Rust    Rusty
666     SlugBug Pink    Cranky

Press any key to continue
```

Figure 14-28. The InsertCommand Property in action

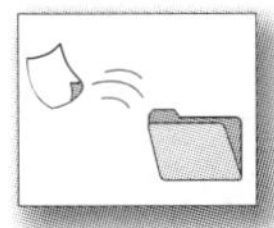

SOURCE CODE *The InsertRowsWithSqlAdapter project can be found under the Chapter 14 subdirectory.*

Updating Existing Records Using the SqlDataAdapter

Now that you can insert new rows, look at how you can update existing rows. Again, start the process by obtaining a connection (using the SqlConnection type) and creating a new SqlDataAdapter. Next, set the value of the UpdateCommand property, using the same general approach as when setting the value of the InsertCommand. Here is the relevant code in Main():

```
Sub Main()
    ' Step 1: Create a connection and adapter.
    Dim cn As SqlConnection = New _
    SqlConnection("server=(local);uid=sa;pwd=;database=Cars")
    Dim dAdapt As SqlDataAdapter = _
    New SqlDataAdapter("Select * from Inventory", cn)
    ' Step 2: Establish the UpdateCommand.
    dAdapt.UpdateCommand = New SqlCommand("UPDATE Inventory SET " & _
    "Make = @Make, Color = @Color, PetName = @PetName " & _
    "WHERE CarID = @CarID", cn)
```

```
        ' Step 3: Build parameters for each column in Inventory table.
        Dim workParam As SqlParameter
        workParam = dAdapt.UpdateCommand.Parameters.Add _
        (New SqlParameter("@CarID", SqlDbType.Int))
        workParam.SourceColumn = "CarID"
        workParam.SourceVersion = DataRowVersion.Current
        workParam = dAdapt.UpdateCommand.Parameters.Add(New _
        SqlParameter("@Make", SqlDbType.VarChar))
        workParam.SourceColumn = "Make"
        workParam.SourceVersion = DataRowVersion.Current
        workParam = dAdapt.UpdateCommand.Parameters.Add(New _
        SqlParameter("@Color", SqlDbType.VarChar))
        workParam.SourceColumn = "Color"
        workParam.SourceVersion = DataRowVersion.Current
        workParam = dAdapt.UpdateCommand.Parameters.Add(New _
        SqlParameter("@PetName", SqlDbType.VarChar))
        workParam.SourceColumn = "PetName"
        workParam.SourceVersion = DataRowVersion.Current
        ' Step 4: Fill data set (with PK).
        Dim myDS As DataSet = New DataSet()
        dAdapt.Fill(myDS, "Inventory")
        PrintTable(myDS)
        ' Step 5: Change row.
        Dim changeRow As DataRow = myDS.Tables("Inventory").Rows(1)
        changeRow("Make") = "FooFoo"
        changeRow("Color") = "FooFoo"
        changeRow("PetName") = "FooFoo"
        ' Step 6: Send back to database and reprint.
        Try
            dAdapt.Update(myDS, "Inventory")
            myDS.Dispose()
            myDS = New DataSet()
            dAdapt.Fill(myDS, "Inventory")
            PrintTable(myDS)
        Catch e As Exception
        Console.Write(e.ToString())
        End Try
    End Sub
```

Figure 14-29 shows the output.

```
C:\Apress Books\VB.NET\Code\Chapter 14\UpdateR...
Here is what we have right now:
CarID   Make    Color   PetName
0       BMW     Red     Chucky
1       FooFoo  FooFoo  FooFoo
2       Viper   Red     Zippy
3       BMW     Pink    Buddha
4       Colt    Rust    Rusty
666     SlugBug Pink    Cranky

Here is what we have right now:
CarID   Make    Color   PetName
0       BMW     Red     Chucky
1       FooFoo  FooFoo  FooFoo
2       Viper   Red     Zippy
3       BMW     Pink    Buddha
4       Colt    Rust    Rusty
666     SlugBug Pink    Cranky

Press any key to continue
```

Figure 14-29. Updating existing rows

SOURCE CODE *The UpdateRowsWithSqlAdapter project is found under the Chapter 14 subdirectory.*

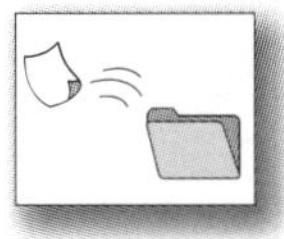

Autogenerated SQL Commands

At this point you can use the data adapter types (OleDbDataAdapter and SqlDataAdapter) to select, delete, insert, and update records from a given data source. Although the general process is not rocket science, it is a bit of a bother to build up all the parameter types and configure the InsertCommand, UpdateCommand, and DeleteCommand properties by hand. As you would expect, some help is available.

One approach is to use the SqlCommandBuilder type. If you have a DataTable that is composed from a single table (not from multiple joined tables), the SqlCommandBuilder automatically sets the InsertCommand, UpdateCommand, and DeleteCommand properties based on the initial SelectCommand! In addition to the no-join restriction, the table must have been assigned a primary key, and this column must be specified in the initial SELECT statement. The benefit is that you have no need to build all those SqlParameter types by hand.

To illustrate, assume you have a new Windows Forms example, which allows the user to edit the values in a DataGrid. When finished, the user may submit changes back to the database using a Button type. First, assume the following constructor logic:

```
Public Class Form1
    Inherits System.Windows.Forms.Form
    Private cn As SqlConnection = New _
    SqlConnection("server=(local);uid=sa;pwd=;database=Cars;")
    Private dAdapt As SqlDataAdapter
    Private invBuilder As SqlCommandBuilder
    Private myDS As DataSet = New DataSet()
    Private dataGrid1 As System.Windows.Forms.DataGrid
    Private WithEvents btnUpdateData As System.Windows.Forms.Button

    Public Sub New()
        MyBase.New()
        'This call is required by the Windows Form Designer.
        InitializeComponent()
        ' Create the SELECT SQL statement.
        dAdapt = New SqlDataAdapter("Select * from Inventory", cn)
        ' Auto generate the INSERT, UPDATE and DELETE statements.
        invBuilder = New SqlCommandBuilder(dAdapt)
        ' Fill and bind.
        dAdapt.Fill(myDS, "Inventory")
        dataGrid1.DataSource = myDS.Tables("Inventory").DefaultView
    End Sub
End Class
```

Beyond closing the connection on exiting, that's it! At this point the SqlDataAdapter has all the information it needs to submit changes back to the data store. Now assume that you have the following logic behind the Button's Click event:

```
Private Sub btnUpdateData_Click(ByVal sender As System.Object, _
ByVal e As System.EventArgs) Handles btnUpdateData.Click
    Try
        dataGrid1.Refresh()
        dAdapt.Update(myDS, "Inventory")
    Catch ex As Exception
        MessageBox.Show(ex.ToString())
    End Try
End Sub
```

As usual, you call Update() and specify the DataSet and table to update. If you take this out for a test run, you see something like Figure 14-30.

Windows Data Adapter Client

Inventory

CarID	Make	Color	PetName
1	FooFoo	FooFoo	FooFoo
2	Viper	Red	Zippy
3	BMW	Pink	Buddha
4	Viper	Rust	Killer
89	Yugo	Purple	(null)
666	SlugBug	Pink	Cranky
876	Pinto	Brown	Beanie
78	Saab	(null)	(null)

Submit Changes

Figure 14-30. Extending our DataSet with new DataRows

Excellent! I am sure you agree that autogenerated commands are far simpler than working with the raw parameters. Like all things, of course, there are tradeoffs. Specifically, if you have a DataTable composed from a join operation, you cannot use this technique. Also, as you have seen, when you work with parameters in the raw, you have a much finer level of granularity.

SOURCE CODE *The WinFormSqlAdapter project is included under the Chapter 14 subdirectory.*

Filling a Multitabled DataSet (and Adding DataRelations)

To wrap things up, let's come full circle and build a final Windows Forms example that mimics the application you created during the first half of this chapter. The GUI is simple enough. In Figure 14-31 you can see three DataGrid types that hold the data retrieved from the Inventory, Orders, and Customers tables of the Cars database. In addition, the single Button pushes any and all changes back to the data store:

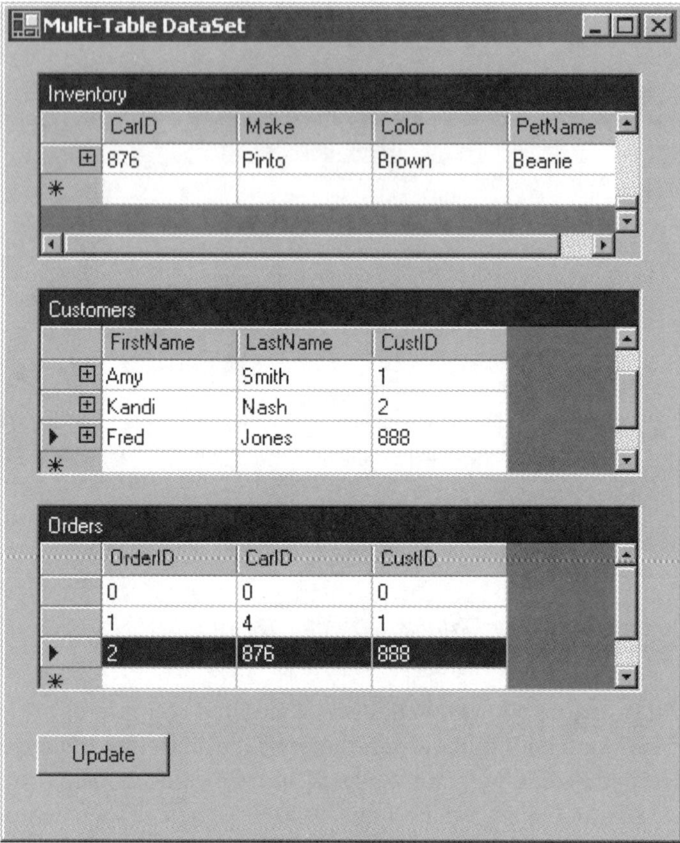

Figure 14-31. A multitable DataSet on display

To keep things even simpler, use autogenerated commands for each of the three SqlDataAdapters (one for each table). First, here is the Form's state data:

```
Public Class Form1
    Inherits System.Windows.Forms.Form
    Private custGrid As System.Windows.Forms.DataGrid
    Private inventoryGrid As System.Windows.Forms.DataGrid
    Private WithEvents btnUpdate As System.Windows.Forms.Button
    Private OrdersGrid As System.Windows.Forms.DataGrid
    ' Here is the connection.
    Private cn As SqlConnection = New _
    SqlConnection("server=(local);uid=sa;pwd=;database=Cars;")
    ' Our data adapters (for each table).
    Private invTableAdapter As SqlDataAdapter
    Private custTableAdapter As SqlDataAdapter
```

```
    Private ordersTableAdapter As SqlDataAdapter
    ' Command builders.
    Private invBuilder As SqlCommandBuilder = New SqlCommandBuilder()
    Private orderBuilder As SqlCommandBuilder = New SqlCommandBuilder()
    Private custBuilder As SqlCommandBuilder = New SqlCommandBuilder()
    ' The dataset.
    Private carsDS As DataSet = New DataSet("Cars")
End Class
```

The Form's constructor does the grunge work of creating your data-centric member variables and filling the DataSet. Also note that there is a call to a private helper function, BuildTableRelationship(), as shown here:

```
Public Sub New()
...
    cn.Open()
    ' Create adapters.
    Try
        invTableAdapter = New SqlDataAdapter("Select * from Inventory", cn)
        custTableAdapter = New SqlDataAdapter("Select * from Customers", cn)
        ordersTableAdapter = New SqlDataAdapter("Select * from Orders", cn)
    Catch e As Exception
        MessageBox.Show(e.Message)
    End Try
    ' Auto gen commands.
    invBuilder = New SqlCommandBuilder(invTableAdapter)
    orderBuilder = New SqlCommandBuilder(ordersTableAdapter)
    custBuilder = New SqlCommandBuilder(custTableAdapter)
    ' Fill tables into DS.
    Try
        invTableAdapter.Fill(carsDS, "Inventory")
        custTableAdapter.Fill(carsDS, "Customers")
        ordersTableAdapter.Fill(carsDS, "Orders")
    Catch e As Exception
        MessageBox.Show(e.Message)
    End Try
    ' Build relations.
    BuildTableRelationship()
End Sub
```

The BuildTableRelationship() helper function does just what you would expect. Recall that the Cars database expresses a number of parent/child relationships. The code looks identical to the logic seen earlier in this chapter, as shown here:

```
Private Sub BuildTableRelationship()
    ' Create a DR obj.
    Dim dr As DataRelation = New DataRelation("CustomerOrder", _
    carsDS.Tables("Customers").Columns("CustID"), _
    carsDS.Tables("Orders").Columns("CustID"))
    ' Add to the DataSet.
    carsDS.Relations.Add(dr)
    ' Create another DR obj.
    dr = New DataRelation("InventoryOrder", _
      carsDS.Tables("Inventory").Columns("CarID"), _
      carsDS.Tables("Orders").Columns("CarID"))
    ' Add to the DataSet.
    carsDS.Relations.Add(dr)
    ' Fill the grids!
    inventoryGrid.SetDataBinding(carsDS, "Inventory")
    custGrid.SetDataBinding(carsDS, "Customers")
    OrdersGrid.SetDataBinding(carsDS, "Orders")
End Sub
```

Now that the DataSet has been filled and disconnected from the data source, you can manipulate each table locally. To do so, simply insert, update, or delete values from any of the three DataGrids. When you are ready to submit the data back for processing, click the Form's Update Button. The code behind the Click event should be clear at this point, as shown here:

```
Private Sub btnUpdate_Click(ByVal sender As System.Object, _
ByVal e As System.EventArgs) Handles btnUpdate.Click
    Try
        invTableAdapter.Update(carsDS, "Inventory")
        custTableAdapter.Update(carsDS, "Customers")
        ordersTableAdapter.Update(carsDS, "Orders")
    Catch ex As Exception
        MessageBox.Show(ex.Message)
    End Try
End Sub
```

Once you update, you can find each table in the Cars database correctly altered.

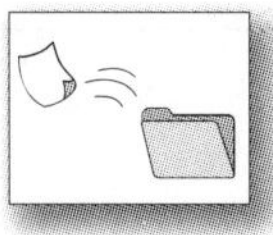

SOURCE CODE *The MultiTableDataSet project is included under the Chapter 14 subdirectory.*

Bring in the Wizards!

At this point you have had the chance to work with the DataSet type and the related classes provided by the OleDb and SqlClient managed providers 'in the raw'. Although this did entail a good amount of typing on your part, the good news is that you now have a solid understanding of how to interact with ADO.NET. Nevertheless, let's close this chapter by spending some time checking out the numerous data manipulation tools provided by VS.NET. Given your work up until this point, you should have no problem reading (and augmenting) the generated code.

Establishing a Data Connection

To begin, create a brand new Windows Application named VSDataWizards. Now, open the Server Explorer window (using the View menu) and right click on the 'Data Connections' node to establish a connection with the Cars database (Figure 14-32).

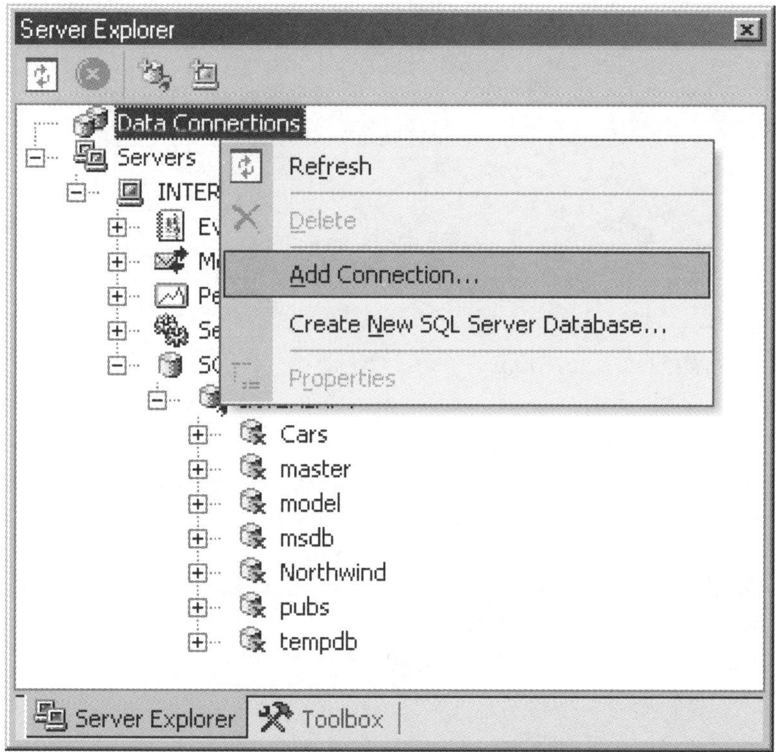

Figure 14-32. Creating an active connection

As you can see (Figure 14-33), this menu option launches the all-familiar Data Link wizard (a common staple in earlier editions of VB). Go ahead and connect to the Cars database and close the tool.

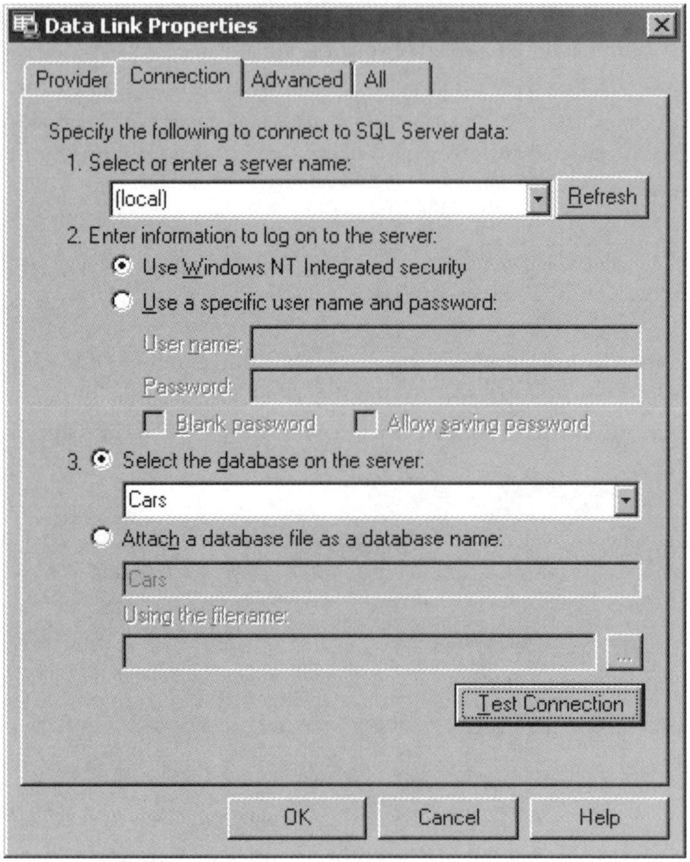

Figure 14-33. The Data Link tool

At this point, you will find a new connection under the Data Connections node. As you can see from Figure 14-34, you are able to view each object (i.e., tables, stored procedures, diagrams, and whatnot) defined by the Cars database. As you would expect, if you double-click on a given item, a corresponding window is opened within the IDE to allow you to view and edit a particular database object (provided you have the right security credentials!).

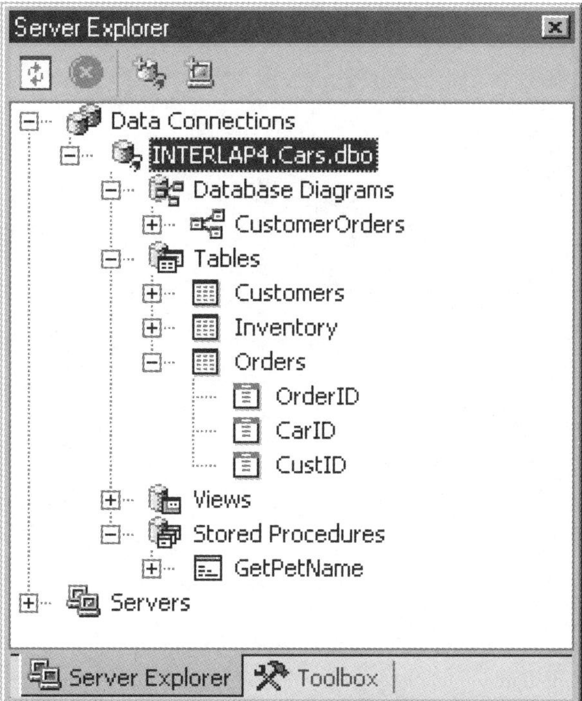

Figure 14-34. The Cars connection

Understand that when you create a connection to a database, you have not altered your code base in any way. However, this is a mandatory step when preparing to make use of the other intergraded data Wizards.

Creating a SQL Connection at Design Time

As you have seen earlier in this chapter, the System.Data.SqlClient.SqlConnection type defines a ConnectionString property, which contains information regarding a programmatic connection to a given data source. While it is not too difficult to build a connection string by hand, the IDE provides a number of tools to assist you in this regard. To illustrate, activate the Data tab from the Toolbox window, and place a SqlConnection component onto your design time Form (Figure 14-35).

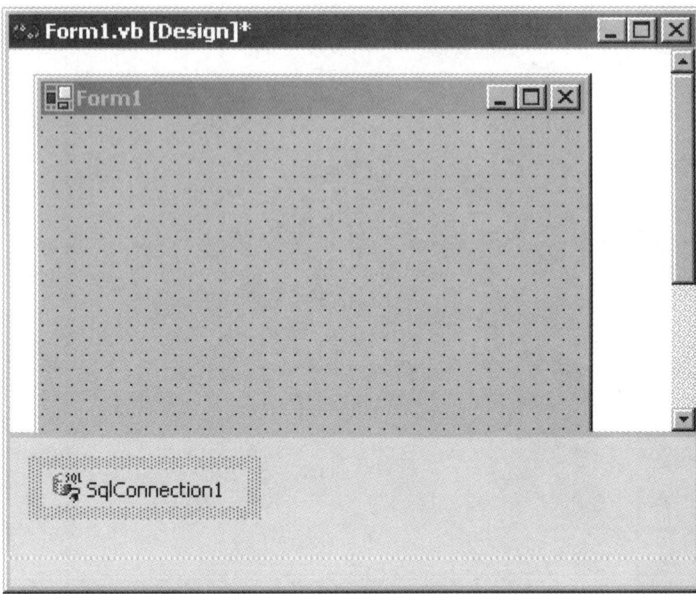

Figure 14-35. The SqlConnection component

Once you have done so, select this item from the Icon Tray, and using the Properties window, select the name of your Cars connection from the ConnectionString property drop down list (Figure 14-36).

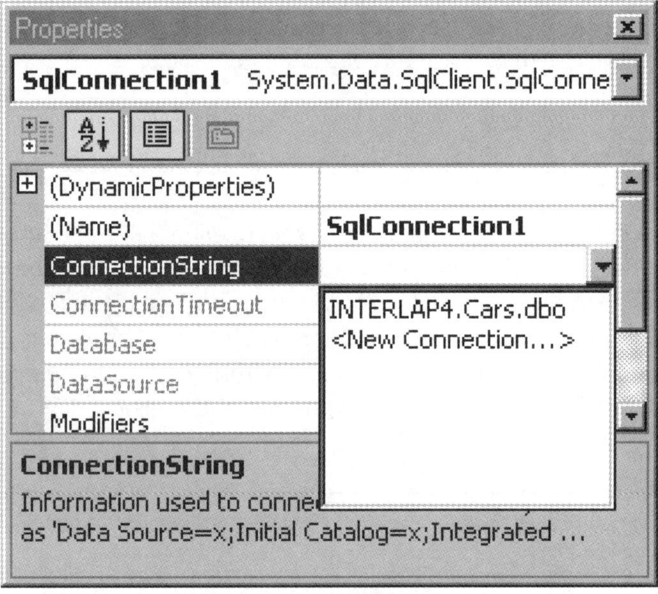

Figure 14-36. The SqlConnection component at work

At this point, you are pleased to see that a valid connection string has been created on your behalf (within the #region code block):

```
...
Friend WithEvents SqlConnection1 As System.Data.SqlClient.SqlConnection
...
<System.Diagnostics.DebuggerStepThrough()> Private Sub InitializeComponent()
        Me.SqlConnection1 = New System.Data.SqlClient.SqlConnection()
        '
        'SqlConnection1
        '
        Me.SqlConnection1.ConnectionString = "data source=(local);"& _
        initial catalog=Cars;" & _
        integrated security=SSPI;persist security info=False;" & _
        "workstation id=INTERLAP4;packet size=4096"
```

Building a Data Adapter

The VS .NET IDE also provides an integrated Wizard that takes care of the grunge work that is necessary to build Select, Update, Insert, and Delete commands for a given SqlDataAdapter (or OleDbDataAdapter). As you have already seen, writing this code by hand can be a bit on the verbose side. To take this tool out for a test drive, place a SqlDataAdapter component onto your Icon Tray. This action will launch the Data Adapter Configuration Wizard. Once you click past the initial Welcome screen, you will be asked which data connection should be used to configure the data adapter (Figure 14-37).

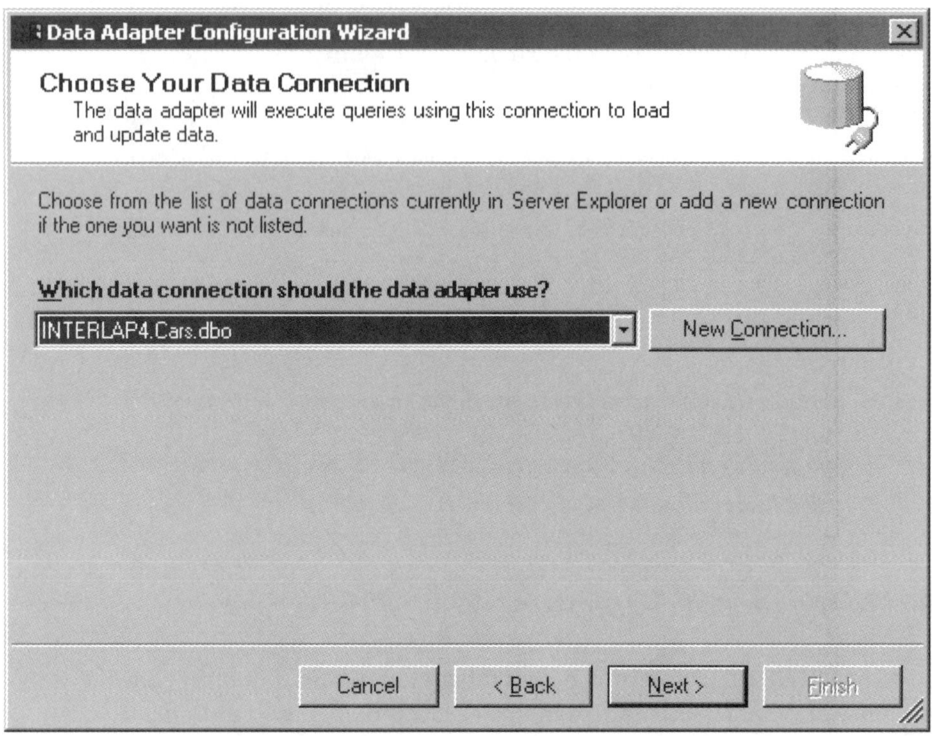

Figure 14-37. Selecting the connection

The next step allows you to configure how the data adapter should submit data to the data store (Figure 14-38).

As you can see from Figure 14-38, you have three choices. If you want to move data between the data store and the DataSet using stored procedures, you may instruct the Wizard to generate new Insert, Update, and Delete functions based on an initial Select statement or as an alternative, choose prefabricated stored procedures. Your final option is to have the Wizard build SQL queries. I'll assume you will check out the generated stored procedures at your leisure, so simply select "Use SQL Statements" for the time being.

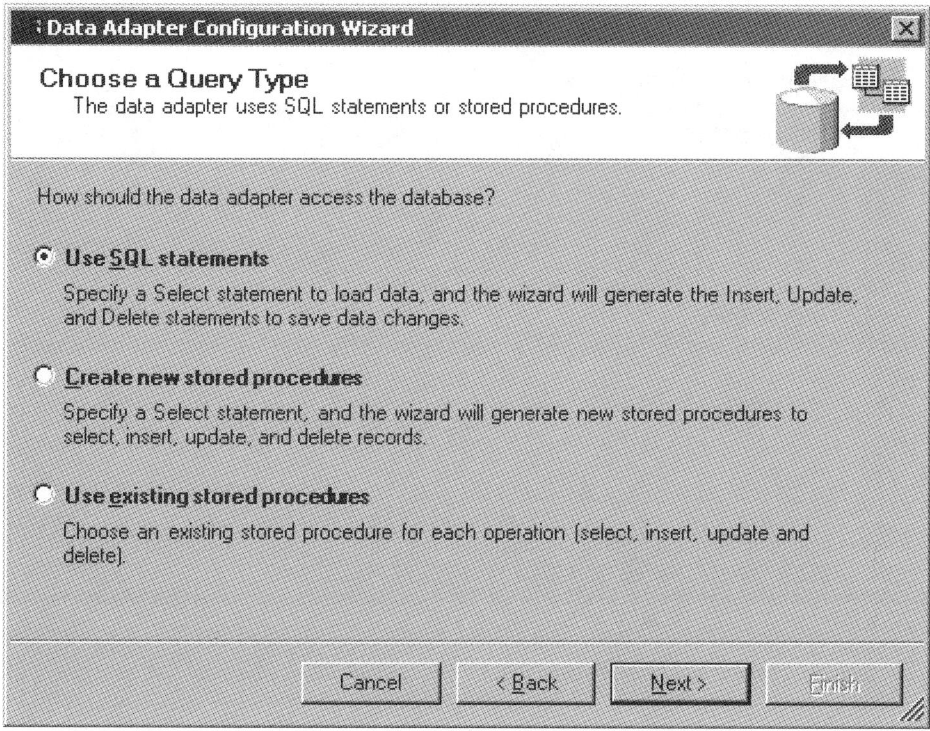

Figure 14-38. Configuring the behavior of your data adapter.

The next step of the tool asks you to specify the SQL Select statement that will be used to build the set of SQL queries (Figure 14-39). Although you may simply type in the SQL Select by hand, you can also activate the Query Builder tool (which should look familiar to many Visual Basic developers).

At this point, you are provided with a final confirmation of the work done on your behalf. Now, open your code window and check out the InitializeComponent() method. As you can see, the new SqlCommand data members are configured automatically. I won't bother to list each aspect of the

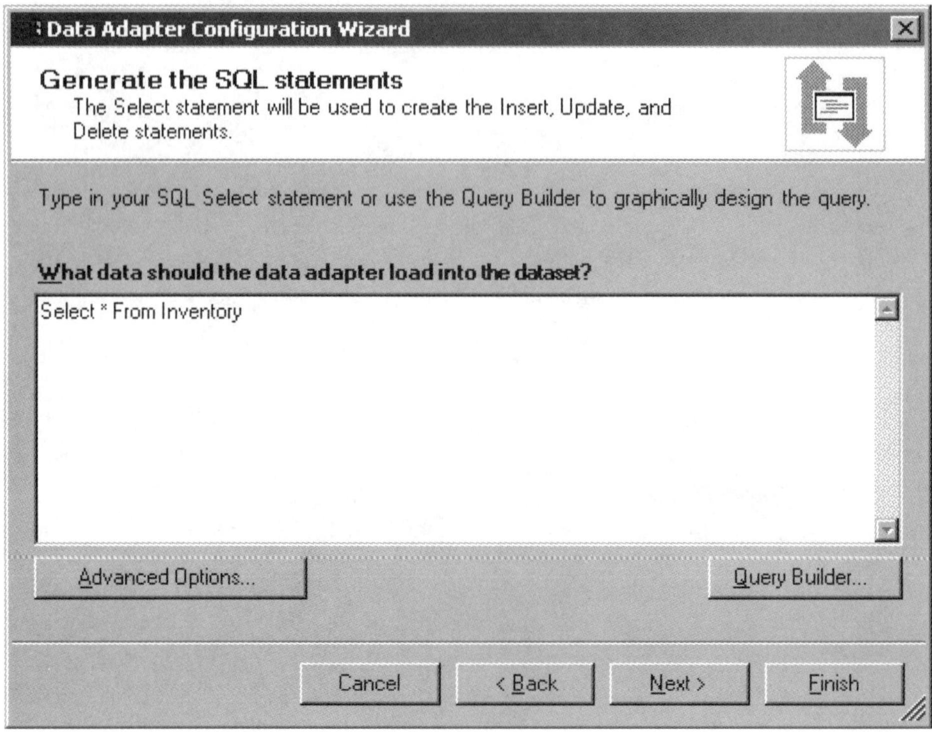

Figure 14-39. Specifying the initial Select.

generated code, as you have already manually written the same syntax by hand during the chapter. However, here is a partial snapshot:

```
Public Class Form1
    Inherits System.Windows.Forms.Form
. . .
    Friend WithEvents SqlDataAdapter1 As System.Data.SqlClient.SqlDataAdapter
    Friend WithEvents SqlSelectCommand1 As System.Data.SqlClient.SqlCommand
    Friend WithEvents SqlInsertCommand1 As System.Data.SqlClient.SqlCommand
    Friend WithEvents SqlUpdateCommand1 As System.Data.SqlClient.SqlCommand
    Friend WithEvents SqlDeleteCommand1 As System.Data.SqlClient.SqlCommand
    . . . .
    'SqlSelectCommand1
    '
    Me.SqlSelectCommand1.CommandText = _
    "SELECT CarID, Make, Color, PetName FROM Inventory"
    Me.SqlSelectCommand1.Connection = Me.SqlConnection1
    '
```

```
    'SqlInsertCommand1
    '
    Me.SqlInsertCommand1.CommandText = _
    "INSERT INTO Inventory(CarID, Make, Color, " & _
    PetName) VALUES (@CarID, @Make, @Color," & _
    " @PetName); SELECT CarID, Make, Color, _
    PetName FROM Inventory WHERE (CarID = @Se" & _
    "lect_CarID)"
    Me.SqlInsertCommand1.Connection = Me.SqlConnection1
    Me.SqlInsertCommand1.Parameters.Add(New     _
    System.Data.SqlClient.SqlParameter("@CarID",  _
    System.Data.SqlDbType.Int, 4, _
    System.Data.ParameterDirection.Input, False, _
    CType(0, Byte), CType(0, _
    Byte), "CarID", System.Data.DataRowVersion.Current, Nothing))
...
```

Hopefully, things look quite familiar.

Using the Configured Data Adapter

At this point you are free to make use of any of the tricks you have learned about during the chapter to obtain and manipulate a DataSet. By way of a simple test, place a DataGrid widget onto the main Form, and show the inventory table on start-up. All you need is the following constructor logic (note that the connection was opened implicitly on your behalf when the data adapter comes to life . . . be sure to close the connection when you are finished).

```
Public Sub New()
    MyBase.New()
    'This call is required by the Windows Form Designer.
    InitializeComponent()
    ' Fill the grid (close In the Dispose() method)!
    Dim ds As New DataSet()
    SqlDataAdapter1.Fill(ds, "Inventory")
    DataGrid1.DataSource = ds.Tables("Inventory")
End Sub
```

Which gives us the expected output as shown in Figure 14-40.

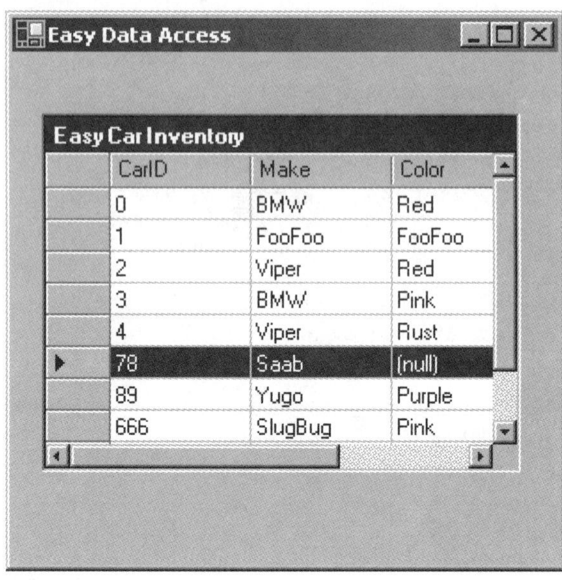

Figure 14-40. Not bad for 4 lines of code!

So, as you can see, VB .NET still provides a generous amount of design time support that makes interacting with ADO.NET extremely painless. To be sure, you will most likely take advantage of this design time support, however given your work in this chapter, you should feel quite confident that you can alter the Wizard generated code as you see fit.

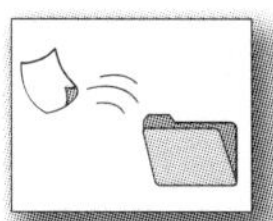

SOURCE CODE *The VSDataWizards project is included under the Chapter 14 subdirectory.*

Summary

ADO.NET is a brand-new data access technology developed with the disconnected *n*-tier application firmly in mind. The System.Data namespace contains most of the core types you need to programmatically interact with rows, columns, tables, and views. As you have seen, the System.Data.SqlClient and System.Data.OleDb namespaces define the types you need to establish an active connection.

The centerpiece of ADO.NET is the DataSet. This type represents an in-memory representation of any number of tables and any number of optional interrelationships, constraints, and expressions. The beauty of establishing relations on your local tables is that you are able to programmatically navigate between them while disconnected from the remote data store.

Finally, this chapter examined the role of the data adapter (OleDbDataAdapter and SqlDataAdapter). Using this type (and the related SelectCommand, InsertCommand, UpdateCommand, and DeleteCommand properties), the adapter can resolve changes in the DataSet with the original data store.

CHAPTER 15

Web Development and ASP.NET

UNTIL NOW, ALL OF YOUR example applications have used Windows Forms or console-based front ends. In this chapter, you begin to explore how the .NET platform facilitates the construction of browser-based presentation layers. To begin, you will review some basic Web atoms, including HTML, HTTP requests (POST and GET), the role of client-side scripting (using JavaScript), and classic ASP. *Of course, if you are already "Web aware," feel free to skim or skip this section entirely* (I italicize this caveat to prevent the casual reader from making the faulty assumption that this chapter is only concerned with basic HTML).

With the initial Web primer out of the way, the remainder of this chapter focuses on ASP.NET proper. As you will see, ASP.NET supports a far more robust programming model than classic ASP. For example, you can now partition your HTML presentation logic and business logic into discrete locations using a technique called *Codebehind.* Furthermore, building Web applications with ASP.NET enables you to use "real" programming languages such as VB .NET and C#, rather than interpreted scripting languages (in fact, server-side scripting is effectively dead under .NET). As you examine the architecture of an ASP.NET Web application, you learn about the almighty Page type and the classic ASP–like Request, Response, Session, and Application properties.

After this point, the chapter shifts focus to examine the role of ASP.NET Web controls, data binding, and server-side event handling. To pull together the material presented in this chapter, I wrap up by building a minimal and complete Web application. Once you have absorbed the following material, you are in a perfect position to examine the topic of the next chapter: ASP.NET Web services.

Web Applications and Web Servers

Before diving into the ASP.NET framework, let's take some time to review the basic architecture of a simple Web application and explore some core Web-centric technologies in the process (again, feel free to skim this section if you are already Web-aware). To begin, a *Web application* can be understood as a collection of related files (*.htm, *.asp, *.aspx, image files, and so on) and related components (.NET or classic COM binaries) stored on a Web server.

A *Web server* is a software product in charge of hosting your Web applications and it typically provides a number of related services such as integrated security, File Transfer Protocol (FTP) support, mail exchange services, and so forth. Internet Information Server (IIS) is Microsoft's enterprise-level Web server product. Currently, IIS is in its fifth version (IIS 5.0) and has been integrated as part of the Windows 2000 operating system.

When you create classic ASP as well as ASP.NET Web applications, you will be required to (directly or indirectly) interact with IIS. Be aware, however, that IIS is *not* automatically selected when you install Windows 2000 Professional Edition. Therefore, you may be required to manually install IIS before proceeding through this chapter. To install IIS, simply access the Add/Remove Program applet from the Control Panel folder and select Add/Remove Windows Components.

Assuming you have IIS properly installed on your workstation, you can launch IIS from the Administrative Tools folder (again located in the Control Panel folder). For this chapter you are only concerned with the Default Web Site node (see Figure 15-1).

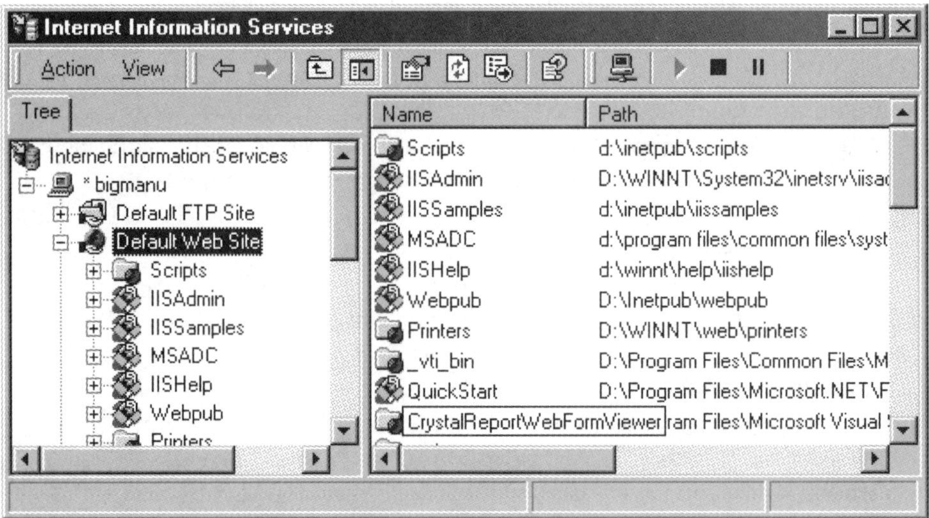

Figure 15-1. The IIS Manager applet

Understanding Virtual Directories

A given IIS installation is able to host numerous Web applications, each of which typically resides in a *virtual directory*. Each virtual directory is mapped to a physical directory on the local hard drive. Therefore, if you create a new Web application named FrogsAreUs, the outside world navigates to your site using a Universal Resource Locator (URL) such as `http://www.FrogsAreUs.com/`

(assuming your site's IP address has been registered with the world at large). Internally, however, the Web application may map to a physical directory such as "C:\FrogsSite," which contains the set of files that constitute the Web application.

To illustrate, let's create a simple Web application named Cars. The first step is to create a new folder on your machine to hold the collection of files that constitute this new site (for example, C:\CarsWebSite). Once this is done, you need to create a new virtual directory to host the Cars site. There are many ways to accomplish this using the IIS applet—one of which is to simply right-click the Default Web Site node and select "New | Virtual Directory" from the context menu (see Figure 15-2).

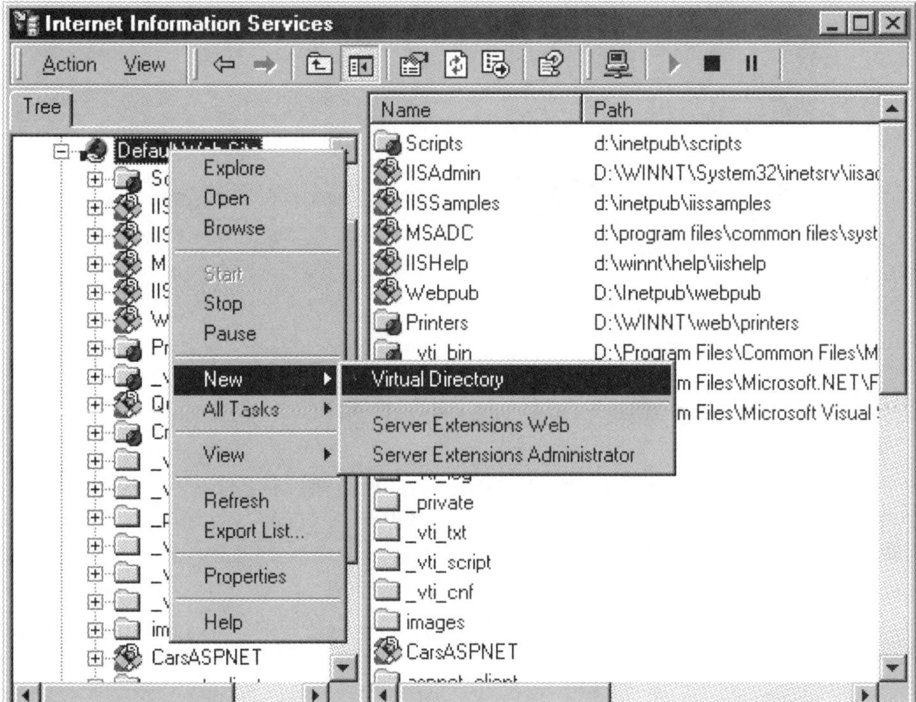

Figure 15-2. Creating a virtual directory

This menu selection launches an integrated Wizard. Skip past the welcome screen and give your Web site a name (Cars). Next, you are asked to specify the physical folder on your hard drive that contains the various files and images that represent this site (in this case, C:\CarsWebSite).

The final step of the wizard prompts you for some basic traits about your new virtual directory (such as read/write access to the files it contains, the ability to view these files from a Web browser, the ability to launch executables [e.g., CGI applications], and so on). For this endeavor, the default selections are just fine.

(As you would hope, you can always modify your selections after running this tool using the Properties window.) Once you are finished, you see that your new virtual directory has been registered with IIS (see Figure 15-3).

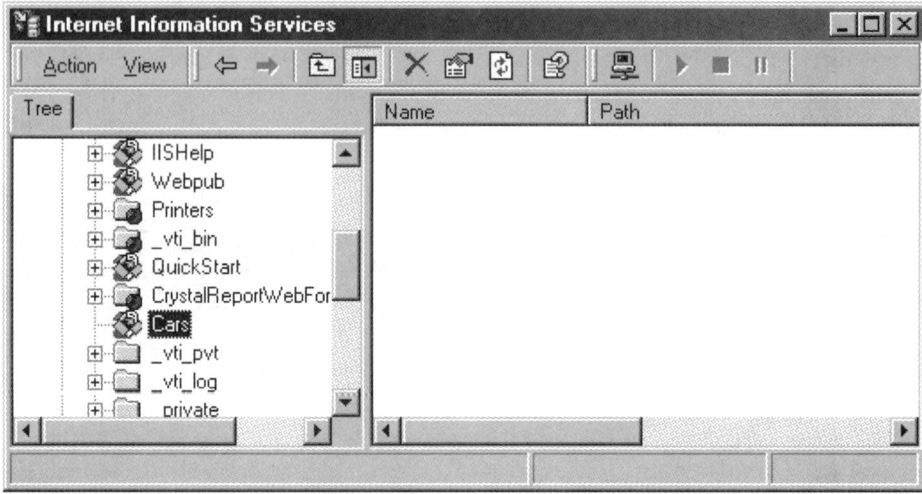

Figure 15-3. Your new virtual directory

The Basic Structure of an HTML Document

Now that you have a virtual directory, you need to create the Web application itself. When you build Web applications, you cannot escape the use of Hypertext Markup Language (HTML). As you know, HTML is a standard markup language used to describe how text, images, links, and various HTML GUI widgets are rendered by the hosting Web browser. While it is true that modern IDEs (including VS .NET) have built-in tools that hide most of the raw HTML from view, you still need to feel comfortable with basic HTML syntax as you work with ASP.NET, so let's review.

A given HTML file consists of a core set of markup tags used to specify the fact that it is an HTML file, define general document information (title, file metadata, and so forth), and establish the body of the document (i.e., the collection of text, images, tables, and links). Keep in mind that HTML tags are not case-sensitive. Therefore, in the eyes of the hosting browser, <HTML>, <html>, and <Html> are identical.

To get started, open the VS .NET IDE and insert an empty HTML file using the "File | New | File. . ." menu selection and save this file under your physical directory as default.htm. If you examine the new *.htm file created by the IDE, you find the following skeletal definition:

```
<!DOCTYPE HTML PUBLIC "-//W3C//DTD HTML 4.0 Transitional//EN">
<html>
     <head>
          <title></title>
          <meta name="GENERATOR" content="Microsoft Visual Studio.NET 7.0">
     </head>
     <body>
     </body>
</html>
```

A given HTML tag is opened using the <*X*> notation and closed with a corresponding </*X*> (slash) tag. Although the syntax of HTML allows for a degree of laziness (closing end tags are not absolutely required in many cases), it is good practice to always close a tag with the </*X*> syntax.

The <html> and </html> tags are used to mark the beginning and end of your document. As you may guess, Web browsers use these tags to understand where to begin applying the rendering formats specified in the body of the document.

The <head> tags are used to hold any metadata about the document itself. Here, the HTML header uses some <meta> tags that describe the origin of this file (MS Visual Studio .NET 7.0). Currently, your page has no title, so modify this HTML file to look like the following:

```
<!DOCTYPE HTML PUBLIC "-//W3C//DTD HTML 4.0 Transitional//EN">
<html>
     <head>
          <title>HTML is unavoidable</title>
          <meta name="GENERATOR" content="Microsoft Visual Studio.NET 7.0">
     </head>
     <body>
     </body>
</html>
```

The <title> tag is used to specify the text string that should be placed in the title bar of the hosting Web browser. After you save this file and open it in a browser, you see something like the window in Figure 15-4. (Note the caption of the window.)

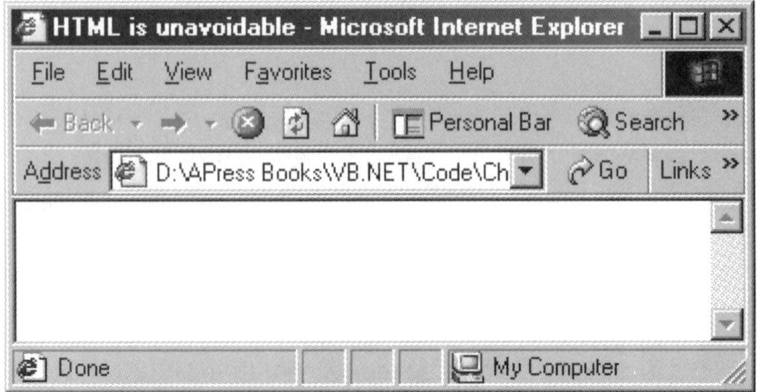

Figure 15-4. The <title> tag in action

The real action in an HTML file takes place in the <body> tag set. Nestled within these tags is any number of additional tags used to render and format textual or graphical information. While an exhaustive examination of every HTML tag is (way) beyond the scope of this book, the next several pages document some of the core tags you are bound to run into when working with ASP.NET Web applications.

Basic HTML Text Formatting

One obvious use of an HTML file is to display textual messages. In HTML, text elements are typically placed within the <body> tag set. For example, assume that you are building a login page for a given Web application, as shown here (note the HTML comment syntax):

```
<body>
    <!-- Prompt for user -->
    The Cars Login Page
</body>
```

Notice that in this case, you did not surround the text block with additional tags. When the browser finds a line of untagged text, it pumps out the textual information exactly as written. Thus, if you update the <body> as shown here:

```
<body>
    <!-- Prompt for user -->
    The Cars Login Page
    Please enter your user name and password.
</body>
```

You find that the browser does not add the expected line break (see Figure 15-5).

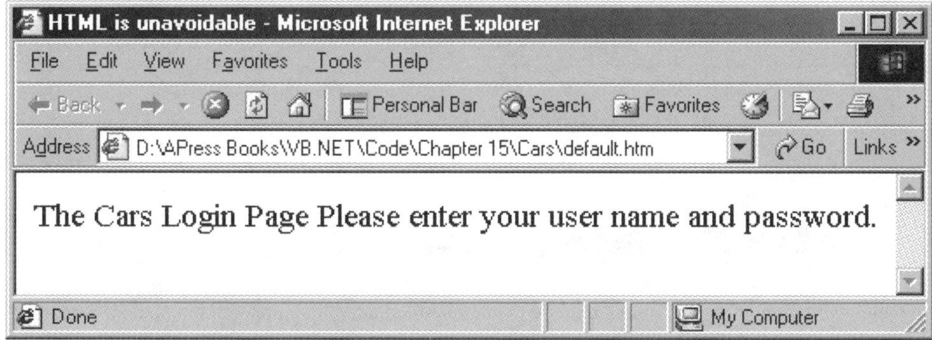

Figure 15-5. Untagged textual information omits line breaks

To flow text over multiple lines, you need to use the <p> and </p> (paragraph) tags, which instruct the browser to begin a new paragraph, as shown here:

```
<body>
    <!-- Technically, you do not need to close a paragraph with </p> -->
    The Cars Login Page
    <p>Please enter your user name and password.</p>
</body>
```

Figure 15-6 shows the new output.

Figure 15-6. The <p> tag begins a new paragraph

To insert a new blank line (rather than begin a new paragraph), use the
 (BReak) tags instead (see Figure 15-7):

```
<body>
    <!-- Insert a break without a blank line -->
    The Cars Login Page
    <br>Please enter your user name and password.</br>
</body>
```

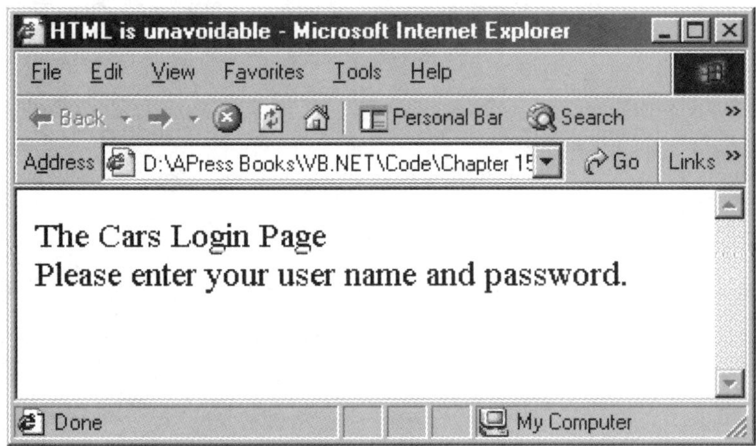

Figure 15-7. The <br> tag simply starts a new line.

Now that you can add multiple lines of text (with carriage returns), you may want to add some bold or italic formatting using the <b> and <i> tags. For example, to apply bold formatting to the first line of text and italicize specific words in the second line, you could write the following (see Figure 15-8 for output):

```
<body>
    <!-- Bold and italic formatting -->
    <b>The Cars Login Page</b>
    <br>Please enter your <i>user name</i> and <i>password</i>.
</body>
```

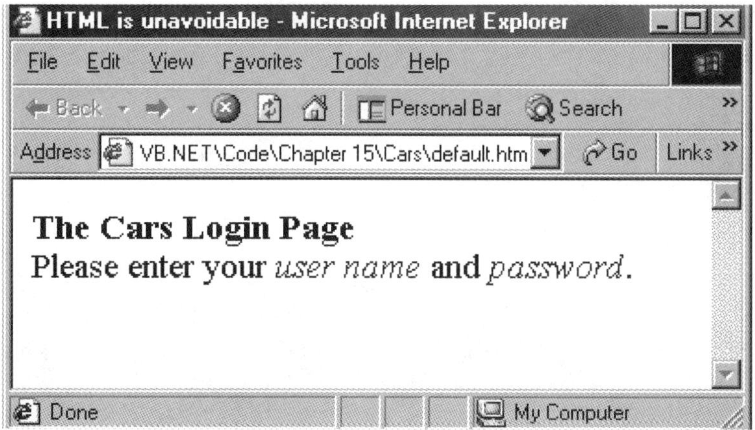

Figure 15-8. Bold and italic text

Working with Format Headers

The final textual formatting issue you examine is the use of the various heading tags. Using <h1>, <h2>, <h3>, <h4>, <h5>, and <h6> tags, you can alter the size of the rendered text. The <h1> tag is your largest possible option, while <h6> marks the smallest format. Here is an example:

```
<body>
    <!-- Prompt for user -->
    <h1>The Cars Login Page</h1>
    <br><h3>Please enter your <i>user name</i> and <i>password</i>.</h3>
</body>
```

Finally, you can apply the <center> tag (as well as left, right, and justify) to force a block of text to be centered in the browser's client area, as shown here:

```
<body>
    <!-- Prompt for user -->
    <center>
    <h1>The Cars Login Page</h1>
```

```
    <br><h3>Please enter your <i>user name</i> and <i>password</i>.</h3>
    </center>
</body>
```

Figure 15-9 shows the end result. (Notice that as you resize the browser, the text remains centered.)

Figure 15-9. Working with HTML header tags

Visual Studio .NET HTML Editors

So far, your simple HTML page is rather bland. To help spruce things up, let's take a moment to explore some of the design-time tools supplied by the VS .NET IDE. First and foremost, you may configure various aspects of the page itself using the Properties window. To do so, select the DOCUMENT object and hack away (see Figure 15-10).

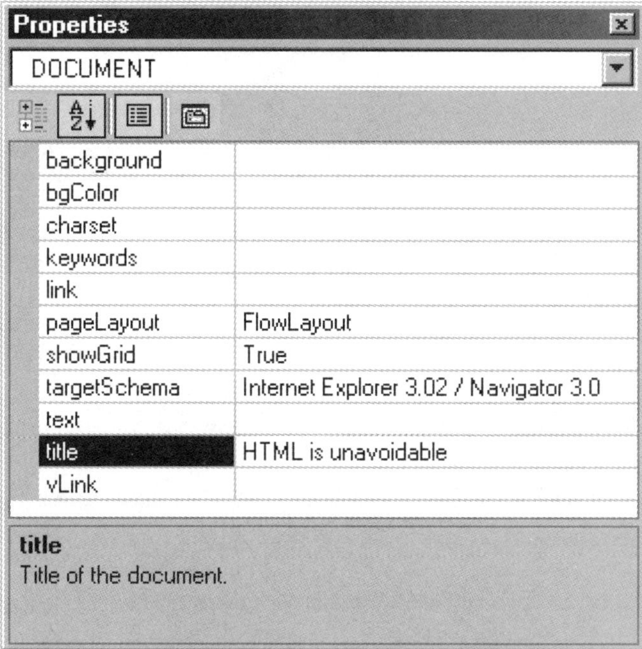

Figure 15-10. Visual editing of an HTML document begins here

For example, if you modify the bgColor property (which sets the background color of the page), the underlying HTML file is updated automatically, as shown in Figure 15-11.

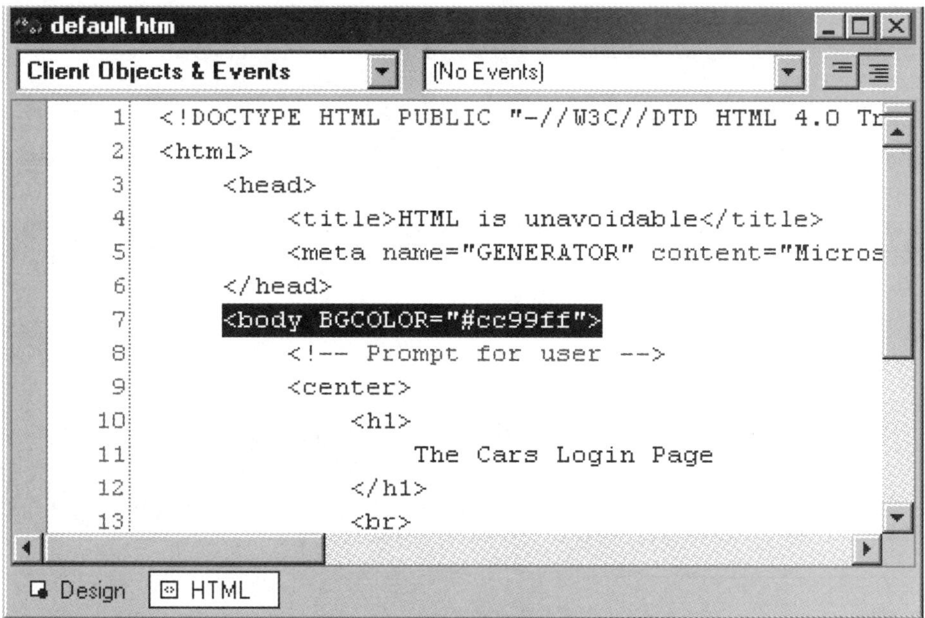

Figure 15-11. Design-time modifications are recorded as HTML

The IDE also provides an HTML Formatting toolbar (shown in Figure 15-12), which allows you to modify the appearance of your text (color, font, header size, bullet points, and so on).

Figure 15-12. The HTML Formatting toolbar

You can build up the verbiage of your page using a word processor–like approach, with the difference being that raw HTML is generated under the hood. As you build your Web pages during this chapter, I assume you will take the time to play around with various formatting options and examine the underlying HTML tags.

HTML Form Development

Now that you have had an initial look at the layout of a basic HTML page, you can explore how to facilitate some user interaction. As you see later in this chapter, the ASP.NET framework supplies a number of Web Form controls, which are responsible for generating raw HTML tags automatically. The beauty of using the Web Form control set is the fact that you (as a Web developer) can build the UI of the returned page without concern for the underlying HTML. Understand that the controls you are about to briefly examine are *not* .NET Web Form controls but simply a set of built-in widgets used during HTML form development.

An *HTML form* is simply a named group of related UI elements used to gather user input, which is then transmitted to the Web application via HTTP. (You see exactly how in just a bit.) Do not confuse an HTML form with the literal client area displayed in a browser. In reality, an HTML form is more of a *logical grouping* of widgets placed in the <form> and </form> tag pairs, as shown here:

```
<form name = MainForm id = MainForm>
     <!--Add UI elements here -->
</form>
```

Here you have created a form and assigned the ID and friendly name to MainForm. While this is technically optional, get in the habit of doing so. Later in this chapter, you will find this useful when working with client-side scripting, where you frequently need to identify controls by name.

Typically, the opening <form> tag supplies an action attribute, which specifies the URL to submit the form data to, as well as the method of transmitting the data itself (posting or getting). You examine this aspect of the <form> tag in just a bit. For the time being, let's look at the sorts of items that you can place in an HTML form.

HTML Controls

The VS .NET IDE provides an HTML Toolbox option that allows you to select each HTML-based UI widget (see Figure 15-13).

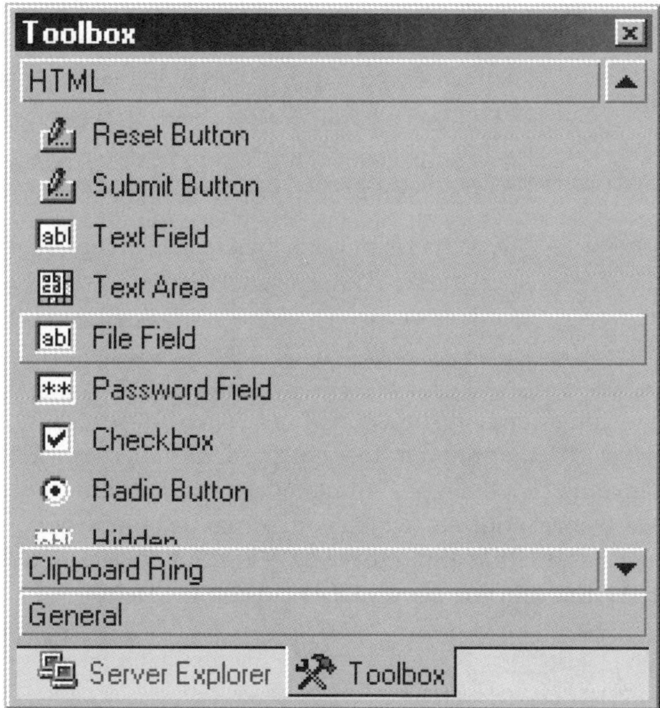

Figure 15-13. The HTML controls

Table 15-1 gives a rundown of some of the more common items.

Table 15-1. Common HTML GUI Types

HTML GUI WIDGET	MEANING IN LIFE
Button	A button that does not support the type attribute used to trigger a SUBMIT or RESET. This sort of button can be used to hit a block of client-side script code or any other logic that does not require a trip to the Web server.
Checkbox Radio Button Listbox Dropdown	Standard UI selection elements.
Image	Allows you to specify an image to render onto the form.
Reset Button	This button element has its type attribute set to RESET. This instructs the browser to clear out the values in each UI element on the page to their default values.
Submit Button	This button element has its type attribute set to SUBMIT, which sends the form data to the recipient of a request.
Text Field Text Area Password Field	These UI elements are used to hold a single line (or multiple lines) of text. The Password Field renders input data using an asterisk (*) character mask.

As an interesting side note, be aware that the .NET base class libraries supply a number of managed types that correspond to these raw HTML widgets. Understand that the types contained within this namespace are *not* ASP.NET Web Form controls (which you formally examine later in this chapter). For further information about these HTML wrapper classes, refer to the System.Web.UI.HtmlControls namespace using online Help.

Building the User Interface

The first step in building a user interface using HTML widgets is to declare a <form> segment of the HTML document. Thus, add the following markup to your existing file:

```
<html>
    <head>
        <title>HTML is unavoidable</title>
            <meta NAME="GENERATOR" Content="Microsoft Visual Studio">
            <meta HTTP-EQUIV="Content-Type" content="text/html">
```

```
    </head>
    <body bgcolor="#66ccff">
        <!-- Prompt for user -->
        <center>
        <h1>The Cars Login Page</h1>
        <br><h3>Please enter your <i>user name</i> and <i>password</i>.</h3>
            <!-- Build a form to get user info -->
            <form name=MainForm >
            </form>
        </center>
    </body>
</html>
```

At this point, you can either flip back to design mode and drag and drop the HTML widgets onto the form, or you can add the corresponding HTML tags by hand. In general, each HTML widget is described using a "name" attribute (used to identify the item programmatically) and a "type" attribute (used to specify which UI element you are interested in placing in the <form> declaration).

Depending on which UI widget you are manipulating, you find additional attributes specific to that particular item. As you expect, each UI element and its attributes can be modified using the VS .NET IDE Properties window. The UI you build contains two text fields (one of which is a Password widget), as well as two button types (one for submitting the form data and the other to reset the form data to the initial default values). Here is the associated HTML (by the way, " " identifies a single blank space):

```
<form name=MainForm >
    <p>User Name:
    <input name = txtUserName type = text></p>
    <p>Password:
    <input name = txtPassword type = password></p>
    <input name = btnSubmit type = submit value = Submit>
    <input name = btnReset type = reset value = Reset>
</form>
```

Notice that you have assigned relevant names to each widget (txtUserName, txtPassword, btnSubmit, and btnReset). Of greater importance, note that each input button has an extra attribute named "value" that marks these buttons as UI items that automatically clear all fields to their initial values (value = Reset) or send the form data to the recipient (value = Submit). Other UI elements may also take a value attribute. For example, you can set the value of the txtUserName text box as shown in Figure 15-14.

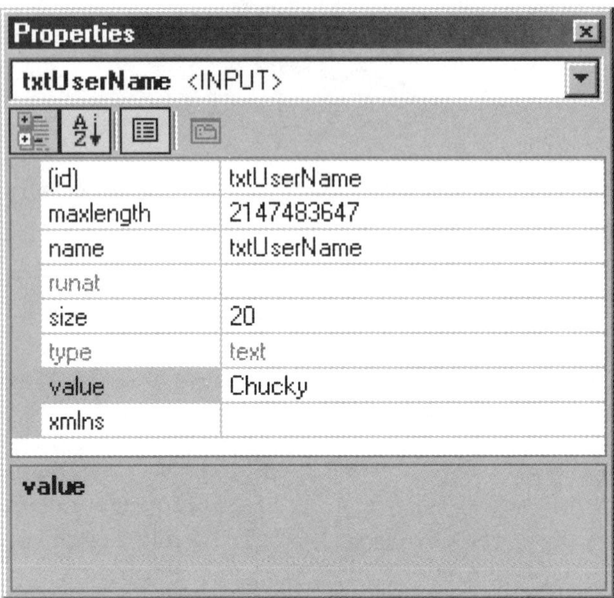

Figure 15-14. Setting a widget's value

The string "Chucky" is now the default value of the txtUserName UI widget. To test out your application, save your changes and open the *.htm file. Notice that when you enter values into the Text Box items and click the Reset button, the UI elements are reassigned their default values. Figure 15-15, then, displays your creation thus far.

Figure 15-15. An extremely boring Web page

Adding an Image

The final raw HTML UI topic here is how to incorporate images into your HTML documents. Like other aspects of HTML, images are marked using tags—specifically, <img>, as shown here:

```
<img alt="You gotta log in to see this!" src="car.gif" border=4>
```

The "alt" (alternative) attribute is used to specify a textual equivalent to the graphic image specified by the "src" (source) attribute. This text blurb is used as pop-up text when the cursor is placed over the image or, in browsers that do not support graphical images, as a textual alternative. The border attribute is optional, but it is used here to render an outline around your image. Be aware that the value assigned to the src attribute may be a hard-coded path or (as you have here) a relative path. This approach assumes that the images used are in the same directory as the *.htm files making use of them. Figure 15-16 shows the update.

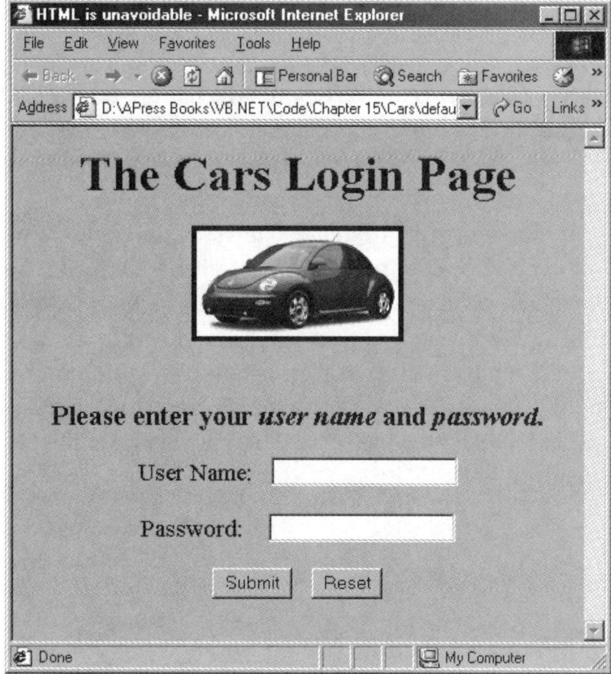

Figure 15-16. A slightly more interesting Web page

The Role of Client-Side Scripting

Now that you have a better understanding of how to construct an HTML form, the next issue to examine is the role of client-side scripting. The inherent evil of a Web application is the need to make frequent calls to the server machine to update the HTML rendered into the browser. Of course, while round trips are unavoidable, you should always be aware of ways to minimize travel across the wire. One technique that reduces round trips is using client-side scripting to validate user input before submitting the form data to the recipient.

For example, currently you require the end user to enter a password and user name. If either field were left blank, you would not want to allow a submission of the form's data to occur. Of course, HTML alone cannot help in this endeavor, as HTML is only concerned with the display of content. To augment the functionality of standard HTML, you must use a given scripting language (or, if necessary, any number of scripting languages).

There are many scripting languages. Two of the more popular ones are VBScript and JavaScript. VBScript is a subset of the Visual Basic 6.0 programming language. Be aware that Microsoft Internet Explorer (IE) is the only Web browser that has built-in support for client-side VBScript support. Thus, if you want your HTML pages to work correctly in any commercial Web browser, do *not* use VBScript for your client-side scripting logic.

The truth is that VBScript is effectively dead as of the release of the .NET platform. The reason is simple: Unlike classic ASP, ASP.NET does not use scripting languages at all. Rather, ASP.NET pages use full-fledged programming languages (VB .NET, C#, and so on) to perform server-side logic.

The other popular scripting language is JavaScript. Be very aware that JavaScript is in no way, shape, or form a subset of the Java language. While JavaScript and Java have a somewhat similar syntax, JavaScript is not a full-fledged programming language and thus is far less powerful than Java itself. The good news is that all Web browsers support JavaScript, which makes it a natural candidate for client-side validation. (As an interesting side note, understand that JavaScript is standardized as ECMAScript, whereas JScript is the Microsoft implementation of JavaScript.)

A Client-Side Scripting Example

To begin understanding client-side scripting, you first need to examine how to intercept events from HTML GUI widgets. Assume you have a new and very simple HTML page that looks like Figure 15-17.

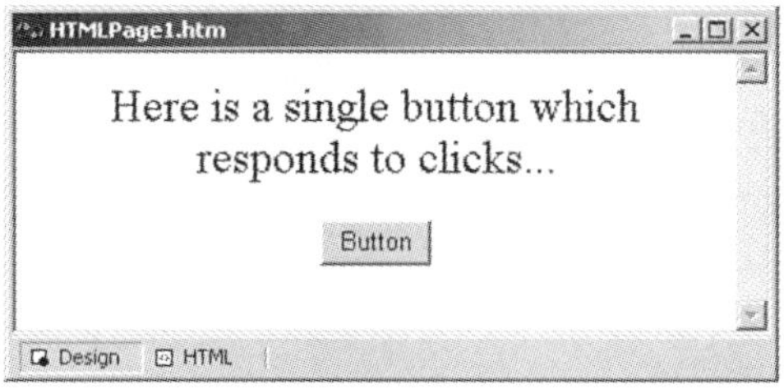

Figure 15-17. A new HTML page

Next, you need to assign a valid ID and name to the button using the Properties window (testBtn will do the trick). To capture the Click event for this button, activate the HTML view and select your button from the left drop-down list. Using the right drop-down list box, select the "onclick" event, as shown in Figure 15-18.

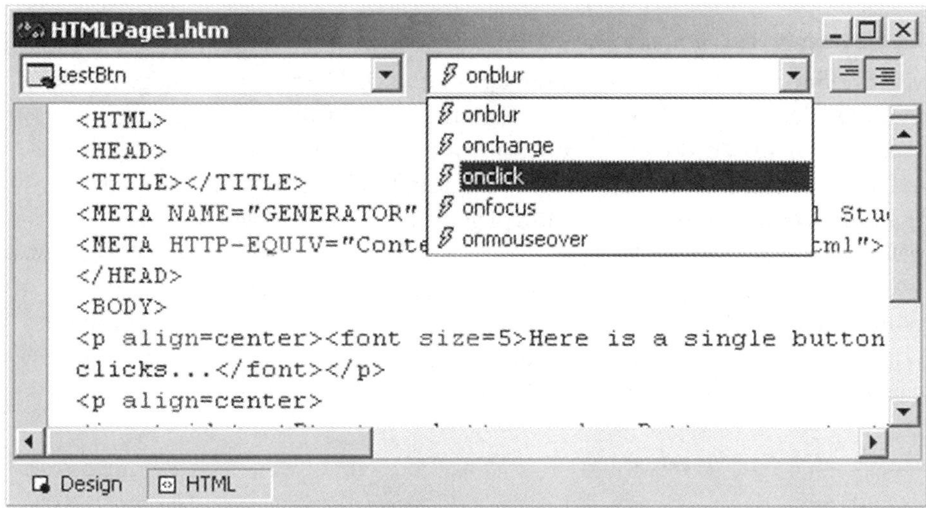

Figure 15-18. Capturing HTML widget events

Once you do this, you will find two major HTML updates (shown in bold):

```
<html>
    <head>
    <title></title>
. . .
    <script id=clientEventHandlersJS language=javascript>
        <!--
```

```
        function testBtn_onclick() {
        }
        //-->
    </script>
    </head>
    <body>
        <p align = center>
        <font size = 5>
        Here is a single button which responds to clicks. . .
        </font></p>
        <p align = center>
        <input id =testBtn type=button value=Button name=testBtn
        language=javascript onclick="return testBtn_onclick()">
        </p>
    </body>
</html>
```

As you can see, a new <script> block has been added to your HTML header, with JavaScript specified as the language of choice. Note that the scripting block has been placed with HTML style comments. The reason for this is simple. If your page ends up on a browser that does not support client-side scripting, the code will be treated as a comment block and ignored. Of course, your page may be less functional, but the upside is that the page will not blow up when it is rendered into the hosting browser.

Next, notice that the attribute set for the HTML button has a new member named onclick, which is assigned to the return value of the JavaScript function. In this way, when the button is clicked, this method is automatically invoked. By way of a simple example, if you update the function as shown here:

```
<script id = clientEventHandlersJS language = javascript>
<!--
function testBtn_onclick()
{
     // JavaScript function call (a message box).
     alert("Hey, stop clicking me. . .");
}
//-->
</script>
```

you will see a message box pop up when you click the button (see Figure 15-19).

Figure 15-19. IE alert

Validating the default.htm HTML Page

Now, let's update your current default.htm page to support some client-side validation. The goal is to ensure that when the user clicks the Submit button, a JavaScript function is called that checks each text box for empty entries. If this is the case, you issue an alert that instructs the user to re-enter the required data.

First, assign an onclick event for the Submit button to a JavaScript method named ValidateData(). Within the logic of this method, check each text box for empty strings, as shown here:

```
<script language = javascript>
<!-- Scope the names of the text boxes with the name of the form!
function ValidateData()
{
      // If they forget either item, pop up a message box.
      if((MainForm.txtUserName.value = = "") ||
      (MainForm.txtPassword.value = = ""))
      {
            alert("You must supply a user name and password!");
            return false;
      }
      return true;
}
-->
</script>
. . .
<input id = btnSubmit onclick = "return ValidateData()" type = submit
  value = Submit name = btnSubmit>
```

While you're at it, add another JavaScript method named GetTheDate(), which is called when the page is loaded to display the time and date when the user logs on. To call this function requires a separate <script> tag, which uses the write() method of the Internet Explorer Document object to pump out a block of text, as shown here:

```
<html>
    <head>
    <title>HTML is unavoidable</title>
    <script language = javascript>
    <!-- Here are the JavaScript methods for this form.
    function ValidateData()
    {
        if((MainForm.txtUserName.value = = "") ||
            (MainForm.txtPassword.value = = ""))
            {
              alert("You must supply a user name and password!");
              return false;
            }
            return true;
    }
    function GetTheDate() { return Date(); }
    -->
    </script>
    </head>
<body bgColor=#66ccff>
<!-- Prompt for user -->
<center>
<h1>The Cars Login Page</h1>
<h2>Today is: </h2>
<script language=javascript>
     document.write(GetTheDate());
</script>
<br>
<h3>Please enter your <i>user name</i> and <i>password</i>.</h3>
    <!-- Build a form to get user info -->
    <form name=MainForm>
         <p>User Name:   <input type=text name=txtUserName></p>
         <p>Password:
         <input type=password name=txtPassword></p>
         <input id=btnSubmit onclick=ValidateData() type=submit
         value=Submit name=btnSubmit>
         <input type=reset value=Reset name=btnReset>
        </form>
        </center>
    </body>
</html>
```

Submitting the Form Data (GET and POST)

At this point you have been exposed to a number of Web-centric design techniques. Now that you have a simple Web front end, you need to examine the very important issue of submitting this data to a Web application. When you build an HTML form, you typically supply an action attribute to specify the recipient of the incoming data. Possible receivers include mail servers, other HTML files, an Active Server Page (classic or .NET), and so forth. For this example, you make use of a classic ASP file (which you build in just a moment). First, update your HTML file by specifying the following attribute in the opening <form> tag, as shown here:

```
<form name=MainForm
action="http://localhost/Cars/ClassicASPPage.asp" method = "GET">
      ...
</form>
```

This additional attribute specifies that when the Submit button for this form is clicked, the form data should be sent to an ASP page (named ClassicASPPage.asp) located under the Cars virtual directory located on the current machine (i.e., localhost). When you specify "method = GET" as the mode of transmission, the form data is appended to the query string as a set of name/value pairs. The other method of transmitting form data to the Web server is to specify "method = POST," as shown here:

```
<form name=MainForm
action="http://localhost/Cars/ClassicASPPage.asp" method = "POST">
      ...
</form>
```

In this case, the form data is not appended to the query string, but instead is written to a separate line sent with the HTTP header. In this way, the form data is not directly visible to the outside world and is therefore a bit more secure. (More important, POST is not limited by character length.) For the time being, assume you have specified the GET method of form data transfer.

Parsing a Query String

To understand exactly how the receiving ASP file can extract the form's data, you need to examine the format of a query string. When you submit form data using the GET action, you see a slightly mangled text string appearing in your browser's Address box. Here is an example:

```
http://localhost/Cars/ClassicASPPage.asp?
txtUserName=Chucky&txtPassword=somepassword&btnSubmit=Submit
```

One core feature of this (and any) query string is the question mark (?) delimiter. On the left side of the "?" is the address of the recipient (your ASP page). On the right side is a string composed of any number of name/value pairs (such as txtUserName=Chucky).

As you can see, each name/value pair is separated by an ampersand (&). This particular query string was quite simple to parse, given that you have not injected any blank spaces in the process. However, if the user name is changed from "Chucky" to "Chucky Chuckles," you find the following query string:

```
http://localhost/Cars/ClassicASPPage.asp?txtUserName=
Chucky+Chuckles&txtPassword=somepasswork&btnSubmit=Submit
```

Notice how extra spaces are marked with a plus sign (+). Thus, if you have five spaces between "Chucky" and "Chuckles," you find the following:

```
http://localhost/Cars/ClassicASPPage.asp?txtUserName=
Chucky+++++Chuckles&txtPassword=somepassword&btnSubmit=Submit
```

In addition to handling spaces, query strings represent various oddball characters (e.g., nonalphanumeric characters such as ^ and ~) as their hexadecimal ASCII equivalents. Thus, if you resubmit to the ASP page using "Hello^77" as the password, you find the following:

```
http://localhost/Cars/ClassicASPPage.asp?txtUserName=
Chucky++++Chuckles&txtPassword=Hello%5E77&btnSubmit=Submit
```

Building a Classic Active Server Page

To receive the form data, you now need to build the ClassicASPPage.asp file. First, insert a new Active Server Page file using VS .NET (see Figure 15-20). Be sure the filename you assign to this new item is the same name specified in your form's action attribute (and also be sure to save this file into the folder to which your virtual directory has been mapped).

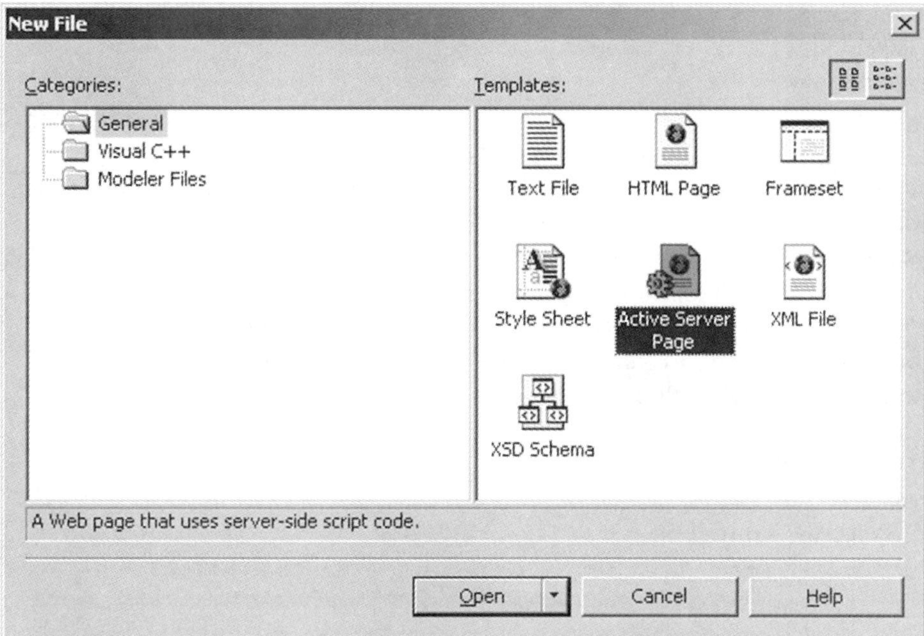

Figure 15-20. Inserting a classic ASP file

A classic Active Server Page is a hodgepodge of HTML code and server-side scripts. If you have never worked with classic ASP, understand that the goal of ASP is to dynamically build HTML on the fly using server-side scripting. For example, you may have a scripting block that reads a table from a data source (using ADO) and returns the rows as generic HTML.

For this example, the ASP page uses the intrinsic ASP Request object to read the values of the incoming query string and render them as HTML (thus just echoing the input). Here is the relevant script (note the use of <% . . . %> to mark a block of script):

```
<%@ Language=VBScript %>      <!-- VBScript A-OK on the server side -->
<HTML>
<HEAD>
<META NAME="GENERATOR" Content="Microsoft Visual Studio 7.0">
</HEAD>
<BODY>
<!-- Send back the info they gave us -->
<center>
     <h1>You said: </h1>
     <b>User Name: </b><%= Request.QueryString("txtUserName") %><br>
     <b>Password: </b><%= Request.QueryString("txtPassword") %><br>
```

```
</center>
</BODY>
</HTML>
```

The first thing to be aware of is that an *.asp file begins and ends with the standard <html>, <head>, and <body> tag pairs. Here you use the Request object, which like any classic COM type supports a number of properties, methods, and events. You call the QueryString() method to examine the values contained in each HTML widget (submitted via "method = GET"). Also note that the <%= . . .%> notation is a shorthand way of saying "Insert the following into the HTTP response." To gain a finer level of flexibility, you could use the ASP Response object directly. Here is an example:

```
<!-- Send back the info they gave us -->
<center>
     <h1>You said:</h1>
     <b>User Name: </b><%= Request.QueryString("txtUserName") %><br>
     <b>Password: </b>
     <%
          dim pwd
          pwd = Request.QueryString("txtPassword")
          Response.Write (pwd)
     %>
</center>
```

The Request and Response objects of classic ASP provide a number of additional members. Furthermore, class ASP also defines a small number of additional objects (Session, Server, Application, and ObjectContext) that you can use while constructing your Web application. You don't examine the functionality of these classic ASP items here. However, later in this chapter you find that the same behavior is supplied using properties of the ASP.NET Page type.

In any case, to trigger the ASP logic, simply launch your default.htm page from a browser and submit the information. After the script is processed, you are returned a brand-new (dynamically generated) HTML file (see Figure 15-21).

Granted, this current example is not very sexy. Nevertheless, you should be able to understand the key principle behind ASP (and thus ASP.NET) programming: Given some data submitted by an HTML form, you can use code to dynamically return content to the user.

Figure 15-21. The dynamically generated HTML

Responding to POST Submissions

Currently, your default.htm file specifies GET as the method of sending your form's data to the receiving *.asp page. Using this approach, the values contained in the various GUI widgets are appended to the end of the query string. It is important to note that the ASP Request.QueryString() method is *only* able to extract data submitted via the GET method. If you change your method of data transfer to "action = POST" and rerun your Web application, you will be saddened to find an empty response (see Figure 15-22).

Figure 15-22. The QueryString() method can only process information submitted using HTTP GET.

This is due to the fact that the form data has now been sent as part of the HTTP header, rather than as appended textual information. The good news is that this same information can be obtained using the Request.Form collection. To submit your data using the POST technique, you can update your *.asp file as shown here:

```
<BODY>
<!-- Send back the info they gave us -->
<center>
    <h1>You said:</h1>
    <b>User Name: </b><%= Request.Form("txtUserName") %><br>
    <b>Password: </b>
    <%
        dim pwd
        pwd = Request.Form("txtPassword")
        Response.Write (pwd)
    %>
</center>
</BODY>
```

Once you update your *.asp file, you see that you can read the incoming data again. This time, however, the values are not appended to the URL, as shown in Figure 15-23.

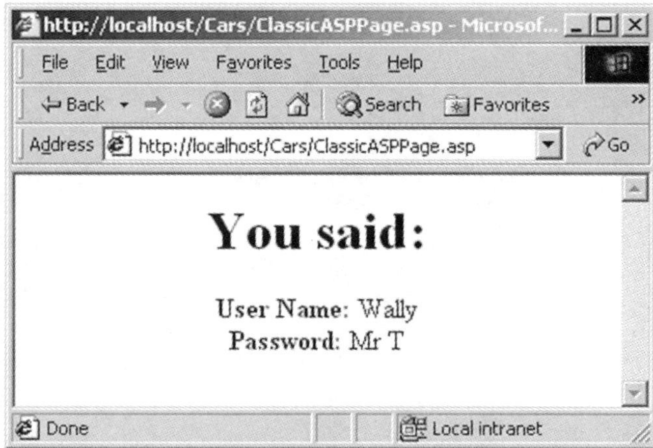

Figure 15-23. POSTed data can be processed using Request.Form.

Figure 15-24 illustrates each technique used to submit form data to a recipient and the corresponding technique to obtain this data from a classic ASP Web application.

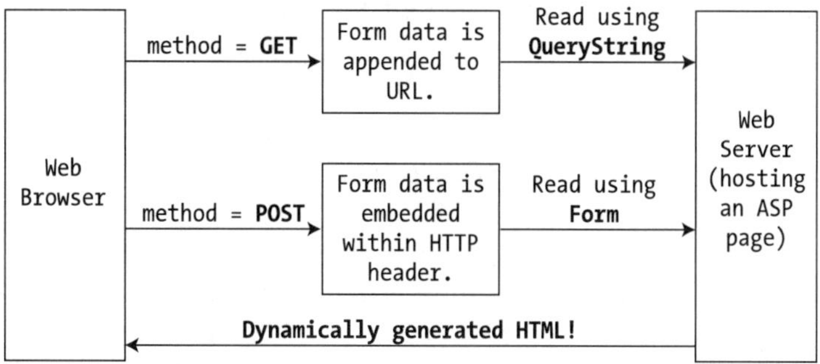

Figure 15-24. Submitting data to an ASP page using HTTP GET and POST

Building Your First Official ASP.NET Application

Before you finish this review of basic Web atoms, open the default.htm file and update the opening <form> tag as shown here (note the .aspx file extension):

```
<form name=MainForm action="http://localhost/Cars/ClassicASPPage.aspx"
method=post ID=Form1>
```

Then, change the file extension of your classic ASP file to *.aspx and rerun the application. You should see no difference at all (see Figure 15-25).

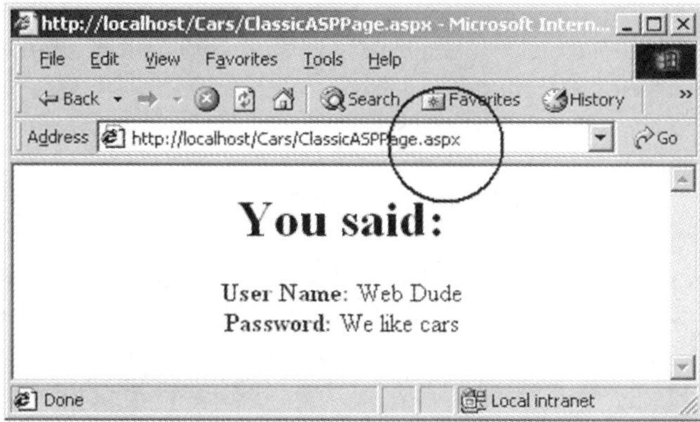

Figure 15-25. An ASP.NET application

Congratulations! You have just created your first ASP.NET application (by virtue of the *.aspx file extension). As you can see, all of the techniques presented thus far are valid in the world of ASP.NET. At this point you should (hopefully) feel more comfortable working with Web-based applications and understand how each of these building blocks interrelate. With this Web review out of the way, you can spend the remainder of this chapter examining the framework of ASP.NET.

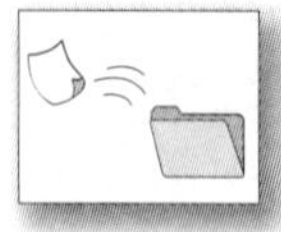

SOURCE CODE *The HTMLCars project is included under the Chapter 15 subdirectory.*

Some Problems with Classic ASP

While many successful Web applications have been created using classic ASP, this architecture is not without its downside. Perhaps the biggest downfall of ASP proper is the very point that makes it a powerful platform: scripting languages. While it is true that the ASP scripting parser is sophisticated enough to cache the compiled script after the first use, scripting languages such as VBScript and JavaScript are interpreted, typeless entities that do not really lend themselves to robust OO programming techniques.

Another problem with classic ASP is the fact that an *.asp page does not yield very modularized code. Given that ASP is a blend of HTML and script in a *single* page, most ASP Web applications are a confused mix of two very different programming techniques. While it is true that classic ASP allows you to partition related code into distinct files, the underlying object model does not support true separation of concerns. In an ideal world, a Web framework would allow the presentation logic (i.e., HTML code) to remain separate from the business logic (i.e., functional code).

One final issue is the fact that classic ASP demands a good deal of boilerplate, redundant script that tends to repeat between projects. Almost all Web applications need to validate user input, render rich HTML content, and so on. In classic ASP, *you* are the one in charge of adding the appropriate server-side scripting code for these tasks. Ideally, a Web framework (rather than a human) would be in charge of such details.

Some Benefits of ASP.NET

ASP.NET addresses each of the previously mentioned limitations (and more) of classic ASP. First and foremost, ASP.NET files (*.aspx) do not use interpreted scripting languages. As mentioned earlier, ASP.NET allows you to use "real" programming languages such as VB .NET, JScript .NET, and C#. Because of this, you can apply each technique you have learned throughout this book directly to your Web development efforts. As you may expect, *.aspx pages can make programmatic use of the .NET class libraries as well as access the functionality provided by custom assemblies.

Next, ASP.NET applications provide numerous ways to decrease the amount of code you need to write to begin with. For example, through the use of server-side Web controls, you can build a browser-based front end using various GUI widgets that emit raw HTML under the hood. Other Web controls are used to perform automatic validation of your GUI items (which decreases the amount of client-side script you are responsible for authoring).

Beyond the simplification of your coding efforts, ASP.NET offers many practical bells and whistles. For example, all ASP.NET Web applications use the integrated VS .NET IDE (a huge improvement from debugging scripting logic using Visual InterDev). To begin seeing these and other benefits in action, let's begin by examining the core ASP.NET namespaces.

The ASP.NET Namespaces

The .NET class libraries contain numerous namespaces that represent Web-based technologies. Generally speaking, these namespaces can be grouped into three major categories: core Web atoms (e.g., HTTP types, configuration types, and security types), GUI (Web Form controls), and Web services (which are described in Chapter 16). While a full examination of each item would require a book on its own, you can certainly come to terms with the functionality offered by the core namespaces described in Table 15-2.

Table 15-2. ASP.NET Namespaces

WEB-CENTRIC NAMESPACE	MEANING IN LIFE
System.Web	System.Web defines core types that enable browser/Web server communication (such as request and response capabilities, cookie manipulation, and file transfer).
System.Web.Caching	This namespace contains types that facilitate caching support for a Web application.
System.Web.Configuration	This namespace contains types that allow you to configure your Web application in conjunction with the project's Web configuration file.
System.Web.Security	Security support for a Web application.
System.Web.Services System.Web.Services.Description System.Web.Services.Discovery System.Web.Services.Protocols	These namespaces provide the types that allow you to build Web services (which are examined in Chapter 16).
System.Web.UI System.Web.UI.WebControls System.Web.UI.HtmlControls	These namespaces define a number of types that allow you to build a GUI front end for your Web application.

The Core Types of System.Web

The System.Web namespace defines the minimal and complete set of types that allow a browser-based client to communicate and interact with the Web server. Table 15-3 is a quick rundown of some items of interest, many of which are examined in greater detail throughout this chapter.

Table 15-3. Core Types of the System.Web Namespace

SYSTEM.WEB TYPE	MEANING IN LIFE
HttpApplication	Defines the members common to all ASP.NET applications. As you soon see, the global.asax file defines a class derived from HttpApplication.
HttpApplicationState	Enables developers to share global information across multiple requests, sessions, and pipelines in an ASP.NET application.
HttpBrowserCapabilities	Enables the server to compile information on the capabilities of the browser running on the client.
HttpCookie	Provides a type-safe way to access multiple HTTP cookies.
HttpRequest	Provides an object-oriented way to enable browser-to-server communication (e.g., used to gain access to the HTTP request data supplied by a client).
HttpResponse	Provides an object-oriented way to enable server-to-browser communication (e.g., used to send output to a client).

Creating a Simple VB .NET Web Application

To get the ball rolling, you build a small test project and examine the overall structure of the ASP.NET framework. First, create a new VB .NET Web Application project workspace named FirstWebApplication (see Figure 15-26).

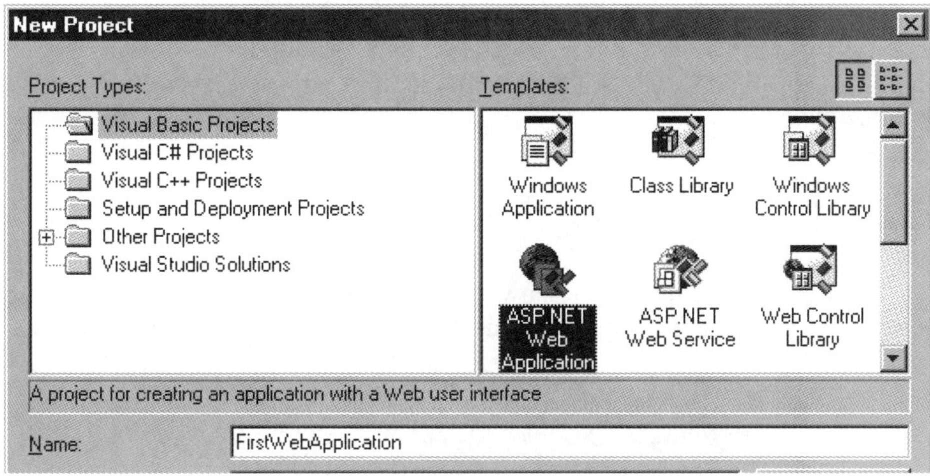

Figure 15-26. Creating your initial ASP.NET application

Before you click the OK button, take a minute to notice that the Location text box does not map to a specific folder on your hard drive, but rather to the URL of the machine hosting this Web application. By default, VS .NET solution files (*.sln and *.suo) are stored under the "My Documents\Visual Studio Projects" subfolder, while your source code is stored under the generated virtual directory.

After you create the new project workspace, notice that a design-time template has been opened automatically (see Figure 15-27).

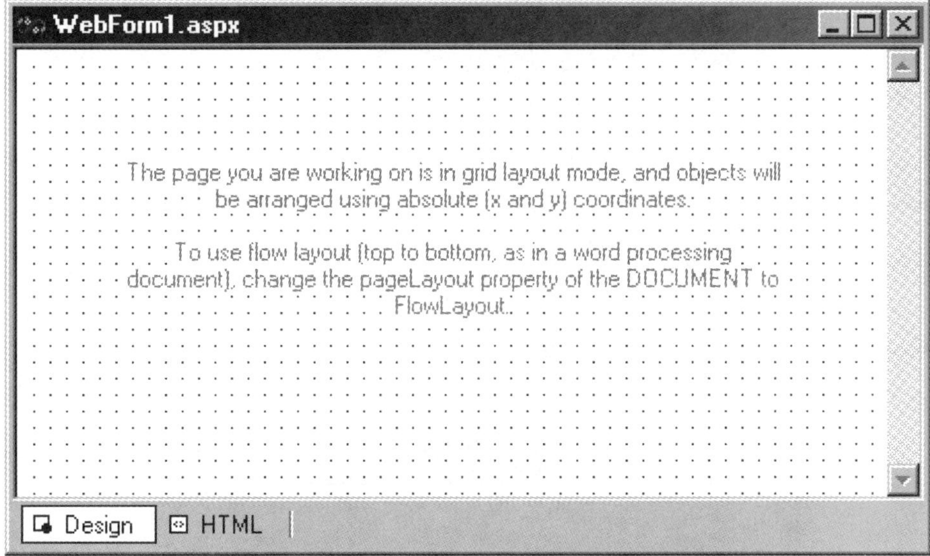

Figure 15-27. The design-time template

Much like a Windows Forms application, this template represents the visual appearance of the *.aspx file you are constructing. The difference, of course, is that you are using HTML-based Web Forms controls rather than Win32-based Windows Forms controls.

Examining the Generated Files

Now, examine the Solution Explorer window shown in Figure 15-28. As you can see, you have been given a number of new files and external assembly references.

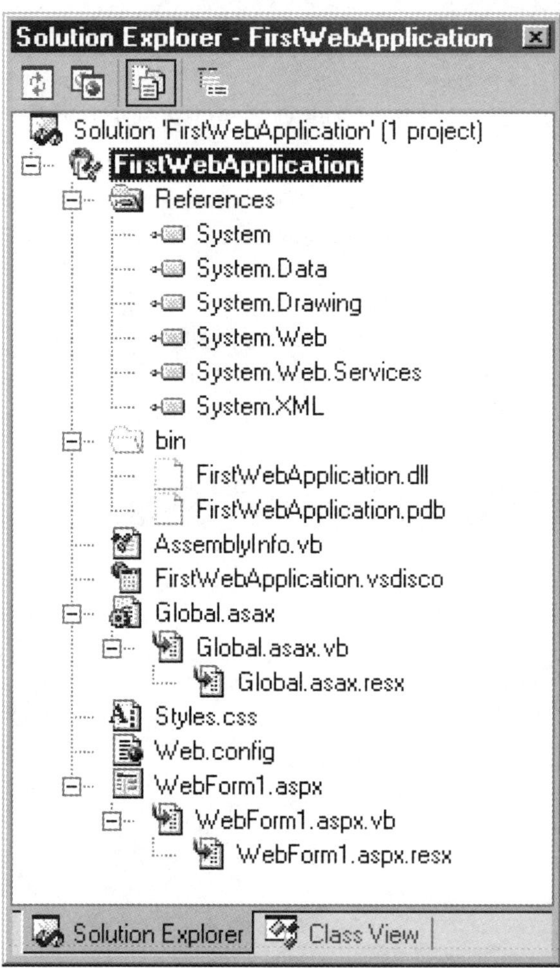

Figure 15-28. Initial files of an ASP.NET application

Table 15-4 documents the basic role of each of these generated files.

Table 15-4. ASP.NET Project Workspace Files

GENERATED FILE	MEANING IN LIFE
AssemblyInfo.vb	Like any VS .NET project workspace, the assemblyinfo.vb file is used to hold assembly-level attribute definitions.
*.vsdisco	As you see in Chapter 16, Discovery of Web Services (or DISCO) files are used to allow the outside world to discover the set of Web services available from a given Web application.
Global.asax, Global.asax.vb, Global.asax.resx	These files are used to handle application-level events and interact with the incoming HTTP request (and outgoing HTTP response).
Styles.css	Defines a default HTML CSS style sheet for a new Web Application project.
Web.config	As you recall from Chapter 7, *.config files are used to control runtime behaviors for a given application.
*.aspx, *.aspx.vb, *.aspx.resx	These files constitute the design-time template and the associated Codebehind file.

Examining the Generated Virtual Directory

If you open IIS, you see that a new virtual directory (FirstWebApplication) has been automatically created on your behalf, as shown in Figure 15-29.

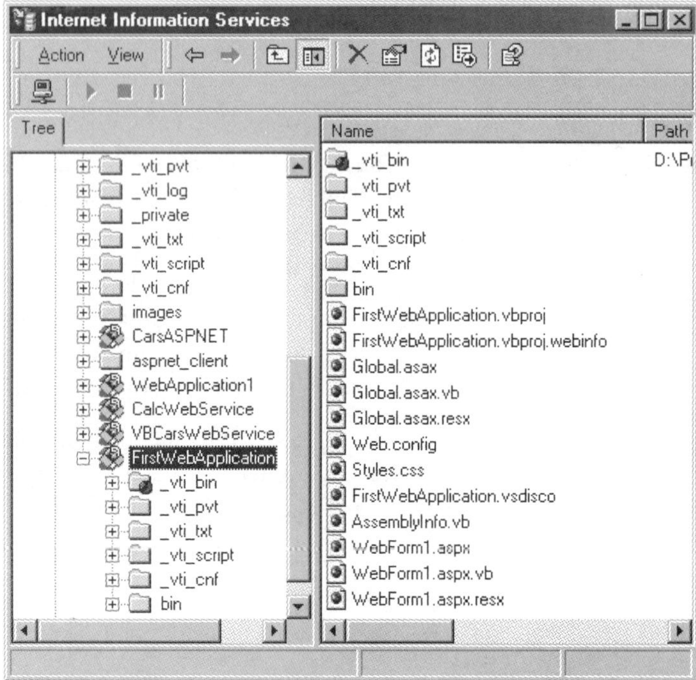

Figure 15-29. The new (automatically created) virtual directory

As you can see, the source files in the workspace have been included in the generated virtual directory. The physical folder to which this virtual directory is mapped can be located under a subdirectory under <drive>:\Inetpub\wwwroot (see Figure 15-30).

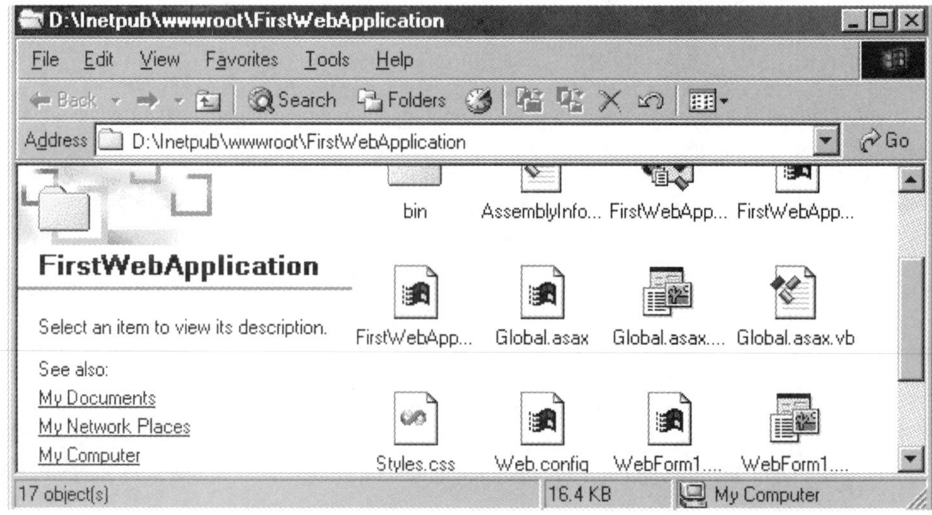

Figure 15-30. The physical file containing your project files

Examining the Initial *.aspx File

If you examine the HTML behind your *.aspx file, you see that you have been given the minimal set of tags that establish a basic HTML form. The first point of interest is the *runat* attribute appearing in the opening <form> tag. This attribute is the heart and soul of ASP.NET and is used to mark an item as a candidate for processing by the ASP.NET runtime, as shown here:

```
<%@ Page Language="vb" AutoEventWireup="false" Codebehind="Web Form1.aspx.vb"
Inherits="FirstWebApplication.Web Form1"%>
<!DOCTYPE HTML PUBLIC "-//W3C//DTD HTML 4.0 Transitional//EN">
<html>
    <head>
        <title></title>
            <meta name="GENERATOR" content="Microsoft Visual Studio.NET 7.0">
            <meta name="CODE_LANGUAGE" content="Visual Basic 7.0">
            <meta name="vs_defaultClientScript" content="JavaScript">
            <meta name="vs_targetSchema"
content="http://schemas.microsoft.com/intellisense/ie5">
    </head>
    <body MS_POSITIONING="GridLayout">
        <form id="Form1" method="post" runat="server">
        </form>
    </body>
</html>
```

The initial code block establishes a number of traits regarding the current page. First, you can see the name of the language used behind the scenes to construct your page (VB .NET).

The Codebehind attribute names the VB .NET file that represents the file containing the underlying business code. On a related note, the Inherits attribute is used to specify the name of the class that represents the Page-derived type defined in the file specified by the Codebehind attribute. (You examine these topics further in just a bit.)

Adding Some Simple VB .NET Logic

If you compile and run new Web application at this point, the ASP.NET engine returns an empty page. To remedy this situation, let's modify the body of your *.aspx file to return some textual information that specifies various aspects regarding the incoming HTTP request (the System.Web.UI.Page.Response property is investigated in more detail later in this chapter):

```
<body MS_POSITIONING="GridLayout">
    <h1>
        <b>I am:</b>
    </h1>
    <%=Me.ToString() %>
    <h1>
        <b>You are:</b>
    </h1>
    <%= Request.ServerVariables("HTTP_USER_AGENT") %>
    <form id="Form1" method="post" runat="server">
    </form>
</body>
```

Once you are done, compile and run the project. An HTML page is returned (see Figure 15-31) that documents the agent who sent this request, as well as the string name of the entity receiving the request (the name of your page).

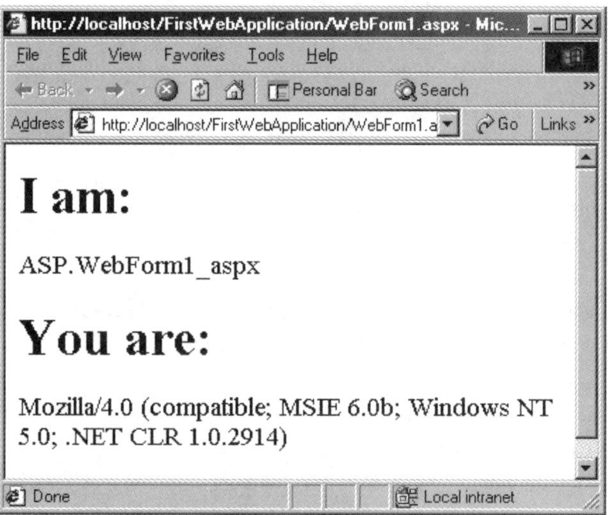

Figure 15-31. Documenting who's who

So far, it looks like ASP.NET is functionally identical to classic ASP. In fact, if you worked through the sample classic ASP application earlier in this chapter, things should look quite familiar. The only difference thus far is the fact that what you used to regard as the Request *object* is now a *property* of the Page base class. Also, as you can see, you are *not* writing script code in your <%. . .%> tags, but full-fledged VB .NET code, as shown here:

```
<%=Me.ToString() %>
```

The Architecture of an ASP.NET Web Application

Now that you have had a chance to build a simple Web application, you can begin digging a bit deeper into the architecture itself. The first major point of interest is the mysterious Codebehind attribute in the initial script block, as shown here:

```
<%@ Page Language="vb" AutoEventWireup="false"
Codebehind="Web Form1.aspx.vb"
Inherits="FirstWebApplication.Web Form1"%>
```

The major difference between classic ASP and ASP.NET is that the *.aspx page, which is requested by an external client, is represented by a unique VB .NET class identified by the Codebehind attribute. When the client requests a particular *.aspx page, an object of this class is instantiated (and manipulated) by the ASP.NET runtime. Notice, however, that this VB .NET file is not shown in the Solution Explorer. To access the Codebehind file, simply right-click the *.aspx file and select View Code. Here is the initial code block:

```
Public Class Web Form1
    Inherits System.Web.UI.Page
#Region " Web Form Designer Generated Code "
    'This call is required by the Web Form Designer.
    <System.Diagnostics.DebuggerStepThrough()> Private Sub InitializeComponent()
    End Sub
    Private Sub Page_Init(ByVal sender As System.Object, _
    ByVal e As System.EventArgs) Handles MyBase.Init
        'CODEGEN: This method call is required by the Web Form Designer
        'Do not modify it using the code editor.
        InitializeComponent()
    End Sub
#End Region
    Private Sub Page_Load(ByVal sender As System.Object, _
    ByVal e As System.EventArgs) Handles MyBase.Load
        'Put user code to initialize the page here
    End Sub
End Class
```

The default skeleton code is not too complicated. The constructor of the Page-derived class establishes an event handler for the Init event. The implementation of this handler calls InitializeComponents(), which establishes another event handler for the Load event (more details on a Page's life cycle in just a bit).

The System.Web.UI.Page Type

To understand the purpose of this autogenerated class, let's begin by examining the System.Web.UI.Page base class. The Page class defines the properties, methods, and events common to all pages processed on the server by the ASP.NET runtime. Table 15-5 describes some (but by no means all) of the core properties.

Table 15-5. Properties of the Page Type

SYSTEM.WEB.UI.PAGE PROPERTY	MEANING IN LIFE
Application	Gets the HttpApplicationState object provided by the runtime.
Cache	Indicates the Cache object in which to store data for the page's application.
IsPostBack	Gets a value indicating if the page is being loaded in response to a client postback, or if it is being loaded and accessed for the first time.
Request	Gets the HttpRequest object that provides access data from incoming HTTP requests.
Response	Gets the HttpResponse object that allows you to send HTTP response data back to a client browser.
Server	Gets the HttpServerUtility object supplied by the HTTP runtime.
Session	Gets the System.Web.SessionState.HttpSessionState object, which provides information about the current request's session.

As you can see, the Page type defines properties that correlate to the intrinsic object model of classic ASP. In addition to defining a number of inherited methods (which you typically do not need to interact with directly), Page also supplies the critical events described in Table 15-6.

Table 15-6. Events of the Page Type

SYSTEM.WEB.UI.PAGE EVENT	MEANING IN LIFE
Init	This event is fired when the page is initialized and is the first step in the page's life cycle.
Load	Once initialized, the Load event is fired. Here, you can configure any Web Form controls with an initial look and feel.
Unload	Occurs when the control is unloaded from memory. Controls should perform any final cleanup before termination.

You examine the life cycle of an ASP.NET Page type in greater detail later in this chapter.

The *.aspx/Codebehind Connection

In addition to this boilerplate code, the VB .NET class represented by the Codebehind tag can be extended with any number of custom properties and methods that can be called (indirectly) by the <%. . .%> code blocks in your *.aspx file. As you recall, classic ASP requires you to define your custom functionality directly in the *.asp file. Thus, your pages were a jumble of HTML tags and VBScript (or JavaScript) code. Because of this, the *.asp files were hard to read and even harder to maintain and reuse.

Furthermore, recall that the whole approach of classic ASP was not terribly object oriented. ASP.NET has resolved these problems by providing a way for you to truly separate the logic that dynamically generates the returned HTML (the *.aspx) file from the implantation of your page's logic (e.g., the *.aspx.vb file).

Now, one slightly odd concept is that when you are writing code in the *.aspx file, you can reference the custom methods and properties defined in the *.aspx.vb file. Let's see a simple example.

Assume you want to build a simple function that obtains the current time and date. You may do so directly in your Page-derived class as shown here:

```
Public Class Web Form1
    Inherits System.Web.UI.Page
     ' Generated code. . .
. . .
   Public Function GetDateTime()
       Return DateTime.Now.ToString()
   End Function
End Class
```

To reference this method in your *.aspx code, you can simply write the following:

```
<body>
     <!-- Get the time from the VB .NET class -->
     <% Response.Write(GetDateTime())%>
. . .
     <form method="post" runat="server" ID=Form1>
     </form>
</body>
```

You can also make reference to the inherited Page members directly in your VB .NET class. Thus, you can also write this:

```
Public Class Web Form1
     Inherits System.Web.UI.Page
      ' Generated code. . .

     Public Sub GetDateTime()
          Response.Write("It is now " & DateTime.Now.ToString())
     End Sub
End Class
```

And then you simply call the following:

```
<!-- Get the time -->
<% GetDateTime() %>
```

Working with the Page.Request Property

As you saw earlier in this chapter, the basic flow of a Web session begins with a client logging onto a site, filling in user information, and clicking a Submit button maintained by an HTML form. In most cases, the opening tag of the form statement specifies an action and method attribute, which specifies the file on the Web server that is sent the data in the various HTML widgets and the method of sending this data (GET or POST). Here is an example:

```
<form name=MainForm action="http://localhost/default.aspx" method=get ID=Form1>
```

In ASP.NET, the Page.Request property provides access to the data sent by the HTTP request. Under the hood, this property manipulates an instance of the

HttpRequest type. Table 15-7 lists some core members (which should look strangely familiar to you if you are coming from a classic ASP background).

Table 15-7. Members of the HttpRequest Type

SYSTEM.WEB.HTTPREQUEST MEMBER	MEANING IN LIFE
ApplicationPath	Gets the virtual path to the currently executing server application.
Browser	Provides information about incoming client's browser capabilities.
ContentType	Indicates the MIME content type of an incoming request. This property is read-only.
Cookies	Gets a collection of client's cookie variables.
FilePath	Indicates the virtual path of the current request. This property is read-only.
Files	Gets the collection of client-uploaded files (multipart MIME format).
Filter	Gets or sets a filter to use when reading the current input stream.
Form	Gets a collection of Form variables.
Headers	Gets a collection of HTTP headers.
HttpMethod	Indicates the HTTP data transfer method used by the client (GET or POST). This property is read-only.
IsSecureConnection	Indicates whether the HTTP connection is secure (i.e., HTTPS). This property is read-only.
Params	Gets a combined collection of QueryString + Form + ServerVariable + Cookies.
QueryString	Gets the collection of QueryString variables.
RawUrl	Gets the current request's raw URL.
RequestType	Indicates the HTTP data transfer method used by the client (GET or POST).
ServerVariables	Gets a collection of Web server variables.
UserHostAddress	Gets the IP host address of the remote client.
UserHostName	Gets the DNS name of the remote client.

You saw the members of the HttpRequest type earlier in this chapter. For example, when you spit out various characteristics of the incoming HTTP request, you used what looked to be an object named Request, as shown here:

```
<b>You Are: </b><%= Request.ServerVariables("HTTP_USER_AGENT") %>
```

What you are really doing is accessing a property on the returned HttpRequest type, as shown here:

```
<h1>
    <b>You are:</b>
</h1>
<%
    Dim r as HttpRequest
    r = Me.Request
    Response.Write(r.ServerVariables("HTTP_USER_AGENT"))
%>
```

See the connection? Now, let's check out the Request.Response property (and the related HttpResponse type).

Working with the Page.Response Property

The Response property of the Page class provides access to an internal HttpResponse type. This type defines a number of properties that allow you to format the HTTP response sent back to the client browser. Table 15-8 lists some core properties (which again should look familiar if you have a classic ASP background).

Table 15-8. Properties of the HttpResponse Type

SYSTEM.WEB.HTTPRESPONSE PROPERTY	MEANING IN LIFE
Cache	Returns the caching semantics of the Web page (e.g., expiration time, privacy, and vary clauses).
ContentEncoding	Gets or sets the HTTP character set of output.
ContentType	Gets or sets the HTTP MIME type of output.
Cookies	Gets the HttpCookie collection sent by the current request.
Filter	Specifies a wrapping filter object to modify the HTTP entity body before transmission.

Table 15-8. Properties of the HttpResponse Type (continued)

SYSTEM.WEB.HTTPRESPONSE PROPERTY	MEANING IN LIFE
IsClientConnected	Gets a value indicating whether the client is still connected to the server.
Output	Enables custom output to the outgoing HTTP content body.
OutputStream	Enables binary output to the outgoing HTTP content body.
StatusCode	Gets or sets the HTTP status code of output returned to the client.
StatusDescription	Gets or sets the HTTP status string of output returned to the client.
SuppressContent	Gets or sets a value indicating that HTTP content will not be sent to the client.

Also, consider the methods of the HttpResponse type described in Table 15-9.

Table 15-9. Methods of the HttpResponse Type

SYSTEM.WEB.HTTPRESPONSE METHOD	MEANING IN LIFE
AppendHeader()	Adds an HTTP header to the output stream.
AppendToLog()	Adds custom log information to the IIS log file.
Clear()	Clears all headers and content output from the buffer stream.
Close()	Closes the socket connection to a client.
End()	Sends all currently buffered output to the client, and then closes the socket connection.
Flush()	Sends all currently buffered output to the client.
Redirect()	Redirects a client to a new URL.
Write()	Writes values to an HTTP output content stream.
WriteFile()	Overloaded. Writes a file directly to an HTTP content output stream.

Perhaps the most important aspect of the HttpResponse type is the ability to write to the HTTP output stream. As you have seen, you may directly call the Write() method or inline an output request using the <%= . . . %> notation (like classic ASP). Thus, you can manipulate this object from your *.aspx file as shown here:

```
<h1>
    <b>You are:</b>
</h1>
<%
    Dim r as HttpRequest
    r = Me.Request
    Dim rs as HttpResponse
    rs = Me.Response
    rs.Write(r.ServerVariables("HTTP_USER_AGENT"))
%>
```

The preceding code is exactly equivalent to the following:

```
<%= Request.ServerVariables("HTTP_USER_AGENT") %>
```

Understanding the Application/Session Distinction

One aspect of Web-based programming that may be new to desktop application developers is the distinction between application and session *state*. Recall that a Web application can be understood as a collection of all related files located under a virtual directory. ASP.NET provides the HttpApplication type to represent the common methods, properties, and events for a given Web application. As you see soon, the globals.asax file defines a single type (named Global) that derives from the HttpApplication base class.

Closely related to HttpApplication is the HttpApplicationState type. This class enables you to share global information across multiple sessions in an ASP.NET application. A *Web session* expresses one user's interaction with the Web application. For example, if 20,000 users are logged on to the Cars site, 20,000 sessions are in process.

In ASP.NET, each session retains stateful information for a given user, programmatically represented by the HttpSessionState type. In this way, each user has an allocated block of memory that represents the user's unique interaction with the Web application. (After all, if two users have logged on to the Cars site, user A may want a brand-new BMW while user B may want a 1970 Colt.) The relationship between a Web application and Web sessions is shown in Figure 15-32.

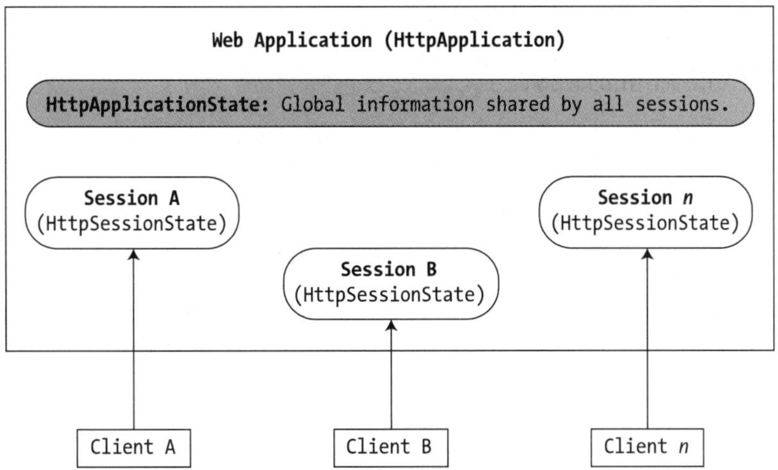

Figure 15-32. Application and session state

Under classic ASP, the notions of application and session state are represented using distinct COM objects (Application and Session). Under ASP.NET, a Page-derived type defines identically named *properties* (Page.Application and Page.Session), which expose the underlying HttpApplicationState and HttpSessionState types.

Working with the Page.Application Property

The Application property of the Page class provides access to the underlying HttpApplicationState type. As mentioned earlier, HttpApplicationState enables developers to share global information across multiple sessions in an ASP.NET application. Table 15-10 describes some core properties.

Table 15-10. Properties of the HttpApplicationState Type

HTTPAPPLICATIONSTATE PROPERTY	MEANING IN LIFE
AllKeys	Enables user to retrieve all application state object names in a collection
Count	Gets the number of item objects in the application state collection
Keys	Returns a NameObjectCollectionBase.KeysCollection instance containing all the keys in the NameObjectCollectionBase instance
StaticObjects	Exposes all objects declared via an <x runat=server></x> tag in the ASP.NET application file

When you need to create data members that can be shared among all active sessions, you need to establish a simple name/value pair (e.g., firstUser = "chuck") and insert it into the internally maintained KeysCollection. To do so, use the class indexer as shown here:

```
Private Sub Page_Load(ByVal sender As System.Object, _
ByVal e As System.EventArgs) Handles MyBase.Load
    ' Create an application-level data member.
    Application("AppString") = "Initial App Value"
End Sub
```

Later, when you need to reference this value, simply extract it using the same property, as shown here:

```
Public Sub GetAppVariable()
    Dim appVar As String = "App: " & Application("AppString")
    Response.Write(appVar)
End Sub
```

Working with the Page.Session Property

As mentioned earlier, a *session* is little more than a given user's interaction with a Web application. To maintain stateful information for a particular end user, use the Session property (which as luck would have it works just like the Application property). For example, assume you have updated the current Web Form1.aspx.vb file to include a subroutine that returns a session-level variable named SessionValue:

```
Public Class Web Form1
    Inherits System.Web.UI.Page
. . .
    Private Sub Page_Load(ByVal sender As System.Object, _
    ByVal e As System.EventArgs) Handles MyBase.Load
        ' Create an application-level data member.
        Application("AppString") = "Initial App Value"

        ' And a session-level data member.
        Session("SessionValue") = New Random().Next().ToString()
    End Sub
    Public Sub GetAppVariable()
        Dim appVar As String = "App: " & Application("AppString")
        Response.Write(appVar)
    End Sub
    Public Sub GetSessionVariable()
        Dim sesVar As String = "Session: " & Session("SessionValue")
        Response.Write(sesVar)
    End Sub
End Class
```

Given that the session variable is assigned a random number within the Page_Load handler, you should be able to launch a number of Web sessions and indeed find that the browser displays the same application-level variable and unique session values. To test this, update your *.aspx.vb file as follows and launch three or four sessions of this Web application:

```
<body MS_POSITIONING="GridLayout">
. . .
    <h1>
        Application variable is:
    </h1>
    <% GetAppVariable() %>
    <h1>
        Session variable is:
    </h1>
    <% GetSessionVariable() %>
    <form id="Form1" method="post" runat="server">
    </form>
</body>
```

Figures 15-33 and 15-34 show two possible results.

Figure 15-33. Same application, session 1

Figure 15-34. Same application, session 2

The Globals.asax File and HttpApplication Type

Each and every ASP.NET application contains a file named Globals.asax. If you open this page using the Solution Explorer, you are presented with a design-time template. Don't be tricked into thinking that this design-time template is directly visible from a given Web session, however. Rather, the role of the Globals.asax file is to function as a central location to place any and all global-level variables, events, and objects that may be used by the Page-derived types. Seen in this light, the design-time template is nothing more than a convenient way to configure global design-time components such as an ADO.NET SqlConnection, or perhaps a GUI widget that is shared between all pages of your Web application (for example, a PictureBox widget that contains your company's logo).

When you add items to the design-time template, the corresponding VB .NET member declarations are added to the associated Globals.asax.vb file (i.e., the CodeBehind file). The initial code behind the Globals.asax.vb file defines a class type named Globals, which derives from System.Web.HttpApplication. Furthermore, your class type has been configured to respond to a subset of possible application-level events.

```
Imports System.Web
Imports System.Web.SessionState
Public Class Global
    Inherits System.Web.HttpApplication
' #Region code. . .
    Sub Application_BeginRequest(ByVal sender As Object, ByVal e As EventArgs)
        ' Fires at the beginning of each request
    End Sub
    Sub Application_AuthenticateRequest(ByVal sender As Object, _
    ByVal e As EventArgs)
        ' Fires upon attempting to authenticate the use
    End Sub
    Sub Application_Error(ByVal sender As Object, ByVal e As EventArgs)
        ' Fires when an error occurs
    End Sub
    Private Sub Global_Disposed(ByVal sender As Object, _
    ByVal e As System.EventArgs) Handles MyBase.Disposed
    End Sub
End Class
```

In addition to the autogenerated application-level events, the HttpApplication type defines 15 additional events, each of which can be handled using the Base Class Events option of the VB .NET code window. Although you do not typically need to handle each and every possible event, Table 15-11 runs through the purposes of the core items of interest. Just understand that these events are used to process the details of incoming HTTP requests and outbound HTTP responses.

Table 15-11. Events of the HttpApplication Type

HTTPAPPLICATION EVENT	MEANING IN LIFE
BeginRequest	This event is raised whenever an incoming HTTP request is detected.
AuthenticateRequest	This event is raised once the ASP.NET runtime is ready to perform authentication upon the incoming request. As you might suspect, this is a fine place to add any additional authentication code.
Error	The handler for this event functions as a catch-all for any unhandled exception within the Webapplication.
EndRequest	When this event is raised, this is your last chance to tweak the outgoing HTTP response before the generated HTML is returned to the recipient.
Start	This event is called the very first time the Web application is loaded by the ASP.NET runtime. This is a handy place to make global database connections, as well as initialize any global-level variables.
End	This event is raised just before the Web application is terminated. As you may expect, this is an ideal place to deallocate any global resources that were acquired within the OnStart event handler.

Figure 15-35 illustrates the flow of these core application-level events.

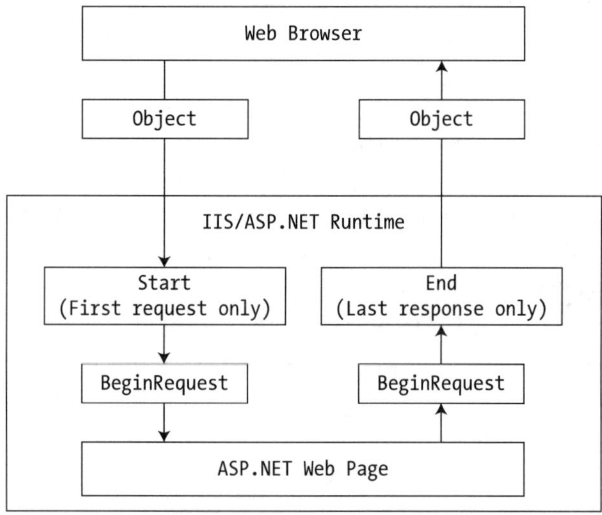

Figure 15-35. The flow of core HttpApplication-level events

The Life Cycle of a Page-Derived Type

Now that you have a better understanding of the life cycle of a Web application, you can examine the flow of events that occur in the Page-derived type itself. Figure 15-36 illustrates the order of events.

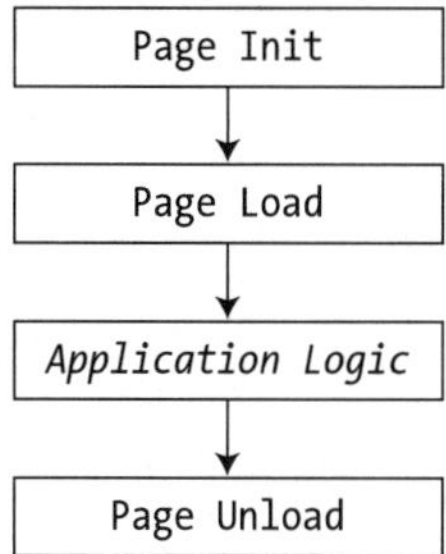

Figure 15-36. Page event sequence

The Init Event

When a page is loaded for the first time, the Init event is fired. VB .NET Web applications handle the Page_Init event within the collapsed #Region code block, which by default does little more than call InitializeComponent().

```
Public Class Web Form1
    Inherits System.Web.UI.Page
#Region " Web Form Designer Generated Code "
. . .
    Private Sub Page_Init(ByVal sender As System.Object, _
    ByVal e As System.EventArgs) Handles MyBase.Init
        'CODEGEN: This method call is required by the Web Form Designer
        'Do not modify it using the code editor.
        InitializeComponent()
    End Sub
#End Region
End Class
```

Within the scope of the Page_Init event handler, all Web controls are assigned their default values (which typically means the values you assigned using the VS .NET Properties window).

The Load Event

The Load event will be fired each and every type time a given ASP.NET Web page is executed in response to an incoming HTTP POST or GET request. Typically speaking, the Load event is where you programmatically populate and manipulate any Web control maintained by the Page-derived type. Again, when you create a new ASP.NET Web application, the Load event is automatically handled.

```
Public Class Web Form1
    Inherits System.Web.UI.Page
...
    Private Sub Page_Load(ByVal sender As System.Object, _
    ByVal e As System.EventArgs) Handles MyBase.Load
        'Put user code to initialize the page here
    End Sub
End Class
```

As you see a bit later in this chapter, ASP.NET defines the concept of *ViewState*. The ViewState is an encoded representation of the values assigned to each Web control, which is persisted *automatically* between page loads. Given this fact, understand that when the Load event is fired, the default values assigned to your Page's set of Web controls are replaced by the values assigned by a given user during postback.

The IsPostBack Property

If you read the previous description of the Load event, you may see a dilemma. As mentioned, the Load event is where you should programmatically fill and tweak Web controls before they are returned to the hosting browser for view. Assume you have a Page-derived type that maintains a TextBox type and a single Button that is configured as follows:

```
Public Class Web Form1
    Inherits System.Web.UI.Page
    Protected WithEvents Button1 As Button
    Protected WithEvents txtFirstName As TextBox
...
    Private Sub Page_Load(ByVal sender As System.Object, _
    ByVal e As System.EventArgs) Handles MyBase.Load
        'Fill TextBox with initial value.
```

```
        txtFirstName.Text = "Please enter your name"
    End Sub
    Private Sub Button1_Click(ByVal sender As System.Object, _
    ByVal e As System.EventArgs) Handles Button1.Click
        ' This server-side event will trigger a postback. . .
    End Sub
End Class
```

When the user first logs on to this page, the value of the TextBox shows "Please enter your name." However, if the user changes this value and clicks the Button type (to initiate a postback), the changes are overridden by the default logic of the Load event. Clearly, what is needed is a way to determine if the page has been loaded for the first time or if it is a result of a postback operation. As luck would have it, the Page.IsPostBack property provides this very functionality. Thus, you can update the Load event handler as follows:

```
Private Sub Page_Load(ByVal sender As System.Object, _
ByVal e As System.EventArgs) Handles MyBase.Load
    'Fill TextBox with initial value only upon first request.
    If Not IsPostBack Then
        txtFirstName.Text = "Please enter your name"
    End If
End Sub
```

Now, when the user enters a new value into the txtFirstName TextBox Web control, this value is retained between all postings within this Web session. Again, this functionality makes use of the ViewState, which is defined in just a moment.

The Unload Event

Finally, you have the Unload event. As you can guess by its name, this event is fired whenever the page is removed from memory, and it is an excellent place to clean up any allocated resources. By default, this event is not handled within your Page-derived type. However, much like a Windows Forms application, you may do so by selecting Base Class Events from the drop-down object list, as shown in Figure 15-37.

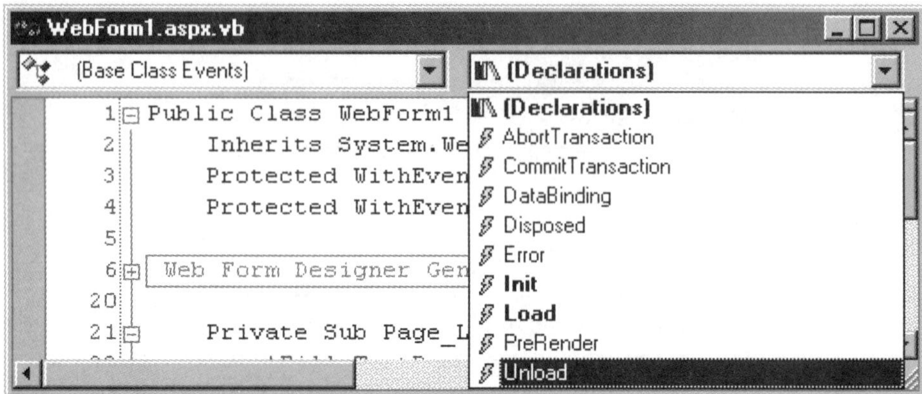

Figure 15-37. Handling the Unload event

Understanding ViewState

Web applications by their very nature are *stateless*. As the client submits HTTP requests to the Web server, all stateful information (such as the values retained within a TextBox or the entries within a DataGrid) is not "remembered" between postings. Under classic ASP, the Web developer was forced to incorporate a good deal of code to ensure that form-level data was cached and reused between Web requests. Under ASP.NET, however, a page is able to retain its state between post-backs using the *ViewState* technique. In a nutshell, when an ASP.NET Web page responds to an HTTP request, a hidden form field named __ViewState is inserted into the response stream. This field is little more than an encoded string that represents all stateful information as name/value pairs.

To illustrate, assume you again have a Page-derived type that allows the user to enter a value within a TextBox and trigger a postback using a Button Web control (see Figure 15-38).

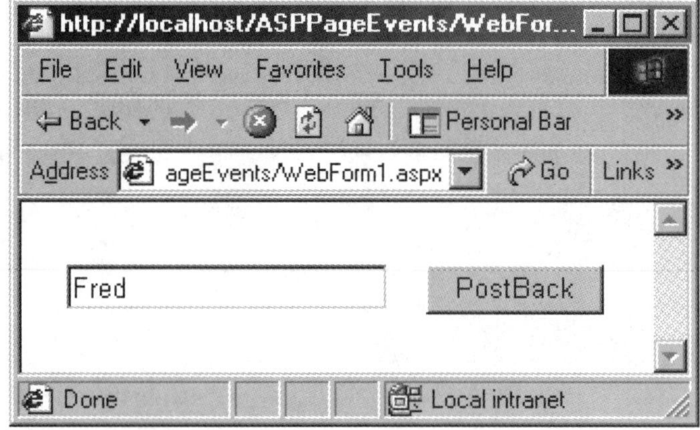

Figure 15-38. Entering stateful data within the context of a stateless Web page

When the user resubmits the page by clicking the Button type, a name/value pair for this TextBox is placed into the ViewState string. Thus, if you open up the source for the returned *.aspx page, you find the following:

```
<form name="Form1" method="post" action="Web Form1.aspx" id="Form1">
<input type="hidden" name="__VIEWSTATE" value="dDwxNDg5OTk5MzM7Oz4=" />
```

Of course, this value is not very human-friendly. Nevertheless, the ASP.NET runtime will read this string to rehydrate the Web controls with the current values whenever the HTML form is submitted to the Web server. In this way, a page (not the server) contains stateful information on its own terms.

Disabling ViewState

In this simple example, the physical size of the ViewState string is quite manageable. Imagine, however, that you have a more complex page that contains numerous Web controls, each of which may contain a user-supplied value. In this case, the size of the hidden ViewState field may swell to such a point that you are downloading a large amount of data back to the rendering Web browser (which may affect performance).

By default, each and every Web control you place onto a Page has its ViewState enabled. However, if you want to disable the capability for a given control (or two) to store its state within the ViewState string, you may do so by setting the EnableViewState property to False, as Figure 15-39 shows.

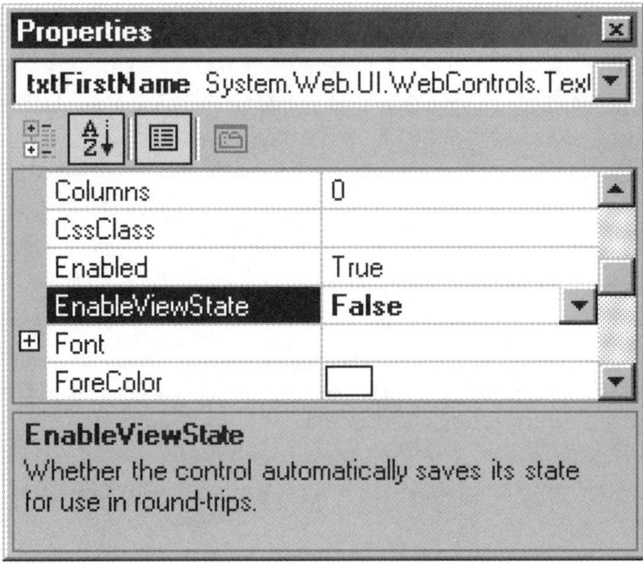

Figure 15-39. Disabling ViewState for the TextBox control

If you want to disable the ViewState mechanism for all Web Controls on a given page, you may modify the @Page directive as follows:

```
<%@ Page Language="vb" AutoEventWireup="false"
Codebehind="Web Form1.aspx.vb" Inherits="ASPPageEvents.Web Form1"
EnableViewState = False%>
```

Debugging and Tracing ASP.NET Applications

If you have worked with Visual InterDev, you understand the pain associated with debugging classic ASP applications. The good news is that when you build ASP.NET Web projects, you can use the same debugging techniques you do with any other sort of VS .NET project type. Thus, you can set breakpoints in script blocks as well as any VB .NET class files (see Figure 15-40), start a debug session (press F5), and step through your code.

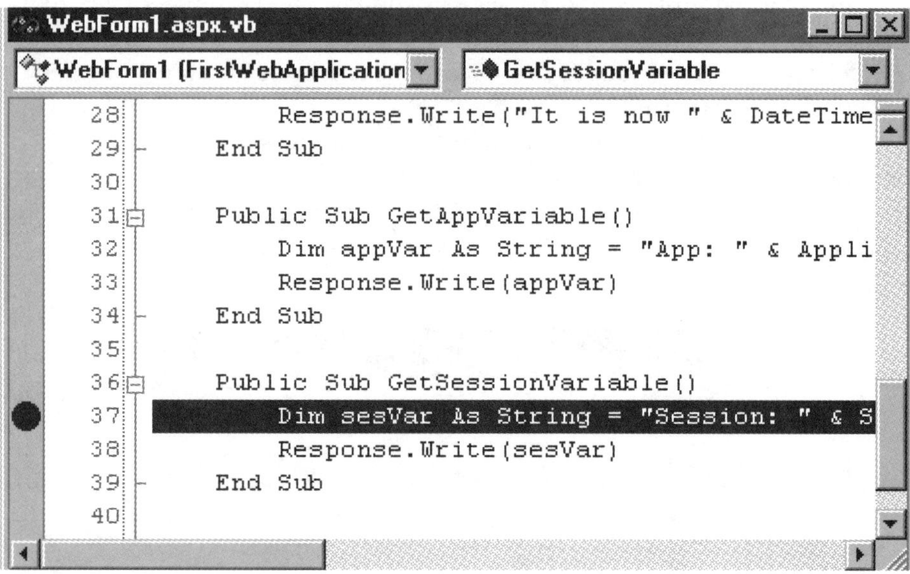

Figure 15-40. Establishing break points

Also, you can enable tracing support for your *.aspx files by specifying the trace attribute in your opening script block, as shown here:

```
<%@ Page Language="vb" AutoEventWireup="false"
Codebehind="Web Form1.aspx.vb"
Inherits="FirstWebApplication.Web Form1"
trace = "true"%>
```

When you do so, the returned HTML contains trace information regarding the previous HTTP response (see Figure 15-41).

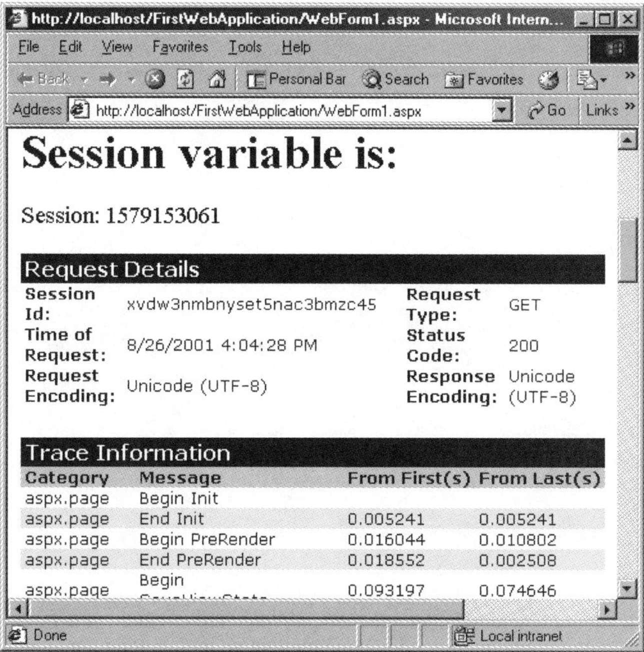

Figure 15-41. Enabling trace information

To insert your own trace messages into the mix, you can use the Trace type. Any time you want to log a custom message (from a script block or VB .NET source code file), simply call the Write() method, as shown here (see Figure 15-42 for output):

```
<%
    Dim r as HttpRequest
    r = Me.Request
    Dim rs as HttpResponse
    rs = Me.Response
    Trace.Write("App Category", "About to determine agent. . .")
    rs.Write(r.ServerVariables("HTTP_USER_AGENT"))
%>
```

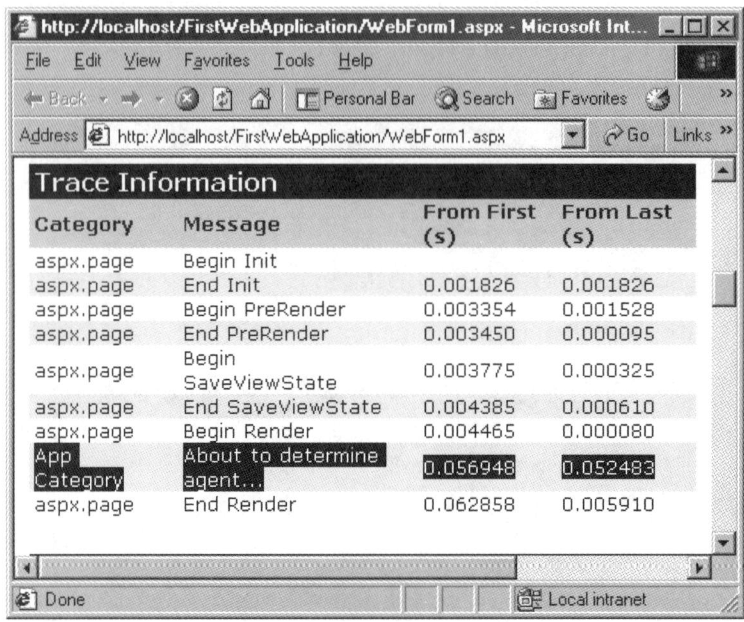

Figure 15-42. Logging custom trace messages

So, to recap the story thus far, ASP.NET Web applications have a look and feel similar to that of classic ASP, given that you still work with Response, Request, Session, and Application properties (rather than objects). Unlike classic ASP, ASP.NET provides a technique termed Codebehind, which allows you to separate your presentation logic from the raw underlying business logic (which may be written using any .NET-aware programming language). While working with the HttpRequest and HttpResponse types are a step in the right direction, your first crack at a feature-rich thin client leaves much to be desired. Next, let's take a tour of the Web-centric GUI widgets.

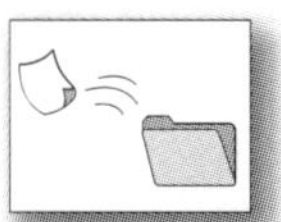

SOURCE CODE *The *.aspx, *.aspx.resx, and *.aspx.vb files for the FirstWebApplication are included under the Chapter 15 subdirectory.*

Understanding the Benefits of Web Form Controls

One major benefit of ASP.NET is the ability to assemble the user interface of your Web pages using the GUI types defined in the System.Web.UI.WebControls namespace. These controls (which go by the name server controls, Web controls, or Web Form controls) are *extremely* helpful in that they automatically generate the necessary HTML tags required by the browser.

For example, in classic ASP, if you author a Web page that needs to display a series of text boxes, you basically need to type the HTML tags directly into the ASP page. However, in ASP.NET, you simply design your Web form using the design-time template and intrinsic Web Form controls. For example, if you want to place a TextBox widget onto the design-time Web Form, the following tags are generated on your behalf:

```
<form id="Form1" method="post" runat="server">
    <asp:TextBox id="TextBox1" style="Z-INDEX: 101;
    LEFT: 26px; POSITION: absolute; TOP: 23px" runat="server">
    </asp:TextBox>
</form>
```

When the ASP.NET runtime encounters widgets with this attribute, the correct HTML is inserted into the response stream automatically. Thus, if you run your Web application and view the generated source code (simply right-click anywhere in the browser and select View Source), you find the following:

```
<input name="TextBox1" type="text" id="TextBox1" style="Z-INDEX: 101; LEFT: 26px;
POSITION: absolute; TOP: 23px" />
```

Granted, in this situation, it looks as if the Web Form controls required more markup than the raw HTML widget definition. However, not all controls are as trivial as a simple TextBox. For example, some Web controls encapsulate full-blown calendars, ad rotators, HTML tables, data grids, and so forth. In such a case, the Web Form controls can save you from writing dozens of lines of raw HTML code.

Another benefit is that each ASP.NET control has a corresponding class in the System.Web.UI.WebControls namespace and can therefore be programmatically manipulated from your *.aspx file as well as the associated Page-derived class (e.g., the VB .NET class marked by the Codebehind attribute). On a related note, Web controls also host a number of events that can be processed on the *server* (more on this later).

The final core benefit of using Web Form controls (rather than raw HTML controls) is the fact that ASP.NET provides a whole set of controls to validate the user-supplied data. Therefore, you do not need to generate client-side JavaScript routines to validate the data (although you are still free to do so).

Working with Web Form Controls

When you build Web Application projects, notice that your Toolbox window has an active tab named Web Forms, as Figure 15-43 shows.

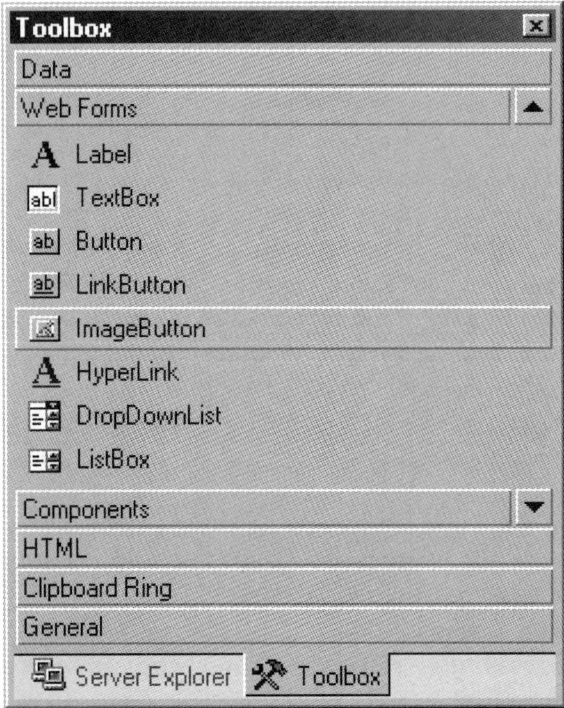

Figure 15-43. The Web controls

Understand that each server control can be configured using the Properties window of the VS .NET IDE. Given your work with Windows Forms earlier, you should have no problem understanding the build of a given widget's property set. For example, if you have a text box control (which I have assigned the ID of txtEMail), you will find the choices shown in Figure 15-44.

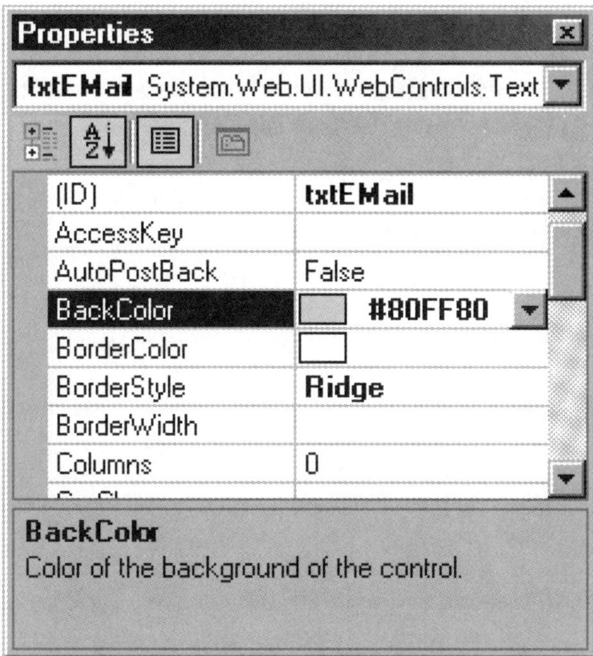

Figure 15-44. Like Windows Forms controls, Web Form controls are configured using the Properties window

As you configure a given WebControl using the Properties window, your changes are written directly to the *.aspx file. As an example, if you select the txtEMail text box and modify the BorderStyle, BorderWidth, BackColor, BorderColor, and ToolTip properties, the opening <asp:textbox> tag has a number of new name/value pairs representing your selections, as shown here:

```
<asp:TextBox id="txtEMail" style="Z-INDEX: 101; LEFT: 26px;
POSITION: absolute; TOP: 23px" runat="server" BorderStyle="Ridge"
BackColor="#80FF80">
</asp:TextBox>
```

Again, the result is plain old HTML:

```
<input name="txtEMail" type="text" id="txtEMail"
style="background-color:#80FF80;border-style:Ridge;
Z-INDEX: 101; LEFT: 26px; POSITION: absolute; TOP: 23px" />
```

Formalizing the Web Control

Now let's examine exactly how these server controls are represented in the *.aspx file. A given WebControl is defined using an XML-like syntax in which the opening element tag is always <asp: *controlType* runat="server">. The closing tag is simply </asp: *controlType*>. Thus, you find that each control is represented in the *.aspx file using syntax such as the following:

```
<form id="Form1" method="post" runat="server">
    <asp:TextBox id="txtEMail" style="Z-INDEX: 101; LEFT: 26px;
    POSITION: absolute; TOP: 23px" runat="server" BorderStyle="Ridge"
    BackColor="#80FF80">
    </asp:TextBox>
    <asp:Button id="btnClickMe" style="Z-INDEX: 102; LEFT: 34px;
    POSITION: absolute; TOP: 69px" runat="server" Text="Click Me">
    </asp:Button>
</form>
```

The runat="server" attribute marks this item as a server-side control and informs the ASP.NET runtime that this item needs to be processed before returning the response stream to the browser to generate the necessary HTML. Now, open the Codebehind window. You notice that you now have a number of new member variables that represent each server control. As you can see, the names of these variables are the same as those of the ID element defined in the *.aspx file:

```
Public Class Web Form1
    Inherits System.Web.UI.Page
    Protected WithEvents btnClickMe As System.Web.UI.WebControls.Button
    Protected WithEvents txtEMail As System.Web.UI.WebControls.TextBox
. . .
End Class
```

In this way, you can programmatically manipulate your items using VB .NET code in the *.aspx file or in your custom-defined routines in the Page-derived class.

The Derivation of Web Form Controls

All of the ASP.NET server-side controls ultimately derive from a common base class named System.Web.UI.WebControls.WebControl. WebControl in turn derives from System.Web.UI.WebControls.Control, which in turn derives from System.Object. For example, the derivation of the Web Form Button type is shown in Figure 15-45.

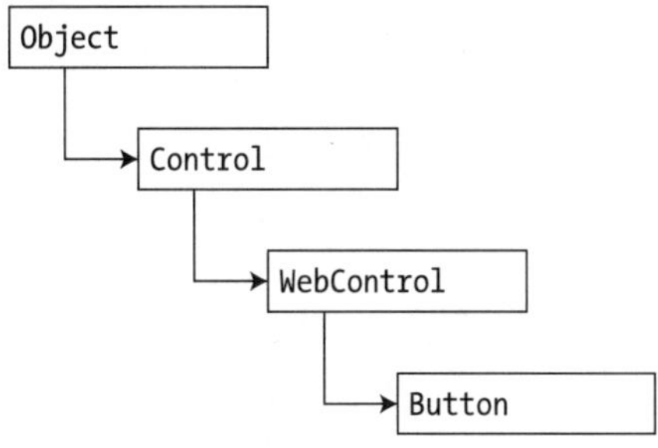

Figure 15-45. Base classes of a Web Control

Control and WebControl each define a number of properties common to all server-side controls. To help gain an understanding of your inherited functionality, consider the partial set of Control properties described in Table 15-12.

Table 15-12. Properties of the Control Base Class

CONTROL PROPERTY	MEANING IN LIFE
ID	Gets or sets the identifier for the control. Setting the property on a control allows programmatic access to the control's properties as well as the chance to respond to events sent by the control.
EnableViewState	Gets or sets a value indicating whether the control should maintain its view state and the view state of any child control it contains when the current page request ends (more on this later).
Page	Gets the Page object that contains the current control.
Visible	Gets or sets a value that indicates if a control should be rendered on the page.

As you can tell, the Control type provides a number of non-GUI-related behaviors. WebControl also defines some additional properties described in Table 15-13 that allow you to configure the look and feel of the server-side widget.

Table 15-13. Properties of the WebControl Base Class

WEBCONTROL PROPERTY	MEANING IN LIFE
BackColor	Gets or sets the background color of the Web control.
BorderColor	Gets or sets the border color of the Web control.
BorderStyle	Gets or sets the border style of the Web control.

Table 15-13. Properties of the WebControl Base Class (continued)

WEBCONTROL PROPERTY	MEANING IN LIFE
BorderWidth	Gets or sets the border width of the Web control.
Enabled	Gets or sets a value indicating if the Web control is enabled.
Font	Gets font information for the Web control.
ForeColor	Gets or sets the foreground color (typically the color of the text) of the Web control.
Height Width	Gets or sets the height and width of the Web control.
TabIndex	Gets or sets the tab index of the Web control.
ToolTip	Gets or sets the tool tip for the Web control to be displayed when the cursor is over the control.

Categories of Web Form Controls

While all the types in the System.Web.UI.WebControls namespace are GUI related, you can break down their functionality into four broad categories:

- Intrinsic controls
- Rich controls
- Data-centric controls
- Input validation controls

Given your work with Windows Forms controls earlier in this book, you should feel right at home. Just remember that while Windows Forms types encapsulate the raw Win32 API from view, Web Form controls encapsulate the generation of raw HTML tags.

Working with the Intrinsic Web Form Controls

To begin, let's examine some of the intrinsic controls. These types are basically .NET components that have a direct HTML widget counterpart. (If there is no direct counterpart, the Web Form control sends back HTML tags that simulate one.) For example, to display a list of items for the end user (see Figure 15-46), you can construct a Web Form ListBox (and the related ListItems), as shown here:

```
<asp:ListBox id=ListBox1 runat="server" Width="86" Height="69">
    <asp:ListItem Value="BMW">BMW</asp:ListItem>
    <asp:ListItem Value="Jetta">Jetta</asp:ListItem>
    <asp:ListItem Value="Colt">Colt</asp:ListItem>
    <asp:ListItem Value="Grand Am">Grand Am</asp:ListItem>
</asp:ListBox>
```

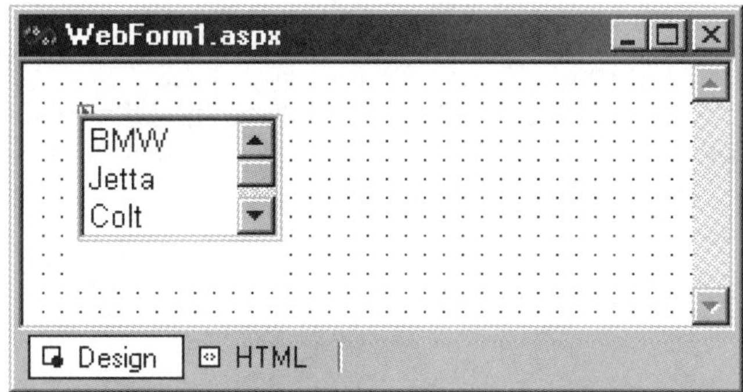

Figure 15-46. Building a ListBox

When the controls are processed by the ASP.NET runtime, the resulting HTML (which is, of course, displayed in the browser) looks something like this:

```
<select name="ListBox1" id="ListBox1" size="5" style="height:69px;width:86px;">
    <option value="BMW">BMW</option>
    <option value="Jetta">Jetta</option>
    <option value="Colt">Colt</option>
    <option value="Grand Am">Grand Am</option>
</select>
```

Table 15-14 describes some of the core intrinsic Web Form controls.

Table 15-14. A Sampling of Intrinsic Web Form Controls

INTRINSIC WEB FORM CONTROL	MEANING IN LIFE
Button ImageButton	Various button types.
CheckBox CheckBoxList	A basic check box (CheckBox) or a list box containing a set of check boxes (CheckBoxList).
DropDownList ListBox	These types allow you to construct standard list box items.
ListItem	Image.
Panel Label	These types represent containers for static text and images (as well as a way to group them).
RadioButton RadioButtonList	A basic radio button type (RadioButton) or a list box containing a set of radio buttons (RadioButtonList).
TextBox	Text box for user input. May be configured as a single-line or multiline text box.

Working with these intrinsic controls is more or less just like working with their Windows Forms equivalents. Given that the VS .NET IDE provides the Properties window to configure a selected widget, your task is even simpler. Therefore, rather than walking through each and every intrinsic control, let's spend time looking at a few common configurations.

Creating a Group of Radio Buttons

Radio button types tend to work as a group in which only one item in the group can be selected at a given time. For example, if you are interested in the UI shown in Figure 15-47, you can write the following script in the body of your form:

```
<body>
<p><font size=5><em>How shall we contact you?</em></font></p>
<p>
    <asp:RadioButton id=RadioHome runat="server"
    Text="Contact me at home" GroupName="ContactGroup">
```

```
    </asp:RadioButton></p>
<p>
    <asp:RadioButton id=RadioWork runat="server"
     Text="Contact me at work" GroupName="ContactGroup">
    </asp:RadioButton></p>
<p>
    <asp:RadioButton id=RadioDontBother runat="server"
    Text="Don't bother me. . ." GroupName="ContactGroup">
    </asp:RadioButton></p>
</body>
```

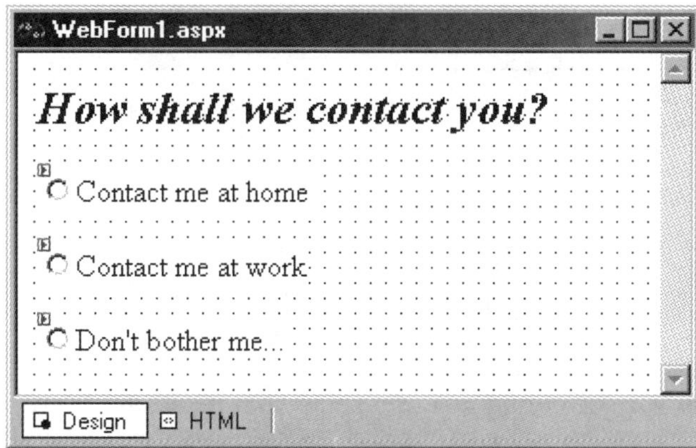

Figure 15-47. Building a set of related radio buttons

Notice that each RadioButton type has a GroupName attribute. Given that each item has been mapped to the same group (ContactGroup), each is mutually exclusive.

Creating a Scrollable, Multiline TextBox

Another common widget is a multiline text box (see Figure 15-48).

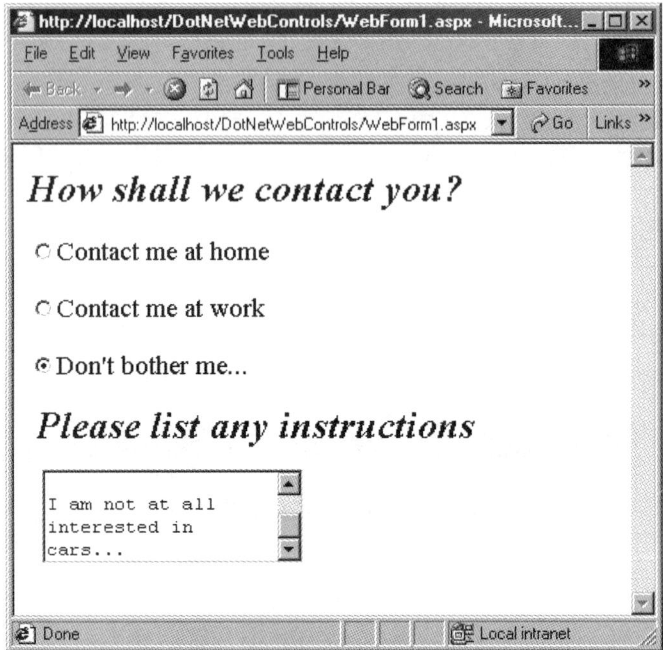

Figure 15-48. A multiline TextBox

As you may expect, configuring a text box to function in this way is simply a matter of adding the correct attribute set to the opening <asp:TextBox> tag. Consider this example:

```
<asp:TextBox id="TextBox1" style="Z-INDEX: 102; LEFT: 20px;
    POSITION: absolute; TOP: 228px" runat="server" Height="66px"
    Width="184px" TextMode="MultiLine">
</asp:TextBox>
```

When you set the TextMode attribute to MultiLine, the TextBox automatically displays a vertical scroll bar when the content is larger than the display area. The remaining intrinsic controls are rather self-explanatory, so take the time to check out their property set.

The Rich Controls

Rich controls are also widgets that emit HTML to the HTTP response stream. The difference between these types and the set of intrinsic controls is that they have no direct HTML counterpart. Table 15-15 describes two rich controls.

Table 15-15. Rich WebControl Widgets

WEB FORM RICH CONTROL	MEANING IN LIFE
AdRotator	This control allows you to randomly display text/images using a corresponding XML configuration file.
Calendar	This control returns HTML that represents a GUI-based calendar.

Working with the Calendar Control

The Calendar control is a widget for which there is no direct HTML equivalent. Nevertheless, this type has been designed to return a batch of HTML tags that simulate such an entity. For example, suppose you place a Calendar control on your Web Form as shown here:

```
<asp:Calendar id=Calendar1 runat="server"></asp:Calendar></p>
```

You find that a *huge* amount of raw HTML has been generated automatically. To test things for yourself, place a Calendar type on your design-time template, save the *.aspx file, and navigate to the correct virtual directory. Once you get back the response, right-click the browser and select View Source (see Figure 15-49).

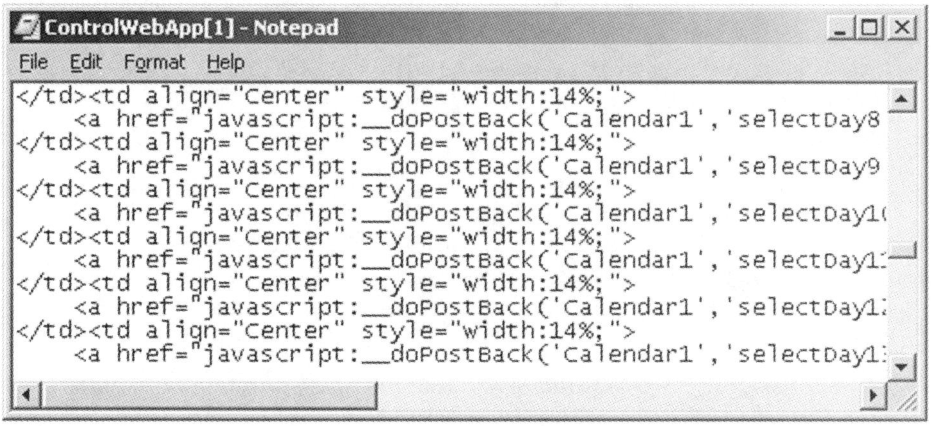

```
ControlWebApp[1] - Notepad
File  Edit  Format  Help
</td><td align="Center" style="width:14%;">
    <a href="javascript:__doPostBack('Calendar1','selectDay8
</td><td align="Center" style="width:14%;">
    <a href="javascript:__doPostBack('Calendar1','selectDay9
</td><td align="Center" style="width:14%;">
    <a href="javascript:__doPostBack('Calendar1','selectDay1(
</td><td align="Center" style="width:14%;">
    <a href="javascript:__doPostBack('Calendar1','selectDay1:
</td><td align="Center" style="width:14%;">
    <a href="javascript:__doPostBack('Calendar1','selectDay1:
</td><td align="Center" style="width:14%;">
    <a href="javascript:__doPostBack('Calendar1','selectDay1:
```

Figure 15-49. The Calendar Web control emits complex HTML

Like its Windows Forms counterpart, the server-side Calendar control is highly customizable. One member of interest is the SelectionMode property. By default, the Calendar control only allows the end user to select a single day (e.g., SelectionMode = Day). You can change this behavior by assigning this property to any of the following alternatives:

- None: No selection can be made (e.g., the Calendar is just for display purposes).
- DayWeek: User may select a single day or an entire week.
- DayWeekMonth: User may select a single day, an entire week, or an entire month.

For example, if you choose DayWeekMonth, the returned HTML renders an additional leftmost column (to allow the end user to select a given week) as well as a selector in the upper left (to allow the end user to select the entire month). Here is the full configuration, which is shocking until you recall that each attribute was configured using the VS .NET IDE's Properties window:

```
<asp:Calendar id=Calendar1 runat="server" SelectionMode="DayWeekMonth"
DayNameFormat="FirstLetter" BackColor="White"
SelectorStyle-ForeColor="#336666" SelectorStyle-BackColor="#99CCCC"
NextPrevStyle-Font-Size="8pt" NextPrevStyle-ForeColor="#CCFF99"
TodayDayStyle-BackColor="#99CCCC" DayHeaderStyle-Height="1px"
DayHeaderStyle-ForeColor="#336666" DayHeaderStyle-BackColor="#99CCCC"
Font-Size="8pt" Font-Names="Verdana" Height="200"
OtherMonthDayStyle-ForeColor="#999999" TitleStyle-Font-Size="11pt"
TitleStyle-Font-Bold="True" TitleStyle-ForeColor="#CCFF99"
TitleStyle-BackColor="#003399" ForeColor="#003399" BorderColor="#3366CC"
 Width="221" SelectedDayStyle-ForeColor="#CCFF99"
SelectedDayStyle-BackColor="#009999"
TodayDayStyle-ForeColor="White" BorderWidth="1px"
TitleStyle-BorderStyle="Solid" TitleStyle-BorderWidth="1px"
TitleStyle-BorderColor="#3366CC" WeekendDayStyle-BackColor="#CCCCFF"
SelectedDayStyle-Font-Bold="True" CellPadding="1">
</asp:Calendar>
```

Figure 15-50 shows the output as rendered in Microsoft Internet Explorer.

Figure 15-50. The client-side Calendar UI

Working with the AdRotator

Although classic ASP also provided an AdRotator control, the ASP.NET variation has been substantially upgraded. The role of this widget is to randomly display a given advertisement at some position in the browser. When you place a server-side AdRotator widget on your design-time template, the display is a simple placeholder. Functionally, this control cannot do its magic until you set the AdvertisementFile property to point to the XML file that describes each ad.

The format of the advertisement file is quite simple. For each ad you want to show, create a unique <Ad> element. At a minimum, each <Ad> element specifies the image to display (ImageUrl), the URL to navigate to if the image is selected (TargetUrl), mouseover text (AlternateText), and the ad weight (Impressions). For example, assume you have a file (ads.xml) that defines two possible ads, as shown here:

```
<Advertisements>
    <Ad>
        <ImageUrl>SlugBug.jpg</ImageUrl>
```

```
        <TargetUrl>http://www.Cars.com</TargetUrl>
        <AlternateText>Your new Car?</AlternateText>
        <Impressions>80</Impressions>
    </Ad>
    <Ad>
        <ImageUrl>car.gif</ImageUrl>
        <TargetUrl>http://www.CarSuperSite.com</TargetUrl>
        <AlternateText>Like this Car?</AlternateText>
        <Impressions>80</Impressions>
    </Ad>
</Advertisements>
```

Once you set the AdvertisementFile property correctly (and ensure that the images and XML file are in the correct virtual directory), one of these two ads is randomly displayed when users navigate to the site:

```
<asp:AdRotator id=AdRotator1 runat="server" Width="470"
 Height="60" AdvertisementFile="ads.xml">
</asp:AdRotator>
```

Thus, you might find the output shown in Figure 15-51.

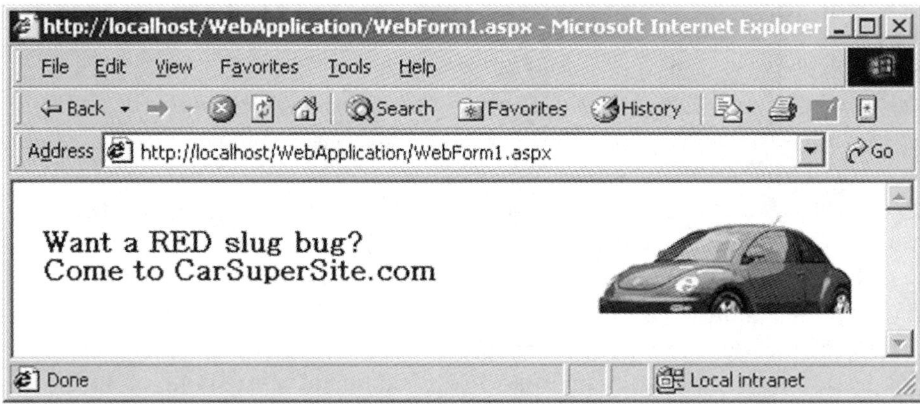

Figure 15-51. One possible ad for the Volkswagen Beetle

Or perhaps you might find something like Figure 15-52.

Figure 15-52. Another possible ad for the Volkswagen Beetle

Be aware that the Height and Width properties of the AdRotator are used to establish the size of your ads. In this example, each ad is the default 60 × 470 pixels. If your ads are larger (or smaller) than the AdRotator's size, you find skewed images.

Data-Centric Controls

Web Form defines a number of widgets that generate HTML based (in part) on a connection to a data store. As you may expect, these controls can be fed into ADO.NET DataSets, just like their Windows Forms counterparts. Table 15-16 gives a partial list of Web Form data controls.

Table 15-16. Web Form Data Controls

WEB FORM DATA CONTROL	MEANING IN LIFE
DataGrid	A widget that displays ADO.NET DataSets in a grid.
DataList	A widget bound to a given data source.

In addition to these core data-centric Web Form types, be aware that most intrinsic controls can be configured to display information obtained from a data store or user-defined type (UDT). You examine how to bind to custom types in just a moment, but first let's examine the process of binding a DataSet to the Web-centric DataGrid widget.

Filling a DataGrid

Far and away one of the most common tasks in Web development is reading a data source for information and returning said data in a tabular format. Using classic ASP, this was accomplished by obtaining an ADO Recordset and building an HTML table on the fly using various HTML tags. You can achieve the same end result using the Web Form DataGrid with minimal fuss and bother.

To illustrate, let's assume that when a user navigates to a given *.aspx page, you want to read the Cars database (which you developed in Chapter 14) and return the results. Your first task is to write an event handler for the Load event of the page class. Once you do so, you can create a DataSet object and bind it directly to the DataGrid. Here is the corresponding VB .NET code (understand that DataGrid1 is the name of the server-side widget you dropped onto your design-time form):

```
' Don't forget to specify an Imports directive for System.Data.SQL!
Private Sub Page_Load(ByVal sender As System.Object, _
ByVal e As System.EventArgs) Handles MyBase.Load
    ' Fill the DataGrid with the Inventory table.
    Dim sqlConn As SqlConnection = New SqlConnection()
    sqlConn.ConnectionString = "data source=.; initial catalog=Cars;" & _
                "integrated security=sspi;"
    Dim dataAdapt As SqlDataAdapter = _
            New SqlDataAdapter("Select * from Inventory", sqlConn)
    Dim ds As DataSet = New DataSet()
    dataAdapt.Fill(ds, "Inventory")
    ' Bind to data grid.
    DataGrid1.DataSource = ds.Tables("Inventory").DefaultView
    DataGrid1.DataBind()
End Sub
```

The output is very satisfying (see Figure 15-53).

More on Data Binding

As you have seen, the DataGrid control provides the DataSource and DataBind() members to allow you to render the contents of a given DataTable. This is obviously a great boon to the enterprise developer. However, most Web Form controls (as well as Windows Forms controls) also allow you to bind other sources of data to a given widget.

Assume that you have a well-known set of values represented by a simple string array. Using the same technique you use to bind to DataGrid types, you

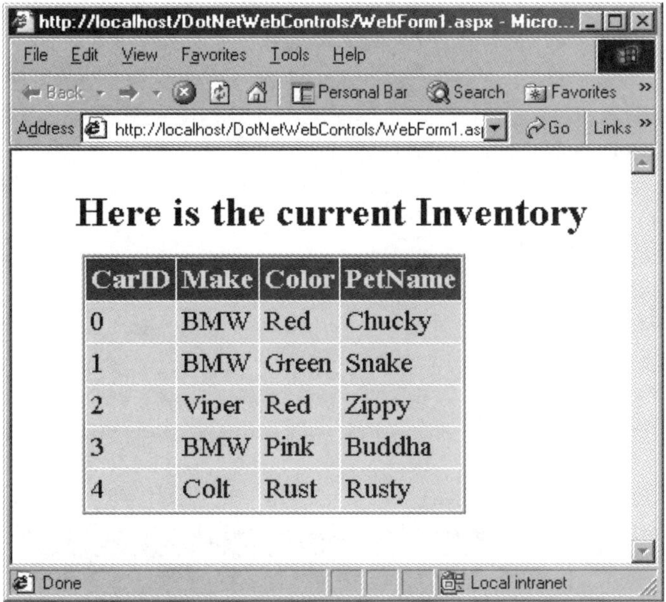

Figure 15-53. Filling a Web Forms DataGrid using a data adapter

can attach an array to a GUI type. If you place an ASP.NET ListBox control (with the ID of lstSalesPeople) on your *.aspx page, you can update the Page_Load() event handler as shown here:

```
Private Sub Page_Load(ByVal sender As System.Object, _
ByVal e As System.EventArgs) Handles MyBase.Load
...
    ' Create an array of data to bind to the list box.
    Dim salesFolk() As String = _
    {"Sally", "Hank", "Ottis", "Alphonzo", "Cage", "TB"}
    lstSalesPeople.DataSource = salesFolk
    lstSalesPeople.DataBind()
End Sub
```

The output is shown in Figure 15-54.

Recall that all .NET arrays map to the System.Array type. Also recall that System.Array implements the IEnumerable interface. The fact is that any type that implements IEnumerable can be bound to a GUI widget. Therefore, if you update your simple string array to an instance of the ArrayList type, the output is identical, as shown here:

```
Private Sub Page_Load(ByVal sender As System.Object, _
ByVal e As System.EventArgs) Handles MyBase.Load
. . .
    ' Now use an array list.
    Dim salesFolk As ArrayList = New ArrayList()
    salesFolk.Add("Sally")
    salesFolk.Add("Ottis")
    salesFolk.Add("Alphonzo")
    salesFolk.Add("Cage")
    salesFolk.Add("TB")
    lstSalesPeople.DataSource = salesFolk
    lstSalesPeople.DataBind()
End Sub
```

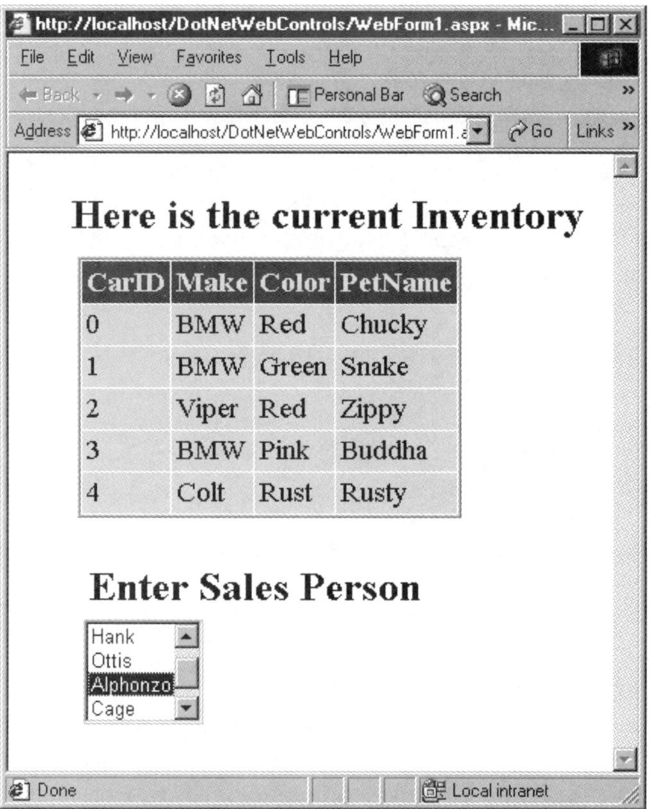

Figure 15-54. Binding data to common Web Form controls

Understanding Server-Side Event Handling

Before you examine the set of Validation controls, you need to come to understand the ASP.NET Web Control event model. As you have seen, one common approach to handling events fired by HTML GUI widgets is through the use of client-side JavaScript. In any case where your event handling requires any rendering logic, browser alerts (e.g., message boxes), or other direct interaction with the browser's object model, this is the way to go. However, other times you have a particular ASP.NET widget that performs non-GUI processing (such as performing a numerical calculation, editing a data table, and so on).

While you are still free to use client-side scripting for these purposes, ASP.NET does offer another alternative. Each Web Form control responds to its own set of events, which can be configured to process event handlers *on the server.* In this way, you are able to keep all event logic within the Codebehind file and keep your business logic truly separate from the HTML GUI presentation tags.

Working the Web Control events is almost identical to the process of handling events for Windows Forms controls. To illustrate, assume you have placed a Calendar control on your design-time template, and you want to determine which day has been selected by the user. Given that the Web Control's are declared WithEvents by default, you can simply make use of the code window (see Figure 15-55).

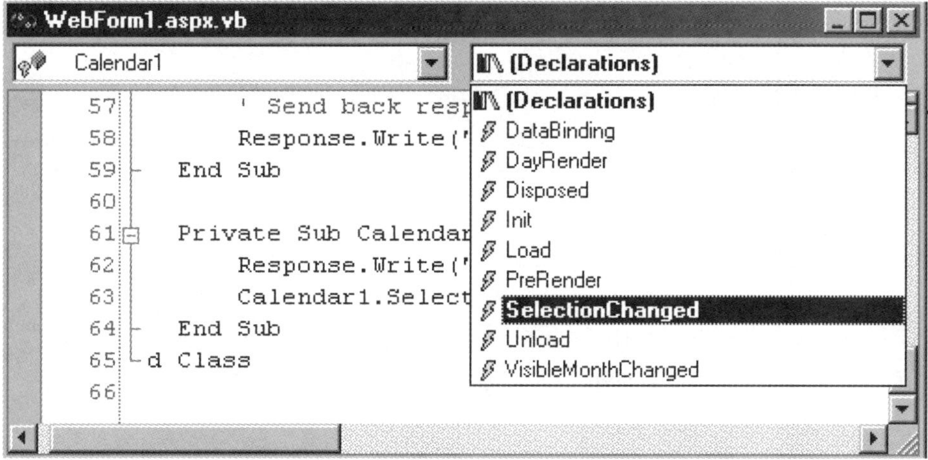

Figure 15-55. Establishing server-side events

You can capture the SelectionChanged event and act accordingly, as shown next:

```
Private Sub Calendar1_SelectionChanged(ByVal sender As System.Object, _
ByVal e As System.EventArgs) Handles Calendar1.SelectionChanged
    Response.Write("<h5>Your car will be delivered on:  " & _
    Calendar1.SelectedDate.Date + "</h5>")
End Sub
```

Now when the user triggers the SelectionChanged event (by clicking a given date), the browser makes a postback to the server to call the correct event handler. Figure 15-56 shows the end result.

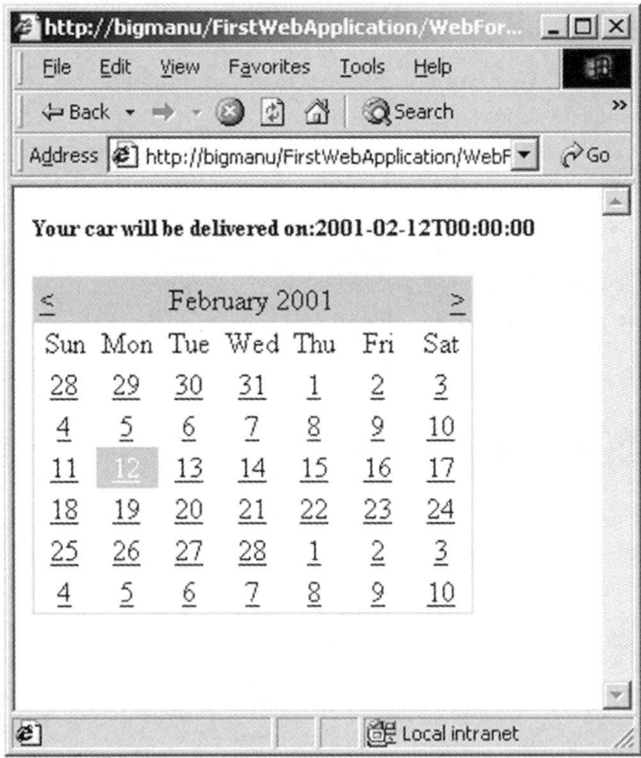

Figure 15-56. Server-side event handling

Even though ASP.NET provides the ability to handle GUI widget events on the Web server, you need to be aware of the obvious drawback: This increases the number of postbacks to the remote machine and therefore degrades the performance of your Web application. However, on the upside, when used prudently server-side event handling leads to more modular and maintainable code.

Validation Controls

The final conceptual set of Web Form controls are termed *validation controls.* Like their Windows Forms equivalents, these types are used to ensure that the data submitted by the user is well formatted based on your application logic. Table 15-17 gives a rundown of the core validation controls.

Table 15-17. Validation Controls

WEB FORM VALIDATION CONTROL	MEANING IN LIFE
CompareValidator	Validates that the value of an input control is equal to a given value of another input control.
CustomValidator	Allows you to build a custom validation function that validates a given control.
RangeValidator	Determines that a given value is in a predetermined range.
RegularExpressionValidator	Checks if the value of the associated input control matches the pattern of a regular expression.
RequiredFieldValidator	Ensures that a given input control contains a value (and is thus not empty).
ValidationSummary	Displays a summary of all validation errors of a page in a list, bulleted list, or single paragraph format. The errors can be displayed inline and/or in a pop-up message box.

To illustrate the basics of working with validation controls, assume that the current Page-derived type now supports three TextBox types that allow the user to sign up for a car-centric e-newsletter in addition to a single Button type that allows the user to submit the form data by way of a server-side event handler (see Figure 15-57).

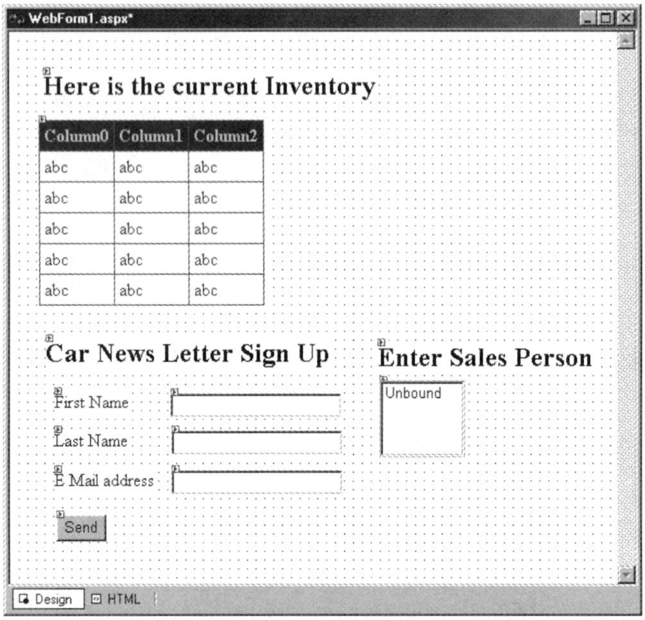

Figure 15-57. A simple Web UI

The Click event handler simply echoes a response to the output stream:

```
Private Sub Button1_Click(ByVal sender As System.Object, _
ByVal e As System.EventArgs) Handles Button1.Click
    ' Send back response.
    Response.Write("Data received. . .")
End Sub
```

Next let's examine how to use the Web Form validation controls. To illustrate, assume that you want to ensure that the txtEMail text box contains information (before the form is submitted to the Web server). At design time, you can simply place a RequiredFieldValidator widget on your form. Using the Properties window, you can set the ErrorMessage property to a given value (which is displayed when the validation fails), as well as establish the ID of the control this widget is in charge of validating using the ControlToValidate property (see Figure 15-58).

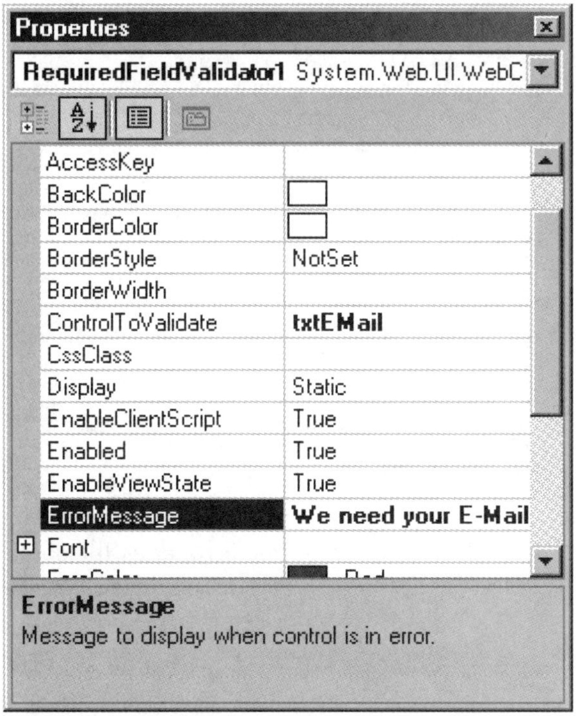

Figure 15-58. *Configuring data validation*

Under the hood, the *.aspx logic is as follows:

```
<asp:RequiredFieldValidator id=RequiredFieldValidator1 style="Z-INDEX: 109;
LEFT: 351px; POSITION: absolute; TOP: 204px"
runat="server"
ErrorMessage="We need your e-mail Address!"
ControlToValidate="txtEMail">
</asp:RequiredFieldValidator>
```

Now, rebuild and run the application once again. At this point, you should not see any noticeable changes. However, when you attempt to click the Send button before you fill in the txtEMail text box, your error message is suddenly visible, as shown in Figure 15-59.

Figure 15-59. The RequiredFieldValidator at work

After the user has submitted all required form data, the confirmation response is visible at the top of the page, as shown in Figure 15-60.

Figure 15-60. Successful posting

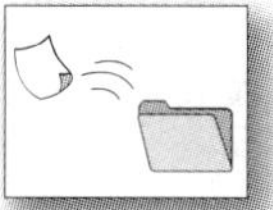

SOURCE CODE *The *.aspx, *.aspx.resx, and *.aspx.vb files for the AspNetWebControls project are included under the Chapter 15 subdirectory.*

Code in the validation section is OK and output matches figures 15-59 and 15-60.

A Complete ASP.NET Example

At this point, you have seen various stand-alone pieces of ASP.NET Web applications. Let's close this chapter by pulling things together by building a minimal but complete Web application named (of course) VbNetCarWebApp (see Figure 15-61).

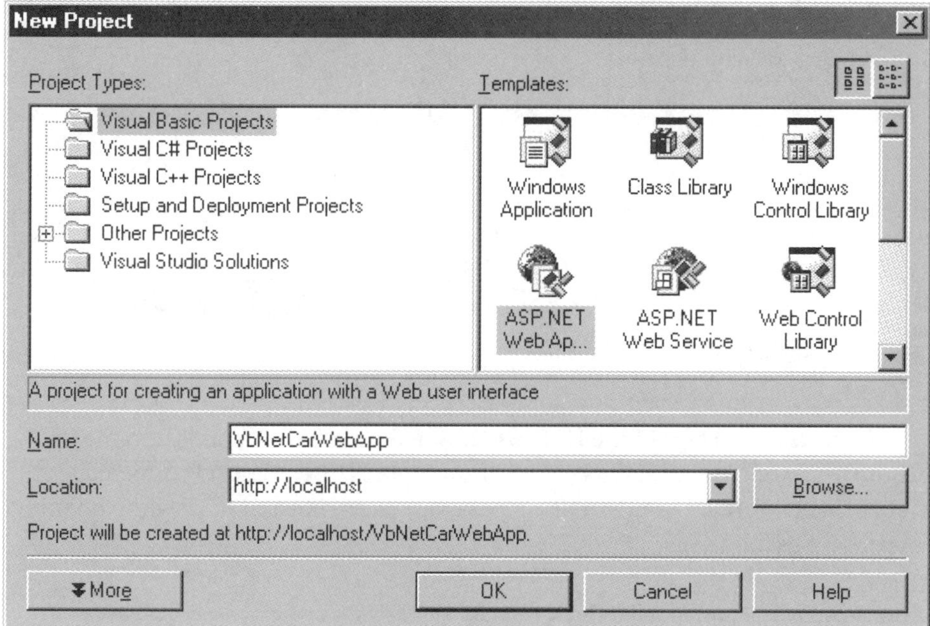

Figure 15-61. The Cars Web application

Building the Logon Page

This Web application consists of two Web pages. First, you have a logon page that allows the user to supply a user ID and password. Once the password has been verified from a fixed set of user names, the user may enter the main page of the Web site where he or she is able to view, add, or remove records from the Inventory table of the Cars database.

To begin, open the IIS manager applet and locate your newly created virtual directory. Right-click the node from the Tree view and select Explore. Now, using the Windows Explorer, place the default.aspx and car.gif files that you created during the opening HTML review section of this chapter and place them into your virtual directory as shown in Figure 15-62 (if you skipped that section, no problem—the downloadable source code contains these same files).

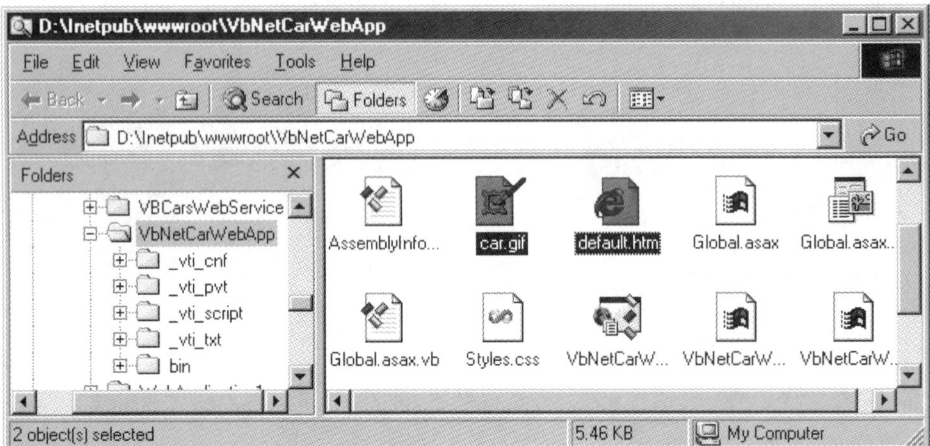

Figure 15-62. Adding the login page

Next, you need to edit the HTML contained within the default.htm file to ensure that when the user clicks the Submit button, the request is directed to the WebForm1.aspx file. Using VS .NET, open your *.htm file and update the opening <form> tag as follows:

```
<form name="MainForm" action="http://localhost/VbNetCarWebApp/WebForm1.aspx"
method="post" ID="Form1">
```

Add each of these files to your current project by selecting the View All Files button from the Solution Explorer, and then right-click each file and select Include in Project. Finally, enable the default.aspx file as the Start Page (see Figure 15-63).

Validating the Password

The next step is to process incoming form data to ensure that the current user has submitted a valid password. First, open the SQL Server Enterprise Manager tool and add a new table to the Cars database named "Passwords." This table

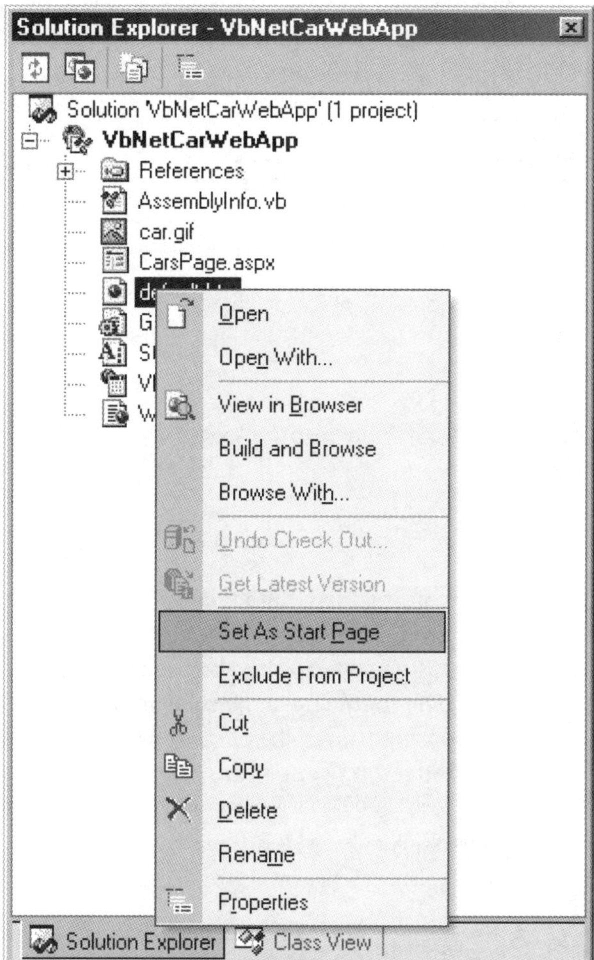

Figure 15-63. Setting the Start Page

contains two columns (UserName and Password), both of which map to a Char data type 20 characters in length. For test purposes, add two or three initial records, as shown in Figure 15-64.

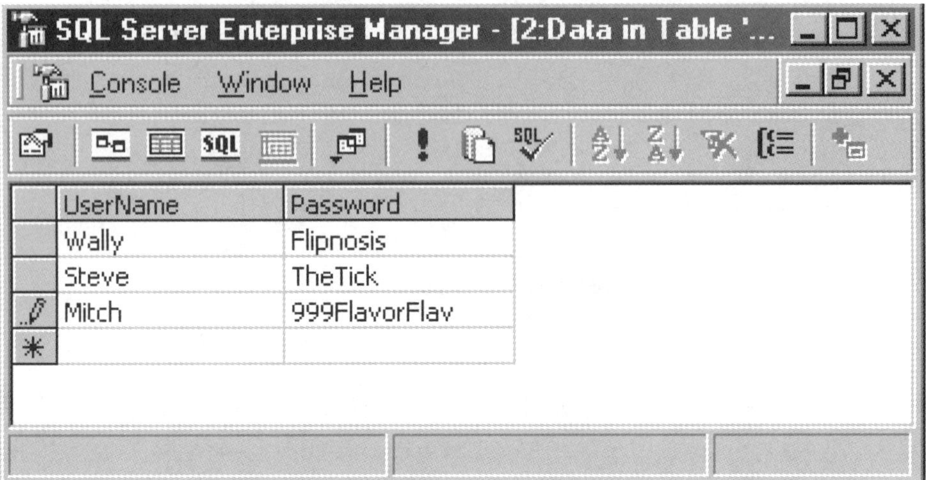

Figure 15-64. The Passwords table

The validation of the incoming form data takes place within the Form_Load event handler of the Page-derived type. Using the Request property, extract the incoming form data and test the user-supplied password against the values held within the Passwords table. The following is the relevant code (without excessive error checking). Note that to keep things simple and well focused, you assume the incoming UserName is indeed present within the Passwords table.

```
Private Sub Page_Load(ByVal sender As System.Object, _
ByVal e As System.EventArgs) Handles MyBase.Load
If Not IsPostBack Then
    ' Get user name and password.
    Dim user As String = Request.Form("txtUserName")
    Dim SendPwd As String = Request.Form("txtPassword")
    ' Build connection.
    Dim cn As New SqlConnection()
    cn.ConnectionString = "data source=(local);initial catalog=Cars;" & _
    "integrated security=SSPI;persist security info=False;" & _
    "workstation id=BIGMANU;packet size=4096"
    Dim sql As String = "Select * From Passwords Where UserName ='" & _
    user & "'"
    ' Fill dataset.
```

```
    Dim da As New SqlDataAdapter(sql, cn)
    Dim ds As New DataSet("Passwords")
    da.Fill(ds, "Passwords")
    ' Check password.
    Dim CorrectPwd As String = ds.Tables(0).Rows(0).Item("Password")
    If CorrectPwd.Trim() <> SendPwd Then
        Response.Redirect("default.htm")
    Else
        ' Helper function (next step. . .)
        RefreshGrid ()
    End If
    cn.Close()
End If
End Sub
```

As you can see, if the user fails to supply the correct password, he or she is simply redirected back to the logon page using the Response.Redirect() methods. On the other hand, if the user does enter the correct information, he or she is granted access to the Cars Page, which is currently blank.

Building the CarsPage

Using the design-time template, construct a user interface that allows the user to insert a new automobile into the Inventory table (four text boxes should do the trick). As well, the user needs to have the ability to remove a car from the same table (yet another text box) and view all items (via a DataGrid). Figure 15-65 shows one possible GUI (you are not trying to win any user interface awards here).

Notice that you have added a SqlConnection component to the Icon Tray to facilitate your ADO.NET endeavors (see Chapter 14 for details).

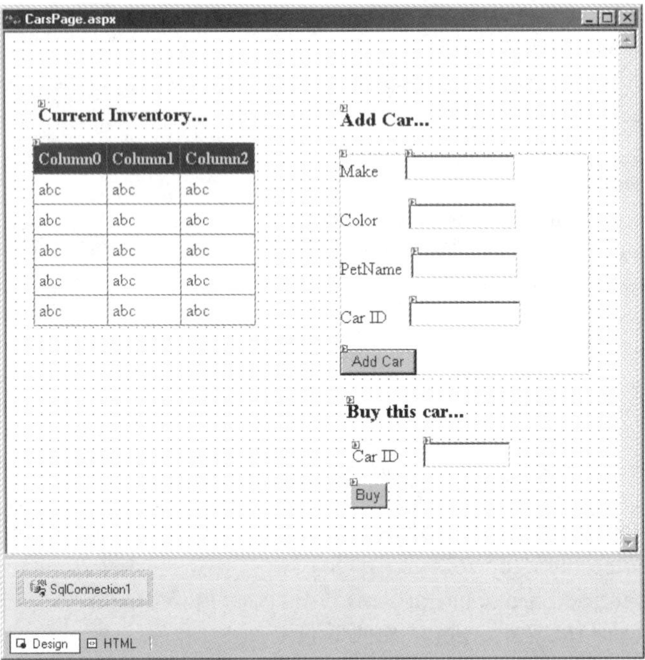

Figure 15-65. The GUI of the main page

Adding a New Car Record

Using the VS .NET IDE, generate an event handler for the Add a Car button's Click event. The goal here is to establish a connection to the Cars database and insert a new record based on the incoming form data. For the most part, this is straight ADO.NET DataSet logic. However, be aware that you need to build the SQL query on the fly using the values contained within the GUI widgets. Here is the code.

```
Private Sub btnAddCar_Click(ByVal sender As System.Object, _
ByVal e As System.EventArgs) Handles btnAddCar.Click
    SqlConnection1.Open()
    ' Build SQL string based on incoming data.
    Dim id As String = Me.txtID.Text
    Dim c As String = Me.txtColor.Text
    Dim m As String = Me.txtMake.Text
    Dim pn As String = Me.txtPetName.Text
    Dim carToInsert As String = _
          "INSERT INTO Inventory Values(" & id & ",'" & m & "','" & _
          c & "','" & pn & "')"
    ' Insert, refresh grid, and send back a simple response.
```

```
    Dim createCMD As SqlCommand = New SqlCommand(carToInsert, SqlConnection1)
    createCMD.ExecuteNonQuery()
    RefreshGrid()
    Response.Write("<h3>Thank you for adding a new " + m + "</h3>")
    ' Clear out edit fields.
    Me.txtID.Text = ""
    Me.txtColor.Text = ""
    Me.txtMake.Text = ""
    Me.txtPetName.Text = ""
    SqlConnection1.Close()
End Sub
```

If you now run this Web application, you are able to enter new Car records into the Inventory table and view the confirmed insertion. For example, Figure 15-66 shows the result of adding a rusty Colt named Clunker.

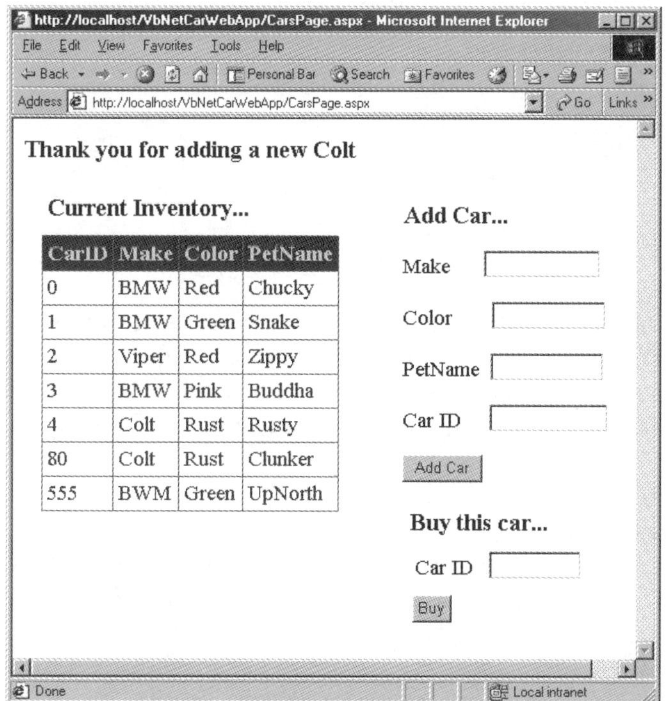

Figure 15-66. Adding Cars

Removing Records

Again using the VS .NET IDE, create a server-side event handler for the Buy Button type. The task is to extract the form data and use it to build a SQL query string. At this point, it is simple ADO.NET logic, as shown here:

```
Private Sub Button1_Click(ByVal sender As System.Object, _
ByVal e As System.EventArgs) Handles Button1.Click
    SqlConnection1.Open()
    ' Build SQL.
    Dim carToKill As String = "Delete From Inventory where CarID =" & "'" & _
    txtCarToBuy.Text & "'"
    Dim killCMD As SqlCommand = New SqlCommand(carToKill, SqlConnection1)
    killCMD.ExecuteNonQuery()
    RefreshGrid()
    Response.Write("<h3><b>Thank you for buying Car #" + _
    txtCarToBuy.Text + "</b></h3>")
    ' Clear out edit fields.
    Me.txtID.Text = ""
    Me.txtColor.Text = ""
    Me.txtMake.Text = ""
    Me.txtPetName.Text = ""
    SqlConnection1.Close()
End Sub
```

As you may expect, when the user enters a given Car ID, the entry is removed from the DataGrid, and the confirmation message in Figure 15-67 is displayed.

Finally, as you have seen, each server-side event handler calls a helper function named RefreshGrid(), which I assume requires little explanation.

```
Private Sub RefreshGrid()
    Dim ds As DataSet = New DataSet()
    ' Create a data set command object to get the inventory.
    Dim da As SqlDataAdapter = _
        New SqlDataAdapter("Select * From Inventory", _
        SqlConnection1)
    ' Use the data set command object to fill the dataset.
    da.Fill(ds, "Inventory")
    DataGrid1.DataSource = ds.Tables("Inventory")
    DataGrid1.DataBind()
End Sub
```

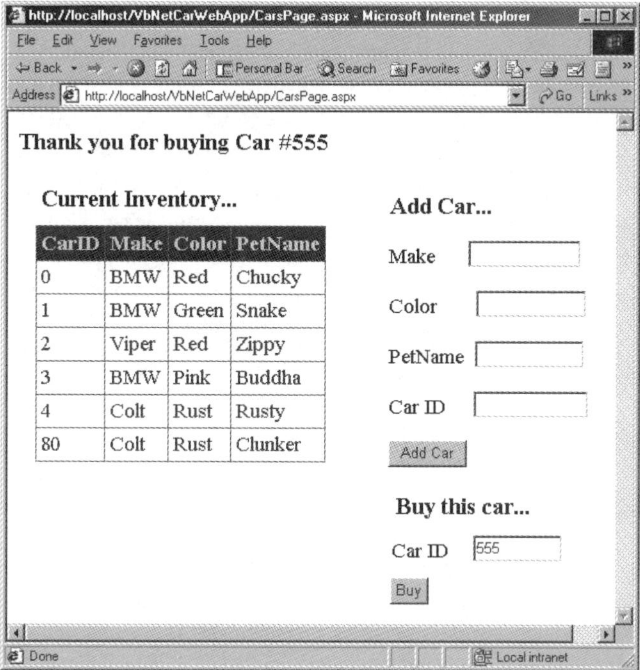

Figure 15-67. Removing Cars

So there you have it. The bare bones of an ASP.NET Web application. One current limitation of this Web application is that you have not added any additional logic to remove an entry from the related Customer and Order tables of the Cars database. Therefore, if you attempt to remove a record from the Inventory table, which is referenced in these child tables, you are thrown an exception. I'll leave it as a task for the interested reader to extend the current ADO.NET logic.

Of course, there are a number of bells and whistles you may choose to add to this project to make it more full featured (make use of validation widgets, build a more attractive GUI, and whatnot). Nevertheless, you should be at the point where you can navigate around the ASP.NET framework. Next up is the related topic of ASP.NET Web services.

SOURCE CODE *The *.aspx, *.aspx.resx, and *.aspx.vb files for the VbNetCarWebApp project are included under the Chapter 15 subdirectory.*

Summary

Building Web applications requires a different frame of mind than you use to assemble traditional desktop applications. In this chapter, you began with a quick and painless review of some core Web atoms, including HTML, HTTP, the role of client-side scripting, and server-side scripts using classic ASP.

The bulk of this chapter was spent examining the architecture of an ASP.NET application. As you have seen, each *.aspx file in your project has an associated System.Web.UI.Page-derived class. Using this code behind approach, ASP.NET allows you to build more reusable and OO-aware systems. Furthermore, you have seen that the core properties defined by the Page type (Session, Application, Request, and Response) provide access to an underlying object instance. This chapter concluded by examining the use of Web Form types. These GUI widgets are in charge of emitting HTML tags to the client side.

CHAPTER 16

Building (and Understanding) Web Services

IN MANY WAYS, this chapter represents the summation of all the topics you have explored over the course of this book. Here you examine the construction and consumption of ASP.NET Web services. Simply put, a Web service is a unit of managed code (typically installed under IIS) that can be remotely invoked using HTTP requests.

As you will see, Web services consist of three supporting technologies: the Web Service Description Language (WSDL), an invocation protocol (HTTP GET, HTTP POST, or SOAP), and a discovery service (*.vsdisco files). You begin by building a simple Calculator Web service and from there you create an automobile-centric Web service that can return ADO.NET DataSets, ArrayLists, and custom class types.

Once you have been exposed to the core building blocks of .NET Web services, the chapter concludes by showing how to build a proxy class (using VS .NET as well as the wsdl.exe utility) that can be consumed by Web-based, console-based, and Windows Forms clients.

Understanding the Role of Web Services

From a high level, one can define a Web service as a unit of code that can be activated using HTTP requests. Now, let's think this one through a bit. Historically speaking, remote access to binary units required platform-specific (and sometimes language-specific) protocols. A classic example of this approach would be DCOM. DCOM clients access remote COM types using tightly coupled RPC calls. CORBA also requires the use of a tightly coupled protocol to activate remote types. EJB (Enterprise Java Beans) requires a specific protocol and (by and large) a specific language (Java). The problem with each of these remoting architectures is that they are proprietary protocols, which typically require a tight connection to the remote source.

As you already know, .NET is extremely language agnostic. Using VB .NET, VB .NETC#, or any other .NET-aware language, you can build types that can be consumed and extended across language boundaries. Using Web services, you can access your language-neutral assemblies using nothing but HTTP. Of all the protocols in existence today, HTTP is the one specific invocation protocol that all platforms tend to agree on.

Thus, using Web services, you (as a Web service developer) can use any language you want. You (as a Web service consumer) can use standard HTTP to invoke methods on the types defined in the Web service. The bottom line is that you suddenly have true language and platform integration. It is not about COM or Java or CORBA anymore. It is all about HTTP and your programming language of choice. As you will see, SOAP (Simple Object Access Protocol) and XML are also key pieces of the Web services architecture, which are used in conjunction with standard HTTP.

Like any .NET assembly, a Web service contains a number of classes, interfaces, enumerations, and structures that provide black box functionality to remote clients. The only real restriction to be aware of is, with Web services, you should avoid the use of any server-side GUI logic. Rather, Web services typically define business objects that execute a unit of work (e.g., perform a calculation, read a data source and return the results, or whatnot) for the consumer and wait for the next request.

One aspect of Web services that might not be readily understood is the fact that the Web service consumer does not necessarily need to be a browser-based client. As you will see, Console-based and Windows Forms-based clients can consume a Web service just as easily. In each case the client indirectly interacts with the Web service through an intervening proxy. The proxy (which is described in detail later in the chapter) looks and feels like the real remote type and exposes the same set of members. In this way, the client is able to interact with the proxy as if it were just another locally scoped class type. Under the hood, however, the proxy code really forwards the request to the Web service using standard HTTP.

The Anatomy of a Web Service

Web services are typically hosted by IIS under a unique virtual directory, much like a standard ASP.NET Web application (as seen in Chapter 15). However, in addition to the managed code that constitutes the exported functionality, a Web service requires some supporting infrastructure. In a nutshell, a Web service typically requires the following:

- An invocation protocol (e.g., HTTP GET/HTTP POST or SOAP)
- A description service (so that clients know what the Web service can do)
- A discovery service (so that clients know the Web service exists)

You examine the details behind each requirement in this chapter. However, just to get into the correct frame of mind, here is a brief overview of each supporting technology.

Previewing the Invocation Protocol

Much like an ADO.NET DataSet, information is transmitted between a Web service consumer and a Web service as XML. As mentioned, HTTP is the protocol that transmits this data. More specifically, you can use the HTTP GET, HTTP POST, or SOAP protocols to move information between consumers and Web services. By and large, SOAP is your first choice, for as you will see, SOAP messages can contain XML descriptions of very complex types (custom classes, ADO.NET DataSets, arrays of objects, and so forth).

Previewing Web Service Description Services

For a Web service consumer to use a remote Web service, it must fully understand the exposed members. For example, the client must know that there is a method named Foo() that takes three parameters of type {String, Boolean, Integer} and returns a class type named Bar before it can invoke it. Again, XML steps up to the plate to offer a generic way to describe the Web service. Formally, the XML schema used to describe a Web service is termed the Web Service Description Language, or WSDL. Fortunately, WSDL is readable by humans, unlike other description languages (after all, WSDL is just XML).

Previewing Discovery Services

In the previous chapter, you briefly studied *.vsdisco (an abbreviation for DISCOvery of Web Services) files. These files are XML-based files and allow a client to dynamically discover the Web services exposed from a given URL. Understand that a client in this sense could be a block of code you are currently authoring or a design time Wizard. You see the syntax of a *.vsdisco file at the end of this chapter.

An Overview of the Web Service Namespaces

As you would imagine, each of these requirements are supported by various .NET types, contained in the namespaces described in Table 16-1.

Table 16-1. Web Service Namespaces

WEB SERVICE CENTRIC NAMESPACE	MEANING IN LIFE
System.Web.Services	This namespace contains the minimal and complete set of types needed to build a Web service.
System.Web.Services.Description	These types allow you to programmatically interact with WSDL.
System.Web.Services.Discovery	These types (used in conjunction with a *.vsdisco file) allow a Web consumer to programmatically discover the Web services installed on a given machine.
System.Web.Services.Protocols	The XML-based data that is exchanged between a Web consumer and a Web service may be transmitted using one of three protocols (HTTP GET, HTTP POST, and SOAP). This namespace defines a number of types that represent these invocation protocols.

Examining the System.Web.Services Namespace

Despite the rich functionality provided by the .NET Web services namespaces, for most projects the only types you need to directly interact with are defined in the System.Web.Services namespace. As you can see from Table 16-2, the number of types is quite small.

Table 16-2. Members of the System.Web.Services Namespace

SYSTEM.WEB.SERVICES TYPE	MEANING IN LIFE
WebMethodAttribute	Adding the <WebMethod> attribute to a method in a Web service makes the method callable from a remote client using HTTP.
WebService	Defines the optional base class for Web services.
WebServiceAttribute	The WebService attribute may be used to add information to a Web service, such as a string describing its functionality. The attribute is not required for a Web service to be published and executed.
WebServiceBindingAttribute	Declares the binding protocol a given Web service method is implementing.

Building a Simple Web Service

Before diving much further into the details, let's build a simple example. (Don't worry, you construct a more exotic Web service later in the chapter). Fire up Visual Studio .NET and create a new VB .NET Web service project named CalcWebService (Figure 16-1).

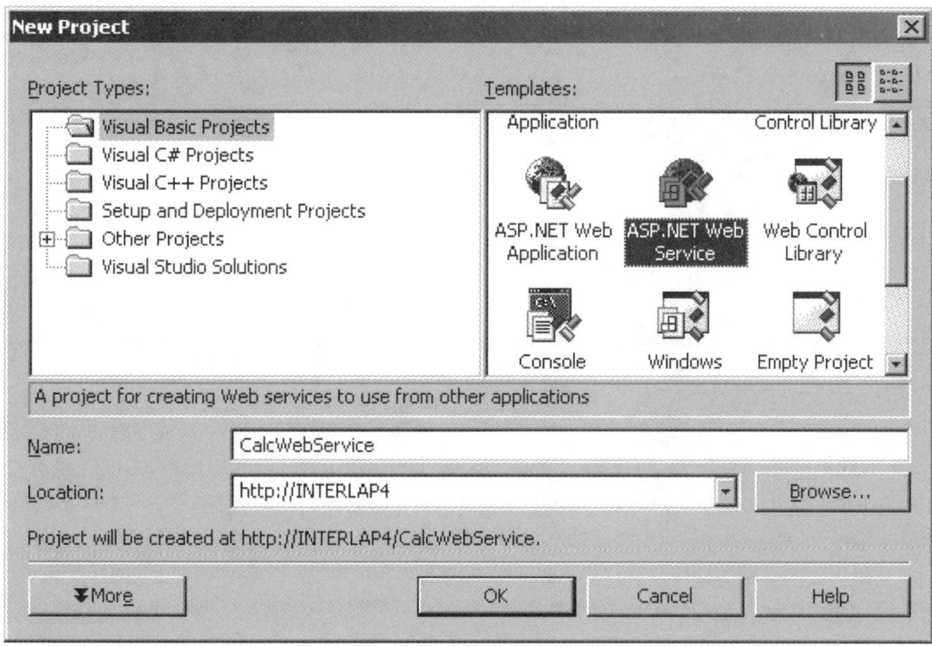

Figure 16-1. Creating a Web service project workspace

Like an ASP.NET application, Web service projects automatically create a new virtual directory under IIS (Figure 16-2) and store your project files under the \My Documents\Visual Studio Projects subdirectory.

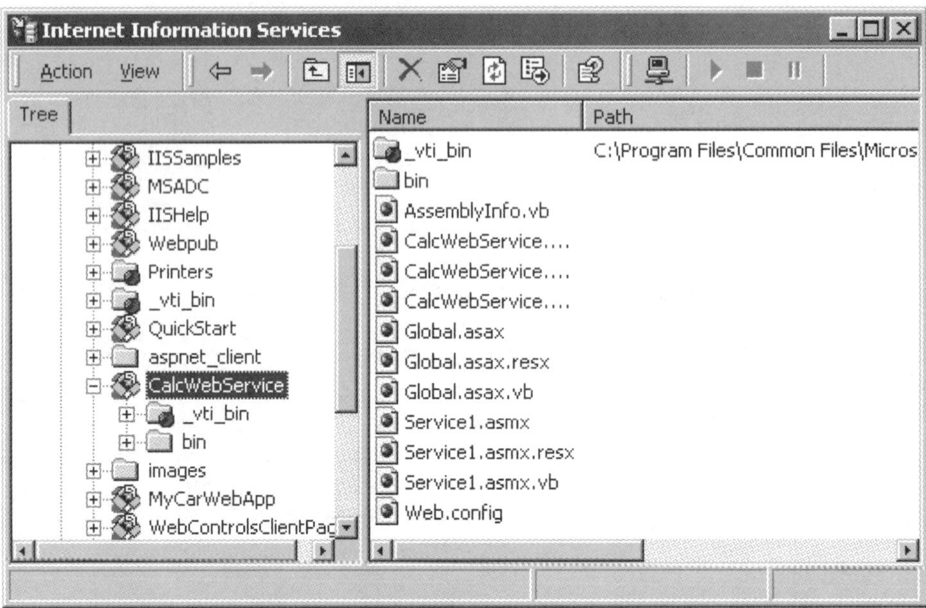

Figure 16-2. Web services are installed under the care of IIS

In light of the configuration of a Web service project, if you want to use the downloadable source code during this chapter, begin by creating a new project workspace and simply import the predefined class. In any case, when you examine the Solution Explorer (Figure 16-3), you should feel right at home with these new project files, given the material presented in Chapter 15.

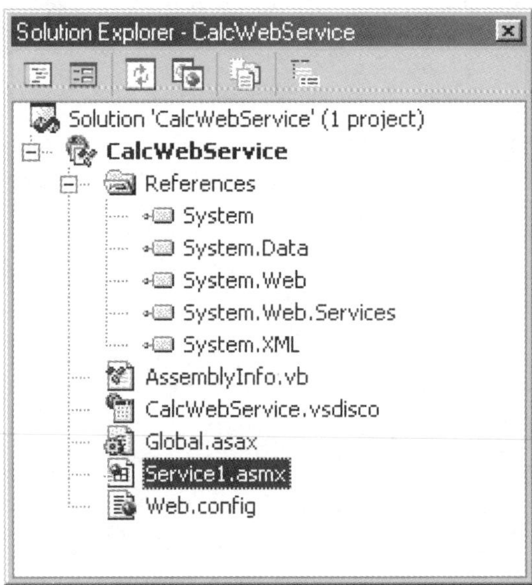

Figure 16-3. Initial project files

The Global.asax and Web.config files serve the same purpose as (and look identical to) an ASP.NET application. As you recall from Chapter 15, the Global.asax file allows you to respond to global-level events. Web.config allows you to declaratively configure your new Web service (again using XML notation). The items of interest to us at this point are the *.asmx, *.asmx.vb, and *.vsdisco files as described in Table 16-3.

Table 16-3. Core Files of a VS.NET Web Service Project

WEB SERVICE PROJECT FILE	MEANING IN LIFE
*.asmx *.asmx.vb	These files define the methods of your Web service. Like an *.aspx file, each *.asmx file has a corresponding *.vb file to hold the code behind.
*.vsdisco	Again, this file extension is short for "DISCOvery of Web Services" and contains an XML description of the Web services at a given URL.

The Code Behind File (.asmx.vb)*

A *.asmx file represents a given Web service in your current project workspace. To view the code behind the design time template, select the View Code option to check out the corresponding *.asmx.vb class definition, as shown here:

```
Imports System.Web.Services

Public Class Service1
    Inherits System.Web.Services.WebService
#Region " Web Services Designer Generated Code "
    Public Sub New()
        MyBase.New()
        'This call is required by the Web Services Designer.
        InitializeComponent()
        'Add your own initialization code after the InitializeComponent() call
    End Sub

    'Required by the Web Services Designer
    Private components As System.ComponentModel.Container

    'NOTE: The following procedure is required by the Web Services Designer
    'It can be modified using the Web Services Designer.
    'Do not modify it using the code editor.
```

```
    <System.Diagnostics.DebuggerStepThrough()> Private Sub InitializeComponent()
        components = New System.ComponentModel.Container()
    End Sub

    Protected Overloads Overrides Sub Dispose(ByVal disposing As Boolean)
        'CODEGEN: This procedure is required by the Web Services Designer
        'Do not modify it using the code editor.
    End Sub

#End Region
    ' WEB SERVICE EXAMPLE
    ' The HelloWorld() example service returns the string Hello World.
    ' To build, uncomment the following lines then save and build the project.
    ' To test this Web service, ensure that the .asmx file is the start page
    ' and press F5.
    '
    '<WebMethod()> Public Function HelloWorld() As String
    ' HelloWorld = "Hello World"
    ' End Function

End Class
```

As you can see, the only real point of interest is the fact that you derive from a new base class: WebService. You examine the members defined by this type in just a moment. For the time being, just understand that Web services have the *option* of deriving from this base class type. In fact, if you comment out the overridden Dispose() method and derive directly from System.Object, the Web service still functions correctly, as shown here:

```
' I'm still a Web service!
Public Class Service1
...
End Class
```

Adding Some Simple Functionality

For this initial Web service, let's keep things short and sweet and add four methods that allow the outside world to add, subtract, multiply, and divide two integers. As you would expect, methods that you want to make available via HTTP requests must be declared Public. In addition to this (obvious) fact, each method must support the <WebMethod> attribute. Therefore, you can update your initial class as shown here:

```
Public Class Service1
    Inherits System.Web.Services.WebService
...
    <WebMethod()> _
    Public Function Add(ByVal x As Integer, ByVal y As Integer) As Integer
        Return x + y
    End Function
    <WebMethod()> _
    Public Function Subtract(ByVal x As Integer, ByVal y As Integer) As Integer
        Return x - y
    End Function
    <WebMethod()> _
    Public Function Multiply(ByVal x As Integer, ByVal y As Integer) As Integer
        Return x * y
    End Function
    <WebMethod()> _
    Public Function Divide(ByVal x As Integer, ByVal y As Integer) As Integer
        If (y = 0) Then
            Throw New DivideByZeroException("Dude, can't divide by zero!")
        End If
        Return x / y
    End Function
End Class
```

Testing Your Web Service

Once you compile your Web service, you can execute it using the Visual Studio .NET IDE. (Simply run or debug the application.) By default, your machine's active browser functions as a makeshift client, showing an HTML view of the methods marked with the <WebMethod> attribute. See Figure 16-4 for a test run.

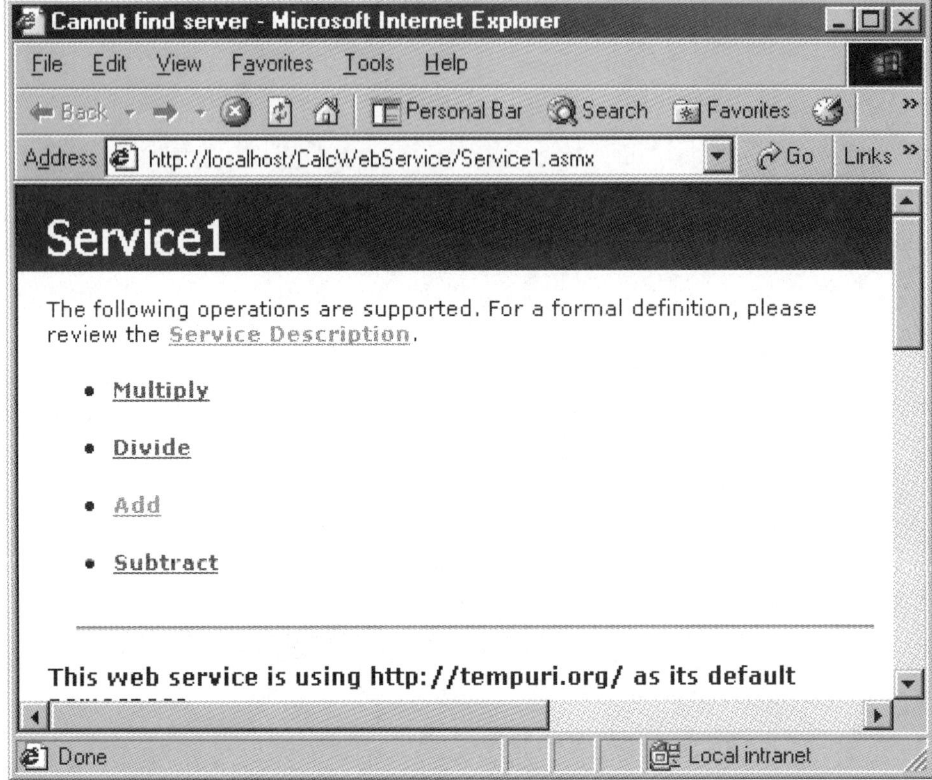

Figure 16-4. IE provides a quick way to test your Web services

In addition to listing each method defined in a given Web service, you can also invoke each method directly from within the browser. For example, click the Add link and enter some text values (Figure 16-5). As you can see, the rendered HTML provides TextBox types to allow user input.

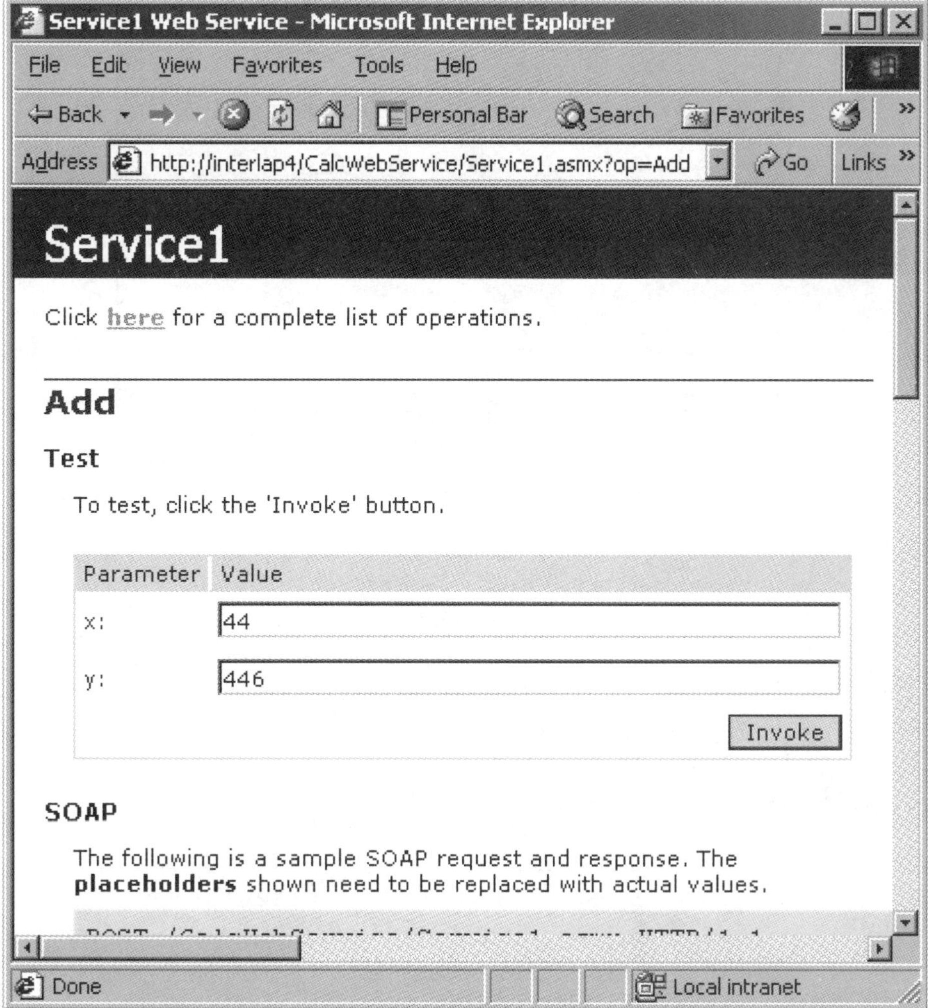

Figure 16-5. IE allows you to invoke a Web method with specific parameters

When you invoke the method, the result (490) is returned via an XML attribute (Figure 16-6).

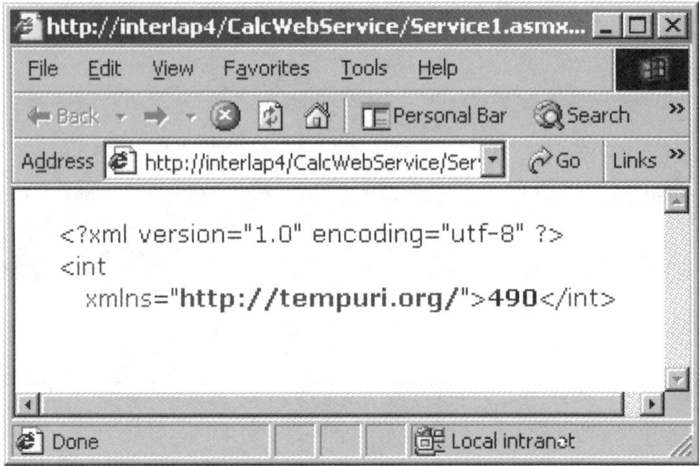

Figure 16-6. The end result

One point of interest is how the information is sent to the Web service. If you check out the generated query string, you find the following:

```
http://interlap4/CalcWebService/CalcService.asmx/Add?x=44&y=446
```

Notice that the URL is composed of the name of the method to be called (Add) followed by the incoming parameter names (and values).

As you can see, it is relatively simple to build and test a simple Web service. Later in this chapter you build some more exotic Web services. Before you do, let's examine some further details behind the Web service architecture.

The WebMethodAttribute Type

The WebMethod attribute must be applied to each method you want to expose to the outside world through HTTP. Like most attributes, the WebMethod type may take a number of optional constructor parameters, each of which is specified as a named argument. For example, to describe the functionality of a particular Web method, you can use the following syntax:

```
' The calculator Web methods.
<WebMethod(Description:="Yet another way to add numbers!")> _
   Public Function Add(ByVal x As Integer, ByVal y As Integer) As Integer
    Return x + y
End Function
```

In some respects, setting the Description aspect of the WebMethod attribute is analogous to the IDL [helpstring] attribute. If you compile and test once again, you see something like Figure 16-7.

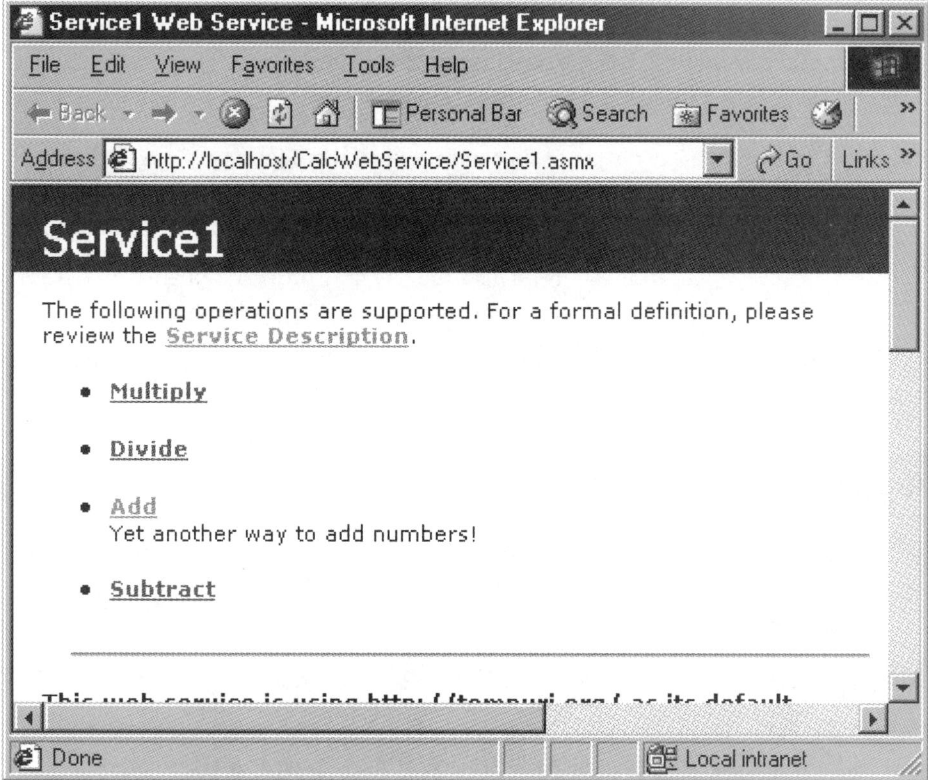

Figure 16-7. The end result of setting the WebMethod.Description property

Under the hood, the WSDL contract has been updated with a new <documentation> attribute (more on WSDL in just a bit), as shown here:

```
<operation name="Add">
    <documentation>Yet another way to add numbers!</documentation>
    <input message="s0:AddSoapIn" />
    <output message="s0:AddSoapOut" />
</operation>
```

In addition to the Description aspect, you can also configure the WebService attribute type using any of the core properties described in Table 16-4.

Table 16-4. Properties of WebServiceAttribute

WEBSERVICEATTRIBUTE PROPERTY	MEANING IN LIFE
Description	Used to add a friendly text description of your Web method.
EnableSession	By default, this property is set to true, which configures this method to maintain session state (as discussed in Chapter 15). You may disable this behavior if you set it to false.
MessageName	This property can be used to configure how a Web method is represented in WSDL, to avoid name clashes.
TransactionOption	Web methods can function as the root of a COM+ transaction. This property may be assigned any value from the System.EnterpriseServices.TransactionOption enumeration.

The MessageName Property

One item of special interest is the MessageName property. To illustrate, assume your Web calculator now defines an additional method that can add two Doubles, as shown here:

```
' The calculator Web methods.
<WebMethod(Description:="Add 2 Integers!")> _
Public Function Add(ByVal x As Integer, ByVal y As Integer) As Integer
    Return x + y
End Function
<WebMethod(Description:="Add 2 Doubles!")> _
Public Function Add(ByVal x As Double, ByVal y As Double) As Double
    Return x + y
End Function
```

If you were to compile your updated class, you would be happy to find no generated errors. However, when you request access to the Web service, you find the following complaint:

```
Both Double Add(Double, Double) and Int32 Add(Int32, Int32)
use the message name 'Add'. Use the MessageName property
of the WebMethod custom attribute to specify unique message
names for the methods.
```

One requirement of WSDL is that each < soap:operation soapAction > element (used to define the name of a given Web method) must be uniquely named. However, the default behavior of the WSDL generator is to generate the < soap:operation soapAction > name *exactly* as it appears in the source code definition. (That's why you ended up with two Web methods named Add().) To resolve the name clash, you can either rename your method or simply use the MessageName property to establish a unique name, as shown here:

```
' The calculator Web methods.
<WebMethod(Description:="Add 2 Integers!")> _
Public Function Add(ByVal x As Integer, ByVal y As Integer) As Integer
    Return x + y
End Function
<WebMethod(Description:="Add 2 Doubles!", MessageName:=" AddDoubles")> _
Public Function Add(ByVal x As Double, ByVal y As Double) As Double
    Return x + y
End Function
```

With this, you can see that each WSDL description is now unique:

```
<operation name="Add">
    <documentation>Add 2 Integers!</documentation>
    <input message="s0:AddSoapIn" />
    <output message="s0:AddSoapOut" />
</operation>
<operation name="Add">
    <documentation>Add 2 Doubles!</documentation>
    <input name="AddDoubles" message="s0:AddDoublesSoapIn" />
    <output name=" AddDoubles" message="s0:AddDoublesSoapOut" />
</operation>
```

The Description Property

On a related note, the WebServiceAttribute also provides a Description property to allow you to document the overall functionality of the Web service itself, as shown here:

```
[WebService( Description = "The painfully simple web service" )]
public class Service1 : System.Web.Services.WebService
{
. . .
}
```

If you rerun the application, you see something like Figure 16-8.

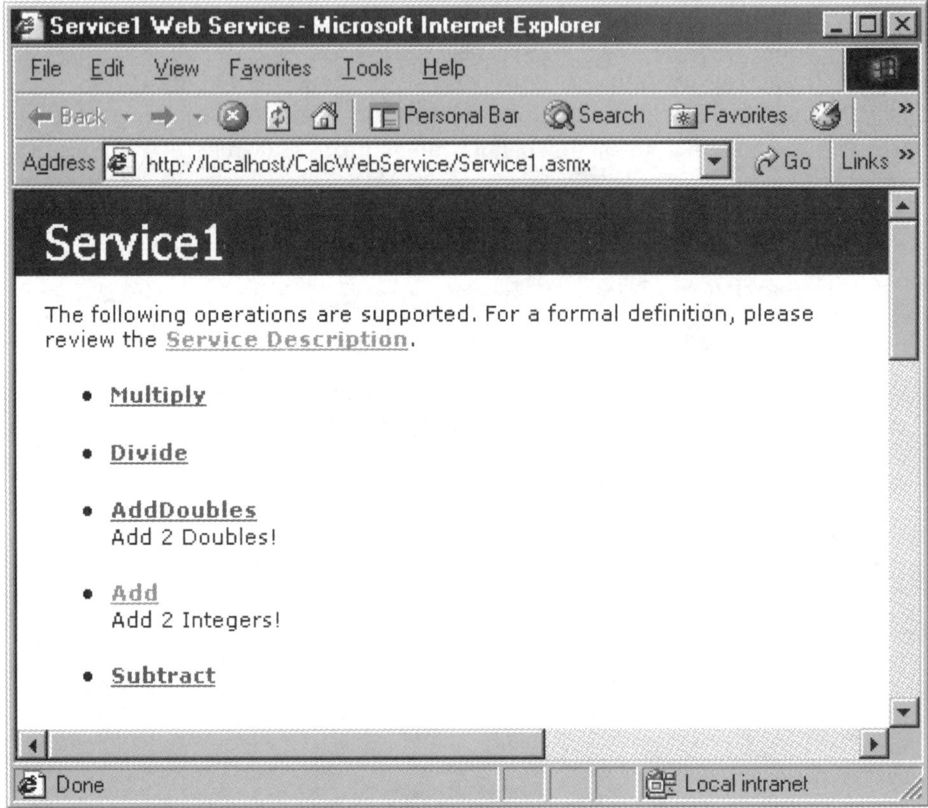

Figure 16-8. The WebServiceAttribute describes the nature of your creation

The System.Web.Services.WebService Base Class

As mentioned earlier in this chapter, .NET Web services are free to derive directly from System.Object. However, by default, Web services developed using Visual Studio .NET automatically derive from the WebService base class. The functionality provided by this type equips your Web service to interact with the same types used by the ASP.NET object model (Table 16-5).

Table 16-5. Core Properties of the WebService Base Type

SYSTEM.WEB.SERVICES.WEBSERVICE PROPERTY	MEANING IN LIFE
Application	Gets a reference to the application object for the current HTTP request.
Context	Gets the ASP.NET Context object for the current request, which encapsulates all HTTP-specific contexts used by the HTTP server to process Web requests.
Server	Gets a reference to the HttpServerUtility for the current request.
Session	Gets a reference to the SessionState.HttpSessionState instance for the current request.
User	Gets the ASP.NET server User object, which can be used to authenticate a given user.

As you recall from Chapter 15, the Application and Session properties allow you to maintain stateful data during the execution of your ASP.NET Web applications. Web services provide the exact same functionality. For example, assume your CalcWebService maintains an application-level variable (and is thus available to each session) that holds the value of PI, as shown here:

```
Public Class Service1
    Inherits System.Web.Services.WebService
    Public Sub New()
        MyBase.New()
        'This call is required by the Web Services Designer.
        InitializeComponent()
        'Assign an app level variable.
        Application("SimplePI") = 3.14
    End Sub
...
    <WebMethod()> _
    Public Function GetSimplePI() As Double
        Return CType(Application("SimplePI"), Double)
    End Function
End Class
```

Understanding the Web Service Description Language (WSDL)

Now that you have seen a simple Web service in action, let's talk a bit about how your Web methods are described under the hood. COM programmers understand that IDL is a metalanguage used to define each aspect of a COM item. .NET programmers understand that compilers that produce managed code also emit full and complete metadata that completely describes all types in the assembly. When a binary image (COM or .NET) is described in language-neutral terms, you essentially establish a contract that the client can read to understand method-calling conventions, type names, base types, supported interfaces, and so on.

In the same spirit of IDL and .NET metadata, Web services are also described using a metalanguage named *WSDL*. WSDL is a block of XML that fully describes how external clients can interact with the Web services on a given machine, the methods they support, and the syntax of the various invocation protocols (GET, POST, and SOAP).

When you test your Web services from your browser of choice, you will see a link entitled Service Description (Figure 16-9).

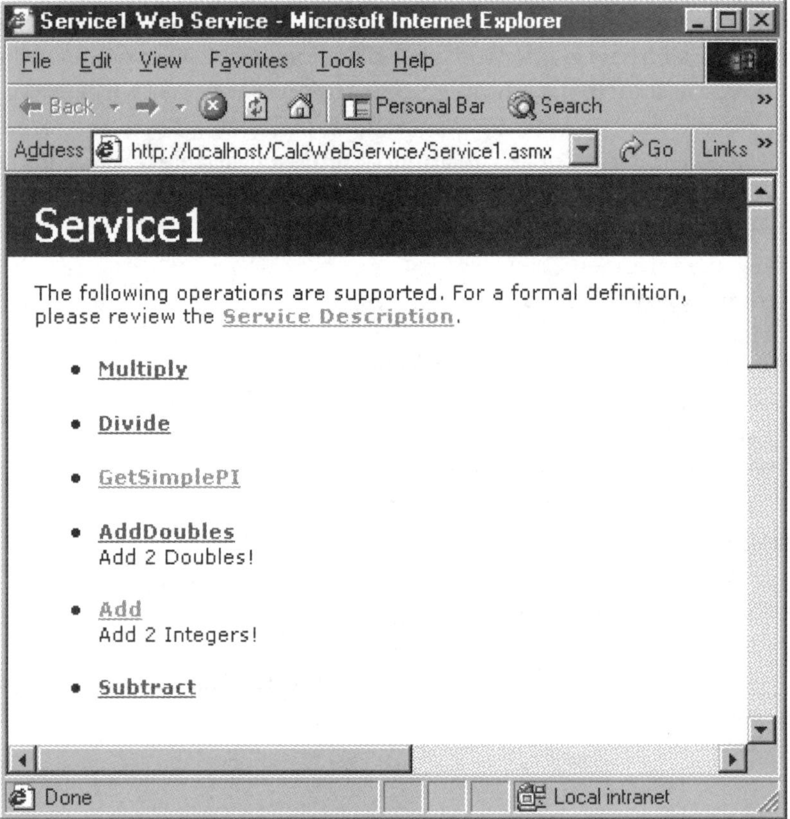

Figure 16-9. This link allows you to view the underlying WSDL

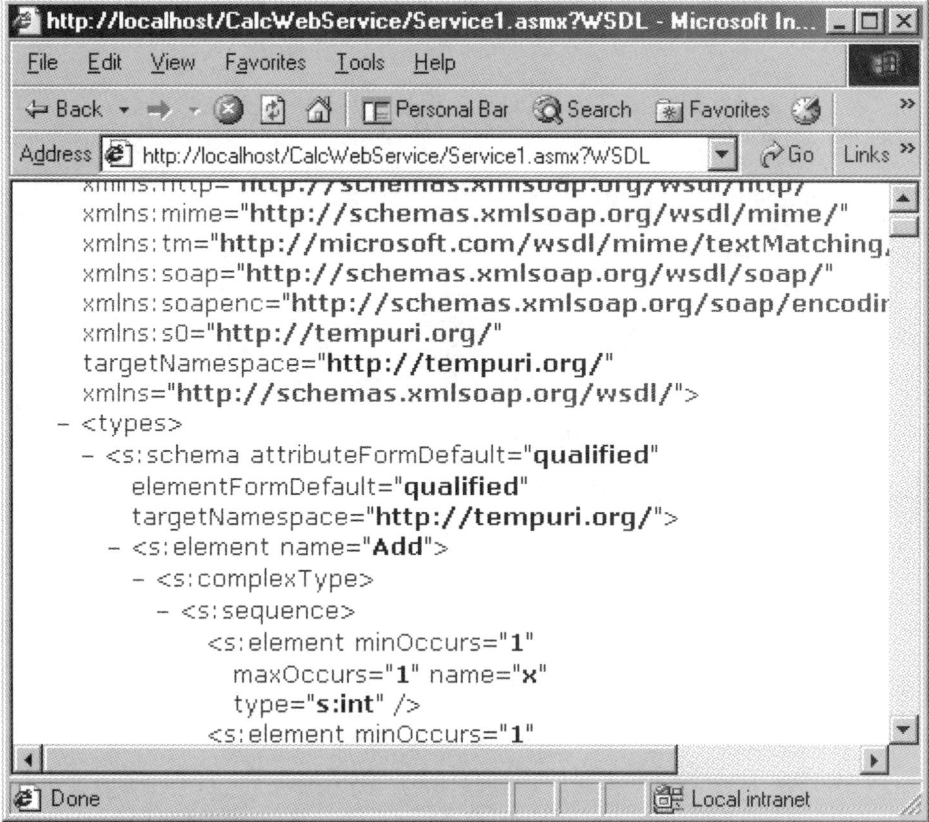

Figure 16-10. The raw WSDL

When you select this link, a separate window opens that describes the contract defined by the current Web service (Figure 16-10).

Although you can always choose to remain blissfully unaware of the exact WSDL syntax, let's run through some basics. First of all, a WSDL contract is opened and closed using the <definitions> tag. After the opening tag comes a set of nodes that define the various invocation protocols, as shown here:

```
<?xml version="1.0" ?>
<definitions xmlns:s="http:www.w3.org/2000/10/XMLSchema"
xmlns:http="http:'schemas.xmlsoap.org/wsdl/http/"
        xmlns:mime="http:'schemas.xmlsoap.org/wsdl/mime/"
        xmlns:urt="http:'microsoft.com/urt/wsdl/text/"
        xmlns:soap="http:'schemas.xmlsoap.org/wsdl/soap/"
        xmlns:soapenc="http:'schemas.xmlsoap.org/soap/encoding/" xmlns
        xmlns:s0="http:'tempuri.org/" targetNamespace="http:'tempuri.org/"
        xmlns="http:'schemas.xmlsoap.org/wsdl/">
...
```

Next you find the WSDL definition for each Web method defined by the Web service in terms of the GET, POST, and SOAP invocation protocols (Figure 16-11).

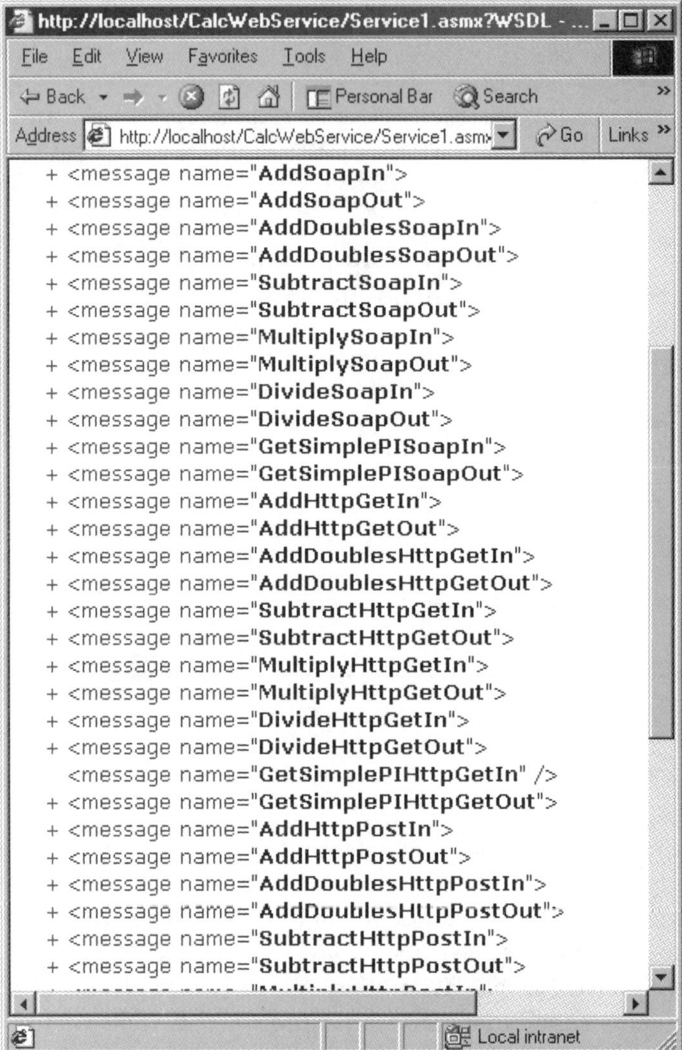

Figure 16-11. Each Web method has a GET, POST, and SOAP pair

As you can see, each Web method has an "In" and "Out" variation. Therefore, the Subtract() Web method has six unique <message name> tags: one In/Out pair for HTTP POST, one pair for HTTP GET, and another pair for SOAP. For example, here is the WSDL definition for Subtract when using the HTTP POST protocol:

```
<message name="SubtractHttpPostIn">
     <part name="x" type="s:string" />
     <part name="y" type="s:string" />
    </message>
<message name="SubtractHttpPostOut">
     <part name="Body" element="s0:int" />
</message>
```

If you examine the SOAP description of the same method, you find the following:

```
<message name="SubtractSoapIn">
    <part name="parameters" element="s0:Subtract" />
</message>
<message name="SubtractSoapOut">
    <part name="parameters" element="s0:SubtractResponse" />
</message>
```

Again, much like other metalanguages, WSDL is typically of direct interest only if you are building something along the lines of a custom parser or object viewer utility. If this is your lot in life (or if you are just interested in playing with some new toys), you should take the time to explore the System.Web.Services.Description namespace. Here you find a plethora of types that allow you to programmatically manipulate WSDL. If you are not interested in this endeavor, simply understand that WSDL fully describes the calling conventions (and transport protocols) that enable an external client to call the Web methods defined by a given Web service.

Web Service Invocation Protocols

As you know, the purpose of a Web service is to return XML-based data to a consumer, using the HTTP protocols. Specifically, a Web server bundles this data into the body of an HTTP message and transmits it to the consumer using one of three specific techniques (Table 16-6).

Table 16-6. Web Service Invocation protocols

TRANSMISSION PROTOCOL	MEANING IN LIFE
HTTP GET	GET submissions append parameters to the query string of the current URL.
HTTP POST	POST transmissions embed the data points into the header of the HTTP message rather than appending them to the query string.
SOAP	SOAP is an invocation protocol that specifies how to submit data across the wire using XML.

While each approach leads to the same result (calling a remote method using HTTP), your choice of invocation protocol determines the types of parameters (and return types) that can be sent between each interested party. The SOAP protocol offers you the greatest form of flexibility (as you soon see). However, for completion let's begin by examining the use of standard GET and POST encoding.

Transmitting Data Using HTTP GET and POST

As described in Chapter 15, HTTP GET transmissions are sent to the recipient by appending name/value pairs to the end of the receiving URL. Recall that a question mark (?) is the character that signifies the separation of the page from the named set of parameters. HTTP POST transmissions also represent incoming data as a set of name/value pairs, which are placed in the body of the HTTP message. When you use GET or POST transmissions, the end result looks identical. The returned data is expressed in simple XML notation, taking the form <*type*>VALUE </ *type*>.

Although GET and POST verbs may be familiar constructs, you must be aware that this method of transportation is not rich enough to represent such complex items as structures or object instances. When you use GET and POST verbs, you can only interact with Web methods using the types listed in Table 16-7.

Table 16-7. Supported POST and GET Data Types

SUPPORTED GET/POST DATA TYPES	MEANING IN LIFE
Enumerations	GET and POST verbs support the transmission of System.Enum types. These are represented as a static constant string.
Simple Arrays	You can construct arrays of any primitive type.
Strings	GET and POST transmit all numerical data as a string token. *String* really refers to the string representation of CLR primitives such as Int16, Int32, Int64, Boolean, Single, Double, Decimal, DateTime, and so forth.

To build an HTML form that submits data using GET or POST semantics, you specify the *.asmx file as the recipient of the form data. As a simple example, assume the following *.htm file creates a UI that allows the end user to enter two numbers to send to the Subtract() method of the CalcWebService, using the GET protocol:

```
<!DOCTYPE HTML PUBLIC "-//W3C//DTD HTML 4.0 Transitional//EN">
<html>
    <head>
        <title></title>
        <meta name="GENERATOR" content="Microsoft Visual Studio .NET 7.0">
    </head>
    <body>
        <form method='GET'
            action='http://localhost/CalcWebService/Service1.asmx
            /Subtract' ID="Form1">
        <p>
            First Number: <input id="Text1" name="x" type="text">
        </p>
        <p>
            Second Number <input id="Text2" name="y" type="text">
        </p>
        <p>
            <input id="Submit1" type="submit" value="Submit" NAME="Submit1">
        </p>
        </form>
    </body>
</html>
```

A few points of interest. First, the action attribute points to not only the *.asmx file, but also the name of the method to invoke. Next, notice that the name attribute is used to identify the name of each parameter. (Recall that Subtract() takes two integers named *x* and *y*.)

Figure 16-12 shows the result of entering 300 and 3 as input data.

Figure 16-12. Subtracting numbers a la HTTP GET

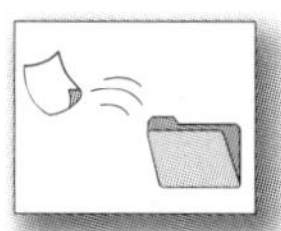

SOURCE CODE *The CalcWithGET HTML page is included under the Chapter 16 subdirectory.*

Transmitting Data Using SOAP

A far sexier alternative to moving information between a consumer and Web service is to use SOAP, which can represent complex types (in XML notation) as shown in Table 16-8.

Table 16-8. SOAP Types

ADDITIONAL SOAP DATA TYPES	MEANING IN LIFE
ADO.NET DataSets	Although the DataSet is just another class, it is important to point out that this type is supported via SOAP.
Complex Arrays	You may build arrays of classes, structures, and XML nodes.
Custom Types	Using SOAP, you can build Web methods that expose custom types.
XML Nodes	Your Web methods may expose XML nodes that are transported as XML!

Although a complete examination of SOAP is outside the scope of this text, understand that SOAP was designed to be as simple as possible. Given this, SOAP itself does not define a specific protocol and can thus be used with any number of existing Internet protocols (HTTP, SMTP, and others).

In a nutshell, the SOAP specification contains two aspects. First is the envelope (which can conceptually be understood as the box containing the relevant information). Second, you have the rules that are used to describe the information in that message.

Recall, that when you use SOAP to call your Add() method, the SOAP definition looks like this:

```
<message name="AddSoapIn">
    <part name="parameters" element="s0:Add" />
</message>
<message name="AddSoapOut">
    <part name="parameters" element="s0:AddResponse" />
</message>
```

To illustrate open the WSDL window for your CalcWebService. Toward the end of the page, you find three XML nodes describing the GET, POST, and SOAP bindings, as shown in Figure 16-13.

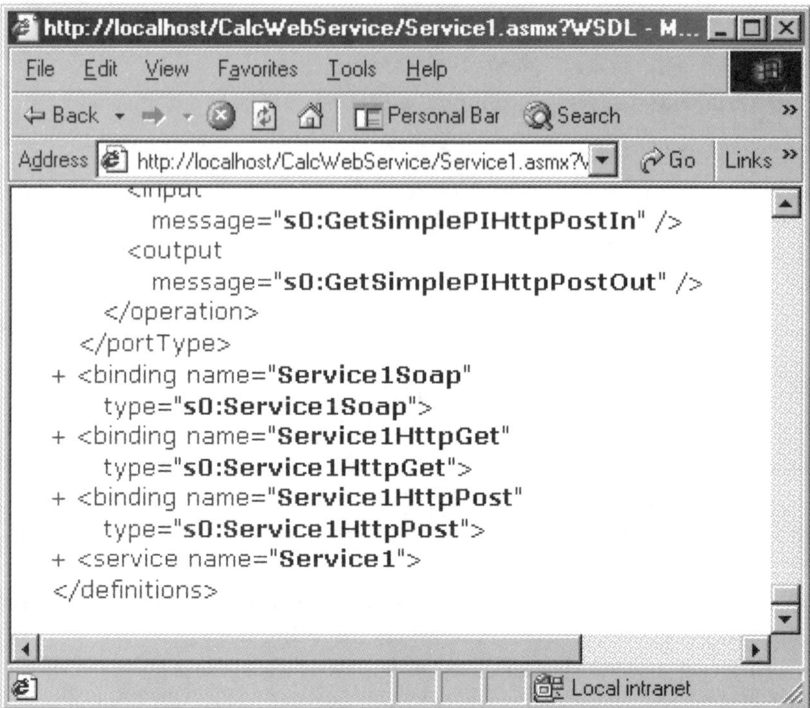

Figure 16-13. Bindings

If you expand the SOAP binding for your Web service, you find the following description for the Add() method (note the input and output tags):

```
<operation name="Add">
    <soap:operation soapAction="http://tempuri.org/Add" style="document" />
<input>
    <soap:body use="literal" />
</input>
<output>
    <soap:body use="literal" />
</output>
</operation>
```

While it is edifying to understand what is being sent back and forth across the wire, the good news is that the internals of a SOAP message are hidden from view (as you will notice during the remainder of this chapter).

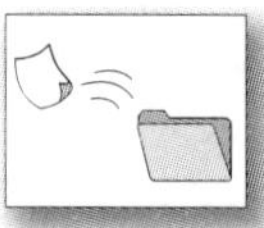

SOURCE CODE *The CalcService.asmx.vb file can be found under the Chapter 16 subdirectory.*

WSDL into VB .NET Code (Generating a Proxy)

At this point, you should feel fairly comfortable with the composition of a .NET Web service. The next step is to understand how to build clients that can consume these services. As you have seen, WSDL is used to describe Web methods in XML syntax. However, it would be undesirable to construct clients that *manually* request a WSDL definition and *manually* parse each node to establish a connection to the remote service. A much-preferred approach is to leverage a tool that can generate a proxy to the Web method.

Proxies can be simply defined as types (classes in this case) that look and feel exactly like the remote entity they pretend to be. If you have a background in classic DCOM, this should sound familiar. The COM client makes calls on the proxy class, which packages up the incoming parameters and sends them to the receiving stub. The stub in turn unpackages the request and hands off the request to the "real" COM object.

The same general behavior takes place when a consumer uses a remote Web service. The key difference is that accessing a Web service does *not* depend on a propriety binary format, specific platform, or given programming language. All that is required is an awareness of HTTP and XML.

Generating a Web service proxy is quite simple. First, you can use a standalone command-line tool named wsdl.exe. As an attractive alternative, the Visual Studio .NET IDE allows you to reference a Web service using a friendly wizard. Let's examine each approach.

Building a Proxy Using wsdl.exe

The wsdl.exe command-line tool generates a code file that represents the proxy to the remote Web service. At a minimum, you need to specify the name of the proxy file to be generated and the URL where the WSDL can be obtained, as shown here (update your path accordingly and type the command on a single line):

```
wsdl.exe /l:VB /out:c:\calcproxy.vb http://localhost/calcwebservice/
Service1.asmx?WSDL
```

If all is well, you see what appears in Figure 16-14.

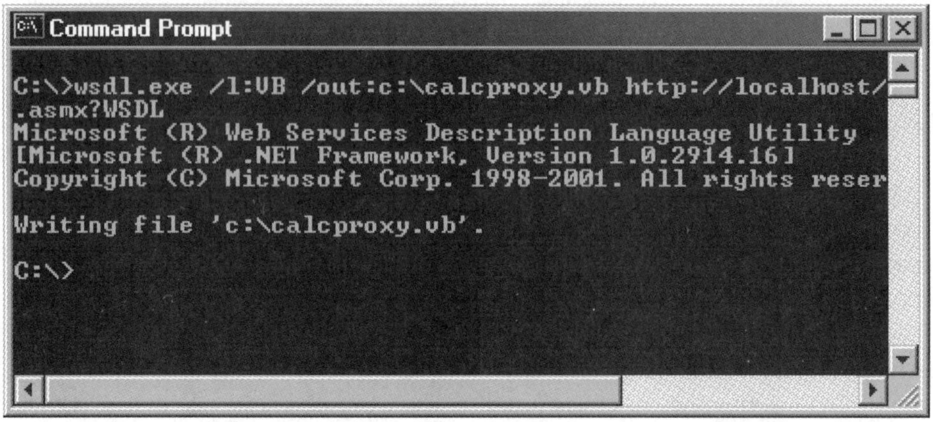

```
C:\>wsdl.exe /l:VB /out:c:\calcproxy.vb http://localhost/
.asmx?WSDL
Microsoft (R) Web Services Description Language Utility
[Microsoft (R) .NET Framework, Version 1.0.2914.16]
Copyright (C) Microsoft Corp. 1998-2001. All rights reser

Writing file 'c:\calcproxy.vb'.

C:\>
```

Figure 16-14. Generating a proxy class with wsdl.exe

The wsdl.exe utility generates C# code by default. If you choose to have your proxy written in VB .NET or JScript.NET syntax, you can use the optional /l: (Language) flag (as seen in the previous command). Table 16-9 lists some of the more interesting command-line options

Table 16-9. Various Flags of the wsdl.exe Utility

WSDL.EXE FLAG	MEANING IN LIFE
/l[anguage]:	Specifies the language to use for the generated proxy class. You can specify CS (default), VB, or JS as the language argument.
/n[amespace]:	Specifies the namespace for the generated proxy or template. The default namespace is the global namespace.
/out:	Specifies the file in which to save the generated proxy code. The tool derives the default file name from the service name. The tool saves generated datasets in different files.
/protocol:	Specifies the protocol to implement. (The default is SOAP.) You can specify SOAP, HttpGet, HttpPost, or a custom protocol specified in the configuration file.

Examining the Proxy Code

If you have ever examined the underlying stub and proxy code for classic ORPC (DCOM) request/response, you will be extremely happy to find a simple, readable VB .NET class file. First comes the class definition (note the use of the WebServiceBinding attribute), as shown here:

```
Option Strict Off  ' Ug...the default behavior as of Beta2...
Option Explicit On

Imports System
Imports System.Diagnostics
Imports System.Web.Services
Imports System.Web.Services.Protocols
Imports System.Xml.Serialization
<System.Web.Services.WebServiceBindingAttribute _
(Name:="Service1Soap", [Namespace]:="http://tempuri.org/")> _
Public Class Service1
    Inherits System.Web.Services.Protocols.SoapHttpClientProtocol

    <System.Diagnostics.DebuggerStepThroughAttribute()> _
    Public Sub New()
        MyBase.New
        Me.Url = "http://localhost/calcwebservice/Service1.asmx"
    End Sub
    ...
End Class
```

As you can see, the constructor of this proxy class maintains the URL of the remote Web service and stores it in the inherited URL property. Also notice that your immediate base class is of type SoapHttpClientProtocol. This type specifies most of the implementation for communicating with a SOAP Web service over HTTP. (The remaining functionality comes from numerous base classes.) Table 16-10 describes some interesting inherited members.

Table 16-10. Core Inherited Properties

INHERITED MEMBERS	MEANING IN LIFE
BeginInvoke()	Starts an asynchronous invocation of a method of a SOAP Web service.
EndInvoke()	Ends an asynchronous invocation of a method of a remote SOAP Web service.
Invoke()	Synchronously invokes a method of a SOAP Web service.
Proxy	Gets or sets proxy information for making a Web service request through a firewall.
Timeout	Gets or sets the timeout (in milliseconds) used for synchronous calls.
URL	Gets or sets the base URL to the server to use for requests.
UserAgent	Gets or sets the value for the user agent header sent with each request.

Of course the real meat of the generated proxy is the method implementations themselves. The generated proxy code defines synchronous and asynchronous members for each Web method defined in the Web service. As you are aware, synchronous method invocations are blocked until the call returns. Asynchronous method inoculations return control to the calling client immediately after receiving the invocation request. When the processing has finished, the runtime makes a callback to the client. Here is the synchronous Add() implementation:

```
<System.Diagnostics.DebuggerStepThroughAttribute(),  _
System.Web.Services.Protocols.SoapDocumentMethodAttribute _
("http://tempuri.org/Add", _
Use:=System.Web.Services.Description.SoapBindingUse.Literal, _
ParameterStyle:= _
System.Web.Services.Protocols.SoapParameterStyle.Wrapped)>  _
Public Overloads Function Add(ByVal x As Integer, ByVal y As Integer) As Integer
    Dim results() As Object = Me.Invoke("Add", New Object() {x, y})
    Return CType(results(0),Integer)
End Function
```

Each Web method is marked with the SoapDocumentMethod attribute. Also, notice that the Add() method has the same signature as the original Web method. As far as clients are concerned, when they call the Add() method, the logic is executed directly. Of course in reality the incoming parameters (along with the named method) are sent to SoapHttpClientProtocol.Invoke(). At this point, the HTTP request is sent to the correct URL.

One update you will want to make for the generated proxy file is to wrap the class in a namespace definition, as shown here, as the wsdl.exe utility will not do this on your behalf unless you explicitly specify the /n flag. Here is the update:

```
namespace TheCalcProxy
<System.Web.Services.WebServiceBindingAttribute _
(Name:="Service1Soap", [Namespace]:="http://tempuri.org/")>  _
Public Class Service1
    Inherits System.Web.Services.Protocols.SoapHttpClientProtocol
     . . .
End Class
End Namespace
```

Building the Assembly

Before you can create clients that use your Web service, you need to build an assembly to contain the proxy type (or as an alternative, simply include the generated class into a given client project workspace). Assuming you want to place your proxy into a self describing DLL, you can use the VB .NET compiler directly or select a new VB .NET Code Library using Visual Studio.NET. Either way, you must be sure to add references to the System.Web.Services.dll and System.Xml.dll references, as shown in Figure 16-15.

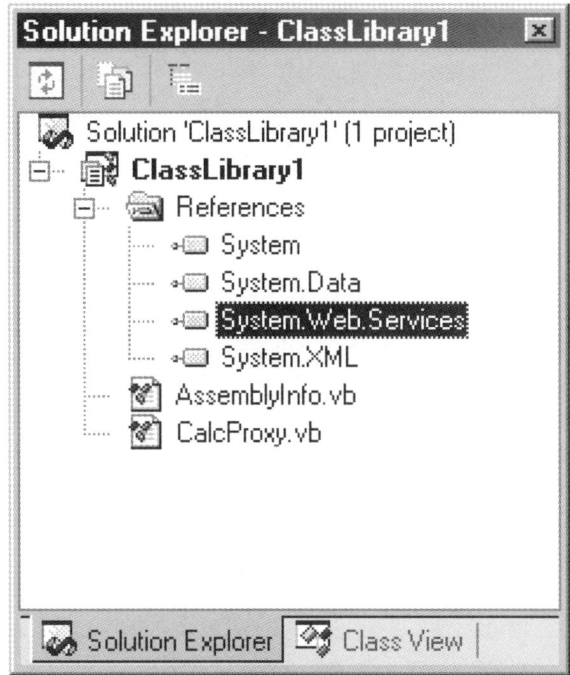

Figure 16-15. Proxies must reference System.XML.dll and System.Web.Services.dll

The result is a new library that contains your proxy class (Figure 16-16).

Figure 16-16. Your proxy, wrapped in a .NET assembly

Building a Client

At this point, you can create a new Form-based, ASP.NET, or Console-based application, add a reference to your assembly and write some code. (In each case you need to ensure that a reference to System.Web.Services.dll is included.) To keep things simple, here is a Console-based client that tests various aspects of the calc Web service:

```
' Don't forget to set a reference to
' System.Web.Services.dll!
Imports ClassLibrary1.TheCalcProxy
```

```
Module Module1
    Sub Main()
        ' Work with the Web service.
        Dim w As Service1 = New Service1()
        Console.WriteLine("100 + 100 is {0}", _
                          w.Add(100, 100))
        Try
            w.Divide(0, 0)
        Catch e As DivideByZeroException
            Console.WriteLine(e.Message)
        End Try
    End Sub
End Module
```

Figure 16-17 shows the output. (Notice that your custom exception message has been passed along as an inner exception.)

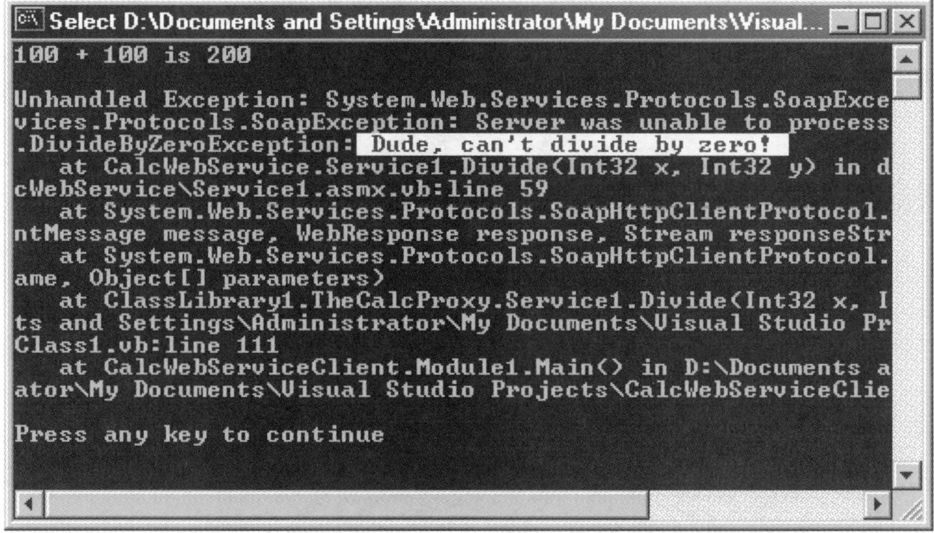

Figure 16-17. A console Web service consumer

SOURCE CODE *The CalcWebServiceClient project can be found under the Chapter 16 subdirectory.*

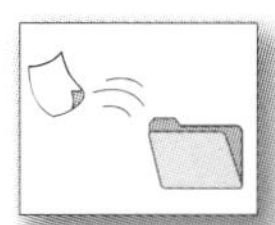

Generating a Proxy with VS.NET

Working with the wsdl.exe utility and raw VB .NET compiler is a bit clumsy. The only real benefit of using the wsdl.exe command-line tool is that it allows you to directly specify a given invocation protocol (GET, POST, or SOAP) using the /protocol flag. In contrast, Visual Studio .NET only creates proxies that respond to the SOAP protocol (which is typically what you want anyway).

To illustrate how to build proxies using VS.NET, let's build a Windows Forms client application. Assume you have a simple user interface that allows the user to define two values passed to the various methods (Add(), Subtract(), and so on). Once your GUI has been established, you can add a Web reference to your project (Figure 16-18).

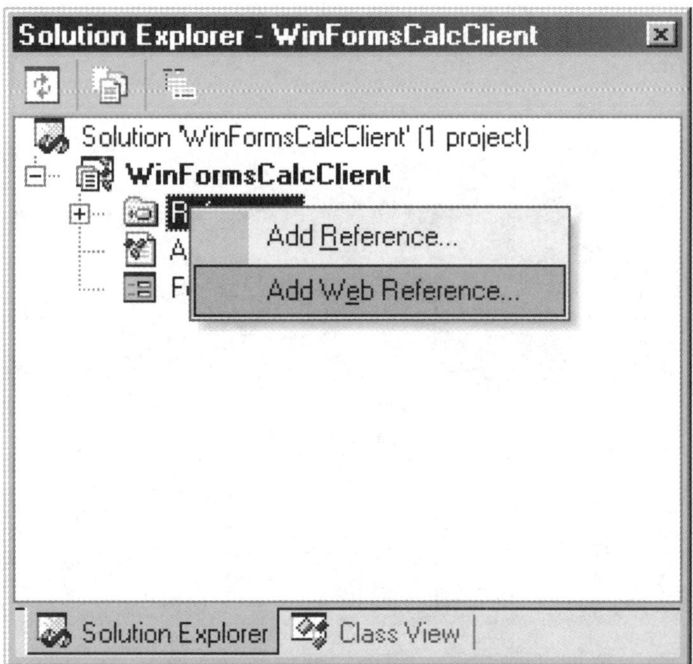

Figure 16-18. Adding a Web reference automatically generates the proxy file

When you elect to add a Web reference, this will launch a simple tool that allows you to view the Web services at a given URL. Assuming you have selected the "Web References on Local Web Server" link, you are presented with a list of all Web services on your local machine (Figure 16-19).

Now, select the CalcWebService, and add the reference. A new Web References node has been added to your Solution Explorer window

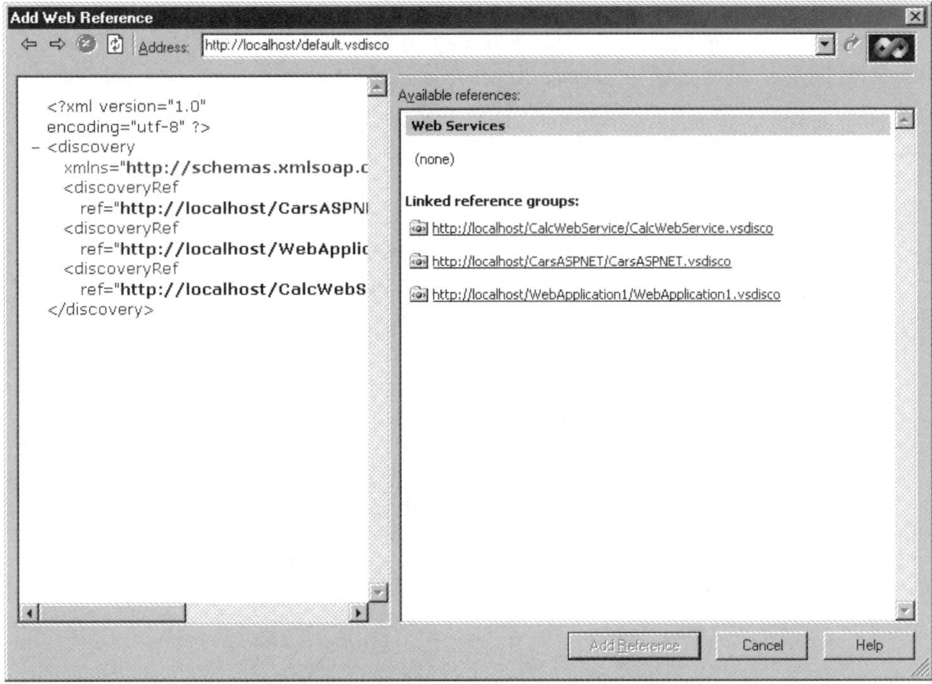

Figure 16-19. The CalcWebService

(Figure 16-20). Note that the name of the generated namespace is based on the URL at which the Web service was located.

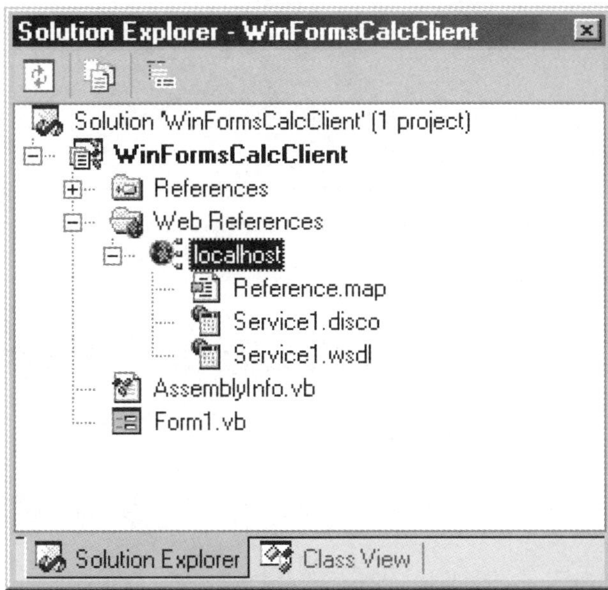

Figure 16-20. The Web References node

At this point, you are ready to specify work with the Service1 type directly (note that the name of the generated namespace is the name of the machine hosting the Web service), as shown here:

```
Public Class Form1
    Inherits System.Windows.Forms.Form
    Private ws As New localhost.Service1()
...
    ' Check out the InteliSense!  You're overloaded Add() method
    ' came through!
    Private Sub btnAdd_Click(ByVal sender As System.Object, _
    ByVal e As System.EventArgs) Handles btnAdd.Click
        txtAns.Text = ws.Add(Integer.Parse(txtNumb1.Text), _
        Integer.Parse(txtNumb2.Text))
    End Sub
```

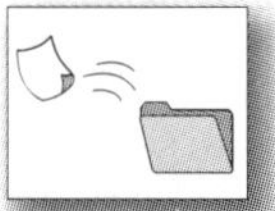

SOURCE CODE *The WinFormsCalcClient can be found under the Chapter 16 subdirectory (you will have to reference your own version of the Calc Web service!)*

A More Interesting Web Service (and Client)

So much for Math 101. The real power of Web services becomes much more evident when you build Web methods that return complex types, unlike the very simple CalcWebService example you have been examining. Thus, you need to build a more interesting Web service that can return ADO.NET DataSets, custom types, and arrays of types. As you recall, this is facilitated through the use of SOAP.

Create a new VB .NET Web service project workspace named VBCarsWebService. Your first goal is to create a Web method that returns an ADO.NET DataSet, containing the full set of records in the Inventory table. Let's call this Web method GetAllCars(). The return value is (of course) a DataSet. To begin, drag a SqlConnection component (renamed to SqlCarsConnection) onto the design time representation of your *.asmx.vb code file (Figure 16-21).

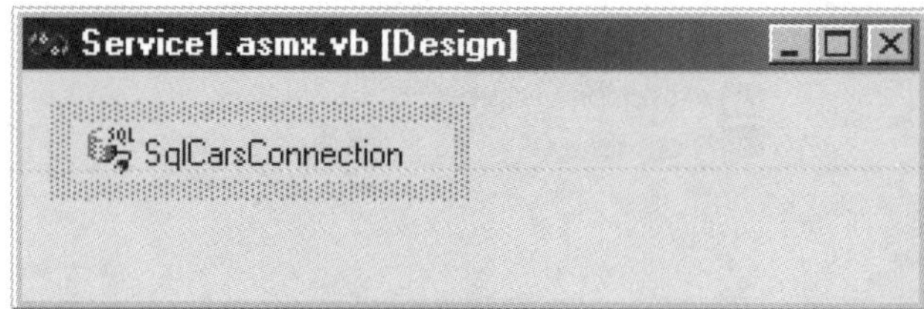

Figure 16-21. Design time data connections

Using the Properties window, build a connection string that hooks you into the Cars database you created in Chapter 14 (take a peek back to this chapter if you need a refresher on using the Data Link tool).

The implementation logic fills the DataSet using an SqlDataAdapter type, as shown here:

```
' Don't forget to import System.Data.SqlClient.
<WebMethod()> _
Public Function GetAllCars() As DataSet
    ' Fill the DataGrid with the Inventory table.
    Dim dataAdp As SqlDataAdapter = _
          New SqlDataAdapter("Select * from Inventory", SqlCarsConnection)
    Dim ds As DataSet = New DataSet()
    dataAdp.Fill(ds, "Inventory")
    Return ds
End Function
```

If you now create a Windows Forms client (and add a reference to this Web service), you can call the GetAllCars() method and attach the returned DataSet to a DataGrid widget (Figure 16-22), as shown here:

```
Private Sub btnGetCars_Click(ByVal sender As System.Object, _
ByVal e As System.EventArgs) Handles btnGetCars.Click
    Dim ws As New localhost.Service1()
    Dim ds As DataSet = ws.GetAllCars()
    DataGrid1.DataSource = ds.Tables("Inventory")
End Sub
```

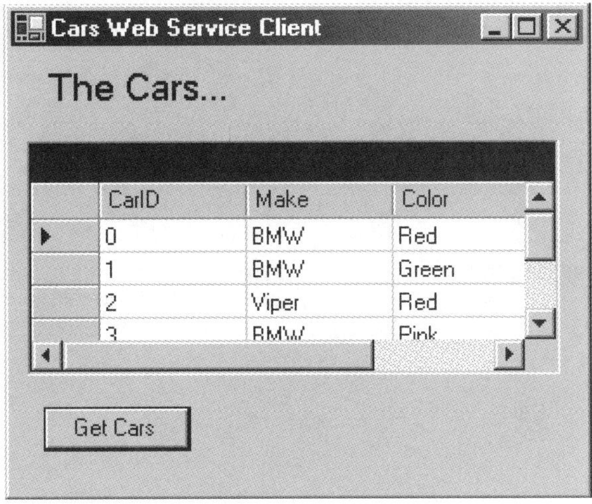

Figure 16-22. Obtaining a DataSet from the Car Web service

Serializing Custom Types

The SOAP protocol is also able to easily transport XML representations of custom data types automatically. To illustrate, let's build the *final* Car type of the book (thank me later). Insert a new class named Car in your current VBCarsWebService application. This iteration is simple: You have two public fields (to represent the pet name and max speed) and an overloaded constructor to set the data. Also notice the very important detail, the use of the XmlInclude attribute (defined in the System.Xml.Serialization namespace), as shown here:

```
Imports System.Xml.Serialization
<XmlInclude(GetType(Car))> _
Public Class Car
    Public Sub New()
    End Sub
    Public Sub New(ByVal n As String, ByVal s As Integer)
        petName = n
        maxSpeed = s
    End Sub
    Public petName As String
    Public maxSpeed As Integer
End Class
```

Technically speaking, the process of transforming the stateful data of an object into an XML representation is termed *serialization*. Given that XML itself has no clue what a car type is, you must mark each custom type to be serialized as XML can be included using the XmlIncludeAttribute type.

Next, define a Private ArrayList data member (carList) and fill it with some initial cars in the constructor of your Web service, as shown here:

```
Public Class Service1
    Inherits System.Web.Services.WebService
    Private carList As New ArrayList()
...
    Public Sub New()
        MyBase.New()
...
        'Fill car list with sample data.
        carList.Add(New Car("Zippy", 170))
        carList.Add(New Car("Fred", 80))
        carList.Add(New Car("Sally", 40))
    End Sub
```

Now let's add two additional Web methods. GetCarList() returns the entire array of autos. GetACarFromList() returns a specific car from the array list based on a numerical index. The implementation of each method is simple, as shown here:

```
' Return a given car from the list.
<WebMethod()> _
Public Function GetACarFromList(ByVal carToGet As Integer) As Car
    If (carToGet <= carList.Count) Then
        Return CType(carList(carToGet), Car)
    End If
    Throw New IndexOutOfRangeException()
End Function
' Return the entire set of cars.
<WebMethod()> _
Public Function GetCarList() As ArrayList
    Return carList
End Function
```

Enhancing Your Windows Forms Client

The next task is exercising the GetACarFromList() and GetCarList() members from our client application. Given that your Web service is a .NET assembly at heart, understand that the definition of the car type has been described in the assembly's metadata. (You need to update the Web reference using the Solution Explorer.) To illustrate, you can create a given car as shown here:

```
Private Sub btnCarACar_Click(ByVal sender As System.Object, _
ByVal e As System.EventArgs) Handles btnCarACar.Click
    Try
        Dim ws As New localhost.Service1()
        Dim c As localhost.Car

        c = ws.GetACarFromList(Integer.Parse(txtCarFromArrayList.Text))
        MessageBox.Show(c.petName, "Car " & txtCarFromArrayList.Text _
                 & " is named:")
    Catch
        MessageBox.Show("No car with that number. . .")
    End Try
End Sub
```

Figure 16-23 shows a test run. (Remember that you are referencing the ID of the car in the ArrayList, not the Inventory table!)

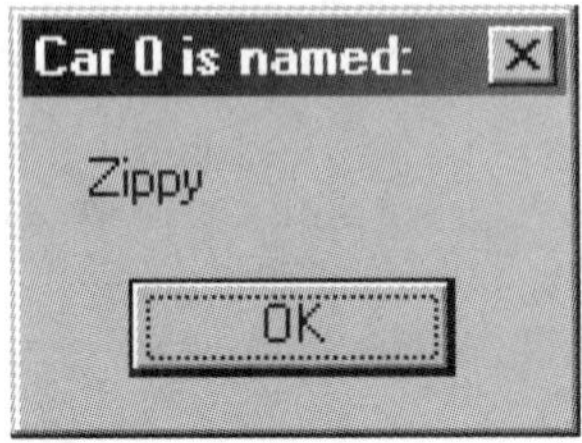

Figure 16-23. Grabbing a car from the ArrayList

As far as the ArrayList returned from GetCarList() is concerned, you can hold the entire set of items in an object array and cast accordingly, as shown here:

```
Private Sub btnGetAll_Click(ByVal sender As System.Object, _
ByVal e As System.EventArgs) Handles btnGetAll.Click
    Dim ws As New localhost.Service1()
    Dim objs() As Object = ws. GetCarList()
    Dim petNames As String
    ' Print out pet name of each item in array.
    Dim i As Integer
    For i = 0 To UBound(objs)
        ' Extract next car!
        Dim c As localhost.Car = CType(objs(i), localhost.Car)
        petNames &= c.petName & vbLf
    Next
    MessageBox.Show(petNames, "Pet names for cars in array list:")
End Sub
```

Figure 16-24 shows the output.

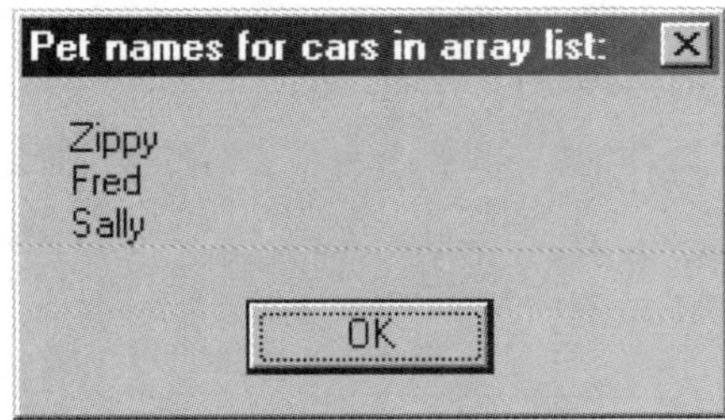

Figure 16-24. Grabbing all members in the ArrayList

Serialization of Custom Types (Further Details)

When a custom type is serialized into XML, you are essentially storing the stateful data from the object for later use. For example, if you were to run your VBCarsWebService using your default browser and select the GetAllCars() method, you would find the XML representation shown in Figure 16-25.

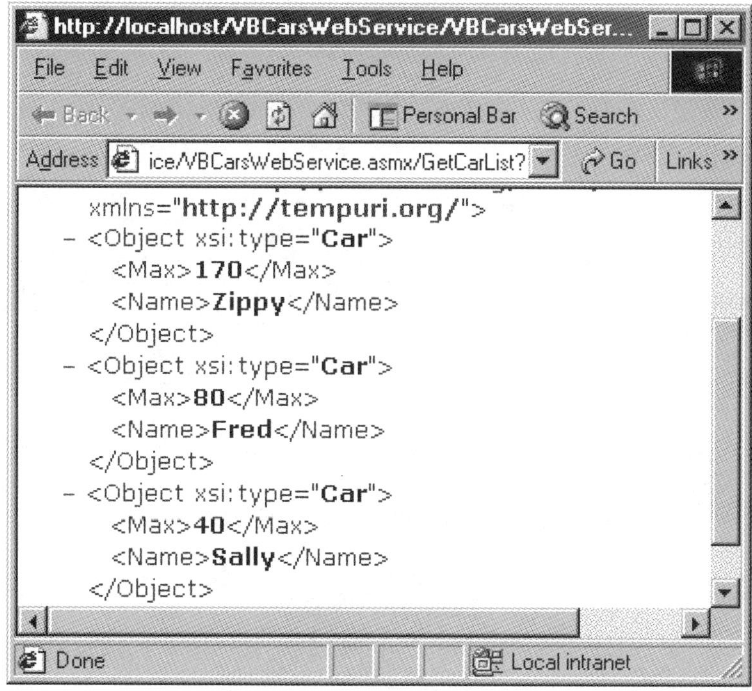

Figure 16-25. The ArrayList as XML

Therefore, for the runtime to serialize a given member of a custom type, it must somehow have *access* to the underlying value. As you recall, the car you previously created supported two Public fields, as shown here:

```
<XmlInclude(GetType(Car))> _
Public Class Car
. . .
    Public petName As String
    Public maxSpeed As Integer
End Class
```

If you were to change each of these members to Private as shown here:

```
<XmlInclude(GetType(Car))> _
Public Class Car
. . .
    ' Serialize me?
    Private petName As String
    Private maxSpeed As Integer
End Class
```

When you test the GetCarList() method once again, you find an ArrayList with three cars. However, each item would have *no state data* expressed in the XML. (Figure 16-26).

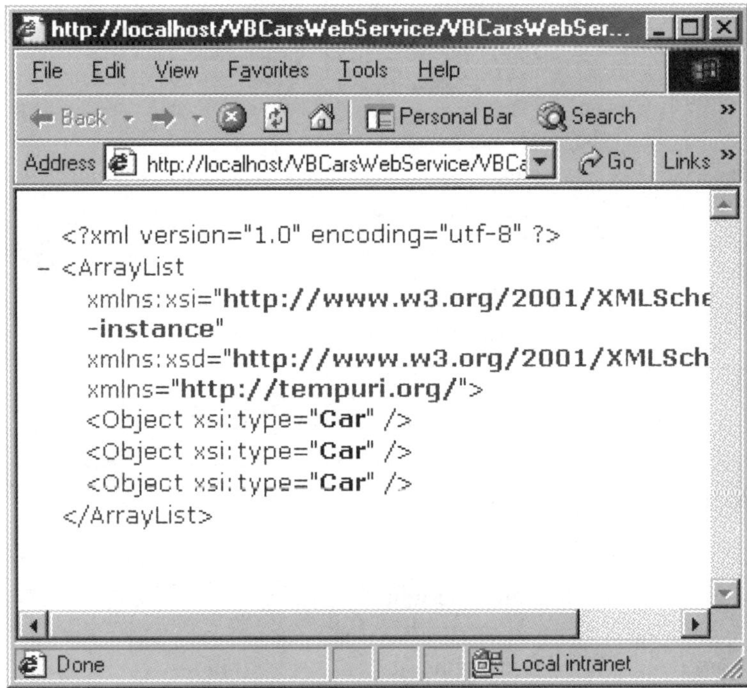
http://localhost/VBCarsWebService/VBCarsWebSer...
File Edit View Favorites Tools Help
Back Personal Bar Search
Address http://localhost/VBCarsWebService/VBCa Go Links
<?xml version="1.0" encoding="utf-8" ?>
- <ArrayList
xmlns:xsi="http://www.w3.org/2001/XMLSche
-instance"
xmlns:xsd="http://www.w3.org/2001/XMLSch
xmlns="http://tempuri.org/">
<Object xsi:type="Car" />
<Object xsi:type="Car" />
<Object xsi:type="Car" />
</ArrayList>
Done
Local intranet

Figure 16-26. Private members are not serializable

The reason is simple enough. The runtime could not access this private data! The short answer is, if you want the value of your types to be serialized into an equivalent XML representation, you must either supply Public fields or better yet, provide access to Private data using a corresponding property, as shown here:

```
<XmlInclude(GetType(Car))> _
Public Class Car
    Public Sub New()
    End Sub
    Public Sub New(ByVal n As String, ByVal s As Integer)
        petName = n
        maxSpeed = s
    End Sub
    ' Preserve encapsulation!
    Private petName As String
    Private maxSpeed As Integer
    Public Property Name() As String
        Get
            Return petName
        End Get
        Set(ByVal Value As String)
            petName = Value
        End Set
    End Property
    Public Property Max() As Integer
        Get
            Return maxSpeed
        End Get
        Set(ByVal Value As Integer)
            maxSpeed = Value
        End Set
    End Property
End Class
```

In summary, building types that are available through a Web service is more or less just like building any VB .NET data type. The only real points to be aware of are that you need to mark the type with the <XmlInclude> attribute and that only publicly accessible points of data (or public properties) can be represented in the underlying XML.

SOURCE CODE *The CarsWebService.asmx.vb file and CarClient project can be found under the Chapter 16 subdirectory.*

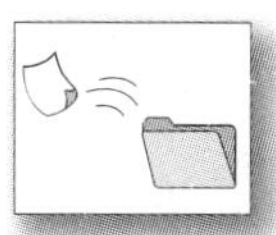

Understanding the Discovery Service Protocol

The final topic of this chapter is to address the cleverly named *.vsdisco file (which you recall is an abbreviated form of DISCOvery of Web Services). Whenever a remote (or local) client is interested in using a Web service, an obvious step is to determine which Web services exist on a given machine. While the .NET class library defines the types that allow you to examine registered Web services programmatically, discovery services are also required by numerous design time CASE tools (such as the Add Web Reference Wizard).

The *.vsdisco file is used to describe each Web service in a given virtual directory and any related subfolders. When you create a new Visual Studio .NET Web project, you automatically receive a *.vsdisco file that looks like this:

```
<?xml version="1.0" ?>
<dynamicDiscovery xmlns="urn:schemas-dynamicdiscovery:disco.2000-03-17">
<exclude path="_vti_cnf" />
<exclude path="_vti_pvt" />
<exclude path="_vti_log" />
<exclude path="_vti_script" />
<exclude path="_vti_txt" />
<exclude path="Web References" />
</dynamicDiscovery>
```

The <dynamicDiscovery> tag signifies that the *.vsdisco file is to be processed on the server to return an XML description for each Web service in a given virtual directory. In addition to the <dynamicDiscovery> tags, you can also see that a number of irrelevant paths have been excluded from this search. To illustrate, launch IE and navigate to the VBCarsWebService.vsdisco file (Figure 16-27).

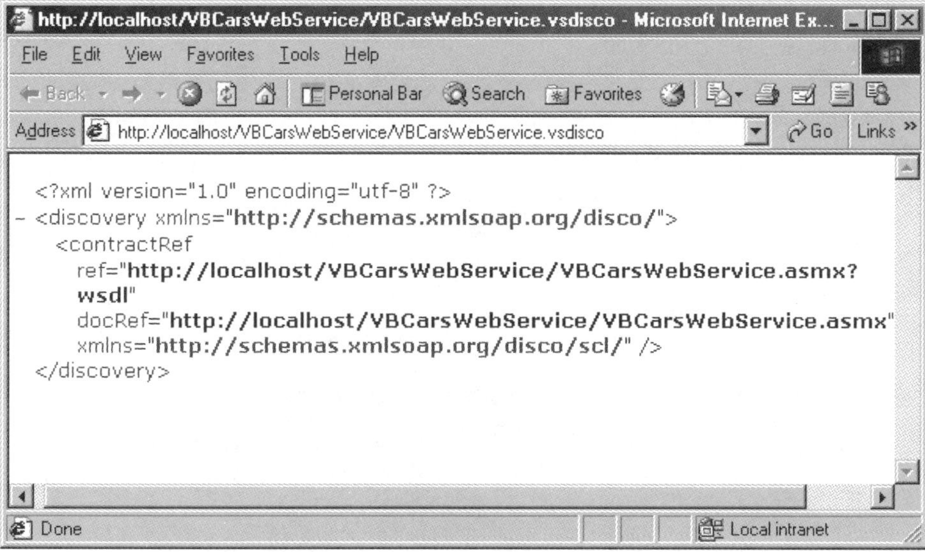

*Figure 16-27. The *.vsdisco file provides discovery services*

Adding a New Web Service

Understand that a single *.vsdisco file describes each and every Web service installed under a given virtual directory. Assume you have added another Web service to your current CarWebService project using the "Project|Add Web Service . . ." menu selection named MotorBike.asmx.

The MotorBike class defines a single Web method, as shown here:

```
<WebMethod()> _
Public Function GetBikerDesc() As String
    Return "Name: Tiny. Weight: 374 pounds."
End Function
```

If you recompile the application and once again specify the *.vsdisco file from IE, you have Figure 16-28.

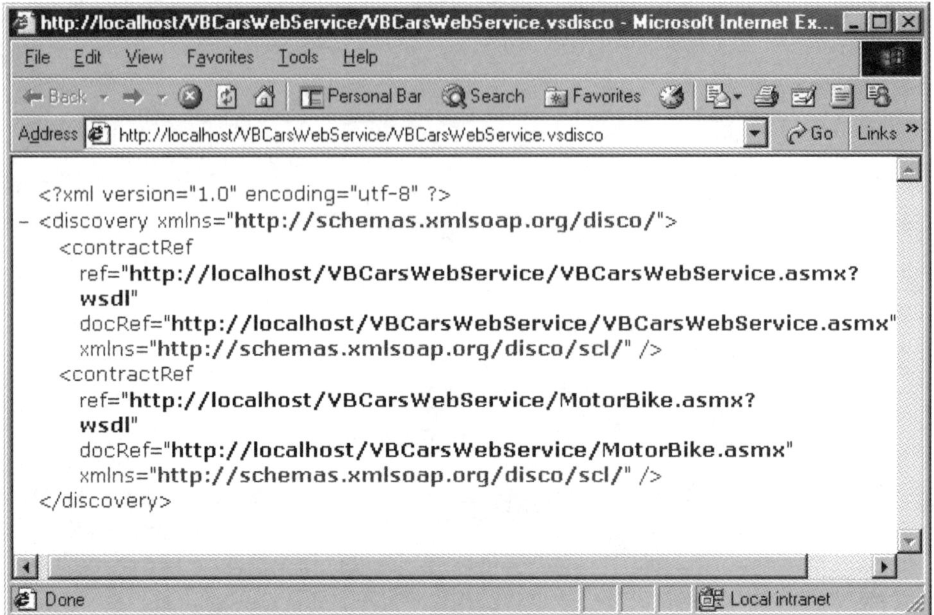

*Figure 16-28. *.vsdisco files describe all Web services under a given virtual directory*

As you can see, you now have two <contractRef> nodes, one for automobiles and one for motorcycles. Granted, viewing the results of a disco query from within IE is not all that fascinating. Recall however that this same file is used with the Add Web Reference Wizard. Furthermore, you could also programmatically obtain this same information using various WSDL-centric .NET types. However, I will leave this task as an exercise for any interested readers.

Summary

This chapter has exposed you to the core building blocks of .NET Web services. The chapter began by examining the core namespaces (and core types in these namespaces) used during Web service development. As you have seen, Web services require three interrelated technologies: a lookup mechanism (*.vsdisco files), a description language (WSDL), and an invocation protocol (GET, POST, or SOAP).

Once you have created any number of <WebMethod>-enabled members, you can interact with a Web service through an intervening proxy. The wsdl.exe utility generates such a proxy, which can be used by the client like any other VB .NET type. As you have seen, by default wsdl.exe generated VB .NET code using SOAP as the method of transport. This can be adjusted using various command-line switches. This chapter explored how you can expose custom types from a Web service using the <XmlInclude> attribute.

Index

Apress Titles

ISBN	PRICE	AUTHOR	TITLE
1-893115-01-1	$39.95	Appleman	Appleman's Win32 API Puzzle Book and Tutorial for Visual Basic Programmers
1-893115-23-2	$29.95	Appleman	How Computer Programming Works
1-893115-97-6	$39.95	Appleman	Moving to VB. NET: Strategies, Concepts, and Code
1-893115-09-7	$29.95	Baum	Dave Baum's Definitive Guide to LEGO MINDSTORMS
1-893115-84-4	$29.95	Baum, Gasperi, Hempel, and Villa	Extreme MINDSTORMS
1-893115-82-8	$59.95	Ben-Gan/Moreau	Advanced Transact-SQL for SQL Server 2000
1-893115-99-2	$39.95	Cornell/Morrison	Programming VB .NET: A Guide for Experienced Programmers
1-893115-71-2	$39.95	Ferguson	Mobile .NET
1-893115-90-9	$44.95	Finsel	The Handbook for Reluctant Database Administrators
1-893115-85-2	$34.95	Gilmore	A Programmer's Introduction to PHP 4.0
1-893115-17-8	$59.95	Gross	A Programmer's Introduction to Windows DNA
1-893115-62-3	$39.95	Gunnerson	A Programmer's Introduction to C#, Second Edition
1-893115-10-0	$34.95	Holub	Taming Java Threads
1-893115-04-6	$34.95	Hyman/Vaddadi	Mike and Phani's Essential C++ Techniques
1-893115-50-X	$34.95	Knudsen	Wireless Java: Developing with Java 2, Micro Edition
1-893115-79-8	$49.95	Kofler	Definitive Guide to Excel VBA
1-893115-56-9	$39.95	Kofler	MySQL
1-893115-87-9	$39.95	Kurata	Doing Web Development: Client-Side Techniques
1-893115-75-5	$44.95	Kurniawan	Internet Programming with VB
1-893115-19-4	$49.95	Macdonald	Serious ADO: Universal Data Access with Visual Basic
1-893115-06-2	$39.95	Marquis/Smith	A Visual Basic 6.0 Programmer's Toolkit

ISBN	PRICE	AUTHOR	TITLE
1-893115-22-4	$27.95	McCarter	David McCarter's VB Tips and Techniques
1-893115-76-3	$49.95	Morrison	C++ For VB Programmers
1-893115-80-1	$39.95	Newmarch	A Programmer's Guide to Jini Technology
1-893115-58-5	$49.95	Oellermann	Architecting Web Services
1-893115-81-X	$39.95	Pike	SQL Server: Common Problems, Tested Solutions
1-893115-20-8	$34.95	Rischpater	Wireless Web Development
1-893115-93-3	$34.95	Rischpater	Wireless Web Development with PHP and WAP
1-893115-24-0	$49.95	Sinclair	From Access to SQL Server
1-893115-94-1	$29.95	Spolsky	User Interface Design for Programmers
1-893115-53-4	$39.95	Sweeney	Visual Basic for Testers
1-893115-29-1	$44.95	Thomsen	Database Programming with Visual Basic .NET
1-893115-65-8	$39.95	Tiffany	Pocket PC Database Development with eMbedded Visual Basic
1-893115-59-3	$59.95	Troelsen	C# and the .NET Platform
1-893115-26-7	Troelsen		Visual Basic .NET and the .NET Platform
1-893115-54-2	$49.95	Trueblood/Lovett	Data Mining and Statistical Analysis Using SQL
1-893115-16-X	$49.95	Vaughn	ADO Examples and Best Practices
1-893115-83-6	$44.95	Wells	Code Centric: T-SQL Programming with Stored Procedures and Triggers
1-893115-95-X	$49.95	Welschenbach	Cryptography in C and C++
1-893115-05-4	$39.95	Williamson	Writing Cross-Browser Dynamic HTML
1-893115-78-X	$49.95	Zukowski	Definitive Guide to Swing for Java 2, Second Edition
1-893115-92-5	$49.95	Zukowski	Java Collections

Available at bookstores nationwide or from Springer Verlag New York, Inc. at 1-800-777-4643; fax 1-212-533-3503. Contact us for more information at sales@apress.com.